Communications
in Computer and Information Science 269

P. Venkata Krishna   M. Rajasekhara Babu
Ezendu Ariwa (Eds.)

Global Trends in Computing and Communication Systems

4th International Conference, ObCom 2011
Vellore, TN, India, December 9-11, 2011
Proceedings, Part I

Springer

Volume Editors

P. Venkata Krishna
VIT University
School of Computing Science and Engineering
Vellore 632014, TN, India
E-mail: pvekatakrishna@vit.ac.in

M. Rajasekhara Babu
VIT University
School of Computing and Engineering
Vellore 632014, TN, India
E-mail: mrajasekharababu@vit.ac.in

Ezendu Ariwa
London Metropolitan University, UK
E-mail: e.ariwa@londonmet.ac.uk

ISSN 1865-0929 e-ISSN 1865-0937
ISBN 978-3-642-29218-7 ISBN 978-3-642-29219-4 (eBook)
DOI 10.1007/978-3-642-29219-4
Springer Heidelberg Dordrecht London New York

Library of Congress Control Number: 2012934198

CR Subject Classification (1998): I.2, H.3, H.4, C.2, I.4, I.5

Typesetting: Camera-ready by author, data conversion by Scientific Publishing Services, Chennai, India

Printed on acid-free paper

Springer is part of Springer Science+Business Media (www.springer.com)

Preface

Welcome to the fourth edition of the International Conference ObCom 2011—Recent Trends in Computing, Communication and Information Technology. Computing, communication and information technology are hand-in-glove responsible for the majority of innovations and novel transformations that occur around the world. Starting from how data are stored, processed and consumed, there have been several optimizations taking place in different geographical locations. In order to tap the cutting-edge solutions from different streams of computing, ObCom was launched in the year 2003. The Conference ObCom 2004 was eventually made available to the computing community in the year 2004 and it promoted the exploitation of parallelism and distribution in order to achieve better functionalities and performance in certain classes of computer applications. The next version of ObCom was in 2006 and it was focused on the theme "Mobile, Ubiquitous and Pervasive Computing." The theme was chosen to script the challenges and issues while designing and building the new spectrum of human–computer interfaces prevalent in mobile, ubiquitous and pervasive computing.

The ObCom 2011 conference addressed issues associated with computing, communication and information. Its aim was to increase exponentially the participants' awareness of the current and future direction in the domains and to create a platform for researchers, leading industry developers and end users to interrelate. The conference began with keynote address on the first day and continued on the second and third day with invited lectures by leading researchers in academia and industry.

We have grown into an international conference of high influence by catering to independent technical communities—the research/academic body and the industry/practices body. The academic–industry synergy will eventually make technologies available at large. A glance at the participants' record reveals an equal mix of high-caliber research academics and dominant industry engineers and managers in the software industry. ObCom 2011 was fortunate to attract people who are experts in their area of interest.

ObCom's research paper selection process is unique and is praised for its thoroughness and fairness in representation of the best practices in the research community. ObCom had a large Program Committee, both form the host country and other developed countries, with a cross-section of skills and talents across computing and engineering disciplines. The Program and Advisory Committee increased gradually to fulfill the needs of the conference. The received papers were reviewed by several expert critics (about two or more reviews per paper), while the Organizing Chair kept a close watch on review quality and reviewer thoroughness. Conflicts of interest were made transparent and handled to avoid disputes. Thus, every research paper accepted at ObCom 2011 was carefully examined and discussed among a body of world-class researchers. The conference accepted 173 papers from 842 submissions, which includes keynote and invited papers.

Research papers are just one element of ObCom 2011. We had several tracks making up the conference and catering to different segments of the community. In conjunction, we had an international ObCom student conference, OSIC 2011, dealing with research papers of UG, PG and PhD students, a PhD Forum exclusively for doctoral students to present their research challenge and find out its feasibility with a huge research panel of ObCom participants. Poster presentations, workshops, and keynotes completed the event. Each of these had its own committee and processes for review and selection of papers.

The principal objective of this proceedings volume is to collect the cutting-edge results in the field of computing, communication and information technology. Accordingly, we selected papers representing such works.

The proceedings consist of invited paper dealing with the review of performance models of computer and communication systems and contributed papers dealing with the issues of networking, cloud computing, fuzzy logic, mobile communication, image processing, navigation systems, biometrics and Web services covering literally all the vital areas of the computing domains.

The conference as a whole was pulled off with an extremely engaged and committed team, and we thank those people involved in addressing the various needs of the conference. Recognition is given on our website with their respective roles and titles. The list might not cover many whose work was valuable for the conference.

Thanks to Alfred Hofmann, Leonie Kunz and other members of the editorial team of Springer CCIS for their kind cooperation during the publication process.

Sincere thanks to our VIT University Chancellor G. Viswanathan, Vice President (Administration), Sankar Viswanathan, Vice President (Operations) G.V. Sampath, Vice President (University Affairs), Sekar Viswanathan, Vice President (Chennai campus), G.V. Selvam, Vice Chancellor V. Raju, Pro-Vice Chancellor (Vellore campus), S. Narayanan, and Pro-Vice Chancellor (Chennai campus), Anand A. Samuel for their valuable suggestions and encouragement.

Lastly, thanks to everyone who attended this conference making it bigger in all respects.

P. Venkata Krishna
M. Rajasekhara Babu
Ezendu Ariwa

Organization

Chief Patron

G. Viswanathan	Chancellor, VIT University

Patrons

Sankar Viswanathan	Vice President, Administration
G.V. Sampath	Vice President, Operations
Sekar Viswanathan	Vice President, University Affairs
G.V. Selvam	Vice President, Chennai campus

Co-Patrons

V. Raju	Vice Chancellor
S. Narayanan	Pro-Vice Chancellor (Vellore campus)
Anand A. Samuel	Pro-Vice Chancellor (Chennai campus)

Convenor(s)

M. Khalid	VIT University, Vellore
Margret Anouncia S.	SCSE, VIT University, Vellore

Conference Chair

P. Venkata Krishna	VIT University, Vellore

Technical Chair

Ezendu Ariwa	London Metropolitan University, UK

Technical Co-chair(s)

Sumanth Yenduri	University of Southern Mississippi, USA
H.R. Vishwakarma	VIT University, Vellore, India

Honorary Chair

Rajkumar Buyya	The University of Melbourne, Australia

Publicity Chair

Ezendu Ariwa	London Metropolitan University, UK

Sponsorship Co-chairs

S.R. Pullobhotla	PAT, VIT University, India
Samuel Rajkumar V.	PAT, VIT University, India
Singaravelan M.	CTS, VIT University, India

International Advisory Board

Bettina Harriehausen-Mühlbauer	Fachbereich Informatik, Germany
Kam-Hoi Cheng	University of Houston, USA
Phil Prins	Seattle Pacific University, USA
Suiping Zhou	NTU, Singapore
Pramod Kumar Meher	NTU, Singapore
Pururav Thoutireddy	California Institute of Technology, USA
Jaspal Subhlok	University of Houston, USA
Boleslaw K. Szymanski	Rensselaer Polytechnic Institute, USA
Hans Martin Gündner	UAS Esslingen, Germany
Eberhard Kienzle	UAS Esslingen, Germany
Gareth J. Monkman	UAS Regensburg, Germany
Wolfgang Köster	UAS Darmstadt, Germany
Arno G. Kostka	Technical University of Darmstadt, Germany
Hermann Hartig	Technische Universität Dresden, Germany
Uwe Wloka	UAS Dresden, Germany
Axel Toll	UAS Dresden, Germany
H.-W. Philippsen	UAS Bremen, Germany
Richard Aubele	UAS Esslingen, Germany
Lothar Issler	UAS Esslingen, Germany
Albrecht Eßlinger	UAS Esslingen, Germany
Bertold Deppisch	University of Technology, UAS Karlsruhe, Germany
Frieder Keller	University of Technology, UAS Karlsruhe, Germany
Christine Roueche	Esigelec, France
Robin Pollard	Monash University, Australia
Mike Mannion	Glasgow Caledonian University, UK
John MacIntyre	David Goldman Informatics Centre, UK
T. Radhakrishnan	Concordia University, Canada
Dheeraj Sanghi	IIT, Kanpur, India
Phalguni Gupta	IIT, Kanpur, India

D. Janakiram	IIT-M, Chennai, India
Sudip Misra	IIT, Kharagpur, India
S.C. Misra	IIT, Kharagpur, India
Manfred Goetze	University of Applied Sciences, Germany
B. Srinivasan	Monash University, Australia
Sumanth Yenduri	University of Southern Mississippi, USA
Ram Chakka	Research & Development, MIET, Meerut, India
Lim Chee Peng	Universiti sains Malaysia (Science University of Malaysia), Penang, Malaysia
Palaniappan Ramaswamy	University of Essex,UK
Loo Chu Kiong	University of Malaya, Kuala Lumpur, Malaysia
Vijanth Sagayan a/l Asirvadam	University Technology Petronas, Malaysia
Vijay Devabhaktuni	The University of Toledo, USA
Shonali Krishnaswamy	Monash University, Australia
Asai Asaithambi	University of North Florida, USA
K. Baskaran	Deakin University, Australia
Wanlei Zhou	Deakin University, Australia
Lynn Batten	Deakin University, Australia
Sita Ramakrishnan	Monash University, Australia
Sita Venkatraman	University of Ballarat, Victoria, Australia

Local Advisory Board

B.V.A. Rao	
M. Khalid	SCSE, India
D. Subhakar	VIT University, India
K. Chidambaram	VIT Community Radio and Proctoring Scheme, VIT University, India
M. Adithan	Academic Staff College, VIT University, India
S.R. Pullobhotla	PAT, VIT, India
K. Kannabiran	Students' Welfare, VIT University, India
Margret Anouncia S.	SCSE, VIT University, Vellore, India
Ayee Goundan	Aethros, India
Asoke K. Talukeder	IIIT-B
Deependra Moitra	Infosys, Bangalore, India
P.C.P. Bhat	Philips Innovations Center, Bangalore, India
Pethuru Raj	Project Manager, India
Sundaresan Krishnan	Infosys, Mysore, India
K. Chandrasekharan	NIT, Suratkal, India
H.R. Vishwakarma	VIT University, Vellore, India
E. Bhaskaran	Dy. Director of Industries and Commerce, India

Technical Program Committee

Abdul Gaffar H.	SCSE, VIT University, Vellore, India
Anthoniraj A.	SCSE, VIT University, Vellore, India
Arunachalam V.	SENCE, VIT University, Vellore, India
Balamurugan B.	SITE, VIT University, Vellore, India
Bhagyavathi M.	SCSE, VIT University, Vellore, India
Bhulakshmi Bonthu	SCSE, VIT University, Vellore, India
Chandra Mouli P.V.S.	SCSE, VIT University, Vellore, India
Dhinesh Babu L.D.	SITE, VIT University, Vellore, India
Ganapathy G.P.	CDMM, VIT University, Vellore, India
Ganesh Gopal D.	SCSE, VIT University, Vellore, India
Ilango P.	SCSE, VIT University, Vellore, India
Jaisankar N.	SCSE, VIT University, Vellore, India
Kalaivani D.	SCSE, VIT University, Vellore, India
Kamalakannan J.	SITE, VIT University, Vellore, India
Kannadasan R.	SCSE, VIT University, Vellore, India
Kauser Ahmed P.	SCSE, VIT University, Vellore, India
Kumar K.	SCSE, VIT University, Vellore, India
Lakshmanan K.	SCSE, VIT University, Vellore, India
Madhu Viswanatham V	SCSE, VIT University, Vellore, India
Manjula R.	SCSE, VIT University, Vellore, India
Suresh Thanga Krishnan	SCSE, VIT University, Vellore, India
Muhammad Rukunuddin Ghalib	SCSE, VIT University, Vellore, India
Rajasekhara Babu M.	SCSE, VIT University, Vellore, India
Ramesh Babu K.	SCSE, VIT University, Vellore, India
Ravikanth A.S.V.	SAS, VIT University, Vellore, India
Saleem Durai M.A.	SCSE, VIT University, Vellore, India
Samuel Rajkumar V.	PAT, VIT University, Vellore, India
Sendhil Kumar K.S.	SCSE, VIT University, Vellore, India
Singaravelan M.	CTS, VIT University, Vellore, India
Sivanesan S.	SCSE, VIT University, Vellore, India
Swarnalatha P.	SCSE, VIT University, Vellore, India
Thirunavukkarasu A.	SMBS, VIT University, Vellore, India
Tripathy B.K.	SCSE, VIT University, Vellore, India
Vijaya Rajan V.	SCSE, VIT University, Vellore, India
Vijayasherly V.	SCSE, VIT University, Vellore, India
Viswanathan P.	SITE, VIT University, Vellore, India
Vivekanandashanmuganathan P.	SMBS, VIT University, Vellore, India
Andrews Samraj P.	SCSE, VIT University, Chennai, India
B. Sarojini	Avinashilingam University, India
A. Srinivasan	MNM Jain Engineering College, Chennai, India
Maragatham Natraj	Avinashilingam University for Women, India
S.N. Sivanandam	Karpagam College of Engineering, India

K. Sankaranarayanan	Easa College of Engineering and Technology, India
R.M. Somasundaram	SNS College of Engineering, India
G. Thokappia Arusu	Jayam College of Engineering and Technology, India
R. Pugazendi	KSR Arts College, India
Kannan Ramakrishnan	Multimedia University, Malaysia
Shohel Sayeed	Multimedia University, Malaysia
Lim Chee Peng	Universiti Sains Malaysia, Malaysia
Zubeir Izaruku Daffala	Colleges of Applied Sciences, Oman
G. Prakash	Intel Engineering College, India
B. Baskara Rao	RGMCE, India
S.S. Gantayat	GIET, India
H.K. Tripathy	CSIR-IMMT, India
D. Mohanthy	NII, India
Mohanakrihsna Varma	Kukman University, Korea
Shoba Bindhu	JNTUA, India
K. Komathy	Eswary Engineering College, India
T.S. Pradeep Kumar	VIT University, Chennai, India
V. Saritha	VIT University, Vellore, India
Ch. Pradeep Reddy	VIT University, Vellore, India

Organized by

School of Computing Science and Engineering

VIT®
UNIVERSITY
(Estd. u/s 3 of UGC Act 1956)

Vellore-632 014, Tamil Nadu, India.
www.vit.ac.in

Table of Contents – Part I

Table of Contents – Part II

Steady State Solution to CPP/M/1 Queue with Working Vacations Used in Internet Engineering

Tien V. Do[1] and Ram Chakka[2,*]

[1] Department of Telecommunications,
Budapest University of Technology and Economics,
H-1117, Magyar tudósok körútja 2., Budapest, Hungary
do@hit.bme.hu
[2] Meerut Institute of Engineering and Technology (MIET),
Meerut, India 250005
ramchakka@yahoo.com

Abstract. In order to extend the application opportunities of queues with working vacation to to the performance evaluation of practical systems with bursty traffic, we introduce the CPP/M/1 queue with working vacations. In this queue customers arrive in a batch having a geometric size distribution. We present a method and give closed form expressions for the steady state probabilities. We also show that a stochastic decomposition property exists for the CPP/M/1 queue with working vacations.

Keywords: Vacation queue, CPP, batch arrivals, performance evaluation.

1 Introduction

Vacation queues have formed an intensive research topic in queueing theory for years ([1,2,3,4,5,6,7,8,9,10,11]). Recently, queues with working vacations have obtained an attention in the work of [3], [12], and [2], which are motivated by the performance analysis of Wavelength Division Multiplexing (WDM) optical systems . However, most of the work assume the Poisson arrival model [1,2,3,5] or single arrival model [4], which limits the application of vacation queues to the performance evaluation of practical systems.

The Compound Poisson Process is a process, where the inter-arrival times follow the General Exponential distribution (GE). The GE distribution is the only distribution of least bias, if only the mean and variance are reliably computed from the measurement data (c.f. [13]). It has been shown in the recent work by [14,15] that the CPP is accurate enough to model Internet traffic (i.e.: CPP parameters were estimated from the captured Internet traffic) and to be used for the performance evaluation in telecommunication systems. Therefore,

* Corresponding author.

P.V. Krishna, M.R. Babu, and E. Ariwa (Eds.): ObCom 2011, Part I, CCIS 269, pp. 1–10, 2012.

we introduce the CPP/M/1 queue with working vacations in order to extend the application opportunities for vacation queues (e.g.: to evaluate the optical system presented in [3] with bursty traffic). We derive closed form expressions for the steady state probabilities in a simple and comprehensible manner. We also show that a stochastic decomposition property exists for the CPP/M/1 queue with working vacations.

The rest of the paper is organized as follows. In Section 2, we present the solution for the steady state probabilities of the CPP/M/1 queue. In Section 3, we prove the stochastic decomposition property of the CPP/M/1 queue. In Section 4, we show a numerical example to demonstrate the impact of the CPP on the performance of the system.

2 CPP/M/1 Queue with Working Vacations

We consider the CPP/M/1 queue with working vacations and First In First Out (FIFO) service principle. The customer arrival process is the Compound Poisson Process (CPP) with parameters (λ, ω). Note that $0 \leq \omega < 1$. The probability distribution function of inter-arrival times τ for customers is defined by $\Pr(\tau = 0) = \omega$ and $\Pr(0 < \tau < t) = (1-\omega)(1-e^{-\lambda t})$. Therefore, the arrival process can be seen as batch-Poisson, with batches arriving at each point having geometric size distribution. Specifically, the probability that a batch is of size s is $(1-\omega)\omega^{s-1}$.

The service rate is μ_b when the system is not on a vacation. The single server takes a working vacation at the times when the queue is empty. The vacation duration is exponentially distributed with parameter θ. During the vacation periods the arriving customers are served with rate μ_v. At the end of the vacation period, there are two possibilities: (i) the server takes another vacation if the queue is empty, (ii) the service rate will be μ_b otherwise.

The overall average arrival rate of customers is $\frac{\lambda}{1-\omega}$ and the ergodicity condition for the CPP/M/1 queue without vacation is $\frac{\lambda}{1-\omega} < \mu_b$, which is the same condition for the CPP/M/1 queue with working vacations.

The state of the system at any time t can be specified completely by two integer-valued random variables.

- $I(t) = \begin{cases} 0 \text{ if the server is on a working vacation at time } t \\ 1 \text{ if the server is not on a working vacation at time } t \end{cases}$
- $J(t)$ represents the number of customers in the system at time t, including any in service.

The system is now modeled by a continuous time discrete state Markov process, $Y = \{I(t), J(t)\}$, on a rectangular lattice strip. We denote the steady state probabilities by $\{\pi_{i,j}\}$, where $\pi_{i,j} = \lim_{t\to\infty} Prob(I(t) = i, J(t) = j)$, and let $\mathbf{v}_j = (\pi_{0,j}, \pi_{1,j})$. It is clear that $\pi_{1,0} = 0$.

A continuous time Quasi-Birth-and-Death (QBD) process is formed when one-step transitions of the Markov chain Y from states are allowed to states in the same level or in the two adjacent levels. Due to the batch arrivals, the matrix-geometrix solution method can not directly applied to obtain the steady state probabilities. In what follows, we present a method to find the steady-state probabilities.

The possible transitions of the Markov chain are identified as follows.

(a) $A_j(i,k)$ denotes the purely phase transition from state (i,j) to state (k,j) $(0 \le i,k \le 1; j = 0,1,\ldots)$. This transition happens when the server returns from vacation. A_j's denote the matrices, where the elements are $A_j(i,k)$.

$$A_0 = \begin{bmatrix} 0 & 0 \\ 0 & 0 \end{bmatrix}; \ A_j = A = \begin{bmatrix} 0 & \theta \\ 0 & 0 \end{bmatrix} \ \forall j \ge 1.$$

(b) $B_{j,s}(i,k)$ is the $s-$step upward transition from state (i,j) to state $(k,j+s)$ $(0 \le i,k \le 1; j = 0,1,\ldots)$. These transitions are caused by the arrivals of customers. $B_{j,s} = [B_{j,s}(i,k)]$ matrices are introduced, where the elements are $B_{j,s}(i,k)$.

$$B_{j,s}(i,k) = \begin{cases} B_{j,s}(i,i) = (1-\omega)\omega^{s-1}\lambda \ \text{ if } j \ge 1, i = k = 0..1, s \ge 1; \\ B_{0,s}(0,0) = (1-\omega)\omega^{s-1}\lambda \ \text{ if } j = 0, i = k = 0, s \ge 1; \\ B_{0,s}(1,1) = 0 \text{ if } \ j = 0, i = k = 1, s \ge 1; \\ 0 \ \text{ otherwise.} \end{cases}$$

(c) $C_j(i,k)$ is the one$-$step downward transition from state (i,j) to state $(k,j-1)$ $(0 \le i,k \le 1; j = 1,\ldots)$. These transitions are caused by the departure of customers from the system. C_j's are the matrices, where the elements are $C_j(i,k)$.

$$C_1 = \begin{bmatrix} \mu_v & 0 \\ \mu_b & 0 \end{bmatrix}; \ C_j = C = \begin{bmatrix} \mu_v & 0 \\ 0 & \mu_b \end{bmatrix} \ \forall j \ge 2.$$

Let us introduce the following notations

$$\Lambda = Diag[\lambda,\lambda]; \quad \Omega = Diag[\omega,\omega].$$

Therefore, we can write

$$\begin{aligned} B_{j,s} &= B_s = Diag[(1-\omega)\omega^{s-1}\lambda, (1-\omega)\omega^{s-1}\lambda] = \Omega^{s-1}(E-\Omega)\Lambda \ (j \ge 1); \\ B_{0,s} &= Diag[(1-\omega)\omega^{s-1}\lambda, 0]; \\ \Lambda &= \sum_{s=1}^{\infty} B_s; \\ \mathbf{v}_0 B_{0,s} &= \mathbf{v}_0 B_s. \end{aligned}$$

For $j \ge 1$, the balance equation is written as follows

$$\sum_{s=1}^{j-1} \mathbf{v}_{j-s} B_s + \mathbf{v}_0 B_{0,j} + \mathbf{v}_j \left[A^* - \Lambda - C\right] + \mathbf{v}_{j+1} C = 0,$$

where

$$A^* = \begin{bmatrix} -\theta & \theta \\ 0 & 0 \end{bmatrix}.$$

Equivalently, we obtain

$$\sum_{s=1}^{j} \mathbf{v}_{j-s} B_s + \mathbf{v}_j \left[A^* - \Lambda - C \right] + \mathbf{v}_{j+1} C = 0 \ \ (j \geq 1).$$

Substituting $B_s = \Omega^{s-1}(E - \Omega)\Lambda$, we can write

$$\sum_{s=1}^{j} \mathbf{v}_{j-s} \Omega^{s-1}(E - \Omega)\Lambda + \mathbf{v}_j \left[A^* - \Lambda - C \right] + \mathbf{v}_{j+1} C = 0 \ \ (j \geq 1). \quad (1)$$

Therefore, it can be written

$$\sum_{s=1}^{j-1} \mathbf{v}_{j-1-s} \Omega^{s-1}(E - \Omega)\Lambda + \mathbf{v}_{j-1} \left[A^* - \Lambda - C \right] + \mathbf{v}_j C = 0 \ \ (j \geq 2). \quad (2)$$

Multiplying equation (2) with Ω and then subtract the result from equation (1), we obtain

$$\mathbf{v}_{j-1}(E - \Omega)\Lambda + \mathbf{v}_j \left[A^* - \Lambda - C \right] + \mathbf{v}_{j+1} C - \mathbf{v}_{j-1} \left[A^* - \Lambda - C \right] \Omega - \mathbf{v}_j \Omega C = 0 \ \ (j \geq 2),$$

$$\mathbf{v}_{j-1}[\Lambda - A^*\Omega + C\Omega] + \mathbf{v}_j \left[A^* - \Lambda - C - C\Omega \right] + \mathbf{v}_{j+1} C = 0 \ \ (j \geq 2),$$

$$\mathbf{v}_{j-1} Q_0 + \mathbf{v}_j Q_1 + \mathbf{v}_{j+1} Q_2 = 0 \ \ (j \geq 2), \quad (3)$$

where $Q_0 = [\Lambda - A^*\Omega + C\Omega]$, $Q_1 = A^* - \Lambda - C - C\Omega$, $Q_2 = C$.

$Q(x) = Q_0 + Q_1 x + Q_2 x^2$ is defined as the characteristic matrix polynomial associated with equations (3). If (x, ψ) is an eigenvalue-eigenvector pair of $Q(x)$

$$\psi Q(x) = 0, \ \ det[Q(x)] = 0,$$

then $\mathbf{v}_j$ $(j \geq 1)$ can be expressed as a linear combination of certain eigenvalue-eigenvector pairs and appropriate coefficients.

Since

$$Det[Q(x)] = Det \begin{bmatrix} q_{00}(x) & \theta x - \theta\omega \\ 0 & q_{11}(x) \end{bmatrix} = Q_{00}(x) Q_{11}(x),$$

$$q_{00}(x) = \lambda + \mu_v \omega + \omega\theta - (\lambda + \mu_v + \mu_v \omega + \theta)x + \mu_v x^2$$

$$q_{11}(x) = \lambda + \mu_b \omega - (\lambda + \mu_b + \mu_b \omega)x + \mu_b x^2 = (1 - x)(\lambda + \mu_b \omega - \mu_b x),$$

$Q(x)$ has four eigenvalues

$$x_1 = \frac{1}{2\mu_v} \left(\lambda + \mu_v + \mu_v \omega + \theta - \sqrt{(\lambda + \mu_v + \mu_v \omega + \theta)^2 - 4(\lambda + \mu_v \omega + \omega\theta)\mu_v} \right),$$

$$x_2 = \frac{1}{2\mu_v} \left(\lambda + \mu_v + \mu_v \omega + \theta + \sqrt{(\lambda + \mu_v + \mu_v \omega + \theta)^2 - 4(\lambda + \mu_v \omega + \omega\theta)\mu_v} \right),$$

$$x_3 = \lambda/\mu_b + \omega, \ \ x_4 = 1.$$

Based on [16], the necessary and sufficient condition for the ergodicity of the Markov process Y that the number of eigenvalues of $Q(x)$ inside the unit disk is 2.

We have $\omega < 1$, therefore $\lambda + \mu_v + \omega\theta < \lambda + \mu_v\omega + \theta$ is valid. As a consequence

$$\sqrt{(\lambda + \mu_v + \mu_v\omega + \theta)^2 - 4(\lambda + \mu_v\omega + \omega\theta)\mu_v} > \sqrt{(\lambda + \mu_v + \mu_v\omega + \theta)^2 - 4(\lambda + \mu_v\omega + \theta)\mu_v},$$

$$\sqrt{(\lambda + \mu_v + \mu_v\omega + \theta)^2 - 4(\lambda + \mu_v\omega + \omega\theta)\mu_v} > |\lambda + \mu_v\omega + \theta - \mu_v|,$$

$$-\sqrt{(\lambda + \mu_v + \mu_v\omega + \theta)^2 - 4(\lambda + \mu_v\omega + \omega\theta)\mu_v} < -|\lambda + \mu_v\omega + \theta - \mu_v|,$$

$$x_1 < \frac{1}{2\mu_v}(\lambda + \mu_v + \mu_v\omega + \theta - |\lambda + \mu_v\omega + \theta - \mu_v|) \leq 1.$$

In the similar way $|x_2| > 1$, which means that in order to satisfy the ergodicity condition $x_3 < 1$ should hold, which is stated above.

Note that $\mathbf{\Psi}_1 = \{1, (\theta\omega - \theta x_1)/q_{11}(x_1)\} = \{1, \psi_{11}\}$ is the eigenvector of $Q(x)$ for eigenvalue x_1, and $\mathbf{\Psi}_3 = \{0, 1\}$ is the eigenvector of $Q(x)$ for eigenvalue x_3. Therefore, the steady state probabilities can be expressed as follows

$$\begin{aligned} \mathbf{v}_j &= a\mathbf{\Psi}_1 x_1^{j-1} + b\mathbf{\Psi}_3 x_3^{j-1} \ (j \geq 1), \\ \pi_{0,j} &= a x_1^{j-1} \ (j \geq 1), \\ \pi_{1,j} &= a\psi_{11} x_1^{j-1} + b x_3^{j-1} \ \ (j \geq 1), \end{aligned} \tag{4}$$

where a and b are the coefficients to be determined.

We have the balance equation for $J(t) = 1$ as follows.

$$\mathbf{v}_0 B_{0,1} + \mathbf{v}_1 [A^* - \Lambda - C] + \mathbf{v}_2 C = 0.$$

Then, a and b can be written as an expression in the term of $\pi_{0,0}$

$$\begin{aligned} a &= \frac{\pi_{0,0}\lambda(1-\omega)}{\lambda + \mu_v + \theta - x_1\mu_v}, \\ b &= \frac{\pi_{0,0}\lambda^2(1-\omega)\theta}{\mu_b(1-x_1)(\lambda + \mu_b\omega - \mu_b x_1)(\lambda + \mu_v + \theta - \mu_v x_1)}. \end{aligned} \tag{5}$$

Finally, $\pi_{0,0}$ can be determined from the normalization equation

$$\pi_{0,0} + \sum_{j=1}^{\infty}(\pi_{0,j} + \pi_{1,j}) = \pi_{0,0} + \frac{a}{1-x_1} + \frac{a\psi_{11}}{1-x_1} + \frac{b}{1-x_3} = 1.$$

Note that the balance equation $\mathbf{v}_0(A_0 - Diag[\lambda, 0]) + \mathbf{v}_1 C_1 = 0$ for $J(t) = 0$ is also satisfied.

The average number of customers in the system is easily obtained based on equation (4) as

$$E(J) = \frac{a\psi_{11} + a}{(x_1 - 1)^2} + \frac{b}{(x_3 - 1)^2}.$$

Thus the average time spent in the system is computed based on Little's formula as

$$E(W) = \frac{E(J)(1-\omega)}{\lambda}.$$

Proposition 1. *The following relationship is valid between the coefficients and the eigenvalues:*

$$\frac{a\psi_{11}x_3 + bx_1}{a\psi_{11} + b} = \omega. \qquad (6)$$

Proof. From equation (5), the expression of ψ_{11} and x_3, we obtain

$$\frac{b}{a} = \frac{\lambda\theta}{\mu_b q_{11}(x_1))} = \frac{\lambda\theta\psi_{11}}{\mu_b(\theta\omega - \theta x_1)} = \frac{\psi_{11}(x_3-\omega)}{\omega - x_1},$$

which follows equation (6). ◇

Remark 1. When $\omega = 0$, the CPP/M/1 queue with working vacations becomes the M/M/1 queue with working vacations. We observe that the quantitative r (see [2]) is x_1, and $\rho = \lambda\mu_b^{-1}$ is x_3 for $\omega = 0$, respectively. After a simple algebra, we can verify that $K = a/x_1 = a/r$. Utilizing $\sum_{j=0}^{k-1} r^j \rho^{k-1-j} = \frac{r^k - \rho^k}{r-\rho}$, it is easy to see that the stationary distribution expressed in [2] is the same as the steady state probability distribution given in (4).

An alternative way is to follow the same argument presented in [17] to obtain the rate matrix

$$R = \begin{bmatrix} \mathbf{\Psi}_1 \\ \mathbf{\Psi}_3 \end{bmatrix}^{-1} .diag(x_1, x3). \begin{bmatrix} \mathbf{\Psi}_1 \\ \mathbf{\Psi}_3 \end{bmatrix},$$

which yields equation (2) of [2] after the simple algebraic step.

3 Stochastic Decomposition

The classical vacation queues without batch arrival have the stochastic decomposition property for the queue length. We show that the stochastic decomposition exists for the present queue with batch arrivals.

Lemma 1. *If the ergodicity condition for the CPP/M/1 queue with working vacations holds, the queue length J can be decomposed into the sum of two independent random variables*

$$J = J_0 + J_d,$$

where J is the queue length of the CPP/M/1 queue without vacations and J_d is the additional queue length due to vacations. J_d has the probability generating function

$$G_{J_d}(z) = \frac{\pi_{0,0}}{\mu_b \pi_0}\left(\frac{2\mu_b - (2\mu_b\omega - 2\mu_v\omega + 2x_1\mu_v)z}{1 - zx_1}\right),$$

where $\pi_0 = \frac{\mu_b - \lambda - \omega\mu_b}{\mu_b - \omega\mu_b}$.

Proof. The probability generating function of $J(t)$ is as follows:

$$\begin{aligned} G(z) &= \sum_{j=0}^{\infty} z^j \pi_{0,j} + \sum_{j=1}^{\infty} z^j \pi_{1,j} \\ &= \pi_{0,0} + \sum_{j=1}^{\infty} [a x_1^{j-1} z^j + a\psi_{11} x_1^{j-1} z^j + b x_3^{j-1} z^j] \\ &= \pi_{0,0} + \frac{az + a\psi_{11} z}{1 - z x_1} + \frac{bz}{1 - z x_3} \\ &= \frac{F(z)}{(1 - z x_1)(1 - z x_3)}, \end{aligned}$$

where

$$F(z) = \frac{\pi_{0,0}}{\mu_b}(1 - \omega z)(2\mu_b - (2\mu_b\omega - 2\mu_v\omega + 2x_1\mu_v)z).$$

Since the probability generating function of the number of customers in the CPP/M/1 queue without vacations is (e. g.: by letting $\mu_b = \mu_v$ and $\theta = 0$)

$$G^*(z) = \pi_0 \frac{1 - \omega z}{1 - z x_3}. \tag{7}$$

Therefore,

$$G(z) = G^*(z) G_{J_d}(z). \diamond$$

In what follows we prove a conditional stochastic decomposition property in the CPP/M/1 queue with working vacations.

Lemma 2. *If the ergodicity condition for the CPP/M/1 queue with working vacations holds, the conditional queue length* $J_b = lim_{t\to\infty}\{J(t)|I(t) = 1\}$ *given that the server is not on the working vacation can be decomposed into the sum of two independent random variables*

$$J_b = J_0 + J_c,$$

where J_0 *is the queue length of the CPP/M/1 queue without vacations and* J_d *is the additional queue length due to vacations.* J_c *has the probability generating function*

$$G_{J_c}(z) = K \frac{z}{1 - z x_1}$$

where

$$K = \frac{(1 - x_1)(a\psi_{11} + b)}{(1 - x_1 - \pi_{0,0}(1 - x_1) - a)\pi_0}.$$

Proof. The probability that the server is on the vacation is

$$\pi_{0,0} + \sum_{j=1} \pi_{0,j} = \pi_{0,0} + \frac{a}{1 - x_1}.$$

The probability generating function of J_b can be expressed as follows

$$
\begin{aligned}
G_{J_b}(z) &= \sum_{j=0}^{\infty} P\{J_b = j\} z^j \\
&= \sum_{j=1}^{\infty} \frac{1}{1-\pi_{0,0}-\frac{a}{1-x_1}} (a\psi_{11} x_1^{j-1} + b x_3^{j-1}) z^j \\
&= \left(\frac{1-x_1}{1-x_1-\pi_{0,0}(1-x_1)-a}\right)\left(\frac{a\psi_{11} z}{1-zx_1} + \frac{bz}{1-zx_3}\right) \\
&= \left(\frac{1-x_1}{1-x_1-\pi_{0,0}(1-x_1)-a}\right)\left(\frac{z(a\psi_{11}+b-(a\psi_{11}x_3+bx_1)z)}{(1-zx_1)(1-zx_3)}\right) \\
&= \left(\frac{(1-x_1)(a\psi_{11}+b)}{1-x_1-\pi_{0,0}(1-x_1)-a}\right)\left(\frac{z}{1-zx_1}\right)\left(\frac{1-z(a\psi_{11}x_3+bx_1)/(a\psi_{11}+b)}{1-zx_3}\right) \\
&= K\left(\frac{z}{1-zx_1}\right) G^*(z) = G_{J_c}(z) G^*(z)
\end{aligned}
$$

based on equation (6). ◇

4 Numerical Example

In this Section, we illustrate the importance of the use of the CPP to model real traffic. The proposed model can be used to evaluate the performance of the practical systems with more accurate consideration of real traffic by the CPP process than by Poisson process. We assume the optical system presented in [3]) is fed by Internet traffic. To estimate the parameters of the input process, we use the Auckland traffic trace [18].

- If we approximate the arrival process of packets in the traffic trace with the CPP process, then the parameters are $\lambda = 610$ [1/s] and $\omega = 0.4$.
- If we assume the arrivals follow the Poisson process, then the interarrival times are exponentially distributed with parameter 1016 (i.e.: $\lambda = 1016.67$ [1/s] and $\omega = 0$).

In Fig. 1, we plot the distribution of the number of packets in the system with $\mu_b = 1500$ [1/s], $\mu_v = 500$ [1/s] and $\theta = 100$ [1/s]. It can be observed that the CPP input traffic has a stronger impact on the tail of the distribution of the number of packets than the Poisson input traffic. That is, the CPP process can better take into account the impact of the bursty traffic on the performance of the system than the Poisson process.

We plot the average number of customers in the system versus μ_b and μ_v (the same parameter value are kept except μ_b and μ_v) in Figures 2. The impact of the bursty traffic on the change of parameters on the average number of customers is clearly observed as well.

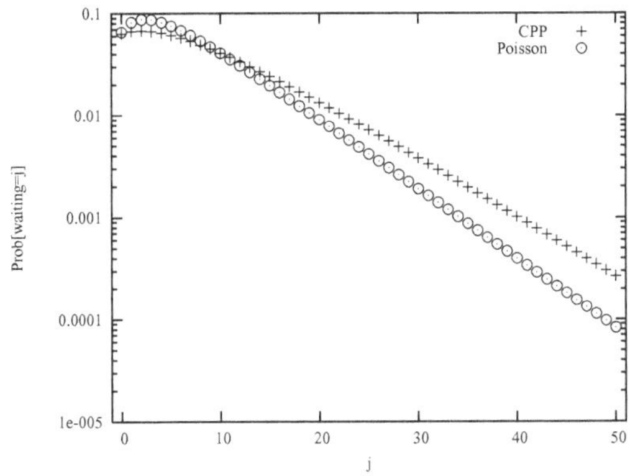

Fig. 1. Distribution of the number of packets in the system with working vacation

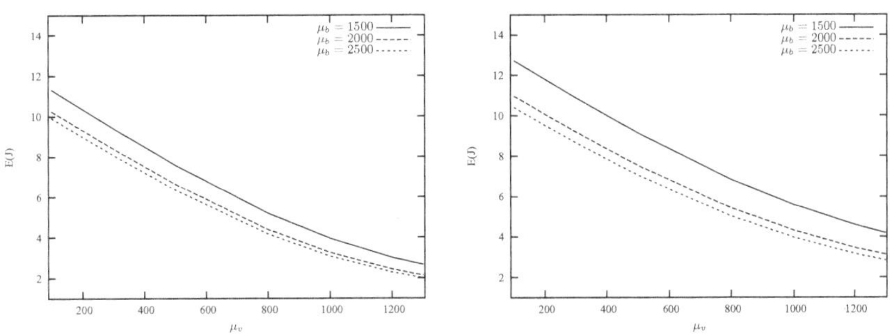

(a) Poisson (b) CPP

Fig. 2. Average number of customers in the system

Acknowledgement. This work is connected to the scientific program of the "Development of quality-oriented and harmonized R+D+I strategy and functional model at BME" project. This project is supported by the New Széchenyi Plan (Project ID: TÁMOP-4.2.1/B-09/1/KMR-2010-0002).

References

1. Doshi, B.T.: Queueing systems with vacations – a survey. Queueing Syst. Theory Appl. 1(1), 29–66 (1986)
2. Liu, W., Xu, X., Tian, N.: Stochastic decompositions in the M/M/1 queue with working vacations. Oper. Res. Lett. 35, 595–600 (2007)
3. Servi, L.D., Finn, S.G.: M/M/1 queues with working vacations (M/M/1/WV). Perform. Eval. 50(1-4), 41–52 (2002)
4. Tian, N., Zhang, Z.G.: Stationary Distributions of GI/M/c Queue with PH Type Vacations. Queueing Syst. Theory Appl. 44(2), 183–202 (2003)
5. Zhang, Z.G., Tian, N.: Analysis on queueing systems with synchronous vacations of partial servers. Perform. Eval. 52(4), 269–282 (2003)

6. Wu, D.-A., Takagi, H.: M/G/1 queue with multiple working vacations. Perform. Eval. 63(7), 654–681 (2006)
7. Li, J.-H., Tian, N.-S., Liu, W.-Y.: Discrete-time GI/Geo/1 queue with multiple working vacations. Queueing Syst. Theory Appl. 56(1), 53–63 (2007)
8. Chae, K.C., Lim, D.E., Yang, W.S.: The GI/M/1 queue and the GI/Geo/1 queue both with single working vacation. Perform. Eval. 66(7), 356–367 (2009)
9. Li, J.-H., Tian, N.-S., Zhang, Z.G., Luh, H.P.: Analysis of the M/G/1 queue with exponentially working vacations–a matrix analytic approach. Queueing Syst. Theory Appl. 61(2-3), 139–166 (2009)
10. Yu, M.M., Tang, Y.H., Fu, Y.H.: Steady state analysis and computation of the GI[x]/Mb/1/L queue with multiple working vacations and partial batch rejection. Comput. Ind. Eng. 56(4), 1243–1253 (2009)
11. Zhang, Z.G.: A note on workload control for an under-utilized server of M/G/1 system. Comput. Ind. Eng. 56(1), 28–32 (2009)
12. Li, J.-H., Tian, N.-S.: The discrete-time GI/Geo/1 queue with working vacations and vacation interruption. Applied Mathamatics and Computation 185, 1–10 (2007)
13. Kouvatsos, D.: Entropy Maximisation and Queueing Network Models. Annals of Operations Research 48, 63–126 (1994)
14. Do, T.V., Chakka, R., Harrison, P.G.: An integrated analytical model for computation and comparison of the throughputs of the UMTS/HSDPA user equipment categories. In: MSWiM 2007: Proceedings of the 10th ACM Symposium on Modeling, Analysis, and Simulation of Wireless and Mobile Systems, pp. 45–51. ACM, New York (2007)
15. Do, T.V., Krieger, U.R., Chakka, R.: Performance modeling of an apache web server with a dynamic pool of service processes. Telecommunication Systems 39(2), 117–129 (2008)
16. Mitrani, I., Chakka, R.: Spectral expansion solution for a class of Markov models: Application and comparison with the matrix-geometric method. Performance Evaluation 23, 241–260 (1995)
17. Do, T.V., Chakka, R.: An Efficient Method to Compute the Rate Matrix for Retrial Queues with Large Number of Servers. Applied Mathematics Letters 23, 638–643 (2010)
18. Auckland Internet Traffic Capture, `http://www.wand.net.nz/wand/wits/auck/6/20010612-060000-e1`

Elastic Virtual Machine for Fine-Grained Cloud Resource Provisioning

Wesam Dawoud, Ibrahim Takouna, and Christoph Meinel

Hasso Plattner Institute,
Potsdam University,
Potsdam, Germany
firstname.lastname@hpi.uni-potsdam.de

Abstract. Elasticity is one of the distinguishing characteristics associated with Cloud computing emergence. It enables cloud resources to auto-scale to cope with workload demand. Multi-instances horizontal scaling is the common scalability architecture in Cloud; however, its current implementation is coarse-grained, while it considers Virtual Machine (VM) as a scaling unit, this implies additional scaling-out overhead and limits it to specific applications. To overcome these limitations, we propose Elastic VM as a fine-grained vertical scaling architecture. Our results proved that Elastic VM architecture implies less consumption of resources, mitigates Service Level Objectives (SLOs) violation, and avoids scaling-up overhead. Furthermore, it scales broader range of applications including databases.

Keywords: virtualization, elasticity, auto-scaling, cloud computing.

1 Introduction

The rapid growth of E-Business and the frequent changes in the sites contents and the customers interest pose the need for rapid and dynamic scaling of resources. Fortunately, Cloud computing Infrastructure as a Service (IaaS) model, based on Virtualization technologies such as Xen [4]; VMWare [3]; and KVM [14], enables agile and dynamic provisioning of resources. However, current scalability implementation offered by IaaS providers, e.g. Amazon EC2 [5] and GoGrid [1], has the following limitations: first, it uses VM as a scaling unit, which is course-grained scaling that can cause unnecessary over-provisioning. Second, it implies running additional load-balancer VM instance. Third, multi-instances scaling architecture is limited to specific application and can't scale-out applications like databases which do not support clustering or synchronization; applications which are not designed to be distributed (singleton applications); or applications with expensive licenses.

Typically, web applications and services consist of three tiers: web tier, application tier, and database tier. The incoming requests go through these tiers to get back with the results. According to the application characteristics, each tier may cast an intensive demand to specific tier resources making it a bottleneck.

P.V. Krishna, M.R. Babu, and E. Ariwa (Eds.): ObCom 2011, Part I, CCIS 269, pp. 11–25, 2012.

For example, Amza et al. implemented a benchmark that simulates the behavior of online bookstore such as amazon.com, bulletin board websites, and auction websites [6]. Analyzing these benchmarks shows that the CPU of database tier of online bookstore is the bottleneck, while for auction sites and bulletin board, the CPU of the web-tier is the bottleneck. Unfortunately, the dependency between these tiers propagates degradation in performance of one tier to the whole application, therefore, to cope with traffic load and eliminate bottlenecks of multi-tier applications, the first step is to detect the bottleneck tier, and then to scale it dynamically.

In this paper, we propose a fine-grained scaling architecture. That is Elastic VM architecture. It implements the scalability characteristic into VM resources level (e.g. Number of cores, CPU capacity (%), and Memory (MB)). The architecture can be implemented into any tier. If any of these tiers turned to be a bottleneck, the Elastic VM scales vertically to cope with workload demand. To compare our architecture with current multi-instances architecture, we implemented both architectures locally, and considered the parameters that control both *Amazon Elastic Load Balancing* and *Amazon Auto Scaling models.* For workload simulation, we installed RuBBoS benchmark [6] which is a simple bulletin board benchmark implemented as two-tiers system.

In the next section, we explain in details the proposed Elastic VM scaling architecture and compare it to the conventional multi-instances scaling architectures. In section 2, we describe our experiment setup and analyze the results. In section 4, we compare our research to related work. Finally, in section 5, we conclude our work and point out our extended research.

2 Scalability Architectures

This section starts with an overview of the current scalability architecture in the cloud infrastructure using multi-instances. This is followed by an overview of our proposed Elastic VM scalability architecture. Afterwards, we compare both architectures performance analytically. Finally, we discuss how the implementation of each architecture influences its performance.

2.1 Multi-Instances Architecture

Implementation of scalability in the current (IaaS) providers, like Amazon and GoGrid, is illustrated in figure 1(a). Users' requests are directed to a load-balancer (i.e. balancer) which forwards it to the available web servers (i.e., VM1 to VMn) according to a specific load balancing policy (e.g., Round Rubin).

To maintain a determined QoS, a controller monitors instances of the web-tier, if the monitored performance metrics (e.g., CPU utilization) of current group of instances exceeded a user specific threshold, controller will provision more instances to maintain QoS. On the other hand, if the performance metrics exceed a user specified lower threshold, it will release some instances to reduce cost.

2.2 Elastic VM Architecture

Elastic VM is a VM that runs a modified kernel that supports on-the-fly resources scaling feature without interrupting the service or rebooting the system. In addition, the hypervisor is extended with interfaces that enable modifying VMs resources by programming languages.

Figure 1(b) illustrates implementation of Elastic VM into two-tier system (i.e., web-tier and database tier). As in multi-instances architecture, a controller monitors tiers performance and scale Elastic VM resource dynamically to cope with workload demand.

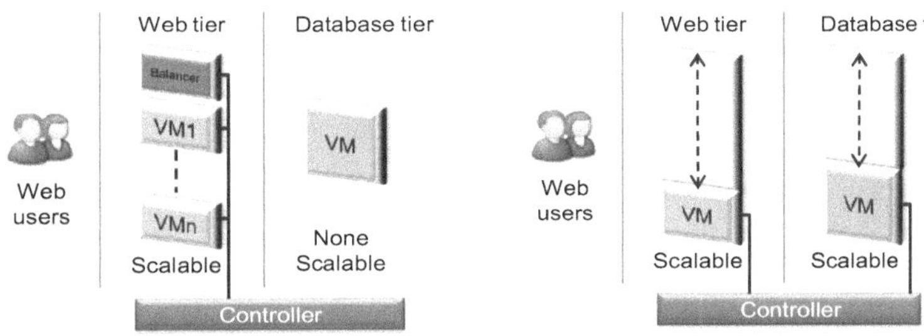

(a) Multi-instances Scaling Architecture (b) Elastic VM Scaling Architecture

Fig. 1. Multi-instances vs. Elastic VM Scaling Architecture

2.3 Multi-Instances vs. Elastic VM Response Time

In this section we analyze the average response time of both Multi-instances and Elastic VM using the queuing analytical model. The analyzed time is the waiting time spent by the packet in the queue until being served added to the service time. Each VM instance with one virtual CPU (vCPU) is modeled as a single-server queue (M/M/1), while the Elastic VM with several vCPUs is modeled as a single queue with multiple servers (M/M/c).

According to Kendall's notation [16], M is a notation for Markovian (exponential) distribution, which means that both the inter-arrival time and service time are exponentially distributed. The mathematical model that describes M/M/c model is as the following:

System utilization ρ is calculated by:

$$\rho = \frac{\lambda}{c * \mu} \tag{1}$$

The probability of having zero request in the system:

$$P_0 = \left[\sum\nolimits_{n=0}^{c-1} \frac{\lambda^n}{n!} + \frac{\lambda^c}{c!(1-\lambda/c)}\right]^{-1} \tag{2}$$

Expected average queue length:

$$E(m) = P_0 \frac{\rho^{c+1}}{c.c!} \frac{1}{(1-\rho/c)^2} \tag{3}$$

Expected average number of requests in the system:

$$E(n) = E(m) + \rho \tag{4}$$

Expected average total time spent by a request in the system:

$$E(v) = E(n)/\lambda \tag{5}$$

Expected average waiting time spent by a request in the queue:

$$E(w) = E(v) - 1/\mu \tag{6}$$

An example to compare the average response time of Multi-instances architecture with Elastic VM architecture is as follows:

First, consider a multi-instances architecture running 4 VMs instances in parallel, each machine is modeled as a single queue served by one server (vCPU). Assuming that each vCPU has the capacity to serve 100 req/sec and the total traffic rate to the whole system is 320 req/sec distributed fairly by the load balancer to be 80 req/sec for each VM instance. In this case the VM utilization $\rho = \frac{80}{100} = 80\%$, hence, *the average response time* = 0.05 and the *waiting time* = 0.04 calculated by equations 5 and 6 in consequence where c=1, λ =80, and μ =100.

Second, consider the same traffic directed to Elastic VM with 4 vCPUs (i.e., c=4), in this case, the system utilization is calculated as $\rho = \frac{320}{4*100} = 80\%$, while *the average response time* = 0.017 and *the average waiting time* = 0.007 calculated by equations 5 and 6 where c=4, λ =320, and μ =100.

The above example, is repeated for different values of c while keeping systems utilization equals 80%, the results are presented in table 1.

Table 1. An Elastic VM with different number of vCPUs (i.e., c) compared with a Static VM with one vCPU (i.e., c=1)

c	1	2	3	4	5	6	7	8
λ	80	160	240	320	400	480	560	640
Average response time (seconds)	0.05	0.027	0.02	0.017	0.015	0.014	0.013	0.013
Average wait time (seconds)	0.04	0.018	0.01	0.007	0.006	0.004	0.003	0.003

As shown in table 1, a single VM with multiple vCPUs, as in Elastic VM implementation, performs better than multiple of VMs instances each with one vCPU running in parallel, even though there is the same total number of vCPUs in both systems. In section 3, we observe how this behavior could influence the system performance in real environments.

2.4 Elastic VM vs. Multi-Instances Architecture Implementation

By analyzing the scaling architectures implementations characteristics of both Elastic VM and Multi-Instances architecture, we can summarize pros and cons of each architecture as in table 2:

Table 2. Comparison between Mutli-instances and Elastic VM architecture implementation

Mutli-instances	Elastic VM
It implies running load-balancer (i.e., additional consumption of resources)	No need for running additional machine as a Load-balancer
Scalability is limited to specific tiers	It is applicable to any tier
It uses VM as a scaling unit (coarse-grained scale)[1]	It is fine-grained scaling while it implements scaling by the real units of resources
Scaling-down can interrupt sessions-based web connections	It supports sessions-based web connections
Booting time of VMs, to scale-out, increases the overhead	It eliminates the overhead caused by booting VMs
Scale-out overhead, cause SLO violation and decrease the throughput	Scale-up vertically maintains better performance, less violation of SLO, and higher throughput
Both software and hardware load-balancer can be a single point of failure	Elastic VM itself could be a single point of failure [2]
It supports all small, medium, and big business	Currently, Elastic VM scaling is limited to host machine capacity, which limits Elastic VM to small and medium business [3]

[1] One solution is to have smaller VM instances (e.g., Amazon micro-instance), however, this solution could reduce the probability of over provisioning, but do not eliminate it totally.

[2] Compared to static machines, Elastic VM ability to scale-up make it more resistance to failure that could be caused by overloading, this characteristic makes it a recommended replacement to static load-balancer instances as an example.

[3] If a global policy is enabled to reallocate VMs according to host utilization, it will be possible to move VMs with lower load into another hosts to make more room for the overloaded Elastic VM to scale-up. Moreover, integrating both Elastic VM and Multi-instances architecture together can come up with fine-grained scaling architecture which is unlimited to one physical host.

One of the challenging issues in Elastic VM is that some applications could be unaware of dynamic resources scaling, especially memory scaling, fortunately, many researches are directed to optimizing applications parameters according to available resources like [9], [8], [15], [19], and [18]. Such approaches can be incorporated into our architecture to tune applications parameters for optimum performance after each scaling.

3 Experimental Setup

For the sake of the practical comparison between multi-instances and our Elastic VM scaling architectures, we implemented a similar architecture to Amazon Elastic Load Balancing and Amazon Auto Scaling models considering the same parameters that supposed to be defined by user. These parameters and the corresponding values, which are used within our experimental setup, are listed in table 3.

Table 3. Most significant parameters that control Amazon Scaling Model

Parameter description	Value
Minimum number of running instances	1
Maximum number of running instances	4
Monitored metric	CPU Utilization
Monitored metrics' measurement period	5 seconds
Lower threshold of measured metric	80
Upper threshold of measured metric	90
Breach duration	60 seconds
Lower breach increment	-1
Upper breach increment	1

Table 3 can be translated by our implementation as follows: The minimum number of running instances at anytime is 1 VM instance, and the maximum is 4 instances. The measured metric is CPU utilization, which is measured every 5 seconds. Before any scaling-down, a check for the new utilization to be less than 80% should be done with the following simple equation:

$$CPU_{next}^{util} = CPU_{current}^{util} * number\_of\_instances / (number\_of\_instances - 1) \quad (7)$$

The scaling-out is triggered when VM instances utilization exceeds 90%. To prevent oscillating which maybe caused by changing CPU utilization quickly, a specific period of time (Breach duration) is left to give the system a chance to reach a stable state after each scale. Finally, the last two parameters in table 3 determine the scaling step size.

In addition to above parameters, during our experiments, we discovered many modifications that can improve the performance of current auto-scaling implementation within the cloud. First, the current implementation of the Multi-instances auto-scaling in Amazon Ec2 considers only one breach duration value for both scaling-out and scaling-down. In our implementation, it is split into two values: breach-out duration for scaling-out, and breach-down duration for scale-down. The small breach-out duration value enables a rapid scale-out. Rapid scale-out is very import to cope with sudden surge of the traffic. On the other hand, breach-down duration should always be larger than breach-up duration to prevent uncertain scale-down, which could be more harmful to the system performance.

The same aforementioned parameters described are applied to Elastic VM scaling architecture but instead of changing VMs instances number, Elastic VM is scaled by changing the number of vCPUs and the memory size.

Testbed Setup: Our experiment conducted on a testbed of two machines (Client and Server) connected by 1 Gbps Ethernet. Server machine has Intel Quad Core i7 Processor, 2.8 GHz and 8GB of Memory. It runs Xen 3.3 with kernel 2.6.26-2-xen-686 as hypervisor. On the hypervisor, VMs with Linux Ubuntu 2.6.24-19 are hosted. Some of these hosted VMs run Apache 2.0 as a web server in prefork mode. One of them has additional mod_proxy extension installed to enable load balancing. Furthermore, a single VM machine runs MySql to host benchmark database.

Workload Generation: To evaluate our architecture, we installed RuBBoS benchmark [6]. RuBBoS is a bulletin board benchmark that implements the essential bulletin board features of the Slashdot site [2]. The benchmark is implemented as two tiers: front-end tier which is a web-server that enables PHP modules, and a back-end tier which is a database stores users information, posts, and comments. The user discussions are started as threads, each thread has a story at its root and many comments for that story. There are two types of users in RuBBoS: *Regular users* who mainly browse, start threads, and submit comments. *Moderators* who can review stories and rate comments in addition to the basic features available to regular users.

The workload is generated by RuBBoS clients which is written in Java. Each RuBBoS client emulates hundreds of HTTP clients. An HTTP client issues a sequence of requests with thinking time of 7 seconds, according to clause 5.3.1.2 of the TPC-W v1.8 specification [17]. One of the important parameters in RuBBoS benchmark client is the *workload_number_of_clients_per_node* parameter. It determines number of running threads that will be initiated in each RuBBoS benchmark client machine. Each thread emulates one user behavior, so for generating variant workload, we set different value of *workload_number_of_clients_per_node* for each workload step.

Utilization window: During the experiments, we noticed small periods of low CPU utilization appear among high CPU utilization values. The bad influence of such values appears when the system exceeds breach-down period. In this case, any uncertain low CPU utilization can instantly trigger a false scaling-down. The false scale-down reduces the system capacity and ability to cope with current workload. From our observation, this sudden low CPU utilization values are unavoidable, while it could be one of the workload characteristics, as we will seen in section 3.1. As a solution, we had a window of 10 values that stores a sorted list of the last CPU utilization. The second highest value of this window (i.e., 90th) is considered as the current CPU utilization. This maintains rapid scale-out but add confidence to scale-down triggers. Each point of the utilization window is measured by calculating the average CPU utilization for 5-seconds period of time.

3.1 Web-tier Scalability

The goal of the following experiments is to compare web-tier scalability using Multi-instances with web-tier scalability using Elastic VM scalability architecture. The comparison includes total throughput and SLO violation. For this experiment we assume (20 ms maximum response time) as a SLO. It is measured as the difference between the moment of packet arrival to network interface of physical host until the moment of getting out with the result. Response time is relatively small; this is because it excludes any delay caused by the network.

To experiment web-tier scalability without any influence from database-tier, we ran RuBBoS benchmark [6] with *browse_only_no_search_transitions* traffic pattern. This traffic pattern is selected because it casts high workload to web-tier and a low workload to database-tier which prevents database-tier from being a bottleneck at any stage of the experiment.

Web-tier Scalability Implemented by Multi-Instances: In this part of the experiment, we implement the scalability into web-tier using Multi-instances scalability architecture. To experiment this setup, we ran the step traffic seen in figure 2(d). Each step shows the number of users (sessions) initiated by RuBBoS client host. The number of sessions seen in figure 2(d) is scaled-down by 4 to fit in the figure. Each instance of web-tier VMs is set up with one virtual CPU, and 1 GB of memory.

Load-balancer: The load-balancer is a VM instance set up with one virtual CPU and 512MB of RAM. The load-balancer software is Apache web server with *mod_proxy_balancer* module enabled. Apache load-balancer has a static configuration files that describe available web servers. During load-balancer running, it checks periodically these servers availability. If one of these web servers is turned down, the load-balancer will spend time to discover and stop forwarding traffic to it. Therefore, to improve the load-balancer response with the possible rapid change of the available VMs, we designed an interface that allows the controller to update the load-balancer configuration files dynamically with each change in number of VMs.

At the start of this part of the experiment, a single VM web-server instance was able to cope with workload of 200 sessions. But, at second 300, as in figure 2(d), when the sessions number jump from 200 to 400, the CPU utilization of the instance was very high. Accordingly, the controller provisioned more VMs instance rapidly to cope with traffic surge. At second #444, the CPU 90th utilization was 50% which allows the controller to scale-down to 3 VMs. At second

#516, the CPU utlization still low, and the scale-down breach time period is passed (i.e. 60 seconds). This allows the contoller to scale down to 2 VMs. Along the remaining experiment run, the controller continue to scale-out rapidly and scale-down slowly to cope with traffic's variation.

Utilization window: With the help of utilization window, the uncertain low values of the CPU utilization (e.g., CPU utilization at seconds 444, 936, and 1884) are filtered by utilization window. This saves the system from the oscillating and adds more stability to scaling-down process.

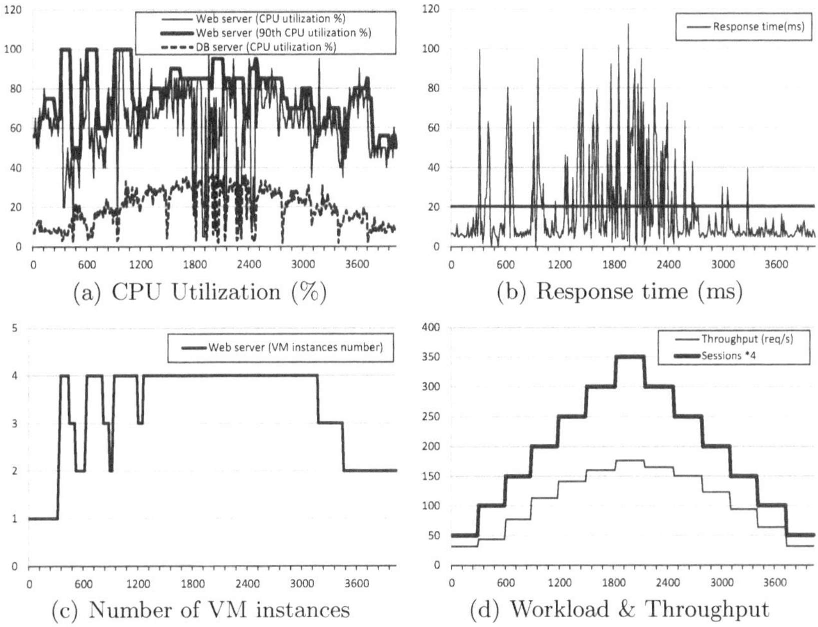

(a) CPU Utilization (%) (b) Response time (ms)

(c) Number of VM instances (d) Workload & Throughput

Fig. 2. Multi-instances Architecture implemented into web-tier

Analyzing response time curve at figure 2(b) shows a high number of violations to SLO, it reaches 23.4% of the total experiment run time. SLO violations are caused by the booting time overhead of the VMs instances which delays its ability to cope quickly with the traffic surge. Also, figure 3(d) shows a decrease in the throughput of the ramp-up step traffic compared with the ramp-down step traffic. For example at step 400 sessions, the throughput for ramp-up step is 44 req/sec, while it is supposed to be 64 req/sec. This is also because of the VMs booting time overhead.

Web-tier Scalability Implemented by Elastic VM: In this part of the experiment, we implement web-tier scalability using Elastic VM. To test this setup scalability, we ran the same step traffic described in the first part of this experiment.

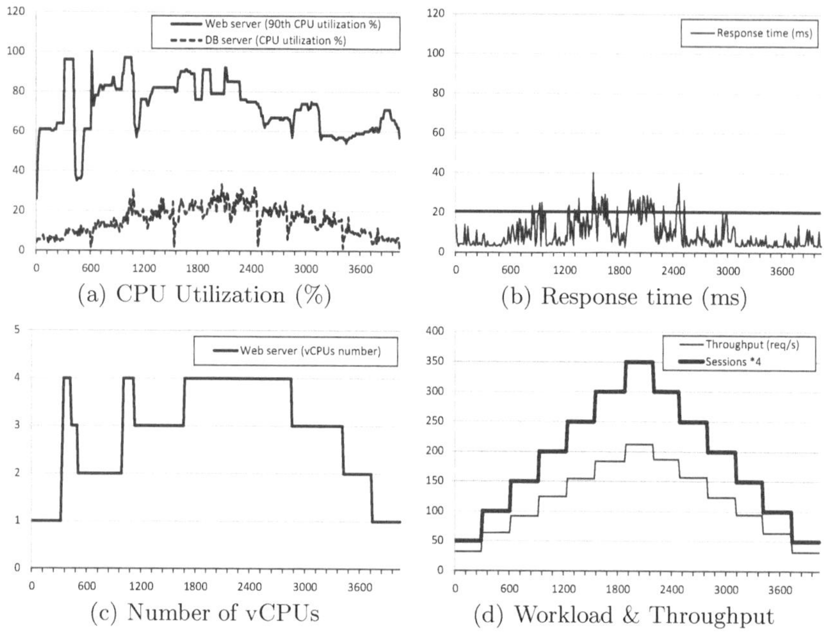

(a) CPU Utilization (%) (b) Response time (ms)

(c) Number of vCPUs (d) Workload & Throughput

Fig. 3. Elastic VM implemented into web-tier

Observing response time at figure 3(b) shows that proposed Elastic VM architecture was able to mitigate SLO violation, (i.e., 12.5%) of experiment run time. It is half the SLO violations in case of Multi-instances architecture. Also, figure 3(d) shows that average throughput (req/sec) for each ramp-up step almost equals average throughput of the equivalent ramp-down step. In other words, symmetry of throughput curve in figure 3(d) means that the scaling-up with Elastic VM does not degrade the throughput.

To compare the two architectures performance, we assume that the Elastic VM is the reference, and calculate the degradation in performance in the case of Multi-instances architecture. The results are illustrated in table 4.

By analyzing results in table 4, we come to the following observations: First, Elastic VM throughput is always better than Multi-instances architecture in case of ramp-up traffic (left side of figure 2(d)), because it copes faster with traffic surge. Second, for high level values of traffic (i.e., 1000, 1200, and 1400), Elastic VM throughput is also better than Multi-instances, this observation confirms the theoretical analysis in section 2.3 where an Elastic VM with 4 vCPUs implies less response time compared with 4 VMs instances running in parallel, this also enables Elastic VM to serve more requests and maintain higher throughput.

3.2 Elastic VM as a Scalable DB Server

In this part of experiment, we will study Elastic VM scalability as a database server. To make database tier the bottleneck, we tuned RuBBoS benchmark with traffic

Table 4. Throughput degradation in Multi-instances architecture

Sessions Number	Elastic-VM throughput (req/sec)	Multi-instances throughput (req/sec)	Multi-instances throughput degradation (%)
200	32	32	0
400	64	44	31
600	92	77	16
800	125	113	10
1000	155	141	9
1200	184	160	13
1400	212	176	17
1200	187	165	12
1000	157	150	4
800	124	123	1
600	95	94	1
400	64	64	0
200	32	32	0

pattern that implied more search requests to put more workload on the database, therefore, the requests type was as the following: StoriesOfTheDay (12%), ViewStory(14%), SearchInStories (25%), and the remaining was distributed as same as the default_user_traffic pattern designed by RuBBoS benchmark.

Figure 4(a) shows that web server was never the bottleneck of any of workload sessions, while database server CPU utilization touch a high value of CPU utilization many times, the controller reacts by increasing number of vCPUs rapidly to cope with traffic surge, and then slowly decrease them to a suitable value. In figure 4(d) we notice some violation to SLO accompany the workload increase, however, the violations did not exceed 5.2% of the experiment run time.

To express the benefit of Elastic VM scalability in database-tier, we compare above result with non-scalable database tier. We initiated the same workload into the same setup but replaced Elastic VM with a static VM (i.e., two virtual CPUs). The number of the vCPUs is calculated by getting the average of the number of running vCPUs in the previous experiment after excluding intervals of high number of vCPUs which are caused by rapid scaling-up behavior of the controller. The average is 1.9 which can be rounded to 2 vCPUs.

Figure 5(b) shows many violations to SLO caused by the high utilization of database CPU for the traffic sessions higher than 800 as shown in figure 5(a). SLO violation time is 28% of the experiment run time, which is five times the SLO violation in case of Elastic VM as a database. The throughput also degrades for the traffic sessions 800 and 1000 by values 12% and 16% compared with the throughput of Elastic VM for the same traffic session number. In spite of the fact that the improvement in Elastic VM was on account of the price (number of vCPUs), but we should remind that we are manipulating the worst case (high traffic surge). Usually, real traffic contains periods of time (e.g., Midnight time) that implies low-workload. For these periods of time, Elastic VM reduces the resources consumption to the minimum.

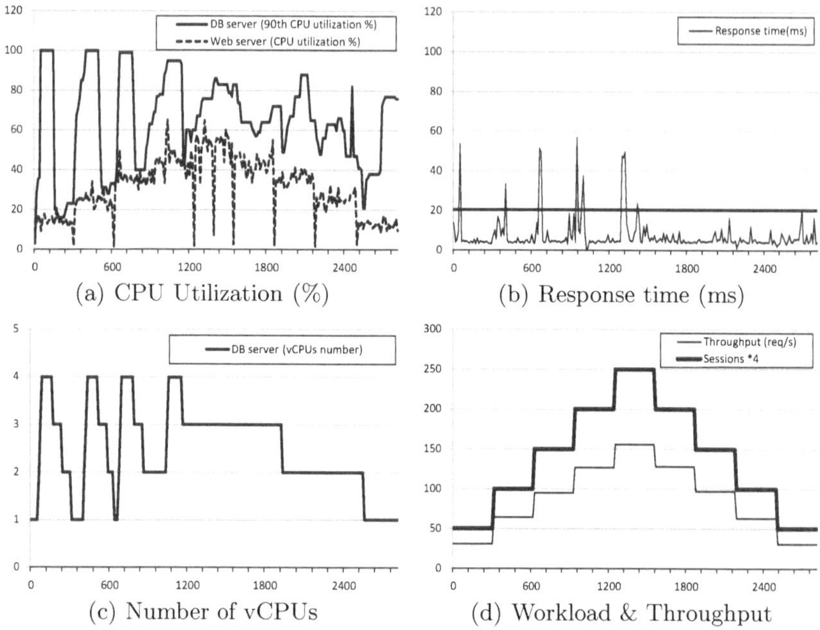

Fig. 4. Elastic VM implemented into database tier

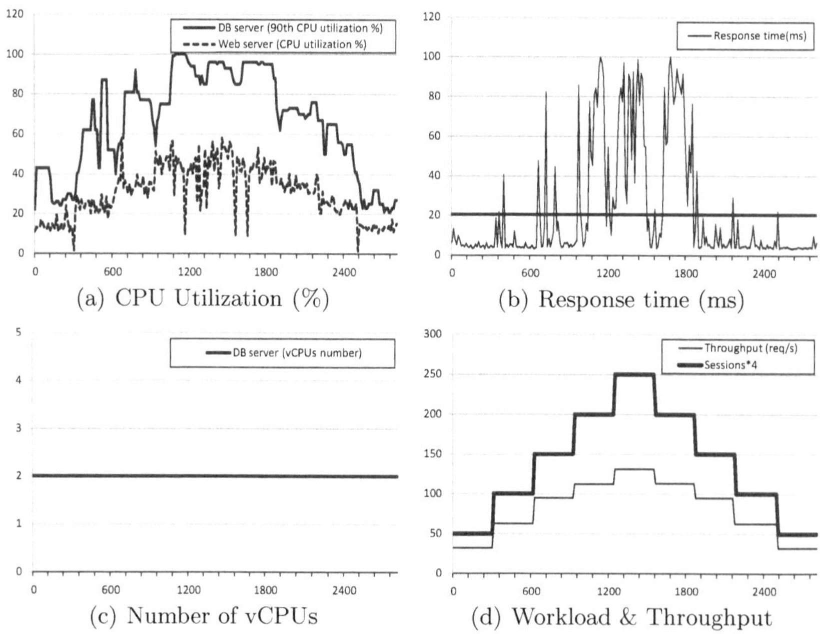

Fig. 5. Static VM implemented into database tier

4 Related Work

On the topic of detecting bottleneck tier, and provisioning adequate resources dynamically to mitigate SLO violation, the work of [11] implemented a prototype using Multi-instances scaling architecture, and developed a heuristic and active profiling of the CPU of virtual machines. The approach considers scaling database layer horizontally but do not discuss associated challenges that could affect the approach feasibility and performance specifically in database tier (e.g., data replication and synchronization). Moreover, the work presents scale-up algorithm with no scale-down.

To predict next workload and provision enough resources to cope with workload surge, the work in [13] implements two feedback controllers integrated with Kalman filter. The first controller, the Basic Controller (BC), predicts separately the necessary CPU allocation for each tier. The second controller, the Process Noise Covariance Controller (PNCC), extends BC by considering the coupling between multi-tier components. The experiment results express how PNCC cope better to the workload changes and therefore maintain better response time. However, the system is sensitive to the workload distribution, for example, it can not track the variables with noise that is not essentially normally distributed.

Many researchers presented analytical models to describe different tiers behavior, for example, [7] presents multi-tier model based on a network of queues, while each queue represents a different tier. The model is able to predict the mean response time for a specific workload. Scalability of this model is realized by dispatching new instances at each tier except the database tier which is not replicable in this model. The dispatching is initiated by a dispatcher at each tier. The dispatcher does not only provision or release VM instances but also balance the load.

By regression analysis of CPU utilization and service time to predict the bottlenecks, authors of [10] demonstrated an approach for performance modeling of two-tier applications (web and database). Despite the lack of dynamic scaling, this approach helps understanding application behavior for optimum capacity planning.

Using queuing theory models along with optimization techniques, [12] presented off-line techniques to predict system behavior and automatically generate optimal system configurations. The result is a rule set that can be inspected by human system administrators and used directly with a rule-based system management engines. In previous work [9], we implemented an online heuristic controller to tune apache controller for variant workload and dynamic resources provisioning, where the experiment results showed improvement in the system performance, reduction of SLO (e.g., response time) violation, and maintenance of a high throughput.

Amazon EC2 Spot Instances [5] is a way to provide VMs with a lower price. It is developed to serve customers who are in need for high computational power but for none online systems (e.g., Image and video processing, conversion and rendering; Scientific research data processing; and Financial modeling and analysis). Amazon EC2 Spot Instances was one of the motivating ideas to our research. Nowadays, Amazon static *Large EC2* instance costs $0.34 per hour, while static *Extra Large EC2* instance costs $0.68 per hour. Implementing Elastic VM can emerge the following service: *Elastic Large to Extra Large EC2* instance which costs for example $0.40 per hour. The lower case is to have a Large EC2 instance, and the upper case is to expand it to Extra Large EC2. As in Amazon EC2 Spot Instances, the idea behind the cost reduction is the dependency on the free capacity in cloud provider. Such approach depends on the probability of having free resources in the same zone, which is not guaranteed. However, having a global workload management plan that runs a complement workload on the same zone, considering the daylight differences around the world, increases the probability of having free resources in the same host.

5 Conclusion and Future Work

In this paper, we proposed an Elastic VM scalability architecture and compared it with existing Multi-instances scalability architecture. The presented work suggests modifications to current Multi-instances architecture that increases its stability and improve performance. Experiment results proved that Elastic VM reduces the provisioning overhead, mitigates SLOs violations, and maintains a higher throughput. Moreover, it enables scaling applications, such as databases, with lower cost and complexity.

Our immediate future work includes developing a global management policy for VMs management. It does not only consider scaling VMs in place but also relocation of VMs to physical hosts with less utilization. We also study integrating both Multi-instances and Elastic VM scaling architecture to enable rapid and fine-grained scaling architecture which is unlimited to one physical host. Moreover, we study the influence of the Elastic VM architecture on the current pricing models in cloud environments.

References

1. GoGrid, `http://www.gogrid.com/`
2. Slashdot, `http://slashdot.org/`
3. VMWare, `http://www.vmware.com/`
4. Xen hypervisor, `http://www.xen.org/`
5. Amazon: Amazon Elastic Compute Cloud, `http://aws.amazon.com/ec2/`
6. Amza, C., Cecchet, E., Ch, A., Cox, A.L., Elnikety, S., Gil, R., Marguerite, J., Rajamani, K., Zwaenepoel, W.: Bottleneck Characterization of Dynamic Web Site Benchmarks (2002)
7. Bhuvan Urgaonkar, G.P.: An analytical model for multi-tier internet services and its applications. In: Proc. of the ACM SIGMETRICS 2005, pp. 291–302 (2005)
8. Chess, Y.D., Hellerstein, J.L., Parekh, S., Bigus, J.P.: Managing Web server performance with AutoTune agents. IBM Systems Journal 42(1), 136–149 (2003)

9. Dawoud, W., Takouna, I., Meinel, C.: Elastic VM for Cloud Resources Provisioning Optimization. In: Abraham, A., Lloret Mauri, J., Buford, J.F., Suzuki, J., Thampi, S.M. (eds.) ACC 2011. CCIS, vol. 190, pp. 431–445. Springer, Heidelberg (2011), doi:10.1007/978-3-642-22709-743
10. Dubey, A., Mehrotra, R., Abdelwahed, S., Tantawi, A.: Performance modeling of distributed multi-tier enterprise systems. ACM SIGMETRICS Performance Evaluation Review 37(2), 9 (2009)
11. Iqbal, W., Dailey, M.N., Carrera, D.: SLA-Driven Dynamic Resource Management for Multi-tier Web Applications in a Cloud. In: 2010 10th IEEE/ACM International Conference on Cluster, Cloud and Grid Computing, CCGRID 2010, pp. 832–837. IEEE, Washington (2010)
12. Jung, G., Joshi, K.R., Hiltunen, M.A., Schlichting, R.D., Pu, C.: Generating Adaptation Policies for Multi-tier Applications in Consolidated Server Environments. IEEE (June 2008)
13. Kalyvianaki, E., Charalambous, T., Hand, S.: Self-adaptive and self-configured CPU resource provisioning for virtualized servers using Kalman filters. In: Proceedings of the 6th International Conference on Autonomic Computing - ICAC 2009, p. 117. ACM Press, New York (2009)
14. KVM: Kernel Based Virtual Machine
15. Liu, X., Sha, L., Diao, Y., Froehlich, S., Hellerstein, J.L., Parekh, S.: Online Response Time Optimization of Apache Web Server (2003)
16. Sayyad, M.B., Chatterjee, A., Nalbalwar, S.L., Subramanian, K.T.: Novel Approach to Improve QoS of a Multiple Server Queue. Int'l J. of Communications, Network and System Sciences 3(1), 83–86 (2010)
17. TPC-W: Transactional web e-Commerce benchmark, `http://www.tpc.org/tpcw/`
18. Tran, D.N., Huynh, P.C., Tay, Y.C., Tung, A.K.H.: A new approach to dynamic self-tuning of database buffers. ACM Transactions on Storage 4(1), 1–25 (2008)
19. Wiese, D., Rabinovitch, G., Reichert, M., Arenswald, S.: Autonomic tuning expert. In: CASCON 2008. ACM Press, New York (2008)

A Theoretical Approach to a Better Tag Cloud Visualization

Achin Mishra[1] and Raj Pati Mishra[2]

[1] Department of Computer Science and Engineering,
National Institute of Technology, Rourkela,
Odisha-769008
achin.mishra.cse@gmail.com
[2] R&D-ES,
NPCIL,
Mumbai-400094
rpmishra@npcil.co.in

Abstract. Tag Cloud is an arrangement of metadata emerging with increase in bookmarking called tagging. It is a method to visually produce the socially linked information on websites. It represents an idea with which different tags are co-related. Differences in font sizes, weight, color and the relation between tags displayed introduce a whole new dimension of search for information on web. Efficacious cloud visualization is necessary to draw attention of the users. In this paper, various tag cloud presentation techniques are discussed aiming the effects of a visually better tag cloud by changing certain properties along with a different proposed technique.

Keywords: Tag Cloud, Social Bookmarking, Similarity Measures.

1 Introduction

A Tag Cloud is a visual representation of text, mostly to put metadata tags and keywords on websites in order to perceive freely without main text. They are predominantly single words, but more than one word tags are also being entertained in the market. There are certain physical appearance features which help to distinguish tag clouds like alphabetical order of tags, and the importance of every tag is displayed with a pattern in font size or colour. This format is very helpful in seeing the most prominent tags. Most of tags are alphabetically arranged for locating a term in the cloud to determine its relative prominence. When used in website navigation tools, these words are hyperlinked to items ascribed to the tag. It is a whole new approach to create metadata with the growth of social bookmarking [3]. Tag Cloud has become a helpful tool in easy retrieval and navigation of tagged data. They have risen with an exceptional increase in collaborative tagging which is trite on social softwares and websites such as flickr, del.icio.us, Technorati etc [1].

P.V. Krishna, M.R. Babu, and E. Ariwa (Eds.): ObCom 2011, Part I, CCIS 269, pp. 26–31, 2012.

Fig. 1. Tag Cloud of Technorati

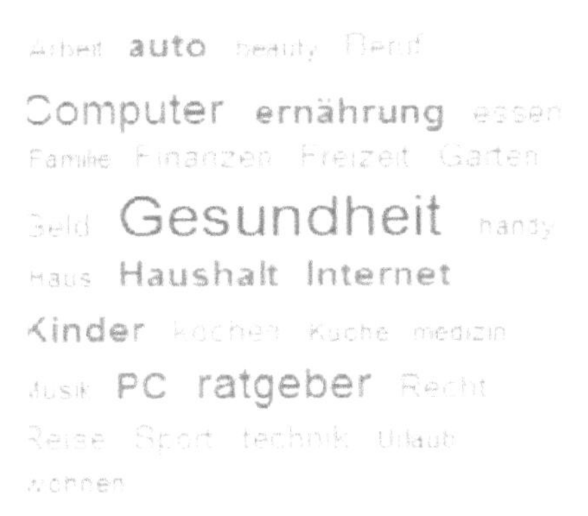

Fig. 2. Other Tag Cloud example

Clouds have produced results helping people to get a high-understanding of the data and to help people in normal exploration [4]. These clouds don't include visualization features like pie or bars but it targets in merging tags or terms. The most pervasive technique used is to map the frequency of a tag to the font size of the term in the tag cloud. The key feature enhanced in this technique is to make the tag emerge from rest of the items showing the importance it holds. Other methods involve the user responses. If a particular tag is clicked many times after it is suggested, that particular tag finds its relevance with the content and helps to have effective tag cloud contents later. Apart from showing the word from text content, parts of the text are also selected to appear in the tag cloud, hence aiming for a better visualization [5].

Tagging has not limited itself to websites only but to various softwares which provide platforms for teaming. Like Novell Vibe OnPrem, a major initiative in the field of teaming, has implemented tagging for the posts or workspaces. One can have the extension to this software, as it is an open source, to have a Tag Cloud with it.

There are various kinds of tag clouds in the market. Dubinko and others present an approach to tag cloud formation which has evolved over time [2]. Shaw has proposed a tag cloud which is portrayed like a graph, where tags are represented and distributed nodes and similarity measures are weights of the edges connecting the tags [6].

But Bielenberg and Zacher [7] present a tag cloud in a circular form where distance from the center and the font size of tags display the relative importance of the tags. The proposed algorithm finds its root in this suggested circular tag cloud along with automated tag clustering introduced by Grigory Begelman[8] et al.

In this paper, I have studied various visualization properties and clustering methods, and suggested a possible approach for comprehensible cloud visualization. I have then talked about the databases and other data structures that were introduced in my experimental works to have a clear understanding behind the scene.

2 Benefits of Tag Cloud

It is lucid in information representation and not any inkling is required to understand it. Most of the websites place it just below their main page to provide an idea to the user about the popular items which are currently enthralling a huge mass. Discussing the advantages it holds and the reason it has flourished, Rivadeneira and his team had categorized four different tasks in sight to accomplish this [4]:-

2.1 Search: Finding the user's target becomes a little more specific. This helps the user to have detailed information about his target.

2.2 Browsing: Exploring the websites become easy. User can casually look into the contents and browse through other recent related topics of his interest.

2.3 Recognition or Matching: Recognizing the whole cloud as data which is a metadata of a subject.

2.4 Impression Formation and Impression Presentation: The cloud can be studied to have an overview of the desired subject. Less prominent tags also provide the details which can be closely speculated as how they affect the subject.

3 Need for a Comprehensible Tag Cloud

The existing tagging techniques in the market have following limitations [8]:

1) Search is limited: Searching in tag space is bounded for people searching from various backgrounds as lexical relations are not taken into consideration.
2) Exploration is limited: Although a great visualization paradigm, we believe that with today's tagclouds it is hard to find more than one or two tags to click on. Tags are not grouped, there is too much information, so that you find lot of related tags scattered on the tag cloud. One or two popular topics and all their related tags tend to dominate the whole cloud.

If we could automatically and dynamically cluster tags, we could provide a better and stronger service. Searching and exploring would be much efficient than the usual.

4 Complex Nature

Visual properties are dealt differently by the people. To demonstrate this, I, informally, asked around 15 students to go through the tag cloud in Figure 1 and choose the most striking one with reasoning. Some chose "top post xeni", some "comics" and others book. When the reasons were asked, they commented on the color and size of the tags, and also how much the selected ones stored their interests and curiosity. No one considered "video" even though it was the largest in font size. Hence, awareness about the visual properties is not the sole criterion for a comprehensible tag cloud because it is not seen by everyone with parity with what the designer intended to make it look like.

5 Visual Properties

This is the list of interesting font and textual properties for the study:-

1. **Font Size:** Large sizes create an impact on users. This has the strongest effect on the users in comparison to any other property.
2. **Color:** It plays a certain role in influencing the choice of the user. The intensity of color of the tags and the color itself directs the users to make their biased choice of the tags.
3. **Font Weight:** This has a reliable effect and underscores the importance of tags. The most pervasive tags are held in bold display so as to help the user reconcile his thoughts before further processing.

Other features like Position, Number of Pixels and Number of Characters do hold minor responsibilities in a Tag Cloud.

6 Proposed Algorithm

The proposed algorithm takes care of the following features: Multidimensional Space of Data, Distances between nodes/tags suggesting their relative importance and an algorithm which computes similarity based upon weights. Grigory Begelman [8] suggested an algorithm. On similar roots, I have devised an algorithm which could serve for a better retrieval of tags and the display features.

Taking up two tables like this: *Table Tags (id: unique ID of tags, text: tag name, URL: hyperlink associated to the tag)* and *Table Edge (start_id: unique ID of tag, end_id: unique ID of tag, weight: weight of an edge, primary key (start_id, end_id)).* Each tag is considered as a node of a graph. Edge table holds the edges and a weight which is equal to the number of times the two tags have appeared together, with a common post. If two tags have appeared for the same tagging space, then there exists an edge between two nodes/tags.

As just evaluating these weights would cause the popular tags only to get selected every time, there should be some mapping technique which is provided by five different similarity measuring functions: Matching, Dice, Jaccard, Overlap and

Cosine. For simplicity, dice is selected for mapping and the weight of each edge is calculated. Then K means algorithm is implemented giving me clusters of similar weights (only one parameter in consideration).

Now, a feasible solution could be in choosing the right points to cut the graph. Here the similarity numbers are taken in account. Therefore it would be easy to cluster it by cutting where the graph edges' weights are small. The "edge" table could be sorted and ordered by weight value and we can prune the graph by:-

$$(E / T) * k \qquad (1)$$

where E = total no. of edges
T = total no. of tags
k = a positive integer k

Other thing that could be done is arranging the tags in the cloud in a radial manner. The inner circle would be according to the token generated from the Search String and the reciprocal of the similarity multiplied with a positive constant will give us the radius to which the tag should be placed from the centre or the central tag.

The main key here is the distance from the centre. This will show the relation between different tags and help to visually create an effect on the user about the importance of tags, and thus emphazing better visual features.

7 Results

The circular Tag cloud has provided a different horizon for the research in better visualization of a tag cloud. It leaves an impact on the viewer just by placing the right tags at the right position measured in the back in terms of similarity measures. This acknowledges the requirements of the user by considering valid suggestions from the user.

8 Conclusion

Various properties and the shapes of the tag cloud are prominent parameters in determining features of tags and the cloud. Alphabetization aiding users, Font size, Color, Position of the tags etc help to navigate through the tag cloud easily and produce relevant results to the user. Tag clouds have indeed lessened the burden of searching and exploring contents by just displaying them before the users; wrapped up in a single term. Modern approaches and techniques are now the fundamentals towards a henceforth, comprehensible tag cloud.

References

1. Bateman, S., Gutwin, C., Nacenta, M.: Seeing things in the cloud: The Effect of visual features on Tag Cloud Selections, pp. 193 (2008)
2. Dubinko, M., Kumar, R., Magnani, J., Novak, J., Raghavan, P., Tomkins, A.: Visualizing Tags over Time. In: WWW Conference (2006)

3. Halvey, M., Keane, M.T.: An Assessment of Tag Presentation Techniques. In: WWW Poster Paper, pp. 1313–1314. WWW Press (2007)
4. Rivadeneira, A.W., Gruen, D.M., Muller, M.J., Millen, D.R.: Getting our head in the clouds: toward evaluation studies of tagclouds. In: CHI, pp. 995–998 (2007)
5. Souto, V.T.: Decisions, ideas and text clouds. Information Design Journal, 165 (2009)
6. Shaw, B.: Utilizing Folksonomy: Similarity Metadata from the Del.icio.us System, Project Proposal (December 2005), http://www.metablake.com/webfolk/web-project.pdf
7. Bielenberg, K., Zacher, M.: Groups in social software: Utilizing Tagging to Integrate Individual Contexts for Social Navigation. In: Digital Media, Universitat Bremen (2006)
8. Begelman, G., Keller, P., Smadja, F.: Automated Tag Clustering: Improving search and exploration in the tag space. In: WWW Conference (2006), http://www.pui.ch/phred/automated_tag_clustering/

Core Temperature Depends on the Processing Load of the Core and the Temperature of Adjacent Core-A Regression Analysis

Subrata Sinha

Centre for Bioinformatics Studies, Dibrugarh University, Dibrugarh-786004, India
subratasinha@indiatimes.com

Abstract. In a multi core CPU, the temperature of a core is an important aspect of study. In this paper an attempt has been made to examine the dependency of core temperature on the utilization of core and temperature of adjacent core. The study was conducted in dual core architecture. The utilization rate and temperature of both the cores are recorded and regression analysis has been made on the data. The result shows the core temperature depends more on the temperature of other cores than the utilization of the core itself.

Keywords: Core temperature, dual core, LCMP.

1 Introduction

In a multicore processor, the temperature behaviour of cores is very important aspect of study. Temperature of core not only affects performance but also power, reliability and cost of the embedded system [1]. The overall theme of this area of research is to control the chip temperature through task migration among cores [2]. Task needs to be migrated to the coolest neighbour core[6]. In this paper an attempt has been made to study the relation between core temperature and utilization of a dual core chip. The result motivates us to further work on Large Chip Multiprocessor (LCMP). The most challenging issue in LCMP is that task migration to reduce the overall temperature of the chip [2]. The result motivates us not to migrate the task to a core whose adjacent core is heavily loaded with any other task.

2 Method

The experiment was performed in Linux environment. To record the temperature lm_sensors used.The lm_sensors package includes a collection of modules for general SMBus access and hardware monitoring [3]. To record the core utilization mp_stat is used, it reports processor related statistics. A Linux shell script is written to record the temperature of cores and its processing load in percentage. Script which will read temperature of cores and utilization rate of cores at an interval of 1 second for 440 seconds .The script is given below.

P.V. Krishna, M.R. Babu, and E. Ariwa (Eds.): ObCom 2011, Part I, CCIS 269, pp. 32–36, 2012.

```
i=0
while [ $i -lt 440 ];
do
  sensors
  mpstat -P ALL 1 1
  i=$((i+1))
done
```

Fig. 1. Script Code

Above code when executed produces output in the format given below (sample given for one second)

```
coretemp-isa-0000
Adapter: ISA adapter
Core 0:     +32.0°C  (high = +100.0°C, crit = +100.0°C)

coretemp-isa-0001
Adapter: ISA adapter
Core 1:     +32.0°C  (high = +100.0°C, crit = +100.0°C)

Linux 2.6.31.5-127.fc12.i686.PAE (localhost.localdomain)   07/07/2010   _i686_   (2 CPU)

02:54:59 AM  CPU   %usr  %nice   %sys %iowait   %irq   %soft  %steal  %guest   %idle
02:55:00 AM  all   0.00   0.00   0.00    0.00   0.00    0.00    0.00    0.00  100.00
02:55:00 AM    0   0.00   0.00   0.00    0.00   0.00    0.00    0.00    0.00  100.00
02:55:00 AM    1   1.01   0.00   0.00    0.00   0.00    0.00    0.00    0.00   98.99

Average:     CPU   %usr  %nice   %sys %iowait   %irq   %soft  %steal  %guest   %idle
Average:     all   0.00   0.00   0.00    0.00   0.00    0.00    0.00    0.00  100.00
Average:       0   0.00   0.00   0.00    0.00   0.00    0.00    0.00    0.00  100.00
Average:       1   1.01   0.00   0.00    0.00   0.00    0.00    0.00    0.00   98.99
```

Fig. 2. Output of script code

To filter the required values from the raw reading fields the another script FinalResult is written is run. The coding of the script file is provided as below

```
sed '/Average/d' MyTempReading.txt > MyTempReading1.txt
sed '/CPU/d' MyTempReading1.txt>MyTempReading2.txt
sed '/all/d' MyTempReading2.txt>MyTempReading3.txt
sed '/Adapter/d' MyTempReading3.txt>MyTempReading4.txt
sed '/coretemp/d' MyTempReading4.txt>MyTempReading5.txt
cut -c1-25 MyTempReading5.txt | tr '(hi' ' ' >MyTempReading7.txt
cat MyTempReading7.txt | tr '[+]' ' ' > MyTempReading8.txt
cat MyTempReading8.txt | grep Core >CoreTempReading.txt
cat MyTempReading8.txt | grep M >CoreUtilReading.txt
cat CoreTempReading.txt | tr -s ' ' ' ' > CoreTempReading1.txt
cat CoreTempReading1.txt | cut -c1-4,6-7,9- > CoreTempReading2.txt
cut -c19-26 CoreUtilReading.txt > CoreUtilReading2.txt
./a.out > TempResult.txt
cat TempResult.txt | tr ':' ' ' > TempResult1.txt
cut –c1-10,13- TempResult1.txt > FinalResult.txt
```

Fig. 3. Script to filter the output in a proper format

The script includes a c program object code, The program is used to read data from two files core temperature and core utilization and outputs in one file in a concise manner.

```
#include<stdio.h>
int main()
{
    FILE *fp1,*fp2;
            char c1[30],c2[30];
    int a=5;
    fp1=fopen("CoreTempReading2.txt","r");
    fp2=fopen("CoreUtilReading2.txt","r");
    while((fscanf(fp1,"%s",c1))!=EOF)
    {
                    printf("%s " ,c1);
                    fscanf(fp2,"%s",c2);
                    printf("%s\n" ,c2);
    }
    fclose(fp1);
    fclose(fp2);
    return 0;
}
```

Fig. 4. C Program code called from the script code

The script result in output in the following format

Table 1. Output snapshot of few records

Core No.	Tempr(in Celcius)	Utilization %
Core0	35.0	100.00
Core1	35.0	7.07
Core0	36.0	100.00
Core1	36.0	30.69
Core0	37.0	100.00
Core1	37.0	98.00
Core0	38.0	100.00
Core1	38.0	98.00
Total 440 readings were taken and statistical analysis was conducted.		

3 Statistical Analysis

Regression analysis includes any techniques for modeling and analyzing several variables, when the focus is on the relationship between a dependent variable and one or more independent variables.More specifically,regression analysis helps one understand how the typical value of the dependent variable changes when any one of the independent variables is varied,while the other independent variables are held fixed[4]. So regression analysis was carried out considering T2(temperature of core 2) as dependent variable and T1(temperature of core 1) and U2(utilization of core 2) as independent variable.Data was analysed in SPSS 17.0 and the result is as follows:

3.1 Regression Model

A linear regression model with two predictor variables can be expressed with the following equation:

$$Y = \beta_0 + \beta_1 X_1 + \beta_2 X_2 + E$$

The variables in the model are Y, the response variable; X1, the first predictor variable; X2, the second predictor variable; and E, the residual error, which is an unmeasured variable. The parameters in the model are B0, the Y-intercept; B1, the first regression coefficient; and B2, the second regression coefficient. The model summary is given below.

Table 2. Model Summary(b)

Model	R	R Square	Adjusted R Square	S.E of the Estimate
1	.951(a)	.904	.904	1.09989

a Predictors: (Constant), U2, T1
b Dependent Variable: T2
The regression model gives a good fit as the R square is very near to 1.

3.2 ANOVA

An "Analysis of Variance" table provides statistics about the overall significance of the model being fitted.The ANOVA table also shows that the regression model fits well with the data (p-value : 0.000) and higher F value.

Table 3. Model Fit

Model	Sum of Squares	Df	Mean Square	F	Sig
Regression	5016.26	2	2508.13	2073.24	.000
Residual	529.87	338	1.21		
Total	5546.14	440			

Table 4. Regression Coefficient

Model	Unstandardized Coefiicient		Standardized Coefficient	T	Sig
	B	Std. Error	Beta		
(Constant)	4.55	.698		6.53	.000
T1	.860	.017	.824	51.32	.000
U2	.068	.004	.252	15.69	.000

4 Result

The results shows that the regression coefficients of core 1 is 0.86 i.e. with 1 unit increase of temperature in core 1 the temperature of core 2 (T2) increases 0.86 units which is statistically significant (p-value : .000). The regression coefficients for utilization of core 2 is 0.068 i.e., with 1 unit increase of utilization of core 2, the temperature of core 2 increases by 0.068 unit which is also statistically significant.

$$T2 = 4.558 + .86\,T1 + .068\,U2$$

The model described above is for dual core architecture.

5 Conclusion

The result shows the core temperature depends more on the temperature of adjacent core than the utilization of the core itself. The result motivates us to further work on task migration of Large Chip Multiprocessor. The most challenging issue in LCMP is the task migration to reduce the overall temperature of the chip. The result motivates us not to migrate the task to a core whose adjacent core is heavily loaded with any other task.

References

1. Xie, Y., Hung, W.-L.: Temperature-Aware and Task Allocation and Scheduling for Embedded Multiprocessor System-on-Chip(MPSoC) Design. Journal of VLSI Signal Processing 45, 177–189 (2006)
2. Carta, S., Mereu, F., Acquaviva, A., De Micheli, G.: MiGra:A Task Migration Algorithm for Reducing Temperature Gradient in Multiprocessor Systems on Chip. In: International Symposium on System-on-Chip, pp. 1–6 (2007) ISBN 978-1-4244-1368-3
3. `http://www.lm-sensors.org/browser/lm-sensors/trunk/progs`
4. Montgomery, D.C., Peck, E.A., Vining, G.: Introduction to Linear Regression Analysis, 3rd edn. John Wiley and Sons, Newyork (2003)
5. Carta, S., Mereu, F., Acquaviva, A., Micheli, G.: MiGra: A Task Migration Algorithm for Reducing Temperature Gradient in Multiprocessor Systems on Chip. In: Proceedings of SOC 2010, pp. 1–6 (2010)
6. Wu, G., Xu, Z., Xia, Q., Ren, J., Xia, F.: Task Allocation and Migration Algorithm for Temperature constrained Real-time Multi-Core Systems. In: Green Computing and Communications (GreenCom), 2010 IEEE/ACM Int'l Conference on & Int'l Conference on Cyber, Physical and Social Computing (CPSCom), pp. 189–196 (December 2010)

Ligand Binding Studies of Caspase 3 Protein with Compounds of *Bacopa monneri* - A Target Protein Responsible for Alzheimer's Disease (AD)

Surabhi Johari[1], Subrata Sinha[1], Sewali Bora[1],
Sagarika Biswas[2], and Khushboo Gupta[1]

[1] Center for Bioinformatics Studies, Dibrugarh University, Dibrugah, Assam
[2] Institute of Genomics and Integrative Biology, (CSIR Lab), Mall Road,
Delhi University, North Campus, New Delhi
surabhibiotech1@gmail.com

Abstract. Alzheimer's disease (AD) is a type of dementia that causes problems with memory, thinking and behaviour. It has been discovered that APP (amyloid precursor protein) is a precusor molecule whose proteolysis generate amyloid ß (Aß) amino acid peptide. Aß is an amyloidogenic peptide that forms senile plaques found in the brains of AD. Evidence suggests that senile plaques are formed due to the activation of Caspases particulary caspases CASP 3 and CASP 4. *Bacopa monneri* has been in use since early as a brain tonic to enhance memory development, however how the components of *Bacopa monneri* function is yet unknown .In this paper an attempt has been made to establish the components activities insilico with CASP 3. We found that among the screened seven compounds Ligand 6 interacts potentially with CASP 3 and has passed all the properties of drug with drug likeliness 0.95, drug score 0.69 , highly soluble, highly permeable, non mutagenic, non tumerogenic and non irritant.

Keywords: Alzheimer's Disease, Caspases, CASP 3, *Bacopa monneri*, Ligand.

1 Introduction

Neurodegenerative disorders (NDD) are characterized by presence of some abnormal protein aggregates resulting in progressive and fatal disorders [1]. Alzheimer's disease (AD) a NDD disease is a type of dementia that causes problems with memory thinking and behavior [2]. Research is being made that activation of caspases is responsible for Neurodegenerative disorder associated with AD [2].It is also found that caspases also play a role in promoting pathogenic mechanism of this disease. There is a considerable evidence that activation of caspases results in formation of beta amyloid and neurofibrillary tangles (NFTs)[3]. As the activation of caspases is at the proximal end and is not associated with neurodegeneration [4]they can be used as potential therapeutic targets for the treatment of AD.

The KEGG pathway entry hsa05010 also shows that the caspases are responsible for celldeath which causes due to aggregation of oligomeric amyloid precursor. [6]. The CASP 3 is present at the proximal end in cytoplasm whose activation results in

P.V. Krishna, M.R. Babu, and E. Ariwa (Eds.): ObCom 2011, Part I, CCIS 269, pp. 37–43, 2012.

apoptosis [2].Thus inhibiting CASP 3 protein may also inhibit formation of amyloid β which further affects disease development and spread through the brain region .

Although current medications cannot cure Alzheimer's or stop it from progressing , they help to lessen the symptoms ,such as memory loss and confusion .The people are given two types of medications –Cholinesterase inhibitors (Aricept , Exelon ,Razadyne and Cognex) and memantine (Namenda) to treat AD symptoms[6]. These medications provide relief for a limited period of time with some side effects such as nausea, vomiting and sometimes liver damage[7].

In India for PD most of the time herbal medications "*Bacopa Monnieri*" also referred as "Brahmi" has been used in the Ayurvedic system of medium centuries [8]. Traditionally it was used as a brain tonic to enhance memory development learning and concentration and provide relief to patients with anxiety or epileptic disorder [9]. .Bacopa herb contains many compounds including – Bacopaside I BacopasideII, , Bacopaside III, Bacopaside IV, Bacopaside V, Bacopaside X, BacopasideN2, Bacopasaponin F, Bacopasoponin E, Bacopaside N1, Luteolin, Apigenin, Butalinic acid,Wogonin,Oroxindin, Pseudojujubogenin and Jujubogenin glycosides which is supposed to have ability to increase mental ability [9]. However how the components of *Bacopa Monnieri* interact with the various proteins of AD is yet unknown. Therefore in this paper we attempt to establish drug likeliness of the various components of *Bacopa monnieri* insilco, by interaction studies of the components with the CASP 3 one way responsible for AD.

2 Materials and Methods

2.1 Protein and Ligand Preparation

Referring the various literatures and KEGG pathway database [6] we found that probably inhibition of CASP 3 may effectively reduce the AD symptoms .The Caspase gene (Gene id 836) [10] on chromosome 4 location 4q34 which encodes the protein CASP 3 (apoptosis related cysteine peptidases) was observed and retrived from Protein data bank (PDB) (http://www.rcsb.org/pdb/) with PDB id 3KJF [11] . The active sites of protein were identified by Molegro Virtual Docker [12&13]. The 3D structure of components of *Bacopa monnieri* and its physiochemical properties were retrived from Chemspider Database for identifying its drug likeliness [14]. The components were filtered on the basis of Lipsinki's rule of five using OSIRIS (http://www.organicchemistry.org/prog/peo/) [15] and Molinspiration [16] that satisfy Structure Activity Relationship (SAR) properties.

2.2 Optimisation of Protein and Ligand

The protein CASP 3 downloaded from PDB (PDB id 3KJF) was prepared for docking by deleting all hetero atoms, ligands and water molecules and optimized by minimization of energy by using AutoDock Vina [17] The grid parameter was set and the obtained structure was saved as .pdbqt. **Ligands**- Ligands designed was obtained from Chemspider as mol format and was optimized by using AutoDock Vina. Later, all the optimized ligands were saved in .pdbqt format.[18,19&20]

2.3 Molecular Descriptors

The molecular descriptors of screened 6 components of *Bacopa monnieri* were predicted by loading them into an online server, OSIRIS property explorer [15]. This prediction process depends on comparison between precomputed set of structural moieties whose properties are already known and the structural moieties of loaded molecules. Molecular descriptors like clogP, solubility, drug score and side effects such as mutagenicity, carcinogenicity and teratogenicity were determined. To calculate the overall drug score, OSIRIS combined logP, logS, molar mass, drug-likeness and toxicity risks into a single number to predict the molecule's over all drug potential.

2.4 Docking Studies

All the 6 ligands , including Aricept were docked with CASP 3 protein in the software AutoDock Vina (MGL Tools for Ligand Docking) [17] using a genetic algorithm and simulated annealing approach to explore wide range of ligand conformational flexibility and rotational flexibility of selected receptor hydrogens . In the aspect of producing binding energy estimates, the AutoDock Vina computes minimum binding energy with Ligand 6 as compared to other ligands [19]. The compound binding site was defined within a 10 Å radius around the binding sites of CASP 3. Standard default parameter settings were used to evaluate the protein-ligand interactions [20].

2.5 Visualization of Docked Complex

The docked complex was visualized in Pymol [21] showing how the ligand interacts with the protein CASP 3.

3 Results and Discussion

Target CASP 3 (Pdb id 3KJF) was downloaded from Protein Data Bank (PDB) Fig 1. It is a Peptidase binding protein consisting of two polymers (Polymer1 and Polymer 2) having molecular weight 30101.32 belonging to Caspase Domain (PFam Accession no PF00656) .It was screened for its active site cavities by using by Molegro virtual docker. There was 1 predicted active site with site volume 215 Cubic Angstroms and Protein Volume: 17228 Cubic Angstroms. The cavity point was

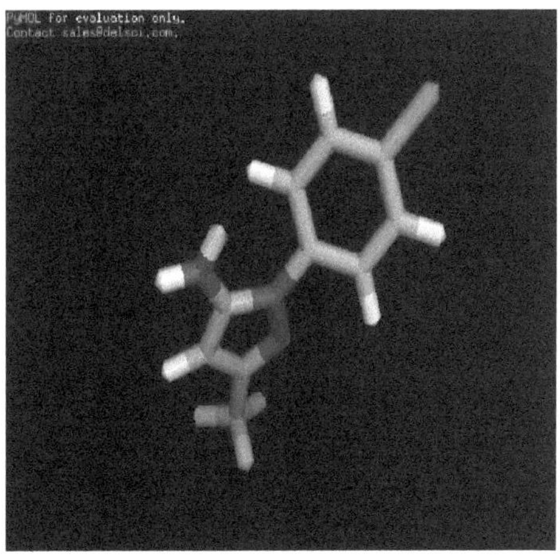

Fig. 1. The CASP 3 Protein (PDB id 3KJF) obtained from Protein data bank

22, - 13, 16 in x,y,z coordinates. CASP 3 protein downloaded from RCSB PDB server is prepared by removing water and other hetero molecules and it was geometrically optimized by Autodock Vina. All the ligands are optimized to its least possible energy conformation. All the components of *Bacopa monnieri* were screened for its toxicity properties. Among them the best components showing maximum drug likeliness are listed in Table 1 where we found that Ligand 6 (Fig 2) is the most important component of *Bacopa monnieri* having the properties non mutagenic,non tumerogenic ,non irritant and no reproductive effect and highly permeable (clogP=5.05) ,very soluble (-5.64) as per the range of clogP(<2.5) [22] and solubility (<1) [23].whereas the other components of *Bacopa monnieri* such as Ligand 2 was (mutagenic and tumerogenic, drugscore=0.12) ,Ligand 3 (mutagenic ,drug score=0.17) and Ligand 5(drug score=0.47) were found to be bad drug candidates. It was found that Ligand 6 follow lipsnski rule of five and was able to form docked complex with CASP 3 protein . The Ligand 6 showed maximum binding affinity with CASP 3 protein (Fig 3) No literature references described about the drug candidature of these components. It is assumed that Ligand 6 is having much higher external hydrogen bonding energy that leads to better binding than any other ligands. Ligand 6 also shows good drug score when compared to other ligands as it shows higher H-bond & VanderWaal's interactions.

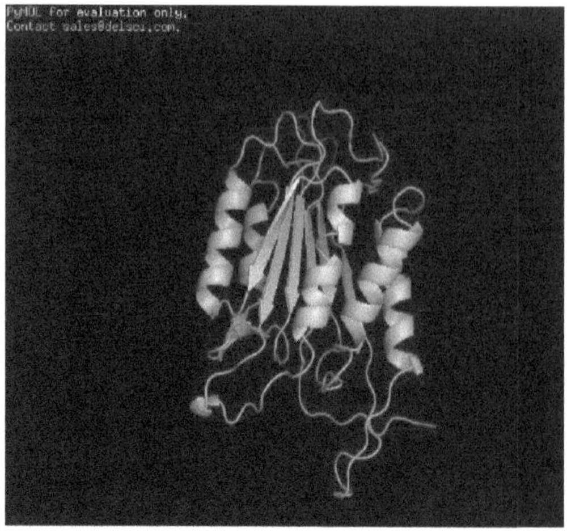

Fig. 2. Ligand 6 designed by Mervin Sketch

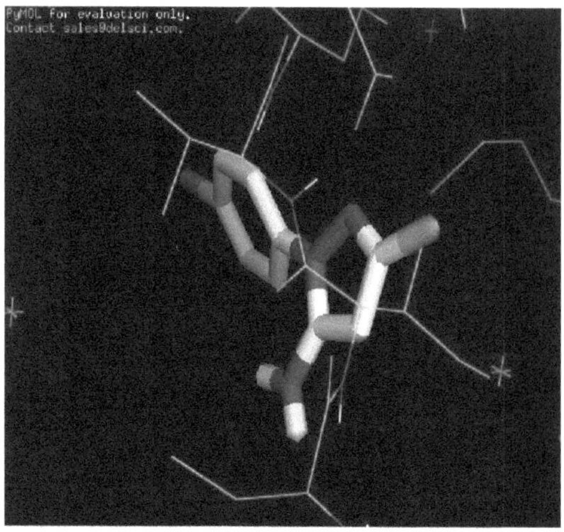

Fig. 3. The ligand 6 inside the cavity of protein CASP 3

Table 1. Physiochemical Properties of Ligands obtained by Molinspiration and OSIRIS

Ligand	IUPAC name	Structure	Mutagenic	Tumorogeni	Irritant	Reproductiv	cLogP	Solubility	M.Wt	Drug	Drug Score
1	Aricept 2-[(1-benzylpiperidin-4-yl)methyl]-5,6-dimethoxy-2,3-dihydroinden-1-one	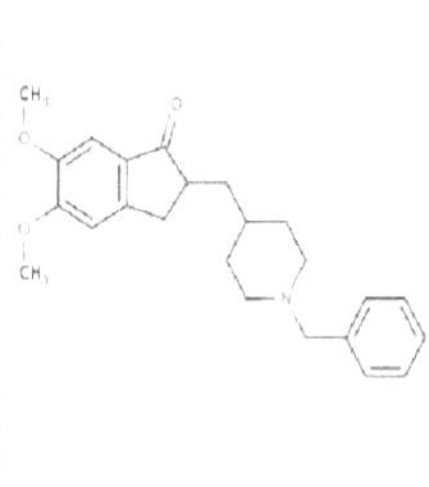	No	No	No	No	4.4	4.3	415	7.29	0.63
2	2-methyl-4-([1,3]oxazolo[4,5-b] pyridine-2-yl)analine	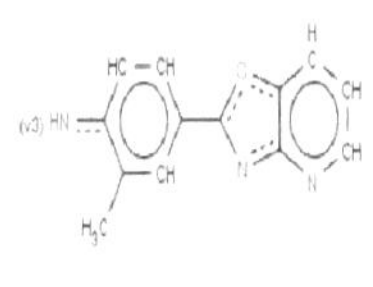	Yes	Yes	Yes	No	2.15	5.08	225.0	11.08	0.1
3	2-chloro-5-([1,3]oxazolo[4,5-b]pyridine-2-yl)analin	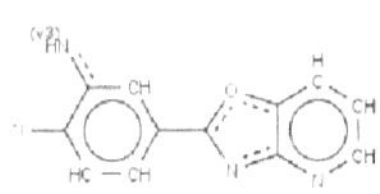	Yes	Yes	Yes	No	2.45	-5.47	245.0	-3.96	0.17
4	3,5,7-trimethoxy-2-(4-methoxyphenyl)-4H-chromen-4-one	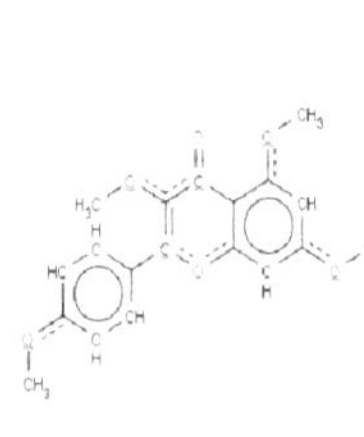	No	No	No	No	3.14	-3.86	342.0	-1.73	0.44
5	1-(1,5-dimethyl-1H-pyrozol-4-yl)-N-methylmethanami	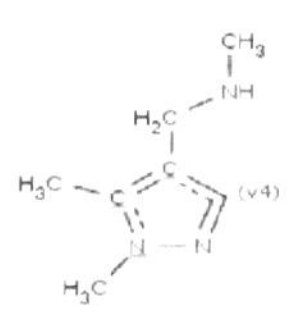	Yes	Yes	No	No	0.8	-0.66	153.0	6.54	0.47

Table 1. (*Continued*)

Ligand	IUPAC name	Structure	Mutagenic	Tumorogenic	Irritant	Reproductive	cLogP	Solubility	M.Wt	Drug Likeness	Drug Score
6	5amino-3methyl-1-(4-chlorophenyl)pyrozol	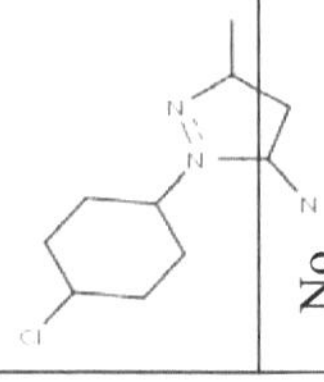	No	No	No	No	1.9	-3.06	207.0	0.95	0.69

4 Conclusion

The interactions between CASP 3 protein and the ligands were studied by using various computational methods. Based on binding energy, and hydrogen bond formed, docking results were analyzed. The results were compared to find out the best ligand which can dock with the CASP 3. Based on these observations, Ligand 6 has high values to inhibit the CASP 3 among the ligands and Aricept (Ligand 1). Thus the *in silico m*ethod adopted in the present study helped in identifying the ligands using the commercial software and online tools for the treatment of neurodegenerative Alzheimer's disorder. This method reduces the time and cost in designing a drug as well as in analyzing the drug likeliness before it enters the clinical trials.

References

1. Brown, R.C., Lockwood, A.H., Sonawane, B.R.: Neurodegenerative Diseases: An Overview of Environmental Risk Factors. Environmental Health Perspectives 113(9), 1250–1256 (2005); © 2005 National Institute of Environmental Health Sciences
2. Rohn, T.T., Head, E.: Caspases as Therapeutic Targets in Alzheimer's disease: Is It Time to "Cut" to the Chase? Int. J. Clin. Exp. Pathol. 2(2), 108–118 (2009); published online (June 10, 2008)
3. Selkoe, D.J.: Alzheimer's Disease: Genes, Proteins, and Therapy. Physiological Reviews 81(2) (April 2001)
4. Rohn, T.T.: The role of caspases in Alzheimer's disease; potential novel therapeutic opportunities. Apoptosis 15(11), 1403–1409 (2010)
5. Rohn, T.T., Head, E.: Caspase activation in Alzheimer's disease: early to rise and late to bed. Rev. Neurosci. 19(6), 383–393 (2008)

6. KEGG, http://www.genome.jp/keggbin/highlight_pathway/map05012/parkinson's
7. Drug treatments for Alzheimer's disease. Alzheimer's Society
8. Kartika, B., et al.: Herbal treatment of Parkinsons: A review. IISPRR 5(3), article-034 (December 2010)
9. Bacopa monniera: Monograph. Alternative Medicine Review 9(1), 79–85 (2004), http://www.thorne.com/altmedrev/.fulltext/9/1/79.pdf
10. National Center for Biotechnology Information, http://www.ncbi.nlm.nih.gov
11. Protein Data Bank, http://www.rcsb.org/pdb/home/home.do
12. Thomsen, R., Christensen, M.H.: MolDock: A New Technique for High-Accuracy Molecular Docking. J. Med. Chem. 49(11), 3315–3321 (2006)
13. Gehlhaar, D.K., Verkhivker, G., Rejto, P.A., Fogel, D.B., Fogel, L.J., Freer, S.T.: Docking Conformationally Flexible Small Molecules Into a Protein Binding Site Through Evolutionary Programming. In: Proceedings of the Fourth International Conference on Evolutionary Programming, pp. 615–627 (1995)
14. Chem Spider, http://www.chemspider.com
15. OSIRIS Property Explorer, http://www.organicchemistry.org/prog/peo/
16. Molinspiration, http://www.molinspiration.com
17. Trott, O., Olson, A.J.: AutoDock Vina: improving the speed and accuracy of docking with a new scoring function, efficient optimization and multithreading. Journal of Computational Chemistry 31, 455–461 (2010)
18. Mervin Sketch Suite, http://www.chemaxon.com/products/marvin/marvinsketch/
19. Randic, M.: Chem. Phys. Lett. 211, 478–483 (1993)
20. Lucic, B., Lukovits, I., Nikolic, S., Trinajstic, N.: J. Chem. Inf. Comput. Sci. 41(3), 527–535 (2001)
21. PyMol a Molecular Visualization System, http://www.pymol.org/
22. Jouyban, A., Fakhree, M.A.A., Shayanfar, A.: Solubility Prediction Methods for Drug/Drug Like Molecules. Recent Patents on Chemical Engineering 1, 220–231 (2008)
23. Gertz, M., Kilford, P.J., Houston, J.B., Galetin, A.: Drug Lipophilicity and Microsomal Protein Concentration as Determinants in the Prediction of the Fraction Unbound in Microsomal Incubations. Drug Metabolism and Disposition 36(3), 0090-9556/08/3603-535–542

Protein Ligand Interaction Studies of DJ-1 Protein Responsible for Parkinson's Disease and Chemical Analogues of *Bacopa monnieri* (Brahmi) Compounds

Subrata Sinha, Surabhi Johari, Khushboo Gupta, and Sewali Bora

Center for Bioinformatics Studies, Dibrugarh University, Dibrugah, Assam
surabhibiotech1@gmail.com

Abstract. Parkinson's disease (PD) is a neurodegenerative disorder characterized by progressive loss of dopaminergic neurons of substantia nigra . It has been discovered that DJ1 is a protein responsible for oxidative stress which causes aggregation of α synuclein fibrils further resulting in formation of Lewy bodies. These Lewy bodies serve as a marker for neuronal degeneration . Therefore probably inhibiting the DJ1 may reduce the formation of Lewy bodies thus decreasing the epidemiology of PD. *Bacopa monnieri* has been in use since early as a brain tonic to enhance memory development, however how the components of *Bacopa monnieri* functions is yet unknown. In this paper an attempt has been made to establish the component's activities insilico with DJ1 that is responsible for Lewy bodies' formation. We found that among the screened seven components, Jujubogenin glycosides interacts potentially with DJ1 but its drug like behavior was not satisfied so an analogue of Jujubogenin glycosides was designed which has passed all the properties of drug with drug likeliness 2.89 , drug score 0.65, highly soluble, highly permeable, non mutagenic, non tumerogenic and non irritant.

Keywords: Parkinson's disease, DJ1, *Bacopa monnieri*, Analogue, Jujubogenin glycosides.

1 Introduction

A genetic study suggests that physiological effects of PD is in degeneration of a part of the brain called substania nigra ,through the loss of dopaminergic neurons which produce hormone dopamine [1]. The research is carried out in mice and drosophila to investigate protein DJ1 and its interactions with other genes [2]. It is known that mutations in the DJ-1 gene cause early onset autosomal receesive PD [3]. It was found that DJ1 is involved to promote neuron survival in aging cells which help us to study the cause of PD and its possible drugs [2].

The KEGG pathway entry hsa05012 also shows that the DJ1 protein is responsible for oxidative stress which causes aggregation of α Syn fibrils [4]. This aggregation of fibrils form lewy bodies which is considered as marker for neuronal degeneration

P.V. Krishna, M.R. Babu, and E. Ariwa (Eds.): ObCom 2011, Part I, CCIS 269, pp. 44–50, 2012.

[5].Thus inhibiting DJ1 protein may also inhibit formation of lewy body which further affects disease development and spread through the brain region.

At present there is no cure for Pakinson's disease but a variety of medications provides relief from the symptoms [6]. Usually patients are given levodopa combined with carbidopa. Nerve cells can use levodopa to make dopamine and replenish the brain's dwindling supply [6] .Other drugs such as bromocriptine, pramipexole and ropinirole mimic the role of dopamine in the brain, causing the neurons to react as they would to dopamine [7]. An antiviral drug amantdine also appears to reduce symptoms [4].

In India for PD most of the time herbal medications "Bacopa Monnieri" also referred as "Brahmi" has been used in the Ayurvedic system of medium centuries [8]. Traditionally it was used as a brain tonic to enhance memory development learning and concentration and provide relief to patients with anxiety or epileptic disorder [8]. .Bacopa herb contains many compounds including – Bacopaside I Bacopaside II, , Bacopaside III, Bacopaside IV, Bacopaside V, Bacopaside X, Bacopaside N2, Bacopasaponin F, Bacopasoponin E, Bacopaside N1, Luteolin, Apigenin, Butalinic acid, Wogonin , Oroxindin, Pseudojujubogenin, Jujubogenin glycosides which is supposed to have ability to increase mental ability [9]. However how the components of Bacopa Monnieri interact with the various proteins of PD is yet unknown. Therefore in this paper an attempt has been made to establish drug likeliness of the various components of Bacopa monnieri insilico, by interaction studies of the components with the DJ1 one way responsible for PD.

2 Materials and Methods

2.1 Protein and Ligand Preparation

Referring the various literatures and KEGG pathway database [4] we found that probably inhibition of DJ1 may effectively reduce the PD symptoms .The PARK 7 gene (accession number 11315) [10] on chromosome location 1p36.23 which encodes the protein DJ 1 was observed and retrived from Protein Data Bank (PDB) (http://www.rcsb.org/pdb/) with PDB id 3EZG [11] . The active sites of protein were identified by Molegro Virtual Docker [12&13].

The 3D structure of components of *Bacopa monnieri* and its physiochemical properties were retrived from Chemspider Database for identifying its drug likeliness [14]. The components were filtered on the basis of Lipsinki's rule of five using OSIRIS ((http://www.organicchemistry.org/prog/peo/) [15] and Molinspiration [16] that satisfies Structure Activity Relationship (SAR) properties.

2.2 Optimisation of Protein and Ligand

The protein DJ downloaded from PDB (PDB id 3EZG) was prepared for docking by deleting all hetero atoms, ligands and water molecules and optimized by minimization of energy by using AutoDock Vina [17] .The grid parameter was set and the obtained structure was saved as .pdbqt. **Ligands**- Ligands designed was obtained from Chemspider as mol format and was optimized by using AutoDock Vina. Later, all the optimized ligands were saved in .pdbqt format.The analogs were designed using Mervin sketch [18,19&20].

2.3 Molecular Descriptors

The molecular descriptors of screened five components of *Bacopa monnieri* were predicted by loading them into an online server, OSIRIS property explorer [15]. This prediction process depends on comparison between precomputed set of structural moieties whose properties are already known and the structural moieties of loaded molecules. Molecular descriptors like clogP, solubility, drug score and side effects such as mutagenicity, carcinogenicity and teratogenicity were determined. To calculate the overall drug score, OSIRIS combined logP, logS, molar mass, drug-likeness and toxicity risks into a single number to predict the molecule's over all drug potential.

2.4 Docking Studies

All the 7 ligands , including Levodopa and were docked with DJ1 protein in the software AutoDock Vina (MGL Tools for Ligand Docking) [17] using a genetic algorithm and simulated annealing approach to explore wide range of ligand conformational flexibility and rotational flexibility of selected receptor hydrogens . In the aspect of producing binding energy estimates, the AutoDock Vina computes minimum binding energy with Jujubogenin glycosides as compared to other ligands [6]. The compound binding site was defined within a 10 Å radius around the binding sites of DJ1. Standard default parameter settings were used to evaluate the protein-ligand interactions [6].

2.5 Visualization of Docked Complex

The docked complex was visualized in Pymol [21] showing how the ligand interacts with the protein DJ1.

3 Results and Discussion

Target DJ1 (Pdb id 3EZG) was downloaded from Protein Data Bank (PDB) Fig 1 .It is RNA binding protein consisting of A chains having molecular weight 20881.20 belonging to class alpha beta and DJ-1_Pfp protein family (PFam Accession no PF01965).

Table 1. Toxicity Property of Ligands : OSIRIS Property Explorer

Ligand	Mutagenic	Tumorogenic	Irritant	Reproductive	ClogP	Solubility	Molecular weight	Drug likeness	DrugScore
Wogonin	No	No	No	No	1.38	-2.85	284.0	1.71	0.83
Levodopa	No	No	No	No	0.94	-1.26	198	1.78	0.9
Luteolin	Yes	Yes	No	Yes	2.4	-2.56	286.0	1.9	0.32
Oroxondin	Yes	No	No	No	-1.03	-2.48	464	0.44	0.5
Apigenin	No	No	No	Yes	2.42	-2.13	272	0.52	0.44
Jujubogenin – glycosides (JG)	No	No	No	No	5.05	-5.64	472	0.37	0.32
Analogue of(JG)	No	No	No	No	2.97	-4.52	376	2.08	0.65

It was screened for its active site cavities by using by Molegro virtual docker. There was 1 predicted active site with site volume 255 Cubic Angstroms and Protein Volume: 17228 Cubic Angstroms. The cavity point was 30, - 11, 9 in x,y,z coordinates (Fig 2). DJ1 protein downloaded from RCSB PDB server is prepared by removing water and other hetero molecules and it was geometrically optimized by Autodock Vina. All the ligands are optimized to its least possible energy conformation. All the components of *Bacopa monnieri* were screened for its toxicity properties.

Among them the best components showing maximum drug likeliness are listed in Table 1 and Graph 1 where we found that Jujubogenin glycosides (JG) is the most important component of

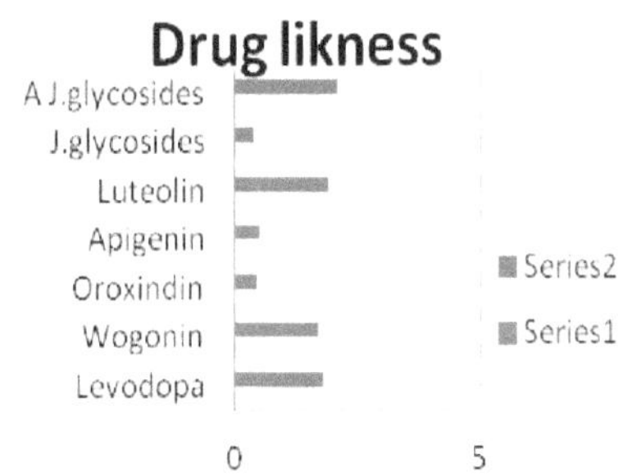

Graph 1: Drug Likeliness Graph

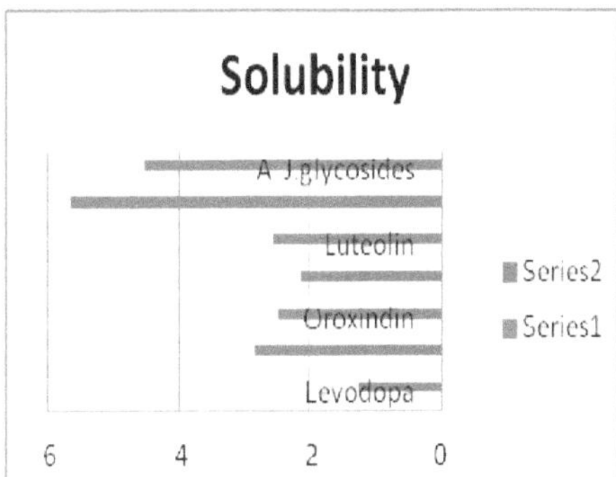

Graph 2 : Solubility Pattern Graph

Bacopa monnieri having the properties non mutagenic,non tumerogenic ,non irritant and no reproductive effect and highly permeable (clogP=5.05) ,very soluble (-5.64) as per the range of clogP(<2.5) [23] and solubility (<1) [22] as shown in Graph 2 and 3 .Whereas the other components of *Bacopa monnieri* such as Luteolin was (mutagenic and tumerogenic, drugscore=0.32), Oroxandin (mutagenic ,drug score=0.5) and Apigenin (reproductive effect , drug score=0.44) were found to be bad drug candidates It was found that JG inspite of following lipsnski rule of five but was not able to form docked complex with DJ 1 protein . So efforts were made to design analog of JG (Fig 3). The analogue showed maximum binding affinity with DJ-1 protein (Fig 4).

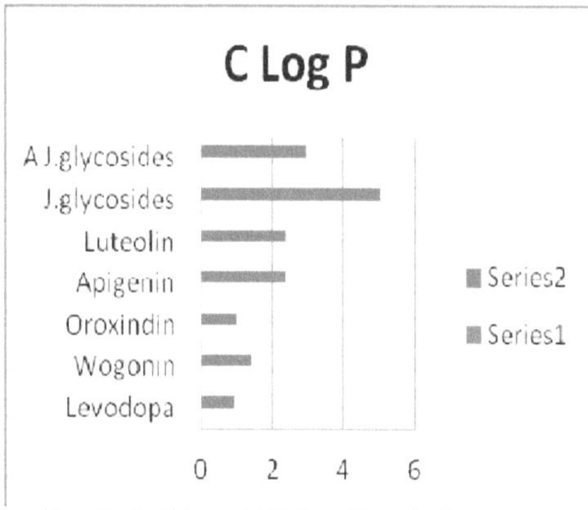

Graph 3: Lipophilicity Graph Pattern

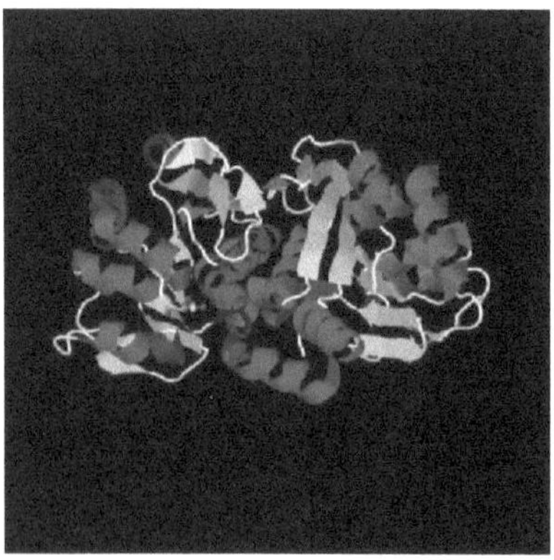

Fig. 1. The DJ1 Protein (PDB id 3EZG) obtained from Protein data bank

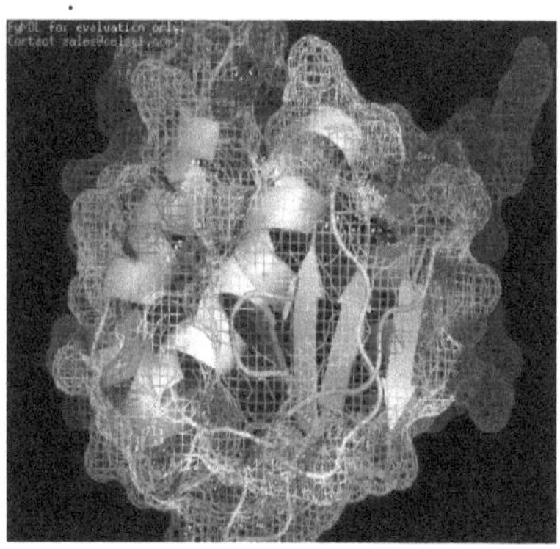

Fig. 2. Predicted Active Sites by Molegro Virtual docker visualized by PyMol. (Green)

No literature references described about the drug candidature of these components. It is assumed that analog of JG is having much higher external hydrogen bonding energy that leads to better binding than any other ligands. JG also shows good drug score when compared to other ligands as it shows higher H-bond & Vander Waal's interactions.

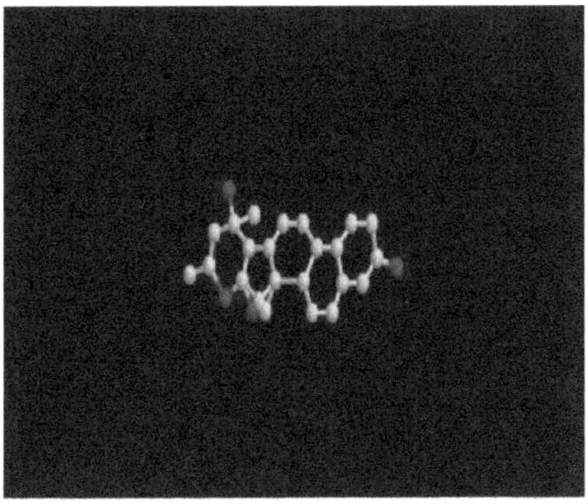

Fig. 3. Analogue of Jujubogenin glycosides (JG) designed by Mervin Sketch

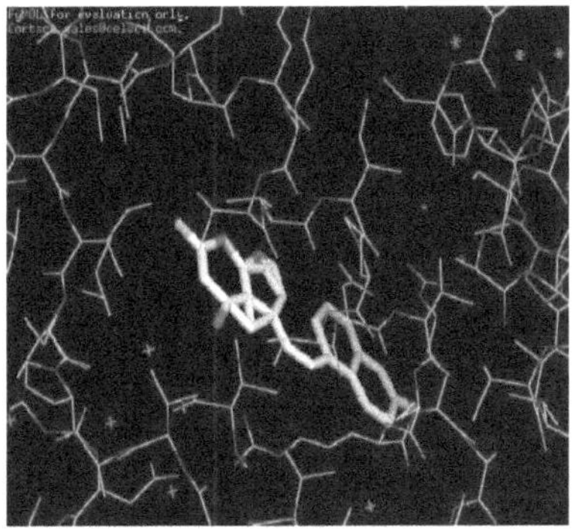

Fig. 4. The ligand (JG) inside the cavity of protein DJ 1

4 Conclusion

The interactions between DJ1 protein and the ligands were studied by using various computational methods. Based on binding energy, and hydrogen bond formed, docking results were analyzed. The results were compared to find out the best ligand which can inhibit the property of the DJ1. Based on these observations, analog of JG is the most potent ligand among the other ligands . Thus the *in silico m*ethod adopted in the present study helped in identifying the ligands using the commercial software and online tools for the treatment of neurodegenerative Parkinson's disorder. This method reduces the time and cost in designing a drug as well as in analyzing the drug likeliness before it enters the clinical trials.

References

1. Suzzane, L., Alexis, B.: Parkinson's Disease:from monogenic forms to genetic susceptibility factors. Human Molecular Genetics 18(1), 48–59 (2009)
2. Aron, L., et al.: Pro-Survival Role of Parkinsons Associated Gene DJ-1 Revealed in Trophically Impaired Dopaminergic Neurons. PLoS Biology 8(4), e1000349 (2010), doi:10.1371/journal.pbio.1000349
3. Xu, J., et al.: The Parkinson's Disease-associated DJ-1 Protein is a transcriptional co-activator that protects against neuronal apoptosis. Human Molecular Genetics 14(9), 1231–1241 (2005), doi:10.1093/hmg/ddi134
4. KEGG. `http://www.genome.jp/keggbin/highlight_pathway/map05012/parkinson's`
5. Hiroo, Y., Jie, S.: Absence of Dopaminergic neuronal degeneration and oxidative damage in aged DJ-1 deficient mice. Molecular Neurodegeneration Biomed. Central 2(10) (2007), doi:10.1186/1750-1326-2-10

6. Devi, M.L.V., et al.: Analogues of Carbidopa: Insilico Design and development of Novel Dopa Decarboxylase inhibitor in the treatment of Parkinson's Disease. IPSR 3(4), 1176–1181 (2011)
7. National Institute of Neurological Disorders and Stroke, NINDS Parkinson's Disease Information Page: National Institue of Health
8. Kartika, B., et al.: Herbal treatment of Parkinsons: A review. IISPRR 5(3), article-034 (December 2010)
9. Bacopa monniera: Monograph. Alternative Medicine Review 9(1), 79–85 (2004), http://www.thorne.com/altmedrev/.fulltext/9/1/79.pdf
10. National Center for Biotechnology Information, http://www.ncbi.nlm.nih.gov
11. Protein Data Ban, http://www.rcsb.org/pdb/home/home.do
12. Thomsen, R., Christensen, M.H.: MolDock: A New Technique for High-Accuracy Molecular Docking. J. Med. Chem. 49(11), 3315–3321 (2006)
13. Gehlhaar, D.K., Verkhivker, G., Rejto, P.A., Fogel, D.B., Fogel, L.J., Freer, S.T.: Docking Conformationally Flexible Small Molecules Into a Protein Binding Site Through Evolutionary Programming. In: Proceedings of the FourthInternational Conference on Evolutionary Programming, pp. 615–627 (1995)
14. Chem Spider, http://www.chemspider.com
15. OSIRIS Property Explorer, http://www.organicchemistry.org/prog/peo/
16. Molinspiration, http://www.molinspiration.com
17. Trott, O., Olson, A.J.: AutoDockVina: improving the speed and accuracy of docking with a new scoring function, efficient optimization and multithreading. Journal of Computational Chemistry 31, 455–461 (2010)
18. http://www.chemaxon.com/products/marvin/marvinsketch/
19. Randic, M.: Chem. Phys. Lett. 211, 478–483 (1993)
20. Lucic, B., Lukovits, I., Nikolic, S., Trinajstic, N.: J. Chem. Inf. Comput. Sci. 41(3), 527–535 (2001)
21. PyMol a Molecular Visualization System, http://www.pymol.org/
22. Jouyban, A., Fakhree, M.A.A., Shayanfar, A.: Solubility Prediction Methods for Drug/Drug Like Molecules. Recent Patents on Chemical Engineering 1, 220–231 (2008)
23. Gertz, M., Kilford, P.J., Houston, J.B., Galetin, A.: Drug Lipophilicity and Microsomal Protein Concentration as Determinants in the Prediction of the Fraction Unbound in Microsomal Incubations. Drug Metabolism and Disposition 36(3), 0090-9556/08/3603-535–542

Towards Development of an Intelligent Framework for Managing Authorization Service in Ubiquitous Enterprise Computing Environment

Supreet Kaur[1] and Kawaljeet Singh[2]

[1] Punjabi University, Regional Centre for IT & Management, Mohali, India
skaur.gujral@gmail.com
[2] UCC, Punjabi University, Patiala, India
singhkawaljeet@rediffmail.com

Abstract. Traditional security mechanisms and models may not provide adequate guarantees to deal with the new exposures and vulnerabilities of emerging Ubiquitous computing environment. Ubiquitous Computing environment characteristics make the security problem complex and challenging. In this paper we discuss how computationally intelligent based approach can be used to design an intelligent model for managing security issues related to authorization service in ubiquitous enterprise computing environment.

Keywords: Access Control, Computational Intelligence, Ubiquitous Computing.

1 Introduction

Ubiquitous computing, a concept proposed by Mark Weiser [1] is seen as a fundamental development direction for the 21st century's computing technology. Ubiquitous Enterprise Computing Environment has the four main characteristics i.e. Computing everywhere, Content everywhere, Connectivity everywhere and Context Aware Service. All of these trends make ubiquitous computing environment convenient and powerful but at same time also brings with them new challenges to the security of enterprise computing. To meet the security challenges, traditional security mechanisms and models may not provide adequate guarantees to deal with the new exposures and vulnerabilities. Therefore, the traditional forms of computer security need to be reexamined and enhanced for realization of secure Ubiquitous enterprise computing environments.

2 Ubiquitous Computing Security

In this section we talk about the major challenges for securing Ubiquitous enterprise computing environment. An Enterprise Users expect high degree of information availability anytime and anywhere as needed, leading to serious security risks and

P.V. Krishna, M.R. Babu, and E. Ariwa (Eds.): ObCom 2011, Part I, CCIS 269, pp. 51–60, 2012.

authorization problems. Realization of secure authorization service in Ubiquitous Enterprise computing environment is one of the major areas of focus among research community. In this context some important issues that need to be addressed are

User Mobility and Ubiquity. Ubiquitous Enterprise computing environment consists of large no. of network entities and most of the interactions are ad-hoc in nature. The authorization decision may need to be taken on the basis of partial, potentially unreliable or out of date information.

Multiple Enterprise Administrative Domains. Numerous network entities, roaming across different domains in ubiquitous network, are usually unknown to the Local Domain system.

Distributed Authorization Architecture. Ubiquitous enterprise computing environments often cannot use a centralized authorization control model because the users requesting resources and the resources themselves are not known a priori.

Context Awareness. In ubiquitous computing environment the authorization decision process should be able to capture the different and dynamic context and situational information and integrate them with users, devices and resources.

Any security solution for secure authorization service in Ubiquitous Computing Environment should take the above issues into consideration. In this paper computational intelligence approach based solution is proposed to address the challenges and dynamism of Ubiquitous Computing environment.

3 Computational Intelligence for Ubiquitous Computing Security

Computational Intelligence (CI) is a fairly new research field with competing definitions. In Computational Intelligence - A Logical Approach [2], the authors define CI as "Computational Intelligence is the study of the design of intelligent agents - An intelligent agent is a system that acts intelligently. What it does is appropriate for its circumstances and its goal, it is flexible to changing environments and changing goals, it learns from experience, and it makes appropriate choices given perceptual limitations and finite computation."

In ubiquitous enterprise computing environment Computational Intelligence can play an important role to solve the security problems related to authorization service. The main challenge of Ubiquitous computing environment is to control access to service and information only to authorized users. In this work we propose to design an intelligent authorization framework consisting of intelligent authorization infrastructure and context infrastructure. The authorization infrastructure makes decision intelligently to grant access rights based on both contexts and policies specified with a flexible specification language. The context infrastructure provides contexts at various levels of abstraction. The major challenge is imposed by the heterogeneous characteristics of the context information in Ubiquitous computing environment. Context is key element that controls authorization privileges in Ubiquitous computing environment .To establish authorized relationship between entities that need services and entities that provide services, novel methods and techniques are required for processing of context information. Characteristics of computational intelligence (CI) systems, such as adaptation, fault tolerance, high computational speed and error resilience in the face of heterogeneous, noisy and complex context information fit the requirements of building a good authorization model to meet the dynamic authorization requirements of ubiquitous enterprise computing environment.

4 Proposed Framework

The research methodology proposed is based on Hybrid Computational Intelligence approach. It is well known that intelligent systems, which can provide human-like expertise such as domain knowledge, uncertain reasoning, and adaptation to a noisy and time-varying environment, are important in tackling practical computing problems. Hybridization of different intelligent systems is an innovative approach to construct computationally intelligent systems consisting of artificial neural network, fuzzy inference systems and other evolutionary computation techniques.

Hybrid systems combine two or more individual technologies (fuzzy logic, neural networks and genetic algorithms) for building intelligent systems. The individual technologies represent the various aspects of human intelligence that are necessary for enhancing performance. However, all individual technologies have their constraints and limitations. Having the possibility to put two or more of them together in a hybrid system increases the system's capabilities and performance, and also leads to a better understanding of human cognition. Hybrid architectures are classified into the following four categories

Combination. Typical hybrid architecture of this kind is a sequential combination of neural networks and rule or fuzzy rule-based systems.

Integration. This architecture usually uses three or more individual technologies and introduces some hierarchy among the individual subsystems. For example, one subsystem may be dominant and may distribute tasks to other subsystems.

Fusion. A tight-coupling and merging architecture usually based on the strong mathematical optimization capability of genetic algorithms and neural networks. When other techniques incorporate these features, the learning efficiency of the resulting system is increased.

Association. The architecture that includes different individual technologies, interchanging knowledge and facts on a pair wise basis.

In this paper we propose to use Association based Hybrid Architecture. The processes in the proposed framework would include learning i.e. the acquisition of context information and policy rules as data cases .These data cases is to be used as training data for learning with computationally intelligent agents. The results are to be applied to an intelligent authorization inference framework for automating the authorization service in ubiquitous computing environment. The next process is reasoning i.e. including the policy rules to reach approximation or definite decision. The final process is self correction for reliable authorization service.

Main focus of our work is to investigate the idea of intelligent and dynamic resource access management in ubiquitous computing environment. Through this investigation we will demonstrate how generic Authorization system by application of intelligent processing can be adapted into intelligent system. We term the framework as Ubiquitous Intelligent Authorization framework (Ubiq-IAF). At the core of the Ubiq-IAF, there is an intelligent authorization engine (IAE) that should be flexible enough to support the diversity of user communication in Ubiquitous Computing Environment. Secondly it should be reconfigurable to adapt to the dynamic nature of communication in Ubiquitous Computing environment. Thirdly it should have intelligence to sense the multiple environment attributes, understanding context, time diversity and spatial diversity options. Lastly it should be capable of Learning from experience and Knowledge and adapt the authorization process to improve required quality of security service. A typical computational intelligent system is illustrated in Fig. 1. These systems take the input through sensors and respond to the input through actuator.

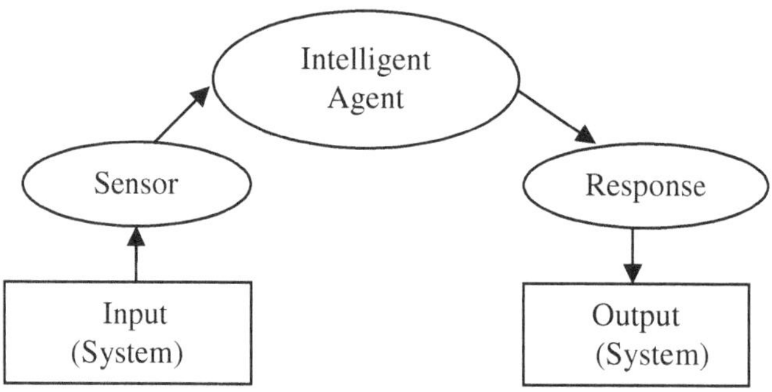

Fig. 1. Typical Computational Intelligent agent diagram for providing Authorization service with intelligence

The intelligent agent provides the learning and intelligent algorithms that understand the environment so as to adjust the mode of user interaction i.e. type of access etc. To meet the design goal of Ubiq-IAF, IAE at a minimum is required to perform the three main functions i.e. Coordination of set of sensors inputs, Learning cum Decision making system and Monitoring feedback improve decision making For Authorization system to become intelligent we have to address many aspects in Ubiquitous computing and Computational Intelligence. IAE is the application of Computational Intelligence and adaptation to Ubiquitous Computing environment. We implement IAE as a processing engine to translate observation about the environment to intelligent authorization action. We begin with description of the design of IAE. The IAE is the intelligent core of Ubiq-IAF described by Fig. 2.

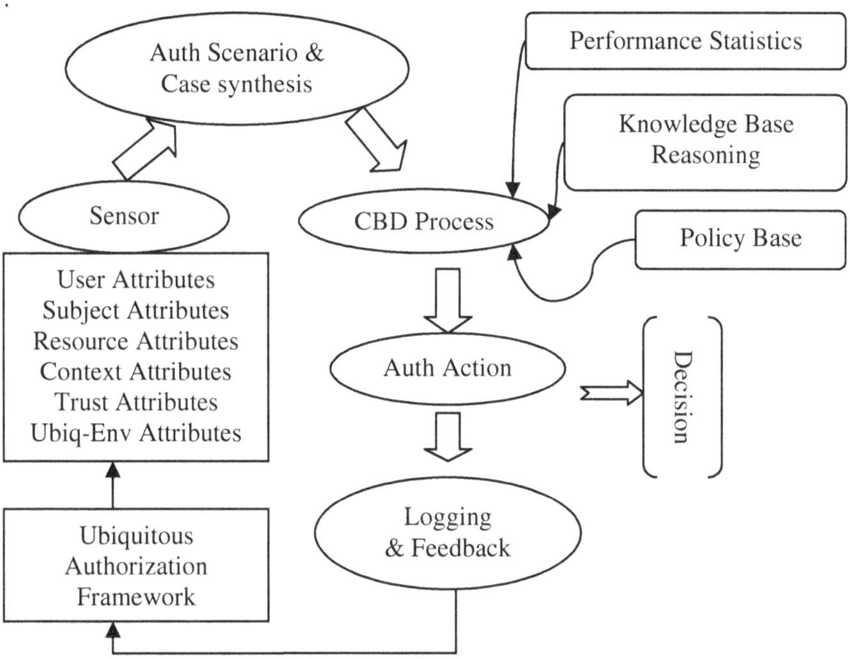

Fig. 2. The Intelligent Authorization Engine process cycle with Observation module, learning module and Decision making module

The Ubiq-IAF provides the input to the sensor and receives output from decision module. The sensors are labeled with no. of domain of information useful for IAE. The sensor passes the information to the IAE which is composed of intelligent processing units and Learning algorithm. The results of IAE are then used to control the final output of Ubiq-IAF.We use the above theoretical aspect of the IAE process cycle to develop the IAE architecture.

4.1 Intelligent Authorization Engine

As a part of the Intelligent Authorization Architecture (Fig. 3), four main components have been identified i.e. Environmental Data Sensor, Authorization Policy Engine, IAE Core Manager and Authorization Decision System. Each Component is launched as a separate process as it allows low coupling between processes. This architecture design enables the testing of different types of algorithm and processes to realize each component. To coordinate among the various components, IAE core manager (ICM) is also proposed. IAE core manager is required to handle the inputs from the other system components to develop the intelligent capabilities.

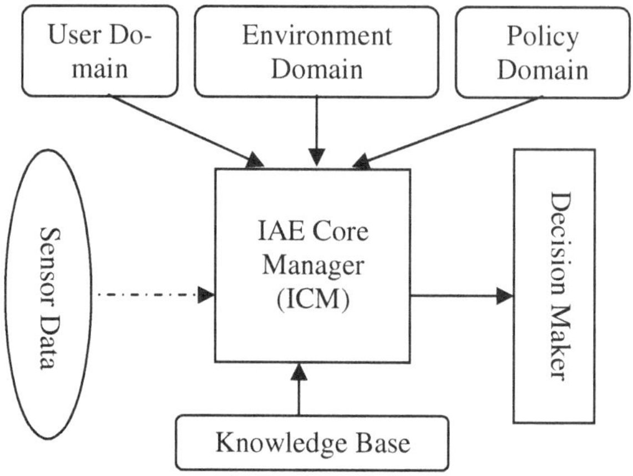

Fig. 3. The Intelligent Authorization Engine architecture

In Figure 3 a generic architecture for Intelligent Authorization Engine (IAE) is presented. The IAE relies on information from the sensors, user, environment and policy domain for authorization management. The user domain inputs act as basis for authorization requirements that need to be evaluated by IAE. These requirements include access to different resources, services and application offered by computing environment. The sensor and environment input provide the context according to which IAE adapts it behavior. The dynamic property of these input needs to be continuously monitored by IAE and adjust its behavior. The environment and sensor input play a significant role in building intelligence and optimizing the decision making process of IAE.The input from the policy domain help the authorization system to constraint its access process as interpreted by the security policy engine. The policy engine enforces the policies as per access control security requirement of the organization policy. The input from the knowledge base provides past Knowledge that helps IAE to optimize its decision making process. The past knowledge includes database of observed authorization request cases and action taken to respond to those cases. In order to better understand the functionality of IAE, the details of the various system components is described in next section.

4.2 Intelligent Authorization Engine Components

In this section we provide more detail about the purpose and role of each system component. We begin with Environmental Data Sensor [EDS] component. The main role of the environment data sensor is to collect the context/trust/user/environmental data. The EDS is an important component of IAE as it provides data based on which the intelligent core manager builds its intelligence and learn how to use knowledge gained from the sensing mechanism to aid the decision process.

Sensors collect the data from the surrounding environment and transferred it to the intelligent core manager. Sensors get initialized on request from the Intelligent Core

Manager, and perform its data collection process. This is followed by packaging of data in XML format that contains the semantics to describe the sensor data. SOAP (Simple Object Access Protocol) is standard protocol for providing the communications between the sensor and the core manager. Each sensor device has a XML template file associated with it which when combined with the sensor data generates XML document. XPath Query language can be used to query this document.

4.3 IAE Data Management Architecture

We proposed to use XML for information encoding. The main advantage of XML is that it allows encoding of raw data from various sources and sensors that is both human and machine readable. XML has a standardized format and method of verifying format via a document type definition .This feature make it suitable candidate to be used as policy specification framework for access control management

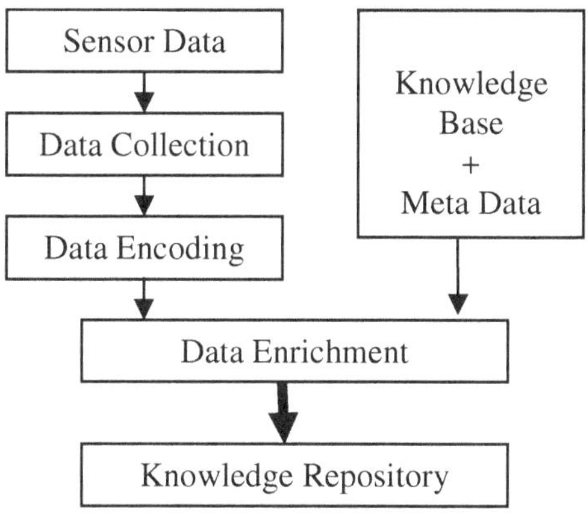

Fig. 4. The Intelligent Authorization Engine Data Processing frameworks

Moreover being open and simple standard, many tools are available to read and write it with library support for almost all programming languages. Figure 4 describes the IAE Data Processing framework. The raw data captured through sensors is semantically enriched by wrapping them into XML tags with their corresponding attributes names. In comparison to flat text representation approach, XML has a power of representing data in organized manner. XML structure offers efficient and flexible representation of data and metadata with support of standard query language like XQuery and XPath. Further enrichment of captured data is done with information from other sources like User Context and Environment Domain in context with source data. This leads to semantically enriched knowledge repository which along with policy base leads to efficient authorization and decision making.

4.4 IAE Computational Intelligence

We also reviewed computationally intelligent techniques in the literature which can possibly be deployed in hybrid mode to implement on Intelligent Access Control Mechanisms. The first popular technique is the expert system i.e. Rule Based Approach. The bottlenecks occur in this technique due to need for domain expert to define all knowledge, action and behavior of the expert system. This same principle also limits any refinement, thereby limiting the flexibility of the system to new situation, constraints and information. We found techniques based on Bayes' theorem which uses past experience to enhance future decisions. Another technique is based on Neural Networks. In the context of intelligent application design, neural network provide a reliable mechanism for detection and classification. The collection of artificial neurons and learning algorithm allow network to build and adapt to represent and process data in interesting ways. Next technique that is reviewed is implementation of Bayes' law i.e. Hidden Markov Model (HMM).A HMM is a processing tool that uses past data to help predict future actions.HMM can potentially be used in hybrid mode with other technique to model the system with state based approach. Another technique is fuzzy logic which deals extensively with uncertainty in decision making and analysis. Fuzzy logic requires establishing rules related to a specific situation in which it is used but is far more flexible and powerful as compare to expert systems. Another important technique that we studied is case based reasoning (CBR).CBR based systems use past knowledge to learn and improve future actions.

Next technique we studied is based on evolutionary algorithms, specifically genetic algorithm. Genetic Algorithm offers significant amount of flexibility in handling large search space faced in dynamic environment and situations. The technique based on unsupervised learning algorithm in Neural Network theory can be useful for active learning. After studying various computational intelligence (CI) based approach we conclude that CI based approach provides viable techniques and tools for design of intelligent systems framework. In later phases, we will use and develop these ideas more deeply in the design of IAE framework.

5 Related Work

In literature survey we found an emerging trend towards research on security aspect of ubiquitous computing environment. The various studies that have been done in relation to security aspect of ubiquitous computing is outlined below. Weiser, M.[3] suggests that, due to the trends of unobtrusive technology and more intrusive information, the next phase of computing technology will develop nonlinearly. Al-Muhtadi et al.[4] present a ubiquitous security mechanism that integrates context-awareness with automated reasoning to perform authentication and access control in ubiquitous computing environments. Brezillon et al. [5] presented a new model for specifying context-based security policies for pervasive computing environment. Sampemane et al.[6] studied the problem of access control for new emerging environments, which are called Active Spaces. Zhefan et al.[7] proposes a security management middleware in ubiquitous computing environments.Song-hwa Chae et al.[8] proposed new access control model supporting time and location dimensions. Fang Pu et al.[9] presented a context access control model based on UCONABC which not only focuses on authorization, but also introduces obligations, and conditions. Hong, S. et al.[10] proposed a method and framework of user-centric and efficient access control to handle personal privacy within ubiquitous computing environment by using both proposed model based on core component of RBAC model and privacy policies. Wang, H. et al.[11] presented a usage control model to protect services and devices in ubiquitous computing environments, which allows the access restrictions directly on services and object documents. Kulkarni et al.[12] presented a context-aware RBAC (CARBAC) model for pervasive computing applications. Cai et al.[13] proposed a novel ANN-based (Artificial Neural Network) service selection model (called the ANNSS model). Gavrilov [14] proposed usage of hybrid intelligent systems based on combination of neural networks and rule based techniques for development of smart environment like ubiquitous computing environment. Kyu et al.[15] proposed the mechanism that a user is able to automatically access to resource by means of context aware on ubiquitous computing environments. . Hung et al. [16] proposed Activity-Oriented Access Control (AOAC) model, aiming to support user's activity in ubiquitous environments. Sejong [17] proposed a new access control model termed the Ubi-RBAC model. It is based on the RBAC model and adds new components such as space, space hierarchy, and context constraints.

Our work proposed is section 4, takes into consideration the concept of computational intelligence and with emphasis on hybridization of various evolutionary computing learning techniques for the development of effective authorization system for ubiquitous computing environment.

6 Conclusion

We have presented a framework that comprises of components and processes to achieve correct authorization decision for ubiquitous computing environment. The schema of intelligent authorization engine has been described for automating the authorization service in ubiquitous computing environment. The inclusion of concept of computational intelligence makes the framework more reliable in terms of decision making and adapting to the dynamic characteristics of Ubiquitous Computing. Future work shall include formalizing a model based on the proposed framework and evaluating the framework for access control requirements of Ubiquitous computing environment.

References

1. Weiser, M.: The computer for the 21st century. Scientific America 23, 49–104 (1991)
2. Poole, D., Mackworth, A., Goebel, R.: Computational Intelligence - A Logical Approach. Oxford University Press, Oxford (1998)
3. Weiser, M.: Some computer science problems in ubiquitous computing. Communications of the ACM 7, 75–84 (1993)

4. Al-Muhtadi, J., Ranganathan, A., Campbell, R., Mickunas, M.D.: Cerberus: a contextaware security scheme for smart spaces. In: 1st IEEE International Conf. on Pervasive Computing and Communications, pp. 489–496. IEEE Press (2003)
5. Brezillon, P., Mostefaoui, G.K.: Context-based security policies: a new modeling approach. In: 2nd IEEE Annual Conference on Pervasive Computing and Communications Workshops, pp. 154–158. IEEE Press (2004)
6. Sampemane, G.: Access Control for Active Spaces. Doctoral Thesis. UMI Order Number: AAI3199131. University of Illinois at Urbana-Champaign (2005)
7. Zhefan, J., Kanghee, L., Sangok, K., Hyunchul, B., Sangwook, K., Soongju, K.: Design of a Security Management Middleware in Ubiquitous Computing Environments. In: 6th International Conference on Parallel and Distributed Computing, Applications and Technologies, pp. 306–308 (2005)
8. Chae, S.-H., Kim, W., Kim, D.-K.: Role-Based Access Control Model for Ubiquitous Computing Environment. In: Song, J.-S., Kwon, T., Yung, M. (eds.) WISA 2005. LNCS, vol. 3786, pp. 354–363. Springer, Heidelberg (2006)
9. Fang, P., Daoqin, S., Qiying, C., Haibin, C., Fan, Y.: Pervasive Computing Context Access Control Based on UCON_ABC Model. In: International Conference on Intelligent Information Hiding and Multimedia Signal Processing, pp. 689–692 (2006)
10. Hong, S., Cho, E., Moon, C., Baik, D.: RBAC-Based Access Control Framework for ensuring Privacy in Ubiquitous Computing. In: 2006 International Conference on Hybrid Information Technology, pp. 278–283 (2006)
11. Wang, H., Zhang, Y., Cao, J.: Access control management for ubiquitous computing. Future Gener. Comput. Syst., 870–878 (2008)
12. Kulkarni, D.: A Context-aware role-based access control in pervasive computing systems. In: 13th ACM Symposium on Access Control Models and Technologies, pp. 113–122 (2008)
13. Cai, H., Pu, F., Huang, R., Cao, Q.: A novel ANN-based service selection model for ubiquitous computing environments. J. Network Computer Application 4, 944–965 (2008)
14. Gavrilov, A.V.: Hybrid Rule and Neural Network Based Framework for Ubiquitous Computing. In: 4th International Conference on Networked Computing and Advanced information Management, pp. 488–492 (2008)
15. Kim, K.I., Ko, H.J., Hwang, H.S., Kim, U.M.: Context RBAC/MAC Access Control for Ubiquitous Environment. In: Kotagiri, R., Radha Krishna, P., Mohania, M., Nantajeewarawat, E. (eds.) DASFAA 2007. LNCS, vol. 4443, pp. 1075–1085. Springer, Heidelberg (2007)
16. Hung, L., Shaikh, R., Jameel, H.: Activity-oriented access control for ubiquitous environments. In: 6th IEEE Conference on Consumer Communications and Networking Conference, pp. 1402–1406. IEEE Press (2009)
17. Sejong, O.: New role-based access control in ubiquitous e-business environment. J. Intell. Manuf. 5, 607–612 (2010)

ANOVA Discriminant Analysis for Features Selected through Decision Tree Induction Method

N. Gayatri, S. Nickolas, and A.V. Reddy

Department of Computer Applications, National Institute of Technology, Tiruchirappalli, India
gayatrinandam@yahoo.co.in, nickolas@nitt.edu, reddy@nitt.edu

Abstract. Feature selection plays an important role in recent years as the selected features improve the classification accuracy of the classifiers in software defect predictions. For improving the quality of the defect prediction model, effective features must be selected. Many feature selection algorithms have been developed for the improvement of defect prediction models. In this paper, we have used ANOVA Discriminant Analysis (ADA) to statistically prove that the features selected through Decision Tree Induction (DTI) approach are effective for defect predictions and only these features can be used for further use. ADA computes the means of variables and it selects the significant features from the groups iteratively for better results. By using ADA, it is found that the features selected through the DTI approach have higher discriminating power than others and the accuracy of the classifiers also increases when this feature set is used for many classifiers. Hence it is said that the selected feature set alone can be used for defect prediction instead of original feature set. It is also observed that the attributes selected through DTI are same as attributes used by ADA. Hence, these are proved to be significant. Wilk's Lambda is taken as the significant measure. It shows the Discriminant power of the features i.e. discriminating power is high when Wilk's lambda is low.

Keywords: Feature selection, Software defect prediction, ANOVA Discriminant analysis, Wilk's- lambda.

1 Introduction

Software Quality comprises of several quality activities such as testing, verification, inspection and software fault predictions. Metrics are potentially very valuable for providing standards for efficient software quality outcome. Software fault prediction is one of the quality assurance activities where the fault detection in early stage can result in better and quality outcome of the product [1]. Recently machine learning and statistical techniques have been used as the software fault prediction models to enable timely identification of fault prone modules so that the quality can be increased and good prediction models can be constructed. Classification, Clustering are some of the data mining /Machine learning techniques [2] which are used for the software fault prediction. This paper uses ADA for classification for fault predictions. The metrics data is collected from very large databases. These databases may contain data that

P.V. Krishna, M.R. Babu, and E. Ariwa (Eds.): ObCom 2011, Part I, CCIS 269, pp. 61–70, 2012.

may be redundant, incomplete, imprecise or inconsistent, which can affect predictive accuracy of data mining model. So, mining the software metrics may require more data reduction. All the features that are present in the dataset are not required for building good model. The inclusion of irrelevant or noisy features makes knowledge discovery difficult and also result in poor accuracy or poor prediction of the model. So, the optimal features should be selected to build the best model for better accuracy. This conveys that feature selection plays a vital role in classification or prediction for building good model.

This paper focus on giving the statistical proof for the features selected through the decision tree induction approach [8] which is a wrapper approach. In literature, some authors have discussed that filter approach outperforms the wrapper approach and it is highly computational. But the features selected through this approach gives high accuracy when compared with original features [11]. Hence using ADA, we get the same accuracy when compared to original feature set and the discriminating power of the selected features is also high when compared to others. So, we conclude that the features selected through DTI approach, even though little computational intensive, give better accuracy and only these features can be used for further defect predictions for finding more fault prone module in early phase of defect prediction. Wilk's lambda is taken as the performance measure to find the significance of the each and every variable. Five public datasets from promise repository have been taken and ADA is used on them and evaluated.

This paper is organized as follows: following section presents the related work. Section 3 explains in detail the ADA, CDF used for performance evaluation. Dataset Descriptions and Analysis of the experiments performed and results are discussed in the section 4. This is followed by the conclusion at the end.

2 Related Work

In order to use data mining techniques effectively, data pre-processing is essential [2]. Feature selection is one of the important steps in pre-processing of data. The basic job of feature selection is to reduce the number of features. The inclusion of unwanted and noisy features in the dataset gives low accuracy, less comprehensibility and high computational complexity. These data must be cleaned and by doing so gives good comprehensibility and better performance. From the literature, many feature selection techniques have been studied, applied for different domains and found to be improving the performance of the classifiers.[3][4]. Various feature selection techniques include Correlation based feature selection, Principal Component Analysis, Attribute Oriented induction, Information Gain, Chi squared evaluation, Support Vector Machines (SVM) etc. Feature selection is based on different measures such as information measures, distance measures and dependence measures to find the goodness of individual features. The attributes are ranked according to their values on these measures [5].

In previous studies, two approaches have been given for feature selection problem: The Filter model and The Wrapper model. Filter model chooses features by heuristically determined relevant knowledge where as Wrapper model selects features by feedback of the classifier's evaluation. Research shows that wrapper model outperforms the filter model by comparing the predictive power on unseen data [6]. Wrappers use classification accuracy on training dataset as a measurement of how well a subset of features formed and thus turns the feature selection problem into optimization problem. Many researchers have developed various feature selection techniques using different evaluation and searching criteria. One can simply choose M features as the selected feature subset in any order from the original attribute set. M is determined according to some domain knowledge or a user specified threshold value [7]. Recursive Feature Elimination is also one of the feature selection techniques. It selects the best or relevant features by recursively eliminating the irrelevant features based on ranking of the attributes and predictive accuracy.

This paper is the extension of our previous work [8] where the features selected are through DTI (Decision Tree Induction) approach and the statistical significance is evaluated using ADA. ADA is a supervised classification technique, which predicts the vector that is best in discriminating positive from negative cases [9]. The main advantage of ADA is that analysis of variance (ANOVA) estimates Wilk's λ statistics based on grouping class variable. The features selected through the DTI approach has discriminating power when ADA is used and also these features when used in classification give better accuracy comparatively ,and thus the selected features are better and enough for further defect predictions.

3 Proposed Work

In our previous work [8], we have selected 14 features from set of 21 features of metric data and found that accuracy of classifiers increased when thee 14 features are used when compared to 21 features. These 14 features are selected through DTI approach based on the rules [8]. In this paper, we found the discriminating power of those selected features using ADA is high when compared to other features, by knowing the Wilk's lambda of each feature.

ANOVA DA uses more than one independent categorical variable and a single dependent continuous variable. ADA is a supervised dimension reduction technique and predicts discriminant function coefficients such that these coefficients discriminate positive from negative cases effectively. ANOVA is a special case of the general linear model as shown in Equation (1).

$$y = Xb + e \tag{1}$$

where y is a dependent variable (DV), X is a matrix of predictors or independent variables (IV), b is a vector of regression coefficients (weightings) and e is a vector of error terms.

ANOVA is a procedure that determines whether differences exist between two or more population means by analyzing within group and between group variances. Wilk's λ is defined as the ratio of sum of squares within-group to the total sum of squares. So, the smaller the Wilk's lambda better is the classification [12].

Standardized CDF score is also given using ANOVA DA which compares the relative contribution of each variable to the overall Discriminant function. Standardized coefficients are useful to look at each factor relative to the others. The standardized CDF coefficients for each feature are shown in Table 3. The generalized CDF score is calculated for each module using the feature values (*f*1, *f*2, …, *fn*) and CDF coefficients (*c*1, *c*2, …, *cn*) is shown in Equation (2),

$$\text{CDF score} = f1 * c1 + f2 * c2 + \ldots\ldots + fn * cn + \text{Constant} \tag{2}$$

Here we have used ADA classifier to find the accuracy for all 21 features and also for selected 14 features. The accuracy is almost same or little bit high when 14 selected features are used. Hence, we can understand that only 14 features can be taken instead of 21 features so that the time for collection of remaining data can be reduced and also these metrics can be used effectively for quality outcome.

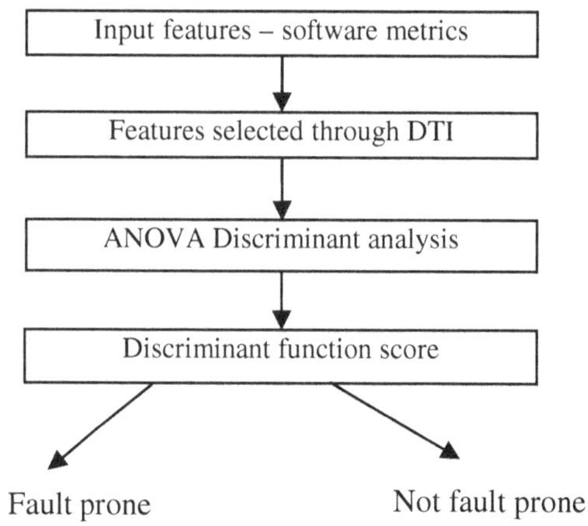

Fig. 1. Architecture of Proposed work

4 Experimental Results

Two data sets from Promise repository have been tested to prove that the attributes selected through decision tree approach are statistically significant and all the variables have high discrimination power independent of the datasets. The features selected trough DTI method are given in table 2. The performance measure is Wilk's lambda which gives the significance of the variables, i.e. if the variable has low lambda value then it has high discriminating power. For ANOVA Discriminant classification and experimental analysis, SPSS package is used.

4.1 Datasets Description

The datasets were taken from the NASA projects. We used two public datasets called KC1, CM1 belonging to several NASA projects [10]. KC1 dataset, which is implemented in C++ programming language, belongs to a storage management project for receiving/processing ground data. It has 2109 software modules, 15% of which are defective. CM1 belongs to a NASA spacecraft instrument project developed in C programming language. CM1 has 498 modules of which 10% are defective. Table 1 gives overview of the datasets.

Table 1. Datasets descrption

Dataset name	Attributes	modules	Defective	Percentage%
CMI	21	498	49	9.83%
KC1	21	2109	326	15.4%

Table 2. Attributes selected through DTI method

Attributes	Description
loc	McCabe's line count of code
v(g)	McCabe's cyclomatic complexity
ev(g)	McCabe's essential complexity
iv(g)	McCabe's design complexity
l	Halstead "program length'
d	Halstead "difficulty"
i	Halstead "intelligence"
b	Halstead "delivered bugs"
loCode	Halstead's line count
loComment	Halstead's count of lines of comments
loCode And Comment	Lines of code and comment
uniq_opnd	Unique operands
total_opnd	Total operands
loBlank	Halstead's count of blank lines

The Wilk's lambda, significance and CDF score are tabulated in tables separately for each dataset, for the original feature set and selected features set. From these, it can be found that the removed features have high wilk's lambda and low discriminating power than others. The wilk's lambda values for original feature set for two datasets are given in tables 9 and 10 and provided at the end of the paper. The CDF score is calculated using the equation 2. Using this, the modules are classified as defect prone or not defect prone.

From Tables 5 AND 6 it can be observed that almost all features have Wilk's λ statistic less than 0.95 except for some features. Thus, these features have high discriminating power compared to other features. The standardized canonical Discriminant Function (CDF) coefficients for each feature is shown in Table 2.

It can be rewritten using CDF coefficients present in Table 5 and 6 as

CDF score = loc * (.884) + v(g) * (-2.565) +.........+b * (.904) + constant for CMI dataset
CDF score = loc * (.245) + v(g) * (-1.805) +.........+b * (.408) + constant for KC1 dataset

In Table 3and 4, the CDF value evaluated at each group mean for each defect type is shown. The average CDF score is 0.595. Thus, modules whose CDF score less than 0.595 are classified as defective and CDF score greater than 0.595 are classified as not defective for CMI dataset. The average CDF score for KC1 dataset is 0.773 and modules are classified accordingly. Figures 2 and 3 show the graphical representation of CDF score classifying them as defective and non defective modules.

Table 3. CDF at group centroids for CMI dataset

Defects	Function
0	-0.146
1	1.336

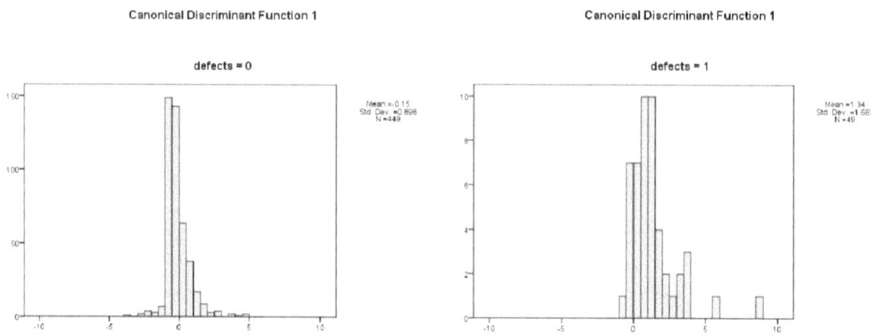

(a) (b)

Fig. 2. CDF Score for (a) defects = 0 and (b) defects = 1 for CMI dataset

Table 4. CDF at group cancroids for KC1 dataset

Defects	Function
0	-0.213
1	1.164

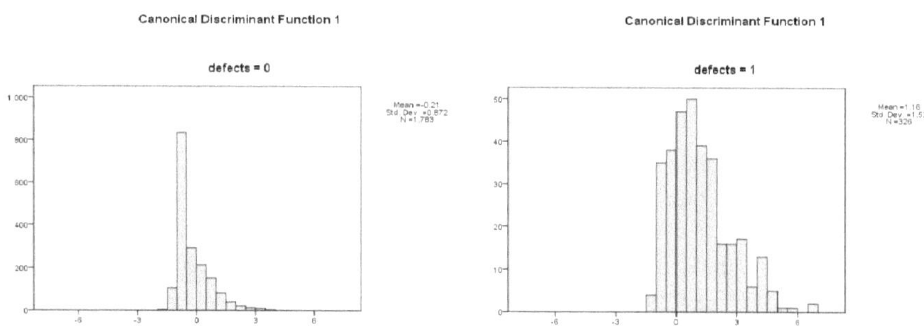

(a) (b)

Fig. 3. CDF for (a) defects = 0 and (b) defects = 1 for KC1 dataset

Table 5. Tests of Equality of Group Means for CMI dataset for 14 features

Features	Wilk's Lambda	Function	Sig.
Loc	.939	.884	.000
v(g)	.972	-2.565	.000
evg	.989	-.351	.019
ivg	.959	.599	.000
d	.972	.269	.000
locoed	.996	-.337	.160
locomment	.909	.795	.000
l	.982	.617	.000
uniq_opnd	.932	.236	.000
i	.924	-1.097	.000
tot_opnd	.955	-.396	.000
loblank	.970	.073	.000
branchcount	.971	1.045	.000
b	.954	.904	.000

Table 6. Tests of equality of group means for KC1dataset for 14 features

Features	Wilk's Lambda	Function	Sig
Loc	.879	.245	.000
vg	.913	-1.805	.000
e(vg)	.958	-.226	.000
ivg	.913	1.038	.000
d	.850	1.448	.000
locoed	.883	-.633	.000
locomment	.946	.093	.000
loblank	.895	.090	.000
l	.946	-.391	.000
uniq_opnd	.850	1.142	.000
i	.882	-1.224	.000
tot_opnd	.869	.177	.000
branchcount	.911	.588	.000
b	.885	.408	.000

The Wilk's lambda and CDF score graph are given for two datasets i.e. CMI and KC1 The overall Wilk's lambda and chi-square value are given for two datasets and tabulated in the table7, this shows the significance of the overall feature set.

Table 7. Overall Wilk's lambda for all datasets

Datasets	Wilk's lambda	chi-square	Df	Sig
CMI	.836	87.405	14	.000
KC1	.801	465.293	14	.000

The overall accuracy for all datasets is given using ADA in the following table 8. When compared this with the previous results [11], it gives the almost same or little better classification accuracy which is measured in terms of Receiver Operating Characteristic (ROC) value. ADA classifiers is also used for features selected through other feature selection technique named SVM Attribute Evaluation method and found that the accuracy for feature set selected through DTI is almost equal and comparable and can be said that those DTI features has high significant power which is proved statistically using ADA.

SVM Attribute Evaluation method evaluates the worth of an attribute by using an SVM classifier. Attributes are ranked by the square of the weight assigned by the SVM. Attribute selection for multiclass problems is handled by ranking attributes for each class separately using a one-vs-all method and then "dealing" from the top of each file to give a final ranking.

Table 8. Accuracy of Datasets when ANOVA DA is used

Datasets	Accuracy		
	For 21 features	For 14 features(DTI)	SVM 14
CMI	90.2%	90.2%	91.8
KC1	77.8%	85.9%	85.5

The results of the paper show that the Wilk's lambda for the selected features is less and the discriminating power of is high when compared with the original features. The significance of features is also high independent of datasets i.e., data of that features. The other important thing is to observe that the accuracy for all the 21 features and the selected 14 features is same when ADA is used and it is understood that the features selected using statistical classifier is same as the features selected trough the DTI approach and thus those selected features are statistically proved as significant, so in that case we need not go for collection of remaining 7 attributes and there we can save

Table 9. Tests of equality of group means for CMI dataset for 21 features

	Wilk's lambda	F	Significance
loc	.939	32.079	.000
vg	.972	14.188	.000
evg	.989	5.534	.019
ivg	.959	21.241	.000
n	.954	23.816	.000
v	.957	22.120	.000
l	.982	8.873	.003
d	.972	14.436	.000
i	.928	38.309	.000
e	.990	4.788	.029
b	.954	24.089	.000
t	.990	4.788	.029
locode	.996	1.976	.160
locomment	.909	49.616	.000
loblank	.970	15.402	.000
locodeandcomment	.998	1.122	.290
uni_op	.938	32.859	.000
uniq_opnd	.932	36.423	.001
tot_op	.954	23.824	.000
tot_opnd	.955	23.341	.000
branchcount	.971	14.702	.000

Table 10. Tests of equality of group means for KC1 dataset for 21 features

	Wilk's lambda	F	Significance
loc	.879	291.095	.000
vg	.913	201.691	.000
evg	.958	92.581	.000
ivg	.913	201.877	.000
n	.874	304.021	.000
v	.885	274.563	.000
l	.946	120.819	.000
d	.850	372.264	.000
i	.882	280.668	.000
e	.927	165.771	.000
b	.885	273.630	.000
t	.927	165.772	.000
locode	.883	278.217	.000
locomment	.946	120.806	.000
loblank	.895	246.479	.000
locodeandcomment	1.000	.054	.816
uni_op	.851	367.926	.000
uniq_opnd	.850	370.505	.000
tot_op	.878	291.819	.000
tot_opnd	.869	318.859	.000
branchcount	.911	205.085	.000

the time and use resources effectively The overall accuracy when compared to [11] is almost same or better using ADA classification. In [11] the performance measure taken was Receiver Operating Characteristic (ROC) value and the performance of DTI,SVM attribute evaluation method and original feature set is are compared in terms of ROC value Hence, we conclude that these features can be formed as separate set and these alone can be used for further software defect predictions.

5 Conclusion

Selection of relevant features is very important in data mining for effective classification of the classifiers. If selected features have high discriminating power, then it is understood that these features actively participate in the final class distribution and the final accuracy of the classifiers. In this paper, using ANOVA Discriminating Analysis (ADA), it is shown that the features selected through decision tree induction (DTI) approach have high discriminating power. Wilk's lambda is used as the performance measure. If Wilk's lambda is low, then discriminating power of that variable is high and significance of that variable is below 0.005. From the results, it is observed that Wilk's lambda is low for the features selected trough DTI approach independent of datasets and it can be concluded that those features have high discriminating power. If these selected features alone are used for classification, then they give better accuracy with many classifiers for defect predictions. Hence, these alone can be used for further defect predictions and also it is proved that the selected feature are significant statistically using ADA. In future, these features can be used for classification with many other classifiers and can be combined with other features to obtain better classification accuracy.

References

1. Fenton, N.E., Pfleeger, S.L.: Software Metrics, A Rigorous & Practical Approach. International Thomson Computer Press, London (1997)
2. Han, J., Kamber, M.: Data Mining: Concepts and Techniques. Morgan Kaufmann Publishers, San Francisco (2001)
3. Almuallim, H., Dietterich, T.G.: Efficient algorithms for identifying relevant features. In: Proceedings of Ninth Canadian Conference on Artificial Intelligence. Morgan Kaufmann, Vancouver (1992)
4. Siedlecki, W., Skalansky, J.: Om automatic feature selection. Int. J. Pattern Recog. Art. Intell. 2(2), 197–220 (1988)
5. Sabzevari, H., Soleymani, M., Noorbrakhsh, E.: A Comparison between Statistical and Data Mining methods for credit scoring in case of limited data available
6. John, G.H., Kohavi, R., Pfleger, K.: Irrelevant Features and Subset Selection Problem. In: Proceedings of the Eleventh International Conference of Machine Learning, pp. 121–129. Morgan Kaufmann Publishers, San Francisco (1994)
7. Liu, Y., Schumann, M.: Data mining feature selection for credit scoring models. Journal of the Operational Research Society 56, 1099–1108 (2005)
8. Gayatri, N., Nickolas, S., Reddy, A.V.: Performance analysis and Enhancement of Software Quality Metrics using Decision Tree based Feature Extraction. International Journal of Recent Trends in Engineering 2, 54–56 (2009)
9. Duda, R.O., Hart, P.E., Stork, D.G.: Pattern Classification, 2nd edn. John Wiley & Sons, New York (2001)
10. Promise Software Engineering, `http://www.promise.site,uttowa.ca/SERpository`
11. Gayatri, N., Nickolas, S., Reddy, A.V.: Performance Analysis of decision Tree Induction feature selection Method for Software defect Predictions. International Journal of Software Engineering 1(1), 61–71 (2010) ISSN 0974-3162
12. Surediran, B., Vadivel, A.: A hybrid classifier for mammogram mass classification using various new geometric shape and margin features. International Journal of Rapid manufacturing 2(1/2) (2011)
13. Gondra, I.: Applying machine learning to software fault-proneness prediction. The Journal of System and Software, 186–195 (2008)
14. Lessmann, S., Baesens, B., Mues, C., Pietsch, S.: Benchmarking Classification Models for Software Defect Prediction: A Proposed Framework and Novel Findings. IEEE Transactions on Software Engineering 34(4), 485–496 (2008)
15. Hall, M.A., Holmes, G.: Benchmarking Attribute Selection Techniques for Discrete Class Data mining. IEEE Transactions on Knowledge and Data Engineerng 15, 1437–1447 (2003)

Developing an Efficient Mechanism for Retrieving Documents Using Automatically Generated Metadata

Sayanti Bandyopadhyay[1,*], and Amit Kumar Bandyopadhyay[2]

[1] University Institute of Technology, University of Burdwan, Burdwan, 713104 W.B., India
bandyopadhyay.sayanti@gmail.com

[2] Department of Library and Information Science, University of Burdwan, Burdwan, 713104 W.B., India
amitkrb@yahoo.com

Abstract. Efficient generation of metadata and retrieval is becoming highly challenging with the increase in volume of resources. Huge recall with low precision is the problem of most document retrieval systems. Effective automatic generation of metadata can reduce time required in creating metadata manually. This paper attempts to develop a search algorithm to retrieve documents using automatically generated metadata. The fifteen elements of Dublin Core Metadata are discussed and addition of another element consisting of popular search keywords for retrieving the document has been suggested. The keywords in the suggested extended metadata element can be grouped according to geographic location for personalizing the search results. Precision increment and recall decrement can be achieved by retrieving books of specific topic-ids for which maximum words match with the searched keywords. Different stemming mechanisms for the search keywords have also been discussed. A flowchart of the proposed algorithm is given at the end.

Keywords: Document retrieval, automatic metadata generation, Dublin Core metadata.

1 Introduction

Information retrieval systems in the context of digital libraries bring in a huge volume of results where the actual relevant ones are very few.

It is difficult to achieve precision and recall at the same time as generally the two goals have a conflicting nature. Trying to achieve more relevant results i.e. increasing recall would result in a large number of documents being retrieved with increase in the number of non relevant results as well, thus decreasing the precision.

Herein lays the requirement of effective metadata generation and a mechanism for retrieval of desired results. But, manual creation of metadata is a time taking procedure. Automatic metadata generation is a feasible option for many digital documents, reducing time consumed in manual creation.

* Corresponding author.

P.V. Krishna, M.R. Babu, and E. Ariwa (Eds.): ObCom 2011, Part I, CCIS 269, pp. 71–79, 2012.

1.1 Objective

The objective of the present paper is to develop a query string search algorithm to retrieve documents using automatically generated metadata for having increasing precision of search results.

2 Metadata

Metadata is defined as data providing information about one or more other pieces of data, such as:

- means of creation of the data, purpose of the data, time and date of creation.
- creator or author of data, standards used.

2.1 Metadata Structures

Metadata is typically structured according to a standardized concept using a well defined metadata scheme, including: metadata standards and metadata models. Tools such as controlled vocabularies, taxonomies, thesauri, data dictionaries and metadata registries can be used to apply further standardization to the metadata.

2.2 Metadata Syntax

Metadata syntax refers to the rules created to structure the fields or elements of metadata. A single metadata scheme may be expressed in a number of different markup or programming languages, each of which requires a different syntax. For example, Dublin Core may be expressed in plain text, HTML, XML, etc. Metadata can be stored either *internally*, in the same file as the data, or *externally*, in a separate file. Metadata that is embedded with content is called *embedded metadata*. A data repository typically stores the metadata *detached* from the data.

3 Dublin Core Metadata

The Dublin Core Metadata Element Set is a vocabulary of fifteen properties for use in resource description. [1]

3.1 Dublin Core Metadata Element Set

1. *Title*: Title of the resource given by author/creator.
2. *Creator*: Author/creator person(s), organization(s) for the intellectual content of the resource.
3. *Subject*: Subject, keyword. The topic, keywords, phrases that describe the resource.
4. *Description*: Annotation, abstract etc.

5. *Publisher:* Publisher (person or institution)
6. *Contributor*: Contributing person or institution.
7. *Date*: The date of the resource made available in the present form.
8. *Type*: Resource type-category such as home page, novel, poem, working paper, report, essay, dictionary etc.
9. *Format*: Format, file type, also physical medium data representation such as text, HTML, ASCII, executable application, JPEG image.
10. *Identifier*: Resource identification URL, URN, ISBN etc.
11. *Source*: Resource physical or digital from which the present resource was derived.
12. *Language*: Language of the resource, language of the intellectual content of the resources.
13. *Relation*: Relationship to other works e.g. Images of documents, chapters in books.
14. *Coverage*: Geographic or temporal coverage.
15. *Rights*: Rights management statement, copyright. URL or other URI appropriate.

3.2 The Dublin Core Metadata Elements Are Broadly Categorized into Three Categories

1. Elements related to the content of the resource:
   Title, subject, description, source, language, relation, coverage
2. Elements related to intellectual property:
   Creator, publisher, contributor, rights
3. Elements related to instantiation of the resources:
   Type, format, identifier, date.

4 Metadata Generation

The elements related to the content of the resource are our main focus when we are concerned with automatic metadata generation. It is not difficult to retrieve the other information directly from the digital documents for generation of metadata.

"Most frequent words are function words; least frequent words are obscure while mid range words are content bearing" [2]. Thus the words in the document which occur in mid frequency range are generally the keywords.

All words are to be passed through stemming algorithm before being stored as metadata for the concerned document in a database.

Implementation of another element is suggested in the present paper for metadata generation along with the fifteen elements present in Dublin Core.

Many a times keywords searched by users for retrieving a document are not exactly as expected while metadata is generated. The search queries can greatly vary according to the geographic positions (region of the client searching for a document). Thus to get an accurate search result the user's psychology has to be understood. This may be achieved by personalizing the search according to the person's geographic location. Geographic location extraction is important as the same word may be used more frequently in a different context in some place while it may imply something else in another place. Hence a separate element which would include a list of most frequently used query strings to access the document can be optimal. It's logical to make a database in which the words stored are the frequently used strings when searching for the particular book. The database table can have columns for geographic location, keywords and their corresponding popularity i.e. the number of times these keywords have been used to retrieve the document. If a query search result is clicked on for downloading a document then the query strings used can be matched with a database containing a list of words that has been earlier searched to retrieve the document. If a keyword match is found the concerned keyword's popularity is increased by one and the database is arranged according to decreasing order of popularity of the keywords. Thus the words that are most frequently used to retrieve the document will stay at the top and those which are least used will stay at the base. These keywords should be placed into an appropriate position of the table according to its geographic position. Next time when a keyword is searched the database with the most relevant geographic will be given priority for matching with metadata keywords. Thus retrieval will be more efficient. Older search keywords which have become obsolete and have minimum popularity can be deleted if the corresponding dates of search are also stored. Both the search query string to be matched and keyword generated should follow steps like stemming algorithm, conflation algorithm etc.

Synonym matching and regional language translations can be included for matching the searched string with the keywords in metadata.

Conventional search techniques assume:-

the user knows the exact word usage in the document
how a word is used in different contexts
what are the correct spellings of different words
the user has a precise goal and can represent it into a query accurately.

But these assumptions are often false.

5 Implementing Query String Search Algorithm to Retrieve Documents Using Automatically Generated Metadata

```
  1. Query string, author name, publisher name and
other information are entered.

  2. Match the name or title of the book and/or
author name and/or publisher name:

  (a) If there is an exact match, a catalogue with
the book and its various volumes (if present) is
returned.
```

(b) If author name and/or publisher name is specified then search metadata list of books of that particular author and/or publisher for keyword or query string match.

Go to Step 2. (c).v).

(c) Else if author name and/or publisher name is not specified:

i) Remove words like {is, are, a, an, the, that, in, on, to, and, or.....} from the auxillary list to get the kernel words.

ii) Pass the query string through stemming algorithm.

iii) Extract geographic location from where the search is being done from the IP address of the visitor.

iv) If there are two or more words in the remaining stemmed query strings then match them with the word list for different topic id s.

- If any topic-d is found such that two or more words from the query string match with its word list then set that topic-id (for which maximum words match) to highest priority and others to lower priority according to the number of word match.

- Else if no such topic-d has been found get synonyms of the query strings. If any topic-d is found such that two or more word's synonym from the synonym list for each word match with the word list of a topic-id then set that topic-id (for which maximum words match) to highest priority and others to lower priority according to the number of word match.

v) If any topic id priority has been set then search book metadata list only belonging to those topic-ids for query string match.

Else search in metadata list of all books for query string match.

```
  Search the extended metadata list for the specif-
ic geographic location and time span as well.

      •If any match is found between the query
        strings and metadata, then return book ca-
        talogue in order of maximum match.

      •If no match is found, match the query string
        synonyms with the words in the metadata
        list excluding the extended metadata list.
        Display the catalogue of the books in de-
        creasing order of match.

      •If no result is being returned after all
        this, perform sound-ex operation on the ex-
        act query string searched (query string be-
        fore stemming).
  Return catalogue of books having words in their
metadata list which sound similar to the searched
words.
       End if.
  vi)      If the resulting document retrieved is
downloaded, update popularity of the keyword
searched. If topic id preference is set, update the
popularity of keyword in word list of topic-id.
```

[For flow chart see fig. 1 at the end.]

6 Stemming of Kernel Words

Stemming of kernel words can be achieved by lexicon searching technique or by applying stemming algorithms.

Lexicon search involves searching the lexicon for a keyword from the kernel string and returning the root word. Lexicon search stems the kernel string efficiently and precision can be enhanced. However this occurs at the cost of time factor.

7 Some Common Stemming Algorithms

Trivial Algorithms - This algorithm involves truncating words at N-th position. This algorithm works as a base for other stemming algorithms [3].

"S"-stemmer – This algorithm conflates singular and plural forms of nouns in English language.

It states some rules for stemming words longer than three characters.

```
IF a word ends in "ies", but not "eies" or "aies"
THEN "ies" -> "y"
ELSE IF a word ends in "es", but not "aes", "ees" or
"oes"
THEN "es" -> "e"
ELSE IF a word ends in "s", but not "us" or "ss"
THEN "s" -> NULL
```

Lovins Algorithm - This algorithm describes twenty nine conditions each associated to two hundred ninety four endings and suggests thirty five transformation rules. This algorithm is fast but fails in certain cases.

Porter's Algorithm and Snowball Framework – This algorithm gives five steps for word transformation. Each step consists of a set of rules in the form: <condition> <suffix> -> <new suffix> [4].

Paice/Husk Algorithm - This is an iterative algorithm. There are approximately 120 rules indexed by the last letter of the suffix. On each iteration, it tries to find an applicable rule is searched for by the last character of the word. The iteration terminates if there is no such rule or if a word starts with a vowel and there are only two letters left or if a word starts with a consonant and there are only three characters left. Otherwise the process repeats [5].

Dawson Algorithm - It is a modification of Lovins algorithm. It follows the longest match process and has a very comprehensive list of English suffixes and transformation rules. The suffixes are stored in the reversed order indexed by their length and last letter. The rules define if a suffix found can be removed [6].

Statistical Algorithms:

N-gram Stemming Algorithm - The algorithm analyses all N-grams. Inverse document frequency (IDF) is used to find out the stem words as variation of word roots are more frequent than morphological invariants [7].

HMM Algorithm - HMMs are finite-state automata with transitions defined by probability functions. Since probability of each path can be computed, it is possible to find the most probable path in the automata graph. Each character comprising a word is considered as a state. All possible states is divided into two groups (roots and suffixes) and two categories: initial (which can be roots only) and final (roots or suffixes). Word building is signified by state transitions. For any given word, the most probable path from initial to final states will produce the split point (a transition from roots to suffixes). Then the sequence of characters before this point can be considered as a stem [8].

YASS Algorithm (Suffix Stripper) - Conflation can be viewed as a clustering problem with a-prior unknown number of clusters. Usually such problems can be solved

with a hierarchical algorithm having a distance measure function for cluster elements.Then the resulting clusters are considered as equivalence classes and their centroids as stems [9].

Corpus-Based Stemming –

This algorithm uses statistical properties of a corpus to correct heavy stemming. Equivalence class of words is formed. Then conflated words are "separated back" according to their co-occurrence in corpora [10].

Context Sensitive Stemming – Word distributional similarity is found based on Corpus. Stemming candidates are found using Porter's algorithm. Ultimately some of them are finalized. Obtained forms are used to expand a search query on non-transformed index [11].

8 Conclusion

Efficient generation of metadata and retrieval is becoming more and more challenging with the increase in volume of resources and documents in digital library. The steps proposed in this article for retrieval of documents in digital library by matching query string with metadata is expected to have high precision in comparison to other conventional techniques. However, the storage requirement increases as popular keywords are maintained according to geographic location. Improvements can be made if the popular keywords are further grouped according to the age group of the searcher.

References

1. DCMI Dublin Core Metadata, `http://dublincore.org`
2. Smeaton, A.F.: Natural Language Processing & Information Retrieval, `http://www.compapp.dcu.ie/~asmeaton/asmeaton.html`
3. Frakes, W.B.: Term Conflation for Information Retrieval. In: 7th Annual International ACM SIGIR Conference on Research and Development in Information Retrieval, pp. 383–389 (1984)
4. Porter, M.F.: An Algorithm for Suffix Tripping. Program. 14, 130–137 (1980)
5. Paice, C.D.: Another Stemmer. ACM SIGIR Forum 24, 56–61 (1990)
6. Dawson, J.: Suffix Removal and Word Conflation. ALLC Bulletin 2, 33–46 (1974)
7. Mayfield, J., McNamee, P.: Single N-gram Stemming. In: 26th Annual International ACM SIGIR Conference on Research and Development in Information Retrieval, pp. 415–416 (2003)
8. Melucci, M., Orio, N.: A Novel Method for Stemmer Generation based on Hidden Markov Models. In: 12th International Conference on Information and Knowledge Management, pp. 131–138 (2003)
9. Majumder, P., Mitra, M., Parui, K.S., Kole, G., Mitra, P., Datta, K.: YASS: Yet another Suffix Stripper. ACM Transactions on Information Systems 25 (2007)
10. Xu, J., Croft, B.W.: Corpus-based Stemming using Co-occurrence of Word Variants. ACM Transactions on Information Systems 16, 61–81 (1998)
11. Funchun, P., Ahmed, N., Xin, L., Yumao, L.: Context Sensitive Stemming for Web Search. In: 30th Annual International ACM SIGIR Conference on Research and Development in Information Retrieval, pp. 639–646 (2007)

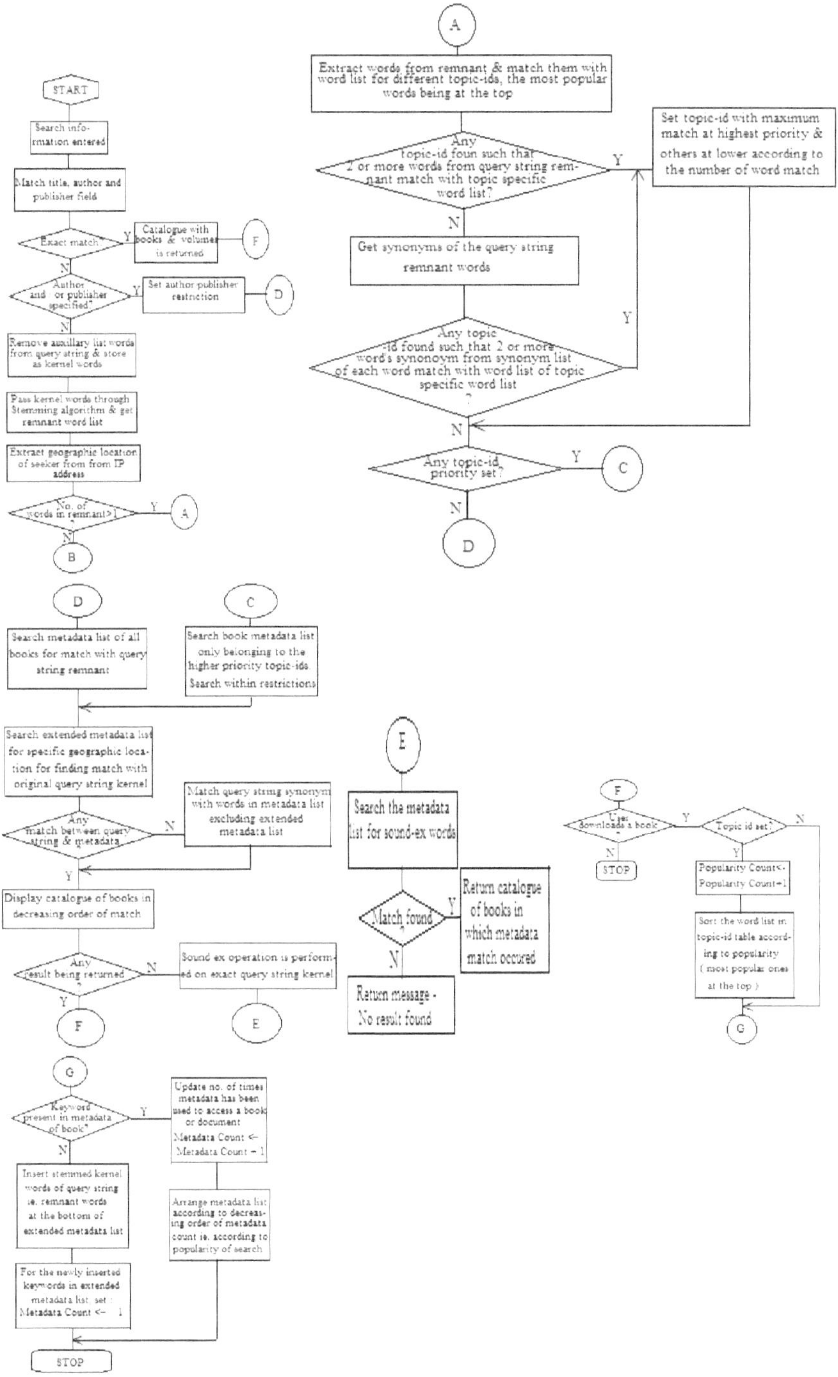

Fig. 1. Flow Chart for Document Retrieval Using Automatically Generated Metadata

Filtering Semantic Information at Client Side Using Semantic Enriched Tool

Anand Kumar, S.K. Jain, Saurabh Parmar, and Gagandeep Kaur

Computer Engineering Department,
National Institute of Technology, Kurukshetra, 136119, India
{anandncst777,saurabh.parmar08,deep.gagan102}@gmail.com,
skj_nith@yahoo.com

Abstract. The Semantic Web is a "web of data" that enables machines to understand the semantics, or the meaning, of information on the World Wide Web. The semantic web is a vision of information that is understandable by computers. This is what the Semantic Web is all about, describing things in a way that computers applications can understand it. Web browsers retrieve content and display it. Web browsing involves two tasks, finding the right web page and making sense of its content. So far much less attention has been paid to the interpretation of its content. In this paper we describe the tools which support the interpretation of web pages semantically without altering the original web page. It brings semantic interpretation to classical web pages by dynamically – i.e. during browsing – selecting ontologies that contain semantic descriptions of the main terms of the web page.

Keywords: semantic web, ontology, browsing.

1 Introduction

The Semantic Web is a "web of data" that enables machines to understand the semantics, or meaning, of information on the World Wide Web (WWW)[1].

Sentences like these two can easily be understood by people. (1) The Beatles was a popular band from Liverpool and (2) John Lennon was a member of the Beatles. But the question arises, how can they be understood by computers? We know statements are built with syntax rules. The syntax of a language defines the rules for building the language statements. But how can syntax become semantic? This is what the Semantic Web is all about, describing things in a way that computers applications can understand it. The Semantic Web is not about links between web pages. The Semantic Web describes the relationships between things (like A is a part of B and Y is a member of Z) and the properties of things (like size, weight, age, and price).

Relationships are keys to the semantics and hence the Semantic Web.. It involves publishing in languages specifically designed for data: Resource Description Framework (RDF), Web Ontology Language (OWL), and Extensible Markup Language (XML). HTML describes documents and the links between them.

P.V. Krishna, M.R. Babu, and E. Ariwa (Eds.): ObCom 2011, Part I, CCIS 269, pp. 80–90, 2012.

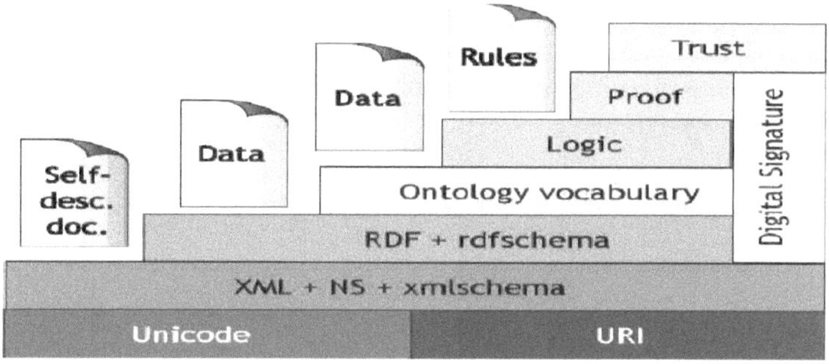

Fig. 1. Semantic Web components

1.1 Web Browser

Surfing the web is made possible by web browsers. Web browsers retrieve content and display from remote web servers. Web pages are written using a simple language called HyperText Markup Language (HTML). The primary purpose of a web browser is to bring information resources to the user. Web browsing involves two basic tasks:

1. Finding the right web page and
2. Making sense of its content.

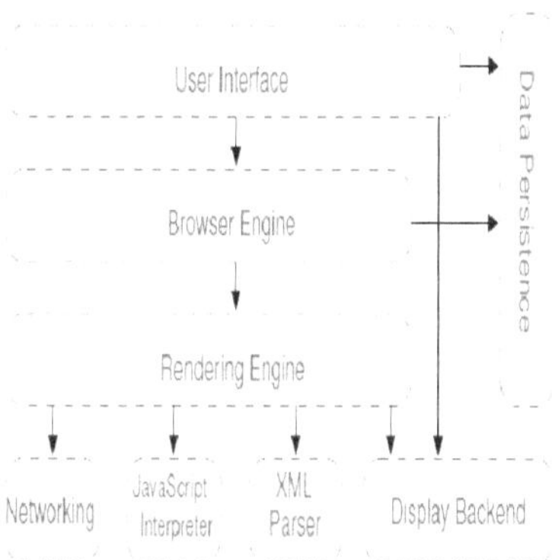

Fig. 2. Reference architecture of web browser

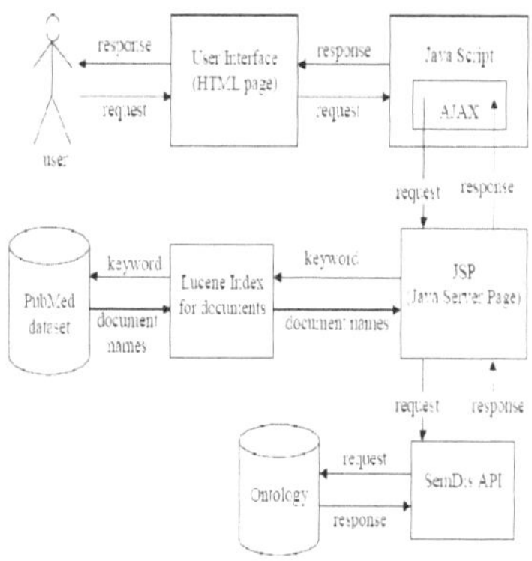

Fig. 3. Architecture of Semantic Web Browser

A lot of research has gone into supporting the task of finding web resources by means of 'standard' information retrieval mechanisms. Less work has been done on the second task – supporting the interpretation of web pages. Many web browser are available today's date to retrieve the information but no one is fully semantically enriched which provide semantic information to the user. To develop a newly semantic web browser is difficult task in comparison of developing a new semantic tool which added as a layer to the existing web browser to provide semantic information. There are pre-existing semantic tools, which provide the support to the interpretation of web pages. It acts as a complementary knowledge source, which a user can call upon to gain instantaneous access to the background knowledge relevant to a web resource.

1.2 Plug-in

In computing, a **plug-in** (or extension) is a set of software components that adds specific abilities to a larger software application. If supported, plug-ins enables customizing the functionality of an application. For example, plug-ins are commonly used in web browsers to play video, scan for viruses, and display new file types. Well-known plug-ins examples include Adobe Flash Player and QuickTime [5].

As shown in the figure 4, the host application provides services which the plug-in can use, including a way for plug-ins to register themselves with the host application and a protocol for the exchange of data with plug-ins.

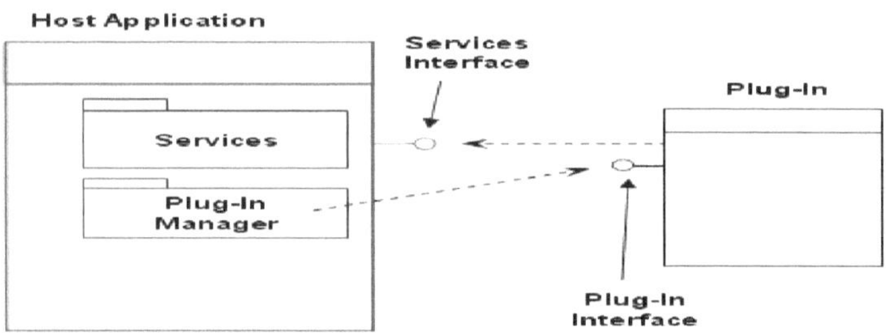

Fig. 4. Plug-In Framework

2 Ontology

An ontology is a data model that represents a set of concepts within a domain and the relationships between those concepts. Ontology defines a common vocabulary for researchers who need to share information in a domain. It includes machine-interpretable definitions of basic concepts in the domain and relations among them. Ontology construction, or ontology learning, is an important task in Artificial Intelligence, Semantic Web and Knowledge Management. It is the process of building an ontology, a data model that represents a set of concepts within a domain and the relationships between those concepts [8].

2.1 Ontologies and Semantic Information Retrieval

A new approach is emerging – the semantic approach. This approach aims to use meta-data – data about data – in order to answer the users' requirement in a more satisfactory way for Data Retrieval and navigation Ontologies can be very useful in improving the process in two ways:

1. It allows to abstract the information and represent it explicitly- highlighting the concepts and relations and not the words used to describe them.
2. Ontologies can possess inference functions, allowing more intelligent retrieval. [9]. We can interprate the web page by two technologies by
3. By Annotation
4. By complementary knowledge source.

In Annotation technologies [10, 11, 12] allow users to associate meta-information with web resources, which can then be used to facilitate their interpretation. While such technologies provide a useful way to support group-based and shared interpretation, they are nonetheless very limited; mainly because the annotation is carried out manually.

2.2 Algorithm Pseudo Code

Algorithm to annotate the text

```
Tokenize the text in words
For i=1 to #of words DO
{ LongestTerm=word[i]
While(LongestTerm is in MeSH term)
{ If(LongestTerm + Next_Term is in MeSH terms)
{ Longestterm=LongestTerm + next_term
}//End if
}//End while
If(LongestTerm is in MeSH term)
{ Annotateterm(LongestTerm);
//End for
//End if
Return annotated text;
```

Second technique is complementary knowledge source, which a user can call upon to gain instantaneous access to the background knowledge relevant to a web resource. it automatically associates a semantic layer to a web resource, rather than relying on a manual annotation. This process relies on the availability of an ontology [13].

3 Semantically Enriched Tool

There are many existing techniques which provide semantic information to the users in their own way to help them to find the specific and required information. Every user having their own requirement and it is very difficult to provide all requirements of the users at single platform, So that each technique having their own specific users to provide benefit to the users. In a seminal study of how users browse the web, Tauscher and Greenberg [22] presented the following statistics on the types of actions users may carry out:

1. 58% of pages visited are revisits,
2. 90% of all user actions are related to navigation
3. 30% of navigation actions are through the 'Back' button
4. Less than 1% of navigation actions use a history mechanism

A fairly obvious conclusion from such statistics is that web users need support in capturing what they have seen previously. So there is a need arise to create such type of technique which capture most of user and provide useful information what they required most of the times in Semantic form. So there is a need arise to create such type of technique which capture most of user and provide useful information what they required most of the times. This supposes to automatically relate the major terms present in the text of the web page to semantic entities, dynamically discovered in ontologies available on the web. In order to achieve this goal, It has to handle following major tasks:

1. Identifying relevant terms in the currently browse web page.
2. Selecting online ontologies to interpret the domain terms. This task constitutes one of the major differences from Magpie
3. Relating the text to semantic information. The goal here is to associate the terms of the domain, found in the text of the web pages, with the relevant semantic information.

3.1 Browsing with the Tool

At the left side of the panel the entities are populated dynamically and it depends upon the current web page that user open or browse. These entities mainly populated from the ontology part it shrink or increase according to the current web page. From this user comes to know which are the entities supported by the ontology for the present page. While in magpie we have to manually set the entity, while on changing the page it may or may not work because may be that page did not attach with this type of ontology. It works for particular domain of knowledge.

On the top of left panel there are some option available which are helpful in refining the page. Options are:

1). Expand all 2). Expand none 3). Highlight all 4). Highlight none 5). Accumulator 6). Storage 7). Search

On clicking on the expand button all the entities present at the left panel will expand and the related information will be collected under this particular entity. For example suppose we click on city entity. Then all the names of the city will collect under city entity and it also show its occurrence in the current web page. In the second part of its functionalities, let suppose we want to store the information of the specific entity item, on clicking the particular entity information to store, the next page will open to store the information locally at the client side. On that page some entity related information present and we have to fill according to it. Let suppose we click on the book entity and want to store the information related to the book.Then we have to fill some information like: (1) Book name (2) Date (3) Publication (4) Author (5) Title.

And then we will save it. We can also save it with our own choice tag which will helpful for future use to retrieve information. Now the question arises we can also bookmark the required page, then what is the need of it to save information separately but in the book mark we save the whole page, not the specific information that required. While in it we get only the required information and no need to search the whole page again. This all stored information can be searched with little time and did not have to browse the different pages from different sites. we get all the information at one place only. We can search the stored information when required by single click .we can search it by the given tag and get the required information of different web pages at on place. We can also search it by another way as shown in the figure. We search it by the entity name. We choose some entity from the group of entity and then make search to get the required data. Let suppose we select the entity author, book and publication. For example we want to search the DRAMA book of ramchandra author whose publication is Springer. From that we get the required data that is stored in the storage at client side only. From this search only those data will be fetch which are related with the three entity.

Fig. 5. All the entities at left panel are represented by different color

Fig. 6. Related information of particular entity is collected under that entity with the occurrence number in the current page

Fig. 7. Left panel act as a accumulator to store the related information under that category

Fig. 8. Search the particular entity name to know in detail about it

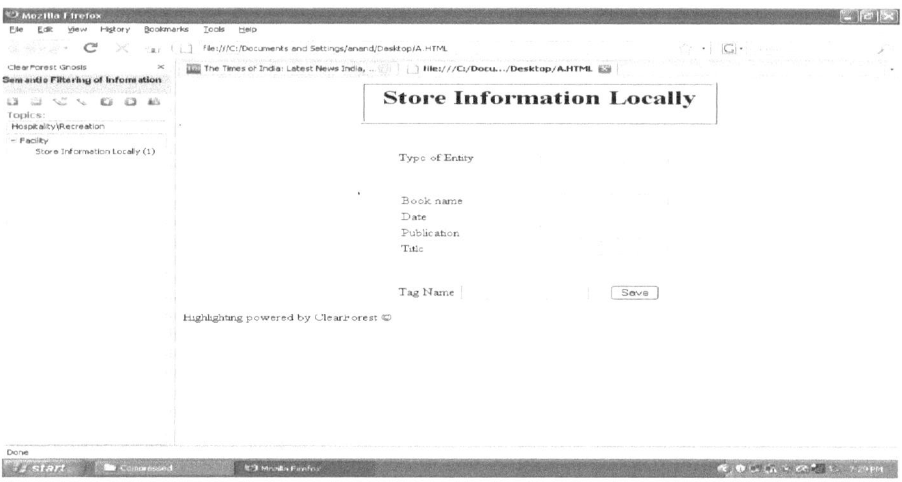

Fig. 9. Storage of information locally

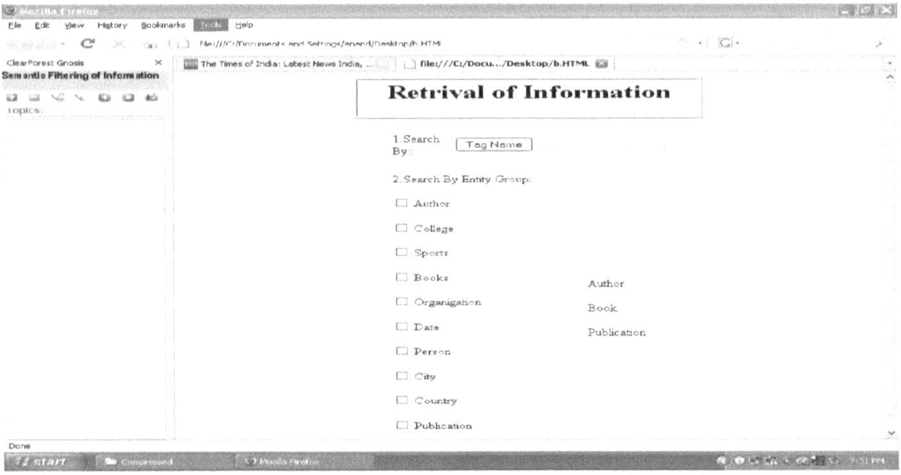

Fig. 10. Retrieval of Information

4 Advantages of the Proposed Tool

1. **Selecting Online Ontologies to Interpret the Domain Terms.** This task constitutes one of the major differences between Magpie and proposed tool. Magpie requires for the user to manually select the appropriate ontology for semantic browsing. This is an important limitation since the user may not be familiar with ontologies and has to be aware of the existence of the appropriate ontology, matching the domain of the currently browsed document.
2. **Collection of Information in Semantic form.** Collecting structured information from various web pages and web sites, motivated by the need to re-purpose such information on the client side in order to cater to the individual user‘s needs and preferences.
3. **Search the Collected Information.** User can search the required information at client side storage when required. User searches the required document or data by the tag keyword or by the group of entities.

5 Conclusion and Future Work

5.1 Conclusion

In this paper, we have presented the design and development of a tool, a semantic browser that supports the semantic interpretation of web documents through the dynamic selection of relevant knowledge from online ontologies. Its one of the features is the automatic selection, presentation and invocation of web services on the basis of the semantic information attached to the recognized terms. It is developed as an extension of a classical web browser, and populates ontologies dynamically and provides access of semantic information. It achieves this by extending standard web browsers with standard mark-up languages, without altering the layout of the web page. The key principle is that it's on the user how they access the relevant information through this tool. By adopting it, users immediately gain flexibility in the ways they use existing Web information without ever leaving their familiar web browser. As it consume Web information, they automatically produce Semantic Web information at the client side in structured format. Through the information collected at client side, the information they have collected merges together smoothly, giving rise to higher-ordered patterns and structures. This, we believe, is how the Semantic Web might emerge from the Web.

5.2 Future Work

We can further improve this tool to provide greater extent of relevant and semantic information to the users.

Scopes of improvement are:

1. Each time when new pages are visited there are numerous calls occur in the selection of related ontologies. It is more time consuming and also more computation required to find the ontology that are scattered on web. So we have to work it on to make it more efficient and reliable.
2. We can work to share this semantic information with one another. For this we have to create central database of semantic information which is accessible for all users which are connected in that network.

References

1. Tim, B.-L., Yuhsin, C., Lydia, C., Dan, C., Ruth, D., James, H., Adam, L., David, S.: Tabulator: Exploring and analyzing linked data on the semantic web (2006) (42 citations — 0 self)
2. Campbell, L.M., MacNeill, S. (July 08, 2010)
3. Eixelsberger, W., Ogris, M., Gall, H., Bellay, B.: Software architecture recovery of a program family. In: Proceedings of the 20th International Conference on Software Engineering (ICSE 1998), pp. 508–511 (1998)
4. Grosskurth, A., Godfrey, M.W.: A Reference Architecture for Web Browsers. In: ICSM 2005, Proceedings of the 21st IEEE International Conference on Software Maintenance, pp. 661–664 (2005)
5. Plug-in (May 05, 2011), `http://en.wikipedia.org/wiki/Plug-in_(computing)`
6. Orgun, B., Dras, M., Nayak A., James, G.: Approaches for semantic interoperability between domain ontologies, vol. 25(3), pp: 179–196
7. Hui, Y., Jamie, C.: Human-Guided Ontology Learning. In: Second Workshop on Human-Computer Interaction and Information Retrieval (HCIR 2008). Microsoft Research, Redmond (2008)
8. Asuman, D., Gokce, L., Yildiray, K., Ibrahim, C.: Exploiting Web Service Semantics: Taxonomies vs. Ontologies CoRR cs.DB/0212051 (2002)

9. Sini, M., Salokhe, G., Pardy, C., et al.: Ontology-based navigation of bibliographic metadata: example of the Food, Nutrition and Agriculture Journal. In: International Conference on Solid Dielectrics, Winchester, Hampshire UK, July 8-13, pp. 1–13 (2007) (published) (conference paper)
10. Ovsiannikov, I.A., Arbib, M.A., Mcneill, T.H.: Annotation Technology. International Journal of Human-Computer Studies 50(4), 329–362 (1999)
11. Vargas-Vera, M., Motta, E., Domingue, J., Lanzoni, M., Stutt, A., Ciravegna, F.: MnM: Ontology Driven Semiautomatic and Automatic Support for Semantic Markup. In: Gómez-Pérez, A., Benjamins, V.R. (eds.) EKAW 2002. LNCS (LNAI), vol. 2473, pp. 379–391. Springer, Heidelberg (2002)
12. Gruber, T.R.: A Translation approach to Portable Ontology pecifications. Knowledge Acquisition 5(2), 199–221 (1993)
13. Sadiq, W., Kumar, S.: Web Service Description (Usage Scenarios). In: World Wide Web Consortium (2002), `http://www.w3.org/TR/2002/WDwsdescusecases-20020604`
14. Motta, E.: Reusable Components for Knowledge Modelling. Frontiers in AI and Applications. IOS Press, The Netherlands (1997)
15. Tauscher, L., Greenberg, S.: How People Revisit Web Pages: Empirical Findings and Implications for the Design of History Systems. International Journal of Human Computer Studies 47(1), 97–138 (2001)

4-Bit Serial-Parallel Multiplier and Bit-Level Systolic Architecture for Implementation of Discrete Orthogonal Transforms

M.N. Murty[1*], S.S. Nayak[2], B. Padhy[3], and S.N. Panda[4]

[1] Department of Physics, NIST, Berhampur-761008, Orissa, India
mnarayanamurty@rediffmail.com
[2] Department of Physics, JITM, Centurion University, Paralakhemundi-761200, Orissa, India
[3] Department of Physics, Khallikote (Auto) College, Berhampur-760001, Orissa, India
[4] Department of Physics, Gunupur College, Gunupur-765022, Orissa, India

Abstract. Highly efficient arithmetic operations are necessary to achieve the desired performance in many real-time systems and digital image processing applications. In all these applications, one of the important arithmetic operations frequently performed is to multiply and accumulate with small computational time. In this paper, a serial - parallel multiplier, which can be used to perform either signed or unsigned multiplications, is presented. In this multiplier one factor $B(n)$ is fed serially with word length n=4 while the other $A(m)$ is stored in parallel with number of bits m=4. Baugh-Wooley algorithm necessitates complementation of last bit of each partial product except the last partial product in which all but the last bit are complemented. In the proposed algorithm all bits of the last partial product are complemented. This modification results in considerable reduction in hardware compared to Baugh-Wooley multiplier. This multiplier can be used for implementation of discrete orthogonal transforms, which are used in many applications, including image and signal processing. Also a fully pipelined 2-D bit-level systolic architecture is presented for efficient implementation of discrete orthogonal transforms using a serial-parallel matrix-vector multiplication scheme. A comparison with similar structures has shown that the proposed structure requires less computation time.

Keywords : signal processing, serial-parallel multiplier, discrete orthogonal transforms, systolic architecture.

1 Introduction

In digital signal processing (DSP) numerous arithmetic operations require the extensive use of multiplications. The multiplier is therefore an essential part of any DSP

* Corresponding author.

P.V. Krishna, M.R. Babu, and E. Ariwa (Eds.): ObCom 2011, Part I, CCIS 269, pp. 91–99, 2012.

circuit. In the past much attention has been paid to the development of multiplication strategies, among others the algorithms of Booth [1], Chen [2], Wallace[3], Braun[4] and Baugh-Wooley[5] are most popular. A number of DSP applications demand high-speed multiplication while others require less hardware and moderate speed. Performance is greatly affected by the multiplication strategy and the type of multiplier used. A serial multiplier is employed to minimise the chip area and hence the hardware cost. On the other hand, a parallel multiplier presents a high speed but is expensive in terms of silicon area. A serial-parallel multiplier is a good trade-off between a time consuming serial multiplier and an area consuming parallel multiplier. In this device one factor is entered serially and the other is stored in parallel with a fixed number of bits. The multiplier is therefore designed for a given word length.

This paper proposes a serial-parallel multiplier designed to achieve precision with 4 bits. This multiplier is configured to accept and produce unsigned or signed two's complement numbers. The hardware used in this multiplier is less compared with Baugh-Wooley multiplier [5]. This multiplier can be used for implementation of discrete orthogonal transforms (DOTs).

DOTs are used in speech and image processing applications. The discrete Fourier transform (DFT) and the discrete Hartley transform (DHT) are popular orthogonal transforms. Of all the sinusoidal transforms, the discrete cosine transform (DCT) is most efficient transform for the compression of speech and image data. All these transforms are based on matrix-vector multiplication.

The systolic arrays are used in the design and implementation of high performance digital signal processing equipment. The systolic array concept can also be exploited at bit level in the design of individual VLSI chips. Bit-level systolic arrays exhibit a number of attractive features such as :

i) The basic processing element (PE) is small.
ii) The computation time of the PE is small.
iii) The highly regular structure of the circuits renders them comparatively easy to design and test.

The computation time of the proposed bit level systolic architecture for DOT based matrix-vector product is less compared to similar structures [6]-[8].

The rest of the paper is organised as follows. The multiplication algorithm is presented in Section-2. The proposed serial-parallel multiplier is presented in Section-3. Section-4 deals with the systolic architecture for implementation of discrete orthogonal transforms. Finally we conclude our paper in Section-5.

2 Multiplication Algorithm

Consider two unsigned fixed-point numbers $A(m) = a_{m-1},\ldots, a_0$ and $B(n) = b_{n-1}, \ldots, b_0$ represented by m and n bits, respectively. The product of these numbers is given by.

$$P = A(m)\ B(n)$$

In two's complement, $A(m)$ and $B(n)$ can be represented as

$$A(m) = -a_{m-1}2^{m-1} + \sum_{i=0}^{m-2} a_i 2^i \quad (1)$$

and

$$B(n) = -b_{n-1}2^{n-1} + \sum_{j=0}^{n-2} b_j 2^j \quad (2)$$

Then the product of these two's complement operands can be written as

$$P = \left[-a_{m-1}2^{m-1} + \sum_{i=0}^{m-2} a_i 2^i\right]\left[-b_{n-1}2^{n-1} + \sum_{j=0}^{n-2} b_j 2^j\right]$$

$$= a_{m-1}b_{n-1}2^{m+n-2} + 2^{n-1}\sum_{i=0}^{m-2} 2^i(-a_i b_{n-1})$$

$$+ 2^{m-1}\sum_{j=0}^{n-2} 2^j(-a_{m-1}b_j) + \sum_{i=0}^{m-2}\sum_{j=0}^{n-2} 2^{i+j} a_i b_j$$

Using the relation $A + \bar{A} = 1$ from Boolean algebra,

$$P = (-\overline{a_{m-1}b_{n-1}} + 1)\, 2^{m+n-2} + 2^{n-1}\sum_{i=0}^{m-2} 2^i(\overline{a_i b_{n-1}} - 1)$$

$$+ 2^{m-1}\sum_{j=0}^{n-2} 2^j(\overline{a_{m-1}b_j} - 1) + \sum_{i=0}^{m-2}\sum_{j=0}^{n-2} 2^{i+j} a_i b_j$$

$$= \sum_{i=0}^{m-2}\sum_{j=0}^{n-2} 2^{i+j} a_i b_j + 2^{n-1}\sum_{i=0}^{m-2} 2^i\, \overline{a^i b_{n-1}}$$

$$+ 2^{m-1}\sum_{j=0}^{n-2} 2^j\, \overline{a_{m-1}b_j} - 2^{m+n-2}\, \overline{a_{m-1}b_{n-1}}$$

$$+ 2^{m-1} + 2^{n-1} - 2^{m+n-2} \quad (3)$$

Equation (3) can be mapped into a systolic architecture.

3 Proposed Serial - Parallel Multiplier

For $m = n = 4$, (3) can be written as

$$P = 2^0 a_0 b_0 + 2^1(a_1 b_0 + a_0 b_1) + 2^2(a_2 b_0 + a_1 b_1 + a_0 b_2)$$
$$+ 2^3(\overline{a_3 b_0} + a_2 b_1 + a_1 b_2 + \overline{a_0 b_3})$$
$$+ 2^4(\overline{a_3 b_1} + a_2 b_2 + \overline{a_1 b_3} + 1) + 2^5(\overline{a_3 b_2} + \overline{a_2 b_3}) - 2^6(\overline{a_3 b_3} + 1) \quad (4)$$

The multiplication algorithm (4) resulting from (3) for a word length 4 is illustrated by the multiplication table shown in Table 1. The partial product terms are formed by ANDing each multiplicand bit with each multiplier bit. For a two's complement multiplication, one NAND and three AND operations are performed in each of the first three rows of the bit product, and four NAND operations in the fourth row. The final product is computed by adding '1' to the fifth and the seventh columns along with all partial product terms.

Figure 1 shows the steps of multiplication procedures for four bit tow's complement numbers.

The 2's complement serial - parallel multiplier comprising of a logic unit and an adder unit is shown in Fig. 2. The logic unit consist of three AND gates, one NAND gate, and three XOR gates. In this multiplier $A(m)$ is stored in parallel and $B(n)$ is entered serially from the least-significant bit to the most-significant bit. A flip-flop (FF) saves the carry bit and a full adder adds the result of the partial product. The output of the multiplier is obtained from the adder unit using a carry-save and add-shift technique (the CSAS technique) together with one control signal Q. In the first three and last two clock cycles Q=0, but in the fourth, fifth and sixth clock cycles Q=1. The extra '1' for the fifth and seventh columns are automatically provided by the control signal Q. Four zeros are appended to the left of the MSB of $B(n)$ for input / output synchronisation. The excessive carry-out bit out of (2n-1) bit product is ignored.

Table 1. 4 X 4 Bit Two's Complement Multiplication

			b_3	b_2	b_1	b_0
			a_3	a_2	a_1	a_0
			$\overline{a_3b_0}$	a_2b_0	a_1b_0	a_0b_0
		$\overline{a_3b_1}$	a_2b_1	a_1b_1	a_0b_1	
	$\overline{a_3b_2}$	a_2b_2	a_1b_2	a_0b_2		
$\overline{a_3b_3}$	$\overline{a_2b_3}$	$\overline{a_1b_3}$	$\overline{a_0b_3}$			
1		1				
P_6	P_5	P_4	P_3	P_2	P_1	P_0

			1	1	0	1	(-3)
			0	1	0	1	(5)
			1	1	0	1	
		1	0	0	0		
	1	1	0	1			
1	0	1	0				
1		1					
1	1	1	0	0	0	1	(-15)

			1	0	1	1	(-5)
			1	1	0	0	(-4)
			0	1	0	0	
		0	1	0	0		
	1	0	0	0			
0	0	1	1				
1		1					
0	0	1	0	1	0	0	(20)

Fig. 1. Steps in computation of -3 x 5 and -5 x -4

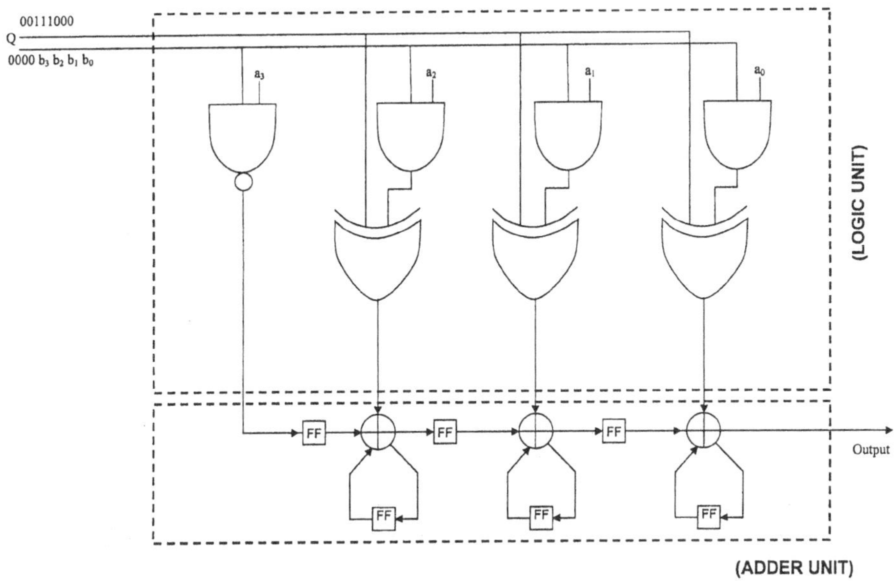

Fig. 2. Serial - Parallel 4-bit multiplier

4 Proposed Architecture

This section describes the methodology used in the design and implementation of DOTs based on the proposed multiplication algorithm using a systolic architecture implementation strategy.

4.1 Mathematical Background

Let $\boldsymbol{A}$ be the N x N kernel matrix of an orthogonal transform and $\boldsymbol{B} = [B_0, B_1, \ldots, B_{N\text{-}1}]^T$ be an N vector. The transformed vector $\boldsymbol{Y}$ is given by

$$\boldsymbol{Y} = \boldsymbol{AB} = [y_0, y_1, \ldots, y_{N\text{-}1}]^T \tag{5}$$

Such that

$$y_\ell = \sum_{k=0}^{N-1} A_{\ell k} B_k \quad \text{for } \ell = 0, 1, .., N\text{-}1 \tag{6}$$

The elements of the kernel matrix $\boldsymbol{A}$ and the data matrix $\boldsymbol{B}$ be represented by the 2's complement code as

$$A_{\ell k} = -a_{\ell k}^{n-1} 2^{n-1} + \sum_{i=0}^{n-2} a_{\ell k}^{i} 2^{i} \tag{7}$$

and

$$B_k = -b_k^{n-1} 2^{n-1} + \sum_{j=0}^{n-2} b_k^{j} 2^{j} \tag{8}$$

Where $a^i_{\ell k}$ and b^j_k are the ith bit of $A_{\ell k}$ and jth bit of B_k, respectively, which are either 0 or 1. Substituting (7) and (8) in (6), we get according to (3)

$$\begin{aligned} y_\ell = \sum_{k=0}^{N-1} \Bigg[& \sum_{i=0}^{n-2}\sum_{j=0}^{n-2} 2^{i+j} a^i_{lk} b^j_k + 2^{n-1}\sum_{i=0}^{n-2} 2^i \overline{a^i_{lk} b^{n-1}_k} \\ & + 2^{n-1}\sum_{j=0}^{n-2} 2^j \overline{a^{n-1}_{\ell k} b^j_k} - 2^{2n-2}\overline{a^{n-1}_{\ell k} b^{n-1}_k} + 2^n - 2^{2n-2} \Bigg] \end{aligned} \tag{9}$$

N-point discrete orthogonal transform output given by (9) may be computed by a systolic architecture.

4.2 Proposed Systolic Architecture

From (6), we have for N=3

$$\begin{aligned} y_0 &= A_{00}B_0 + A_{01}B_1 + A_{02}B_2 \\ y_1 &= A_{10}B_0 + A_{11}B_1 + A_{12}B_2 \\ y_2 &= A_{20}B_0 + A_{21}B_1 + A_{22}B_2 \end{aligned} \tag{10}$$

Equation (9) can be mapped into the proposed systolic architecture as shown in Fig. 3 for the case of N=3 and the matrix -vector product (10) can be implemented by this structure. It consists of three identical blocks. Each block has three identical processing elements (PEs). Function of each PE is shown in Fig. 4. Each PE comprises a serial - parallel multiplier M as shown in Fig. 2, a flip-flop (FF) for saving the carry bit and a full adder that adds the result of the partial product and the result generated from the previous PE.

The input words B_0, B_1 and B_2 are fed to a 3-stage parallel - serial S shift registers of each block. The vector elements b^j_k are fed in a parallel / serial fashion bit by bit with LSB first while the matrix elements $a^i_{\ell k}$ are fed in parallel fashion and remain fixed in their corresponding PE cell during the entire computation of the operation. The data in the S shift registers are bit-serially shifted out with least significant bit first, staggered by one addition delay 'T_A' with respect to the preceding location of the shift register. Q signal is provided to each PE for regulating the multiplications. Each bit of the final product of the PE is fed to the full adder of the preceding PE so that the corresponding output of each PE are added to compute the desired output.

The proposed systolic architecture for implementation of N-point discrete orthogonal transform consists of N number of S shift registers and N^2 number of PEs.

The area complexity of the structure for N-point transform is $O(N^2)$ as the area of the shift registers can be treated small compared with the area of the PEs.

The entire computation process can be carried out in $(2n-1)$ clock cycles with structure area of N^2 PEs. The first transform component y_0 is available after $(N+2n-2)$ clock cycles. The second transform component y_1 and third transform component y_2 are computed in every $(2n-1)$ clock cycles. The set up time to load the input words in the parallel - serial shift registers is ignored in the estimation of computation time. The latency is $(N+2n-2)T$.

Table 2 gives the comparison of the proposed structure with some similar architectures. It can be seen that the proposed architecture requires less computation time when compared with the structures in [6] - [8].

Table 2. Comparison Of Proposed Matrix - Vector Structure With Some Existing Structures

Features	Proposed Structure	Structure of [6]	Structure of [7]	Structure of [8]
Computation time	$(2n-1)\,T$	$(2n)T$	$(2n)T$	$(2nN)T$
Area complexity	$O(N^2)$	$O(N^2)$	$O(N^2)$	$O(N)$

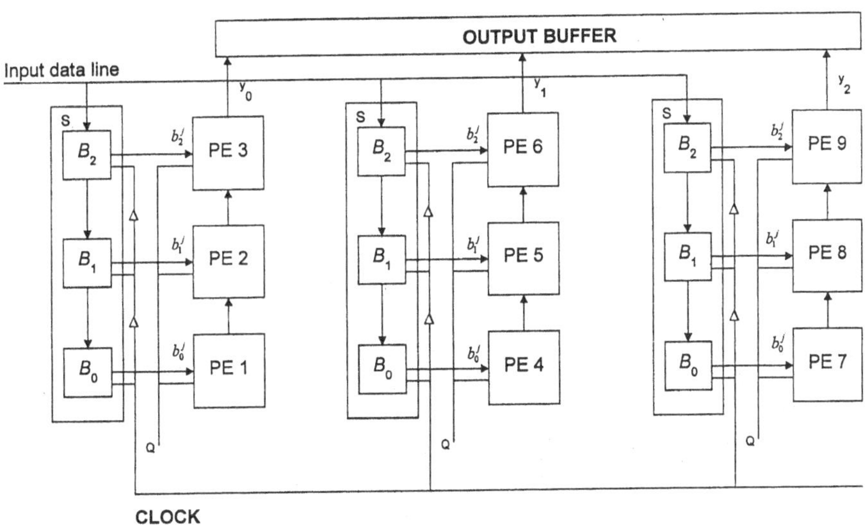

Fig. 3. Systolic architecture for implementation of DOT based matrix-vector product for N=3. Δ implies delay of duration T_A.

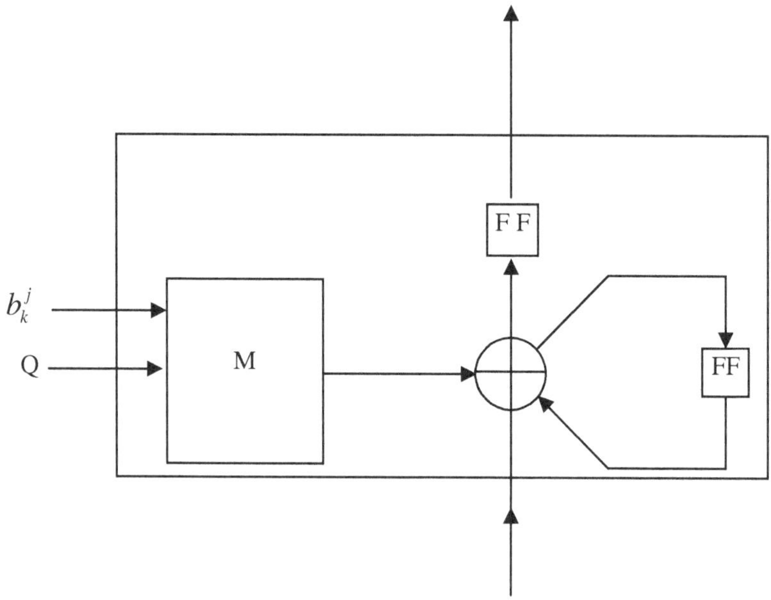

Fig. 4. Processing element of systolic architecture

5 Conclusion

A serial - parallel multiplier, which can perform either signed or unsigned multiplications, is proposed. The hardware used in this multiplier is less compared with Baugh - Wooley multiplier. Also we have presented a bit - level systolic architecture for the computation of discrete orthogonal transforms, which are central in many signal / image processing applications. The computation time of the proposed architecture is less when compared with some existing structures. Due to simplicity and regularity, the proposed systolic architecture is suitable for VLSI implementation of discrete orthogonal transforms.

References

1. Booth, A.D.: A signed binary multiplication technique. Q. J. Mech. Appl. Math. 4, part-2, 236–240 (1951)
2. Chen, T.C.: A binary multiplication scheme based on squaring. IEEE Tans. C-20, 678–680 (1971)
3. Wallace, C.S.: A suggestion for a fast multiplier. IEEE Trans. EC-13, 14–17 (1964)
4. Braun, E.L.: Digital computer design. Academic Press, New York (1963)
5. Baugh, C.R., Wooley, B.A.: A two's complement parallel array multiplication algorithm. IEEE Trans. C-22(1-2), 1045–1047 (1973)

6. Nayak, S.S., Meher, P.K.: High throughput VLSI implementation of discrete orthogonal transforms using bit-level vector - matrix multiplier. IEEE Trans. Circuits Syst. II. Analog and Digital Signal Processing 46(5), 655–658 (1999)
7. Nayak, S.S., Murty, M.N., Panda, H.: Bit - level systolic implementation of discrete orthogonal transforms. Signal Processing 81, 2437–2443 (2001)
8. Amira, A., Bouridane, A., Milligan, P., Belatreche, A.: Design of efficient architectures for discrete orthogonal transforms using bit level systolic structures. IEE Proc. - Comput. Digit. Tech. 149(1), 17–24 (2002)

Sound Data Compression Using Different Methods

Pravin Y. Kumbhar and Shoba Krishnan

Dept. of Electronics and Telecommunication,
Vivekanand Education Society, Institute of Technology, Mumbai University,
Mumbai, Maharashtra

Abstract. This paper is about the methods of sound data compression. The development of audio data compression has significantly made our lives easier. The technological progress has facilitated the process of recording audio on different media such as CD-Audio. In recent years, much has been achieved in the field of audio and speech compression. Many standards have been established In order to compare methods of sound data compression I have used Adobe Audition 3.0 software and computer program of the sound compression system from manufacturers' side. They are characterized by more better sound quality at lower bit rate. It allows recording the same CD-Audio formats using "lossy" or lossless compression algorithms in order to reduce the amount of data surface area at almost noticeable difference in the quality of the recording. To illustrate the problem, I have used the graphs of the spectrum and musical composition spectrograms. The comparison has been done on the basis of uncompressed music track from the original CD-Audio) lines before and after the abstract. This document is in the required format.

Keywords: sound data compression, mp3, FLAC, Lossless compression algorithm, Lossy compression algorithm.

1 Introduction

Nowadays, it is possible to store audio data on various media such as hard drive, audio cd ,data disc,MP3 disc, or portable flash memory. Due to the technological progress, it has been noticed that the audio data takes up too much memory space. Placing various audio files without using compression algorithms on the Internet would be useless. What is more cell phones without compression are not capable of communication in better quality. It is noticeable how fast the data compression has become ubiquitous in our lives and yet it has been an interest of only small group of engineers and scientists for many years.

1.1 Definition

Sound compression is a form of data compression. Data compression is the process of encoding information using fewer bits than the original representation would use. Compression is useful because it helps reduce the consumption of expensive

P.V. Krishna, M.R. Babu, and E. Ariwa (Eds.): ObCom 2011, Part I, CCIS 269, pp. 100–108, 2012.

resources, such as hard disk space or transmission bandwidth.Data compression is a change of recording information in such a way to reduce the volume of the collection. Audio compression algorithms are implemented in computer software as audio codec Therefore, it is a shift of the same set of information using fewer bits. The use of compression can be found in multimedia devices, DVD movies, digital television, data transmission, the Internet, etc. Consequently, specifically optimized audio lossless and lossy algorithms have been created. Lossy algorithms provide greater compression rates and are used in mainstream consumer audio devices. In both lossy and lossless compression, information redundancy is reduced, using methods such as coding, pattern recognition and linear prediction to reduce the amount of information used to represent the uncompressed data.

1.2 Modeling and Coding

One's requirements decide what type of compression he applies. However, the choice between lossy or lossless method also depends on other factors. One of the most important is the characteristics of data that will be compressed. For instance, the same algorithm, which effectively compresses the text may be completely useless in the case of video and sound compression. It is worth remembering that compression is an experimental science. The best option is chosen depending on the nature of the redundancy present in the data. Designing of algorithms' compression for different data is divided into two stages. The first stage is called modelling. Due to this, the information of any redundancy occurring in the data is described by a model. The next step is encoding the description of the model and the description that informs about the differences in data related to the model. This process is done by using the binary alphabet. Any type of media file, such as, music, images and videos, can be stored in either lossy or lossless formats. The files in lossless formats usually consume much more storage space than in lossy formats . This would allow them to carry around more music at slight loss of quality. Lossless formats are, however, best for archives, who maintain enormous collection of music tracks. Music stored in lossless formats can easily be converted to lossy formats if required. . Lossless formats usually preserve the exact quality of media files that was present in the original source. Subsequent encoding in other lossless formats will also cause very minor degradations at best. For example, you could rip a song from an audio CD using Windows Media Lossless format, and later re-encode it using FLAC.

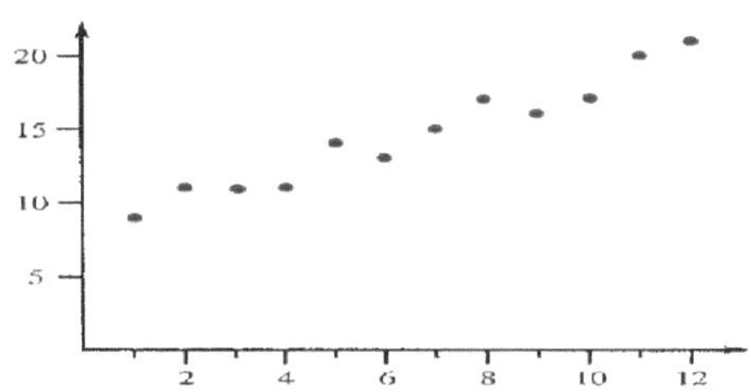

Fig. 1. String data

1.3 Lossless Compression Algorithms

The figure 2, depicts the approach taken by all the compression algorithms. The raw signal is approximated by some kind of "prediction" algorithm, the parameters of which are selected to produce a wave quite similar to the input waveform. Those parameters are different for each frame (say 256 samples) of audio and are packed into a minimum number of bits in the output file (or stream, in a real-time application).

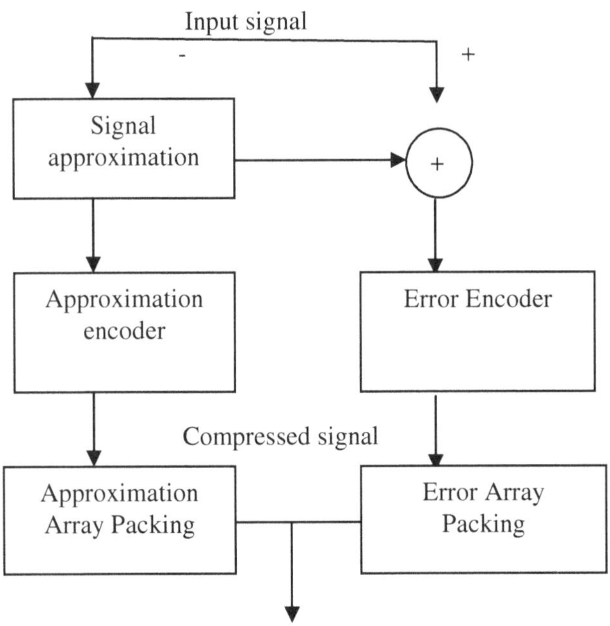

Fig. 2. Lossless algorithm

Meanwhile, the difference between the "predicted" waveform and the real signal is packed into as small a number of bits as possible. The predictor is replicated in the decoder - and it must work from prediction parameters. The predicted value is added to the "error" value to create the final exactly correct value for that sample. Then the prediction algorithm is run again, based on the newly decoded sample and some previous ones, to predict the next sample.

1. signal approximation

A signal is decomposed to a linear combination of normalized Gaussian functions. Since both the sampling steps and bandwidth are data-adaptive, the new scheme tends to concentrate the signal to a smaller dimension. The new scheme could be very useful for speech processing applications and many other signal processing applications as well.

2. Approximation encoder

An encoder is a device, circuit, transducer, software program, algorithm or person that converts information from one format or code to another, for the purposes of standardization, speed, secrecy, security, or saving space by shrinking size.

3. Approximation Array Packing

A packing array is a $b \times k$ array, A with entries $a_{i,j}$ from a g-ary alphabet such that given any two columns, i and j, and for all ordered pairs of elements from a g-ary alphabet, (g_1, g_2), there is at most one row, r, such that $a_{r,i} = g_1$ and $a_{r,j} = g_2$. Further, there is a set of at least n rows that pair wise differ in each column they are disjoint. A central question is to determine, for given g, k and n, the maximum possible b. We examine the implications when n is close to g. We give a brief analysis of the case $n = g$ and show that $2g$ rows is always achievable whenever more than g exist. We give an upper bound derived from design packing numbers when $n = g - 1$. When $g+ 1 \leq k$ then this bound is always at least as good as the modified Plotkin bound of. When the associated packing has as many points as blocks and has reasonably uniform replication numbers, we show that this bound is tight. In particular, finite geometries imply the existence of a family of optimal or near optimal packing arrays. When no projective plane exists we present similarly strong results. This article completely determines the packing numbers, $D(v, k, 1)$, when v < \frac{k(k-1)}{2}.Most any compression algorithm will get close to the minimum entropy needed to encode the integers, for example, Huffman coding, but accessing it like an array will be non-trivial. The advantage of Huffman or LZW is that they create codebooks in such a way that the length of the codes can be derived from the output bit stream without actually storing the lengths. These techniques allow you to get very close to the Shannon limit.

4. Error Encoder

It means that unknown or unsupported video/audio codec is specified. Input to error encoder is the summation of input signal and signal approximation .from output of encoder we conclude that video/audio is supported or unsupported.

5. Error Array Packing

Input from error encoder and mix with output of Approximation Array Packing its combines gives the compressed signal.

Lossy Compression Algorithms

Lossy compression reduces the number of bits needed to express a particular information. Reconstructed information usually is not identical to the original. There is some loss of information and distortion. However, a better compression ratio is gained than in lossless compression. An inability of an exact reconstruction is not an obstacle. In some applications this is not a must, for example sending the speech signal does not require the exact value of each sample. Assuming a certain quality of reconstruction, diverse distortions and differences in relation to the original are allowed. If, for instance, the speech quality signal has to be the phone quality, some loss of information can be permitted. When there is a need to receive the speech signal of CD quality, some loss of information (relatively small) is also acceptable. While designing algorithms for lossy compression, some methods are needed to measure its quality. Due to the different areas of applications, a number of concepts has been introduced to describe and measure the compression quality Sound can often be compressed at 10:1 with imperceptible loss of quality. This can be done with the following methods AAC, ATRAC, WMA.

Advanced Audio Coding (AAC)

Advanced Audio Coding (AAC) is a standardized, Lossy compression and encoding scheme for digital audio. Designed to be the successor of the MP3 format, AAC generally achieves better sound quality than MP3 at similar bit rate.AAC has been standardized by ISO as part of the MPEG-2 and MPEG-4 specificationsThe MPEG-2 audio tests showed that AAC meets the requirements referred to as "transparent" for the ITU at 128 Kbit/s for stereo, and 320 Kbit/s for 5.1 audio.

AAC's Improvements over MP3

Advanced Audio Coding is designed to be the successor of the *MPEG-1 Audio Layer 3*, known as MP3 format, which was specified by ISO/IEC in 11172-3 (MPEG-1 Audio) and 13818-3 (MPEG-2Audio). Blind tests show that AAC demonstrates greater sound quality and transparency than MP3 for files coded at the same bit rate.

Improvements Include

- More sample frequencies (from 8 to 96 kHz) than MP3 (16 to 48 kHz)
- Up to 48 channels (MP3 supports up to two channels in MPEG-1 mode and up to 5.1 channels in MPEG-2 mode)
- Arbitrary bit-rates and variable frame length. Standardized constant bit rate with bit reservoir.
- Higher efficiency and simpler filter bank (rather than MP3's hybrid coding, AAC uses a pure MDCT)
- Higher coding efficiency for stationary signals (AAC uses a block size of 1024 or 960 samples, allowing more efficient coding than MP3's 576 sample blocks)

Overall, the AAC format allows developers more flexibility to design codecs than MP3 does, and corrects many of the design choices made in the original MPEG-1 audio specification. This increased flexibility often leads to more concurrent encoding strategies and, as a result, to more efficient compression. However, in terms of whether AAC is better than MP3, the advantages of AAC are not entirely decisive, and the MP3 specification, although antiquated, has proven surprisingly robust in spite of considerable flaws. AAC and HE-AAC are better than MP3 at low bit rates (typically less than 128 kilobits per second). This is especially true at very low bit rates where the superior stereo coding, pure MDCT, and better transform window sizes leave MP3 unable to compete. However, as bit rate increases, the efficiency of an audio format becomes less important relative to the efficiency of the encoder's implementation, and the intrinsic advantage AAC holds over MP3 no longer dominates audio quality.Also, in terms of comparison, due to its popularity, MP3 format was much more explored than AAC, and there are fewer available AAC codecs than MP3 ones.

Adaptive Transform Acoustic Coding

It is a family of proprietary audio compression algorithms developed by Sony. In order to deliver on a tangible product that could encode at high speeds and with minimal power consumption. This is in contrast to other codecs developed on computers with no regard for the constraints of portable hardware. This is reflected in the design of the ATRAC codecs, which tend to emphasize processing smaller numbers of samples at a time to save memory at the cost compression efficiency and additional multiplies. These trade-offs are entirely logical on DSP systems, where memory is often at a premium compared to multiplier performance.

Windows Media Audio (WMA)

It is an audio data compression technology developed by Microsoft. The name can be used to refer to its audio file format or its audio codecs. It is a proprietary technology that forms part of the Windows Media framework. WMA consists of four distinct codecs. Standard is the NBC Olympics website which uses WMA 10 Pro in its low-bitrate mode at 48 kbit/s.

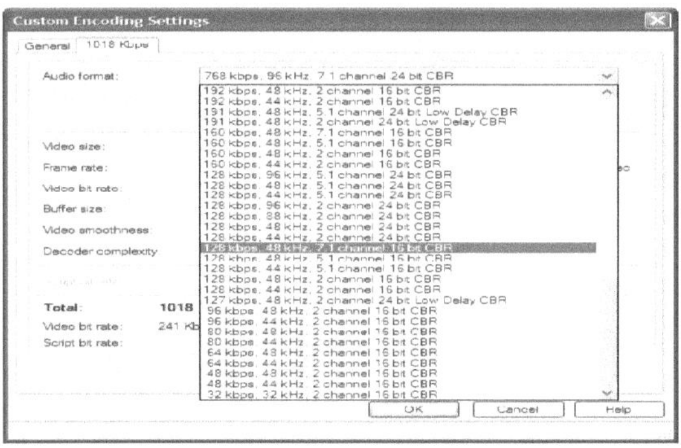

Above figure shows Screenshot of Windows Media Encoder 9 Series displaying new encoding options for Windows Media Audio 10 Professional. Its purpose is to provide a visual representation for the new encoding options available for Windows Media Audio 10 Professional.

Windows Media Audio Voice (WMA Voice) is a lossy audio codec that competes with Speex (used in Microsoft's own Xbox Live online service[]),ACELP, and other codec. Designed for low-bandwidth, voice playback applications, it employs low-pass and high-pass filtering of sound outside the human speech frequency range to achieve higher compression efficiency than WMA.

Measures of Quality Compression

Compression algorithms can be assessed using different criteria, for example, measuring the complexity of the algorithm, speed of action, memory, which is required for the algorithm implementation , the degree of compression and data similarity after decompression to the original data. The degree of compression is a measure of how effectively an algorithm can be compressed. It is the ratio of the number of bits needed to represent the data before compression to the number of bits that is needed to represent data after the process. Using a lossy compression, the data obtained after decompression differ from the original. To determine the effectiveness of the algorithm, some ways are needed to measure these differences. Such differences are called the distortion. Lossy compression is usually used to compress data, which originally took the form of the analog, for instance audio, video sequence. Encoding analog signal is often referred to as a continuous wavelet encoding. The ultimate arbiter, that can assess the quality of sound signal waveform encoding, is a man. Due to the fact that such assessments are difficult to reproduce mathematically, some models are applied. One of these schemes is the psycholinguistic model. Further terms such as fidelity and quality are used to detect differences between the original and decompressed signal. If the fidelity or quality of decompression (reconstruction) is large, it means that such data does not differ significantly from the original data.

Analysis and Comparison of Audio Data Compression Standards

In my analysis I used four systems of lossy compression and two of lossless compression. I have compared every described standard with the uncompressed source file, deriving from the original CD. I have based my analysis of selected files on a specific criterion. I took into account the psychoacoustic qualities, therefore a human hearing. For the study I have used Adobe Audition 3.0. demo version that is a professional music program for processing and analysis of an audio sound. The results are presented using the two most important tools: a graph showing the spectrum of acoustic signal (Fig. 2) and the spectrogram that is the signal amplitude spectrum diagram (Fig. 3). The main problem in lossy compression systems was weak transfer of high frequencies. This effect occurred at lower data rates because the algorithms use the filters, which cut the high frequency band depending on the bandwidth, such as 16kHz upwards. The lower the rate, the less bandwidth system offers us. The best lossy compression system has turned out to be little known Muse pack, offering exemplary sound quality at 210kbps bit rate. As far as lossless compression is concerned, Monkey's Audio has been the top-quality system offering compression grade of 67.39%.

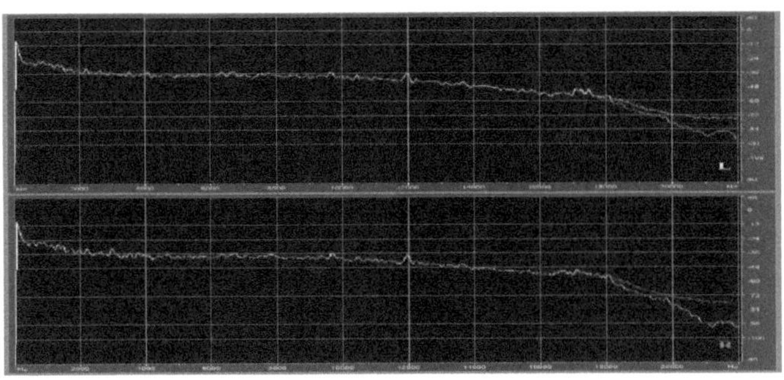

Fig. 3. The spectrum of a musical composition after applying MP3 compression at 320kbps

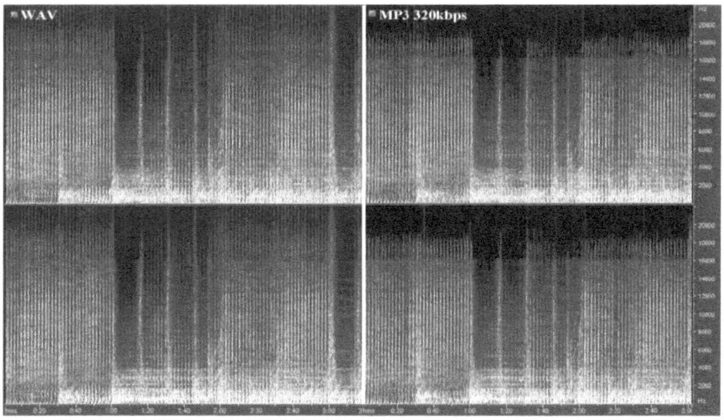

Fig. 4. Spectrogram of a musical composition after applying MP3 compression at 320 kbps

The following table shows the results of compression using chosen standards that apply lossy compression. Comparative criterion is the degree of compression, the compressed file size and sound quality after compression of the original WAV file size 64.1 MB. (Table 1)

Table 1. Compression using chosen standards that apply lossy compression

Compression system	Compression ratio	Compressed size	Sound quality
MP3 320 kbps	22.62%	14.5MB	Very good
MP3 128 kbps	9%	5.81 MB	Good
MP3 96 Kbps	6.79%	4.35 MB	Low
WMA 320 Kbps	22.62%	14.15 MB	Very good
WMA 128 kbps	9.13%	5.85 MB	good
WMA 96 kbps	6.86%	4.4 MB	low
Ogg Vorbis 320 kbps	22.78%	14.6 MB	high
Ogg Vorbis 128 kbps	9.2%	5.9 MB	Very good
Ogg Vorbis 96 kbps	6.9%%	4.42 MB	Good
Ogg Vorbis 64 kbps	4.6%	2.95 MB	Low
Musepack 210 kbps	15%	9.62 MB	High
Musepack 180 kbps	12.8%	8.22 MB	Very good
Musepack 130 kbps	9.6%	6.18 MB	Good
Musepack 90 kbps	6.72%	4.31 MB	acceptable

Table 2. Compression using given standards that apply lossless compression

Compression system	Compression ratio	Compressed size
Monkey's Audio tryb „Extra High"	67.39%	43.2MB
Monkey's Audio tryb „High"	67.86%	43.5MB
Monkey's Audio tryb „Normal"	68.02%	43.6MB
Monkey's Audio tryb „Fast"	69.89%	44.8MB
FLAC tryb „8"	69.58%	44.6MB
FLAC tryb „5"	70.2%	45.0MB
FLAC tryb „0"	75.19%	48.2MB

Next table presents the results of compression using given standards that apply lossless compression. In this case, the comparison criterion is the degree of compression and file size after compression of the original WAV file size 64.1 MB. The sound quality after decompression in all cases is the same, consistent with the original. (Table 2)

2 Conclusion

Many standards have been created that are characterized by increasingly higher sound quality at lower data rates. Their efficiency and capabilities have increased significantly. A big space of available memory gives a possibility to save a huge amount of music compressed by different codec using a lossy method, such as MP3, WMA, Muse pack, and lossless method, such as increasingly popular standard for FLAC. Indeed, without compression large amounts of audio data could be moved. However, by using the compression, saving the data is 10 times more efficient with a slight, almost imperceptible loss of quality. After this analysis, I conclude that using the audio compression that uses systems applying the lossless compression, allows to reduce the audio data without any loss in quality by 30%. In this way a perfect copy of the original is received. Using lossy compression schemes, one can obtain the file size of about 90% smaller than the original, with an appreciable loss of quality. Thus obtained files, thanks to their small size, suit perfectly for transmission over the Internet. The second option is to get the file decreased about 80% with obtaining high-quality music recording, with no noticeable differences by an average listener.

References

1. Sayood, K.: Data compression. Introduction. RM, Warsaw (2002)
2. Buryn, W.: Digital audio. Multichannel Systems, Wiki, Warsaw (2004)

A Non Redundant Compact XML Storage for Efficient Indexing and Querying of XML Documents

Mohammed Atique[1] and A.D. Raut [2]

[1] Deptt. of Computer Science, Sant Gadge Baba Amravati University, Amravati
[2] I.T. Deptt. J.D.I.E.T., Yavatmal
atuldraut@gmail.com

Abstract. XML is self describing and extensible. It is stored in the form of text document which makes it a cross platform technology independent of hardware and software. Because of such unique features XML is now recognized as standard for data storage and exchange over the net. Moreover size of XML database has also increased considerably. With such growing presence of XML in database technology there is ever increasing need to design compact non redundant storage for XML which can be effectively utilized for efficient indexing and querying of XML. The proposed technique (NRCX) stores the structure (path) and contents separately in the form of structure index and contents index respectively. The structure index provides id for all unique paths in the XML document. All data items for particular path id are grouped and stored together. This technique uniquely blends the path and the contents without the necessity of storing the path information repeatedly. This approach dramatically reduces the storage requirement for XML. The implementation of this technique and comparison with other techniques confirms our claim.

Keywords: non redundant storage, structure index, content index.

1 Introduction

XML is widely accepted standard for storage and exchange of data over the internet. Most importantly the size of XML has also increased dramatically. This gives rise to development of non redundant compact storage of XML data which will ultimately help the development of efficient indexing and querying technique to query large repositories of XML database. For this reason we propose a novel non redundant technique for efficient storage of XML document

Most of the techniques implemented so far for storing and querying of XML either made use of inverted list or tree structure representation of XML. Both of these techniques require large amount of memory for storing of XML and complex query algorithm to query XML. [1][2] Our technique makes use of a non tree or non inverted tree based representation and successfully reduces the storage requirement. It not only reduces the storage requirement but also stores the data in such a way that it can be directly utilized by the query algorithm i.e. the complexity of query algorithm is reduced. It eliminates the complex join algorithms which were required in case inverted list representation. [3][4] This technique creates two types of indices for

P.V. Krishna, M.R. Babu, and E. Ariwa (Eds.): ObCom 2011, Part I, CCIS 269, pp. 109–113, 2012.

compact and non redundant storage of XML. The first type of index is the structure index. This structure index is a compact summarization of all root to leaf paths in an XML document and assigns a unique path id to all the paths in the structure index. The other type of index created is the content index which stores the contents. It groups and stores at one place all the data for all the paths having the same id i.e. all the similar paths. Thus all the data items for all similar paths can be found at one location and moreover the structure information is not repeated. This greatly reduces the storage requirement for XML.

The rest of the paper is organized as fallows. Section2 discusses the related work. Section 3 describes our technique. Section 4 reports the experimental results and section 5 concludes.

2 Related Work

Till date several storage techniques have been implemented for storing of XML documents. These can be classified as queriable and non queriable. Among the non queriable techniques includes XMill[5], XMLPPM[6] etc. XMill achieves a good compression ratio and does not require a DTD. But the main drawback of XMill is that it requires decompression before querying. Hence the query response time is more in case of XMill. XMLPPM achieves higher compression than XMill but requires longer compression time. Inverted list techniques and techniques using tables to store XML data are somewhat nearer to queriable techniques as it does not require decompression before querying. The main drawback of inverted list techniques and techniques using tables is that it requires complex join operation for querying. [7][8]

Xgrind [9], Xpress [10], XQuec [11], Tbitmap [12], PCIDindex [13], RFX [14], ISX [15] etc are some of the queriable XML compression techniques. Xgrind has lower compression ratio as compared to Xmill. Both Xgrind and Xpress require two scans over the document and hence requires longer compression time. Moreover both of these techniques does not support set based queries such as the join queries. XQuec's compression factor is slightly inferior to that of Xgrind and comparable to that of Xpress but XQuec has grater query capabilities than Xgrind. The Tbitmap technique represents XML data in the form of a tree and assigns a bitmap to nodes of the tree. If the number of nodes increases the tbitmap requires more space and processing time. PCIDindex uses dewey id for nodes. Again the dewey id of node becomes very long if the number of nodes in the tree increases considerably. This results in requirement of more memory space. ISX is compact XML storage engine to store XML in a more concise structure, but it is a schema aware storage technique.

3 Non Redundant Compact XML (NRCX) Storage

This technique first constructs a path index. This path index is a compact summarization of the entire XML document. To facilitate Xpath queries containing parent child or ancestor descendant relationship it stores all the unique paths in the XML document without considering the attributes or its values on the path. Consider the following fragment of a sample XML document which illustrates the creation of two types of indices.

```
<studentdata>
  <student >
     <college>jdiet</college>
     <deptt> it </deptt>
     <year> iii </year>
     <name>abc</name>
  </student>
  <student >
     <college>dbnce</college>
     <deptt> cse </deptt>
     <year> ii </year>
     <name>xyz</name>
  </student>
</studentdata>
```

The structure index for the above XML document is as given below

Path	id
/studentdata/student/college	1
/studentdata/student/deptt	2
/studentdata/student/year	3
/studentdata/student/name	4

As mentioned earlier the path id acts as a link between the path and the contents on that path. The content index for the above XML is as shown below.

Path id	Contents
1	jdiet,dbnce
2	it,cse
3	iii,ii
4	abc,xyz

Thus from the above content index it is clear that the structure or path information is not repeated several times but the path information is stored only once. Moreover all the data items on particular path are stored together. An important feature of the content index is that it retains the ordering of the original XML document. For example the path /studentdata/student/college, this path appears twice in the sample XML document and may appear several times in the actual XML document. This path is stored only once and using its id (id=1) the contents are stored and can be accessed directly. The contents on this path are jdiet, dbnce and most importantly these contents are stored in document order at one place without repeating the path information. This technique works extremely well with document centric XML document and particularly if the elements of XML document does not contain attributes. It requires further enhancement for data centric XML document.

Although not implemented efficient query processing algorithm can be implemented to evaluate xpath queries which makes use of the path and the content index.

4 Experimental Results

We have implemented our technique on Intel Pentium IV dual core 3.0 GH processor with 1 GB of DDR Ram with VB.NET running on Windows XP platform. Some benchmark XML databases were considered for comparison with other techniques for compact storage of XML. Table 1 shows the results of implementation of our technique and comparison with the results of other previously implemented and tested techniques. The results of other techniques have been reported directly from the reference cited by [14].

Table 1. Storage Size of RFX, ISX, XMill, Xgrind, NRCX

Bench Mark Database	Source Data (MB)	RFX (MB)	ISX (MB)	XMILL (MB)	XGRIND (MB)	NRCX (MB)
Mondial	1.7	1	1	0.3	0.6	0.189
Orders	5.1	3	3	0.5	1.3	1.821
Shakespeare	7.5	5.1	5.3	0.9	2.1	3.7
Lineitem	30.8	15.8	21	3.7	8.6	7.021

As seen from the above table NRCX requires less amount of memory i.e. the compression ratio is better in case of NRCX. Since the size of structure and content index is small for small to medium size XML documents(1 to 100MB) the entire contents of both the index can be processed in main memory. This will significantly reduce the query response time for an xpath expression. The way the structure index is organized and stored greatly helps in finding quick response to different types of xpath queries. The simple xpath expression can be directly answered by using the structure index. The xpath queries beginning with // can be answered by just storing the paths in reverse order and performing the prefix matching which can be performed by single index look up of the structure index to get the index id. Once the id is obtained all the contents present on the path can be obtained in a single I/O operation.

5 Conclusion

In this paper we proposed a non redundant compact XML (NRCX) storage for storing XML. The experimental result shows that our technique achieves a better compression ratio. In addition to this it provides several other desirable features. The stored data is queriable i.e. it does not require decompression. It maintains the document order and the size of structure index is small even for very large XML documents. As mentioned earlier this technique is suitable for document centric XML document and requires further work for data centric XML documents.

References

[1] Al-Khalifa, S., Jagdish, H.V., Koudas, N., Patel, J.M., Srivastava, D., Wu, Y.: Structural Joins: A Primitive For Efficient Xml Query Pattern Matching. In: 18th International Conference on Data Engineering (ICDE), San Jose, CA, February 26-March 1, pp. 141–152 (2002)
[2] Bruno, N., Koudas, N., Srivastava, D.: Holistic Twig Joins: Optimal XML Pattern Matching. In: 21st ACM SIGMOD Int. Conference on Management of Data (SIGMOD), pp. 310–321 (2002)
[3] Bunaman, P., Grohe, M., Christioph, K.: Path Queries on Compressed XML. In: 29th VLDB Conference, Berlin Germany (2003)
[4] Kaushik, R., Krishnamurthy, R., Naughton, J.F., Ramkrishnan, R.: On the Integration of Structure Index and Inverted List. In: 2004 ACM SIGMOD International Conference on Management of Data, Paris, France, June 13-18, pp. 779–790 (2004)
[5] Liefke, H., Suciu, D.: XMill: An Efficient Compressor for XML Data. In: ACM SIGMOD International Conference on Management of Data, pp. 153–164 (2000)
[6] Cheney, J.: Compressing XML with multiplexed hierarchical PPM models. In: Proceedings of the IEEE Data Compression Conference, pp. 163–172 (2000)
[7] Chan, Z., Gehrke, J., Korn, F., Koudas, N., Shanmugasundram, J., Srivastava. D.: Index Structures for Matching XML Twigs using Relational Query Processor. In: 21st International Conference on Data Engineering Workshop ICDEW, Tokyo, Japan, April 5-8, pp. 1273–1283 (2005)
[8] Totarinov, I., Vigals, S.D., Beyer, K., Shanmugasundram, J., Shekita, E., Zhang, C.: Storing and Querying Ordered XML using a Relational Database System. In: ACM SIGMOD Int'l Conference on Management of Data, Madison Wisconsin USA, June 3-6, pp. 204–215 (2002)
[9] Tolani, P., Haritsa, J.: XGRIND: A Query-Friendly XML Compressor. In: 18th International Conference on Data Engineering (ICDE), pp. 225–234. IEEE Computer Society (2002)
[10] Min, J., Park, M., Chung, C.: XPRESS: A Queriable Compression for XML Data. In: Proceedings of the ACM SIGMOD International Conference on Management of Data, San Diego, California (2003)
[11] Arion, A., Bonifati, A., Costa, G., Aguanno, S.D., Manolescu, I., Pugliese, A.: XQueC: Pushing queries to compressed XML data. In: 29th International Conference on Very Large Data Bases (2003)
[12] Huang, Y.F., Wang, S.-H.: An efficient XML Processing based on combining T bitmap and Index Techniques. In IEEE Symposium on Computers and Communication ISCC, Marrakech, Morocco, July 6-9, pp. 858–863 (2008)
[13] Ying, L., Yun, M.S.: Applying Dewey Encoding to Construct XML Index for Path and Keyword Query. In: First International Workshop on Database Technology and Application, Wuhan, Hubie, China, April 25-26, pp. 553–556 (2009)
[14] Senthilkumar, R., Varshinee, P., Kannan, A.: Designing and Querying a Compact Redundancy Free XML Storage. J. The Open Information System Journal 3, 98–107 (2009)
[15] Wong, R., Lam, F., Shui, W.: Querying and maintaining a compact XML storage. In: 16th International Conference on World Wide Web, Banff, Alberta, Canada (2007)

EduCloud: An Institutional Cloud with Optimal Scheduling Policies

L. Shyamala and Saswati Mukherjee

Dept. of Information Science and Technology, College of Engineering, Anna University, Guindy, Chennai-25, India
lshyamlabi@gmail.com, msaswati@yahoo.com

Abstract. Cloud computing is an internet based distributed computing technology becoming an adoptable technology for many of the organizations with its dynamic scalability and usage of virtualized resources as a service. It will likely have a significant impact on the educational environment in the future. Cloud computing is an excellent alternative for educational institutions which are especially under budget shortage in order to operate their information systems effectively without spending any more capital for the computers and network devices. Technically cloud computing can be described as virtual centralization of distributed systems. Universities can take advantage of this to perform various academic and administrative tasks effectively. In this paper, we review the role of cloud environment in the educational arena in detail, especially in the universities where the use of computers are more intensive and what can be done to maximize the utilization of resources available in the infrastructure.

Keywords: Cloud computing, Virtualization, Scheduling, Education.

1 Introduction

Access to state-of-the-art computational facilities is essential for a wide range of computation-driven science disciplines and computational science research and education programs [1]. Cloud Computing is currently one of the new technology trends (broadband internet, fast connection and virtualization) widely accepted by the industry and is slowly becoming popular in educational institutions. It is being predicted that it would have a significant impact on teaching and learning environment. Cloud computing is becoming an adoptable technology for many of the organizations with its dynamic scalability and usage of virtualized resources as a service through the Internet. It would have a significant impact on the educational environment in the future. One of the hallmarks of cloud computing is that it enables users to interact with systems, data, and each other in a manner that minimizes concern about the underlying technology.

1.1 Need for Private Cloud

Every new technology starts from the academicians and later establishes in the industry. With the advancement of technical education and establishment of reputed

P.V. Krishna, M.R. Babu, and E. Ariwa (Eds.): ObCom 2011, Part I, CCIS 269, pp. 114–123, 2012.

technical institutions, it becomes imperative on the institution's side to provide the necessary infrastructure and updated technical knowledge to the students. However, with growing rate of students per year, providing state of the art facility to all of students, thereby ensuring effective utilisation of resources available is fast becoming a challenging task. Time and space, availability of good and well- equipped laboratory facilities with licensed software, accommodation of student per licensed software are some of the constraints that such Institutions face. These challenges lead to the additional burden on capital investments of resources. One easy avenue to reduce such cost is use of pirated software, which should be strictly prohibited, especially in educational institutions, for ethical reasons. A solution to this lies in buying costly licensed software and sharing among different departments. Unfortunately this leads to the laboratory allocation problem.

At its extreme end, this may force some institutions to modify the curriculum based on student strength to accommodate all the required students in the prescribed laboratories. Changing curriculum to avoid laboratory collision degrades the quality of education. Unfortunately, these same laboratory resources (software, hardware), that can hardly accommodate all the students in one department may sometime remain underutilised due to low demand in other department. Hence an adoptable technology which could solve these problems is the need of the hour.

Even as educational institutions already struggle under cost constraints, challenging budgetary times have been forecasted to persist across higher education for the next few years and hence this spurs activities in all levels to find a solution or alternate way to cut down the cost [2]. Both cloud computing and open source software promises to cut IT infrastructure costs, diminishes vendor dependence and reduces licensing fees. Open source software (OSS) is a flexible means for sharing, viewing and modifying computer code. Open source software is a revolutionary licensing framework, even though the use of OSS may require dedicated servers. This implies that the whole resources are fully dedicated to the hosted users only. This, however, has a major disadvantage that it does not provide the scalability and optimum resource utilization. These techniques are also limited to a set of machines on the same network or specific computers that have been linked, with platform incompatibility as a problem.

Cloud computing is an innovative, cost-effective delivery model [3]. Cloud Computing uses the virtualization technique in order to achieve its criteria [4]. In cloud, the concept is to deliver virtual servers with a specific configuration details with specific operating system, applications and services. The physical location of cores (Processors/computation power), software, and data access and storage space is immaterial to the users. In cloud, users work with web based services rather than local storage and software. With Web OS users can store, find, and manage files and services from a web desktop. Storing applications, files etc. on server rather on user's PC or laptop secures data from hard disk crash and hence users have less worry about their backup.

In a typical educational institution scenario, laboratories and servers are typically underutilized during the nights, weekends and semester breaks [5]. In addition, these resources are on high demands mainly towards the end of a semester. Cloud set up can also help minimize such underutilizations and to utilize the existing infrastructure in a more efficient way.

Students, teachers and administrative personnel have the opportunity to quickly and economically access various application platforms and resources through the web pages on-demand. This automatically reduces the cost of organizational expenses and offers more powerful functional capabilities. For universities, migrating to cloud-based services provides them with the ability to offer improved collaboration and research capabilities.

A further consideration is the type of cloud such institutions need. We argue that in university/educational setup, private cloud is a better option than the public cloud. The reason for this is three-fold. The first is that these institutions already are operating and hence have paid heavily on a certain amount of infrastructure. Setting up a private cloud provides such institutions an option of utilizing the existing infrastructure thereby providing better control over the resources.

The second reason is that there is hardly any additional cost/approval process required for setting up the cloud. Since for such institutions a private cloud is built on top of the existing infrastructure, it is not the usual "pay-as-you-go" model. Hence cost is not considered as a major factor. The main idea behind cloud set up in university is for the maximised utilisation of resources and eliminating the idleness of hardware, reducing the cost on investing resources by making a centralised utilisation model.

Third and final reason for setting up a private cloud is security. Certain activities such as admission process of new students and policies thereof, examinations/tests conducted for existing students and all research activities require confidentiality and cannot tolerate a breach in security. Private cloud helps to achieve this with a certainty that public cloud lacks.

Architecture for an institutional cloud CloudIA has been described in Frank Doelitzscher [5]. Hochschule Furtwangen University (HFU) established own private cloud infrastructure for staff and student for the purpose of creating on-demand infrastructures, running e-Learning applications, and allowing access to external users for collaboration purposes. Many similar initiatives have been started that explore the benefits of private cloud.

In this paper, we propose a private cloud set up for educational institutions. Private cloud needs special scheduling mechanism to efficiently manage all the requirements of an organization, and hence we have investigated the scheduling mechanism for private cloud.

1.2 Need of Effective Job Scheduling

Scheduling is a key concept in computer multitasking, multiprocessing operating system and real-time operating system designs. To derive maximum advantage out of cloud infrastructure, we need an effective scheduling technique in place, which will help in effective utilisation of resources and will also satisfy the computing needs of the users. Scheduling refers to the way processes are assigned to run on the available CPUs, since there are typically many more processes running than there are available CPUs. This assignment is carried out by software known as a scheduler and dispatcher. Efficiency of a scheduler is measured mainly with throughput, latency, turnaround time, response time and fairness. While throughput is the number of processes that complete their execution per time unit, latency is a measure of time delay experienced in a system. Turnaround time is the total time between submission of a process and its completion, while response time is the amount of time it takes from when a request was submitted until the first response is produced. Fairness ensures that equal CPU time is given to each process.

The rest of this paper is organized as follows, section 2 gives the proposed Architecture, and proposed scheduling for Educloud, and section 3 provides some related work on University clouds, related work in job scheduling. Finally, section 4 concludes the paper and shows future work.

2 Proposed Architecture

The proposed architecture includes virtual server, virtual network and scheduling functionality on the Cloud Management System (CMS). Fig.1. shows a general overview of this architecture that builds on top of an existing hardware infrastructure. It consists of three computer pools (PC Pool, Research Pool and Server Pool), that are located at different locations and use separate IP subdomains within the university. The PC and Server pools are used by students and staff for teaching purposes during the day. The Research Pool is used for research and development purposes.

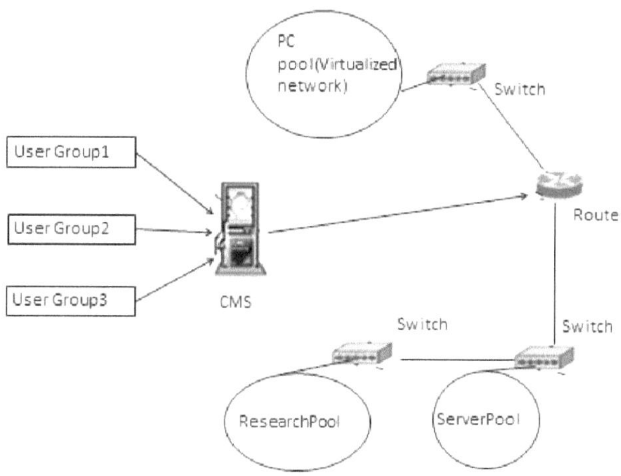

Fig. 1. Overview of Institute Cloud

Cloud Management System(CMS) acts as a Cloud controller. This handles tasks such as managing users, group permission, resource managing, job scheduling etc. CMS is responsible for regulate resource supply through SLA(Service Level Agreement), monitoring and management of resources, ensuring the privacy, recovery, integrity and security of user data and transactions security.

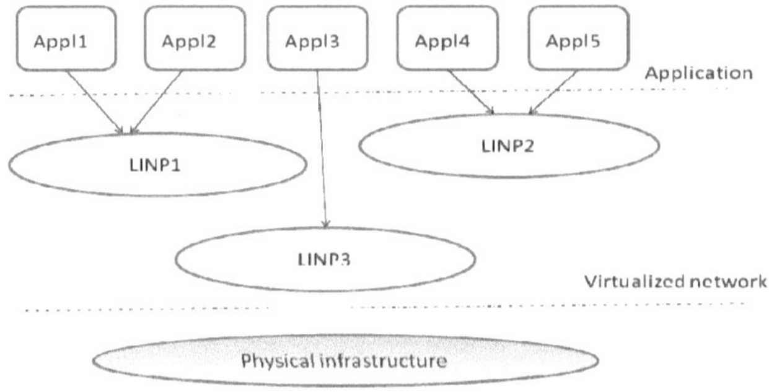

LINP:Logically Isolated Network Partitions

Fig. 2. Architecture of Virtual Network

Fig. 2. shows virtual networks. Network virtualization is a useful technology to achieve better utilization of infrastructures in terms of reusing a single physical or logical resource for multiple other network instances, or to aggregate multiples of these resources to obtain more functionality. They are only logically isolated networks, over a common infrastructure. Each such virtual network can provide the user network services similar to those provided by the common infrastructure as a non-virtualized network.

Universities face the challenge of managing a rapidly growing strength of student, introduction of new courses with a data center that was originally designed to handle a fraction of the actual workload. In this situation, servers are deployed at a 1:1 ratio (one server for one application). While this model can provide a reliable environment, server utilization rates are typically low and valuable floor or rack space is inefficiently used. To combat these issues, a growing trend is to implement a virtualization solution.

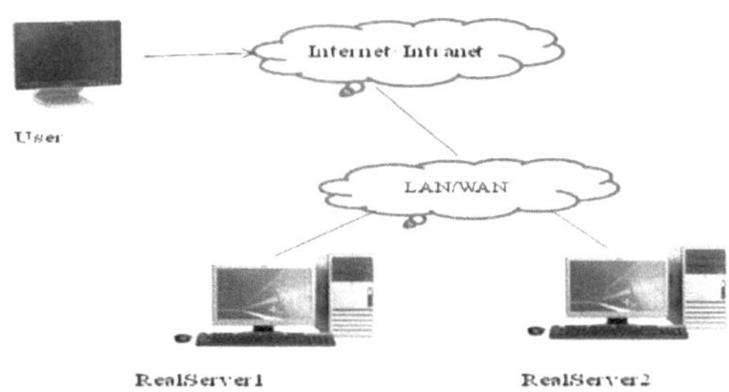

Fig. 3. Virtual Server

Fig.3. shows Virtual server, it is a highly scalable and highly available server built on a cluster of real servers. The virtual server environment, propagating a "build it once, deploy it to many" philosophy. New servers can now be built and old ones decommissioned in a fraction of the time it took before. In real world terms, server provisioning time has been reduced 75 percent and reboot time has dropped to under 30 seconds. Other benefit is that the virtualization solution provided includes additional manageability and improved application availability by allowing for:

- Automatic optimization and allocation of entire pools of resources for maximum hardware utilization, flexibility, and availability.
- Proactive migration of virtual machines away from failing or under-performing servers.
- Centralized management through VirtualCenter's single interface to manage and monitor the virtual environment.

2.1 Scheduling Algorithm

Many companies and institutions take advantage of technology in their own data centres to evolve a private cloud. Since private clouds have some unique characteristics and special requirements, it is still a challenging problem to effectively schedule requests onto compute nodes, with multiple objectives to meet. The scenario of jobs in a public cloud and private cloud are different. There is further difference in case of organisational private cloud and institutional private cloud. The basic characterisation of cloud can be much more personalised in the case of institutional cloud.

In educational cloud, typical characteristics may be that the end users are well defined, usage pattern can be predicted well in advance, deadline of jobs can be predicted with fare accuracy, service of cloud can be defined etc.. Jobs that could be submitted to the cloud may be virtual laboratory, virtual class room, e-learning, online exams, research work, batch jobs like report generation, database updation etc. Users will be students, faculty, administrator, technical and administrative staff etc. Hence the jobs to be scheduled can be modelled in different way for the maximum utilization of resources where the constraints on resources, peak hour, and priority exist. In this paper, we consider an Infrastructure-as-a-Service (IaaS) cloud system for providing virtual lab to the students,staff, research scholars. In cloud computing, there are three different modes of renting the computing capacities,

- Advance Reservation (AR): Resources are reserved in advance. They should be available at a specific time. Ex: Students lab decided for that particular semester.
- Best-effort: Resources are provisioned as soon as possible. Requests are placed in a queue. Ex. request by a scholar for specific software like MATLAB for research work.
- Immediate: When a client submits a request, either the resources are provisioned immediately, or the request is rejected, based on the resource availabilities. Ex .request from a staff to train on any specific Software.

A virtual machine is an abstract unit of storage and computing capacities provided in a cloud. The provision of these computational resources is in the form of virtual machines (VMs) deployed in a provider's data center.

Different jobs are kept in different user groups to maintain a certain order of uniformity in the scheduling jobs and therefore, are allotted their respective usergroupID. Every user can contribute to any number of jobs depending upon the type and number of operations to be performed by that particular instance of process. Jobs are assigned a particular ID, JobID by their respective group which also bear a unique jobID. Both JobID and usergroupID are used in the scheduler for scheduling the resources.

A lease of resource is implemented as a set of VMs. The allocated resources of a lease can be described by a tuple (n, m, d, b), where n is number of CPUs, m is memory in megabytes, d is disk space in megabytes and b is the network bandwidth in megabytes per second. For the AR mode, the lease also includes the required start time and the required execution time. For the best-effort and the immediate modes, the lease has information about how long the execution lasts, but not the start time of execution.

For example, online exams and Virtual labs schedule are known in advance. Hence advance reservation can be done. Student gets priority during regular time, batch jobs gets least priority can be run during the idletime of resources where can adopt backfilling strategy. Dynamic requests are set by seeing the availability of resources of AR datacentre if present or to the other resource pool. Hence the algorithm aims for the maximum utilization of the resources.

3 Related Work

3.1 Related Work on Institutional Cloud

Cloud computing infrastructures accelerated the adoption of different technological innovations in academia and its facilities and resources could be accessed by the colleges as on–demand. Praveena & Betsy [6] provided a comprehensive introduction to the application of cloud in universities. Mitchell [7] provided an overview of existing learning architectures, and raised questions about how educational institutions are managing the cloud computing resources. He also brought reasonable explanations for the challenge of indexing web resources for optimum discoverability by students and educators. Tuncay Ercan [2] discussed statistically the need of cloud computing in many fields and the usage in education institutions. All these papers discussed about the usage of public cloud in educational institutions.

BlueSky cloud framework [8], developed by Xi'an Jiaotong University (China), enables Physical machines to be virtualized and allocated on-demand for e-Learning systems. Virtual Computing Laboratory (VCL) [9], developed by North Carolina State University (USA), enables students to reserve and access virtual machines (VMs) with a basic image or specific applications environments, such as Matlab and Autodesk.

Satish Srirama et al. [10] discussed SciCloud, a project studying the scope of establishing private clouds at universities to solve computationally intensive scientific, mathematical, and academic problems.

These works shows the scope of establishing a private cloud on already existing Physical resources. Junjie Peng et al. [11] provide the various platforms for constructing the private cloud over the existing infrastructure. Existing data center investment considerations should take into account that real-world cloud architectures will be heterogeneous with a mix of virtual and physical platforms with the applications that run on them. By design, these cloud architectures will also be able to accommodate larger scale than existing data centres.

3.2 Related Work in Job Scheduling

Managing and supplying computational resources to user applications is one of the main challenges for the high performance computing community. Users submit their applications as jobs to a resource management system responsible for job scheduling and resource allocation. Usually jobs are scheduled by user requirements. New scheduling strategies need to be proposed to overcome the problems faced by cloud systems between user and resources [12].

The open-source implementation of Eucalyuptus [13], scheduling policies such as FIFO, Round Robin, Greedy scheduling is used by the master node to distribute waiting tasks to computing nodes. Junjie Peng [14] discusses how the virtualisation techniques could improve the resource allocation problems. Gerasoulis and Yang [15], in the context of Directed Acyclic Graph (DAG) scheduling invparallel computing environments, named grouping of jobs to reduce communication dependencies among them as clustering. Nithiapidary Muthuvelu et al. [16] presented a scheduling strategy that performs dynamic job grouping activity at runtime.

A job scheduling strategy that encompasses the job grouping concept coupled together with bandwidth-aware scheduling is proposed and evaluated by T.F.Ang et al. [17]. The proposed scheduling strategy focuses on grouping independent jobs with small processing requirements into suitable jobs with larger processing requirements and schedules them in accordance with indeterminist network conditions.

Selvarani et. al. [18] proposed an improved cost-based scheduling algorithm for making efficient mapping of tasks to available resources in cloud. This scheduling algorithm measures both resource cost and computation performance, it also improves the computation/communication ratio by grouping the user tasks according to a particular cloud resource's processing capability and sends the grouped jobs to the resource.

Sandeep Tayal [19] proposed an optimized algorithm based on the Fuzzy-GA optimization, which makes a scheduling decision by evaluating the entire group of task in the job queue. Jiayin Li et. al. [20] proposed a feedback preemptible task scheduling algorithm to generate scheduling with the shortest average execution time of jobs.

4 Conclusion

Cloud computing is an exciting development and it provides significant alternative to today's educational perspective. Students and administrative personnel have the opportunity to quickly and economically access various application platforms and resources through the web pages on-demand. This automatically reduces the cost of organizational expenses and offers more powerful functional capabilities. Cloud computing has the potential to revolutionize the computing facilities institutions provided to their students in a cost effective way. There are different open source technologies which are available to build private cloud within college, school campuses. This Private Cloud can offer students with desired computational facilities on demand without any expense. In this paper, we present a optimal job scheduling mechanism in IaaS cloud systems for personalising the scheduling based on the usage pattern. In future we will explore more scheduling algorithms which will help us to customize cloud environment in most efficient way.

Acknowledgements. This research is supported by Anna Centenary Research Fellowship from Anna University, Chennai, India.

References

1. Oberg, M., Woitaszek, M., Voran, T., Tufo, H.M.: System architecture supporting high-performance and cloud computing in an academic consortium environment. Computer Science - Research and Development 26, 3–4 (2011)
2. Ercana, T.: Effective use of cloud computing in educational institutions. WCES, Procedia Social and Behavioural Sciences 2(2), 938–942 (2010)
3. Cappos, J., Beschastnikh, I., Krishnamurthy, A., Anderson, T.: Seattle: a platform for educational cloud computing. SIGCSE Bull. 41(1), 111–115 (2009)
4. `http://www.virtualization.sys-con.com`
5. Doelitzscher, F., Sulistio, A., Reich, C., Kuijs, H., Wolf, D.: Private Cloud for Collaboration and e-Learning Services: from IaaS to SaaS, vol. 91(1), pp. 1–20 (2011)
6. Praveena, K., Betsy, T.: Application of Cloud Computing in Academia. IUP Journal of Systems Management 7(3), 50–54 (2009)
7. Mitchell, P.: Learning architecture: issues in indexing Australian education in a Web 2.0 world. Indexer 26(4), 163–169 (2008)
8. Dong, B., Zheng, Q., Qiao, M., Shu, J., Yang, J.: BlueSky Cloud Framework: An E-Learning Framework Embracing Cloud Computing. In: Proceedings of the 1st International Conference on Cloud Computing (CloudCom 2009), China (2009)
9. Vouk, M., Averritt, S., Bugaev, M., Kurth, A., Peeler, A., Schaffer, H., Sills, E., Stein, S., Thompson, J.: Powered by VCL – Using Virtual Computing Laboratory (VCL) Technology to Power Cloud Computing. In: Proceedings of the 2nd International Conference on the Virtual Computing Initiative (ICVCI 2008) (2008)
10. Srirama, S., Batrashev, O., Vainikko, E.: SciCloud: Scientific Computing on the Cloud. In: 10th IEEE ACM International Conference on Cluster Cloud and Grid Computing, pp. 579–580. IEEE (2010)
11. Hu, F., Qiu, M., Li, J., Grant, T., Tylor, D., McCaleb, S., Butler, L., Hamner, R.: A Review on Cloud Computing: Design Challenges in Architecture and Security. CIT 19(1), 25–55 (2011)
12. de Assunção, M.D., di Costanzo, A., Buyya, R.: A cost-benefit analysis of using cloud computing to extend the capacity of clusters. Springer Science &Business Media, LLC (2010)
13. Nurmi, D., Wolski, R., Grzegorczyk, C., Obertelli, G., Soman, S., Youseff, L., Zagorodnov, D.: The eucalyptus open-source cloud computing system. In: Proceedings of the 2009 9th IEEE/ACM International Symposium on Cluster Computing and the Grid, CCGRID 2009, pp. 124–131. IEEE Computer Society, Washington (2009)

14. Li, J., Qiu, M., Niu, J., Chen, Y., Ming, Z.: Adaptive resource allocation for preemptable jobs in cloud systems. In: ISDA, pp. 31–36 (2010)
15. Gerasoulis, A., Yang, T.: A comparison of clustering heuristics for scheduling directed graphs multiprocessors. Journal of Parallel and Distributed Computing 16(4), 276–291 (2002)
16. Muthuvelu, N., Liu, J., Soe, N.L., Venugopal, S., Sulistio, A., Buyya, R.: Dynamic Job Grouping-Based Scheduling for Deploying Applications with Fine-Grained Tasks on Global Grids. In: Conferences in Research and Practicein InformationTechnology (AusGrid 2005), vol. 44 (2005)
17. Ang, T.F., Ng, W.K., Ling, T.C., Por, L.Y., Liew, C.S.: A Bandwidth-Aware Job Grouping-Based Scheduling on Grid Environment. Proceedings of Information Technology Journal 8(3), 372–377 (2009)
18. Selvarani, S., Sudha Sadhasivam, G.: Improved Cost Based Algorithm For Task Scheduling In Cloud Computing. In: IEEE International Conference on Computational Intelligence and Computing Research, ICCIC (2010)
19. Tayal, S.: Tasks Scheduling optimization for the Cloud Computing Systems. International Journal of Advanced Engineering Sciences And Technologies (IJAEST) 5(2), 111–115 (2011)
20. Li, J., Qiu, M., Niu, J., Gao, W., Zong, Z., Qin, X.: Feedback Dynamic Algorithms for Preemptable Job Scheduling in Cloud Systems. In: Web Intelligence, pp. 561–564 (2010)

Resource Discovery for Grid Computing Environment Using Ant Colony Optimization by Applying Routing Information and LRU Policy

S. Nirmala Devi[1] and A. Pethalakshmi[2]

[1] Department of Computer Science,
Government Arts College for Women, Salem – 8,
Tamilnadu, India
devi.dharu@gmail.com
[2] Department of Computer Science,
MVM Government Arts College for Women, Dindigul,
Tamilnadu, India
pethalakshmi@yahoo.com

Abstract. Grid computing can be defined as the agreement between the virtual organization to share the resources viz., data, processor, peripheral devices, network, storage, web services to achieve the high performance. The resources are dynamic and heterogeneous in nature. Hence proper mechanisms are needed to discover those resources. Various studies were available on resource discovery as centralized, distributed, hierarchical, etc. Among these, we propose an approach which uses the ACO (Ant Colony Optimization) and routing information to discover the resources in the grid environment. The LRU (Least Recently Used) is employed here, anticipating the balance in resource utilization. This paper defines the grid computing and resources and makes a literature study over the available algorithms. Finally, we propose an algorithm which is a hybrid approach with ACO and routing information with LRU policy.

Keywords: Grid Computing, Resource Discovery, Swarm Intelligence, Ant Colony Optimization, Routing Table, LRU.

1 Introduction

Grid Computing yields high performance between agreed nodes in the virtual organization. The organizations cooperate and work together to achieve high performance. Thus the grid computing can be defined as the agreement between the organizations to form a virtual environment to share the resources of any type to achieve the efficient utilization of those resources in dynamic and heterogeneous setup. The resources can be database server, processor, peripheral devices, and network and web services. The environmental set up is shown in figure 1, which depicts the way that the virtual organizations can communicate with each other. The grid environment considered here is with three virtual organizations viz., A, B and C. The virtual organizations collaborate and work. These virtual organizations would have the participating nodes.

P.V. Krishna, M.R. Babu, and E. Ariwa (Eds.): ObCom 2011, Part I, CCIS 269, pp. 124–133, 2012.

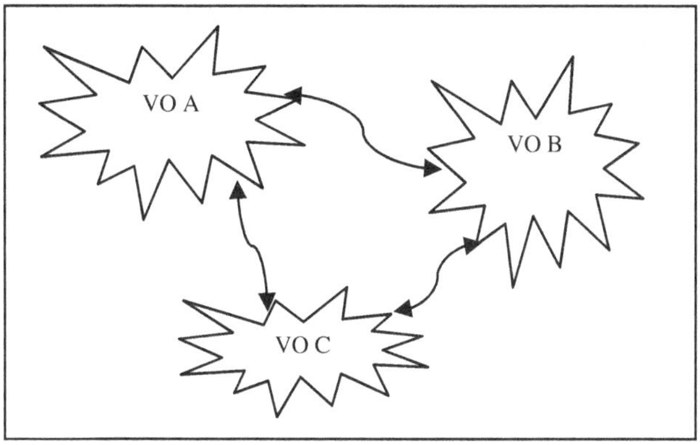

Fig. 1. Grid Environment

These nodes accept the problem from the user and try to solve the problem by itself or through sending it to other nodes. The nodes can also enter and leave the environment as it is dynamic and also the nodes can be any type. The grid computing environment provides the dynamic and heterogeneous resources and environment. The Virtual organization is depicted in the figure 2. The sample virtual organization in figure 2 has 6 nodes, database server and other resources like r1 and r2 to accomplish a particular task.

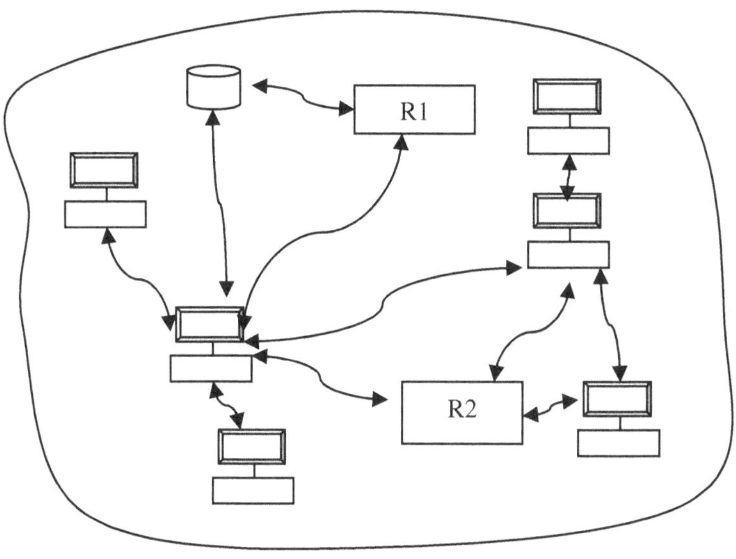

Fig. 2. Virtual Organization

2 Resources

Grid environment considers any kind of resources as computing resources, data resources, storage resources, service resources, network resources and web resources. All these resources are heterogeneous and dynamic in nature. And efficient utilization of resources is required for the problem solving in grid environment.

- The computing resources include the processors for performing the operations. By means of sharing the processors the advantage of parallel processing is arrived in grid environment.
- The specific data grids are also available. The grid environment shares the data across the virtual organizations. The large volume of data such as the spatial data is required to be in grid environment.
- The storage resource means that the data or information could be stored in the available node/storage to enable the easy retrieval and storage.
- The service resource can be of any nature like software or even providing the peripheral devices such as printer, scanner etc.,
- The network resource can be the network bandwidth in the grid. In grid environment, the message passing is being considered as the pillar. To enable this, the bandwidth and other supporting services are also termed under network resource.
- The web services provide the heterogeneity to the grid environment. The platform-independent nature induces the grid to make use of this service.
- These resources are of dynamic in nature as it can enter or leave the environment at any time. Similarly, the resources are heterogeneous in nature as it belongs to any environment or platform.

3 Literature Study

There were various approaches available for discovering these resources which are discussed below.

3.1 Centralized Approach

In centralized approach, the participating nodes would register their resources with the registry. The registries here are maintained using UDDI (Universal Description Discovery and Integration) or LDAP (Lightweight Directory Access Protocol) since the grid environment is built on the web services. Normally the disadvantage in this system is the failure of centralized node or link, may lead to the severe consequences and it also sometimes necessitates the maintenance of replication. And this would increase the overhead and it is also not possible. This even increases the communication cost.

In [10], the GMD Web based grid service publication directory system is maintained for resource discovery. In this method, there were two key components as

GMD Portal manager and GMD query web service. The GMD portal manager is a centralized one and every entry is made in this which employs the tomcat server.

In [1], the centralized and hierarchical architectures are used to discover the resource.

3.2 Decentralized Approach

The decentralized approach can also be used to maintain the details of the resources. In [2], the dynamic hash tables are used to maintain the details about the resources at multiple sites. But this requires frequent data updating. This follows the query approaches as RLQ and RUQ. RLQ is the query issued to the broker service to locate the resources and RUQ is the update query sent by the participating site about its available resources. In [11], the system is divided into groups as inter groups, intra groups etc and also the penalty functions are implemented by applying the distributed approach.

3.3 Ontology Based Approach

Ontology means representing related information as a set of concepts. Then retrieving information based on match making process.

In [3], the match making algorithm is used to retrieve the information about the resources. The main actions involved are advertising, matching, notification and claiming for the resources. Here the matchmaker protocol is composed of the publishing protocol and notification protocol.

3.4 Peer-to-Peer Approach

Peer to peer refers to the approach where every participating node have equal preference and it can act both as server and client at a time. This modeling could also be used in grid as there is no client server approach available in the grid and each participating node can serve and request the process.

The peer to peer approach also makes use of DHT with indexing features. In [4], the P2P uses the network organization, Data organization and d- dimensional query routing.

In [15], the comparative study is made between the structured P2P systems and unstructured P2P systems for resource discovery. And various parameters such as scalability, dynamicity, reliability, range queries, multiattribute queries and dynamic attribute queries were considered.

3.5 Routing Based Approach

The routing approach makes use of message routing concepts [5]. In [13] the link state routing protocol OSPF (open shortest path first) was improved for resource discovery and location. The routing table data is considered and the shortest path to the resource is identified and made use. This facilitates the higher query efficiency and less communication traffic

3.6 Agent Based Approach

Current researches are focusing on agent based approaches to discover the resources. The agents collect resources that match the resources required and inform to the source and even it leaves the information for other agents [6] [7] [8]. In [15], the agent based approach is evaluated on various parameters as scalability, dynamicity, reliability, range queries. And it has been arrived that the agent based system is suitable for small or medium scale environment rather than on large scale environments. The dynamicity is tolerable but it is not reliable and all the query approaches are supported by this agent approach.

3.7 Hybrid Approaches

Certain researches are on hybrid approaches, combines the approaches to reap the benefits of both the approaches. In [14] the P2P approach and ontology approach is combined for resource discovery. And the authors have also notified that the energy utilization is reduced to 10% from 40%.

4 Proposed Approach

The proposed is a hybrid approach which makes use of the ant colony optimization technique with the routing information. And also it considers the resource utilization policy, only the resources which were least recently used are given precedence over the others.

4.1 Ant Colony Optimization

Ants while searching for food paths, it would leave behind the pheromone. So that other ants would also follow the same the path to find the food. The more pheromone released is the shortest path. Hence the ants used to form a line and march towards the food. The similar technique applied here is called ant colony optimization.

4.2 Routing Information

The routers used to maintain the routing information while forwarding packets in the network. A similar approach is employed here. A resource routing table is maintained by each and every participating node in the network to support the resource discovery. The resource routing table maintains the address of the requesting node, agent id, resource request id, type of resource and number of hops crossed.

4.3 LRU (Least Recently Used)

The efficient resource utilization includes the balanced utilization of resources. Some resources may be frequently used and some other may not be used that much often. Hence this algorithm also handles the issue by way of utilizing the balanced usage of resources as it also makes use of the LRU policy.

5 Data Structures Used

The data structures used by the proposed algorithm are maintained at agent and nodes in the grid environment and those were explained below.

5.1 Data Structure Used by Agent

Once the request is generated, the agent would have the information with it. It would have the address of the requesting node, the id generated for the particular request, the timestamp when the agent is created. This is given in the below table 1.

Table 1. Data Structure maintained by agent

S.No	DataField	Description
1	raddress	This is the address of the node which has generated the request for the resource
2	request id	This is the unique id generated whenever a request is made and it is local to the particular node
3	agent id	The agent generated would also have an id this is also generated locally by the requesting node
4	rtimestamp	The timestamp denotes the time at which the agent is generated
5	resourcetype	The required resource type should be given at the time generating the agents
6	Hopcount	This value is periodically updated whenever the agent passes through a hop. This is used to determine the distance the agent is travelling

In addition to this the agent need to maintain another table which denotes the availability of the resources. This is given in the below table 2.

Table 2. Data Structure Maintained by agent regarding the resource identified

S.No	DataField	Description
1	id	The unique id generated whenever a matching resource is found by the agent
2	address	The address of the node where the request match is found
3	LRU	The least recently used value

5.2 Data Structure Maintained at the Participating Node

Certain information is needed to be maintained at the participating node also. The node used to maintain the following data structures in addition to the details regularly maintained. The following table 3 indicates the major details maintained by the nodes in the grid environment.

Table 3. Data Structure to get the LRU value

S.No	DataField	Description
1	resourceid	The unique id generated whenever a resource is entered in the environment.
2	resourcetype	The type of the resource
3	returntimestamp	This is to get the LRU value of the resource

In addition to the above data, the node would also maintain the routing information, since other agents could read the details from this part and this is shown in table 4.

Table 4. Data Structure maintained by node for the agents

S.No	DataField	Description
1	resourceid	The unique id from the agent
2	raddress	The address of the requesting node
3	rtimestamp	The requested timestamp
4	resourcematcing	The details regarding the resource matching
5	Hopcount	The number of hops travelled

6 Algorithm Used

In the proposed approach, whenever a request is made for a resource, the agent will be generated and flooded in the grid to fetch the resource and it is pictured in figure 3. Here the resource request is made and then the agents were generated and put in the grid. The agents were denoted in the dashed lines and the connectivity through the solid lines and it is bidirectional. The below is the algorithm

Step 1. The user submits a job to the system.
Step 2. The resources required are identified by the system.
Step 3. Depending upon the required number of resources and the strength of the grid the agents are created to trace the resources.
Step 4. Whenever the agent crosses a hop, it would leave update the tables in it and also in the node.
Step 5. When the agent identifies the resource it would update the resource information including the LRU and proceed.
Step 6. When the agents return with the required information.
Step 7. The decision regarding the resource selection would be made based on the LRU.

Thus the algorithm considers the way the agent identifying the resource. Similarly the need for timestamp is to frequently discarding the agent, after a lapse of time. Similarly the timestamp is also maintained in the tables at the node and this is to avoid the overload in the database. After a lapse of time this table will also be discarded.

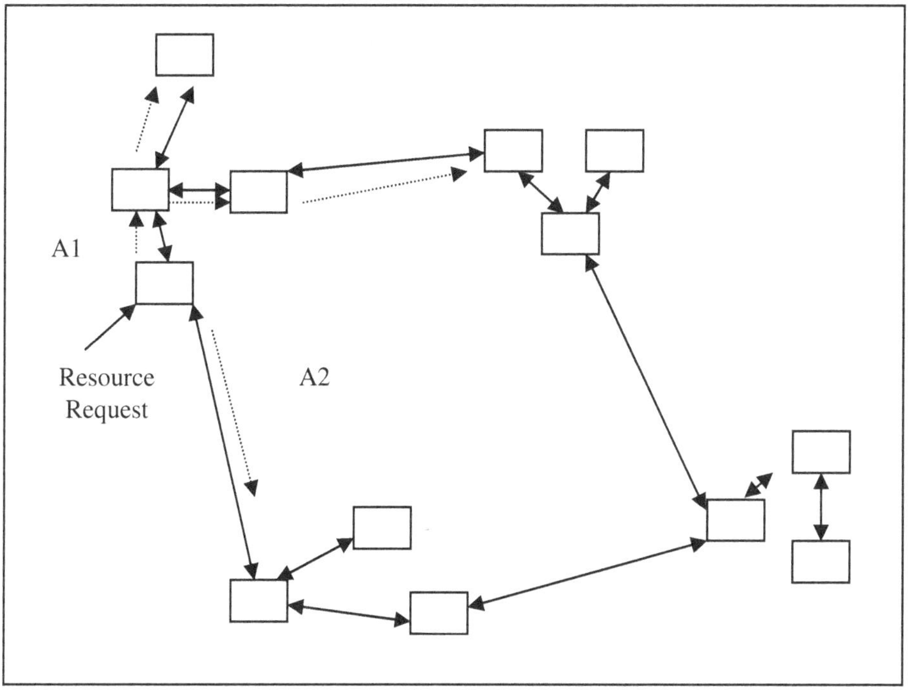

Fig. 3. The agent generation and the movement in a sample grid environment

6.1 Submission of Job by the User

The user submits the job to a particular node in the grid. The job may require to do a computation, request a service or to retrieve particular information.

6.2 Resource Identification

The node which receives the job would decide on the resources required for the solving the problem. It has to decide on various issues like resource type, number of resources for each type and anticipated resource locking period.

6.3 Agent Generation

Once the resources are identified the agents can be generated. The number of agents generated typically depends on the number of resources required. The agents would carry the information as raddress, request id, agent id, rtimestamp, resource type and hopcount.

6.4 Node Behavior

The node has to maintain the information regarding the agents visiting. After a lapse of time the information should be automatically deleted. The participating node would register the source node details, the agent details and also the resource details with timestamp.

6.5 Resource Details at Node

The node also maintains the resource details whenever a resource enters or leaves the environment. And even the details regarding the service time is maintained, to get the least recently used information.

7 Experimental Setup

This ongoing research is simulated in gridsim. There were 1000 nodes created in the grid environment using the gridinit method. And 100 resources were also created. These were done by way of creating the PE's i.e., processing elements. The resource characteristics are defined and these were assigned with the machine list created. The agents could be created to do the activities. The successful execution of the research project would surely result in efficient utilization of resources and leads to the performance enhancement in grid environment.

8 Conclusion

The grid environment affords the efficient execution of problems in limited time span. Its goal is also to provide the necessary resources which are located anywhere in the grid. There were various approaches available to identify the resources available. By means of employing the agents the grid environment would get the more relevant and reliable information regarding the resource in the grid. The agent employment also relieves the designer from complex programming.

References

1. Cokuslu, D., Hameurlain, A., Erciyes, K.: Grid Resource discovery based on centralized and hierarchical architecture. International Journal for Infonomics 3(1) (March 2010)
2. Ranjan, R., Chan, L., Harwood, A., Karunasekera, S., Buyya, R.: Decentralized Resource Discovery service for Large scale federated database

3. Dhindsa, K.S., Dogra, N., Kumar, M.: Resource Discovery in grid environment using ontology based approach. In: Proceedings of 2nd National Conference on Challenges and Opportunities in Information Technology, RMIT – IET, March 29, pp. 100–103 (2008)
4. Ranjan, R., Harwood, A., Buyya, R.: A study on peer-to-peer based discovery of grid resource information
5. de Mello, R.F., Senger, L.J., Yang, L.T.: A Routing Load Balancing Policy for Grid Computing Environments. In: Proceedings of 20th International Conference on Advances Information Networking and Applications (AINA 2006) (2006)
6. Forestiero, A., Mastroianni, C., Spezzano, G.: An Agent Based Semi-informed Protocol for Resource Discovery in Grids. In: Alexandrov, V.N., van Albada, G.D., Sloot, P.M.A., Dongarra, J. (eds.) ICCS 2006, Part IV. LNCS, vol. 3994, pp. 1047–1054. Springer, Heidelberg (2006)
7. Singh, B., Bawa, S.: Grid Resource Discovery using Natural Mobile Agents. International Journal of Computer Science and Network Security 8(11) (November 2008)
8. Srinivasan, T., Siddharth Jonathan, J.B., Seshadri, J., Chandrasekhar, A.: A Swarm Intelligence based Task Allocation Algorithm (SITA) for the computational Grid
9. Joseph, J., Fellenstein, C.: Grid Compting. IBM Press
10. Yu, J., Venugopal, S., Buyya, R.: Grid Market Directory: A Web Services based Grid Service Publication Directory,
`http://arxiv.org/ftp/cs/papers/0302/0302006.pdf`
11. Oppenheimer, D., Albrecht, J., Patterson, D., Vahdat, A.: Design and implementation tradeoffs for wide – area resource discovery,
`http://sword.cs.williams.edu/pubs/hpdc05.pdf`
12. Forestiero, A., Mastroianni, C., Spezzano, G.: An Agent Based Semi-informed Protocol for Resource Discovery in Grids. In: Alexandrov, V.N., van Albada, G.D., Sloot, P.M.A., Dongarra, J. (eds.) ICCS 2006. LNCS, vol. 3994, pp. 1047–1054. Springer, Heidelberg (2006)
13. Liu, Y., Wang, S.: Grid Resource Discovery Mechanism based on OSPF routing protocol. In: Control and Design Conference (2008)
14. Xiong, Z., Zhang, X., Liu, L.: Resource Management Model and Resource discovery algorithm for P2P Grid. Journal of Networks 6(8), 1187–1194 (2011)
15. Hamemeurtain, A., Cokuslu, D.: Resource Discovery in Grid Systems: A Survey. Int. J. Metadata, Semantics and ontologies 5(3) (2010)

Service Oriented Architecture for Governing Engineering Colleges

Neelavathi Suryamurthy[1] and Vivekanandan Kalimuthu[2]

[1] Perunthalivar Kamarajar Institute of Engineering and Technology, Karaikal
neelabaski@gmail.com
[2] Department of CSE, Pondicherry Engineering College, Puducherry
k.vivekanandan@pec.edu

Abstract. In today's world, more and more organizations are adopting automation. Educational institutions are also willing to have such automated environment. The challenge is to find a solution that is extendible, flexible and fits well with the existing legacy systems. Replacing legacy systems to cope with the new architecture is not only costly but also introduces the risk of malfunctioning. Service Oriented Architecture (SOA) is recommended which provides a relatively cheap and more cost-effective solution in addressing the problems and challenges of combing legacy system with new architecture. This Paper is focused on Service Oriented Architecture for e-governance of engineering institution. A e-governance based on SOA model is proposed and the services needed for the institution are implemented. Systems are developed for engineering institution which provided the services in student attendance system, staff attendance system, project maintenance system, alumni association system, library management system, laboratory management system, department information system, student information system, conference maintenance system, training and placement system, hostel management system, internal mark maintenance system, time table and syllabus system, fees maintenance system and scholarship maintenance system. The services needed for the above systems are implemented using .NET and J2EE. The services are used to implement applications like due certificate details, eligibility of a student for examination, eligibility of a student for campus interviews, etc.

Keywords: Service Oriented Architecture, E-governance, Business Application Model, Service Orientation, Service Composition.

1 Introduction

Departments in educational institutions comprise students, staff, and non-teaching staffs. Automation is required to provide operational efficiency and reduce human errors. But the existing systems have low operational efficiency and have vulnerability of human errors [4]. The draw backs in the existing legacy system is that systems are very big and trying to keep them up to date with new trends is very difficult [1]. And implementing new technology for automation will not only increase implementation cost but also leads to malfunctions. So we go for Service Oriented Architecture concept.

P.V. Krishna, M.R. Babu, and E. Ariwa (Eds.): ObCom 2011, Part I, CCIS 269, pp. 134–143, 2012.

Service Oriented Architecture provides many benefits in various fields [2]. The use of Service Oriented Architecture is proposed for an engineering institution. Generally, engineering institutions have only isolated computing systems at the department level and replacing legacy systems to cope with the new architecture is also costly. So a model is developed using Service Oriented Software Architecture which integrates the existing legacy systems to provide complete automation through services [3].

The objective of our work is to develop a model using Service Oriented Architecture (SOA) for e-Governance of an engineering institution. It provides services like list of students with 100 percent attendance, project done under a domain, due certificates from library, laboratory, hostel for a particular student, etc using .NET and J2EE. Using these base services, the applications such as due certificate details, eligibility of a student for appearing examination, progress report for students, etc are developed. The use of Service Oriented Architecture (SOA) establishes interoperability and reusability of services among the various existing isolated systems [5].

2 Service Oriented Architecture

Service Oriented Architecture for e-Governance of engineering institution is being implemented in Pondicherry Engineering College to develop new services faster and to provide seamless integration.

Pondicherry Engineering College is an institution sponsored by the Union Territory of Pondicherry. The college was started in the year 1984 and it has more than ten degree courses namely Chemical Engineering , Civil Engineering, Computer Applications (MCA), Computer Science & Engineering, Electronics and Communication Engineering, Electrical and Electronics Engineering, Electronics & Instrumentation Engineering and Information Technology .

The service orientation and Service Oriented Architecture (SOA) are not new or revolutionary concepts. It is the next stage of evolution in the distributed computing [4]. SOA is defined as "Service Oriented Architecture (SOA) is a paradigm for organizing and utilizing distributed capabilities that may be under the control of different ownership domains [4]." SOA includes the previously proven and successful elements from past distributed paradigms. These elements are combined with the design approaches to leverage recent technology in distributed computing [2].

In SOA, the loosely coupled systems do computing in terms of services. SOA separates functions into distinct units, or services, which developers make accessible over a network in order to allow users to combine and reuse them in the production of applications. These services communicate with each other by passing data from one service to another [8], or by coordinating an activity between two or more services. They use the well established standards [9].

This approach is based on the design principles of loose coupling, which is a principle by which the consumer and service are insulated from changes in underlying technology and behavior, Interoperability[4] the principle which provides the ability to support consumers and service providers that are of different programming languages on, different operating systems with different communication capabilities,

Encapsulation that allows the potential consumer to be insulated from the internal technology and even the details of behavior of service, Discoverability which is used to realize the benefit of reuse [7].

Service Oriented Architecture creates an opportunity for legacy systems to be made available for implementation without replacing them with new ones [3]. A Service Oriented Architecture (SOA) model is developed for an Engineering institution and the services required for the automation of the college is proposed.

3 Business Application Model

The collective logic [4] that defines and drives an enterprise can be divided into business logic and application logic. Business logic is a documented implementation of the business requirements that originate from an enterprise's business areas [3]. Application logic is an automated implementation of business logic organized into various technology solutions. Service-orientation applies to enterprise logic. It introduces new concepts that augment the manner in which this logic is represented, viewed, modeled, and shared. The concepts introduced by service-orientation [4] are realized through the introduction of services. They establish a high form of abstraction wedged between traditional business and application layers. This allows for the service layer to consist of multiple layers of abstraction.

Fig.1 shows how individual services are implemented for the application like due certificate details. The services in Laboratory management system, Library management system and Hostel management system are utilized to implement the No Due Certificate application. This application is implemented using J2EE.After verifying the authorization of the user with username and password, the register number is obtained as input. The no due service of Laboratory management system provides the due details of user concerned with Laboratories. Similarly, no due service of Library management system and Hostel management system provides the respective due details.

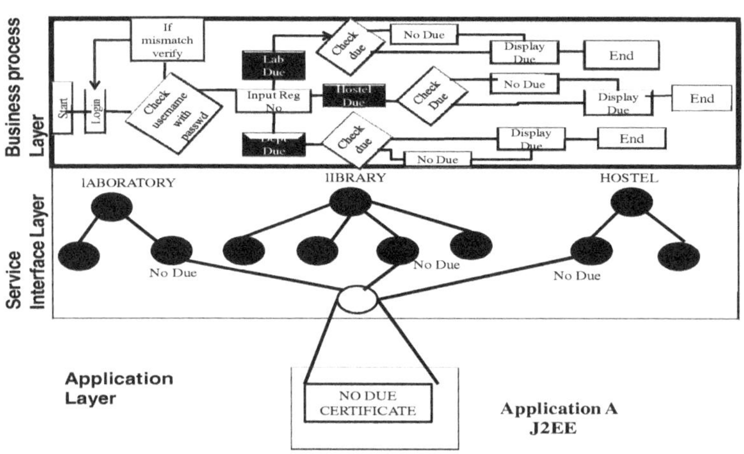

Fig. 1. Business application model for No Due Certificate

Fig.2 shows the implementation of eligibility of a student for appearing examination. The services from student attendance system and student information system are used to implement this application. It is implemented using .Net. After verifying the authorization of the user with username and password, the register number is obtained as input. The services namely attendance percentage of a particular student and list of students with less than 75% attendance from student attendance system is combined with the service from student information system. The combination of three services will provide the list of candidates who are eligible for appearing examination.

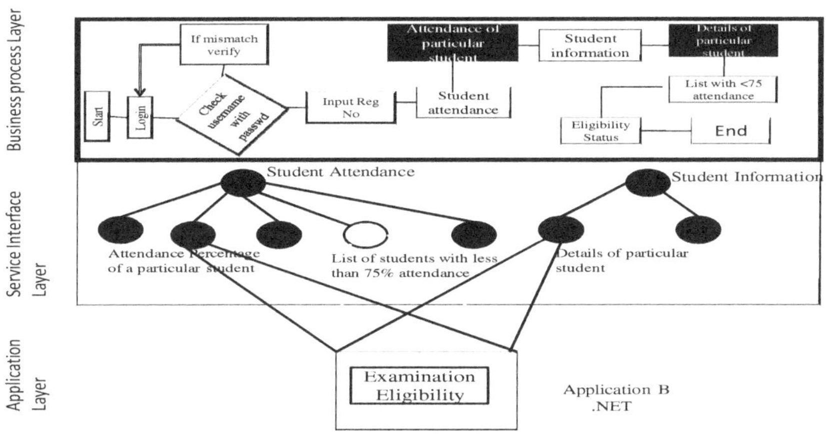

Fig. 2. Business application model for Examination Eligibility

Fig.3 shows the business application model for campus eligibility of a student. It is a legacy application leveraged by using SOA. After verifying the authorization of the

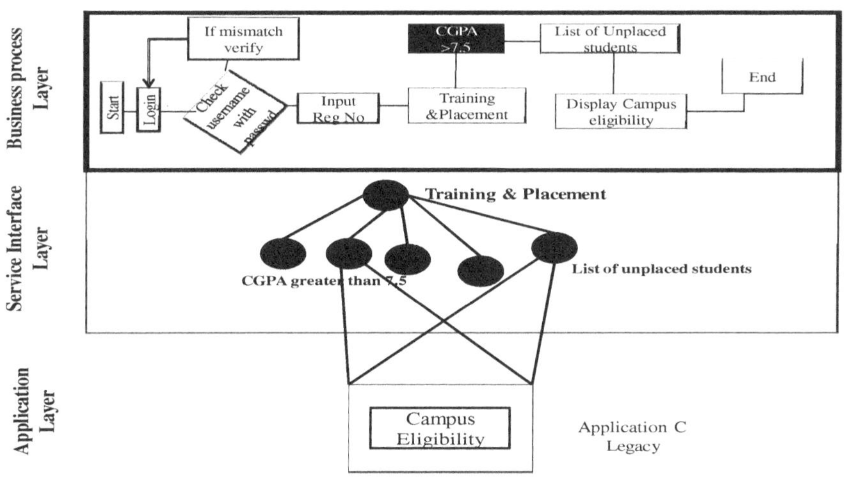

Fig. 3. Business application model for Campus Eligibility

user with username and password, the register number is obtained as input. Training and placement system provides the services namely CGPA greater than 7.5 and list of unplaced students which are used for building the campus eligibility application.

The below Table 1 shows the services provided by the systems. The services are implemented using .NET and J2EE. The services are used to implement applications like due certificate details, eligibility of a student for examination, eligibility of a student for campus interviews, etc.

Table 1. Applications developed by service composition

Application Developed	Systems Used	Services offered
Due certificate details	Laboratory management system Library management system Hostel management system	No due service No due service No due service
Examination eligibility	Student attendance system Student information system	Attendance percentage of a particular student Details of a particular student
Campus eligibility	Training and placement	CGPA greater than 7.5 List of unplaced students

3.1 Architecture Diagram

The overall architecture model in the Fig.4 shows all the systems connected via Ethernet. Here any system may act the service provider or the service consumer. Any service request or service response is done through XML format using SOAP protocol.

The student attendance system provides the services that are helpful in finding the regular student, the students eligible for examination, etc. The internal mark maintenance system helps in maintaining the internal marks of each class, each student under each subject, etc. Student's information system is very useful for knowing about the personal details of each student. It is used mainly by the faculties and the administration. The Department library management system is very helpful for students and the staff for finding the availability of books in library. Staff daily attendance system helps in marking and maintaining the daily of each staff. It helps to generate the leave records of the faculties.

The alumni association system is mainly used to trace down the students who had passed out of college and refers the topper in each out going batch. The time table and syllabus system is useful in providing the time table of each class, the teachers handling each class, electives of each semester, etc. The training and placement cell system helps in maintaining all the placement cell records such as details of companies visited in an academic year, details of placed students in a company, etc. The Laboratory inventory system is an inventory system that helps in maintaining records of the equipments available in the laboratories. The aim of Scholarship maintenance system is for identifying the eligible candidates for scholarship and provides them financial assistance during their course of study. The Hostel information system provides information about the hostel students in each class. It is also useful in providing no due certificates for them. The Department information system is very helpful in providing information about each department. It also provides list of faculties present in each department. The Project Maintenance system is exclusively used to view the types of projects done by the students in each department in each year. The Fees maintenance system helps in providing the fees structure for each class. It is also useful in providing the defaulters list who had abstained from paying fees. The Conference maintenance system is useful for students and staffs to get information about the conferences and enroll themselves in these conferences.

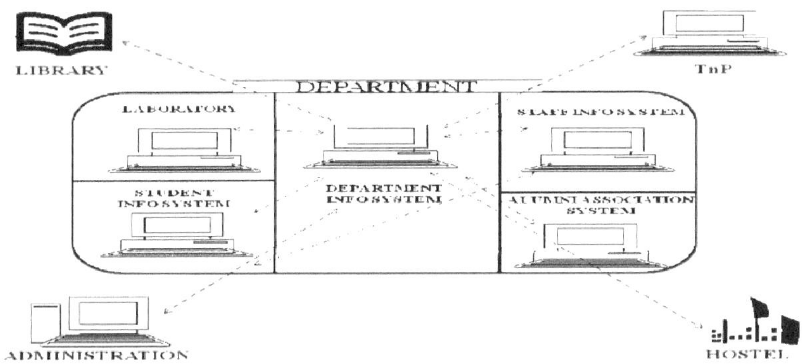

Fig. 4. Overall system architecture

3.2 Services Implemented for the Systems

If a service-oriented architecture is to be effective, we need a clear understanding of the term service. A service is a function that is well-defined, self-contained, and does not depend on the context or state of other services. The following Table 2 shows the services provided by the systems. The services are implemented using .NET and J2EE. The services are used to implement applications like due certificate details, eligibility of a student for examination, eligibility of a student for campus interviews, etc. They provide various functionalities for the different departments of the engineering institution. The following services provided by the systems can be composed in different possibilities as per the need, to design different Business application model.

Table 2. List of services implemented by systems

S.No	Systems Developed	Services Provided
1	Student attendance system	Attendance Percentage of all subjects for a class Subject wise attendance Percentage for a class List of students with 100% attendance List of students with less than 75% attendance Attendance Percentage of a particular student with his register number
2	Internal mark maintenance system	Subject wise internal marks for a class Internal marks of all subjects for a semester Internal marks of a particular student
3	Student information system	Details of a particular student (e.g. register No) Batch wise student details (e.g. 2006-2010)
4	Department library management system	List of books available in library under a category Details of a particular book List of books taken by a particular student No due certificate for a student in library
5	Staff daily attendance system	Particular teachers leave details Attendance details of a teacher
6	Alumni association system	Passed out student details batch wise Toppers list in a particular batch
7	Time table and syllabus system	Time table of a semester Subjects handled by teachers Elective subjects for a semester Subjects for a particular semester
8	Training and placement cell system	Companies visited in an academic year Number of students placed in a year List of students placed in a particular company in a year List of students placed in a particular year List of students with a particular range of CGPA
9	Laboratory inventory system	List the equipments available in a particular lab No due certificate for a student in a lab
10	Scholarship maintenance system	List of scholarships available List of students receiving a particular scholarship List of students in a department receiving a particular scholarship
11	Hostel information system	List of hostellers in a class No due certificate for a student in hostel
12	Department information system	Details of the function conducted by the department Details of a particular teacher List all Professors' details List all Assistant Professor's details List all Lecturers' details
13	Project maintenance system	Projects done under a domain Projects done in the current year Projects done in any given year
14	Fees maintenance system	Exam fees structure List of students who have not paid the exam fees Tuition fees structure List of students who have not paid the tuition fees
15	Conference maintenance system	List the available conferences List of people attending a particular conference

4 Service Implementation

Due Details Application with Service Composition shown below in Fig. 5 displays the due details of a particular student after entering his register number. The display of due details is an exact scenario of service composition where no due service from Hostel Information System, Laboratory Inventory System and Department library management system is composed together. Similarly, Business application model for Examination eligibility is created by composing the two services Attendance percentage of a particular student and list of students with less attendance with student detail service of Student Information System. Likewise, the application model for campus Eligibility is achieved by composing services from Training and placement system.

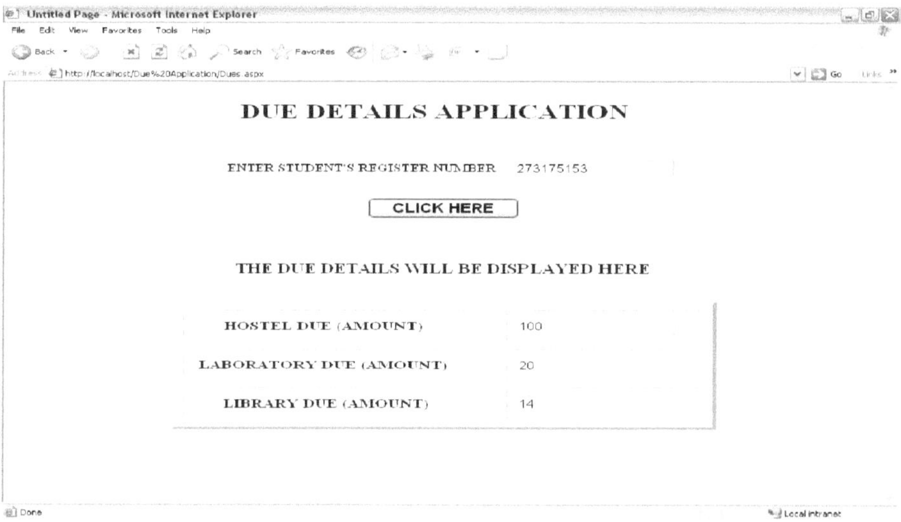

Fig. 5. Displaying the Due Details

5 Results and Discussions

The potential benefits and the intital results from our implementation of service-oriented architecture in Engineering Institution are highly promising. We have automated systems for Student's attendance, Internal mark maintenance, Student's information, Department information, Department library management system, Staff daily attendance, Alumni association, Time table & syllabus systems. Services of these systems perform request-reply for information sharing and it is been automated. The work developed is subjected to below discussions as shown in Table 3.

Table 3. Advantages of automated systems in terms of attributes

Compatibility	The services developed for the systems namely Laboratory management system, Library management system, Hostel management system, student attendance system, student information system etc. can be integrated to implement applications thereby ensuring interoperability and reusability of services.
Complexity	The existing system at Pondicherry Engineering college have only isolated computing systems at the department level which has low operational efficiency and is vulnerable of human errors [4]. Hence replacing the existing legacy systems with the new architecture is costly and also increases the risk of malfunctioning.
Advantages	The model developed using Service Oriented Architecture integrates the Student attendance system and Student information system to develop business application model for examination eligibility. Similarly the services in training and placement are integrated for the application Campus eligibility.

6 Conclusion

Service Oriented Architecture integrates with the existing legacy systems to provide complete automation through services and in turn reduces the implementation cost and maintenance cost. The services help to automate isolated systems. In this work we have automated the engineering institution and prototype is developed considering major use cases involved in an engineering institution.

In future, if all educational institutions construct this type of system then we can form an interconnection and make an overall e-Governance for education department. It is also planned to couple the system with biometrics and additional control equipments to cater for misuse and deceit. The integration, deployment and testing part is to be done in the future.

References

1. Shaikh, A., Muniba, M., Muhammad, M., et al.: The Role of Service Oriented Architecture in Tele-Medicine Healthcare System. IEEE Computer Society, Japan (2009)
2. Adegboyego, O., Tomasz, J., Elsa, E.: Domain models and enterprise application framework for developing electronic public services. UNU- IIST report no. 369 (2007)
3. Viswanath, S., Austin, L.: Adoption of Service Oriented Architecture (SOA) for Enterprise Systems in Education. Public Draft 1.0 (2009)
4. Phan, C.: Service Oriented Architecture (SOA) - Security Challenges and Mitigation Strategies. IEEE Computer Society (2007)
5. Erradi, A., Anand, S., Kulkarni, N.: Evaluation of strategies for Integrating legacy application as services in a service oriented architecture. In: IEEE International Conference on Services Computing (2006)

6. Bosin, A., Dessi, N., Pes, B.: Extending the SOA Paradigm to e- science environments. Sciencedirect Future Generation Computer System 27 (2011)
7. Li, Y., Chen, H., Zheng, X., et al.: A Service Oriented Travel Portal and Engineering Platform. International Journal of Expert Systems with Applications 38
8. Callaway, R.D., Viniotis, Y., Rodriguez, A.: An Autonomic Service Delivery Platform For Service Oriented Network Environments. IEEE Transactions on Services Computing 3(2) (April-June 2010)
9. Menasce, D.A., Gomaa, H., Malek, S., Sousa, J.P.: Sassy: A Famework for Self-Architecting Service-Oriented Systems. Publication of IEEE Software

A Device Middleware-Based Smart Home Environment for Ambient Health Care

Veeramuthu Venkatesh[1], Pethuru Raj[2], and V. Vaithayanathan[1]

[1] Department of Computer Science, SOC,
SASTRA University, India
[2] Enterprise Architect, Sify Software Ltd., Tidel Park, Chennai, India

Abstract. The growing elderly population in the developed countries is increasingly forced to live independently. They are being remotely monitored, reminded, recommended and cared by a stream of care givers, providers, doctors, etc. The enabling technologies and devices are also growing fast. Firstly the room or house wherein the patient lives has been equipped and saturated with a host of multifaceted, multi-channel, multimedia, and multimodal sensors / actuators, robots, displays, appliances etc. Another noteworthy development is the powerful emergence of communication protocols and connectivity solutions, web-enabled devices, device-specific and agnostic services. To enable these diverse participants, to find one another, correspond and collaborate together dynamically and cognitively to understand the prevailing situation and needs of the patient, conceive and construct composite services for patient-centric, sophisticated and smart. In short, smart environments, wherein the ambient intelligence is the norm, are being created and sustained leveraging calm, cognitive and catalytic technologies.

Keywords: Assisted Living, Device Profile Web Services(DPWS), Pervasive Computing, Ubiquitous Healthcare.

1 Introduction

Leading information technology (IT) players and professionals are collaboratively working towards the realization of the smart planet vision. It is widely recognized that IT is the greatest enabler of the aspects and the automation requirements associated with the vision and the mission. Predominantly besides software services and applications, cloud infrastructures and platforms, the vast and varied device space has to see quite a lot of paradigm and pioneering shifts. That is, disappearing, sentient and smart sensors, actuators, controllers, chips, robots, displays, communication and computing instruments are to be manufactured in plenty and hence their contributions will be immense and immeasurable for the vision in sync up with the cyber systems along with wireless sensor network [1]. Here the vision is to develop a flexible and futuristic architecture for deriving a host of specific smart (home) environments [2], [3], [4], [5], [6] .

P.V. Krishna, M.R. Babu, and E. Ariwa (Eds.): ObCom 2011, Part I, CCIS 269, pp. 144–153, 2012.

1.1 Envisioning the Technology Landscape

Due to the faster maturity and stability of device discovery, connectivity, integration and orchestration technologies, the mission of establishing and sustaining a cornucopia of smart zones is getting easier. Due to multiplicity and heterogeneity [7], [8] of devices, there came a number of standards in order to bring a kind of semblance to the device chaos. Service oriented device architecture (SODA) [7] is the device-centric service oriented architecture concept gaining a greater value and adoption as the service paradigm in the enterprise space is shining. In other words, service oriented architecture (SOA) is for the enterprise space where as SODA is for the embedded space, which is incidentally vast and varied. Device profile for web services (DPWS) [9] is the first and foremost standard that fully complies with the ideas and ideals of SODA.

There is another popular and pioneering approach called as the open service gateway initiative (OSGi) [10], which is Java-centric. However DPWS [9] is technology-neutral. Also DPWS, being the industry-strength standard, there are of best-of-breed implementations in different languages. Also implementations could be tweaked and twisted according to the target devices. That is, if the target platform is very minuscule, then the micro version of DPWS implementation can be smartly utilized.

Zigbee [11] is the communication protocol standard for the sensor world. There are a growing array of sensors and actuators with varying capacities and capabilities. Zigbee technology [12] has become so popular and pervasive for building next-generation sensor-based applications. The arrival of slim and sleek devices has led to fresh opportunities and possibilities especially in the vast domain of personal health care. Zigbee is the unifying standard and technology and hence we have chosen it for our ambient healthcare system.

1.2 The Problem Area and the System Descriptions

Patient Tele-monitoring is a common practice in the pervasive telemedicine discipline in both indoor and outdoor environments [13], [14]. Especially the ageing societies in the developed nations are looking for mission-critical and sustainable IT solutions to promote healthy yet independent lifestyles for elderly as far as possible. Thereby the field of Ambient Assisted Living (AAL) [15],[16],[17],[18] has become so demanding these days. Considering all these, we have come out a Zigbee-based smart sensor network (SSN) that takes care of all the functional requirements of the AAL system.

The ultimate system comprises Zigbee sensors to sense the environment and to communicate the data captured and extracted to the central corporate server. The processing, analysis and mining happens at this cyber server in order to decide and dictate the best course of actions in order to simplify and streamline the daily lives of debilitated and deficient people. We have conceptualized an extensible architecture to accommodate future changes and challenges in the subject as well as in the technology domain. Our architecture is capable of capturing events proactively and hence real-time interactions could happen.

1.3 The Solution Distinctions

The primary focus is on the design challenges of ambient home care systems. These systems invariably aid and assist aged and incapacitated people who need continuous monitoring and medication. This system is for those insisting independent living. These systems are capable of gathering environmental and personal information in order to produce and provide a set of services: information about the need for food supply or the appliances' status, storage of environmental and energy consumption data, security alarms, medication prompting, health monitoring and alerts, etc.

This AAL system facilitates older and needy people to live in their own home environment safely and securely. This significantly increases their autonomy and decision-making abilities by assisting them in carrying out their activities through the exemplary usage of intelligent products and the provision of remote services including care services. Most efforts towards building ambient assisted living systems for the elderly people are based on developing pervasive devices and use Ambient Intelligence (AmI) concepts to integrate these devices together to construct an active, aware, augmented and articulate environment.

This paper describes how to develop and deploy a Zigbee-based sensor network at a home environment. The middleware created is based on DPWS. The hugely potential service paradigm is an excellent option for crafting competent ambient care systems and their components. All the individual components enabled with Zigbee are made as services so the device middleware can find, bind and use to generate newer and nimbler services for patients and participants in the environment. The parameter values obtained are hosted on the local host. This architecture helps one to monitor the patients or elderly motion at home.

2 Why Device Profile for Web Service (DPWS)?

In SOA, interoperability of different platforms is established through the definition of common communication protocol and message exchange standards. Several middleware are designed using the SOA technology to list a few UPnP, JiNi, OSGi, DPWS and many others; Service oriented architecture (SOA) is an open concept which supports plug-and-play capabilities of heterogeneous software and hardware components. The SOA addresses issues such as addressing, discovery, description and eventing.

The most popular architecture based on SOA is the Device Profile for Web Service (DPWS).The big advantage of DPWS is its reliance on web service. Microsoft has included DPWS in their operating system called Windows Vista. DPWS apart from utilizing web service also includes other standards such as ws-policy, ws-addressing, ws-eventing etc.

2.1 WS-Policy

Policies mostly define QoS characteristics and security considerations which are necessary for service .communication Service users have to choose and comply with one of the offered policy alternatives which consist of several policy assertions from the policy document.

2.2 WS-Addressing

The main objective of WS-Addressing is to provide an addressing mechanism for Web services as well as messages in a transport-neutral matter. By introducing the concept of endpoint references (EPR) WS-Addressing overcomes the lack of SOAP's independence of underlying transport protocols and secondly support of asynchronous message exchange. Endpoint references are structures defined to address Web services endpoints. The address property within endpoint references is mandatory and its value could be an HTTP-based URL.

2.3 WS-Discovery

It's a protocol based on IP multicast for enabling services to be discovered automatically. Discovery introduces three different types of endpoint namely the target service, the client and the discovery proxy. Target services are Web services offering themselves to the network. Clients may search for target services and discover them dynamically. Discovery proxy is an endpoint enabling discovery in spanned networks since simple discovery is limited to a multicast group and hence to local managed networks only. Basically it defines four operations and they are: probe, probe match, hello and bye messages. Probe is used whenever one needs to identify another service in the network. ProbeMatch as the name implies, identifies the service and sends a response to the device which probed for its presence. Hello is sent when a device comes to the network for the first time and bye is sent when one device leaves the network.

2.4 WS-Transfer

This is a specification that defines the data types and operations to retrieve metadata associated with an endpoint. This metadata describes what other endpoints are needed to know to interact with the described endpoint. This is very similar to HTTP messages like Get, Put and Delete. WS-Transfer can contain arbitrary XML data, WS-policy and the like.

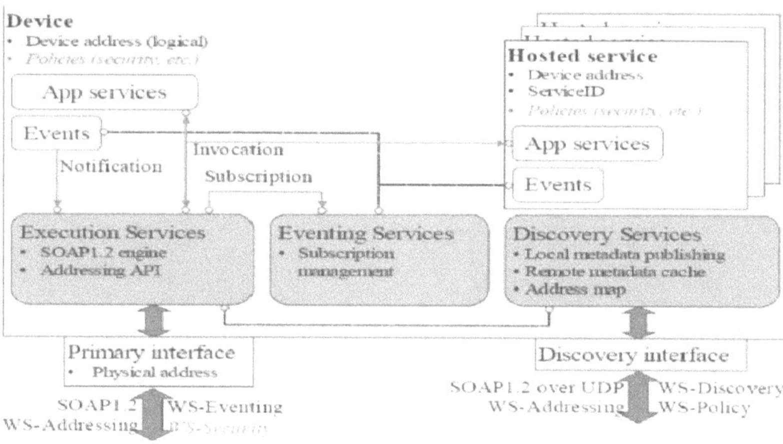

Fig. 1. DPWS working

2.5 WS-Eventing

WS-Eventing defines a protocol for managing subscriptions for a Web service based on the eventing mechanism. This protocol defines three endpoints: subscriber, event source and subscription manager.

3 The System Architecture Layer

Device Layer - At the user end, there are a wider variety of slim and sleek input / output terminals. That is, any kind of devices, appliances, instruments, touch screens, and systems can be used at the client level. These devices are multifaceted in the sense that they can handle multimedia, multimodal gestures, multi-channel etc.

Channel Layer - Then the architecture talks about multiple channels such as intranet, internet, extranet, wireless connectivity, etc.

Middleware Layer – All the right and relevant transformations and enhancements are being accomplished at this layer in order to enable services to find one another in their vicinity as well as remote services over the network, bind and use in order to produce competent services.

The Service Repository Layer – Here all the services participating in the interactions are being stored and managed here.

The Cyber Server Layer – All the cyber applications and services are being deployed in high-end servers in order to guarantee enterprise-class qualities.

The Data Layer – The data are always enabling contemplating and taking intelligent decision. Here too, services utilize the streaming as well as persistent data effectively in order to help them to formulate better and bigger things. There are adapters, connectors, drivers and gateways in order to simplify connectivity and integration.

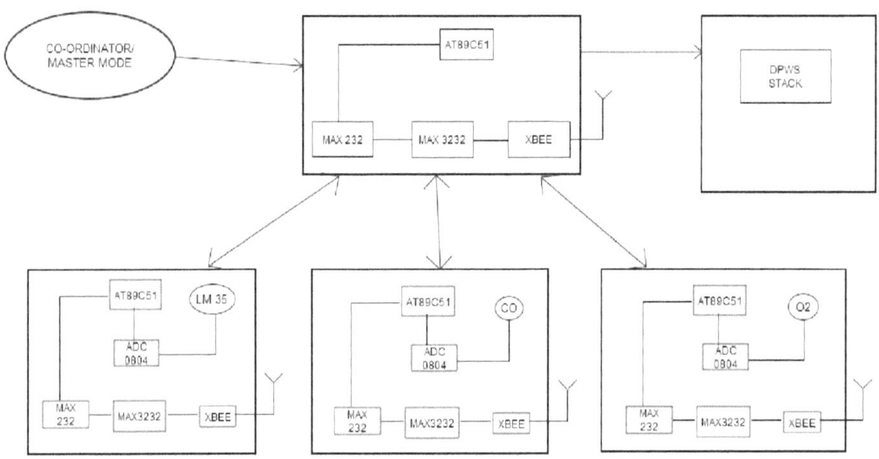

Fig. 2. Architecture of the model designed

The proposed implementation have been using the following sensors

Oxygen sensor

The basic function of an oxygen sensor is to measure the proportion of oxygen in the gas or liquid being analysed. The original sensing element is made with a thimble-shaped zirconia ceramic coated on both the exhaust and reference sides with a thin layer of platinum and comes in both heated and unheated forms. They are used to measure respiration or rate of production of oxygen. Oxygen sensors are used in oxygen analyzers which find a lot of use in medical applications such as anesthesia monitors, respirators and oxygen concentrators. Oxygen sensors can be used along with carbon dioxide sensors to help improve the characterization of soil respiration. Moreover, they are used widely marine biology.

Carbon-dioxide sensor

A carbon dioxide sensor or CO2 sensor is an instrument for the measurement of carbon dioxide gas. Measuring carbon dioxide is important in monitoring indoor air quality and many industrial processes. For air conditioning applications these kind of sensors can be used to monitor the quality of air and the tailored need of fresh air, respectively. In applications where direct temperature measurement is not applicable NDIR sensors can be used. The sensors absorb ambient infrared radiation (IR) given off by a heated surface.CO2 sensors are also able to determine how many people are in a room and then adjust the air conditioning accordingly.

Temperature sensor

A temperature sensor is a machine that measures heat radiation. There are a variety of types of temperature sensor, and different methods are suited to different situations. They are of two types namely contact sensors and non contact sensors. Temperature sensors can give a specific readout and are often used in industrial manufacturing sectors such as steel, glass and ceramics. A thermocouple is a device which falls under this category and it consists of two different conductors that produce a voltage proportional to a temperature difference between either end of the pair of conductors. The main use of temperature sensor is in medical industry to measure body temperature and that device is called a thermometer.

4 The Sensor-Based AAL System

We have implemented a Zigbee home network. Zigbee, which is an IEEE 802.15.4 compliant technology and here XBee mote has been created, enabled and used. They can transmit parameters of interest based on the user requirements within 30m indoor .The motes are created with Philips micro-controller which is 8-bit.For initial study of how the DPWS architecture works, we have four wireless ZigBee enabled sensors. Initially we configure one of the four Xbee to act as the coordinator. Coordinator is the one which performs all the manipulations of the data it receives from other sensors. Other three motes are configured to be the end devices.

For a regular time interval the coordinator receives values from a single sensor. Based on the value received the cluster head or the coordinator take necessary actions. The main objective is to utilize the concept of service orchestration. We have connected the cluster head to a laptop. The laptop houses the developed middleware. The coding of DPWS that is the middleware is done using C# language in .Net Micro Framework. The coordinator upon receiving the value transmits the same to the middleware. The middleware displays the values on a local host.

Fig. 3. Picture of the XBee mote

4.1 Program Code

```
<Project DefaultTargets="Build"
xmlns=http://schemas.microsoft.com/developer/msbuild/2003
 ToolsVersion="3.5">
  <PropertyGroup>
    <AssemblyName>TemperatureClient</AssemblyName>
    <OutputType>Exe</OutputType>
    <RootNamespace>TemperatureClient</RootNamespace>
    <ProjectTypeGuids>{b69e3092-b931-443c-abe7-
7e7b65f2a37f};{FAE04EC0-301F-11D3-BF4B-
00C04F79EFBC}</ProjectTypeGuids>
    <ProductVersion>9.0.30729</ProductVersion>
    <SchemaVersion>2.0</SchemaVersion>
    <ProjectGuid>{76E6952A-A5D6-4FAF-BA63-
47A78B0C0445}</ProjectGuid>
    <TargetFrameworkVersion>v3.0</TargetFrameworkVersion>
    <NetMfTargetsBaseDir
Condition="'$(NetMfTargetsBaseDir)'==''">$
(MSBuildExtensionsPath)\Microsoft\.NET Micro
Framework\</NetMfTargetsBaseDir>
  </PropertyGroup>
  <PropertyGroup Condition="'$(Configuration)|$(Platform)'==
'Debug|AnyCPU' ">
```

```
<DebugSymbols>true</DebugSymbols>
<DebugType>full</DebugType>
<Optimize>false</Optimize>
<OutputPath>bin\Debug\</OutputPath>
<DefineConstants>DEBUG;TRACE</DefineConstants>
<ErrorReport>prompt</ErrorReport>
<WarningLevel>4</WarningLevel>
<Reference Include="MFDpwsClient" />
<Reference Include="MFDpwsExtensions" />
<Reference Include="MFWsStack" />
<Reference Include="Microsoft.SPOT.Hardware" />
<Reference Include="Microsoft.SPOT.Native" />
<Reference Include="System.IO" />
<Reference Include="System.Xml" />
```

5 The Future Work

This work can be further extended in several directions. The possibilities are definitely infinite and mindboggling. Here primarily we are trying to read the values that are published in the local host from a remote location. This is a kind of monitoring from the remote location.

We have used the same type of sensors. That is, all the sensors are Zigbee sensors only and hence this is a homogeneous network. This has therefore significantly made our work simpler and faster. There is very little for protocol translation, data transformation, message mediation and enrichment. All the middleware requirements are being taken care of by .NET micro framework. The next task planned is to use disparate sensors and actuators in order to create a more complicated network that in turn will be more people-centric. That is, we are going to use several types of sensors from different manufacturers. Also different sensor platforms will be used. When we move to this heterogeneous setup, there is a need for a host of technical services such as discovery, adaptation, intermediation, aggregation, security, arbitration, performance monitoring, etc.

6 Conclusion

Any automated healthcare applications are always given extreme importance due to the sliding healthcare scenario. The computing, communication, sensing and actuation technologies facilitate in deriving context-aware, converged, dynamic, on-demand and highly available applications.

In the experiments conducted, the results that were obtained are very satisfactory .We were able to co-ordinate four wireless sensors and we successfully invoked another sensor based on the processing done at the coordinator. We are consistently working towards a heterogeneous network of smart sensors in order to enhance the value and verve of next-generation smart applications.

References

1. Yick, J., Mukherjee, B., Ghosal, D.: Wireless sensor network survey. Computer Networks 52, 2292–2330 (2008)
2. Chan, M., Estéve, D., Escriba, C., Campo, E.: A review of smart homes—Present state and future challenges. Computer Methods and Programs in Biomedicine, 55–81 (2008)
3. Abowd, G.D., Mynatt, E.D.: Designing for the human experience in smart environments. In: Cook, D.J., Das, S.K. (eds.) Smart Environments: Technology, Protocols, and Applications, pp. 153–174. Wiley, Chichester (2005)
4. Mozer, M.C.: Lessons from an adaptive home. In: Cook, D.J., Das, S.K. (eds.) Smart Environments: Technology, Protocols, and Applications, pp. 273–298. Wiley, Chichester (2005)
5. Abdulrazak, B., Mokhtari, M., Feki, M.A., Ghorbel, M.: Integration of home networking in a smart environment dedicated to people with disabilities. In: Proceeding of the IEEE International Conference on Information & Communication Technologies, pp. 125–126 (2004)
6. Augusto, J.C., Nakashima, H., Aghajan, H.: Ambient intelligence and smart environments: A state of the art. In: Nakashima, H., Aghajan, H., Augusto, J.C. (eds.) Handbook of Ambient Intelligence and Smart Environments, pp. 3–31. Springer, New York (2010)
7. Leguay, J., Lopez-Ramos, M., Jean-Marie, K., Conan, V.: Service oriented architecture for heterogeneous and dynamic sensor networks. In: Proc. of the Second International Conference on Distributed Event-Based Systems (DEBS 2008), pp. 309–312. ACM, New York (2008)
8. El Kaed, C., Denneulin, Y., Ottogalli, F.-G., Mora, L.F.M.: Combining Ontology Alignment with Model Driven Engineering Techniques for Home Devices Interoperability. In: Min, S.L., Pettit, R., Puschner, P., Ungerer, T. (eds.) SEUS 2010. LNCS, vol. 6399, pp. 71–82. Springer, Heidelberg (2010)
9. OSGi Alliance, OSGi Alliance. OSGi Service Platform, Release 3 (2003), `http://www.osgi.org` (last visited July 24, 2007)
10. Sleman A., Moeller, R.: Integration of wireless sensor network services into other home and industrial networks using device profile for web services (DPWS). In: The 3rd International Conference on Information and Communication Technologies (ICTTA), pp. 1–5 (2008)
11. Zigbee Alliance, ZigBee Specification (Rev. 17) (January 2008), `http://www.zigbee.org`
12. Zhang, Q., Yang, X.-L., Zhou, Y.-M., Wang, L.-R., Guo, X.-S.: A wireless solution for greenhouse monitoring and control system based on ZigBee technology. Journal of Zhejiang University - Science A, 1584–1587 (2007), doi:10.1631
13. Hongliang, R., Meng, M.Q.-H., Chen, X.: Physiological information acquisition through wireless biomedical sensor networks. In: IEEE International Conference on Information Acquisition, pp. 483–488 (2005)
14. Venkatesh, V., Raj, P., Gopalan, K., Rajeev, T.: Healthcare Data Fusion and Presentation using Service- Oriented Architecture (SOA) Orchestration Mechanism. IJCA Special Issue on Artificial Intelligence Techniques - Novel Approaches & Practical Applications 2, 17–23 (2011)
15. Venkatesh, V., Raj, P., Vaithayanathan, V., Prashanth Kumar, M.: A Pragmatic Note on Knopflerfish-based Ambient Assisted Living (AAI) Systems Engineering. International Journal of Computer Applications 19(8), 42–47 (2011)

16. Ní Scanaill, C., et al.: A Review of Approaches to Mobility Telemonitoring of the Elderly in Their Living Environment. Annals of Biomedical Engineering 34(4), 547–563 (2006)
17. Carneiro, D., Novais, P., Costa, R., Neves, J.: Case-Based Reasoning Decision Making in Ambient Assisted Living. In: Omatu, S., Rocha, M.P., Bravo, J., Fernández, F., Corchado, E., Bustillo, A., Corchado, J.M. (eds.) IWANN 2009, Part II. LNCS, vol. 5518, pp. 788–795. Springer, Heidelberg (2009)
18. Sánchez-Pi, N., Molina, J.M.: A Centralized Approach to an Ambient Assisted Living Application: An Intelligent Home. In: Omatu, S., Rocha, M.P., Bravo, J., Fernández, F., Corchado, E., Bustillo, A., Corchado, J.M. (eds.) IWANN 2009. LNCS, vol. 5518, pp. 706–709. Springer, Heidelberg (2009)

Computer Oriented Process for Treating Second Order Differential Equations with Singular Coefficient at the First Derivative Term

A.S.V. Ravi Kanth* and K. Aruna

Fluid Dynamics Division, School of Advanced Sciences,
VIT University, Vellore- 632 014, Tamilnadu, India
asvravikanth@yahoo.com, k.aruna@vit.ac.in

Abstract. This paper applies the computer oriented process for solving second order differential equations with singular coefficient at the first derivative term. The original differential equation is modified at the singular point and then the differential equation is treated by using spline in tension. To test the efficiency of the proposed method both homogeneous and non-homogeneous singular boundary value problems are considered.

Keywords: Differential equation, singular coefficient, spline in tension.

1 Introduction

In this paper, we consider the second order differential equations with singular coefficient at the first derivative term is of the form

$$y''(x) = \frac{k}{x}y'(x) + b(x)y(x) + c(x), 0 \leq \ x \leq \ 1 \tag{1}$$

subject to the boundary conditions

$$y'(0) = 0, y(1) = \alpha \tag{2}$$

These equations arise naturally in different fields of applied mathematics and engineering, such as electrodynamics, theory of thermal explosions, fluid dynamics geo physics, optimal control theory etc. There has recently been much attention devoted to the search for better numerical method for determining a solution of singular boundary value problems. Some of the notable contributions in the study of singular boundary value problems are finite difference approximations [1-4], B-splines [5], sinc Galerkin and homotopy perturbation method [6], modified homotopy analysis method [7], differential transform method [8] and variational iteration method [9]. In this paper, we presented a spline in tension method for the numerical solution of the second order differential equations with singular coefficient at the first derivative term is of the form (1)-(2). The original differential equation is modified at the singular point and then the proposed

* Corresponding author.

method is employed to solve the differential equation. Computed orientation process is given in section 2 and in section 3 computational results are presented to demonstrate the applicability of the method.

2 Computed Orientation Process

Consider a class of second order differential equation having singular coefficient at the first derivative term is of the form (1)-(2). We first modify the equation(1) at the singular point at $x = 0$ by using L' Hospital rule and (1)-(2) is transformed into

$$y''(x) = p(x)y'(x) + q(x)y(x) + r(x) \tag{3}$$

$$y'(0) = 0, y(1) = \alpha \tag{4}$$

where

$$p(x) = \begin{cases} 0, & x = 0 \\ \frac{k}{x}, & x \neq 0 \end{cases}$$

$$q(x) = \begin{cases} \frac{b(0)}{1-k}, & x = 0 \\ b(x), & x \neq 0 \end{cases}$$

$$r(x) = \begin{cases} \frac{c(0)}{1-k}, & x = 0 \\ c(x), & x \neq 0 \end{cases}$$

We develop a smooth approximate solution of (3) using tension splines. For this purpose we discretize the interval [0, 1] divided into a set of grid points $x_i = ih$, $i = 0, ..., N$ with $h = \frac{1}{N}$. A function $S(x, \tau)$ of class $C^2[a, b]$ which interpolates $y(x)$ at the mesh point x_i depends on a parameter τ, reduces to cubic spline in $[a, b]$ as $\tau \to 0$ is termed as parametric cubic-spline function [10]. The spline function $S(x, \tau) = S(x)$ satisfying in $[x_i, x_{i+1}]$, the differential equation,

$$S''(x) - \tau S(x) = [S''(x_i) - \tau S(x_i)]\frac{(x_{i+1} - x)}{h} + [S''(x_{i+1}) - \tau S(x_{i+1})]\frac{(x - x_i)}{h} \tag{5}$$

where $S(x_i) = y_i$ and $\tau > 0$ is termed as cubic spline in tension. Solving the equation (5) and determining the arbitrary constants from the interpolatory conditions $S(x_i) = y_i$ and $S(x_{i+1}) = y_{i+1}$. After writing $\lambda = h\sqrt{\tau}$, we get

$$\begin{aligned} S(x) = & \frac{h^2}{\lambda^2 \sin h\lambda}[M_{i+1} \sin h\lambda \frac{(x - x_i)}{h} + M_i \sin h\lambda \frac{(x_{i+1} - x)}{h}] \\ & - \frac{h^2}{\lambda^2}[\frac{(x - x_i)}{h}(M_{i+1} - \frac{\lambda^2}{h^2}y_{i+1}) + \frac{(x_{i+1} - x)}{h}(M_i - \frac{\lambda^2}{h^2}y_i)] \end{aligned} \tag{6}$$

Differentiating equation (6) and using continuity conditions which lead to the tridiagonal system

$$h^2(\lambda_1 M_{i-1} + 2\lambda_2 M_i + \lambda_1 M_{i+1}) = y_{i+1} - 2y_i + y_{i-1}$$

$$i = 1(1)N - 1 \tag{7}$$

where $\lambda_1 = \frac{1}{\lambda^2}(1 - \frac{\lambda}{\sin h\lambda})$, $\lambda_2 = \frac{1}{\lambda^2}(\lambda \cot h\lambda - 1)$, $M_i = S''(x)$. The condition (7) ensures the continuity of the first order derivatives of the spline $S(x, \tau)$ at interior nodes. we rewrite (1) in the form $M_i = p(x_i)y'(x_i) + q(x_i)y(x_i) + r(x_i)$ and substituting into equation (7), and using the following approximations for first order derivatives of y:

$$y'_{i-1} \cong \frac{-y_{i+1} + 4y_i - 3y_{i-1}}{2h} \tag{8}$$

$$y'_{i+1} \cong \frac{3y_{i+1} - 4y_i + y_{i-1}}{2h} \tag{9}$$

$$\begin{aligned} y'_i \cong & \frac{1 + 2h^2\omega q_{i+1} + h\omega(3p_{i+1} + p_{i-1})}{2h} y_{i+1} - 2\omega(p_{i+1} + p_{i-1})y_i \\ + & \frac{-1 - 2h^2\omega q_{i-1} + h\omega(3p_{i-1} + p_{i+1})}{2h} y_{i-1} + h\omega(r_{i+1} - r_{i-1}) \end{aligned} \tag{10}$$

we get the following three term recurence relaation, which gives the approximation $y_1, y_2, \dots, y_{N-1}$ of the solution $y(x)$ at the points $x_1, x_2, \dots, x_{N-1}$.

$$\begin{aligned} &(-\frac{3}{2}h\lambda_1 p_{i-1} + h^2\lambda_1 q_{i-1} - h\lambda_2 p_i(1 + 2h^2\omega q_{i-1} - h\omega(p_{i+1} + 3p_{i-1})) \\ &+\frac{1}{2}\lambda_1 h p_{i+1} - 1)y_{i-1} + (2\lambda_1 h p_{i-1} - 4h^2\lambda_2\omega p_i(p_{i+1} + p_{i-1}) + 2h^2\lambda_2 q_i \\ &-2h\lambda_1 p_{i+1} + 2)y_i + (-\frac{1}{2}h\lambda_1 p_{i-1} + h^2\lambda_1 q_{i+1} + h\lambda_2 p_i(1 + 2h^2\omega q_{i+1} \\ &+h\omega(3p_{i+1} + p_{i-1})) + \frac{3}{2}\lambda_1 h p_{i+1} - 1)y_{i+1} = -h^2((\lambda_1 - 2\lambda_2 h\omega p_i)r_{i-1} \\ &+2\lambda_2 r_i + (\lambda_1 + 2\lambda_2 h\omega p_i)r_{i+1}), \qquad i = 1, \dots, N-1 \end{aligned} \tag{11}$$

The boundary condition $y'(0) = 0$ can be written in discretized form as

$$\begin{aligned} &(3h^2\lambda_1 p_1 p_{-1} + 3h^4\lambda_1\lambda_2 q_0 p_{-1} - 2h^3\lambda_1 q_{-1} p_1 + 2h^4\lambda_1^2 p_1 q_{-1} - 2h^5\lambda_1\lambda_2 q_{-1} q_0 \\ &-h^2\lambda_1 p_1 + 2h^3\lambda_1^2 p_1^2 - h^4\lambda_1\lambda_2 p_1 q_0 + 2h - 4h^2\lambda_1 p_1 - 2h^3\lambda_1^2 p_{-1} p_1 \\ &+2h^4\lambda_1\lambda_2 q_0 p_1 - 2h^3\lambda_1^2 p_1^2 + 2h^2\lambda_1 p_1)y_0 + (-3h^2\lambda_1 p_{-1} + \frac{9}{2}h^3\lambda_1^2 p_{-1} p_1 \\ &+3h^4\lambda_1^2 p_{-1} q_1 + 2h^3\lambda_1 q_{-1} - 3h^4\lambda_1^2 p_1 q_{-1} - 2h^5\lambda_1^2 q_{-1} q_1 + \lambda_1 h^2 p_1 \\ &-\frac{3}{2}h^3\lambda_1^2 p_1^2 - \lambda_1^2 h^4 p_1 q_1 - 2h + 3h^2\lambda_1 p_1 + 2h^3\lambda_1 q_1 - \frac{1}{2}h^3\lambda_1^2 p_{-1} p_1 \\ &+\frac{3}{2}h^3\lambda_1^2 p_1^2 + h^4\lambda_1^2 q_1 p_1 - h^2\lambda_1 p_1)y_1 = -h^4\lambda_1 r_{-1} p_1 - 2h^4\lambda_1\lambda_2 r_0 p_1 \\ &-h^4\lambda_1^2 r_1 p_1 - 3h^4\lambda_1^2 r_1 p_{-1} - 3h^4\lambda_1\lambda_2 p_{-1} r_0 + 2h^4\lambda_1 q_{-1} + 2h^5\lambda_1^2 q_{-1} r_1 \\ &+2h^5\lambda_1\lambda_2 q_{-1} r_0 + h^4\lambda_1^2 p_1 r_1 + h^4\lambda_1\lambda_2 r_0 p_1 - 2h^3\lambda_1 r_1 - 2h^3\lambda_2 r_0. \end{aligned} \tag{12}$$

By expanding (11) in a Taylor series about x_i, and using (3) we obtain the following local truncation error:

$$T_o(h) = h^4(\frac{\lambda_1}{3} - 2\lambda_2(\frac{1}{6} + 2\omega))p_i y'''(x_i) + \frac{h^4}{12}(1 - 12\lambda_1)y''''(\mu^i) + O(h^6) \tag{13}$$

It can be seen easily that $T_o(h) = O(h^4)$ for any choice of $\lambda_1 + \lambda_2 = \frac{1}{2}$ and for any value of ω and $T_o(h) = O(h^6)$ for $\lambda_1 = \frac{1}{12}$, $\lambda_2 = \frac{5}{12}$ and $\omega = -\frac{1}{20}$. Thus, we have proved the following.

Theorem. Let $y(x) \in C^2[a,b]$, then our method provides a second order convergent approximation for solution $y(x)$ of the boundary value problem (1) - (2) for any choice of λ_1, λ_2 and ω with $\lambda_1 + \lambda_2 = \frac{1}{2}$ and fourth order convergent solution for $\lambda_1 = \frac{1}{12}$, $\lambda_2 = \frac{5}{12}$ and $\omega = -\frac{1}{20}$.

3 Computational Results and Conclusions

To test the efficiency of the proposed method, we applied a spline in tension method for a class of second order differential equations with the singular coefficient at the first derivative term is of the form (1) - (2) whose exact solution are known. The computational result shows that proposed method is fourth order for the specific choice of λ_1 and λ_2. The accuracy of the method is tested by calculating the error norms $L_\infty = \overset{max}{i} \ |y_i - \tilde{y}_i|$, $L_2 = \sqrt{\sum_{i=1}^{N}(y_i - \tilde{y}_i)^2}$, where y and $\tilde{y}$ denote the exact and the approximate solution respectively.

Example 1: Consider Bessel's equation of order zero

$$y''(x) + \frac{1}{x}y'(x) + y(x) = 0 \tag{14}$$

subject to the boundary conditions

$$y'(0) = 0, \ \ y(1) = 1. \tag{15}$$

The exact solution for the problem is $y(x) = \frac{J_0(x)}{J_0(1)}$. In Table 1, we compared the maximum absolute errors and the order of convergence obtained by the proposed method and the method in [11] and also errors for different values of h obtained by the proposed method and the B-spline method are presented in Table 2, which shows the supremacy of our method.

Example 2: Now, consider the following non-homogeneous singular boundary value problem

$$y''(x) + \frac{2}{x}y'(x) - 4y(x) = -2, 0 < x \leq 1, \tag{16}$$

subject to the boundary conditions

$$y'(0) = 0, \ \ y(1) = 5.5. \tag{17}$$

The exact solution for the problem is $y(x) = 0.5 + \frac{5\sinh 2x}{x\sinh 2}$. Errors obtained by the proposed method and the B-spline method are given in Table 3 and it shows that the computational errors obtained by the proposed method are much smaller than the errors obtained by the B-spline method.

Example 3: Finally, we consider the singular boundary value problem

$$y''(x) + \frac{1}{x}y'(x) = (\frac{8}{8-x^2})^2 \tag{18}$$

subject to the boundary conditions

$$y'(0) = 0, \quad y(1) = 0. \tag{19}$$

The exact solution for the problem is $y(x) = 2\log(\frac{7}{8-x^2})$. In Table 4, we presented the errors for the proposed method and B-spline method. It is evident from results that the proposed method approximates the exact solution very well.

Table 1. Comparison of computational maximum absolute errors and computed order of convergence for the proposed method and the method in [11]

N	20	40	80	160	320
$\lambda_1=\frac{1}{6},\lambda_2=\frac{1}{3}$					
Method in [11]	1.95(-5)	6.31(-6)	1.70(-6)	4.34(-7)	1.09(-7)
Order	1.62	1.89	1.96	1.99	1.99
Proposed Method	5.04(-5)	1.29(-5)	3.25(-6)	8.15(-7)	2.04(-7)
Order	1.96	1.99	1.99	1.99	2.00
$\lambda_1=\frac{1}{12},\lambda_2=\frac{5}{12}$					
Method in [11]	4.47(-5)	8.62(-6)	1.96(-6)	4.77(-7)	1.84(-7)
Order	2.37	2.13	2.03	1.51	2.64
Proposed Method	2.43(-6)	1.78(-7)	1.26(-8)	8.75(-10)	6.08(-11)
Order	3.77	3.81	3.85	3.84	4.00

Table 2. Comparison of error norms for the present method and the B-spline method

h	B-spline method		Proposed method	
	L_∞Norm	L_2 Norm	L_∞ Norm	L_2Norm
0.1	1.1×10^{-4}	2.7×10^{-4}	3.1×10^{-5}	5.5×10^{-5}
0.02	4.5×10^{-6}	2.3×10^{-5}	7.6×10^{-8}	1.9×10^{-7}
0.02	2.8×10^{-5}	9.2×10^{-5}	2.4×10^{-6}	4.9×10^{-6}

Table 3. Computational errors for the B-spline method, the present method and the exact solution for $h = 0.05$

x	Exact solution	B-spline method	Proposed method
0	3.257206	3.0×10^{-4}	2.9×10^{-5}
0.1	3.275624	3.0×10^{-4}	1.0×10^{-5}
0.2	3.331322	2.9×10^{-4}	3.8×10^{-6}
0.5	3.740271	2.6×10^{-4}	3.6×10^{-7}
0.9	5.006766	9.0×10^{-5}	7.9×10^{-8}

Table 4. Absolute errors for the B-spline method, the proposed method and the exact solution for $h = 0.05$

x	Exact solution	B-spline method	Proposed method
0.00	-0.2670628	-2.7×10^{-5}	5.5×10^{-6}
0.05	-0.2664377	-2.7×10^{-5}	5.5×10^{-6}
0.10	-0.2645612	-2.7×10^{-5}	4.2×10^{-6}
0.20	-0.2570377	-2.6×10^{-5}	2.9×10^{-6}
0.9	-0.2035654	-2.2×10^{-5}	1.2×10^{-6}

Acknowledgments. The authors would like to thank Defence Research and Development Organisation, Governement of India for providing the financial support under the grant number ERIP/ER/0903823/M/01/1285.

References

1. Chawla, M.M., Katti, C.P.: A Finite Difference Method for a Class of Singular Two Point Boundary Value Problems. IMA J. Numer. Anal., 4457–466 (1984)
2. Gustafsson, B.: A Numerical Method for Solving Singular Boundary Value Problems. Numer. Math. 21, 328–344 (1973)
3. Jamet, P.: On the Convergence of Finite Difference Approximations to One Dimensional Singular Boundary Value Problems. Numer. Math. 14, 355–378 (1970)
4. Abu-Zaid, I.I., Gebeily, M.A.: A Finite Difference Method for Approximating the Solution of a Certain Class of Singular Two-Point Boundary Value Problems. Arab. J. Math. Sci. 1(1), 25–39 (1995)
5. Caglar, N., Caglar, H.: B-spline Solution of Singular Boundary Value Problems. Appl. Math. Comput. 182(2), 1509–1513 (2006)
6. Al-Khaled, K.: Theory and Computation in Singular Boundary Value Problems. Chaos Solitons Fractals 33(2), 678–684 (2007)
7. Sami Bataineh, A., Noorani, M.S.M., Hashim, I.: Approximate Solutions of Singular Two-Point BVPs by Modified Homotopy Analysis Method. Phys. Lett. A 372, 4062–4066 (2008)
8. Ravi Kanth, A.S.V., Aruna, K.: Solution of Singular Two-Point Boundary Value Problems using Differential Transformation Method. Phys. Lett. A 372, 4671–4673 (2008)
9. Ravi Kanth, A.S.V., Aruna, K.: He's Variational Iteration Method for Treating Nonlinear Singular Two-Point Boundary Value Problems. Comput. Math. Appl. 60, 821–829 (2010)
10. Prenter, P.M.: Splines and Variational Methods. Wiley, New York (1975)
11. Rashidinia, J., Mahmoodi, Z., Ghasemi, M.: Parametric Spline Method for a Class of Singular Two-Point Boundary Value Problems. Appl. Math. Comput. 188(1), 58–63 (2007)

Text Dependent Speaker Identification and Speech Recognition Using Artificial Neural Network

Suma Swamy[1], Shalini T.[2], Sindhu P. Nagabhushan[2], Sumaiah Nawaz[2], and K.V. Ramakrishnan

[1] Department Of Electronics & Communications Engineering, Anna Technological University, Coimbatore
[2] Department of Computer Science & Engineering, Sir M. Visvesvaraya Institute of Technology, Bangalore
{suma_swamy,shalinit927}@yahoo.com,
{sindhu2990,summi1989}@gmail.com, ramradhain@rediffmail.com

Abstract. Speaker Identification deals with the process of automatically recognizing the speaker based on his or her speaking one or more specific phrases, like passwords, PIN codes etc which acts as authenticator. Text Dependent Speaker Identification system makes use of mel frequency cepstrum coefficients to process the input signal and vector quantization approach to identify the speaker. Speech Recognition system is implemented using Linear Predictive Coding and Back Propagation technique of Hyperbolic Tangent Function under Artificial Neural Networks. The above tasks are implemented using MATLAB.

Keywords: MFCC, VQ, Mel scale, LPC, BNN.

1 Introduction

A Speaker Identification system uses digitized speech signal [1] and consists of two main modules, viz A speaker specific feature extractor followed by a speaker modelling technique for generalized representation of extracted features. [2].

2 Methodology

2.1 Speaker Identification

An illustrative speaker Identification system is shown in figure.1. Speech recognition system is divided mainly into two major units: 1. Speech signal processing. 2. Speech pattern recognition technique. The first unit consists of speech starting and end point detection, windowing, filtering, calculating the Linear Predictive Coding (LPC) and Cepstral Coefficients. The second unit consists of pattern recognition system using Artificial Neural Network (ANN). The feature extractor uses a standard LPC Cepstrum coder. The structures of the neural network is designed with Multi Layer Perceptron approach and tested with 1, 2, 3 hidden layers using the Tangent hyperbolic function for the speech recognition system [5].

P.V. Krishna, M.R. Babu, and E. Ariwa (Eds.): ObCom 2011, Part I, CCIS 269, pp. 160–168, 2012.

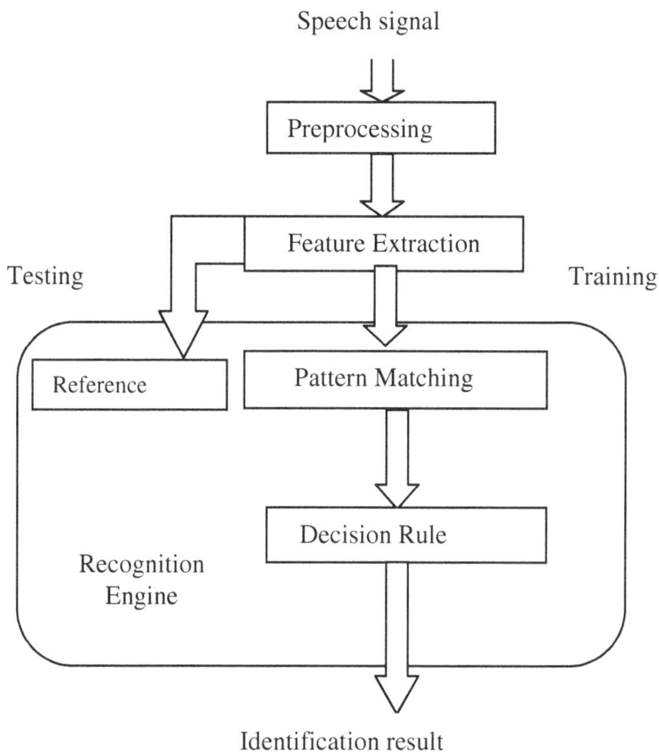

Fig. 1. Speaker Identification System [6]

Feature Extraction Using MFCC. The endpoint detection algorithms implemented is a conventional short-time or spectral energy based which is very sensitive to speech artifacts and break down quickly in the presence of noise. In preprocessing, filtering is used to filter out any surrounding noise. Endpoint detection is a process of selecting only a desired speech interval. To achieve good performance pitch, duration information, use of adaptive thresholds and zero crossings rate resulted in improved performance.

Feature extraction is done using MFCC. MFCC is a representation of a short-term power spectrum of a sound, based on a linear cosine transform of a log power spectrum on a non-linear Mel scale of frequency. MFCC's are derived as follows:

Compute the Fourier transform of a signal:

$$\int_{-\infty}^{\infty} F(k)e^{2\pi ikx}dk. \tag{1}$$

This gives the frequencies present in the input speech signals. Map the power of the spectrum obtained above on to the Mel scale using triangular overlapping windows.

$$m = (1000/\log (2)) (\log (f/1000+1)) \tag{2}$$

Compute the logs of the powers at each of the Mel frequencies. Compute the discrete cosine transform of the list of Mel log powers as if it were a signal. A discrete cosine transform (DCT) expresses a sequence of finite data points in terms of a sum of cosine functions oscillating at different frequencies. The formula for DCT is:

$$x_k=\Sigma\ x_n\cos\ [\pi/n\ (n+0.5)\ k] \tag{3}$$

where n=0, 1,...N-1 and k=0,1........N-1.

The N real numbers $x_{o....}\ x_{n-1}$ transforms into the real numbers $X_0\ ......X_{n-1}$.The MFCC's are the amplitudes of the resulting spectrum.

Pattern Matching Using Vector Quantization. In VQ-based approach, clustering the speaker's feature vectors in K non-overlapping clusters forms the speaker models. The codebook effectively reduces the amount of data by preserving the essential information of the original distribution [4]. The matching function in VQ-based speaker recognition is typically defined as the quantization distortion between two vector sets $X=\{x_1,x_2.......x_T\}$ and $C=\{c_1,c_2.....c_k\}$ Consider a feature vector xi generated by the unknown speaker, and a codebook .The quantization distortion of the vector with respect to C is given by

$$d_q=(x_i,c)=\min_{cj\epsilon C}d(x_i,c_j) \tag{4}$$

where d(. , .) is a distance measure defined for the feature vectors. The code vector c_{j*} for which d (x_i, cj_{*}) is minimum and the nearest neighbour of x_i in the codebook C. The average quantization distortion DQ is defined as the average of the individual distortions

$$D_Q(X, C) = 1/T\ \sum_{i=1}^{T} dq\ (xi, C) \tag{5}$$

The equation is not symmetrical .In this work the assumption is made that the first argument of DQ is the sequence of the unknown speaker's feature vectors, and the second argument is a known speaker's codebook. The feature vectors are passed to the decision logic and then the speaker is identified [5].

2.2 Speech Recognition

Figure 2 shows a block diagram of the general procedure for speech recognition.

The preprocessing involves several steps: normalization, parameterization, feature extraction.

Normalization-The magnitude normalization step attempts to eliminate the variability in the input speech signal.

Parameterization-The parameterization step involves converting the speech signal into a set of statistical parameters that maximize the likelihood of choosing the right output features corresponding to the input signal.

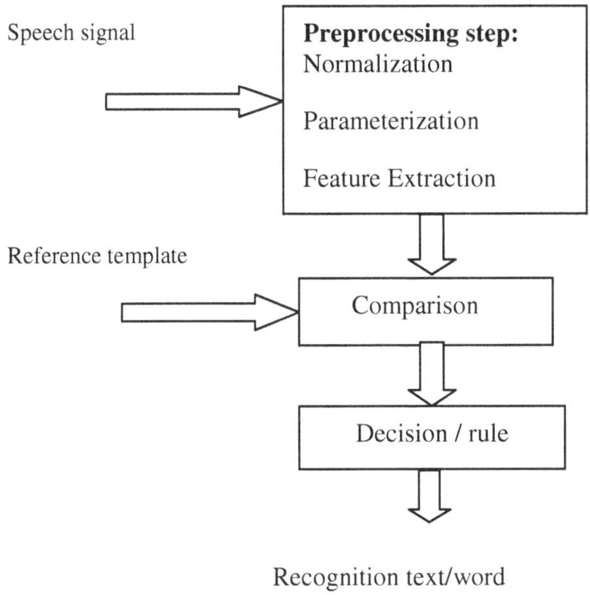

Fig. 2. Block Diagram of Speech Recognition [7]

The speech signal is fed into a pre-processor, which generates a test template based on the features. The test template is then compared with a set of pre-stored reference templates. The reference template that most closely matches the test template is determined based on predetermined decision rules [6].

Similarity Comparison and Detection- When neural networks accomplish the ASR, the comparison and decision steps are performed through training. The neural network is trained by presenting examples of the reference templates. A learning algorithm based on the delta rule is used to minimize a global error function between the current output and the desired output. Once the network is "trained", i.e., the error or the delta weight term ($w_{ijnew}- w_{ijold}$) is less than a pre-set threshold, a final set of weight values are obtained and used as the network characteristics. The test signal is then passed through this network with fixed weight values; the word corresponding to the highest value in the output vector is the word being recognized. The recognition rate is then calculated based on the percentage of correctly identified outputs [6].

Preprocessing and Feature Extraction. The input vector to the back-propagation neural network consists of linear predictive coding coefficients, a., error variance, E, short time energy function, E. short time average zero crossing rate, Z., and voiced/unvoiced discrimination, VAL.

Segmenting the speech signal is done by a method that divides the speech signal into a fixed number of frames with variable length. This is done to deal with the non-uniform word length in the speech recordings. The digitized speech signal is segmented into 10 frames of 10 to 40 milliseconds each depending on the length of a given word in the vocabulary. Each frame is weighted by a hamming window [6].A brief summary of the processing steps is given in figure 3.

The method of Feature extraction used is LPC. The algorithm used to compute the LPC coefficients is the covariance method, which requires solving a set of least square based normal equations.

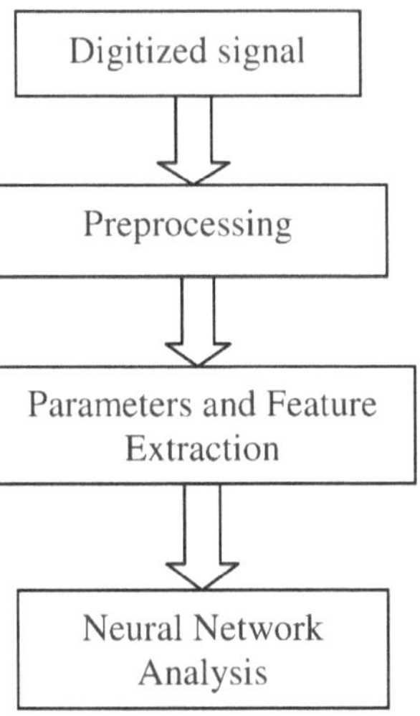

Fig. 3. Block Diagram of Preprocessing step [6]

Pattern Matching Using Back Propagation under Artificial Neural Networks (BNN)

Multi-Layered Perceptron (MLP). In this work, MLPs have been adapted for speech recognition. A general neural structure is shown in figure 4. MLP consists of three layers: an input layer, an output layer, an intermediate or hidden layer.

Processing elements or neurons in the input layer only act as buffers for distributing the input signal x_i to neurons in the hidden layer. Each neuron j in the hidden layer sums up its input signals x_i after weighting them with the strengths of the respective connections w_{ji} from the input layer and computes its output y_j as a function f of the sum, viz., [6]

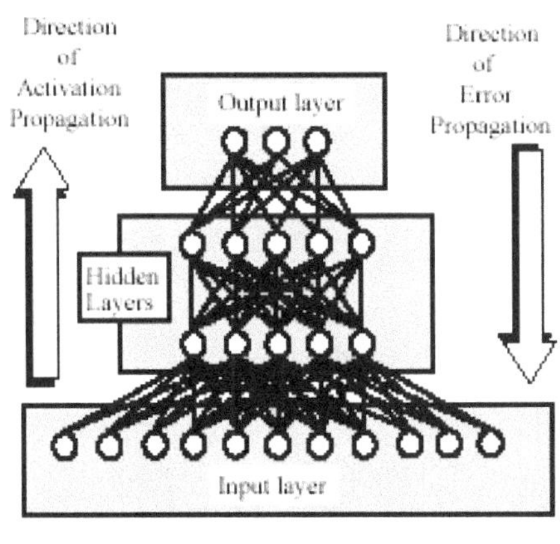

Fig. 4. Multilayer Perception [5]

$$Y_j=f(\Sigma\, w_{ji}\, x_i) \tag{6}$$

Training a network consists of adjusting its weights using a training algorithm. The training algorithms adopted in this study optimize the weights by attempting to minimize the sum of squared differences between the desired and actual values of the output neurons, namely:

$$E= \tfrac{1}{2}\, \Sigma\, (Y_{dj}-Y_j)^2 f \tag{7}$$

Where Y_{dj} is the desired value of output neuron j and Yj is the actual output of that neuron. Each weight w_{ji} is adjusted by adding an increment $.w_{ji}$ to it. w_{ji} is selected to reduce E as rapidly as possible. The adjustment is carried out over several training iterations until a satisfactorily small value of E is obtained or a given number of epochs are reached. The computation of w_{ji} depends on the training algorithm adopted. Training process is ended when the maximum number of epochs is reached. The learning algorithm used in this work is summarized briefly.

Back Propagation Using Hyperbolic Tangent Function

1) *Training Set-* A collection of input-output patterns that are used to train the network.
2) *Testing Set-*A collection of input-output patterns that are used to assess network performance.
3) *Learning Rate-* A scalar parameter, analogous to step size in numerical integration, is used to set the rate of adjustments.
4) *Network Error–*

Total-Sum-Squared-Error (TSSE)[5]

$$\text{TSSE}= 0.5 \sum_{patterns} \sum_{outputs} (\text{desired} - \text{actual})^2 \tag{8}$$

Root-Mean-Squared-Error (RMSE)-

$$\text{RMSE} = \sqrt{\frac{2 * \text{TSSE}}{\#patterns * \# outputs}} \tag{9}$$

The Back Propagation algorithm looks for the minimum of the error function in weight space using the method of gradient descent. The combination of weights that minimizes the error function is considered to be a solution of the learning problem. These neurons receive signals from the neurons in the preceding layer, l-1. The net input at any neuron is given by the following formula

$$n_j^{(l)} = \sum a_i^{(l-1)} * w_{ij}^{(l)} + b_j^{(l)} \tag{10}$$

where $j=1, 2, 3\ldots.N_l$

The algorithm for Back Propagation is shown below:

1. Set α. Initialize weights and biases.
2. For step time t=1, 2.... repeat the following steps until convergence.
3. Set a (0) = x(t), randomly picked from training set.
4. For l=1, 2,...L where L=Total number of layers.

Compute for n=1, 2.... N_L

$$S_{(n)}^{(L)} = 2(a_n^{(L)} - t_n(t))\ \dot{F}^{(L)}(n_n^{(L)}) \tag{11}$$

5. For l=L-1,....,2,1 and j=1,2,...Nl, compute

$$S_j^{(l)} = \dot{F}^{(l)}(nj)^{1}\, \Sigma\, w_{ji}^{(l+1)}\, S_i^{(l+1)} \tag{12}$$

6. For l=1, 2,...L update

$$w_{ij}^{(l)}(t+1) = w_{ij}^{(l)}(t) - \alpha\, a_i^{(l-1)}(t)\, s_j^{(l)}(t) \tag{13}$$
$$b_i^{(l)}(t+1) = b_i^{(l)}(t) - \alpha\, s_i^{(l)}(t)$$

3 Result Analysis

The comparative results for a finite set of words with sigmoid function under Artificial Neural Networks [7] for speaker identification in bar chart is shown in Figure 5. The overall efficiency for speaker identification using back propagation with hyperbolic tangent function is 91%.

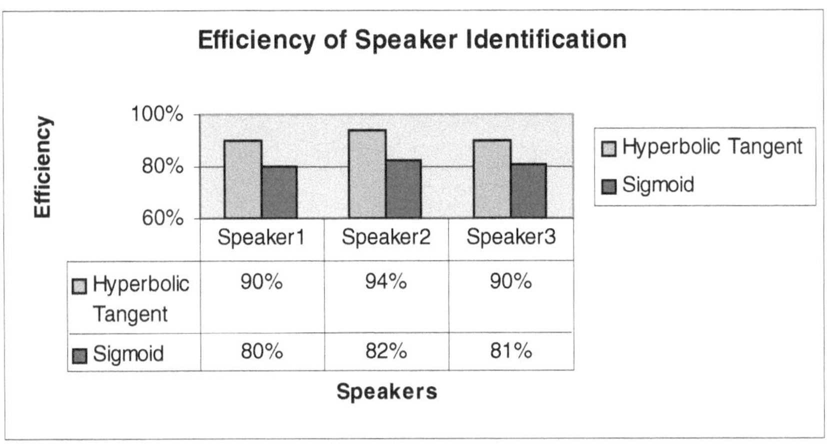

Fig. 5. Bar chart for Speaker Identification

The efficiency for Speech recognition for finite set of words i.e close, move and right in bar chart is shown in Figure 6.the letters c, m and r refers to close, move and right respectively.

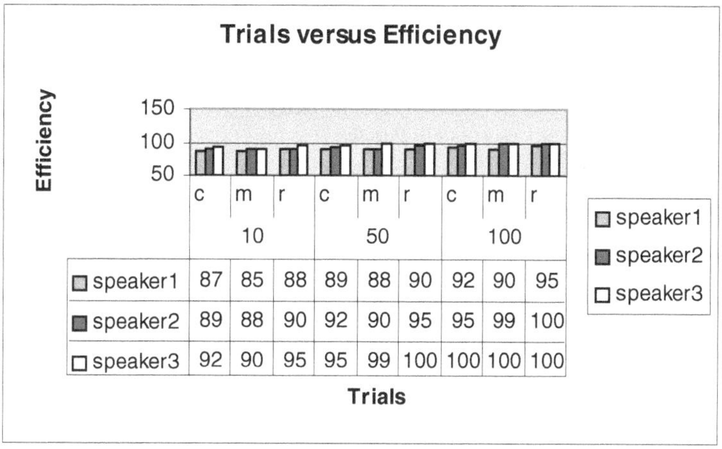

Fig. 6. Bar chart for Speech Recognition

Hence, the overall efficiency for speech recognition for three words is 98%.

4 Conclusion

This present work implements Speaker Identification using MFCC and Vector Quantisation for feature Extraction and Pattern Matching respectively and then it recognizes the spoken word. using LPC and Neural networks. The efficiency is 91% for speaker Identification and 98% for 3 words. Speech recognition with three nodes is taken in the hidden layer to obtain better efficiency. LPC and Back Propagation with sigmoid function give the efficiency of only 81% for three speakers. ANN under Hyperbolic Tangent function has enhanced efficiency in comparison with the sigmoid function. This work can be extended to multiple speakers and large vocabulary in future. It can also be enhanced to text independent speaker identification.

Acknowledgements. The author acknowledges Anna Technological University, Coimbatore for the encouragement and the permission to publish this paper. The author would like to thank the Principal of Sir M Visvesvaraya Institute of Technology, Dr.M.S.Indira for her constant encouragement and would like to thank Prof. Dilip.K.Sen, Head of the Department, CSE/ISE for his invaluable guidance and suggestions from time to time.

References

1. Gatica-Perez, D., Lathoud, G., Odobez, J.-M., McCowan, I.: Audiovisual probabilistic tracking of multiple speakers in meetings. IEEE Transactions on Speech and Audio Processing 15(2), 601–616 (2007)
2. Faundez-Zanuy, M., Monte-Moreno, E.: State-of-the-art in speaker recognition. IEEE Aerospace and Electronic Systems Magazine 20(5), 7–12 (2005)
3. Kyung, Y.J., Lee, H.S.: Bootstrap and aggregating VQ classifier for speaker recognition. Electronics Letters 35(12), 973–974 (1999)
4. Linde, Y., Buzo, A., Gray, R.M.: An algorithm for vector quantizer design. IEEE Trans. Commun. 28(1), 84–95 (1980)
5. Pawar, R.V., Kajave, P.P., Mali, S.N.: Speaker Identification using neural Networks. World Academy of Science, Engineering and Technology (December 2005)
6. Le, C.G.: Application of a back propagation neural network to isolated-word speech recognition (June 1993)
7. Love, B.J., Vining, J., Sun, X.: Automatic Speech Recognition using Neural Networks (Spring 2004)
8. Moore, B.: Hearing. Academic Press, Inc. (1995) ISBN 0-12-505626-5

Efficient Probabilistic Query Ranking in Uncertain Databases

Divya Katukoori, K. Bhima, T. Aruna Sri,
S. Hemanth Chowdary, and Sujoy Bhattacharya

Department of Information Technology,
Padmasri Dr. B.V. Raju Institute of Technology, Narsapur, A.P.
bhima_mnnit@yahoo.co.in, {divya.mswe,hemanth79s}@gmail.com,
it.arunasritalluri@bvrit.ac.in, Sujoy.b@bvrit.ac.in

Abstract. Large databases with uncertainty became more common in many applications.In many modern applications, there are no exact values available to describe the data objects. Instead, the feature values are considered to be uncertain. This uncertainty is modeled by probability distributions instead of exact feature values and that are assumed to be mutually-exclusive. A typical application of such an uncertainty model are moving objects where the exact position of each object can be determined only at discrete time intervals. The objective is to rank the uncertain data according to their distance to a reference object. In the existing system, a framework is used for efficient computation of probabilistic similarity ranking queries in uncertain vector databases, each object is ranked in object instance wise and it is clustered and again ranking to the objects is performed, which results in log-linear i.e, O(nlogn). In this paper, we propose the Radix algorithm in order to increase the performance to O(n).we theoretically as well as experimentally show that it reduces this to a linear-time complexity while having the same memory requirements, facilitated by incremental accessing of the uncertain vector instances in increasing order of their distance to the reference object.

Keywords: Uncertain Database, probabilistic ranking, aggregation, sorting.

1 Introduction

The emergence of many recent applications involving uncertain data, led to a great deal of research in the field of managing uncertain data. The reasons for uncertainty in data differ from one application to another: in sensor and radio frequency identification RFID data, uncertainty is due to measurement errors, in information extraction, uncertainty comes from the inherent ambiguity in natural language text, in business intelligence, uncertainty is tolerated because of the high cost of data cleaning and in privacy, uncertainty is purposely inserted to hide sensitive attributes of individuals. Uncertainty in the data can be caused due to a number of reasons. First, recording data involves uncertainty by nature either caused by imprecise sensors or by imprecision induced by the discretization, which is necessary to record the data. Second, uncertainty obviously occurs in prediction tasks, e.g. weather forecasting, stock market prediction, and traffic jam prediction. There are two models for capturing uncertainty

P.V. Krishna, M.R. Babu, and E. Ariwa (Eds.): ObCom 2011, Part I, CCIS 269, pp. 169–177, 2012.

of objects in a high dimensional space. In the continuous uncertainty model, the uncertain values of an object are represented by a continuous probability distribution function (pdf) within the vector space. This type of representation is often used in applications where the uncertain values are assumed to follow a specific pdf, e.g., a Gaussian distribution. In the discrete uncertainty model, each object is represented by a discrete set of alternative values, and each value is associated with a probability.

The main motivation of this representation is that, in most real applications, data are collected in a discrete form (e.g., information derived from sensor devices). In this paper, we adopt the discrete uncertainty model. For an uncertain data object, some or even all describing feature values are not exactly known. However, it is possible to make conclusions about uncertain data objects by describing the uncertain values using probability distributions. Various top-k query approaches have been proposed generating un-ambiguous rankings from probabilistic data. Examples are U-topk, U-kRanks , PT-k, Global top-k , and expected rank In this paper, A framework that, given a database with uncertain vector objects, computes the rank probabilities of the object instances (e.g., a1) in linear time to the total number of instances of all objects.assuming that the instances are accessed in increasing distance order to the query object q (e.g., with the help of a nearest neighbor search algorithm).

Definition 1. (Uncertain Vector Objects): An uncertain vector object o corresponds to a finite set of alternative points in a d-dimensional vector space, called object instances, each associated with a probability value, i.e., o = {(x, p), where x € R^d, and p € [0,1]} is the probability that o has position x. The probabilities of the object instances represent a discrete probability distribution of the alternative points, such that the condition ∑(x,p)€o p <= 1 holds. The collection of instances of all objects forms the uncertain database D. Note that the condition ∑(x,p)€o p < 1 implies existential uncertainty, meaning that the object may not exist at all. We assume that the database objects are already given in the discrete representation as specified above. In case of an uncertain database where the uncertain objects are represented by a continuous probability function (pdf), the generally applicable concept of sampling can be used to transform the objects to the discrete representation as defined above. Given a database of uncertain vector objects, our goal is to compute for each object instance and for the first k rank positions, the probability of the object to be in that position.

Definition 2. (Rank Probability): Given a query point q, an instance x 2 D, belonging to object o, and a rank i € {1,..... ,k}, the probabilistic rank p_ rankq : (D×{1,..... ,k}) → [0,1] reports how likely (i-1) objects O'≠ o are closer to q than x, i.e., the probability that x is at the ith ranking position according to the distance (i.e., dissimilarity) between x and q. Contributions and Outline The main contributions of this paper can be summarized as follows:

A framework based on iterative distance browsing that efficiently supports probabilistic similarity ranking in uncertain vector databases. We present a novel and theoretically founded approach for computing the rank probabilities of each object. We prove that our method reduces the computational cost of the rank probabilities from $O(n^2)$, achieved by the best currently known method, to O(n). We show how diverse state-of-the-art probabilistic ranking models can use our framework to accelerate computation. We conduct an experimental evaluation, using real and synthetic data, which demonstrates the applicability of our framework and verifies our theoretical findings.

2 Related Work

Uncertain data management has been established as an important branch of research within the database community, with increasing tendency. Existing approaches in this field of modelling of, managing of and query processing on uncertain data can be categorized into diverse directions, including probabilistic databases indexing of uncertain data [9], [3], [6] and probabilistic query processing [7], [11], [6], [12], [5], [4], [8].. In the general model, the possible worlds are constrained by rules that are defined on the tuples in order to incorporate object (tuple) correlations. The ULDB model proposed and used in the Trio system supports uncertain tuples with alternative instances which are called x-tuples. Relations in ULDB are called xrelations containing a set of x-tuples. Each x-tuple corresponds to a set of tuple instances which are assumed to be mutually exclusive, i.e. no more than one instance of an x-tuple can appear in a possible world instance at the same time. This probabilistic data model closes the gap between two prevalent uncertainty models, the tuple uncertainty [11] and the attribute uncertainty [7]. An x-tuple is able to model an object with attribute value uncertainty; i.e., the instances of an x-tuple represent the probability value distribution of the corresponding uncertain attribute.

In this paper, we adopt this concept to model uncertain vector objects. An uncertain vector object would correspond to an x-tuple of alternative uncertain instances of the object. Several approaches for indexing uncertain vector objects have been proposed [10], [3], [5], [7]. They mainly differ in the uncertainty model supported and in the type of supported similarity queries. In [6], the Gauss-tree is introduced, which is an index for managing large amounts of uncertain objects with their uncertain attribute represented by a Gaussian distribution function. The proposed system aims at efficiently answering identification queries like "Give me all persons in the database that could be shown on a given image with a probability of at least 10%". Additionally, [6] proposed probabilistic identification queries which are based on a Bayesian setting. Later, in [6] an approach for incrementally retrieving the k most likely uncertain objects that might be placed in a given query interval is proposed.

We can categorize existing probabilistic querying approaches according to the uncertainty model they use. While probabilistic similarity queries over uncertain vector data are dedicated to the attribute value uncertainty model [7],probabilistic top-k query approaches are usually associated with tuple uncertainty data in probabilistic databases [8], [4]. There exists a third probabilistic query category concerning spatially extended uncertain data as proposed in. But there is only little work in this direction. To the best of our knowledge, only addresses probabilistic ranking according to our problem definition. We can categorize existing probabilistic querying approaches according to the uncertainty model they use. While probabilistic similarity queries over uncertain vector data are dedicated to the attribute value uncertainty model [9], [12], probabilistic top-k query approaches are usually associated with tuple uncertainty data in probabilistic databases [8], [4]. There exists a third probabilistic query category concerning spatially extended uncertain data as proposed in [10]. But there is only little work in this direction.

To the best of our knowledge, only [2] addresses probabilistic ranking according to our problem definition. There, a divide and conquer method for accelerating the computation of the ranking probabilities is proposed. Although the proposed approach achieves a significant speed-up compared to the naïve solution incorporating each possible database instance, its runtime is still exponential. Related to our ranking problem, significant work has been done in the field of probabilistic top-k query processing.Soliman et al. [8] were the first who studied such problems on the x-relations model of [4]. They proposed two ways of ranking uncertain tuples. In the first, uncertain top-k (U-Topk) query, the objective is to find the k-permutation of the most likely tuples to be the top-k. In our setting, this corresponds to finding the top-k most probable object instances (belonging to different objects) in all possible worlds. The uncertain k-ranks query (U-kRanks) reports a probabilistic ranking of the tuples (again, not the x-tuples).

3 Probabilistic Ranking Framework

In the Existing system ,a framework basically consists of two modules which are performed in an iterative way: The first module (distance browsing) incrementally retrieves the instances of all objects in order of their distance to q. This can be achieved with the help of a multi-dimensional index (e.g., an R_-tree index), using an incremental nearest neighbor search algorithm [12].

The second module computes the probabilistic ranks p_rankq(o_j,i) of each object instance oj reported from the distance browsing for all $1 \leq i \leq k$. This step is the main focus of this paper, because of its potentially high computational cost.

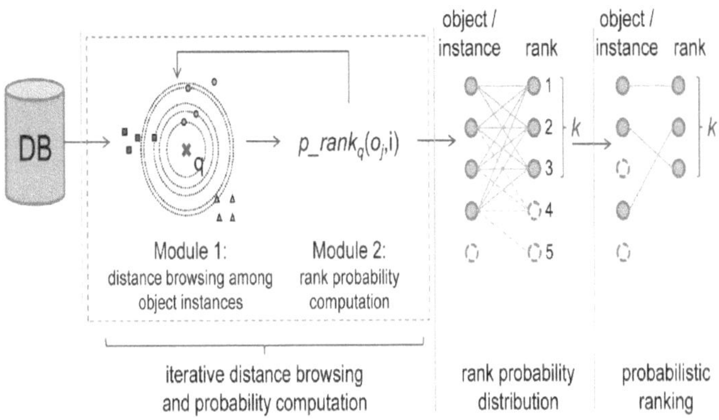

Fig. 1. Probabilistic Ranking Framework

The computation of the probability distributions is iteratively processed within a loop. First, we initialize a distance browsing among the object instances starting from a given query point q. For each object instance fetched from the distance browsing (Module 1), we compute the corresponding rank probabilities (Module 2) and update the rank probability distributions generated from the probabilistic ranking routine. Note that the rank probabilities of the object instances (i.e., tuples in the x-relations model) reported from the second module can be optionally aggregated into rank probabilities of the objects (i.e., x-tuples in the x-relations model). The probability that an uncertain vector object o = {(x1, p1)..... (xs, ps)} is at the ith ranking position according to the distance between o and a reference query object q is p_rankq(o,i)=$\sum_{l=1....s}$pl.p_rankq(xl,i). framework can be used to compute the object-based rank probabilities by maintaining a list of objects, each object is ranked in instance wise and it is aggregated and again ranking to the objects is performed, which results in log-linear i.e, O(nlogn).

In this paper, we use a Radix algorithm and improve this method to a linear time and space complexity algorithm. The objective is to find a non-ambiguous ranking where each object or object instance is uniquely assigned to one rank. a novel polynomial algorithm concept that achieves a linear runtime complexity in contrast to the best-known existing approach that solve the same problem with quadratic runtime complexity and log-linear time complexity. By using this algorithm, aggregation of objects is avoided i.e, ranking to the object instance and again ranking to the object is avoided .instead, as the sorting is already performed in an order, ranking to the individual object will be performed which leads the time complexity to O(n).it is applicable even for large databases as linear time is often viewed as a desirable attribute for an algorithm.

4 Framework for Probabilistic Similarity Ranking Using Radix Algorithm

In the proposed system, we introduce radix algorithm for sorting the key values of the object which have been resulted from module1.i.e,data objects which have fetched from the database, to that distance browsing is calculated using nearest neighbor search algorithm as distance between the object instances. In the module 2, sorting will be performed to the object based up on the difference of that.in the post processing step individual unique ranking to the object or object instance will be performed.

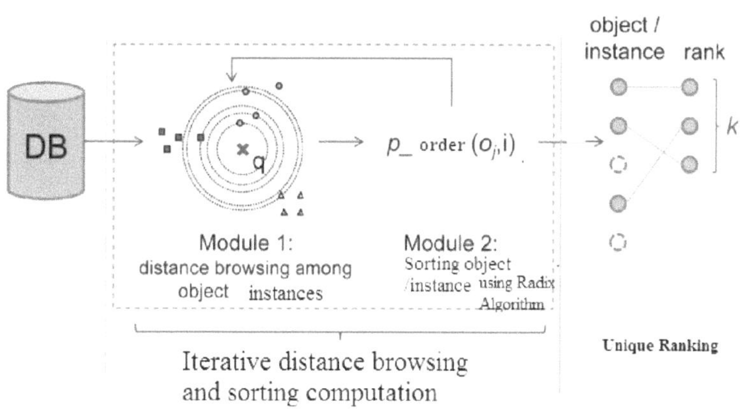

Fig. 2. Framework for probabilistic similarity ranking

Radix Sorting Algorithm

Radix sort is a sorting algorithm that sorts integers by processing individual digits. Because integers can represent strings of characters and specially formatted floating point numbers, radix sort is not limited to integers. Two classifications of radix sorts are least significant digit (LSD) radix sorts and most significant digit (MSD) radix sorts. LSD radix sorts process the integer representations starting from the least significant digit and move towards the most significant digit. MSD radix sorts work the other way around. MSD sorting algorithm has particular application to parallel computing, as each of the subdivisions can be sorted independently of the rest. Radix sort is not a comparison-based sort, so theoretical limit of O(NlogN) is not applicable. Computational complexity of radix sort is O(NK), where N is the number of values and K is the number of subdivisions. This complexity holds for worst, best and mean cases. Space complexity is O(NK).

The magic of Radix Sort lies in finding the key to shuffle the items. For integer data, the key is each individual digits. In a group of data, there can be up to ten bins for each digit (0 - 9). Thus we isolate each individual digit of each data, and place into the corresponding bin. When we start, we start with the least significant digit and work our way up to the most significant digit.

Let the following number be the objects differences key values which have been generated from module1:

LSD-Radix Sort

12	34	42	32	44	41	34	11	32	23	87	50	77	58	08

Input is an array of 15 integers. For integers, the number of buckets is 10, from 0 to 9. The first pass distributes the keys into bins by the least significant digit (LSD). When the first pass is done, we have the following.

0	1	2	3	4	5	6	7	8	9
50	41	12	23	34			87	58	
	11	42		44			77	08	
		32		34					
		32							

We collect these, keeping their relative order:

50	41	11	12	42	32	32	23	34	44	34	87	77	58	08

Now we distribute by the next most significant digit, which is the highest digit in our example, and we get the following.

0	1	2	3	4	5	6	7	8	9
08	11	23	32	41	50		77	87	
	12		32	42	58				
			34	44					
			34						

When we collect them, they are in order.

08	11	12	23	32	32	34	34	41	42	44	50	58	77	87

✓ Running time for this example is:
  - $T(n) = \Theta\ (d(n+k))$
- k = number of bins = 10(0 to 9).
- n = number of elements to be sorted = 15
- d = digits or maximum length of element = 2

✓ Thus in our example, the algorithm will take
$T(n) = \Theta\ (d(n+k))$
$= \Theta\ (2(15+10))$
$= \Theta\ (50)$ execution time.

Pseudo code of Radix sort is:

Radix Sort (Sorting array A[size])

Create all of the bins.

From the least significant digit to the most significant digit
{
For each element (from the first to the last)
{
Isolate the value of the significant digit.
Store the element in the bin with the matching significant digit value.
}
For each bin (from the first to the last)
{
Retrieve all of the elements and store them back into the array.
}}
Destroy all of the bins.

5 RunTime Analysis

Run time table	No precomputed D	Precomputed D
Ours	O(nlogn+kn)loglinear	O(kn) linear
[1]	$O(kn^2)$quadratic	O(nlogn+kn) loglinear
[4]	$O(kn^2)$	$O(kn^2)$ quadratic
[2]	Exponential	Exponential
[3]	Exponential	Exponential

Table 1. Of notations used in this Work

D	An uncertain database
q	a query vector in respect to which a probabilistic ranking is computed
D	A distance browsing of **D** with respect to q
k	The ranking depth that determines the no. of ranking positions of the ranking query result.
AOL	Active object list
$P_i(x)$	The probability that an instance x of object X is assigned to the ith ranking position i, i.e, the probability that exactly i-1 objects in (**D**/{X})are closer to q than x.
$P_i(X)$	The probability that object X is assigned to the ith ranking position i, i.e,the probability that exactly i-1 objects in (**D**/{X})are closer to q than X.
P(X=x)	The probability that an uncertain vector object X matches a given vector point of instance x.
S	A set of objects that have already been seen.i.e, the set that contains an object X,if atleast one instance X has already been returned by the distance browsing D
N	Cardinality of D

6 Conclusion

In the previous paper, A framework is used for efficient computation of probabilistic similarity ranking queries in uncertain vector databases, each object is ranked in instance/object wise and it is aggregated and again ranking to the object/instance's is performed, which results in loglinear i.e,O(nlogn).

In this paper,We introduced a Radix sort algorithm concept that achieves a **linear** runtime complexity in contrast to the best-known existing approach that solve the same problem with quadratic runtime complexity. Our concepts are theoretically and empirically proved to be superior to all existing approaches.

In an experimental evaluation, we showed that our approach scales very well and, thus, is applicable even for large databases as linear time is often viewed as a desirable attribute for an algorithm. As future work, we plan to extend the concepts proposed in this paper to further uncertainty models and can also improve the performance to O(log n) by using spatial pruning techniques.

References

[1] Bernecker, T., Kriegel, H.-P., Mamoulis, N., Renz, M., Zuefle, A.: Scalable Probabilistic Similarity Ranking in Uncertain Databases (September 2010)

[2] Bernecker, T., Kriegel, H.-P., Renz, M.: ProUD: Probabilistic Ranking in Uncertain Databases. In: Ludäscher, B., Mamoulis, N. (eds.) SSDBM 2008. LNCS, vol. 5069, pp. 558–565. Springer, Heidelberg (2008)

[3] Soliman, M., Ilyas, I., Chen-Chuan Chang, K.: Top-k Query Processing in Uncertain Databases. In: Proc. 23rd Int'l Conf. Data Eng. (ICDE 2007), pp. 896–905 (April 2007)

[4] Yi, K., Li, F., Kollios, G., Srivastava, D.: Efficient Processing of Top-K Queries in Uncertain Databases. In: Proc. 24th Int'l Conf. Data Eng. (ICDE 2008), pp. 1406–1408 (April 2008)

[5] Böhm, C., Pryakhin, A., Schubert, M.: Probabilistic Ranking Queries on Gaussians. In: Proc. Int'l Conf. Scientific and Statistical Database Management, pp. 169–178 (2006)

[6] Cheng, R., Singh, S., Prabhakar, S.: U-DBMS: A Database System for Managing Constantly-Evolving Data. In: Proc. 31st Int'l Conf. Very Large Data Bases, VLDB 2005 (2005)

[7] Soliman, M., Ilyas, I.: Ranking with Uncertain Scores. In: Proc. 25th Int'l Conf. Data Eng. (ICDE 2009), pp. 317–328 (March/April 2009)

[8] Yi, K., Li, F., Kollios, G., Srivastava, D.: Efficient Processing of Top-K Queries in Uncertain Databases with X-Relations. IEEE Trans. Knowledge and Data Eng. 20(12), 1669–1682 (2008)

[9] Cheng, R., Kalashnikov, D., Prabhakar, S.: Evaluating Probabilistic Queries over Imprecise Data. In: Proc. ACM SIGMOD, pp. 551–562 (2003)

[10] Cheng, R., Xia, Y., Prabhakar, S., Shah, R., Vitter, J.: Efficient Indexing Methods for Probabilistic Threshold Queries over Uncertain Data. In: Proc. 30th Int'l Conf. Very Large Databases (VLDB 2004), pp. 876–887 (2004)

[11] Cormode, G., Li, F., Yi, K.: Semantics of Ranking Queries for Probabilistic Data and Expected Results. In: Proc. 25th Int'l Conf. Data Eng. (ICDE 2009), pp. 305–316 (March/April 2009)

[12] Kriegel, H.-P., Kunath, P., Pfeifle, M., Renz, M.: Probabilistic Similarity Join on Uncertain Data. In: Li Lee, M., Tan, K.-L., Wuwongse, V. (eds.) DASFAA 2006. LNCS, vol. 3882, pp. 295–309. Springer, Heidelberg (2006)

A Parameterized Framework of Trust Computation for Grid Resource Broker

M. Ashok and S. Sathiyan

Department of IT, Rajalakshmi Institute of Technology, Chennai, TN, India
{ashok.m,sathiyan.s}@ritchennai.edu.in

Abstract. Now a days the power of distributed computing is explored the ventures of grid computing and cloud computing. Grid computing is used to solve any large scale scientific problems by integrating geographically distributed ideal resources. Cloud computing is the next generation of grid computing and also it is an on demand version of grid computing. Especially in grid computing, the research on identifying best resources is still on its way. In this paper, we are contributing a methodology to identify the best resources for computational grid. The proposed solution will focus and extract the trust of the resource with more accuracy.

Index Terms: Cloud, Grid, Resource, Trust.

1 Introduction

High performance computing (HPC) is the only driving environment to yield solutions for large scale scientific problems such as Tsunami Engineering simulation, Earthquake Engineering simulation etc in those days. Initially cluster computing makes remarkable changes in the HPC field. Later the growth of computer network leads to the innovation of high speed networks which integrates its power with distributed computing. From 1960 onwards, the field of grid computing started to emerge. At the initial stage, grid computing solved the long running iterative tasks only. On its complete growth and enhanced infrastructures, it marks its step on large scale simulations of scientific problems.

There are varieties of research challenges cumulate on this field. They are resource discovery, resource co-allocation, scheduling, rescheduling, reservation of resources, service level negotiation for agreement resource management and more that turned up for discovering the best resources which helps the resource provider as well as the resource broker. Now we have introduced a new parameter in this paper for identifying the trusted resource with concentrating more on accuracy of the esources. Rest of the paper is organized as follows: Section II illustrates the related work, Section III dictates the trust calculation, Section IV compares the existing literature with the proposed solution and Section V concludes the paper with future research directions.

P.V. Krishna, M.R. Babu, and E. Ariwa (Eds.): ObCom 2011, Part I, CCIS 269, pp. 178–181, 2012.

Section VI moving on future research direction indentified more accurate Trust computation.

2 Related Work

Buyya et al [2] had used availability as the parameter for the prediction of load in enterprise grids. Sathish and Sanjay [3] used the parameter as communication characteristics and also later [4] they used CPU utilization, bandwidth, availability for scheduling tightly coupled parallel applications on clusters. Marcos [5] used load as the parameter for intergrid resource provisioning. Jay & team [6] used availability and bandwidth as parameters for performance prediction. Keshav & Liang [7], [11] used network load and bandwidth as parameters for MPI processing. ThamaraiSelvi [8] used bamdwidth, availability, latency and job execution rate as parameters for trusted resource identification. Gupta & team [10] used time and machine availability as parameters for mapping parallel applications. Ashok and Vasundra [1] moved with more accuracy on Trust computations using failure rate of the resources.

3 Trust Computation

From the literature survey, we have collected five parameters such as bandwidth of the network, availability of the systems, job execution rate of the resource and latency of the resource and failure rate of the resources. Here we are introducing a new parameter termed to be Hack rate of the resource. Hack rate is defined as the ratio between number of jobs submitted to a resources that has been hacked to the total number of jobs allocated to the resource. The reason to introduce 'hack rate' is whenever a resource has been has been exposed on internet there are much more possibilities to be hacked by the hackers through worms or other hacking techniques. This will surely lead to steal the information that is being running on the resources. Hence when more number of jobs has been hacked that leads the trust on the resources to fall down.Now the real trust on the resource is calculated by subtracting the sum of failure rate and hack rate from the original trust computation value. The individual parameter calculation of bandwidth, availability, job execution rate, latency and failure rate are illustrated in the work of Ashok and Vasundra.

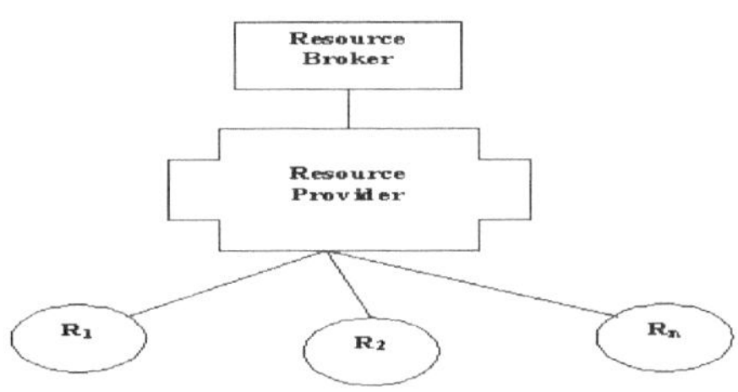

Fig. 1. Depicts the basic infrastructure of the grid computing environment

3.1 Algorithm

```
Trust Compute ( )
{
 Identify the bandwidth (B), availability (A), job execution rate (J),
latency (L) and  failure rate (F) of resources.
 for each resource do
   trust= (B * A * J * L) – (F+H);
 end for
}
```

4 Performance Comparison

From the proposed work the accuracy of the resource is still more molded to have more trust on computation compared to the existing work of Ashok et al. As our research is on initial stage, we have restricted the number of resources up to 100. fig 2. illustrates for 30 resources.

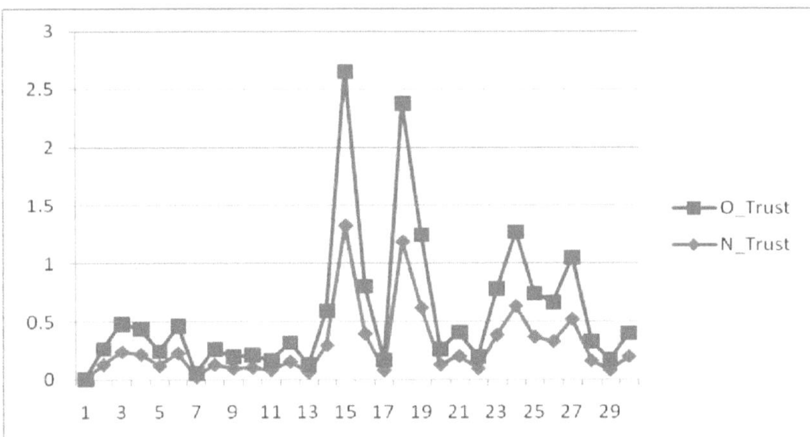

Fig. 2. Trust Comparison between proposed and existing Systems

5 Conclusion and Future Directions

Our work entirely concentrating on the identification of best resource for job execution by holding the strategy on resource hacking management. The newly introduced parameter which helps the trust computation from a different dimension. The task of job scheduling comprises of two tasks viz allocation of resources, scheduling and by keeping this as outline the proposed work will initiate more research directions. On the future extension of our work we will use the parameters trust, failure rate and hack rate to predict the job schedule in a computational grid.

References

1. Ashok, Vasundra: An Enhanced Framework to compute the Trustworthiness of Resources in Grid Computing environment. In: Proceedings of Intl. Conference on Advances in Mathematical and Computational Methods, vol. II, pp. 115–117 (2011)
2. Rahman, Hassan, Buyya: Jaccord Index based Availability Prediction in Enterprise Grids. In: ICCS, pp. 2701–2710 (2010)
3. Sundari, Satish, Ravi: Grids with multiple batch systems for performance enhancement of multi component and parameter sweep parallel applications. FGCS, pp. 217–227 (2010)
4. Sanjay, Sathish: A strategy for scheduling tightly coupled parallel applications. Concurrency and Computation: Practice and Experience, 2491–2517 (2009)
5. Marcos, Buyya: Performance analysis of allocation policies for intergrid resource provisioning. Information and Software Technology, 43–55 (2009)
6. Jay, Sanjay, Sathish: Performance Modeling based on Multidimensional Surface Learning for Performance Predictions of Parallel Applications in Non Dedicated Environments. IISc, 45/SERC (2007)
7. Keshav, Liang: An Efficient MPI (2007)
8. ThamaraiSelvi & Team: A Framework for Trust Management System in Computational Grids, DIT, New Delhi (2007)
9. Gupta, Paul, Mostafa: A Reputation System for Peer to Peer Networks. ACM (2003)
10. Tracy & Team: A Comparison of Eleven Static Heuristics for Mapping a class of Independent Tasks on to Heterogeneous Distributed Computing Systems, pp. 810–837. Academic Press (2001)
11. Keshav, Liang: Application Oriented Adaptive MPI. Micro Grid (2001)

Energy and Path Aware Ant Colony Optimization Based Routing Algorithm for Wireless Sensor Networks

Hamed Orojloo[1], Reza Askari Moghadam[2], and Abolfazl T. Haghighat[3]

[1] Payam Noor University, Tehran, Iran
hamed.orojloo@gmail.com
[2] Tehran University, Tehran, Iran
askari@pnu.ac.ir
[3] Islamic Azad University, Qazvin Branch, Qazvin, Iran
haghighat@qazviniau.ac.ir

Abstract. Maximizing the network lifetime is a common objective of sensor network researches, because of the battery limitation in each sensor. Furthermore, the shortest and optimal path between sender and receiver needs to be found, so that the network can operate efficiently and provide the largest benefits for its users. In this paper, we will present energy and path aware ant colony optimization based routing algorithm for wireless sensor networks (EPWSN). This algorithm with use of presented competency function and effective definition of its parameters can increase the system efficiency. In this algorithm new pheromone update operator is designed to integrate energy consumption, hop count and path length into routing choice. Finally, simulation result shows that the proposed algorithm in comparison with the previous ant colony based routing algorithm (ACLR, traditional ACA), achieves lower path cost, obtains more balanced transmission among the node, reduces the energy consumption of the routing and extends the network lifetime. Therefore the proposed algorithm has a greater performance in comparison with other ant colony routing algorithm.

Keywords: wireless sensor network, routing algorithms, ant colony optimization, energy consumption, network lifetime.

1 Introduction

Wireless Sensor Networks (WSNs) consist of small nodes with sensing, computation, wireless communications capabilities and an energy source which can be a small battery. Many sensor nodes forward a data packet and transmit it to the base station called "sink node" or "BS" standing for Base Station [8]. These sensors have the ability to communicate either among each other or directly to an external BS. The sensor nodes are very limited in terms of their battery capabilities. For this reason, energy efficiency is a critical factor in routing protocol design [1]. Also since we often use these networks in rough and inaccessible environments such as battlefields, forests and so on, normally there is low possibility to change or recharge the defective

P.V. Krishna, M.R. Babu, and E. Ariwa (Eds.): ObCom 2011, Part I, CCIS 269, pp. 182–191, 2012.

or dead nodes. Hence, the main difference between WSNs and other classic wireless networks is that WSNs are depletion to energy. Moreover the performance of WSNs severely depends on lifetime of the network [7].

The main problem that must be resolved by a routing algorithm is to find a path from the sink to the destination node [8]. Finding the shortest path between source node and destination node is one of the most important problems in WSNs.

In some category of routing algorithms, software agents are used to make a route between the source and the sink node. Ant Colony Optimization (ACO) algorithms is a basic agent-based routing algorithm which is inspired by the motion pattern of the ants. Over the last two decades, ant colony optimization has emerged as a leading Meta heuristic method for the solution of combinatorial optimization problems [12].

In this paper, we will propose an energy and path aware ant colony optimization based routing algorithm for wireless sensor networks. The energy, hop count and the length of path are combined to affect the pheromone concentration in optimization path, which can avoid network congestion and fast consume of energy of individual node. Then it can prolong the lifetime of the whole network. In this algorithm, parameters such as the distance to the destination node and energy with effective definition are used to choose the next step in the current travel. This algorithm also tries to choose the shortest path between source and destination node. We compare this prepared algorithm with Ant Colony Optimization-Based Location-Aware Routing for Wireless Sensor Networks (ACLR) that presented in [1, 6], and traditional ant colony optimization based routing algorithm ACA [1, 3, 5, 9, 13], and see that the proposed algorithm reduce the consumption of energy and decrees the length of path in comparison of these routing algorithms. Simulation results show that the approach is effective and efficient in finding high-quality solutions for maximizing the lifetime of WSNs and minimizing the average cost of path.

2 Related Work

Some of the resent researches about ant colony routing algorithm in wireless sensor networks are presented as following:

In [1] is proposed a Routing Algorithm for Wireless Sensor Networks Using Ant Colony Optimization that present a comparison of two Ant Colony-based routing algorithms, taking into account current amounts of energy consumption under different scenarios and reporting the usual metrics for routing in wireless sensor networks. In [2] is proposed an Energy Aware Ant Colony Algorithm for the Routing of wireless Sensor Networks that when the ant chooses the next node, not only the distance of sink node, but also the residual energy of next node and the path of the average energy are taken into account. This algorithm is compared with traditional ACA algorithm and gets more improvement in balance the energy consumption of nodes and extends the network lifetime. In [4] the authors proposed the a fair comparison of low energy adaptive clustering hierarchy (LEACH) and ant colony applied on LEACH on the basis of the death of first node in the wireless sensor networks and are shown that when the ant colony algorithm is applied on existing LEACH protocol, the network lifetime has improved. In [6] the authors proposed the called Ant Colony Optimization-Based Location-Aware Routing Algorithm (ACLR) which is a flat and location awareness algorithm. It fuses the residual energy and the global and local location information of nodes, to define the probability to select the next node for the ants. In [9] the authors proposed an Ant Colony optimization algorithm and apply it to energy control and congestion control on wireless sensor network route. In this algorithm, the pheromone and the energy of the node are combined to affect the pheromone consent ration in optimization path, which can avoid network congestion and fast consume of energy of individual node. Then it can prolong the lifecycle of the whole network. In [10] is proposed a Predication mode based Routing Algorithm based on ACO (PRACO) to achieve the energy-aware data-gathering routing structure in wireless sensor networks. This algorithm by checking the load factor in heuristic factor and guided by novel pheromone updating rule, artificial ants can foresee the local energy state of networks and the corresponding actions could be adaptively taken to enhance the energy efficiency in routing construction.

However, none of these algorithms consider average energy, length of established path and hop count traveled by ants in pheromone update operator and most of them don't consider location information of nodes in their probability function to selection of next-hop node. In proposed algorithm, in order to optimize of the routing quality, we achieve the tradeoff between route hops, location of nodes and energy consumption.

3 System and Energy Model

WSN can be represented by a weighted undirected connectivity-graph $G(V,E)$. Where: V is the set of sensor nodes and E is the set of links between these nodes [1, 7]. Any node in WSN area has a set of neighbors that are placed in wireless communication coverage of the node. We use the Euclidean distance for calculate the distance between two node in WSN area. Nodes are deployed in certain area uniformly.

Generally, sensors consume energy when they sense, receive and transmit data. Communication characteristics and energy consumption models affect the advantages and performance of protocol. The wireless transmission and energy consumption model defined in the reference [14] is used in this paper. In this model, the transmitter has power control abilities to dissipate minimal energy to send data to the receiver. In order to achieve an acceptable signal-to-noise ratio (SNR), the energy consumption of the transmitter is given by:

$$\begin{cases} E_{TX}(n,d) = n(E_{elec} + \varepsilon_{fs} d^2) & d < d_0 \\ E_{TX}(n,d) = n(E_{elec} + \varepsilon_{mp} d^4) & d \geq d_0 \end{cases} \tag{1}$$

Where, n is the number bit of the message and d is the distance. E_{elec} is the energy dissipated per bit to run the transmitter or the receiver circuit, and ε_{fs}, ε_{mp} is the energy dissipated per bit to run the transmit amplifier depending on the distance between the transmitter and receiver. If the distance is less than a threshold d_0, the free space (FS) model is used; otherwise, the multipath (MP) model is used. The energy consumption of the receiver is given by:

$$E_{RX}(n) = n(E_{elec}) \tag{2}$$

4 Design of Proposed ACO Based Routing Algorithm (EPWSN)

In our schemes we aim at building a system that would ensure that total energy dissipation is divided equally among all the nodes of the network. It is need to achieve the tradeoff between route hops, location of nodes and energy consumption.

In EPWSN algorithm, the neighbor candidate list for each node is comprised of nodes that are placed in wireless communication coverage of the node and also are nearer to destination node in comparison of current node. Ants start from a source node and move through neighbor repeater nodes and reach final destination node. In this algorithm, for calculating the packet transfer probability to the next hop neighbor, the residual energy of node, pheromone value and location of nodes are considered. Every ant selects the next-hop node from its candidate list in current travel. Ant k in node i choose the next node j to move to, according to a probabilistic decision rule:

$$P_{ij}^{k}(t) = \frac{[\psi_{ij}(t)]^{\alpha} \times [\varepsilon_{ij}(t)]^{\beta} \times [\eta_{ij}(t)]^{\gamma}}{\sum_{l \in C(i)} [\psi_{il}(t)]^{\alpha} \times [\varepsilon_{il}(t)]^{\beta} \times [\eta_{il}(t)]^{\gamma}}. \tag{3}$$

In this equation, $P_{ij}^{k}(t)$ is the transfer packets probability, $\psi_{ij}(t)$ is pheromone metric, $\varepsilon_{ij}(t)$ is the location metric, and $\eta_{ij}(t)$ is the energy metric; α, β, γ are the three constant exponents associated with the algorithm. $C(i)$ present the candidate list of node i.

Definition of probability function parameters in ACLR

ACLR [1, 6] algorithm uses the same probability function as (3). But the energy metric proposed by ACLR, has the following definition:

$$\eta_{ij}(t) = \frac{e_j(t)}{\sum_{l \in C(i)} e_l(t)} \tag{4}$$

Where e_j is the energy level of node j in time t and $C(i)$ present the candidate list of node i. This equation only considers current energy level of nodes in candidate list. The location function proposed in ACLR, ε_{ij} is defined by:

$$\varepsilon_{ij} = \left(\frac{d_{ob}}{d_{oi} + d_{ij} + d_{jb}}\right) \times \left(1 - \frac{d_{ij}}{\sum_{l \in C(i)} d_{il}}\right). \tag{5}$$

Where d_{ob} is the distance between source node and destination node, d_{oi} is the distance between source node and node i, d_{ij} and d_{jb} have the same definition.

Definition of probability function parameters in EPWSN

The energy metric proposed by EPWSN, has the following definition:

$$\eta_{ij}(t) = \frac{(E - e_j(t))^{-1}}{\sum_{j \in C(i)} (E - e_j(t))^{-1}} \tag{6}$$

Where E is the initial energy of nodes and $e_j(t)$ is the current energy level of receiver node j in time t. This equation cause that the node with lower energy consumption in candidate list, has higher probability for selection. In this algorithm, we apply A* approach for selection of next-hop node in current travel. Therefore the location function proposed in EPWSN, ε_{ij} is defined by:

$$\varepsilon_{ij} = \frac{1/(dist + d_{ij} + d_{jb})}{\sum_{l \in C(i)} 1/(dist + d_{il} + d_{lb})}. \tag{7}$$

Where $dist$ is the distance traveled by ant from source node, d_{ij} is the Euclidean distance between node i (current node) and node j (that is one of the node in candidate list of i) and d_{jb} is the Euclidean distance between node j (that is in candidate list of node i) and destination node b. If there is not any next-hop neighbor to select, then ant k returns to the previous-hop node and that node is added to the contraindication list of the ant k.

Pheromone rule

In ACLR algorithm, the pheromone $\psi_{ij}(t)$ will be update at the end of each searching period in the way of:

$$\Delta\psi_{ij}^{k} = \frac{d_{ob}}{(d_{oi} + d_{ij} + d_{jb})L^{k}}. \tag{8}$$

Where d_{ob}, d_{oi}, d_{ij} and d_{jb} have same meaning as that of (5). L^k is the length of the route that is found by the ant k in the current round travel (the number of node visited by ant k). This equation are shown that the ACLR algorithm only consider distance for pheromone enhancement.

In EPWSN algorithm, after all ants have completed their tour, each ant deposits a quantity of pheromone given in this equation:

$$\Delta\psi_{ij}^{k} = (hop_{\max} - hop_{count_k} + \upsilon) * (pathL_{\max} - pathL_k + \omega) * E_{avg_k} \quad (9)$$

Where $hop_{\max}$ represents the maximum number of nodes that traveled by ants in their path from beginning of the algorithm, hop_{count_k} represents the number of hops for ant k in network from source node to destination node (the number of nodes visited by ant k), $pathL_{\max}$ is the maximum traveled distance by ant so far and $pathL$ is the traveled distance by current ant. ϑ, ω are control constant and E_{avg_k} is average energy of nodes visited by ant k. This equation achieves the tradeoff between route hops, location of nodes and energy consumption.

The amount of pheromone concentration on each connection between nodes in EPWSN algorithm is defined as follow:

$$\psi_{ij}(t+1) = (1-\rho) \times \psi_{ij}(t) + \frac{\Delta\psi_{ij}}{hop_{count_k} \times pathL_k} \quad (10)$$

Where hop_{count_k} and $pathL_k$ have the same meaning as that of (9) and ρ is pheromone evaporation rate. In this algorithm, we assume that, the concentration of pheromone cannot be reducing to zero or negative value and pheromone become no lower than default value.

When the ant k has returned to the source node, the ant k is eliminated. Algorithm is repeated until all ants have been eliminated. This loop performed until algorithm reaches a certain number of iterations.

After definition of design issue of proposed algorithm, the EPWSN algorithm is defined as follow:

Algorithm 1 (EPWSN algorithm)

Start
Initialize the network size $m \times n$ and number of sensor nodes, number of ants and number of iterations; distribute nodes uniformly in this area
Initialize the default pheromone level of links between network nodes and also the energy level of each node;
A set of ants placed in source node
  for (i=1 **to** iteration number)
    begin
      for (j=1 **to** ant number)
        begin
          Cnode (Current node) = source node
          while Cnode!= destination node
            begin

```
                    Calculate P_ij^k(t) probability function for nodes in candidate
    list of Cnode according to formula (3)
                    Choose the next-hop node
                    Cnode= next-hop node
                End while
          End for
     Modify the path density of pheromone according to formula (10), (9)
   End for
End
```

5 Simulation Parameters

For all algorithms, the basic node energy is a random amount between 0.5 and 1; and the nodes are distributed randomly in a quadrangle square perimeter. The ACLR algorithm parameters are defined as follows: $\alpha = 1, \beta = 1, \gamma = 1$ and the proposed algorithm parameters are defined as follows:

$$\alpha = 1.5\beta = 1.5, \gamma = 1.5, \vartheta = \omega = 0.001.$$

The parameters used in stimulation, are defined in Table 1. In this table, R is the wireless communication radius of sensors, ρ is pheromone evaporation rate, $\psi_{ij}(0)$ is the initial pheromone level for every pair of adjacent nodes, E is the initial energy for network nodes. On the assumption that, m sensor nodes are randomly laid in the monitor area of the simulation model and the value of m is among 125 to 250. The parameters used in stimulation, are as following.

Table 1. Simulation Parameters

Parameter	Values
Network Size	100*100 m^2
R	20m
Number of Nodes	125-250
Ant number	20
ρ	0.8
$\psi_{ij}(0)$	0.01
E	rand [0.5,1]J
E_{elec}	50nJ/bit
ε_{fs}	10pJ/bit/m2
ε_{mp}	0.0013pJ/bit/m4
E_{da} data aggragation	50nJ/bit/signal
d_0	87m

6 Simulation Results

The simulation mainly compares new proposed routing algorithm EPWSN, with the ACLR and ACA routing algorithms in the average energy consumption, network lifetime and average path length in a network with a fixed size of (100×100) with a different number of nodes. The result of energy consumption after running 100s independent experiments of these three algorithms, for 6 sets of different network nodes is shown in figure 1. As figure 1 shows the energy consumption in EPWSN is less than other algorithms. This accounts for using average energy parameter in pheromone update operator. Furthermore, it is due to EPWSN routing algorithm considered the energy factors when the data packets select the next hop node, and they transfer packets according to the probability of distance and the weight of energy. Thus, a single node is avoided to death early because of excessive energy consumption. As figure 2 shows the network lifetime in EPWSN is considerably more compared to the ACLR and ACA. This accounts for using combined parameters such as average energy and hop count in pheromone update operator and using a candidate selection function with effective parameters definition for energy and location.

Simulation results are shown that the proposed algorithm out performs ACLR and ACA in case of network lifetime. The energy consumption of the network is saved to extend the network lifetime. The result for average length of founded path for these algorithms is shown in figure 3. It can be seen that the average length of path in the proposed EPWSN algorithm is lower than that of ACLR and traditional ACA. This accounts for using path length parameter in pheromone update operator and probability function.

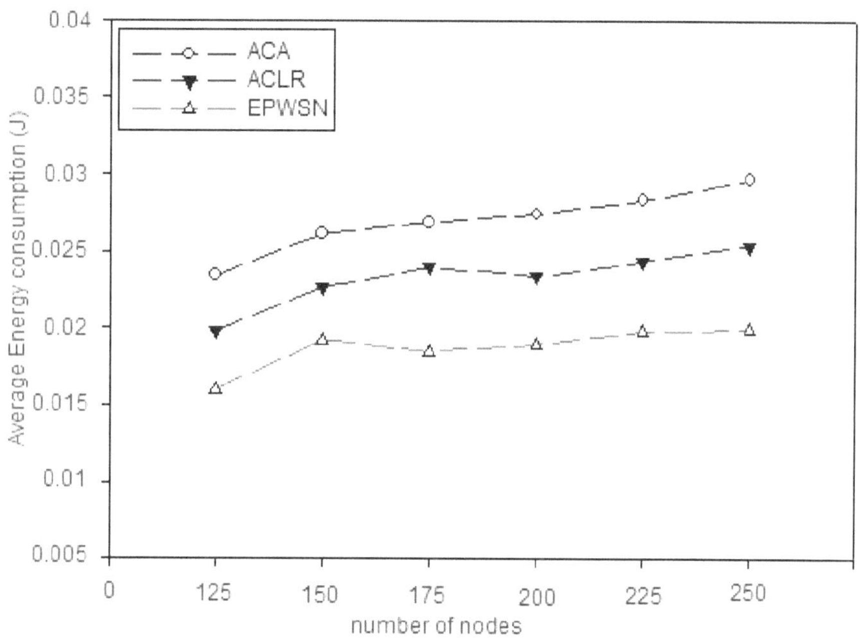

Fig. 1. Average Energy consumption

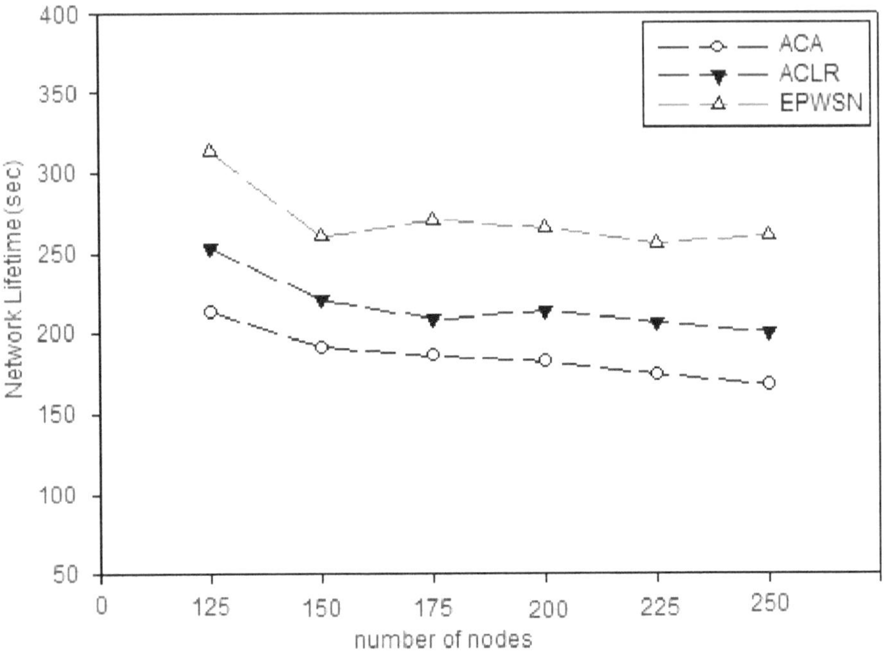

Fig. 2. Network Lifetime

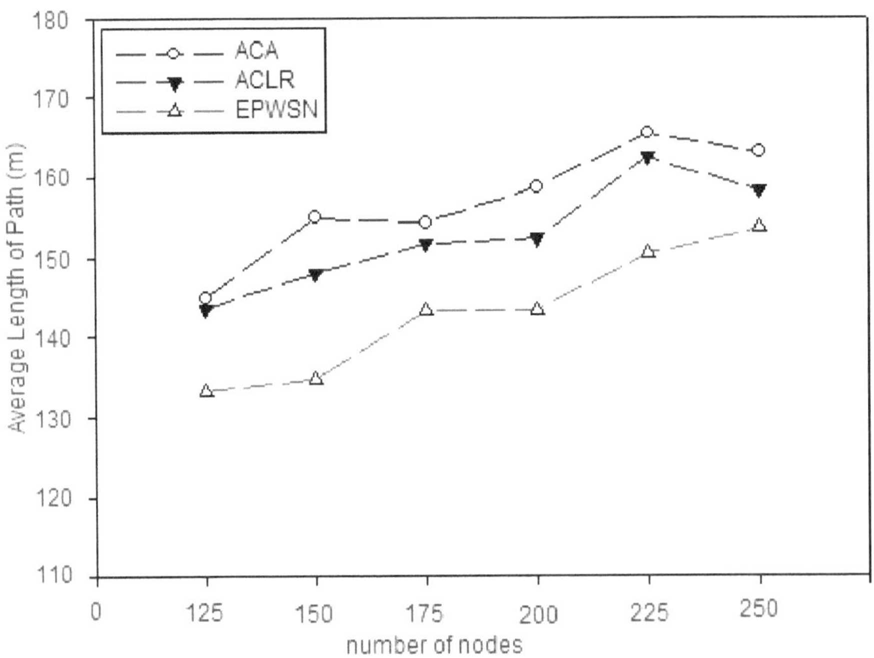

Fig. 3. Length of path

7 Conclusion

In this paper, we have proposed an ant colony based routing algorithm. We have shown that this algorithm with use of presented probability function and new pheromone update operator, can increase the system efficiency, obtain more balanced transmission among the node, and reduce the length of path and energy consumption of the routing. This algorithm is achieved by using ACO algorithm to optimize routing paths and also can prolong the network lifetime. The experimental results showed that the algorithm leads to very good results in different WSN.

References

1. Domínguez-Medina, C., Cruz-Cortés, N.: Routing Algorithms for Wireless Sensor Networks Using Ant Colony Optimization. In: Sidorov, G., Hernández Aguirre, A., Reyes García, C.A. (eds.) MICAI 2010, Part II. LNCS (LNAI), vol. 6438, pp. 337–348. Springer, Heidelberg (2010)
2. Cheng, D., Xun, Y., Zhou, T., Li, W.: An Energy Aware Ant Colony Routing Algorithms for the Routing of Wireless Sensor Networks. In: Chen, R. (ed.) ICICIS 2011, Part I. CCIS, vol. 134, pp. 395–401. Springer, Heidelberg (2011)
3. Camilo, T., Carreto, C., Sa Silva, J., Boavida, F.: An Energy–Efficient Ant-Based Routing Algorithm for Wireless Sensor Networks. In: Dorigo, M., Gambardella, L.M., Birattari, M., Martinoli, A., Poli, R., Stützle, T. (eds.) ANTS 2006. LNCS, vol. 4150, pp. 49–59. Springer, Heidelberg (2006)
4. Agarwal, T., Kumar, D., Prakash, N.R.: rolonging Network Lifetime Using Ant Colony Optimization Algorithm on LEACH Protocol for Wireless Sensor Networks. In: Meghanathan, N., Boumerdassi, S., Chaki, N., Nagamalai, D. (eds.) NeCoM 2010. CCIS, vol. 90, pp. 634–641. Springer, Heidelberg (2010)
5. Jiang, X., Hong, B.: ACO Based Energy-Balance Routing Algorithms for WSNs. In: Tan, Y., Shi, Y., Tan, K.C. (eds.) ICSI 2010. LNCS, vol. 6145, pp. 298–305. Springer, Heidelberg (2010)
6. Wang, X., Li, Q., Xiong, N., Pan, Y.: Ant Colony Optimization-Based Location-Aware Routing for Wireless Sensor Networks. In: Li, Y., Huynh, D.T., Das, S.K., Du, D.-Z. (eds.) WASA 2008. LNCS, vol. 5258, pp. 109–120. Springer, Heidelberg (2008)
7. Enami, N., Moghadam, R.A., Haghighat, A.: A Survey on Application of Neural Networks in Energy Conservation of Wireless Sensor Networks. In: Özcan, A., Chaki, N., Nagamalai, D. (eds.) WiMo 2010. CCIS, vol. 84, pp. 283–294. Springer, Heidelberg (2010)
8. Eftekhari, P., Shokrzadeh, H., Haghighat, A.T.: Cluster-Base Directional Rumor Routing Protocol in Wireless Sensor Network. In: Das, V.V., Vijaykumar, R. (eds.) ICT 2010. CCIS, vol. 101, pp. 394–399. Springer, Heidelberg (2010)
9. Zong, Z., Tian, Z., Li, Z., Xu, P.: An Ant Colony Optimization Competition Routing Algorithm for WSN. In: IEEE 2008 (2008) 978-1-4244-2108-4/08
10. Houang, R., Chen, Z. Xu, G.: Energy-aware Routing Algorithm in WSN using Predication-mode. In: IEEE 2010 (2010) 978-1-4244-8223-8/10
11. Rivero, J., Cuadra, D., Calle, J., Isasi, P.: Using the ACO algorithm for path searches in social networks. Springer Science+Business Media, LLC (2011)
12. Kolavali, S.R., Bhatnagar, S.: Ant Colony Optimization Algorithms for Shortest Path Problems. In: Altman, E., Chaintreau, A. (eds.) NET-COOP 2008. LNCS, vol. 5425, pp. 37–44. Springer, Heidelberg (2009)
13. Okdem, S., Karaboga, D.: Routing in Wireless Sensor Networks Using Ant Colony Optimization. In: Proceedings of the First NASA/ESA Conference on Adaptive Hardware and Systems. IEEE (2006)
14. Heinzelman, W.R., Chandrakasan, A., Balakrishnan, H.: Energy efficient communication protocol for wireless sensor networks. In: Proceedings of the 33rd Hawaii International Conference on System Science, vol. 2 (2000)

A Data Profile-Based Contention-Free MAC Protocol for the Patient Monitoring Systems on WBANs

Hongkyu Jeong[1], Min-Gon Kim[2,*], and Hong-Shik Park[2]

[1] Department of High Tech. Medical System, Kyungil University
hongkyu.jeong@gmail.com
[2] Department of Electrical Engineering, KAIST
kmg0803@gmail.com,parkhs@ee.kaist.ac.kr

Abstract. The patient monitoring system is one of the essential medical systems to help medical team monitoring the vital signs of patients for 24 hours and giving emergency treatment at the critical abnormal condition. Recently, Wireless Body Area Networks (WBANs) are applied to this situation for making the patients comfortable and the medical team convenient. However, existing candidate MAC protocols for WBAN are not appropriate to satisfy the requirements of the patient monitoring systems. To resolve this issue, we propose a Data Profile-based Contention-free MAC (DPC-MAC) protocol, which can synchronize the slave nodes by piggybacking synchronization information to ACK/NACK packets without beacon packet transmission. In addition, the DPC-MAC schedules the superframe resources based on the data profile of slave nodes. Through the performance comparison, the proposed DPC-MAC protocol radically reduces the average latency, extends the network lifetime, and diminishes the average link occupancy compared to the existing candidate MAC protocols.

Keywords: Wireless body area network, patient monitoring system, latency, network lifetime, link occupancy.

1 Introduction

Recently, one of the major problems faced by human being is expending aging societies. According to the U.S. Census Bureau, worldwide population of elderly people aged 65 and over are expected to be more than double by 2025 [1]. Due to the increase of the elderly people population and extension of life duration, medical expense has been increasing continuously. This mostly comes from that the occurrence possibility of chronic diseases (e.g., heart disease, diabetes, cancers, and arthritis) and degenerative diseases increases as human being grows older. In addition, the number of patients having critical cardiovascular disease and/or malignant tumor increases as people grows older, and thereby many of

* Corresponding author.

P.V. Krishna, M.R. Babu, and E. Ariwa (Eds.): ObCom 2011, Part I, CCIS 269, pp. 192–201, 2012.

them have to stay in Intensive Care Units (ICUs). Most patients in ICUs have no consciousness or movement restriction. This situation results in the needs of huge number of doctors and nurses to monitor the patients for 24 hours, but the number of trained doctors and nurses cannot catch up with these needs. Therefore, the efficient medical system can be one of the promising solutions, in particular the patient monitoring systems.

Based upon Wireless Body Area Networks (WBANs), patient monitoring systems monitor significant vital signs, such as heart movement, O2 and CO2 rate in blood, blood pressure, body temperature, and blood sugar, and notify doctors and nurses when the vital signs become abnormal. The state-of-the-art patient monitoring systems have several characteristics; first, they consists of sensors, which are directly attached on human body, and a management node with monitor. The management node synthesizes data received from sensors and shows every vital information via a monitor. Second, each sensor detects the vital signs, processes them, and generates data periodically as a form of analog signals through wired links. However, because of complex wire connections between sensors and management node, patients are inconvenient in their daily life and medical team also can meet some trouble to manage the patient monitoring systems. To resolve this problem, wireless sensor network technologies have the potential to offer convenient and cost-effective solution. A recent report by ON World titled "WSN for Healthcare" supported the value of wireless sensor network technologies since it estimated that wireless sensor networks can reduce annual health-care costs by US$25 billion by 2012.

One of the most candidate technologies for constructing WBAN is the IEEE 802.15.4, which is the standard of physical layer and Medium Access Control (MAC) protocol to support low data rate, short-range Wireless Personal Area Networks (WPANs). The IEEE 802.15.4 provides beacon-enabled mode based on synchronous MAC protocol and non-beacon-enabled mode based on asynchronous MAC protocol. If the generated traffic is cyclic and heavy, the synchronous MAC protocols including beacon-enabled mode of the IEEE 802.15.4 are generally efficient in the viewpoint of energy-saving and latency reduction[2]. This positive effect can be achieved by receiving a beacon message per every superframe cycle for synchronization and transmitting data based on the reserved period without sleeping time. On the other hand, the asynchronous MAC protocols including non-beacon-enabled mode of the IEEE 802.15.4 and the DB-MAC[3] can effectively reduce energy consumption by evading periodical synchronization procedure between the slave and management nodes under a low level of data traffic load. In addition, the asynchronous MAC protocols also can minimize the latency if the protocol adaptively operates on the condition of traffic alteration.

Fundamentally, in WBAN, the latency and the network lifetime are the most important factors to guarantee real time and seamless transmission of vital signs. Taking into consideration this issue, we proposes a Data Profile-based Contention-free MAC (DPC-MAC). To begin with, the DPC-MAC lets the master (or management) node maintain a data profile table about data generation

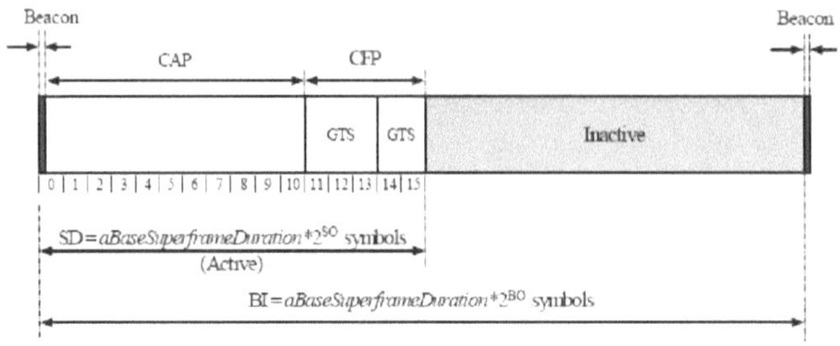

Fig. 1. IEEE 802.15.4 Superframe Structure

cycle per slave (or sensor) node. That is to say, the master node knows when the slave nodes generate data. Thus, it is possible for the master node to reserve wireless resource based on the data profile, and slave nodes can deliver their data to the master node at the reserved period without additional resource allocation procedure. Next, the DPC-MAC lets slave nodes synchronize with the master by using not a beacon packet but an acknowledgement (ACK or Negative ACK) packet. When the master node receives a data from slave node, it responses with an ACK or a NACK packet. At this moment, the master node inserts synchronization information with offset value (from the start time of the superframe) by padding it to an ACK or a NACK packet. Simulation results show that the DPC-MAC achieve a smaller average latency and extended network lifetime. In addition, it requires a lower level of the average link occupancy.

The following sections of this paper are organized as follows. In Section 2, we describe the synchronous MAC as well as the asynchronous MAC protocol to highlight the need of enhancing the existing candidate MAC protocols. In Section 3, we present our proposal with an operational mechanism. In Section 4, we evaluate the performances of the proposed DPC-MAC protocol compared to the existing candidate MAC protocols. Then we conclude the paper in Section 5 with our contribution.

2 Related Work

2.1 Synchronous MAC Protocol

The IEEE 802.15.4 is, as we aforementioned, the world standard describing physical layer and MAC layer for low data rate, short-range wireless personal area networks (WPANs). Though WPAN includes bigger area than Wireless Body Area Network (WBAN), which is currently under discussion at IEEE standardization groups, WPAN technology, especially the IEEE 802.15.4 MAC protocol, is commonly used for biomedical sensor networks by controlling power and adapting network structure to star topology [2,4]. The IEEE 802.15.4 supports beacon-enabled mode as a type of synchronous MAC, where this mode consists of Contention Access Period (CAP) and Contention Free Period (CFP) as shown in Figure 1. The CAP is utilized for resource reservation to transmit data from

Table 1. Technical Requirements of Selected BAN Applications[6]

Application	Target data rate	No. of nodes	Topology	Setup time	BER	Desired battery lifetime
ECG	72 kb/s	<6	Star	< 3 s	10^{-10}	> 1 week
EEG	86.4 kb/s	<6	Star	< 3 s	10^{-10}	> 1 week
O2/CO2/BP/ temperature	<10 kb/s	<12	Star	< 3 s	10^{-10}	> 1 week

slave nodes to the master node with slotted-CSMA approach including a back-off period. And the CFP is a reserved period for each slave with TDMA approach.

Figure 1 shows the IEEE 802.15.4 superframe structure[5]. The active period (CAP and CFP) (or Superframe Duration (SD)) and Beacon Interval (BI) are defined as follows:

$$BI = aBaseSuperframeDuration \times 2^{BO}, \quad (1)$$

$$SD = aBaseSuperframeDuration \times 2^{SO}, \quad (2)$$

where aBaseSuperframeDuration is calculated by multiplying aBaseSlotDuration to aNumSuperframeSlots, BO is the beacon order, and SO is the superframe order ($0 \leq SO \leq BO \leq 14$). The BI and SD are determined through communication between slave nodes and a master node in the step of network initialization. As we aforementioned briefly, slave nodes competitively try to send a packet to the master node in order to reserve Guaranteed Time Slots (GTSs) and each slave node is awaken during active period. On the other hand, slave nodes turned off their radio modules to minimize power consumption in the inactive period. And if multiple slave nodes are contending at the CAP, they try to communicate with the master node after a random back-off period.

Power consumption and latency are somewhat in the relation of trade-off. That is, if BI interval is longer, power consumption can be reduced while latency to complete data transmission can be increased. On the contrary, if BI interval is shorter, latency can be decreased with relatively high power consumption. Thus, these parameters should be controlled based on the network condition and application requirements. As a consequence, the IEEE 802.15.4 beacon-enabled mode is efficient in the viewpoint of energy consumption and latency reduction if the application has heavy and periodic traffic pattern. However, receiving a beacon packet per each superframe still can be a burden of this MAC protocol.

2.2 Asynchronous MAC Protocol

In order to reduce energy consumption caused by periodic beacon packet reception at the synchronous MAC protocols and to achieve rapid data transmission via adaptive polling cycle (i.e., sleeping and listening time), some asynchronous MAC protocols [3,7] are proposed.

Contrary to the IEEE 802.15.4 non-beacon-enabled MAC protocol, which supports CSMA/CA approach to transmit a data packet without a cyclic period, the asynchronous MAC protocols have a sleep and wake-up period. And they control the cycle length of the periods according to a policy of the MAC protocols in order to reduce energy consumption. For example, if there is no arriving data packet, asynchronous MAC protocols let the node go to sleep for a period. After the period, the slave node wakes up and checks whether a packet arrives during a period (i.e., listening period). If there is no arriving packet, the slave node extends the sleep period. Otherwise, the slave node reduces the sleep period. Therefore, the asynchronous MAC protocols can control the sleep interval based on the traffic condition, so that they can optimally save the energy consumption. In addition, since the asynchronous MAC protocols do not need to wait for the next superframe period to transmit a data packet, it can reduce the latency based on the adaptive control of the polling cycle.

Among the asynchronous MAC protocols, the DB-MAC[3] was recently proposed for adaptively setting the preamble length as well as channel polling cycle according to traffic condition. Basically, the DB-MAC increases the channel polling cycle if there is no data transmission, or decreases the channel polling cycle if there is a data transmission. Thus, the DB-MAC is appropriate not only for constant traffic pattern but also bursty traffic pattern throughout network lifetime. For instance, if the traffic pattern is constant, the channel polling cycle(i.e., periodic listening interval) eventually reaches an almost ideal value. On the other hand, if the traffic pattern is bursty in the long term, the channel polling cycle becomes larger during inactive period as well as shorter rapidly during active period. Therefore, the DB-MAC achieves a low level of latency and high energy-saving through adaptive polling cycle control based on the traffic pattern.

3 Proposed Data Profile-Based Contention-Free MAC

Since slave nodes in the IEEE 802.15.4 beacon-enabled mode should receive a beacon packet per every superframe to synchronize with master node, contend among slave nodes at the CAP, and wake up during whole active period. In the case of the DB-MAC, it cannot avoid frequent preamble transmission because of the traffic pattern of the patient monitoring systems. Therefore, we proposed a Data Profile-based Contention-free MAC (DPC-MAC) protocol, which achieves low energy consumption as well as high latency reduction compared to the aforementioned MAC protocols.

3.1 Description of the DPC-MAC

Before mentioning the DPC-MAC, reminding the characteristics of the patient monitoring systems is helpful to understand the value of the DPC-MAC. Table 1 shows the technical requirements of selected BAN applications discussing at the IEEE standardization groups. Especially, the patient monitoring systems display the vital signs of various applications simultaneously such as ECG, EEG, EMG, O2/CO2 rate, temperature, and blood glucose and alarm if a vital sign is detected as an abnormal state based on the predefined threshold value. The vital signs detected by slave nodes are processed by sampling, modulating, and

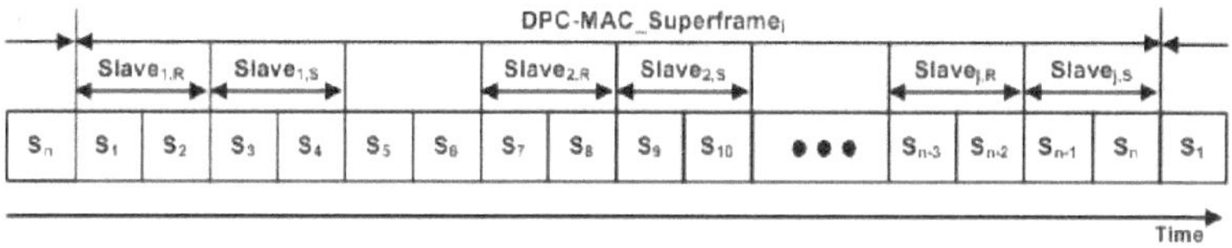

Fig. 2. DPC-MAC Superframe

packetizing per a pre-defined period. That is, each application has own packet generation cycle, but the cycle is independent among applications.

In order to achieve a better energy conservation in the environment of the patient monitoring systems, we propose a Data Profile-based Contention-free MAC (DPC-MAC) protocol. The DPC-MAC has several characteristics as follows: first, the DPC-MAC is operated based on the data profile of the slave nodes, where the profile includes packet generation cycle, and packet size. Then the master node maintains the profile information as a profile table and update it when a slave node joins or leaves the network. By utilizing the profile table, the DPC-MAC allocates time-slots for slave nodes in the superframe. In the case of overlapping of allocated time-slots between slave nodes, the DPC-MAC adjusts properly by temporarily reallocating the time-slot position of a slave node and announces the temporary alteration to the related slave node by inserting the alternation message to an ACK or a NACK packet. From this, the DPC-MAC can provide contention-free communication, so that it guarantees reliability, which is one of the most essential requirements for biomedical sensor networks.

Second, the DPC-MAC does synchronize via not a beacon packet but an ACK(or a NACK) packet. The slave node receives an ACK(or a NACK) packet from the master node as a confirmation of transmitted packet, and this operation is essential for reliable communication and rapid retransmission. Therefore, the DPC-MAC can deliver the synchronization information by piggybacking it to the ACK/NACK packet with an offset value from the start of the superframe cycle. Moreover, the DPC-MAC lets slave nodes operate an window-based synchronization approach, which inserts incoming synchronization information into a window with the First-In-First-Out method, and averages the values in the windows for the accurate timing estimation. In the results, the slave nodes can maintain accurate synchronization timing. The number of windows is dependent on the policy of the network operator.

Third, the DPC-MAC schedules superframes based on the data profile of slave nodes. For the specific description of the DPC-MAC scheduling, the following symbols and notations pertain for the remainder of the article as shown in Table 2. Figure 2 shows an example of the DPC-MAC scheduling. A superframe consists of multiple time-slots. The master node allocates time-slots for each

Table 2. Symbols and Notations

DPC-MAC_Superframe$_i$	Superframe number counted from zero to i
$Slave_{j,R}$	Number of requested time-slots for slave node j
$Slave_{j,S}$	Number of spare time-slots for slave node j

slave node per each superframe or per multiple superframes depending on the traffic pattern of the slave node. Since the network traffic load is normally lower than maximum link capacity, the master node has some amount of spare capacity, and thereby allocates the spare capacity($Slave_{j,S}$) just following requested traffic($Slave_{j,R}$) for slave nodes ($Slave_j$). As a results, the slave nodes allocated spare time-slots can reduce latency to complete data packets by retransmitting data packets if transmitted packets are lost. How to allocate $Slave_{j,S}$ is dependent on the amount of total spare capacity as well as Quality of Service (QoS) policy of network operator, so it is out of scope of this paper. In addition, allocated time-slots are utilized for slave node to transmit data packets and to receive an ACK or a NACK packet, basically including guard-time between time-slots.

4 Performance Evaluation

This section evaluates the performance of the proposed DPC-MAC regarding the average latency between the slave nodes and the master node, the remaining energy state of the slave nodes, and the average link occupancy compared to the IEEE 802.15.4 MAC and the DB-MAC.

4.1 Assumptions

The results were obtained with the following assumption: (i) network topology is a star structure, where slave nodes are connected to a master node. For the clear performance comparison of the MAC protocols, a slave node is mainly operated; (ii) an ECG application (shown in the Table 1) is utilized for the performance comparison, where data packet is generated every 10 ms; (iii) the beacon interval of the IEEE 802.15.4 is differentiated between two types (20 ms and 50 ms) and the DB-MAC has seven types of channel polling interval: 4, 8, 16, 32, 64, 128, 256, and 512 (ms); (iv) in the case of the DPC-MAC, the master node schedules the superframe resource based on the data profile of slave nodes; (v) the event-driven simulation is run until the remaining energy of the slave node is fully exhausted and repeated for 30 times to obtain the average values. The parameters used in the simulation are summarized in Table 3.

Table 3. Simulation Properties

Symbol	Description	Value	Unit
E_F	Full remaining energy states of slave nodes	10^4	joule
LS_A	Average link speed of slave nodes	250	kbps
P_{Tx}	Power consumed in transmitting	52.2	mW
P_{Rx}	Power consumed in receiving or listening	56.4	mW
P_S	Power consumed in sleeping	3	μ W
T_{Sen}	Average carrier sense time	2	ms
L_D	Length of data packet	90	Bytes
L_R	Size of ACK/NACK	5	Bytes
S_P	Size of short preamble for the DB-MAC	15	Bytes

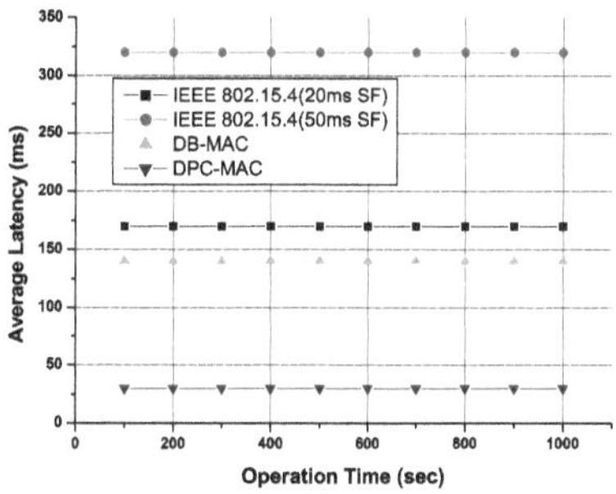

Fig. 3. The average latency of slave nodes

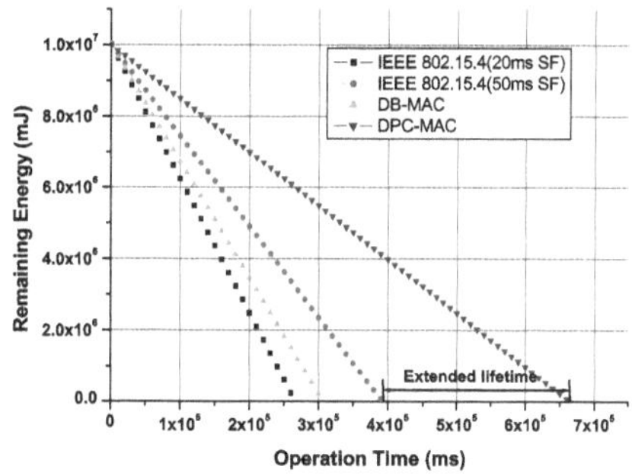

Fig. 4. The remaining energy state of slave nodes

4.2 Performance Evaluation

As we aforementioned before, we evaluate the performance of the proposed DPC-MAC in the viewpoint of the average latency, remaining energy, and average link occupancy compared to the IEEE 802.15.4 MAC (beacon-enabled mode) and the DB-MAC.

Figure 3 shows the average latency, where the DB-MAC is superior to the IEEE 802.15.4 MAC protocol because the DB-MAC does not wait for the next superframe cycle in order to transmit a data packet. And the DPC-MAC is radically superior to the DB-MAC because the DPC-MAC schedules the superframe based on the data profile of slave nodes, and thereby additional delay is not required without data transmission time. Figure 4 presents the remaining energy state, where the IEEE 802.15.4 MAC protocol with 50 ms superframe cycle outperforms the DB-MAC because asynchronous MAC protocols cannot avoid the energy consumption of the preamble transmission, especially amplified in the application generating data constantly. On the other hand, the DPC-MAC extremely reduces the energy consumption by only waking up during data generation and transmission time without resource reservation procedure.

For the performance comparison of the average link occupancy, it is necessary to define the term of link occupancy. The link occupancy means the utilized link capacity in order for a slave node to transmit data packets including shared link capacity for resource reservation among slave nodes. Therefore, the more the master node has spare link capacity, the better the master node accepts the network join request of other slave nodes. And the average link occupancy (L_{occup}) per MAC protocol is achieved by:

$$\text{[the IEEE 802.15.4]}\ L_{occup} = T_{beacon} + T_{CAP} + \sum_i T_{CFP_i}, \tag{3}$$

$$\text{[the DB-MAC]}\ L_{occup} = T_{superframe}/2 + \sum_i T_{data_i + ACK/NACK_i}, \tag{4}$$

$$\text{[the DPC-MAC]}\ L_{occup} = \sum_i T_{data_i + ACK/NACK_i}, \tag{5}$$

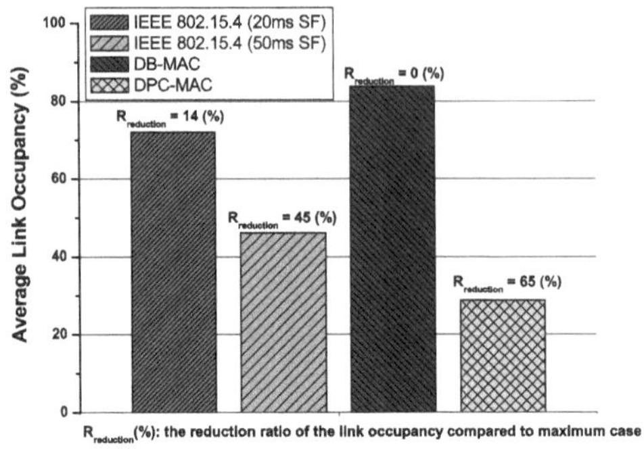

Fig. 5. The average link occupancy of slave nodes

where i is the identification of slave nodes.

Figure 5 illustrates that the IEEE 802.15.4 MAC protocol is superior to the DB-MAC since the DB-MAC has to occupy some amount of link capacity for preamble transmission. In addition, the DPC-MAC dramatically achieves 65% average link occupancy reduction compared to maximum case (i.e., DB-MAC). This is because the DPC-MAC does not require link capacity for resource reservation as well as preamble transmission.

As a consequence, the DB-MAC is superior to the IEEE 802.15.4 MAC protocol in the viewpoint of latency. On the other hand, the IEEE 802.15.4 with 50 ms beacon interval is superior to the DB-MAC in terms of remaining energy and average link occupancy. Therefore, each protocol has both advantage and demerit simultaneously. Because of these fundamental limitations, we proposed the DPC-MAC protocol and it thoroughly outperforms the IEEE 802.15.4 and the DB-MAC in the viewpoint of average latency, remaining energy, and average link occupancy.

5 Conclusion

Patient monitoring systems are one of the essential medical systems to reduce the burden of doctors and nurses to monitor their patients for 24 hours, especially at the ICUs. In order to make patients comfortable and make medical team convenient, sensor nodes should be connected in the form of WBAN. However, existing various MAC protocols have limitations to achieve excellent performance in the viewpoint of average latency, remaining energy, and average link occupancy for the patient monitoring systems. Therefore, we proposed the DPC-MAC protocol, which delivers synchronization information with offset time by piggybacking to ACK/NACK packet and applies data profile of slave nodes to schedule the resource of superframe. Through these operations, the DPC-MAC can avoid resource reservation and synchronization procedure. In the result, the proposed DPC-MAC radically outperforms the IEEE 802.15.4 MAC protocol and the DB-MAC protocol in the viewpoint of average latency, remaining energy, and average link occupancy. Moreover, this approach can be one of the promising solutions for designing advanced biomedical sensor network, especially for the patient monitoring systems.

Acknowledgment. This work was supported in part by (1) the Kyungil University Grant, (2) the KCC, Korea, under the R&D program supervised by the KCA (KCA-2011-(09913-05003)) and (3) the MKE(The Ministry of Knowledge Economy), Korea, under the ITRC(Information Technology Research Center) support program supervised by the NIPA(National IT Industry Promotion Agency)" (NIPA-2011-(C1090-1111-0013)).

References

1. U.S. Census Bureau, `http://www.census.gov/`
2. Shrestha, B., et al.: IEEE 802.15.4 MAC with GTS Transmission for Heterogeneous Devices with Application to Wheelchair Body-Area Sensor Networks. IEEE Transaction on Information Technology in Biomedicine (99), 1–11 (2011)
3. Stone, K., et al.: Efficient Duty Cycling through Prediction and Sampling in Wireless Sensor Networks. Wireless Commun. and Mobile Comput. 7(9), 1087–1102 (2007)
4. Timmons, N.F., et al.: An Adaptive Energy Efficient MAC Protocol for the Medial Body Area Networks. In: Wireless VITAE 2009, pp. 587–593 (2009)
5. Part 15.4: Wireless Medium Access Control (MAC) and Physical Layer (PHY) Specifications for Low-Rate Wireless Personal Area Networks (WPANs). IEEE Std 802.15.4-2006, `https://mentor.ieee.org/802.15/`
6. Zhen, B., et al.: TG6 Technical Requirements documents. IEEE P802.15-08-0644-09-0006, `https://mentor.ieee.org/802.15/`
7. Buettner, M., et al.: X-MAC: a Short Preamble MAC Protocol for Duty-Cycles Wireless Sensor Networks. In: Proc. ACM Sensys (November 2006)

Switching of a Sixteen Electrode Array for Wireless EIT System Using a RF-Based 8-Bit Digital Data Transmission Technique

Tushar Kanti Bera and J. Nagaraju

Department of Instrumentation and Applied Physics, Indian Institute of Science Bangalore, Bangalore – 560012, Karnataka, India
solarjnr@isu.iisc.ernet.in

Abstract. Surface electrode switching of 16-electrode wireless EIT is studied using a Radio Frequency (RF) based digital data transmission technique operating with 8 channel encoder/decoder ICs. An electrode switching module is developed the analog multiplexers and switched with 8-bit parallel digital data transferred by transmitter/receiver module developed with radio frequency technology. 8-bit parallel digital data collected from the receiver module are converted to 16-bit digital data by using binary adder circuits and then used for switching the electrodes in opposite current injection protocol. 8-bit parallel digital data are generated using NI USB 6251 DAQ card in LabVIEW software and sent to the transmission module which transmits the digital data bits to the receiver end. Receiver module supplies the parallel digital bits to the binary adder circuits and adder circuit outputs are fed to the multiplexers of the electrode switching module for surface electrode switching. 1 mA, 50 kHz sinusoidal constant current is injected at the phantom boundary using opposite current injection protocol. The boundary potentials developed at the voltage electrodes are measured and studied to assess the wireless data transmission.

Keywords: electrical impedance tomography, EIT, wireless-EIT, Radio Frequency (RF), surface electrode switching, opposite current injection protocol, digital data transmission, phantoms, boundary potential data.

1 Introduction

Electrical Impedance Tomography (EIT) [1-3] is an image reconstruction technique in which the electrical conductivity or resistivity of a conducting domain is reconstructed from the surface potential developed by a current signal injected at the domain boundary. EIT finds good applications in different areas of science and technology due to its several advantages [1-3] over other computed tomographic techniques [4]. As a nondestructive testing modality, electrical impedance tomography has been extensively researched in clinical diagnosis [5-8], biomedical engineering [9] and biotechnology [10]. Wireless data acquisition (Fig.-1) has many advantages and hence it is sometimes preferred in medical EIT systems for electric isolation

P.V. Krishna, M.R. Babu, and E. Ariwa (Eds.): ObCom 2011, Part I, CCIS 269, pp. 202–211, 2012.

property and maximum patient safety. Surface electrodes are required to be switched in a particular fashion depending on the current injection protocol used in EIT. Analog multiplexers are used for electrode switching in modern digital EIT hardware [11]. Parallel digital bits are required to operate the multiplexers for electrode switching. More the electrodes in an EIT system, more digital bits are required to operate the suitable multiplexers. In wireless EIT, required parallel digital data are transmitted wirelessly from the computer end and it is received at the phantom side. Hence, more the digital bits required to operate the suitable multiplexers in EIT, more number of channels are required in encoder/decoder ICs.

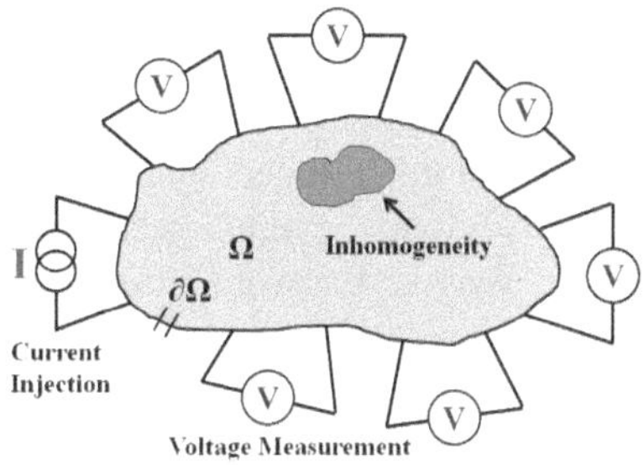

Fig. 1. Current injection and voltage measurement in EIT

In this context a Radio Frequency (RF) transmission technology [12] based digital data transmission technique operating with 8 channel encoder/decoder is proposed to switch the surface electrodes of a 16-electrode wireless EIT system. 8-bit parallel digital data are generated and transmitted through the wireless transmission module (Fig.-2) and then the 8-bit data are converted to the 16-bit parallel digital data required for the multiplexer operation in the 16-electrode EIT system. 8-bit parallel digital data collected from the receiver module are converted to 16-bit digital data by using binary adder circuits and then used for switching the surface electrodes in opposite current injection protocol.

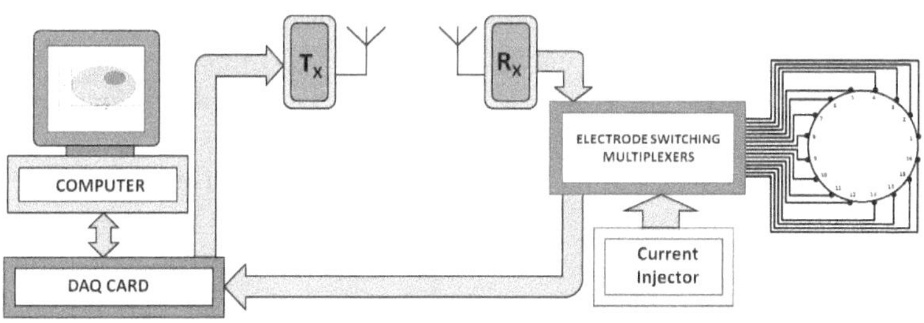

Fig. 2. A wireless digital data transmission scheme developed with Radio Frequency (RF) based transmitter (Tx) and receiver (Rx) modules for a 16-electrode EIT

8-bit parallel digital data are generated using NI USB 6251 card in LabVIEW platform and sent to transmission module which transmits the 8-bit digital data digital data to the receiver side. Receiver module supplies the 8-bit parallel digital data bits to the binary adder circuits. Binary adder circuits convert the 8-bit parallel digital data to the 16-bit digital data and fed to the four multiplexers in electrode switching module. 1 mA, 50 kHz sinusoidal current is injected at the phantom boundary using opposite current injection protocol and the boundary potentials developed at the voltage electrodes are measured and studied to assess the performance of the wireless data transmission module.

2 Materials and Methods

2.1 Analog Instrumentation

An analog EIT instrumentation [13] consists of constant current injector (Fig.-3), electrode switching module, signal conditioners and data acquisition system is used for boundary data collection. Constant current injector consists of a Voltage Controlled Oscillator (VCO) and a Voltage Control Current Source (VCCS) as shown in Fig.-3.

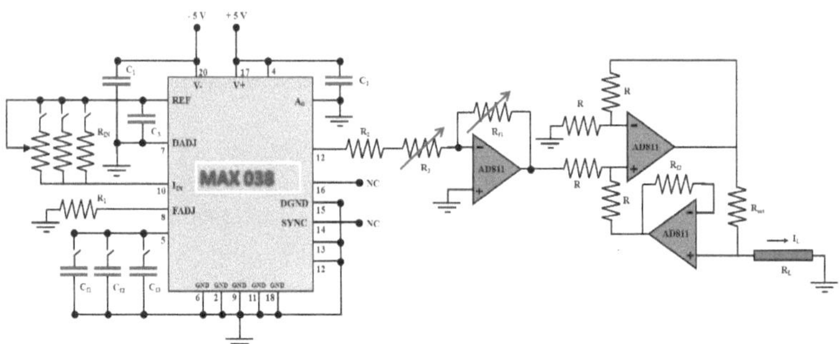

Fig. 3. Schematic of the constant current injector developed with a voltage controlled oscillator and modified Howland constant current source

The VCO consists of a variable frequency function generator IC (MAX038, Maxim Inc. USA) and supplies the input signal to the VCCS. MAX038 is a high-frequency, precision function generator producing accurate, high-frequency triangle, sawtooth, sine, square, and pulse waveforms with a minimum of external components [14]. VCO generates signal with different frequency bands depending on the value of C_F. Frequency of the VCO output is a function of R_{IN} and C_F with a positive dc supply of ±5 volts [13]. Different capacitors are connected and individually switched for different frequency bands. For a particular frequency, one capacitor is connected as C_F using single pole single throw DIP switches along with an adjusted value of R_{IN}. Changing the value of the R_{IN} and C_F in the VCO circuit a sinusoidal voltage signal of a very high bandwidth (10 Hz-10 MHz) is achieved [13] which is suitable for a multi frequency EIT application. VCCS is basically a modified Howland constant current generator (Fig.-3) which is fed by the VCO. VCCS is developed with two AD811 ICs (Analog Devices Inc. USA) [15]. AD811 is a high speed wideband current feedback operational amplifier which is suitably used in modified Howland current source with a feedback resistor of 750 Ω [15] in voltage follower circuit of the VCCS (Fig.-3). A signal conditioner block consisting a 50 Hz notch filter and a narrow band pass filter with a center frequency of 50 kHz is used for improving the signal to noise ratio of the measured potential.

An electrode switching module is developed with high speed CMOS analog multiplexers (MUX) (CD4067BE). Four 16:1 MUXs are used for current electrode and voltage electrode switching with their similar pins (Pin-1 through Pin-16) shorted and connected to the corresponding electrodes on the phantom. The electrode switching module is developed with four CD4067 ICs; two for current electrode switching and another two for voltage electrode switching. 4-bit parallel digital data are used to operate one multiplexer and hence, 16-bit parallel digital data are used to operate four 16:1 MUXs. Current electrodes are switched with two multiplexer named as current electrode multiplexers (MUX-I_1 and MUX-I_2). Voltage electrodes are switched with two multiplexer named as voltage electrode multiplexers (MUX-I_1 and MUX-I_2). Positive terminal of the current source is connected to the input terminal of MUX-I_1 where as the other point of the VCCS is connected to the input terminal of MUX-I_2. Similarly, the positive terminal of the voltage measuring probe is connected to the input terminal of MUX-V_1 where as the other point of the voltage measuring probe is connected to the input terminal of MUX-V_2.

2.2 RF Transmitter/Receiver Module

A wireless RF transmission system (Fig.-4a) is developed using ASK (Amplitude Shift Keying) based transmitter/receiver (T_x/R_x) pair operating at 433 MHz. 8-bit parallel digital data are generated in DAQ card and fed it to the encoder IC (HT640) in the transmitter module. Encoder converts the parallel data into serial format and then feeds it to the transmitter block which transmits the serial data to the receiver end (Fig.-4a). Receiver receives the serial data and supplies it to the decoder IC (HT648L) which converts the serial data into parallel data again.

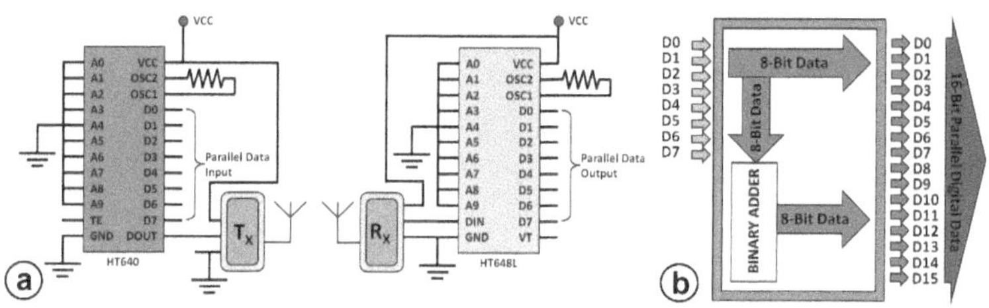

Fig. 4. (a) RF transmitter (Tx)/receiver (Rx) module, (b) Schematic of the binary adder circuit

2.3 Binary Adder Circuit

8-bit parallel digital data received from the wireless transmission module are converted to the 16-bit digital data using the binary adder circuits (Fig.-4b). 8-bit parallel digital data ($D_7D_6D_5D_4D_3D_2D_1D_0$) collected from the receiver module and fed to the binary adder circuits. In binary adder circuit the 8-bit parallel digital data are converted into 16-bit digital data ($D_{15}D_{14}D_{13}D_{12}D_{11}D_{10}D_9D_8D_7D_6D_5D_4D_3D_2D_1D_0$) required for the multiplexer operation. 8-bit parallel digital data are summed with another 8-bit digital data ($S_7S_6S_5S_4S_3S_2S_1S_0$). $S_7S_6S_5S_4S_3S_2S_1S_0$ data are defined by the type of current injection protocol used in the EIT system. Binary adder outputs (16-bit parallel digital data) are fed to the multiplexer (MUX-I_1 MUX-I_2, MUX-V_1 and MUX-V_2) used for switching the surface electrodes in opposite current injection protocol.

2.4 Data Acquisition System

The data acquisition system consists of a NI USB-6251 DAQ card which collects the boundary data through the multiplexer board connected to the surface electrodes. Data acquisition software is written in LabVIEW and interfaced with the DAQ card through PC. 8-bit parallel digital data are generated using NI USB 6251 card in LabVIEW platform and sent to transmission module which transmits the 8-bit digital data digital data to the receiver side. Receiver module supplies the 8-bit parallel digital data bits to the binary adder circuits. Binary adder circuits convert the 8-bit parallel digital data to the 16-bit digital data and fed to the four multiplexers in electrode switching module.

2.5 EIT-Phantom

A reconfigurable practical phantom (Fig.-5a) is developed with a shallow glass tank (150 mm diameter) and sixteen stainless steel electrodes [16] equally spaced on the tank inner wall (Fig.-5a) and fixed on tank wall using steel paper clips. Sixteen identical electrodes (rectangular shape, 34 mm × 10 mm) are cut from a 50 μm thick high quality stainless steel (type 304) sheet. All the electrodes are connected to the EIT electronic hardware through the low resistivity flexible multi-strand copper wires with steel crocodile clips (Fig.- 5a).

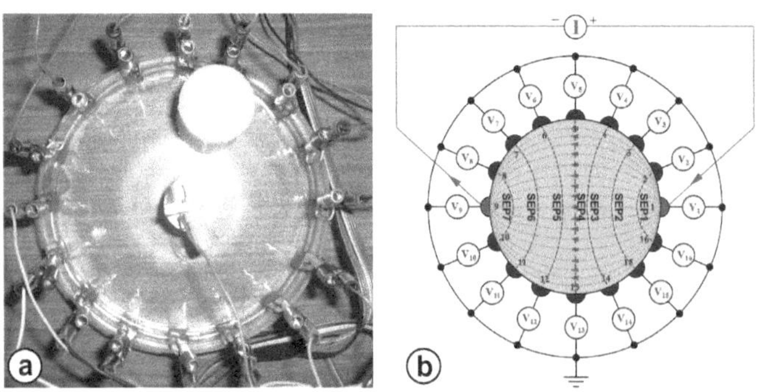

Fig. 5. (a) Practical phantom with nylon inhomogeneity near electrode no. 4, (b) Boundary potential measurement for opposite current injection

The phantom tank is filled with a 0.9% (w/v) NaCl solution and a cylindrical stainless steel rod of 25 mm diameter is put at the phantom center (Fig.- 5a). The stainless steel rod, called common mode electrode (CME) [17] in EIT, is connected to the ground point of the EIT electronics to reduce the common mode error [18] of the circuits.

2.6 Data Collection

1 mA, 50 kHz sinusoidal constant current is injected to the phantom boundary with and without inhomogeneity and the electrode potentials are collected using opposite current injection protocol (Fig.-5b). Nylon cylinders are put as the inhomogeneity near electrode no. 3, 5 and 7 and the current signal is injected through the electrode switching module. The boundary potentials developed at the surface electrodes placed on the phantom boundary are collected using opposite current injection protocol (Fig.-5b) and sent to the PC for the analysis. RMS potentials on all the electrodes are measured for first eight current projections and the voltage data set (contains 128 voltage data for a sixteen electrode system) are saved as a *.txt* file in PC for computation. Boundary data for first eight current projections are sufficient to produce impedance image (due to reciprocity principle) and that is why the other eight current projections are not required [16]. The boundary potentials (V_1 through V_{16} in Fig.-5b) developed at the surface electrodes (E_1, E_2, E_3, ..., E_{15} and E_{16}) are collected for the first eight current projections. The potential profile of symmetric electrodes (SEP) [19] of the phantom is also studied for evaluating the boundary data profile of the EIT system. The axis through the current electrodes divides the electrodes (excluding the current electrodes) in two sets (all are symmetrically placed in space) which are called symmetric electrode pair [19]. The equipotential lines and the SEPs are shown in the Fig.-5b. All the electrodes in a SEP are symmetrically placed in space with respect to the axis through the current electrodes divides the electrodes (Fig.-5b). All the SEPs of a 16 electrode system for current projection 1 are shown in Fig.-5b and 6a.

	First Seven measurements	Next Seven Measurements
SEP1	Electrode 2	Electrode 16
SEP2	Electrode 3	Electrode 15
SEP3	Electrode 4	Electrode 14
SEP4	Electrode 5	Electrode 13
SEP5	Electrode 6	Electrode 12
SEP6	Electrode 7	Electrode 11
SEP7	Electrode 8	Electrode 10
SEP8	Electrode 9	Electrode 9

(a)

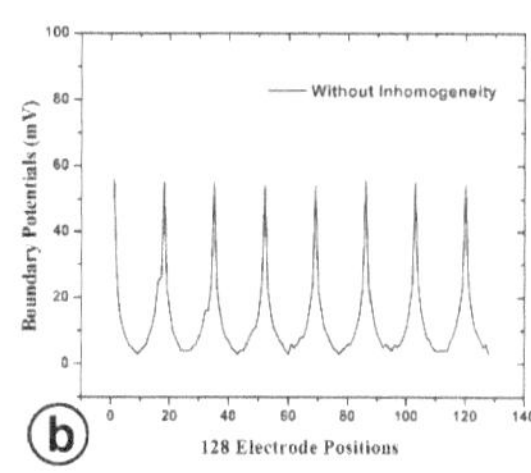

Fig. 6. (a) Symmetric electrode pairs (SEP) of a 16 electrode EIT system in current projection 1, (b) Boundary potentials for homogeneous medium

3 Results and Discussion

The boundary potentials developed for homogeneous medium (NaCl solution) show that (Fig.-6b) the surface potential profile changes in similar fashion as it changes for a wired EIT system in opposite method. It is observed that the potential profiles of all the current projections are symmetric (Fig.-6b) which indicates that the circular phantom system is symmetric and stabile. It is reported that [16] for opposite method, only first 128 voltages measured for first eight projections are independent data and hence are sufficient to reconstruct the inhomogeneities due to the reciprocity principle [16]. Hence the all the boundary potentials are collected for the first eight current projections and the 128 voltage data are studied (Fig.-6b). Consequently the acquisition time in this case reduces to 50 % of the full acquisition time of the 16-electrode EIT system. The potential of the SEPs (Fig.-7a) also shows that the experimental phantom is symmetric with respect to the current injection axis. It is observed that the standard deviation of SEP1, SEP2, SEP3, and SEP4 are less than 1.0 whereas the standard deviation of SEP5, SEP6, SEP7, and SEP8 are zero (Fig.-7b).

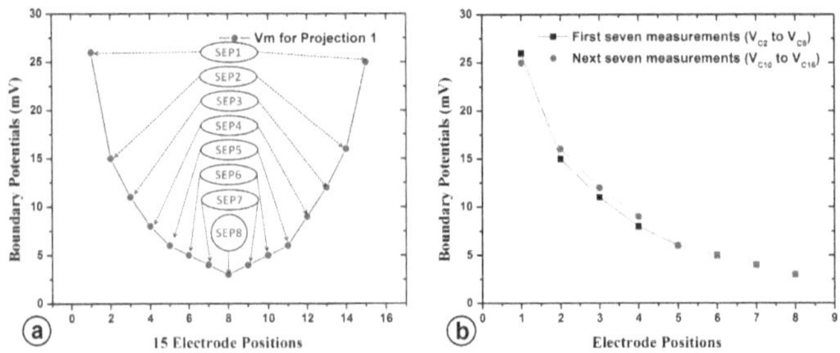

Fig. 7. (a) Boundary potentials in current projection 1 for the homogeneous medium, (b) SEP electrode potentials for first seven measurements and next seven measurements

Circular nylon inhomogeneities are placed at the different electrode positions (Figs.-8a, 9a and 10a) and the RMS boundary potentials are measured using data acquisition system. Boundary data profiles (Figs.-8b, 9b and 10b) of their corresponding phantom configurations (Figs.-8a, 9a and 10a respectively) show that the maximum potential (V_{ei}) of the boundary data for a phantom with inhomogeneity placed near N^{th} electrode occurs in $[((N-1) \times 16) + N]^{th}$ data point in the boundary potential data matrix.

The maximum potential (V_{ei}) point in the boundary potential data matrix is the potential of the electrode which is positioned near the inhomogeneity provided the

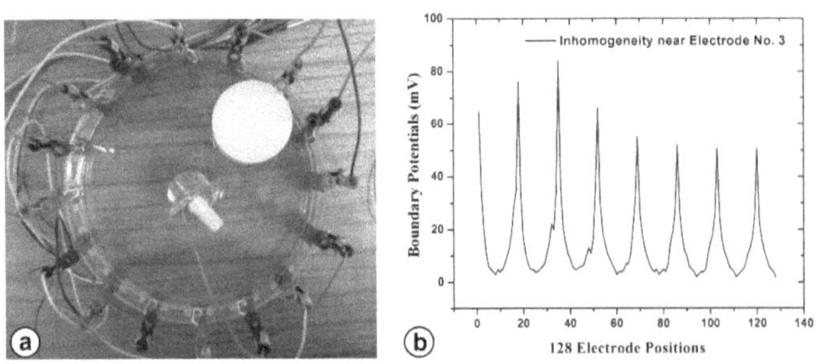

Fig. 8. (a) Practical phantom with nylon cylinder at electrode no. 3, (b) boundary potentials

positive terminal of the current source is connected to the same electrode. The voltage drop across the current path along the inhomogeneity and the electrode is found maximum because of the high resistance of inhomogeneity and the high electrode contact impedance. It is also observed that for all the inhomogeneity positions boundary data are successfully generated by the system. Boundary potentials measured with nylon inhomogeneity are found satisfactory for all the at electrode positions (Fig.-8a, 9a and 10a). Potential curves with nylon cylinder at electrode 3 (Fig.-8a) show that the high voltage peak is appeared at the $[((3\text{-}1) \times 16) + 3]^{th}$ position or 35th data point (Fig.-8b) of the data matrix (in 3rd projection loop). Hence it is understood that the inhomogeneity is positioned at the electrode number 3. Potential curves with inhomogeneity at electrode 5 (Fig.-9a) also show that the high voltage peak is appeared at the 69th data point (Fig.-9b) of the data matrix (in 5th projection loop) which clearly indicates the presence of inhomogeneity at 5th electrode position. Similarly boundary data (Fig.-10b) for inhomogeneity at electrode 7 (Fig.-10a) show that the high voltage peak comes at the 103th data point (Fig.-10b) of the data matrix (in 7th projection loop). Hence it is understood that the inhomogeneity is positioned at the electrode number 3.

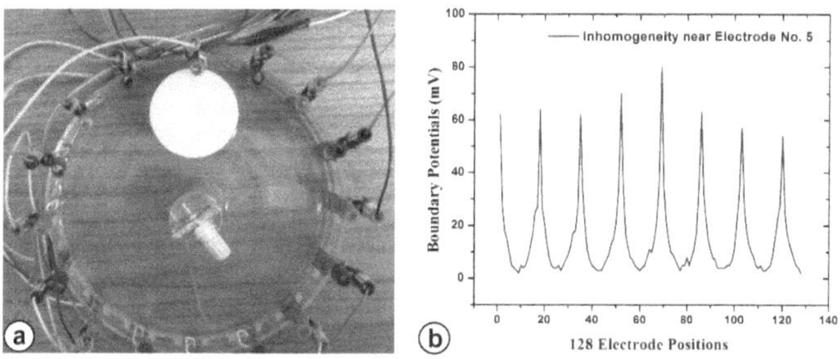

Fig. 9. (a) Practical phantom with nylon cylinder at electrode no. 5, (b) boundary potentials

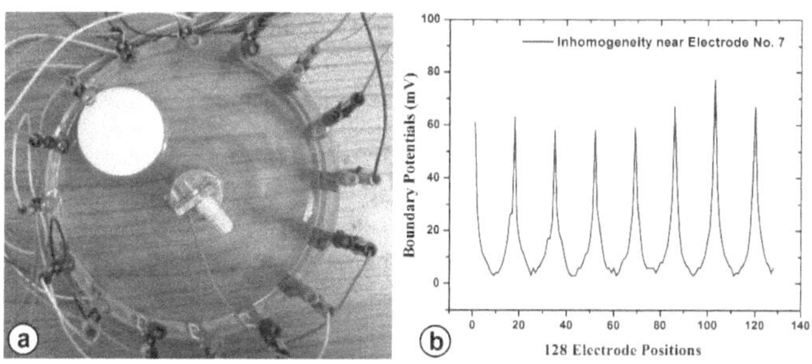

Fig. 10. (a) Practical phantom with nylon cylinder at electrode no. 7, (b) boundary potentials

4 Conclusions

Surface electrode switching of 16-electrode wireless EIT is proposed and studied using a Radio Frequency (RF) based digital data transmission technique operating with 8 channel encoder/decoder ICs. Transmitter/receiver module developed is successfully interfaced with the USB based DAQ system through the analog multiplexers based electrode switching module. USB based data acquisition system properly generate digital data required for multiplexer operation. 8-bit parallel digital data are generated by DAQ card and sent to the transmission module which transmits the digital data bits to the receiver. Receiver module feeds the parallel digital bits to the binary adder circuits and the 16-bit data obtained at the adder outputs are fed to the multiplexers of the electrode switching module for surface electrode switching. Results show that the wireless module successfully transmits and receives the parallel data for switching the voltage and current electrodes wirelessly. 1 mA, 50 kHz sinusoidal constant current is injected to the phantoms with different inhomogeneity configurations using opposite current injection protocol. The boundary potentials developed at the surface electrodes are measured and studied to assess the wireless data transmission. Boundary data collected from practical phantom show that the multiplexers are operating in the required sequence in opposite current protocol. The voltage picks obtained at the proper positions in the boundary data matrix proved that the sequential operation of multiplexers and successful wireless transmission of digital bits. The developed wireless digital data transmission module can be used for wireless EIT-data acquisition system.

References

[1] Webster, J.G.: Electrical impedance tomography. Adam Hilger Series of Biomedical Engineering. Adam Hilger, New York (1990)

[2] Metherall, P.: Three Dimensional Electrical Impedance Tomography of the Human Thorax, PhD Thesis, University of Sheffield (January 1998)

[3] Denyer, C.W.L.: Electronics for Real-Time and Three-Dimensional Electrical Impedance Tomographs, PhD Thesis, Oxford Brookes University (January 1996)

[4] Bushberg, J.T., Seibert, J.A., Leidholdt Jr., E.M., Boone, J.M.: The Essential Physics of Medical Imaging, 2nd edn. Lippincott Williams & Wilkins, ISBN-10: 0683301187

[5] Li, Y., et al.: A Novel Combination Method of Electrical Impedance Tomography Inverse Problem for Brain Imaging. IEEE Transactions on Magnetics 41(5) (May 2005)

[6] Bagshaw, A.P., et al.: Electrical impedance tomography of human brain function using reconstruction algorithms based on the finite element method. NeuroImage 20, 752–764 (2003)

[7] Murphy, D., Burton, P., Coombs, R., Tarassenko, L., Rolfe, P.: Impedance Imaging in the Newborn. Clin. Phys. Physiol. Meas. 8(suppl. A), 131–140 (1987)

[8] Hope, T.A., Iles, S.E.: Technology review: The use of electrical impedance scanning in the detection of breast cancer. Breast Cancer Res. 6, 69–74 (2004)

[9] Brown, B.H.: Medical impedance tomography and process impedance tomography: a brief review. Measurement Science & Technology 12, 991–996 (2001)

[10] Linderholm, P., et al.: Cell Culture Imaging Using Microimpedance Tomography. IEEE Transactions on Biomedical Engineering 55(1) (January 2008)

[11] Arpinar, V.E., Eyuboglu, B.M.: Microcontroller controlled, multifrequency electrical impedance tomograph. In: Proceedings of the 23rd Annual International Conference of the IEEE Engineering in Medicine and Biology Society (2001)

[12] Voldman, S.H.: ESD: RF Technology and Circuits. John Wiley & Sons Ltd, The Atrium (2006)

[13] Bera, T.K., Nagaraju, J.: A Multifrequency Constant Current Source for Medical Electrical Impedance Tomography. In: Proceedings of the IEEE International Conference on Systems in Medicine and Biology 2010 (IEEE ICSMB 2010), Kharagpur, India, December 16-18, pp. 278–283 (2010), doi:10.1109/ICSMB.2010.5735387
[14] Data Sheet, MAX038-High-Frequency Waveform Generator. Maxim Integrated Products, Inc., CA 94086
[15] Data Sheet, AD811 - High Performance Video Op Amp, Analog Devices, Inc.
[16] Bera, T.K., Nagaraju, J.: Resistivity Imaging of A Reconfigurable Phantom With Circular Inhomogeneities in 2D-Electrical Impedance Tomography. Measurement 44(3), 518–526 (2011), doi:10.1016/j.measurement.2010.11.015
[17] Bera, T.K., Nagaraju, J.: A Stainless Steel Electrode Phantom to Study the Forward Problem of Electrical Impedance Tomography (EIT). Sensors & Transducers Journal 104(5), 33–40 (2009)
[18] Rosell, J., Riu, P.: Common-mode feedback in electrical impedance tomography. Clin. Phys. Physiol. Meas. 13(suppl. 4), 11–14 (1992)
[19] Bera, T.K., Nagaraju, J.: Studying the Boundary Data Profile of A Practical Phantom for Medical Electrical Impedance Tomography with Different Electrode Geometries. In: Proceedings of The World Congress on Medical Physics and Biomedical Engineering-2009, Munich, Germany, September 7-12. IFMBE Proceedings, vol. 25/II, pp. 925–929 (2009)

An Artificial Bee Colony Algorithm for the Minimum Average Routing Path Clustering Problem in Multi-hop Underwater Sensor Networks

Venkateswara Rao Dokku and Alok Singh

Department of Computer and Information Sciences,
University of Hyderabad, Hyderabad 500 046, India
dvrao.584@gmail.com, alokcs@uohyd.ernet.in

Abstract. Given a set of sensor nodes and a set of sinks placed randomly in an Euclidean plane, the minimum average routing path clustering problem (MARPCP) seeks a subset of sensors to function as cluster heads such that each sensor node is adjacent to at least one cluster head, and the expected hop distance from a node to its nearest sink in the clustering-based routing scheme is minimized. This problem is of particular concern in underwater sensor networks. This paper proposes a new approach to this problem based on Artificial Bee Colony (ABC) algorithm. Computational results show the effectiveness of our proposed approach.

Keywords: Artificial Bee Colony Algorithm, Swarm Intelligence, Clustering Based Routing Scheme, Underwater Sensor Networks.

1 Introduction

Underwater Sensor Networks (USN) provides an attractive alternative for observing the oceanic environments which otherwise considered as an arduous and expensive task. USNs are now-a-days regarded as a promising solution for a broad range of underwater monitoring requirements in both civilian and military domains [1, 2].

A USN consists of a network of static sensor nodes and one or more underwater sinks. The underwater sinks are responsible for transmitting the data gathered by USN to out-of-water sinks such as ships or buoys, which in turn transmit it to a designated station for processing. Usually, an underwater sensor node costs several times more than a conventional sensor node. An underwater sink must be different from the normal underwater sensor nodes as it has to communicate over a longer range which requires more transmission power and hardware support. Therefore, its cost is even more than an underwater sensor node. As a result USNs are normally sparser than the conventional sensor networks [1]. Moreover, only few underwater sinks are provided in a typical USN.

Apart from cost considerations, energy efficiency is even a bigger concern for USN than conventional sensor networks because of the following two reasons: First of all, replacing the battery in underwater environment is extremely difficult and/or

P.V. Krishna, M.R. Babu, and E. Ariwa (Eds.): ObCom 2011, Part I, CCIS 269, pp. 212–219, 2012.

expensive. Secondly, underwater sensor nodes have to use acoustic channels for communication which consume five times more energy than radio signals. Actually, normal radio signals can not travel far inside water. Though very low frequency radio signals can be used, they consume much more energy and require each node to be equipped with a very large antenna [1, 2]. One way to save energy is to divide the sensor nodes into clusters. Each cluster will have a cluster head which is responsible for sending the data collected from all sensors in that cluster to its nearest underwater sink. All other sensors in the cluster will simply send their data to the clusterhead. The clusterhead may fuse the data collected from more than one sensor and send it as a single message. This can reduce the number of messages transmitted in the network significantly thereby reducing the energy consumption. The clusterhead will send its messages to the nearest underwater sink through a multihop path consisting of zero or more clusterheads. In this scheme a message has to pass through the corresponding clusterhead if it has to pass through any node of a cluster because the routing information will be maintained only at cluster heads and other nodes passively forward the message received on its one link to another. This routing information needs to be changed only in case of the failure of a clusterhead. Such a policy increases the fault tolerance and minimizes the overhead in error recovery [1, 3].

In this paper, we have considered a relatively new problem in the context of USN called minimum average routing path clustering problem (MARPCP). Given a USN, the MARPCP seeks a subset of sensors to function as cluster heads such that each sensor node is adjacent to at least one cluster head, and, the expected hop distance from a node to its nearest underwater sink in the clustering-based routing scheme is minimized. This problem is introduced by Kim et al. [1]. A proof of NP-Hardness of this problem can be found in [4].

Kim et al. [1] showed that an approximation solution to MARPCP problem in a unit disk graph G induced by sensor and underwater sink nodes can be obtained by solving the minimum weight dominated set problem (MWDSP) in a transformed graph G′ where the weight of a node is equal to the minimum hop distance between that node and nearest underwater sink. Further, they showed that an approximation algorithm for MWDSP is also an approximation algorithm for MARPCP albeit with a bound that is three times loose. As the approximation algorithms based on computation of MWDSP are computationally expensive, they also presented a constant factor approximation algorithm for MARPCP based on maximal independent set computation (MIS).

In this paper, we have proposed an artificial bee colony (ABC) algorithm for the MARPCP problem. To our knowledge this is the first metaheuristic approach for the MARPCP problem. Computational results show the effectiveness of our approach in solving the MARPCP problem.

The remainder of this paper is organized as follows: Section 2 defines the MARPCP problem formally. Section 3 provides a brief introduction to artificial bee colony algorithm. Our ABC approach for the MARPCP problem is presented in section 4, whereas section 5 describes the computational results. Section 6 outlines some concluding remarks and directions for future works.

2 Problem Definition

Following the notational convention used in [1], the minimum average routing path clustering problem (MARPCP) can be formally defined as follows: Given a set $S = \{s_1, s_2, \ldots, s_n\}$ of sensor nodes and a set $U = \{U_1, U_2, \ldots, U_m\}$ of underwater sinks in an Euclidean plane, the MARPCP seeks a subset of sensor nodes $C = \{CH_1, CH_2, \ldots, CH_c\}$ to function as cluster heads such that each sensor node is adjacent to at least one node in C, and, the expected hop distance from a node to its nearest underwater sink in the clustering-based routing scheme is minimized. We have used the same objective function as used in [1], i.e., minimize

$$\sum_{1 \le j \le c} \min_{1 \le k \le m} (Routedist(CH_j, U_k) - 1)$$

under the condition that for each sensor node s_i, there exist a cluster head CH_j such that the hop distance between s_i and CH_j is at most 1. The $Routedist(CH_j, U_k)$ is computed as follows: First a unit disk graph G is constructed on the union of S and U. The minimum hop distance between each pair of adjacent clusterheads and each pair of adjacent clusterhead and underwater sink are determined. Two clusterheads are said to be adjacent, if we can reach one from the other through nodes belonging to the clusters corresponding to those two clusterheads only. Similarly a cluster head and underwater sink is said to be adjacent if we can reach one from the other through nodes belonging to the clusters corresponding to the clusterhead in consideration only. Note that the maximum possible hop distance between two adjacent clusterheads is 3 and the maximum possible hop distance between adjacent clusterhead and underwater sink is 2. Now a new weighted graph G′ on the union of C and U is constructed where edges are based on the concept of adjacency described above and the weight of an edge is the hop distance between its endpoint in G. Then for each clusterhead CH_j, the $Routedist(CH_j, U_k)$ is defined to be a minimum-weight path in G′ from CH_j to the underwater sink U_k consisting of only clusterheads as intermediate nodes.

3 The Artificial Bee Colony Algorithm

Motivated by intelligent foraging behavior of natural honey bee colonies, Karaboga [5] proposed a new metaheuristic technique called the artificial bee colony (ABC) algorithm. It is extended further by Karaboga and Basturk [5, 6, 7, 8, 9], Singh [10] and Pan et al. [11]. In natural honey bee colonies, foraging bees are classified into three types, viz. employed bees, onlooker bees and scout bees. All bees which are presently exploiting a food source are termed as "employed". The employed bees bring loads of nectar from the food source to the hive and may convey the information about their food sources with the onlooker bees. "Onlookers" are those bees which are waiting in the hive for employed bees to convey information about their food sources. "Scouts" are those bees which are looking for a new food source in the vicinity of the hive. The employed bees convey information about their food sources to the onlookers by dancing in a common area in the hive called dance area.

The nature and the duration of a dance are proportional to the nectar content of the food source presently being tapped by the dancing employed bee. Onlookers watch numerous dances before choosing a food source. The probability of choosing a food source is directly proportional to its quality. Therefore, the good food sources attract more onlookers than the poor ones. Whenever a bee, whether it is scout or onlooker, finds a food source it becomes employed. Whenever a food source is exhausted, the associated employed bee abandons it and becomes scout. As soon as a scout finds a new food source, it again becomes employed. Thus, employed and onlooker bees can be seen as performing the job of exploitation, whereas scouts can be seen as performing the job of exploration.

Inspired by this intelligent foraging behavior, Karaboga [5] developed the artificial bee colony (ABC) algorithm. In ABC algorithm each food source represents a feasible solution to the problem under consideration and the nectar content of a food source represents the fitness of the solution being represented by that food source. Karaboga [5] also categorized the colony of artificial bees into same three groups, i.e., employed, onlookers and scouts with similar functions. In ABC algorithm, there are only as many employed bees as there are number of food sources. Normally, the number of onlooker bees is also taken to be equal to the number of employed bees. The employed bee of an exhausted food source abandons it and becomes a scout. As soon as it finds a new food source it again becomes employed. In the ABC algorithm, the action of a scout bee is modeled by generating a new food source (solution) randomly and associating the scout bee in consideration with this newly generated food source to make it employed again. We will use food source and solution interchangeably throughout the description of the ABC algorithm.

The ABC algorithm is an iterative algorithm. The algorithm starts by associating each employed bee with a randomly generated food source. Then, during each iteration, each employed bee determines a new food source in the neighborhood of its currently associated food source and computes the nectar amount of this new food source. If the nectar amount of this new food source is more than that of its currently associated food source, then this employed bee moves to the new food source leaving the old one, otherwise it continues with the old one. The procedure for determining a food source in the neighborhood of a particular food source is problem specific, and, therefore, varies from one problem to another. Once all employed bees have completed this process, they convey information about their food sources with onlookers. Onlookers select the food sources probabilistically according to the nectar amount (fitness) of that food source. The probability p_i of selecting a food source i is determined using the following expression:

$$p_i = \frac{F_i}{\sum_{j=1}^{m} F_j}$$

where F_i is the fitness of the solution corresponding to the food source i and m is the total number of food sources. This selection method is known by the name "roulette wheel" in genetic algorithm community. According to this selection method, higher the fitness of a food source, the probability of its selection will be more. Therefore, richer nectar containing food sources attracts more onlookers than the poorer ones. Once all onlookers select their food sources in the aforementioned way, each of them determines a new food source in the neighborhood of its selected food source in the same manner as employed bees and computes the nectar amount of the new food source. Among all the neighboring food sources determined by the onlookers associated with a particular food source *i* and the food source *i* itself, the best food source is determined. This best food source becomes the new location of the food source *i* in the next iteration. If the solution represented by a food source *i* does not improve for a predetermined number of iterations, say *limit*, then food source *i* is assumed to be completely exhausted and its associated employed bee leaves it to become scout. This scout is again made employed by associating it with a new randomly generated food source. When the new locations of all food sources are determined, then the next iteration of ABC algorithm begins. This process is repeated until the termination criterion is satisfied.

Interested readers may refer to [12] for a survey on ABC algorithm and other algorithms based on bee swarm intelligence.

4 The ABC Algorithm for MARPCP

The main features of our ABC algorithm for MARPCP are described below:

4.1 Solution Encoding and Fitness

We have encoded a solution by the set of its clusterheads. The set of clusterheads forms a dominating set for the unit disk graph induced by sensor and sink nodes. Our fitness function is same as the objective function described in section 2. To compute the value of this fitness function, we have to follow the procedure described in section 2.

4.2 Initial Solution Generation

We have used the algorithm referred to as FAST-MARPCP in [1] for generating initial solutions. We have also used this method for generating a new solution whenever an employed bee becomes a scout.

4.3 Probability of Selecting a Food Source

For selecting the food source for an onlooker, we have used binary tournament selection. In binary tournament selection, two food sources are randomly chosen and the better of the two food sources are selected with the probability p_{onl} and the worse of the two with the probability $(1-p_{onl})$. In the binary tournament selection, the worst food source also gets a chance for selection though with a smaller probability.

4.4 Determination of New Neighboring Food Source

In order to generate a solution in the neighborhood of a particular solution say solution i, first we create a copy i' of solution i and add two nodes that are not there in i' to it. These two nodes are selected randomly. Then we find the set R of those nodes, all of whose neighbors are covered by other nodes. Nodes in set R are deleted one-by-one from the solution to get a neighboring solution.

4.5 Other Features

If a food source (solution) does not improve for a predetermined number of iterations determined by parameter *limit*, then employed bee associated with that food source abandons it and becomes a scout. The parameter *limit* controls the delicate balance between exploration and exploitation and therefore, it is an important control parameter of the ABC algorithm. We have used FAST-MARPCP algorithm of [1] to generate a solution for the scout bee. Another distinguishing feature of our ABC algorithm is that there is no upper limit on the number of scout bees in an iteration, i.e., in an iteration there may not be even a single scout bee, whereas in another iteration there may be several scout bees. In our approach, the number of scout bees in an iteration is equal to the number of those employed bees whose solutions have not been improved over previous *limit* iterations.

5 Computational Results

We have used C programming language to implement our ABC approach and executed it on an Intel core 2 quad system with 4 GB RAM running at 2.83 GHz under Linux platform. We have used a colony of 50 bees out of which 25 are the employed bees and the remaining 25 are the onlookers. We have used $p_{onl} = 0.8$, *limit* = 100. We have executed our ABC algorithm for the 500 iterations. All these parameter values are chosen empirically. For comparison purpose we have also implemented FAST-MARPCP [1]. As ABC algorithm generates 25000 solutions, therefore, to allow a fair comparison, we have run FAST-MARPCP 25000 times, each time with a different random seed, and, reported the best solution obtained.

Since there are no standard benchmark instances for this problem, we have generated our own instances. In all these instances we have assumed that all sensors and underwater sinks are randomly located in a 500×500 square area. Communication range is fixed to 100. Number of nodes in these instances varies from 100 to 500 with an increment of 100. We have generated 5 instances for each of the 5 different node sizes. Therefore, we have a total of 25 instances. Each instance name is of the form $n.i$, where n is the number of nodes in that instance and i is the sequence number of the instance in its size.

Table 1 compares the results of our ABC approach against the multiple runs of FAST-MARPCP. Table 1 clearly shows the superiority of our ABC approach. Our ABC approach obtained better solution on all 25 instances. As far as running time is concerned both approaches require roughly the same time. This is due to the fact that most of the execution time of both the approaches is spent on fitness evaluation.

Table 1. Results of the FAST-MARPCP and the ABC algorithm

Instance	FAST-MARPCP Cost	FAST-MARPCP Time (Sec.)	ABC Approach Cost	ABC Approach Time (Sec.)
100.1	89	1045.000	65	1030.810
100.2	110	1036.060	78	1061.800
100.3	94	1027.660	75	1045.140
100.4	103	1056.320	78	1030.510
100.5	98	1048.150	88	1073.100
200.1	136	1216.020	109	1223.280
200.2	127	1150.580	100	1185.160
200.3	172	1236.630	122	1231.830
200.4	148	1228.610	123	1256.160
200.5	134	1169.800	100	1171.330
300.1	150	1292.560	121	1303.860
300.2	137	1296.350	113	1319.440
300.3	153	1268.310	125	1321.970
300.4	144	1289.800	115	1306.230
300.5	166	1314.230	125	1344.180
400.1	137	1204.860	109	1224.070
400.2	120	1173.360	107	1203.450
400.3	127	1211.030	102	1244.900
400.4	118	1211.780	107	1207.970
400.5	125	1237.480	103	1235.250
500.1	121	1215.510	104	1251.110
500.2	128	1244.210	104	1295.020
500.3	136	1234.000	108	1228.120
500.4	147	1247.460	107	1287.480
500.5	110	1188.690	88	1175.000

6 Conclusions

In this paper, we have proposed an artificial bee colony algorithm for solving the Minimum Average Routing Path Clustering Problem (MARPCP) in under water sensor networks. We have compared the performance of our proposed approach against the FAST-MARPCP algorithm proposed in [1]. Computational results show the effectiveness of our approach.

As our approach is the first metaheuristic approach for the MARPCP problem, it will serve as the baseline approach for future metaheuristic approaches for the same problem. As a future work we intend to develop similar approaches for other related clustering problems in wireless sensor networks.

Acknowledgments. The authors are thankful to the Department of Science and Technology, Government of India for providing financial support to carry out this work.

References

1. Kim, D., Wang, W., Ding, L., Lim, J., Oh, H., Wu, W.: Minimum average routing path clustering problem in multi-hop 2-D underwater sensor networks. Optimization Letters 4, 383–392 (2010)
2. Akyildiz, I.F., Pompili, D., Melodia, T.: Underwater acoustic sensor networks: research challenges. Journal of Ad Hoc Network 3, 257–279 (2005)
3. Belding-Royer, E.M.: Multi-level hierarchies for scalable ad hoc routing. Wireless Networks 9, 461–478 (2003)
4. Wang, W., Kim, D., Wilson, J., Thuraisingham, B., Wu, W.: A better approximation algorithm for minimum average routing path clustering problem in multi-hop 2-D underwater sensor networks. Discrete Mathematics, Algorithms and Applications 1, 175–191 (2009)
5. Karaboga, D.: An idea based on honey bee swarm for numerical optimization. Technical Report TR06, Computer Engineering Department, Erciyes University, Turkey (2005)
6. Basturk, B., Karaboga, D.: An artificial bee colony (ABC) algorithm for numeric function optimization. In: IEEE Swarm Intelligence Symposium 2006, Indianapolis, Indiana, USA, May 12-14 (2006)
7. Karaboga, D., Basturk, B.: A powerful and efficient algorithm for numerical function optimization: artificial bee colony (ABC) algorithm. Journal of Global Optimization 39, 459–471 (2007)
8. Karaboga, D., Basturk, B.: Artificial Bee Colony (ABC) Optimization Algorithm for Solving Constrained Optimization Problems. In: Melin, P., Castillo, O., Aguilar, L.T., Kacprzyk, J., Pedrycz, W. (eds.) IFSA 2007. LNCS (LNAI), vol. 4529, pp. 789–798. Springer, Heidelberg (2007)
9. Karaboga, D., Basturk, B.: On the performance of artificial bee colony (ABC) algorithm. Applied Soft Computing 8, 687–697 (2008)
10. Singh, A.: An artificial bee colony algorithm for the leaf-constrained minimum spanning tree problem. Applied Soft Computing 9, 625–631 (2009)
11. Pan, Q.-K., Tasgetiren, M.F., Suganthan, P.N., Chua, T.J.: A discrete artificial bee colony algorithm for the lot-streaming flow shop scheduling problem. Information Sciences 181, 2455–2468 (2011)
12. Karaboga, D., Akay, B.: A survey: Algorithms simulating bee swarm intelligence. Artificial Intelligence Review 31, 61–85 (2009)

Zero Knowledge Proof in Secret Sharing Scheme Using Elliptic Curve Cryptography

Anusuya Sardar, Subba Rao Y.V., and RukmaRekha N.

Department of Computer and Information Sciences, University of Hyderabad, Hyderabad, India
{yvsrcs,rrcs}@uohyd.ernet.in

Abstract. In this paper a secured secret sharing scheme has been proposed where the dealer (who distribute shared secrets among the participants and reconstruct the shared secret key) is verified using zero knowledge proof concept by the participants. To protect authenticity of the participants and confidentiality of the secret shares being transferred through the network a signcryption scheme based on elliptic curve cryptography (ECC) which incorporates both the digital signature and encryption scheme in a logical single step is used. It reduces computational cost and communication overhead. As we are using elliptic curved-based zero-knowledge proof, it provides privacy and security more than other existing techniques. The improvement of security is due to the complexity of solving the discrete logarithm problem over elliptic curves.

Keywords: Threshold Secret Sharing, elliptic curve cryptography, trusted dealer, zero-knowledge proofs, authentication, verification, security, signcryption.

1 Introduction

The proposed scheme uses elliptic curve-based zero knowledge proof for verification of trustworthiness of the dealer. Our approach provides higher efficiency and better security and privacy. The proposed scheme also uses elliptic curve cryptography based signcryption scheme [8] which fulfill both the function of digital signature and public key encryption in a logically single step and with a cost significantly lower than the traditional " Signature-then-encryption" to protect the authenticity and confidentiality of the secret shares of the participants transferred through the insecure wireless environment . The paper organization – Some related work is mentioned in section 2. Zero knowledge proof and ZKP for the DL problem are described in section 3. VSS Scheme using ECC Based Signcryption is described in section 4. A new verification scheme using elliptic curve-based zero knowledge proof is presented in section 5. The conclusion and future work is in section 6.

2 Related Work

A.Basu and I.Sengugpta proposed various techniques for dealer verification [8]. Most of the applications have been implemented using other than zero-knowledge proof

P.V. Krishna, M.R. Babu, and E. Ariwa (Eds.): ObCom 2011, Part I, CCIS 269, pp. 220–226, 2012.

techniques for verification purposes. Most of these solutions reveal more information in order to achieve verification.

Our scheme is proposing implementing ZKP using elliptic curve in verification of the dealer. This will increase the security level also, due to the fact that solving the discrete log problem over elliptic curves takes exponential time, as oppose to sub exponential time for discrete logarithm problem [12].

3 Zero-Knowledge Proof

A zero-knowledge proof is an interactive way that a "prover" can prove possession of a certain piece of information (secret) to a "verifier" without revealing it.

General Structure of ZK Protocols –

P: Prover, V: Verifier
P → V: witness
P ← V: challenge
P → V: response

3.1 Properties of Zero-Knowledge Proof

- **Completeness:** If the prover knows the secret, the honest verifier will be convinced of this fact by the prover.
- **Soundness:** If the prover does not know the secret, she cannot convince the honest verifier that she knows the secret, except with some small probability.
- **Zero-knowledge:** If the statement is true, no cheating verifier learns anything about the secret.

3.2 Classical Problems

The problem that cannot be solved in polynomial time but a potential solution can be verified in polynomial time, can be used for the zero-knowledge proof.

There are various classical problems that involve zero-knowledge proofs. These include discrete logarithm problem, square root of an integer modulo n, graph isomorphism, and Integer factorization. In general, these problems belong to a class of problems known as NP problems. There is no known efficient (polynomial time) algorithm to solve any of such problems. However the solution can be verified in polynomial time. Among these we present discrete logarithm problem [13], to be compared to the same problem using elliptic curves.

3.3 Zero Knowledge Proof for the Discrete Logarithm (DL) Problem

If the equation is $b^a = c$ then a is called the discrete logarithm to base b of c. If b and c are known then it is difficult to compute a in a finite field.

Suppose, p: large prime, g : generator for the multiplicative group Z_p, and b: number $\in Z_p$, the Prover wants to prove in zero-knowledge that she knows x such that $g^x = b \pmod p$, without revealing the secret x.

We will present two existing approach. One is Iterative protocol of zero-knowledge proof of the discrete log problem [12] and another is One-round ZKP of DL problem [13].

Initially, Prover and Verifier both know the generator g and b. The Prover claims that she also knows x, the discrete log of b.

Prover (P) (g,b,p,x)		Verifier (g,b,p)
Prover generates random r P calculate $h = g^r \bmod p$ And sends h to V	h ⟹	
	⟸ C	V flips a coin C = H or T
If C = H P sends r to V	r ⟹	Check $g^r = h$
If C = T, P sends $m = x + r$	m ⟹	Check $g^m = b.\ h$
Steps 1-4 are repeated until Verifier is convinced that Prover must know x (with probability $1\text{-}2^{-k}$, for k iterations).		

Fig. 1. Iterative ZKP of Discrete log problem

Thus if prover doesn't know x, the discrete log of b, she can only cheat for any one of the 2 outcomes. By repeating this, verifier can be convinced by the prover.

Prover (P) (g, b, p, x)		Verifier(V) (g, b, p)
	⟸ c	Verifier generates random r V calculate $c = g^r \pmod p$ And sends c to P
Prover calculates $y = c^x \pmod p$ sends y to V	y ⟹	
		Verifier accept if $y = b^r \pmod p$

Fig. 2. One-Round ZKP of Discrete log problem

In one round zero knowledge proof, the protocol runs in one round. The one-round ZKP overcomes the iteration problem. The one-round ZKP is more suitable than the iterative approach. The one round ZKP has better execution-time complexity – saves local computations, less communication cost – exchanges much less information in terms of bits and less latency – exchange fewer messages over the network.

4 Verifiable Secret Sharing Scheme Using ECC Based Signcryption

Atanu Basu and Indranil Sengupta presented a new scheme "Verifiable (t, n) Threshold Secret Sharing Scheme Using ECC Based Signcryption" that give high security and less complexity [8]. This scheme prevents cheating from participants as well as from trusted dealer (which distributes shared secrets and reconstruct shared secret key).

There are three phases in their scheme –

—System Initialization phase (Setup)
—Verification of Dealer
—Reconstruction of secret key

In System Initialization phase, the participants register to the dealer and dealer chooses a secure elliptic curve over finite field, the group private key d_G, the corresponding group public key Q_G. Dealer also chooses its own private key d_D and corresponding public key Q_D and computes private key d_i and the corresponding public key Q_i of each participant and computes secret share, d^s_i for participant P_i and sends to each participant.

In the next phase, when participant need to send their secret share to the dealer then to verify of the dealer, generally participants request for the (t-1) number of the coefficients of the polynomial from the dealer. But in our scheme the dealer is verified using zero knowledge proof based on Elliptic Curve discrete logarithm problem by participants.

In the reconstruction phase, after verification Participants generate signcrypted message of their shares and send to the dealer and dealer performs unsigncryption to retrieve the shares and reconstructs the secret key from the set of shares.

5 Proposed Approach

In our approach the dealer is verified using zero knowledge proof based on elliptic Curve discrete logarithm problem by participants. Here in the verification algorithm dealer wants to prove in zero knowledge that she knows the group private key d_G such that $Q_G = (d_G . B) \bmod q$.

Where Q_G is the Group public key, B is the Base point, d_G is the Group private key (Secret that is not revealed) and q is the order of base point.

Here we have proposed two verification algorithms –

a) The iterative approach of zero-knowledge proof based on elliptic curve discrete logarithm problem.
b) One round zero-knowledge proof based on elliptic curve discrete logarithm problem.

a) In the iterative approach, initially Dealer and participant both know the B, Q_G, q. Now Dealer generates random r where $r \in [1, q - 1]$ and computes $A = (r. B) \bmod q$. Dealer sends A to Participant. Then Participant flips a coin and sends the outcome to Dealer. If it is heads, Dealer sends r to Participant and participant verifies $r. B = A$. If it is tails, Dealer sends $x = (d_G + r)$ to Participant and participant verifies $x. B = Q_G + A$. These steps are repeated until Participant is convinced that Dealer must know d_G with probability of $(1\text{-}2^{-k})$, where k is the number of times these steps are repeated.

	P : Prover , V : Verifier	Dealer (P)	Participant (V)
0		B, Q_G, q, d_G	B, Q_G, q
1	Dealer generates random r	r	
2	Dealer computes $A = (r. B) \bmod q$ and sends A to Participant.	A	A
3	Participant flips a coin c = H or T	c	$c \in [H, T]$
4	If c = H, Dealer sends r to Participant	r	Verifies : $r. B = A$
5	If c = T, Dealer sends $x = d_G + r$	x	Verifies : $x. B = Q_G + A$
6	Steps 1-5 are repeated until Participant is convinced that Dealer must know d_G (with probability $1\text{-}2^{-k}$, for k iterations).		

Fig. 3. Iterative approach of ZKP based on ECDLP

b) In one round zero-knowledge protocol, initially Dealer and participant both know the B, Q_G, q. First, Participant generates a random y and computes $C = y.B \pmod q$. Participant sends C as a challenge to Dealer. Dealer responds by computing $A = d_G .C \pmod q$ and sending A to Participant. Participant can verify the Dealer's response by $A = y. Q_G \pmod q$. The improvement of security is due to the complexity of solving the discrete logarithm problem over elliptic curves and the protocol does not reveal any information about the secret group private key d_G because solving for d_G is infeasible.

	P : Prover , V : Verifier	Dealer (P)	Participant (V)
0		B, Q_G, q, d_G	B, Q_G, q
1	Participant generates a random y		Y
2	Participant computes C = y.B (mod q) and sends C to Dealer.	C	C = y.B
3	Dealer computes A = d_G .C (mod q) and sends A to Participant.	A = d_G .C	A
4	Participant verifies that		A = y. Q_G (mod q)

Fig. 4. One round ZKP based on ECDLP

6 Conclusion and Future Work

Zero-Knowledge Proof is a strong mechanism in an Authentication System. In this paper, we proposed an approach using elliptic curve-based zero-knowledge proofs in a verifiable secret sharing scheme. The drawback in the previous verification approach [8] is, the coefficients (a_j,B) of the polynomial are disclosed to the participants for the verification of the dealer. So after knowing all the values, the participants can easily demand to other participants that he is the honest dealer. Then the system may be no longer secure. To overcome this drawback we have proposed zero knowledge proof based on elliptic curve discrete logarithm problem for verification of the Dealer in the Secret Sharing Scheme that gives more security than the previous approach [8]. It prevents the Dealer to capture the attack efficiently. Also it is based on the elliptic curve cryptography, so it is more efficient than RSA based system. Zero-knowledge proofs techniques are powerful tools in such critical applications for providing both security and privacy at the same time. The improvement of security is due to the higher complexity of solving the discrete logarithm problem over elliptic curves.

The proposed approach covers the following key requirements:

Authentication— It provides user authentication via proven the possession of an authentication secret.

Privacy — The private information (group private key) is not revealed. Only the possession of such information is checked.

Low Cost — One round ZKP reduces computation and communications cost of such system.

Ease of Use — The authentication process is performed easily by Participants.

The same approach can be experimented with other problems like the square root of an integer modulo n, graph isomorphism and integer factorization.

References

1. Shamir, A.: How to share a secret. Communications of the ACM 22(11), 612–613 (1979)
2. Zheng, Y., Imai, H.: How to construct efficient signcryption schemes on elliptic curves. Information Processing Letters 68(5), 227–233 (1998)
3. Feldman, P.: A Practical Scheme for Non-interactive Verifiable Secret Sharing. In: Proc. IEEE Symp. Foundations of Computer Science, pp. 427–437 (1987)
4. Pedersen, T.P.: Non-Interactive and Information-Theoretic Secure Verifiable Secret Sharing. In: Feigenbaum, J. (ed.) CRYPTO 1991. LNCS, vol. 576, pp. 129–140. Springer, Heidelberg (1992)
5. Han, Y., Yang, X., Sun, J., Li, D.: Verifiable Threshold Cryptosystems Based on Elliptic Curve. In: Proc. of ICCNMC 2003, pp. 334–337. IEEE Computer Society (2003)
6. Peng, C., Li, X.: Threshold Signcryption Scheme Based on Elliptic Curve Cryptosystem and Verifiable Secret Sharing. IEEE (2005)
7. Chao, Qun, Fen: An improved authenticated (T,N) threshold , signature encryption scheme based on ECC. IEEE (2006)
8. Basu, A., Sengupta, I.: Verifiable *(t, n)* Threshold Secret Sharing Scheme Using *ECC* Based Signcryption (2010)
9. Cao, Z.-F., Li, J.-G., Li, J.-Z.: A new *(t, n)* threshold signature encryption scheme with specified receiver. Journal of China Institute Communications 24(5), 8–12 (2003)
10. Dai, Y.-J., Yang, C.: (t, n) threshold signature encryption scheme base on elliptic curve cryptosystem. Application Research of Computer 21(9), 142–146 (2004)
11. Stinson, D.: Cryptography: Theory and Practice
12. Almuhammadi, S., Sui, N.T., McLeod, D.: Better Privacy and Security in E-Commerce: Using Elliptic Curve-Based Zero-Knowledge Proofs. In: 2004 IEEE International Conference on E-Commerce Technology (CEC 2004), pp. 299–302 (2004)
13. Almuhammadi, S., Neuman, C.: Security and Privacy Using One-Round Zero-Knowledge Proofs. In: 2005 IEEE International Conference on E-Commerce Technology (CEC 2004) (2005)
14. Han, Y., Yang, X., Hu, J.: Threshold signcryption based on elliptic curve (IEEE). IEEE (2009)
15. Zheng, Y.L.: Signcryption and Its Application in Efficient Public Key Solutions. In: Proceedings of Information Security Workshop, pp. 201–218 (1997)
16. Dai, Y., Yang, C.: A (t,n) threshold signcryption scheme based on ECC. Aplication Research of Computers 9, 142–143, 146 (2004)

On the Design and Realization of Non-Synchronous Frequency Hopping Spread Spectrum for Securing Data over Mobile and Computer Networks

Javaid A. Sheikh[1,*], Shabir A. Parah[1], and G. Mohiuddin Bhat[2]

[1] Deptt. of Electronics and I.T., University of Kashmir, Srinagar - India
[2] University Science Instrumentation Centre, University of Kashmir, Srinagar - India
sjavaid_29ku@yahoo.co.in

Abstract. We propose and investigated the novel scheme of non-synchronous method of Frequency Hopping Spread Spectrum modulation and demodulation scheme. The frequency hopping spread spectrum is most widely used spread spectrum technique in wideband wireless communications due to its numerous advantages like elimination of near far effect in cellular mobile communications. The strict timing synchronization is major requirement in frequency hopping spread spectrum. The hopping pattern at transmitting as well as receiving end should be synchronous to each other. This can be achieved to use same spreading codes both at transmitting and receiving end. In practical communication systems it is very difficult to achieve code synchronization when the signal is supposed to transmit over frequency selective channels. In this paper a novel scheme has been proposed in which two Frequency Modulation (FM) demodulators (CXA1619BS) one at transmitting end and another at receiving end have been used to produce voice signal having same frequency and amplitude, due to random behavior of voice signal (only unvoiced part was taken) a chaotic signal was generated and used as spreading code. The digitally controlled chaos oscillator has been used for spreading code generation. Since in two different geographical regions FM signals received at transmitting as well as receiving end at the same time are having same frequency and amplitude, therefore do not require synchronous codes for proper detection of received data. So the proposed technique solves one of the major problems of synchronization in practical communication systems. The proposed scheme was tested experimentally using hardware module and results are presented in the form of various waveforms.

Keywords: Frequency Hopping Spread Spectrum, Synchronization, FM demodulator, chaotic signal oscillator.

1 Introduction

Wireless personal communication systems enable geographically dispersed users to exchange information using a portable terminal, such as a hand held transceiver.

* Corresponding author.

P.V. Krishna, M.R. Babu, and E. Ariwa (Eds.): ObCom 2011, Part I, CCIS 269, pp. 227–236, 2012.

Often, the system engineer's design objective is to maximize the transmission rate and number of simultaneous users (capacity) under the constraints of robustness, power consumption and hardware complexity. The tradeoffs among capacity, reliability, signal power, and cost of equipment can be complex.

Future generations of wireless personal communication systems will be based on digital transmission technology. Digital technology has important advantages over traditional analog technology. With digital technology, radio communication systems can be designed to meet more stringent transmission reliability requirements. Furthermore, digital technology enables more efficient sharing of channel resources when multiple users need to access the system through a common channel simultaneously. The use of radio telephones has evolved rapidly and grown explosively in the last few decades. This evolution of wireless systems can be viewed to have occurred in different stages. The main force driving the evolution is an increasing public demand for wireless services. To meet this ever increasing demand, better communication technologies are required to increase network capacity, to improve quality of service (QOS), and to introduce new service features.

As the public appetite for wireless services gets bigger, the capacity of first generation systems, even with improvements, soon became insufficient to satisfy the demand in some areas. This led to the development of the second generation digital wireless systems, built in the 1980's and the 1990's. In this period, digital technology is implemented to improve the system capacity several times over traditional analog systems. At this stage, vehicular cellular radio and cordless telephone are developed and optimized separately to provide service to users with different mobility patterns and communication needs. The typical vehicular radio systems include Global System for Mobile Communications (GSM) in Europe and Digital AMPS (IS-54) in the United States; the typical cordless telephone systems include CT-2 in Europe and some spread spectrum products in the United States.

Among second generation systems, one of the new technologies used to boost system capacity is Code Division Multiple Access (CDMA). CDMA, based on spread spectrum technology, is developed to utilize the available spectrum more efficiently in multi-cell networks. The history of spread spectrum (SS) communications can be traced all the way back to its military origin during early phases of World War II [1]. In military applications, spread spectrum technology is used to combat intentional jamming by an enemy transmitter. The approach to defeat jamming is to transmit over many signal coordinates with large-bandwidth signals, such that the jammer cannot achieve large jammer-to-signal power ratio in all the coordinates. The anti-jamming properties of SS signals are well investigated and documented [4].

Since spread-spectrum uses large-bandwidth signals that result in the apparent inefficient use of the radio spectrum, people had assumed that commercial applications of SS radios were impractical [1][4]. Cooper and Nettleton, in 1978, were the first ones to recognize that digital spread-spectrum radio had a potentially higher capacity for mobile radio applications than the analog narrowband radios used at that time [6]. More research on digital SS mobile radio soon followed in 1980. By the late 1980's and early 1990's, advances in Very-Large-Scale Integrated (VLSI) circuit technologies has made low-cost implementation of spread-spectrum radio possible while the popularity of mobile radio has spurred the market demand for high-capacity systems. These factors contributed to a renewed interest in the application of spread-spectrum technology for mobile radio. The widespread commercial development of SS wireless systems today is sparked by two key events. One of the events is the 1985 FCC ruling which allows the unlicensed use of spread spectrum radio in ISM bands, which include the 902 to 928 MHz band. Another key event is the well-publicized Qualcomm Direct Sequence Spread Spectrum (DS/SS) and frequency Hopping Spread Spectrum (FH/SS) CDMA system which has led to the adoption of a second U.S. digital cellular standard, IS-95 [8]. Commercial spread-spectrum radios are now being used in indoor office applications, such as wireless local area networks (WLANs), and wireless cordless phone (PBX) systems. Among the interesting outdoor applications is the Federal Emergency Management Agency's (FEMA) experimental use of spread-spectrum radios to transmit digital video. In some situations, unlicensed spread spectrum radio is used as an emergency backup to wired lines and in many cases; they are used as a more economical substitute for digital leased lines.

In this paper a novel scheme based on chaotic Frequency Hopping Spread Spectrum (CFH-SS) has been used. The fast hopping spread spectrum is presently the most widely used technique for both commercial and military applications. However, the implementation of this scheme demands high speed frequency synthesizers and moreover code synchronization between transmitter and receiver at high frequency is very difficult to achieve. The proposed scheme does not require strict timing synchronization and hence can be used for securing data over computer and mobile networks. The Frequency Modulated (FM) signal available at the transmitter and receiver has been demodulated using CXA1619BS module to generate similar synchronization signals after using adequate signal processing techniques at the transmitter and receiver ends.

2 Chaos in Secure Communications

Chaos theory is applied in many scientific disciplines: Mathematics, Programming, Computer science, Physics, Engineering and Robotics. Chaotic behavior has been observed In the laboratory in a variety of systems including electrical circuits and electronic circuits as proposed by numerous researchers. Chaos theory provides a new way of looking at complexity in nature and enables us to analyze 'Random process' that were thought to be completely unsolvable. Recent development in this field has turned to practical applications in a variety of disciplines such as secure communications, Crytography, spread spectrum modulation as spreading signal.

Communications is an application Chaos theory is aimed to provide security and spreading in the transmission of information performed through telecommunications technologies. In chaos communications security (i.e., privacy) is based on the complex behavior. Some properties of Chaotic dynamics, such as complex behavior, noise like dynamics (Pseudorandom noise) and Spread Spectrum, are used to encode data, on the other hand, being chaos a deterministic phenomenon, it is possible to decode data using this determinism. In practice, implementations of chaos communications devices resort to synchronization of chaos oscillator at both transmitting and receiving end. Since in CDMA based multiple access technology each user is assigned a particular code . One of the major hurdles in Code Division Multiple Access Technology is the synchronization of code used at transmitting end and one utilized at receiving end. For very long, numerous contributions of varying success have been made by researchers around the world for the synchronization of multiple access communication systems. Dynamical (Chaotic) based synchronization method is shown to be capable of providing high quality synchronization, which is essential for multiple access communication technology. The Pseudo-random (PN) Code has been widely used in spread spectrum modulation for achieving synchronization and security besides other applications, but due to lack of complexity of pseudo-random codes it cannot find applications in areas like multiuser communication system, Global Positioning Systems, Radar Tracking Systems.

Chaotic Systems are dynamical systems which show complex behavior. One of the defining attributes of chaotic systems is the sensitive dependence on initial conditions. Time series generated from chaotic systems are wideband in nature and noise like in appearance (Strogatz S.H., 2001). Because of these special properties, chaotic systems are being widely studied for the multi-user secure communication technology. Efficient utilization of bandwidth is the most common technique used for electronically communicating sensitive information. However, this requires that the receiver know the “code” used by the sender to encrypt the message. In classical secure communication systems, this key, which is typically a sequence of numbers, is usually send over a secure channel while the encrypted messages is transmitted over a public channel. It would, be of course very useful, if the key need not to be transmitted at all. The spread spectrum communication has been used in satellite communication for TV broadcasting, Telephony and bundled data tracking, Military communication, and data relay for space missions (Halford K.W. and Brandit-Parce M., 2000). Satellite can provide service to mobile users as well as fixed ground users while the terrestrial networks (fiber and wireless) can only cover terrestrial users on several approaches have recently been proposed for secure communications using synthesized chaotic systems. Chaotic Communications based on the transmission of messages encoded on a chaotic waveform are a subject of great current interest, attracting increasingly intensive research activities compared to conventional communication systems; there are several unique features of chaotic communication systems. Potential benefits of chaotic communications include efficient use of the bandwidth of a communication channel, utilization of the intrinsic non-linearties in communication devices, large signal modulation for efficient use of carrier power, reduced number of components in a system, and security of communication by chaotic encryption. Some of the chaotic circuits available in the literature are as under (a and b).

All the chaotic circuits reported so far are analog in nature, which is very difficult to use in digital communications. In this paper a novel digital method of implementing chaos oscillator has been used both at transmitting and receiving end as shown in figure c.

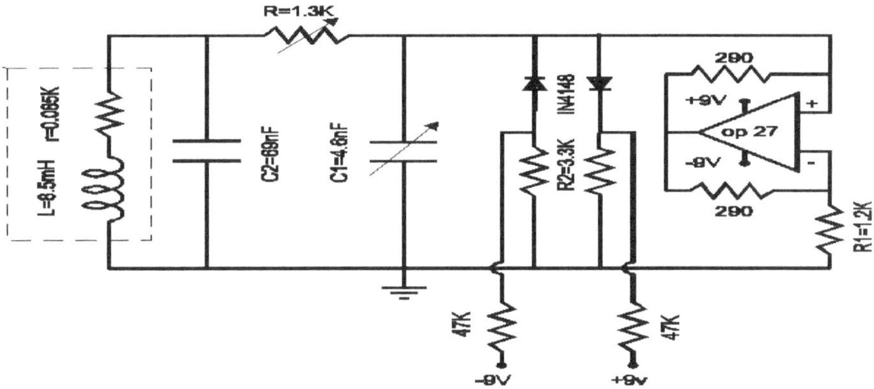

Fig. a. Basic Chaotic Circuit

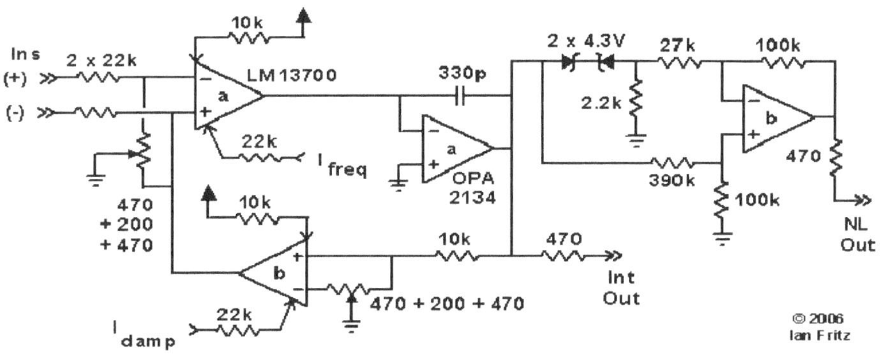

Fig. b. Cyclic Chaotic Circuit

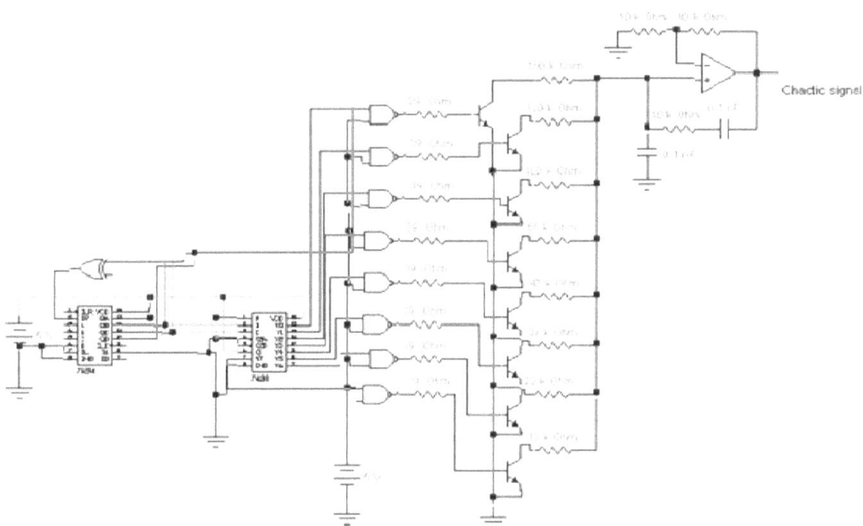

Fig. c. Proposed Digitally controlled Chaos Oscillator

The Proposed technique for chaotic signal generator has been experimentally verified by using readily available non-linear and linear IC's. The conventional PN code generated by Linear Feedback Shift Register (LFSR) has been used for controlling the operation of decoder circuitry consists of array decoder and array of transistors and logic gates to digitally simulate variable resistor for Chaos oscillator which in turn is used to produce output of varying frequency in a random fashion. The decoder and digitally controlled variable resistor have also been implemented using readily available IC's. The resultant chaotic signal generator generates a wide band of from of frequencies from few KHZ to megahertz range.

3 Proposed Non- Synchronous Frequency Hopping Spread Spectrum for Securing Data over Computer and Mobile Networks

The block diagram of the proposed scheme consisting of transmitter and receiver are shown in figures 1 and 2 respectively and the waveforms obtained at various checkpoints are shown in figure 3– 9 respectively. The whole work has been divided into number of blocks. The novel chaotic phenomena have been used to generate random signals. The FM signal of a given frequency has been received with the help CXA1619BS FM receiver. To adjust gain and simultaneously amplify the weak FM signal. The signal is then given to the automatic gain control unit. The circuit also contains a clamping circuitry, which provides the clamped output. The clamped output of the clamper is given as input to the preceding analog to digital converter which makes it compatible with ADC by taking it as a positive voltage reference to the ADC. The ADC provides a digital output, which is fed to the code converter. The code generator works as heart of the system. The most important functional block of code generator is chaos oscillator, which consists of array of AND gates transistor arrays and PN code generator. To generate chaotic signal using chaos oscillator. The amplitude as well as frequency shows variation in accordance with the received signal. In conventional chaos oscillators, the non-linear resistors are used to get the desired result. The non-linear devices like diodes, transistors have been used in chaos oscillators. The value of the simulated resistor is proportional to the digital equivalent of the incoming analog FM signal. The chaos oscillator generates a wide band signal whose frequency varies in a random manner depending upon the incoming information (i.e. demodulated FM signal) and PN code. In this way a new circuit based on frequency modulation signal and pseudo random code is used .The circuitry constitutes the digital AND gates whose one input is the generated PN sequence and another is the ADC output. The output of the AND gates is taken through transistor which is then fed to the inverting terminal of operational amplifier. The output of this operational amplifier is given to another analog to digital converter. This ADC provides a digital signal and act as input to the digital frequency synthesizer, which generates a frequency-hopped signal whose frequency hops over a wide range of frequencies. The important aspect of the resulting hopped signal is that the frequency hops in highly unpredictable manner, which is highly desirable for designing secure message communication system. This frequency hoped signal has been used to modulate incoming data at the transmitter.

At the receiving end the frequency hopped signal has been generated using the same mechanism as at the transmitter and successfully used to demodulate the signal by mixing it with the transmitted signal to get the desired signal.

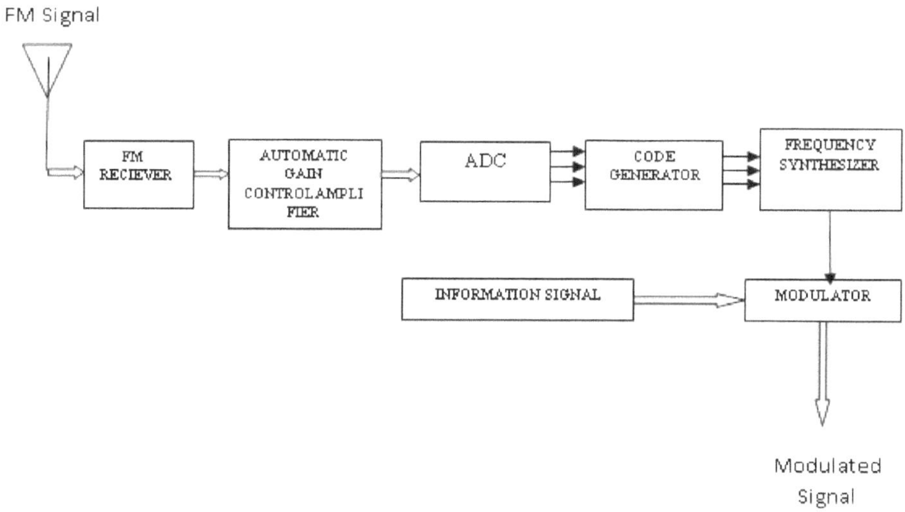

Fig. 1. Schematic of Non-Synchronous FH-SS Transmitter

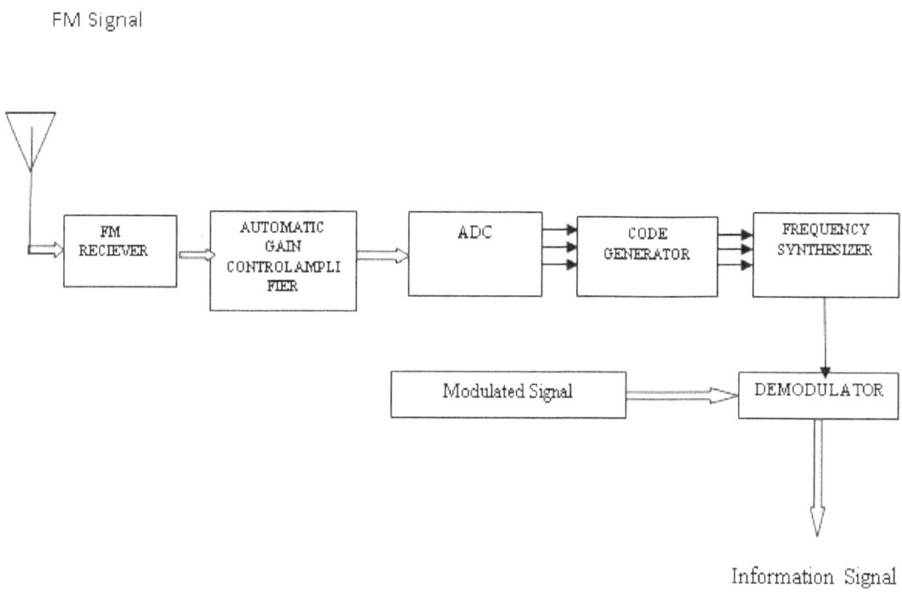

Fig. 2. Schematic of Non-Synchronous FH-SS Receiver

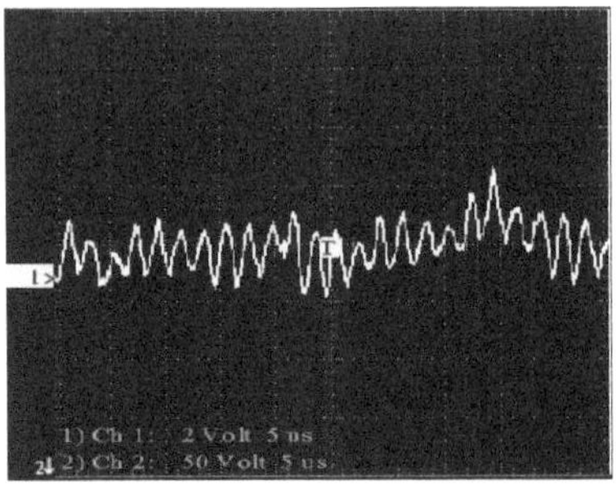

Fig. 3. Wave Form of FM Signal at Transmitter

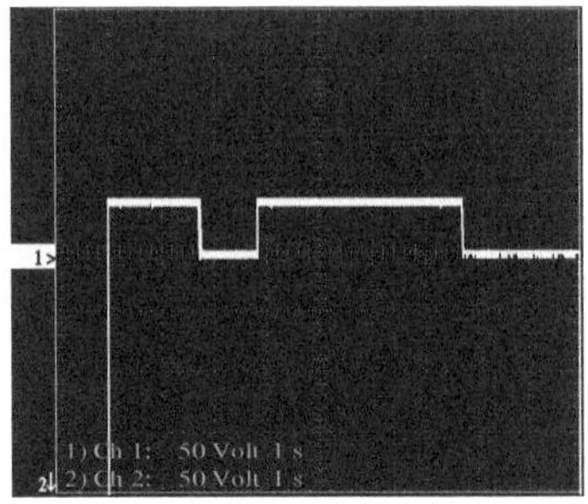

Fig. 4. Digital Equivalent of Chaotic Signal at Transmitter

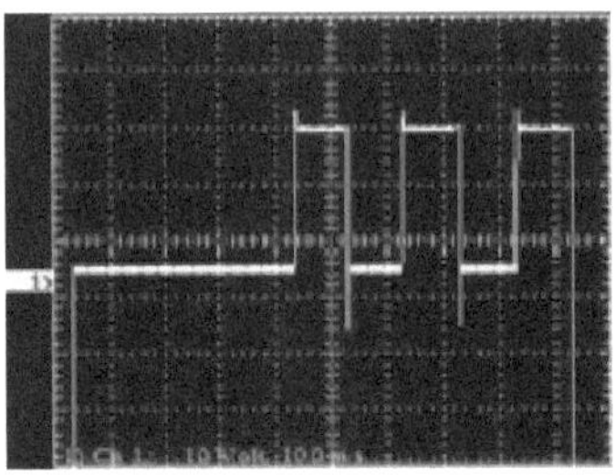

Fig. 5. Waveform of Frequency Synthesizer

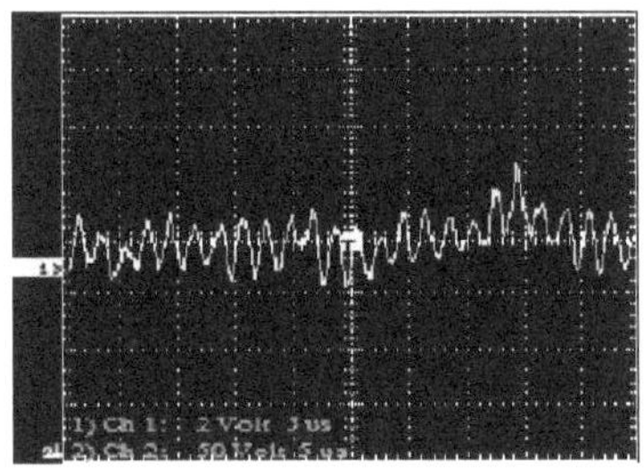

Fig. 6. Wave Form of FM Signal at Receiver

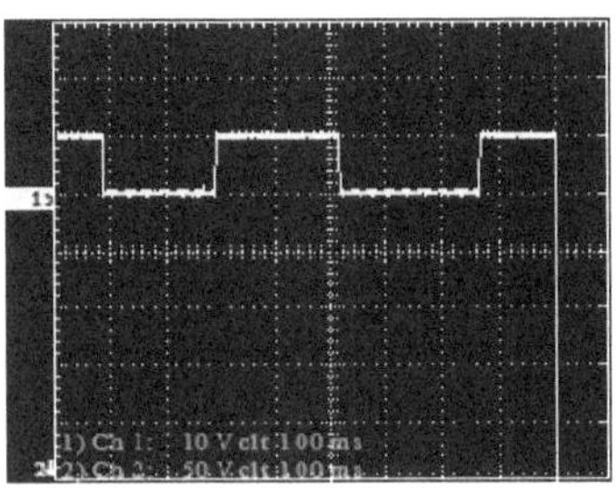

Fig. 7. Digital Equivalent of Chaotic Signal at Receiver

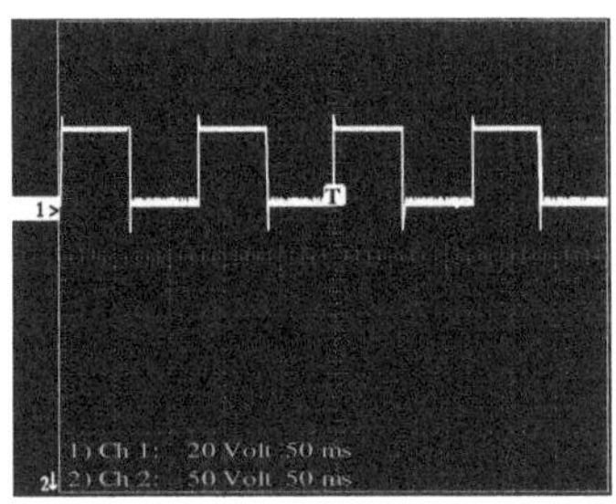

Fig. 8. Waveform of Frequency Synthesizer at the Receiver

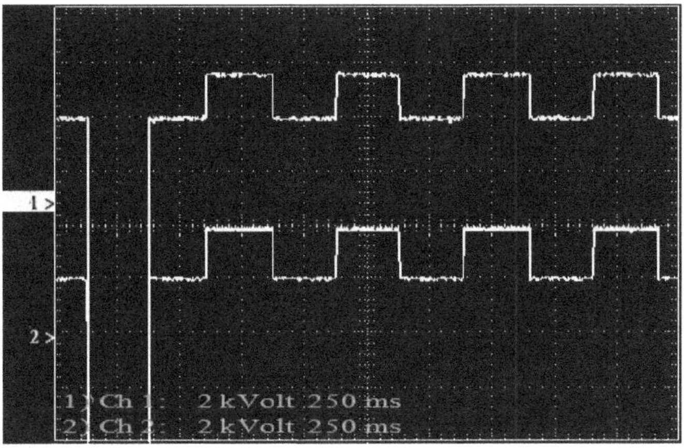

Fig. 9. waveforms of Transmitted and Received signals
Upper: Transmitted
Lower: Received

4 Conclusion

In real world communication scenarios, the transmitter and/or the receiver may be in motion. In a mobile radio situation in which the transmitter is fixed in position while the receiver is moving, the direct line between the transmitter and receiver may be obstructed by buildings. At ultra-high frequencies and above, therefore, the mode of propagation of the electromagnetic energy from transmitter to receiver is largely by way of scattering. The scattering process alters the amplitude as well as phase of the received signal and therefore it is very difficult to properly demodulate the received signal. Moreover to demodulate the received signal a synchronous carrier which should be same in amplitude as well as phase to that of the carrier used at the transmitting end. In this paper a novel scheme has been proposed in which two demodulated FM signals has been used both at transmitting and receiving end to generate same spreading codes having same frequency and phase. By utilizing these spreading codes both at transmitting as well as receiving end eliminates one of the severe problems of synchronization in practical communication systems.

References

1. Miyazaki, N., Komine, T., Hatakawa, Y., Suzuki, T.: Development and Experiments of 100MHz Bandwidth Testbed for IMT-Advanced Systems. In: IEEE 66th Vehicular Technology Conference, VTC-2007, Fall 2007, September 30-October 3, pp. 1317–1321 (2007)
2. Dahlman, E., Gudmundson, B., Nilsson, M., Skold, J.: UMTS/IMT-2000 Based on Wideband CDMA. IEEE Communications Magazine 36, 70–80 (1998)
3. Adachi, F., Grag, D., Takaoka, S., Takeda, K.: Broadband CDMA techniques. IEEE Wireless Commun., Mag. 12(2), 8–18 (2005)

4. Dahlman, E., Beming, P., Knutsson, J., Ovesjo, F., Persson, M., Roobol, C.: WCDMA- The Radio Interface for Future Mobile Multimedia Communications. IEEE Transactions on Vehicular Technology 47(4), 1105–1118 (1998)
5. Third Generation Partnership Project Technical Specification Group Radio Access Network Working Group 1, Spreading and Modulation TS 25.213 V2.1.2 (April 1999)
6. Third Generation Partnership Project Technical Specification Group Radio Access Network Working Group 1, Physical Channels and Mapping of Transport Channels onto Physical Channels (FDD), TS 25.211 V2.2.1 (August 1999)
7. Dinan, E.H., Jabbari, B.: Spreading Codes for Direct Sequence CDMA and Wideband CDMA Cellular Networks. IEEE Communications Magazine 36, 48–54 (1998)
8. Rappaport, T.S.: Wireless Communications: Principles and Practice. Pr entice Hall PTR, Upper Saddle River (1996)
9. Third Generation Partnership Project Technical Specification Group Radio Access Network Working Group 1, Multiplexing and Channel Coding (FDD), TS 25.212 V2.0.1 (August 1999)
10. Alpha Concept Group, Wideband Direct Sequence CDMA (WCDMA) Evaluation Document (3.0), Tdoc SMG 905/97, Madrid, Spain, December 15-19 (1997)
11. Liberti, J.C., Rappaport, T.S.: Analysis of CDMA Cellular Radio Systems Employing Adaptive Antennas. Ph.D dissertation, Virginia Tech, Blacksburg, VA (September 1995)
12. Alamouti, S.M.: A Simple Transmit Diversity Technique for Wireless Communications. IEEE Journal on Selected Areas in Communications 16, 1451–1458 (1998)
13. Goni, U.S., Turkmani, A.M.D.: BER performance of a direct-sequence CDMA system in multipath fading mobile radio channels with Rake reception. In: The Proceedings of Vehicular Technology Conference, June 8-10, vol. 2, pp. 747–751 (1994)
14. Biglieri, E., Prokias, J., Shamai, S.: Fading channels: Information- theoretic and communication aspects. IEEE Trans. Info, Theory 44(6), 2619–2692 (1998)
15. Shannon, C.E.: Communication in the Presence of Noise. Proc. IRE 37, 10–21; reprinted in the Key Papers on Information Theory. J

Improved Object Lookup in Unstructured Peer-to-Peer Overlay Networks

Chittaranjan Hota[1], Gaurav K.[1], Prasanna G.[1], Narayana M.V.S.[1], Hrushikesha Mohanty[2], and Muttukrishnan Rajarajan[3]

[1] Birla Institute of Technology and Science-Pilani, Hyderabad Campus, Hyderabad, India
{hota,f2008437,f2008215,sathya}@bits-hyderabad.ac.in
[2] University of Hyderabad, Hyderabad, India
[3] City University London, London EC1V 0HB
hmcs@uohyd.ernet.in, R.Muttukrishnan@city.ac.uk

Abstract. Effectiveness of unstructured P2P overlays highly depends on the efficiency and scalability of their lookup algorithms. However, how to quickly discover or lookup an object or a file that a peer is looking for in a large scale P2P network with efficiency remains a challenging research problem. In this paper we dynamically select peers with high priority of having objects while reducing the overall network traffic. Our experiments have demonstrated that our method can significantly shorten the search path and result in a higher peer search performance. We achieved a success rate of 85 percentage in locating a file when the number of peers are large in the topology with a reduction of 40 percentage of search traffic.

Keywords: Peer-to-Peer, Overlay Networks, Lookup; Priority, Internet, Backtrack.

1 Introduction

The lookup problem in a P2P overlay refers to finding any given data item in a scalable manner. Lookup in unstructured P2P overlay networks happens by forwarding messages to neighbors. Quickly locating interested objects in such a large P2P system is not a trivial task. However, how to find the right information and resource in a large-scale P2P network has remained a critical problem [1,2]. In an unstructured overlay, nodes share files as per their wish. Files are present at random locations. Unstructured overlays use flooding [3], random walks [4], iterative deepening search [4, 5], modified breadth first search (BFS) [6] etc. to lookup content stored on other overlay peers. Structured overlays use Distributed Hash Table (DHT) as a substrate using which any data object can be located in O (logN) overlay hops on average where N is the number of peers in the system [7]. DHT based overlays use techniques like partitioning id space [8], leaf set [9] etc. for the lookup process. In this work we have addressed the lookup problem in unstructured peer to peer overlays.

P.V. Krishna, M.R. Babu, and E. Ariwa (Eds.): ObCom 2011, Part I, CCIS 269, pp. 237–244, 2012.

The rest of the paper is organized as follows. Section 2 discusses the related work done in unstructured lookup, followed by our algorithm in Sec. 3. Section 4 describes our P2P simulation results, and Sec 5 compares our results with other algorithms. We conclude our work in Section 6.

2 Related Work

Gnutella [3] uses a fully decentralized search mechanism which is known as Flooding. In flooding, the query is forwarded to every neighbor node with a certain TTL limit. Advantage in this approach is that initial results are reported very fast. The disadvantage is that the traffic generated increases exponentially at every hop. Lv et al. [4] propose a method for addressing the TTL selection problem which they call it as 'expanding ring' method. Requester node searches with increasing TTLs until a success is found. The results show that the method reduces the number of messages at the cost of delay in getting the response. The use of random walk method proposed in this paper uses a query forwarded to a randomly chosen neighbor at each hop until the object is found. k-random walkers can be used to reduce the delay. It is claimed that k-walkers after T-steps reach roughly the same number of nodes as 1-walker after kT steps. This way by using k-walkers, the delay is reduced by a factor of k. Zhang et al. [11] propose a local adaptive routing protocol driven by query interest among peers. Our approach here enhances the flooding and random walk by proposing a heuristics to improve the search performance.

3 Proposed Algorithm

3.1 Basic Idea

Let us consider five nodes forming an unstructured network as shown in Fig.2. If a search query is initiated by a node say node "1", then the neighboring node to which this query will be forwarded is decided by a priority function as given below:

$$P(k) = (0.4 \times T) + (0.4 \times N) + (0.2 \times R), \tag{3.1}$$

where, T = Time since the node has joined the network (in seconds), N = Total number of files in the file list of the node, and R = Rating associated with a node.

As we know from the normal behavior of peers, the more time the node is alive,the more it is good for getting the file,it will be more available for sharing files on the network to other peers. The more the number of files shared by a particular node,the more probability that it will have the file to be searched. Rating is used so that no node misuses the network. As an if a node which always takes or downloads files from others, but do not share relevant files (files which are of no use) then every time the node is visited and it doesn't have the file to be searched it's rating decreases by 1. So its priority goes on decreasing and a point will come where the rating decreases beyond certain threshold, and the node is removed from the network. We have taken the priority of rating as half of the other two because of simple reason that the rating is used to remove the greedy nodes whereas the other two parameters (T and N) are used to find the file to be searched.

Initially when a node joins the network, its rating (R) is set to 100, and this rating is incremented or decremented during the course of time based on whether a search query has been successfully evaluated at that node (If the file is found, rating increases by one and if it is not found then rating decreases by one). Another feature included is building up of an advertisement list for a node that initiates the search query. So as the search query traverses through the intermediate nodes to its destination, the file list contents are appended to the advertisement list, which can be used by the node's later search queries, thereby reducing the network congestion and time required to locate the node in future searches. In order to improve the look up process in the advertisement list, the lists of all the nodes in the network are periodically updated at fixed time intervals, removing the contents of the free rider node(s) (Node having the least rating in the topology).

3.2 Finding Neighbors Using Priority

When a node initiates a search query for a file which is located at another node, node with highest priority is selected for forwarding the query. Now that this node again decides the node to which this query will be forwarded on the basis of priority. Likewise, the process continues and finally query reaches desired node where the content is found. During this process, the file list contents of the intermediate nodes are added to the advertisement lists of nodes which initiated the search for future reference.

Now if suppose the same node again initiates the same query, then first the contents of advertisement list are looked up to find if there is a match. For a successful result, the contents are retrieved through the shortest possible path from destination to source.

3.2.1 Algorithms

Algorithm 1. Priority Calculation

```
for each neighbor 'j' adjacent to node 'k'
 {
  if( A[k-1][j] ==1 )
    for (each node in backtrack list 'B')
             if (( 'j' in list 'B') and (j != (k-1)))
                 A[k-1][j] = 1;
               else
                 priority = 0.4*j.time + 0.4*j.file + 0.2*j.rating;
```

```
                A[k-1][j] = priority;
                flag = FALSE;
if( flag is FALSE )
    maximum_priority -> A[k-1][0];
for (each node 'j' in the topology)
    if (maximum_priority < A[k-1][j] )
                    maximum_priority = A[k-1][j];
                    l = j;
   return l;
}
```

Algorithm 2. Search using Priority

```
flag = FALSE;
l = priority_func(k)
if(l exists)
{
   add l to backtrack list B;
   fopen(local_advertisementfile of l);
  while(!eof)
  {
    if(search_query=file_content)
    flag = TRUE; }
  if(flag)
  {
  send ResponseMsg to sourceNode;
  increment the rating of node l by 1;
   }
  else
  {
   fopen(remote_logfile of l)
   while(!eof)
   {
      if(search_query=file_content)
      flag = TRUE;
    }
   if(flag)
     send ResponseMsg to sourceNode;
   else
     forward search to neighbors of node l;
   decrement the rating of node l by 1;
  }
 }
 if (l has no neighbors)
 then backtrack and chose node with second best priority;
 repeat this process for all the nodes in the network}
```

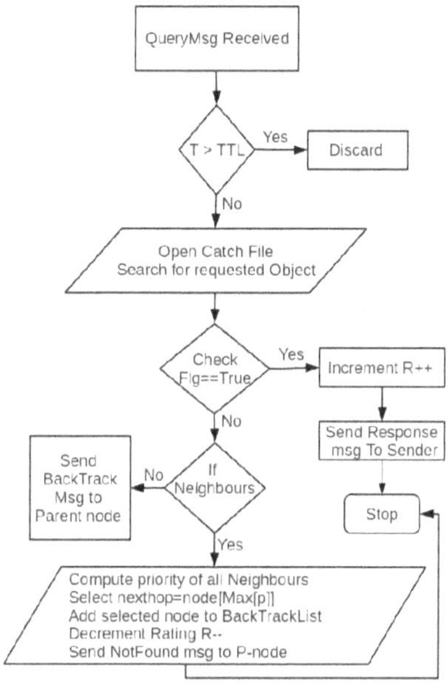

Fig. 1. Flow Diagram for Object lookup search by using priority

4 Simulation

We have used the UNIX Socket - API with C language to build the peer to peer network. Since in peer-to-peer network every node acts as a server as well as a client, so we built an application with create(), accept(), bind(), connect() and listen() functions which are described below. We ran our simulations over Linux machines. We used a random function for the purpose of simulating peers and storing files on the peers. Our peer-to-peer program ran over different Linux machines and we gathered our results by carrying out varied set of nodes in the network from time to time both as number of nodes, and number of files available at different peers. Whenever a new peer joins a network ,it is provided a unique id (socket port number) and the log file is updated with this new peer entry which will be helpful in letting know how much time a node is alive in the network. An initial rating of 100 is provided and its priority is calculated by the no of files it is willing to share with others. This priority dynamically changes from time to time.

As an example let us consider the Fig.2 as a network consisting of five nodes, which have arrived in the overlay at the same time. So, once the topology is set, all the nodes have the same initial rating of 100 as shown in Table 4.1. New nodes are given an initial rating of 100 which increases or decreases depending on whether a file is searched or not. If a node falls below a specific rating (while doing our simulation we set this parameter to 25) then that peer is considered as selfish and removed from the network. Every time a node enters into the network, its log time is stored and time alive is calculated. Every time a node leaves, its entry time from the log file is removed.

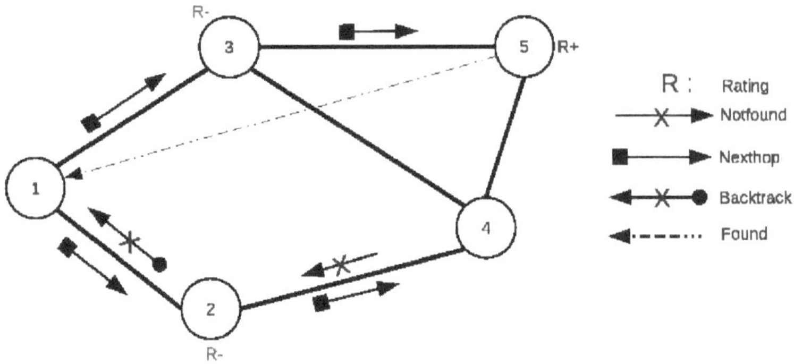

Fig. 2. An example Network with Time alive, Number of files, and Rating

Table 4.1

Node	Time alive	No of files	Rating
Node1	1 sec	5	100
Node2	1 sec	4	100
Node3	1 sec	3	100
Node4	1 sec	3	100
Node5	1 sec	6	100

Table 4.2

Node	Time alive	No of files	Rating
Node1	1.2 sec	5	100
Node2	1.2 sec	4	99
Node3	1.2 sec	3	99
Node4	1.2 sec	3	100
Node5	1.2 sec	6	101

For understanding our approach, we describe here an example. In Fig.2, if node 1 initiates the search query for a file present at node 5 after 1 second, then based on the values of time alive, number of files and rating, node 2 is selected for forwarding the query. Likewise the priority is calculated for neighbor of node 2, and then forwarded to highest priority node, which in this case turns out to be node 3. Finally, node 3 forwards the query to node 5 where the file is found. Thus after a successful match for the file, the table contents would be updated as shown in Table 4.2 (time taken to run the algorithm is 0.2 seconds).

5 Result Analysis

5.1 Traffic as a metric

When we consider the traffic in the network as the number of nodes increases, heuristic based search results in less congestion as compared to flooding and random walk. Fig.3 plots average number of messages (network traffic) in our approach (heuristic search) and other two i.e. Random walk and flooding. When we consider the traffic in the network as the number of nodes increases, heuristic

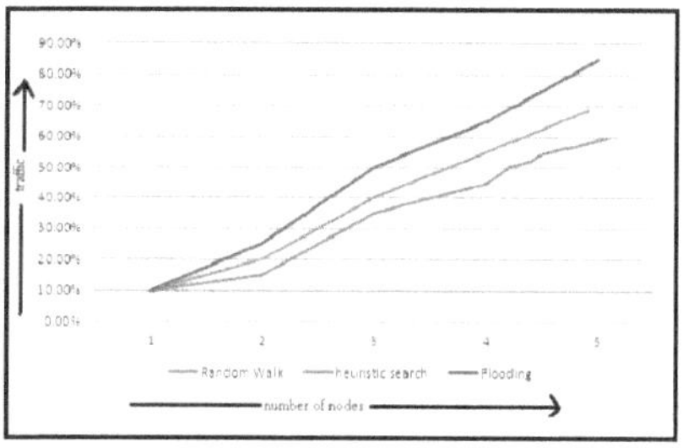

Fig. 3. Number of nodes Vs Network Traffic

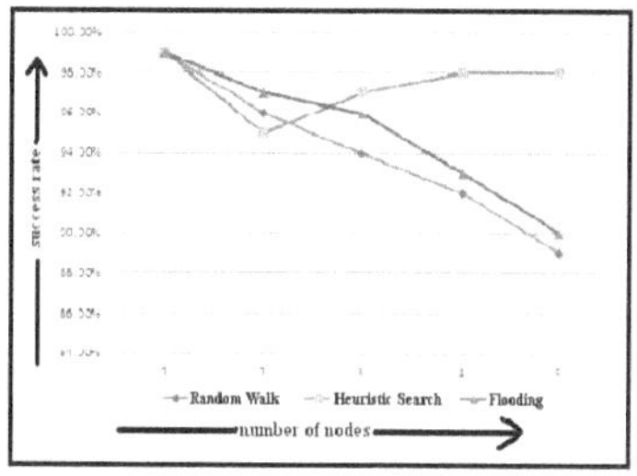

Fig. 4. Number of nodes Vs Success Rate

based search results in less congestion as compared to flooding and random walk. Figure 3 plots average number of messages (network traffic) in our approach (heuristic search) and other two i.e. Random walk and flooding.

5.2 Success Rate as a Metric

Also, the success rate (chances) of finding a file gradually increases for heuristic based search with the number of nodes in the network, which in the case of random walk or flooding is observed as decreasing because of inherent limitations of these two approaches. The simulation results below in Figure 4 justifies this claim.

5.3 Hop Count as a Metric

A simulation using 25 nodes was carried out to compare the number of hops in random walk and heuristic search by taking random searches of files from random sources. As shown in Fig.5, a graph between the number of hops (Y axis) and the number of ticks/search queries (X axis) for random walk (RW) and heuristic search (HS) shows that with the increase in the number of ticks, the hop count decreases for heuristic search. In Fig. 6, the average number of documents found by different queries from peers is plotted and we also found that this count is better as compared to that in the random walk.

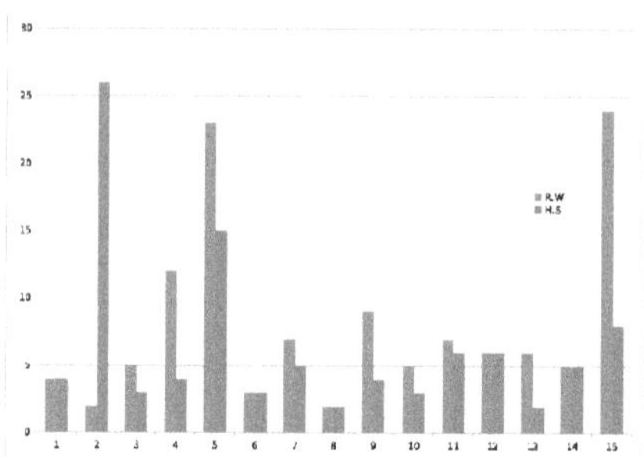

Fig. 5. Hop count Vs Ticks

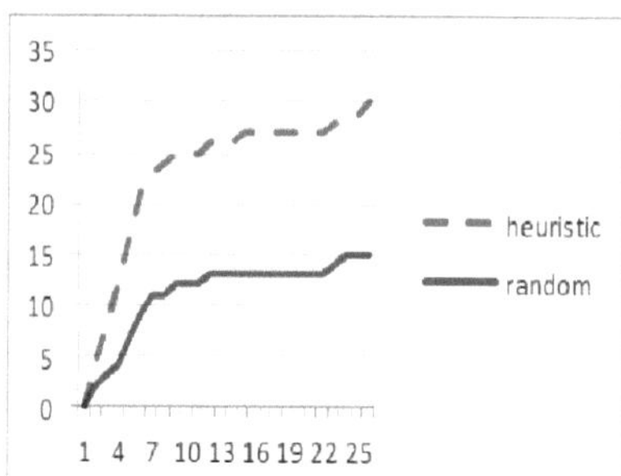

Fig. 6. Average number of documents found

6 Conclusion

In this paper we described a novel approach of using a heuristic function to evaluate the betterness of a neighbor amongst all neighbors while dynamically selecting a path to lookup an object in an unstructured peer-to-peer overlay network. Our simulation results indicate that file lookup success rate in P2P is high (85%) when the number of nodes are large enough while reducing the average traffic in the network to a great extent (40%). Therefore, we safely assume that a heuristic based search algorithm is a better approach to unstructured peer-to-peer lookup problem as compared to flooding or random walk that are extensively used in the literature. We plan to explore these in future.

Acknowledgment. This work was supported in part by Grant number 39/118 (2010) for Scientific research under Major Research Project grant from University Grants Commission, New Delhi, INDIA.

References

[1] Kim, J.K., Kim, H.K., Cho, Y.H.: A user oriented content recommendation system in peer-to-peer architecture. Expert Systems with Applications 34(1), 300–312 (2008)
[2] Yang, S.J.H., Zhang, J., Lin, C., Tsai, J.J.P.: Improving peer-to-peer search performance through Intelligent social search. Expert Systems with Applications, 10312–10324 (2009)
[3] Gnutella Protocol Specification Version 0.4, `http://www9.limewire.com/developer/gnutella-protocol-0.4pdf`
[4] Lv, C., Cao, P., Cohen, E., Li, K., Shenker, S.: Search and Replication in Unstructured Peer-to-Peer Networks. In: Proceedings of the 16th International Conference on Supercomputing, June 22-26. ACM Press, New York (2002)
[5] Yang, B., Garcia-Molina, H.: Improving Search in Peer-to-Peer Networks. In: Proceedings of the 22nd International Conference on Distributed Computing Systems (ICDCS 2002),), Vienna, Austria, July 02-05. IEEE Computer Society, Washington DC (2002)
[6] Kalogeraki, V., Gunopulos, D., Zeinalipour-Yazti, D.: A Local Search Mechanism for Peer-to-Peer Networks. In: Proceedings of the 11th International Conference on Information and Knowledge Management, McLean, November 04-09. ACM Press, New York (2003)
[7] Lua, E.K., Crowcroft, J., Pias, M., Sharma, R., Lim, S.: A Survey and Comparison of Peer-to-Peer Overlay Network Schemes. IEEE Communications Surveys and Tutorials 7, 72–93 (2005)
[8] Stoica, I., Morris, R., Liben-Nowell, D., Karger, D., Kaashoek, M.F., Dabek, F., Balakrishnan, H.: Chord: A scalable peer-to-peer lookup service for internet applications. IEEE/ACM Transactions on Networking 11, 17–32 (2003)
[9] Zhao, B.Y., Huang, L., Rhea, S.C., Stribling, J., Joseph, A.D., Kubiatowicz, J.D.: Tapestry: A global-scale overlay for rapid service deployment. IEEE Journal on Selected Areas in Communications 22, 41–53 (2003)
[10] Mashayekhi, H., Habibi, J.: Combining search and trust models in unstructured peer-to-peer networks. Journal of Supercomputing 53, 66–85 (2010)
[11] Zhang, M., Yang, J.Q.: An efficient searching scheme in unstructured P2P networks. Key Engineering Materials 439-440, 865–869 (2010)

Ontology Construction for Polycystic Kidney Disease

Saurabh Parmar, S.K. Jain, Gagandeep Kaur, and Anand Kumar

Computer Engineering Department,
National Institute of Technology, Kurukshetra, 136119, India
saurabh_1only1@yahoo.co.in, skj_nith@yahoo.com,
{deep.gagan102,anandncst777}@gmail.com

Abstract. Ontologies and knowledge bases are fundamental cornerstones in semantic search systems based on which efficient web services and sophisticated search mechanisms are designed. High quality domain ontologies are essential for successful employment of semantic Web services. However, acquisition of ontologies is difficult and costly, thus hindering the development of this field. In this work, the knowledge acquisition problem in the semantic Web is cast as the task of ontology construction. We construct an ontology for "polycystic kidney disease" from domain text by a pattern based method which requires minimum human intervention. We also create ontology manually to present the evaluation results of the constructed ontology.

Keywords: Ontology, ontology construction, patterns, concept extraction.

1 Introduction

During the past years, a wide range of ontologies has been constructed by a large amount of researchers and developers world-wide. Those ontologies have different purposes and belong to different areas of activities such as management of enterprise knowledge and competences, Bioinformatics, e-commerce, etc. Ontologies are used in these research fields to collect and organize knowledge and adapt semantics to be comprehensible by machines. Some researchers now propose approaches for the construction of ontologies, which are based on patterns that have the advantage of constructing well structured ontologies. These approaches of pattern based method have the advantages of easy and fast construction, also have minimum human intervention. Study says patterns are best suited for domain ontology construction.

Important issues for ontology builders are, reducing the manual tasks required to construct ontologies, reducing the involvement of domain-expert knowledge and constructing well structured ontologies. As a result, this work is focused on construction of ontology for "polycystic kidney disease" by pattern based method and from unstructured text. Tools used are open sources and free to use for educational purposes so that anyone can use and construct ontologies by this method. Polycystic kidney disease is a disease in which multiple cysts form on the single or both kidneys of the suffering person. This disease occurred due to the malfunctioned gene given by the parents to the child so it is also called genetic disease.

P.V. Krishna, M.R. Babu, and E. Ariwa (Eds.): ObCom 2011, Part I, CCIS 269, pp. 245–254, 2012.

The remainder of this paper is structured as follows. First review the background of the ontology construction task. Second we provide brief information about the domain of ontology which is *polycystic kidney disease*. Third we describe approach of ontology construction that is methodology. Fourth we give the results and evaluations of constructed ontology. Finally draws conclusions and discuss future work.

2 Background

This section presents ontology definitions, ontology construction, ontology construction methods and related work along with the ontology construction methods.

2.1 Ontology

The term *ontology* comes from the Greek *ontologia* and means "talking" (-logia) about "being" or "individual" (on / onto-). Gruber (1993) [1], define the ontology as "an explicit specification of a conceptualization" (where a conceptualization "is an abstract, simplified view of the world that we wish to represent for some purpose").

Domain knowledge provided by domain experts includes the understanding of a dataset, relationships among variables, normal range of variables and so on. Ontology captures the domain concepts and their relations; therefore, it provides an alternative knowledge source than domain experts. Domain ontology, provides a common and unambiguous understanding of a domain or both the users and the system to communicate with each other via a set of representational primitives.

2.2 Construction of Ontology

Effective extraction of domain knowledge from sources becomes the major approach to knowledge acquisition. It is necessary to develop methods and techniques that allow reducing the effort necessary for the knowledge acquisition process, being this the goal of the ontology construction. Alexander Maedche and Steffen Staab [10] distinguish different ontology construction approaches focus on the type of source used, like ontology construction from text, ontology construction from the dictionary, ontology construction from the knowledge base, ontology construction from semi-structured schemata and ontology construction from relational schemata.

In this work we have concentrated on the method of ontology construction from text.

2.2.1 Construction of Ontology from Texts

Ontology is extracted from the text by the application of the natural language processing technology. As human language is a primary mode of knowledge transfer, ontology construction from relevant text collections seems indeed a viable option as illustrated by systems like TextToOnto [11], ASIUM [12] and Ontolearn [13].

Methods of Construction of Ontology from Text. Here is the classification of existing ontology learning methods in the literature into six categories based on the techniques deployed, discussed below.

1. Pattern-based Approach - Lexico-syntactic methods exploit regular expressions or repetitive patterns in natural languages. A well-known example is the Hearst-patterns [6] which are originally used to acquire hyponyms from large text corpora. Cimiano et al [4] utilize a method called "Learning by Googling" to exploit the potential of large Web search engines to match patterns. SPRAT [14] combines aspects from traditional named entity recognition. TextOntoEx [15] constructs ontology from natural domain text using a semantic pattern based approach.
2. Association Rule-based Approach - Association rules were initially defined on the database field as follows: "*Given a set of transactions, where each transaction is a set of literals (called items), an association rule is an expression of the form X implies Y, where X and Y are sets of items. The intuitive meaning of such a rule is that transactions of the database which contain X tend to contain Y*" (Agrawall et al., 1993) [8]. The association rules method for ontology learning has been originally described and evaluated in (Maedche and Staab, 2000) [11].
3. Clustering and Classification - Statistical machine learning techniques such as clustering and classification have also been adopted to learn ontologies out of unstructured text. Harris' distributional hypothesis [5] states that similar words tend to occur in similar contexts [2]. D. Faure selected the method of the concept clustering [9], and its basic cluster includes some fixed words phrase, made up of the form of the verb and the preposition.
4. Information Extraction - An IE application will take texts (structured or unstructured) as input and generate structured and unambiguous data. The simplest and most reliable IE technology is named entity recognition and has been deployed in some of the semantic search systems [19, 20].
5. Probabilistic-based Approaches - Probabilistic Latent Semantic Indexing (PLSA) [7] and Latent Dirichlet Allocation (LDA) [3] are both models are based upon the idea that instead of modeling relations between documents and words, documents are modeled as mixtures of topics, where a topic is a probability distribution over words.
6. Data Co-occurrence Analysis - Sanderson et al [11] utilize a method based on an idea that a term A subsumes B if the documents in which B occurs are (or nearly) a subset of the documents in which A occurs.

3 Domain of Ontology Construction

For this work we have chosen the domain named as *polycystic kidney disease*. Polycystic kidney disease (PKD) is a disease in which multiple cysts form on the single or both kidneys of the suffering person. This disease occurred due to the malfunctioned gene given by the parents to the child so it is also called genetic disease. When cysts form in the kidneys, they are filled with fluid. PKD cysts result in reduced kidney function and lead to kidney failure also called end-stage renal disease (ESRD). This disease till now is incurable.

4 Methodology

This section introduces the method of ontology construction. Ontology construction methods are described in section 2.2.1; we use pattern-based method which requires matching of patterns with the concepts extracted from the domain text. This method has three phases to generate concepts and relations as ontology elements.

4.1 Pattern-Based Method

In this work, we used a generalized and improved procedure to create domain ontologies from textual resources while keeping manual intervention to the minimum. In this method first domain text is collected and patterns are generated with the help of tool Text2Onto. Then NLP is performed on domain text and possible concepts and relations are extracted. These concepts are matched with the patterns and matched concepts are accepted with their relations as the final concepts and relations of the ontology.

The whole process can be summarized in following phases:

1. Pattern Generation Phase: - Firstly patterns are generated from the collected domain text with the help of tool Text2Onto with some manual refinement. This is a seed file containing the terms related to the domain. Later this file is used for matching the concepts extracted from the NLP processed text to confirm it as final concept of ontology.

This phase comprises following processes:

a. Text Collection for Domain - To collect text corpus for the domain, research papers and government websites related to domain are used. These data are stored in plain text file for further processing.
b. Pattern Generation - To generate patterns we used concepts given by the tool Text2Onto. Text2Onto is centered on the Probabilistic Ontology Model which stores the results of the different ontology learning algorithms. The output of Text2Onto contains concepts, subclass-of relations and other outputs but we used only concepts to generate the pattern. These patterns are refined and stored in a text file which we called seed file. Table 1 shows some generated patterns.

Table 1. Patterns generated by Text2Onto tool

dialysis, cyst infection, parents, cyst, child, liver, abdomen, fetus, spleen, infection, kidney transplantation, ultrasound imaging, tract infection, cyst growth etc.

2. Concept and Relation Extraction Phase: - Concept extraction is a field of the information extraction domain. In this phase possible concepts and relations between them are extracted from the domain text. For this work natural language preprocessing has performed and then extract noun as possible concepts and verb as their relations by writing pattern matching rules and corresponding action part. These possible concepts and relations are matched with the patterns in next phase. For this task we rely on robust tools from the GATE (General Architecture for Text Engineering) architecture [18] and use following steps:

   a. Document Pre-processing - The collected domain text is processed through a set of state-of-the-art NLP tools: tokenizer, part-of-speech tagger, and syntactic parser. For this purpose we used GATE's built-in IE component set called ANNIE (a Nearly-New Information Extraction System). We have run ANNIE on the domain text and execute algorithm in the following order to have semantically tagged output of text: ANNIE Tokenizer, sentence splitter, POS tagger.
   b. Concept and Relation Discovery - The concept and relation discovery module extracts the concepts and relations of interest using the NLP information extracted from the domain text. For this work, we focus only on noun concepts and their relations.

      Every noun in a sentence is considered to be a potential new concept and the verb between those nouns as a potential relation between concepts. In this work, we consider only those nouns which are generated by following grammatical rules:
      - ❖ Noun composed of many nouns (e.g. kidney disease),
      - ❖ Noun composed of adjective and noun (e.g. genetic disorder),
      - ❖ Noun composed of verb with -ing suffix (e.g. purifying),
      - ❖ Noun contains the preposition (e.g. cysts in liver).

      Even though, nouns can be generated with many grammatical rules more than the above shown rules, but according to some rules entire noun could not be an ontological concept.

      For extracting semantic relations, we use a verb to express the relation between concepts that they are co-occurrence. In this process, the system will extract the verbs that are significant for the interested domain.

      To carry out this step we have used the GATE information extraction system. While GATE comes with a default information extraction system called ANNIE, it is only partially relevant to our purpose. The ANNIE system identifies generic concepts such as person names, locations, organization, dates, etc. Therefore we had to develop and adapt new rules for our system. For this purpose we have used JAPE (Java Annotation Patterns Engine) grammar. A JAPE grammar consists of a set of phases, each of which consists of a set of pattern/action rules.

      For achieving required concepts and relations we have constructed a jape file called *extraction* with extension .jape with the help of any text editor and write our own rule to extract above described nouns as concepts and verbs as relations between those concepts. Output of this step contains XML file from which tags and other annotations are filtered and used for later matching with patterns in the next phase.

3. Pattern Matching: - In this phase possible concepts extracted in previous step are matched with pattern created by Text2Onto. We write matching programs in java for this purpose. Here matching is identified when the whole word from extracted concepts is matched with the word in patterns. Like extracted concept *Polycystic kidney disease* is identified as a match with the pattern *kidney* present in seed file.

Below in fig. 1, we show the abstract pictorial view of the three phases.

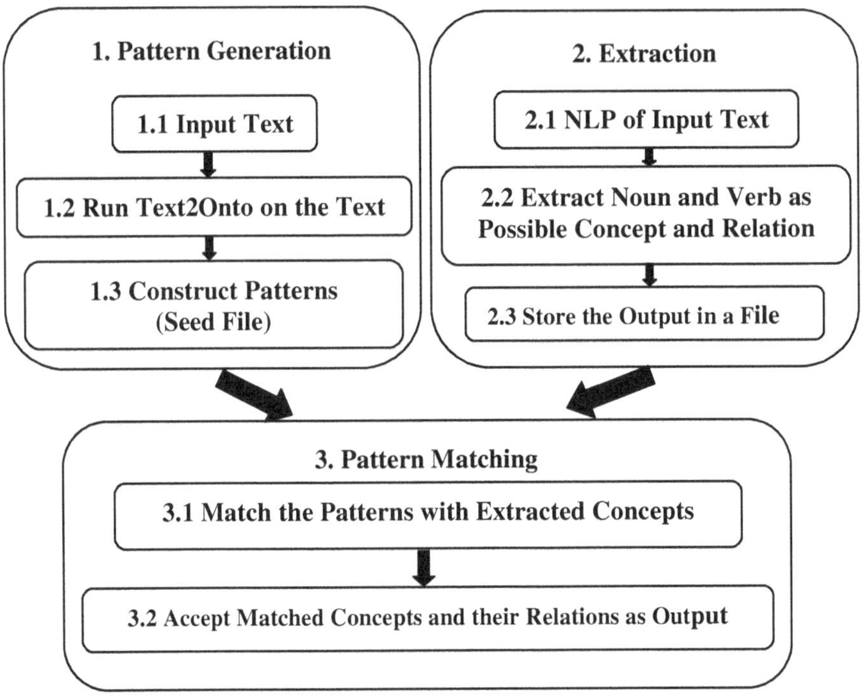

Fig. 1. Abstract view of the methodology

5 Results and Evaluations

This section shows the results of the ontology construction task and the evaluations of the results. Result consists of the concepts and relations of the ontology. The graphical representation of the constructed ontology from these concepts and relations is also shown in this section. We also performed evaluations of constructed ontology which comprises these concepts and relations.

5.1 Results

In this work we have constructed ontology for *polycystic kidney disease* by generating concepts and relations between those concepts from the domain text. In section 4 we have described the phases which are needed for this ontology construction task.

We get the final output after these phases in terms of concepts and relations. The output after execution of three phases, described in section 4.1, is shown in table 2.

Table 2. Ontology concepts and relations between them

Concept	Relation	Concept
polycystic kidney disease	is	genetic disorder
kidney	filters	wastes
kidney failure	is called	end-stage renal disease
genetic disease	occur through	spontaneous mutation
autosomal recessive PKD	has	disease gene
nephrons	are	tiny filtering units
high blood pressure	develop in	patient
ultrasound imaging	detect	cysts in the kidneys

The graphical representation of one part of constructed ontology is shown in fig. 2.

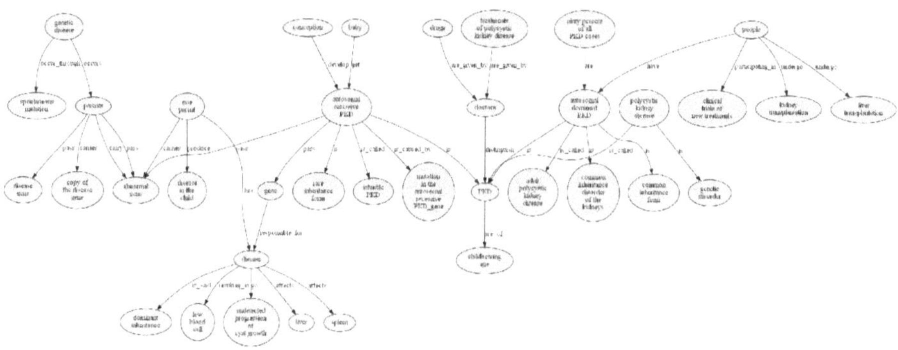

Fig. 2. One part of constructed ontology

We have also handcrafted ontology from the domain text which we called manually constructed ontology for the evaluation of this work. Manually constructed ontology judges and evaluates the performance of generated ontology by used methodology.

5.2 Evaluations

In order to measure the reliability of the constructed ontology, experiments have been conducted for evaluating;

1. The recall, precision and F-measure of the system.
2. Comparison of precision and recall of concepts generated by used method against the concepts generated with the help of tool Text2Onto.

Recall and precision are used for evaluating the relevance of the results obtained by the used method. They are defined by the following formulas:

Recall - A measure of the ability of a system to present all relevant items.

$$\text{Recall} = \frac{\text{number of relevant items retrieved}}{\text{number of relevant items in collection}}$$

Precision - A measure of the ability of a system to present only relevant items.

$$\text{Precision} = \frac{\text{number of relevant items retrieved}}{\text{total number of items retrieved}}$$

F-measure - A measure that combines precision and recall is the harmonic mean of precision and recall, the traditional F-measure or balanced F-score:

$$F = 2 * \frac{\text{precision} * \text{recall}}{\text{precision} + \text{recall}}$$

This is also known as the F_1 measure, because recall and precision are evenly weighted.

In this work we have calculated precision, recall and f-measure of the final concepts and the relations between them by the help of manually constructed concepts and relations which worked as total relevant concepts and relations of the system as used in the formula. Here we considered only those relations which are used to relate two concepts. Table 3 shows the evaluation results.

Table 3. Evaluation results of extracted concepts and relation

	Precision (%)	Recall (%)	F-measure (%)
Concept	60.04	77.9	67.63
Relation	63	71.4	66.9

After calculating precision and recall of our results, we have also calculated precision, recall and f-measure of the concepts generated by the Text2Onto tool. We compare its results with our results. This comparison is shown in the table 4 below.

Table 4. Comparison of our results with Text2Onto in terms of generated concepts

	Manual	Total Extracted	Correct	Precision (%)	Recall (%)	F-measure (%)
Used Method	231	298	180	60.04	77.9	67.63
Text2Onto	231	238	94	39.49	40.6	40.03

It seems that the cleanness of the ontology is not of major importance for the ontology construction task. Even after concepts, that are not included in the final ontology, are often useful to give an insight in the domain itself and to guide the ontology construction task. We should therefore concentrate on increasing the recall of the concept extraction process even at the expense of its precision.

6 Conclusion and Future Scope

This section includes descriptions and concluding remarks of the results and evaluations. It also provides the future scope and directions of this work briefly.

6.1 Conclusion

The semantic Web community has produced a great number of ontology construction methods and techniques, nevertheless, these methods have not been implemented for various domain ontology constructions except a few. Here we construct the ontology for *polycystic kidney disease* by using the text resources with a pattern based method which requires minimum human intervention and manual modification. Initially possible concepts are extracted by writing pattern matching rules and corresponding action part, which is also called linguistically based pattern matching, with the help of JAPE grammar and matched with patterns to have them as final concepts.

We defined evaluation metrics to assess the quality of the constructed ontology using the methodology used in this work. The evaluation shows good results as the precision and recall values of generated concepts and relations are around 60-70%. We also defined evaluation metrics for the concept generated from the tool Text2Onto and compared its results with our results. This comparison shows that the results of used methodology are far better than the results of Text2Onto tool used alone. The results can show better results if the seed file which contains pattern, is constructed more precisely. Even though, method used in this work to construct the ontology is simple and fast; these results show that a good amount of knowledge can be extracted by the method while keeping the manual intervention in the process minimum.

6.2 Future Scope

While the evaluation results show promising performance of the generated concepts and relations, this work has some limitations. Constructed ontology does not deal with the synonym that is required in ontology. Synonym like disease and illness can be used interchangeably so that a search for polycystic kidney illness in place of polycystic kidney disease can give the same results.

Also in extraction task of noun for having possible concept we have not handled noun splitting in which if a conjunction (and, or) or some noun-delimiting punctuation like "," or ":" is found with any noun, split the noun to create two concepts at the point of the conjunction or punctuation. Ontology can be represented by many representation languages like OWL, Frame-based, description logic based etc. This representation task is not performed however the constructed ontology is represented graphically by the node as a concept and edge as a relation between those concepts.

This ontology is not verified by any domain expert. Domain experts are the people who belong from the domain and have enough and sufficient knowledge about the domain. These tasks after completion will lead to a complete and verified ontology however this work will guide to basic ontology construction task for people who are novice in the ontology construction process.

References

1. Gruber, T.: A translation approach to portable ontologies. Knowledge Acquisition 5(2), 199–220 (1993)
2. Biemann, C.: Ontology learning from text: A survey of methods. LDV Forum 20(2), 75–93 (2005)
3. Blei, D.M., Ng, A.Y., Jordan, M.I.: Latent dirichlet allocation. Journal of Machine Learning Research 3, 993–1022 (2003)
4. Cimiano, P., Staab, S.: Learning by googling. SIGKDD Explorations 6(2), 24–33 (2004)
5. Harris, Z.: Mathematical Structures of Language. Wiley (1968)
6. Hearst, M.A.: Automatic acquisition of hyponyms from large text corpora. In: COLING, pp. 539–545 (1992)
7. Hofmann, T.: Probabilistic latent semantic analysis. In: UAI (1999)
8. Agrawal, R., Imielinski, T., Swami, A.: Mining Association Rules between Sets of Items in Large Databases. In: ACM SIGMOD, pp. 207–216 (1993)
9. Faure, D., Poibeau, T.: First experiments of using semantic knowledge learned by ASIUM for information extraction task using INDEX. In: Proceeding of the Workshop on Ontology Learning, 14th European Conference on Artificial Intelligence (ECAI 2000), Berlin (2000)
10. Maedche, A., Volzr, R.: The text-to-onto ontology extraction and maintenance environment. In: Proceeding of the ICDM Workshop on Integrating Data Mining and Knowledge Management (2001)
11. Sanderson, M., Croft, W.B.: Deriving concept hierarchies from text. In: SIGIR, pp. 206–213 (1999)
12. Faure, D., Poibeau, T.: First experiments of using semantic knowledge learned by ASIUM for information extraction task using INTEX. In: Proceedings of the ECAI 2000 Workshop Ontology Learning (2000)
13. Missikoff, M., Navigli, R., Velardi, P.: Integrated approach to web technology learning and engineering. IEEE Computer 35(11), 60–63 (2002)
14. Maynard, D., Funk, A., Peters, W.: SPRAT: a tool for automatic semantic pattern-based ontology population. In: Proceedings of International Conference for Digital Libraries and the Semantic Web, Trento, Italy (2009)
15. Rafea, A., Hassan H.A., Dahab, M.Y.: TextOntoEx: Automatic Ontology Construction from Natural English Text. Intelligence and Machine Learning (2006)
16. Mithun, B., Dan, M., Marta, T., Marian, O.: SemiAutomatic Domain Ontology Creation from Text Resources. In: Proceedings of the Seventh Conference on International Language Resources and Evaluation, LREC (2010)
17. Völker, J., York, S.: Task T3.3 Data-driven Change Discovery, EU-IST Integrated Project (IP) IST-2003-506826 SEKT (2005)
18. Developing Language Processing Components with GATE Version 6 (a User Guide) For GATE version 6.2 (2011)
19. Kiryako, A., Popov, B., Terziev, I., Manov, D., Ognyanoff, D.: Semantic annotation, indexing and retrieval. J. Web Semantics 2(1), 49–79 (2004)
20. Cimiano, P., Völker, J.: Text2Onto. In: Montoyo, A., Muńoz, R., Métais, E. (eds.) NLDB 2005. LNCS, vol. 3513, pp. 227–238. Springer, Heidelberg (2005)

An Intelligent Recommendation System for Individual and Group of Mobile Marketplace Users Based on the Influence of Items' Features among User Profile

Amer A. Sallam, Siba K. Udgata, and Vineet Padmanabhan

Department of Computer & Information Sciences, A.I Lab,
500046, Hyderabad, India
amer.sallam@gmail.com, {udgatacs,vineetcs}@uohyd.ernet.in

Abstract. With the expansion of the wireless services, the number of mobile users has rapidly increased and the quantity of information on the internet and in wireless medium has also increased exponentially. This much information becomes difficult to be monitored by users well as searching for specific data may cost a lot in terms of time. Moreover, in the mobile scenario, only simple search and browsing functions are available due to limited computing power of a mobile phone. Therefore, it is more preferable to let the desirable information find the customers rather than to let them search for specific information when it is needed. This can be realized by integrating personalized user preferences along with justification recommendation system such that necessary information find the mobile user and alleviate the burden of search for that information when it is needed. This paper proposes an effective recommender system that can help consumers formulate better purchasing decision by incorporating support for user features. This system is not only recommends items to user based on their interest, but also attempt to recommend the nearest location place of the item. The proposed framework has the potentiality to increase consumer satisfaction, enhance consumer/company loyalty, and boost overall sales by giving justification and creditability to the products that have high degree of interest to consumers. The results show a significant promise in the system's ability to make accurate recommendations to the users.

Keywords: Mobile Market-Place, User Profile, Items Features, Weight and Similarity, and Intelligent Recommendation.

1 Introduction

The increasing complexity of information on the wired and wireless networks has made the recommender system as essential tools for users in a variety of information seeking or m-commerce activities. Recommender systems help overcome the information overload problem by exposing users to the most interesting items in a brief and clear form, and by offering novelty, surprise and relevance. Currently, there are

P.V. Krishna, M.R. Babu, and E. Ariwa (Eds.): ObCom 2011, Part I, CCIS 269, pp. 255–267, 2012.

several recommendation techniques such as, collaborative filtering recommendation, content-based recommendation, demographic-based recommendation, utility-based recommendation, knowledge-based recommendation and association rule- based recommendation [1]. Recommender systems are applied in a variety of application domains, namely education, business, healthcare, entertainment, and so on. However, such recommender systems have only aimed to enhance their accuracy of recommendations [2] by improving their algorithms, but they also should provide high quality of justification via combining the content influence of item's features along with the data of user and items. The content and rating data are able to disclose the information of features influence among user interest. However, the activities observation of the influence style [3] has shown better accuracy than the nearest neighbor style [4], as it allows users to precisely predict their obvious view of an item. In addition, the rapid growths of recommender systems along with communication technologies have increased the perceived credibility [5], [6] of the marketplace, thus leading users to buy more items. That is considered as a great help from the user's point of view as it facilitates the way of finding interested items. However, the ever-increasing marketplace is still required smarter recommender systems to help users obtain items that best satisfy their interest. To attain this requirement, many recommendation systems have been built for this, especially to assist individual users in filtering and selecting items based on their respective personal preferences.

Undoubtedly, the marketplaces or service providers are usually having multiple groups of users. Therefore, the recommendation systems are expected to not only provide a personalized item for individuals, but also be able to recommend items to multiple users. This paper deals with these requirements, proposing an intelligent model of hybrid justifiable recommender system. This system has the ability of offering a range of justifications for a proposed recommendation made for individual and group of users alike, based on their geographical location and personal preferences. This system is capable to take into account the dependency of features influence among the preferences majority of users, and the reasonability of justification that gives credibility to the recommendation.

The rest of the paper is organized as follows: Section 2 discusses previous work relevant to this paper; Section 3 contains the problem description; Section 4 provides the prototype implementation of the proposed approach; Section 5 discusses result; and Section 6 concludes the paper.

2 Related Work

Recommender systems provide much potential for electronic and mobile commerce applications. Customizing information content upon an individual's needs or groups of users' interests and providing more personalized justifiable recommendation is one of the most important goals of the electronic and mobile commerce activities. However, recommender systems are able to recommend items of interest to users based on preferences they have expressed, either explicitly or implicitly. The explicit processes could be carried through explicit ratings of users who have rated the items in the past.

In such recommendation, the user is required to rate given items for recommending new items that have been highly rated by similar users. This type of recommendation is called Collaborative Filtering (CF), which is observed to be the most widely used recommender systems [7]. It explicitly uses preference information such as product ratings, comments, or registered attributes of interest and also the identification information such as name, address, e- mail and phone number [1]. By contrast, the content of the dynamic information implicitly attempts to provide the dynamic information that describes the situation of items and users rather than to look further on other users' opinions. Such a recommendation is known as content based (CB) [8]. Recently, many researchers have tried to integrate CB with CF [2], [9], [10]. Those hybridized approaches have gained a lot of attention and shown a promising success [5]. In fact, hybrid recommendations were extended to knowledge-based techniques for the purposes of improving the quality of recommendations and reducing the effect of the traditional CF cold-start problem. However, those recommender systems are still in need for involving the justification quality of recommendation that is required in electronic and mobile domains. In an attempt to address this requirement, few recommender systems have been built in recent years to make the recommendations more adequate and serviceable. Further, different mechanisms have been used through those systems to fulfill the needs of justification and enhance the accuracy of recommendation, i.e., nearest neighbor [4], influence style and keyword-based [3]. In fact, our approach aims to provide a list of justifiable recommendations to a group of users by merging users and items features profiles and finding the similarity within sub-clusters of users and the weighted sub-clusters of features as well. Based on the previous recommendations, system is also able to provide a justifiable recommendation for each user based on their location.

3 Problem Description

The problem addressed in this paper is how to provide recommendations for a group of users. Here, we subdivide a mobile market place into distinct subsets of users where any subset may conceivably be selected as groups or individual target. This leads to the creation of a distinct justifiable recommendation according to the particular locations and preferences of specific group. We address this problem by collecting and processing different attributes of users based on their geographical location and rating related information of item feature. Such an issue is meant for finding dependencies among items and users for disclosing their rating behaviors. Then, we apply weighting mechanism on the user's features to show the features that are more interesting to each user. A subsequent step is to find the clusters of similar users and measure the clustering accuracy to provide accurate justifiable recommendation. This is done by observing rating patterns of users in same cluster vs. those from different clusters. Here, we identify items based on their feature similarity that are selected together by sufficiently many users. Finally, we find out the dependencies between user location and item location to give the suitable recommendation based on the common location.

4 The Proposed Approach

4.1 Building User(S) Profile

As shown in Fig. (1-c), user profile $P(U_j, f_n)$ consists of rating data and content data as shown on Fig. (1-a) & (1-b) respectively. Rating data $R(U_n, i_k)$, represents the rating data given by user U for a specific item I whereas content data $C(I_k, f_n)$, represents the features f for an item I. The values of rating data of I could easily reflect and disclose the user's behavior and show the degree of their interest in a particular item. However, such data is still lacking and unable to explain what precisely a user prefers most in a specific item. Therefore, it is necessary to use the content data. Moreover, considering values for such features will help to figure out the features that are more important and preferable by each user.

For instance, combining the features of rating items for each user individually would yield a clear picture with optimal meaning for user profile $P(U_j, f_n)$ and would lead to accurate recommendation. Here, we assigned the minimum value of threshold of rating data as $T_{i=1}$ and threshold content data as $T_{f=0}$ to bring out the most coherent dependencies of items features among user profile. In our proposed model, the equation below is used to build user profile:

$$P(U, f_n) = \sum_{\forall R(U, I_k) \geq T_i} \forall C(I, f) > T_f \text{ whereas } (T_i = 1 \text{ and } T_f = 0) \quad (1)$$

To give an example, user profile of U_6 rated for items I_1, I_4, and I_5 as (2, 3, 5) respectively, and the content features of those items are (I_1=1010, I_3=0110, I_5=1011). Here, it is possible to observe and understand the user behavior by his/her profile, and thereby get to know that f_1 and f_3 are more interesting features to U_6. However, it is clear that f_3 is able to describe the user better than f_1 can.

	I_1	I_2	I_3	I_4	I_5	I_6
U_1	3	-	-	5	-	-
U_2	2	-	5	4	-	3
U_3	4	-	2	2	5	-
U_4	-	3	-	1	-	5
U_5	4	1	-	5	3	2
U_6	2	-	4	-	5	-

	f_1	f_2	f_3	f_4
I_1	1	0	1	0
I_2	0	1	0	1
I_3	0	1	1	0
I_4	0	0	1	0
I_5	1	0	1	1
I_6	1	1	0	1

	f_1	f_2	f_3	f_4
U_1	1	0	2	0
U_2	2	2	3	1
U_3	2	1	4	1
U_4	1	2	0	2
U_5	3	1	3	2
U_6	2	1	3	1

Fig. 1. a)Rating data $R(U_2 i_k)$ b) Content data of features $C(I_2 f_n)$ c) User profile$(U_2 f_n)$

4.2 Assigning Weight

The weighting mechanism on user profile $WP(U, f)$ has been used to find out the dominant features that better describe and distinguish the particular user from the remaining users. As illustrated by the equations below, inverse user frequency (IDF) [11], is used for this purpose

$$WP(U, f) = FF(U, f) * IUF(f). \quad (2)$$

$$IUF(f) = \log(|u|/UF(f))$$

Where, |u| - the total number of users, IUF - inverse user frequency, UF - users frequency in user profile, FF - feature frequency in user profile, If UF=U then UF=UF-0.1.

4.3 Biclustering

To divide users into sub-groups according to their rating by using traditional clustering is not efficient since the traditional clustering algorithms put each user/item in exactly one cluster. Therefore, to ensure that a user may exist in more than one cluster, a degree of overlap between biclusters is introduced to cover all the different preferences of user [12], [13]. In order to provide recommendations to a specific user, it is obligatory to find only the biclusters that have subsets of constant values and represent the users who have similar behavior to that particular user. For this purpose, we use a simple binary inclusion-maximal biclustering algorithm Bi-Max. It is an exact biclustering algorithm based on a divide-and-conquer strategy capable of finding all maximal biclusters in a corresponding graph-based matrix representation [14]. The run-time complexity of Bi-Max is $O(mnb)$, where m is the number of users, n is the number of items, and b is the number of the resulting biclusters.

Thus, in our example, given a set of m users in n items (i.e., an $m \times n$ matrix) as represented in rating data $R(U, i_k)$, the Bi-Max algorithm generates biclusters as a subset of users that have exhibited similar behavior across a subset of items.

Once the biclusters are created, the biclusters of rating data $Br(b,i)$ are generated as the frequency of items i in a bicluster b. To figure out the variety and differences between the features among biclusters, biclusters of content data $Bc(b,f_n)$are constructed based on the summation of features f in content data $C(I, f_n)$ for particular items included in specific bicluster of rating data $Br(b,i_k)$ multiplied by the common frequency for the same items existing in bicluster of rating data $Br(b,i_k)$.Finally, based on bicluster of content data $Bc(b, f_n)$, the weighted bicluster of content data $WC(b, f_n)$ *is* generated, by using inverse document frequency as follows:

$$WC(b, f) = FF(b, f) * IUF(f) \quad (3)$$
$$IUF(f) = \log(|b|/BF(f)).$$

Where, |b| - the total number of biclusters, IUF - inverse user frequency, BF - users frequency in bicluster of content data Bc(b, f_n), FF - feature frequency in bicluster of content data Bc(b, f_n), If UF=|b| then UF=UF-0.1.

4.4 Finding Similarity

As the predictions for an individual can be made by averaging the opinions of the other users in that cluster, similarly, the prediction for groups could be the average across the clusters, weighted by degree of participation, that represent each user in several cluster. However, the nearest neighbor algorithms [15] have obtained better results compared to what the standard clustering techniques do.

Clustering techniques can also be used as a preliminary step for reducing the candidate set in a nearest neighbor algorithm or for distributing nearest-neighbor computation across several recommender engines.

Therefore, in order to identify similar users and justify the recommendation, we measure the similarity between the biclusters b_i which contains strong partial similarity with target user u, considering only the similarity between the set of items/features that are included in b_i and the set of items/features rated by u. Thereafter, the similarity between each test user/group and the generated biclusters is calculated, thus creating the test users' neighborhood, which consists of the most k nearest biclusters. Then, each test user/group is provided with a Top-N recommendation list based on the most frequent items in the neighborhood. In this paper, cosine similarity has been used to measure and find similarity by means of two different ways:

i. By calculating the cosine similarity between a test user and bicluster 'only on the items'. The similarity of users is computed according to their rating behavior on items and the related biclusters as follows:

$$sim_1(u,b) = \frac{\sum R(u,i) \cdot Br(b,i)}{\sqrt{\sum R(u,i)^2} \cdot \sqrt{\sum Br(b,i)^2}} \qquad (4)$$

In the example given in Fig. 1, Sim_1 represents the individual user while the $sim_{1,4}$ represent the group that contains random users, and $sim_{1,2,3,5}$ represent the regular group that has been made during biclustering processes.

ii. By calculating the cosine similarity between a test user and bicluster "only on the features". The similarity of users is computed according to weighted user profile and weighted bicluster of content data as follows:

$$sim_2(u,b) = \frac{\sum wp(u,f) \cdot wc(b,f)}{\sqrt{\sum wp(u,f)^2} \cdot \sqrt{\sum wc(b,f)^2}} \qquad (5)$$

Sim_1 represents the individual user while the $sim_{1,4}$ represent the group that contains random users, and $sim_{1,2,3,5}$ represent the regular group the has been made during biclustering processes.

In our experiment, it has been observed that, the best way to calculate the cosine similarity between individual/group of user u and bicluster b is:

$$\text{Sim}(U, b) = (1\text{-a}).\ \text{Sim}_1 (U, b) + \text{a}\ .\ \text{Sim}_2 (U, b) \qquad (6)$$

Parameter 'a' takes values between [0 and 1]. Thus, it has been noticed that the more "a" increases, the more justifiable recommendation the system is required to give, concentrating on the dominant features because user-features can give more precise recommendations than user-items can. Here, the best result is obtained when "a" was equal to'0.8'.

4.5 Extracting Dominant Features

In this section, we extract the dominant features inside the nearest biclusters for individual/group of test user *u*. Thus, items that contain those dominant features are favored and used in our recommendations.

Here, we compute the dominant features for the items that are selected by user/group with the same biclusters that contain the features and weight as follows:

$$DF(i, f) = Br(b, I)' * WC(b, f), \quad \forall b \in bu \tag{7}$$

Then we calculate the influence of an item in the user's neighborhood as:

$$Influence(i) = \sum DF(i, f) \tag{8}$$

As mentioned in section 4, we have targeted different type of individual/group of users to be tested. Here we have calculated the dominated features for each individual/group that have been taken in section 4 separately.

For individual user we have eliminated those items from influence matrix that their influence is equal to zero, or already has been rated by the test user, and keep the number of items with highest aggregated values that contain the most dominate features. In contrast, for group of users, we retained the zero influence values and the rated item by some of group users, because such values have shown significant enhancement bettering performance of the recommendation among the selected group.

5 Results and Discussion

5.1 Generation of Recommendation and Justification Lists

Regarding the generation of recommendation and justification lists for group and individual users based on items/features and user profile, the generated recommendation consists of Top-N ranked list followed by a justification list of features as illustrated in Figs. (2.1, 2.2, and 2.3). Here, we processed the recommendation of those items with the highest values of influence as follows:

$$RI(u, i) = WP(U, f). \quad C(I, f), \quad \forall i \in DF \tag{9}$$

	f_1	f_2	f_3	f_4
U_1	0.079	0	0.158	0
U_1	1	0	2	0

(a)

	I_2	I_3	I_5	I_6
f_1	0	0	1	1
f_2	1	1	0	1
f_3	0	1	1	0
f_4	1	0	1	1

(b)

	I_2	I_3	I_5	I_6
U_1	0	0.158	0.237	0.079
U_1	=	②	①	③

(c)

Fig. 2.1. a) Test user from weighted user profile WP(U, f) & User profile $P(U, f_n)$ b) Content data C(I, f)', c) recommended items RI(u, i)

$U_{1,4}$	f_1	f_2	f_3	f_4
	0.158	0.158	0.158	0.158
U_1	1	0	2	0
U_4	1	2	0	2

(a)

	I_2	I_3	I_5	I_6
f_1	0	0	1	1
f_2	1	1	0	1
f_3	0	1	1	0
f_4	1	0	1	1

(b)

$U_{1,4}$	I_5	I_3	I_6	I_2
	0.474	0.316	0.474	0.316
U_1	①	③	②	④
U_4	②	③	①	±

(c)

Fig. 2.2. a) Test user from weighted user profile WP(U, f) & User profile P(U, f_n), b) Content data C(I, f)', c), recommended items RI(u, i)

$U_{1,2,3,5}$	f_1	f_2	f_3	f_4
	0.633	0.316	0.952	0.316
U_1	1	0	2	0
U_2	2	2	3	1
U_3	2	1	4	1
U_5	3	1	3	2

(a)

	I_2	I_5	I_3	I_6
f_1	0	1	0	1
f_2	1	0	1	1
f_3	0	1	1	0
f_4	1	1	0	1

(b)

$U_{1,2,3,5}$	I_2	I_5	I_3	I_6
	0.632	1.901	1.268	1.265
U_1	④	①	②	③
U_2	±	①	±±	②
U_3	②	±±	±	①
U_5	±	±±±	①	±±

(c)

Fig. 2.3. a) Test user from weighted user profile WP(U, f) & User profile P(U, f_n), b) Content data C(I, f)', c), recommended items RI(u, i)

N.B. The numbers in tables of recommended items show the order of the recommendation list, and the symbol `±' exposes user interest in rated items.

5.2 The Justification of Recommendation

Reviewing the features of user profile against the features of recommended system is essential to make the justification of recommendation more reasonable and understandable by service provider as well as by the user.

Here it is obvious from the results of the recommendation list how the features of recommended items are coherent and similar to the features of user profile. The proposed system has been implemented to work with different test cases that may have different sizes as below:

Individual User: The recommended items for U_1 are I_1, I_5, and I_2 successively. By exploring the features of these items with the profile features of the tested user, the coherent match appears. This similarity is much closer among the recommended items that have highest values of influence. In contrast, the values revealing poor influence are evidence of the poor matching between the features of both those items and the tested user. Both the high and low values can be taken to interpret the significance of the role of influence among the features. In addition, the list of recommended items for U_1 has assigned the highest rank of recommendation to I_1, which has more weight on f_1 and f_3. Those features are the most desirable ones and are highly accepted by U_1, that actually meets the requirements of the interest of the test user, whose attention is on drawn most to the same features. The system is also seen to be intelligent enough to suggest I_5 as the second option holding f_1 which is considered as one of the highly preferable features by the same user. On the other hand, the system suggests I_2 as a last resort when there are no matching features between the item and user. I_2 is not excluded from the recommendation list intentionally so as to show the capability of the system's understanding as well as to show the effects of such influence on the group recommendation. In this way, it is obvious that our system has the ability to grasp the user's needs and recommend items according to the user's interest with a high degree of accuracy.

Random group: Before giving an explanation for group recommendation we should emphasize that the items that got poor influence value with individual user are not supposed to be eliminated during building the recommendation for groups. When these values have been eliminated less accuracy of recommendations has been observed. Therefore, those values play important roles to improve the accuracy and the quality of recommendations for the group. In other words, the influence among items' features and users' profiles has strong effect on the group recommendations, unlike individuals. For instance, the influence value of I_2 was zero during the recommendation of individual user. Therefore, in this case, such an item can be neglected having no effect on the recommendation accuracy. In contrast, the same cannot be eliminated in group recommendation case as it has a different value that could enhance the recommendation accuracy. This reflects the needs for involving those items rated by some users of the group or get zeros' influence values during building the recommendation's processes. In this section, the system has recommended the items $\{I_5, I_3, I_6, I_2\}$ and $\{I_5, I_3\}$ for the users U_1 and U_4 respectively. Items $\{I_5, I_3, I_6\}$ have been recommended for U_1 and for the reasons that have been mentioned above in the individual case. However, for the same user, I_2 also has been recommended in this case as a fourth option. As such, we can observe how the influence of features among the group users could effect and improve the recommendation of group accuracy. For U_4, items $\{I_5, I_3\}$ have been recommended which contains f_1, f_4 and f_2 respectively. By taking those into account, we can observe that those features are interested to the same user. Thereafter, we can eliminate the rated items by the same user from his/her list or leave them in case it may hold the new version of the same items that has been rated.

Biclustered group: For instance, we have taken the bicluster (b_1: $U_{b1}=\{U_1, U_2, U_3, U_5\}$) that has been generated during biclustering processes to check out the accuracy of recommendation for such case. The system shows a good result for such case as well. It is clear that the influence values are changeable from case to case for the same user due to items influence among the group. However, that change does not affect the sequence of recommended items or the justification of top-n ranked listed. This can also be considered as another aspect of this system ability to serve under different circumstances. For this group, the recommended items has been listed as $\{I_5, I_3, I_6, I_2\}$, $\{I_5, I_6, I_2\}$, $\{I_6, I_2\}$, $\{I_3, I_2\}$ *for users* U_1, U_2, U_3, *and* U_5 respectively. By figuring out the list of recommendation for each user, we observed that all those entire items have been recommended based on user interest. As mentioned above, the items that have been rated by user could be excluded or kept the same to introduce a recommendation to the specific user about the new generation of item he/she got it before.

Real data: Moreover, we have performed experiments with a real data set (MovieLens). These data sets were collected by the GroupLens Research [16] Project at the University of Minnesota. This data set consists of 100,000 ratings from 943 users on 1682 movies. The range of rating is between 1 (bad) and 5 (excellent). Each user has rated at least 20 movies. Movies are classified according to their 19 genres and these genres are the features of the movies in our data set. The 19 genres are: Unknown, Action, Adventure, Animation, Children's, Comedy, Crime, Documentary, Drama, Fantasy, Film-Noir, Horror, Musical, Mystery, Romance, Sci-Fi, Thriller, War, Western. '1' under a particular genre indicates that movie is of that genre and '0' indicates it is not; movies can be in several genres at once. For instance, we selected a random user among 943 users of the data-set and the system has recommended two movies to this user which exactly matches his/her the interest.

5.3 Generation of Recommendation and Justification Lists for Group and Individual User Based on Location for Items and Users

Finally, we have constructed the user location profile *UL(U,lm)*. An example of user location profile is given in Fig. 3-a, where $U_{1\text{-}6}$ are users and $L_{1\text{-}4}$ represent the pin code of the areas that users usually exist in. The same thing has been done for item location in Fig. 3-b, where $I_{1\text{-}6}$ are items and $L_{1\text{-}4}$ represent the pin code of the areas that items are available in. The null cells (no exact locations) are presented with dash.

	L_1	L_2	L_3	L_4
U_1	1	8	5	3
U_2	5	2	7	-
U_3	2	6	3	4
U_4	-	1	2	4
U_5	1	4	3	8
U_6	8	5	4	6

	L_1	L_2	L_3	L_4
I_1	-	5	2	7
I_2	5	2	6	3
I_3	4	-	1	5
I_4	8	1	4	3
I_5	6	8	5	4
I_6	2	-	3	-

Fig. 3. a) User location b) Item location

The system has been subjectively designed not only to generate the intelligent recommendation in respect to user interest, but also to help users find the closest place that surely contains their item of interest. The recommended location has been generated as follows:

$$Rl(U, I) = Il(I, l) \cap Ul(u, l) \tag{10}$$

In our examples, the recommendation location is computed as the intersection between user location and the location for every item that was recommended to him/her.

However, the location of user may change and continuously be updated according to user movement, but the recommendation will fire and take place according to the last updates. The recommendation locations for the different users targeted during recommendation have been listed in the given recommendation for each user.

5.4 Evaluation Metrics

First, we have divide our data into two disjoint sets; the training set and the test set. The algorithm employed by the system works only on the training set and generates a ranked list of recommended items, which we will refer to as the top-N set. The main goal is to scan through the test set, representing the portion of the initial data set which was not used by the Recommender System, and match items in the test set with items included in the generated top-N set. Items that appear in both sets will become members of a special set, called the hit set. The existing studies of recommendation systems use several different measures to evaluate the quality of recommendation produced [17]. The metrics we adopted and used to calculate the performance of our recommender systems are recall and precision measure which is one of popular evaluation metrics in information retrieval systems. We can now define recall and precision for top-N recommendation systems in the following way:

1. Recall describes the idea of all items, which are relevant to the query that are successfully retrieved. Here, it can be defined as the ratio of relevant retrieved items over the relevant items.

$$Recall = \frac{Relevant\ Retrieved\ Items}{Relevant\ Items} \quad (11)$$

2. Precision describes the measure of only those items, which are relevant to the user's information need. Therefore, we have used the precision for measuring the correctness of recommendation as the ratio of the relevant retrieved items to the number of retrieved recommended items (top-N set size).

$$Precision = \frac{Relevant\ Retrieved\ Items}{Retrieved\ Item\ (Top-N)} \quad (12)$$

The following Figs. (4 and 5) are represents the values of recall and precision for recommended items and locations respectively in our running examples.

	Individual User	Random Group		Biclustered Group			
	U_1	U_1	U_4	U_1	U_2	U_3	U_5
Recall	1	1	0.66	1	1	1	1
Precision	0.75	1	0.50	1	0.75	0.50	0.50

Fig. 4. Precision and recall for the recommendation items

	U_1				U_2		U_3		U_4		U_5
	I_2	I_3	I_5	I_6	I_2	I_5	I_2	I_6	I_2	I_5	I_2
Recall	0.50	0.50	0.50	0.25	0.50	0.50	0.50	0.50	0.50	0.25	0.50
Precision	0.50	0.50	0.50	0.33	0.50	0.50	0.50	0.50	0.50	0.33	0.50

Fig. 5. Precision and recall for the recommendation locations

That is, precision represents the probability that recommended items/locations are chosen for each user. The difference among the different groups was rather small, and our system consistently resulted in better recommendations for all group sizes that have been taken in our examples.

The result for the MovieLens data set for different values of 'a' which was used in Equation (6) is shown in Fig. 6. As expected, precision decreases when 'a' increase. This decrease is less steep because in this data set, there is no deviation between the feature profiles of the users and their rating behavior.

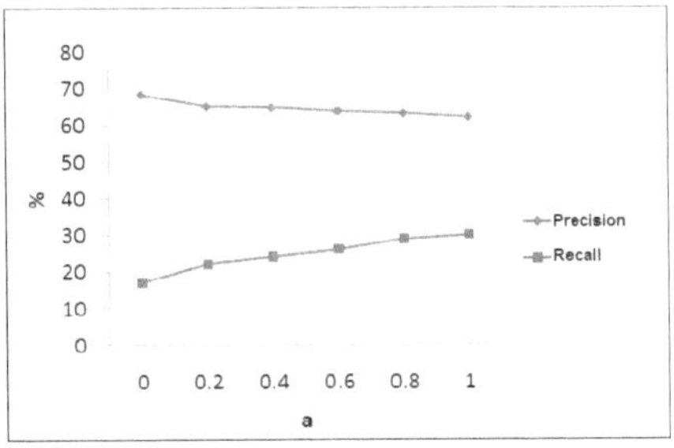

Fig. 6. Precision and recall versus 'a' for MovieLens

However, our method attains good precision because the similarity measure is based on nearest bicluster and thus, being able to detect partial matching of users preferences and can provide accurate recommendations.

6 Conclusions

In this paper, we proposed a method for intelligent recommendation system that can serve for both individuals and groups of mobile marketplace users based on the influence of items features, user location, and user rating. The novelty of this method is the ability to recommend items for individual/group of users with applicable justifications based on their profile. Understanding the influence of user rating and items features among user profiles subjectively captures the quantification of recommendation.

The framework is implemented and evaluated using synthetic and real-life data sets and has shown good results. The generated recommendations have been categorized as individual, groups that contain random users, and group, which consists biclusters that have been built during clustering processes. By exploring the features of the recommended items with the profile features of the tested user the coherent match appears. This similarity is much closer among the recommended items that have highest values of influence. In contrast, the values that reveal poor influence are evidence of the poor matching between the features of both recommended items and the tested user. Both the high and low values can be taken to interpret the significance of the role of influence among the features.

In addition, the list of recommended items for tested users has assigned the highest rank of recommendation to the items that are most desirable ones and are highly accepted by user which actually meets the requirements of the interest of the tested user, whose interest is for the same features. In this way, it is obvious that our system has the ability to grasp the user needs and recommend items according to the user interest.

Moreover, this system has been designed with the goal of providing accurate, low-cost item recommendations. Where searching for particular item costs is prohibitively expensive and takes a lot of time especially in mobile market place domain, this system can provide a better alternative. It generates not only justifiable recommendation but also applicable recommendations for the customers of mobile marketplace based on their location.

References

1. Schafer, J.B., Konstan, J.A., Riedl, J.: E-commerce recommendation applications. Data Mining and Knowledge Discovery 5(1/2), 115–153 (2001)
2. Salter, J., Antonopoulos, N.: Cinema screen recommender agent: Combining collaborative and content-based filtering. Intelligent Systems Magazine 21(1), 35–41 (2006)
3. Bilgic, M., Mooney, R.: Explaining recommendations: Satisfaction vs. promotion. In: Proc. Recommender Systems Workshop, IUI Conf. (2005)
4. Umyarov, A., Tuzhilin, A.: Improving Collaborative Filtering Recommendations Using External Data. In: Eighth IEEE International Conference on Data Mining, ICDM 2008 (2008)
5. Greco, G., Greco, S., Zumpano, E.: Collaborative Filtering Supporting Web Site Navigation. AI Communications 17, 155–166 (2004)
6. Ardissono, L., Goy, A., Petrone, G., Segnan, M., Torasso, P.: INTRIGUE: personalized recommendation of tourist attractions for desktop and handset devices. Application Artificial Intelligent 17(8-9), 687–714 (2003)
7. Gong, S.: A Collaborative Filtering Recommendation Algorithm Based on User Clustering and Item Clustering. Journal of Software 5(7), 745–752 (2010)
8. Weng, S.-S., Liu, M.-J.: Feature-based recommendations for one-to-one marketing. Journal of Expert Systems with Applications 26, 493–508 (2004)
9. Melville, P., Mooney, R.J., Nagarajan, R.: Content-Boosted Collaborative Filtering for improved Recommendations. In: Proc. AAAI Conf., pp. 187–192 (2004)
10. Iaquinta, L., Gentile, A.L., Lops, P., de Gemmis, M., Semeraro, G.: A Hybrid Content-Collaborative Recommender System Integrated into an Electronic Performance Support System. In: 7th International Conference on Hybrid Intelligent Systems (2007)
11. Wu, H.C., Luk, R.W.P., Wong, K.F., Kwok, K.L.: Interpreting TF-IDF term weights as making relevance decisions. ACM Transactions on Information Systems 26(3) (2008)
12. Madeira, S.C., Oliveira, A.L.: Biclustering Algorithms for Biological Data Analysis: A Survey. IEEE Transactions on Computational Biology and Bioinformatics 1(1), 24–45 (2004)
13. Mirkin, B.: Mathematical Classification and Clustering. Kluwer Academic Publishers (1996) ISBN 0792341597
14. Prelic, A., et al.: A systematic comparison and evaluation of biclustering methods for gene expression data. Bioinformatics 22(9), 1122–1129 (2006)
15. Breese, J., Heckerman, D., Kadie, C.: Empirical analysis of predictive algorithms for collaborative filtering. In: Proceedings of the Uncertainty in Artificial Intelligence Conference, pp. 43–52 (1998)
16. `http://www.grouplens.org`
17. Herlocker, J.L., Konstan, J.A., Terveen, L.G., Riedl, J.T.: Evaluating collaborative filtering recommender systems. ACM Transactions on Information Systems 22(1), 5–53 (2004)

An Efficient Mechanism to Avoid Additional Nesting in Nested Network Mobility

M. Dinakaran[1,*] and P. Balasubramanie[2]

[1] School of IT & Engineering, VIT University, India
dinakaran.m@vit.ac.in
[2] School of Computer Applications, Kongu Engineering College, India
pbalu_20032001@yahoo.co.in

Abstract. A vehicle today needs Internet connectivity which consists of many mobility based devices, built in computers, and various devices carried on by the passengers. These devices are connected to the Internet to provide entertainment to passengers, to execute some official works and to provide connectivity to its base network too. Through Network Mobility (NEMO) by IETF, connectivity can be provided. Some times the movable networks may work based on nesting concept also, during that scenario the regular limitation like Sub-optimality due to additional packet size and packet counts are increasing. In order to overcome the additional limitation due to nested network mobility, we are proposing a new mechanism to avoid the additional nesting to reduce the same additional packet size and delays.

Keywords: Nested Mobile IP, Nested NEMO, Movable networks.

1 Introduction

In this fast moving world everyone wants instant access to the data on the fly. When a group of nodes moves together through a vehicle, NEMO protocol [1] is needed to support the network so that the connectivity can be maintained through a point of attachment. NEMO provides connectivity, even the point of attachment changes from one location to another location [2]. In NEMO a separate router called Mobile Router (MR) will take care of changing its attachment point on the Internet, and provides movement transparency to nodes behind. As the vehicle moves it obtains Internet connectivity through wireless access points deployed on road signs and traffic lights. Network mobility is supported to maintain the connectivity with the networks from transportation systems such as vehicles, trains and airplanes.

The mobile networks under mobile networks with its respective home agents (HA) and mobile routers form a topology known as nested NEMO. Due to nesting of Mobile Routers these data packets must go through multiple home agents and several levels of encapsulation, which causes problems such as suboptimal routing and overhead caused by multiple encapsulation. Suboptimal routing is a state at which packets

* Corresponding author.

P.V. Krishna, M.R. Babu, and E. Ariwa (Eds.): ObCom 2011, Part I, CCIS 269, pp. 268–276, 2012.

are routed through a path other than the direct routing between two attachment points on the Internet. In the NEMO Basic Support protocol, packets address to a MNN are always routed with the path via the HA of the MR [3]. When the MR is away from home, such path can often be considered as suboptimal. When the communication involves one or more mobile networks, the number of HAs increases, and therefore it causes the path to be more suboptimal [4]. When the communication involves a nested mobile network, the path could become even more suboptimal. Figure 1 gives an idea about nested network mobility.

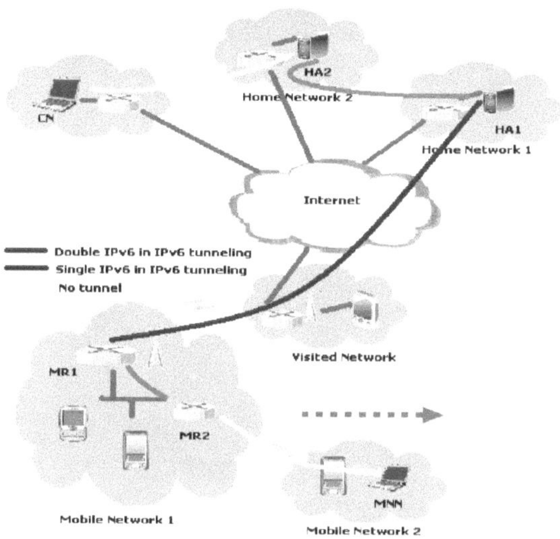

Fig. 1. Nested Network Mobility

In Nested mobile IPv6 network, packets forwards many MR's HA and it causes Sub optimal routing and multiple encapsulations overhead. There are many concepts proposed such as 'Reverse Routing Header', 'Recursive binding update', 'Prefix Delegation for route optimization' but the degree of optimization in these methods are still sub optimal in some cases. So a good solution is to be proposed to solve sub optimal routing and multiple encapsulations overhead in nested mobile network [5].

2 Literature Survey

2.1 Reverse Routing Header

Reverse routing header is technique based on a single tunnel between the Mobile Router to its Home Agent, using IPsec encapsulating security payload (ESP) [6] in order to ensure the privacy of the data transfer between MNN and CN. The tunnel between home agent and mobile router is only one, even the nesting level increase. It launches a new routing header called Reverse Routing Header (RRH) to execute a source routing in the mobile structure. This mechanism is an extension of Loose

Source and Record route in IPv4. It records the route of the data traveled in nested mobile environment.

RRH uses the mechanism of source routing technique to route the packets in optimal path for the nested mobile networks, while sending the packets from MNN to CN [7]. The Mobile Router (MR) which is connected to MNN allocates 'n' number of RRH's to the previous Mobile Router (MR) along with the tunnel header.

Consider a nested mobile scenario in which MNN of mobile network 3 sends a data to CN. The nested mobile scenario is updated in the following figure 2 and the regular NEMO basic support protocol will handle the data transfer between MNN and CN with the following encapsulated levels. This increases the processing delay, packet loss possibility and over head etc.,

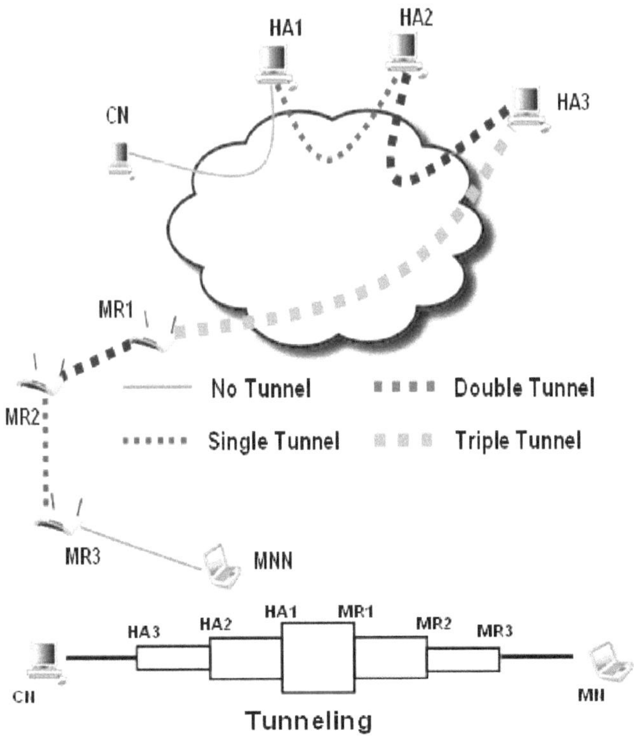

Fig. 2. Nested NEMO

In RRH scheme, when MNN sends the message to CN the MR3 (as per the example), which is the first router on the path initiates the tunneling. It will follow the RRH mechanism as per the header format and number of slots [7].

The last Mobile Router (MR) inserts its home address in slot 1. The destination address of the outer IPv6 header is the HA of last Mobile Router (MR), and the source address is the care-of address of last MR. When the packet arrives at previous Mobile Router (MR) the Mobile Router (MR) swaps the source address with its care-of address, and records the original source address in next slot of the RRH it is similar for all Mobile Router (MR) that is connected in nested mobile network. The packet is then tunneled to the HA of 'n'th MR. Once 'n'th MR HA receives this packet, it notices the RRH and finds the packet being tunneled from the 'n'th MR. the HA then decapsulates and forwards the packet to CN [8]. The following figure 3 refers RRH format for the example nested mobile network scenario.

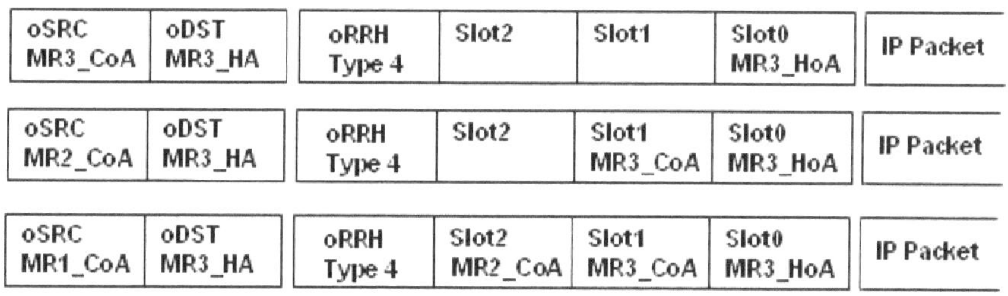

Fig. 3. Reverse Routing Header format

The HA also creates a Binding Cache for 'n'th MR, including the entries recorded in the RRH and the source address of the outer IPv6 header. This Binding Cache allows packets to the MNN to be tunneled using the RRH for the opposite direction. The RRH protocol leaves the MNN and the CN untouched and only the intermediate MRs and the HA are required with the modification. RRH protocol offers the optimal route while achieving security equivalent to the NEMO Basic Support protocol.

2.2 Recursive Binding Update

Recursive Binding Update is helpful to utilize the binding information of the MR contained in the binding cache of the CN. When the CN wants to send a packet to the Visiting Mobile Node (VMN), and if the binding is present, the CN adds a type 2 routing header to the packet. The current Mobile IPv6 draft incorporates a restriction which requires that a type 2 routing header must have only one intermediate node [9].

For example a recursive binding update with source routing for route optimization. We modify the type 2 routing header, in order to be able to use several intermediate nodes, so as to obtain the optimal route from the CN to the VMN by recursive searching of the binding cache. The RBU has an advantage in that; it requires no changes to the existing Mobile IP specification, except for the possibility of using multiple type 2 routing headers. R-BU scheme requires minimum modification to both the Mobile IPv6 specification and the NEMO Basic Support protocol to offer the optimal path. Therefore it is easy to integrate to the current specification.

2.3 Prefix Delegation for Route Optimization

The basic idea behind prefix delegation-based route optimization [10] is to let Local Mobile Node (LMN), VMN and MR to obtain CoA from the prefix of the foreign network visited by the Top Level Mobile Router (TLMR), and let the CN know the

CoA. Therefore, CN can send packets to this CoA to have the packets directly (without going through HAs) reach the foreign network visited by TLMR. In simple prefix delegation (SPD) MRs are delegated a prefix, that can be aggregated at TLMR's foreign network prefix, to advertise inside mobile network. MNNs (except LFNs) obtain CoA from the advertised prefix, and send the CoA to their respective HAs and CNs. This scheme defines a new neighbor discovery option, called Delegated Prefix Option, which is used by MRs to delegate prefix to attached MRs [11]. This scheme does not optimize LFNs' route, and consequently packets sent to LFNs have to be tunneled through the HA of the LFNs' MR. Since the care-of address generated at the VMN is directly routable to the AR, use of the prefix delegation (PD) protocols allows bypassing the bi-directional tunnels for communication between the VMN and the CN.

2.4 Neighbor Discovery for IPv6

Neighbor discovery is mechanism used be wireless nodes in order to find the link layer address of the neighbors known to exist on the attached links. Neighbor discovery can also be used to find the neighboring routers that are willing to forward the packets on behalf of the respective nodes. The availability of the neighbors must be maintained by the nodes in ND mechanism [12]. The nodes actively keep the track of which neighbors are reachable and which are not and to detect the changes in the link layer addresses. The node has to implement an immediate vigorous search of alternative neighbor router, if the active neighbor router in path fails. ND uses link-layer multicast for some of its services, as it is possible that on some link types. If a mobile node within a mobile network receives the new prefix information option through RA message and can recognize this option, it may prefer this new prefix information option to the normal prefix information option that contains the mobile network prefix assigned by the mobile router's home network. By performing binding update with the prefix of the access network, the mobile node can optimize the routes between its correspondent nodes and itself [13].

3 Avoiding Additional Nesting in Nested NEMO

The proposed mechanism adds a single flag in the header format of the packet. Assume that there is data transfer from CN to MNN in mobile network 3. The regular Nested NEMO process encapsulates the original data, based on number of levels of nesting. This increases the packet size of the data, which leads the pin ball routing problem which is discussed in the chapter 6. When a message is sent to MNN by CN, MR3 is the mobile router who is the respective agent for the particular network, delivers the packet.

Reversed Routing Header mechanism expects a header level change and adds some extra information to avoid additional nesting levels. Header size is increased to store 3 address of mobile router in the name of slot 0, 1, and 2 apart from RRH Type. Hence this increases the header size also. It includes additional process in the intermediate mobile router nodes by changing the care of address of each mobile router and updates the old mobile routers care of address in the slot address. This increases the processing time in the intermediate nodes.

A new flag field called as 'Nesting' is added in the header. If this flag is set, it's assumed that additional tunneling is not permitted. It makes any intermediate nodes to avoid additional level of encapsulating, which directly means that we can stop the nesting levels. Though the routing follows the same flow, encapsulation is avoided; hence the packet size of the data is limited.

When there is a packet delivery from CN to MNN, MR3 which is the mobile router of MNN starts the process. This is implemented by MR3 when MNN sends a reply to CN or a fresh message transfer from MNN to any CN. The source address is will to be MNN and destination address is CN in the original packet. MR3 will encapsulate the packet and set the flag field of 'Nesting' if the packet is expected to encapsulate one more time. After encapsulation the source address is MR3 CoA and destination address in MR3 Home Agent address. But as per the flow the packet will be captured by MR2 as a next hop. When the packet is delivered to MR2, it will find that the 'Nesting' flag is set. Hence with out any change it will just forward the packet towards MR1 which is the next hop, with out encapsulation. MR1 follows the same process and forwards the packet to its home agent HA1 and from HA1 to HA2 and HA3. The packet will reach HA3 with a single encapsulation as the 'Nesting' flag is set. While the message is delivered HA3, it will decapsulates the packet and delivers it to the CN. This makes the nested NEMO network as normal NEMO, by avoiding additional tunnels. The following figure 4 illustrates the proposed header format.

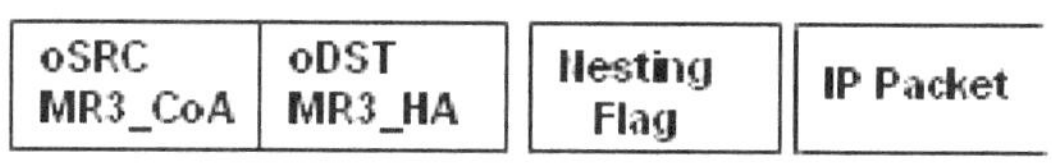

Fig. 4. Proposed header format

This mechanism didn't expect any architecture level changes. In order to identify the intermediate nodes or next hops it's assumed that the regular IPv4 routing mechanism is followed. In IPv4 the packet transfer between hops will identified with physical address. The source and destination IP address will remain unchanged.

4 Performance Analysis

The proposed system and the existing mechanism are simulated using NS2 simulation tool in linux environment and the following results were observed [14]. Packet loss and packet delay are the two parameters considered to evaluate the efficiency of the systems. On comparing the existing system trace files with the proposed system trace file it is evident that the proposed system improves the efficiency.

NS2 is used to simulate both the scenarios. From the simulated scenario the output is recorded in a separate file with .tr extension. From the resultant file the total number of packets transferred, total number of packets dropped, packets source and destination node were predicted. The data is given in Table 1.

Table 1. Packet Loss

	Existing System	Proposed System
Total Packet transferred	5751	4549
Total packet Loss	454	47
Time required (seconds)	10	9
Packet Loss Percentage	7.89%	1.03%

The following graph in figure 5 shows the Packet Loss during the packet transfer in the existing system. The total number of packet lost during packet transfer from correspondent node to the mobile network node is plotted in y axis and the time is plotted in x axis. The packets that are dropped are represented by dots. The dots are over crowded which depicts that the packet loss in the existing system is high. As the packet loss increases the quality of service decreases. Increased packet loss causes jitters and poor video display which is annoying for the user.

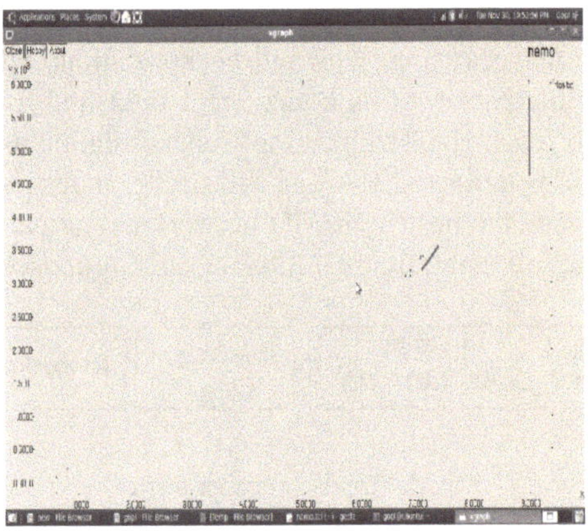

Fig. 5. Packet Loss in Nested NEMO

The following graph in figure 6 shows the Packet Loss during Packet Transfer in proposed System. The dot in the Xgraph is very less when compared to the preceding graph. This depicts that the packet loss is meager in the proposed system. There by assuring more reliable packet transfer in the new proposed system.

The following graph in Figure 7 shows the Packet transfer Delay in the Existing System. The delay in packet transfer is more in the existing system. The time taken to reach the destination is high.

The following graph in figure 8 shows the Packet transfer Delay in the Proposed System. The packet delay is less when compared with the previous graph. Thus the proposed system is far better than the existing system.

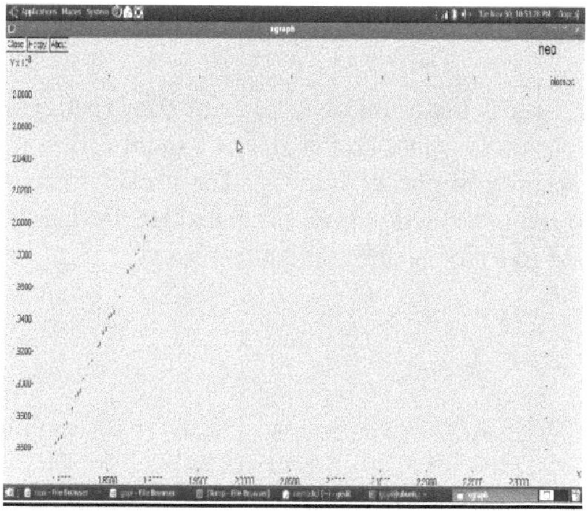

Fig. 6. Packet Loss in Proposed System

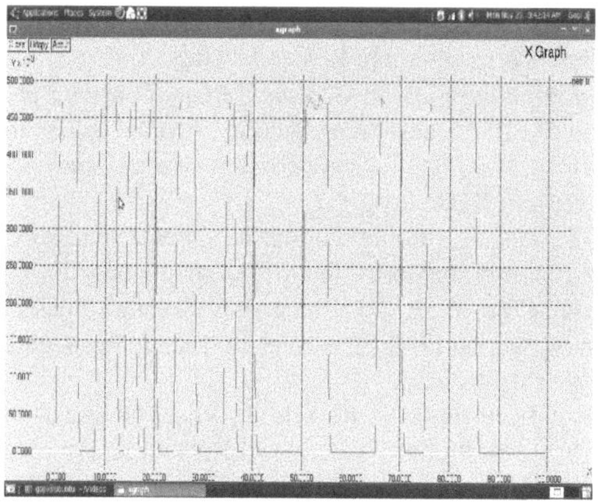

Fig. 7. Packet delay in Existing system

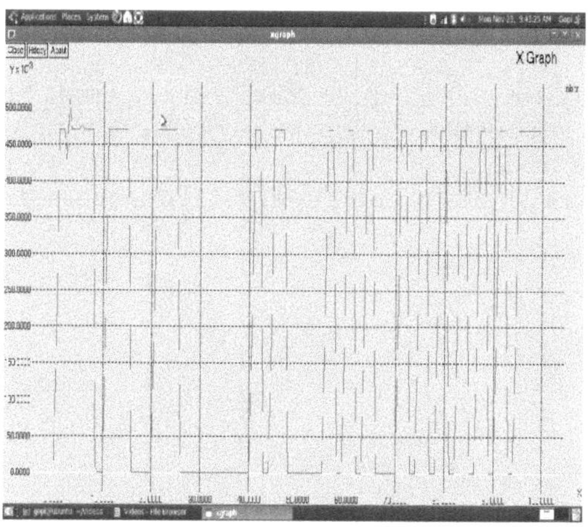

Fig. 8. Packet delay in Proposed System

5 Conclusion

The proposed system curbs major disadvantages of the existing system. It minimizes the delay time and packet loss and proves that it's more efficient. Future works may be carried on over security in packet delivery. The packets may be authenticated before being routed to the inner nodes from the root-MR. Further the packet delay can be even more reduced so as to enhance the video quality.

References

[1] Devarapalli, V., Wakikawa, R., Petrescu, A., Thubert, P.: Nemo Basic Support Protocol, draft-ietf-nemo-basic-support- 02.txt (December 2003)
[2] Johnson, D., Arkko, J.: Mobility Support in IPv6, RFC 3775 (2) (June 2004)
[3] Thubert, P., Ohnishi, H., Paik, E.: Taxonomy of Route Optimization models in the NEMO, NEMO working group-Internet draft (August 25, 2005)
[4] Ng, C., Thubert, P., Watari, M., Zhao, F.: Network Mobility Route Optimization Problem Statement, Network Working Group, RFC 4888 (July 2007)
[5] Ernst, T.: Network Mobility Support Goals and Requirements, RFC 4886 (October 2004)
[6] Kent, S., Atkinson, R.: IP Encapsulating Security Payload (ESP), IETF RFC 2406
[7] Thubert, P., Molteni, M.: IPv6 Reverse Routing Header and its application to Mobile Networks, Internet Draft (February 2007)
[8] Cho, H., Kwon, T., Paik, E.: Route Optimization Expected Properties and Performance Metrics for Nested Mobile Networks, Internet Draft (January 19, 2007)
[9] Cho, H., Paik, E.K., Choi, Y.: R-BU : Recursive Binding Update for Route Optimization in Nested Mobile Networks. In: IEEE Vehicular Technology Conference, vol. 3 (October 2003)
[10] Lee, K.-J., Jeong, J.-H., Park, J.-S., Kim, H.-J.: Route Optimization for Mobile Nodes in Mobile Network based on Prefix Delegation. IEEE Journal (February 2004)
[11] Qureshi, R., Shahriar, A., Atiquzzaman, M.: Performance of prefix delegation based route optimization schemes for NEMO. In: Military Communications Conference (November 2008)
[12] Narten, T., Nordmark, E., Simpson, W.: Neighbor Discovery for IP Version 6 (IPv6), IETF RFC2461
[13] Kuntz, R., Montavont, J., Noel, T.: Multiple mobile routers in NEMO: How Neighbor Discovery can assist default router selection. Personal Indoor and Mobile Radio Communications (2008)
[14] Network Simulator 2 (NS2), http://www.isi.edu/nsnam/ns/

Design of Secure Communication Model for Virtual Environment

R. Anand[1], S. Saraswathi[2], V.R. Sindu[1], and B. Sandhya[1]

[1] Computer Science and Engineering, Dhaanish Ahmed College of Engineering, Anna University, Chennai, Tamil Nadu
[2] Information Technology, Pondicherry Engineering College, Pondicherry University, Pondicherry
{nowhereanand,swathimuk,sindupretty}@yahoo.com, samyuktha.zinky13@gmail.com

Abstract. This structural design mainly concentrates on the concept of Virtualization. This architecture is an innovative approach towards the virtualization technology. This mainly depends on 'Virtual Service', providing the optimal implementation of Virtual Hardware, Virtual Machine, Virtual Applications, Virtual Trust, Virtual Security and Virtual Space. This Virtual Space contains collection of virtual machines which run on virtual hardware environment containing virtual applications. During communication between the virtual applications, Virtual Security has been ensured along with virtual trusted connection. This architecture also aims to increase the speed of transmission and minimize the malware threat.

Keywords: virtualization, Virtual Trust, Virtual Applications.

1 Introduction

Virtualization is the process of decoupling hardware from the operating system on a physical machine. A Virtual Machine (VM) is the virtualized representation of a physical machine that is run and maintained on a host by a software virtual machine monitor or hypervisor [1]. VMs have significant security implications. A primary concern is to ensure whether the proper virtual environment is operating within a VM and the VM is configured properly. Another concern is of virtual machines specific vulnerabilities that can be exploited to mount attacks specialized to subvert the built in defenses of the guest operating systems.

The security and integrity of the VMs in the cloud becomes a major concern as more organizations turn to cloud virtualization solutions. We wish to place a level of trust in the VM, so that it will perform its intended task without compromising or losing the data it is processing. In the below context existing security, trust and privacy implementations have been discussed. Security model that has been implemented in each virtual machine calls via hypervisor. This implementation provides trusted communication between the virtual machine and privacy on each virtual machine thereby providing secured virtual environment [2] as shown in the fig 1 below:-

P.V. Krishna, M.R. Babu, and E. Ariwa (Eds.): ObCom 2011, Part I, CCIS 269, pp. 277–283, 2012.

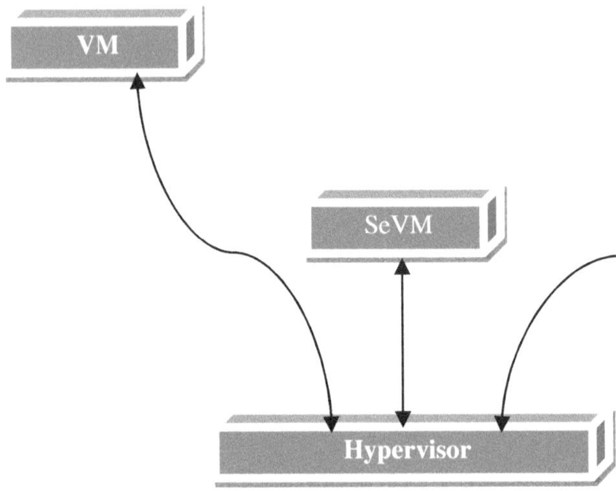

Fig. 1. Existing virtual environment security techniques

Security program implements cost-effective counter measures that mitigates the vulnerabilities that will potentially lead to loss. Certain security policies and procedures are adopted in the virtual environment to secure the data and information in VM's. Physical, technical and administrative security policies provide security in virtual environment [2][3]. This virtualization is laden with trust issues. The client not only trust the data centre operator but also each of the individual clients that are co-located in the facility and each third party server provider of the operator. Clients are assured that their sensitive information is protected against compromise/loss and that their application is available when demanded. Trust among VM's provides secure transfer of data between the virtual machines [4].

Trusted Computing Platform uses a trusted component to provide a foundation for trust for software processes. The trust relationship is established and provides trust worthy services among the virtual machines using certain trust models. Privacy in VM's is attained by encrypting the information and by legal sharing of information. When personal information is collected VM will not transfer the personal information to third parties without consent aspects under limited conditions there by privatizing the VM's. There are two types of applications used in virtual machines of existing virtual environment. One is installed application and the other is portable application.

An installed application in virtual machines is a software package that refers to computer software packed in an archive format to be installed by a package management system or a self-sufficient installer. These installed applications have entries in the registry. It requires disk space on the computer and is costly to upgrade. Portable applications in virtual machines take up a little space. They don't need to be installed in the computer that we use. They don't leave any trace in the computer. They depend on the Operating system [4][5].

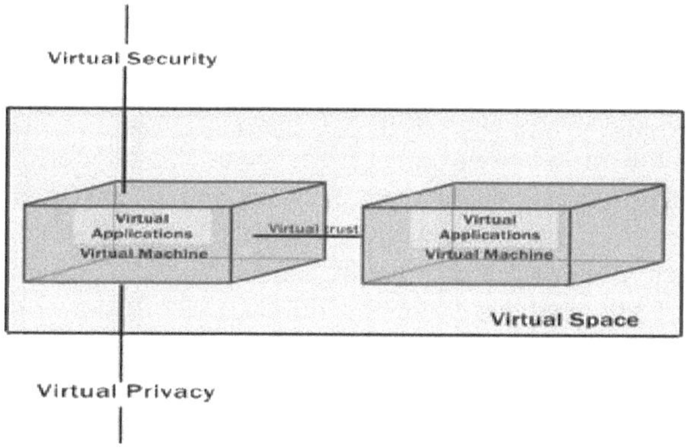

Fig. 2. Proposal model of virtual environment and secured communication between virtual machines

Portable applications are simply copied in a particular folder or drive for access and it does not store program settings in the windows registry. Though the security is well furnished in these models it uses several times more resources than the proposal virtualization scheme and is a heavy weight process that reduces the performance of the system[6][7].

The proposal virtualization scheme provides the implementation of other following terms such as Virtual Applications, Virtual Trust, Virtual Security and Virtual Space in a virtual environment as shown fig 2. Virtual machine is a complete duplication of a real machine and there can be number of virtual machines in an operating system which in turn has number of virtual applications with virtual security, virtual trust.

Virtual privacy is provided among the client machines so that any client is secure from any other client machines. By means of virtual security one virtual machine is isolated from other virtual machines that run in the general operating systems of a physical machine. The virtual security is also provided among the virtual applications. The virtual privacy isolates one virtual machine from any another virtual machines. The virtual privacy in each isolated virtual machine provides secure communication between virtual applications.

2 Proposed System

A virtual machine is an isolated OS installation within a normal operating system of a physical machine. A virtual machine has no direct correspondence to any real hardware. A virtual machine is the appearance of a machine which does not physical exists. Each virtual machine uses a virtual instruction set which the user has access to, and then the virtual machine "maps" these virtual instructions to the real instruction set of the computer.

VM consists of a virtual application in order to maximize the performance of the application, and makes the appliance smaller and possibly more secure. In this context, virtual machines have virtual application which provides data security, virtualization, and virtual privacy among these virtual applications. The client machines and other PDA's depend on the VM in order to access the virtual application in a virtual infrastructure. Administrator of VM restricts the client to access the application in a variety of ways. This authorization is provided by the Application server as administrator and the trusted virtual connections are established between the applications.VM is widely used by cloud computing. Thus, in order to provide security for cloud computing it is necessary to securely identify the kernel of VM.

Generally virtual machine is a software implementation of a machine that executes program like a physical machine. The process of creating a VM assigns a default virtual hardware platform to the VM. Virtual hardware assignments include memory, processor cores, optical drives, network adapters, I/O ports, a disk controller and one or more virtual hard disks (VHDs). Perhaps, the most interesting attribute of a virtual hardware platform is its versatility, because an administrator can adjust the levels of each resource, adding more memory and additional processor cores, allocating another VHD or assigning more network adapter ports. Increasing resource levels will normally boost that workload's performance or responsiveness (especially on older physical servers) or allow the VM to support more users.

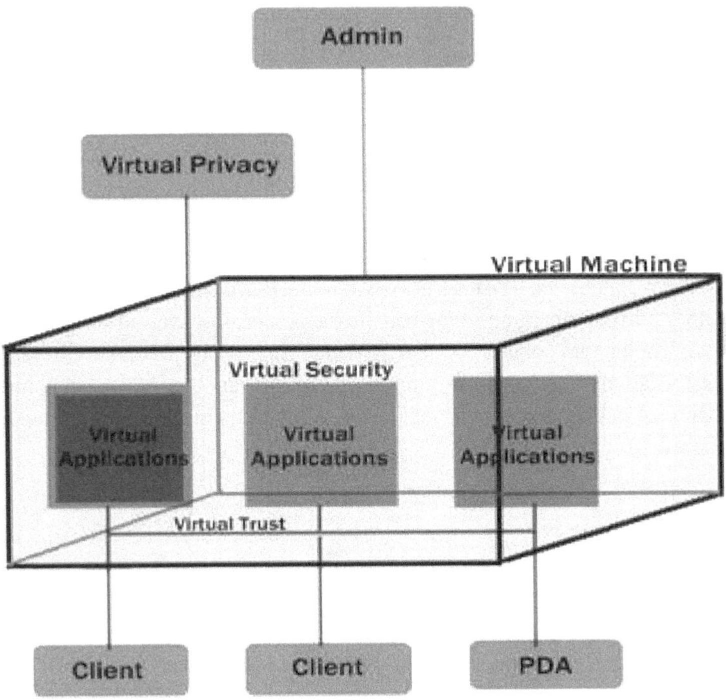

Fig. 3. Trusted connection between virtual applications of proposed model

Virtual application is optimized to run on virtual infrastructure. The application software along with just enough operating systems is combined inside a virtual machine container in a manner that maximizes the performance of the application by minimizing the system software to the smallest set of packages. Packages of code resides on the server but the details about how they are to be invoked in order to create the functionality that adds up to the application get passed to the server as and when needed, but the application does not reside on the server. The incoming request must either include application logic or information where to locate such logic in a repository.

Virtual privacy is provided among the client machines so that any client is secure from any other client machines. By means of virtual security one virtual machine is isolated from other virtual machines that run in the general operating systems of a physical machine. The virtual security is also provided among the virtual applications. The virtual privacy isolates the client's machines of a single virtual machine and virtual machines from each other.

With virtualization, a single physical machine can be divided or partitioned into multiple VMs (E.g. Server Consolidation). This provides each VM with better security isolation and each partition is protected from the possibility of Denial of Service (DoS) attacks from other partitions and also the security attacks in one VM are completely isolated and contained from affecting the other VM.

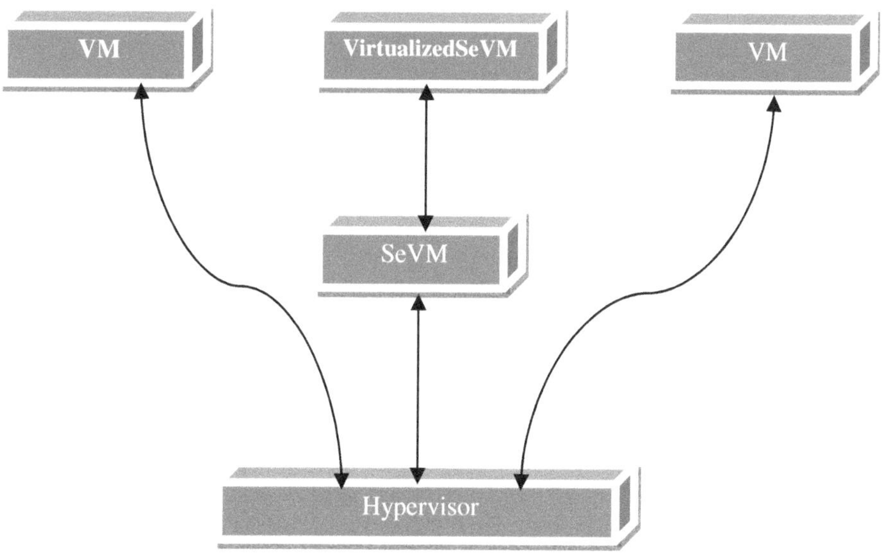

Fig. 4. Proposed security between virtual machines

Security services must be independent of any platform, adaptable to constantly changing environments, and supportive of a virtualized environment. To meet all these seemingly divergent requirements, virtual security must maintain compatibility with the service offerings provided in the virtualized environment.

Virtual trust can provide the following features in the virtualization environment, such as the strong authentication in Virtual Applications, Secured Virtual Machines and Secured Virtual Storage. Virtual privacy, virtual security and virtual trusted connections are provided between the virtual machines. Virtualization takes place in the virtual space which increases the performance, trusted connections between the machines and thus provides a greater data security.

3 Conclusion

It is already been a known fact that the virtual machines restrict the software to a contained environment. Malware crashes and other disasters are limited to just the one instance of the virtual machine. Sometimes installing an application corrupts another application. Whereas virtual application helps to reduce the risk of application conflict with virtual security techniques. Since all virtual mechanisms are a light weight processes the performance of virtual environment is improved. Virtualization reduces the capital cost by increasing energy efficiency and requiring less hardware while increasing the server to admin ratio. Since all these virtualization activities are performed in the virtual space the performance is high and the client request is processed at a short time period.

References

[1] Cacheiro, J.L., Fernández, C., Freire, E., Díaz, S., Simón, A.: Providing Grid Services Based on Virtualization and Cloud Technologies. In: Lin, H.-X., Alexander, M., Forsell, M., Knüpfer, A., Prodan, R., Sousa, L., Streit, A. (eds.) Euro-Par 2009. LNCS, vol. 6043, pp. 444–453. Springer, Heidelberg (2010)

[2] Benzina, H., Goubault-Larrecq, J.: Some Ideas on Virtualized System Security, and Monitors. In: Garcia-Alfaro, J., Navarro-Arribas, G., Cavalli, A., Leneutre, J. (eds.) DPM 2010 and SETOP 2010. LNCS, vol. 6514, pp. 244–258. Springer, Heidelberg (2011)

[3] Cafaro, M., Aloisio, G.: Grids, Clouds, and Virtualization. Computer Communications and Networks, 1–21 (2011)

[4] Teixeira, R.A., Cavenaghi, M.A., Lobato, R.S., Spolon, R.: Proposal of an On-demand Software Deployment System Based on Application Streaming, Virtualization Techniques and P2P Transport. In: Özcan, A., Chaki, N., Nagamalai, D. (eds.) WiMo 2010. CCIS, vol. 84, pp. 417–424. Springer, Heidelberg (2010)

[5] Zhang, Y., Su, G., Zheng, W.: Converting Legacy Desktop Applications into On-Demand Personalized Software. IEEE Transactions on Services Computing 3, 306–321 (2010)

[6] Chen, B., Xiao, N., Cai, Z., Wang, Z., Wang, J.: Fast, On-Demand Software Deployment with Lightweight, Independent Virtual Disk Images. In: Grid and Cooperative Computing, vol. 1, pp. 16–23 (2009)

[7] Ku, K.-I., Choi, W.-H., Chung, M., Kim, K., Kim, W.-Y., Hur, S.-J.: Method for distribution, execution and management of the customized application based on software virtualization. In: Advanced Communication Technology (ICACT), vol. 1, pp. 493–496 (2010)

[8] Van Do, T., Krieger, U.R.: A Performance Model for Maintenance Tasks in an Environment of Virtualized Servers. In: Fratta, L., Schulzrinne, H., Takahashi, Y., Spaniol, O. (eds.) NETWORKING 2009. LNCS, vol. 5550, pp. 931–942. Springer, Heidelberg (2009)

[9] Zhang, B., Wang, X., Lai, R., Yang, L., Wang, Z., Luo, Y., Li, X.: Evaluating and Optimizing I/O Virtualization in Kernel-based Virtual Machine (KVM). In: Ding, C., Shao, Z., Zheng, R. (eds.) NPC 2010. LNCS, vol. 6289, pp. 220–231. Springer, Heidelberg (2010)
[10] Xie, W., Navathe, S.B., Prasad, S.K., Fisher, D., Yang, Y.: Optimizing Peer Virtualization and Load Balancing. In: Li Lee, M., Tan, K.-L., Wuwongse, V. (eds.) DASFAA 2006. LNCS, vol. 3882, pp. 357–373. Springer, Heidelberg (2006)
[11] He, R., Lacoste, M., Leneutre, J.: Virtual Security Kernel: A Component-Based OS Architecture for Self-Protection. In: Computer and Information Technology (CIT), pp. 851–858 (2010)
[12] Wu, H., Ding, Y., Winer, C., Yao, L.: Network security for virtual machine in cloud computing. In: Computer Sciences and Convergence Information Technology (ICCIT), pp. 18–21 (2010)
[13] Huang, D., Ata, S., Medhi, D.: Establishing Secure Virtual Trust Routing and Provisioning Domains for Future Internet. In: GLOBECOM 2010, pp. 1–6 (2010)
[14] Peng, S., Het, J., Dai, F.: Trust Propagation Model for Federated Virtual Commnunities. In: Communications and Information Technologies, pp. 402–406 (2008)
[15] Ma, S.-G., Yang, J.-H., Ma, S.-G.: Research on trust model in optimal resource allocation for a virtual organization. In: E -Business and E -Government (ICEE), pp. 1–4 (2011)

An Enhanced Probabilistic Encryption Algorithm for Secured Data Transmission

K. Adi Narayana Reddy[1], V. Madhu Viswanatham[2], and B. Vishnu Vardhan[3]

[1] Department of CSE, Hyderabad Institute of Technology and Management, Hydearabad, India
[2] School of Computing Science and Engineering,VIT University,Vellore, India
[3] Department of CSE, JNTU, Jagityala, India

Abstract. In this paper, we propose a modification probabilistic encryption algorithm by generating Basins (sub keys) dynamically. A probabilistic encryption produces more than one cipher text for the same plaintext. In probabilistic encryption, we use a secret shared key matrix. We multiply this key matrix with a matrix formed from ternary vector and then apply a sign function on the product, which generates a sequence. From this sequence we generate Basins using equality. In our paper we propose a mod with modulo base value to generate the Basins. As the base value changes, the number of Basins also changes.

Keywords: Probabilistic Encryption, Basins, Ternary vector, Mod function.

1 Introduction

The new probabilistic encryption algorithm is based on the concept of polyalphabetic substitution cipher which is an improvement over monoalphabetic cipher. Polyalphabetic substitution cipher is a symmetric encryption algorithm. In 1467, Leon Battista Alberti developed the earliest form of polyalphabetic cipher. Later on more modern forms were devised which changes substitution for each letter. In 1518, Johannes Trithemius first published a progressive-key system, where keys are used one after the other in normal form.. In 1553, Giovan Batista Belaso invented Vigenere cipher algorithm. The auto key system, where a key starts the choice of alphabet, but the message itself determines the alphabets to use in later parts of the message. In 1585, B D Vigenere proposed modern form of autokey cipher. The probabilistic encryption algorithm [1] has been introduced for public key cryptosystem. A new probabilistic encryption [2] has been introduced for symmetric key cryptosystem. A new probabilistic encryption [7] encrypts a plaintext by selecting key from basins. This produces more than one cipher text for the same plaintext. But the Basins are generated based on equal values[3]. In this paper we propose a new method for generating Basins.

The paper is organized section wise in the following way: section 2 briefly introduces probabilistic encryption algorithm. Section 3 presents a modified

P.V. Krishna, M.R. Babu, and E. Ariwa (Eds.): ObCom 2011, Part I, CCIS 269, pp. 284–290, 2012.

probabilistic encryption algorithm. Section 4 discusses security analysis. Section 5 concludes the proposal.

2 A Probabilistic Encryption Scheme

In public key cryptosystem a cryptanalyst always gain some information bt the encryption of random plaintext with public key. Georg J. Fuchsbauer [1] proposed a probabilistic public key bit-encryption scheme. With probabilistic encryption algorithms a cryptanalyst can no longer encrypt random plaintext looking for correct cipher text, since multiple cipher text will be developed for one plaintext. A probabilistic encryption [5, 6, 7, 8] produces more than one cipher text for the same plaintext.

2.1 Algorithm

2.1.1 Key Generation

- A random matrix is used as shared key. Let it be A
- Considers the sequence from 0 to n, where n is positive integer
- Converts each element of the sequence into ternary form of a given digit number
- Represents these values in matrix form of (n+1) X (digit number). Let it be T
- 1 is subtracted from all the elements of matrix T
- The result of the matrix T is multiplied with shared key matrix A
- A sign function is applied on the elements of the product matrix TA. The sign function converts all positive values to 1, negative values to -1, and zero to 0
- 1 is added to all the elements of the results of above sign function
- Converts each row into decimal form and generates a sequence S

2.1.2 Basins Generation

- Considers the rows starting from 0 to n
- Considers the converted sequence corresponding rows
- Reads the starting element of row and stores the row first element and corresponding converted element from the sequence in a basin
- Compare the elements of basin with the elements of sequence. If there is a match, stores the corresponding row elements in the basin. Neglects already visited elements
- Repeats the above step with the remaining elements of the basin and store them in the same basin. This will form one basin

- Goes the next row element which is not visited earlier
- If a basin is having one or less number of elements we neglect that basin

2.1.3 Encryption

- Plaintext characters numbered from 0
- Each plaintext character is converted to set of basins from chosen base value
- Each basin is replaced by values from basins in random
- This produces corresponding cipher text

2.1.4 Decryption

- Writes the cipher text in numeric equivalent
- Writes the equivalent basins for numeric value
- Writes the decimal value for the basins
- Converts into equivalent characters

2.2 Example

1. Consider the sequence from 0 to 26
2. Convert the sequence into ternary form of a 3 digit number
3. Represent above ternary form in 27 x 3 matrixes. Let it be T
4. Subtract 1 from all the elements of T. Store the result in T
5. Consider a random matrix

$$A = \begin{bmatrix} 2 & 5 & -6 \\ 3 & 1 & 3 \\ 4 & -2 & -3 \end{bmatrix}$$

6. T = T * A
7. Apply sign function on the result matrix T
8. Add 1 to all the elements of the above resultant matrix T
9. Convert each row of the matrix T to decimal form to generate sequence

The generated sequence S = 2 0 0 18 0 3 18 18 6 20 2 6 20 13 6 20 24 6 20 8 8 23 26 8 26 26 24

2.2.1 Generation of Basins

n	0	1	2	3	4	5	6	7	8	9	10	11	12	13
s	2	0	0	18	0	3	18	18	6	20	2	6	20	13

n	14	15	16	17	18	19	20	21	22	23	24	25	26
s	6	20	24	6	20	8	8	23	26	8	26	26	24

Now identify similar values of sequence and put the n values in the basins
The generated basins are
Basin B (0) = (0, 1, 2, 4, 10)
Basin B (1) = (3, 5, 6, 7, 8, 9, 11, 12, 14, 15, 17, 18, 19, 20, 21, 23)
Basin B (2) = (16, 22, 24, 25, 26)

2.2.2 Encryption

Consider a base value 3
Plaintext: “adi ”
Assign a to 1, b to 2 . . . z to 26

a	d	i
1	4	9
001	011	100
B(0)B(0)B(1)	B(0)B(1)B(1)	B(1)B(0)B(0)

Pick random numbers from basins

1 2 5   4 8 12   15 1 10

Cipher text

a b e   d h l   o a j

2.2.3 Decryption

Cipher text	a b e	d h l	o a j
	1 2 5	4 8 12	15 1 10
	B(0)B(0)B(1)	B(0)B(1)B(1)	B(1)B(0)B(0)
Plaintext	1	4	9
	a	d	i

In this, firstly, we choose key matrix then we generate a sequence. From this sequence we generate Basins using equal values. This method generates fixed number of basins. If the base value is 4 and character to be encrypted is ‘d’, then we cannot encrypt the character using the above Basins. In this paper we propose a mod with modulo base value in place of equal values.

3 Proposed Modification

The algorithm uses a sign function on the product of matrix formed by ternary vectors and shared key matrix to generate the sequence. The sign function converts all positive values to 1, negative values to -1 and zero to 0. It is difficult to find key matrix since sign function is not invertible. In our proposed scheme we use the same method for generation of key. For the generation of Basins, we use mod with modulo base value. This makes confusion to the adversary to the information of Basins. The Basin generation algorithm as follows

3.1 Generation of Basins

1. Chose a base value
2. r = (S[n] + n) % base value , where S[n] is the sequence generated to corresponding rows of the key generation procedure and n is the corresponding row
3. Based on remainder r we place the corresponding row value n in the Basins b(r).
4. In this algorithm we are mixing the row n and corresponding converted value to confuse the cryptanalyst. We can generate Basins (sub keys) dynamically by choosing different base values. We assume that the base value is greater than 2.

3.1.1 Example

We use data of the previous example

n	0	1	2	3	4	5	6	7	8	9	10	11	12	13
S	2	0	0	18	0	3	18	18	6	20	2	6	20	13

n	14	15	16	17	18	19	20	21	22	23	24	25	26
S	6	20	24	6	20	8	8	23	26	8	26	26	24

The generated basins are

If base value =3

Basin B(0) = (3, 3, 10, 19, 22, 25)

Basin B(1) = (1, 4, 7, 16, 20, 23)

Basin B(2) = (0, 2, 5, 8, 9, 11, 12, 13, 14, 15, 17, 18, 21, 24, 26)

If base value =4

Basin B(0) = (4, 5, 6, 12, 14, 15, 19, 23, 25)

Basin B(1) = (1, 3, 7, 11, 12, 16, 20, 21, 22)

Basin b(2) = (0, 2, 8, 9, 13)

Basin b(3) = (17, 18, 24, 26)

In this we can chose base value from that we generate basins. If we change the base value basins also changes. This provides dynamism in basins generation.

4 Security Analysis

In this modification we are generating basins dynamically by choosing base value. This scheme produces more than one cipher text for the same plaintext. Assume a cryptanalyst has certain cipher text Ci. Even if he/she guesses correctly when she encrypts message the result will be completely different Cj. He/She cannot compare Ci and Cj so she cannot know where the guessed message is correct. The algorithm provides almost equal security at low computational overhead. The algorithm is free from differential and linear cryptanalysis.

5 Conclusion and Future Work

This scheme is more secure and the computational overhead less than the existing system to generate the Basins. The size of the cipher text is more than the plaintext. In future the size can also be reduced.

References

1. Fuchsbauer, G.J.: An Introduction to Probabilistic Encryption. Osjecki Matematicki List 6, 37–44 (2006)
2. Guo, D., Cheng, L.M., Cheng, L.L.: A New Symmetric Probabilistic Encryption Scheme Based on Chaotic Attractors of Neural Networks. Applied Intelligence 10(1), 71–84 (1999)
3. Baker, H., Piper, F.: Cipher Systems. North Wood Books, London (1982)
4. Chien-Chiang, I.: Efficient improvement to XTR and two padding schemes for probabilistic trapdoor one way function (2005)
5. Krishna, A.V.N.: A New Algorithm in Network Security. In: Proc. of International Conference on CISTM 2005, Gurgoan, India (July 2005)

6. Krishna, A.V.N., Pandit, S.S.N., Vinay Babu, A.: A Generalized Scheme for Data Encryption Technique using a Randomized matrix key. Journal of Discrete Mathematical Sciences and Cryptography 10, 73–81 (2007)
7. Krishna, A.V.N., Vinay Babu, A.: Training of New Probabilistic Encryption Scheme using a Optimal Matrix Key. Georgian Electronic Scientific Journal: Computer Science and Telecommunications (2) (2009)
8. Krishna, A.V.N., Vinay Babu, A.: Web and Network Communication Security Algorithms. Journal of Software Engineering 1(1), 12–14 (2006)

JavaScript Application Framework for Mobile Devices

Raghu R. and Shobha K.R.

Dept. of Telecommunication, MSRIT,
Bangalore, India
raghu.25.12@gmail.com

Abstract. This paper presents the concept of JavaScript Application Framework (JSAF) which is a Platform Independent Model (PIM). This Paper aims at developing an application framework using web developing languages which supports the usage on all platforms making it easy for the developers to use the application framework to develop applications. JSAF is used for creating applications for Mobile Devices which supports a Browser which can render advanced web developing languages such as JavaScript, HTML5 and CSS3. The JSAF provides all the basic User-Interface (UI) widgets required for the Application Development to the Application developer. The JSAF Application is rendered on a Browser which will load JSAF framework prior to the Application. JavaScript Application Framework has the Multitasking feature and Cross Application Communication feature. JavaScript Application Framework is developed at Samsung India Software Operations and proprietary.

Keywords: Application Framework, Mobile Applications, JavaScript, HTML, CSS.

1 Introduction

Mobile application development is the process by which application software is developed for small low-power hand held devices such as personal digital assistants, enterprise digital assistants or mobile phones. These applications are either pre-installed on phones during manufacture, or downloaded by customers from various mobile software distribution platforms.

The life span of mobile application software in market is usually very short and it causes unstructured mobile application software.

A common architecture for mobile application software which is named as *Application Framework* is used to support agile software development. The Framework is defined following PIM (Platform Independent Model) in MDD (Model Driven Development) [1] to satisfy the need of supportability from one mobile application to various mobile platforms.

Mobile Applications are the most important part of the Smartphones. With the rise in the Mobile Application Market, there is a requirement to develop applications for each Mobile Platform such as iOS, Android, Blackberry OS, Symbian OS and Windows Phone. iOS applications are programmed in C, C++ and objective C has 16.7% market share. Android applications are programmed in Java has 25.5% market

P.V. Krishna, M.R. Babu, and E. Ariwa (Eds.): ObCom 2011, Part I, CCIS 269, pp. 291–299, 2012.

share.. Blackberry OS applications are programmed in Java has 14.8% market share. Windows Phone is programmed in C++ has 2.8% market share as per 3rd quarter 2010 Market Share [2].

Each Platform uses different programming languages for creating applications which needs a developer to learn the programming languages of the particular platform to create an application. There is a need for a Platform Independent application framework which can be used to develop an application with minimum required programming languages and works on all the Platforms.

The goal of JavaScript Application Framework platform is to allow developers to develop platform independent mobile applications with open web standards and leverage advantages of both conventional web applications and native applications. Cross Platform Applications can be developed using the JavaScript Application Framework for different Mobile Platforms available in the Market. The open web standards for web application development are HTML, CSS and JavaScript.

JavaScript is a light-weight scripting language with object-oriented capabilities. It has some dynamic features such as objects modification in runtime through properties added dynamically. JavaScript is a prototype-based, object-oriented scripting language that is dynamic and has first-class functions [3].

HTML, which stands for Hypertext Markup Language is the predominant markup language for web. A markup language is a set of markup tags, and HTML uses markup tags to describe web pages.[4]

Cascading Style Sheets (CSS) is a style sheet language used to describe the presentation semantics (the look and formatting) of a document written in a markup language. It's most common application is to style web pages written in HTML and XHTML [5] Transformations for code generation.

In chapter 2, describes the Layered View based on JavaScript Application Framework (JSAF). In chapter 3, explains Software Architecture Design of JSAF. Chapter 4 describes the widgets supported in JSAF. Chapter 5 describes the 3 different features of JSAF framework. Chapter 6 discusses about the Results .Chapter 7 gives conclusion based on Results.

2 Layered View

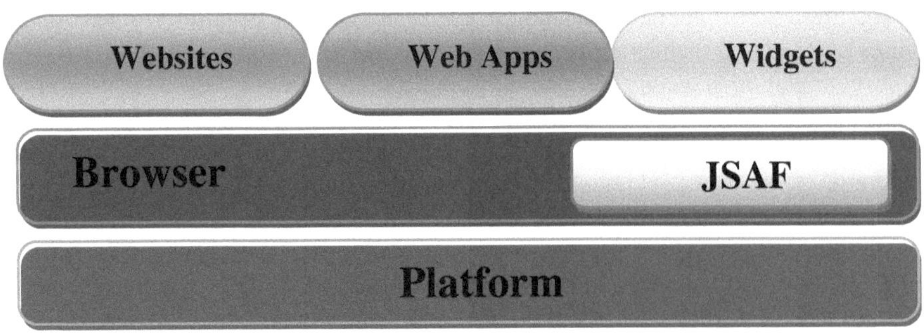

Fig. 1. Layered View of Architecture

Figure 1 describes the Layered View of Architecture. A **platform** is a crucial element in software development. A platform might be simply defined as a place to launch software.

A **Browser** is a software application for retrieving, presenting, and traversing information resources on the World Wide Web. An *information resource* is identified by a Uniform Resource Identifier (URI) and may be a web page, image, video, or other piece of content. Hyperlinks present in resources enable users to easily navigate their browsers to related resources.

The **JavaScript Application Framework** is loaded into the Browser. The new web applications are created on this browser. Widgets are the part of the JavaScript Application Framework which gives the basic required widgets for creation of new application to the third party Developers.

A **website** is a collection of related web pages, images, videos or other digital assets that are addressed relative to a common Uniform Resource Locator (URL), often consisting of only the domain name.

WebApps are the Web Applications created by Web Developers for this JavaScript Application Framework.

Widgets are the part of the JavaScript Application Framework which gives the basic required widgets for creation of new application to the third party Developers.

3 Software Architecture Design

3.1 Design Considerations

Design Goal

Usability is the main goal of this Software system, since this framework will be used by 3rd party application developers. The framework should provide easy to use and consistent Application Programming Interfaces. Framework should be extensible and highly maintainable.

To achieve the usability and extensibility the framework is based on the Model-View-Controller (MVC) based application model [6]. Many GUI frameworks have been developed based on MVC architectural pattern and it is highly proven model. The mobile applications are structured and packaged in MVC model.

Application Model

Figure 2 describes the JSAF application model and distinguishes it from a typical web application.

View consists of UI descriptions which are in HTML and CSS for a JSAF application. Controller is mainly responsible for initialization of setup, initialization of model and handling user actions. And model consists of the application data. In our application controllers are called assistants.

The JSAF Application model as shown in Figure 3 is based on Pages and Views. Page corresponds to one window and view corresponds to content displayed inside the page. A page can have multiple views to be displayed. An application can have multiple pages in it. At any given point a page can have only one 'active' view; similarly an application can have only one 'active' page at a given time. An application can have multiple entry points, and multiple pages can be useful to provide multiple entry points to an application.

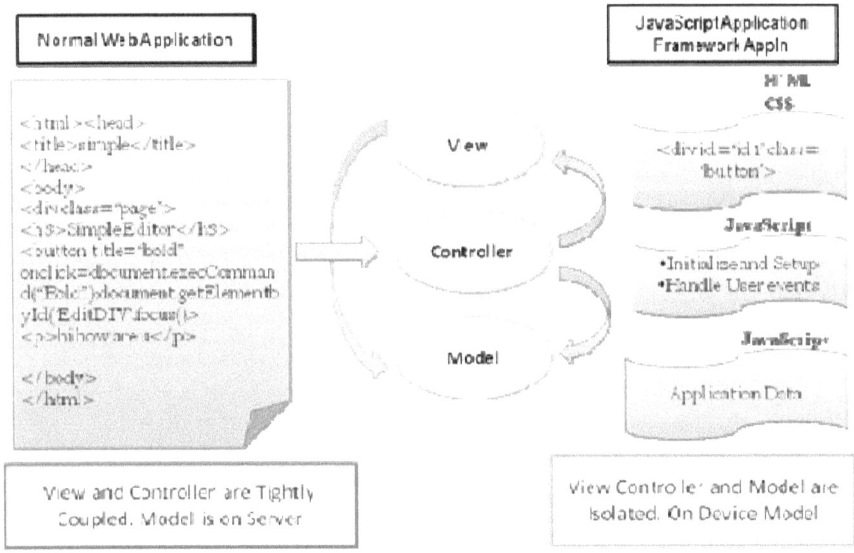

Fig. 2. MVC architecture in Normal Web Application and JSAF Application Framework

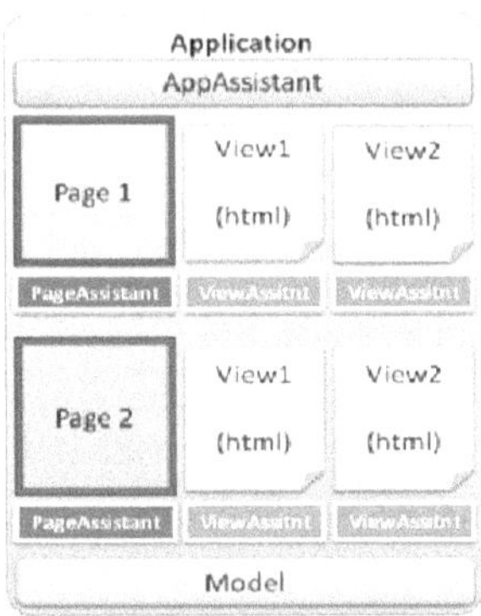

Fig. 3. Application model

Application Launch

As a result of launching an application, the root (faceless) window is created, which is supplied with the URL for the application. The URL will point to the application's base document, containing a <script> reference to the framework script file (JSAF.js).When an application is launched, a new DOM page is created and the application's base document (index.html) is loaded. This document must request loading of JSAF.js

```
<script type="text/javascript" src="/JSAF/framework/scripts/JSAF.js">
```

After loading JSAF.js, the execution flow of framework takes control. It initializes and loads all the framework files and application sources.

4 JSAF Widgets

Widget is a generic type of software application comprising portable code intended for one or more different software platforms. The term often implies that either the application, user interface, or both, are light, meaning relatively simple and easy to use. Widgets often take the form of on-screen tools.

Although some widgets are instantiated automatically or on request, most are instantiated by the framework when it finds a `<div>` element in a view that has the `Jsaf-Widget` attribute specified. This attribute names a widget class in the `Jsaf.Widget` namespace. When a widget is instantiated, the framework creates a `Widget Controller` instance for the <div> element.The widget controller takes care of instantiating a widget assistant containing the actual widget implementation, and other standard widget setup work.

The Different Widgets supported in JSAF are Application Menu, Command Menu, Popup Menu / Sub Menu, View Menu, Text Fields, Dialog Box, Progress Bar, Progress Pill, Progress Slider, Progress Spinner, Spinner, Lists, Slider, Checkbox, Scroller, Buttons, Radio Group and Color Picker.

5 JSAF Framework

JSAF framework provides 2 different approaches for application development and another feature called Cross Application Communication

1) Single Page Multiple View
2) Multiple Page Multiple View
3) Cross Application Communication

5.1 Single Page Multiple View

Figure 4 represents Single Page Multiple View which has Single page and multiple number of views which is placed one after the other in the Application. Each View has a separate View Assistant and Page has a Page Assistant.

Example for Single Page Multiple View application can be taken as an Alarm Clock in which when we click on the Clock it goes to the new view asking to set an alarm clock .Only one view is visible at a time.

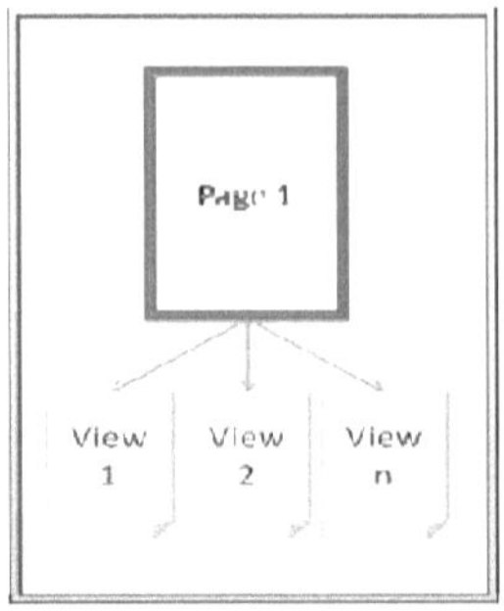

Fig. 4. Single Page, Multiple View

5.2 Multiple Page Multiple View

Multiple Page and Multiple View implementation is as shown in Figure 5 which has multiple page assistants for each page and multiple view assistants for each view as shown earlier.

We have Multiple Page and Multiple Views which has multiple page assistants for each page and multiple view assistants for each view as shown earlier.

We can take E-Book library as an application example where we have a large no of eBooks when we are viewing some page of an eBook and we want to refer another page in another eBook then we can just go back to the main page without disturbing the present page condition. From main page we can check the required eBook page in that page. So it would help in Multitasking and we can apply it for different applications also as each application starts with a page .Each application can be accessed in between if we want to go to that application.

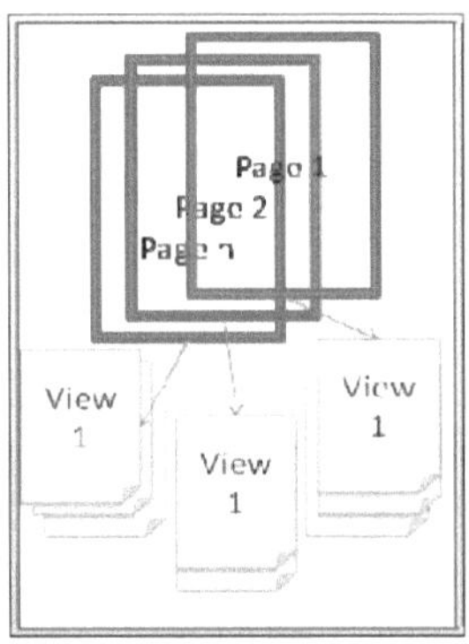

Fig. 5. Multiple Page, Multiple View

5.3 Cross Application Communication

In Cross Application communication there is a communication between two apps .From the Figure 6 we can see that the Application App1 is in a page with view1.From view1 we can directly jump to the view2 of App2 without going to view1 of App2.To reduce the complexity for the user who has to access both the applications separately can use the Cross Application Communication in which second application required view is accessed through first application directly without entering the application separately.

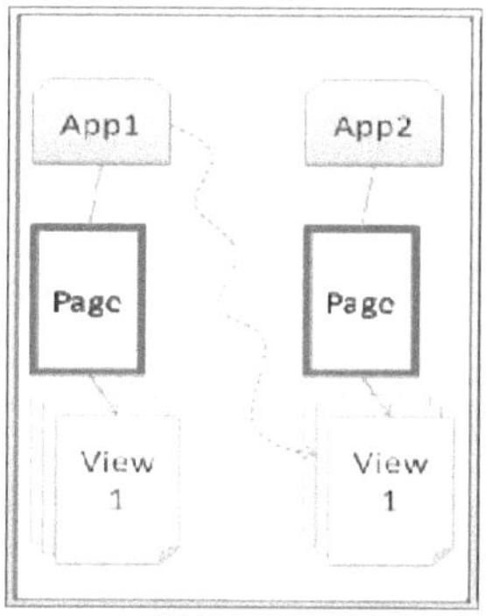

Fig. 6. Cross Application Communication

6 Results

6.1 Single Page Multiple View

In Single Page Multiple View, we have a Single page in which multiple views are displayed one over the other just like a stack. When we push a view, the view displaying presently will be pushed with a new view that has been called. When we pop a view, the present view is popped out and the old view is displayed. In any Page only one active view is possible. Date Picker application shown below in Figure 7 depicts the Single Page Multiple View.

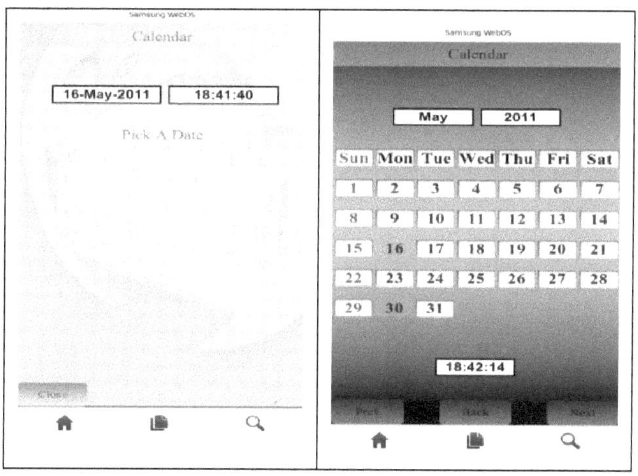

Fig. 7. Single Page Multiple View

6.2 Multiple Page Multiple Views

In Multiple Page, Multiple View we have Multiple Single Pages .In each page there are multiple views. Here also, there is only one active view in foreground. E Magazine Application shown in Figure 8 depicts multiple page and multiple Views.

Fig. 8. Multiple Page Multiple Views

6.3 Cross Application Push

In Cross Application push, there is communication between two applications .We can access a different application with different view directly from the present application.

In the Results, the Cross Application Communication between birthday list application and Calendar application is shown.

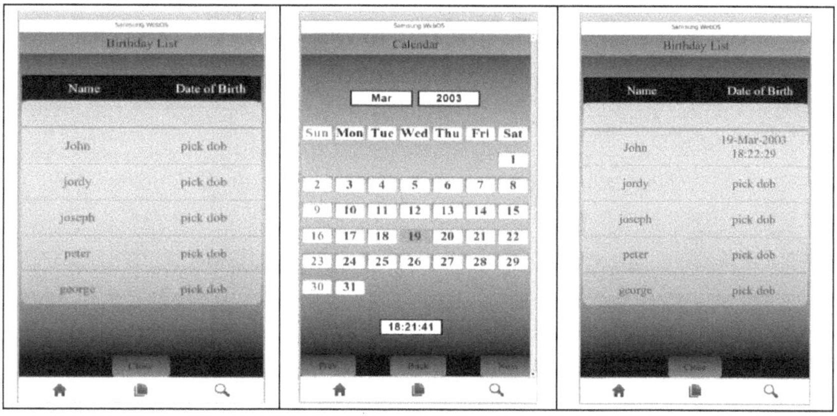

Fig. 9. Cross Application Communication

7 Conclusion

The JavaScript Application Framework is designed for mobile devices of any platform. There is a wide range of widget APIs available in JSAF which can be used directly in the developer's application once the JSAF is loaded in the browser of the Mobile, the widgets are also loaded into the Browser. The widget has to be instantiated to be displayed on the Mobile screen. The applications are purely created from web developing languages HTML, CSS and JavaScript.

Lots of Web Applications can be incorporated into mobile using JSAF. There is no need to learn any procedure oriented or object oriented language for Web Developers to create an application for Mobile Device instead they can use the JavaScript itself to create applications with the help of JSAF. Almost all device native applications can be implemented with JavaScript Application Framework.

References

1. Choi, Y., Yang, J.-S., Jeong, J.: Application Framework for Multi Platform Mobile Application Software Development, pp. 208–213 (2009)
2. Gartner Says Worldwide Mobile Phone Sales Grew 35 Percent in Third Quarter 2010; Smartphone Sales Increased 96 Percent. Gartner, Inc. (November 2010), `http://www.gartner.com/it/page.jsp?id=1466313`
3. Hamilton, N.: The A-Z of Programming Languages: JavaScript, pp. 1–6 (June 2008)
4. Musciano, C., Kennedy, B.: HTML & XHTML: The Definitive Guide, 5th edn., pp. 15–19. O'Reilly Media (2002)
5. Meyer, E.A.: Cascading Style Sheets: The Definitive Guide, 3rd edn., pp. 3–11. O'Reilly Media, Inc. (2006)
6. Reenskaug, T.: Applications programming in Smalltak-80(TM): How to use Model-View-Controller (1979)

A Centralized Priority Based RWA Protocol for WDM Networks

T.K. Ramesh, A. Nageswara Reddy, G.V.L. Praveen Kumar, K. Biju, and P.R. Vaya

Department of ECE
Amrita Vishwa Vidyapeetham, Bengaluru, India
tk_ramesh@blr.amrita.edu, {ambatinagesh,biju24n}@gmail.com,
praveengvl5@hotmal.com, pr_vaya@blr.amrita.edu

Abstract. In this protocol we use appropriate RWA methodologies depending on the priority and speed of the incoming traffics to identify the optimal lightpaths. As request arrives, centralized management system (CMS) identifies the traffic class depending on their priority and speed. Accordingly CMS uses appropriate RWA methodologies to identify the optimal lightpaths. To give more importance to high priority request the available wavelength set is divided into two subsets, called P set of higher order wavelengths and C set of remaining wavelengths. Protocol first tries to find an optimal lightpath for high priority request using wavelengths from subset C, else finds out using P. Lightpaths for low priority traffics are found by only using subset C. Further for survivability backup lightpath is maintained. The selection of backup lightpath is done in such a way that there is no shared link between the primary and backup lightpath. By simulation results, we have shown high priority requests have low blocking probability.

Keywords: Blocking probability, centralized management system, grooming, priority, RWA, traffic speed, WDM networks.

1 Introduction

Demand for networks of higher data rate with assured security and effective bandwidth utilization at a reasonable cost necessitates the use of optical networking. Optical networks have extremely high bandwidth of around 50 Tbps within very low bit error rates [1]. However, the demand for point to point communication per application is not typically as much, as the rate at which an end user can access the network is limited by "electronic bottleneck"[2]. Therefore to better utilize the entire bandwidth of an optical fiber it is always best to divide the remarkable bandwidth of an optical fiber into multiple non-overlapping optical channels of suitable data rates called lightpaths.

The development of wavelength division multiplexing (WDM) and optical fiber amplifier like erbium doped fiber amplifier (EDFA) made the possibility of dividing the huge bandwidth of optical fiber into many non-overlapping lightpaths and of amplifying several optical signals at the same time without converting them first to

P.V. Krishna, M.R. Babu, and E. Ariwa (Eds.): ObCom 2011, Part I, CCIS 269, pp. 300–307, 2012.

electrical domain respectively [3]. Hence WDM networks are capable of broadcasting multiple channels on a single fiber for longer distances. WDM network consists of nodes interconnected by point-to-point fiber links in an arbitrary topology. A message is sent from one node to another node using a wavelength continuous route called a lightpath, without requiring any optical-electronic-optical conversion and buffering at the intermediate nodes. This process is known as wavelength routing [4]. The requirement that the same wavelength must be used on all the links along the selected route is known as the wavelength continuity constraint (WCC) [5].

A RWA protocol selects a good lightpath to satisfy a connection request so as to improve the network performance [6]. Different RWA protocols have been proposed in the literature to choose the best pair of route and wavelength. They differ in their policies for selecting route and wavelength. The cost of a route is usually computed based on its hop count, delay, or congestion. If there is no wavelength which is free on all the links of a route, then the cost of the route is infinity. Otherwise, its cost is finite. The RWA problem is NP-complete [7] i.e. it is computationally intractable or, in other words, the only known protocol that find an optimal solution require exponential time in the worst case.

RWA protocol assumes either centralized or distributed control for selecting routes and wavelengths [8]. In the case of a centralized control, a central controller is assumed to be available. It keeps track of the state of the network. In the case of distributed control, no central controller is used. The whole network status information which includes the details of wavelength usage and existing lightpaths is not known to any node in the network.

Traffic grooming addresses the gap between the bandwidth capacity of wavelengths and the bandwidth requirement of connections. With the improvement of optical technology, the capacity of a single wavelength reaches optical carrier OC-192 (10 Gbps). On the other hand, the bandwidth of a connection request may be less than that, possibly OC- 48 (2.5 Gbps) or even lower. To make efficient use of the wavelength bandwidth, traffic grooming [9] is needed to pack connections at sub wavelength granularities effectively onto wavelength channels.

Since each lightpath can carry a huge mount of traffic, failures in such networks may seriously damage end-user applications. Therefore, it is very important to have networks that are capable of preventing such failures; these are known as survivable networks [10]. In survivable WDM networks, the lightpath known as primary lightpath carries traffic during normal operations. In case a primary lightpath fails, the traffic is rerouted over a new lightpath known as the backup lightpath.

2 Protocol Overview

We propose a priority based RWA protocol which uses centralized management scheme for the establishment of optimal lightpaths on the basis of number of available free wavelengths.

Initially we classify the traffic flows into four classes depending on their priority and speed. Thus most important data with high priority high speed (HPHS) and high priority low speed (HPLS) are considered as class-I and class-II flow remaining data with least priority high speed (LPHS) and least priority low speed (LPLS) are considered as class-III and class-IV flows. For this case, different suitable RWA methodologies and multiple lightpaths need to be maintained to provide the choice of selecting the suitable RWA methodologies as per the traffic classes and best lightpath, based on the changing traffic load conditions respectively.

In this priority based RWA protocol the available wavelength set is divided into two subsets, called P set of higher order wavelengths and C set of remaining wavelengths. RWA protocol tries to finds an optimal lightpath for class-I and class-II traffics using wavelengths from subset C, if connection is established then updates the routing table status else finds out using wavelengths from subset P. If connection is established then updates the routing table status else call is blocked. Optimal lightpath for class-II and class-IV traffics are found by only using wavelengths from subset C, if connection is established then updates the routing table status else call is blocked.

Here a restorable connection is realized by establishing two link-disjoint lightpaths. One lightpath is called primary lightpath, which is used to carry traffic under normal condition; the other lightpath is called backup lightpath, which is used to carry traffic when the primary lightpath fails. To reduce the spare capacity reservation for a backup lightpath, the technique of backup sharing is used. In backup sharing, two backup lightpaths can share the same wavelength on a common link if their primary lightpaths are link-disjoint. The sharing is possible since under the single link failure assumption two link-disjoint primary lightpaths cannot fail simultaneously, therefore their backup lightpaths will not be needed at the same time.

In addition traffic grooming is used for low speed traffics i.e. for class-II and class-IV traffics. In our analysis we considered the speed of low speed traffics as 2.5 Gbps and high speed traffics as 10 Gbps. As the rate of each wavelength channel is assumed to be 10 Gbps our proposed protocol tries to groom a maximum of four low speed traffics in a single wavelength channel.

3 Centralized Priority Based RWA Protocol (CPRP)

In order to give more importance to High priority requests, our protocol uses any of the existing free wavelengths (C and P sets respectively) for establishing the lightpath but for low priority requests it uses only from the C set. In our analysis out of 40 wavelengths we considered C with 27, P with 11 and remaining two wavelengths for control signals.

3.1 Establishment of Optimum Primary Lightpath

Depending on the type of traffic on the basis of priority and speed CMS establishes optimal primary lightpaths as follows:

High priority high speed (HPHS): On the basis of number of available free wavelengths.

High priority low speed (HPLS): On the basis of number of available free wavelengths and the protocol tries to groom up to four low speed traffics on this lightpath.

Low priority high speed (LPHS): On the basis of number of free wavelengths.

Low priority low speed (LPLS): On the basis of number of available free wavelengths and the protocol tries togroom up to four low speed traffics on this lightpath.

3.2 Establishment of Backup Lightpath

CMS follows above steps to find backup lightpath. But the selection of backup lightpath is done in such a way that there is no common link between backup and primary lightpath. However backup lightpaths can share the same wavelength on a common link if their primary lightpaths are link-disjoint.

3.3 Protocol

Step1: Source node intimates the CMS about the requests.
Step2: Depending on the request type CMS identifies the optimal primary and backup lightpaths as follows:

3.4 For HPHS Request

(i) CMS identifies all the possible lightpaths.
(ii) In each lightpath CMS calculates the number of free wavelengths from sub set C
(iii) Lightpath with more number of free wavelengths is considered as primary lightpath.
(iv)If no lightpath is available with free wavelengths then CMS calculates the number of free wavelengths from sub set P.
(v) Lightpath with more number of free wavelengths is considered as primary lightpath.
(vi)If no lightpath is available with free wavelengths then the request is blocked.
(vii) If primary lightpath is established CMS identifies the backup lightpath in such a way that there will not be any shared link between primary and backup lightpath.

3.5 For HPLS Request

(i) CMS first tries to groom with existing HPLS and LPLS traffics in sub set C else tries to groom withHPLS traffics in sub set P

(ii) If connection (primary lightpath) is established CMS identifies the backup lightpath in such a way that there will not be any shared link between primary and backup lightpath.
(iii) If step (i) fails then CMS repeats steps (i) to (vii) of HPHS requests.

3.6 For LPHS Request

CMS repeats steps (i), (ii), (iii), (vi) and (vii) of HPHS requests.

3.7 For LPLS Request

(i) CMS tries to groom with existing HPLS and LPLS traffics in sub set C.
(ii) If connection (primary lightpath) is established CMS identifies the backup lightpath in such a way that there will not be any shared link between primary and backup lightpath.
(iii) If step (i) fails then CMS repeats steps (ii), (iii), (vi) and (vii) of HPHS requests.

4 Simulation Results

In this section, we examine the performance of our CPRP with an extensive simulation study based upon the MATLAB 7.10.0(R2010a) simulator. For the analysis of our algorithm we used a NSF network (Fig.1) of 14 nodes and 21 links. Various simulation parameters are as given in table1.

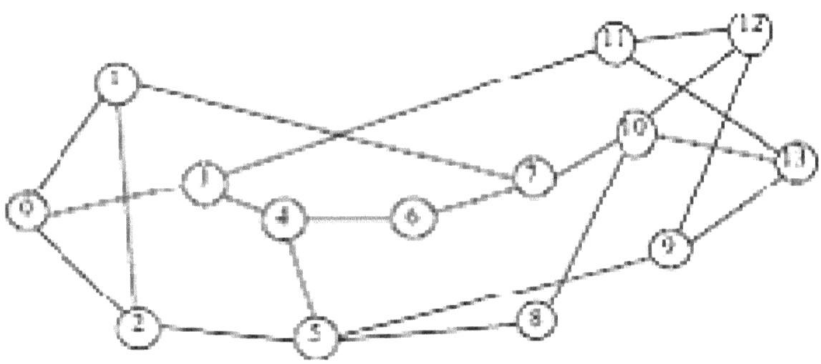

Fig. 1. NSF Network with 14 Nodes and 21 Links

Table 1. Simulation Parameters

Connection Management Scheme	Centralized
Topology	NSFNET
Number of Nodes	14
Number of Links	21
Number of Wavelengths	40
Channel Bandwidth	10 Gbps
Traffic types	4
High Speed Data Rates	10 Gbps (OC-48)
Low Speed Data Rates	2.5Gbps(OC-92)

In our experiments, we considered each type (HPHS, HPLS, LPHS, and LPLS) 25 connection requests arrive for every two seconds. In this experiment, we varied the time interval as 2, 4, 6....20 seconds and measured the blocking probability. Table 2 gives the number of each type calls rejected for every 25 connection requests per two seconds and its blocking probability.

4.1 Formula

Where Blocking Probability (BP) = Number of Connection Rejected/ Total Number of Requests Arrived

Table 2. Blocking Probability

Request Type	T=0	T=2	T=4	T=6	T=8	T=10	T=12	T=14	T=16	T=18	T=20
HPHS REJ	3	5	5	4	8	4	3	0	4	5	4
LPHS REJ	9	15	14	21	18	18	15	14	11	20	18
HPLS REJ	2	3	4	2	6	6	2	3	1	2	3
LPLS REJ	6	8	5	8	10	11	8	9	7	6	6
HPHS BP	0.12	0.2	0.2	0.16	0.32	0.16	0.12	0	0.16	0.2	0.16
LPHS BP	0.36	0.6	0.56	0.84	0.72	0.72	0.6	0.56	0.44	0.8	0.72
HPLS BP	0.08	0.12	0.16	0.08	0.24	0.24	0.08	0.12	0.04	0.08	0.12
LPLS BP	0.24	0.32	0.2	0.32	0.4	0.44	0.32	0.36	0.28	0.24	0.24

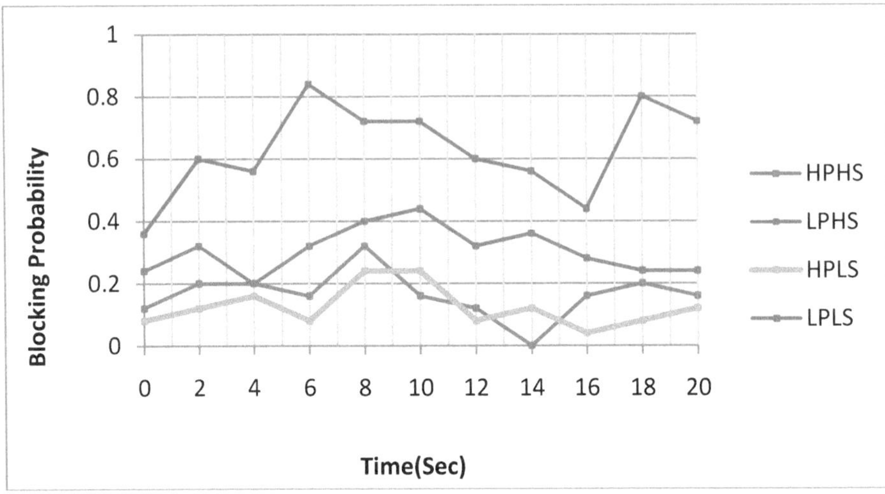

Fig. 2. Shows the blocking probability obtained for HPHS, HPLS, LPHS, and LPLS type connection requests with our CPRP scheme. It shows that the blocking probability of high priority traffic is significantly less than the low priority traffics.

5 Conclusion and Future Works

It is always best to make use of appropriate RWA methodologies as for every different traffic requests. For this case an appropriate RWA protocol has to be designed which has to make use of different appropriate RWA strategies as for every traffic requests. In this paper we have proposed a priority based routing protocol taking into consideration four classes of traffics based on priority and speed. Based on the number of free wavelengths the CMS selects the optimal lightpath with more number of free wavelengths. When there is a failure occurs along the lightpath, it adaptively shifts the traffic through the backup lightpath. In this RWA protocol in order to give more importance to high priority request the available wavelength set is divided into two subsets, called P set of higher order wavelengths and C set of remaining wavelengths. In addition traffic grooming is used for low speed traffics. By simulation results, we have shown that high priority requests have low blocking probability in comparison to low priority requests.

As centralized protocols are not scalable to large networks because of the performance bottleneck and it is also a case of single-point failure, which is not desirable. In our future work we would like to divide the network into sectors and to use single backup CMS which will take over if any of the sector CMS fails.

References

1. Shepherd, F.B., Vetta, A.: Lighting Fibers in a Dark Network. IEEE Journal on Selected Areas in Communications 22(9), 1583–1588 (2004)
2. Almeida, R.T.R., de Calmon, L.C., Olivieira, E., Segatto, M.E.V.: Design virtual topologies for large optical networks through an efficient MILP formulation. Optical Switching and Networking 3(1), 2–10 (2006)

3. Siva Ram Murthy, C., Gurusamy, M.: WDM Optical Networks, Concepts, Design and Algorithms. Eastern Economy Edition (2004)
4. Chlamtac, I., Ganz, A., Karmi, G.: Lightpath Communications: An Approach to High Bandwidth Optical WAN's. IEEE Transactions on Communications 40(7), 1171–1182 (1992)
5. Ramaswami, R., Sivarajan, K.N.: Routing and wavelength assignment in all-optical networks. IEEE/ACM Transactions on Networking 3(5), 489–500 (1995)
6. Zang, H., Jue, J.P., Mukherjee, B.: A Review of Routing and Wavelength Assignment Approaches for Wavelength-Routed Optical WDM Networks. Optical Networks 1(1), 47–60 (2000)
7. Tornatore, M., Lucerna, D., Pattavina, A.: Improving Efficiency of Backup Reprovisioning in WDM Networks. In: Proceedings of IEEE INFOCOM (2008)
8. Ramesh, T.K., Konda, S.K., SwarajTeja, M., Harshadeep, Vaya, P.R.: An Adaptive Reliable Multipath Centralized RWA Algorithm for All-Optical WDM Networks. CiiT International Journal of Networking and Communication (4) (April 2011)
9. Zhu, K., Mukherjee, B.: Traffic grooming in an optical WDM mesh network. IEEE J. Sel. Areas Communication 20(1), 122–133 (2002)
10. Ramamurthy, S., Sahasrabuddhe, L., Mukherjee, B.: Survivable WDM Mesh Networks. Journal of Light Wave Technology 21(4) (April 2003)

Low-Power Area Efficient Reconfigurable Pipelined Two's Complement Multiplier with Reduced Error

R. Sakthivel[1], M. Vanitha[2], and Harish M. Kittur[1,*]

[1] School of Electronics Engg, Vellore Institute of Technology University, Vellore, 632014, Tamilnadu, India
rsakthivel@vit.ac.in
[2] School of Information Technology and Engineering, VIT University

Abstract. This paper describes reconfigurable two's complement multiplier using Baugh Wooley's algorithm supporting six modes of operation. A fixed width Baugh Wooley multiplier is used as prototype for the architecture. Error reduction technique based on bias compensation vector is introduced in the design to achieve a low error fixed width product. Clock gating technique and zero input method is used to obtain a power efficient design. A power reduction of 8.14% and 7.39% is achieved for the current design compared to other non-reconfigurable and reconfigurable techniques. Also a higher clock frequency of 200 MHz is supported by the current architecture compared to other reconfigurable structure which supports 100 MHz for the same reconfigurable two's complement multiplication. Area of the proposed power efficient architecture is also reduced by 32.64% compared to the previous reconfigurable architecture.

Keywords: Baugh Wooley, Reconfigurable, Clock gating, Two's complement multiplication.

1 Introduction

Multiplication is a very important operation in any VLSI application. About 40% of the total power consumed by a processor is dissipated in arithmetic computational operations. Increasing demand for portable computing and digital signal processing makes the design of power efficient multipliers indispensable in modern VLSI design. Most of the basic multipliers either follow Booth [1] or Baugh Wooley [2] algorithm. For most of the DSP applications we need fixed width multipliers [3]. Fixed width multipliers also called single precision multipliers are studied in [3], [4], [5]. The multipliers discussed in [3] and [4] are not reconfigurable architectures. Reconfigurable architectures are presented in [5], [6], [7] and [8]. The work in [6], [7], [8] focuses on construction of reconfigurable multipliers with full-precision prototypes. Four configuration modes are presented in [5] with pipelining technique. In the present work we improve this design to support six configuration modes with

* Member, *IEEE.*

P.V. Krishna, M.R. Babu, and E. Ariwa (Eds.): ObCom 2011, Part I, CCIS 269, pp. 308–321, 2012.

lesser power consumption than [5]. Sub word multiplication results in a large error when compared to truncating n least significant bits of a full precision multiplier. Considerable work has been done in [3], [4], [5], [9], [10] to reduce this error by statistical means. Error compensation bias vector discussed in [10] is employed in the design to reduce the error.

This work aims at design of a pipelined, reconfigurable, power-efficient, low-error Baugh Wooley multiplier. The paper is organized as follows: section 2 gives a brief description of Two's complement parallel array multiplication algorithm, section 3 gives an insight into fixed width multiplication and bias compensation for low error implementation of a Baugh Wooley multiplier, section 4 gives the architecture of a reconfigurable Baugh Wooley multiplier. In section 5 power reduction schemes are discussed for the proposed architecture and results are presented in section 6. A brief conclusion closes the paper.

2 Two's Complement Parallel Array Multiplication Algorithm

Two's complement representation of a binary number adds complexity to the multiplier algorithm because the sign of the number is embedded in the number itself [2]. The algorithm for two's complement multiplication is presented in [2]. The algorithm's principal advantage is that all the partial products are positive.

Let us consider two numbers X and Y:

$$X = (x_{n-1} \ldots x_0) = -x_{n-1}2^{n-1} + \sum_{i=0}^{n-2} x_i 2^i \; (1); \; Y = (y_{n-1} \ldots y_0) = -y_{n-1}2^{n-1} + \sum_{i=0}^{n-2} y_i 2^i \quad (2).$$

A full precision product XY is given by:

$$XY = x_{n-1}\, y_{n-1}\, 2^{2n-2} + \sum_{i=0}^{n-2} \sum_{j=0}^{n-2} x_i\, y_j 2^{i+j} - x_{n-1} \sum_{j=0}^{n-2} y_j 2^{j+n-1} - y_{n-1} \sum_{i=0}^{n-2} x_i\, 2^{i+n-1} \quad (3)$$

To avoid the usage of subtractor cells, negative terms can be rewritten as:

$$x_{n-1} \sum_{j=0}^{n-2} y_j 2^{j+n-1} = x_{n-1}(-2^{2n-2} + 2^{n-1}) + \sum_{j=0}^{n-2} y'_j 2^{j+n-1} \quad (4)$$

This way XY becomes: $XY = x_{n-1}\, y_{n-1}\, 2^{2n-2} + \sum_{i=0}^{n-2} \sum_{j=0}^{n-2} x_i\, y_j 2^{i+j} + x_{n-1}(-2^{2n-2} + 2^{n-1}) +$

$$\sum_{j=0}^{n-2} y'_j 2^{j+n-1}) + y_{n-1}(-2^{2n-2} + 2^{n-1} + \sum_{i=0}^{n-2} x'_j 2^{j+n-1}) \quad (5)$$

The final equation is given by:

$$XY = -2^{2n-1} + (x'_{n-1} + y'_{n-1} + x_{n-1}\, y_{n-1})\, 2^{2n-2} + \sum_{i=0}^{n-2} \sum_{j=0}^{n-2} x_i\, y_j 2^{i+j} + (x_{n-1} + y_{n-1})\, 2^{n-1} - x_{n-1} \sum_{j=0}^{n-2} y_j 2^{j+n-1} + \sum_{j=0}^{n-2} x_{n-1}\, y'_j 2^{j+n-1} + \sum_{i=0}^{n-2} y_{n-1}\, x'_i 2^{j+n-1} \quad (6)$$

The above equation represents the Baugh Wooley's algorithm for Two's complement parallel array multiplication [2]. Fig 1 is the pictorial representation of Baugh Wolley's multiplication algorithm for n=6 and m=4.

3 Low Error Fixed Width Multipliers

When two numbers are multiplied, a double-word length product is produced. In applications where only the single-precision product is required, the double-word length result is rounded to single precision. Hence, in single-precision applications, it is not necessary to compute the least significant part of the product exactly. Instead, it is only necessary to estimate the carries generated in the computation of the least significant part that will ripple into the most significant part of the product. This will produce single-precision multiplier with significantly reduced circuit complexity [11].

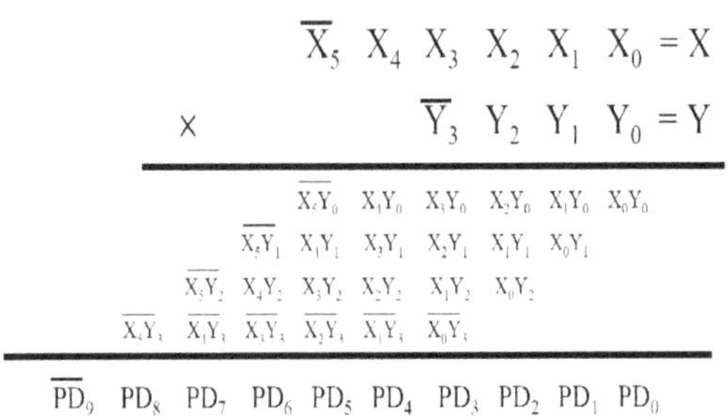

Fig. 1. Baugh Wolley's Algorithm for two's complement array multiplication

The main disadvantage of such a less complex single precision multiplier is that it introduces a significant error in the actual product term. This error could refrain the design from its usage in DSP applications where a more accurate value close to the expected value is desired. There are many statistical techniques that can be employed to reduce this error. Compensation vector method is used to reduce the error [7]. This method has showed better performance compared to the other techniques. The compensation vector for τ=m=n=v, where τ, m, n and v are clearly defined in [7], is given by:

$$P = (X_{v-2}Y_1 + \ldots + X_1Y_{v-2}) + 1 \quad (7)$$

The compensation vector is fed as carry input for the most significant part.

4 Reconfigurable Fixed-Width Baugh Wooley Multiplier

Reconfigurable fixed width Baugh Wooley Multiplier is discussed in [5] with four operation modes. Effort is made to increase the number of operating modes to six.

The prototype for the proposed reconfigurable architecture is a fixed width multiplier. Fig. 2(a) shows the partial products generated by the prototype. The three modules denoted by mul1, mul2 and mul3 are used to achieve the six modes of operation (Table 1). To achieve these modes of operation various configuration parameters are to be set. The details of the Configuration Parameters (CP) are given in the corresponding Fig for each mode. M3 and M6 are not discussed in the basic prototype architecture but are incorporated here in the design of the power efficient multiplier architecture.

4.1 Mode 1 (M1) – One *n x n* Fixed Width Multiplier

In mode 1 the multiplier receives two n bit data and gives an n bit product. All the three multipliers are utilized in this mode of operation. The partial products are independently generated and then summed up to get the final result (Fig. 2(b)).

Table 1. Operation modes for the proposed reconfigurable structure

TABLE 1

Mode of Operation (M)	Function Description
M1	One n x n fixed width multiplier
M2	Two n/2 x n/2 fixed width multiplier
M3	One n/2 x n/2 fixed width multiplier
M4	One n/2 x n/2 full precision multiplier
M5	Two n/4 x n/4 full precision multiplier
M6	One n/4 x n/4 full precision multiplier

Compensation vector is generated according to the above described method and is added as carry in at the final stage. To avoid addition of this compensation bit twice (from both MUL1 and MUL2) a control circuit has been introduced in MUL1 which results in the proper selection of the compensation bit according to the mode of operation.

4.2 Mode 2 (M2) – Two n/2 x n/2 Fixed Width Multipliers

Two n/2 bit numbers are received as input and two n/2 bit numbers are presented as output (Fig. 3c). This mode utilizes only MUL1 and MUL2 for its operation. To make use of MUL1 and MUL2 for this mode of operation we need to set some of the partial products of the MUL1 and MUL2 to some predefined values. The configuration parameters are as mentioned in the Fig 3(b).

4.3 Mode 3 (M3) – One n/2 x n/2 Fixed Width Multiplier

Mode two invokes two multipliers for its operation. For some of the smaller applications we don't need to perform two multiplication operations at a time. In such cases we make use of only one of the multiplier MUL1 to arrive at the result. This mode of operation reduces the power consumption of the multiplier which is discussed in the next section.

4.4 Mode 4 (M4) – One n/2 x n/2 Full Precision Multiplier

MUL 3 alone is used for operation in this mode. Two n/2 bit numbers are multiplied and an n bit product is given as output. The partial product array diagram for mode 4 is shown in the fig.5 along with the mode settings.

4.5 Mode 5 (M5) – Two n/4 x n/4 Full Precision Multipliers

Mode 5 (M5) widely used in lower resolution operation serves as performing two n/4x n/4 full-precision multiplications. Under the minimum number of modules and partial product configuration setting constraints, we make use of the MUL3 to fulfill the M5 operation. The parameter settings for the operation in this mode are explained in fig 7(b).

4.6 Mode 6 (M6) – One n/4 x n/4 Full Precision Multiplier

Similar to M3, M6 is an extension to M5 which uses lesser resources compared to M5 to arrive at multiplication of only one set of inputs. This mode is also an added advantage for low power applications where only a part of the entire architecture is invoked.

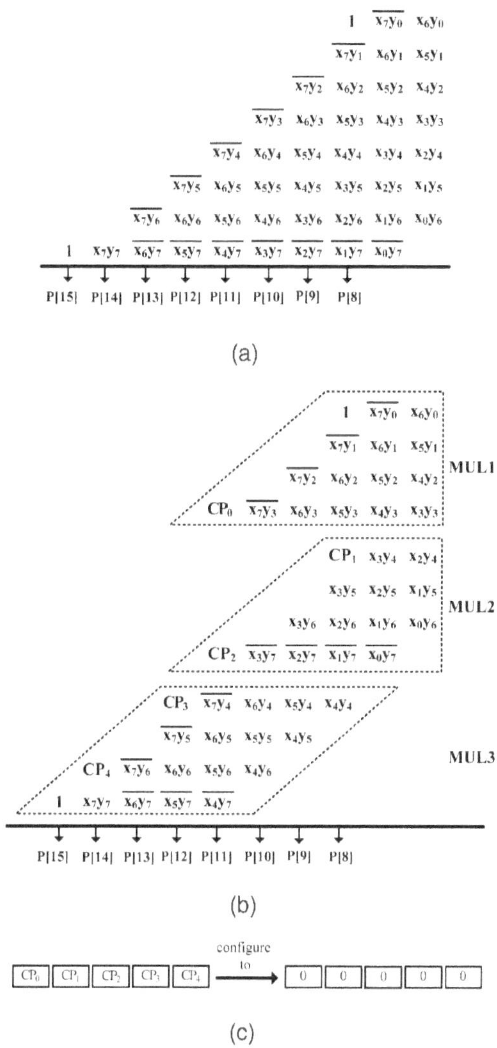

Fig. 2. (a) Partial products for fixed width multiplication, (b) Partial Products for M1, (c) Configuration parameters [5]

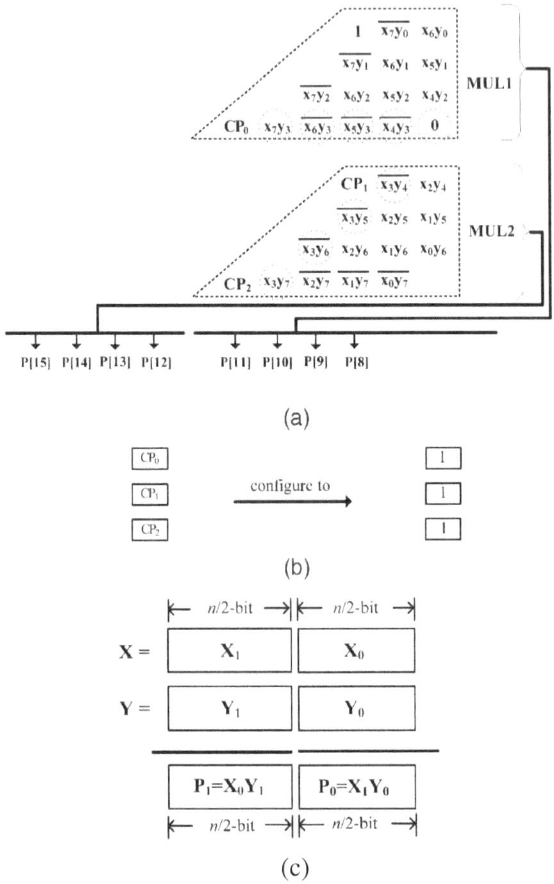

Fig. 3. (a) Partial products for M2, (b) Configuration Parameters for M2, (c) Input and output relations for M2

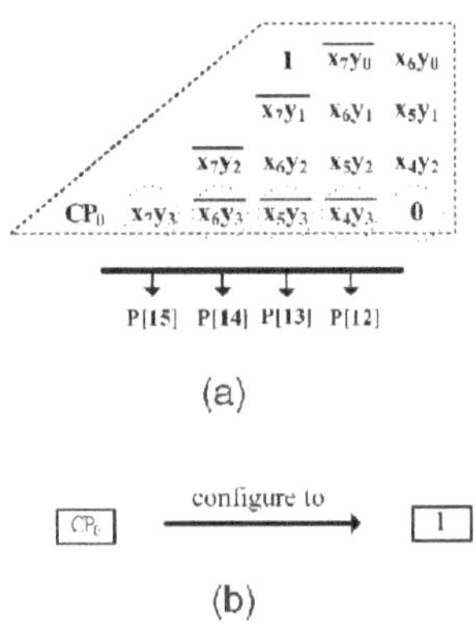

Fig. 4. (a) Partial products for M3, (b) Configuration Parameters for M3

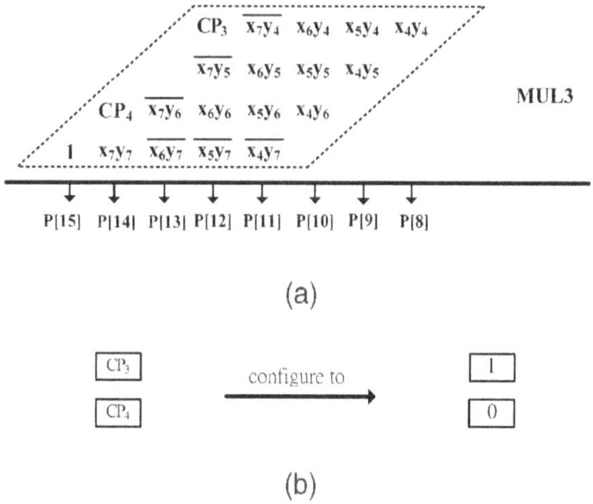

Fig. 5. (a) Partial products for M4, (b) Configuration Parameters for M4

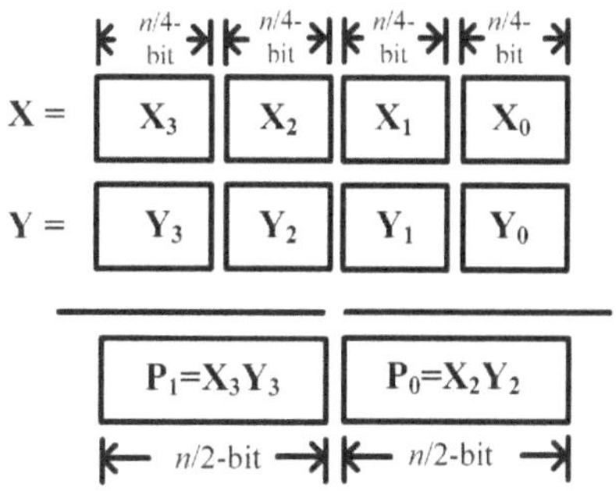

Fig. 6. Input Output relations for M4

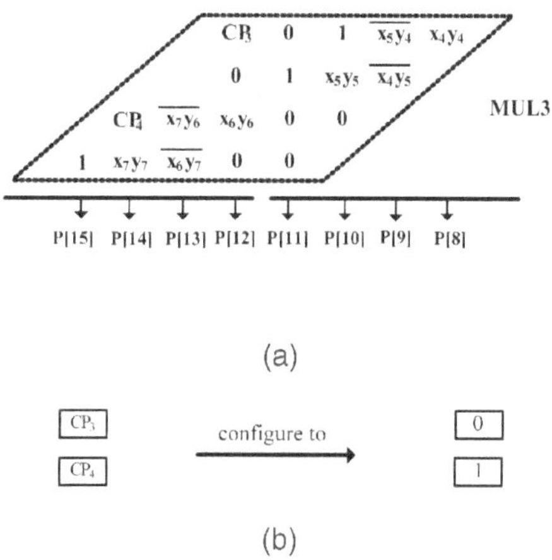

Fig. 7. (a) Partial products for M5, (b) Configuration parameters for M5

Keeping the above mentioned operating modes and reconfigurable architecture a pipelined structure [7] is proposed to arrive at the functionality. Fig 9 (a) gives an overview of the architecture. Further each block is elaborated in the corresponding Figures. The architectures of MUL1, MUL2 and MUL3 are also elaborated (Fig. 9(e, f, g)). Further AND and NAND in the MUL architecture represent AND and NAND gates respectively. Other blocks used in the MUL architecture are elaborately shown as the independent modules in Fig 9(h). It can be clearly seen that the entire architecture is divided into three stages. Stage 1 decodes the operating conditions (op) for different modes of operation. Modes M3 and M6 are not included in the prototype architecture but are introduced in the next section to reduce the power consumption of the prototype multiplier.

Signal op is used to determine the type of multiplication performed; either n x n fixed width or n/2 x n/2 fixed width or n/2 x n/2 full precision or n/4 x n/4 full precision. In stage two each MUL module performs independent multiplication operation according to the multiplicand inputs and the decoded control signals from the stage 1. The product from each MUL is then sent to stage 3 for final addition. MUX in the final stage is used to select the output of the multipliers based on the input control signals.

5 Power Efficient Architecture

The reconfigurable structures discussed in section 4 are power in-efficient because they invoke all the hardware resources during the operation. To make the architecture power efficient we introduce clock gating and zero input techniques. Also control signal n is introduced in the design to achieve M3 and M6 modes of operation. Control signal n determines number of multiplication operations. n=0 implies only one multiplication operation and n=1 implies two multiplication operations. The control signal n has no significance when used in M1 or M4 modes.

5.1 Clock Gating

Clock gating is applied to second and third stages of the architecture to achieve power saving. Correspondingly gating registers are introduced in the design. According to our requirement the registers are disabled based on the mode of operation.

1. If multiplier is operated in M1 mode then MUL1, MUL2 and MUL3 are conditionally disabled based on the zero inputs to the multiplier.
2. For operation in M2 mode MUL3 is disabled.
3. For operation in M3 mode MUL2 and MUL3 are disabled.
4. For operation in M4 mode MUL1 and MUL2 are disabled.
5. For operation in M5 mode MUL1 and MUL2 are disabled.
6. For operation in M6 mode MUL1 and MUL2 are disabled and MUL3 is partially disabled by disabling the gated register: gated_reg_s3_b (Fig. 8(a)).

The main disadvantage of this scheme is the redundant hardware that is generated. The duplicated registers increase the area of the architecture.

Table 2. Quanlitative Comparison of other Reconfigurable Multiplier

	[10]	[9]	[5]	Proposed work
Prototype architecture	Array multiplier and two's complement multiplier	array multiplier and MAC	Two's complement multiplier	Two's complement multiplier
Number of operating modes	4	4	4	6
Precision provided	Full-precision	Full-precision	Full-precision, Fixed-width	Full-precision, Fixed-width

Table 3. Quantitative comparison of the results obtained with the results reported by non-reconfigurable and other reconfigurable architectures

Power Consumption, Timing and Chip Area	Non-Reconfigurable Pipelined Fixed-Width Multiplier [10]	Non-Power Efficient Reconfigurable Pipelined Fixed-Width Multiplier [5]	Power Efficient Reconfigurable Pipelined Fixed-Width Multiplier [5]	Basic Reconfigurable Low-Error Pipelined Multiplier (our work)	Power Efficient Reconfigurable Low-Error Pipelined Multiplier (our work)
Timing	100 MHz	100 MHz	100 MHz	200 MHz	200 MHz
M1 Power Consumption	1.609 mW	1.845 mW	2.145 mW	1.913 mW	2.461 mW
M2 Power Consumption	N/A	1.822 mW	1.607 mW	1.886 mW	1.834 mW
M3 Power Consumption	N/A	N/A	N/A	1.872 mW	1.437 mW
M4 Power Consumption	N/A	1.815 mW	1.389 mW	1.822 mW	1.154 mW
M5 Power Consumption	N/A	1.657 mW	1.242 mW	1.642 mW	1.031 mW
M6 Power Consumption	N/A	N/A	N/A	1.636 mW	0.954 mW
Average Power Consumption	1.609 mW	1.785 mW	1.596 mW	1.795 mW	1.478 mW
Area Consumed	$9072 um^2$	$11342\ um^2$	$13456\ um^2$	$8546\ um^2$	$9051\ um^2$

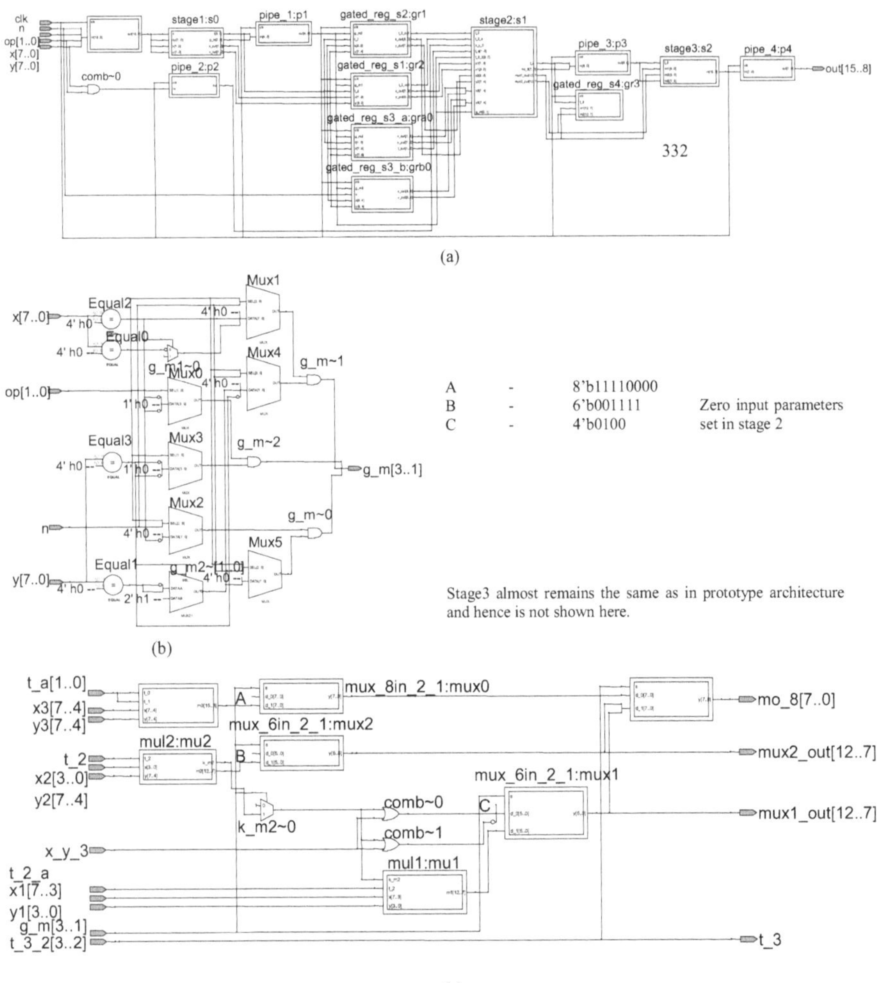

Fig. 8. (a) Power efficient multiplier architecture, (b) Detailed view of decoder in stage1 used to select the multiplier, (c) Stage 2 elaborated.

5.2 Zero Input

As mentioned above for MUL1, MUL2 and MUL3 can be conditionally disabled based on the zero inputs they receive. The conditions for zero value of input are:

1. If X[7:4] is zero, input registers of MUL1 and MUL3 can be disabled.
2. If X[3:0] is zero, input registers of MUL2 can be disabled.
3. If Y[7:4] is zero, input registers of MUL2 and MUL3 can be disabled.
4. If Y[3:0] is zero, input registers of MUL1 can be disabled.

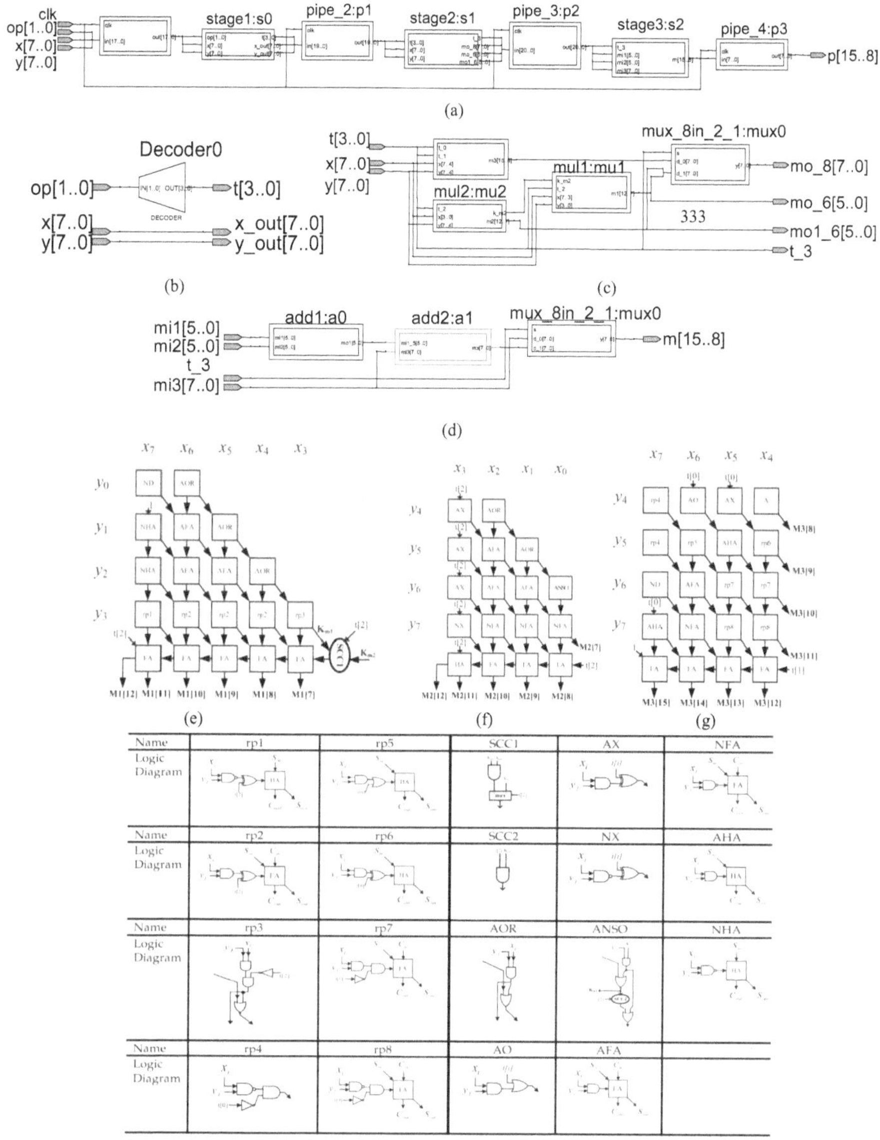

Fig. 9. (a) Prototype for fixed width two's compliment multiplier, (b) Stage 1 elaborated, (c) Stage 2 elaborated, (d) Stage 3 elaborated, (e) MUL1, (f) MUL2, (g) MUL3, (h) Each block of MUL elaborated [5]

Although one of the input operands to the multiplier is zero the product of the multiplication module is not zero, because some of the partial products are complemented in the multiplication algorithm. The actual product outputs of the MUL3 and MUL2 should be $(11110000)_2$ and $(001111)_2$ respectively [5]. The output of MUL1 in such case is not same in all cases because the output depends on the partial product vector. In such case the actual product of MUL1 in the disabled condition is {0100, x_3y_3 & K_{m2}, $(x_3y_3$ & $K_{m2})'$ } [5]. The control unit CU is used to treat Km2 = 1 when MUL2 is disabled [7]. Latch L is used to keep the present value of when MUL1 is disabled. For the operations other than M1 mode, input registers of ADD1 can be disabled.

Based on the above stated conditions the input signal is decoded and g_m1, g_m2 and g_m3 are generated (fig. 8(b)) which control the gated registers of MUL1, MUL2 and MUL3 respectively (fig. 8(c)). The gated register at stage 3 is controlled by t[3] which is 1 only in the operation mode M1.

6 Results and Comparison

The architecture is modeled in Verilog HDL. Concerning the chip implementation, we adopt cell based design flow with typical 1.13 and tpz973gtc 230 technology libraries and implement the reconfigurable multiplier in TSMC 180nm CMOS process. Cadence rc complier is used to synthesize the RTL design of the proposed reconfigurable architecture. Table 2 gives the qualitative comparison among different reconfigurable multipliers. It is difficult to compare the current work with other reconfigurable multipliers in a quantitative way due to different modes of operation, number of operation modes, operating frequencies and different prototype multiplier architectures. [5] mentions four modes of operation and the results obtained here are in close agreement with those presented in [5]. Fig. 8 shows the power comparison of different module in different modes. Due to the inclusion of M3 and M5 the average power of the architecture is considerably reduced. The power efficient architecture described in this paper showed a 8.14% lesser power consumption compared to non reconfigurable structure reported in [5]. Also 7.39% lesser average power is consumed compared to the power efficient multiplier proposed in [5]. The frequency of operation is doubled as compared to the other reconfigurable architectures. Although only 8 bit multiplier is studied here the same methodology can be extended to n=16, 32 and 64. The average power is expected to further decrease when implemented for n=16, 32, 64 [5]. The power is calculated by giving random vectors as inputs to the multiplier for the clock frequency of 200 MHz. The proposed architecture also consumes lesser area compared to the area reported in [5]. Area is reduced by 24.33% for the prototype and 32.64% for the power efficient architecture.

7 Conclusion

In this paper we present a pipelined, reconfigurable, power-efficient, low error two's complement multiplier using Baugh Wooley's multiplication algorithm. Two additional operation modes are proposed other than the four mentioned in [5] to achieve six modes of operation. With the addition of the two more operating modes the average power of the multiplier is significantly reduced. We employed clock gating and zero input techniques for achieving better power efficiency. Though only 8 bit architecture is described in the paper same design can be extended to 16, 32 and 64 bits with modifications in the design. A similar technique can be adopted for simple array multiplier by changing the basic prototype structure described in section 3. In spite of doubling the frequency of operation the power consumption of M1 and M2 is only slightly greater then the previously proposed ones. The power consumption of modes 3, 4, 5 and 6 are definitely lower than previously reported values.

References

1. Booth, A.D.: A Signed Binary Multiplication Techniques. Quarterly J. Mechanics and Applied Math. 4, 236–240 (1951)
2. Baugh, C.R., Wooley, B.A.: A Two's Complement Parallel Array Multiplication Algorithm. IEEE Trans. Computers 22(12), 1045–1047 (1973)
3. Jou, J.M., Kuang, S.R., Chen, R.D.: Design of Low-Error Fixed-Width Multiplier for DSP applications. IEEE Trans. Circuits and Systems 46(6), 836–842 (1999)
4. Kidambi, S.S., El-Guibaly, F., Antoniou, A.: Area-Efficient Multipliers for Digital Signal Processing applications. IEEE Trans. Circuits and Systems 43(2), 90–94 (1996)
5. Tu, J.-H., Van, L.-D.: Power-Efficient Pipelined Reconfigurable Fixed-Width Baugh-Wooley Multipliers. IEEE Trans. Computers 58(10) (October 2009)
6. Van, L.D., Yang, C.C.: Generalized Low-Error area-Efficient Fixed-Width Multipliers. IEEE Trans. Circuits and Systems I 52(8), 1608–1619 (2005)
7. Tsai, M.-H.: DSP Processor Approaches for The synchronization in DMT based VDSL. Dissertation report submitted at National Central University, Taiwan (October 2002)
8. Lim, Y.C.: Single-Precision Multiplier with Reduced Circuit Complexity for Signal Processing Applications. IEEE Trans. Computers 41(10), 1333–1336 (1992)
9. Wey, C.L., Li, J.F.: Design of Reconfigurable Array Multipliers and Multiplier-Accumulators. In: Proc. IEEE Asia-Pacific Conf. Circuits and Systems, pp. 37–40 (December 2004)
10. Krithivasan, S., Schulte, M.J.: Multiplier Architectures for Media Processing. In: Proc. IEEE Asilomar Conf. Signals, Systems, and Computers, vol. 2, pp. 2193–2197 (November 2003)
11. Tsao, Y.-L., Chen, W.-H., Tan, M.-H., Lin, M.-C., Jou, S.-J.: Low-Power Embedded DSP Core for Communication Systems. EURASIP J. Applied Signal Processing, 1355–1370 (January 2003)

RWA Protocol for Larger WDM Networks

T.K. Ramesh, R. Janani, S. Prannoy Kiran, T. Swapna, and P.R.Vaya

Department of ECE
Amrita Vishwa Vidyapeetham, Bengaluru, India
tk_ramesh@blr.amrita.edu, {prannoy.s91,swapnalucky15}@gmail.com,
jananijn294@gmail.com

Abstract. In this paper we present the design of a RWA protocol for larger WDM network (RPLN), consisting of 'N' sector networks, each with a centralized management system (CMS). A backup central CMS of high capacity is maintained to share the work and to takeover if any of the sector CMS fails. As per the connection request, the central CMS decides inter or intra sector transmission. In the case of intra transmission, the sector CMS identifies the optimal lightpaths based on number of free wavelength and distance. For inter transmission, it acts as a node for the central CMS. The central CMS acts as the backup CMS if anyone of the sector CMS fails. By this we introduce a new concept of *centralized-centralized-distributed*. RPLN overcomes the single point failure and performance bottleneck of a large network with single CMS. Furthermore grooming is also used to improve the blocking probability of connection requests.

Keywords: Blocking probability, CMS, grooming, large WDM network.

1 Introduction

Demand for networks of higher data rate with guaranteed security and effective bandwidth utilization necessitates the use of optical networking. These networks have extremely high bandwidth of around 50 Tbps within extremely low bit error rates [1].

However, the demand for point to point communication per application is not typically as much, as the rate at which an end user can access the network is limited by "electronic bottleneck"[2]. Therefore to better utilize the entire bandwidth of an optical fiber it is always best to divide the remarkable bandwidth of an optical fiber into multiple non-overlapping optical channels of suitable data rates called lightpaths.

The invention of wavelength division multiplexing (WDM) and optical fiber amplifier like erbium doped fiber amplifier (EDFA) made the possibility of dividing the huge bandwidth of optical fiber into many non-overlapping lightpaths and of amplifying several optical signals at the same time without converting them first to electrical domain correspondingly. In a WDM network, end users communicate with one another via WDM channels, which are referred to as lightpaths [3]. Protocols used for selecting routes and wavelengths to establish lightpaths is known as a routing and wavelength assignment (RWA) protocol. Many problems in wavelength routed WDM.

P.V. Krishna, M.R. Babu, and E. Ariwa (Eds.): ObCom 2011, Part I, CCIS 269, pp. 322–328, 2012.

Demand for networks of higher data rate with guaranteed security and effective bandwidth utilization necessitates the use of optical networking. These networks have extremely high bandwidth of around 50 Tbps within extremely low bit error rates [1].

However, the demand for point to point communication per application is not typically as much, as the rate at which an end user can access the network is limited by "electronic bottleneck"[2]. Therefore to better utilize the entire bandwidth of an optical fiber it is always best to divide the remarkable bandwidth of an optical fiber into multiple non-overlapping optical channels of suitable data rates called lightpaths.

The invention of wavelength division multiplexing (WDM) and optical fiber amplifier like erbium doped fiber amplifier (EDFA) made the possibility of dividing the huge bandwidth of optical fiber into many non-overlapping lightpaths and of amplifying several optical signals at the same time without converting them first to electrical domain correspondingly. In a WDM network, end users communicate with one another via WDM channels, which are referred to as lightpaths [3]. Protocols used for selecting routes and wavelengths to establish lightpaths is known as a routing and wavelength assignment (RWA) protocol. Many problems in wavelength routed WDM networks have RWA as a sub problem .Therefore, it is mandatory to use a good routing and wavelength assignment protocol to establish lightpaths in an efficient manner so as to improve network performance in terms of blocking probability of connections. In addition as each lightpath can carry a huge amount of traffic, failures in such networks may seriously damage end-user applications.

Therefore, it is very important to have networks that are capable of preventing the failures; these are known as survivable networks [4]. In survivable WDM networks, the lightpath known as primary lightpath carries traffic during normal operations. In case a primary lightpath fails, the traffic is rerouted over a new lightpath known as the backup lightpath. Lightpath establishment in WDM networks can use either distributed or centralized management scheme. In distributed scheme, no central controller is assumed to be present. The global state information of the network, which includes the details of wavelength usage and existing lightpaths, is not known to any node in the network. It is the responsibility of the source node to identify and to establish the optimal lightpath with the limited information available with it. So this scheme is used as the backup scheme in case of any failure of the main CMS so as to have an uninterrupted service. So, before the race condition occurs in the distributed, the backup CMS has to be replaced. In centralized scheme, when a demand arrives at the source node, the node sends the demand information to a CMS, which runs a centralized routing protocol to compute a primary and backup lightpath pair for the demand [5]. The advantage of this approach is that wavelength channels can be utilized in an efficient way, as the central node keeps the up-to-date network state information. But as the traffic load increases, the control traffic to and from the controller increases substantially and the central controller requires sufficient buffer and processing power to handle the request and also in a large network, the central controller becomes the performance bottleneck. It is also a case of single-point failure, which is not desirable, i.e. the failure of the CMS can bring down the entire network [6]. In our protocol we have overcome the problem of performance bottleneck by dividing the larger networks into sectors of smaller networks called global networks. A backup CMS is used to overcome the single point failure of centralized scheme with single CMS. For better utilization of bandwidth RPLN uses grooming method which in turn improves the blocking probability of connection requests.

2 A RWA Protocol for Larger Network (RPLN)

Large network: It is a WDM network consisting of 'N' sector networks, each with certain number of nodes within the performance bottleneck of the centralized management scheme with single CMS. In our analysis we considered N = 4 and each sectors with NSFNET 14 node 21 link. The block schematic is as follows:

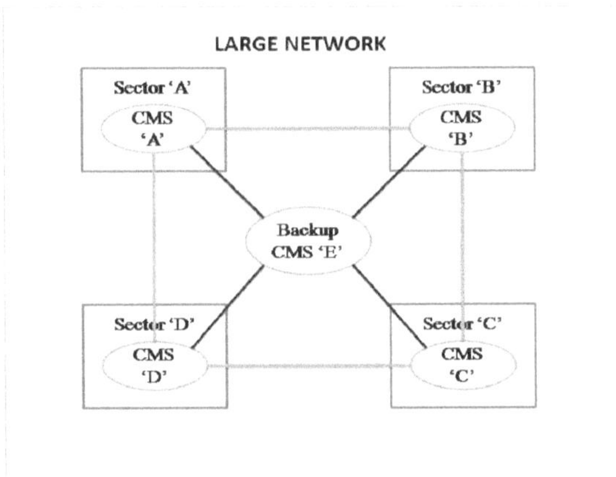

Fig. 1.

The additional CMS ('E') is of very high capacity which acts as a backup for sector CMSs, i.e., if any of the sector CMS fails CMS 'E' will takeover, and also it involves in the data transmission between the sectors. This CMS is of very high capacity and it also participates in routing from the source to destination. In any case of failure of this CMS, the distributed links between the sectors provides the backup lightpaths with uninterrupted data transmission.

2.1 Data Transmission

The data transmission in the large WDM networks is of two types:

I. Within the sector (INTRA)
II. Between the sectors (INTER)

In our analysis we used centralized management scheme for INTRA and INTER type of connection requests and distributed management schemes as our backup in any case of failure of the main CMS 'E'.

2.2 Algorithm

Step1: Request arrives at a node.
Step2: Central CMS identifies INTRA or INTER transmission.
Step3: For INTRA transmission, sector CMS identifies the optimal primary and backup lightpath using the following techniques.

(i) Number of free wavelengths
(ii)Shortest distance algorithm

Step3(a1): Lightpath with least distance and maximum number of free wavelengths are selected as primary lightpath and very next lightpath acts as backup lightpath.
Step3(a2): If the primary lightpath fails, the data will be routed through the backup lightpath and very next lightpath is considered as new backup lightpath.

Step3(b1): For INTER transmission source node transfer the request to the sector CMS and then from there to the central CMS.

(b2): The center CMS finds the destination sector.
(b3): Sector CMS identifies optimal primary and backup lightpath.
(b4): CMS checks for the possibility of grooming if the arrived request is equal to or less than 5Gbps else it follows the normal procedure.
(b5): The center CMS allocates the path between the source of the sector CMS to the destination of the remote CMS.

Step4: If any of the CMS fails in any of the sectors, the central CMS replaces that CMS establishing a distributed network between the sectors.

Step5: If the center CMS itself fails, the transfer continues through the distributed links between the sectors.

3 Simulation Results

We have studied the performance of our RPLN protocol using MATLAB 7.10.0(R2010a) simulator. For the analysis, we used west part of NSFNET in each sector, which is of 14 nodes and 21 links as shown in figure 2. Various simulation parameters of west part of NSFNET are as given in table1.

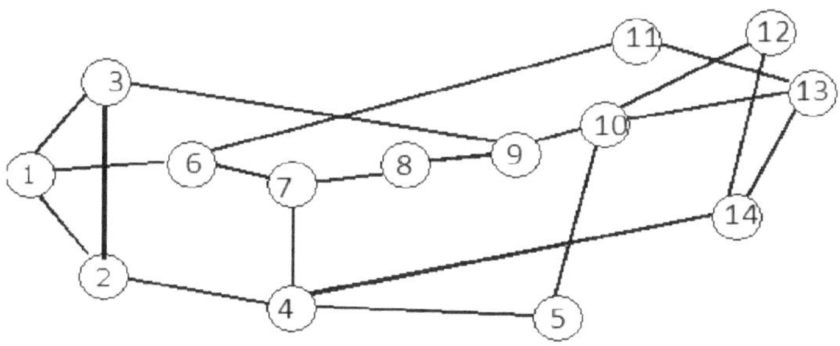

Fig. 2. NSF Network with 14 Nodes and 21 Links

Table 1. Simulation Parameters

Connection Management Scheme	Centralized/distributed
Topology	NSFNET
Number of Nodes	21
Number of Links	21
Number of Wavelengths	40
Channel Bandwidth	10 Gbps
Traffic types	2
High Speed Data Rates	10 Gbps (OC-48)
Low Speed Data Rates	2.5Gbps (OC192)

Table 2. Number of calls rejected

	T=2	**T=4**	**T=6**	**T=8**	**T=10**	**T=12**	**T=14**	**T=16**
With Grooming	8	13	23	21	36	60	51	74
Without grooming	10	16	24	40	64	85	114	128

Table 3. Blocking Probability

	T=2	**T=4**	**T=6**	**T=8**	**T=10**	**T=12**	**T=14**	**T=16**
With Grooming	40	32.50	38.30	0.2625	0.4	0.5	0.36	0.4625
Without grooming	50	40	40	0.75	0.64	0.7	0.814	0.8

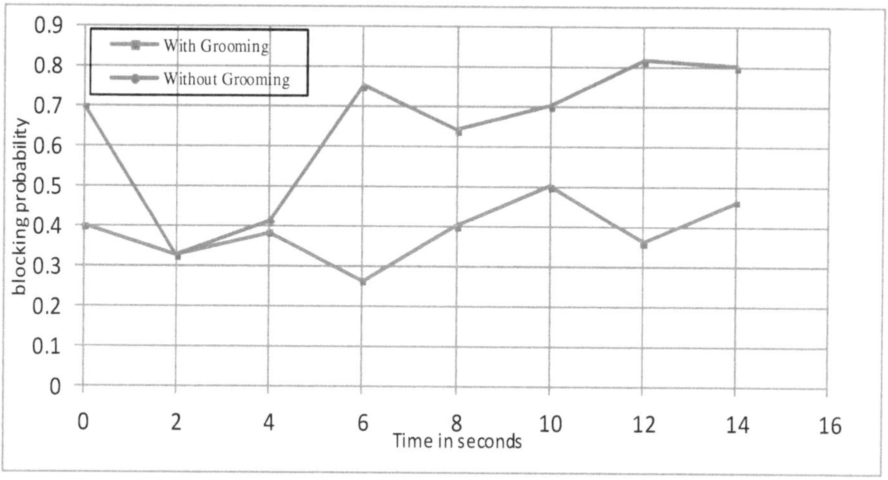

Fig. 3. Shows the Blocking Performance of RPLN with and without grooming as per the simulation results recorded in table 2. Traffic grooming concept is used to improve the bandwidth utilization, i.e. we can send more than one request in a single wavelength at the same time. There by efficiently utilizing the bandwidth.

4 Conclusion

In this paper we proposed a RWA protocol for larger WDM networks (RPLN) which gives better performance compared to the large centralized networks. As the network with N number of nodes is divided into sub-networks, the number of nodes in each network decreases which increases the network performance. In general for optimal lightpath calculation, number of free wavelengths is used to distribute the load in the network and to reduce congestion; but that may lead to large setup time if the distance between the nodes is more. Similarly if we use only shortest distance for the optimal lightpath calculation, it may result in more congestion in the network. To avoid these, we use both the parameters for the calculation in order to achieve less congestion and minimum setup time in the network. Our approach is more reliable because if any of the sector CMS fails the backup CMS takeover the entire process. In addition grooming is applied to reduce the request rejections.

References

1. Shepherd, F.B., Vetta, A.: Lighting Fibers in a Dark Nework. IEEE Journal on Selected Areas in Communications 22(9), 1583–1588 (2004)
2. Siva Ram Murthy, C., Gurusamy, M.: WDM Optical Networks. Prentice Hall of India, Private Ltd, New Delhi (2004)
3. Singh, P., Sharma, A.K., Rani, S.: Routing and wavelength assignment strategies in optical networks. Optical Fiber Technology 13, 191–197 (2007)

4. Ramamurthy, S., Sahasrabuddhe, L., Mukherjee, B.: Survivable WDM Mesh Networks. Journal of Light Wave Technology 21(4) (April 2003)
5. Ruan, L., Luo, H., Liu, C.: A Dynamic Routing Algorithm With Load Balancing Heuristics for Restorable Connections in WDM Networks. IEEE Journal on Selected Areas in Communications 22(9) (November 2004)
6. Shen, L., Ramamurthy, B.: Centralized vs. Distributed Connection Management Schemes under Different Traffic Patterns in Wavelength-Convertible Optical Networks (2002)

Integration of SMS Security Systems in Cloud Computing

Mohan Kumar C.M.[1], Raj Sudheer Dangeti[2], and Jeganathan L.[3]

[1] School of Computing Science & Engineering
VIT University-Chennai Campus, Chennai-600048, India
cmmohankumar@vit.ac.in
[2] Data Centre & Virtualisation Specialist,
CISCO Systems, Bangalore, India
rajsudheer.it@gmail.com
[3] School of Computing Science & Engineering
VIT University-Chennai Campus, Chennai – 600025, India
jeganathan.l@vit.ac.in

Abstract. The main motive of this paper is to patch up one of the security problems in the Public CLOUD COMPUTING, to accesses the Virtual Machines (VM)'s by authorized owner only and to secure the cloud resources from the un-authorized users through SMS alert systems. The SMS service is dedicated to Cloud setup which can be integrated independent of work load manager (like condor, novello, other orchestrators etc). Though there are number of cloud security solutions that allow the users to use the allocated VM's or resources by the authorized owner like AAA, we are still facing of intrusion in the pubic clouds

Keywords: Virtual Machine, SMS, Cloud Computing, Virtualization.

1 Introduction

Cloud computing, the hottest buzzword in the IT area, has been frequently discussed in workshops, conferences and many articles published in Journals and Magazines. Nevertheless, to define cloud computing is not an easy task, confusion still remains about what exactly the definition of cloud computing is from different perspectives; there are more than a dozen definitions for cloud computing in Academia.

But the following features of cloud computing defined among them are common:

_ Cloud computing is a computing platform to enable resource sharing in terms of scalable infrastructures, middleware and application development platforms and applications.

_ New computer technologies, such as service oriented architecture, virtualization, high power enterprise servers and high band width, support to realize cloud computing platforms.

P.V. Krishna, M.R. Babu, and E. Ariwa (Eds.): ObCom 2011, Part I, CCIS 269, pp. 329–335, 2012.

_ Typically, services provided in clouds can be grouped into 3 categories: software as a service (SaaS), platform as a service (PaaS), and infrastructure as a service (IaaS).

Cloud computing enables users to store and process all their data on the web via the Internet, with no doubts, security is one of main significant concerns. A more fundamental reason preventing companies from moving to cloud computing is that the cloud computing platform is inherently less secure than the traditional network infrastructure. Security must be integrated into every aspect of cloud computing platforms to make users trust that their data is secure.

One of biggest challenges of security issues in the design of a cloud computing platform is that of virtual machine (VM) instance interconnectivity. In this paper, we focus on network security for virtual machines.

2 Proposed Solution

Here we discuss and analyze the network secure problems existed in VMs, and then present a novel virtual network model which can control the inter-communication among VM instances running on the hypervisor with higher security.

To provide the security and best access to the resource allocated based on the privileges, and by allowing the end user and administrator with instant authentication and alert systems via SMS for smooth flow of access if there is any intrusion. This second level is user level authentication. The SMS service in the public cloud is integrated to workload manger and portal to send SMS via SMS gateway. An SMS of the 12 character code is generated and passed to individual VM; the VM that is going to access will send SMS with code to the user, trying to access the resource. The end user will be prompted to enter the code with display of the phone number that is sent (this can be invisible also) for the authentication before the access of traditional authentication. The architecture of the solution is shown in Fig.1.

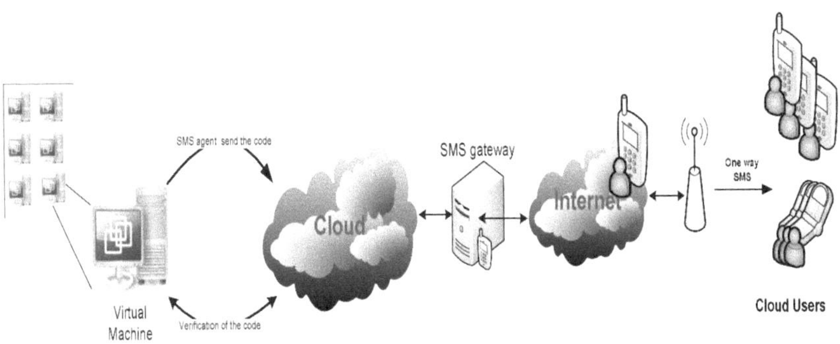

Fig. 1. Architectural Diagram of the Proposed Solution

Fig.2 shows how SMS codes are generated. The abbreviation of the code is also given here in Fig.2. In Fig.3 the sample SMS code generated is given.

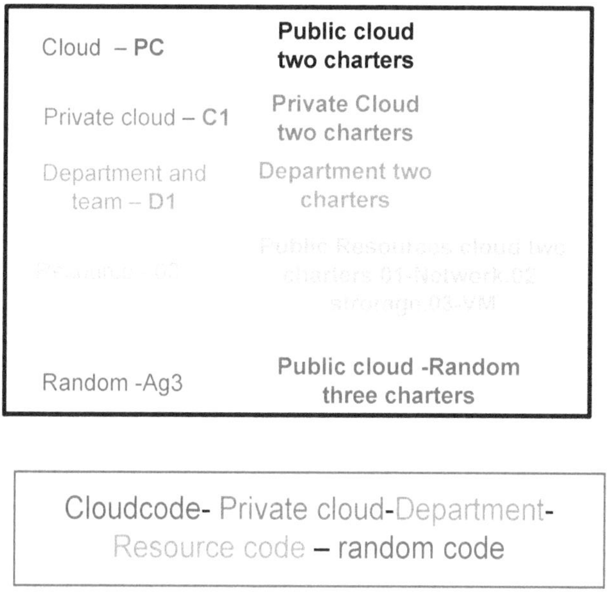

Fig. 2. SMS Coding Process

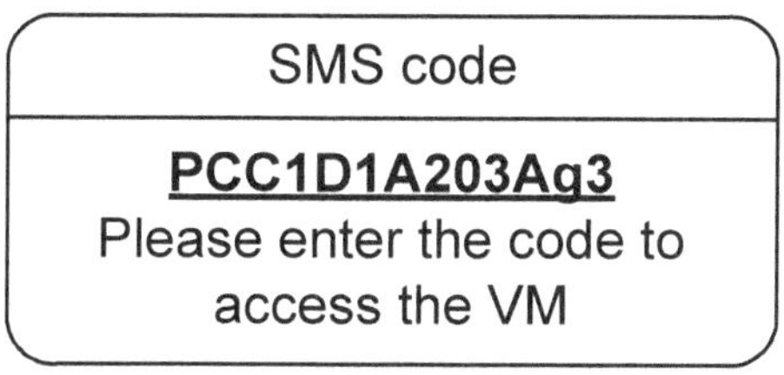

Fig. 3. Generated SMS code

The SMS service is integrated with all components of the workload management, from the layers of the hardware integration and VM's repository ,which can be done without major code changes by adding pieces of code in all the system component API's or plug-in (network ,storage ,server etc integration to workload manger). SMS will be sent as per the workflow to alert the administrator and to the user, in case of the resource shortage or intrusion or failure etc.

3 Work Flow

The Fig. 4 narrates the work flow of accessing cloud resources using VMware Integrated with SMS alter Systems. Here the user ties to login the cloud using the user name & password. The credentials are sent to the cloud user database where the user details like name of the user, mobile number are stored. The SMS agent generates the access code for the user based on the type resource access request.

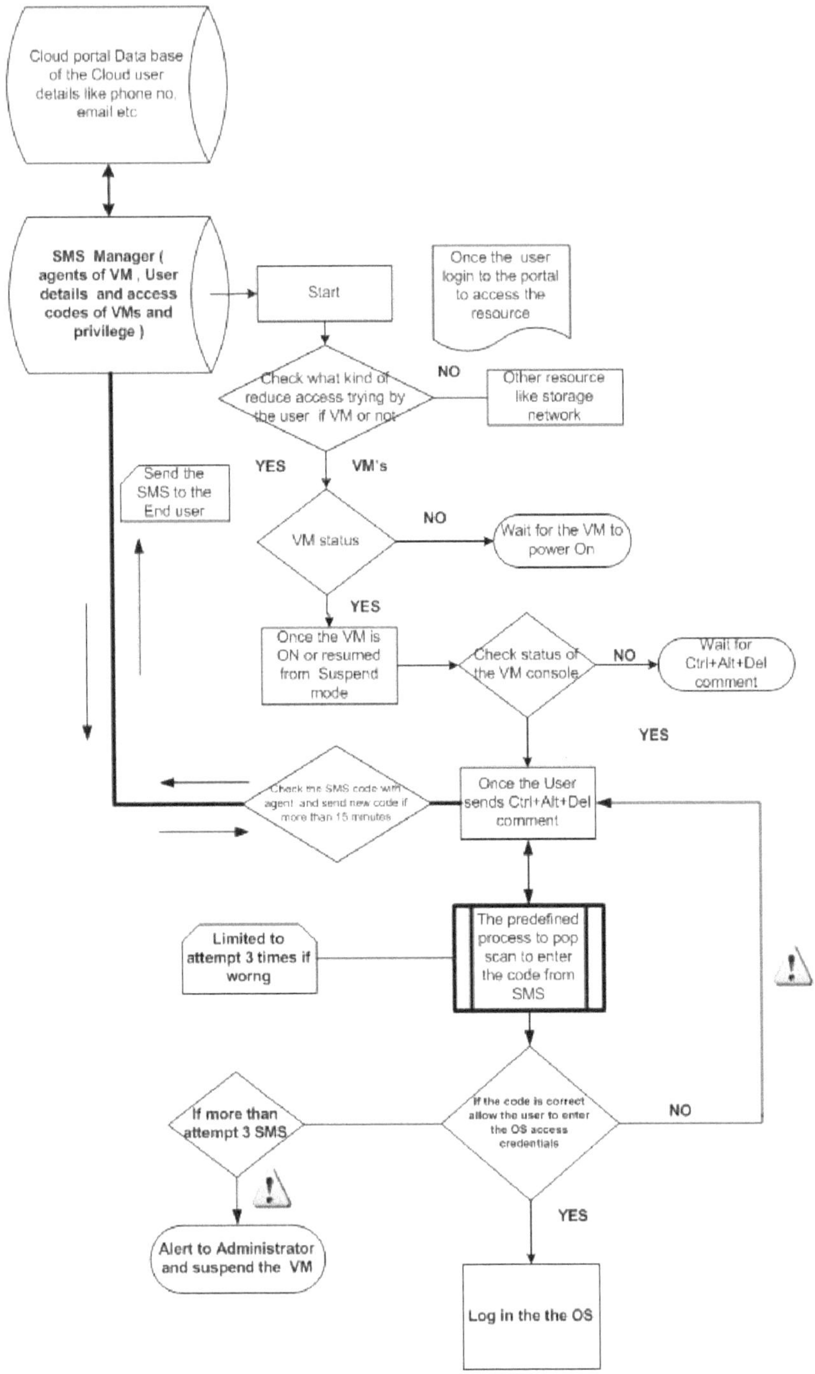

Fig. 4. Work Flow of Cloud Access

The agent then sends the access code to the user's mobile number. The User on login keys-in the access code received via SMS on his / her mobile. The access code entered is matched with the code generated. If the code matches, the user will be logged in and will have access to resources based on the access privilege. If the access code entered by the user doesn't match with the access code generated by the SMS agent, in 3 attempts, an SMS alert is send to the user's mobile indicating that there is an unauthorized access with his user name.

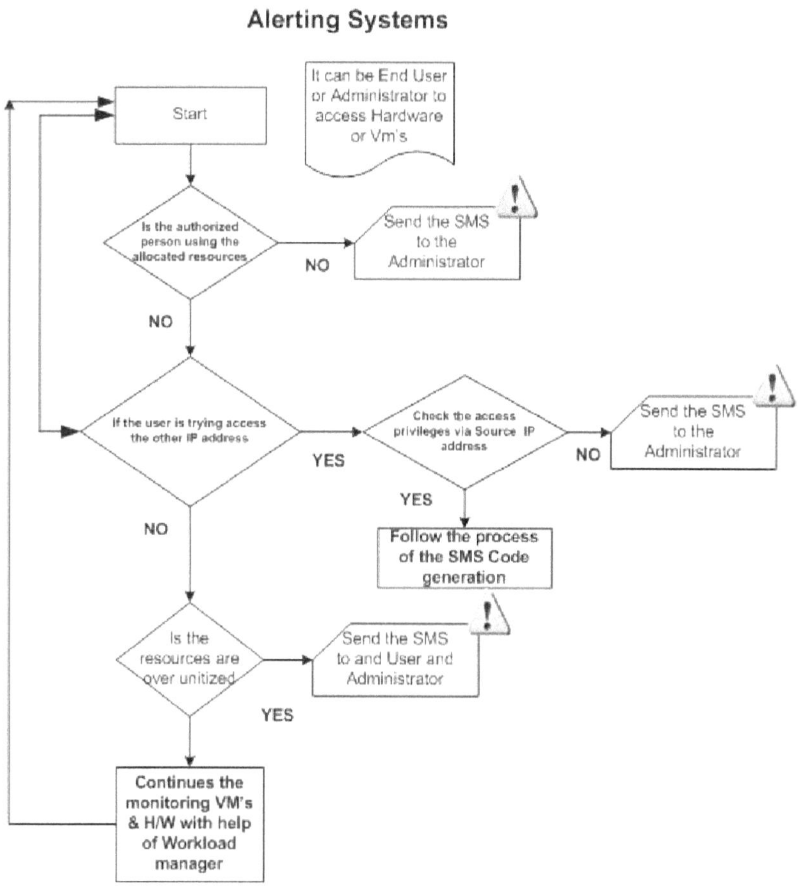

Fig. 5. SMS Alert work flow

We can further integrate this with Microsoft Exchange server and active sync as well.

Fig. 5 explains how SMS alerts are send to the user. Alerts are sent to the user in 3 instances.

a. Unauthorized access to VM.

b. Unauthorized access to resources where the user doesn't have access privileges after user logged in VM.

c. When resources are over utilized.

This model can be used not only for the resource access alert system but also for process triggering like logs, analysis, updates etc and event scheduling by enabling two way SMS service in the gateway.

4 Conclusion

A survey shows that security is the most significant user's concerns in cloud computing. In this paper, we focus on the security of virtual machines which is a key technology of cloud platforms. We propose a solution to integrate SMS with Virtual Machines to access VM's by authorized users there by restricting the access for an intruder. The same solution can be extended to secure any resource in cloud. The proposed model is in the conceptual level only and is not tested hence no test results available.

References

1. Pervez, Z., Lee, S., Lee, Y.-K.: Multi-Tenant, Secure, Load Disseminated SaaS Architecture. In: Proceedings of the 12th International Conference on Advanced Communication Technology (ICACT), Phoenix, USA, pp. 214–219 (2010)
2. Pastaki Rad, M., Sajedi Badashian, A., Meydanipour, G., Ashurzad Delcheh, M., Alipour, M., Afzali, H.: A Survey of Cloud Platforms and Their Future. In: Gervasi, O., Taniar, D., Murgante, B., Laganà, A., Mun, Y., Gavrilova, M.L. (eds.) ICCSA 2009. LNCS, vol. 5592, pp. 788–796. Springer, Heidelberg (2009)
3. Sun Microsystems, Inc. Introduction to Cloud Computing Architecture.White Paper, 1st edn. (June 2009)
4. Gruman, G., Knorr, E.: What cloud computing really means. InfoWorld. Electronic Magazine (April 2008)
5. Armbrust, M., Fox, A., Griffith, R., Joseph, A.D., et al.: Above the Clouds: A Berkeley View of Cloud Computing. EECS Department, University of California, Berkeley (2009)
6. Vaquero, L.M., Rodero-Merino, L., Caceres, J., Lindner, M.: A break in the clouds: towards a cloud definition. SIGCOMM Comput. Commun. Rev. 39, 50–55 (2009)
7. Geelan, J.: Twenty one experts define cloud computing. Virtualization. Electronic Magazine (August 2008)
8. Whyman, B.: Cloud Computing. Information Security and Privacy Advisory Board, pp. 11–13 (December 5, 2008)
9. Security-as-a-Service - The next growth area for cloud computing (October 26, 2009)
10. Nurmi, D., Wolski, R., Grzegorczyk, C., Obertelli, G., Soman, S., Youseff, L., Zagorodnov, D.: The Eucalyptus Open-source Cloudcomputing System. In: 9th IEEE/ACM International Symposium on Cluster Computing and the Grid, pp. 124–131 (2008)

11. Virtualization Concept and History (January 24, 2010)
12. Amazon Elastic Compute Cloud (Amazon EC2), http://aws.amazon.com/ec2/
13. MacDonald, N.: Security considerations and best practices for securing virtual machines. Gartner, Inc. (March 2007)
14. Reiser, H.P.: Security Challenges with Virtualization (December 2009)
15. Virtualization: What are the security risks? (January 22, 2008)
16. Kirch, J.: Virtual Machine Security Guidelines Version 1.0. The Center for Internet Security (September 2007)
17. SMS integration Process, http://www.sms-integration.com/p_30-solutions-sms.html

Identity Based Cryptosystem: A New Paradigm in Public Key Infrastructure

S. Kuzhalvaimozhi[1] and G. Raghavendra Rao[2]

[1] Department of Information Science and Engineering,
National Institute of Engineering
Mysore-570 008
kuzhali_mozhi@yahoo.com
[2] Department of Computer Science and Engineering
National Institute of Engineering
Mysore-570008

Abstract. Identity Based Cryptosystem (IBC) is a new paradigm in the field of cryptography. Using IBC two users can communicate in secured manner without the need for exchanging of public or private keys and without keeping any key directories to store the public keys. IBC systems have the advantage of having any unique identity string as the public key, like an email address, phone numbers, etc. This system removes the requirement for certificates and associating a name with a public key. Thus eliminates some of the practical problems related with the traditional public key cryptosystems. In this paper we proposed the algorithm to implement the Identity Based Encryption System.

Keywords: Identity Based Cryptosystem, Public Key Infrastructure, Bilinear Map.

1 Introduction

In traditional crypto schemes, Public Key Infrastructure (PKI) is one of the popular approach, where individual users generate their own key pairs. The private keys are with the people who created the pair and share their public keys to a public key server. To encrypt a message everyone can get the authenticated public key from the certificate server as illustrated in Fig. 1. Suppose Alice wishes to send an encrypted message to Bob. It is required that the message should be authenticated and reach securely to Bob. If Bob had not generate a key pair for him, uploaded it to a key server, or if Alice cannot find Bob‘s public key, she will not be able to encrypt the message and send it to Bob.

Problems with the traditional Public Key Cryptosystems (PKCs) are use of very long keys, typically 1024 bits, the cost involved in managing the infrastructure needed [7] and authenticate public keys. Digital certificates are used in these systems to connect an identity of a person or a machine to a public key. But in the practical system, the distribution and revocation of keys and constant checking of

P.V. Krishna, M.R. Babu, and E. Ariwa (Eds.): ObCom 2011, Part I, CCIS 269, pp. 336–341, 2012.

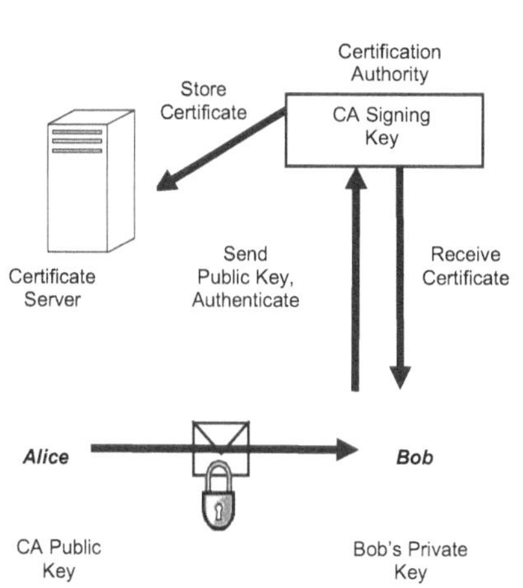

Fig. 1. Traditional Public Key System

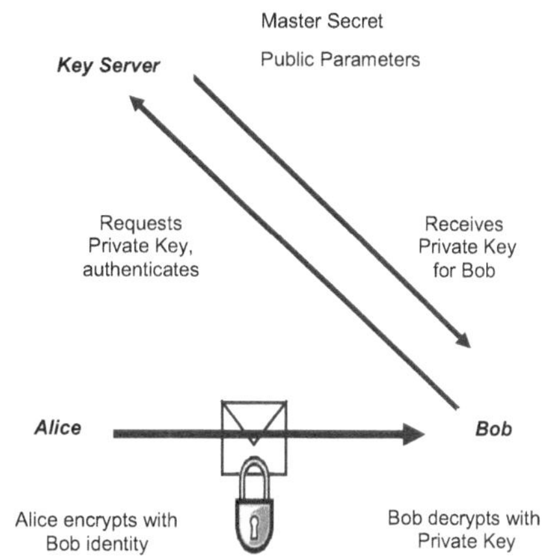

Fig. 2. Identity Based Cryptosystem

these certificates produce difficulties. At the same time the IBC will not replace the conventional PKI. But it might prove to be a complementary technology.

In 1984 Dr. Shamir[4] proposed the idea of public key encryption scheme called Identity Based Cryptosystems. His main motivation was to reduce the usage of the certificate. The design and implementation of an Identity-Based Encryption (IBE) system was a long-standing open problem in cryptography. Boneh and Franklin[2] proposed the first secure and practical IBE system in 2001. The advantage of IBE system is that users can choose any arbitrary string as their public key.

IBE goal is to reduce the complexity to bring an entity into the crypto system. In the past, work on IBE has been mathematical. It has developed a new public-key cryptosystem in that the public key generated [1] from some arbitrary bit string that is the identity. Thus, a name, an email address, a binary object such as a picture or sound can be considered equivalent to a public key. The IBE system can be thought of as a function of the form $K = IBE(ID)$ that produces keys from identities and other system parameters, without loss of generality.

The functionality of IBE would be extremely practical. Anyone could encrypt the messages and send it to anyone, without worrying about their keys. On the other side the receiver can not decrypt the messages without the private key. The main component of identity-based encryption is going to be private key computations at the receiver side. It should not be possible to calculate the corresponding the private key from the public identity without any additional trapdoor information such as master secret and public parameters as illustrated in Fig. 2. Otherwise, anyone could perform the same computation and the system would offer no security.

To calculate a private key, a cryptographic secret is needed. The calculation can only be done by a trusted server which has this secret. Each entity in the system sends his/her identity to a trusted third party called the Private Key Generator (PKG), to obtain the private key. The PKG is capable of keeping the global trapdoor information secret and efficiently deliver to any valid user. As a consequence, the level of trust on the PKG that is required is even stronger than the level of trust required for public-key certificates.

2 Preliminaries

Here in this section, we briefly present the background concepts which help in understanding the Identity-based cryptosystems.

Bilinear pairing is an important primitive for many cryptographic schemes. Many elegant cryptographic schemes have been formulated utilizing the properties of these bilinear pairings. Let G_1 be an additive group of prime order q, generated by p , and let G_2 be a multiplicative group with the same order q. We assume that there is a bilinear map e from $G_1 \times G_1 \rightarrow G_2$ with the following properties:

(1) Bilinearity: Which means that given elements $A_1, A_2, A_3 \in G_1$, we have that
$e(A_1 + A_2, A_3) = e(A_1, A_3) \times e(A_2, A_3)$ and
$e(A_1, A_2 + A_3) = e(A_1, A_2) \times e(A_1, A_3)$.
In particular, for $e(aA_1, bA_2) = e(A_1, A_2)^{ab}$, a,b $\in Z_q^*$ where Z_p denotes all positive integer which is less than p. Z_p^* denotes multiplicative group modulo p.

(2) Non-degeneracy: Which means that there exists $A_1, A_2 \in G_1$ such that $e(A_1, A_2) \neq 1_{G_2}$, where 1_{G_2} is the identity of G_2.

(3) Computability: Which means that there exists an efficient algorithm to compute $e(A_1, A_2)$ $\forall A_1, A_2 \in G_1$.

Decision Diffie-Hellman is easy: The Decision Diffie-Hellman problem (DDH). Given aP, bP, cP $\in G_1$. If we want to decide whether cP = abP, we can easily determine by checking e(P, cP) = e(aP, bP).

Computational Diffie-Hellman is hard: The Computational Diffie-Hellman problem (CDH). Given P, aP, bP $\in G_1$, if we want to compute abP $\in G_1$, it is assume to be hard.

Since the Decision Diffie-Hellman problem (DDH) in G1 is easy, we cannot use DDH to build our cryptosystems. Instead, the security of our IBE system is based on a variant of the Computational Diffie-Hellman assumption (CDH).

3 Related Work

Shamir's original system was based upon RSA encryption. The system proposed by Shamir is a signature-only system. He was unable to extend the proposed system to an encryption system. Between 1984 and 2001, a number of IBE systems were created, but they all had limitations, such as requiring large amounts of computation on the part of the PKG. In 2001, two new proposals were published, improving on previous work. Clifford Cocks created a scheme based upon quadratic residues[3].

Cocks's system encrypts bit-by-bit, and requires expansion of the message; for a 1024-bit modulus and a 128-bit bulk encryption key, 16K of data must be transferred. With modern networks, this is a completely acceptable overhead. Dan Boneh and Matt Franklin created a scheme based upon Weil Pairings [2]. Pairing-based systems [10] use bilinear maps between groups to establish a relationship whereby hashes of the identity create the encryption scheme.

Gentry also described Certificate-Based Encryption that uses an IBE system with certificates to create a hybrid approach[6] that essentially makes the identity not be a name, but a well-defined certificate. In a conceptually related approach, Al-Riyami and Paterson [8] have their Certificateless Public Key Cryptography.

4 Identity Based Encryption

In this paper we explain the algorithms to implement the Identity Based Encryption. IBE usually consisting of four algorithms namely, System Setup, Key Extraction, Encryption, and Decryption and three types of players, a Private Key Generator PKG, sender S, and receiver R.

1. System Setup: This algorithm is responsible for generating a master key and global system parameters. IBE systems rely upon a trusted central authority called Private Key Generator (PKG) who manages the parameters with which keys are created. The PKG uses the following steps to generate the system parameters.

- picks an elliptic curve, a master secret key ***msk*** where $msk \in Z_p^*$ and system parameters ***param*** on the curve using a random number generator.
- Then PKG calculates $msk \bullet param$. The operator $\bullet$ is multiplication of integers with points on elliptic curve.
- The key generation center publishes the system parameter $msk \bullet param$ to all the users and keeps the key ***msk*** secret. In this step calculating $msk \bullet param$ is easy, but for a given ***param*** finding the value of ***msk*** is practically impossible.

2. Encryption: This algorithm uses the receiver's identity (ID) as a public key to encrypt the messages.

- The sender first hashes receiver's identity $\boldsymbol{ID}$(for example, the ID can be Bob@nie.ac.in) to a point on the elliptic curve.
- The sender picks a random number $\boldsymbol{r}$
- calculates a key $\boldsymbol{k} = e(r \bullet ID, msk \bullet param)$.
- The sender then sends the encrypted message $C = E_k[M]$ to receiver.
- The PKG also sends $r \bullet param$ to the receiver.

3. Key Extraction: This algorithm generates the private key for the receiver involved in the message transaction. Using the system parameters, receiver identity ID and the master secret , it generates the private key of receiver. This algorithm is run by the key generation center on behalf of a user that requests his own private, after checking that the user matches with his claimed identity. When the Receiver receives the message, he may not yet have a private key. The following are the steps followed by PKG for the key extraction.

- To get a private key, the receiver authenticates to the PKG.
- The key server, after authenticating the Receiver, calculates $msk \bullet ID$ and returns it to the Receiver.
- the receiver can get the key k by calculating: $k = e(msk \bullet ID, r \bullet param)$.

4. Decryption: This algorithm decrypts messages and obtain the plaintext message M using the corresponding private key.

- $M = D_k[C]$

5 Conclusion

In this paper Identity Based Encryption is investigated. We also presented the algorithm to implement the IBE. IBC is an extension to the public key infrastructure environment, which is used to reduce the trouble of certificate management between the users. Email encryption, ecash, evote are some of the applications where IBC can be directly applied. However, a major weak point [5] of this system is key generation by a single entity PKG . To avoid this problem, several key generation authorities can be assigned. They cannot compromise the system without help from the other authorities. IBE can be further extended for digital signatures, group signature by which authentication can be provided.

References

1. Boneh, D., Boyen, X.: Secure Identity Based Encryption Without Random Oracles. In: Franklin, M. (ed.) CRYPTO 2004. LNCS, vol. 3152, pp. 443–459. Springer, Heidelberg (2004)
2. Boneh, D., Franklin, M.: Identity-Based Encryption from the Weil Pairing. SIAM J. of Computing 32(3), 586–615 (2003); In: Kilian, J. (ed.) CRYPTO 2001. LNCS, vol. 2139, pp. 213–229. Springer, Heidelberg (2001)
3. Cocks, C.: An Identity Based Encryption Scheme Based on Quadratic Residues. In: Honary, B. (ed.) Cryptography and Coding 2001. LNCS, vol. 2260, pp. 360–363. Springer, Heidelberg (2001)
4. Shamir, A.: Identity Based Cryptosystems and Signature Scheme. In: Blakely, G.R., Chaum, D. (eds.) CRYPTO 1984. LNCS, vol. 196, pp. 47–53. Springer, Heidelberg (1985)
5. Gagne, M.: Identity-Based Encryption: a Survey. RSA Laboratories Cryptobytes 6(1) (Spring 2003)

6. Gentry, C.: Certificate-Based Encryption and the Certificate Revocation Problem. In: Biham, E. (ed.) EUROCRYPT 2003. LNCS, vol. 2656, pp. 272–293. Springer, Heidelberg (2003)
7. Ellison, C., Schneier, B.: Ten risks of PKI: What you're not being told about public key infrastructure. Computer Security Journal 16(1), 1–7 (2000)
8. Al-Riyami, S.S., Paterson, K.G.: Certificateless Public Key Cryptography. In: Laih, C.-S. (ed.) ASIACRYPT 2003. LNCS, vol. 2894, pp. 452–473. Springer, Heidelberg (2003)
9. Crampton, J., Lim, H.W., Paterson, K.G.: What can identity-based cryptography offer to web services? In: Proceedings of the 2007 ACM Workshop on Secure Web Services, SWS 2007, Fairfax, Virginia, USA, November 02, pp. 26–36. ACM, New York (2007)
10. Paterson, K.: Cryptography from pairings: a snap-shot of current research. Information Security Technical Report 7(3), 41–54

An Efficient Take-Back Call Admission Control Scheme for 3G/WLAN Integrated Cells

S. Nanda Kumar, Sibaram Khara, and T. Velmurugan

School of Electronics Engineering, VIT University
Vellore-632014, T.N., India
{snandakumar,tvelmurugan}@vit.ac.in, sianba@rediffmail.com

Abstract. Capacity increases and call dropping probability decreases in a 3G cell with embedded WLAN(s) (i.e., mixed cell). Two factors reduce the 3G traffic. One, users initiate new calls through WLANs and two, ongoing sessions are handed over from 3G to WLAN. As a result, call blocking probability in 3G system decreases and overall system capacity increases with increasing WLAN coverage. It is observed that call dropping rate in an entire mixed cell decreases as long as the call blocking probability in WLAN remains less than that in the 3G system. But new call arrival rate in WLAN also increases with increasing call intercepting (CI) probability of WLAN (i.e., probability with which WLAN shares a call in a mixed cell). Thus call blocking probability in WLAN increases. At higher values of CI probability, the blocking probability of WLAN becomes more than that in the 3G system duo to rise in new calls. At this juncture, call dropping rate increases with increasing CI probability. We propose an efficient take-back call admission control (TB-CAC) scheme in which a mobile station always prefers to access WLAN and the blocked calls of WLAN are immediately taken back by 3G systems. Proposed TB-CAC scheme shows considerable improvement of call dropping rate under increasing CI probability of WLAN.

Keywords: Mixed cell, blocking probability, dropping probability, call intercepting (CI), call admission control (CAC), new call, horizontal handoff (HH), vertical handoff (VH), mobile station (MS).

1 Introduction

Heterogeneous radio access technology (RAT) is a key issue of next generation wireless networks [1]. Third generation (3G) cellular network and wireless local area network (WLAN) are the two important technologies for integrated wireless heterogeneous network [2]. A mobile station (MS) can have choices to select one of multiple available RATs. This will provide ubiquitous wireless connectivity and better load balancing among different RATs [3]. Higher bit rate can be provided to the users by handing over the call from 3G to WLAN [4]. Joint spectrum of 3G and integrated WLAN can handle more users with lower call dropping probability [5]. In a pure 3G cell, i.e., a 3G cell without integrated WLAN, two types of calls occur; new

P.V. Krishna, M.R. Babu, and E. Ariwa (Eds.): ObCom 2011, Part I, CCIS 269, pp. 342–352, 2012.

calls and horizontal handoff (HH) calls. In a mixed cell (i.e., 3G cell with integrated WLAN) three types of calls occur; new calls, HH calls and vertical handoff (VH) calls. VH calls are generated in 3G system due to moving of sessions to the outside of WLAN coverage. Vertical handover from WLAN to 3G is required to support session-mobility with wider range. In WLAN coverage too there may be three types of calls; new, HH, VH calls.

Integrated WLAN(s), in a 3G cell, absorbs considerable amount of new and handoff traffic. The capacity of a 3G cell with 25% coverage of integrated WLAN(s) becomes three times [6]. There are number analytical models [7], [8], [9] for joint spectrum management of 3G and WLAN to provide low dropping probability to the incoming calls. Tang and Lee [7] shows that a small fraction of WLAN spectrum can be reserved for handling the blocked HH calls(s) of 3G system. It is able to reduce the dropping probability HH calls potentially. But the scheme restricts the vertical movement from WLAN to 3G and sometimes users do not use WLAN although it resides in WLAN coverage. Call intercepting (CI) probability is defined as the probability with which integrated WLAN intercepts a new call or an ongoing session in a mixed cell. CI probability helps estimate net traffic in 3G and WLAN system of a mixed cell [10]. The study in [6] shows that the cell capacity increases three fold with CI probability of 0.25. Articles [5], [6] and [11] show tunnel-WLAN based CAC scheme to maximize the usage of WLAN bandwidth. Thus it reduces the traffic load in the 3G system. It potentially reduces the call dropping probability in 3G. A call is said to be dropped if it blocked and subsequently lost in the system. The user has to re-initiate new call. The call blocking probability of WLAN increases with increasing CI probability. At some increasing values of CI the WLAN traffic becomes so heavy that its blocking probability becomes more than that of the 3G system. Under such scenario the overall call dropping rate again increases with increasing CI probability. Therefore, blocked calls of WLAN must be transferred to 3G to reduce the call dropping probability. We propose an enhanced CAC scheme in which blocked calls of WLAN are transferred to 3G. We propose a modified CAC scheme in which users always preferably access WLAN and blocked calls of WLAN are immediately taken back by 3G system. This is called take-back CAC (TB-CAC) scheme. In this scheme, a call is dropped if there is no channel in both 3G and WLAN systems.

Proposed TB-CAC scheme removes the restriction on horizontal and vertical movements of calls. It allows the users to access WLAN on priority as long as it can provide desired throughput. The denied new calls of WLAN automatically access 3G. We use the 'make before break' VH handoff scheme from 3G to WLAN. This facilitates an MS to retain the ongoing 3G connection in the event of denial of VH calls in WLAN. Call dropping rate becomes independent of blocking probability of WLAN. We consider 'break before make' scenario for VH from WLAN to 3G. A blocked call in 3G-only coverage (i.e., 3G coverage without WLAN hotspot) is necessarily dropped because. TB-CAC scheme improves call dropping rate by 16% with respect to tunnel-WLAN model [5], [6], [11].

2 Traffic Budget

Figure 1 shows the call flow between 3G and WLAN in a mixed cell. New and HH call arrival rates are λ_n and λ_h , respectively. We consider steady state condition in which the incoming and outgoing HH arrival rates are equal for a mixed cell. We assume all WLANs are identical and isolated [6]. According to [10], all WLANs of a mixed cell can be represented by a single WLAN. Say P^w is the CI probability of all WLAN hotspots. Unless specified, by WLAN we mean all WLANs in a mixed cell.

2.1 Traffic in 3G System

New and HH call arrival rates in 3G-only coverage are $\lambda_n^g = \lambda_n(1-P^w)$ and λ_h . The VH calls in 3G-only coverage are generated due to moving of ongoing calls from WLAN to 3G-only coverage. For simplicity, we assume that vertically handed over sessions in WLAN (3G) do not initiate again vertical handoffs in 3G (WLAN). Successful new calls in WLAN can initiate VH calls in 3G. So, VH call arrival rate in 3G system is $\lambda_v = \lambda_n^w(1-b)P^{wg}$. New call arrival rate in WLAN is λ_n^w , blocking probability of WLAN is b and P^{wg} is vertical handoff probability from WLAN to 3G.

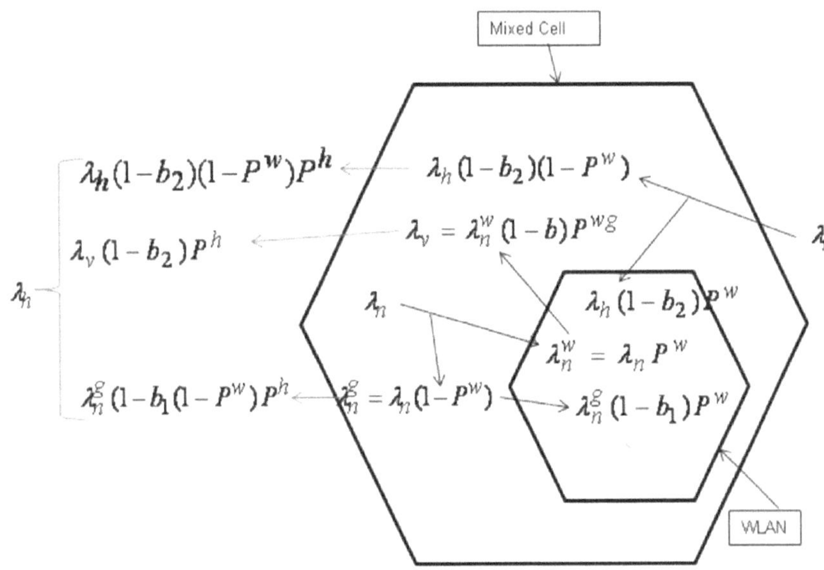

Fig. 1. Traffic flow for a mixed cell

2.2 Traffic in WLAN System

In WLAN, we consider only two types of calls, new and VH calls. New call arrival rate in WLAN is $\lambda_n^w = \lambda_n P^w$. VH calls in WLAN are generated in two scenarios. One, Successful new calls of 3G system may initiate VH calls in WLAN when the users move into it. Two, successful HH calls of 3G system may initiate VH call in WLAN. Total VH call arrival rate in WLAN is $\lambda_v^w = \lambda_n^g (1-b_1)P^w + \lambda_h (1-b_2)P^w$. Where b_1 and b_2 are blocking probability of new and HH calls in 3G system. If $P^w = 0$ then new and HH call arrival rates remain λ_n and λ_h, respectively.

3 Tunnel-WLAN Scheme

In this model, a user residing in WLAN hotspot is called WLAN user. This user first tries to access WLAN. The model assumes that WLAN has sufficient bandwidth. So, 3G does not take care of WLAN users. The rate of incoming HH calls is equal to that of outgoing HH calls across 3G cell-boundary. From Figure 1, we write the following equation for HH call arrivals.

$$\lambda_h = \lambda_n^g (1-b_1)(1-P^w)P^h + \lambda_h (1-b_2)(1-P^w)P^h + \lambda_n^w (1-b)P^{wg}(1-b_2)P^h$$

$$\lambda_h = \left(A_1 \lambda_n^g + A_2 \lambda_n^w \right)$$

$$A_1 = \frac{(1-b_1)(1-P^w)P^h}{1-(1-b_2)(1-P^w)P^h} \text{ and } A_2 = \frac{(1-b)P^{wg}(1-b_2)P^h}{1-(1-b_2)(1-P^w)P^h}$$

$$\frac{dA_1}{dP^w} = \frac{-(1-b_1)P^h}{\left[1-(1-b_2)(1-P^w)P^h\right]^2} \text{ and } \frac{dA_2}{dP^w} = \frac{-(1-b_2)P^h}{\left[1-(1-b_2)(1-P^w)P^h\right]^2}$$

HH arrival rate in a mixed cell always decreases with increasing CI probability.

New call blocking rate

$$\lambda_{nb}^{ttl} = \lambda_n (1-P^w)b_1 + \lambda_n P^w b = \left((1-P^w)b_1 + P^w b \right)\lambda_n$$

$$\frac{d}{dP^w}\left(((1-P^w) + P^w b)\lambda_n \right) = (b-b_1)\lambda_n$$

The above derivative becomes positive for $b > b_1$ and total blocking rate of new calls in mixed cell increases with increasing CI probability. Therefore, in a tunnel WLAN model, there must be sufficient bandwidth or limited number of users in WLAN to maintain $b < b_1$ so that overall new call dropping rate decreases with CI probability.

HH call blocking rate: HH blocking rate in 3G is $\lambda_h b_2$. Since HH rate itself decreases with increasing CI probability the blocking rate of HH also decreases accordingly.

VH call blocking rate: The blocked VH calls of 3G and WLAN are necessarily dropped. Total VH call blocking rate in a mixed cell is given as follows.

$$\lambda_{vb}^{ttl} = \lambda_h (1-b_2) P^w b + \lambda_n (1-P^w)(1-b_1) P^w b + \lambda_n P^w (1-b) P^{wg} b_2$$

$$\frac{d}{dP^w}\left[\lambda_{vb}^{ttl}\right] = \lambda_h (1-b_2) b + \left((1-2P^w)(1-b_1) b + (1-b) P^{wg} b_2\right)\lambda_n$$

The above derivative guaranteed to be positive for $P^w < 0.5$. This implies that VH dropping rate increases with increasing CI probability for $P^w < 0.5$. From the above analysis we see that new and vertical call blocking rate increases and HH call blocking rate decreases with increasing CI probability. In the following section we derive the total call blocking rate in a mixed cell.

Total call blocking rate in 3G (λ_b^g) is as given below.

$$\lambda_b^g = \lambda_n^g b_1 + \lambda_h b_2 + \lambda_v b_2$$

$$\lambda_b^g = \lambda_n \left((1-P^w) b_1 + P^w (1-b) P^{wg} b_2\right) + \lambda_h b_2 \tag{2}$$

Total call blocking rate in WLAN is given by the following.

$$\lambda_b^w = \lambda_n P^w b + \lambda_n (1-P^w)(1-b_1) P^w b + \lambda_h (1-b_2) P^w b \tag{3}$$

Sum of equations (2) and (3) gives the total blocking rate in entire mixed cell, $\lambda_b^{ttl} = \lambda_b^g + \lambda_b^w$ which is given by the following.

$$\lambda_b^{ttl} = \begin{bmatrix} \left((1-P^w)b_1 + P^w(1-b)P^{wg}b_2 + P^w b + (1-P^w)(1-b_1)P^w\right)\lambda_n \\ +\left(b_2 + (1-b_2)P^w b\right)\lambda_h \end{bmatrix}$$

$$\lambda_b^{ttl} = y_1\lambda_n + y_2\lambda_h$$

$$y_1 = (1-P^w)b_1 + P^w(1-b)P^{wg}b_2 + P^w b + (1-P^w)(1-b_1)P^w b \text{ and}$$

$$y_2 = b_2 + (1-b_2)P^w b$$

$$\frac{dy_1}{dP^w} = (b-b_1) + (1-b)P^{wg}b_2 + b(1-b_1)(1-2P^w)$$

$$\frac{dy_1}{dP^w} = +ve \text{ if } b > b_1 \text{ and } P^w < 0.5\text{, and } \frac{dy_2}{dP^w} = (1-b)b_2 = +ve$$

Therefore, y_1 and y_2 increases with increasing CI probability. This implies that total blocking rate increases with increasing call CI probability of WLAN. To reduce dropping rate, blocking probability in WLAN must be maintained less than that in 3G system. This can be done either by deploying more number of WLANs or restricting the number of calls in WLAN.

Equations should be punctuated in the same way as ordinary text but with a small space before the end punctuation mark.

4 Proposed TB-CAC Scheme

In the proposed TB-CAC scheme, am MS checks whether there is WLAN coverage (Fig 2). This can be done by sensing the WLAN beacon signal. An MS always tries to access WLAN if valid beacon is available. A call may be accepted or denied by WLAN access point (AP). This depends on the number of users that are already accessing WLAN. If no other user can be tolerated in WLAN within the threshold throughput (at user level) the call can be denied by AP. This can be done by issuing a negative WLAN association response message to MS. Otherwise a call can be admitted by the AP by issuing positive WLAN association response. 3G coverage prevails in WLAN too. So, the blocked (new) calls of WLAN can be diverted to the 3G system (Fig 2). Thus a blocked new call is taken back by the 3G system. A denied handoff call in WLAN retains the 3G connection. It performs a 'make before break' handoff scheme. Since WLAN and 3G are different radio interfaces, the session can be handed over only after affirming the bandwidth availability in WLAN. In case the VH call WLAN cannot be supported by WLAN it is taken back by 3G. If a call is blocked in 3G it is dropped and the user has to initiate again a new call.

The TB-CAC enables the maximum usage of WLAN. Calls are diverted to 3G only when WLAN is unable to handle the call. So, the CAC allows the WLAN to absorb the traffic load of 3G to the maximum extend. 3G can handle more users outside WLAN coverage.

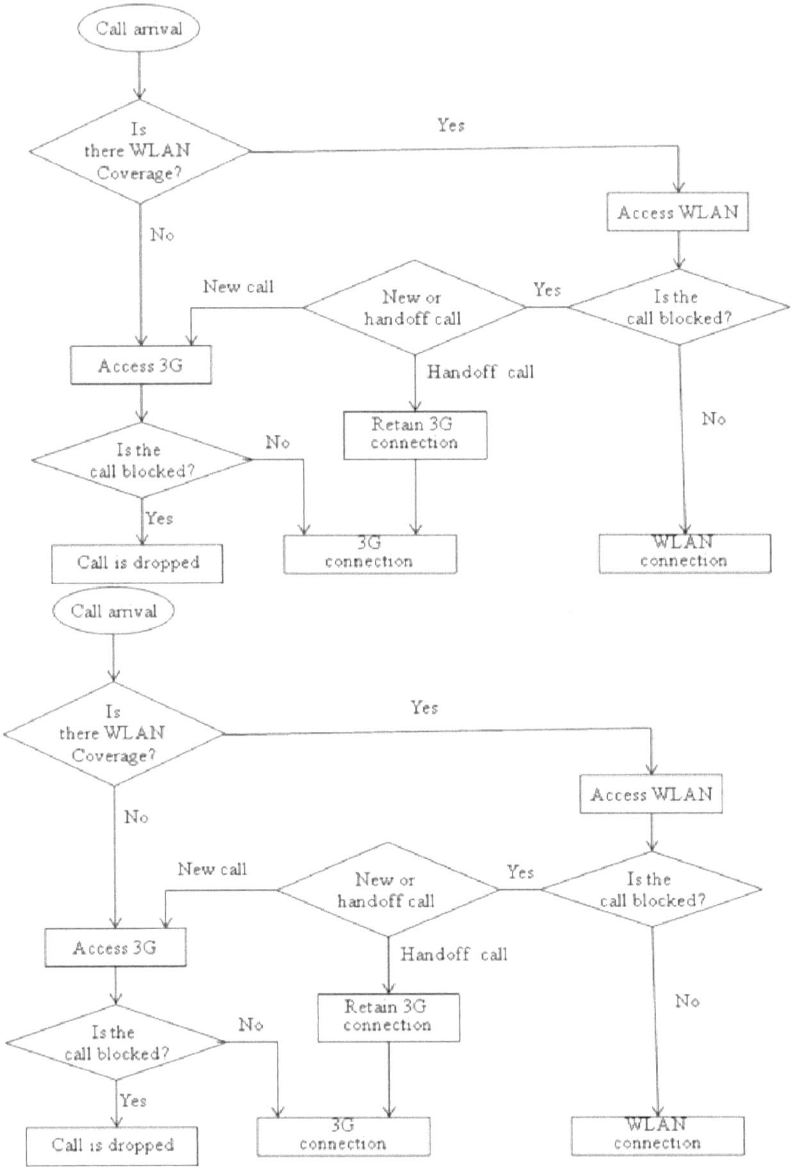

Fig. 2. Flow chart of TB-CAC scheme

5 Performance Analysis

According to the TB-CAC scheme, the call dropping rate is sum of the following calls.

i. Rate of blocking of calls in 3G system in 3G-only coverage (λ_{dn}^{g})

ii. Rate of blocking of new calls in 3G system in WLAN coverage (λ_{dn}^{gw})

iii. Rate of blocking of HH calls in 3G in 3G-only coverage (λ_{dh}^{g})

iv. Rate of blocking of VH calls in 3G system in 3G-only coverage (λ_{dv}^{g})

The total call dropping rate in a mixed cell is given by the following.

$$\lambda_{d}^{ttl} = \lambda_{dn}^{g} + \lambda_{dn}^{gw} + \lambda_{dh}^{g} + \lambda_{dv}^{g}$$

$$\lambda_{dn}^{g} = \lambda_{n}(1-P^{w})b_1\,,\ \lambda_{dn}^{gw} = \lambda_{n}P^{w}bb_1\,,\ \lambda_{dh}^{g} = \lambda_{h}b_2\,,\lambda_{dv}^{g} = \lambda_{n}P^{w}(1-b)P^{wg}b_2$$

$$\text{and } \lambda_{dv}^{w} = 0$$

$$\lambda_{d}^{ttl} = \left((1-P^{w})b + P^{w}bb_1 + P^{w}(1-b)P^{wg}b_2\right)\lambda_{n} + \lambda_{h}b_2$$

$$\frac{d}{dP^{w}}(\lambda_{d}^{ttl}) = \left\{-1+\left(b+(1-b)P^{wg}a\right)\right\}b_1 \tag{4}$$

Here, $a = b_2 / b_1 \le 1$. Since b and P^{wg} are less than unity, $\left(b+(1-b)P^{wg}a\right) < 1$. a is always less than unity since some channels are reserved for handling handoff calls in the CAC. For non-prioritized CAC, $a = 1$. It implies that in equation (4) $\frac{d}{dP^{w}}(\lambda_{d}^{ttl}) = -ve$.

Therefore, total call dropping rate in a mixed cell always decreases with increasing CI probability of WLAN.

In the tunnel-WLAN model of WLAN-first CAC scheme, the MSs always access WLAN on priority. But, WLAN users are not visible to 3G. As a result, the blocked calls of WLAN are not taken back by 3G. Although, the technique enhances the WLAN usage, call dropping rate increases also increases. Call dropping rate decreases *if and only if* the blocking probability of WLAN is less than that in 3G system.

6 Numerical Results

We provide the numerical results for comparing between the tunnel-WLAN and TB-CAC schemes under increasing CI probability. We assume $\lambda_n = 30$, $b_1 = 0.02$, $b_2 = 0.015$, $b = 0.01$, $P_h = 0.01$, $P^{wg} = 0.01$. Figure 3(a) shows that call dropping rate, in a mixed cell, decreases by only 2% when CI probability increases from 0.20 to 0.30. But in TB-CAC scheme it decreases by 12%. The call dropping rate decreases in both the cases for $b < b_1$. But the blocked calls of WLANs are not taken over by 3G system. So, in tunnel-WLAN, the decreasing rate of call dropping is less than that in TB-CAC scheme.

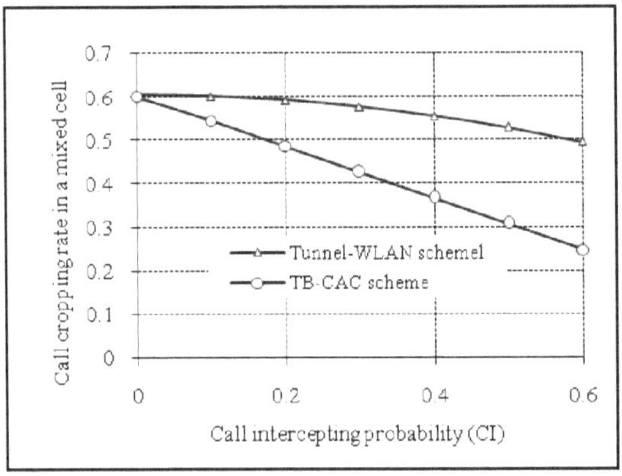

Fig. 3. (a) Call dropping rate vs. CI probability ($b < b_1$).

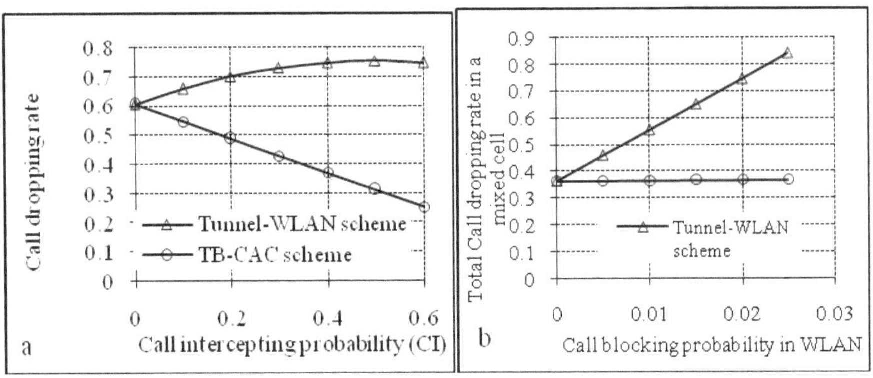

Fig. 4. (a) Call dropping rate vs. CI probability ($b > b_1$) and (b) Call dropping rate vs. call blocking probability of WLAN ($P^W = 0.40$)

Figure 4(a) shows that call dropping rate for $b > b_1$. The call dropping rate in tunnel-WLAN scheme increases by 4% when CI probability increases from 0.20 to 0.30, but in TB-CAC scheme in decreases by 12%. With increasing CI probability the number of users in WLAN increases. So, call dropping rate also increases. However, dropping rate can be decreased by bringing down the blocking probability of WLAN. This can be done by enhancing the WLAN bandwidth. Therefore, tunnel-WLAN performance would be good for bandwidth rich WLAN. Moreover, in tunnel-WLAN scheme, dropping 3G bandwidth is not used with full extent. Call dropping may occur even when 3G channels are available. In tunnel-WLAN scheme, the call dropping rate slightly decreases when CI probability exceeds 0.50.

In TB-CAC scheme, a call in WLAN is dropped when it is blocked in both the systems. Therefore, the increasing blocking probability of WLAN does not affect the call dropping probability. Figure 4(b) shows that call dropping rate in a mixed cell remains almost constant under increasing blocking probability of WLAN. Here the total traffic and CI probability is kept fixed. The call dropping rate in tunnel-WLAN scheme increases with increasing blocking probability of WLAN.

7 Conclusion

In this article, we propose a new take-back call admission control scheme in which blocked calls of WLANs are taken back by 3G system. Thus, in WLAN, a call can be dropped if it is blocked in first in WLAN and then in 3G. The block calls of WLANs alternatively and automatically access 3G. The call blocking rate is not affected by increasing blocking probability of WLAN. The performance of this CAC is better when WLAN does not have capability of handle the increasing traffic. TB-CAC scheme improves the call dropping rate by 16% over tunnel-WLAN based call admission scheme.

References

[1] Ferrus, R., Sallent, O., Agusti, R.: Interworking in Heterogeneous Wireless Networks: Comprehensive Framework and Future Trends. Proc. of IEEE Wireless Communicatin 17(2), 22–31 (2010)

[2] Salkintzis, A.K.: IP Multimedia in Next Generation Mobile Networks: Services, Protocols, and Technologies. IEEE Wireless Communications 9(5), 56–57 (2002)

[3] Cheng, D., Wang, X., Elhakeem, A.K.: Load Sharing with Buffering over Heterogeneous Networks. In: Proc. of 62nd VTC-2005-Fall, September 25-28, vol. 4, pp. 2602–2606 (2005)

[4] Doufexi, A., Tameh, E., Nix, A., Armour, S.: Hotspot Wireless LANs to Enhance the Performance of 3G and Beyond Cellular Networks. IEEE Communication Magazine 41(7), 58–65 (2003)

[5] Khara, S., Misra, I.S., Saha, D.: Performance Analysis of a UMTS Cell with Underlying Tunnel-WLANs. In: Garg, V., Wattenhofer, R., Kothapalli, K. (eds.) ICDCN 2009. LNCS, vol. 5408, pp. 389–394. Springer, Heidelberg (2008)

[6] Liu, H., Bhaskaran, H., Raychaudhuri, D., Verma, S.: Capacity Analysis of a Cellular Data System with UMTS/WLAN Interworking. In: Proceeding of IEEE VTC 2003, vol. 3, pp. 1817–1821 (2003)

[7] Tang, S., Li, W.: Modeling and Evaluation of the 3G Mobile Networks with Hotspot WLANs. Proceeding of Int. Journal of Wireless and Mobile Computing (IJWMC) (2006)

[8] Song, G., Cuthbert, L., Schormans, J.: Modelling Cellular/Wireless LAN Integrated Systems with Multi-Rate Traffic Using Queueing Network. In: WiCOM 2008 (2008)

[9] Choi, Y., Kim, H., Han, S.-W., Han, Y.: Joint Resource Allocation for Parallel Multi-Radio Access in Heterogeneous Wireless Networks. IEEE Transaction on Wireless Communication 9(11), 3324–3328 (2010)

[10] Khara, S., Misrha, I.S., Saha, D.: An Improved WLAN-first Access Scheme for UMTS/WLAN Integrated System. In: Proc. of ACM Symposium on Advanced Computing (SAC 2010), Sierre, Sitzerland, March 22-26, pp. 630–634. ACM, NY (2010) ISBN:978-1-60558-639-7

[11] Bejoui, T., Mokdad, L.: Adaptive Hybrid Call Admission Control Policy for UMTS with Under Lying Tunnel-WLANs Heterogeneous Networks. In: Proc. of IEEE ICC 2009, Dresden, June 14-18 (2009)

A Case Study on Various Routing Strategies of VANETs

Santhosh Jayachandran, Johnson Doraisami Jothi, and Siva Rama Krishnan

School of I.T. and Engineering, VIT University, Vellore, Tamil Nadu
{santhosh.4121,jothi.johnson}@gmail.com, siva.s@vit.ac.in

Abstract. Vehicular Ad Hoc Networks (VANET) is a subclass of Mobile ad hoc networks which provides a distinguish approach for intelligent transport system (ITS). The survey of routing protocols in vanet is important and necessary issue for smart ITS. The existing routing protocols for VANET are not efficient to meet every traffic scenarios. Thus design of an efficient routing protocol has taken significant attention. So, it is very necessary to identify the pros and cons of routing protocols which can be used for further improvement or development of any new routing protocol.. The paper discusses the advantages and disadvantages of VANETs routing protocols. Many researchers have proposed various routing strategies in VANETS. In this paper, we identify certain drawbacks in existing protocols and we propose new methodology to overcome the same.

Keywords: FSR, AODV, DSR, PBR, VADD, TORA, GRANT, Geocast, VANET.

1 Introduction

The main goal of VANET is providing safety and comfort for passengers. Each vehicle equipped with VANET device will be a node in the Ad-hoc network and can receive & relay other messages through the wireless network. Collision warning, Road signal arms and in place traffic view will give the driver essential tool to decide the best path along the way. VANET or Intelligent Vehicular Ad-Hoc Networking provides an intelligent way of using vehicular networking .VANET integrates multiple Ad-Hoc networking technologies such as WiFi IEEE 802.11 b/g, WiMaX 802.16, Bluetooth, and ZigBee for easy accurate effective and simple communication between vehicles on dynamic mobility.

VANET helps in defining safety measures in vehicles, streaming communication between vehicles. With the sharp increase of vehicles on roads in the recent years, driving becomes more challenging and dangerous. Roads are saturated; safety distance and reasonable speeds are hardly respected. The leading car manufacturer decided to jointly work with govt. agencies to develop solution aimed at helping drivers on the roads by anticipating hazardous events or bad traffic areas. This paper summarizes the pros and cons of unicast routing protocols which can be used for better understanding of the routing protocols and future improvement can be made.

P.V. Krishna, M.R. Babu, and E. Ariwa (Eds.): ObCom 2011, Part I, CCIS 269, pp. 353–362, 2012.

2 Characteristics

2.1 Mobility Modeling

The mobility pattern of vehicles depends on traffic environment, roads structure, the speed of vehicles, driver's driving behavior and so on.

2.2 Frequent Disconnected Network

From the highly dynamic topology results we observe that frequent disconnection occur between two vehicles when they are exchanging information. This disconnection will occur most in sparse network.

2.3 Battery Power and Storage Capacity

In modern vehicles battery power and storage is unlimited. Thus it has enough computing power which is unavailable in MANET. It is helpful for effective communication & making routing decisions.

2.4 Communication Environment

The communication environment between vehicles is different in sparse network & dense network. In dense network building, trees & other objects behave as obstacles and in sparse network like high-way this things are absent. So the routing approach of sparse & dense network will be different.

2.5 Interaction with Onboard Sensors

The current position & the movement of nodes can easily be sensed by onboard sensors like GPS device. It helps for effective.

3 Routing Protocols

The characteristic of highly dynamic topology makes the design of efficient routing protocols for VANET is challenging. The routing protocol of VANET can be classified into two categories such as Topology based routing protocols & Position based routing protocols.

4 Advantages and Disadvantages of Topology Based Routing protocols

Topology based routing protocols use link's information within the network to send the data packets from source to destination. Topology based routing approach can be further categorized into proactive (table-driven) and reactive (on-demand) routing.

4.1 Proactive Routing Protocol

Proactive routing protocols are mostly based on shortest path algorithms. They keep information of all connected nodes in form of tables because these protocols are table based. Furthermore, these tables are also shared with their neighbors. Whenever any change occurs in network topology, every node updates its routing table.

Advantages:
- No Route Discovery is required.
- Latency is minimum or low for real time applications.

Disadvantages:
- Unused paths occupy a significant part of the available bandwidth.

4.1.1 Fisheye State Routing

FSR is a proactive or table driven routing protocol where the information of every node collects from the neighboring nodes. Then calculate the routing table. It is based on the link state routing & an improvement of Global State Routing.

Advantages
- FSR reduces significantly the consumed bandwidth as it exchanges partial routing update information with neighbors only.
- Reduce routing overhead.
- Changing in the routing table will not occur even if there is any link failure because it doesn't trigger any control message for link failure.

Disadvantages
- Dull efficiency or performance in small ad hoc networks.
-Distant node knowledge is less known.
-The increase in network size the storage complexity and the processing overhead of routing table also increase.
- Insufficient information for route establishing.

4.2 Reactive Routing Protocol

Reactive routing protocol is called on demand routing because it starts route discovery when a node needs to communicate with another node thus it reduces network traffic.

Advantages
-To update routing table not require periodic flooding the network. Flooding requires when it is demanded.
-Beaconless so it saves the bandwidth.

Disadvantages
- High latency for route finding
- Excessive flooding of the network causes disruption of nodes communication.

4.2.1 AODV

Ad Hoc On Demand Distance Vector routing protocol is a reactive routing protocol which establish a route when a node requires to send data packets. It has the ability of unicast & multicast routing. It uses a destination sequence number (DestSeqNum) which makes it different from other on demand routing protocols.

Advantages

- An up-to-date path to the destination because of using destination sequence number.
- It reduces excessive memory requirements and the route redundancy.
- AODV responses to the link failure in the network.
- It can be applied to large scale ad-hoc network.

Disadvantages

-Time consumption in connection setup & initial communication to establish a route compared to other approaches.
-If intermediate nodes contain old entries it can lead inconsistency in the route.
-For a single route reply packet if there has multiple route reply packets this will lead to heavy control overhead.
- Because of periodic beaconing it consume extra bandwidth.

4.2.2 Dynamic Source Routing

The Dynamic Source Routing (DSR) protocol presented in which utilize source routing & maintain active routes. It has two phases route discovery & route maintenance.

Advantages

-To obtain route between nodes, it has small overload on the network. It uses caching which reduce load on the network for future route discovery.
-No periodical update is required in DSR.

Disadvantages

-If there are too many nodes in the network the route information within the header will lead to byte overhead.
-Unnecessary flooding burden the network.
-In high mobility pattern it performs worse.
-Unable to repair broken links locally.

4.2.3 Temporally Ordered Routing Protocol (TORA)

Temporally Ordered Routing Protocol is based on the link reversal algorithm that creates a direct acyclic graph towards the destination where source node acts as a root of the tree. In TORA packet is broadcasted by sending node, by receiving the packet neighbor nodes rebroadcast the packet based on the DAG if it is the sending node's downward link.

Advantages
-It creates DAG (Direct acyclic graph) when necessary.
-Reduce network overhead because all intermediate nodes don't need to rebroadcast the message.
-Perform well in dense network.
-It is not used because DSR & AODV perform well than TORA.

Disadvantages
-It is not scalable.

5 Advantages Disadvantages of Geographic Routing Protocols

Geographic routing is a routing that each node knows it's own & neighbor node geographic position by position determining services like GPS. It doesn't maintain any routing table or exchange any link state information with neighbor nodes. Information from GPS device is used for routing decision.

Advantages
- Route discovery & management is not required.
-Scalability.
-Suitable for high node mobility pattern.

Disadvantages
-It requires position determining services.
-GPS device doesn't work in tunnel because satellite signal is absent there.

5.1 DTN

Delay Tolerant Network (DTN) uses carry & forward strategy to overcome frequent disconnection of nodes in the network. In carry & forward strategy when a node can't contact with other nodes it stores the packet & forwarding is done based on some metric of nodes neighbors.

5.1.1 VADD (Vehicle-Assisted Data Delivery)

Vehicle-Assisted Data Delivery is based on the idea of carry & forward approach by using predicable vehicle mobility. Among proposed VAAD protocols H-VAAD shows better performance.

Advantages
-Comparing with GPSR (with buffer), epidemic routing and DSR, VADD performs high delivery ratio.
-It is suitable for multi-hop data delivery.

Disadvantages
- Due to change of topology & traffic density it causes large delay.

5.1.2 Geographical Opportunistic Routing (GeOpps)

Geographical Opportunistic Routing (GeOpps) protocol utilizes the navigation system suggested routes of vehicles for selecting the forwarding node which is closer to the destination. During this process if there is any node which has minimum arrival time the packet will be forwarded to that node.

Advantages

-By comparing with the Location-Based Greedy routing and MoVe routing algorithm GeOpps has high delivery ratio.
-To find a vehicle which is driving towards near the destination GeOpps need few encounters.
- The delivery ratio of GeOpps rely on the mobility patterns & the road topology but not dependent on high density of vehicles.

Disadvantages

-Privacy is an issue because navigation information is disclosed to the network.

5.2.1 Greedy Perimeter Stateless Routing (GPSR)

Greedy Perimeter Stateless Routing selects a node which is closest to the final destination by using beacon. It uses greedy forwarding algorithm if it fails it uses perimeter forwarding for selecting a node through which a packet will travel.

Advantages

-To forward the packet a node needs to remember only one hop neighbor location.
-Forwarding packet decisions are made dynamically.

Disadvantages

-For high mobility characteristics of node, stale information of neighbors' position are often contained in the sending nodes and neighbor table.
-Though the destination node is moving its information in the packet header of intermediate node is never updated.

5.2.2 GPSR+AGF

In GPSR we see that stale information of neighbour's position is often contained in the sending nodes neighbor table. For this reason an approach which is called Advanced Greedy Forwarding (AGF) is proposed.

Advantages

- Though the destination node is moving its information in the packet header of intermediate node is updated.
-Stale nodes of neighbor table can be detected.

Disadvantages

- To find the shortest connected path it may not give desired optimal solution.

5.2.3 PBR-DV

PBR-DV consists of various approaches such as a greedy, position-based and a reactive, topology-based routing strategy & if packet falls in local maximum it uses AODV approach recovery.

Advantages

- No comparison is done with any other routing protocol so uncertain about packet delivery ratio & overhead.

Disadvantages

-For non-greedy part excessive flooding is required.

5.2.4 Greedy Routing with Abstract Neighbor Table (GRANT)

To avoid local maximum Greedy Routing with Abstract Neighbor Table (GRANT) applies extended greedy routing algorithm concept. Abstract Neighbor Table of GRANT divides the plane into areas and includes per area only one representative neighbor.

Advantages

-In city scenario with obstacles this extended greedy routing approach works well than as usual greedy approach.

Disadvantages

- VANET has a high mobility characteristics but the performance evaluation of GRANT is done on static traces.

-The overhead of beacon and possible inaccuracy in packet delivery are not measured.

5.3.1 Greedy Perimeter Coordinator Routing (GPCR)

Greedy Perimeter Coordinator Routing is a position-based routing protocol uses greedy algorithms to forward packet based on a pre-selected path which has been designed to deal with the challenges of city scenarios. No global or external information like static map does not require in GPCR.

Advantages

- Does not require any global or external information.

-For representing the planar graph it uses the underlying roads though it is based on the GPSR.

-It has no as usual a planarization problem like unidirectional links, planar sub-graphs & so on.

Disadvantages

- Depends on junction nodes.

-There has a problem in the Junction detection approach in which first approach fails on curve road & second approach fails on a sparse road.

5.3.2 GpsrJ+

GpsrJ+ is a position based routing protocol which reduces the dependency on junction node. By using digital maps GpsrJ+ recovers from the local maximum. It uses two hop neighbors information for detecting appropriate junction turns & to calculate a good routing path.

Advantages

-The packet delivery ratio of GPCR increases which is managed by GPSRJ+.
-The number of hops in the recovery mode of GPSR is reduced by 200%.
- An expensive planarization strategy is not required in GPSRJ+.

Disadvantages

- Not appropriate for the delay sensitive applications.
- It did not apply on realistic city map that are not necessarily grids.
- It has used simple line trajectory but realistic roads follow a more complex trajectory.

5.3.3 CAR (Connectivity-Aware Routing)

For city and/or highway environment Connectivity-Aware Routing (CAR) is designed which uses AODV for path discovery and uses PGB for data dissemination mode. It uses guard concept to maintain the path.

Advantages

-No digital map is required.
-It has no local maximum problem.
- CAR ensures to find the shortest connected path because CAR has higher packet delivery ratio than GPSR and GPSR+AGF.

Disadvantages

-Unnecessary nodes can be selected as an anchor.
-It cannot adjust with different sub-path when traffic environment changes.

5.3.4 Greedy Traffic Aware Routing protocol (GyTAR)

Greedy Traffic Aware Routing protocol gives a new concept of intersection-based routing protocol which aims to reduce the control message overhead & end-to-end delay with low packet loss.

Advantages

- For high mobility topology changes rapidly and often occurring network fragmentation which is efficiently handle by GyTAR.
-Performance shows that throughput, delay and routing overhead\ are better than GSR.

Disadvantages

- GyTAR depends on roadside units because it assumes that the number of cars in the road will be given from road side units.

-Gytar cannot avoid void.

5.3.5 GSR (Geographic Source Routing) GSR

Routing was proposed for vehicular ad hoc networks in city environments which is the combination of position-based routing with topological knowledge.GSR uses greedy forwarding along a pre-selected shortest path & this path is calculated by using Dijkstra algorithm.

Advantages

- Packet delivery ratio of GSR is better than AODV & DSR.
- GSR is scalable than AODV & DSR.

Disadvantages

-This protocol neglects the situation like sparse network where there are not enough nodes for forwarding packets.

-GSR shows higher routing overhead than GyTAR because of using hello messages as control messages.

Routing Protocols	**Drawbacks**
GPSR	Frequent network disconnection. Routing loops. Too many hops. Routing in wrong direction.
GSR	End to end connection is difficult in low traffic density.
GPCR	End to end connection is difficult in low traffic density.
A-STAR	Routing paths are not optimal and results in large delay of packet transmission
MDDV	Large delay if the traffic density varies by time.
VADD	Large delay due to varying topology and varying traffic density.
PDGR	Too many hops. Large delay if the traffic density is high. Low packet delivery ratio. Frequent network disconnection.

6 Conclusion and Future Work

In this paper, we have investigated the pros and cons of different routing protocols for inter-vehicle communication in VANET. By studying different routing protocol in VANET we have seen that further performance evaluation is required to verify performance of a routing protocol with other routing protocols based on various traffic scenarios. Comparison can be done among the routing protocols in the Overlay and so on. GSR is not compared with other position based routing protocol. A predictive algorithm is used which adapts to traffic dynamics and an oblivious algorithm is tested which offers provable worst-case bounds.

The future perspectives for VANET routing protocols should include following:

1. Improve reliability of Protocols and to reduce delivery delay time and the number of packet retransmission.
2. Efficient algorithm that is competitive and often outperforms the predictive algorithm.
3. Comfort messages are usually tolerant of delay, Network bandwidth is generally reserved for emergency messages. It is worth to develop an efficient geo cast routing protocol for comfort applications with delay tolerant capabilities with low bandwidth utilization.

References

[1] Lee, K.C., Lee, U., Gerla, M.: Survey of Routing Protocols in Vehicular Ad Hoc Networks. In: Advances in Vehicular Ad-Hoc Networks: Developments and Challenges. IGI Global (October 2009)

[2] Franz, W., Hartenstein, H., Mauve, M. (eds.): Inter- Vehicle-Communications Based on Ad Hoc Networking Principles-The Fleet Net Project. Universitatverlag Karlsuhe, Karlshue (2005)

[3] Perkins, C., Belding-Royer, E., Das, S.: Ad hoc On-Demand Distance Vector (AODV) Routing (July 2003)

[4] Ericson: Communication and Mobility by Cellular Advanced Radio, ComCar project (2002), http://www.comcar.de

[5] Festag, A., et al.: NoW-Network on Wheels: Project Objectives, Technology and Achievements. Proceedings

[6] Reichardt, D., Miglietta, M., Moretti, L., Morsink, P., Schulz, W.: CarTALK 2000 – safe and comfortable driving based upon inter-vehicle-communication. In: Proc. IEEE IV

[7] Morris, R., Jannotti, J., Kaashoek, F., Li, J., Decouto, D.: CarNet: A scalable ad hoc wireless network system. In: 9th ACM SIGOPS European Workshop, Kolding, Denmark (September 2000)

[8] Pei, G., Gerla, M., Chen, T.-W.: Fisheye State Routing: A Routing Scheme for Ad Hoc Wireless Networks. In: Proc. ICC 2000, New Orleans, LA (June 2000)

High Utility and Low Cost Microcontroller Based Data Acquisition System for Antenna Encoders

Vikalp Paharia, Harshul Gandhi, and Astha Jain

Electronics and Communication , Computer Scince and Engineering,
Dept. of Information Technology, MANIT Bhopal, M.P., India
{asthajain.nitb,gandhi.harshul.88,vikalppaharia3}@gmail.com

Abstract. Satellite communication is very vital for the high speed communication. In order to communicate with satellite efficiently proper tracking is required by an antenna. The status of the antenna can be obtained from switching between the two different encoders giving data of two different quantities – Angular and Elevation and displayed on LCD, transmitted to a PC and also available for processing. This data can be further used to change the antenna positions to required state by rotating motors and again fetching the data. Thus, a whole control system can be made. The system consists of a two ATmega16 microcontrollers and several other ICs. It has been noted that this system performs satisfactorily and provides necessary variations and has easy switching characteristics.

Keywords: Data Acquisition system, Microcontroller, Variable frequency/clock generation, Antenna encoder monitoring.

1 Introduction

Satellite communication is a widely used mode of communication in the modern world. Common users find its application in every sphere of life be it mobile phones, satellite television, navigation etc. It forms an integral part of the information and broadcasting technology we use in the advanced world. The advancement in satellite communication field has revolutionized the world. The developments in microcontroller provide an efficient method of developing a data acquisition system. Various earth stations across the globe function on these data acquisition systems.

It's evident that in satellite communication we need an Earth Station with antenna to receive the data from satellite. For this purpose it is essential to keep a track of the position of the antenna to ensure correct reception of data and proper tracking of satellite. In the past, there have been many publications on data acquisition, but the quest for advancement in precision and diversity is never satiated. There are numerous such features that are noticed while comprehending these publications. All of these have unique utilities and new features that keep emerging all the time.

The working in one mode only, that is, either RS 232 of RS 485 decreases the efficiency of the system. The encoders require clock to latch and transmit the data. The inability to change the clock frequency limits the range of communication.

P.V. Krishna, M.R. Babu, and E. Ariwa (Eds.): ObCom 2011, Part I, CCIS 269, pp. 363–369, 2012.

The lack of changing delay between consecutive clocks restricts the required diversity in data processing time and data communication time. The absence of ability to change the number of pulses hinders sensitivity because the number of pulses sets the sensitivity of data by fixing the number of bits in data. The incapability to customize the clock characteristics does not allow the user to change the encoder that is connected to the system. The deficiency of readily available parallel data restricts the fast processing feature. The deficit of Graphical User Interface to set the clock characteristics forces direct human efforts. The lack of GUI to calculate angle from data also increases human involvement.

The scope of improvements mentioned above and the ease of operation encourages the development of the system. Several challenges came across in synchronizing the units, establishing communication channel and microcontroller coding. This Data Acquisition System is developed to work on both RS – 232 and RS – 485 protocols. It uses microcontroller ATmega16 and various other ICs. It has the facility of changing the frequency of clock (used in synchronous communication), number of pulses in a pulse train and the delay between consecutive pulse trains. The onboard switches are also employed for the control of these variations. The clock is generated by using TIMER0. The serial data is converted to parallel data and then read on another ATmega16, displayed on a LCD and sent to PC with the help of [5]. The latched data can be used for fast parallel processing as well. The external inputs for setting the frequency, delay and number of pulses are provided by a Clock controller GUI made on C#. The data on PC is also received and showed on Position display GUI.

Data acquisition system developed can operate RS 232 as well as RS 485 increasing the applicability. The variation in frequency of clock required by the encoder and number of pulses in a pulse train with variable delay between consecutive pulse-train is of great use. This feature enables the user to set frequency according to range of data transfer. The number of pulse are adjusted as per the different encoders to which clock will be given. These variations provide a feature of switching between different encoders on the same setup. The user can also vary the delay between consecutive pulse trains as per the time required for the data processing between consecutive sets of data received. Sometimes there is a need of parallel data for faster processing as well. Parallel Data feature proves to be very useful. Apart from this, a scope for on-board switches to control the frequency and other variations also increases the versatility.

2 Description

2 (A) Operation of the Data Acquisition Unit

The developed data acquisition system is categorized into 3 units –

a) Graphical User Interface/switch controlled frequency generation and clock conversion in Data Acquiring unit.

b) Serial to Parallel data conversion and latch unit.
c) Data display on LCD and Graphical User Interface in Display unit.

In the Data Acquiring Unit, the reception of the signals is controlled by specifying the frequency, number of pulses and delay between the subsequent set of pulses through a Graphical User Interface (illustrated in section B-i) or the on-board switches. The clock is generated by microcontroller-1 running on 12 MHz with the above specified attributes using Timer-0 peripheral. The interfacing of the GUI with the hardware is done using the parallel port. This is an enhancement of data reception system implemented in [1] which does hold feature of varying the above parameters (frequency, number of pulses and delay) using GUI. The microcontroller works on RS232 protocol for data communication and encoders in use operates on RS422/RS485 protocol. The generated clock is converted for the system to function at required protocol. This unit generates both RS 232 and RS 485 level clocks at the same time. This experimental set up bears the advantages of [1] over Kalaitzakis [2] and Wu [4].

The second unit converts the received serial synchronous data to parallel data. This conversion is carried out by IC HD74LS164. Each HD74LS164 has 8 output data pins. Therefore, to acquire a maximum of 24 bit data three such ICs are integrated in series in the unit. This parallel data is latched using IC 74LS374 to ensure the reception of data bits without any loss. This data is also available for parallel processing which is an advantage over various existing systems which read the data on I2C.

Table 1. Four of the 64 combinations of bits that can be formed

BINARY DATA(INPUT)	00101000	11010000	11110100	10011100
NO OF PULSE	14	24	24	19
FREQUENCY	200 KHz	150 KHz	250 KHz	150 K Hz
DELAY	30 MS	10MS	20MS	40MS
ACQUIRED DATA	1101001101 1101	1100010110100 11101101101	1100110100101 01101010011	11011100100 11101001
ANGLE	273.27	277.95	288.57	310.23

In the third unit the data from latch unit is fed to digital Input-Output lines of microcontroller ATmega16. The data is read, processed for calculations and the output is displayed on a LCD and Graphical User Interface (illustrated in section B-ii). The interfacing of this GUI with PC is done on a RS 232 level using USART through serial port. The output contains the received data bits and the azimuth angle.

The formula for calculation of angular value is –

$$\text{Angle in Degree} = \frac{\text{Decimal Equivalent of Acquired Data}}{2^n} \times 360 \qquad (1)$$

Where n : no. of bits

2 (B) Graphical User Interface Detail

i.) **Clock Controller:** The first Graphical User Interface is developed in C# language over Microsoft Visual Studio. This Graphical User Interface is used to send various values of frequency, number of pulses and delay in the form of binary data over the parallel port to the data acquisition unit. The combination of 1s and 0s depict different values of above said parameters. Different combinations of binary digits are attained simply by clicking on the button which toggles the value of variable associated with it. Once the *SEND* button is clicked, the 8 bit binary data is converted into its corresponding decimal value. Fig 1 shows the user interface which sets the three parameters this information is sent to the system in the form of 8 bit binary data which appears on the buttons (6 bits + 2 bits set to 0 always). The value of each parameter corresponding to the combination of bits set is shown below the buttons.

The data is sent over parallel port using *Output* function defined in *InteropServices* class with address of port and decimal value, so attained, as the parameters to it.

Since we can send 8 bits at a time through parallel port, no of different values (as high as 2^8) of above said quantities (Frequency, No of pulses and Delay) can be set using this Graphical User Interface which accounts for broader scale utility of this Data Acquisition System.

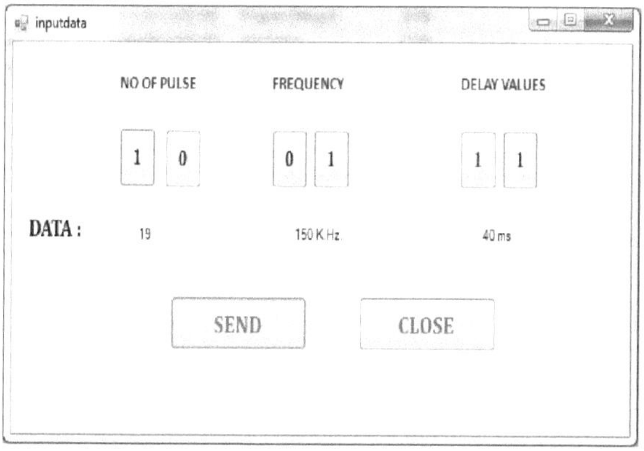

Fig. 1. Clock Controller GUI

ii.) **Position Display:** The other Graphical User Interface which is being used in this system is also developed using C# language. This Graphical User Interface starts receiving data from the Serial Port of computer, to which the microcontroller is connected, on the click event of START button installed on it (Fig 2). The serial communication is established between computer and microcontroller using USART periphery of ATmega16. This Graphical User Interface also shows the value of angle (in degrees) which is being calculated by applying formula (1) on the binary data so received.

Fig 2 shows the output for the input data depicted by the forth column of Table I and also shown in Fig 1.

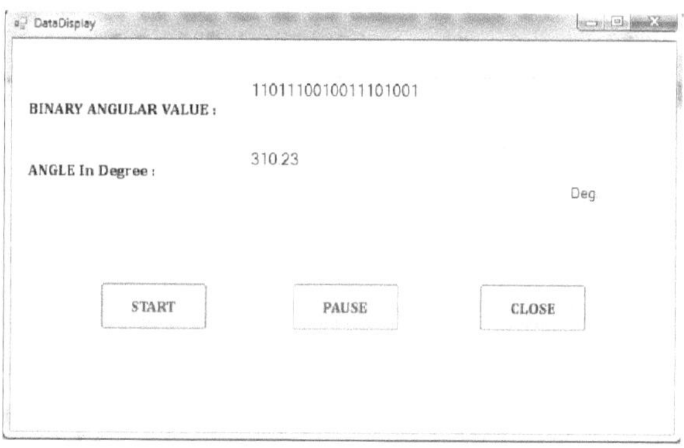

Fig. 2. Data Displaying GUI

2(C) Schematic of the System (Fig 3.)

(1) Data Acquiring Unit

a) Clock Generator - The TIMER 0 of microcontroller ATmega16 is the clock generator.

b) Switches - The 6 DIP toggle switches provide the 6 bit data.
c) RS 485 level convertor - The IC SN75174 is used to give clock and clock bar.
d) Encoder - It latches and transmits the data giving the antenna position.
e) RS 232 level convertor- The IC SN75175 is used to fetch data.
f) GUI - The Clock Controller GUI developed on C# is a standalone executable file.

(2) Serial to Parallel Convertor and Latch Unit

a) Serial to parallel convertor circuit -
Three HD74LS164 ICs are cascaded and used to convert the serial data.
b) Latch unit-
The IC 74LS374 is used to latch the data when it is clocked.

(3) Display Unit

a) GUI via USART- The Data Display GUI developed on C# is a standalone executable file.
b) LCD - It is 40x4 size liquid crystal display.
c) PC via parallel port- The latched data is available on a 25 pin parallel port .

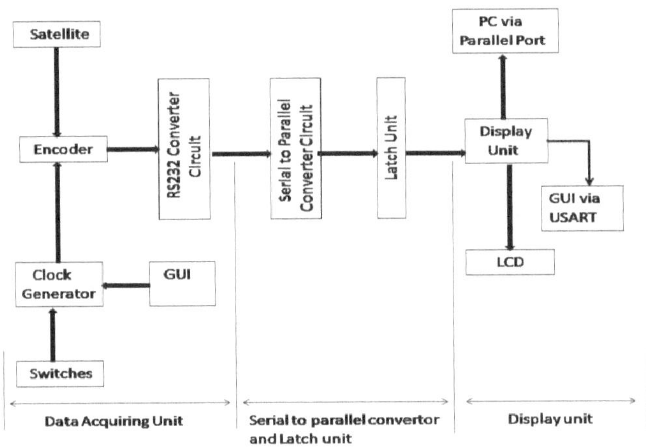

Fig. 3. Schematic of the System

3 Conclusion

The system is found to work successfully on the experimental set up. The experimental results prove the stated advantages of data acquisition system developed. The diverse applicability of system in various respects is verified during the observation. The precision and accuracy of the system is also within the acceptable limits. There is a scope of using I2C technique and reducing the hardware. Microcontrollers working on both RS 485 and RS 232 protocol can also be used to reduce hardware and IC's used. The 2 different GUI's can be integrated under 1 application. The RS 232 module used for serial communication can be replaced by USB to serial convertor.

References

1. Demirtas, M., Sefa, I., Irmak, E., Colak, I.: Low-Cost and High Sensitive Microcontroller Based Data Acquisition System for Renewable Energy Sources. In: SPEEDAM, International Symposium on Power Electronics, Electrical Drives and Automation. IEEE (2008)
2. Koutroulis, E., Kalaitzakis, K.: Development of an integrated data-acquisition system for renewable energy sources systems monitoring. Renewable Energy 28, 139–152 (2003)
3. Kalaitzakis, K., Koutroulis, E., Vlachos, V.: Development of a data acquisition system for remote monitoring of renewable energy systems. Measurement 34, 75–83 (2003)
4. Wu, S., Kotak, D., Fleetwood, M., Tomato, H.: Distributed data acquisition and monitoring system for an integrated energy application. In: IEEE international Conference on Systems, Man and Cybernetics, vol. 3, pp. 2590–2594 (2005)
5. Sankule, S.: Beginners guide to embedded systems and robotics (2009)

Design of WDM Optical Networks for the Analysis of Cross Phase Modulation and Self Phase Modulation

Sugumaran S., Vamsi Nath Reddy P., Sirivella V.S.M. Reddy, and Arulmozhivarman P.

School of Electronics Engineering, VIT University, Vellore, Tamilnadu, India

Abstract. Wavelength Division Multiplexing (WDM) is a boon of Light wave Technology as it increases the transmission capacity and enhances the transmission distance by using optical amplification. The capacity of the present system is limited by the noise generated by the amplifiers and interactions due to nonlinearities like Cross Phase Modulation (XPM), Self Phase Modulation(SPM), Four Wave Mixing(FWM) and Stimulated Raman Scattering(SRS). This paper focuses on the design of WDM Network in order to analyze the effect of XPM on the optical transmission rate. Also the papers focus on the suppression methods that can be used in order to remove the degrading effects of these non linearity's.

Keywords: Wavelength division multiplexing, Fiber Non Linearity's, Self Phase Modulation, Cross Phase Modulation.

1 Introduction

In the modern world of technology, data rates up to 40 Gb/s are becoming a reality and the bandwidth centered applications such as teleconferencing, telemedicine have already begun to make their presence in the commercial market. New business models based on novel telecommunication technologies continue to dramatically change the way people live and work nowadays. People want to be always connected, with ultra-high speed data transfer, with high-quality video streaming and without face-to-face meeting. These bandwidth hungry applications attract the need for optical communications in which the fiber can theoretically provide infinite bandwidth. In order to satisfy such needs, one of the solutions that can be put into effect is the concept of WDM (Wavelength Division Multiplexing) which involves transmitting multiple wavelengths spaced very close to each other thereby providing higher bandwidth efficiency. As a result of closely spaced wavelengths, there will be crosstalk and other detrimental effects [1-8].

2 Impact of Fiber Nonlinearities on Transmitted Optical Power

The insatiable demand for information capacity is ultimately limited by the Kerr effect in the transmission fibre, the refractive Index of the fiber is both intensity and

P.V. Krishna, M.R. Babu, and E. Ariwa (Eds.): ObCom 2011, Part I, CCIS 269, pp. 370–379, 2012.

frequency dependent. Nonlinear Kerr effect is dependence of the refractive index of the fiber on the power that is propagating through it. This effect is responsible for the generation of non linear effects like Four Wave Mixing (FWM), Stimulated Raman Scattering (SRS), Self Phase Modulation (SPM), Cross Phase Modulation (XPM)[8]. In this paper, we report the nature and extent of nonlinear interaction between signal and noise generated by the amplifiers in WDM Optical network.

2.1 Self Phase Modulation (SPM)

Phase modulation of an optical signal by itself is known as *self-phase modulation (SPM)*. SPM is primarily due to the self-modulation of the pulses. Generally, SPM occurs in single-wavelength systems. At higher bit rates, however, SPM tends to cancel dispersion. SPM increases with high signal power levels. In fiber plant design, a strong input signal helps overcome linear attenuation and dispersion losses. However, consideration must be given to receiver saturation and to nonlinear effects such as SPM, which occurs with high signal levels. SPM results in phase shift and a nonlinear pulse spread. As the pulses spread, they tend to overlap and are no longer distinguishable by the receiver. The acceptable norm in system design to counter the SPM effect is to take into account a power penalty that can be assumed equal to the negative effect posed by XPM. A 0.5-dB power margin is typically reserved to account for the effects of SPM at high bit rates and power levels [1-14]. In fibers, the refractive index always has some dependence on the optical intensity which is the optical power per effective area. This relation can be given as,

$$N = n_0+n_2I= n_0+n_2P/A_{eff} \quad (1)$$

where n_0 is the ordinary refractive index ,n_2 is the non-linear refractive index co-efficient,A_{eff} is the effective core area, and P is the power of the optical signal. This non-linearity is called as Kerr nonlinearity. This produces Kerr effect in which the propagating signal is phase modulated by the carrier. This leads to a phenomenon called Self-phase modulation that converts power fluctuations into phase fluctuations in the same wave [8].

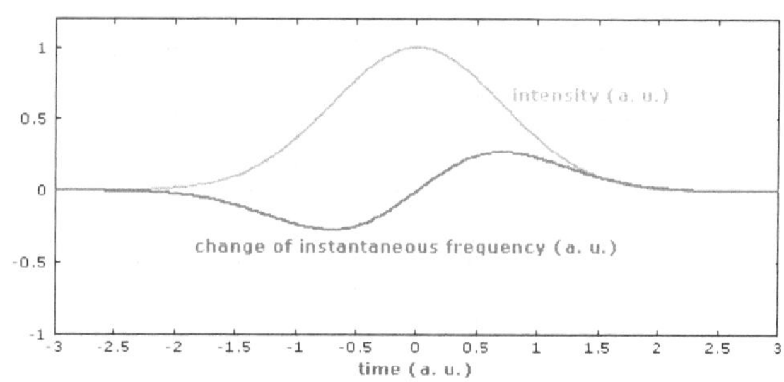

Fig. 1. Instantaneous frequency of an initially unchirped pulse which has experienced self-phase modulation. The central part of the pulse exhibits an up-chirp.

An optical pulse propagating through fiber experiences degradation that may cause communication errors limiting the overall system performance. Fiber loss, dispersion and nonlinearity are the main factors that lead to such degradation even in single mode fibers (SMFs). For single channel communications, group velocity dispersion (GVD) and self-phase modulation (SPM) are the most significant dispersion and nonlinear effects respectively. SPM arises due to intensity dependence of refractive index; it introduces chirp that causes pulse spectrum broadening. These phenomena impose limits on the transmission rate and overall performance of the optical communications; therefore it is highly desired to mitigate these effects in fiber optic communication. This produces higher refractive index at the peak of the pulse when compared to the edges of the pulse. This produces a time varying phase change $d\theta/dt$. Due to this change, the frequency of the optical signal undergoes a frequency shift from its initial value. This effect is known as frequency chirping, in which different parts of the pulse undergo different phase change Fig. 1 shows the frequecy chirping effect [3, 8-14]. The rising edge experiences a shift towards the higher frequency and the trailing edge experiences a shift towards the lower frequency. Since this effect depends heavily on the signal intensity, SPM has more effect on high intensity signal pulses. In case of fibers which have the GVD effects, the pulse broadens which leads to difficulty in the receiver side to decode the signal. When the chromatic dispersion is negative, the edges of frequencies which experienced higher shifts tend to move away from the centre of the pulse. The edges of frequencies which experienced lower shifts tend to move away from the centre in the opposite direction. Thus this GVD affected pulse will be broadened at the end of the fiber. The chirping worsens due to this effect. Thus SPM can worsen the performance of the optical system in case of long haul transmission [1].

2.2 Cross Phase Modulation

High power optical amplifiers and dispersion management enable increased length of inter-amplifier spans in multi-channel high bit-rate transmission systems. The bit-rate - distance product is limited by the combined effects of fiber dispersion and non-linear effects due to the high launched power into the fiber. In dispersive fiber, the combined effects of self-phase modulation (SPM), cross-phase modulation (XPM) and four-wave mixing (FWM) affect the transmission performance. Phase modulation due to XPM has significant influence on a WDM system as it affects channels over a continuous wavelength range and is converted into amplitude distortion by residual dispersion [6-10]. Only little work has been done investigating the XPM induced pulse distortion systematically in dependence of a wide range of parameters [5]. In this paper we present the experimental and theoretical investigation of a XPM impaired system depending on fiber dispersion. Cross-phase modulation is a consequence of an intensity dependent refractive index in silica fibers (Kerr effect) [4]. A signal at wavelength λ_k experiences a nonlinear phase shift depending on the optical power at different wavelengths. For a WDM system consisting of M channels the total nonlinear phase shift $\Delta\phi_k^{NL}$ of the considered channel k is (factor 2 for parallel polarization):

$$\Delta\phi_k^{NL} = \gamma \cdot L_{eff} \cdot \left(P_k + 2 \cdot \sum_{i \neq k}^{M} P_i \right) \qquad (2)$$

The first contribution in this expression $\Delta\phi_k^{NL}$ is due to SPM depending on the power of the detected channel alone. The summation takes into account XPM arising from the optical power in the neighboring channels where the integrated power in the fiber is relevant for the total phase shift. Amplitude modulation of the pump channels results in phase modulation $\Delta\phi(t)$ of the probe channel due to XPM. This nonlinear frequency chirp is converted into amplitude fluctuation in a dispersive fiber. The effect of XPM also depends on the wavelength separation between the signal channel and the neighbouring channel. If the channels are separated widely, then the XPM effects are relatively weak because the two bit streams walk-off from each other quickly. In case of the DWDM systems, the channel wavelength separation is very narrow which leads to strong XPM effect. Since XPM results in a inter channel crosstalk, its effect, to some extent, also depends on the bit pattern of the two channels.

3 Considerations for Simulating the Effects of SPM AND XPM

A model of WDM Optical network system has been simulated using Optsim software. The Optsim simulator used to provide block-based designs, which are interconnected with the wires. The tool is useful in analyzing nonlinear effects with respect to dispersion, noise, jitter etc. In this section, we will discuss simulations of design models for different nonlinear effects namely SPM, XPM in sample mode because these are time varying nonlinear effects. Sample mode deals with time domain simulations.

3.1 Self Phase Modulation

The design model contains transmitter, receiver and fiber channel blocks.

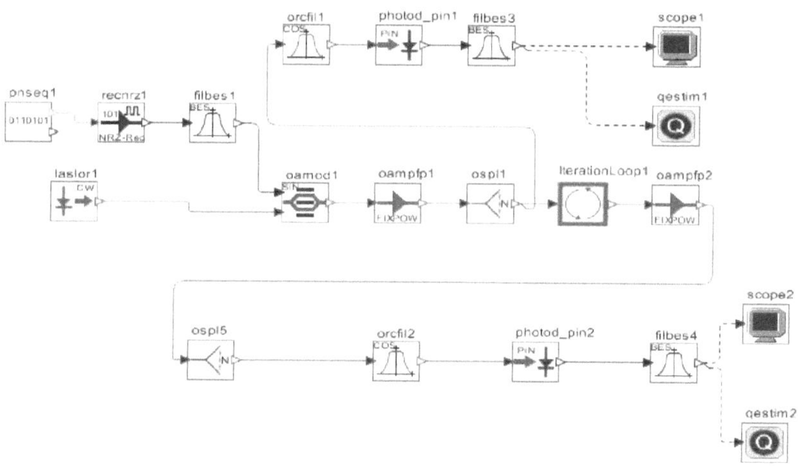

Fig. 2. Block diagram Self Phase Modulation

3.1.1 Transmitter Block

The transmitter block contains Random data generator, Non Return to Zero (NRZ) modulation, Bessel filter, continuous wave laser, Mach-Zehnder amplitude modulator, booster, and optical splitter component blocks. Random data generator is used to generate bits randomly, which are transformed to signal using modulation techniques. Commonly used modulation techniques are Non Return to Zero (NRZ) and Return to Zero (RZ). In NRZ, all 1's are represented by positive voltage and all 0's are represented by negative voltage. In RZ, signal returns to zero for each pulse with respect to logic level (1 or 0). Here we used NRZ modulation (Digital signaling) technique to generate a signal. The CW laser block is used to generate the optical light signal wave. Wavelength, frequency, power of the signal is initialized and phase parameter of the signal is set to random in this block. The output of the NRZ modulator is sent to Bessel's filter. The filter is used to preserve the shape of the wave when transmitted within in the pass band mainly with the phase response .The configuration of filter is set to "low pass filter" which passes all frequencies with respect to cutoff frequency (3db frequency in this filter configuration) and attenuates high frequency signals than cutoff. In this design, 3db frequency is same as bit rate to ensure every signal is passed through filter and preserve the shape. The output of filter and CW laser are sent to amplitude Mach-zehnder modulator, which is an electro-optical modulator used to modulate the light wave with respect to transmitted electrical signal and generates an optical signal at the output of modulator. Chirp factor of the signal is defined in the modulator block. The modulated signal is sent to booster (an optical amplifier), which is used to boost power of the signal with the factor set in booster block configuration. This amplified signal is sent to optical splitter which is then sent onto many sub design models with equal division of optical power if the losses are set to zero. The design shown in the Fig.2 has only one sub design. To generalize the things, optical splitter is used in the above design so that we can add sub designs in the future for the same design. An optical scope is connected at the output of optical splitter to observe the optical signal.

3.1.2 Fiber Channel

Fiber channel in the design is shown in Fig.3 as iterative loop component. The iterative loop component consists of fiber, fiber compensating technique component and In-line optical amplifier. The components in the iterative loop block are shown.

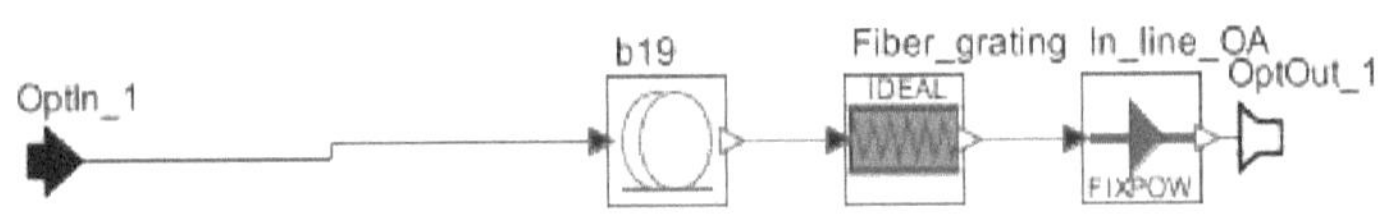

Fig. 3. Configuration setup for iterative loop component

The iterative loop is used to resend the signal within the block depending on iteration number. Iteration number is set in the iterative block properties. Iteration number repeats the process of sending the signal through fiber. When the components are made as a compound block, they need to be connected by input and output ports inside the compound block. Use of an iterative loop makes the design more reliable and aids in observe of the quality of output signal by increasing the fiber length.

The Figure 3 also has input and output port within the compound block. The input optical signal is send over the fiber. The fiber has few important parameters, which needs to be considered and configured. They are Length of the fiber, losses, dispersion coefficient, nonlinear effects and nonlinear coefficient. Output of the fiber is sent to fiber grating, which is used to compensate the distortion of signal by inducing dispersion after each stage. Fibers grating compensator is used to reflect particular wavelengths of light and transmits others, achieved by varying refractive index (varying intensity of light). Dispersed signal is then sent to an Inline optical amplifier to amplify signal.

3.1.3 Receiver Block

The main blocks of the receiver system are raised the cosine Gaussian optical filter, a photodiode, a Bessel filter and an electrical oscilloscope. The raised cosine filter is used for pulse shaping to minimize intersymbol interference. The output signal from fiber channel will be an input to raised cosine filter. Filter configuration is set to band pass filter. The band pass filter is used to transmit all the frequencies within the specified range. The photodiode is used to convert an optical signal into an electrical signal. Output of photodiode is sent to Bessel's filter, whose 3db frequency is configured to 80% of the bit rate because the NRZ modulator roll off factor (slope) is 0.8 as it is the property of the ideal modulator that it generates 80% of the input value at the output depending on switching between levels (0 and 1) [9]. Electrical scope is used to capture the output electrical signal, eye pattern. Eye pattern measurements are collected in time domain. All the Component blocks are connected through wires.

3.2 Cross Phase Modulation

Cross phase design model is similar to Self-phase design except the transmitter block has two WDM (wavelength division multiplexing) channels. Design model is shown in Fig 4. Cross phase modulation is nonlinear phase change due to optical signal in other channel.

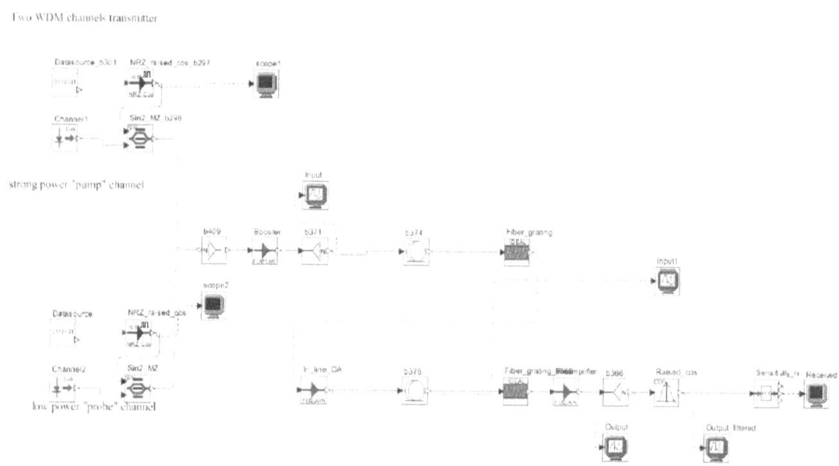

Fig. 4. Block diagram Cross Phase Modulation

3.2.1 Transmitter Block

There are two channels named high and low power channels to differentiate the input signals from each channel. Cross phase modulation is advantageous over the SPM is because it has two channels with the same bit rate. These two signals are combined with light wave to form an optical signal with respect to the each channel. The two optical signals are then combined to form a single optical signal representing two signals. The optical signal having two signals is carried to booster block to amplify the signal.

3.2.2 Fiber Channel

The fiber channels contain fiber, fiber grating and optical amplifier with fixed gain. Optical Amplifier with fixed gain (Inline optical amplifier) is not to amplify signal but to focus on fiber transmission properties. Optical signal shown in Fig. 4 is transmitted over the fiber channel and dispersion due to fiber is compensated at each stage of the fiber and there is a two stage fiber channel outputs are measure using oscilloscope blocks. The signal is dispersed due to the cross phase modulation effects over the fiber channel.

3.2.3 Receiver Block

Dispersed optical signal is transmitted through Cosine raised Gaussian filter which behaves as band pass filter as per the configuration of filter. The filter outputs the signal, by passing the frequencies specified in the filter block configuration. The signal is shown in the Fig 4. The signal generated by band pass filter is sent to a sensitive receiver, which acts as a PIN photo diode, converts optical signal to electrical signal. The output electrical signal is captured using an oscilloscope.

4 Simulation Results and Discussion

4.1 Self Phase Modulation

The basic simulation parameters of the SPM design and its simulation results are discussed in this section. The transmission rate is set to 10 Gb/s. Fiber length is set to 100km, wavelength is set to 1550nm, so frequency is equal to 193.4 THz. The filtered electrical input signal shown in Fig 5 is combined with the light wave to generate an input optical signal. The optical signal transmitted over the fiber channel get distorted due to non linearity's arises in fiber channel. The dispersion effect has been observed in Fig. 6 and the dispersion in the fiber channel has been compensated using the fiber grating technique. But due to the SPM effect in fiber, pulse broadening is observed at the output. Dispersed optical signal shown in Fig. 6 is then sent to receiver unit to convert optical signal to electrical signal. The output electrical signal is captured using electrical scope.

The transmitted signal power decreases as the signal travels through the design, output signal power is less than the transmitted signal but the signal phase and shape is preserved. From Fig. 7, we can observe that the amplitude of the signal is decreases with the decrease in power, which is observed in output optical pulse. The loss of power causing attenuation of the signal with respect to amplitude, results in distortion of signal. The eye pattern is shown in Fig. 8.

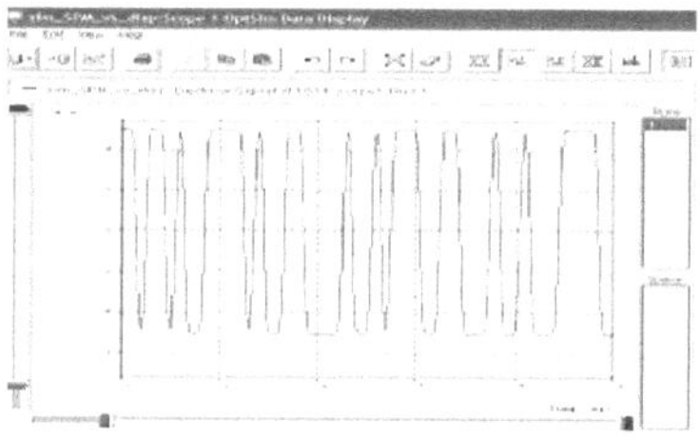

Fig. 5. Input electrical signal of SPM

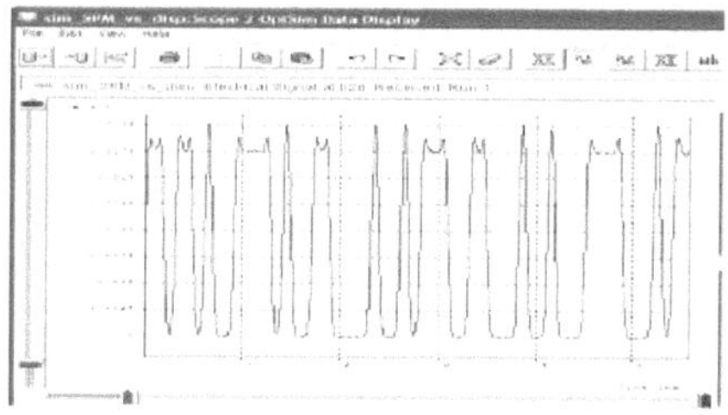

Fig. 7. Output electrical signal of SPM

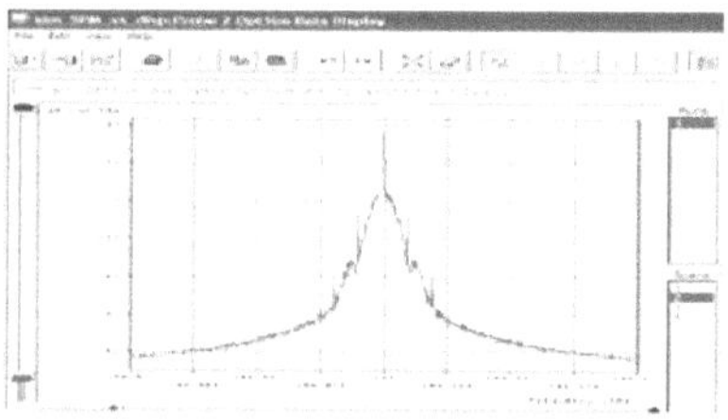

Fig. 6. Optical Signal received after fiber second iteration

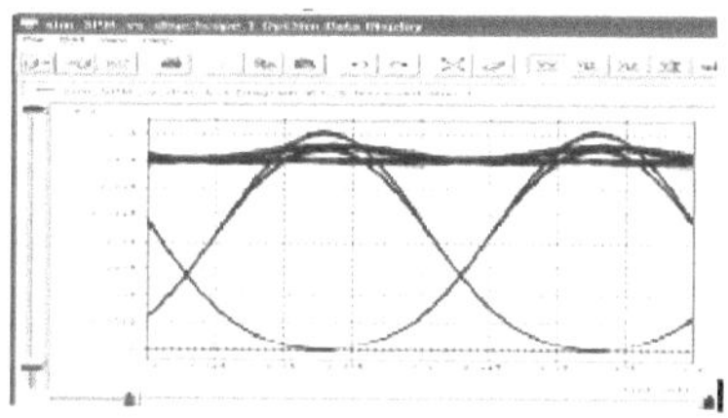

Fig. 8. Eye pattern of SPM

Eye pattern is generated by overlapping the samples of signals. The eye jitter shown in Fig.8 is very less which implies noise level or distortion in the signal is very less. There is no zero level noise in the eye pattern as the distortion is at the higher level of the signal and the lower level of the signal is received without distortion.

4.2 Cross Phase Modulation

The basic simulation parameters of the XPM design and its simulation results are discussed in this section. The transmission rate is set to 10 Gb/s. Fiber length is set to 100km, wavelength is set to 1550nm, so frequency is equal to 193.4 Thz. The high power channel is 100 mV and the low power channel is 10mV. The combined input signal waveform of high power channel and low power channels is shown in Fig 9.

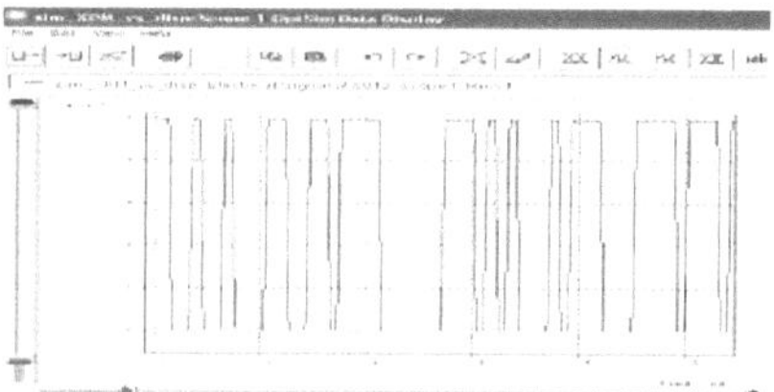

Fig. 9. Combined input of XPM Electrical signal

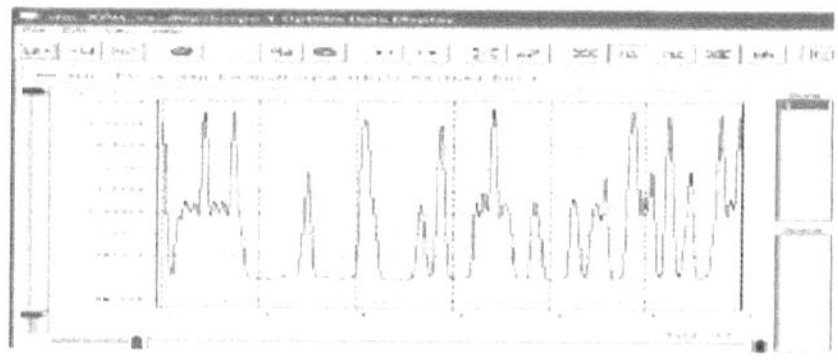

Fig. 11. Output electrical signal of XPM

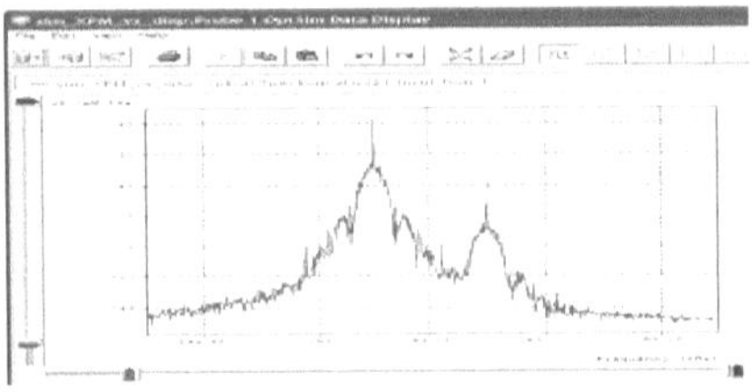

Fig. 10. Optical signal resulted from two different channals

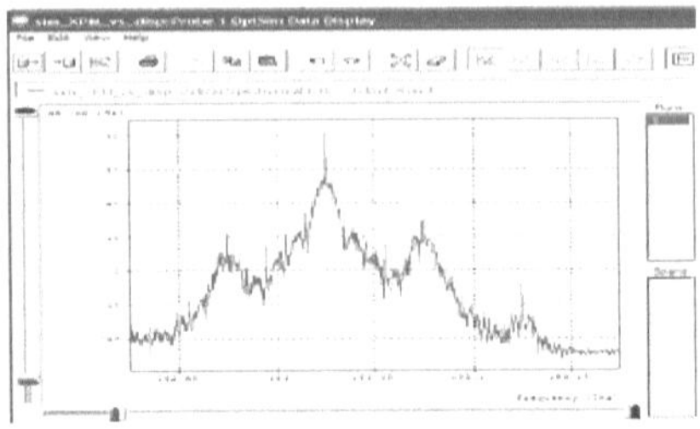

Fig. 12. Dispersed optical signal

Fig.10 displays the optical signal resulted from two different channels, and Fig.11 indicates the output of the electrical signal from the XPM block measured using oscilloscope. The received signal indicates loss of amplitude reduction of the signal, which results from the distortion in fiber channel.

Fig.12 shows the dispersed optical signal from the XPM receiver block, and Fig.13 indicates the eye pattern of the corresponding XPM signal received in the output block.

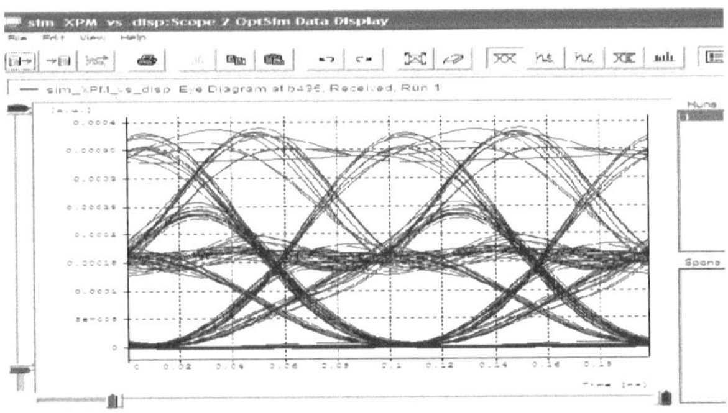

Fig. 13. Eye pattern of XPM

Fig.13 shows the eye pattern of XPM signal output block

5 Conclusion

In this paper we designed and analysis the nonlinear effects of SPM and XPM in a WDM optical fiber network for high data transmission and the corresponding results are indicated. The beam broadening effects in SPM has been studied; also we addressed the suppression methods that can be used in order to remove the degrading effects of these nonlinearities.

References

[1] Bergano, N.S.: Wavelength division multiplexing in long haul transoceanic transmission systems. Journal of Light Wave Technology 23(12), 4125–4139 (2005)
[2] Singh, M.L., Hudiara, I.S.: A piece wise linear solution for nonlinear SRS effect in DWDM fibre optic communication systems. J. Microwave Optoelectron 3(4), 29–38 (2004)
[3] Thele, H.J., Killey, R.I., Bayvel, P.: Transmission Limitations in Optical WDM Networks due to Cross Phase Modulation. The Institution of Electrical Engineers (1998)
[4] Trischitta, P.R., Marra, W.C.: Applying WDM technology to undersea cable networks. IEEE Communication Magazine 36(2), 62–66 (1998)
[5] Kikuchi, N., Sekine, K., Sasaki, S.: Analysis of Cross-Phase Modulation (XPM) Effect on WDM Transmission Performance. Electron. Lett. 33(8), 653–654 (1997)
[6] Rapp, L.: Experimental Investigation of Signal Distortions Induced by Cross-Phase Modulation Combined with Dispersion. IEEE Photon. Technol. Lett. 9(12), 1592–1594 (1997)
[7] Saunders, R.A., Patel, B.L., Harvey, H.J., Robinson, A.: Impact of Cross-Phase Modulation for WDM Systems over Positive and Negative Dispersion NZ-DSF and Methods for its Suppression. Electron. Lett. 32(24), 2206–2207 (1996)
[8] Ogata, T., Yasuhiro, A., Koga, T., Matsuoka, I.: Observation of Bit-Error Rate Impairment due to Dynamic Cross-Phase Modulation in 2.5GbiUs WDM Transmission Systems with Standard Fiber. In: Tech. Digest OFC 1996, San Jose, vol. 2, pp. 42–44 (1996)
[9] Yu, A., O'Mahony, M.J.: Optimization of wavelength spacing in a WDM transmission system in the presence of fibre nonlinearities. IEEE Proceedings-J. Optoelectron 142(4), 190–196 (1995)
[10] O'Mahony, M.J., Simeonidou, D., Yu, A., Zhou, J.: The design of a European optical network. J. Lightwave Technol. 13(5), 817–828 (1995)
[11] Kikuchi, N., Sasaki, S.: Analytical evaluation technique of self-phase modulation effect on the performance of cascaded optical amplifier systems. J. Lightw. Technol. 13(5), 868–878 (1995)
[12] Chraplyvy, A.R.: What is the actual capacity of single mode fibres in amplified lightwave systems. IEEE Photon. Technol. Lett. 5, 665–668 (1993)
[13] Marcuse, D., Chraplyvy, A.R., Tkach, R.W.: Effect of fibre nonlinearity on long-distance transmission. J. Lightwave Technol. 9, 121–128 (1991)
[14] Giles, C.R., Desurvire, E.: Propagation of signal and noise in concatenated erbium-doped fiber optical amplifiers. J. Lightwave Tech. 9(2), 47–154 (1991)

An Energy Efficient Event Based Hierarchical Clustering Algorithm for Wireless Sensor Networks

Chiranjib Patra[1], Arindam Mondal[2],
Parama Bhaumik[2], and Matangini Chattopadhyay[3]

[1] Department of Information Technology, Calcutta Institute of Engineering and Management, Tollygunge, Kolkata, India
chiranjibpatra@gmail.com
[2] Department of Information Technology, Jadavpur Unversity, Kolkata, India
an.arindam@gmail.com
[3] Department of Education Technology, Jadavpur Unversity, Kolkata, India
chttpdhy@yahoo.com

Abstract. WSN's present a new challenge in current research works due to their unlimited potential. Sensor nodes operate with limited battery power, which is seldom replaced or recharged. So, energy utilization is an important constraint in designing routing protocols in WSN. In this paper, we proposed an event based hierarchical cluster based routing algorithm with the objective of reducing the energy consumption for creating the routing topology and thus maximize the lifetime of Wireless Sensor Networks. The performance of the proposed protocol has been examined and evaluated through a simulation study. The simulation results clearly show that it has a better performance than EECDS.

Keywords: EECDS, hierarchical cluster, Topology.

1 Introduction

Constant evolution of communication equipments enables wireless networks, one of the most emerging technologies, to use smaller and cheaper sensors to monitor specific events. These tiny sensor nodes are composed of three major parts: sensor device, processing element, and communication device. Obviously, these small devices have limitations in energy consumption, memory, and transmission bandwidth. This is the main reason why most of the research on WSNs has concentrated on the design of energy and computationally efficient algorithms and protocols, and the application domain has been restricted to simple data- oriented monitoring and reporting applications. The main goal of a WSN is to collect data from the environment and send it to a reporting site where the data can be observed and analyzed.

P.V. Krishna, M.R. Babu, and E. Ariwa (Eds.): ObCom 2011, Part I, CCIS 269, pp. 380–385, 2012.

Some of the related protocols are:

The R&M protocol [4] is a location-based protocol based on the concepts of relay region and the enclosure of a node.

The Local Minimum Spanning Tree (LMST) protocol [5] is another relevant location-based topology control protocol that works in a distributed manner and only needs local information about the topology.

Another location-based protocol is the Geographical Adaptive Fidelity (GAF) algorithm presented in [6]. GAF is designed based on several observations: First, nodes spend considerable energy sending and receiving packets, and also while in idle state. In order to save more energy, radios must be turned off to conserve energy due to overhearing and idle listening. Second, GAF utilizes network and application layer information to turn the radios off, as these layers provide better information about when the radio is not needed. Third, in highly dense networks, multiple paths exist between nodes, so some intermediate nodes can be turned off without compromising connectivity.

The K-Neigh protocol, introduced in [7], pretends to build a K-neighbour graph with exactly the same characteristics as the theoretical definition: each node will be connected with the closest k neighbours. In this protocol nodes are assumed to be able to calculate the distance between them and their neighbours.

One of the most widely known routing based topology construction mechanisms is the Common Power (COMPOW) protocol presented in [8]. COMPOW's main objective is to find the minimum common transmission level that will produce a routing table with the same entries as the one found using the maximum transmission level.

In the hierarchical topology construction approach, a communication hierarchy is created in which a reduced subset of the nodes is selected and given more responsibilities on behalf of a simplified and reduced functionality for the majority of the nodes. This approach has the potential to greatly simplify the network topology and the opportunity to save additional energy by assigning useful functions to the reduced subset of nodes, such as information aggregation and filtering, and routing and message forwarding.

The important protocols in this category are:

The Energy Efficient Connected Dominating Set (EECDS) proposed in [3], uses the colouring approach to create the maximal independent sets, and then connect the independent sets using connector nodes.

The Distance-2 (D2) Colouring algorithm [9] -The authors present the idea of building a Well Connected Dominating Set (WCDS), which is defined as a CDS with low size, low degree and low stretch properties.

In our protocol we are using the local information, such as the position of the nodes to calculate the distances between them. We are also reducing the communication range of the nodes to its farthest neighbour, so that all the neighbours remain covered. Thus reducing the energy required for the construction of the topology.

The rest of the paper is organized as follows. In section II, we present the Features of our protocol. In Section III the Assumptions are stated. Section IV describes our proposed Algorithm. Comparative analysis of the proposed approach with the existing one is presented in section V. Finally in section VI, we conclude the paper and highlight some direction towards future work.

2 Features of the Protocol

The following are the features of the proposed protocol:

1. Each node has exactly one parent.
2. Doing so the Qos features are affected by reducing the redundancy caused due to clustering.
3. The energy wasted or precipitated due to unnecessary transmission is cut off due to avoidance of redundant clustering.
4. As the connectivity between the nodes is based on the limited value of communication radius, therefore, the message transmission is error free and the noise value due to signal strength drop is minimized.

3 Assumptions of the Protocol

The proposed protocol is a hierarchical topology construction protocol based on the growing tree technique. The idea is to illustrate some common message exchange sequences, the use of timeouts, and how the modification of the status of the node modifies the execution of the protocol. The protocol works based on the following assumptions:

- The nodes know their positions but have no list of neighbours.
- Every node starts in an unvisited state.
- The sink is the initiator of the process.
- The protocol ends when every node is in active mode or in sleeping mode.

4 The Algorithm

Step1:

- The sink node initiates the protocol sending a Hello message to all the nodes in its communication range. It includes its address and level (number of hops from the sink), which in the case of the sink it is equal to 0.
- The sender node programs a timeout to stop listening for answers from its neighbours

Step 2:

- All unvisited nodes on the transmission range of the sender node that received the Hello message answer back with a Reply message, set the sender as their default gateway, and change their status to In-Process mode, but the visited ones will not respond.
- The receiver nodes calculate their distances from the sender node and send it as the metric in the Reply message.
- The receiver nodes at the same time set a timeout in case they do not receive an acknowledgment from their default gateway (the sender node).

Step 3:

- Once the timeout of the sender expires, this node checks the list of neighbours that answered back with the Reply message.
- If the sender node did not receive any answer back, it turns itself off and changes its status into a Sleeping mode.
- If the sender node received at least one answer back, it goes into Active mode.
  i. Adds the neighbours as its Children.
  ii. Sorts the children based on their metric.
  iii. Reduces the communication range of the node (the sender) to the distance between that node and its farthest child.
  iv. Declares itself as Parent and sends an unicast message to each one of them in the sorted order to let them know they were selected.

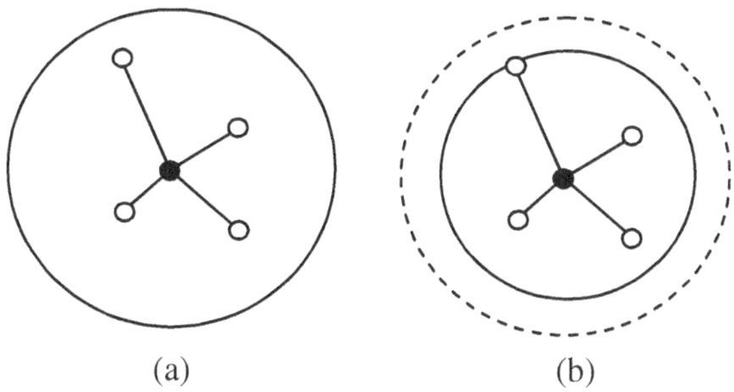

Fig. 1. (a) Maximum Communication Range (b) Reduced Communication Range

Step 4:

- Once a node receives the confirmation message from its default gateway, it waits a random amount of time and sends its own Hello message to discover new unvisited nodes.
- If the timeout of a node in In-Process mode expires, it means that the node was not selected, so it turns itself off and goes into Sleeping mode.

5 Simulation

The above protocol was simulated using Atarraya[1], a generic, Java-based, event-driven simulator for topology control algorithms in wireless sensor networks. The advantage of using Atarraya is its GUI, which is based on the real-time display of the network during execution of the routing protocol.

For testing and comparison we compare our new protocol with standard Energy Efficient Connected Dominating Set (EECDS) protocol as reference. Our comparisons were connected to various issues like:

1. Energy Spent Ratio
2. Reserved Energy in Tree

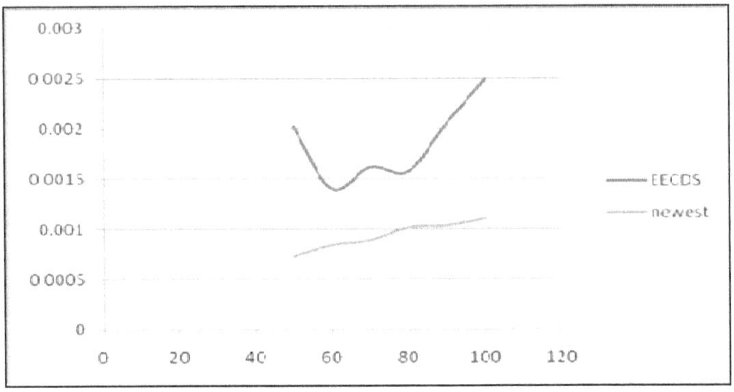

Fig. 2. Plot between Number of Nodes versus Energy SpentRatio

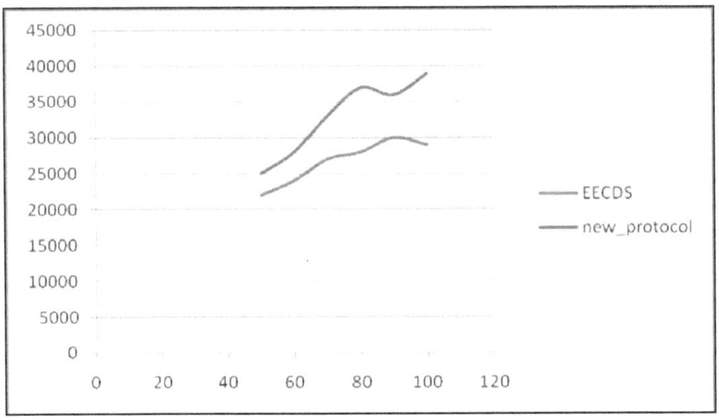

Fig. 3. Plot between Numbers of Nodes versus Reserved Energy in the Tree

The Energy Efficient Connected Dominating Set (EECDS) algorithm creates a maximal independent set in the first phase, and then selects gateway nodes to connect the independent sets during the second phase.

The main disadvantage of the EECDS algorithm is its message complexity. In both phases of the algorithm, competition is used to determine the best candidates to be included in the independent sets and the final tree. This process is very costly in terms of message overhead because each node has to consult its neighbors for their status in order to calculate its own metric.

The execution stages of the new protocol does not require any phase, hence it inherits all the advantages of simple, yet robust features of any other simple routing protocol.

6 Conclusions and Future Work

From the simulation results it can be seen that this routing protocol can be implemented for small to medium scale sensor nets but to be tested and modified for larger networks like mesh network, sonar net etc.

Some advanced clustering techniques using neural nets and fuzzy can be implemented keeping the features of our protocol intact. The relative advantages over our protocolcan be enhanced by using the above techniques.

One disadvantage of the hierarchical approach is that the selected subset of nodes will work more than their unselected neighbours, and will see their batteries drained sooner. Therefore, this approach must be accompanied by a good topology maintenance function that will rotate the role of the nodes with the final goal of spending their energy evenly and extending the network lifetime.

References

[1] Wightman, P.M., Labrador, M.A.: Atarraya: A Simulation Tool to Teach and Research Topology Control Algorithms for Wireless Sensor Networks. In: Simutools 2009 Proceedings of the 2nd International Conference on Simulation Tools and Techniques ICST (Institute for Computer Sciences, Social-Informatics and Telecommunications Engineering). ICST, Brussels (2009)

[2] Wightman, P.M., Labrador, M.A.: Topology Control in Wireless Sensor Networks. Springer, Heidelberg (2009)

[3] Yuanyuan, Z., Jia, X., Yanxiang, H.: Energy efficient distributed connected dominating sets construction in wireless sensor networks. In: Proceeding of the 2006 ACM International Conference on Communications and Mobile Computing, pp. 797–802 (2006)

[4] Rodoplu, V., Meng, T.H.: Minimum energy mobile wireless networks. IEEE J. Sel. Areas Commun. 17(8), 1333–1344 (1999)

[5] Li, N., Hou, J.C., Sha, L.: Design and analysis of an MST-based topology control algorithm. In: Proceedings of IEEE INFOCOM, pp. 1702–1712 (2003)

[6] Xu, Y., Heidemann, J., Estrin, D.: Geography-informed energy conservation for ad hoc routing. In: Proceedings of the 7th Annual International Conference on Mobile Computing and Networking, pp. 70–84 (2001)

[7] Blough, D.M., Leoncini, M., Resta, G., Santi, P.: The K-Neigh protocol for symmetric topology control in ad hoc networks. In: Proceedings of the 4th ACM International Symposium on Mobile AdHoc Networking and Computing, pp. 141–152 (2003)

[8] Narayanaswamy, S., Kawadia, V., Sreenivas, R., Kumar, P.: Power control in ad hoc networks: theory, architecture, algorithm and implementation of the COWPOW protocol. In: Proceedings of the European Wireless Conference, pp. 156–162 (2002)

[9] Parthasarathy, S., Gandhi, R.: Fast distributed well connected dominating sets for ad hoc networks. Technical Report CS-TR 4559, University of Maryland (2004), http://citeseer.ist.psu.edu/parthasarathy04fast.html

Throughput Improvement in Mobile OFDM System with Pilot Free Adaptive Modulation

K. Vinoth Babu, G. Ramachandra Reddy, Sunit Gupta,
Pratul Chauhan, and Pratik Patel

School of Electronics Engineering
Vit University
Vellore, Tamil Nadu, India- 632014
vinothbabu.k@vit.ac.in

Abstract. Orthogonal Frequency Division Multiplexing (OFDM) is an emerging multicarrier modulation scheme, which has been adapted for several wireless local area network (WLAN) systems and IEEE 802.16a (WIMAX) systems. The quality of service and performance sensitivity of different wireless services varies according to the channel, so the conventional OFDM is unsatisfactory. In this paper, we introduce an adaptive modulation scheme in association with OFDM systems. By using different modulation techniques we can send variable number of bits per symbol depending on the channel quality to achieve better throughput. We also remove the pilot bits from the transmitted data to increases the bandwidth efficiency. We propose a method to estimate the channel quality and Signal-to-Noise ratio (SNR) directly, without using any pilot bits.

Keywords: Adaptive Modulation, Orthogonal Frequency Division Multiplexing (OFDM), fading channels, Signal-to-Noise ratio (SNR), kurtosis estimation and Channel capacity.

1 Introduction

Orthogonal Frequency Division Multiplexing (OFDM) is prominently used for wireless communication system. OFDM technology gives a high data capacity and spectral efficiency for the wireless systems. OFDM is a multi- carrier technique in which the entire spectrum is split into narrow-band subcarriers and the information is transmitted in parallel on these subcarriers. Each subcarrier occupies a small frequency interval for which the frequency response is almost constant, thus each symbol experiences an approximately flat fading channel, thereby leading to more reliable networking services. The subcarrier signals are sent through time dispersive channel, which results in different time and frequency synchronization errors for each subcarrier, thereby having different Signal-to-noise ratio (SNR).

Adaptive modulation is an important technique in a mobile communication network for effective utilization of wireless communication channels. By using adaptive modulation we can increase the transmission rate. It can be used as matching

P.V. Krishna, M.R. Babu, and E. Ariwa (Eds.): ObCom 2011, Part I, CCIS 269, pp. 386–391, 2012.

modulation schemes to the time varying channel conditions. To know the desired modulation, we first find the channel capacity and the SNR of each subcarrier. In the OFDM system there are some severely faded channels which will have more errors when compared with others. Adaptive modulation can be used to observe reliable performance across all subcarriers. After identifying the sub-carriers with low - error probability, we use an alternate mode to re-modulate these subcarriers. Thus we can achieve a higher data rate by re-modulating the subcarriers.

Generally, to estimate channel quality pilot signals are inserted in the subcarriers and these pilots are known at the receiver and are thus used for correcting the magnitude and the phase shift of the received symbols. In this paper we use kurtosis for blind estimation of the channel without using the pilots thus increasing the overall throughput of the system.

The paper is arranged as follows, Section 2 describes about OFDM system model. Section 3 describes blind channel quality estimation. Simulation results are presented in section 4. Finally conclusions are given in section 5.

2 OFDM System Model Description

A general OFDM system model is presented in Fig.1. [9] In this OFDM system there are N subcarriers and the symbol period is T. The transmitter section converts digital data to be transmitted, into amplitude and phase of subcarriers. It then transforms N modulated data symbols into a time domain using Inverse Fast Fourier Transform (IFFT).

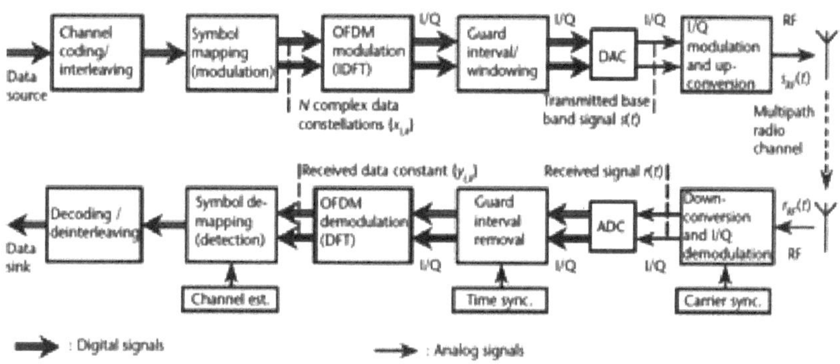

Fig. 1. OFDM System Model

A large number of modulation schemes are available that allows the number of bits transmitted per carrier per symbol to be varied. If an arbitrary modulation scheme is considered, for example, Quadrature Amplitude Modulation (QAM), the complex-valued OFDM symbol $x_{t,n}$ is represented by

$$x_{i,n} = \sum_{k=0}^{N-1} X_{i,k} e^{\frac{j2\pi kn}{N}}, \quad n = 1,2,3..........N-1 \tag{1}$$

where $X_{i,k}$ denotes the transmitted information symbol for the kth subcarrier in the ith OFDM block. The effect of inter symbol interference (ISI) on an OFDM signal can be reduced by the addition of guard intervals to the start of each symbol. It eliminates time-offset errors in the receivers. The guard intervals contain last one fourth samples of OFDM symbols. The receiver section performs the reverse operation of the transmitter by using Fast Fourier Transform (FFT) to analyze the signal in frequency domain. In this paper multipath Rayleigh fading channel is considered, which is modeled as the impulse response function having L propagation paths and is given by

$$h(t,\tau) = \sum_{i=1}^{L} \alpha_i(t)\delta(\tau - t_i), \quad i = 1,2,3........L \tag{2}$$

where $\alpha_i(t)$ is the random process with a Rayleigh distribution and t_i is the i_{th} delay. The transmitted signal passes through linear time-variant channel $h(t,\tau)$ and is further corrupted by zero-mean additive white Gaussian noise (AWGN) with certain variance. The time-variant constraint ensures that the channel is constant during one OFDM symbol period. The received data symbol $R_{i,k}$ of the i_{th} OFDM block is given by

$$R_{i,k} = X_{i,k} H_k + N_{i,k} \tag{3}$$

where H_k is the frequency response at the k_{th} subcarrier and N_{ik} is the AWGN channel noise.

3 Blind Channel Quality Estimation

For analyzing OFDM system performance, a perfect knowledge of channel is required which can be used to find upper limit of OFDM system performance. Such perfect channel knowledge will not be available and needs to be estimated. In adaptive modulation system, different methods are used to determine the channel quality, which are channel SNR, radio signal strength and average SNR for each subcarrier [2], [4]. In this paper, we take average SNR as the channel quality parameter.

This is provided by higher order moments [4], [7]. For determining average SNR, estimation rule for every subcarrier is same, thus we ignore the subcarrier index k.

The second order moment of R_i, for each subcarrier can be denoted as M_2 and is given by

$$M_2 = E[|R_i|^2] = E[|X_i H_i + N_i|^2] \tag{4}$$

The fourth order moment of R_i for each subcarrier can be denoted as M_4 is given by

$$M_4 = E[|R_i|^4] = E[|X_i H_i + N_i|^4] \tag{5}$$

The Kurtosis of R_i is denoted as K_r which is given by [8]

$$K_r = \frac{M_2}{M_4} \tag{6}$$

Similarly, the kurtosis of T_i is denoted as K_t. Average SNR, denoted as A_{snr}, is given by [1]

$$A_{snr} = \frac{(K_r - 2)}{(K_t - K_r)} + \frac{\sqrt{(4-2K_r)^2 - (K_t - K_r)(2-K_r)}}{2(K_t - K_r)} \tag{7}$$

This average SNR estimated using equation (7) depends on data of regular information symbols and does not requires extra pilot information; hence it leads to throughput improvement.

After getting the SNR values for each subcarrier we use the Shannon's channel capacity theorem to find the appropriate number of bits to be loaded in each subcarrier. The maximum number of bits that can be loaded in each subcarrier is given by equation

$$C = \frac{T_u}{T_s} \log_2(1 + A_{snr}) \tag{8}$$

where T_u and T_s represents the useful symbol duration with and without Guard interval respectively. Here T_u = 12.8 µs and T_s = 16 µs.

We calculate the energy requirement of each subcarrier using the SNR and channel capacity of each subcarrier. The equation to find energy is given by [10]

$$E = \frac{(2^C - 1)}{A_{snr}} \tag{9}$$

4 Simulation

In Fig.2 we consider sixty four sub-carriers through which some random data corresponding to 16 QAM is sent and using the kurtosis estimation method we calculate the SNR values for the sub-carriers. Since channel is frequency selective, it is observed that SNR is different for different subcarriers.

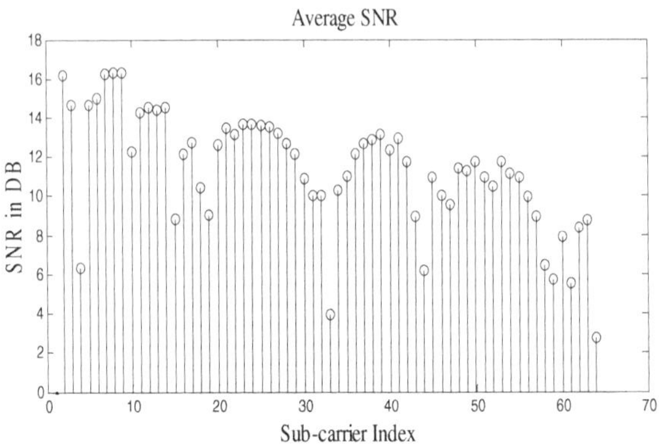

Fig. 2. Comparision of Average SNR for each subcarrier

Using the results obtained in above graph we plot the channel capacity or the bit loading for each sub-carrier. Fig.3 represents the no of bits that can be loaded in each subcarrier. As represented in the graph the sub-carriers with high SNR values can be loaded with more information bits as the noise level in them is less. On the other hand the sub-carriers with low SNR values implies high level of noise, therefore they can be loaded with less number of bits.

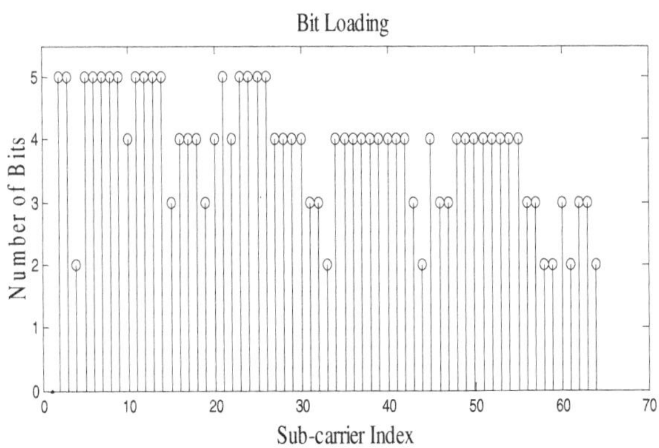

Fig. 3. Bit loading graph for each subcarrier

We also plot the energy requirement for all the sub carriers and is shown in Fig.4. This graph shows that the energy requirement for subcarriers with lower SNR values is comparatively higher than that of subcarriers with high SNR values.

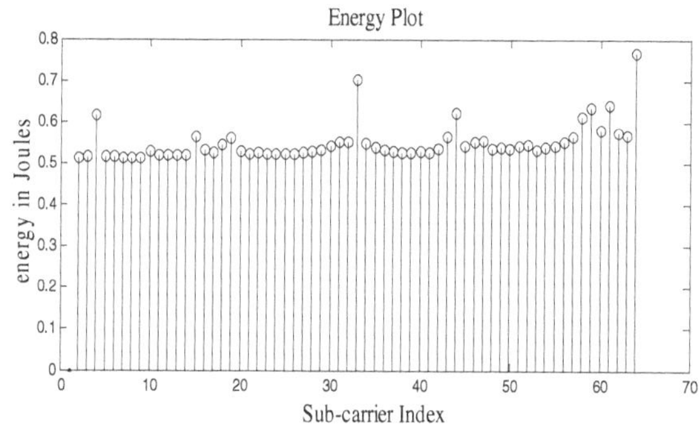

Fig. 4. Energy plot for each subcarrier index

5 Conclusion

In this paper, we have proposed a new adaptive modulation scheme which does not require the pilot bits for channel estimation [1]. Thus, the band-width efficiency of the OFDM system gets increased and by estimating the channel capacity for each sub-carrier we can vary the number of bits loaded in each of them. By using this method we were able to vary the bit rate. The bit rate obtained using our adaptive blind channel method is nearly 20 Mbps. Thus, the effect of noise on the information stream can be minimized and the overall throughput can be enhanced.

References

1. Huang, X., Wu, H.-C.: Novel Pilot-Free Adaptive Modulation for Wireless OFDM Systems. IEEE Transactions on Vehicular Technology 57(6) (November 2008)
2. Wong, C.H., Hanzo, L.: Upper-Bound Performance of a Wide-Band Adaptive Modem. IEEE Transactions on Communications 48(3) (March 2000)
3. Chow, P.S., Cioffi, J.M., Bingham, J.A.C.: A Practical Discrete Multitone Transceiver Loading Algorithm for Data Transmission over Spectrally Shaped Channels. IEEE Transactions on Communications 43(2/3/4) (February/March/April 1995)
4. Chung, J.Y., Guo, F., Ng, S.X., Hanzo, L.: Burst-by-burst Adaptive Joint-Detection CDMA/H.26L BasedWireless Video Telephony using TTCM and LDPC Code
5. Matzner, R., Englberger, F.: An SNR Estiiriatioii -Algorithrn Using Fourth-Order Moments, Institute for Coinmiin. Eugineeiing ET3, Federal Armed Forces University Munich, 85577 Neubiberg, Germany "Siemens AG, 81359 Munich, Germany
6. Rappaport, T.S.: Wireless Communications, Principles and Practice, 2nd edn. Prentice–Hall, Englewood Cliffs (2002)
7. Benedict, T., Soong, T.: The joint estimation of signal and noise from the sum envelope. IEEE Trans. Inf. Theory IT-13(3), 447–454 (1967)
8. Mood, A.M., Graybill, F.A., Boes, D.C.: Introduction to the theory of statistics. McGraw Hill, New York (1974)
9. Prashad, R.: OFDM for Wireless Communications Systems. Artech House universal personal communications series (2000)
10. Haykin, S.: Communication Systems, 4th edn. Wiley, India (2010)

Trust Based Certificate Authority for Detection of Malicious Nodes in MANET

Manoj V., Raghavendiran N., Aaqib M., and Vijayan R.

School of Information Technology and Engineering, VIT University,
Vellore-632014, India

Abstract. In MANET, mobile nodes are prone to various security attacks due to their dynamic changing topology, open medium and are constrained by limited energy, bandwidth and computational power. Most of the currently existing security algorithms designed for these MANETs are insecure, inefficient, and have low detection accuracy for nodes misbehavior. A novel trust based Certificate Authority concept is introduced to transmit data packets only through trusted nodes and isolate malicious nodes in the MANET. The proposed trust management scheme incorporates battery power consumption and packet integrity aspect in addition to direct and indirect trust values. Experimental results are presented with Qualnet Simulator 5.0. The proposed framework has shown better results in detecting malicious nodes and building a secure network.

Keywords: Trust, MANET, Security Attacks, Trust based Certificate Authority, Malicious detection, Secure MANET, Certificate Authority.

1 Introduction

1.1 Trust

Mobile Ad hoc Network (MANET) is a decentralized, infrastructure-less network where wireless nodes move arbitrarily. The nodes communicate directly to nodes in transmission range, and multi-hop communication with nodes out of range. Trust is defined as a set of relations among entities participating in a protocol. It is the degree of belief about the behavior of entities. Establishing trust relationships among participating nodes is vital for secure transmission of packet. Trust establishment mechanisms provide an incentive for cooperation among the nodes. Trust is not static it is dynamic and is dependent on context.

2 Security Attacks in MANET

Gray hole attack can advertise its route as a valid path with the motivation of intercepting the packets. The packets that pass through the attacked node are dropped with certain probability. A wormhole attack follows the tunneling process. Group of nodes

P.V. Krishna, M.R. Babu, and E. Ariwa (Eds.): ObCom 2011, Part I, CCIS 269, pp. 392–401, 2012.

collaborate to encapsulate and exchange messages between them leading to short-circuit of normal flow of packets. This type of forwarding can eat the energy of the nodes at a large extent. In black hole attack, the node advertises as a valid path to the destination and intercepts every packet without forwarding and can generate fake information. The possible changes the attack can accomplish is to modify the packet or can delay the packet without forwarding. Jelly fish attack can enter into the forwarding group and can delay the packets unnecessarily for a specific time and then forwards the packet resulting in performance degradation of the network and increase the traffic flow of packets. Denial of service attacks aim at the complete disruption of the routing function and the entire operation of the ad-hoc network. In a routing table overflow attack the malicious node floods the network to consume the resources. .In resource consumption attack, a malicious node deliberately tries to consume the resources (e.g. battery power, bandwidth, etc.) of other nodes in the network. The attacks could be in the form of unnecessary route request control messages, very frequent generation of beacon packets, or forwarding of stale information to nodes.

3 Related Works

The watchdog mechanism, based on a node supervising all its local neighbors, is one of the basic security mechanisms. It is able to detect both malicious attacks and selfish behaviors without significant overhead. The Watchdog component [1] is responsible of monitoring the received messages with the purpose of making sure that it has forwarded the message without alteration. When intermediary nodes forward the message to its neighbor, it can also verify that the next hop correctly retransmit the message, the node can be termed as trusted or malicious.

The proposed trust management framework in [2] includes Trust agent, Recommendation agent and the Combiner. In this paper the Trust agent derives trust levels from events that are directly experienced monitored by a node. The Recommendation agent shares trust information about nodes with other nodes in the network. The Combiner computes the final trust in a node based upon the information it receives from the trust and recommendation agents.

The energy of mobile nodes in adhoc networks are powered by batteries with limited energy. Hence the nodes with minimal energy can turn into selfish nodes. In this research work [3], the proposed scheme discriminates the selfish and the malicious nodes. The total expenditure at a node is calculated by a devised formula considering the energy spent on transmission and the reception of data packets, acknowledgments and on other nodes.

Fuzzy logic based functions gives accurate results rather than approximate, fixed and exact. Fuzzy logic variables may have trust values that range in degree between 0 and 1. In the proposed scheme [2] trust decision is based on fuzzy logic. If the evaluated trust is greater than or equal to the threshold trust, then that particular node is called as a trustworthy [4], else it will be treated as untrustworthy and excluded from all future network operations.

Packet modification by malicious nodes is a security threat in MANET. The overview of SAODV protocol [5] provides security mechanisms based on non-invertible hash functions and public key cryptography. In this paper [8] energy consumption of the security protocols and cryptographic algorithms are analyzed. RSA utilizes minimal energy for verification, while Digital Signature Algorithm and Diffie Hellman consume more energy. Hash algorithms are the least complex of the cryptographic algorithms and should intuitively incur the least energy cost.

A Novel Approach for Providing Security in VANET uses Certificate Authority [6]. Central authority (CA) nodes are responsible for assigning public and private keys to the requesting nodes in the network. Source nodes requests available CA node for transmission with the destination node. CA validates source and destination nodes and issue certificates for secure transmission.

4 The Proposed Framework

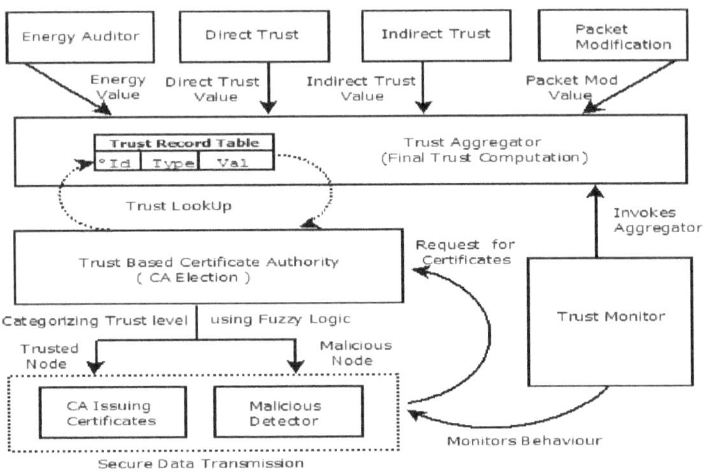

Fig. 1. Proposed Framework

4.1 Energy Audit

Energy is a scarce and non-renewable resource in wireless ad hoc networks. Due to limited resource availability, nodes behave selfishly by saving the battery power without forwarding the packets. The energy spent at each node is monitored by energy audit. The total node energy expenditure at a node due to another node in the network can be calculated follows.

$$E_{Value} = \rho_{n>0}(\rho_{X\equiv Y} E_{T_{ack}} + \rho_{X\neq Y} E_{R_{ack}}) + \rho_{m>0}(\rho_{X\equiv Y} E_{T_{Pck}} + \rho_{X\neq Y} E_{R_{PCK}}) \quad (1)$$

Where

E_{Value} = Energy spent at node Y due to node X
$E_{T_{ack}}$= Energy spent for one acknowledgement
$E_{T_{pck}}$= Energy spent for transmission of one data packet
$E_{R_{ack}}$= Energy Spent for reception of one ACK packet
$E_{R_{pck}}$= Energy spent for reception of one data packet

4.2 Direct Trust

This module monitors neighbors by passively listening to their communication, every node in the network monitors the behavior of every other neighbors. For detecting dropped packet, delayed packet, forwarded packet, this module uses watchdog mechanism to check whether neighbor really forwards the packets or drop them. The collected data is audited by the direct trust monitor.

4.2.1 Direct Trust Agent

Direct trust agent performs the following tasks derivation of trust computation. Node X want to calculate the trust value on node Y termed as $DT_{Value}(K)$

$$K = S - F \tag{2}$$

Here S is a function of successful communication metrics, F is a function of not successful communication metrics. To calculate the direct trust on node Y, node X has to monitor the following statistics. Parameters for the function S are Control packets forwarded, Control packets received. Parameters for function F are packet delay, packet drop. K gives the direct trust value (DT_{Value}) calculated by X on Y.

4.3 Indirect Trust Monitor

Algorithm

Obtaining indirect trust on y from n

1. Node x sends IDTREQ to node(s) n.
2. *If* node n has direct trust value on y, then it will reply back with IDTREP.
3. *Else If* n does not have direct trust value record it will discard the IDTREQ
4. After receiving IDTREP reply from neighbors consider the trust value of the node with maximum direct trust value by applying fuzzy logic.
5. Integrate all the obtained IDT_{value} from neighbors to calculate the Indirect trust value.

Indirect trust means getting the trust value of required node form its neighbors. For obtaining recommendation trust value, the source node will broadcast the request packet regarding the recommendation trust to all its neighboring nodes. Here input for the fuzzy logic is direct trust value of all the replied neighbors. Among all the neighbors, the node with maximum trust value is chosen and recommended trust value is considered for evaluation indirect trust value of X on node Y is denoted as IDT_{Value} .

4.4 Packet Modification Auditor

Packet modification by malicious nodes is a major security threat.If an intermediate node modifies the message content, this modification can be detected and the packet can be discarded. PM_{value} is a positive value at initial stage and if there is modification of request packets by a node its PM_{value} will be decreased. Each node generating a message includes a digital signature generated through its private key and all fields with the exception of the hop count field. In request packets hash chains are applied for the hop count field so that each node, at every hop, can verify that the hop count metric was not maliciously decreased. If a node receives a message, it verifies its authenticity, checking the digital signature content, decrypted through the public key of the node originating the message, is equal to the fields of the received packets. In this way, if an intermediate node modifies the message content, this modification can be detected by the next node receiving the message, the packet can be discarded and its PM_{value} will be decremented. RSA performs signature verification efficiently and incurs least cost compared to other asymmetric algorithms. The huge discrepancy in the energy costs of sign and verify operations in RSA results from the significant difference in the sizes of the keys employed .In our proposed scheme RSA algorithm is implemented due to its efficiency and least energy cost over others.

4.5 Trust Aggregator

The functionality of the trust aggregator is to calculate the final trust value FT_{value} of the target node using direct trust value and recommended trust from the neighbours, Energy value and Packet modification value. For the trust value of each node, a timeout value is assigned. When the timeout expires, Trust Computation is carried out again. Trust aggregator generates a Trust Record Table (TRT) with Node id, trust type and Trust value of each node. Each node maintains a TRT table and every time trust is evaluated TRT table is updated.

$$FT_{Value} = E_{value} + DT_{value} + IDT_{value} + PM_{value} \tag{3}$$

Where FT_{value} = Final trust value

E_{value}=Energy value

DT_{value} = direct trust value

IDT_{value} = indirect trust value

PM_{value}=Packet modification value

4.6 Trust Based Certificate Authority

The proposed framework incorporates a trust based certificate authority approach for detection of malicious nodes and for secured transmission of data. Trust plays a major role in determining behaviour of the nodes. Trust is calculated with the attributes like energy , direct trust from neighbors based on packet delay, packet forward and packet drop, recommendation trust from highly trusted neighbors and packet modification value making the trust value dependable.

Next level of security is provided by electing Trust based Certificate Authority; maximum trusted node in the range. Certificates are issued by the CA, evaluating the trust value of each node. This framework ensures only the trusted nodes to acquire certificates for data exchange isolating the malicious nodes in its range making the system trustworthy.

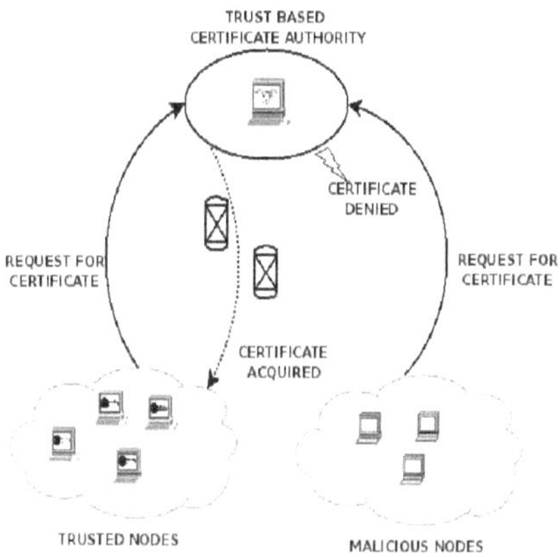

Fig. 2. Certificate Authority

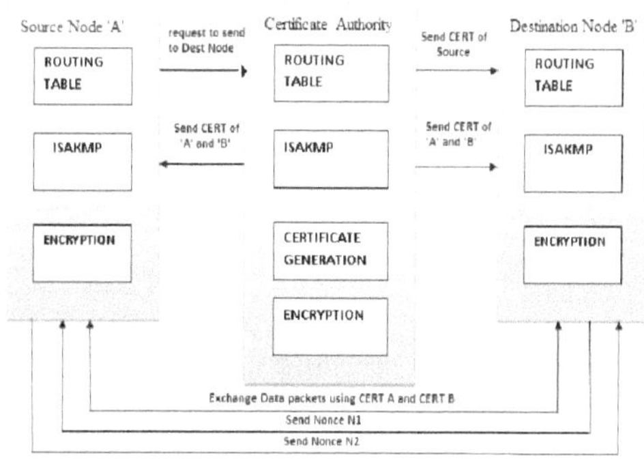

Fig. 3. Message transmission process

4.6.1 CA Election Algorithm

When node j receives an CAREQ packet from node i

Begin

If (FTi > FTj) OR (FTi==FTj) AND (DNi > DNj) ***then***
Accept node i as CA;
else if (FTi < FTj) AND (DNi < DNj) ***then***
Node j remains as CA candidate;
else if (FTi==FTj) AND (DNi==DNj) ***then***
Apply Lowest-ID;

End

FT_i is the final trust value of node i and DN_i is the degree of the neighbour nodes of the node i.

In the proposed scheme, CA Election algorithm is devised, to elect CA node from group of nodes based on the nodes trust value. Each node sends CA request packet (CAREQ) to announce it as CA. CAREQ consists of nodeID and trust value. When a trusted node receives a CAREQ, from one of its neighbours, it executes CA Election algorithm. Any trusted node with the highest trust value will be elected as CA. A single mobile node functioning as a CA will bring the entire MANET to a halt if it moves out of the MANET and also act as a single point of failure if it becomes compromised. Replacement CAs are be used to prevent this security bottleneck.

CA Reply packet (CAREP) is sent back to the requestor node. It consists of node ID and corresponding nodes trust value. If the requestor node is elected as CA node, it maintains the trust value received from the other neighbouring nodes and highest among them will be replacement CA. Timeout value is set to the CA node. When the timeout value expires or CA node fails, CA election algorithm will be invoked again.

4.7 CA Issuing Certificates

Trust levels of the nodes ranges from very untrustworthy to very trustworthy nodes. Fuzzy logic is applied to categorize the trust levels of the nodes to fall either in trusted or malicious range. CA node performs look up from TRT table and retrieves the trust value of the node requesting the certificate. Certificates are issued only for the nodes with trust value above threshold; other nodes are segregated as malicious.

4.7.1 Message Transmission

ISAKMP format provides a consistent framework for security association, key management and authentication which is independent of the key generation technique, encryption algorithm and authentication mechanism. Certificate exchanges and Authentication in our proposed model as shown in Fig 3 follows the procedures as defined in ISAKMP. Before the actual transmission is started among source node, destination node and CA node ISAKMP process is invoked. Source sends a request message to CA node encrypting it with the shared key SKac. On receiving this request the CA node decrypts the message and first checks whether the source and destination nodes are valid. CA node generates CERT A and CERT B, encrypts it with shared keys SKac, SKcb and forwards it to the source and destination nodes. Destination node decrypts and verifies CERT A, CERT B and generates Nonce N1 only if certificates are valid and sends to source node. Source node decrypts and verifies CERT A, CERT B, N1 and generates Nonce N2 only if certificates are valid. Data packet exchanges are initiated for secure transmission with CERT A and CERT B.

4.7.2 Certificate Exchange Algorithm

After the source and destination nodes obtain certificates from CA, it is eligible for packet transmission. Source node uses public key to hash the packet and forwards it to the destination. Only the destination node can verify the packet using its private key. Hash algorithms are least complex of cryptographic algorithms and should incur least energy cost. In this scheme MD4 is used to hash the packet .Once the timestamp value in the certificate expires, the node has to request CA node for the renewal of certificates.

Certificate Exchange Algorithm

	Where
1. Generate Shared Key SKac . 2. Source node request CA E[CREQ(SID,DID,FTValue)SKac] 3. CA node decrypts CREQ looks for SID in ID repository. 4. IF(SID==ID)THEN 5. CA node verifies for SID and checks for DID in its range. 6. Generate PUa,PRa, PUb,PRb, SKbc, CERT A=SID,PRa,PUa,FTvalue,TS. CERT B=DID,PRb,PUb,FTvalue,TS. 7. CA sends CREP as E[(CERT A)SKac] to source node A. 8. CA sends E[(CERT B)SKbc] to destination node B. 9. ELSE DISPLAY("Transmission cannot be granted").	PUa,PUb = Public Key of node A and B. PRa,PRb = Private Key of node A and B. SKac = Shared Key of Source and CA. SKbc = Shared Key of Destination and CA. SID,DID = Source and Destination ID

4.8 Malicious Detector

Node's trust levels that falls below a threshold is marked as malicious and isolated, an alarm is raised to intimate other nodes in the range about the misbehaviour node so as to provide secure transmission. Nodes with low trust level are suspected for being malicious nodes and are prevented from participating in the network for packet transmission. Malicious nodes can never acquire certificates from the CA node and are isolated until its trust level increases and trust monitor calls the trust aggregator to evaluate the trust values.

4.9 Trust Monitor

This module keeps a constant watch on the behaviour of malicious nodes. Malicious nodes are categorized as tolerable and non-tolerable. Non-tolerable nodes are isolated; tolerable nodes are continuously monitored, trust monitor invokes trust aggregator to compute trust of these nodes. Trust aggregator is invoked again while trust value of the nodes with certificate expires.

5 Simulation Analysis and Results

Qualnet5.0 network simulator is used to simulate a wireless network with AODV protocol. Fig 4 shows a scenario with 7 nodes and the traffic flow among them. These nodes are labelled, ranging from Node 0 to Node 7.Constant Bit Rate (CBR) traffic is defined between Node 1 to Node 7, Node 1 to Node 4, Node 3 to Node6, Node 2 to Node 7, Node 5 to Node 7.The simulation detects the malicious nodes based on computed trust values.

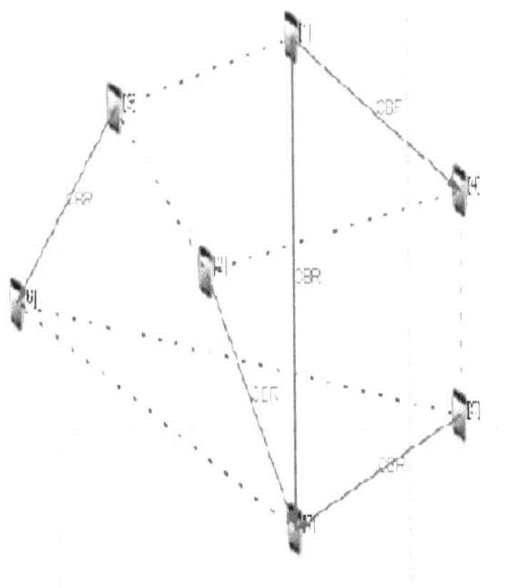

Simulation System Parameters	
Parameter	Default Values
Routing protocol	AODV
Simulation time	1 min
No of nodes	7
Mobility Model	Random Waypoint
Traffic type	CBR
Payload size	512 bytes
`ISAKMP	Enable

Fig. 2. Scenario

The metrics to evaluate the trust of each node are packet forward ratio, packet drop, packet delay. Experimental simulation is based on these parameters and node is marked as trusted and malicious. In this scenario trust value of node 7 is below the threshold and is marked as malicious. Certificate Exchange is through ISAKMP security model. From Fig 4 NODE 7 is malicious and doesn't acquire certificates to forward data packets.

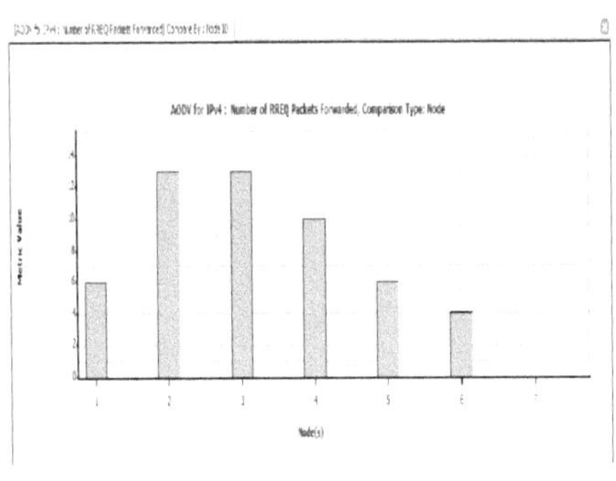

Fig. 3. Data Forwarding Chart

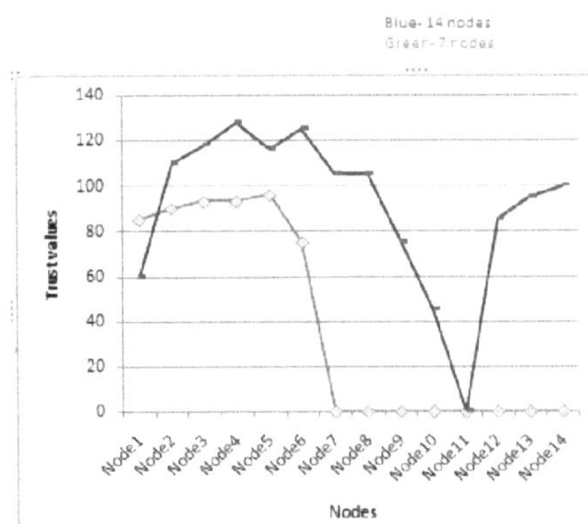

Fig. 4. Malicious Detection

The graph is plotted with two different scenarios (14 and 7 nodes). Threshold of trust value is set as 80 in the above graph and nodes below threshold level are malicious. With the effect to implementation of our framework, Nodes 6,7 in 7 Node scenario model and Node 1,10,11 in 14 Node scenario model are marked as malicious (trust value below 80) and isolated ,building a secure network.

6 Conclusion and Future Work

This novel approach of binding trust and Certification Authority makes the MANET secure and reliable by detecting and segregating the malicious nodes. The proposed framework incorporates two levels of security with trust and certificate authority and is proved to efficient with simulation results in Qualnet. In future performance analysis of the proposed framework with various protocols are experimented and efficiency in detecting malicious nodes will be examined.

References

1. Rossi, A., Pierre, S.: Collusion-resistantReputation-based intrusion detection system for MANETs. IJCSNS International Journal of Computer Science andNetwork Security 9(11) (November 2009)
2. Ghorpade, V.R.: Fuzzy Logic based Trust Management Framework for MANET. DSP Journal 8(1) (December 2008)
3. Vijayan, R., Mareeswari, V., Ramakrishna, K.: Energybased Trust solution for Detecting Selfish Nodes inMANET using Fuzzy logic. International Journal of Research and Reviews in Computer Science (IJRRCS) 2(3) (June 2011)
4. Azzedin, F., Ridha, A., Rizvi, A.: FuzzyTrust for Peer-to-Peer Based Systems. World Academy of Science, Engineering and Technology 27 (2007)
5. De Rango, F.: Improving SAODV Protocol withTrust levels management, IDM and Incentive Cooperationin MANET. In: WTS 2009, Proceedings of the Conference on Wireless Telecommunications Symposium. IEEE Press, Piscataway (2009)
6. Vijayan, R., Singh, S.: A Novel Approach forProviding Security in Vehicular Adhoc Network Through Vehicles Present in the Network. International Journal of Advanced Research in Computer Science 2(1) (January-February 2011)
7. Rajaram, A., Palaniswami, S.: A High CertificateAuthority Scheme for Authentication in Mobile Ad hocNetworks. IJCSI International Journal of Computer Science Issues 7(4(5)) (July 2010)
8. Potlapally, N.R., Ravi, S., Raghunathan, A., Jha, N.K.: A Study of the EnergyConsumption Characteristics of Cryptographic Algorithmsand Security Protocols. IEEE Transactions on Mobile Computing 5(2) (February 2006)
9. Mamatha, G.S., Sharma, S.C.: A Highly SecuredApproach against Attacks in MANETS. International Journal of Computer Theory and Engineering 2(5) (October 2010)
10. Rajesh Babu, M., Selvan, S.: A Lightweight and Attack Resistant Authenticated Routing Protocol For Mobile Adhoc Networks. International Journal of Wireless &Mobile Networks(IJWMN) 2(2) (May 2010)

A Comparative Study on Web Log Clustering Approaches

Sudhamathy G.[1], Sarojini Illango B.[2], and Jothi Venkateswaran C.[3]

[1] Department of Computer Applications, Velammal College of Engineering & Technology, Madurai, Tamil Nadu 625 009, India
sudhamathi10@hotmail.com
[2] Department of Computer Science, Avinashilingam University, Coimbatore -641043, Tamil Nadu, India
balakrishnan.sarojini@gmail.com
[3] Department of Computer Science, Presidency College, Chennai, Tamil Nadu 600 025, India
jothivenkateswaran@yahoo.co.in

Abstract. In the area of Web Usage Mining, the widely used data mining algorithm is the Clustering analysis. Hence we analyzed the most recent work in the field of Web Logs Clustering and made comparison based on their merits and drawbacks with respect to specific application areas. In this work we discuss three different approaches on Web Logs Clustering, namely, Temporal Cluster Migration, Fuzzy Clustering and PSO based Clustering and we conclude on the most efficient algorithm based on the results of experiments conducted with various web log files.

Keywords: Web Usage Mining, Web logs Clustering, Comparison.

1 Introduction

Web usage mining, also known as Web Log Mining, is the process of extracting interesting patterns in web access logs. Analyzing the web access logs of different web sites can help understand the user behavior and the web structure, there by improving the website design. Analyzing and discovering log could help us to find more potential users of the web site and trace service quality of the site. The large majority of methods that have been used for pattern discovery from Web data are clustering methods. Clustering has been used for grouping users with common browsing behavior, as well as grouping Web pages with similar content.

In this paper we study, discuss three different approaches on web logs clustering and analyze their benefits and drawbacks. The three web logs clustering algorithms are: Web logs clustering based on Fuzzy Logic, Temporal Cluster analysis of web log data and the Particle Swarm Optimization based web logs clustering. Based on the experimental evaluation with several web log files and on different parameters we have arrived at a conclusion that the Fuzzy Logic for web logs clustering is the most efficient from different perspectives.

P.V. Krishna, M.R. Babu, and E. Ariwa (Eds.): ObCom 2011, Part I, CCIS 269, pp. 402–411, 2012.

1.1 Related Work

The first approach discussed is a Fuzzy Clustering Algorithm that produces the design mentality of the electronic commerce websites. This algorithm is simple, effective and easy to realize, it is suitable to the web usage mining demand of constructing a low cost B2C website.

The second approach is on temporal web logs clustering. Temporal web usage mining is the analysis of cluster behavior over time and it can reveal additional information on the web site usage. There can be two different temporal changes in cluster analysis - change in cluster compositions and change in cluster memberships. TCMM – Temporal Cluster Migration Matrices is a framework useful for the analysis of changes in nature of the web site usage and loyalty of web site users. TCMM also serves as a visualization tool for analysis of results of temporal data mining.

In the third approach we apply swarm intelligence to the existing web usage clustering techniques and propose the new PSO based Clustering Algorithm for clustering web usage sessions. PSO clustering algorithm is better than the standard K-means clustering algorithm. The efficiency of the data mining algorithms can be enhanced using optimization techniques. One such optimization technique is applying swarm intelligence to data mining techniques. This swarm intelligence takes its inspiration from the social and cognitive properties of the vertebrates and insects. This is implemented using software components called Multi Agent Systems that are communicating in a highly decentralized environment. Their cooperative behavior ensures that they converge on an optimum solution.

2 Approaches to Web Logs Clustering

In this section, let us first discuss the three Web Logs Clustering Approaches before analyzing them on the basis of several parameters.

2.1 Fuzzy Clustering Algorithm

Step1: Collect the web logs from authenticated sources.
Step2: Pre-treat the web logs
 – Clean, format, identify users, sessions, split the web log information into Browser Id, Client IP / User Id, URL and Timestamp.
Step3: Find the count of user's visits to different pages.
Step4: Establish topology of web site by finding:
 a. $V = \{URL_1, URL_2, URL_n\}$ – set of all URLs
 b. $R = \{<URL_1, URL_2>, <URL_2, URL_3>, \ldots\}$
 - ordered hyperlink set of pages
Step5: Establish the matrix of users visiting pages:
 - Value of A_{ij} = No. of time the URL_i visited by the $User_j$
 - Row Vector $B[x, j]$ = situation of all users visiting the URL_x
 - Column Vector $B[i, y]$ = situation of all URLs being visited by the $User_y$
 - Sum of rows S_i = No. of times all users visiting the URL_i
 - Sum of columns S_j = No. of times all URLs being visited by the $User_j$

$$B_{m \times n} = \begin{pmatrix} URL_1 \\ URL_2 \\ \cdots \\ URL_m \end{pmatrix} \begin{pmatrix} User_1 & User_2 & \cdots & User_n \end{pmatrix} = \begin{pmatrix} A_{11} & A_{12} & \cdots & A_{1n} \\ A_{21} & A_{21} & \cdots & \\ & \vdots & & \\ A_{m1} & A_{m2} & & A_{mn} \end{pmatrix}$$

Step6: This matrix can be considered as a relational table and we can use SQL to find the useful information as listed below:

a. First N pages that are mostly accessed
   - Calculate the total no. of times all users visits the pages using the formula

     $$S_i = \sum_{j=1}^{n} A_{ij}$$

   - Compose the aggregate $S = \{S_1, S_2, \ldots S_m\}$, where $i = 1, \ldots m$
   - Arrange the values S_1, S_2 in S in descending order, so that the values in the front of the list represent the most important pages.

b. First N users that has the most visiting time
   - Calculate the time spent by every user visiting all the pages of the web site using the formula:

     $$S_j = \sum_{i=1}^{m} A_{ij}$$

   - Compose aggregate of $S = \{S_1, S_2, \ldots S_n\}$, where $j = 1,\ldots n$
   - Arrange the values of S_1, S_2 in S in descending order, so that the values in the front of the list are the users with most visiting time.

c. Pages which the users are mostly interested in.
   - Calculate the time spent by every user visiting all the pages of the web site using the formula:

     $$S_j = \sum_{i=1}^{m} A_{ij}$$

   - Compose aggregate of $S = \{S_1, S_2, \ldots S_n\}$, where $j = 1,\ldots n$
   - Calculate the rate of a user visiting all the pages of this website as per the formula:

     $$r_{ij} = A_{ij} \Big/ \sum_{j=1}^{n} S_j$$

   - Using this compose a matrix R_{mxn} as below:

     $$R_{m \times n} = \begin{pmatrix} r_{11} & r_{12} & \cdots & r_{1n} \\ r_{21} & r_{22} & \cdots & r_{2n} \\ & \vdots & & \\ r_{m1} & r_{m2} & \cdots & r_{mn} \end{pmatrix}$$

   - Calculate the time the user spends in each page of this web site as per the formula - Settling time = End time – Begin time.
   - Using this compose a matrix T_{mxn} as below

$$T_{m\times n}=\begin{pmatrix} t_{11} & t_{12} & \cdots & t_{1n} \\ t_{21} & t_{22} & \cdots & t_{2n} \\ & \vdots & & \\ t_{m1} & t_{m2} & \cdots & t_{mn} \end{pmatrix}$$

- Take the values from both the above matrices, R & T and arrange them in descending order of the values of rate and time.
- From this we can obtain the pages which the users are mostly interested in.
- That is the visiting rate of these user interested pages are high and the settling time is also longer.

d. Visit characteristics of specific users
  - Each users frequent access path
  - Each users frequent access time

e. Correlated web pages

f. Similar user community

2.2 Temporal Cluster Migration Matrices Algorithm

TCMM = < H, C, n, Ω: H → C_n >, Where, H is the set of users, C is a set of cluster labels and n represents the number of time periods.

Ω: H → C_n is a mapping that describes the sequence of cluster memberships for each user over n time periods.

Web site users are identified by a seven digit number: H = {h | 1000000 <= h <= 9999999}.

The users are grouped into five clusters based on their visiting patterns in a month. These clusters can be named as:

(i) Loyal big visitors (C = 1)
(ii) Loyal moderate visitors (C = 2)
(iii) Semi-loyal big visitors (C = 3)
(iv) Semi loyal moderate visitors (C = 4)
(v) Infrequent visitors (C = 5)

Hence C = {1, 2, 3, 4, 5} – represents the cluster labels;

n = 6; say, the cluster behavior analyzed for six months.

Step1: Collect the web log data of a web site for six months from authenticated sources.

Step2: Pre-treat the web logs
– Clean, format, identify users, sessions, split the web log information into Browser Id, Client Ip / User Id, URL and Timestamp.

Step3: Find the count of pages visited by each user in each month.

Step4: Based on the count of pages visited by each user, the users are categorized into different clusters identified above.

Step5: This clustering is done for each month.

Step6: Using the clustering results the TCMM matrix is constructed as per the format mentioned in Table 1.

Table 1. Sample TCMM Matrix

ID	M1	M2	M3	M4	M5	M6
'2221725'	1	1	2	1	1	2
'6361765'	3	3	3	3	1	3
'7777777'	2	1	1	1	1	3
'7371767'	3	1	2	3	1	3

Step7: Perform analysis on the TCMM table data using SQL and get the below results.

a. Number of loyal big visitors in each month obtained by the below queries.
b. View of overall clustering for a given period.
c. The list of customers who where loyal throughout the study period.
d. Detect the changes in the customer loyalty (Increase in the cluster label during different iterations of clustering)
   (i) Loyalty decreases from 5th Month to 6th Month
   (ii) List of customers whose loyalty declined from fourth month to fifth month and the decline in loyalty sustained in the sixth month.

Step8: The results of the above queries can be visualized in a better way by presenting those using bar graphs and pie charts.

For web personalization we have to concentrate on individual visitors. The company may want to encourage loyal visitors by giving special offers. Another important marketing strategy is to detect the changes in customer loyalty. Business is worried about the attrition rate of their best customers. Let us assume that the cluster labels for the users represent their desire to the business. Then customer's attrition rate will be evident from their increasing cluster labels during repetitive application of clustering. Such a customer may be a potential target for promotional material.

In the result say one customer is always in cluster 3, but moves to cluster 1 in M5 and then again moves to cluster 3 in M6. This is not an indication of potential attrition, but an indication that this customer has the potential to move up to cluster 1. Hence such customers need a different type of campaign than the attrition campaign. Customers who are oscillating between the clusters 1, 2 and 3 can be ignored. Serious indication of attrition is the continued decline of loyalty; that is the customer declined from cluster 1 to cluster 2 and then continued to be in cluster 2 for the subsequent months.

To execute any analysis and to find the result for any set of data, it will be efficient to embed the SQLs in a programming language such as Java. This will help the analyzers to execute more generic and complex queries. TCMM can be applied for a retail ecommerce site or marketing databases.

2.3 PSO Based Clustering Algorithm

PSO stands for Particle Swarm Optimization. Particles represent individual solutions. Swarm is a collection of particles that represents the solution space.

In PSO the swarm is initialized to a uniform solution set. The particles move through this solution space with velocity v. They maintain the best personal position pBest, best position found by a particle and the global best position gBest, best fitness position for all particles. The velocity of the particles is influenced by the social and cognitive components.

- $V_i(t)$ is the velocity of the particle i at time t
- $X_i(t)$ is the position of the particle i at time t
- w is the inertia weight of the particles
- q_1, q_2 are the vectors representing the cognitive and social components
- r_1, r_2 are the random numbers between 0 and 1
- Range of velocities of the particles is $[-V_{max}, V_{max}]$

$$V_i(t+1) = [w*V_i(t)] + [q_1*r_1*(pBest-X_i(t))] + [q_2*r_2*(gBest-X_i(t))] \quad (1)$$

$$X_i(t+1) = X_i(t) + V_i(t+1) \quad (2)$$

Stopping criteria for PSO is the maximum number of iterations reached or minimum error requirement reached.

Web session clustering exploits the two main dimensions of web usage data, the Time dimension and Browsing sequence dimension. As per the parameters listed in the Table 2, the Time and Browsing sequence dimensions can be combined to identify the relative importance of a visit.

The approach discussed in PSO Based Web Session Clustering applies the PSO optimization to the Web Session Clustering. In this approach each Session is considered as a particle.

Step1: Collect the web logs from authenticated sources and pre-treat the web logs – identify sessions.

Step2: Initially a set of particles are created and uniformly mapped to the input sessions.

Each particle consists of the below attributes:

Particle Id - Uniquely identifies a particle.

DistanceFromEachSession - Array that store the distance of a particle to each session at a particular iteration.

WonSessionVectors - Array that represents the session vectors won by a particle at a given iteration.

SessionAttributeValues - Represents the current values of the attributes of the particle in the form of a data vector.

A session vector consists of Session Id, Client Ip address, Count of Pages visited in the session, Session length (End_time – Start-time), Total Bytes downloaded.

Table 2. Web Session Clustering Dimensions – Potential Parameters

	Web Session Clustering Dimensions	
	Time	**Browsing Sequence**
Potential Parameters	Total Session Time	Page Visit Sequence
	Time on Each page	Visit Sequence Similarity
	Average Time per Request	Visit Sequence Length
	% of Session Time on each Page	Topical Sequence of the User

PBest - The position of the nearest session to the particle achieved so far.

Step3: Initialize the particles for the above attributes.

Step4: Now these particles start moving from their initial position, guided by the cognitive and self organizing component. Each position move is considered as one iteration.

Step5: After each iteration the swarm calculates all its parameters and the swarm organizes itself according to the new data vectors won by each particle.

The cognitive component of the algorithm is encoded as:

$$(pBest - X_i(t)) \tag{3}$$

The self organizing component is encoded as:

$$(Y_i(t) - X_i(t)) \tag{4}$$

Where, $Y_i(t)$ is the current value of the particle and $X_i(t)$ is the initial value of the particle. The value of the pBest is calculated based on the particles distance to the current centroid session.

After every iteration, the swarm changes its position by winning the nearest particles. This winning of nearest particle by the swarm is achieved using the Euclidian distance measure.

The Euclidian distance measure is calculated using:

$$d\,(X_n, Z_i) = \| X_n - Z_i \| \tag{5}$$

Step6: The iterations are repeated until there are no significant changes in the position of the particles or the number of maximum iterations reached or no movement of data vectors from one data cluster to another is observed.

3 Critical Evaluation and Analysis

Of the three approaches we can see that the Temporal Cluster Migration Matrices approach is just to categorize the web users into different clusters and to study their cluster migration behavior over a period of time. Thus it does not deal on grouping the web site pages, rank the most interesting pages, frequently accessed web site path and correlated web pages. Hence this approach is mostly suitable for online retail web pages to study the customer behaviors and change the marketing promotion strategies accordingly.

On the contrary the Fuzzy Clustering approach can be applied to study any aspect of E-commerce web sites starting from ranking the users based on their visit time and visit frequency, ranking the web pages based on the visiting rate and time spent on the pages, analyze the users visit characteristics to identifying the correlated web pages. It is an easy to apply and simple approach that provides any required knowledge. It is flexible to adapt to complex analysis as well.

The third approach being different from the rest two approaches is based on the PSO optimization technique that is applied on the web session clustering concept. In this we consider the time and the browsing sequence dimensions of a session and apply the PSO concept iteratively to obtain a more accurate session clusters with less intra cluster distance than the k-means clustering algorithm. Thus this clustering can provide knowledge on the user behavior and common access patterns. Even though it provides all the required knowledge on web usage mining the approach is found to be quite complex and less practical to apply.

Hence after critical evaluation and analysis of the three approaches we can see that the fuzzy clustering logic is simple, effective, and practical to apply and provides all the required knowledge about web usage mining. We can check if the outcome of our analysis holds after experimentation of real time web log data.

4 Experimental Results

To assess the performance of the three clustering approaches we tested the algorithms on the eretailstore web log file for a period of six months, 07/2010 to 12/2010. The logs were processed through the preprocessing steps and were analyzed using the three algorithms. The Fig. 1 shown below shows the bar graph representing the runtime taken for clustering of web logs by the three algorithms. The Fig. 2 shows the optimized efficiency percentage of the three approaches. Fig. 3 compares the memory utilization of Fuzzy, Temporal and PSO algorithms.

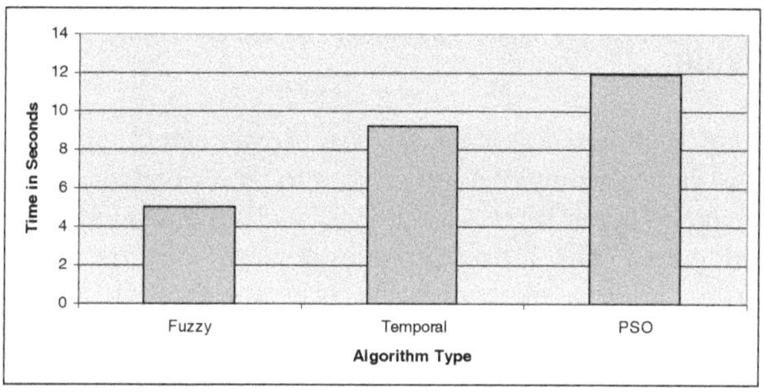

Fig. 1. Run Time Comparison of Fuzzy, Temporal and PSO Approaches

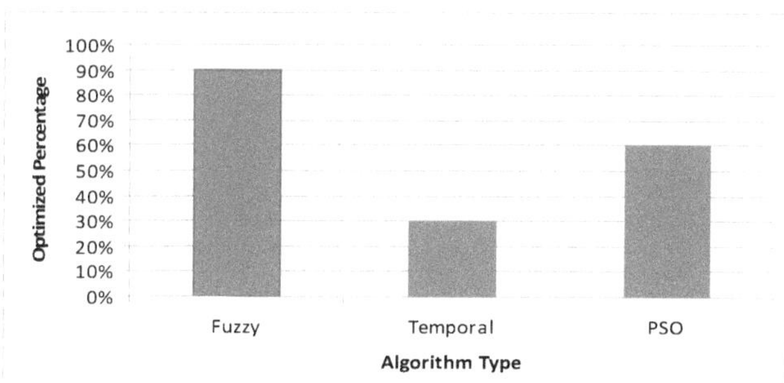

Fig. 2. Optimized Percentage Comparison of Fuzzy, Temporal and PSO Approaches

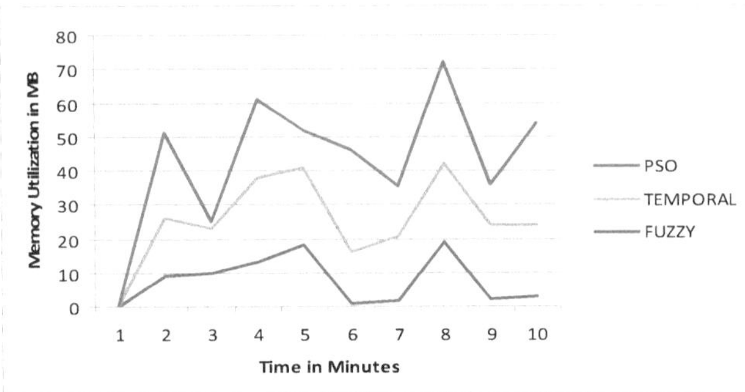

Fig. 3. Memory Utilization Comparison of Fuzzy, Temporal and PSO Approaches

Hence after studying the experimental results we can conclude that our critical evaluation holds good and we can conclude based on various aspects that Fuzzy Web Log Clustering is the efficient approach that can be used for web usage mining, especially for E-commerce sites.

5 Conclusion

With the growth of Web based application, specifically electronic commerce, there is significant interest in analyzing Web usage data to better understand Web usage, and apply the knowledge to better serve users. This has lead to a number of open issues in Web Usage Mining area. This article provides a survey of three web logs clustering approaches focusing on its application to Web Personalization. This survey aims to serve as a source of ideas for people working on personalization of information systems. It proposes the easy, simple, best approach, the Fuzzy Clustering to be used for user behavior pattern discovery. This outcome is based on experimental evaluation of several web log files over periods. For future work we should explore the use of Fuzzy logic along with temporal to explore the interesting dimension of the change in web usage behaviors.

References

1. Han, Q., Gao, X., Wu, W.: Study on Web Mining Algorithm Based on Usage Mining. In: 9th International Conference on Computer-Aided Industrial Design and Conceptual Design, CAID/CD 2008 (November 2008)
2. Lingras, P., Hogo, M., Snorek, M.: Temporal Cluster Migration Matrices for Web Usage Mining. In: Proceedings of IEEE/WIC/ACM International Conference on Web Intelligence (2004)
3. Alam, S., Dobbie, G., Riddle, P.: Particle Swarm Optimization Based Clustering of Web Usage Data. In: IEEE/WIC/ACM International Conference on Web Intelligence and Intelligent Agent Technology, WI-IAT, pp. 451–454 (2008)
4. Chen, M.S., Park, J.S., Yu, P. S.: Efficient Data Mining for Path Traversal Patterns. IEEE Transactions on Knowledge and Data Engineering, 209–221. (March/April 1998)

5. Hong, T., Chiang, M., Wang, S.H.: Mining weighted browsing patterns with linguistic minimum supports. In: IEEE International Conference on Systems, Man and Cybernetics, Yasmine Hammamet, Tunisia (2002)
6. Zaiane, O.R., Xin, M., Han, J.: Discovering Web Access Patterns and Trends by Applying OLAP and Data Mining Technology on Web Logs. In: Advances in Digital Libraries Conf., Santa Barbara, CA, pp. 19–29 (1998)
7. Cooley, R., Mobasher, B., Srivastava, J.: Data preparation for mining world wide web browsing patterns. Knowledge and Information System, 5–32 (1999)
8. Antunes, C., Oliveira, A.: Temporal Data Mining: An Overview. In: Proceedings of KDD 2001 Workshop on Temporal Data Mining (2001), http://www.acm.org/sigkdd/kdd2001/Workshops/ano.pdf
9. Cadez, V., Heckerman, D., Meek, C., Smyth, P., White, S.: Model-based clustering and visualization of navigation patterns on a Web site. Journal of Data Mining and Knowledge Discovery 7(4) (2003)
10. Hogo, M., Snorek, M., Lingras, P.: Temporal Web Usage Mining. In: Proceedings of International Conference on Web Intelligence, IEEE/WIC 2003, pp. 450–453 (2003)
11. Lingras, P., Yan, R., Hogo, M.: Rough Set Based Clustering: Evolutionary, Neural, and Statistical Approaches. In: Proceedings of First Indian International Conference of Artificial Intelligence, Hyderabad, India (2003)
12. Mobasher, B., Cooley, R., Srivastava, J.: Automatic Personalization Based on Web Usage Mining (2000), http://maya.cs.depaul.edu/~mobasher/personalization/
13. Pawlak, Z.: Information Systems: Theoretical Foundations. Information Systems, 205–218 (1981)
14. Perkowitz, M., Etzioni, O.: Adaptive web sites: Conceptual cluster mining. In: Proceedings of the Sixteenth International Joint Conference on Artificial Intelligence (1999)
15. Srivastava, J., Cooley, R., Deshpande, M., Tan, P.: Web Usage Mining : Discovery and Applications of Usage Patterns from Web Data. SIGKDD Explorations, 1–12 (2000)
16. Yao, X.: Research Issues in Spatio-temporal Data Mining (2003), http://www.ucgis.org/Visualization/whitepapers/Yao-KDVIS2003.pdf
17. Fu, Y., Sandhu, K., Shih, M.-Y.: Generalization-Based Approach to Clustering of Web Usage Sessions. In: Masand, B., Spiliopoulou, M. (eds.) WebKDD 1999. LNCS (LNAI), vol. 1836, pp. 21–38. Springer, Heidelberg (2000)
18. Shahabi, C., Zarkesh, A., Adibi, J., Shah, V.: Knowledge Discovery from Users Web-Page Navigation. In: Workshop on Research Issues in Data Engineering, England (1997)
19. Banerjee, A., Ghosh, J.: Click stream clustering using Weighted Longest Common Subsequence. In: Proceedings of the 1st SIAM International Conference on Data Mining: Workshop on Web Mining (2001)
20. Abraham, A.: Natural Computation for Business Intelligence from Web Usage Mining. In: SYNASC 2005, pp. 3–10 (2005)
21. Schockaert, S., De Cock, M., Cornelis, C., Kerre, E.E.: Clustering Web Search Results Using Fuzzy Ants. IJIS 22(5), 455–474 (2007)
22. Chen, J., Zhang, H.: Research on Application of Clustering Algorithm Based on PSO for the Web Usage Pattern. Wireless Communications, Networking and Mobile Computing (2007)
23. Kennedy, J., Eberhart, R.C.: Particle Swarm Optimization. In: Proc. Of IEEE ICNN, Perth, Australia, vol. IV, pp. 1942–1948 (1995)
24. Cohen, S.C.M., de Castro, L.N.: Data Clustering with Particle Swarms. In: IEEE Congress on Evolutionary Computations, Vancouver, BC, Canada (2006)

A New Performance Modelling and Measurement Method for Service-Oriented Cloud Applications (SOCAs)

S. RajaRaajeswari[1], R. Selvarani[2], and Pethuru Raj[3]

[1]Department of Computer Applications, Raja Rajeswari College of Engineering, Bangalore, India
[2] Department of Computer Science and Engineering, M.S. Ramaiah Institute of Technology, Bangalore, India
[3] Enterprise Architect, Sify Software Ltd., Tidel Park, Chennai, India
peter.raj@sifycorp.com

Abstract. Cloud computing has been at the centre of intense discussion particularly for its intrinsic power of bringing out a steady flow of innovations on both the business and the IT domains. Debates on performance, security and reliability form the centre stage of most of these deliberations. Third-party public clouds hosting and delivering scores of social, collaborative, and business acceleration applications to global users are also gaining momentum. On the other hand, the on-premise web, application and database servers are being still sustained due to the lack of unbreakable and impenetrable security capabilities in public cloud infrastructures.

The brewing trend is that a wider variety of legacy, web, enterprise, consumer, social, telecom and embedded services are being deployed and delivered from clouds to global users with all the quality of service (QoS) attributes. That is, next-generation applications are derived out of these distributed and decentralised services. In other words, service oriented cloud applications will become popular and pervasive. In this paper, we have focused on the performance concerns and challenges of SOCAs. We have come out with a few formulae for service utilization, availability and performance in a cloud environment.

Keywords: Cloud Computing, Resource and Product Metrics, Performance Analysis, Federated Cloud, Intercloud, Cloud Integration.

1 Introduction

The leading non-functional requirements (Quality of Service (QoS) attributes) such as elasticity, availability, accessibility, affordability, and ubiquity are the key differentiators of cloud computing. The pioneering cloud model was a result of several matured and enterprise-scale technologies such as consolidation, virtualization, federation, automation, and optimization. Since its inception, the powerful and promising cloud paradigm has shown consistently a promising growth trajectory. Several types of vertical as well as generic clouds are emerging and evolving and hence the number of

P.V. Krishna, M.R. Babu, and E. Ariwa (Eds.): ObCom 2011, Part I, CCIS 269, pp. 412–424, 2012.

cloud services providers (CSPs) is steadily growing. Newer cloud services such as cloud brokerage services (CBS) are promising for cloud-centric business entities. There are a plenty of robust and resilient cloud infrastructures, platforms and tools. A stream of novel use, business and technical cases are being unearthed by professionals and pundits to take the game-changing cloud model to greater heights.

Cloud systems from its original centralised modules are now moving towards distribution and decentralization. With this progressive trend, the need for improved and competent technologies for simplifying and streamlining cloud integration, composition, and collaboration goals is felt across for building next-generation unified, intuitive and interactive cloud environments. As there is more clarity on the cloud principles, there will be convergence and consolidation in the cloud space. That is, there will be a loosely coupled integration among mobile, enterprise, embedded, and cloud spaces. In short, the cloud landscape and ecosystem are bound to grow expeditiously in the days to unfold. We would like to explore, experiment, and expound the performance implications of next-generation clouds, cloud services and applications. The idea is to come out with a measurement method for the performance evaluation of service oriented cloud applications.

2 Next-Generation Cloud Infrastructures

2.1 The Cloud Evolution

The term 'cloud' constantly calls to mind vendors such as Amazon Web Services (AWS), Google AppEngine, Rackspace, or Salesforce.com, the key players in initiating and implementing a cornucopia of cloud-centric IT solutions and services. No doubt these established vendors are certainly the icons and pioneers of the cloud vision. Their efforts and investments are geared for a one-stop shop for all the existing and emerging IT needs of individuals, innovators, and institutions at global level. They are termed as all public cloud service providers (CSPs) and represent one distinct model for deploying, delivering and managing a pile of cloud applications.

However there are other popular models too such as private, hybrid, and community clouds to address diverse information and communication (ICT) needs of small, medium and even large business houses. Thus there are cloud providers and consumers. Due to multiplicity of cloud providers, a new entity (cloud broker) has emerged in the expanding cloud space. Another recent phenomenon is the emergence of cloud auditors. Cloud broker is another specific cloud service procurer and provider. There are automated software solutions for cloud brokers. A typical cloud broker solution is capable of accomplishing the following tasks. The interactions happen via messaging. A broker, which stands on the proven bus architecture, is an advanced version of a standards-compliant messaging server.

- Discovery, Routing & Enrichment
- Integration, & Orchestration
- Aggregation, Arbitration & Intermediation
- Provisioning, Virtualization, & Governance
- Notification, Monitoring, Billing & Management

2.2 Integrated Clouds

Increasingly, enterprise services and applications are being deployed and delivered to worldwide subscribers from cloud infrastructures (Online, on-demand, remote, hosted and off-premise).

However considering the severity of intrinsic security implications, customer, corporate and confidential data are still being securely kept and maintained in enterprise servers (local and on-premise). This situation insists for a standards-based integrator in between the cloud-based applications and the enterprise data stores to enable them to talk to each other through messaging. A popular **module** for cloud integration [1, 3, 4] today is one where an enterprise service bus (ESB)/integration middleware hosted within an enterprise integrates on-premise applications with cloud-based applications.

A **second module** is commonly used as the concept of "Integration as a Service". In this model, the integration infrastructure is hosted within the cloud. Applications that expose service interfaces can be easily integrated using this approach, which also provides the benefits of easy service integration.

2.3 Hybrid Integration Platform

This is the hybrid version of the first two approaches: The traditional (on-location) integration and the SaaS Integration (Integration as a service). The inherent problems of these can be overcome via a hybrid of the two, based on a Peer-to-Peer ESB platform.

2.4 Brokered Clouds

According to Gartner's report, there is a huge market value for cloud brokerage services (CBS) in the years to come. With the surging popularity of cloud computing, a number of unique cloud service providers (small, medium and large) have put their shops and serving up specific as well as generic sets of users.

Individuals, innovators and institutions are moving their offerings to the general public via the cloud medium. A cloud brokerage (CB) creates a robust cloud delivery and management platform to simplify the building and delivery of complex cloud services to cloud service customers. Typically a cloud brokerage is a kind of service provider assisting and associating consumers and providers to arrive at an optimal business decision and execution. Cloud brokerages can conceive newer and nimbler service and pricing models to offer a range of cloud services to their customers and clients to keep up their revenues. A cloud brokerage exposes one or more brokerage application programming interfaces (APIs) that have to be implemented by all the cloud service providers (CSPs) in order to participate and provide their distinctive services to a growing array of cloud users.

The mission of any CB is to discover, compare, select, and aggregate a stream of CSPs to carve out a bevy of people-centric composite services that in turn facilitate the automation of the business process. A CB can aggregate all homogeneous and / or heterogeneous services and applications of geographically distributed CSPs and provide a synchronized and unified information and service portal for worldwide users.

Further on, a CB also can act as a middleman in understanding the needs of consumers precisely, identifying one or more right and relevant CSPs, contributing in getting a good price for the services being provided by the chosen CSP(s), in removing any kind of anomalies and resolving plausible conflicts among CSPs and users and in monitoring, profiling and ensuring the agreed SLAs, in enabling value-added services, etc. CB is a highly available & scalable, high performance and assurance cloud system in the network.

3 Envisioning the Expanding Cloud Ecosystem

The Cloud Computing Reference Architecture (CCRA) authored by IBM [1] consists of five major **actors**. Each actor plays a **role** and performs a set of **activities** and **functions**. Among the five actors, cloud brokers are optional, as cloud consumers may obtain service directly from a Cloud Service Providers [1, 2, 4]. Cloud Carrier is the intermediary that provides connectivity and transport of cloud services from Cloud Providers to Cloud Consumers. Cloud auditor is a party that can conduct independent assessment of cloud services, information system operations, performance and security of the cloud implementation. In a cloud environment, the prominent resources include networks, cloud nodes, virtual machines (VMs), and services.

3.1 Networks

The connectivity occurs in two modes: direct and indirect. The direct network topology can be point-to-point (P2P) (client-to-cloud or cloud-to-cloud (C2C) communication) and the indirect network topology is via a middleware suite. There is a third topology too: a kind of combination of both the direct and indirect connectivity.

3.2 Cloud Nodes

Each cloud node is connected to the network and comprises one or more VMs that host the full software stack including operating system, application server, database systems, and developmental platforms to make and run cloud-based service-oriented applications. This provides instant access to service endpoints and service metadata.

3.3 Cloud Intermediaries

This is a kind of middleware nodes for cloud service connectivity, integration, intermediation, aggregation, arbitration, etc. A cloud intermediary can be a synchronised and unified portal like Yahoo directory for all kinds of diverse, distributed and decentralised cloud services and applications in the ensuing cloud era. There are cloud brokers and service buses to automate the service discovery, message routing, enrichment, and transformation, etc.

3.4 Cloud Services

It denotes both the exposed interfaces and the hidden implementations. The interfaces comprise the input and output parameters, the service signature and the service functionalities. Service interfaces are publicly discoverable and accessible. Service metadata are also accessible for clients through the network. Service implementations are transparent to user agents as any developmental technology and deployment platform can be used to implement and to run the services. Messages are the main building-blocks for service invocations and interactions.

The typical performance metrics are response time and throughput. In a cloud environment, there are several questions including the following ones

- What is the current utilization of cloud networks, intermediaries and nodes?
- How much is it influenced by an invocation of a service's functionality?
- Are service versions managed well?
- What is the performance behaviour of elementary and composite services?

3.5 Service Interaction Scenarios

Services are interoperable and hence seamlessly interactive. There are some standard ways in which services are integrated and composed for creating service composites and for automating business processes. In this section, we are to discuss the key interaction scenarios. This knowledgebase helps to formulate a more precise and perfect performance calculation method.

3.6 Event-Based Service Composition

Event messages are being sourced from different and distributed services in the same or different VMs / PMs and are directed to one or more centralised services. This spontaneously triggers a stream of response messages to different services. That is, several services are involved in accomplishing one or more business processes.

3.7 Service Orchestration

In orchestration, the involved cloud services are under the control of a single endpoint central process (orchestration / controller service). This process coordinates the execution of different operations on the cloud services participating in the process. The invoked services do not bother whether they are involved in a composition process. Only the central process is conscious of this aim, thus, the orchestration is centralized through explicit definitions of operations and the invocation order of cloud services.

3.8 Service Choreography

Choreography does not depend on a central orchestrator. Each cloud service that participates in the choreography has to know exactly when to become active and with whom to interoperate. Choreography is based on collaboration and is mainly used to exchange messages in public business processes. All services which take part in the choreography must be conscious of the business process, operations to execute, and messages to exchange as well as the timing of message exchanges.

3.9 Cloud Brokerage Services

On concluding, novel service interaction patterns are being unearthed in order to facilitate highly sophisticated and smart services realization. In this section, we have discussed the prominent interaction patterns. As we are to investigate the performance problem in the cloud space, all these interaction styles help us to more accurately pinpoint the performance bottlenecks.

4 A Brief on Performance Engineering and Enhancement (PE^2)

Performance is always a key factor for any IT solutions and services. Poor performance causes companies to lose their customers and thereby the brand value too. Because application performance can vary significantly based on its production environment and the delivery infrastructure, businesses must make certain that the performance facet of modern applications is fully geared and optimized when building for deployment on the cloud. Similarly when legacy applications are appropriately modernized and moved from traditional data centres to a cloud centre, the performance criterion has to be given utmost consideration to be effective in their outlooks, offerings, and outputs.

Applications can be tested in cloud and non-cloud environments for base-level performance comparisons. Factors such as disk I/O and RAM access may cause intermittent spikes in performance. However, as with traditional software architectures, overall traffic patterns and peaks in system usage account for the majority of performance issues in cloud computing too. That is, rather than simply moving applications to a cloud environment and flicking the "on" switch, companies should examine performance issues more deeply and diligently. Potential reprogramming constraints of applications getting readied for cloud systems need to be looked into and the capacity planning for the new cloud targets has to be grandly automated to completely and comprehensively optimize application performance in the new hosting environment.

Applications that performed better in the conventional data centre can't be expected to perform identically on a cloud server. These limitations need to be addressed very effectively in the beginning to attain and retain the needed performance in the cloud environment. Researchers across the world are very enthusiastically identifying and articulating the cloud performance issues. There are myriad technology-inspired answers, key guidelines, best practices, and metrics for precise performance evaluation and optimization.

4.1 Performance Definitions

	KPI	Definition	Measurement Unit
Performance	Response Time	Response Time for an atomic or composite Service	Seconds
	Elapsed Time	Completion time for a batch or a background task	Time Units
	Throughput	Number of Transactions or requests processed per an unit of time	Transaction or request count

The main performance characteristic of any network is its throughput. It depends on the network topology. If the peer-to-peer (P2P) topology is leveraged, then the performance is the summation of the throughput of each participating cloud node. When a cloud intermediary is in place for indirect connectivity, the performance is determined for the most part not by the throughput between connected cloud nodes and the intermediary, but by the cloud service bus (CSB)'s internal processing and analysis mechanisms such as message, protocol, and content transformation, brokering, intermediate storage, security enablement, transaction management, concurrency, etc. If the CSB is intra-cloud, there is no network latency. However if the CSB is used in an inter-cloud environment, then the network latencies between the bus and cloud nodes need to be considered.

Performance of a node is first of all characterized by its (current) utilization, defined as fraction of time during which the node is busy with serving incoming requests. Other performance indicators are message rates and network traffic processed by the node. These properties are covered by the metrics at different levels.

4.1.1 Atomic Service Level

As mentioned above, utilization of nodes constitutes from fractions of time used to serve individual requests. That is, the time used to execute certain functionalities in response to incoming messages. In the network throughput context, each of the service functionality is characterized by sizes of input and output messages.

4.1.2 Composite Service Level

If the service under consideration is composite, then the invocation of its functionalities implies a number of cascading calls to subordinate services. These calls cause additional utilization of corresponding nodes. To have an exact picture of the influence of an invocation upon utilizations of all N nodes of the system, each VM should be analysed instead of the consideration of the single node.

4.1.3 Process Level

Processes and workflows represent the greatest abstraction of the service interactions and collaborations towards the efficient accomplishment of business goals and needs.

For accomplishing one or more business processes, generally it involves a series of cloud service providers (CSPs), cloud brokerages (CBs), cloud service buses (CSBs), cloud auditors (CAs), and cloud clients (business process consumers). CSB is the cloud version of enterprise service bus (ESB). CSBs are for service connectivity, integration, composition and collaboration among CSPs. CSB, being a software solution as the prominent cloud integration backbone and engine, can be an ingredient of CSP and / or increasingly as a module of CB. For intra-cloud integration, CSB is a part and parcel of the CSP itself. For inter-cloud integration, CSB can be an important element of CB. Thus the number of concurrent processes running on a cloud environment is a good indicator for measuring up the performance capabilities of the cloud.

5 The Performance Calculation Method

Rud et al, [5, 6] have proposed and used the metrics to calculate/and measure performance of services in services oriented environments. However, a typical cloud environment comprises thousands of cloud servers (physical machines) and each server in turn can be segmented into a number of VMs. Thus the performance calculation has to take this shift in order to arrive at accurate answer. Also as indicated, there are cloud brokers in between cloud users and providers. Also services can be distributed across different VMs as well as physical machines within a cloud as well as distributed clouds.

CS - Cloud Server

VM_n - Set of Virtual Machines available in a Cloud Server $n \in CS$

$S[VM_q]$ – Set of Services provided by each virtual machine $VM_q \in VM_n$

S[*] – Set of services from Cloud

$$S[*] = \bigcup_{VM_q \in VM_n} S[VM_q]$$

M[s] – Set of methods provided by the service $s \in S[VM_q]$

M[VMq] – Set of methods provided by all services of each virtual machine $VM_q \in VM_n$

$$M[VMq] = \bigcup_{s \in S[VM_q]} M[s]$$

M[*] – Set of methods of all services of a Cloud

$$M[*] = \bigcup_{VM_q \in VM_n} M[VM_n]$$

5.1 Process Execution Performance Metrics

The following factors are considered for the formalization of performance metrics of response time of method or functional request from a client. Time taken for a process request from a client machine to different service methods in distributed virtual as well as physical machines:-

Sl. No	Operation Description	Notation
1	Client to discover Cloud Brokerage Service (CBS) (Discovery)	t_D
2	CBS –Client (Transmission)	t_{CS}
3	Client to Cloud services (Transmission)	t_{CT}
4	Service Execution / Processing	t_{SE}
5	Service Response (Transmission)	t_{SR}
6	Service-to-Service Transmission	t_{SS}
7	Service to-multiple Services	t_{SM}
8	Multiple services-to-Service	t_{MS}

Time taken is to be calculated based on the available infrastructure and the size of a particular message or request. The simplest generic case of performance metrics to execute a request from client is **A**verage **T**ime taken to complete a **P**rocess with a fixed **S**ize of **I**nput and **O**utput **M**essage from a **C**lient **R**equest (Total Performance time) is

$$\textbf{Total Performance in Time} \underset{\text{(Multiple Clouds)}}{=} \frac{t_D + t_{CS} + t_{CT} + t_{SE} + t_{SR} + t_{SS} + t_{SM} + t_{MS}}{\text{Number of Average [Methods + Services +VMs]}}$$

$$\textbf{Total Performance in Time} \underset{\text{(One Cloud)}}{=} \frac{t_D + t_{CS} + t_{CT} + t_{SE} + t_{SR}}{\text{Number of Average [Methods + Services + VMs]}}$$

5.2 Measurement of Availability of a Service

For measuring the performance value, availability of services is very vital. A simple measurement of Availability of an Individual Service (AIS) for a client may be calculated as follows:

Total Number of Handling Capacity of a Service (TNHCSR) and Number of Request (NR) received from clients for a service in a VM under a given hardware environment.

$$\text{AIS} = \frac{\text{TNHCSR - NR}}{\text{TNHCSR}} \times 100\%$$

AIS for a particular service from all available services (AIS_{aas}) from a cloud system can be calculated using the following formulae.

$$AIS_{aas} = \frac{TNHCSR \text{ X } \left(\bigcup_{VM_q \subseteq VM_n} S[VM_q] \quad - NR \right)}{TNHCSR \text{ X } \left(\bigcup_{VM_q \in VM_n} S[VM_q] \right)} \text{ x } 100\%$$

Based on this, the service provider may understand about the density of demand for a particular service depends on client requests. In other words, utilization of a particular service may be calculated based on the requests which in-turn helps to plan for the service provider to enhance infrastructure. As an example, the following table shows the availability of a service for usage based on the number of requests.

Sl.No	TNHCSR	NR	Remaining Capacity of AIS in (%)
1	10000	1000	90
2	10000	2500	75
3	10000	3000	70
4	10000	5000	50
5	10000	6000	40
6	10000	7000	30
7	10000	8000	20
8	10000	9500	5
9	10000	10000	0

From this table, the AIS value is ZERO, if TNHCSR and NR are equal which means the service may be available for usage. However performance of that particular service for a given infrastructure will not yield complete potential of performance which indirectly implies that a customer who is using this particular service will not satisfy.

5.3 Measurement of Service Utilization

Maximum service utilization means that a service in a cloud should be used at most by clients without any obscurity within a given infrastructure. This implies that more usage of a service leads to less cost. On contrary to this, if usage of the service by clients is less, the cost will be more for the service. Hence, number of requests in a given period of time, for a service, from clients in a given time measures the service utilization. Therefore the Average Utilization of a Service (AUS) in a cloud may be given as follows:

$$AUS = \frac{AIS_{aas}}{\text{Number of Requests in a given period of time}} \text{ X } 100\%$$

AIS_{aas} denotes the Availability of Individual Service from all available services in a cloud.

$$\text{AUS of a service} = \frac{(\text{Total Number of Services-Number of Services Used})}{\text{Total Number of Services}} \times \text{Number of Requests for Services}$$

Cloud infrastructures are being set up in geographically different locations. A growing array of services and applications are being deployed on these. To realise integrated and composite services, it is mandatory for these diverse clouds to work together. There are efforts for unfolding a host of measures of cloud service discovery, integration and collaboration. As the trend is towards federated clouds and Intercloud, the performance is being taken seriously. Availability and utilization of services play an important role in calculating service and cloud performance. We have brought in a new formulae for calculating availability, utilization and finally performance of service oriented cloud applications.

6 Performance Investigation of an Experimental Cloud

Dealer Management Solution (DMS) is a critical IT solution for manufacturing industries. As industries need to collaborate in real time with all their supply chain partners especially with distributors and dealers to reach out retailers and end-users to sell their products and to collect market intelligence in order to come out with newer and nimbler product offerings to retain customers' loyalty and to explore newer avenues for fresh revenues, the value of automated solution goes up considerably. The system architecture of a typical DMS is given in figure-1.

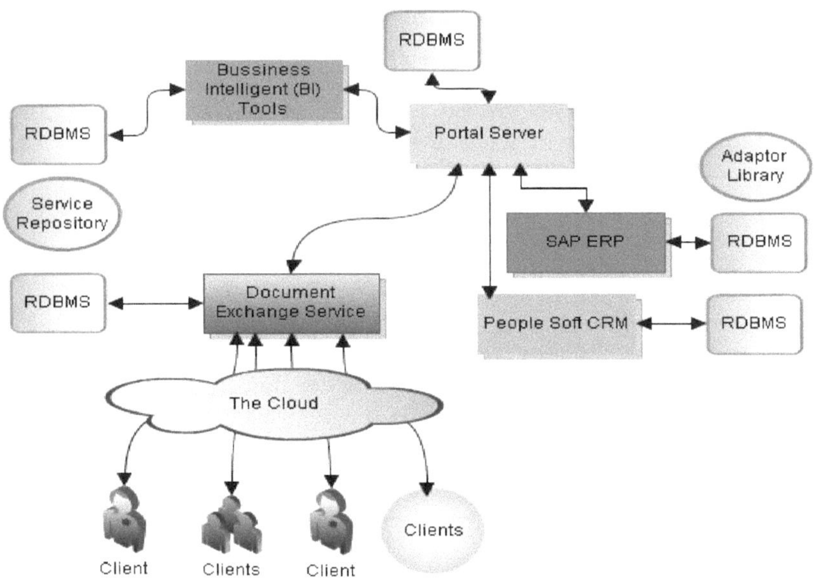

Fig. 1. System Architecture of a Dealer Management Solution

7 The Results

We have set up a private cloud using two personal computers (PCs). The reference architecture of the private cloud is depicted in figure-2.

One is as a cloud controller and the other as node controller. We have leveraged the Eucalyptus package that is enabling to set up infrastructure clouds. We have used the embedded KVM hypervisor for virtual machines within the node controller. We have used the web server (Apache Tomcat) in our own cloud as well as in the traditional server machine in order to host our restful services. We have evaluated the performance of the private cloud based on the formulae indicated above. The DMS is hosted in the cloud and we have employed a couple of browsers to interact with the DMS solution hosted in the cloud. We have put the document exchange service in a virtual machine (VM), SAP, PeopleSoft, and BI in different VMs. The sales portal module is put up in a separate VM whereas the corresponding sales portal solution for clustering purpose is deployed in an another VM. The outputs are on the expected lines.

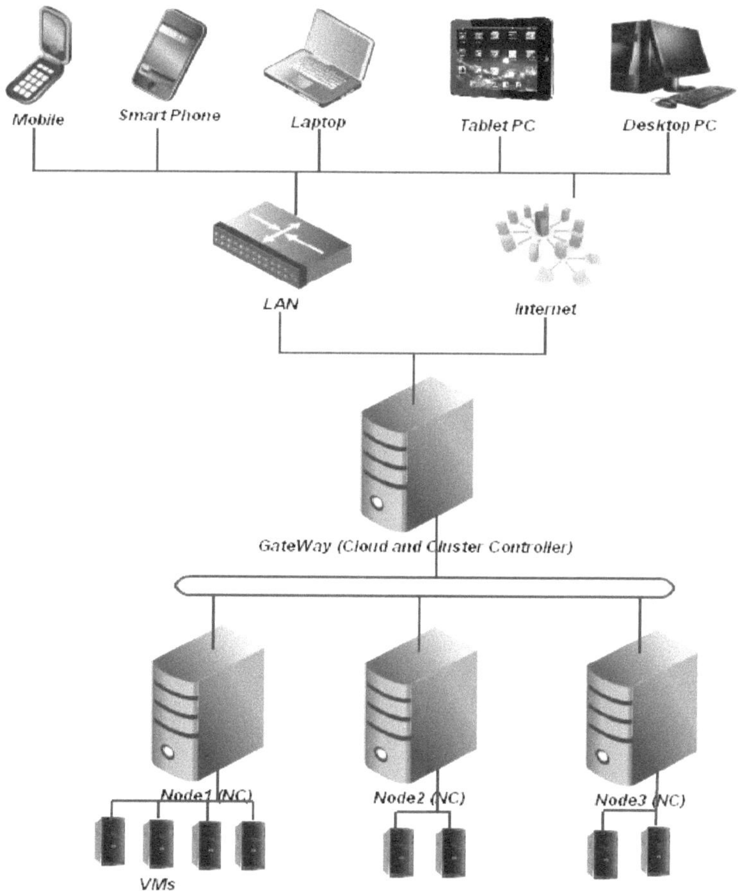

Fig. 2. A Simple Private Cloud Architecture System

8 Conclusion

As widely reported, businesses and IT services deployed and delivered via cloud severs offer a number of unique benefits to businesses as well as consumers. However due to concerns such as security, performance, availability, controllability and visibility, enterprises are hesitating to move their mission-critical applications to cloud infrastructures. As cloud computing represents the commercial side when compared with other computing models such as grid, cluster, peer-to-peer, utility and on-demand paradigms, cloud service providers are leaving no stone unturned to address these valid concerns in well-coordinated ways. Researchers and academicians are too analyzing and articulating the implications induced by these challenges in order to unearth highly competent and technology-based solutions.

In this paper, we have clearly illustrated a number of existing and emerging cloud architectures, reviewed potential future cloud resource deployment strategies and how their interaction will impact on distributed and decentralised clouds towards the vision of Intercloud. As more and more services and applications are modernized and migrated to remote clouds, it is imperative to assess various performance implications and the setback effects they have on cloud computing. We redefined a potential new performance model, setting metric and measurement methods for simplifying the performance calculation, optimization and management.

References

1. http://www.ibm.com/ibm/cloud
2. http://www.oracle.com/us/technologies/cloud/
3. http://www.microsoft.com/en-us/cloud/
4. http://blogs.gartner.com/benoit_lheureux/2010/04/19/solutions-for-cloud-services-integration-saas-integration-proliferate/
5. Rud, D., Schmietendorf, A., Dumke, R.: Resource Metrics for Service-Oriented Infrastructures. In: Intl. Workshop on Software Engineering Methods for Service Oriented Architecture SEMSOA, May 11, pp. 90–98 (2007)
6. Rud, D., Schmietendorf, A., Dumke, R.: Product Metrics for Service-Oriented Infrastructures, Applied Software Measurement. In: Proceedings of the International Workshop on Software Metrics and DASMA Software Metrik Kongress (IWSM/MetriKon), Germany, pp. 161–174. Shaker Verlag (2006)

Defending DoS Attacks Using a Puzzle-Based Approach and Reduction in Traceback Time towards the Attacker

Anup Mathew Abraham[1] and Shweta Vincent[2]

[1] St. Thomas Institute of Science and Technology, Kottayam, Kerala, India
[2] Karunya University, Coimbatore, Tamil Nadu, India

Abstract. In today's world Denial-of-Service attacks have huge impact on network security. DoS attacks are usually launched to make the service of a system unavailable to a person who is authorized to use it. Several methods were introduced for defending Denial-of-Service attacks earlier. In our paper we propose a client-puzzle mechanism approach to defend DoS attacks. Here, intermediate routers can be used for issuing and solving network puzzles of various difficulty levels depending on the intensity of the attack. The target server will be protected by using an intermediate firewall router for issuing the puzzles; this will reduce the load over the server. Likewise intermediate proxy routers can be used for solving the puzzle. But furthermore, this proxy can also be a target of attack. This problem can be overcome by using a hybrid traceback mechanism for the attacking client. This technique helps to find out the attacking node and the router through which the attack packet was forwarded.

Keywords: Client-Puzzle Approach, Flooding DoS Attack, Game Theory, Nash Equilibrium, IP Traceback.

1 Introduction

Security has become one of the primary concerns when an organization connects its private network to the Internet. In a DoS attack, an attacker attempts to prevent legitimate users from accessing information or services from a server. By targeting a computer an attacker may be able to prevent a user from accessing email, websites, online accounts, or other services that rely on the affected computer. The most common and obvious type of DoS attack occurs when an attacker floods a network with unnecessary packets of information.

Network Puzzles can be used for preventing a DoS attack to some extent. Network Puzzles make the attacker client to commit his resources for solving a puzzle before he gets access to the services provided by the server [1]. The service of the server is only provided for clients who are able to solve the puzzle and send the correct solution. The primary function of the server is to produce a puzzle with optimal difficulty. If the difficulty of the puzzle is less the attacker will be able to solve it and initiate an intense attack. If the difficulty of the puzzle is high then the attacker will respond by sending some random answers, the server will have to verify the solution of the

P.V. Krishna, M.R. Babu, and E. Ariwa (Eds.): ObCom 2011, Part I, CCIS 269, pp. 425–433, 2012.

puzzle which causes exhaustion of the defending server's resources. So the puzzle must be of an optimal difficulty.

The network puzzle used will be installed in the server or puzzle issuing router and also in the client machine or intermediate puzzle solving proxy. If the zombies are attacking through a particular proxy then the proxy will be throttled by packets and puzzles. This may cause the legitimate users to wait for long time till the proxy solves the puzzle for the sent packets.

Tracing back is the technique used to identify the attacking node after a DoS attack has occurred [7], [10]. By combining both the client-puzzle technique and traceback an attack over a particular proxy router can be stopped to a certain extent. The packet flow will be halted at the first router which is forwarding the packets. This will reduce the traffic over the proxy router who is solving the puzzle for the clients. The copies of packets used for attacking are sent to other routers in the network so that if similar packets are found then the packets can be dropped at that point itself.

In this paper the second section highlights about the concept of a client-puzzle. The third section elaborates on the system design. The next few sections explain in detail about the use of Game theory, Nash equilibrium in the creation of Network puzzles, and the concept of Traceback. The final section describes about our implementation results and scope of further enhancement.

2 Protocol for Generation of Puzzles

This section describes the concept used in generating puzzles by a server, for being issued to clients that request the server for a connection and its services [1]. The server, upon receiving a request from a client, generates a puzzle and its answer along with a hash of the answer, the server nonce, the puzzle expiration time, the puzzle maturity time, and the flow identifier (Figure 1). The server then sends back to the client: the client cookie, the puzzle and its parameters, the flow identifier, and a server cookie consisting of the above hash, the server's timestamp, the puzzle maturity and expiration times.

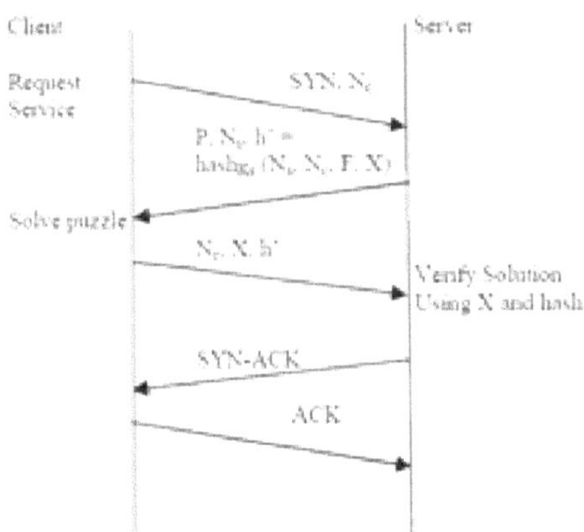

Fig. 1. Puzzle Mechanism (Adapted from [1])

The client, upon receiving the puzzle, calculates the solution and sends back the answer along with the server cookie. Upon receipt of this message, the server takes the server timestamp, uses it to index into the server nonce cache to obtain the server nonce, checks that the nonce has not expired, and verifies the answer by regenerating the hash and comparing it against what the client sent. The Client Nonce used will provide more authenticity to the puzzle protocol. Maturity time for the puzzle is also added to avoid eavesdropping of the puzzle. Expiry time is another feature added to avoid reuse of the same puzzle; it may cause the protection through puzzles.

3 System Design

This section highlights the design of the system worked upon for the implementation of the Client-puzzle mechanism and concept of traceback.

Upon receiving a request from a client for a connection, the defender server produces a puzzle and sends it to the requester. If it is answered by a correct solution, the corresponding resources are then allocated. As solving a puzzle is resource consuming, the attacker client is deterred from perpetrating the attack.

The defense involves a verification stage: every time a request for a service is received, the defender responds with a puzzle, which the attacker must allocate resources to solving before receiving the said services. These two players form the most basic realization of the game (in Game Theory) [1]. Both players have strategies that involve tradeoffs. The attacker must balance the severity of the attack against the amount of resources allocated to carrying it out. The, defender must balance the amount of resources spent defending against an attack and the quality of service it provides to legitimate users.

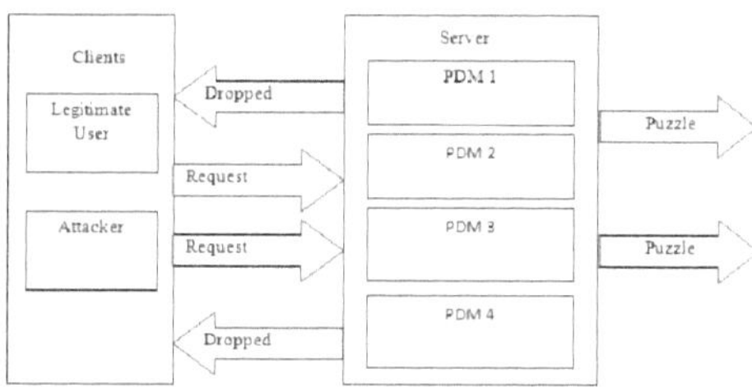

Fig. 2. System Architecture (1/2)

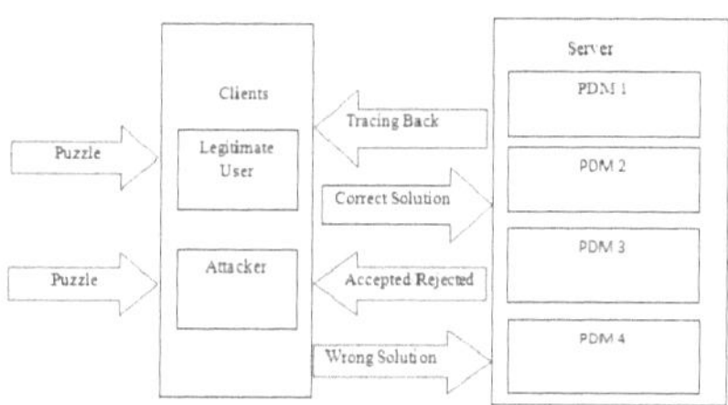

Fig. 3. System Architecture (2/2)

4 Game Theory and Nash Equilibrium

A game is a formal description of a strategic situation. Game theory is the formal study of decision-making where several players must make choices that potentially affect the interests of the other players [1]. A game consists of a set of players, a set of moves available to those players, and a specification of payoffs for each combination of strategies.

Nash equilibrium, also called strategic equilibrium, is a list of strategies, one for each player, which has the property that no player can unilaterally change his strategy and get a better payoff [1]. A payoff is a number, also called utility that reflects the desirability of an outcome to a player, for whatever reason. When the outcome is random, payoffs are usually weighted with their probabilities. In game theory, Nash equilibrium is a solution concept of a game involving two or more players, in which each player is assumed to know the equilibrium strategies of the other players, and no player has anything to gain by changing only his or her own strategy unilaterally. If each player has chosen a strategy and no player can benefit by changing his/her strategy while the other players keep their unchanged, then the current set of strategy choices and the corresponding payoffs constitute Nash equilibrium. Players are in equilibrium if a change in strategies by any one of them would lead that player to earn less than if she remained with her current strategy.

5 Network Puzzles

Until recent times, client puzzles [3] have been used only as an application layer defense against flooding attacks. Yet, client puzzles in the application layer can be easily thwarted if any adjacent or underlying protocol does not provide a similar defense [3]. Network layer puzzles do not preclude the use of higher layer defenses, but rather augment them.

Network puzzles [3] can be selectively applied to all communication from a client. Attacks which use seemingly innocent communication channels for coordination can be thwarted by having difficult puzzles applied to the coordination traffic in addition to the attack traffic. Being able to place puzzle issuers arbitrarily close to the client allows quenching undesirable traffic closer to the source, reducing the wastage of resources deeper within the network. Another issue with puzzles is that the work load required for solving each puzzle must be adjusted to meet the real-time needs of a network. For example, a congested server can throttle its clients using harder puzzles, or a server with a client who is acting maliciously can throttle the individual using more difficult puzzles [5]. Throttling a client cannot be done simply during the establishment of a connection; the need for puzzles may start and stop at any point in a flow's lifetime.

6 Tracing Back

Trace back is a name given to any method for reliably determining the origin of a packet on the Internet [7], [8]. Due to the trusting nature of the IP protocol, the source

IP address of a packet is not authenticated. As a result, the source address in an IP packet can be falsified causing DoS attacks. The problem of finding the source of a packet is called the IP trace back problem.

With router based approaches, the router is charged with maintaining information regarding packets that pass through it. The idea proposed in [8] is to generate a fingerprint of the packet, based upon the invariant portions of the packet and the first 8 bytes of payload.

The concept of packet marking and logging is used as in the Hybird IP traceback approach proposed in [8]. An attack packet is 'marked' by an ingress router as it enters the network as finds its path to the target server. At the next hop, relevant information of this 'marked' packet is 'logged' by the next hop router. This process continues until the target server is reached. Finally once the server goes down, the attacking node can be successfully traced back to using the marking and logging information present in various routers en route.

7 Implementation

There are basically two parts which have been followed in this paper for the implementation of the Network Puzzles. The first part is to create a puzzle issuer which resides in the server. This application is activated when a client tries to connect to the server. The second part is a solver which is on the client machine. The solver solves the puzzle created by the puzzle issuer and sends the solution to the server which is verified by the puzzle issuer. The puzzle solver and issuer are created using Netfilter in Linux. Further, results of time taken to solve network puzzles of various difficulty levels are simulated using NS-2 [13]-[16].

Netfilter and IP tables in Linux are used for creating the network puzzle. Netfilter is the set of hooks within the Linux kernel for intercepting and manipulating network packets. Netfilter is a set of hooks inside the Linux kernel that allows kernel modules to register callback functions with the network stack. A registered callback function is then called back for every packet that traverses the respective hook.

IP tables are a generic table structure for the definition of rule sets. Each rule within an IP table consists of a number of classifiers and one connected action.

In the implementation part two approaches are considered. In the first approach the code is installed in a Linux system. The time taken for creating the puzzle and solving it is studied at various difficulty levels. In the second approach the scenario is simulated in NS-2.

In the first approach, rules are added to the IP table. The rules will act as chains through which the packet has to flow. There is an issuer, a solver, puzzle manager and a nonce manager. The issuer is installed in the firewall router and it issues the puzzle to the client. The solver is installed at the proxy router and it is responsible for solving the puzzle. The puzzle manager controls the difficulty level of the puzzle. This is done based on the number of packets received and the resources left, for solving the puzzle, for the server or firewall router. The nonce manager produces the server nonce and also verifies the client nonce sent by the client.

In the second approach, the various readings of time for solving the puzzles of different difficulty levels are used for simulating the scenario in NS-2. Figure 4 clearly illustrates the scenario of the simulation. Here, node 5 is the end server and node 4 is its proxy. Node 4 is responsible for issuing puzzles to all the clients in the network. Those clients which send request packets at a higher rate are given puzzles of greater difficulty to solve than the rest.

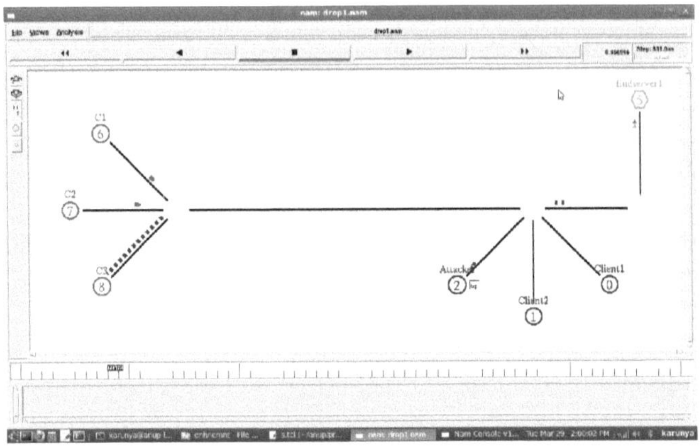

Fig. 4. Attack Scenario for Client-Puzzle Mechanism Simulation in NS-2

Further, an attempt was made to implement the Hybrid IP Traceback mechanism as proposed in [8] and to enhance its application. The enhanced version of HIT has been termed as Enhanced Hybrid IP Traceback mechanism. The simulation scenario consisted of 40 nodes serving as routers in the network. Figure 5 illustrates the scenario generated for the HIT and EHIT mechanism implementation.

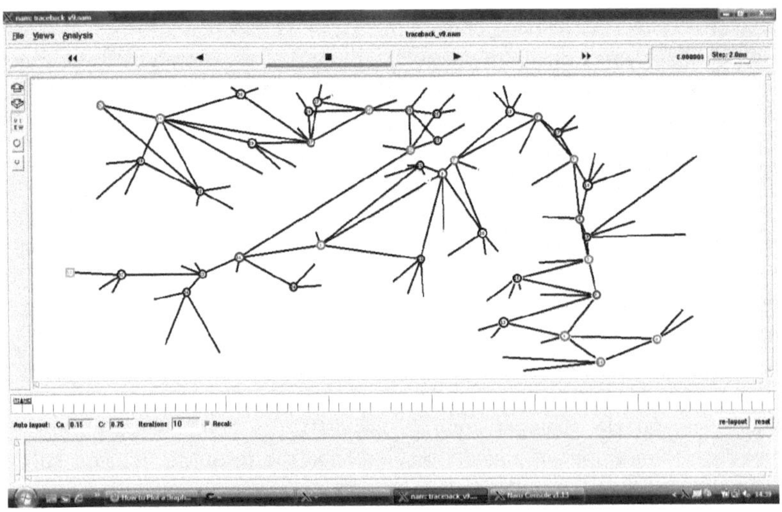

Fig. 5. HIT [8] and EHIT Simulation Scenario in NS-2

Each of the routers is either a marking or logging router. The implementation includes the calculation of time taken for traceback when simple HIT mechanism was used. The enhancement proposed to HIT i.e. EHIT includes sending copies of the attack packet (once the attacker has been identified) to the egress router of the network from which the attacker was detected, so that if the attacker tries to attack from a different host in the same network, the router will compare the packet with the copy of the attacking packet. If matched, the packets from the attacker will not be forwarded. Thus the attack can be thwarted earlier in the second phase of attackc.

8 Result Analysis

The results for Client-Puzzle mechanism were generated for a network that consisted of a set of four clients and a single puzzle-protected server connected on a single VLAN via a Cisco Catalyst 4006 Gigabit switch. Each client and server was a dual 1.8GHz Intel Xeon machine with Gigabit Ethernet interfaces. To measure the baseline performance of the system, clients were configured to flood the server with 64-byte UDP packets while solving all of the puzzles that were received.

The time taken to solve the puzzles of various difficulties was calculated. The response time obtained was plotted versus the difficulty level of the puzzle. Figure 6 clearly illustrates the relation between the response time of solving a puzzle with its difficulty level.

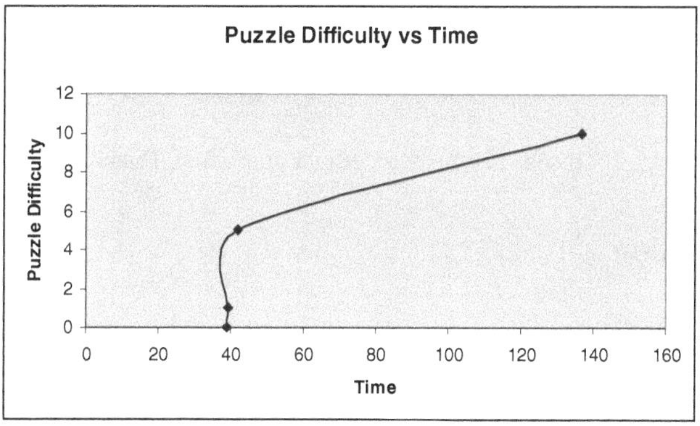

Fig. 6. Plot of Puzzle difficulty vs. Time

Further more, the simulation of HIT and EHIT was carried out and the reslults of simulation time in seconds is tabulated in Table 1. Two attackers, 1 and 2 were chosen belonging to the same network for both the scenario simulations. In case of HIT, the time for tracing back to both the attackers remains similar. In case of EHIT, the attack packet information was propagated to the egress router to whose network attacker 1 belonged; once attacker 1 had been identified. Hence, when attacker 2 from the same network as attacker 1, launched an attack, it could be thwarted faster. This is evident from the tabulated time in Table 1. The figure 7 illustrates the Traceback time requirement graph plotted for HIT and EHIT protocols. This figure clearly illustrates the reduction in tracek back time when EHIT protocol is used.

Table 1. Simulation results of HIT and EHIT in NS-2

PROTOCOL	ATTACKER NO.	TRACEBACK SIMULATION TIME IN SECONDS
HIT	Attacker 1	5.388
	Attacker 2	5.280
Enhanced HIT	Attacker 1	5.380
	Attacker 2	1.772

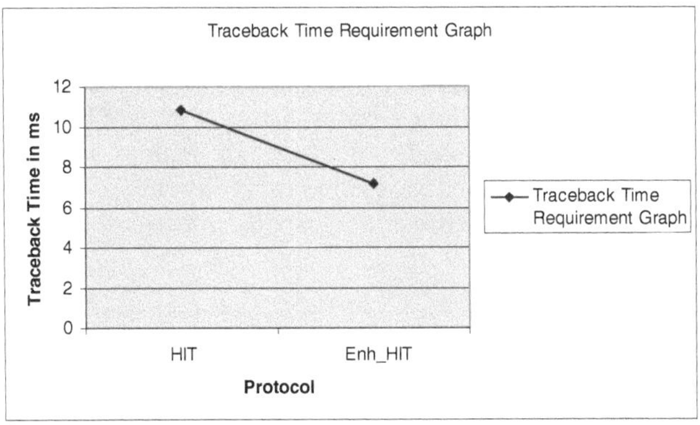

Fig. 7. Traceback time requirement graph for HIT and EHIT

9 Conclusion

A puzzle based mechanism is proposed in this paper and is implemented in Netfilter using IP tables. The server to be protected will issue the puzzles and the client has to solve the puzzle compulsorily to gain access to the server. The method is effective because the puzzle mechanism works at network level. Tracing back provides additional security to the system by helping the server to trace back the attacker to the last router. The puzzle solving proxy router can be protected by this method. By using this method optimal puzzle difficulty can be produced and the Denial of Service attack can be stopped.

Also, the Hybrid IP Traceback mechanism was simulated and a further enhancement for the same was proposed. The simulation results showed that trace back time taken in EHIT is lesser than that for HIT.

Future work would include sending copies of the attack packet to all the nearby routers so that if the attacker tries to attack from a different location the router will compare the packet with the copy of the attacking packet. If matched, the packets from the attacker will not be forwarded. Thus the attack can be solved in the network without even issuing the puzzle or packets reaching the firewall router or proxy router.

References

[1] Fallah, M.S.: A Puzzle-Based Defense Strategy Against Flooding Attacks Using Game Theory. IEEE Transactions on Dependable and Secure Computing 7(1) (January-March 2010)

[2] Waters, B., Jules, A., Halderman, J., Felten, E.: New Client Puzzle Outsourcing techniques for DoS Resistance. In: Proc. ACM Conf. Computer and Comm. Security, pp. 246–256 (2004)

[3] Feng, W., Kaiser, E., Feng, W., Luu, A.: The Design and Implementation of Network Puzzles. In: Proc. 24th Ann. Joint Conf. IEEE Computer and Comm. Societies, pp. 2372–2382 (2005)

[4] Wang, X., Reiter, M.: Defending Against Denial-of-Service Attacks with Puzzle Auctions. In: Proc. IEEE Security and Privacy, pp. 78–92 (2003)

[5] Mahimkar, A., Shmatikov, V.: Game-Based Analysis of Denial of Service Prevention Protocols. In: Proc. 18th Computer Security Foundations Workshop, pp. 287–301 (2005)

[6] Moore, D., Shannon, C., Brown, D.J., Voelker, G.M., Savage, S.: Inferring Internet Denial-of-Service Activity. ACM Trans. Computer Systems 24(2), 115–139 (2006)

[7] Savage, S., Wetherall, D., Karlin, A., Anderson, T.: Practical Network Support for IP Traceback. In: SIGCOMM 2000, Stockholm, Sweden (2000)

[8] Gong, C., Sarac, K.: A More Practical Approach for Single-Packet IP Traceback Using Packet Logging and Marking. IEEE Trasactions on Parallel and Distributed Sysems 19(10) (October 2008)

[9] Savage, S., Wetherall, D., Karlin, A., Anderson, T.: Network Support for IP Traceback. IEEE/ACM Trans. Networking 9(3), 226–237 (2001)

[10] Snoeren, A., Partridge, C., Sanchez, L., Jones, C., Tchakountio, F., Schwartz, B., Kent, S., Strayer, W.: Single-Packet IP Traceback. IEEE/ACM Trans. Networking 10(6), 721–734 (2002)

[11] Al-Duwairi, B., Manimaran, G.: Novel Hybrid Schemes Employing Packet Marking and Logging for IP Traceback. IEEE Trans. Parallel and Distributed Systems 17(5), 403–418 (2006)

[12] Snoeren, A., Partridge, C., Sanchez, L., Jones, C., Tchakountio, F., Kent, S., Strayer, W.: Hash-Based IP Traceback. In: Proc. ACM SIGCOMM 2001 (August 2001)

[13] Wang, J.: ns-2 Tutorial (1), Multimedia Networking Group, The Department of Computer Science, UVA

[14] Wang, J.: ns-2 Tutorial (2), Multimedia Networking Group, The Department of Computer Science, UVA

[15] Wang, G., Xia, Y., Harrison, D.: An NS-2 TCP Evaluation Tool: Installation Guide and Tutorial, NEC Laboratories China, BitTorrent (April 29, 2007)

[16] Wang, G., Xia, Y., Harrison, D.: An NS-2 TCP Evaluation Tool: Installation Guide and Tutorial, NEC Laboratories China, BitTorrent (November 24, 2008)

Cloud and Grid Computing Based Telemedicine Using Computer Communication Network through Internet

S. Saravanan[1], M. AnbuRajan[2], and A. Venkatraman[3]

[1] SRM University, Chennai, India
barathsamraj@yahoo.co.in
[2] BME Dept. SRM University, Chennai, India
anbufelix@yahoo.com.
[3] Mechanical Dept., Pondicherry Engineering college, Pondicherry, India
avr2s@rediff.com

Abstract. Most of the Telemedicine Foundation has limited Telemedicine nodes connection in rural area. But increasing population of countries need unlimited of complexity Telemedicine connection. My research work proposed Cloud and Grid computing based Telemedicine using computer communication network by distributed sharing of Internet for supports increasing complexity of TM nodes connection to implements to rural area for point to point communication and Multipoint to Multipoint connection with communication control This paper examine the evaluation of unlimited TM connection to rural area and analyses the diffusion of Telemedicine nodes by limited connection from model of hierarchical telemedicine network,. [1].[2].[3]

Index terms: Telemedicine, computer network, Distributing sharing, Grid computing, Cloud computing.

1 Introduction

VSAT based telemedicine network is a hierarchical structure of telemedicine network. Mostly telemedicine used in rural area . but needs the following back ground. [1][4][5].

- need network division.
- need License and agreements from Network foundation.
- need of V-Satellite Communication.
- need high frequency , bandwidth allocation with respect distance transmission.
- need high cost for maintenance for TM foundation or division of centre.
- need high filter section circuit for transmission and receiving signal .

The fig 1.model is hierarchical structure of VSAT telemedicine networks model, If the patient 1 has to connect and discuss to Specialist Doctor 4 , the following connectivity of single root path:

P.V. Krishna, M.R. Babu, and E. Ariwa (Eds.): ObCom 2011, Part I, CCIS 269, pp. 434–446, 2012.

Patient 1→ Rural Hospital 1 → Telemedicine division1 → Telemedicine Foundation → Telemedicine Division 2→ Rural Hospital 4 (specialist 4). If failure link root between telemedicine foundation to telemedicine division 2, Patient 1 is not link to Rural Hospital 4 of specialist 4 . It has only one root path , if this root path failure cannot communication between patient 1 to specialist doctor 4..

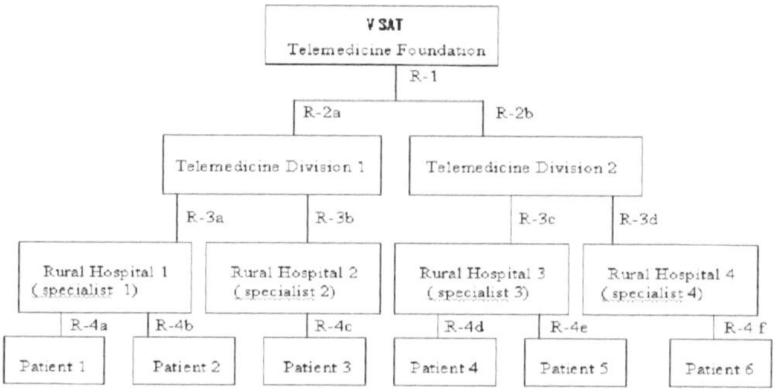

Fig. 1. Hierarchical structure V SAT telemedicine Network

The above hierarchical model of Telemedicine has the following problem in rural areas[1].

- The maintenance cost is very high.
- If the connectivity of foundation is failure depending upon the divisions and hospital specialists are not able to connectivity,.
- need signal strength Antenna for signal transmission and receiving..
- Limited TM Node connection.
- Increasing TM node creates overload increase at Foundation.

2 Method of Cloud and Grid Based Telemedicine Network

My research paper for Telemedicine using Computer Communication Network that is followed cloud and Grid by distributing sharing of Internet method of network , this model supports unlimited TM connection in Rural area and overcome the rooting busy or failure if one root is busy or failure the other root is selected by routing algorithm as shown in fig 2.[1][7][8][9][20].

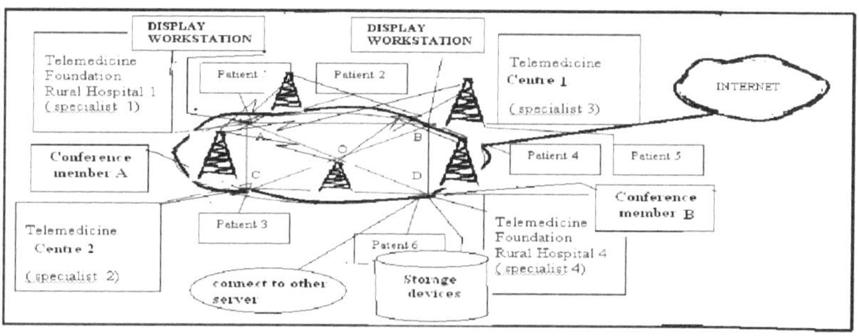

Fig. 2. Model of Cloud and Grid computing based Telemedicine Network through Internet by Telecommunication

If Same patient 1 connect and discuss to Specialist Doctor 4 by point to point communication by IP address, link the following root paths:

Root 1: Patient 1→ Network Point A → Network Point O→ Network Point D→ (specialist 4)

Root 2: Patient 1→ Network Point A → Network Point B →Network Point D→ (specialist 4)

Root 3: Patient 1→ Network Point A → Network Point C→Network Point D→ (specialist 4)

Root 4: Patient 1→ Network Point A → Network Point O→Network Point B→ Network Point D→ (specialist 4)

Root 5: Patient 1→ Network Point A →Network Point C→ Network Point O→ Network Point D→ (specialist 4)

Root 6: Patient 1→ Network Point A →Network Point C→ Network Point O→ Network Point B→ Network Point D→(specialist 4)

Root 7: Patient 1→ Network Point A →Network Point B→ Network Point O→ Network Point D→ (specialist 4)

In Distributed network sharing root paths through internet have seven root paths for connective from patient 1 to Specialist Doctor 4 . So one root path is failure other six root can use by Routing algorithm in Distributed network sharing .

2.1 Advantages of TM Using Computer Communication Networks through Internet by Telecommunication

- all TM nodes act as a telemedicine foundation by implements Cloud and Grid computing..
- all small scale hospitals can be done Telemedicine center..
- no need Antenna with high frequency , Bandwidth allocation for signal transmission and receiving..
- no need high cost for making network foundation.
- mostly avoid filter section Circuit for transmitting and Receiving signal. .
- supports unt limited Channels.

3 Concept of Computer Communication Network by Distributing Sharing

In the application of telemedicine, the medical information usually needs to be distributed among medical doctors and display, archival, and analysis devices. For example in fig.3 is hierarchical structure of Telemedicine Network when Patient A is requested to send data to the medical specialists A and C, by using the traditional method, the patient has to send data to specialist A first and then the same data to specialist C. If a service in the Medical Center A was able to receive the data packages of Patient A and deliver the packages to specialists A and C, the patient's operation would not be simplified. Patient A send data to medical center A then send to Specialist A. then send data to Telemedicine foundation to Medical center B then deliver to Specialist C. [1][18] In Figure 4. is hierarchical network model to implements in Rural hospitals for large TM connection.. Every hospital can link interconnection by distributing sharing of centralized server Hospital in fig 4. .Complexity of large data , biomedical signal and images transmits through centralized server of hospital and heavy work-load increased to centralized server hospitals. The transmission delay also increased by centralized server hospital. If increase large connection in rural area, work load also increase in centralized server hospitals,[1][4][5].

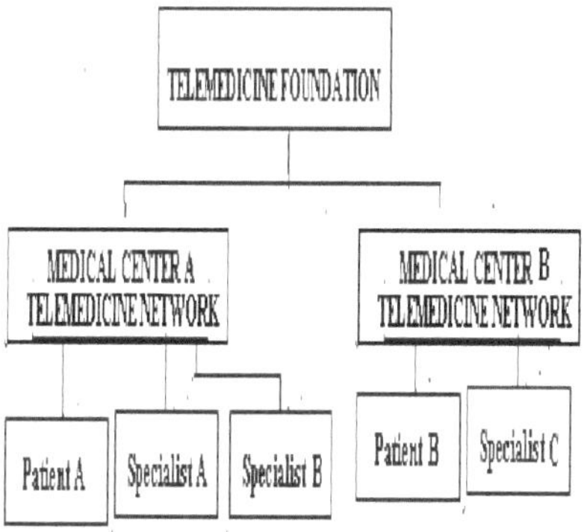

Fig. 3. Hierarchical structure or TM network

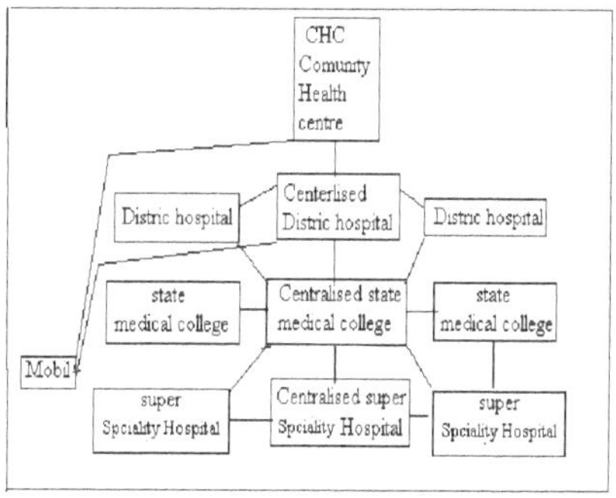

Fig. 4. Limited TM node connection of Hierarchical structure

In Fig 4 is model of hierarchical model of TM network is limited connection of TM node for health care hospital. But increasing the population in India, we need un limited complexity connection Telemedicine node connection to implement to rural area. My research Proposed Cloud and Grid computing based Telemedicine using computer communication network using distributing sharing of Internet for supporting complexity connection of un limited telemedicine node connection with low cost maintenance as shown in figure 5.[1][10][11][12][13[14][14][15][19]. Cloud and Grid

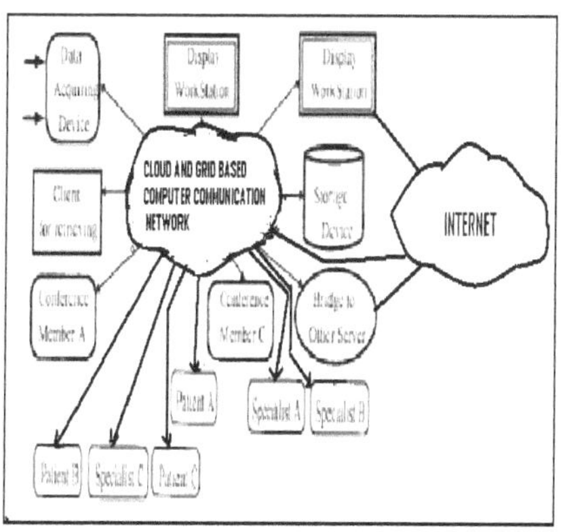

Fig. 5. Cloud and Grid computing based Telemedicine through Internet

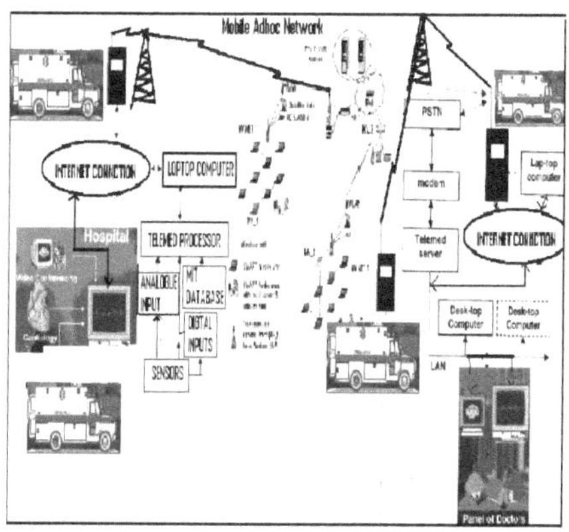

Fig. 6. Cloud and Grid Mobile Telemedicine through Internet

computing based Telemedicine network supports unlimited TM connection and no need centralized server in Model of Cloud and Grid computing based Telemedicine network. Model of Cloud and Grid computing based Telemedicine network. supports complexity of connection with Point to Point , Multi point to Multi Point connection. Cloud and Grid mobile telemedicine using computer communication network as shown in figure 6.

4 Grid Computing Based Telemedicine Network

This Grid computing network service is supports complexity maintenance of Telemedicine using computer communication network by internet with reliability and security assessment[1][21]. Grid computing is a powerful and efficient computational technology which represented as an advanced step for the high speed computer communication network in Telemedicine and high technical specified machines (PC, Desktops, super computers...). Grid computing shares the Telemedicine resources based on different platforms (operating systems), hardware/software architectures, and computer languages, located in different locations depending on architecture of Grid service network to telemedicine Network using open standards and protocols GRID technology as shown in figure 7.

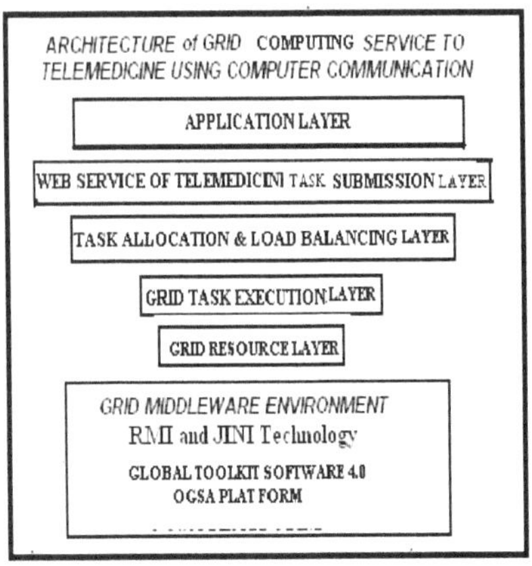

Fig. 7. Architecture of Grid network service

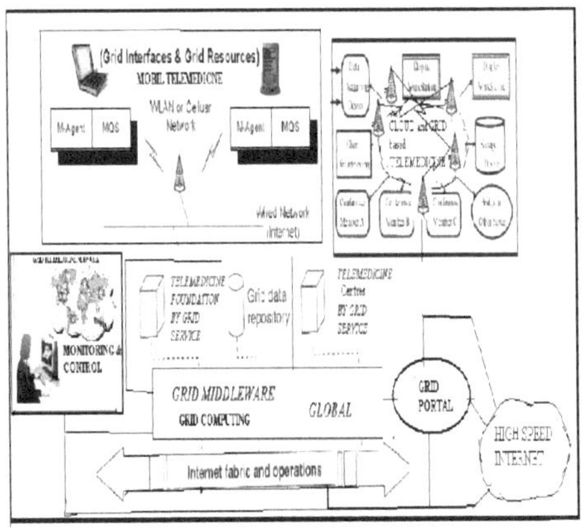

Fig. 8. Monitoring TM Node status by Grid Computing to Telemedicine Network

4.1 The Architecture of Grid Network Service

The Architecture of Grid network service has the following layers

Application layer
Web service Task Submission Layer
Task allocation and Load balancing layer
Grid Task Execution Layer
Grid Resource Layer
Grid Middleware Environment

4.1.1 Application Layer

This Application layer for

- Authorization and Authentication Service Interface of Globus Toolkit are used in Telemedicine for security service.
- Monitoring and control : Monitoring patients details of Bio medical services telemedicine network as shown in figure 8..
- RSA Grid Security Service:: This is the set of services for actually performing the reliability and security assessment of the Telemedicine Node
- Schedule and Execution Service for video conferencing of some discussion of live program
- Registry: It maintains the information and status of all resources and Telemedicine Network service
- Database Management: This service is responsible for access of the database in the Grid Telemedicine service system. This is used for data transfer across the Telemedicine nodes of the whole grid system. GridFTP of the globus toolkit will be used to provide such functionality. will be developed by using JAVA Telemedicine Toolkit Box

4.1.2 Portal

This service provides the uniform web based interface for grid users due to the Grid Telemedicine network system. It also provides the different interfaces forTelemedicine node service submission, result presentation and grid monitoring status. Bio-informaticians are creating Grid Services Portals. These are actual service providers wishing to take advantage of the grid's computational power and data storage capacity. Grid service Portals may be used to run the presently existing algorithms as well as new grid-aware ones. Many biomedical service providers rely on web-based technologies to offer access to their databases and computational resources. Grid service Portal as shown in fig.10.

4.1.3 Web Service Task Submission Layer

Web service submission layer supports Telemedicine nodes of Grid users submit their telemedicine tasks through GCS(Grid computing service) website using web browsing internet access.

- To minimize the TM user's request and response time between the patient and specialist s and specialist to specialist by grid entry point is Grid Agent manager (GAM).
- GAM to direct the Telemedicine nodes tasks , the grid overload and the desired telemedicine user quality of service.
- This layer mechanism supports suitable for mobile Telemedicine devices(3G Mobile phone) and TM using laptops with wireless internet Modem.

4.1.4 TASK Allocation and Load Balancing Layer

- Task allocation mechanism allocate the telemedicine node tasks of TM nodes by GCS for involve information exchange for load balancing request and response between patient to specialist service as shown in fig 9 and 14..
- The load balancing layer propose of load balancing algorithm which consists of the GAM which distributes the Users tasks of load receive from the load balancing layers to the receptor or Tm workers of its pool. The load balancing of TM node status as shown in fig 15.
- Load balancing layer computing the Load balancing to increasing complexity of TM nodes and minimize the congestion (Traffic).
- Load balancing layer Minimize the waiting time and delay time for request and responds, transmitting and receiving information.
- Load balancing layer supports high speed communication of tasks.

4.1.5 Model of Load Balancing Algorithm

Mainly load balancing algorithm needs to Cloud and Grid based telemedicine network for increasing overload of unlimited connection by internet connection Every GAM(Grid Agent Manager) sharing overloads by Grid computing service and minimize the congestion, waiting time, communication delay. The Model of load balancing algorithm implements to Cloud and Grid based Telemedicine through Internet. as shown in figure 9.

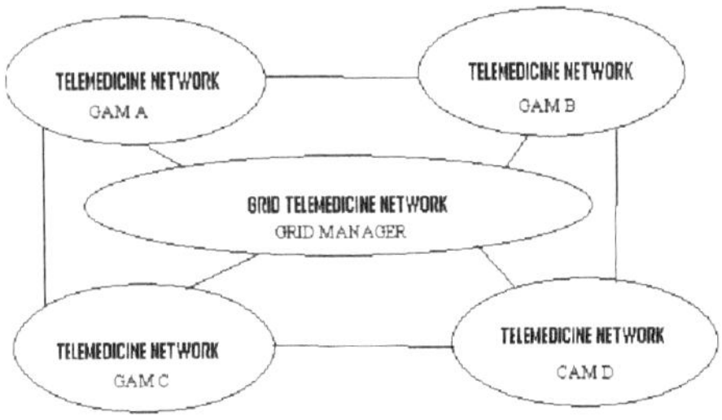

Fig. 9. TM Network load balancing by Grid computing

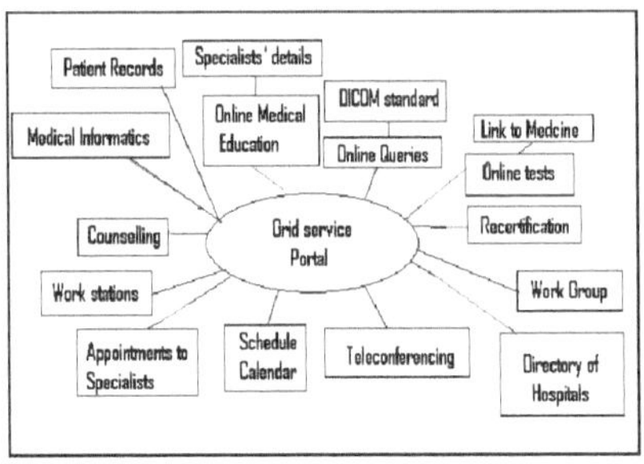

Fig. 10. Grid service Portal

Example: If Grid telemedicine network of Grid Manager consists of GAMs A, B, C, D… are shares TM

Tasks and Overloads by Grid computing. Actual processing capacity of Grid manger at Grid

Telemedicine network of system (APC) =PC*L

if PC=500 Tasks/sec L=30%

APC=500*30/100=150 Tasks/sec (1)

- If implements the Grid Computing Method ,the grid Thresold is assume 80% then Avaliable Grid processing capacity(AVGPC)= GPC-APC =500*80/100 - 150=250 Tasks/sec. (2)

- If Telemedicine Branch GAM A receveived 200 Tasks of TM nodes and it has three undertilized receptors r1,r2,and r5 with AVGPC of 250,300 and 140 tasks/sec respectively then,
- TAPC(Total available processing capacity)= $\sum_{r=1}^{n}$ AVGPC(r) (3)

=250+300+140=690 Tasks/sec
Shares r(1) =(250/690)*200=727 Tasks
Shares r(3)=(300/690)*200=87 tasks
Shares r(5)=(140/690)*200=41 tasks

- If GAM A has N=1000 un process of TM nodes tasks the following GAM load will distribute as follows.

Table 1. Status of GAM"S Load in TM Network

TM Grid Manager in Grid TM Network	Grid TM Network of Grid Agent manager(GAM) of id			
	GAM A	. GAMB	GAB C	GAMD
Status	S	R	R	R
TAPC	1000	700	550	600

Sender(s): Small TAPC and the pool of TM nodes workers are overloaded, need to transfer of load to GAMs.

Receivers: Available TAPC is high, ready to receive new tasks and thus increase the throughput.

Neutral(N): Pool under normal load of Tm nodes.

4.1.6 Grid Task Execution Layer

- GAM B can offer up to 700 tasks/sec but since we can transfer a maximum of 200 tasks /sec over the link connecting GAM A and GAM B then GAM B can only supply 200 tasks/sec.
- GAM C can offer up to 550 tasks/sec and sice the link can offer that amount the GAM C can supply the 550 tasks/sec.
- GAM D offer up to 600 tasks /sec and since the link can offer that amouni the GAM D can supply the 600 tasks /sec .
- Grid total available processing Capacity(GTAPC)=200+550+600=1350 Tasks/sec. Share
- GAM B = (200/1350)*1000=149 Tasks GCS(Grid computing service) allocates the task to suitable TM resources then the task needs to be executed.

- Calculated average TM task size , average task execution time and updated at the GAM levels.
- Determine the computing capacity (number of task per unit of time) at a given computing telemedicine centre

Share GAM C=(550/13508)*1000=407 Tasks
Share GAM D=(600/1350)*1000=444 tasks

4.1.7 Grid Resource Layer

- GAM are building blocks of TM resource monitoring layer and computing different computing sites of networks technologies and different operating system. TM resource status as shown in figure 13.
- GAM in the TM grid system infract and exchanges information to achieve load balancing operation of Tm centre.
- Maintaining the Computers, workstations, clusters of computers in Telemedicine network through Internet.
- Maintaining the Data resource: Grid configurations and log history of the TM events.
- Maintaining Databases of the Telemedicine node data related to generation, transmission and load demand.

4.1.8 Grid Middleware Environment

This layer provides a link between the Grid Telemedicine Network services and grid Telemedicine resources. It provides the access and information about the grid resources to the grid services in third layer. This layer consists of RMI and JINI technology , which provides standard distributed services This layer consists of Globus Toolkit software 4.0, which is standard OGSA platform and provides standard services .as shown in fig 7 and 8.

4.2 Benefits of Grid in Telemedicine Network

- The complicated and complex connectivity of telemedicine network (unlimited connection of rural telemedicine connection of Hospital) global environment leverages a multitude of open standards and technologies in a wide variety of implementation schemes.
- Grid computing adds infinite number of computing Telemedicine nodes into any grid environment So better computing capability and problem resolution Telemedicine tasks within the operational grid environment.
- Grid service telemedicine network using grid computing support with server or without server.
- Load balancing of TM network.
- Maintaining complexity Database of TM data.
- Avoiding congestion and reduced transmission delay .

5 Result and Discussion

The Bio-signal transmission of ECG, EMG, EEG and all image can be transmitted and receiving through Internet by distributed network sharing with live or store and forward method as shown in figure 11 and figure12.. We can avoids noise problem of transmission Bio-signal and all Image through Internet.[17][23] , The same quality of Image are received by Internet IP address with user friendly in rural area TM. The small transfer delay referenced in table 2.

5.1 Maintenance Cost of TM Network

The Maintenance cost of TM network through internet is very low comparably VSAT based TM network[1]. All rural Telemedicine hospital can be implemented low cost maintenance of TM network by Internet.

5.2 Transmission Delay

In hierarchical based TM Network creates Transmission delay by bottom level hospitals to Top level TM foundation through every centralized server of sub division and division layer. [1] in Fig 1 and 4. But Cloud and grid based TM network through Internet supports without any centralized centre server by Internet IP to IP for point to Point or Multipoint to Multipoint communication . So The Transmission delay very less comparably hierarchical based TM Network in Fig 16 and 17.

5.3 Congestion by Overload of Increasing Unlimited TM Connection

Increasing TM hospital by increasing population in India , hierarchical based TM Network Foundation will get overload of increasing unlimited TM connection and creates congestion,. But Cloud and grid based TM through Internet avoids congestion by without any centralized center server and load maintenance by Grid computing (load balancing by Grid computing).

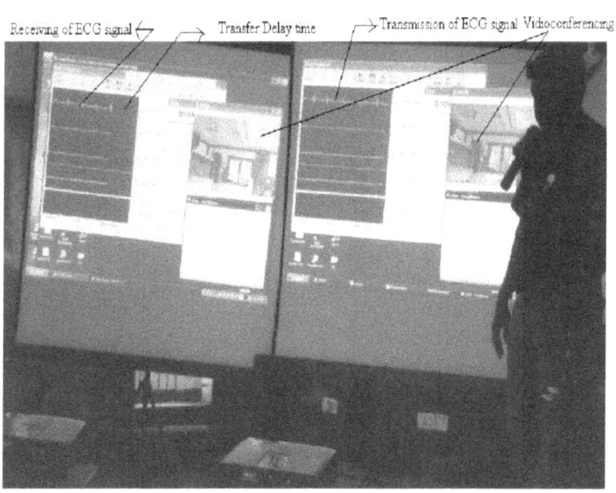

Fig. 11. Live transmission and receiving of ECG signal by Internet

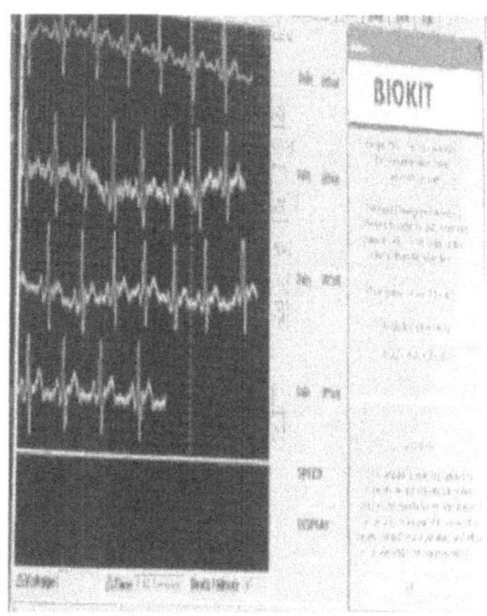

Fig. 12. Receiving of ECG signal by Internet

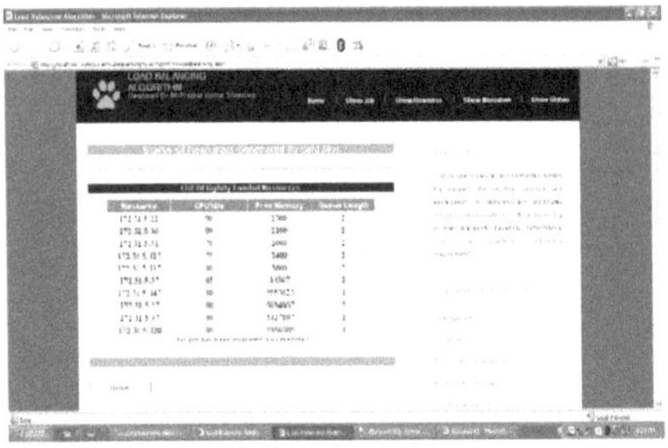

Fig. 13. TM Resource Status by Grid computing

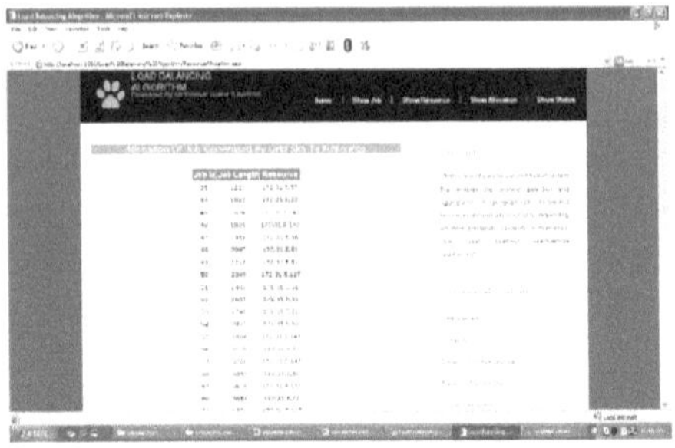

Fig. 14. TM Job allocation by Grid computing

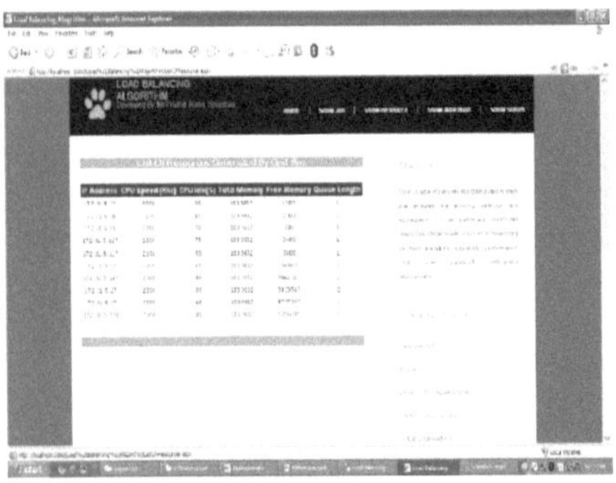

Fig. 15. Load balancing by Grid computing

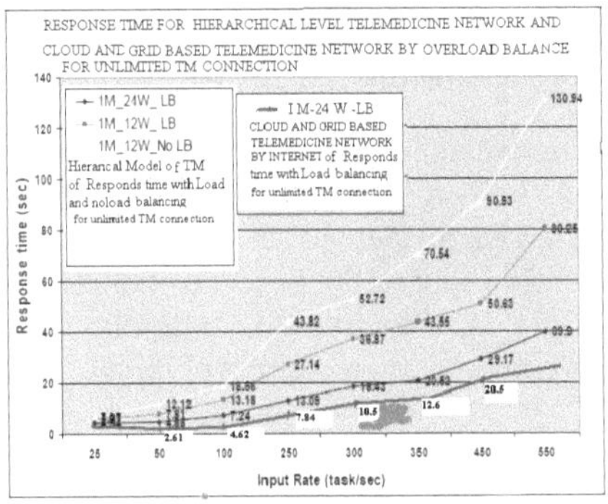

Fig. 16. Response Time of Cloud and grid based TM through internet

Table 2. Transmission delay time of TM using Internet for physiological data and medical image

Data	Internet Speed.	Transfer Delay time
Physiological data	240 KB 3 MB 10 MB 22 MB	0.5 sec 0.1 sec 0.04 sec 0.01 sec
Medical Image	240 KB 3 MB 10 MB 22 MB	1.02 sec 0,1 sec 0.04 sec 0.01 sec

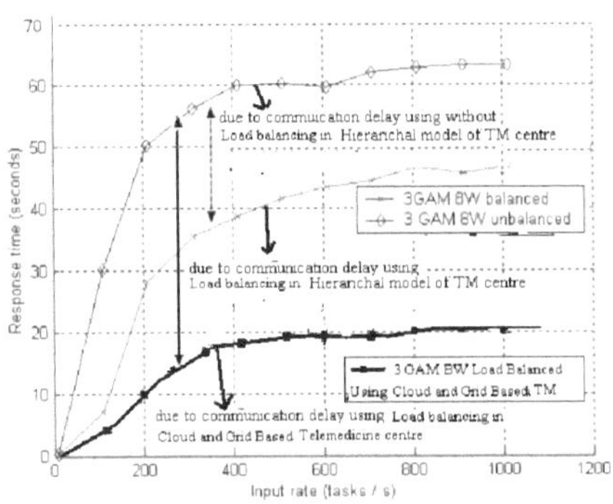

Fig. 17. Average Response Time of Cloud and Grid based TM through Internet

6 Conclusion

Cloud and Grid based telemedicine Network through Internet supports low cost maintenance with unlimited TM connection in rural area. All the small scale hospital can be implemented Telemedicine centre or Foundation by Telecommunication. Grid mobile telemedicine also supports unlimited telemedicine connection in rural area through Internet with Quality assurance.[16][19].

References

1. Saravanan, S., Anbu Rajan, M., Venkat Raman, A.: Telemedicine using computer using computer communication network. International Journal of Computer Science and Communication 2 (June to December 2011)
2. de Toledo, P., Jimenez, S., del Pozo, F., Roca, J., Alonso, A., Hernandez, C.: Telemedicine Experience for Chronic Care in COPD. IEEE Transaction on Information Technology in Biomedicine 10(3) (July 2006)
3. Xue, Y., Liang, H.: Communications, Analysis of Telemedicine Diffusion: The case of China. IEEE Transaction on Information Technology in Biomedicine II(3) (March 2007)
4. Lemma, F., Denko, M.K., Kassegne, S.K.: Hierarchical Model based LAN Architecture and V-SAT based WAN for a National Telemedicine Network in a Developing country: case of Ethiopia (2007)
5. National rural telemedicine Network suggested Architecture and guide lines Ministry of health a family welfare government of India (2005)
6. Martinez, A., Villarroel, V., Seoane, J., del Pozo, F.: Analysis of information and communication need in Rural primary Healthcare in Developing countries. IEEE Transaction on Information Technology in Biomedicine 9(1) (March 2005)
7. Srinivasan III, K.: Webservice and IT Management in Healthcare and Grid computing, hip://mpra.Ub.uni-muenchen.de{70620, MPRA paper No.7082, Postel 09 (February 2008)
8. Nessa, A., Ameen, M.A., ULLah, S., Kwak, K.S.: Applicability of Telemedicine in Bangladesh: Current status and Future Prospects. In: Third 2008 International Conference on Convergence and Hybrid Information Technology, November 8. IEEE Xplore, IEEE Computer Society (2008)
9. Aziz, J.S., Hussein, O.A., Naoom, A.: Design of Telemedicine Systems for Rural and Urban Areas in IRAQ. ARPN Journal of Engineering and Applied Sciences 4(2) (April 2009)
10. Rasid, M.F.A., Woodward, B.: Bluetooth Telemedicine Processor for Multichannel Biomedical Signal Transmission via mobile Cellular Networks. IEEE Transaction on Information Technology in Biomedicine 9(1) (March 2005)
11. Hu, F., Wang, Y., Wu, H.: Mobile telemedicine sensor networks with low-energy data query and network Lifetime considerations. IEEE Transaction on Mobile Computing 5(4) (April 2006)
12. Viswacheda, D.V., Arifianto, M.S., Barukang, L.: SETIT 2007, 4th International conference science of Electronic, Technologies of Information Telecommunications, Tunicia, March 25-29 (2007)
13. Niyato, D., Hossain, E., Diamond, J.: Trlabs and University of MANITOBA, IEEE 802.16 WIMAX-Based broadband wireless access and its Application for telemedicine/ E-health services. IEEE (2007)

14. Pandian, P.S., Safeer, K.P., Shakunthala, D.T.I., Gopal, P., Padaki, V.C.: Journal of Networks 2(6) (December 2007)
15. Zhang, Y., Ansari, N., Tsonoda, H.: Wireless telemedicine service over Integtrated IEEE 802.11 WLAN and IEEE 802.16/WIMAX @ Networks. IEEE (2010)
16. Zvikhachevskaya, A., Markarian, G., Mihaylova, L.: Quality of service consideration for the wireless telemedicine and e-health services. In: IEEE Communication Society –WCNC 2009 Proceedings (2009)
17. Alesanco, A., Garela, J.: Clinical Assesment of wireless ECG Transmission in Real-Time cardio Telmonitoring. IEEE Transaction on Information Technology in Biomedicine 14(5) (September 2010)
18. Bai, J., Hu, B., Zhang, Y., Ye, D.: A communication server for telemedicine applications. IEEE Transaction on Information Technology in Biomedicine (August 06, 2002)
19. Tan, X., Guo, X.-M., Chen, M.: China Design and Realization of Distributed Wireless Telemedicine Monitor Center Based on Virtual Instruments. In: IEEE Transaction on Information Technology in Biomedicine 2009, Third International Conference on ICBBE, June 11-13 (2009)
20. Kim, Y.S.: Anetwork based Telemedicine service. International Journal of Energy, Information and Communications 2(1) (February 2011)
21. Yagoubi, B., Slimani, Y.: Task, load balancing statergy for Grid computing. Journal of Computer Science 3 (2007); Prabhat, K.S., Gupta, S., Yadav, D.S.: Improving performance in load balancing on the grid computing system. International Journal of Computer Application 16 (February 2011)
22. Wu, Y.D., Wei, Z., Yao, H., Zhao, Z., Ngoh, L., Deng, R.H., Yu, S.: Teleoph: A secure real –Time telephthalmology system. IEEE Transaction on Information Technology in Biomedicine 14(5) (September 2010)

AT Command Implementation for a Multimode Wireless Device

Sharana Goud B. and Parimala P.

Dept. of Telecommunication, MSRIT,
Bangalore, India
{sharangoud@gmail.com}

Abstract. This paper presents the concept of AT parser module frame work which is used to test the modem in a wireless device. This Paper aims at developing an AT command framework for a multimode wireless device. AT commands is 3rd Generation Partnership Project standardization. AT commands are supported in several mobile devices. AT commands are used to control the modem in the device. AT commands are used to provide some specific functionality like Packet Switching, Network, *Subscriber Identity Module*, Phonebook, Short Message Service etc., by sending commands and receiving through modem. The objective of this paper is to implement the AT frame work module to communicate between PC and Android java chipset of the device of a multimode wireless device. Device may be a dongle/mobile which supports AT commands. The aim of the paper is to implement the AT frame work module for some of the SMS based AT commands and General AT commands using C language. And also to implement frame works for multiple AT commands. AT command Framework is developed at Samsung India Software Operations and proprietary.

Keywords: AT command Framework, LTE, CDMA, C, Source insight, Ddms.

1 Introduction

Multimode wireless device specified here is a dongle or a mobile which operates with two wireless technologies CDMA and LTE. CDMA and LTE are the two modems used to communicate between device and network.

AT commands are the instructions used to control the modem. AT is the abbreviation of ATtention. AT commands are used to test the device before the release of the device into the market. Testing the device using AT commands is an important and integral part of every device manufacturer. AT commands are used by the programmer to check whether the commands are reaching the network or not in the case of a damaged mobile or non displaying mobile device. Using AT commands we can communicate with the network by connecting the device to computer and we can send and receive SMS, connect to the internet etc.For dongle, AT commands are used to test it because dongle does't has display. AT commands can be used to test the device when the display of the device is not working properly and in case of sending the

P.V. Krishna, M.R. Babu, and E. Ariwa (Eds.): ObCom 2011, Part I, CCIS 269, pp. 447–456, 2012.

multiple SMS. AT commands are used to test the mobile device at the time of manufacturing. Every mobile device supports the AT commands. Before the product is released from company AT framework module should be implemented within the device.

In this paper, implementation of the AT framework module is done for some of the SMS commands and general commands using C language.

CDMA, or *Code Division Multiple Access* [1], is a competing cell phone service technology to GSM, which is the world's most widely used cell phone standard.

LTE (Long Term Evolution) is a fourth generation (4G) wireless standard for broadband mobile technology. This standard is developed to meet long term future requirements of higher data rates, lower latency, better cell coverage an seamless handover.

AT Commands, Many mobile and satellite transceiver units support the sending and receiving of SMS using an extended version of the Hayes command set, a specific command language originally developed for the Hayes Smart modem 300-baud modem in 1977.Common AT commands include AT+CMGS (send message), AT+CMSS (send message from storage), AT+CMGL (list messages) and AT+CMGR (read message). However, not all modern devices support receiving of messages if the message storage (for instance the device's internal memory) is not accessible using AT commands[8].

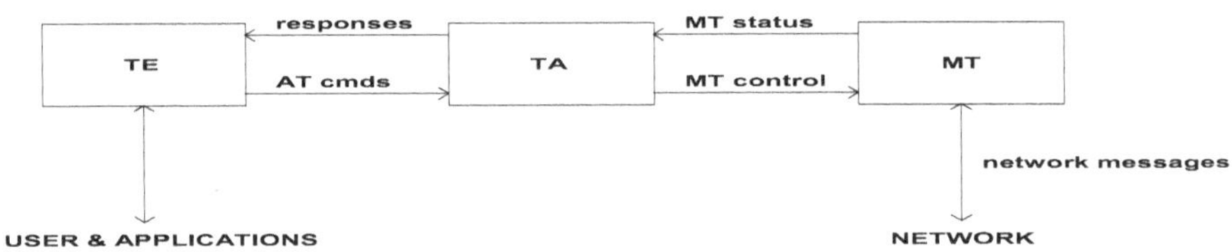

Fig. 1. Setup of General Mobile Communication System

The functional blocks shown in Figure 1.

TE - terminal equipment is the computer in which the applications are running.
TA - It is the Terminal Adopter where the AT commands which are written in hyper terminal are parsed and sent the MT.
MT - It is mobile terminal or the user equipment.

The user application is running on TE (Hyper terminal or some UI application). The commands are entered in the application. And TA is the part where the parsing of the commands are done in such a way that the parsed commands should understood by the mobile. Now once the mobile gets the parsed command, it analyses the command and gives it to the network.The network processes the command and gives it back to the MT and through TA; MT sends the response back to the terminal equipment.

The Technical Specification (TS) of AT commands has been produced by the 3rd Generation Partnership Project (3GPP).

Testing the Communication between the Pc and Modem or Mobile Phone

Suppose you have connected your GSM/GPRS modem or mobile phone to your PC / computer and started a terminal program (such as HyperTerminal on Microsoft Windows). Now you are ready to enter your first command. The first thing that is usually done is to test the communication between the PC and GSM/GPRS modem/mobile phone to confirm that everything is working properly so far. Simply enter "AT" in the terminal program to perform the test. When the GSM/GPRS modem or mobile phone receives "AT", it will send back the final result code "OK" to indicate that it has received your command successfully, like this:

AT

OK

2 USB Dongle Architecture and Implementation

Figure 3.1 above shows the architecture of the system. The system has an application running on PC and a device (Dongle or mobile). There are two ways in which PC and devices can communicate. The one which we are using is USB interface. WMC DLL client and host drivers are supporting applications running on PC. The device has 3 important parts: AP, LTE modem and CDMA modem.

AP has an AT module and Java module. AT module is responsible for parsing the AT commands which are entered from PC (Hyper terminal). AP and both the modems communication is done through Inter Process Communication (IPC).

LTE modem supports only the data service while CDMA supports both data and voice services. The glue layer is responsible to select the appropriate service from the modems. The bidirectional communication between the two modems is for the hand off connection service, when required service is not available with particular modem.

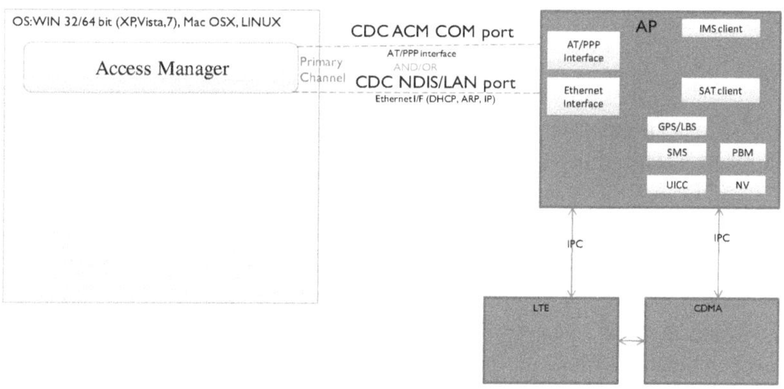

Fig. 2. USB Dongle Architecture

Here, LTE modem is the main modem used by the device. CDMA polls the LTE always, when the LTE network is not available then the current operations are given to CDMA modem because CDMA network is available at many places. So the device is called multimode wireless device. Basically, Verizon wireless company uses the CDMA technology in Verizon devices as we know. Verizon wireless wants to upgrade the network to LTE networks because of high speed requirements today.

In the above figure, VZW access manager is the application in computer and is connected to a device.

The main aim of the project is to implement the AT commands for this device using C language. AT commands are used to test the device modem. So, *AT commands needs to be implemented within the device to test the device*. AT commands are tested using hyper terminal in computer.

AT Command Handling at High Level

Flow chart

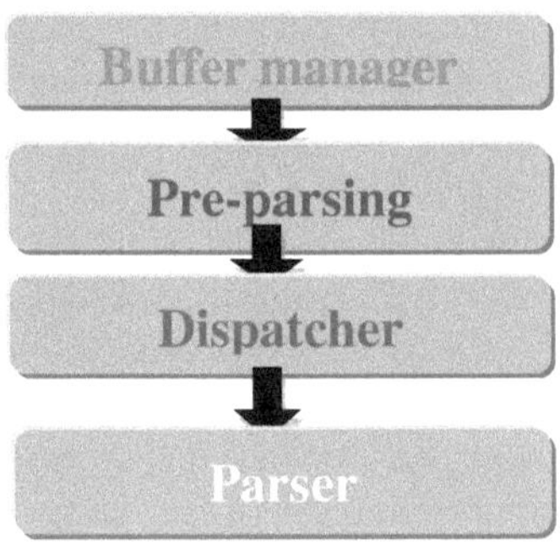

Fig. 3. Flowchart Depicting The At Commands Handling At High Level Using C Language

Buffer manager: - In coming AT command will be buffered in the buffer mode.

Pre-parsing:- given AT command will be split into individual commands and the commands will be stored in command queue.

Dispatcher: - each command in the command queue is dispatched to individual command handler.

Parser: - does the job of parsing the individual command...

Buffer management and pre-parsing modules are implemented in ati-fwcommshandlers.c/h. files in framework. Dispatcher is implemented in ati-fwcommandinterpreter.c/h. files in framework. Parser command parsing is carried out in a no. of different modules depending on the family association of the command.

At Command Line Processing Flow Chart in at Parser

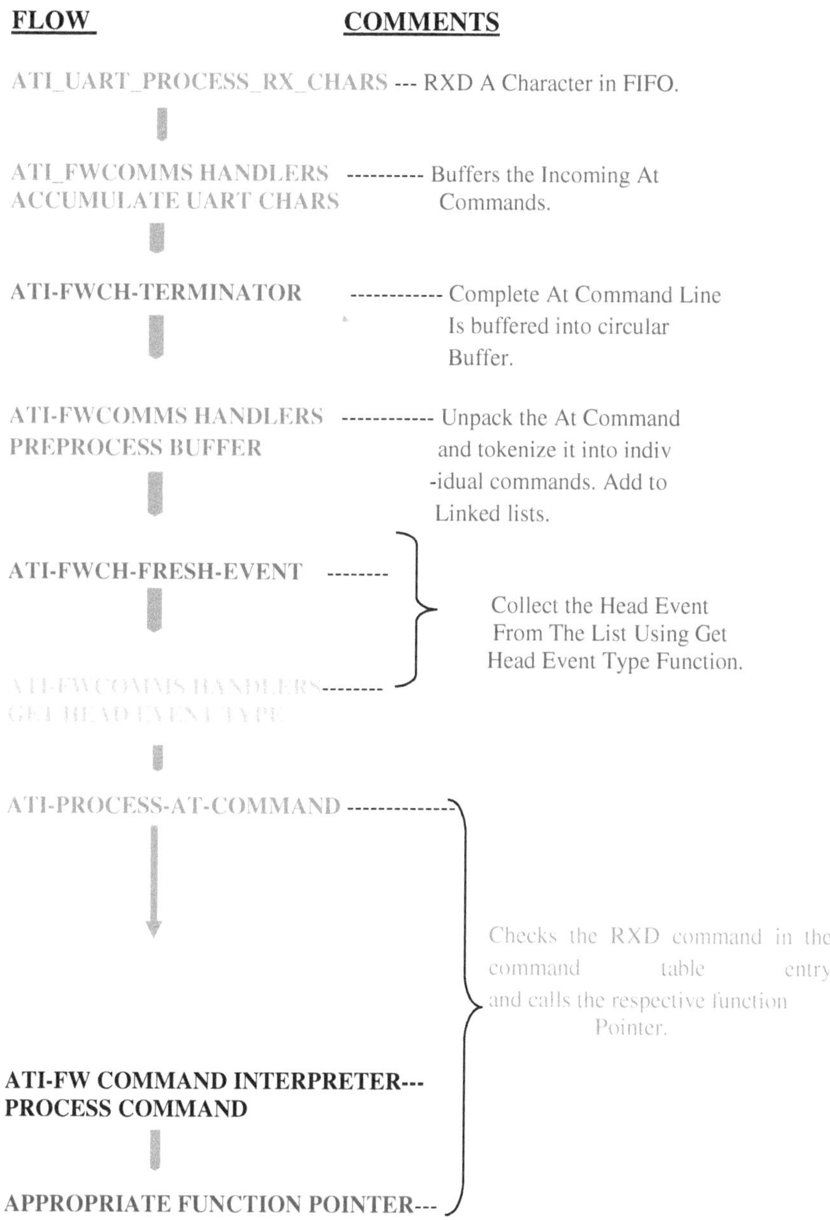

Fig. 4. Flowchart Depicting The AT Commands Line Processing In An AT Parser

Command Flow Diagram: SMS Related

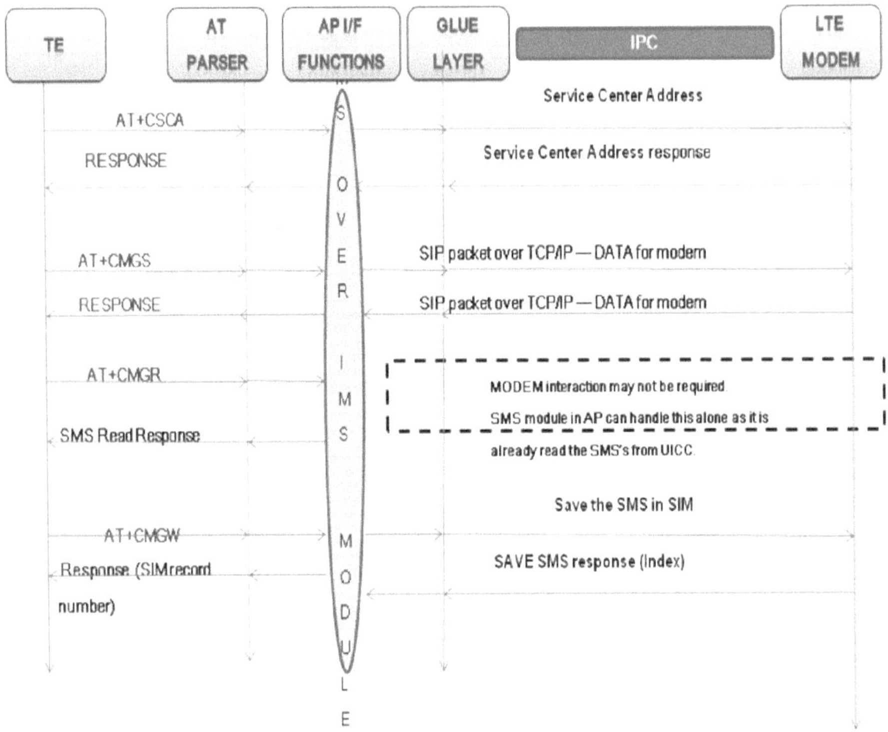

Fig. 5. SMS AT Command Flow Description Of Command Flow Diagram

The above diagram shows the Command flow for sms based AT commands in case of finding service center address (csca), sending SMS over IMS(cmgs), reading SMS from SMS module in AP as it is already read from UICC itself which provides the local storage of messages from which we can read the SMS(cmgr), write or save the SMS in SIM which is present in LTE modem.

3 Test Results

Flashing the Code

Flashing the AT parser code within the device using the odin3 tool is shown below in Steps.

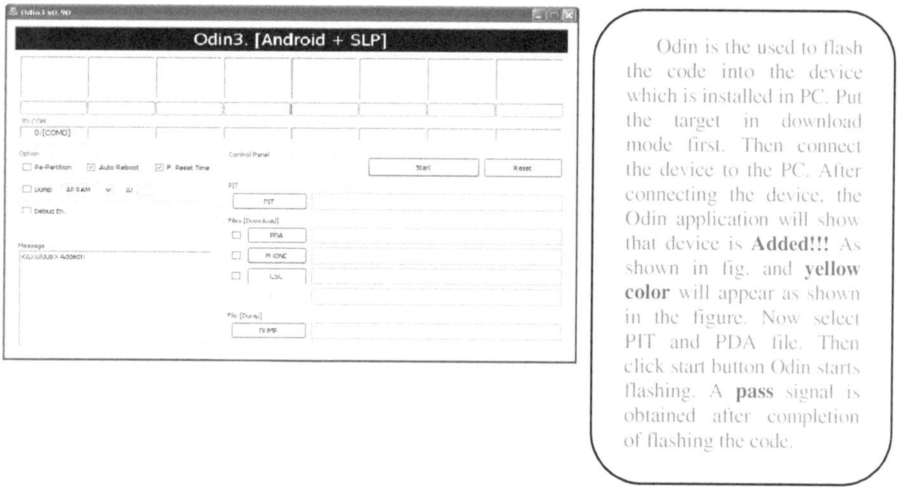

Fig. 6. Odin Application Used For Flashing The Code

Testing a device includes debugging and testing the commands using applications in computer as given below.

Debugging

Dalvik debug monitor is a debugging application which is installed in computer by which we can see logs, on connecting the device to the computer and we can check AT parser flow and errors and can debug. The below figure is the debugging tool as shown.

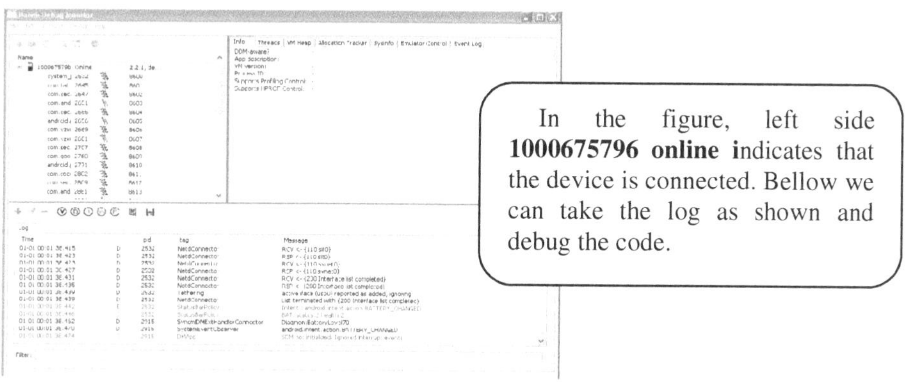

Fig. 7. Dalvik Debug Monitor Tool For Debugging

Testing the Commands Using SGTKEIF

To test the AT commands, two tools are used SGTKEIF and HyperTerminal. SGTKEIF is the testing tool used in the Korea. It is a separate application and we have installed it on computer for testing.

Hyper terminal is also used to test the AT commands. It is used by many companies regularly to test the commands. Hyper terminal is an built in application within the windows XP. By connecting the device to the PC we can test AT commands as shown in below figure.

Fig. 8. Device Used For Flashing And Testing

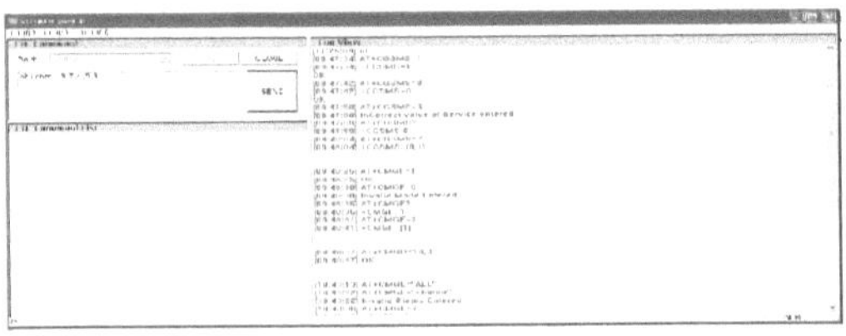

Fig. 9. SGTKEIF Tool Used To Test At Commands In Pc

Testing the Commands Using Hyper Terminal

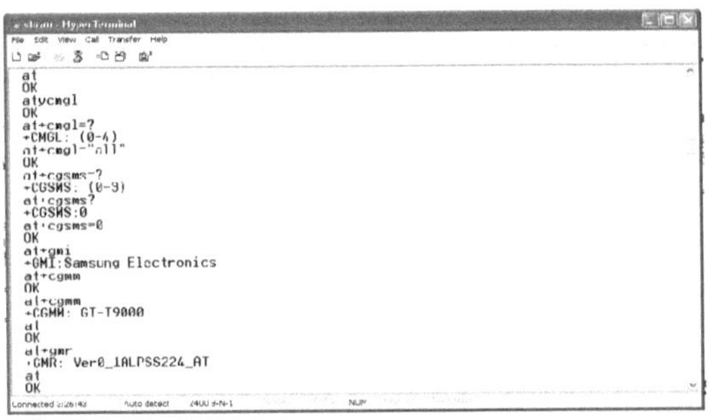

Fig. 10. Hyper Terminal Tool Used To Test At Commands In Pc

RESULTS: Results Got from Hyper Terminal

```
at
OK
at+cmgs=?
at
OK
at+cmgs?
at
OK
at
OK
at+cgsms=?
+CGSMS: (0-3)
at
OK
at+cmgd=0
OK
at+cmgf=?
+CMGF: (1)
at
OK
at+cmgf=1
OK
```

```
at+cmgl=?
+CMGL: (0-4)
at+cmgl="all"
OK
at+cgsms=?
+CGSMS: (0-3)
at+cgsms?
+CGSMS:0
at+cgsms=0
OK
at+gmi
+GMI:Samsung Electronics
at+cgmm
OK
at+cgmm
+CGMM: GT-I9000
at
OK
at+gmr
+GMR: Ver0_1ALPSS224_AT
at
OK
```

```
at+gmm
+GMM: GT-I9000
at
OK
at+gcap
+GACP: LTE1
at
OK
at+cmgs=145,"9945193450"
lti→
OK
at
OK
at
OK
at+cmgs?
at+cmgs=?
at
OK
at+cereg=?
+CEREG: (0-2)
at+cereg=0
CGREG:OK
at+cereg?
CGREG:0
atR:+CEREG: 0
```

```
>at
OK
at+gmi
+GMI:Samsung Electronics
at+cgmm
+CGMM: GT-I9000
at+gmr
+GMR: Ver0_1ALPSS224_AT
```

```
at+cgsms=?
+CGSMS: (0-3)
at+cgsms=0
OK
at+cgsms?
+CGSMS:0
```

```
at+cgsms
parameter error
at+cgsms?
+CGSMS:1
at+cgsms=4
parameter error
at
OK
```

```
at+cnmi=?
+CNMI: (0-3),(0-3),(0-2),(0-2),(0,1)
at+cnmi?
+CNMI: 0,0,0,0,0
at+cnmi=0,2,1,2,1
OK
```

```
at
OK
at+cnmi?
+CNMI: 0,2,1,2,1
at+cgsms
parameter error
at+cgsms=0
OK
```

```
at+cmgf=?
+CMGF: (1)
at+cmgf?0
+CMGF: 0
at+cmgf=?
```

Results Got from SGTKEif Application

```
[17:26:04] at
[09:47:34] AT+CGSMS=1
[09:47:34] +CGSMS=1
OK
[09:47:42] AT+CGSMS=0
[09:47:42] +CGSMS=0
OK
[09:47:50] AT+CGSMS=3
[09:47:50] InCorrect value of Service entered
[09:47:59] AT+CGSMS?
[09:47:59] +CGSMS:0
[09:48:04] AT+CGSMS=?
[09:48:04] +CGSMS: (0,1)

[09:48:25] AT+CMGF=1
[09:48:25] OK
[09:48:30] AT+CMGF=0
[09:48:30] Invalid Mode Entered
[09:48:35] AT+CMGF?
[09:48:35] +CMGF: 1
[09:48:41] AT+CMGF=?
[09:48:41] +CMGF: (1)

[09:49:37] AT+CMGD=10,3
[09:49:37] OK

[10:43:13] AT+CMGL="ALL"
[10:43:22] AT+CMGL="sharan"
[10:43:22] Invalid Status Entered
[10:43:36] AT+CMGL=?
```

```
[09:48:35] AT+CMGF?
[09:48:35] +CMGF: 1
[09:48:41] AT+CMGF=?
[09:48:41] +CMGF: (1)

[09:49:37] AT+CMGD=10,3
[09:49:37] OK

[10:43:13] AT+CMGL="ALL"
[10:43:22] AT+CMGL="sharan"
[10:43:22] Invalid Status Entered
[10:43:36] AT+CMGL=?
[10:43:36] +CMGL: (0-4)

[11:02:38] AT+CMGR=5
[11:02:54] AT+CMGR=?
[11:02:54] +CMGR: (0-127)

[11:03:32] AT+CNMI=1,2,1,2,1
[11:03:39] AT+CNMI?
[11:03:39] +CNMI: 1,2,1,2,1
[11:03:44] AT+CNMI=?
[11:03:44] +CNMI: (0-3),(0-3),(0-2),(0-2),(0,1)
[11:03:52] AT+CNMI=3,7,4,5,3
[11:03:52] Parameters outside the range
```

4 Conclusion

Applications

1. AT commands are used by many wireless device companies for testing the modem.
2. AT commands are used to test the mobile device when the display of the mobile is not available or not working.
3. Due to the use of LTE technology in this device we can speed up the device (dongle) operation. i.e uplink and downlink of the device is increased by the use of LTE.
4. Due to availability of two modems in this device we can use the CDMA Technology also when there is no availability of LTE networks in the required area.
5. IMS Clients are in the AP side hence there is reduced latency.

Future work
As we know we are using LTE technology for high speed data rates. In this project, LTE modem supports only Data services. Implementation of both Data and voice service in LTE modem can be taken as a future work.

References

[1] Maral, G., Bousquet, M.: Satellite Communication, 5th edn. Wiley
[2] Korhonen, J.: Introduction to 3G mobile communications, 2nd edn. Artech House mobile communications series (2003)
[3] Grune, D., Jacobs, C.J.H.: Parsing techniques, 2nd edn.
[4] GCC Compiler documents, http://gcc.gnu.org
[5] Source Insight, http://www.sourceinsight.com
[6] Cdma Documents, http://www.wirelesse2e.com/?s=cdma
[7] LTE documents, http://www.wirelesse2e.com/index.php/category/lte/, http://www.3gpp.org/LTE, http://www.masterltefaster.com/lte10/overview.php
[8] AT commands and 3gpp related documents, http://www.3gpp.org/ftp/Specs/html-info/27005.htm (3GPP TS 27.005 V3.2.0) (3GPP TS 27.007 V3.2.0)

CIMG-BSDS: Image Clustering Based on Bookshelf Data Structure in Web Search Engine Visualization

S.K. Jayanthi [1] and S. Prema[2]

[1] Department of Computer Science,
Vellalar College for Women (Autonomous), Erode, Tamilnadu, India
[2] Dept of Computer Science,
K.S.R College of Arts and Science, Namakkal District, Tamilnadu, India
prema_shanmuga@yahoo.com

Abstract. The Web is nowadays moving from a Web of data to a Web of services. The usage of Web metaphor search engines has been growing at an unstable rate. Due to the uncertainty of query terms and repetitive results, a good clustering of web search results is essential to improve browser experience as well as to improve recovery performance. This paper present an approach for Web Service innovation on Web search, targeted to support flexible and on-demand Web Service usage on the Web. A methodology is focused for building unique service objects from multiple Web resources in public web service. Clustering Image based on Book Shelf Data Structure (CIMG-BSDS) is proposed in this research paper. From the user profile both content based and session based clustering is implemented for effective information retrieval. This system delivers a much better presentation of search results and hence increases the usability of web search engines significantly in visual mode.

Keywords: Web search, Image Clustering, Visualization, Bookshelf Data Structure, Public web service.

1 Introduction

The exponential growth of the number of multimedia documents distributed on the Internet, in personal collections and organizational depositories have brought extensive attention to multimedia search and data management. With Web Service technologies all possible functionalities can be exposed and used in multiple ways. They can be flexibly integrated both in traditional software systems and in Web pages like Web 3.0 style portals. People are using image oriented web search to communicate frequently. With the massive invasion of image clips on the Web, image search has become an increasingly compelling information service that provides users with images relevant to their queries [1]. In terms of relevance and quality, images returned in the first page are not necessarily better than those in the following pages.85 % of the users are not satisfied with the top 10 results.

In summary, this architecture returns much higher quality results yet with similar response time to other systems. The rest of the paper is organized as follows: related

P.V. Krishna, M.R. Babu, and E. Ariwa (Eds.): ObCom 2011, Part I, CCIS 269, pp. 457–466, 2012.

work is discussed in Section 2 and provides some preliminaries on clustering algorithms. Section 3 presents the proposed system by describing the information integration framework, the purpose of each module, and the key comparison .Section 4 explains the Bookshelf Data Structure and Section 5 presents the CIMG-BSDS clustering algorithm. Section 6 reports the results of the experimental study. Finally, Section 7 gives the concluding remarks.

2 Related Work

Currently, there are several commercial Web page search engines that incorporate some form of result clustering. Distribute system divides a document corpus into groups and allow users to iteratively examine the resultant document groups or subgroups for content navigation [2]. Effective bias is necessary for the constraint selection in order to make it a more practical technique [3]. Web image search result clustering algorithms [4] have been proposed to cluster the top returned images using visual and textual features. Garcia et al. [5] explored using the object-action interaction paradigm to improve the usability and accessibility of Web applications. Parallelizing the web search results incorporated with Bookshelf Data Structure owe to the simplistic applicability of the aforementioned strategy, and the use of simple data structure [6].

3 Proposed Work

In this section, the different components of web search results clustering system including acquirement and pre-processing of returned images, preprocessing of context information with a focus on texts, session based clustering method and result visualization are discussed. The proposed system is comprised of a database, processing codes of various algorithms implemented in different languages. The proposed work is designed to achieve (i) More descriptions for public web services using the information captured from related web pages. (ii)Processing of related web pages by duplicate elimination, collected pages are parsed and split into several page segments. (iii) Based on the vector space model, compute the similarity between WSDL file and each fragment. (iv) Finally several text fragments are selected as descriptions of the web service as in Fig.1. With the enhanced descriptions, service consumers can understand the service more easily, efficiently and comprehensively.

3.1 Information from Various Resources

The architecture in this system impersonates the storage and search components of a contemporary Web image search engine. In response to a query request, the query evaluation engine retrieves the document from the backend; the collection may be in the notepad. When supplied with a query, Query engine will send it to web server and will in turn receive a list of images and metadata similarly to the user actually accessing in the existing servers like Yahoo, Google, etc., as in Fig.2.

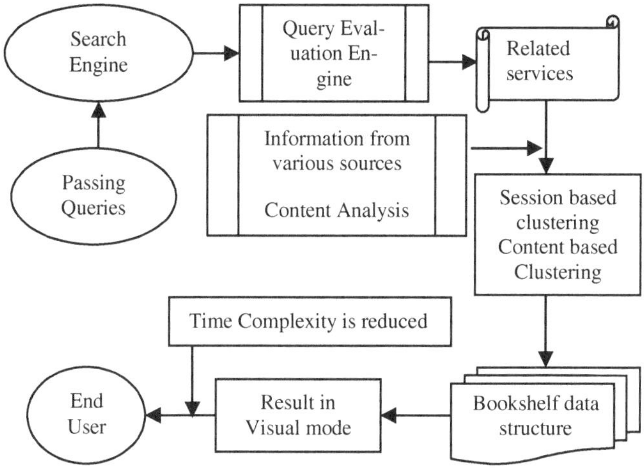

Fig. 1. Semantic web search architecture

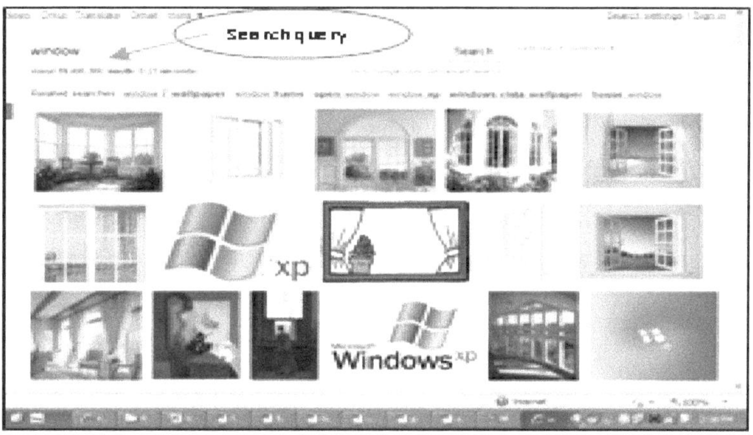

Fig. 2. A search result page showing the flat-ranked list for a "window" query, with multiple semantic categories mixed together

Web search architecture provides an API to its system which enables developers to write content-accessing programs more easily and is essentially a client interface. This information is by default gathered and stored in a local database and indexed by a BSDSC (Book Shelf Data Structure Code) [7].For example an image's title might be "operating systems" while its tags might be "windows", "unix", "dos" which give a good indication that the window search cluster rather than the former window cluster. Based on the code (BSDSC) the retrieved documents are arranged in the book shelf of the data structure proposed.

3.2 Similarity Propagation (SP)

The clustering algorithm for similarity propagation method is proposed in [5].In this algorithm each data point to be clustered is viewed as a node in a network which passes messages to other nodes in order to determine which nodes should be representatives and which nodes should be associated with those representatives. There are two types of messages sent between data point i and candidate representative j: liability l(i, j) and accessibility a(i, j). Availability messages are sent from j to i and reflect how available i is to be assigned to j currently.

$$l(i,j) \leftarrow t(i,j) - \max_{j' | j' \neq j} \{a(i,j') + t(i,j')\} \quad (1)$$

$$a(i,j) \leftarrow \min\left\{0, l(j,j) + \sum_{i' | i' \notin \{i,j\}} \max\{0, l(i',k)\}\right\} \quad (2)$$

For each iteration the evidence accumulates that some points are better representatives. This is handled by initializing a (i, j) to a zero value so that l(i,j) can be calculated in the first iteration. After this the availabilities are calculated and stored to be ready for the next iteration. Responsibility (2) can be thought of as a competitive update where the similarity measure between *i* and j, t*(i, j)*, is subtracted from by j' . That is the greatest similarity value between *i* and every other potential representative, t *(i, j')*, plus the corresponding availability value, *a (i, j')*. It can be seen in (1) that an availability value will not be greater than zero so this factor will either have no effect on responsibility or it will increase it. Intuitively, if some other candidate representative for point *i* is less available, the current candidate representative being analyzed then becomes more responsible and a better fit.

3.3 Computing Similarity Based on Image Content Analysis

Each image can be represented by a sequence of *d*-dimensional frame features obtained from image histograms, in order of appearance. In order to compare two images, the developer may compare their histograms, using a frame-by-frame comparison approach. The hierarchical classification structure based on content analysis supervised learning for image content analysis is given in Fig.3.

3.4 Similarity Measurements

The relationship between sum of squared difference (SSD) and cross correlation template matching approaches are defined as follows:

$$d(u,v) = \sum_{x,y} (f(x,y) - t(x-u, y-v))^2 \quad (3)$$

$$c(u,v) = f(x,y)t(x-u, y-v) \quad (4)$$

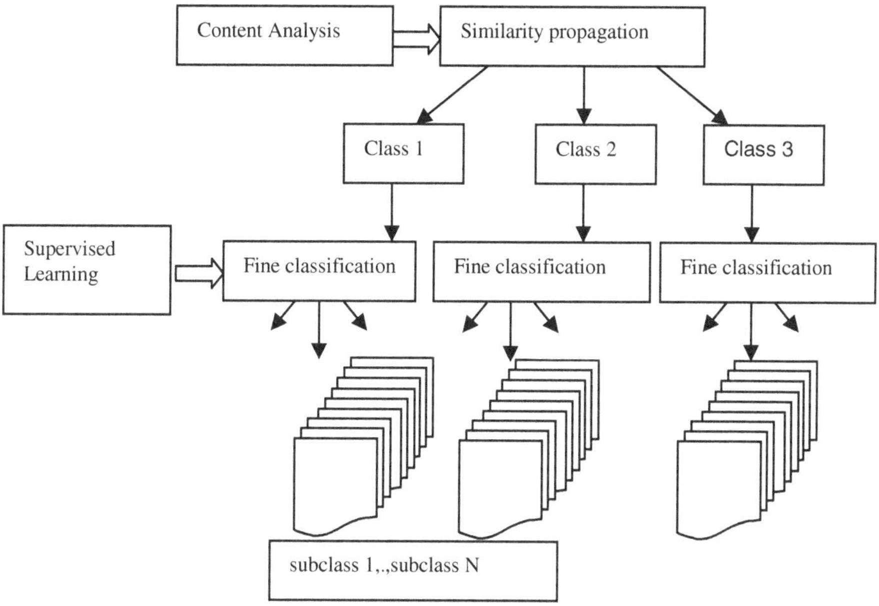

Fig. 3. The hierarchical classification structure based on content analysis supervised learning

Where f is the image, t the template and summation is over positions x, y under the template positioned at u, v. SSD can be viewed as the squared Euclidean distance Expanding (3), (4) yields

$$d(u,v)=\sum_{x,y} f^2(x,y)-2f(x,y)t(x-u,y-v)+t(x-u,y-v)^2 \tag{5}$$

Here fq = fq[0], fq[1],….,fq [n] represents the query feature vector, ft = ft[0], ft[1],….,ft[n] denotes the target feature vector, and n is number of features in each feature vector.

4 Book Shelf Data Structure

Bookshelf data structure [8] as in Fig.4. has been introduced for community information which stores the inverse indices of the WebPages. This data structure is formed by combining a matrix and list with dynamically allocated memory. This is an extended data structure of hash table and bi-partite core [8], which is used to store base domain and sub-domain indices of various communities. A recent study [8] shows that 81.7%of users will try a new search if they are not satisfied with the listings they find within the first 3 pages of results. However it would be too restrictive to only consider the first 30 results (10 results per page). Indeed this study has been done on search engines with linear results visualization (ordered lists) and users may want to see more results on visualizations like web graphs.

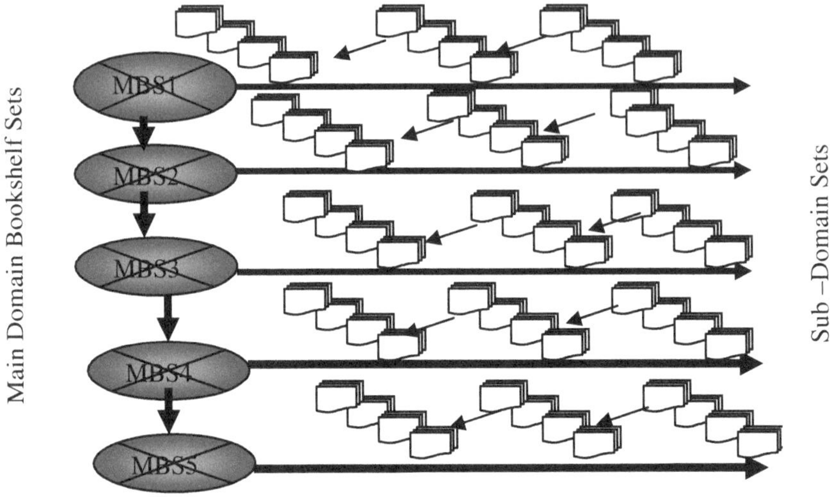

Fig. 4. Bookshelf Data structure

5 CIMG-BSDS Algorithm

5.1 Content Based Clustering

Where dwi(a) and dwi(b) are the weights of the i-th common keyword in the query a, and b respectively and wi(a) and wi(b) are the weights of the i-th keywords in the query a and b respectively. tf * idf is used for keyword weighting.

$$\text{similarity}_{w\_content(a,b)} \frac{\sum_{i=1}^{k} dw_i(a) \times dw_i(b)}{\sqrt{\sum_{i=1}^{m} w_i^2(a) \times \sqrt{\sum_{i=1}^{n} w_i^2(b)}}} \tag{6}$$

5.2 Session-Based Query Clustering

Session-based query clustering is a strategy, which employs the evidences in query sessions to deduce and detect users' search intentions.

$$\text{similarity}_{session\_based}(a,b) = \frac{1}{2} \times \left(\frac{\sum_{i=1}^{m} \left(\max_{j=1}^{n} s(di,dj) \right)}{nd(a)} + \frac{\sum_{j=1}^{n} \left(\max_{i=1}^{m} s(di,dj) \right)}{nd(b)} \right) \tag{7}$$

5.3 Combined Measures

Content-based and Session-based document clustering should be defined to take advantage of both strategies. A simple way to do this is to combine both measures (6), (7) linearly, as follows:

$$\text{similarity}=\alpha^{*}\text{similarity}_{\text{content-based}}+\beta^{*}\ \text{similarity}_{\text{session-based}} \tag{8}$$

Image Clustering based on Book shelf Data Structure is given in the Algorithm below:

```
Algorithm CIMG-BSDS (n,T)
n is an input keyword search      T is the CIMG-BSDS
begin     r=root(T)     increase f(r)
if n = keyword search (r) then exit
  choose Tn=subtree(r) such that s and keyword
      search(mainshelf (Tn)) are comparable
if Tn does not exist then
create a new shelf x for r, keyword
      search (x) =n and f(x) =1
else if main shelf(Tn) ⊂ n then call Construct (n, Tn)
else if n ⊂ mainshelf(Tn) then
create a new node x, as a new shelf of r,
keyword search (x) =s and f(x) = f(root(Tn))+1
else create two nodes x and y, x as the
mainshelf(Tn),n.t.items(x) = n    end.
```

6 Findings and Discussion

Based on user profile the images are clustered. If the user is a Graphics designer he gets the result as in Fig.5 and if he is a interior designer he may gets the result as in Fig.6.The database for the web images are designed in Fig.7. From the document

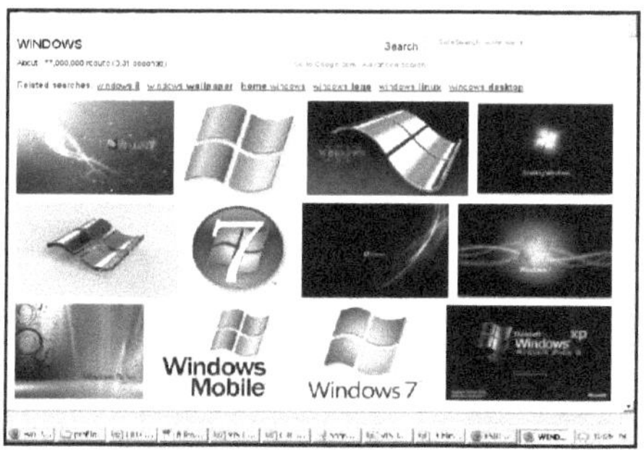

Fig. 5. Clustered results of Windows (OS)

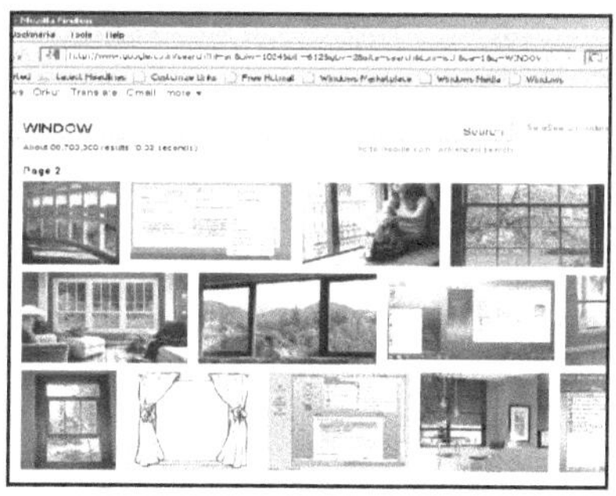

Fig. 6. Clustered results of windows (Interior design)

clustering the lexicon is constructed as in Fig.8.Semantic web search home page is shown in Fig.9. In the home page For example, an interior designer may use the query "windows" to find information about models of the windows, while software engineer may use the same query to find information about window operating systems as in Fig.10. The user after analyzing the result of semantic web search prefers to produce the result in visual mode.

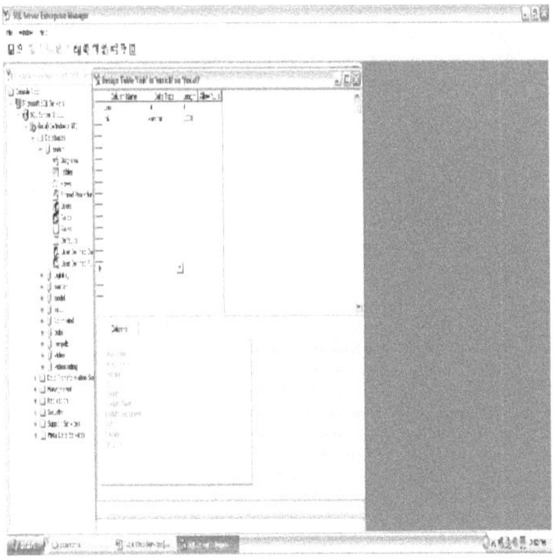

Fig. 7. Table Design

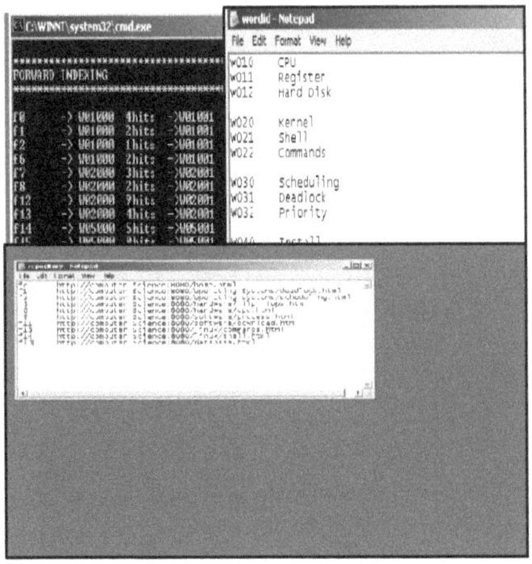

Fig. 8. Lexicon construction

Fig. 9. Semantic search home page

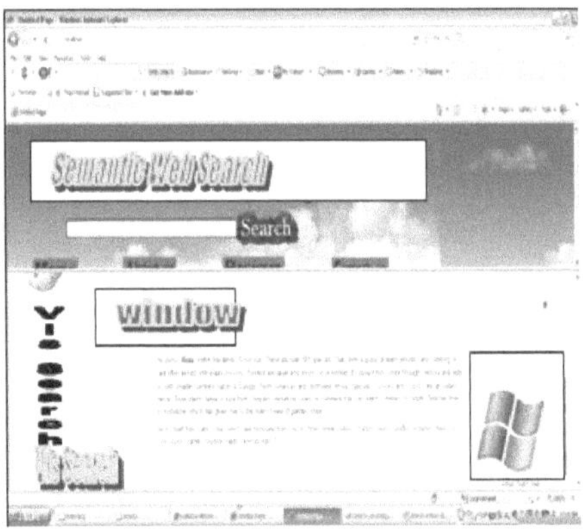

Fig. 10. Vis Search result

The comparison of existing results of Bookshelf Data Structure (BSDS)[8] and the result of Image Clustering based on Bookshelf Data Structure (CIMG-BSDS) is given inFig.11.

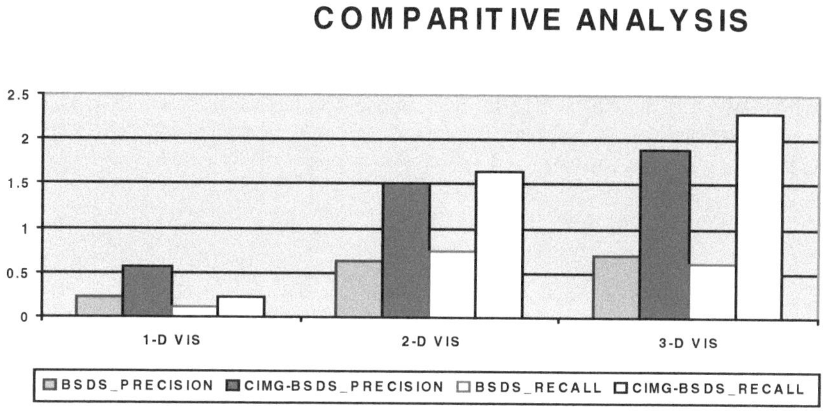

Fig. 11. Comparison of Precision and recall of BSDS and CIMG-BSDS

7 Conclusion

In this paper a methodology for building unique service objects from multiple Web resources is discussed and Clustering Image based on Book Shelf Data Structure (CIMG-BSDS) is proposed .From the user profile both content based and session based clustering are implemented. Based on user profile clustering strategy two different sets of people will receive different sets of results at the same time. This system delivers a much better presentation of search results and hence increases the usability of web search engines significantly in visual mode. To automate the identification of groups of similar pages, the approach has been implemented in a Java prototype. This paper proposes an effective method for organizing and visualizing web search results.

References

1. Gibbon, D.C., Liu, Z.: Introduction to Video Search Engines. Springer, Heidelberg (2008)
2. Cutting, D.R., Karger, D.R., Pedersen, J.O.: Constant interaction-time scatter/gather browsing of very large document collections. In: SIGIR, pp. 126–134 (May 1993)
3. Carpineto, C., Osinski, S., Romano, G., Weiss, D.: A survey of web clustering engines. ACM Comput. Surv. 41(3) (2009)
4. Czajkowski, K., Fitzgerald, S., Foster, I., Kesselman, C.: Grid Information Services for Distributed Resource Sharing. In: 10th IEEE International Symposium on High Performance Distributed Computing, pp. 181–184. IEEE Press, New York (2001)
5. García, R., Gimeno, J.M., Perdrix, F., Gil, R., Oliva, M., López, J.M., Pascual, A., Sendín, M.: Building a usable and accessible semantic Web interaction platform. World Wide Web 13(1-2), 143–167 (2010)
6. Prema, S., Jayanthi, S.K.: Web Search Results Visualization Using Enhanced Branch and Bound Bookshelf Tree Incorporated with B3-Vis Technique. In: 3rd International Conference on Machine Learning and Computing (ICMLC 2011). IEEE Xplore, Singapore (2011) CFP1127J-PRT, ISBN: 978-1-4244-9252-7

7. Prema, S., Jayanthi, S.K.: Facilitating Efficient Integrated Semantic Web Search with Visualization and Data Mining Techniques. In: International Conference on Information & Communication Technologies, pp. 437–442. Springer Transl, Kerala (2010)
8. Prema, S., Jayanthi, S.K.: Referenced Attribute Functional Dependency Database for Visualizing Web Relational Tables. In: International Conference on Network and Computer Science (ICNCS 2011), indexed by the Ei Compendex and Thomson ISI (ISTP). IEEE Xplore, Kanyakumari (2011)

Fuzzy Based Integrated Security Model for Mobile Ad Hoc Network

M.B. Mukesh Krishnan[1] and P. Sheik Abdul Khader[2]

[1] Sathyabama University,
Chennai 600 119, India
mukesh_krishnan@yahoo.com
[2] Department of Computer Application,
B.S. Abdur Rahman University, Vandalur,
Chennai-600 048, India
psaabdul@gmail.com

Abstract. Mobile Ad hoc Network (MANET) which communicates with each other nodes without the basic network infrastructure, all the nodes act as autonomous nodes with self-organization and self-administration, leads to lack of security and selfishness among the nodes. This paper concentrates to provide fuzzy based integrated security model which incorporates Authentication key and Intrusion detection method through fuzzy approach. Authentication key provides effective information security and Intrusion detection provides the security towards the anonymous access. Combining both with fuzzy approach will provide a dual defense to the environment by providing security towards the anonymous access and information security together. The model is implemented by simulating various attacks through the ns/2 simulation and the result are compared with simulation of various authentication key distribution and intrusion detection models and the result shows that integrated security model provide high level of security compared to the stand alone Authentication key based security or Intrusion detection models

Keywords: MANET, Authentication Key, Intrusion Detection, Fuzzy.

1 Introduction

Mobile ad hoc networks (MANET) are networks that do not have an underlying fixed infrastructure and thus have to communicate with each other nodes through self-organization and self-administration. Monitoring of nodes is needed to detect the critical situations as early as possible. The major challenges in MANET are different kinds of communication devices can act as nodes of MANET, varying from tiny sensors to large computers, different mobile nodes can join together and form a network, dynamic network topology, lack of central authority and shared wireless medium for communication this factors will result as security is a major challenge in MANET. Various researches are made but focus is made on different levels separately such as

P.V. Krishna, M.R. Babu, and E. Ariwa (Eds.): ObCom 2011, Part I, CCIS 269, pp. 467–472, 2012.

information security, routing security, transport layer security and application security but integrated security needed so this paper concentrates towards that. The main contributions of this work are towards the analysis of various security issues related to information security and anonymous access. Authentication key distribution provides effective information security and Intrusion detection provides the security towards the anonymous access. Combining both with fuzzy approach will provide a dual defense to the environment by providing security towards the anonymous access and information security together.

The paper is organized as follows, In the next section, we present Security goals issues in MANET. In section 3, we describe Fuzzy Based Integrated security Model for MANET. In section 4 and 5, we present the stimulation setup and performance analysis. Finally, section 6 presents conclusion.

2 Security Goals and Issues in MANET

In any network major security goals are to obtain Availability, Authenticity, Confidentiality, integrity and Non-repudiation there are few issues in MANET. The major issues which pull down us not to obtain them are listed as follows

- Autonomous and infrastructure-less
- Multi-hop routing
- Dynamic network topology
- Device heterogeneity
- Energy constrained operation
- Bandwidth constrained variable capacity links
- Selfishness of the nodes
- Limited physical security
- Network scalability
- Self-creation, self-organization and self-administration

In this paper we analysis all the issues and develop a fuzzy based integrated security model which satisfies all the major security goals.

3 Fuzzy Based Integrated Security Model for MANET

In this section we give a detailed description of our Fuzzy based integrated security model for MANET. First we describe the node evaluation process involved by them. The system starts its function when a new node enters into the group/cluster to attach the node into the group/cluster. The node was evaluated by the Intrusion detection system whether the node is a valid node or a anonymous intruder at the same time the node was also evaluated through the authentication key which checks whether the node is a valid node or not through the validation of the key present in it and updates the key if it is a valid node. Once the node passes this dual check it enter in to the attack monitoring agent which constantly holds a handshake with the cluster head, updates the addition and deletion of new nodes in to the cluster and also holds the attack status of each nodes including the selfish and compromised behavior of the nodes. Attack monitoring agent also updates intrusion detection system about the malicious behavior of the nodes. Then the trust hold was evaluated based on the past malicious behavior of the node based on that node status setting will be done if it exceeds the trust hold level then the node was rejected to join in to the cluster and discarded if it not exceeds the trust hold level then node evaluation database is updated which is used by the attack monitoring agents of the adjacent group/cluster. At last the node added to the group/cluster. By enabling the integrated Authentication key check and Intrusion detection check made and integrate them using the fuzzy based thrust hold evaluation at the entry level of each and every node provide a high level of security.

3.1 Fuzzy Based Trust Estimation

The proposed suggested security model which get the inputs from intrusion detection system and authentication key it uses fuzzy systems to identify malicious network activity. This model combines simple network traffic metrics, node evaluation database which holds the history of node with fuzzy rules to determine the network attacks more over it incorporates the dual security check through logic estimation. There are two main reasons for introducing fuzzy logic along with intrusion detection and authentication key. First, many quantitative features are involved in intrusion detection. Fuzzy set theory provides a reasonable and efficient way to categorize these quantitative features in order to establish high-level patterns. Second, key based authentication security itself is fuzzy. Every nodes compromised behavior is analysis through network traffic behavior analysis of the node such that we analysis the node behavior during network transmission and update in node evaluation database. Based on the database score we cluster the nodes as faith, good, fair and unsecure nodes. To detect the false positive, detection of malicious behavior with faith node is evaluated for authentication key verification if success trace the node attack else discard the node.

Step 1 : Check for new node

Step 2: Evaluate the node using Intrusion Detection System

Step 3 : If evaluation fails discard the node else continue

Step 4: Authenticate the node using valid key

Step 5: If authentication fails discard the node else continue

Step 4: Validate and update the Key

Step 5: Evaluate the node through fuzzy based trust estimation

Step 6: Update node evaluation database

Fig. 1. Node Evaluation Process

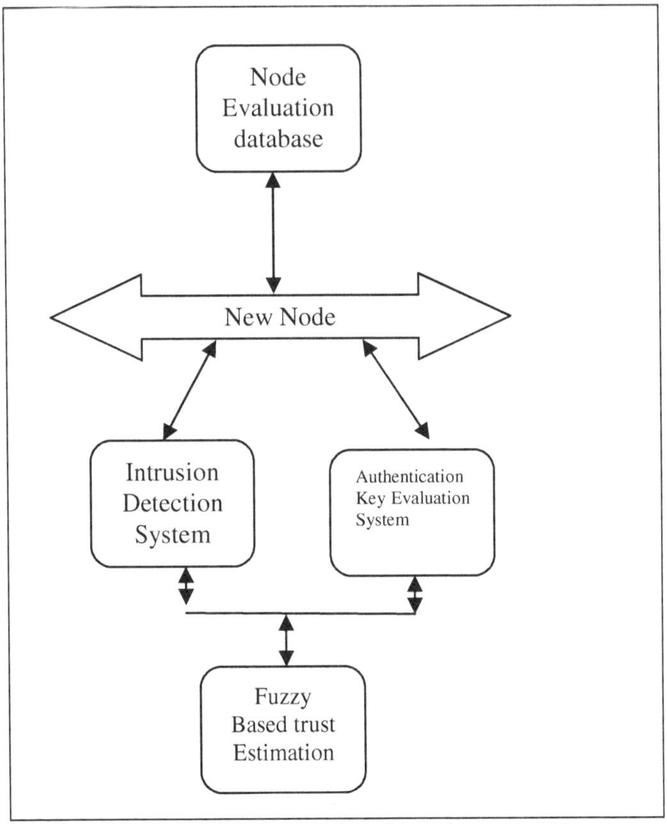

Fig. 2. Fuzzy Based Integrated security Model for MANET

4 Attack Creation and Stimulation Setup

In this section we present the attack creation and stimulation setup. We create 30% of the nodes inside the network as malicious nodes. The malicious nodes are generating invalid key and anomaly node value. These nodes were selected randomly. The randomly selected nodes were made to generate more number of malicious activities. Each malicious node in the network generates a variable type of attacks. The above said operations are done cooperatively by a group of nodes when the a traffic level is very low. When the traffic level is very high the alleged node is directly purge from the network increasing the efficiency of the model and thereby decreasing the time taken for the detection.

Ns/2version 2.34 software is used for the model implementation. The simulations were based on 1500 by 1500 flat space scattered with 100 wireless nodes. The nodes move through the radio – propagation from a random starting point to a destination with a speed ranging from 0-20 m/sec as the destination is reached another destination be targeted after a pause time of 5sec. The MAC layer used for simulations is IEEE 802.11. The Intrusion detection system and authentication key model are incorporated. Traffic sources and the attacks are given as a source input with each data packet of 512 bytes long. all nodes in the network were made the sources and the destinations were spread randomly across the network. The mobility model used is random walk. Duration of the simulations is 900 seconds. Separate simulations were performed for the malicious node created in the network and after the implementation of the Intrusion Detection and authentication key model.

5 Performance Analysis

In this section we describe the stimulation scenarios and analysis the performance. The stimulation was through two scenarios.

In the first scenario nodes enter in to the group/cluster is malicious node which falls under the 30% which we created.

In the second scenario nodes enter in to the group/cluster is malicious node which is formed due the compromised behavior or due to the attacks.

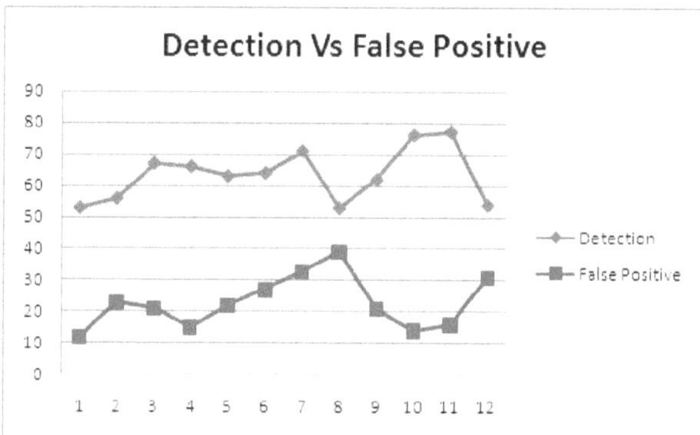

Fig. 3. Malicious node detection vs. False Positive Detection

Through this scenario we calculated the malicious node detection and false positive detections and the result showed that this model detection is 83% and false positive detection is 7%. Similarly we also injected the same type and same count of attacks to various intrusion detection models based on Standalone IDS, Distributed and Cooperative IDS, Hierarchical IDS, Collaborative decision making IDS, Independent decision making IDS and also to the trust hold cryptography model and the result shows that detection percentage ranges between 53% to 77% and the false positive detection ranges between 12% to 39% it shows that Fuzzy Based Integrated security Model for MANET detection node better than other models. We analyzed not only security parameter to ensure this model as a better model, but also analyzed the performance parameter like delay and throughput it also proved the proposed model performs better than other models.

6 Conclusion

Intrusion detection techniques and authentication key act as a defense to safeguard the node from attacks. In this paper we provided the fuzzy based integrated security model which incorporates Authentication key and Intrusion detection method through fuzzy approach. The result analysis proves that this model as a better model which analysis not only security parameters but also performance parameter like delay and throughput it also proved the proposed model performs better than other models.

References

1. Marchang, N., Datta, R.: Collaborative techniques for intrusion detection in mobile ad hoc networks. Elsevier Ad Hoc Networks 6(4), 508–523 (2008)
2. Ma, C.-X., Fang, Z.-M.: A novel intrusion detection architecture based on adaptive selection event triggering for mobile ad-hoc networks. In: IEEE Second International Symposium on Intelligent Information Technology and Security Informatics, pp. 198–201 (January 2009)
3. Jacoby, G.A., Davis, N.J.: Mobile Host-Based intrusion Detection and Attack Identification. IEEE Wireless Communications 14(4), 53–60 (2007)
4. Zhou, L., Ni, J., Ravishankar, C.V.: Efficient key establishment for group-based wireless sensordeployments. In: Proceedings of the ACM Workshop on Wireless Security (2005)
5. Wu, T.-S., Hsu, C.-L.: Cryptanalysis of group-oriented (t, n) threshold digital signature schemeswith traceable signers. Comput. Stand. Interfac. 26(5), 477–481 (2004)
6. Xu, G., Iftode, L.: Locality driven key management architecture for mobile ad-hoc networks. In: Proceedings of the First IEEE International Conference on Mobile and Sensor Networks (2004)
7. Sterne, D., Balasubramanyam, P., et al.: A General Cooperative Intrusion Detection Architecture for MANETs. In: Proceedings of the 3rd IEEE International Workshop on Information Assurance (IWIA 2005), pp. 57–70 (2005)
8. Sun, B., Wu, K., Pooch, U.W.: Alert Aggregation in Mobile Ad Hoc Networks. In: The 2003 ACM Workshop on Wireless Security in conjuction with the 9th Annual International Conference on Mobile Computing and Networking, pp. 69–78 (2003)

An Efficient Authentication Method for Throttling DDoS Attacks

Ch. Rupa[1], J. Madhu Babu[1], P. Siva Prasad[1], and P.S. Avadhani[2]

[1] Dept of CSE, VVIT, Nambur,
Andhra Pradesh, India
{rupamtech,madhubabujanjanam,sivaprasad.mtech}@gmail.com
[2] Dept of CS&SE, Andhra University, Visakhapatnam,
Andhra Pradesh, India
psavadhani@yahoo.com

Abstract. Distributed Denial of Service Attacks has recently emerged as one of the most newsworthy, if not the greatest, weaknesses of the Internet. DDoS attacks aim to deny legitimate users of the services. In this paper, we introduce a novel secure scheme for defending against the DDoS attack. When the number of requests arriving at the victim crosses the threshold value (T), integer factorization solution is invoked and the victim server starts sending encrypted e(n) which is generated by RSA instead of 'n' to all the users. If the user is not an attacker, decrypts the 'n' by using CRT and generate 'p' and 'q' through integer factorization. If the user fails to provide the computational power to decrypt 'n' value as well as to find the factors 'p' and 'q' then consider him as a malicious user.

Keywords: DDoS, Threshold Value, Integer factorization, RSA, CRT.

1 Introduction

As the rapid progressing of modern information technology security is an important technique of many web applications such as E-commerce, portals and secure internet access. A web application is an application has to be accessed over a network such as the internet or intranet. It becomes popular due to more utilization and convenience of using a web browser as a client. At the same time balancing the security parameters is also a typical task. However using a web application as a web client is not be complete secure as it can also be used to send malicious request. Generally in web applications the web client sends a request to the server which takes a less effort to compose. It requires a lot of effort at the server side for composing a response and to process lots of data to transfer to the client.

A web server is designed to accept requests from multiple clients across the internet which makes it difficult to filter requests based on IP address which can be easily accomplished in hardware. Some techniques are particularly useful to web servers as they cannot impose access control, based on usernames and nonce and there are no common patterns in the request sent by the attacker there by rending filtering

P.V. Krishna, M.R. Babu, and E. Ariwa (Eds.): ObCom 2011, Part I, CCIS 269, pp. 473–479, 2012.

ineffective [1, 4]. It is useful to make the web server responsive to legitimate users with reasonable overhead and tolerable failure rates when the server is actively being subject to a denial of service attack (DoS) [1,4].

Generally DDoS attacks are generated by flooding the target servers with unwanted data in unparallel manner. It's a cause to 'capacity overflow'. It has been done by improper configuration of network routers or by performing scurf attacks on the victim servers. This 'Capacity Overflow', followed by Max Out of system resources, which makes the target service unavailable, either temporarily or permanently to the intended users.

In most cases the clients are unauthenticated and even if we impose certain kind of authentication, most applications allow creation of users on the internet which involves little or no manual verification of end-user information provided. Even if we manually verify all the end-users of the application, a single user who bears malice in his heart can inflict all the necessary damage to bring the web application to a grinding halt by sending valid requests through his authenticated account by tweaking the web client a bit. Hence in this paper we proposed an efficient authentication technique by using RSA Chinese Remainder Theorem (CRT) to improve the authentication of the clients [5, 6]. Section 2 consists of description about RSACRT. Section 3 describes proposed technique and section 4 holds the results and analysis of the technique.

2 Integer Factorization

In this section we described the important phrases of integer factorization. The strength of the solution to the throttling [1] lies in the mathematical complexity of the integer factorization problem. Since no algorithms exist to solve this problem in polynomial time the attacker will not try to optimize this computation but will try to get around the computation by finding a hole in the protocol.

2.1 Factoring Problem

Factoring is the act of splitting an integer into a set of smaller integers (factors) which, when multiplied together, form the original integer. For example, the factors of 403 are 13 and 31; the factoring problem is to find 13 and 31 when given 403. Prime factorization requires splitting an integer into factors that are prime numbers; every integer has a unique prime factorization. Multiplying two prime integers together is easy, but factoring the product is much more difficult. No good algorithms exist to solve this problem in polynomial time and the best algorithm which solves this problem in less complexity is general number field sieve in $O(\exp\left(\left({}^{64}/_{9b}\right)^{1/3} \times (log\, b)^{\,2/3}\right))$ for a b -bit integer. For a quantum computer it takes $O(b^3)$ by using Shor's algorithm.

2.2 Threshold Value

The threshold value is the number of requests that a server can handle without straining its resources. It is defined as a predetermined percentage of the maximum number of requests that a server can handle.

Various scenarios where the attacker actively modifies his malicious client and tries to scarf the hosts launching the distributed attack and the countermeasures that we need to have in place to defend against such modifications are discussed in our previous paper [1]. CRT is used to improve the security services to the client regarding authentication. Hence the attacker unable to modifies and scarf the information. This will be described in the following section.

3 RSA with Chinese Remainder Theorem

RSA cryptosystem is the most striking and accepted security technique for many applications. It has to perform modular exponentiation with large exponent and modulus for security consideration. The RSA cryptosystem takes great computational cost. In many RSA applications, user uses a small public key to speed up the encryption operation. However, the decryption operation has to take more computational cost to perform modular exponentiation by this case. Hence an efficient decryption method not only based on Chinese Remainder Theorem (CRT) but also the strong prime of RSA criterion proposed [2, 3]. This RSACRT method only takes 10% computational costs of the traditional decryption method. It also reduces 66% computational costs than that of decryption methods based on CRT only [2, 3]. Two theorems from number theory are required to this efficient authentication method such as Chinese Remainder Theorem (CRT) and Euler's Theorem (also called the Euler-Fermat Theorem)[8].

3.1 Encryption with RSA Algorithm

RSA algorithm is a public-key cryptosystem. It can be described briefly as follows:

Let us consider two large strong primes, p and q. Let $n = p \times q$.

Compute Euler value of n:

$$\emptyset(n) = (p-1) \times (q-1)$$

Find a random number 'e', where $1 < e < \emptyset(n)$and gcd $(e, \varphi(n)) = 1$.

Compute a number d such that $d = e^{-1} mod\ \emptyset(n)$

Cipher text $c = m^e\ mod\ n$ where $m < n$.

3.2 Decryption with CRT Algorithm m

The Chinese Remainder Theorem (CRT) can be used to speed up the calculations for the RSA algorithm. It is four times faster than the existing methods [7]. We can use the CRT to compute $m = c^d\ mod\ n$ more efficiently by the following algorithm.

Compute

$$dP = (1/e)\, mod\ (p-1)$$
$$dQ = (1/e)\, mod\ (q-1)$$
$$qI = (1/q) mod\ p$$

Compute

$$m_1 = c^{dP}\ mod\ p$$
$$m_2 = c^{dQ}\ mod\ q$$
$$h = qI \times (m_1 - m_2)\ mod\ p$$
$$m = m_2 + h \times q$$

Store private key as the quintuple (p, q, dP, dQ, qI).

A special case of the Chinese Remainder Theorem (CRT) can be written as follows.

Case 1: Let p and q be distinct primes and $n = p \times q$. For any pair $(x_1, x_2)$where $0 \le x_1 < p$ and $0 \le x_2 < q$, there is a unique number x where $0 \le x < n$ such that $x_1 = x\ mod\ p$, and $x_2 = x\ mod\ q$. So any integer x ($0 \le x < n$) can be expressed uniquely in its CRT representation(x_1, x_2).

4 Proposed Technique

When the server is facing normal flow of traffic, i.e., the requests (R_i) to the server is less than the threshold value (T), we do not interfere with the web application When the number of requests arriving at the server crosses the threshold value, integer factorization solution [1] is invoked and the server starts sending Encrypted $e(n)$ instead of 'n' to all the users. If the user is not a malicious, decrypts the 'n' by using CRT and generate 'p' and 'q' through integer factorization [1]. If the user fails to provide the computational power to decrypt 'n' value as well as to find the factors 'p' and 'q' then consider him as a malicious user.

4.1 Algorithm

Step 1: Users send requests (R_i) to the server.
Step2: If (Num(R_i) > T) then server sends an encrypted 'n' value to the user.
Step 3: If sender will decrypts that using RSA with CRT then go to step 5 other wise go to step 4.
Step 4: Server considers that request received from attacker.
Step 5: User needs to Factories 'n' into two prime numbers as 'p' and 'q'.
Step 6: If 'p' and 'q' are generated consider them as clients otherwise go to step 4.

5 Results and Analysis

Fig 1 shows the number of requests made by the client/attacker towards increasing number of digits in 'N'.

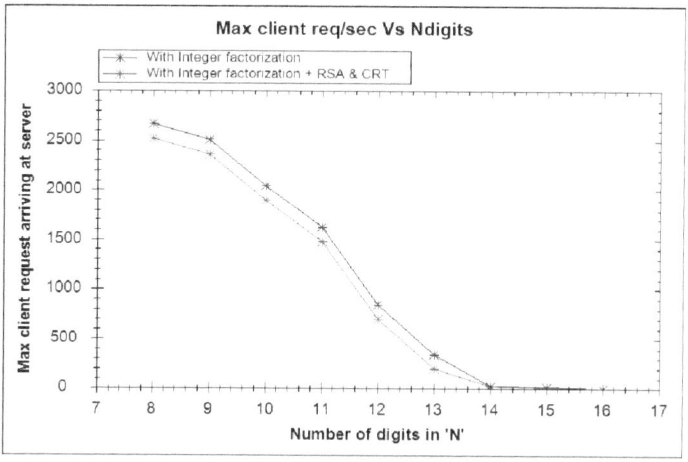

Fig. 1. Max client req/sec Vs 'N' digits

The above graph shows that a client/attacker can send at maximum of 2516 request/second when the server is sending 8 digits encrypted 'N' value and it is nearly zero when the server starts transmitting 16 digit 'N' value.Fig 2, Fig 3 and Fig 4 graphs show the results of overhead on the server while it starts applying the solution.

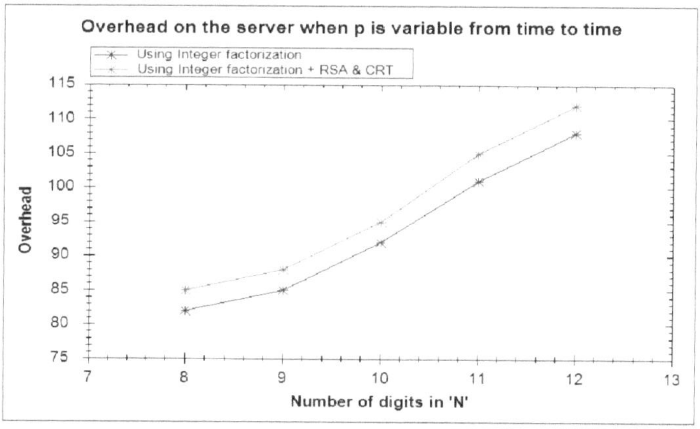

Fig. 2. Overhead on the server when 'p' is variable from time to time

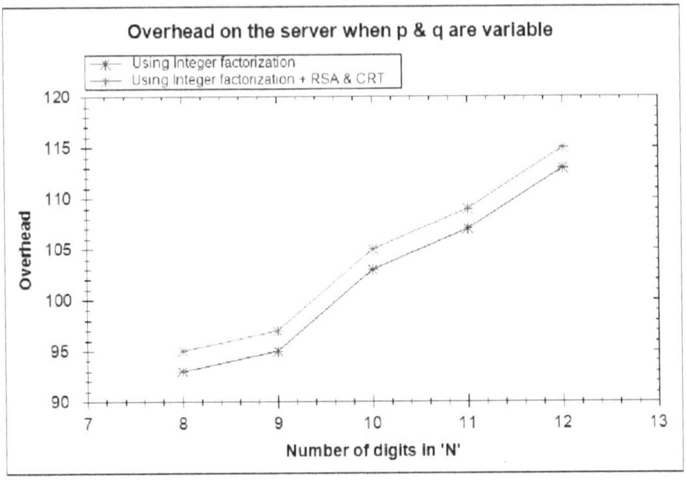

Fig. 3. Overhead on the server when ‘p’ & ‘q’ are variable

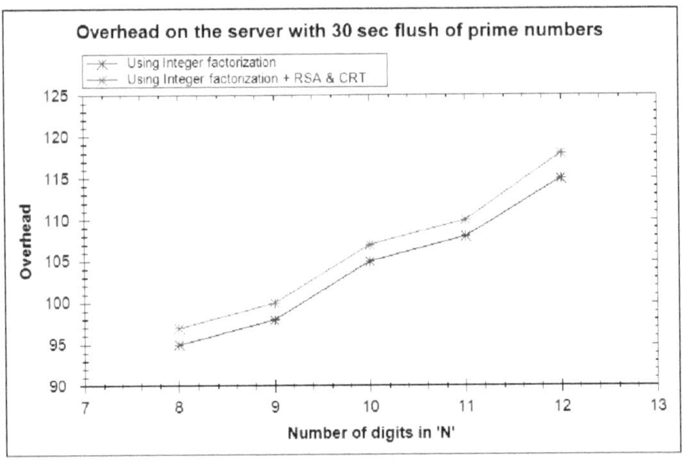

Fig. 4. Overhead on the server with 30 sec flush of prime numbers

At the time of attack, the above graphs are evident that the overhead on the server is negligible when compared with the performance that we achieve by imposing the proposed solution.

6 Conclusion

DDoS attacks are a serious threat. A design of effective ad efficient detection and response strategy is a must. Integer factorization with CRT solution successfully detects and constraints the attacks but has undesired impact on the legitimate flows. Further research is needed to refine the system.

References

1. MadhuBabu, J., et. al: Throttling DDoS attack. In: Secrypt 2009, Italy (2009)
2. Edpegg, J.R.: Chinese Remainder theorem. Wolfram Demonstrations project (2007)
3. Rupa, C., Sridevi, P.: Solution to the Dictionary Attacks using Time-Space Tradeoff with Asymmetric key Cryptography. In: Proceedings in ERTSP organized by Vignan Institute of Information Technology, pp. 120– 124 (2010)
4. Hwang, R.-J., Su, F.-F.: An efficient decryption method for RSA ceryptosystem. In: Proceedings of the 19th International Conference on Advanced Information Networking and Applications (2005)
5. Yen, S.-M., et al.: RSA Speed up with Chinese remainder theorem Immune against Hardware fault crypt analysis. IEEE Transactions on Computers 52(4) (2003)
6. Patra, J.C., et al.: DCT Domain water marking scheme using chaise reminder theorem for image authentication. In: Proceedings in ICME. IEEE (2010)
7. Edpegg, J.R.: Chinese Remainder theorem. Wolfram Demonstrations project (2007)
8. Ogiwara, M.: A method for generating cryptographically strong primes. IEICE Trans., 985–994 (1990)
9. Pinkas, B., Sander, T.: Securing passwords against dictionary attacks. In: Proc. 9th ACM Conference on Computer and Communications Security (CCS), pp. 161–170. ACM (2002)
10. Mori, G., Malik, J.: Recognizing objects in adversarial clutter: Breaking a visual CAPTCHA. In: Proceedings of Conference on Computer Vision and Pattern Recognition (CVPR 2003), vol. 1, pp. 134–141. IEEE Computer Society (2003)

Computational Analysis of Stationary and Transient Distribution of Single Server Queue with Working Vacation

R. Sudhesh[1] and L. Francis Raj[2]

[1] University College of Engineering, Villupuram, Anna University, Chennai, Villupuram-605 103, (T.N.), India

[2] School of Advanced Sciences, Mathematics Division, VIT University, Vellore-632 014, India

rsma@rediffmail.com, francisraj73@yahoo.co.in

Abstract. The classical M/M/1 queue is considered with vacations, in which the server works with different service rates rather than completely stops service during the vacation period. Service times during vacation period, service times during service period and vacation times are all exponentially distributed. An exact transient system size probability distributions and other system characteristics are derived in closed form and also obtained the time-dependent system size probability in the absence of working vacation. Further we deduce the stationary distributions from time-dependent system size probabilities. A numerical illustration is provided by considering various parameters.

Keywords: Transient probabilities, working vacation, generating functions, modified Bessel functions, stationary probabilities.

1 Introduction

During the last two decades, the queueing systems with server vacations have been well investigated due to their wide applications in many areas. In the models with various vacation policies, the server completely stops service in the vacation period, but he can take the assistant work. Doshi [3] presented a methodological overview of the vacation models in different framework by giving an extensive list of references on the subject. Details can be seen in the monograph of Tian and Zhang [10].

Working vacations is a kind of semi-vacation policy and is also a new vacation policy that was introduced by Servi and Finn [8]: a customer is served at a lower rate rather than completely stoping the service during a vacation. In the classical vacation queueing models, during the vacation period the server does not continue on the original work and such policy may cause the loss or dissatisfaction of the customers. For the working vacation policy, the server can still work during the vacation and may accomplish other assistant work simultaneously. So, the working vacation is more reasonable than the classical vacation in

P.V. Krishna, M.R. Babu, and E. Ariwa (Eds.): ObCom 2011, Part I, CCIS 269, pp. 480–489, 2012.

some cases. The vacation period becomes the lower speed operation period of the queueing system. A typical example is often encountered in case of maintenance problem; the idle machine can be utilized for the inspection and preventative maintenance.

Servi and Finn [8] analyzed an M/M/1/ queue with working vacations, denoted as M/M/1/WV, and modeled a wavelength division multiplexing optical access network using multiple wavelengths which can be reconfigured. Xiu et al. [11] studied M/M/1 queue with single working vacation using quasi birth and death process and matrix-geometric solution method, they obtain the distribution of the number of customers in the system, the average number of the customers and the average sojourn time of a customer in the stationary state. Baba [1] extended Servi and Finns M/M/1/WV queue to a GI/M/1/WV queue. Furthermore, Liu et al. [5] obtained the stochastic decomposition structures of the system indices in the M/M/1 queue with working vacations. Recently, Banik et al. [2] studied a finite capacity GI/M/1 queue with multiple working vacations. They developed some important system performance measures such as, the probability of blocking and the expected waiting time in the system. Jain and Jain [4] develop a queueing model with working vacation and server breakdowns, which require a sequence of stages of repair before service is restored. They proposed a matrix-geometric approach for computing the stationary queue length distribution.

Studies in performance analysis of queueing systems and in general, vacation queueing models have traditionally emphasized steady-state or equilibrium performance. Steady state measures of system performance simply do not make sense for systems that never approach equilibrium. Moreover, the steady state results are inappropriate in situations wherein the time horizon of operations is finite. Parthasarathy and Sudhesh [6,7] have used continued fraction and its power series to analytically derive the time-dependent size distribution of the state-dependent birth and death processes both in continuous- and discrete-time Markov chains. Sudhesh [9] has presented time-dependent system size probabilities of a single server queue with system disasters and customer impatience.

In the present investigation, we consider a queueing model with working vacation. In this paper we consider two models namely queue with working vacation (the server is not idle during vacation) and a classical single server queue with exponential vacations (the server is completely idle during vacation) where the server follows an exhaustive service policy. We obtain the time-dependent system size probabilities of the number of customers in the system. We also obtain the time-dependent system size probability in the absence of working vacation. we deduce the distribution of the number of customers in the system of a M/M/1 queue with working vacation in stationary state from the transient system size probabilities. Further, numerical illustrations are presented to visualize the effectiveness of the system.

2 Model Description

Consider a single server queue with arrival rate λ. The server begins a working vacation of random length at the instants when the queue becomes empty, and the vacation duration V follows an exponential distribution with parameter γ. If the system is empty when a working vacation ends, another begins. During the working vacation customers are served at a rate of μ_V. When the server is not on a working vacation customers are served at a rate of μ_B.

We assume that interarrival times, service times, and working vacation times are mutually independent. In addition, the service discipline is first in first out (FIFO).

Let $Q_V(t)$ be the number of customers in the system at time t and let

$$R(t) = \begin{cases} V, & \text{the system is in a working vacation period at time t,} \\ B, & \text{the system is in a regular busy period at time t.} \end{cases}$$

Then $\{Q_V(t), R(t)\}$ is a Quasi birth and death process with the state space

$$\Omega = \{0, 0\} \bigcup \{(j, r) : j \geq 1, r = V \text{ or } B\}.$$

Let $P_{jr}(t)$ be the probability that there are j customers in the system when $r = B$ or V. If $r = B$, the server is not on a working vacation and $r = V$, the server is on working vacation. The various transition rates of the Quasi birth and death process $\{Q_V(t), R(t)\}$ are

$$\begin{aligned} q_{(i-1,V),(i,V)} &= q_{(i,B),(i+1,B)} = \lambda, \quad i = 1, 2, 3, \ldots, \\ q_{(i,V),(i-1,V)} &= \mu_V, \quad i = 1, 2, 3, \ldots, \\ q_{(i,V),(i,B)} &= \gamma, \quad i = 1, 2, 3, \ldots, \\ q_{(1,B),(0,V)} &= \mu_B, \\ q_{(i,B),(i-1,V)} &= \mu_B, \quad n = 2, 3, 4, \ldots. \end{aligned}$$

By the routine procedure, the kolmogorov equations for the time-dependent probabilities are given in the following section.

2.1 Governing Equations

The state probabilities $P_{jr}(t)$ are satisfy the following forward Kolmogorov differential-difference equations:

$$P'_{00}(t) = -\lambda\ P_{00}(t) + \mu_B\ P_{1B}(t) + \mu_V\ P_{1V}(t), \tag{1}$$
$$P'_{1V}(t) = \lambda P_{00}(t) - [\lambda + \mu_V + \gamma] P_{1V}(t) + \mu_V P_{2V}(t), \tag{2}$$
$$P'_{jV}(t) = \lambda P_{j-1,V}(t) - [\lambda + \mu_V + \gamma] P_{jV}(t) + \mu_V P_{j+1,V}(t), \quad j \geq 2, \tag{3}$$
$$P'_{1B}(t) = -[\lambda + \mu_B] P_{1B}(t) + \mu_B P_{2B}(t) + \gamma P_{1V}(t), \tag{4}$$
$$P'_{jB}(t) = \lambda P_{j-1,B}(t) - [\lambda + \mu_B] P_{jB}(t) + \mu_B P_{j+1,B}(t) + \gamma P_{jV}, \quad j \geq 2. \tag{5}$$

with $P_{00}(0) = 1$.

If $\mu_V = 0$ these results specialize to the known decomposition for M/M/1 systems with exponential vacations.

3 Transient Probabilities

In this section, we find the time-dependent system size probabilities of this model by using the generating functions and continued fractions.

3.1 Evaluation of $P_{jB}(t)$

In the analysis below, we express $P_{jB}(t),\ j \geq 1$, in terms of $P_{jV}(t)$.
Define

$$Q(s,t) = \sum_{j=1}^{\infty} s^j P_{jB}(t), \quad Q(s,0) = 0.$$

From (4) and (5),

$$\frac{\partial Q(s,t)}{\partial t} = \left[-(\lambda+\mu_B) + \lambda s + \frac{\mu_B}{s}\right] Q(s,t) + \gamma \sum_{j=1}^{\infty} s^j P_{jV}(t) - \mu_B P_{1B}(t). \quad (6)$$

Solving (6), we find

$$Q(s,t) = \gamma \int_0^t \left[\sum_{m=1}^{\infty} s^m P_{mV}(y)\right] e^{-(\lambda+\mu_B)(t-y)} e^{\left(\lambda s + \frac{\mu_B}{s}\right)(t-y)} dy$$
$$-\mu_B \int_0^t P_{1B}(y) e^{-(\lambda+\mu_B)(t-y)} e^{(\lambda s+\frac{\mu_B}{s})(t-y)} dy. \quad (7)$$

It is well known that, if $\alpha_B = 2\sqrt{\lambda\mu_B}$ and $\beta_B = \sqrt{\frac{\lambda}{\mu_B}}$, then

$$\exp\left[\left(\lambda s + \frac{\mu_B}{s}\right) t\right] = \sum_{j=-\infty}^{\infty} (\beta_B s)^j I_j(\alpha_B t),$$

where $I_j(t)$ is the modified Bessel function of the first kind of order j.

Comparing the coefficients of s^j on both sides of (7) for $j = 1, 2, 3, \ldots$, we see that

$$P_{jB}(t) = \gamma \int_0^t \left[\sum_{m=0}^{j-1} P_{j-m,V}(y) \beta_B^m I_m(\alpha_B(t-y)) + \sum_{m=1}^{\infty} P_{j+m,V}(y) \beta_B^{-m} I_m(\alpha_B(t-y))\right]$$
$$\times e^{-(\lambda+\mu_B)(t-y)} dy - \mu_B \int_0^t P_{1B}(y) \beta_B^j I_j(\alpha_B(t-y)) e^{-(\lambda+\mu_B)(t-y)} dy. \quad (8)$$

The above holds for $j = -1, -2, -3, \ldots$, with the left-hand side replaced by zero. Using $I_{-j}(x) = I_j(x)$, for $j = 1, 2, 3, \ldots$,

$$0 = \gamma \int_0^t \left[\sum_{m=1}^{\infty} P_{mV}(y) \beta_B^{-j-m} I_{j+m}(\alpha_B(t-y))\right] e^{-(\lambda+\mu_B)(t-y)} dy$$
$$-\mu_B \int_0^t P_{1B}(y) \beta_B^{-j} I_j(\alpha_B(t-y)) e^{-(\lambda+\mu_B)(t-y)} dy. \quad (9)$$

Subtraction of (9) from (8) which gives

$$P_{jB}(t) = \gamma \int_0^t \left[\sum_{m=0}^{j-1} P_{j-m,V}(y) \beta_B^m I_m(\alpha_B(t-y)) + \sum_{m=1}^{\infty} P_{j+m,V}(y) \beta_B^{-m} I_m(\alpha_B(t-y)) \right.$$
$$\left. - \sum_{m=1}^{\infty} P_{mV}(y) \beta_B^{j-m} I_{j+m}(\alpha_B(t-y)) \right] e^{-(\lambda+\mu_B)(t-y)}\, dy. \tag{10}$$

Therefore, for $j = 1, 2, 3, \ldots,$

$$P_{jB}(t) = \gamma \int_0^t e^{-(\lambda+\mu_B)(t-y)} \sum_{m=1}^{\infty} \beta_B^{j-m} P_{mV}(y) \left[I_{j-m}(\alpha_B(t-y)) - I_{j+m}(\alpha_B(t-y)) \right] dy. \tag{11}$$

Thus, we expressed $P_{jB}(t)$ in terms of $P_{jV}(t),\ j = 1, 2, 3, \ldots$.

3.2 Evaluation of $P_{jV}(t)$

We will express $P_{jV}(t),\ j \geq 1$ in terms of $P_{00}(t)$.

In the sequel, let $f(s)$ denote the Laplace transform of the function $f(t)$.

On taking the Laplace transforms of the system (1) and (2) and rearranging, we get

$$f_{00}(s) = \frac{1}{s + \lambda - \mu_V \dfrac{f_{1V}(s)}{f_{00}(s)} - \mu_B \dfrac{f_{1B}(s)}{f_{00}(s)}}, \tag{12}$$

and

$$\frac{f_{1V}(s)}{f_{00}(s)} = \frac{\lambda}{s + \lambda + \mu_V + \gamma - \mu_V \dfrac{f_{2V}(s)}{f_{1V}(s)}}, \tag{13}$$

and from (3), for $j = 2, 3, 4, \ldots,$

$$\frac{f_{jV}(s)}{f_{j-1,V}(s)} = \frac{\lambda}{s + \lambda + \mu_V + \gamma - \mu_V \dfrac{f_{j+1,V}(s)}{f_{jV}(s)}}.$$

Iterating the equation, for $j = 2, 3, \ldots,$ we get

$$\frac{f_{jV}(s)}{f_{j-1,V}(s)} = \frac{\lambda}{s + \lambda + \mu_V + \gamma -} \, \frac{\lambda \mu_V}{s + \lambda + \mu_V + \gamma -} \cdots. \tag{14}$$

On utilizing (13) and (14), we arrive at

$$f_{jV}(s) = \beta_V^j \left[\frac{p_V - \sqrt{p_V^2 - \alpha_V^2}}{\alpha_V} \right]^j f_{00}(s), \tag{15}$$

where $p_V = s + \lambda + \mu_V + \gamma$, $\alpha_V = 2\sqrt{\lambda\mu_V}$ and $\beta_V = \sqrt{\frac{\lambda}{\mu_V}}$,

which on inversion yields, for $n = 1, 2, 3, \ldots$,

$$P_{jV}(t) = \lambda\beta_V^{j-1} \int_0^t e^{-(\lambda+\mu_V+\gamma)y}[I_{j-1}(\alpha_V y) - I_{j+1}(\alpha_V y)]\ P_{00}(t-y)dy. \quad (16)$$

From (11) and (15), for $n = 1$,

$$\begin{aligned} \frac{f_{1V}(s)}{f_{00}(s)} &= \beta_V A_V(s), \\ \frac{f_{1B}(s)}{f_{00}(s)} &= \frac{\gamma}{\mu_B} \sum_{m=1}^{\infty} [\beta_V \beta_B^{-1}]^m\ [A_V(s) A_B(s)]^m, \end{aligned} \quad (17)$$

where

$$A_V(s) = \frac{p_V - \sqrt{p_V^2 - \alpha_V^2}}{\alpha_V}; \quad A_B(s) = \frac{p_B - \sqrt{p_B^2 - \alpha_B^2}}{\alpha_B}$$

and $p_B = s + \lambda + \mu_B$.

Substituting (17) in (12), we get after some algebra,

$$f_{00}(s) = \frac{2}{\alpha_V} \sum_{m=0}^{\infty} \left(\frac{\beta_V}{\beta_B}\right)^m \sum_{n_1+n_2+n_3=m} \frac{m!}{n_1!\ n_2!\ n_3!} \left(\frac{\beta_B(\mu_V+\gamma)}{\lambda}\right)^{n_2} \left(\frac{\alpha_V\gamma - \mu_V - \gamma}{\sqrt{\lambda\mu_V}}\right)^{n_3}$$
$$\times \left[A_V(s)^{m+n_3+1} A_B(s)^{n_1+n_3} - \frac{\beta_V}{\beta_B} A_V(s)^{m+n_3+2} A_B(s)^{n_1+n_3+1}\right]$$

On inversion,

$$P_{00}(t) = \frac{2}{\alpha_V} \sum_{m=0}^{\infty} \left(\frac{\beta_V}{\beta_B}\right)^m \sum_{n_1+n_2+n_3=m} \frac{m!}{n_1!\ n_2!\ n_3!} \left(\frac{\beta_B(\mu_V+\gamma)}{\lambda}\right)^{n_2} \left(\frac{\alpha_V\gamma - \mu_V - \gamma}{\sqrt{\lambda\mu_V}}\right)^{n_3}$$
$$\times \left\{\frac{\alpha_V\alpha_B}{4}\left[I_{m+n_3}(\alpha_V t) - I_{m+n_3+2}(\alpha_V t)\right] e^{-(\lambda+\mu_V+\gamma)t} * [I_{n_1+n_3-1}(\alpha_B t) - I_{n_1+n_3+1}(\alpha_B t)]e^{-(\lambda+\mu_B)t}\right.$$
$$\left. - \lambda\mu_B\left[I_{m+n_3+1}(\alpha_V t) - I_{m+n_3+3}(\alpha_V t)\right] e^{-(\lambda+\mu_V+\gamma)t} * [I_{n_1+n_3}(\alpha_B t) - I_{n_1+n_3+2}(\alpha_B t)]e^{-(\lambda+\mu_B)t}\right\}. \quad (18)$$

Hence (11), (16) and (18) completely determine all the state probabilities.

4 M/M/1 Queue with Exponential Vacation

In this section, we consider the server is completely idle during the vacation period. That is, the mean service rate μ_V is zero during the period of working vacation. Therefore, the model is discussed in section 2, reduced to decomposition for M/M/1 systems with exponential vacations. This model known as a well known M/M/1 queue vacation system with exhaustive service. In this model, the server does not take any vacations until the system becomes empty. For this model, we derive the time-dependent system size probabilities.

Let $P_{jB}(t)$ be the probability that there are j customers in the system and server serves customers in the queue. Let $P_{jV}(t)$ be the probability that there are j customers in the system and server is on vacation.

The governing equations of the model are given by

$$P'_{00}(t) = -\lambda\ P_{00}(t) + \mu_B\ P_{1B}(t), \tag{19}$$
$$P'_{1V}(t) = \lambda P_{00}(t) - [\lambda + \gamma] P_{1V}(t), \tag{20}$$
$$P'_{jV}(t) = \lambda P_{j-1,V}(t) - [\lambda + \gamma] P_{jV}(t), \quad j \geq 2, \tag{21}$$
$$P'_{1B}(t) = -[\lambda + \mu_B] P_{1B}(t) + \mu_B P_{2B}(t) + \gamma P_{1V}(t), \tag{22}$$
$$P'_{jB}(t) = \lambda P_{j-1,B}(t) - [\lambda + \mu_B] P_{jB}(t) + \mu_B P_{j+1,B}(t) + \gamma P_{jV}, \quad j \geq 2. \tag{23}$$

and assume that initially the system is empty.

Laplace transform of the equations (20) and (21) gives,

$$f_{jV}(s) = \left(\frac{\lambda}{s + \lambda + \gamma}\right)^j f_{00}(s), \quad j \geq 1.$$

On inversion, we get

$$P_{jV}(t) = \frac{\lambda^j t^{j-1}}{(j-1)!} e^{-(\lambda+\gamma)t} * P_{00}(t), \quad j \geq 1.$$

Laplace transform of (19) gives,

$$f_{00}(s) = \frac{1}{s + \lambda} + \frac{\mu_B}{s + \lambda} f_{1B}(s) \tag{24}$$

From (11), for $j = 1$

$$P_{1B}(t) = \gamma \int_0^t e^{-(\lambda+\mu_B)(t-y)} \sum_{m=1}^{\infty} \frac{1}{\beta_B^{m-1}} P_{mV}(y) \left[I_{m-1}(\alpha_B(t-y)) - I_{m+1}(\alpha_B(t-y))\right] dy.$$

and its Laplace transform is given by

$$f_{1B}(s)(s) = \frac{\gamma}{\mu_B} \sum_{m=1}^{\infty} \left(\frac{\lambda/\beta_B}{s + \lambda + \gamma}\right)^m \left(\frac{p_B - \sqrt{p_B^2 - \alpha_B^2}}{\alpha_B}\right)^m f_{00}(s). \tag{25}$$

Substituting (25) in (24) and after some simple algebra, we see that

$$f_{00}(s) = \sum_{k=0}^{\infty} \frac{\gamma^k}{(s+\lambda)^{k+1}} \left[\sum_{m=0}^{\infty} \left(\frac{\lambda/\beta_B}{s + \lambda + \gamma}\right)^{m+1} \left(\frac{p_B - \sqrt{p_B^2 - \alpha_B^2}}{\alpha_B}\right)^{m+1}\right]^k$$

Inversion yields,

$$P_{00}(t) = \lambda \mu_B \sum_{k=0}^{\infty} \frac{\gamma^k t^k}{k!} e^{-\lambda t} * \left[\sum_{m=0}^{\infty} \frac{(\lambda t/\beta_B)^m}{m!} e^{-(\lambda+\gamma)t} * [I_m(\alpha_B(t-y)) - I_{m+2}(\alpha_B(t-y))] e^{-(\lambda+\mu_B)t}\right]^{*k}$$

where $*$ denotes convolution and '$*k$' denotes k-fold convolution.

Hence we obtained all the transient probabilities for the number of customers in the system.

5 Stationary Analysis

In this section, we obtain the stationary system size distribution of single server queue with working vacation from the time-dependent system size probabilities which we were obtained in the previous section. The steady-state probability distribution π_{nj}, $n = 0, 1, 2, \ldots; j = 0, V, B$ can be found using the well known properties of the Laplace transforms.

It is well known that for steady-state,

$$\rho_V = \frac{\lambda}{\mu_V} < 1, \quad \rho_B = \frac{\lambda}{\mu_B} < 1,$$

and

$$\lim_{t \to \infty} P_{nj}(t) = \pi_{nj} = \lim_{s \to 0} s\hat{f}_{nj}(s), \; n = 0, 1, 2 \ldots; j = 0, V, B.$$

From (15),

$$\pi_{nV} = \lim_{s \to 0} sf_{nV}(s) = \left[\frac{1 + \rho_V + \theta_V - \sqrt{(1 + \rho_V + \theta_V)^2 - 4\rho_V}}{2}\right]^n \pi_{00}.$$

Laplace transform of (11) is

$$f_{nB}(s) = \frac{\gamma f_{00}(s)}{\sqrt{p_B^2 - \alpha_B^2}} \sum_{m=1}^{\infty} \beta_B^{n-m} \left(\frac{p_V - \sqrt{p_V^2 - \alpha_V^2}}{2\mu_V}\right)^m$$
$$\times \left[\left(\frac{p_B - \sqrt{p_B^2 - \alpha_B^2}}{\alpha_B}\right)^{|n-m|} - \left(\frac{p_B - \sqrt{p_B^2 - \alpha_B^2}}{\alpha_B}\right)^{n+m}\right].$$

From this equation, for n=1,2,..., we have

$$\pi_{nB} = \lim_{s \to 0} sf_{nB}(s)$$
$$= \frac{2\gamma\pi_{00}}{\mu_B[1 - \rho_V - \theta_V + \sqrt{(1 + \rho_V + \theta_V)^2 - 4\rho_V}]} \sum_{m=1}^{n} \rho_B^{n-m} \left[\frac{1 + \rho_V + \theta_V - \sqrt{(1 + \rho_V + \theta_V)^2 - 4\rho_V}}{2}\right]^m.$$

Further,

$$\pi_{00} = \frac{\mu_B(1 - A_V)^2(1 - \rho_B)}{\mu_B(1 - A_V)(1 - \rho_B) + \gamma A_V}$$

where $A_V = \dfrac{1 + \rho_V + \theta_V - \sqrt{(1 + \rho_V + \theta_V)^2 - 4\rho_V}}{2}$ and $\theta_V = \dfrac{\gamma}{\mu_V}$.

These stationary distributions agree with the results obtained by Servi and Finn [8]

6 Numerical Illustration

In this section, extensive numerical work is done to depict the behaviour of state probabilities and other performance measure like expected system size in time dependent regime. Figure 1 and Figure 2 depict the variations of the time dependent probabilities of the number of customers in the system when the server is not in working vacation and in working vacation respectively, for the parameters $\lambda = 3, \mu_B = 4, \mu_V = 2.5, \gamma = 0.01$. For the sake of clarity, only a few probability curves are shown. Figure 3 shows time dependent probabilities for the server is in usual working period (not in working vacation) for two different values of $\mu_B = 4$ and 6 and for the same $\lambda = 3, \mu_V = 2.5, \gamma = 0.1$. From this figure, we understand that the system size probability values for $\mu_B = 4$ take larger values than for $\mu_B = 6$.

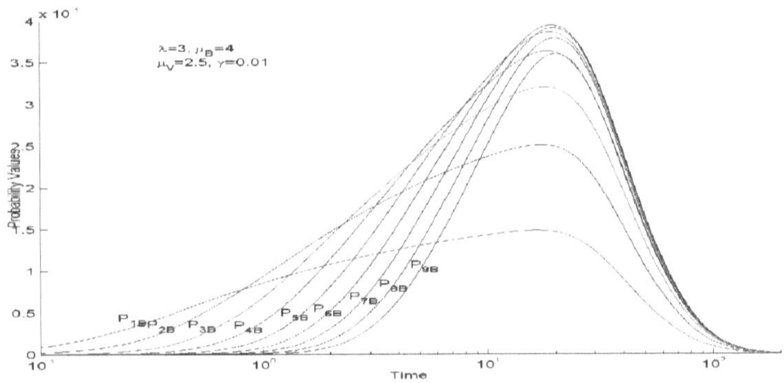

Fig. 1. Probability values for the number of customers in the system when the server is not on working vacation

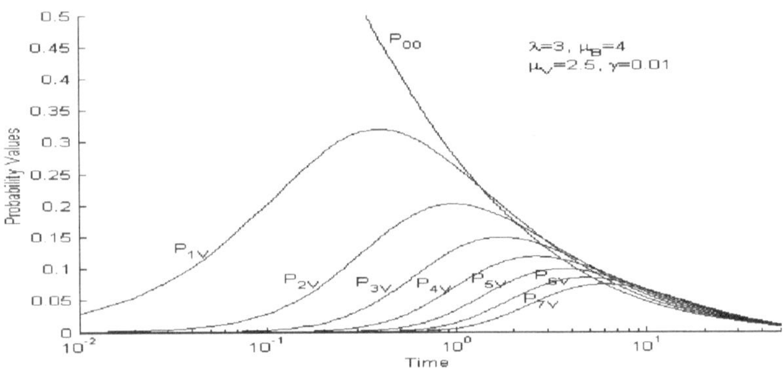

Fig. 2. Probability values for the number of customers in the system when the server is on working vacation

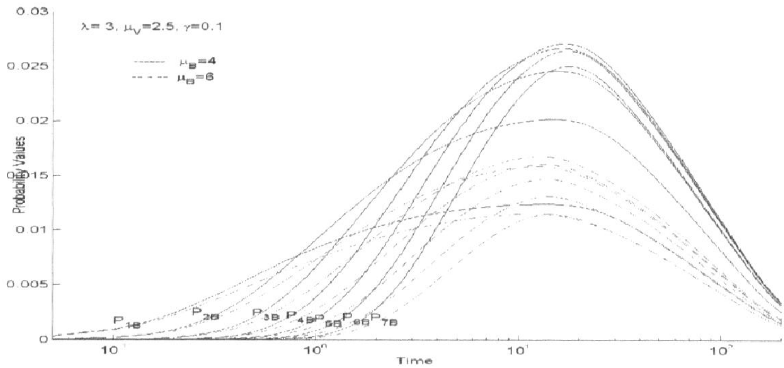

Fig. 3. Probability values for the number of customers in the system for the service rates $\mu_B = 4$ and $\mu_B = 6$

7 Conclusion

In this paper a single server working vacation queueing model is considered. Analytical expressions for time-dependent system size probabilities are derived in closed form. Numerical illustrations are presented to visualize the system performance.

References

1. Baba, Y.: Analysis of a GI/M/1 queue with multiple working vacations. Oper. Res. Letters 33, 201–209 (2005)
2. Banik, A.D., Gupta, U.C., Pathak, S.S.: On the GI/M/1/N queue with multiple working vacations-analytic analysis and computation. Appl. Math. Modelling 31, 1701–1710 (2007)
3. Doshi, B.T.: Queueing system with vacations - a survey. Queueing Syst. 1, 29–66 (1986)
4. Jain, M., Jain, A.: Working vacations queueing model with multiple types of server breakdowns. Appl. Math. Modelling 34, 1–13 (2010)
5. Liu, W., Xu, X., Tian, N.: Stochastic decompositions in the M/M/1 queue with working vacations. Oper. Res. Letters 35, 595–600 (2007)
6. Parthasarathy, P.R., Sudhesh, R.: Exact transient solution of state-dependent birth-death processes. J. App. Math. and Stoc. Analysis 2006, 1–16 (2006)
7. Parthasarathy, P.R., Sudhesh, R.: Exact Transient solution of a discrete time queue with state-dependent rates. American J. Math. and Mgt. Sci. 26, 253–276 (2006)
8. Servi, L.D., Finn, S.G.: M/M/1 queues with working vacations (M/M/1/WV). Perform. Evaluation 50, 41–52 (2002)
9. Sudhesh, R.: Transient analysis of a queue with system disasters and customer impatience. Queueing Syst. 66, 95–105 (2010)
10. Tian, N., Zhang, Z.G.: Vacation Queueing Models: Theory and Applications. Springer, New York (2006)
11. Xiu, C., Tian, N., Liu, Y.: The M/M/1 Queue with Single Working Vacation Serving at a Slower Rate during the Start-up Period. Jornal of Mathematics Research 2, 98–102 (2010)

APD: ARM Deceptive Phishing Detector System Phishing Detection in Instant Messengers Using Data Mining Approach

Mohd Mahmood Ali[1] and Lakshmi Rajamani[2]

[1] Department of CSE, Muffakham Jah College of Engineering & Technology, Banjara Hills, Hyderabad, India
[2] Department of CSE, University College of Engineering & Technology, Osmania University, Hyderabad, India
{mahmoodedu,drlakshmiraja}@gmail.com

Abstract. Deceptive Phishing, is the major problem in Instant Messengers, one is able to disclose sensitive information, including personal information, fact or even patterns that are not supposed to be disclosed, the simplistic solution to address this problem of privacy in Instant Messengers (IM) is presented using Association Rule mining technique a data mining approach. Online criminals have adapted traditional fraudulent schemes like phishing in electronic form. Increasingly, such schemes target an individual's IM where they mingle among masked by honest communications. The targeting and conniving nature of these schemes are an infringement upon an individual's personal privacy as well as a threat to personal safety. In order to focus on privacy preserving the proposed APD (Anti phishing detector) system embeds association rule mining (ARM) technique in IM's to detect deceptive phishing. There are many techniques developed to tackle e-mail phishing, a little research literature not yet done on deceptive phishing in Instant Messengers where the identification of user is often unknown to users. This is one of the motivating factor for the research project described, tested and experimented.

Keywords: Data Mining, Instant Messenger, Deceptive Phishing, Association Rule Mining, Anti Phishing Detector.

1 Introduction

Phishing[1] is a fraudulent trick of stealing victim's personal information by sending spoofed messages through Instant Messengers and e-mails[7] via socially engineered messages. Over the past decades online identity fraud has transformed from being a small scale attack to huge spread syndicated crime as identified in e-mails[7], but no concrete work yet done to detect deceptive phishing in Instant messengers[1], which is one of the fastest means for communication.

Data mining techniques emerged to address problems of understanding ever-growing volumes of information for structured and unstructured data[12], finding frequent patterns within huge data, is done using Association rule mining technique[6].

P.V. Krishna, M.R. Babu, and E. Ariwa (Eds.): ObCom 2011, Part I, CCIS 269, pp. 490–502, 2012.

In Instant messenger[2] phisher tries to find out the password and security related information through questions by pretending as a trustworthy chat-mate. In IM's, deceptive phishing has to be tackled dynamically and there are no robust techniques yet developed to do this, as the existing anti phishing techniques are equipped to deal with static phishing[3][7].

In static Anti-phishing technique, a black list of suspected clients is maintained in centralized black list service[3] which disseminates vetted black list to end clients for enforcement. These techniques are ineffective for Instant Messengers to detect phishing there are two categories of deceptive phishing attacks popularly employed in Instant messengers:

1. Password Phishing Scenarios
2. Security question phishing Scenarios

1.1 Password Phishing Scenarios

1. Hello, My name is Steve, I am a Customer Service Representative, due to recent (insert technical problem here) we lost your password on file. Please send an IM with your password to restore access to IM.
2. Dear IM Members, due to a recent (insert technical problem here), Our records have been damaged, please respond with your password to continue your service from termination.
3. Your screen name is now signed into Instant Messenger in two locations. To sign off other locations, reply to the message with your password.
4. We have noticed you have sent spam links to other members, to stop these messages please type 1 and your password.

All the above four scenario's are designed directly to steal the victims password[4].

1.2 Security Questioning Phishing Scenarios

1. Hey, I have pets too, my dog's name is Tyke, What's your pet's name?
2. Cool, My Favorite Food is Pizza, what's your favorite food?
3. Yaw one of my favorite teachers was Ms. Smith, who was your favorite teacher?
4. I just wanted to see if I know you, what street do you live on again?
5. LOL My dad's middle name is Antoine, what was your dad's middle name?
6. The Yankees? I like the red sox, I hope they aren't your favorite sports team?
7. Aw that's sweet when did you get married?
8. You graduated? Wow! Which high school did you go to?

In the second scenarios the phisher tries to trace out the personal information by acting as a trustworthy person and thereby gain access to his confidential data.

There is no robust technique to deal with such attacks to our knowledge this is the first attempt to apply, Association rule mining technique[10]on the tables/log files extracted from transaction database(TDB) using Information retrieval system[14], when the messages are exchanged between chat-mates in instant messenger shown in table 1.

Our Contribution includes integrating an Instant Messaging System with a Phishing Detection System, using data mining technique of Associative rules[6] and

Information retrieval technique which detects dynamic phishing in Instant messages. The proposed system named as APD(Anti-phishing Detector), detects Phishing in Instant Messengers.

In this paper we proposed, an Anti-phishing system APD that dynamically traces out any potential phishing attacks when messages exchanged between clients of an Instant Messaging System. The current Instant Messaging Systems doesn't have any means to deal with Phishing.

The remainder of this paper is organized as follows: This Section provides an overview of Instant Messaging System and deficiencies exists Section 2 explains the problem statement and work done till date where as Section 3 explains the architecture of the proposed system. Section 4 explains general process followed in the proposed system is explained Section 5 shows experimental results with patterns generated for threshold support and confidence during a traditional Phishing scenario shown in table 1. Section 6 concludes the paper with an outlook to future research directions.

2 Problem Statement in Instant Messaging System and Related Work

As many as 47,324 phishing attacks were analyzed by the APWG[1] in the year 2010, phishers are constantly experimenting and adapting. In a typical phishing scenario, through mail[1] phisher sets up fake website and tricks the people logging to the fake website page and collects confidential and personal information, specifically phishing in e-banking sector[8]. The adoption and use of instant messengers in most of countries became the useful tool in day to day life[9]for quick response, studies of IM text messaging and file transfer frequency reveals the brief discussion in aspects of worms, analysis and countermeasures in IMs[15].

Popular systems such as AOLs Instant Messenger, Microsoft's MSN Messenger, ICQ, Yahoo Messenger, Google Talk, Skype and Internet Relay Chat (IRC) have changed the way we communicate with friends, acquaintances, and business colleagues. Once limited to desktops, popular instant messaging systems are finding their way onto handheld devices and cell phones, allowing users to chat from virtually anywhere. According to IDC[12], the number of corporate instant messaging users is expected to grow to over 500 million by 2012 with an additional 800 million home computer users having IM systems. Unfortunately, while IM systems have the ability to fundamentally change the way we communicate and do business, many of today's implementations pose security challenges. Most IM systems presently in use were designed with scalability rather than security in mind with respect to deceptive phishing attacks. Virtually some freeware IM programs lack encryption capabilities and most have features that bypass traditional corporate firewalls, making it difficult to control instant messaging usage. Some of these systems have insecure password management and are vulnerable to account spoofing and denial-of-service (DoS) attacks. Even worse, no firewall in the market today can scan instant messaging deceptive phishing. While instant messaging may seem like a new technology, it is actually decades old.

The IRC system developed in 1988 by Jarkko Oikarinen3 still in use, this system allows users to form ad-hoc discussion groups to chat peer-to-peer with one another and exchange files seen today in many different messengers that provide the same basic service, without detecting deceptive phishing messages.

The basic Instant Messaging architecture provides functionality of chat, news alerts, and conferences[2][15]. Instant Messaging resources includes Web server, Lightweight Directory Access Protocol(LDAP) server[13]. In this scenario first LDAP server provides user entries for authentication and lookup, second clients download the Instant Messaging resources from web server or System Application Server thirdly clients are always connected to Instant Messaging server through an Instant Messaging multiplexor.

Comparative study of AOL, Yahoo and MSN Instant Messengers with features and functions taxonomy discussed[16] along with protocols used for passing Instant messages. The feature of IM to collect and analyze information in e-learning environment[14] helped the users flexibility of easy learning methodology coupled with presence and availability of management services emerging as killer application in wireless and wire-line networks[19].The filtering and spam detection in IM poured new life to IMs[15]. Integration of IMs in mobile collaborative learning helped the mobile users[17] but ability to detect and filter deceptive phishing is incomplete.

Probabilistic relational algebra for the integration of information retrieval and database systems proposed[18] architecture for personal semantic web information retrieval system by integrating web services and web contents[24] enhanced, Ontology-based intelligent information retrieval system[20] is currently used in web mining.

A Phishing Detection Tool[21], security and identification indicators for browsers against Spoofing and Phishing Attacks[22],[26] is known but detecting and identifying phishing websites in real-time is difficult tasks as it depends on many factors like (URL & Domain Identity) and (Security & Encryption)[23] identifying vulnerabilities which allow these phishing sites to be created and suggest methods to identify common attacks that helped webmasters and their hosting companies to defend their servers[25], Legal Risks For Phishing Researchers[4]. Now-a-days people is using social phishing in IM.

This section describes significant vulnerabilities that are present in common instant messaging systems and the types of attacks that can exploit the users leading to phishing.

3 Proposed Work and System Architecture

In this paper we present an association rule mining technique (Apriori algorithm) to detect Deceptive Phishing, suspicious messages sent using Instant Messenger between two or more or different clients/chatters stored in Transaction Database(TDB) using Information retrieval system technique(stemming, ignore words(IGWDB)) the frequent reoccurring words are extracted from the TDB dynamically using Association rule mining technique and stored in transaction pattern database(TPDB) Table 1 illustrates the scenario with an example then rules are constructed dynamically for the words exists in the TPDB which satisfies the user-defined minimum threshold support and confidence(threshold value)[6]. If the condition is true phish words are pushed to Phishing Database (PDB) then alert message is sent from PDB to clients. It is developed specifically to detect phishing of unusual and deceptive communication in IM's. The proposed method is implemented using java language. In implementation, there are four (4) major functional parts :

1. Storing the Instant Messenger messages in TDB(day to day transaction (or) skewed days)
2. Extracting relevant words, using IRS[11] technique (includes stemming, ignoring words (IGWDB)) from TDB database and storing in TPDB database using Association rule mining Technique eg: I1, I2,….In. For words extracted, including mail-ids.
3. Constructing rules dynamically that satisfies minimum support and minimum confidence threshold value which is user defined.
4. Phishing words are stored in Phishing word database (PDB) and alert to IM client at one side or either side based on APDP-IM installed.

Table 1. Shows the chatting between the two clients and words extracted from them stored in TDB database

T1	I1, I2, I3, I4, I5, I6
T2	I1, I2, I7, I8, I9, I10
T3	I1, I2, I12, I13
T4	I1, I2, I4, I15, I16
T5	I1, I2, 112, I14, I15, I16

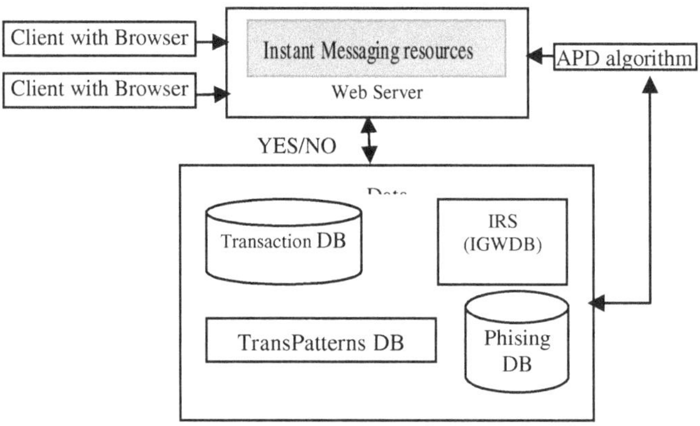

Fig. 1. System architecture of ARMP-IM (3-tier)

The architecture of ARM Phishing detector system includes four (4) main subsystems in figure.1 is 3-Tier Architecture as follows:

1. The Instant Messaging System(web browser).
2. Information Retrieval System.
3. The Databases (TDB, IGWDB, PDB, TPDB).
4. The APD algorithm (Apriori).

3.1 The Instant Messaging System

The component of the system includes:

A. Client machines with browsers.
B. A Web server that provides Instant Messaging Resources.

C. Instant Message Multiplexer to multiplex the communications (only text included).
D. A Directory Server that holds the identities of the clients and helps in authenticating a client.
E. A messaging server that forwards offline line messages whenever the user starts his next session using SMTP [15].

3.2 Information Retrieval System(IRS)

The IRS is used to filter key words from the messages and forward them to the ARM Anti-Phisher component for further processing. Index based Retrieval is a popular approach that most Information Retrieval Systems employ. The IRS follows filtering out the data by break the messages in appropriate form.

A transaction database TDB stores all the messages sent between the clients in TDB database by checking the Ignore words in IGWDB database like words like "of, in, about, although e.t.c" do not have any importance in Information Retrieval. Similarly Stop Words or Stop List contains words that cannot be used for indexing which mostly contains prepositions, articles, adverbs, adjectives and some commonly used words. The removal of keywords improves the retrieval efficiency as unnecessary words are filtered out, noise reduction is the aim of this step.

Stemming of the words is done, it is the process for reducing inflected (or sometimes derived) words to their stem, base or root form. The process of stemming is often called as conflation or Stemmer algorithm. Examples of Stemmers include Brute Force Algorithm, Suffix Stripping algorithms, Lemmatization Algorithms, Stochastic Algorithm or others. A stemmer for English, for example, should identify the string "cats" (and possibly "catlike", "catty" etc.) as based on the root "cat", and "stemmer", "stemming", "stemmed" as based on "stem". A stemming algorithm reduces the words "fishing", "fished", "fish", and "fisher" to the root word, "fish".

Finally the Transaction database (TDB) database filtered data is stored for further processing for Apriori Algorithm.

3.3 The Database

The Apriori algorithm[6] which is the heart of the system, scans the TDB database and checks for phishing patterns if patterns found stores in Transaction Pattern Database TPDB database.

Transaction Pattern database TPDB database is again scanned by using Apriori algorithm[6] for phishing words if phish words are detected, they are stored in Phishing database PDB database.

3.4 Apriori Algorithm

Once the Databases are constructed i.e TDB database, the Apriori algorithm applied twice, firstly to find patterns from TDB database, next to find phishing words from PDB database. Two Level of strong checking is performed, for detecting phishing words, shown figure 3.

In Table 1 shown above captures the transactions in TDB database performed between the two clients are captured and keywords are extracted, unique identification numbers given in above table, totally 16 keywords are extracted from both the chat mates.

The rules extracted from table 1 using Association rules Technique[6], shown as follows, with support=2 and confidence=75% defined by the user are given below. These rules are extracted from the table 1.

The Items in transaction which satisfies support=2 or 20% are[{I1,I2,I12},{I1,I2,I14}, {I1,I2,I15},{I1,I2,I16}]and the confidence=100% which satisfies are {I1^I12=>I2 , I2^I12=>I1, I12=>I1^I2, I1^I14=>I2, I2^I14=>I1, I14=>I1^I2, I1^I15=>I2, I2^I15=>I1 , I15=>I1^I2 , I1^I16=>I2 , I2^I16=>I1 , I16=>I1^I2}.

The chatting messages are identified and detected by the APD system and intimates to the users at the client side when the phishing is found, at one or both the ends, depends on where the APD system is installed, the general process working of APD is shown in figure. 2.

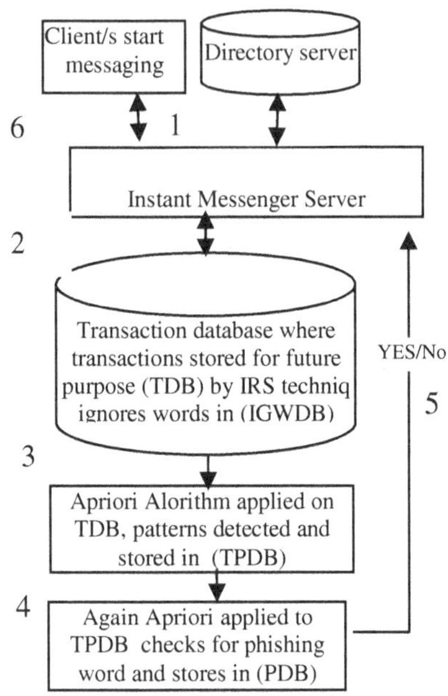

Fig. 2. Shows the overview of the process in which each component of the system interacts with other

The steps of figure 2. are as follows;

1. The client client enabled with a browser establishes a connection with the Instant messaging Server, checks for authentication of the client through the Directory Server. If client is authenticated he can start sending messages.
2. The Instant Messenger Server forwards the messages to transaction database(TDB), where messages exchanged between two clients are stored, by

checking Ignore word database (IGWDB) using IRS technique where filter of words is done.

3. Apriori Alorithm applied on TDB, patterns detected are stored in Transaction pattern database (TPDB).
4. Again Apriori applied to TPDB checks for phishing words and stores in Phishing database (PDB).
5. If phishing words detected, forwards a Yes to the Instant messenger server else No.
6. If Yes is the result, the instant messenger passes an alert message to the victim client about the possible phishing attack else if No is the result the Instant Messenger server proceeds further.

The Working of the ARMP-IM algorithm is shown in figure 3.

Algorithm 1: For storing transactions and reporting to IM client regarding phishing.

Input: Instant Messages in Transaction Database
(TDB)(day to day)
Output: Alert phishing message to IM client if detected

```
1  Do   //Apply IRS for filtering and pick words and push to (TDB)
2  { Do     //Scan TDB for Relevant patterns
            //Apply Apriori technique find patterns from TDB
            // and push to Transaction pattern database (TPDB)
    { Call Apriori and Scan TDB        //generates patterns from TDB and
            //stores in TPDB
3    Push patterns to TPDB }
4  Untill TDB!=NULL
            //Apply apriori find min_support and confidence for TPDB
5  Re-CALL (Apriori algorithm) and apply to TPDB
6  { Derive association rules dynamically for freq_words
7    Calculate confidence//user defined
8    Check the rules satisfying threshold //user-defined
9   If (Confidence satisfies Threshold value)
          // Pick relevant words
          // Push Phishing words in PDB permanently
10 { Scan TPDB and Push words to PDB
11  }While TPDB=PDB //satisfy min threshold support & Conf.
12  }     If detected
13      Report to Instant messenger client as phishing word
14     else
15       Return to IM   // do nothing
16  }
17 Untill TPDB!=NULL
```

Fig. 3. Shows the working of ARMP-IM and detect deceptive phishing messages

4 Implementation and Experimental Results

ARMP-IM implemented using *Apache TomCat 6.0* for Web Server for creating separate sessions for each user with Browser support(*IExplorer 6.5 or higher*), *SQL Server 2005* for Database and *Java 6.0* for Apriori Algorithm for finding frequent patterns, as well as Information retrieval from database using *odbc /jdbc* drivers for connectivity.

The sequence of flow of steps is clearly mentioned in figure 2. when the messages are sent between the chat messages the number of databases dynamically used named as *chatData/TDB*(stores messages between the current chat-mates, *chatData_bkp*(stores historical chat messages),*Ignorewords/IGWDB*(stores ignore words, preposition,etc. which is to be neglected used by IRS), *phishwords/PDB*(stores phishing words detected dynamically), *Transpatters/TPDB*(stores frequent patterns detected). as given in figure 4.

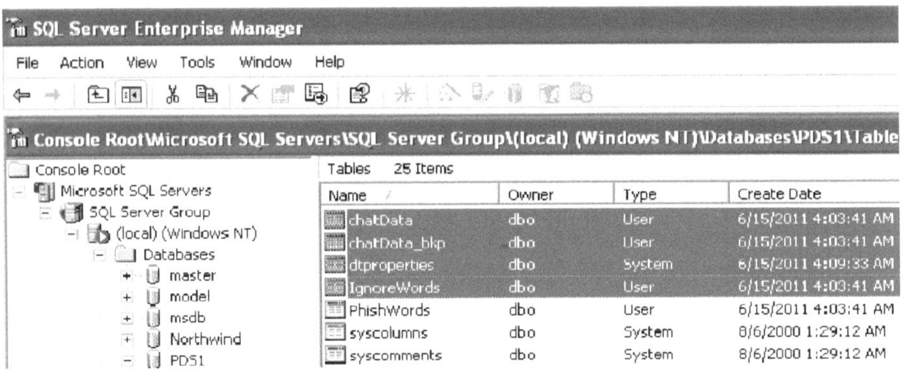

Fig. 4. Shows the Databases(TDB, IGWDB,TPDB,PDB, and ChatbackupDB) which is used by DataProcess

DataProcess program perform the operation of detecting phishing words using TPDB database, which consists of patterns generated between the chat mates using TDB database, DataProcess program consists of Information retrieval technique and Apriori Algorithm, DataProcess program must always be running in active state which generates frequent patterns from the messages and detect phishing words dynamically as shown in figure 5. the phish words detected are updated to PDB database.

3. Periodic deletion of transactions leads to defragmention problem.
4. Instant messengers must be enhanced to detect audio and text phishing collaboratively.

The future looks green as the ARMP-IM can be enhanced to meet the requirements of wireless Instant messengers, mobile Instant Messengers for 3G and 4G Technology. The APDP-IM can be integrated in Instant Messengers if they wish to share the data and avoids Deceptive Phishing attacks we have tested with our own IM system.

References

1. Apwg phishing activity trends (February 2011), http://www.antiphishing.org/reports
2. http://www.docs.sun.com/source/819-0063/im-architecture.html
3. Atighetchi, M., Pal, P.: Attribute-based Prevention of Phishing Attacks Copyright 2009, BBN Technologies (2009)
4. Soghoian, C.: Legal Risks For Phishing Researchers. IEEE Explorer (2009)
5. Chen, K.-T., Huang, C.-R., Chen, C.-S.: Fighting phishing with discriminative key point features. IEEE Internet Community (2010)
6. Agrawal, R., Srikant, R.: Fast algorithms for mining association rules. In: Proceedings of 20th International on Very Large Data Bases VLDB, pp. 487–499. Morgan Kaufmann (1994)
7. Appavu alias Balamurugan, S., Aravind, Athiappan, Bharathiraja, Pandian, M., Rajaram, R.: Association Rule Mining for Suspicious Email Detection: A Data Mining Approach. IEEE
8. Aburrous, M., et al.: Modelling Intelligent Phishing Detection System for e-Banking using Fuzzy Data Mining. IEEE (2009)
9. Rhe, K.Y., Kim, W.-B.: The Adoption and Use of the Internet in South Korea. Journal of Computer-Mediated Communication (2004)
10. Han, J., Kamber, M.: Data mining concepts and techniques, 2nd edn (2006)
11. Kowalski, G.J., Maybury, M.T.: Information storage and retrieval system theory and implementation, 2nd edn. Springer, Heidelberg (2006)
12. The premier global market intelligence firm, http://www.idc.com/research/
13. Salim, M., et al.: Data Retrieval and Security Using Lightweight Directory Access Protocol. In: Second International Workshop on Knowledge Discovery and Data Mining, WKDD (2009)
14. Lee, H., Park, D., Hong, M.: An instant messenger system for learner analysis in e-learning environment. In: SIGITE 2008: Proceedings of the 9th ACM SIGITE Conference on Information Technology Education (2008)
15. Liu, Z., Lin, W., Li, N., Lee, D.: Detecting and filtering instant messaging spam - a global and personalized approach. In: 1st IEEE ICNP Workshop on Secure Network Protocols (NPSec), November 6 (2005)
16. Jennings, R.B., et al.: A study of Internet instant messaging and chat protocols. IEEE Network 20(4), 16–21 (2006)
17. KaiFang, F.: Design and implementation of an instant messaging architecture for mobile collaborative learning. In: ISECS International Colloquium on Computing, Communication, Control, and Management, CCCM 2009 (August 2009)

18. Fuhr, N., Rölleke, T.: A probabilistic relational algebra for the integration of information retrieval and database systems. ACM Transactions on Information Systems, TOIS (January 1997)
19. Debbabi, M., Rahman, M.: The war of presence and instant messaging: right protocols and APIs. In: First IEEE on Consumer Communications and Networking Conference, CCNC 2004 (January 2004)
20. Li, W., Feng, Z., Li, Y., Xu, Z.: Ontology based intelligent information retrieval system. In: Canadian Conference on Electrical and Computer Engineering (May 2004)
21. Yu, W.D., Nargundkar, S., Tiruthani, N.: A Phishing Detection Tool. In: 33rd Annual IEEE International Computer Software and Applications Conference Washington, USA (July 2009)
22. Herzberg, A., Jbara, A.: Security and Identification Indicators for Browsers against Spoofing and Phishing Attacks. ACM Transactions on Internet Technology 8(4), article 16 (September 2008)
23. Aburrous, M., et al.: Modelling Intelligent Phishing Detection System for e-Banking using Fuzzy Data Mining. In: International Conference on CyberWorlds (2009)
24. Yu, H., Mine, T., Amamiya, M.: Architecture for Personal Semantic Web Information Retrieval System integrating we services and web contents. In: Proceedings of the IEEE International Conference on Web Services in 2005, ICWS 2005 (2005)
25. Wardman, B., Shukla, G., Warner, G.: Identifying vulnerable websites by analysis of common strings in phishing URLs. In: eCrime Researchers Summit, eCRIME 2009 (October 2009)
26. Chen, J., Guo, C.: Online Detection and Prevention of Phishing. In: First International Conference on Communications and Networking in China (2006)

Adaptive Duplex Technique for Reduction of Turnaround Time in IEEE 802.22

Kalidoss Rajakani[1] and M.A. Bhagyaveni[2]

[1] Department of ECE, SSN College of Engineering,
Rajiv Gandhi Salai, Kalavakkam, Chennai-603110, India
[2] Department of ECE, Anna University,
College of Engineering, Guindy, Chennai-600025, India
kalidossr@ssn.edu.in, bhagya@annauniv.edu

Abstract. The IEEE 802.22 Wireless Regional Area Network (WRAN) is a first Cognitive Radio (CR) standard to provide wireless broadband services in rural areas for the coverage area of 33 to 100kms. It opportunistically uses the unused UHF/VHF TV bands by using Time Division Duplex (TDD) and Orthogonal Frequency Division Multiple Access (OFDMA) technique. However large Turnaround Time (TT) is the major deployment issues of WRAN system in rural areas. In this paper, we propose an adaptive duplex method that effectively reduces the large Turnaround Time. The results show that Adaptive duplex considerably reduces the amount of TT, increases the efficiency and throughput of the system.

Keywords: Cognitive Radio, Dynamic Spectrum Access, WRAN, IEEE 802.22, Adaptive Duplex Technique, TDD, FDD.

1 Introduction

Due to rapid development in wireless communications, a tremendous number of different communication systems exist in licensed and unlicensed bands, suitable for different demands and applications. Also the demand for additional spectrum is growing faster than technology. Interestingly, most of the recent wireless standards such as IEEE 802.11, IEEE 802.16 are developed from the unlicensed bands. Spectrum measurement report shows that the frequencies below 3 GHz are used only 5.2 % in the US in any given location and at any given time. Surprisingly, heavy spectrum utilization in unlicensed bands while licensed bands often experience low (e.g. TV bands). It informs the term 'limited radio resources' is really an artificial result of the way spectrum is regulated.

FCC (Federal Communications Commission) has defined that the spectrum management policy will be the best solution for this problem. It has made the unused TV spectrum for open use thereby making it a licensed usage for communication. The analog TV channels of frequency range 54-862MHz is available for usage. IEEE 802.22 WG (Working Group) is developing a standard for the purpose of utilizing the unused TV spectrum to provide internet access to rural areas [1]-[5]. In India around

P.V. Krishna, M.R. Babu, and E. Ariwa (Eds.): ObCom 2011, Part I, CCIS 269, pp. 503–511, 2012.

70% consists of rural areas thereby making this application to cause a major impact on the development of the society [3].

The radio spectrum is allocated for many services and this causes spectrum scarcity. This allocated spectrum has to be re-used which makes it necessary to use the concept of spectrum management. The spectrum occupancy measurement of TV bands showed significant underutilization. This underutilization resulted in the formation of TV band Notice of Proposed Rule Making by the FCC, which proposes to allow unlicensed users to operate in the TV broadcast bands. While using the TV bands we must ensure that no harmful interference is caused to the incumbent users, which include TV receivers and FCC Part 74 wireless microphones [6]. These events culminated in the formation of the IEEE 802.22 WG for WRANs in November/2004.

In the past, spectrum allocation was based on the specific band assignments designated for a particular service. Although the fixed spectrum assignment policy generally worked well in the past, there has been a dramatic increase in the access to the limited spectrum for mobile services and application in recent years. This increase is straining the effectiveness of the traditional spectrum policies. The limited available spectrum due to the nature of radio propagation and the need for more efficiency in the spectrum usage necessitates a new communication paradigm to exploit the existing spectrum opportunistically. The inefficient usage of the existing spectrum can be improved through opportunistic access to the licensed bands.

The key enabling technology of dynamic spectrum access is cognitive radio (CR), which is a promising technology that can alleviate the spectrum shortage problem. Cognitive radios have the potential to utilize the large amount of unused spectrum in an intelligent way while not interfering with other incumbent devices in frequency bands already licensed for specific uses [7]. The process of spectrum sensing to detect the free TV channels and the spectrum management policy which defines the usage of unused spectrum can be handled wisely using cognitive radio technology.

In this paper, we discuss the concept of WRAN standard which was developed for the purpose of providing internet access to rural areas and the long Turnaround time problem that exists in it. We also provide a solution for this problem by proposing an adaptive duplex technique. In section II we give a brief overview about IEEE 802.22 standard which includes the physical and MAC layer structures. In section III we describe how the adaptive duplex technique is used to reduce the Turnaround time. The section IV includes the simulation results which show the difference between the Turnaround times of conventional technique and adaptive technique.

2 An Overview of IEEE 802.22

The emerging IEEE 802.22 wireless regional area network uses the same radio spectrum allocated to TV spectrum and aims in providing internet services to rural areas. IEEE 802.22 devices in the TV bands will be unlicensed, which further lowers cost and provides affordable service in rural areas. TV stations operate from channels 2 to 69 in the VHF and UHF portion of the radio spectrum. All these channels are 6 MHz wide, and span from 54-72 MHz, 76-88 MHz, 174-216 MHz, and 470-806 MHz In addition to the TV service, also called primary service, other services such as wireless microphones are also allowed by FCC to operate on vacant TV channels on a non-interfering basis. The cell size ranges from 33 to 100 km and it consists of point to multipoint network consisting of base station and the customer premise equipments. WRAN cell can provide services to 512 users. The downlink rate is about 1.5 Mbps per CPE and uplink rate of 384 Kbps [8]. The maximum coverage of distance is due to the propagation characteristics of the TV frequency bands. As a result of the fact that 802.22 uses cognitive radio technology, it will be possible to ensure that no undue interference is caused to any existing services and users should not suffer any degradation in performance of their terrestrial television reception. Accordingly the use of IEEE 802.22 WRAN technology should enable more efficient use of the spectrum to be made as well as providing new services for users, especially in rural areas. Table 1 lists the specification parameter of IEEE 802.22 standard.

Table 1. Basic IEEE 802.22 standard specification parameters

Parameter	Specification
Typical cell radius (km)	30 - 100 km
Methodology	Spectrum sensing to identify free channels
Channel bandwidth (MHz)	6, (7, 8)
Modulation	OFDM
Channel capacity	18 Mbps
User capacity	Downlink: 1.5Mbps Uplink: 384 kbps

2.1 Physical Layer

The IEEE 802.22 physical layer provides high flexibility in terms of modulation and coding. Two types of channel bonding schemes are introduced in IEEE 802.22: contiguous and non-contiguous. In contiguous channel bonding two or more continuous channels are used to increase the capacity and in non contiguous bonding different free channels are used for transmission. The 802.22 system specifies spectral efficiencies in the range of 0.5 bit/ (sec/Hz) up to 5 bit/ (sec/Hz). If we consider an average of 3 bits/sec/Hz, this would correspond to a total PHY data rate of 18 Mbps in a 6 MHz TV channel [9]-[12]. In order to obtain the minimum data rate per CPE, a total of 12 simultaneous users have been considered which leads to a required minimum peak throughput rate at edge of coverage of 1.5 Mbps per CPE in the downstream direction. In the upstream direction, a peak throughput of 384 kbps is specified, which is comparable to DSL services.

2.2 MAC Layer

The IEEE 802.22 draft MAC layer uses the super frame structure. At the beginning of every super frame the base station sends the special preamble and the super frame control header (SCH) through each and every TV channel that can be used for communication and that meets the incumbent protection. CPEs tuned to any of the channels and who synchronizes and receives the SCH, are able to obtain all the information it needs to associate with the base station. The super frame consists of multiple transmission frames and the structure of frame is shown in the figure 1.Transmission in each frame are time slotted and are based on OFDM subcarriers .A frame consists of the upstream and the downstream sub-frames. During the life time of the super frame, multiple MAC frames are transmitted which may span multiple channels and hence can provide better system capacity, range and multipath diversity.

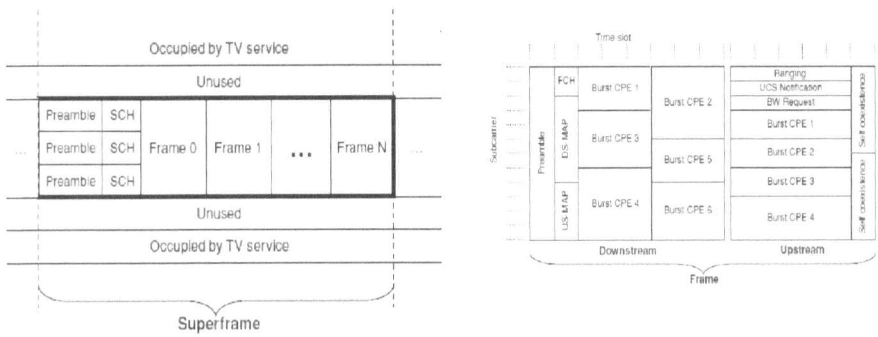

Fig. 1. Super frame structure

2.3 Sensing in IEEE 802.22

IEEE 802.22 entities carry on spectrum sensing to find the free channels. The CPE reports the sensing results to the base station and in turn the base station adjusts the bandwidth and the modulation/encoding rates. The MAC layer performs two types of sensing in either in-band or out of-band measurements: fast sensing and fine sensing. Fast sensing is done at speed of 1ms per channel, this is performed by base station and the CPEs and finally the information is carried to the base station. The fine sensing takes more than 25ms per channel. The sensing and data transmission carried simultaneously affects the quality of service and dynamic frequency hopping (DFH) is performed in parallel with sensing and data transmission in WRAN systems. And in the near future the allocated TV frequency bands would become free due to the increase in DTH (direct to home) services and sensing will not be necessary.

3 Adaptive Duplex Technique

Figure 2 illustrates adaptive duplex technique. The conventional technique used for data transmission in IEEE 802.22 is TDD. This method involves sending data to CPEs in a queue by allocating different time slots. Each CPE receives the data only during its turn. This method works well with wireless networks that consider only short range applications like Wi-Fi and cellular networks. But when it comes to long range networks like WRAN, the turnaround time becomes a major problem. The 802.22 rural networks should target large service areas, for example, up to 100 km in a coverage radius. This means that the difference in the round-trip propagation delay between nearby and edge CPE can be significant.

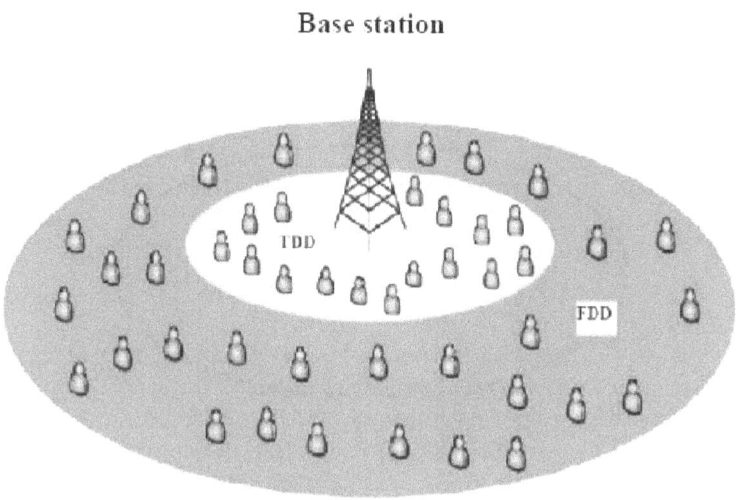

Fig. 2. Adaptive Duplex Technique

Due to the difference in propagation delay from BS to the CPE, different CPE finish the downlink reception at different time instances. Specifically, a nearby CPE can finish its DL reception long before a faraway CPE does. This also means that a nearby CPE is ready to start uplink transmission before a faraway CPE is. However, to guarantee reliable reception at the BS, the UL transmissions from different CPE must be scheduled in a way such that the OFDMA symbol boundaries are aligned at the BS. This makes TDD method to have the drawback of long turnaround time.

Fig. 3 shows the data transmission by conventional TDD technique and it is clear that the UL transmission of CPE 1 has to wait until CPE 4 completes its UL transmission. It shows that the CPE which receives the DL sub frame first will send its UL sub frame at last. This reverse order between DL and UL is the reason for the alignment of OFDMA symbol boundaries at the BS. The nearer CPEs are the most affected by this process of TDD transmission that its turnaround time is long even if they are close to the BS.

The adaptive duplex technique involves the following specifications:

- The data transmission to CPEs in the range 1 (nearer to base station) is done by TDD method.
- The data transmission to CPEs in the range 2 (farer to base station) is done by FDD method. Due to this, the time taken for data transmission in both the ranges is almost equal. Also the overall turnaround time taken is reduced than compared to the conventional TDD method.

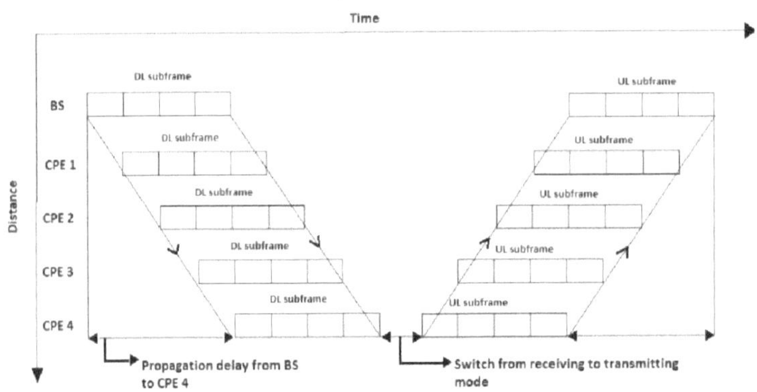

Fig. 3. Data transmission by conventional TDD

Figure 4 shows the data transmission by Adaptive Duplex Technique. Here, TDD technique is used for CPEs 1 and 2 which are nearer to BS and FDD technique for CPEs 3 and 4 which are farer from the BS. In FDD, each CPE is allocated with a unique channel that the data transmission of one CPE doesn't need to wait for other CPEs to complete. Therefore, CPEs 3 and 4 have their UL transmissions independently. This reduces the overall Turnaround time taken for the data transmission.

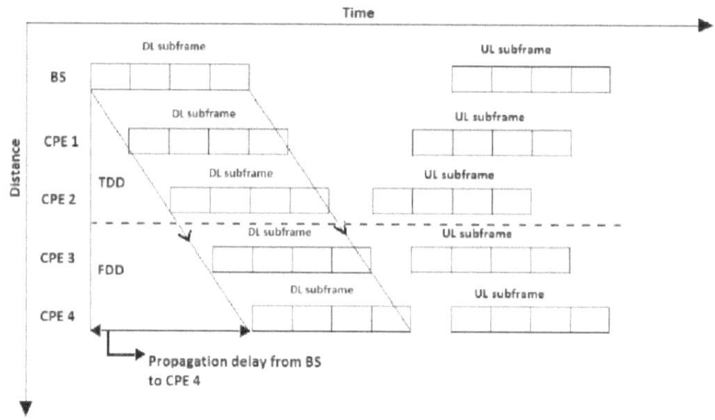

Fig. 4. Data transmission by adaptive Duplex technique

4 Simulation Results

The reduction of turnaround time by adaptive duplex technique can be witnessed using simulation results. The simulation result shows the turnaround time difference between conventional technique and adaptive technique. The variations are shown by the availability of free channels. This result depends on the result of spectrum sensing this is carried out every 2 microseconds. From Fig. 5, it is clearly shown that the turnaround time due to adaptive technique is considerably lesser than that of conventional method. In this case it is considered that the sensing result gives that 25% of the TV channels are free.

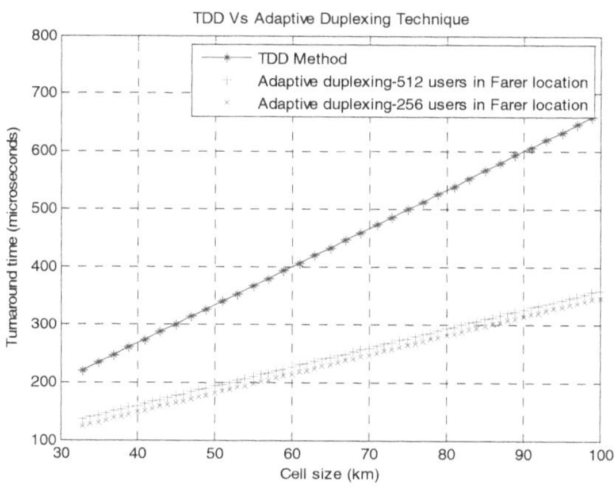

Fig. 5. Cell size vs. Turnaround time (25% channels free)

From Fig. 6, it is clearly shown that even in the worst case of all 512 users lying in the range 2, the overall turnaround time by adaptive duplex technique is considerably lesser. Also if the 512 users are equally distributed in range 1 and range 2 the turnaround time reduces further due to adaptive technique. In this case we consider that the result of sensing shows that 50% of channels are free.

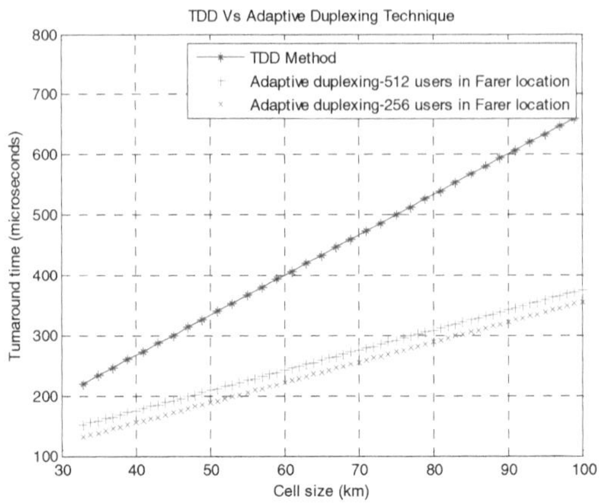

Fig. 6. Cell size vs. Turnaround time (50% channels free)

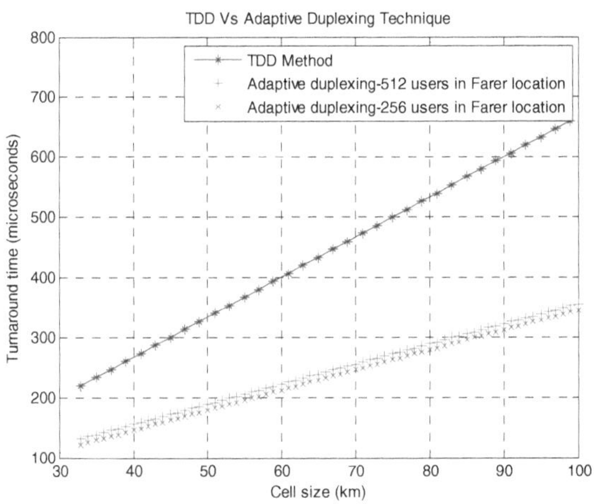

Fig. 7. Cell size vs. Turnaround time (75% channels free)

From Figure 7, it is clearly shown that if the available free channel increases then the turnaround time decreases further. In this case the sensing result shows that 75% of channels are free.

5 Conclusion

The drawback of long turnaround time in conventional TDD method has been reduced considerably using Adaptive Duplex technique. In WRAN, the splitting of range for TDD and FDD while implementing Adaptive technique is flexible. It depends on the range of base station which varies from 33 to 100km and also the number of users within the range covered by base station. The simulation results show that the turnaround time is further reduced by the factor that the availability of free channels increases. This clearly depicts that in future when the analog TV spectrum becomes completely free due to usage of digital DTH services; the Adaptive technique improves the data transmission with high throughput by reducing the turnaround time to greater extent.

References

1. Mitola, J., et al.: Cognitive Radios: Making Software Radios more Personal. IEEE Personal Communications 6(4) (1999)
2. Haykin, S.: Cognitive Radio: Brain-Empowered Wireless communications. IEEE JSAC 23(2) (2005)
3. Liang, Y.C., Hoang, A.T., Hwa, H.: Cognitive Radio on TV Bands: A New Approach to provide Wireless Connectivity for Rural areas. IEEE Wireless Communication 15(3) (2008)
4. Westerveld, R., Prasad, R.: Rural Communication in India Using Fixed Cellular Radio Systems. IEEE Comm. Mag., 70–74 (1994)
5. Liang, Y.-C., et al.: Sensing-Throughput Tradeoff for Cognitive Radio Networks. IEEE Trans. Wireless Comm. 7(4), 1326–1337 (2008)
6. Akyildiz, I.F., Lee, W.Y., Vuran, M.C., Mohanty, S.: Next generation dynamic spectrum access cognitive radio wireless networks a survey. Computer Networks Journal 50(13), 2127–2159 (2006)
7. Cordeiro, C., Challapali, K., Birru, D., Shankar, S.: IEEE 802.22: The first worldwide wireless standard based on cognitive radios. In: IEEE DySPAN, pp. 328–337 (2005)
8. Cordeiro, C., Challapali, K.: CMAC: A cognitive MAC protocol for multichannel wireless networks. In: IEEE DySPAN, pp. 147–157 (2007)
9. Federal Communications Commission, Spectrum Policy Task Force Report, FCC 02-155 (2002)
10. IEEE 802.22 Wireless RAN, Functional Requirements for the 802.22 WRAN Standard, IEEE 802.22-05/0007r46 (2005)
11. FCC, Facilitating Opportunities for Flexible, Efficient, and Reliable Spectrum Use Employing Cognitive Radio Technologies, Notice of Proposed Rule Making and Order, FCC 03-322 (2003)
12. IEEE 802.16 Working Group on Broadband wireless Access, http://www.ieee802.org/16/

WiMAX and WiFi Convergence Architecture to Achieve QoS

G.Vijayalakshmy[1] and G. Shivaradje[2]

[1] Perunthalivar Kamarajar Engineering College
vijipec_03@yahoo.co.in
[2] Pondicherry Engineering College
shivaradje@pec.edu

Abstract. The main challenge in the development of future wireless communication systems is to provide users with a wide range of services across different radio access technologies through a single mobile terminal, while maintaining the quality of service requirements. WiMAX and WiFi are considered as the promising broadband access solutions for wireless MANs and LANs, respectively. In recent works WiMAX is considered suitable as a backhaul service to connect multiple dispersed WiFi 'hotspots'. Hence a new integrated WiMAX/WiFi network has been proposed. In this paper a architecture for integrating IEEE 802.16 with IEEE 802.11 to achieve QoS is proposed. QoS parameters such as throughput, load, delay and network convergence activity are simulated through Opnet 14 for the interworking architecture of WIMAX and WLAN.

Keywords: WiFi, WiMAX, Wireless Access Networks, QoS, Opnet.

1 Introduction

Future wireless networks aim is to provide a universal ubiquitous coverage across different radio technologies through a multi-modal mobile node (MN), while offering a rich range of services with variable bandwidth and quality of service (QoS) anytime and anywhere. These features require connectivity across multiple networks with different radio technologies, over different geographic areas, and access to different types of services. Such connectivity can be provided by 4G architecture which envisions highly flexible and adaptive integration of diverse radio technologies to support built-in capability for seamless interaction in these environments. Nevertheless, integration of heterogeneous networks poses many challenges such as interface selection, seamless handoff mechanisms, coordinated configuration of QoS mechanisms and content adaptation strategies. Any mobile system in such integrated networks have to be able to adapt to changing access networks and changing environments automatically without bothering humans to intervene in order to make mobile computing feasible. To adapt to such changes, the system needs information about the environment, including various information about the access network itself, information about services supported by this access network, as well as more general information about the current context in which the mobile entity resides. The performance of WiMAX/WiFi System under Different Codecs was analyzed previously in the literature. Fixed

P.V. Krishna, M.R. Babu, and E. Ariwa (Eds.): ObCom 2011, Part I, CCIS 269, pp. 512–521, 2012.

topology of Mobile WiMAX is considered in that architecture. Mobility of the Wimax network is not considered. The analysis covered the fixed topology of the nodes because the Mobile WiMAX is not yet under operation in fully commercial domain. There are many variants of future extension which can be done over the VoIP issue [1]. The architectural performance issues of WiMAX over WiFi wireless communication in the term of wireless network design and management which upgrading the upcoming wireless communication technology over a wide region is proposed. Wireless networks are generally less efficient and irregular compared to wired networks, which make quality of service (QoS) provision a bigger challenge for wireless communications. The wireless medium has limited bandwidth, higher packet error rate, and higher packet overheads that in total to limit the capacity of the network to offer guaranteed QoS. In response to the increasing QoS challenge in wireless networks, researchers have made significant modifications in Wireless Fidelity (WiFi) in the legacy IEEE 802.11 standards to make possible QoS to end users. The design constraints at several layers of the IEEE 802.11 restrict its capacity to deliver guaranteed QoS. Recently, the IEEE 802.16 standard, also known as worldwide interoperability for microwave access (WiMAX), has emerged as the strongest contender for broadband wireless technology with promises to give guaranteed QoS to wireless application end users over wifi wireless technology [2]. In Adaptive controlling and classifying IEEES02.16 WiMAX standard and IEEES02.11 Wireless LAN Networks standard Some functions and algorithms in improving wireless networks, especially WiMAX access networks Modules are proposed and functions in analyzing WiMAX and WLAN networks provide a standard link in using and applications of these kinds of networks [3]. Integrated WiFi-WiMAX and WiFi-WiMAX-mesh networks and their performance is compared and discussed in terms of not only throughput and delay but also packet loss. They showed that the mesh architecture has indeed superior performance due to the inherent properties of mesh networking paradigm [4].

A QoS-based vertical handoff scheme for WLAN and WiMAX interworking networks is proposed with aim to provide always best service to users. They also presented a simple, yet efficient method to estimate the available bandwidth in WLAN and WiMAX networks to evaluate the real-time status of the overlay networks and make a handoff decision based on the information. The handoff process will not only be triggered by unaccepted signal strength but also by unsatisfied QoS parameters [5]. A roaming & interworking solution using intermediary entities, called Roaming Interworking Intermediary (RII) is proposed. A generic RII-based interworking and roaming architecture between WiMAX, 3GPP (third Generation Partnership Project) and WLAN networks was presented. They demonstrated and evaluated the robustness, feasibility and efficiency of the proposed architecture through different user scenarios [6]. Some authors addressed the main issues that arise while implementing the interworking mechanisms between different radio access networks. An interworking mechanism based on IEEE 802.21 framework is proposed and described in detail. The concept of autonomic computing in the design of the framework in order to use intelligence to provide flexibility, accessibility and transparency to the mobile is discussed [7]. An integration model and a base station assisted scheduling mechanism to be implemented at the CPE to provide QoS guarantee was implemented. The algorithm were analyzed through extensive simulation and showed that QoS can be provided for real-time and non-real-time traffic over the broadband integrated network [8]. Movement-aware vertical (MAV) handover algorithm between WLAN and Mobile WiMAX for seamless ubiquitous access is addressed. An MAV handover algorithm is proposed to exploit movement pattern for avoiding unnecessary handovers in the integrated WLAN and Mobile WiMAX networks. If a mobile station (MS)'s velocity is high and its movement pattern is irregular, unnecessary handovers likely occur more frequently. Therefore, the MS velocity and moving pattern are important factors for the handover decision procedure. To avoid unnecessary handovers, the MAV handover algorithm adjusts the dwell time adaptively and predicts the residual time in the cell of target base station (BS). Consequently, the adaptive dwell timer of MAV handover algorithm allows an MS a better connection as long as possible [9].

The MSCTI protocol characterized by its multi-homing technique, as vertical handover mechanism between the IEEE S02.16e and the IEEE 802.11e networks, in order to reduce the latency and the interruption during the handover process is discussed. They proposed an interconnection model between the two networks, compare by simulations based on the QoS metrics, the results obtained with the current protocol for the L3 handover: Proxy-Mil) and those with our recommended protocol for the vertical handover case: MSCTP Concerning the mobility scenario [10]. A three-dimensional Markov chain model for the 802.11e enhanced distributed channel access (EDCA) mode is proposed. This model can be used to compute the maximum sustainable throughput and service delay distribution for each priority class when under saturation load. The new framework models the performance impact of major quality-of-service (QoS) specific features (e.g., CWMin, CWMax, AIFS, internal collision resolution) of the 802.11e EDCA mode, and hence can provide an analytical approach to pick the parameter values associated with EDCA to meet the QoS requirements of each priority[11] The concepts of Signaling analysis of SIP-based terminal mobility protocol between WLAN and WMAN is proposed for convergent architecture. [12]. IP level QoS signaling as the key component to support the end to end QoS for various applications. A set of application programmer wireless link friendly IP QoS parameters is proposed for heterogeneous wireless networks [13]. The architecture for mobility management for heterogeneous IP networks were discussed in [14-15]. QoS framework and bearer services for mobile operators were proposed in [16]. Wireless IP model for mobile internet and WLAN model for mobile operators were discussed in [17-18]. Ip multimedia system (IMS) solution for next generation networks is discussed in [19].

The rest of the paper is organized as following: Section 2 describes about IMS Qos provisioning. Section 3 describes architecture for providing interworking between Wimax and Wlan. Section 4 deals with network model and results. Eventually, section 5 ends the paper with conclusion and future work.

2 IMS QoS Provisioning

IP Multimedia Subsystem (IMS) is an architecture that merges the applications and capabilities of the Internet with both wireless and wired access technologies and promotes fixed-mobile convergence. IMS promises true end-to-end handling of multimedia applications; both voice and video, to be used through multiple forms of access, including third generation (3G) wireless devices such as mobile phones and personal digital assistants (PDAs), as well as through traditional Internet access methods, including corporate local-area networks (LANs) and broadband connections. IMS is expected to play major roles in delivering multimedia content to fourth generation (4G) cellular technologies. One of the critical applications of IMS-based QoS, is the successful deployment of Voice over IP (VoIP) on both wired and wireless systems [3]. The ability of a network to support high-quality VoIP calls and the configuration of various hardware and software parameters are important in ensuring caller satisfaction. There are a number of impairment factors that affect the quality of a VoIP system.

2.1 Initial QoS Provisioning

The end-to-end Quality of Service scheme is the correct approach, which ensures correct QoS parameters are passed through different layers. It is vitally important that there are appropriate mappings of QoS parameters between each layer. A true end-to-end QoS handling of the Internet systems, involves all layers; application, transport, network, medium access, and physical layers.

1. IP-level (layer-III or "network layer") QoS handling
2. MAC-level (layer-II) mechanisms for handling QoS and
3. layer-III to layer-II QoS mapping

Behind all this success is the underlying fabric of the Internet: the Internet Protocol (IP). IP was designed to provide best-effort service for delivery of data packets and to run across virtually any network transmission media and system platform. The increasing popularity of IP has shifted the paradigm from "IP over everything," to "everything over IP." In order to manage the multitude of applications such as streaming video, Voice over IP (VoIP), e-commerce, Enterprise Resource Planning (ERP), and others, a network requires Quality of Service (QoS) in addition to best-effort service. Different applications have varying needs for delay, delay variation (jitter), bandwidth, packet loss, and availability [4].

These parameters form the basis of QoS. The IP network should be designed to provide the requisite QoS to applications. To facilitate true end-to-end QoS on an IP-network (for both wireless and wired networks), the Internet Engineering Task Force (IETF) has defined two models: **Integrated Services (IntServ)** and **Differentiated Services (DiffServ)**. IntServ follows the signaled-QoS model, where the end-hosts signal their QoS needs to the network, while DiffServ works on the provisioned-QoS model, where network elements are set up to service multiple classes of traffic with varying QoS requirements [4]. Both models can be driven off a policy base, using the CoPS (Common open Policy Server) protocol. WiMAX standard incorporates QoS features at the MAC layer while the classical WiFi standard does not have QoS specifications. The 802.11e standard introduces QoS in the WiFi MAC layer.

3 Proposed Integrated WiMAX / WiFi Network Architecture

When constructing integrated WiMAX/WiFi networks, one of the most challenging issues facing network designers is that of designing efficient links and Medium Access Control (MAC) layer protocols to optimize the QoS between the WiMAX and the WiFi components of the architecture. Several researchers have recently proposed QoS provisioning mechanisms for integrated WiMAX/WiFi systems.

QoS framework for 802.16/802.11 internetworking applications designed to map the QoS requirements of an application originating in an IEEE 802.11e network to an IEEE 802.16 network. Similarly, a QoS control protocol was also presented to support an integrated QoS for converged networks comprising WiMAX and WiFi systems. To meet QoS, efficient and unified connection-oriented architecture for integrating WiMAX and WiFi technologies in broadband wireless networks is proposed. In the proposed approach, a new wireless Access Point (AP) device, designated as WiMAX/WiFi AP (W2-AP), is developed to manage the WiMAX/WiFi interface.

Fig. 1 presents a classical example of the integrated WiMAX/WiFi network architecture [4]. As shown in fig.1 a single WiMAX Base station BS, operating in a licensed band, serves both multiple WiMAX Subscriber Stations (SSs) and multiple W2-APs within its coverage area. In other words, the WiMAX system provides broadband wireless access to multiple W2-AP devices in a point-to-multipoint (PMP) topology. Each WiFi network is connected to the WiMAX BS through a WiMAX/WiFi (W2)-AP. The connection between the BS and a SS is dedicated to a single user. However, the connection between the BS and each W2-AP is shared amongst all the nodes within the Wireless LAN served by the W2-AP. As a result, the WiMAX network guarantee secured communications service for connecting multiple scattered WiFi nodes to the Internet.

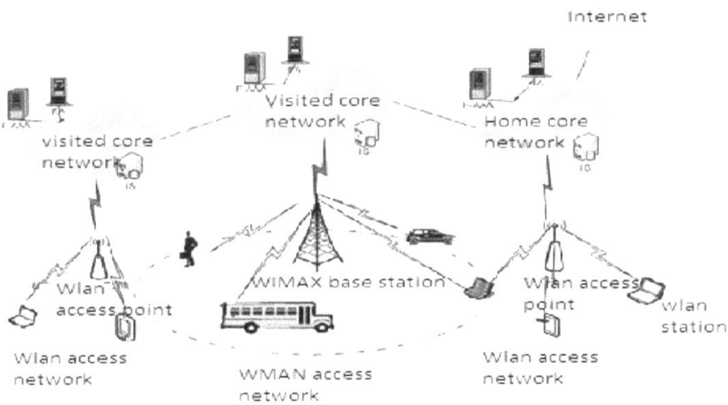

Fig. 1. WiFi-WIMAX Interworking Architecture

4 Results and Discussion with Proposed Network Model

The investigated network topology consists of more realistic scenario structured like a WMAN. The network consists of a center IP cloud which is connected with an application server. There are 10 subscriber stations. under each base station (BS). Each BS is connected to a Point to-Point (PPP) link with a speed of DS3 standard interface with the IP cloud and each BS has the capacity of handling 100 SSs. Here Access point connecting wmax and wlan subscriber station is mobile. Each node is mobile and the access technology is OFDMA 20 MHz TDD duplexing technology. The network topology used in this investigation is shown in Fig. 2.

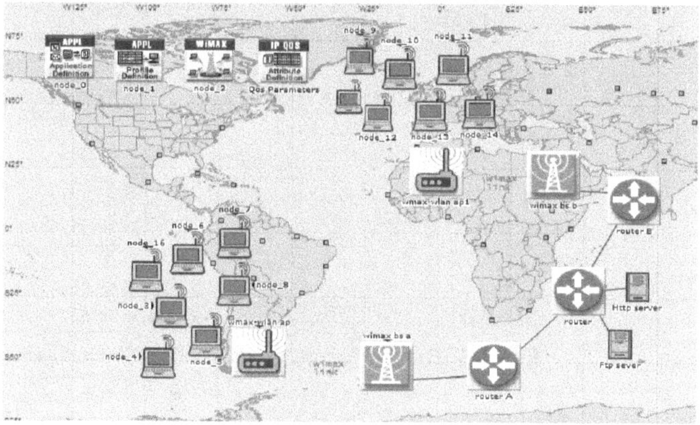

Fig. 2. Network model of WiMax and Wlan interworking

In the experimental results QoS parameters such as load, throughput, delay, network convergence activity for interworked networks were simulated through Opnet. Fig. 3 a) shows WiMAX load (bits/sec) and WiMax throughput in (bits/sec). QoS parameters of the individual network are simulated for the interworking architecture of WiMAX and WLAN Here WiMAX load and WiMAX throughput are same. Eventhough the number of users in WiMAX are increased throughput for the Wimax network remains same.This shows interworked architecture between WiMAX and WLAN maintains the higher throughput in accordance to the network load. Fig. 3 b) shows WiMAX delay in (sec). WiMAX delay is very low nearing 0.08 sec. For increased number of network load in WiMAX the delay parameter is low. This clearly shows the delay is reduced when two networks are interworked together.

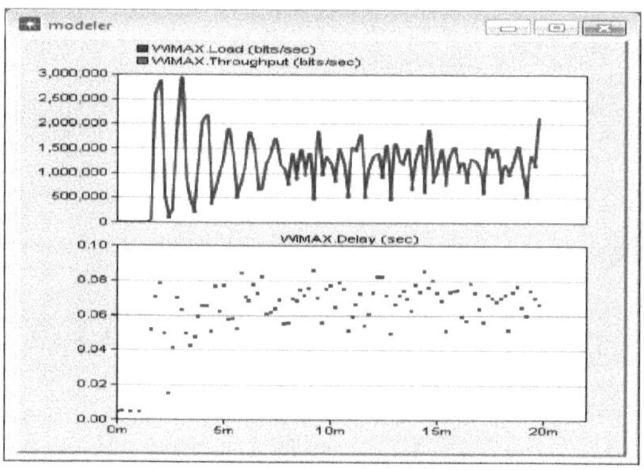

Fig. 3. a)WiMAX load (bits/sec) and WiMax throughput (bits/sec) b) WiMAX delay (sec)

Fig. 4 shows the Routing information protocol network convergence activity for the interworked architecture of WiMAX and WLAN. The convergence parameter is higher reaching unity within small amount of time period. This shows converging activity between WiMAX and WLAN for the interworked architecture is good. The time taken for the whole network convergence is too low. This shows latency time ie. The time taken for the interconnected network to respond is very less so the latency time is also reduced in this architecture.

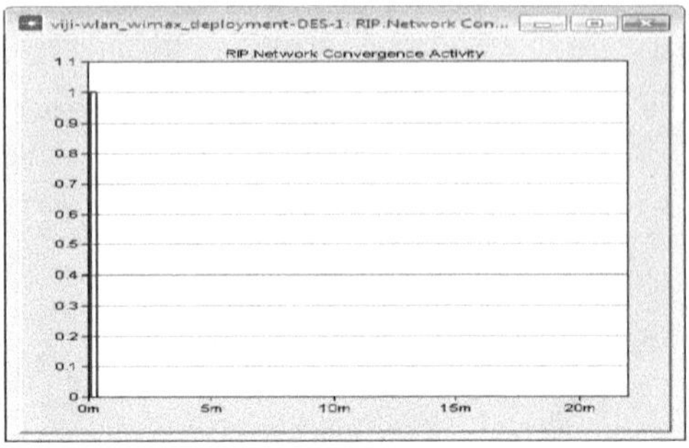

Fig. 4. RIP network convergence activity

Fig. 5 shows WLAN delay and load for the converged architecture. WLAN delay is very low nearing 0.0060 sec for the increased number of users. Fig. 6 shows WLAN throughput in bits/sec. Like WiMAX network, the WLAN netwok load and throughput are nearly same. This again shows the converging compatibility of the two interworking architecture.

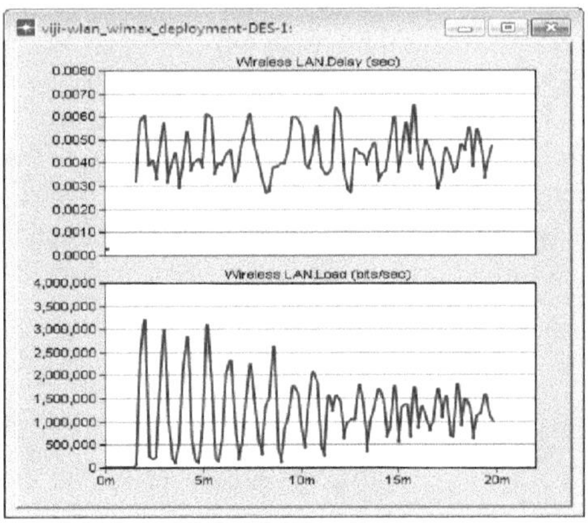

Fig. 5. a) WLAN Delay(sec) b) WLAN Load (bits/sec)

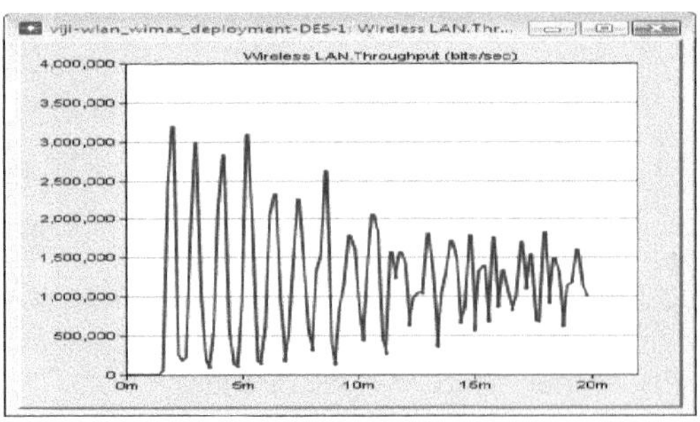

Fig. 6. WLAN Throughput(bits/sec)

Fig. 7 shows WLAN media access delay. The media access delay for WLAN is very low nearing the value (0.0050 to 0.0055)sec. When compared to WLAN network delay it is 0.0060sec. media access delay of WLAN network is still lower than network delay of WLAN. Time required for a head-of-the-line packet in the MAC transmit buffer to gain access to the medium is lower. This shows greater bandwidth and more efficiency in the convergence architecture.

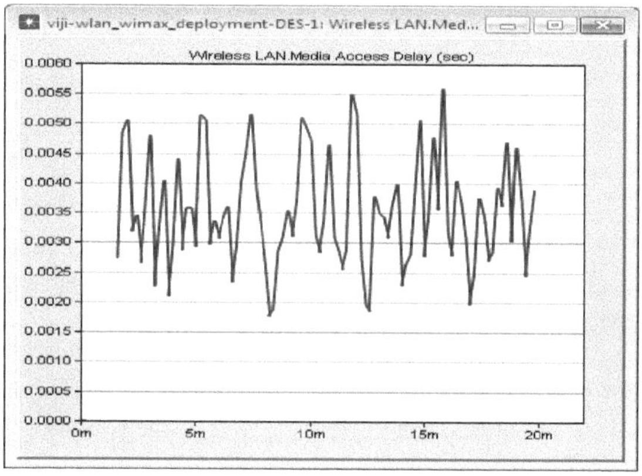

Fig. 7. WLAN media acess delay(sec)

Fig. 8 shows WiMAX delay and WLAN delay in sec for the interworking architecture. It is very low for the both networks. WLAN delay is very less than WiMAX delay. Fig. 9 a) shows HTTP traffic sent (bytes/sec) and HTTP traffic received (bytes/sec). Here HTTP traffic sent and received is nearly same. This shows large throughput and no delay for this type of services. Fig. 9 b) shows HTTP page response time (sec). The time taken for responding is very low. Fig. 9 c) shows FTP traffic sent (bytes/sec) and FTP traffic received (bytes/sec).

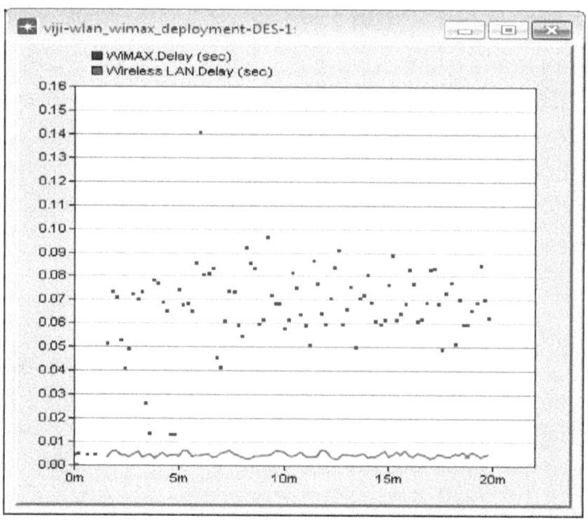

Fig. 8. WiMAX Delay(sec) and WLAN Delay (sec)

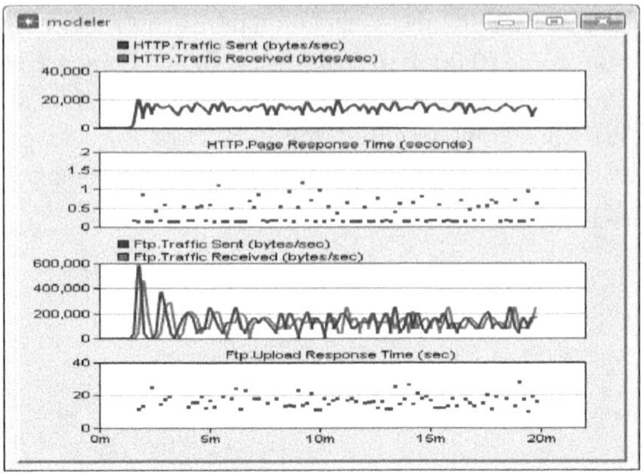

Fig. 9. a) HTTP traffic sent (bytes/sec) and HTTp traffic received (bytes/sec) b) HTTP page response time (sec) c) FTP traffic sent (bytes/sec) and FTP traffic received (bytes/sec) d)FTP upload response time(sec)

FTP traffic sent and received are same. This shows better file transfer without delay. Fig. 9 d) shows FTP upload response time (sec). The upload response is lower but when compared to HTTP response time it is little higher.

5 Conclusion

The rapidly deploying WiFi and the WiMAX represent the two major future wireless technologies. The design of a network architecture that efficiently integrates WiFi and WiMAX networks is a challenging task. To enable efficient use of scarce resources provided by the cellular networks while also maintaining strong service guarantees, QoS model for the integrated WiMAX and WiFi networks. Our proposed model supports the delivery of adaptive real-time flows for end users taking the advantage of high data rate WiFi systems as well as the wide coverage area of cellular networks. The performance of the system is revealed via Opnet simulation. The results show that the convergence architecture scheme effectively exploits system resources. Simulation experiments also indicate that the adaptive multimedia transmission can be made. QoS parameters such as throughput, load, and delay and network convergence activity are simulated. The parameter values shows network convergence is best.

References

1. Shaffatul, I., Mamunur, R.: Performance Analysis of WiMax/WiFi System under Different Codecs. International Journal of Computer Applications 18(6), 13–19 (2011)
2. Singh, S.K., Kumar, A.: Architectural Performance of WiMAX over WiFi with Reliable QoS over Wireless Communication. International Journal of Advanced Networking and Applications 3(1), 1017–1024 (2011)

3. Hamid Reza, A., Abolfazl, T.H.: Adaptive Controlling of IEEE 802.16 WiMAX standard and IEEE 802.11 Wireless. Proceedings of IEEE Communication Society 1 (2010)
4. NavidGhazisaidi, H.K., Saeed, B.M.: Integration of WiFi and WiMAX-Mesh Networks. In: IEEE Conference on Advances in Mesh Networks (2009)
5. Don, M., Maode, M.: A QoS-Based Vertical Handoff Scheme for Interworking of WLAN and WiMAX. Proceedings of IEEE Communication Society (2009)
6. Vamsi, K.G., Nazim, A.: Secure Interworking & Roaming of WiMAX with 3G and Wi-Fi. Proceedings of IEEE Communication Society (2009)
7. Tara, A., Yahiya, T.B., et al.: A cross layer based automatic architecture for mobility and Qos supports in 4G networks. Proceedings of IEEE Communication Society 1, 79–83 (2008)
8. Arul Prasath, G., Raghu, K.R.: Integration of WLAN and WiMAX with Base Station Assisted QoS. Proceedings of IEEE Communication Society (2008)
9. Wonjun, L., Eunkyo, K.: Movement-Aware Vertical Handoff of WLAN and Mobile WiMAX for Seamless Ubiquitous Access. Proceedings of IEEE Transactions on Consumer Electronics 53(4) (2007)
10. Bchini, T., Tabbane, N., Chapul, E., Tabbane, S., Beylot, A.L.: Performance of MSCTP protocol in vertical handover case between IEEE 802.16e and IEEE 802.11e Networks. In: IEEE International Global Information Infrastructure Symposium, pp. 1–4 (2009)
11. Zhifeng, T., Shivendra, P.: Throughput and Delay Analysis for the IEEE 802.11e Enhanced Distributed Channel Access. IEEE Transactions on Communications 54(4) (2006)
12. Chen, J.P., Chen, W.S., Chen, J.Y., Chu, H.T., Hsieh, L.: Signaling analysis of SIP-based terminal mobility protocol between WLAN and WMAN. Communication Systems and Network (2007)
13. Fodo, G., Eriksson, A., Tuoriniemi, A.: Providing Quality of Service in Always Best Connected Networks. IEEE Communication Magazine 41, 154–163 (2003)
14. Chan, P.M.L., et al.: Mobility Management Incorporating Fuzzy Logic for a Heterogeneous IP Environment. IEEE Commun. Mag. 39(12), 42–51 (2001)
15. Munasinghe, K.S., Jamalipour, A.: An Architecture for Mobility Management in Interworked 3G Cellular and WiMAX Networks. IEEE (2008)
16. Eriksson, A., Ohlman, B.: A Framework for Ondemand QoS Bearers over Fixed and Mobile Internet Access. In: PROMS 2000 (October 2000)
17. Dixit, S., Prasad, R. (eds.): Wireless IP and Building the Mobile Internet. Artech House (2002)
18. Ala-Laurila, J., Mikkonen, J., Rinnemaa, J.: Wireless LAN Access Network Architecture for Mobile Operators. IEEE Commun. Mag. 39(11), 82–89 (2001)
19. 19.3GPP.: IP Multimedia Subsystem (IMS). 3GPP TS 23.228 Version 6.10.0 Release 6 (2005)

BPSK Phase Modulation with Novel Prime Codes in OCDMA Networks

Helan Vidhya T., Pavithra S., and Sivasankari S.A.

Department of ECE, Saveetha School of Engineering, Saveetha University, Saveetha Nagar, Thandalam, Chennai-602 105, Tamilnadu, India
{helan.vidhya,pavithrra1286,s.a.sivasankari}@gmail.com

Abstract. In this paper, we simulate the performance of phase modulation in coherent Optical Code Division Multiple Access (OCDMA) systems. An Optical Spreading Sequences, a Prime Code family named Double Padded Modified Prime Code (DPMPC) sequence has been generated and employed because of its flexible code length. The number of active users to be interacted is made high by increasing the Code length value. In this analysis, BPSK format has been deployed where phase modulation has been done with optical signal and Convolutional encoding has been done to the modulated wave for real time error correction and at the receiver side decoding has to be done by using Viterbi algorithm to minimize the bit errors of the output by estimating the original input bits and demodulation of the decoded bits has also done. The Bit error rate analysis is also investigated for this network.

Keywords: Optical Code Division Multiple Access (OCDMA), Double Padded Modified Prime Code (DPMPC), Common Mode Rejection Ratio (CMRR), Binary Phase Shift Keying (BPSK), Convolutional encoding, Viterbi decoding.

1 Introduction

There are various multiple access techniques such as Frequency Division Multiple Access (FDMA), Time Division Multiple Access (TDMA), Code Division Multiple Access (CDMA) techniques. In FDMA, the resources of the channel are shared by dividing them along the frequency coordinates into discrete frequency records. In TDMA, the resources of the channel are shared by dividing them along the time coordinates into disjoint time slots. While in CDMA the channel resources have been shared by the hybrid combination of both FDMA and TDMA. In FDMA, the main disadvantage is the interruption of other frequency components while transmitting data. TDMA is a method for shared medium networks. It allows several users to share same frequency channel by dividing the signal into different time slots. The users transmit one after the other, each using his own time slots. This allows multiple stations to share the same transmission medium while using only a part of its channel capacity. CDMA has been used as a multiple access protocol because of its secure communication. The application of CDMA to the optical domain is called Optical Code Division Multiple Access (OCDMA) [13]. OCDMA has been proposed as a multiple access protocol that takes advantage of its excess bandwidth in a single mode

P.V. Krishna, M.R. Babu, and E. Ariwa (Eds.): ObCom 2011, Part I, CCIS 269, pp. 522–534, 2012.

fiber optic and extra high optical signal processing speed with optical components [4]. Optical-code-division multiplexing access (OCDMA) systems have attracted attention in recent years because of a number of advantages, including their asynchronous access capability, flexibility of user allocation, support of variable bit rates, burst traffic, and security against unauthorized users. It maps low rate electrical or optical signals into high rate optical sequences to achieve random multiple access. The huge bandwidth and extremely low propagation loss offered by optical fibers can be effectively exploited in a multichannel context by grouping several simultaneous transmissions on a common channel. So, signals are designed in such a way that it reduces mutual interferences. OCDMA technique uses specific wavelength or time slot. In order to have high performance OCDMA network, there are two main criteria to be satisfied. First, the receiver should be able to recognize the intended user information in the presence of other interfering users. Second, it should be possible to accommodate more subscribers. Recently, coherent OCDMA has been attracted with the development of compact and reliable en/decoders, where encoding and decoding are based on the phase and amplitude of the optical field instead of its intensity [15].

The remainder of this paper is organized as follows:

Section 2 presents the Phase Modulation of the BPSK signal, proposed DPMPC structure and the encoding and decoding techniques used in the modulation, Section 3 discusses and evaluates the experimental performance results, and Section 4 draws the conclusion.

2 Phase Modulation of BPSK Signal

Phase Modulation is a form of modulation which represents information as a variation in instantaneous phase of the carrier wave. The basic block diagram involved in the process of Phase modulation of BPSK signal is shown in Fig.1. The outgoing data are first BPSK encoded to give in-phase and quadrature phase signals. The BPSK encoded signal has been phase modulated and convolutionally encoded by DPMPC sequences and multiplexed via star couplers and transmitted over star passive optical networks (SPON). This corresponds to multiplication of the optical carrier and enables the system employing codes based on in-phase correlations. While the signal travels through the channel some additive noise gets added with the signal. At the intended receiver as shown in Fig. 1, the inverse process takes place where another decoder is used to decode the received signal at the receiver phase modulator is used to demodulate the received signal using the same DPMPC sequence used for encoding at the transmitter end. Based on the correlation properties of the selected family of prime codes, the signal that has been multiplied by the same code will despread, while signals multiplied by different codes will be further spread in the frequency domain and hence removed. Finally, the demodulated output is detected via balanced detector. Balanced detection removes signal terms common to both the detectors of high CMRR and produces successful decoding for matched delays. This process removes noises and DC components to perfectly detect the in phase and quadrature components and it conserves the phase information [11].

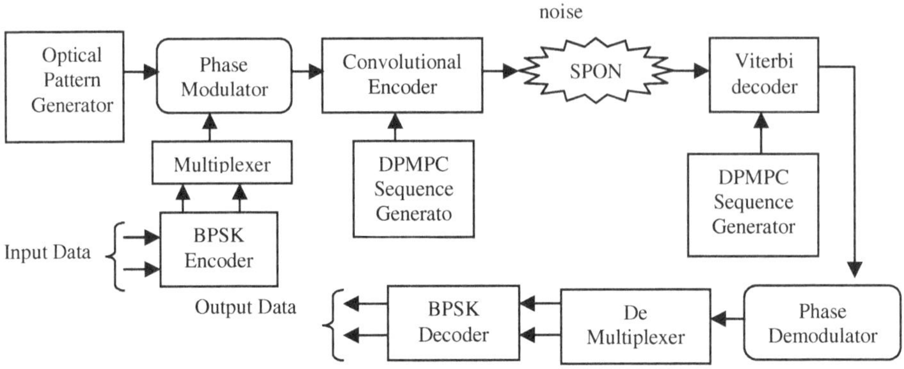

Fig. 1. Coherent OCDMA Phase Modulator

The general form for BPSK follows the equation:

$$S_b(t)=\sqrt{2Eb/_{Tb}}*\cos(2fct+(1+n)),\ n=0{,}1. \quad (1)$$

In a coherent BPSK system, the pair of signals $S_1(t)$ and $S_2(t)$ used to represent binary symbols 1 & 0, respectively is defined by

$$S_1(t)=\sqrt{2Eb/_{Tb}}*\cos 2fct \quad (2)$$

$$S_2(t)=\sqrt{2Eb/_{Tb}}*\cos(2fct+\pi)$$

$$=\ -\sqrt{2Eb/_{Tb}}\ *\cos 2fct \quad (3)$$

Where $0 \le t \le Tb$ and Eb is the transmitted signal energy per bit. Pair of sinusoidal waves that differ only in a relative phase shift of 180° in equations (2) and (3) are referred to as **antipodal signals.**

The signal to noise ratio is derived as follows:

$$\text{SNR (K)}=\frac{1}{\frac{(K-1)}{3N}+\frac{hv}{\eta e\hat{s}^2T}} \quad (4)$$

$$N=P^2+2P$$

Where,

h- Plank's constant= 6.608*10^-34 m²kg/sec
υ- optical frequency
η- quantum efficiency=0.9
e- Charge= 1.602*10 ^ -19 C
$\hat{S}^2$- Average power.
T- Bit interval.
K- Total number of users.
N- Length of signature sequence.
P- Prime Number.

$$\mathrm{BER}_{\mathrm{BPSK}} = Q\left(\sqrt{2 * SNR(K)}\right)$$
$$= erfc\sqrt{SNR(K)} \qquad (5)$$

Where,

Q- Q function.
efrc- complementary error function.

A. Proposed "DPMPC" Structure

As optical spreading sequences a prime code family named Double Padded Modified Prime Code (DPMPC) has been employed because of its flexible code length. In terms of optical signature sequences, DPMPC was extensively introduced in [3],

Table 1. DPMPC Sequences for $P = 5$

Code	Modified Prime Codes					Group Sequences	
C_{00}	10000	10000	10000	10000	10000	10000	01000
C_{01}	00001	00001	00001	00001	00001	00001	10000
C_{02}	00010	00010	00010	00010	00010	00010	00001
C_{03}	00100	00100	00100	00100	00100	00100	00010
C_{04}	01000	01000	01000	01000	01000	01000	00100
C_{10}	10000	01000	00100	00010	00001	00001	00010
C_{11}	01000	00100	00010	00001	10000	10000	00001
C_{12}	00100	00010	00001	10000	01000	01000	10000
C_{13}	00010	00001	10000	01000	00100	00100	01000
C_{14}	00001	10000	01000	00100	00010	00010	00100
C_{20}	10000	00100	00001	01000	00010	00010	00100
C_{21}	00100	00001	01000	00010	10000	10000	00010
C_{22}	00001	01000	00010	10000	00100	00100	10000
C_{23}	01000	00010	10000	00100	00001	00001	00100
C_{24}	00010	10000	00100	00001	01000	01000	00001
C_{30}	10000	00010	01000	00001	00100	00100	00001
C_{31}	00010	01000	00001	00100	10000	10000	00100
C_{32}	01000	00001	00100	10000	00010	00010	10000
C_{33}	00001	00100	10000	00010	01000	01000	00010
C_{34}	00100	10000	00010	01000	00001	00001	01000
C_{40}	10000	00001	00010	00100	01000	01000	00100
C_{41}	00001	00010	00100	01000	10000	10000	01000
C_{42}	00010	00100	01000	10000	00001	00001	10000
C_{43}	00100	01000	10000	00001	00010	00010	00001
C_{44}	01000	10000	00001	00010	00100	00100	00010

[5]–[10], where it has been utilized in incoherent pulse-position modulation (PPM) [5], overlapping PPM [6], coherent heterodyne BPSK system [7], and frequency-shift keying OCDMA system taking advantage of the new multiple access interference (MAI) cancellation technique [8], [9]. To compare with other prime code families, the code length and autocorrelation value in DPMPC increased by 2P and 2, respectively, as a comparison with modified prime code (MPC) [14], and by P and 1 as a comparison with both new MPC and padded MPC. This implies an increase in the chip rate, which makes the proposed code more secure (i.e., less or no interception) and also permits the OCDMA system to operate at higher bit rate and also better detection due to higher correlation differences. DPMPC has P groups, each of which has sequence codes; thus the total number of available sequences is P^2. The code length of each sequence is (P^2+2P) and the code weight is P+2.

The DPMPC structure for GF (5) where GF is the Galois Field, where 5 is the prime number which is P is shown in table 1.

The proposed optical signature sequence (DPMPC) has two fields namely Modified Prime Code and Group Sequence Stream. Modified Prime Code (MPC) field is generated by rotating the bits cyclically in certain order. Group Sequence Stream consists of another two fields. First field is obtained by repeating the bits from the last column of the Modified Prime Code and the second field can be obtained by repeating the last column of the previously coded MPC sequence. It is now clear from where the expression "Double Padded" comes from [5]. The number of users to be interacted is made high by increasing the code length value i.e., P and with little weight i.e., w. This increases the chip rate and achieves best correlation. By reducing the weight (w), code sequence we are sending will be much secured.

B. Convolutional Encoder

Convolutional codes are applied in applications that require good performance with low implementation cost. They operate on data stream and not static block. A Convolutional encoder encodes K information bits to $N>K$ code bits at one time step.Convolutional codes have memory that uses previous bits to encode or decode the following bits. Convolutional codes are extensively used for real time error correction [1], [2]. It is denoted by (n, k, L), where L is code memory depth. Code rate r is determined by input rate and output rate:

$$r = \frac{r\ (input)}{r\ (output)} < 1 \tag{6}$$

Convolutional encoder is a finite state machine (FSM), processing information bits in a serial manner. Thus the generated code is a function of input and the states of the FSM.

C. Viterbi Decoder

The Viterbi decoding algorithm is a state of the art algorithm used to decode Convolutional binary codes (viewed as a trellis tree) used in communication standards. The Viterbi decoder operates by finding the most likely decoding sequence for an input code symbol stream. Viterbi decoding is used as it yields the maximum likelihood decoding of the Convolutional code. In this project, after the encoding process taken place at the transmitter the data are then transmitted to the receiver via some channel where usually some noise gets added. So, Viterbi decoding is the very efficient algorithm to eliminate noises.

3 Experimental Results

The BPSK signal has been generated by giving binary sequences as the input and shown in fig.2 and 3.

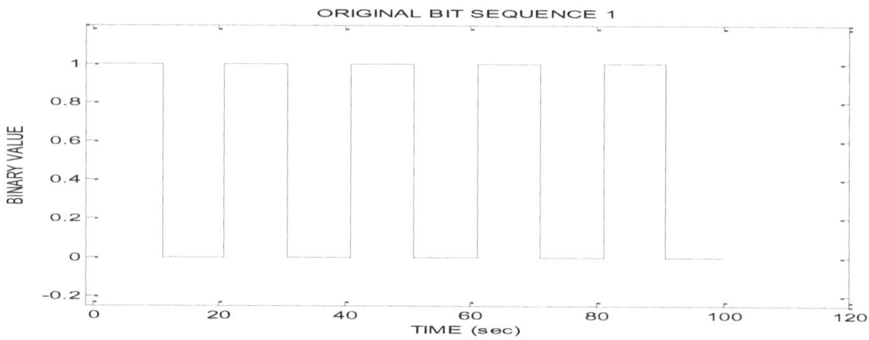

Fig. 2. Given input bit stream 1 for user 1

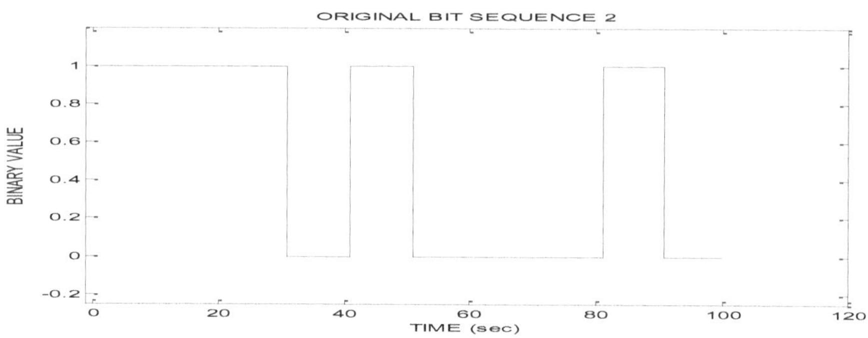

Fig. 3. Given input bit stream 2 for user 2

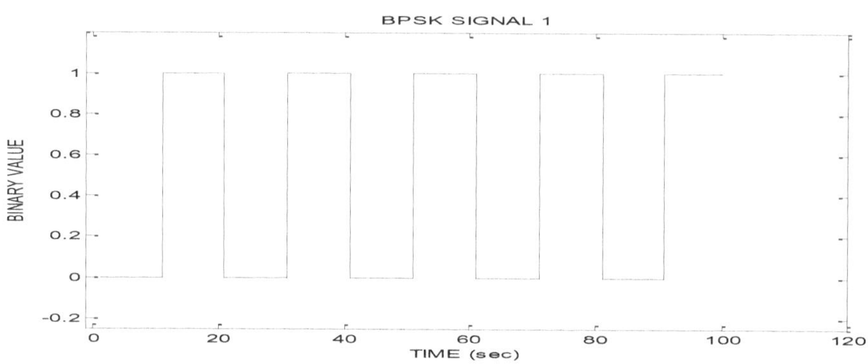

Fig. 4. BPSK signal 1 for user 1

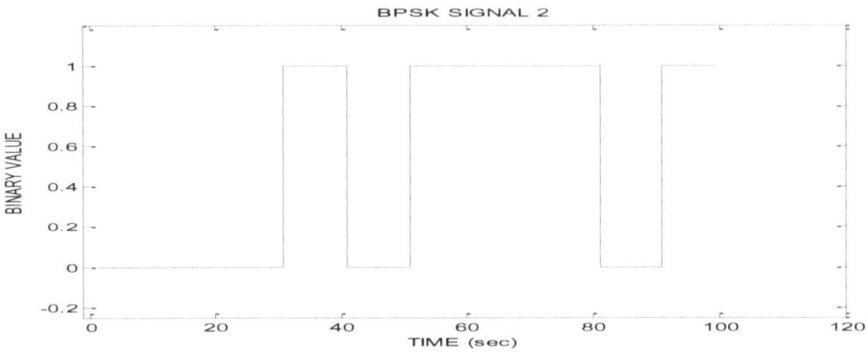

Fig. 5. BPSK signal 2 for user 2

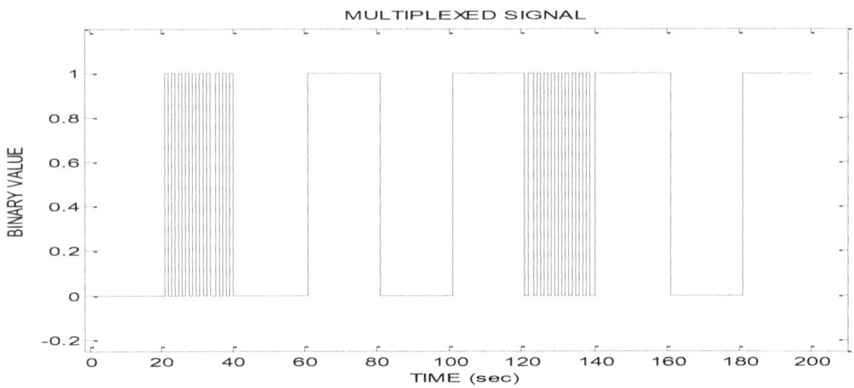

Fig. 6. Multiplexed signal for 2 BPSK signals

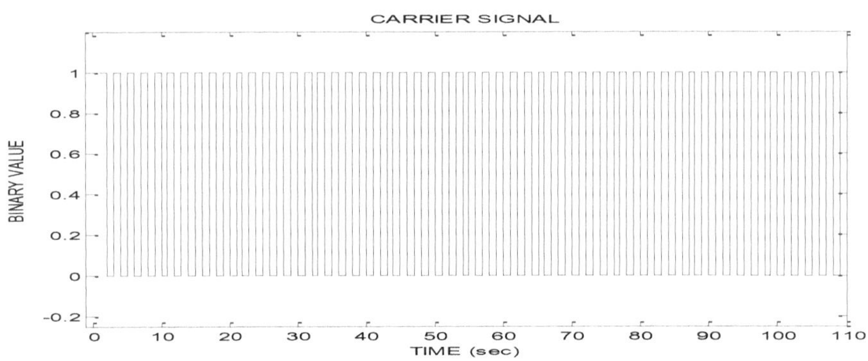

Fig. 7. Carrier signal generated for modulating the BPSK signal

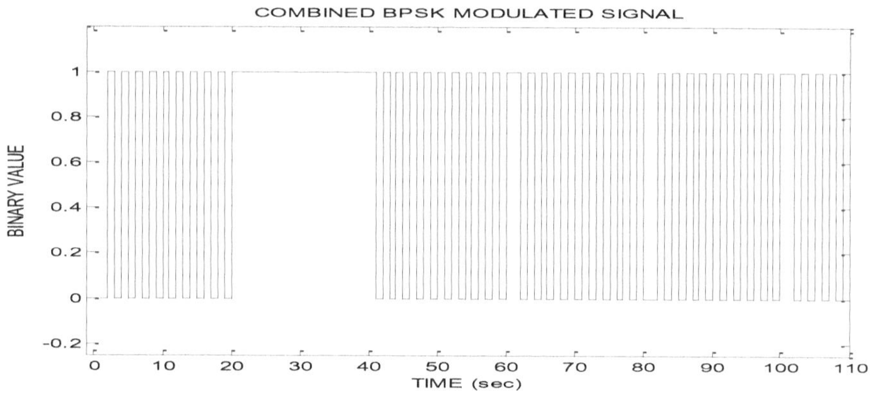

Fig. 8. Modulated BPSK signal

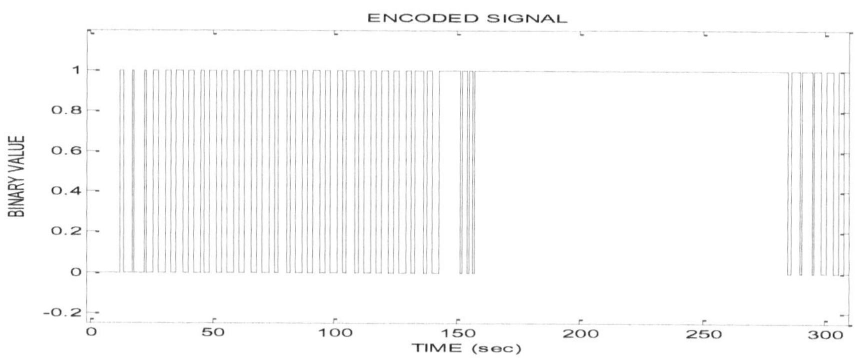

Fig. 9. Encoded signal obtained at transmitter side

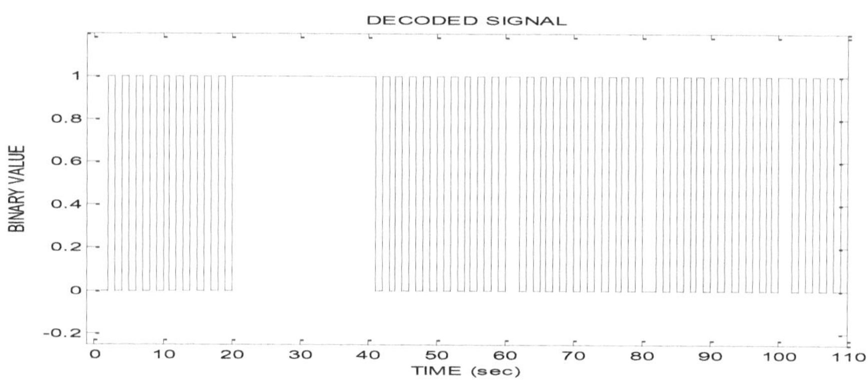

Fig. 10. Decoded signal obtained at receiver side

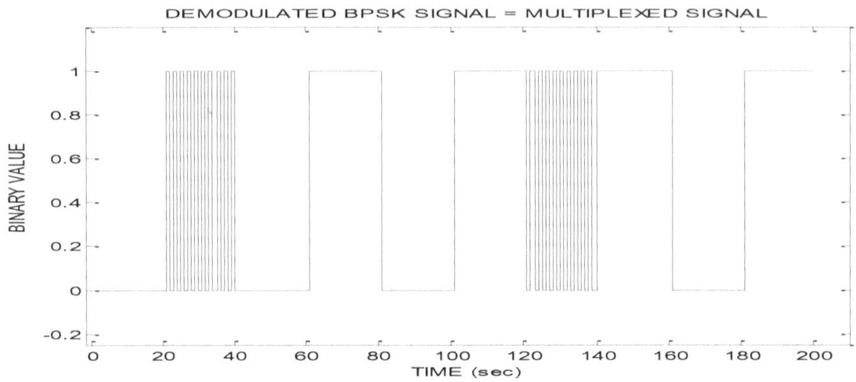

Fig. 11. Demodulated signal at receiver side

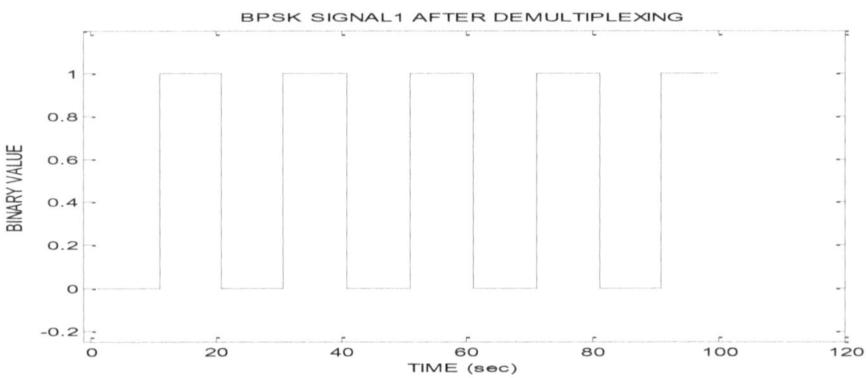

Fig. 12. BPSK signal 1 obtained after demultiplexing

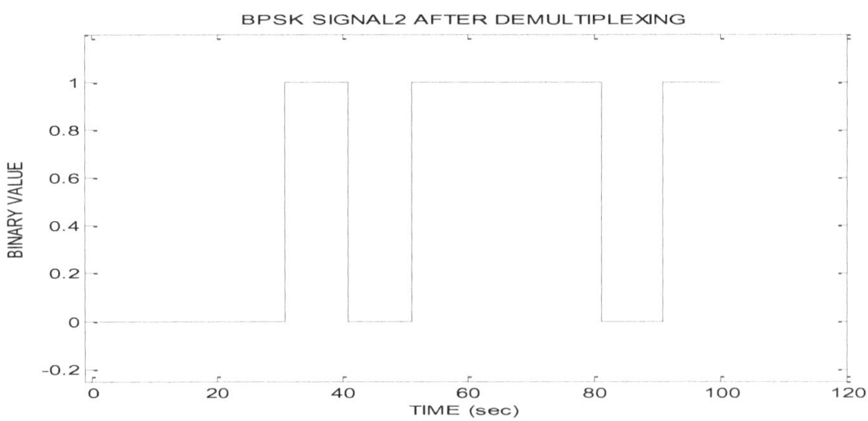

Fig. 13. BPSK signal 2 obtained after demultiplexing

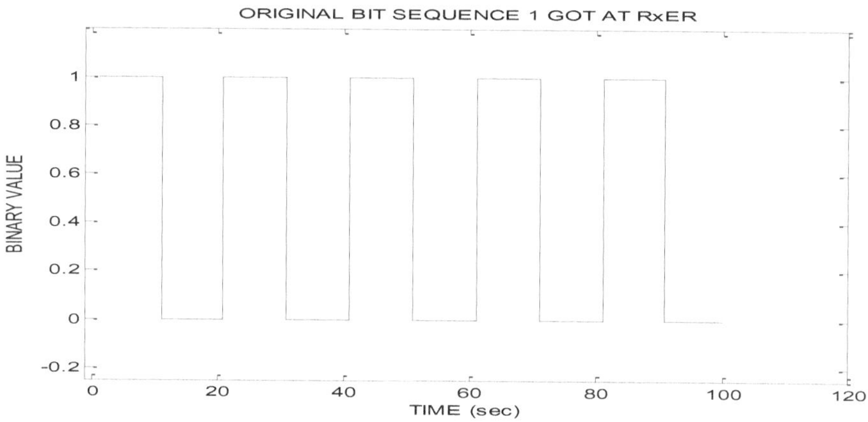

Fig. 14. Original bit sequence 1 obtained at receiver after BPSK decoding

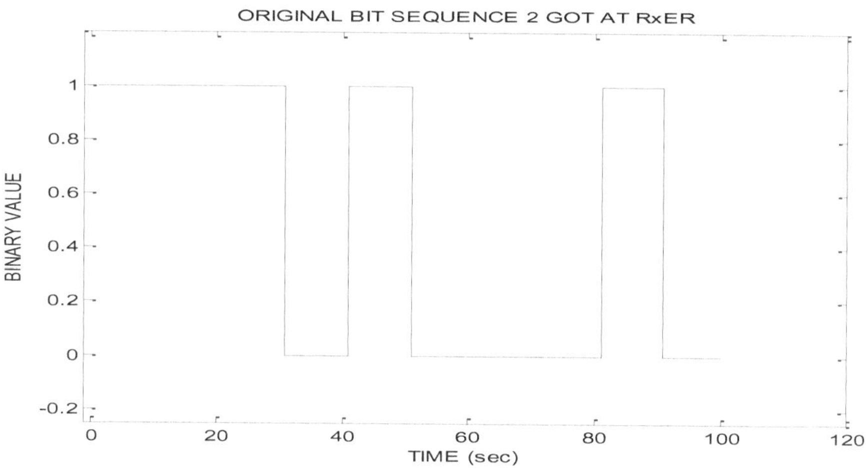

Fig. 15. Original bit sequence 2 obtained at receiver after BPSK decoding

From fig. 16 we can infer that

- As the number of user increases for a fixed Eb/No value, the Bit Error Rate tends to increase.
- For certain fixed number of users, as Eb/No increases the Bit Error Rate tends to decrease. Consider, for 50 users with Eb/No of 15, the BER is less than 10^{-8} and with Eb/No of 12, the BER is 10^{-6}. Hence it can be easily seen that BER decreases as Eb/No increases.

The following graph (Fig. 17) shows, as the length of the code sequence increases the number of users to be interacted also gets increased. For fixed BER of 10^{-3}, for code length of 575 (P=23), the number of users that can be accommodated is 250 and that for 899 (P=29), the number of users that can be accommodated is 400.

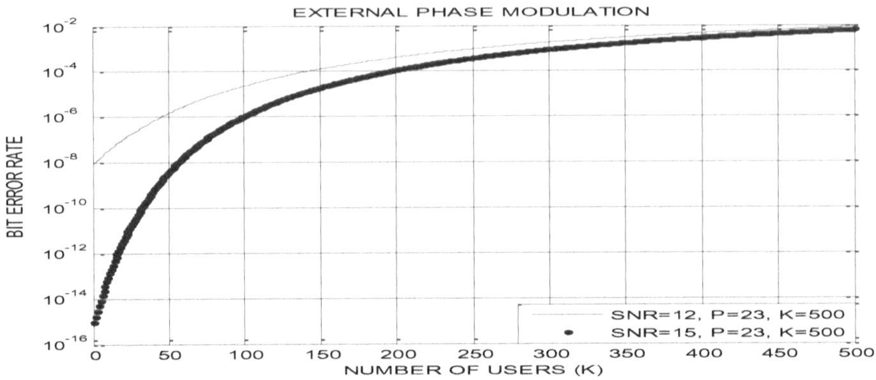

Fig. 16. BER for different number of users

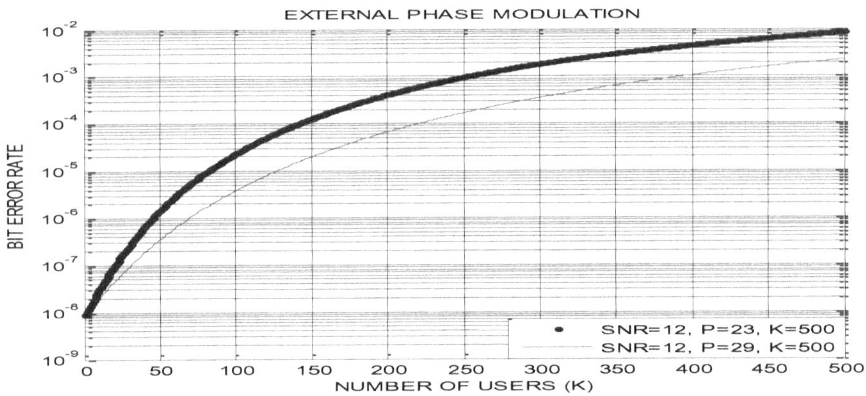

Fig. 17. Proof for increased number of users

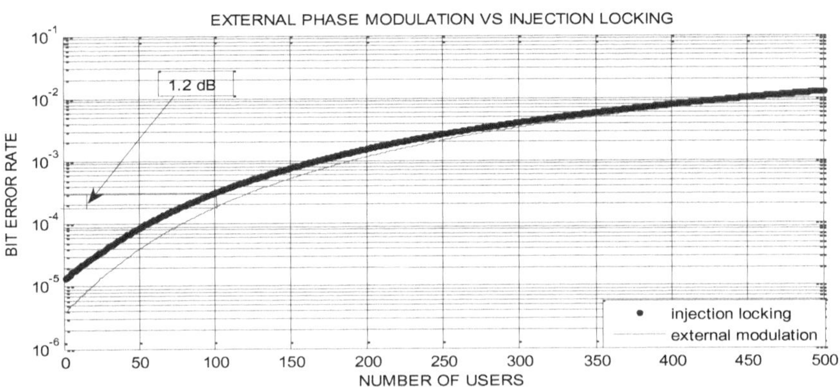

Fig. 18. Performance of BER for External Phase modulation and Injection Locking method

From fig. 18, it can be seen that, for a same BER value, there is degradation in BER equivalent to 1.2 dB. Thus, external modulation method by MZI indicates remarkable performance compared to injection locking method.

4 Summary

The input data given at the transmitter side is converted to obtain BPSK signal following this multiplexing followed by encoding has been done. At the receiver side the reverse process is done to obtain the original signal transmitted by the sender. Thus all the process involved in modulation process has been explained in above screenshots.

5 Conclusion

In this paper, we have discussed the method of phase modulation of BPSK signal and the generation of DPMPC sequences using MATLAB coding. Elimination of noise added to the channel during transmission has been done by Convolutional encoding at transmitter side and decoded by using Viterbi algorithm at the receiver side. The BER (Bit Error Rate) analysis has also discussed.

References

1. Arasteh, D.: Teaching Convolutional Coding Using MATLAB in Communication Systems Course, in Dept of Electronic Engg tech., Southern University, Baton Rouge, LA70813, USA
2. Juleen, L., Kiong, T.S.: Dynamic (2, 1, 8) Convolutional Coding Algorithm for Data Correction and Security Enhancement in an Intelligent Urban Traffic Management System. J. ICGST-CNIR 5(3) (October 2006)
3. Liu, F., Karbassian, M.M., Ghafouri-Shiraz, H.: Novel family of prime codes for synchronous optical CDMA. Opt. Quant. Electron. 39, 79–90 (2007)
4. Massoud Karbassian, M., Ghafouri-Shiraz, H.: Study of Phase Modulations with Dual-Balanced Detection in Coherent Homodyne Optical CDMA Network. J. Lightw. Technol. 26(16) (August 15, 2008)
5. Karbassian, M.M., Ghafouri-Shiraz, H.: Fresh prime codes evaluation for synchronous PPM and OPPM signalling for optical CDMA networks. J. Lightw. Technol. 25, 1422–1430 (2007)
6. Karbassian, M.M., Ghafouri-Shiraz, H.: Capacity enhancement in synchronous optical overlapping PPM-CDMA network by a novel spreading code. In: Proc. GLOBECOM 2007, Washington, DC, November 26-30, pp. 2407–2411 (2007)
7. Karbassian, M.M., Ghafouri-Shiraz, H.: Performance analysis of Heterodyne detected coherent optical CDMA using a novel prime code family. J. Lightw. Technol. 25, 3028–3034 (2007)
8. Karbassian, M.M., Ghafouri-Shiraz, H.: Novel channel interference reduction in optical synchronous FSK-CDMA networks using a data free reference. J. Lightw. Technol. 26(8), 977–985 (2008)

9. Karbassian, M.M., Ghafouri-Shiraz, H.: Frequency-shift keying optical code-division multiple-access system with novel interference cancellation. Microw. Opt. Technol. Lett. 50(4), 883–885 (2008)
10. Karbassian, M.M., Ghafouri-Shiraz, H.: Phase-Modulations Analyses in Coherent Homodyne Optical CDMA Network Using a Novel Prime Code Family. In: Proc. The World Congress on Engg., WCE 2007, London, U.K., July 2-4, vol. 1 (2007)
11. Abtahi, M., Ayotte, S., Penon, J., Rusch, L.A.: Balanced Detection of Correlated Incoherent Signals: A Statistical Analysis of Intensity Noise With Experimental Validation. J. Lightw. Technol. 26(10) (May 15, 2008)
12. Esposito, R., Radicioni, D.P.: CarpeDiem: Optimizing the Viterbi Algorithm and Applications to Supervised Sequential Learning. J. Machine Learning Research 10, 1851–1880 (2009)
13. de Carvalho, V.R., de Almeida, C., Nisenbaum, E.: An Optical CDMA Network Using Incoherent Optical Processing and Bipolar Spreading Sequences
14. Kwong, W.C., Perrier, P.A., Prucnal, P.R.: Performance comparison of asynchronous and synchronous code-division multiple- access techniques for fiber-optical local area networks. IEEE Trans. Commun. 39, 1625–1634 (1991)
15. Wang, X., Wada, N., Cincotti, G., Miyazaki, T., Kitayama, K.: Demonstration of 12-user, 10.71 Gbps truly asynchronous OCDMA using FEC and a pair of multi-port optical-encoder/encoders. In: Proc. ECOC 2005, Glasgow, U.K. (2005), postdeadline paper Thu 4.5.3
16. Painchaud, Y., Poulin, M., Morin, M., Têtu, M.: Performance of balanced detection in a coherent receiver, TeraXion inc., 2716 Einstein Street, Québec, Qc, G1P 4S8, Canada

A Simplified Pricing Model for the 3G/4G Mobile Networks

Reeky Maiti

IEEE Member
reeky.kharagpur@gmail.com

Abstract. The evolution of new technologies in the wireless technological networking environment is expected to provide economic growth as well as support a multitude of interactive and diversified multimedia and traditional services such as voice, e-mail, web-access which require large amount of network resource such as bandwidth to achieve the highest quality level. Economic Growths, Optimal Resource Allocation and End to End QoS guarantee are the key requirements of 4G wireless cellular networks. While the demand for wireless cellular services continues to increase, there is scarcity in the network resource such as bandwidth in the wireless environment which burdens the wireless service provider with a big challenge. Although the service providers feel comfortable with the traditional flat-rate model of pricing which is simple and is a popular way of billing with minimal overhead but it could seriously derelict the long term profitability of the wireless service provider. Under these circumstances in order to meet the key requirements and cope up with the new challenges the study of pricing models have gained a paramount attention in the network research. This article analyzes the existing pricing models and brings out the limitations of the same. A simple pricing model has been proposed in this article keeping in mind the limitations of the traditional pricing models. The proposed pricing model would be capable of ensuring profit of both user and service provider as well as be unbiased to both.

1 Introduction

Over the last decade mobile communication networks have become increasingly pervasive worldwide. The shift of telecommunication towards the wireless networks has become a significant phenomenon in the recent communications. Mobile Networks such as GPRS(General Packet Radio Service), UMTS(Universal Mobile Telecommunications System) and HSDPA(High-Speed Downlink Packet Access) are capable of meeting the user demands [1]. The increase of demands of the multimedia and data services in the recent mobile networks has created a significant challenge of satisfying the users' requirement and at the same time saving the operating costs [2]. Starting from the mid-1990s, a growing attention has developed for the study of sophisticated pricing models for telecommunication services [3]. Pricing for telecommunications has been widely addressed by analyzing a number of pricing models in the context of QoS(Quality of Service) guaranteed networks, mainly with respect to ATM(Asynchronous Transfer Mode) [4], [5], [6]. Wireless Service Providers(WSPs) aim at interconnecting different wireless technologies like (2G, Wideband Code Division Multiple Access(W-CDMA),

P.V. Krishna, M.R. Babu, and E. Ariwa (Eds.): ObCom 2011, Part I, CCIS 269, pp. 535–544, 2012.

UMTS, 802.11b, 802.11g and 802.16e), offering high mobility range and high bandwidth to their customers [7], [8], [9]. The interconnection of wired and wireless networks provide their subscribers with new technologies and a multitude of diversified services for fulfilling their increasing needs [10]. To support these services wireless networks need to support different traffic characteristics with different QoS demands [10]. The concept to use pricing for better allocation of limited network resources is not new [11]. In [12] the authors conclude that pricing plans are the easiest way for operators to limit data consumption. They also say that pricing plans that are too restrictive prevent users from doing much of what they do in wireline connection and will hence constrain market development and revenue opportunity. So, WSPs need to use pricing schemes which can assure the continuous QoS provisioning and monetary benefit [10]. In this paper a very simplified pricing model has been proposed which prices the user based on his perceived QoS as well as the network resource(for e.g bandwidth) consumed by the user and tries to maintain the profit of both user and WSP. The profit of user is that he receives the desired QoS and profit of WSP lies in the maximization of revenue. The proposed pricing model is unbiased in the sense that it charges user according to the network resource usage and on the perceived QoS(in terms of bit-rate in this case). WSP receives money from user based on amount of network resource allocated to user and the service provided. This paper has been organized with the introduction in Section I. Section II analyzes the existing pricing models and describes the limitations of the same. Section III describes the proposed pricing model. Section IV and V describes the simulation results, observations and discussions on the results obtained. The conclusions and future work is given in Section VI.

2 Existing Pricing Models

The existing pricing schemes are described in this section. A lot of study of different pricing schemes has been done by Ahonen, Gizelis and Vergados [10], [13]. The existing pricing schemes can be broadly classified into two categories:- Flat Rate Pricing Schemes and Parameter-based pricing schemes.

Flat Rate Pricing Schemes :- This pricing model sets a fixed price to a session independently of the network condition like traffic variation, usage, capacity, actual time user spends in network, type of service. The disadvantage of this pricing scheme is that this pricing scheme is unable to fulfill the needs of WSP and subscribers because these pricing schemes leads to overpriced events. The flat rate pricing scheme consists of the following pricing models which is described below:-

Unit of time based Charging Model :- Charging in this model is based on the time the connection is open between the user and the service provider. This model is not suitable for GPRS systems as the connection can be left open even if the terminal equipment is turned off. Connection is most of the time in idle state. So, there wouldn't be actually anything to be charged for. Charging based on units of time is suitable for circuit switched technology but is unsuitable for packet switched technology.

Number of Packets based Charging Model :- It is also known as Volume based Charging Model. Here, charging is based on the number of transmitted or received packets. It gives information about customers' network usage and absolute usage of the network. Implementation of packet counting systems and packet data processing systems is very critical and it increases capital expenses. Operational expenses also rise due to large amount of traffic information flow in the network.

Number of Packets based Charging Model :- It is also known as Volume based Charging Model. Here, charging is based on the number of transmitted or received packets. It gives information about customers' network usage and absolute usage of the network. Implementation of packet counting systems and packet data processing systems is very critical and it increases capital expenses. Operational expenses also rise due to large amount of traffic information flow in the network.

Single fee based Charging Model :- In this charging model, one fixed fee per service is charged from the user. These fees might differ depending on the service used. For example, MMS(Multimedia Messaging Service) is based on single fee charging. The disadvantage of this pricing model is if the network consists of lot of different services with different fees then it is really hard for the customer to keep track of expectable expenses.

Paris-Metro Pricing Model :- This pricing model is based on differentiated levels of service. It combines the idea of travel class with network traffic. Subscribers prioritize network traffic by assigning a preferred travel class with an associated cost for their network traffic. Different traffic types(like email, streaming, browsing) may have different priority and different travel classes. The disadvantage of this pricing model is that the possibility of a user to decide tariff class will create overhead to the network. Due to multiple traffic classes, effective multiplexing cannot be done in a Paris-Metro charged network. This model is mathematically very complex to implement.

Responsive Pricing :- In this pricing scheme users are rational with regard to price signals that are relayed to them. This scheme also doesnot address the issue of traffic differentiation for different applications.

Market-based Reservation charging :- This pricing model introduces the model of public auction of bandwidth or network resources. Subscribers maintain a preference profile and place monetary bids for different services which will influence the QoS they receive from their serving network. Network operator routes the network traffic according to subscribers profile. User profiles are administered via a web interface. The disadvantage of this pricing scheme is some subscribers can gain unfair advantage if they bid for certain services at the expense of other subscribers.

Parameter Based Pricing Scheme :-Parameter-based pricing focusses on how WSP will increase offered service and achieve profit maximization and mobile subscriber's satisfaction for the service they receive. Parameter based pricing schemes can be further classified into Static and Dynamic pricing models.

Static Pricing Schemes :- Static Pricing Schemes are those parameter-based pricing schemes which set the prices in a static way and subscribers are charged with a predefined price for the service they use irrespective of the variation of network resources, available bandwidth of the network and the usage of the network resources. In this

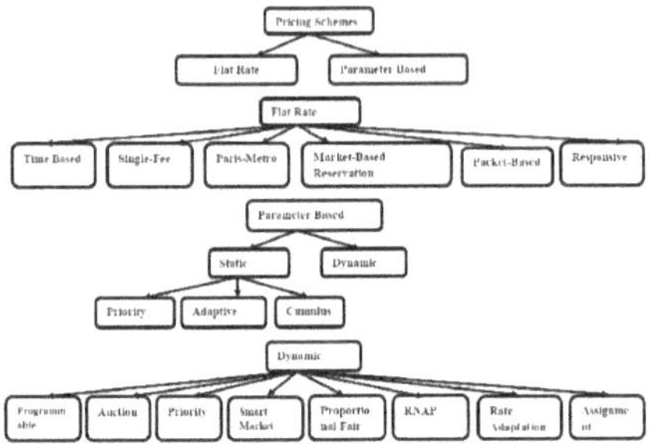

Fig. 1. Classification of Pricing Schemes

pricing scheme, order to set a price to a specific service, the Class of Service(CoS) price is predefined to the subscribers in the Service Level Agreement(SLA). The pricing schemes described below fall under Static Pricing Schemes.

Smart Market :- This was the one of the first proposed pricing schemes by Mackie-Mason and Varian for the internet. It imposes a network congestion dependent per-packet charge. This price per packet changes dynamically with time which makes this pricing scheme a dynamic pricing scheme. Price changes are justified according to the congestion level. This pricing scheme assumes that each packet will have a bid value in its header. The bid value is the rate which the user wants to pay and hence gives some hint to users 'willingness to pay'. It is useful to figure out the optimal amount of extra provisioning needed to improve performance of a running network. It is ideal in terms of pareto-efficiency [14]. It creates a lot of implementation complexities as it requires a lot of extra packet header fields.

Priority Pricing :- It is a pricing scheme with congestion-based pricing proposed by Gupta et al [15], [16]. For each service type within a priority class the service provider maintains a congestion based price which is updated at some time interval T according to network load and congestion and subscribers are given freedom to choose their preferable class of service, their transmission rate and their traffic allocation [17]. This pricing scheme helps in increasing WSP's profit according to subscribers satisfaction as discussed in [18]. Priority selection by subscribers often cause a network capacity overload [10].

Resource Negotiation and Pricing(RNAP) :- Wang and Schulzrine have recently proposed a resource negotiation and pricing framework through which dynamic pricing can be done. It maintains two crucial time intervals to manage service contracting and pricing. One is the negotiation interval to establish contracts between customers and service providers and the second one is the pricing interval for updation of prices. The total charge of customer comprises of three parts:- Usage charge depends on the volume of traffic sent by the user. Holding Charge is the charge made per traffic volume which is not used by the customer although he contracted for it. Congestion charge is made to user when he/she uses the network during congestion. This is some sort of an extra price. The major disadvantage of this scheme is that it involves all the network nodes in price calculation.

Adaptive Pricing :- It uses an algorithm that uses network's historical data like network's offered load, used bandwidth, accepted prices. The disadvantage of this scheme is it fails to assure QoS to user as it doesn't consider QoS parameters of individual users into the pricing methodology.

Cumulus Pricing :- Here some flat-rate-type contract is established between customer and ISP(Internet Service Provider) based on resource requirements specified by the customer. A rough feedback mechanism is there to keep track of user's actual resource consumption. If aggregation of cumulus points over some period exceeds a predefined threshold the whole contract has to be renegotiated. It is basically a service targeted approach and doesn't consider users' perceived QoS.

Dynamic Pricing Schemes :- These type of pricing schemes allow WSPs to modify the mobile subscribers' service priority, according to the variation of the subscribers' demands, leading to a profitable business.

Auction Based :- It is defined as a price of a service that has no standard value, so its value has to be discovered through a bidding process. This scheme doesn't consider user's perceived QoS nor network resource usage.

Assignment Pricing :- It is a method used by WSPs to assign prices to mobile units, based on the BS they belong, their QoS characteristics, and on the power control, aiming to achieve total system utilization. Prices once fixed donot gets updated with change in network conditions.

Rate Adaptation Pricing Scheme :- The prices charged are based on a reservation of resources by users. This pricing scheme incorporates a lot of delay in the feedback of price information from the network to wireless network subscribers. This makes it very unsuitable for the subscribers as they have to wait for long time for the price information.

*Programmable Pricing Schemes :-*It is a method which sets prices to services through a predefined set of rules. It doesn't consider user's perceived QoS nor takes amount of network usage into consideration.

3 Proposed Pricing Model

The previous section brings out the limitations of the various pricing schemes. The amount of resources available for the packet data in mobile networks are not constant and it varies with the propagation characteristics of the radio interface and the utilization of radio channels by other services [19]. So, a unified pricing model needs to evolve which would track both QoS parameters of a particular service as well as take into account the amount of network resource usage. The amount of network resource in this case is the time-frequency grid i.e. the time(in ms)-bandwidth(in Hz) product. It may be termed as a resource block.

Calculating the time-bandwidth product in GSM systems :- In GSM(Global System for Mobile Communications) systems, each TDMA(Time Division Multiple Access) frame consists of 8 time slots. The total time duration of 1 single frame in GSM is 4.615ms. Duration of each time slot is (4.615/8) ms. Total available bandwidth is 200 KHz in 1 time slot of (4.615/8)ms. Resource Block dimension in GSM system is 200KHz*(4.615/8) ms in frequency and time domain. In GSM, per user data-rate is 25 kbps [20]. So, in 0.5769 ms(4.615/8) total number of coded bits sent is 114 bits. Coded bits are the bits sent excluding bits for guard time and start stop bits. So, it can be written 114 coded bits(or say b bits) are sent in 0.5769(4.615/8)ms in 1 time slot utilizing 200 KHz of bandwidth(or say bw amount of bandwidth). So, it can be said that across 200 KHz*0.5769 ms 114 coded bits(equivalent number of bits sent in GSM) are sent in GSM. So, by utilizing 1 resource block(as per dimension in time-frequency domain in GSM) 114 coded bits are sent . In GSM, per user data-rate is 25 kbps(found by calculation). So, by calculation it is found that to send 25 kbits(or y kbs) in 1sec time duration a single resource block needs to be utilized (25*1000/114) i.e 219 times(or m times). In GSM data-rate of user is fixed, it is always 25 kbps so a single resource block will always have to be utilized 219 times in 1 sec to support 25 kbps data-rate. So parameters involved in pricing are number of bits and time-bandwidth product(RB). A single resource block needs to be utilized 219 times in 1 sec to support 25 kbps data-rate for 1 user in GSM. Resource Block dimension is same for every user in GSM systems.

Calculating the time-bandwidth product in LTE systems :- The resource block dimension is different for every user in LTE(Long Term Evolution) systems. User data-rate is not fixed and varies with every time instant and so user's bandwidth requirement also changes with every time instant to support the data-rate. So one user's requirement can be met by allocating one resource block whereas in the same time instant another user needs two resource blocks to be allocated to satisfy the bandwidth requirement. So the resource block utilization will also accordingly vary.

Through calculation, it has been found that in 1 ms time slot over 180 KHz of bandwidth 177 bits(equivalent number of bits sent in LTE) are sent. So the resource block(RB) utilization will also accordingly vary. So, suppose a user has a data-rate of x kbps. So to send x kbs of data in 1 sec a single resource block needs to be utilized (x*1000/177) times, say z times. So now it can be said that x kbs sent across 1 RB(1 ms*180 KHz) in 1 sec by utilizing the RB for z number of times. Here it is taken that user is allocated only one RB, but if the user is allocated more than 1 RB according to his bandwidth requirement then value of equivalent number of bits sent in LTE will change and hence value of z will also be different from the previous case. So, the equivalent number of bits sent and number of times allocated RB is utilized changes from user to user in lte. Sometimes these values are better than GSM, sometimes equal to it. As the bandwidth utilization and number of bits sent varies from user to user two tuning parameters α and β has been introduced which would tune the total cost a user has to pay. α tunes the bandwidth utilization cost or the spectrum cost and β tunes the cost for total number of bits sent or volume cost.

Calculating the Tariff Rates :- Let, the spectrum cost be P_{su} and volume cost p_v. We know as per 3G BSNL(Bharat Sanchar Nigam Limited) tariff rate of data is Rs 0.01/10 KB and voice call rate(STD Off-net Charge) is $80p/min = 1.33p/sec \approx 1p/sec$ [21]. Volume tariff rate will be $p_b = 12.207 * 10^{-6}$ p/bit. $p_{su} = p_{rru} * 2 * 200 * 10^3 * 0.5769 * 10^{-3} * 219$ and $p_v = p_b * 2 * 219 * 114 * 12.207 * 10^{-6}$. $1 = p_{rru} * 2 * 200 * 10^3 * 0.5769 *$

$10^{-3} * 219 + 2 * 219 * 114 * 12.207 * 10^{-6}$. So, spectrum tariff rate, $p_{su} = 7.9 * 10^{-6}$. The tariff rates are calculated for both uplink and downlink transmission.

The values of the tuning factors are assumed to be $\alpha = 1$ and $\beta = 1$. The pricing formula thus will be $P_{tot} = \beta * P_{su} + \alpha * P_v$.

Analytical Framework :- The analytical framework is developed for 20 secs simulation. Weightage Value $\beta = 1$ and $\alpha = 1$ has been assumed in this case.
RB occupied by every user=sum(time-bandwidth product in T_{obs})
Total bits sent for every user = Total bits sent accross RB occupied by every user.
$p_{rru} = 7.9 * 10^{-6} p/Hz - sec$
$p_b = 12.207 * 10^{-6} p/bit$
Spectrum Cost=P_{su} = RB occupied(Hz-sec)* p_{rru}
Volume Cost=P_v=Total bits sent(bits)* p_b
Price all users have to pay after $T_{obs} = 1sec$.
$P_{T_{obs}} = \sum_{t=1ms}^{T_{obs}=1000ms} \sum_{u=1}^{U=400} [P_{su}(t,u) + P_v(t,u)]$
Price all users have to pay after 1 drop=20 secs
$P_{drop} = \sum_{t1=1}^{5sec} [P_{T_{obs}}(d)]$
Price all users have to pay after total simulation time=20 secs(5 secs*4 drop).This will be the total system revenue generated after the entire session(total simulation period)
$P_{T_{sim}} = \sum_{drp=1}^{4} [P_{drop}(drp)]$

4 Simulation Results and Observations

The simulation environment has been set up using CAC(Call Admission Control), Packet Scheduler, SLA(Service Level Agreement) and Revenue Calculation block. CAC block is responsible in taking decisions of admitting new call requests. Packet Scheduler follows two scheduling strategies Dynamic and Semi-Persistent to schedule the VoIP packets for the users. In Dynamic Scheduling strategy user sends a resource request for every VoIP packet, eNodeB allocates uplink resources for every packet and every retransmission separately. VoIP users here can exploit channel diversity in both time and frequency. Semi-Persistent scheduling strategy is a combination of persistent scheduling and dynamic scheduling. Persistent Scheduling is for initial transmissions and Dynamic Scheduling is for retransmissions. Resource Allocation is done on the basis of Max C/I algorithm.

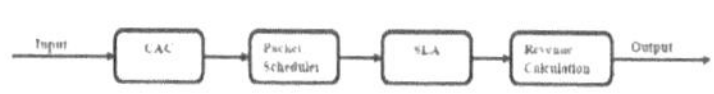

Fig. 2. Schematic Diagram of the Simulation Environment

SLA block is responsible for making the service level agreements between user and WSP. The revenue calculation block is responsible for calculating the amount of money user has to pay to the WSP.

Simulation Parameters :- The simulation parameters are listed below
No.of Users in lte system = 400
No.of Users in gsm system = 200
Total bandwidth available in lte = 5MHz

Total bandwidth available in gsm = 5MHz
Application = VoIP
Total simulation time = 20 secs
Billing Observation Window(T_{obs}) = 1 sec
Duration of each drop = 5 secs
No. of drops = 4
Scheduling Policy = Dynamic,semipersistent
Pricing Formula = $P_{tot} = \beta * P_{su} + \alpha * P_v$

Assumptions :-
All users are using the same application.
All users are existing users in the system. No new service requests are there.
All existing users are having the same session duration and are with same service request i.e all are VoIP users.
Users receive min. required QoS. Service of all existing users cannot be terminated unless session duration has been over.
Here it is assumed that as all are VoIP users so all receive min. required QoS of 16 kbps bitrate.Difference is in the resource(bandwidth in Hz) allocated to them.
Bandwidth sharing is equal in gsm system. All users receive the same amount of bandwidth.5 MHz bandwidth is been shared among 200 users equally irrespective of their requirement.
In lte system, 5 MHz bandwidth is been shared among 400 using a resource allocation policy.Users are allocated bandwidth depending upon their requirement.

Comparison of Revenue in LTE and GSM. The plots of comparison of revenue in GSM and LTE systems is given in figure 3 and 4.

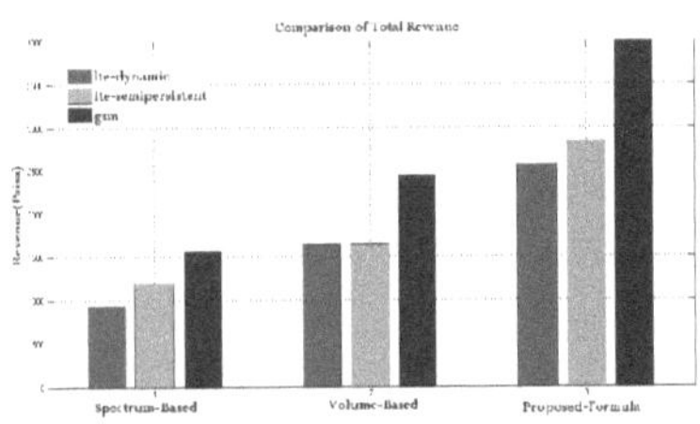

Fig. 3. Comparison of Total System Revenue

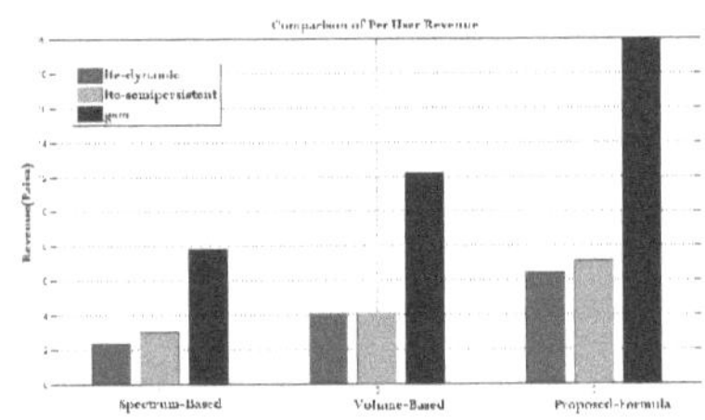

Fig. 4. Comparison of per user revenue

Per user revenue is highest in GSM system and LTE system from proposed pricing scheme compared to other pricing schemes. Per user revenue is more in case of semi-persistent scheduling compared to dynamic scheduling.

Figure 6,7,8 shows the plot of revenue vs SNR, revenue vs distance, revenue vs network usage. SNR(Signal to Noise Ratio) and Revenue has an inverse relationship. As SNR increases revenue degrades and vice versa. As the number of bits received by each user is same so volume cost is constant. Distance and Revenue has a direct relationship. With increase in distance revenue increases.

Revenue increases as network resource usage increases.

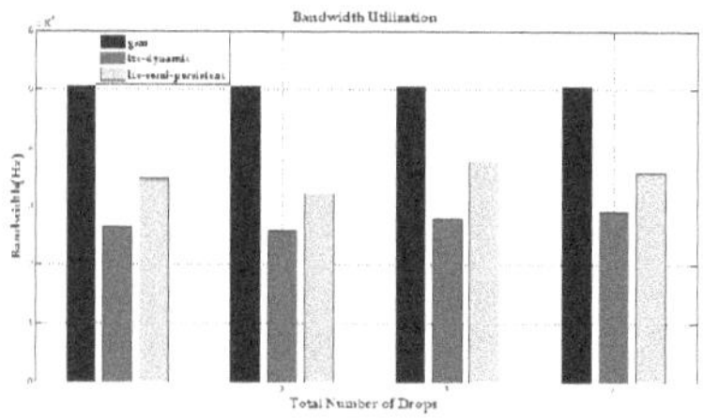

Fig. 5. Bandwidth Utilization

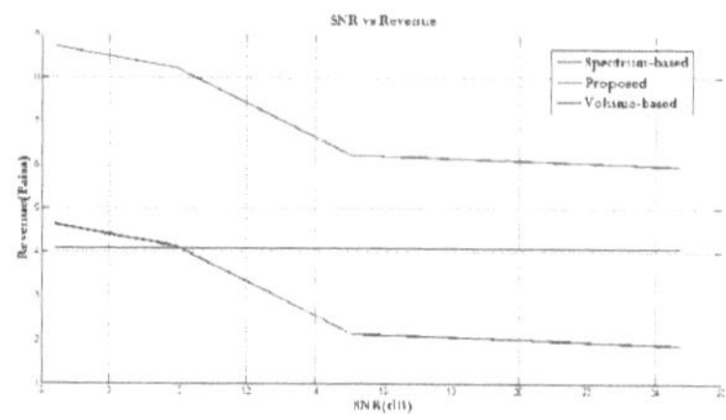

Fig. 6. SNR vs Revenue

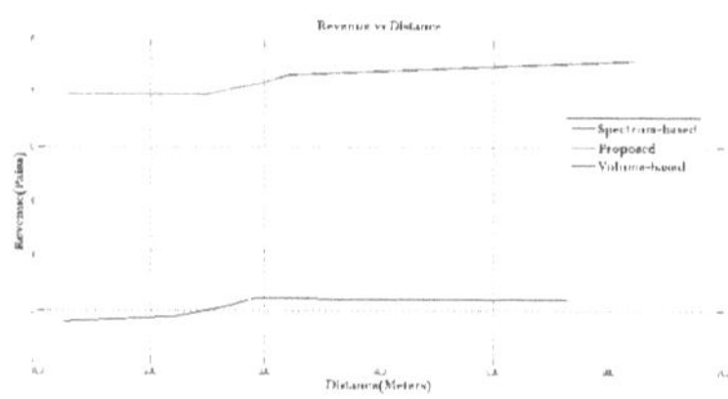

Fig. 7. Distance vs Revenue

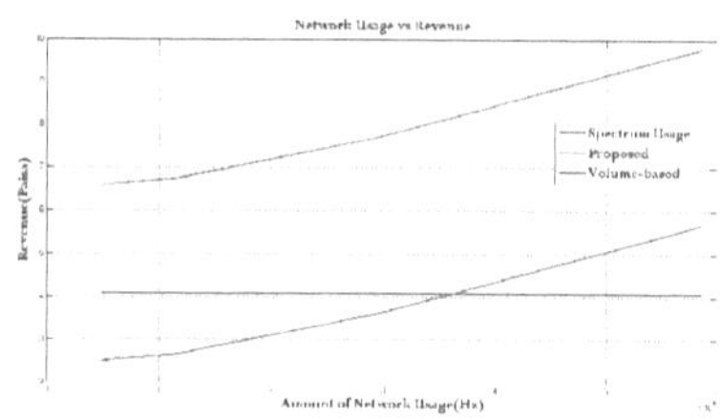

Fig. 8. Network Usage vs Revenue

5 Simulation Results and Discussions

The pricing method developed considered both amount of network resource usage as well as perceived QoS of individual users. As the user pays based on the amount of network resource(in terms of bandwidth in Hz) utilized by him/her and QoS(in terms of bit-rate) perceived and service provider charges user based on the network resource allocation and perceived QoS the proposed pricing scheme is unbiased to both user and WSP. Also users min QoS requirement is satisfied, user pays according to service he receives and service provider receives money according to service he provides to the user so neither the user nor the service provider looses out and profit of both is maintained. Every user pays a different price based on his perceived QoS and network resource usage so dynamic billing is also done.

6 Conclusions and Future Work

In this paper a simple pricing model has been formulated which to some extent is capable of maintaining the profit of both user and service provider and is unbiased to both. User receives his desired QoS and service provider receives the money according to the service he provides to every user. Although this pricing model has been only tested for voice traffic, a comparative analysis of this model with data traffic will be done as a future part of this work. New call arrivals, heterogeneous traffic scenarios has not been considered in this work but will be addressed in the future part of this work.

References

[1] Mouly, M., Pautet, M.-B.: The GSM System for Mobile Communications, Palai, France (1992)
[2] Ghanem, K., Khan, N.D., Mitschele-Thiel, A.: Peak Load Reduction on the Mobile Networks by Applying New Pricing Policies. In: IEEE ISWCS (2007)
[3] Baglietto, M., Bolla, R., Davoli, F., Marchese, M., Mongelli, M.: Integration of Pricing Models between Best-Effort and Guaranteed Performance Services in Telecommunication Networks. Control Engineering Practice 11, 1209–1226 (2003)
[4] Courcoubetis, C., Siris, V.A., Stamoulis, G.: Integration of pricing and flow control for available bit rate services in ATM Networks. In: Proceedings of IEEE Globecom, London, UK, pp. 644–648 (1996)
[5] DaSilva, L.A.: Pricing for QoS-enabled Networks: A Survey. IEEE Communication Surveys (2nd Quarterly) 3(2), 9–20
[6] Kelly, F., Songhurst, D.: Charging Schemes for Multiservice Networks. In: Ramaswami, V., Wirth, P.E. (eds.) Teletraffic Contributions for the Information Age. Elsevier, Amsterdam
[7] Shensheng, T., Li, W.: Performance Analysis of the 3G Network with complementary WLANs. In: GLOBECOM 2005-IEEE Global Telecommunications Conference, vol. 24(1), pp. 2635–2639 (November 2005)
[8] Wang, P., Jiang, H., Zhuang, W.: Performance Enhancement for WLAN Supporting Integrated Voice/Data Traffic. In: ICC 2006-International Conference on Communications, vol. 29(1), pp. 3792–3797 (June 2006)
[9] Lu, K., Qian, Y., Chen, H.: A Secure and Service-Oriented Network Control Framework for WIMAX networks. IEEE Commun. Mag. 45(5), 124–130 (2007)
[10] Gizelis, C.A., Vergados, D.D.: A Survey of Pricing Schemes in Wireless Networks. IEEE Communications Surveys and Tutorials 13(1), first quarter (2011)
[11] Patrick, H.: Pricing for QoS-Based Wireless Data Services and its Impact on Radio Resource Management. Huawei Technologies Co., Ltd.
[12] Mobile Broadband Capacity Constraints and the need for Optimization, Rysavy Research (February 2010)
[13] Ahonen, A.: GPRS Charging Schemes, Networking Laboratory, HUT
[14] Mackie Mason, H.K., Varian, H.R.: Pricing the Internet (1993)
[15] Gupta, A., Stahl, D.O., Whinston, A.B.: Pricing of services on the internet, Technical Report, University of Texas (1997)
[16] Gupta, A., Stahl, D.O., Whinston, A.B.: Priority Pricing of Integrated Services Networks. In: Mcknight, Bailey (eds.) MIT Press (1997)
[17] Marback, P.: Priority service and max-min fairness. IEEE/ACM Trans. Netw. 11(5), 733–746 (2003)
[18] Isiklar, G., Bener, B.A.: A Simple Approach to charging and billing of packetized applications. In: The Proc. IEEE Wireless Communications and Networking Conference, WCNC 2005, New Orleans, March 13-17, vol. 4(1), pp. 2440–2445 (2005)
[19] Golovins, E., Ozianyi, V.G., Ventura, N.: A Novel Pricing Approach to Support QoS in 3G Networks. Computer Networks (52), 1433–1450 (2008)
[20] Rappaport, T.S.: Wireless Communications Principles and Practice, 2nd edn. Prentice Hall of India,
[21] BSNL Launches 3G Revised Tariff (November 5, 2009), Internet `http://www.jharkhand.bsnl.co.in/3Gtariff.pdf` (June 25, 2011)

Performance Analysis and Dispersion Compensation in Ultra Long-Haul 10Gbps Optical System by OPC

Pradeep Doss M.[1], Sridarshini T.[2], and Valliammai M.[3]

[1] Sri Krishna Institute of Technology, Chennai, Tamilnadu
antonypradeep20@gmail.com
[2] Velammal College of Engineering and Technology, Madurai, Tamilnadu
sridharsini@gmail.com
[3] Mount Zion college of Engineering and Technology, Pudukottai, Tamilnadu
classicvalli@gmail.com

Abstract. Dispersion limits the transmission distances and information carrying capacity of Long-Haul optical systems. In this paper, the compensation of Dispersion, an inherent property of all Optical fibers, by optical phase conjugation (OPC) technique is studied. Also, the required number and fashion of OPCs to be introduced in Ultra Long-Haul optical transmission system, to have highly reliable transmission of information, is experimented through simulation in 10Gbps, 30000kms fiber-optic link.

Keywords: Dispersion, Dispersion compensation, Optic-fiber link, Fiber-optic communication, Phase conjugation.

1 Introduction

Communication has its own importance in each and every daily activities and its demand grows rapidly. Recently, a keen interest has been shown towards the research and development of Fiber-optic communication system and its technologies. The most Promising features are its reliable transmission of data, availability of high bandwidth, low power level requirements for input and Minimal losses in the fiber channel over other forms of communication strategy.

In Ultra Long-Haul Fiber-optic communication system with bit rate greater than 2.5Gbps, Chromatic Dispersion plays an major role in degrading the system performance. Various Dispersion compensation techniques have been proposed for optical system whereas, only few were successful so far[7]. OPC proves to be advanced when compared to other methodologies with several advantages.

1.1 Literature Survey

Optical phase conjugation produces an signal spectrum which will be the complex conjugate of the input signal thereby, making the impairments caused due to dispersion

P.V. Krishna, M.R. Babu, and E. Ariwa (Eds.): ObCom 2011, Part I, CCIS 269, pp. 545–549, 2012.

in one half of the channel is exactly compensated by the impairments in the other half of the channel[1]. OPC technique seems to be most fruitful method to compensate Dispersion as well as other effects such as Kerr-effect and fiber non-linear effects[4][5][6]. History of Phase conjugation goes to early 80's. YARIV and FISHER showed that the dispersive nature of fiber can be compensated by the Phase Conjugation Technique[2]. Following them, Chaloemphon and Kazuro demonstrated the design theory of mid-span OPC for Long-distance transmission system. Fig.1 shows the block diagram of the system using midway OPC from Kazuro's design theory[2]. This optical phase conjugated signal is obtained by the process of Four-wave mixing process in a third-order nonlinear medium[2][3].

S.L. Jansen produced a proof-of-principle experiment to indicate the increase in 44% of transmission distance using OPC, when compared to conventional compensation system using DCF[7].

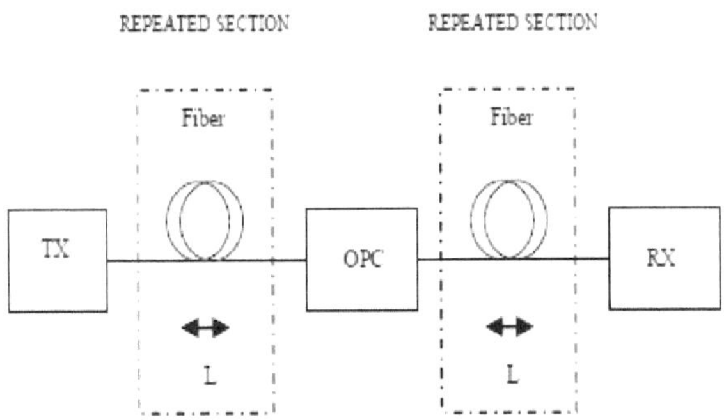

Fig. 1. Long-distance Optical transmission system using midway OPC in Chaloemphon and Kazuro's design theory. *TX* & *RX* denotes the transmitter and receiver sections. *L* is the distance of the optical transmission link.

1.2 In This Paper

OPC, becoming a promising method to compensate for various penalities of optical fiber, the design strategy lies in the further expansion of the optical transmission system with dispersion compensation schemes without disturbing the existing link. In this paper we have analyzed the same for OPC, experimented through simulation for various possible combination over 30,000kms and at 10Gbps fiber-link.

The advantages of OPC are that it can process multiple channels (WDM) and an OPC is transparent to modulation format, data rate and transmission distance[7].

2 Dispersion Compensation by OPC

Consider an optical system with dispersion compensation scheme implemented by mid-span OPC. As mentioned above the main problem lies in addition of length of the fiber-link without degrading the system performance due dispersion due to the addition fiber channel added.

2.1 Experimental Setup

The experimental setup block is depicted in Fig. 2. A Non Return-to-zero (NRZ) Pseudorandom bit sequence is amplitude modulated with optical signal of 1550nm generated by a continuous wave (CW) laser and a Mach-Zehnder modulator. The bit rate is 10Gbps.

Before transmission, the various factors of laser are defined in the simulation parameters. Power of the input optical carrier is set to 5dbm, attenuation is taken to 0.2db/km and length of the fiber-link is considered to be 30,000kms. EDFA amplifier is used in schematic for amplification.

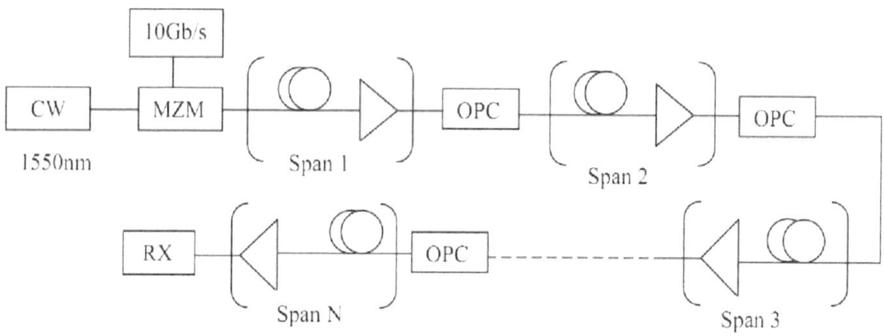

Fig. 2. Experimental optical transmission setup block with OPC

2.2 Implementation of OPC

OPC can also be introduced in an existing system by having it in between the fibers. It is not necessary that an OPC should be exactly at the mid-span to compensate for dispersion.

We have done simulation with introducing OPC at various places in an fiber-link of 30,000kms to have effective dispersion compensation. Results shows the following factors that have to be considered before introducing OPC in an existing system,

i. Inorder to expand an fiber-link, the additional length must be an integral multiple of the total length of the fiber. That is if the total length of the fiber is 2L, then additional length will be of n2L, n is an integer.
ii. OPC can be introduced after a distance of,
   a. 2L from the mid-span OPC which has been already implemented in the existing system. In such systems the total number of OPC implementation will be even.
   b. L from the mid-span OPC, in which the total number of OPC implementation will be odd, as shown in the table 1.

Table 1. Number of OPC required for additional n2L length in existing system of 2L

Value of integer 'n'	OPC after 2L from mid-span	OPC after L from mid-span	Difference
1	1	1	0
2	2	3	1
3	3	5	2
4	4	7	3
5	5	9	4
6	6	11	5
7	7	13	6
8	8	15	7
9	9	17	8
m	m	2m-1	m-1

From table 1. Comparing both the ways by which OPC can be effectively used for dispersion compensation, case b. needs additional (n-1) times the optical phase conjugation technique to be implemented between the fiber-link. Simulation result of which is shown in fig. 3.

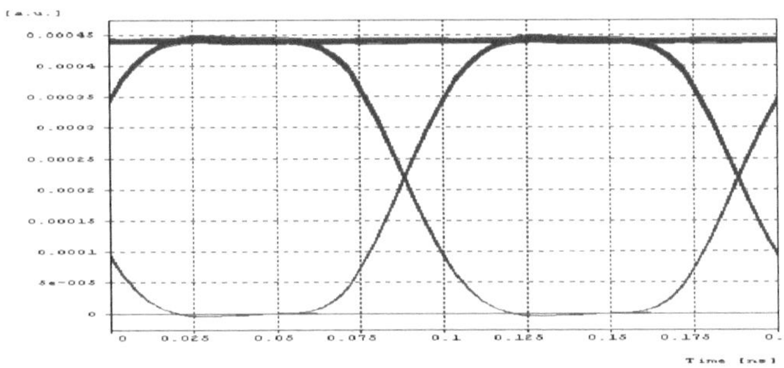

Fig. 3. Eye pattern for Ultra Long-Haul optical transmission dispersion compensated system by optical phase conjugation technique, using the above mentioned criteria

3 Conclusion

OPC resulted in effective compensation of dispersion in an optical system thereby avoiding the reinstallation of existing optical system. OPC can also be experimented for eliminating the need for repeaters and in-line amplifiers within the transmission link by using parallel combination of OPCs in mid-span of the channel. Effective length can be increased with optical phase conjugation. Further investigations are carried on the same technique to be used in Wavelength Division Multiplexing (WDM) and Dense WDM systems and to eradicate Non-linear effects of the fiber-link.

References

1. Watanabe, S., Naito, T., Chikama, T.: Compensation of Chromatic dispersion in a Single mode fiber by optical phase conjugation. IEEE- Photonics Technology Letters 5(1) (January 1993)

2. Lorattanasane, C., Kikuchi, K.: Design theory of long-distance optical transmission systems using midway Optical Phase Conjugation. Journal of Lightwave Technology 15(6) (1997)
3. Inoue, K., Toba, H.: Wavelength conversion experiment using fiber four-wave mixing. IEEE Photon Technology Letter 4 (1992)
4. Yariv, A., Fekete, D., Pepper, D.M.: Compensation for channel dispersion by nonlinear optical phase conjugation. Opt. Lett. 4 (1979)
5. Fisher, R.A., Suydam, B.R., Yevick, D.: Optical phase conjugation for time-domain undoing of dispersive self-phase-modulation effects. Opt. Lett. 8 (1983)
6. Watanabe, S., Shirasaki, M.: Exact compensation for both chromatic dispersion and Kerr effect in a transmission fiber using optical phase conjugation. J.Lightwave Technology 14 (1996)
7. Jansen, S.L., Van den Borne, D., Spinnler, B., Calabro, S., Suche, H., Krummrich, P.M., Sohler, W., Khoe, G.D., de Waardt, H.: Optical Phase Conjugation for Ultra long-Haul Phase-Shift-Keyed Transmission. Journal of Lightwave Technology 24(1) (January 2006)
8. Thirumaran, S., Sivanantharaja, A.: Performance Analysis of Optical Phase Conjugator on Dispersion Compensation in DWDM Systems. In: Optics: Phenomena, Materials, Device, and Characterization, AIP Conf. Proc., vol. 1391, pp. 403–405 (2011)

An Augmented Three-Phase Concept Map Design for an Adaptive Learning System

R. Kavitha[1], A. Vijaya[2], and D. Saraswathi[3]

[1] Dept. of MCA, Aloysius Institute of Management and Information Technology (AIMIT), St. Aloysius College (Autonomous), Mangalore, Karnataka
kavitha.rajamanii@gmail.com
[2] Dept. of Computer Science, Govt. Arts College (Autonomous), Salem-7, Tamilnadu
[3] Dept. of Computer Science, KSR College of Arts and Science, Tiruchengode, Tamilnadu

Abstract. Due to the advancement in information technology and varied learner group, e-learning has become popular. For achieving the adaptivity in learning, predefined concept map is used to provide proper guidance. Many researches propose various approaches in developing concept map by considering only binary numeric grade. Also, weight of concepts in each learning item is not properly considered. In this study, a Three-phase concept map design for adaptivity is proposed. This approach is an efficient one, since the first phase discards all unrelated items which may distract further analysis. Here, Norm-referencing in Item Analysis approach is used to find the item discrimination for elimination of irrelevant items. The second phase, computes all the grade association rules till Large_3 Item Sets. The weight of concept in each learning item is considered and prerequisite concepts are found which is not having any redundancy and cyclic in its map, thereby facilitating the next step of procedure. The final phase constructs the concept map with maximum confidence in a capable manner since most of the surplus computation is abolished in earlier phases. Finally, the concept map can be used in tutoring system, thereby enhancing the adaptivity in e-learning.

Keywords: Concept Map, Concept-Concept Relation, Learning Item-Concept Relation.

1 Introduction

Due to the vast advancement in Information and Communication Technology, E-learning system has become more and more popular. Hence, many adaptive learning and intelligent testing systems have been proposed to offer learners the customized courses. As learning becomes more and more a self-directed experience, the community of learners and educators is looking for tools that support self-driven knowledge acquisition and provide sufficient learning aids to mitigate such losses. The importance of cultivating self-directed learning traits for e-learners supports that concept mapping techniques can serve as one of the effective means for the provision of self-directed learning. Concept maps can serve as the missing bridge between e-learners and their learning needs. It can connect the learner with the content and

P.V. Krishna, M.R. Babu, and E. Ariwa (Eds.): ObCom 2011, Part I, CCIS 269, pp. 550–559, 2012.

provide a wider learner engagement with the intent of providing a learner-centered experience. Researchers have proposed various approaches for developing adaptive learning systems based on concept maps. It is difficult and time consuming to create the concept map of a course. Thus, how to automatically create an exact concept map for a course becomes an interesting research issue. Most proposed methods [1-6] deal only with binary grades of each test item. Also, the existing methods that based on fuzzy set theory [7, 8] do not take into consideration the weight of concept in each question that might be a cause to construct incorrect relationships or exaggerate the degree of relationship. Therefore, in this paper, a Three-Phase Concept Map Formulation is proposed to automatically construct a concept map of a course.

In the first phase, Fuzzy Set Theory is applied to transform the numeric testing records of learners into symbolic. To further refine it, to eradicate the irrelevant quiz from study, Norm-Referenced Theory in Item Analysis is applied to find the Item Discrimination. Then Data Mining approach is used to find its grade fuzzy association rules. The mined grade fuzzy association rules include eight rule types, L-L-L, L-L-H, L-H-L, L-H-H, H-L-L, H-L-H, H-H-L and H-H-H which denote the casual relations between learning concepts of quizzes. For example, a rule type Q1.L→Q2.L→Q3.L means that learners get low grade on quiz Q1 implies that they may get low grade on quiz Q2 and hence it will reflect in Q3 also. Many of the previous studies use single rule type, as L–L type, to analyze the testing data, which may decrease the quality of concept map [9]. Therefore, in the second phase, based upon our observation in real learning situation, multiple rule types are framed till Large_3 Item sets to further analyze the mined rules. Also, redundancy and cyclic between the rules are found and eliminated. In the third phase, based on relevance degree and relationship between quiz and concept, an algorithm is proposed to automatically formulate the concept map. This can be used in the adaptive learning system and thereby refine the learning strategies of learners.

The rest of the paper is organized as follows. Section 2 discusses the related previous research work. Section 3 briefly describes the proposed methodology followed in this study. In Section 4, an example is discussed to illustrate the process of constructing concept maps. The final section concludes the study and discusses the further enhancements.

2 Literature Survey

In the adaptive learning environment, the Concept Map can be used to demonstrate how the learning status of a concept can possibly be influenced by learning status of other concepts and give learners adaptive learning guidance. A conceptual map-based notation, called Concept Effect Relationships (CER), was framed to model the learning effect relationships among concepts. In brief, for two concepts, Ci and Cj, if Ci is the prerequisite for efficiently learning the more complex and higher level concept Cj, then a CER Ci →Cj exists. A single concept may have multiple prerequisite concepts, and can also be a prerequisite concept of multiple concepts. Later, based upon statistical prediction and approach, a CER Builder was proposed in the study [9]. Though the CER Builder is easy to understand, only using single rule type is not enough to analyze the prerequisite relationship among concepts of test items, which may decrease the quality of concept map. In research [7], they proposed a Two-Phase Fuzzy Mining and

Learning Algorithm. The AQR algorithm was applied to find the misconcept map indicating the missing concepts during students learning. However, because the creating misconcept map, which is not a complete concept map of a course, only represents the missing learning concepts, its usefulness and flexibility are decreased. In addition, their approaches generate many noisy rules and only use single rule type to analyze the prerequisite relationship among learning concepts. In the study [10], the first phase applies the fuzzy set theory to transform the numeric testing records of students into symbolic. As known, the numeric testing data are hard to analyze by association rule mining approach. Therefore, a look ahead fuzzy association rules was proposed to mine some rules, which are used to construct the concept maps.

In this proposed study, steps have been taken to avoid redundant, cyclic edges in the initial stage itself and also, since the second phase generates Large_3 Item Set, a lot of spare computations are avoided in next phase. Then, based on the weight of concept in each quiz, the concept map is formulated in an efficient manner.

3 Methodology

The Concept Map Design includes three phases. The first phase is Pruning by Item Discrimination. Only the pertinent quizzes are considered for further analysis. The next phase is Non-Redundant, Non-Cyclic Grade Fuzzy Association Rule Mining Process to generate Large_3 Item Sets. The final phase is the Concept Map Formulation phase.

In the first phase, the learner performances in the quizzes are transformed into matrix form for easy analysis. The weight of each concept in each quiz is depicted in the form of matrix by integrating the degree from different domain experts [10]. It lies within the range of 0 through 1. Based upon Norm-Referencing Theory, the discrimination of item can tell us how good a test item is. If the discrimination of the test item is too low, then it is not discriminating the high and low performers well since, it may not defined properly. It may distract the construction of concept map. The fuzzy set theory is applied to transform the numeric grade into symbolic data. In the fuzzification result, ''Low'', ''Mid'' and ''High'' denote ''Low Grade'', ''Middle Grade'' and ''High Grade'' respectively. Qi .L, Qi . M, and Qi . H denote the value of LOW fuzzy function, MIDDLE fuzzy function, and HIGH fuzzy function for the quiz Qi, respectively. The quiz which has item discrimination below 0.5 is pruned. By the end of the first phase, the data are well pruned by filtering out the useless quizzes and hence, there will not be any anomaly in the further analysis.

In the second phase, apply the fuzzy association rule mining algorithm to find the rules between quizzes. As per this study, Large3_Item sets are developed with confidence above minimum threshold level. Based on grade association rules derived for Large_2 Item Sets, two kinds of Quiz-relationship maps are constructed [10].

1. For the association rules $Q_i.L \rightarrow Q_j.L$, $Q_i.H \rightarrow Q_j.L$ and $Q_i.H \rightarrow Q_j.H$, build the relationship from Q_i to Q_j. The related concepts in Q_i are prerequisite of concepts Q_j.
2. For the association rule, $Q_i.\ L \rightarrow Q_j\ .\ H$, build the relationship from Q_j to Q_i which means the concepts in Q_j are the prerequisite of concepts in Q_i.

The Table 1 shows Prerequisite relation based on rule types involving three item sets.

Table 1. Rule Types with Prerequisite Relation

Rule Types	Prerequisite Relation
$Q_i.L \rightarrow Q_j.L \rightarrow Q_k.L$ $Q_i.H \rightarrow Q_j.L \rightarrow Q_k.L$ $Q_i.H \rightarrow Q_j.H \rightarrow Q_k.L$ $Q_i.H \rightarrow Q_j.H \rightarrow Q_k.H$	$Q_i \rightarrow Q_j \rightarrow Q_k$
$Q_i.L \rightarrow Q_j.L \rightarrow Q_k.H$ $Q_i.L \rightarrow Q_j.H \rightarrow Q_k.H$	$Q_k \rightarrow Q_j \rightarrow Q_i$
$Q_i.L \rightarrow Q_j.H \rightarrow Q_k.L$	$Q_j \rightarrow Q_i \rightarrow Q_k$
$Q_i.H \rightarrow Q_j.L \rightarrow Q_k.H$	$Q_i \rightarrow Q_k \rightarrow Q_j$

Given two quizzes Q1 and Q2, if concepts of Q1 are the prerequisite of concepts of Q2, Learner gets low grade on Q1 implies that he may also get low grade on Q2 or Learner gets high grade on Q2 implies that his grade on Q1 is high. Develop the Prerequisite Relationship PR by segregating the eight L and H rule types with confidence for that specific relation. Construct the Quiz Relationship Map by taking the relationship from PR. While doing so, check for cyclic or redundant edge by the introduction of a new edge relation. If so, only a single edge with maximum confidence value alone is depicted in the map. Also, association rules are developed having Large_3 Item Sets, unnecessary relations are kept away from further analysis. Hence, additional overhead in the next phase is eradicated.

The second phase constructs all the different type of fuzzified grade association rules and Quiz Relationship map is constructed without any redundancy and cycle. Therefore, it gives a well-organized and resourceful yield in the analysis.

The third phase concentrates on concept map formulation. The relevance degree between concepts is composed with the help of quiz relationships in PR. The weight of each concept in each quiz is considered. In order to avoid the extra computation, only the non-zero weights are considered for computation. The relative Quiz-Concept value between concepts is calculated which refers the number of quizzes involved with specific concept. The concept relationship map is formulated by taking all the edges having highest relevance degree of relationship between concepts.

Thus, the concept relationship and prerequisites can be found for any learning item, thereby enhancing the adaptivity in the e-learning which is the main focus of the intelligent tutoring system. Following is the proposed approach towards concept map formulation by 3 phases in steps.

Phase 1:

Step 1: Transform the learner performance into Grade Matrix G.
Step 2: Frame the Quiz-Concept Matrix QC.
Step 3: Classify the learners into High, Medium and Low performers

(3.1) Find the individual score on all quizzes
[Let m=Number of Quizzes, n= Number of learners]

$$STot = \left[\sum_{j=1}^{m} g_{1j} \quad \sum_{j=1}^{m} g_{2j} \quad \cdots\cdots \quad \sum_{j=1}^{m} g_{nj}\right]$$

Where, $1 \leq i \leq n$ and $1 \leq j \leq m$.

(3.2) Find Mean SM, Standard Deviation SD on STot.

Low Performers : $STot_i \leq SM - (SD/2)$

Medium Performers : $STot_i > SM - (SD/2)$ and $STot_i \leq SM + (SD / 2)$
High Performers : $STot_i > SM + (SD / 2)$

Step 4: Fuzzificate the Grade Matrix G into Symbolic data with High, Medium and Low indication

Step 5: Computing Item Discrimination and pruning quizzes

[Weightage for Performance: High=1, Medium = 0.5 and Low=0

Let U and L be the number of high and low performers

U_H, U_M and U_L are the sum of Weightage of High, Medium and Low performance of High performers

L_H, L_M and L_L are the sum of Weightage of High, Medium and Low performance of Low performers]

(5.1) Item Discrimination ID (Q_X)= $\left[\frac{U_H + U_M + U_L}{U}\right] - \left[\frac{L_H + L_M + L_L}{L}\right]$

(5.2) Find all the Q_X with ID (Q_X) < 0.5

(5.3) Frame QC' = QC – Pruned Quizzes

Phase 2:

Step 1: Framing Fuzzy Association Rules among Quizzes

[Input: Min Support Threshold SUP and Confidence CONF

Let C_l be the l- Candidate Item Set and L_l be the l- Large Item Set]

(1.1) While $C_l \neq$ NULL

Generate and insert l- Item Set into C_l

$SUP_l = \max\left(\frac{SUP_1}{l}, SUP_{l-1} - \frac{SUP_1}{(l-1)\times C}\right)$

Where l > 1 and C= Number of Rules in C_{l-1}

$L_l = \{ x \mid Support(x) \geq SUP_l$, for $x \in C_l \}$ and $l = l + 1$

(1.2) Generate the Association rules satisfying CONF into FAGR.

[FAGR : Collection of Fuzzy Association Grade Rules]

Step 2: Construct the Prerequisite Relationship (PR) on Quizzes

(2.1) For each rule in FAGR,

(2.1.1) For all L-L-L, H-L-L, H-H-L and H-H-H Rule types,
Include $Q_i \rightarrow Q_j \rightarrow Q_k$ into PR

(2.1.2) For all L-L-H and L-H-H Rule types,
Include $Q_k \rightarrow Q_j \rightarrow Q_i$ into PR

(2.1.3) For all L-H-L Rule type,
Include $Q_j \rightarrow Q_i \rightarrow Q_k$ into PR

(2.1.4) For all H-L-H Rule type,
Include $Q_i \rightarrow Q_k \rightarrow Q_j$ into PR

Step 3: Framing Quizzes Relationship Map

[Accumulation of Non-Redundant and Non-Cyclic Rules]

(3.1) Create vertices with Quizzes

(3.2) while PR $\neq$ NULL

(3.2.1) Take $Q_i \rightarrow Q_j \rightarrow Q_k$ from PR

(3.2.2) Do Cycle Detection
If so, delete edge with Min Confidence

(3.2.3) Check Redundant edge over $Q_i \rightarrow Q_j$, $Q_i \rightarrow Q_k$ and $Q_j \rightarrow Q_k$
If so, check confidence and label edge with Max Confidence

Phase 3:

Step 1: Find Relevance Degree between Concepts $C_i \rightarrow C_j$, where $1 \leq i \leq P$, $1 \leq j \leq P$

Where, P is the number of concepts

For all Concepts from C_1 to C_P

(1.1) Take $C_i \rightarrow C_j$

(1.2) For all Quiz Relationship from PR

(1.2.1) Take $Q_X \rightarrow Q_Y$, compute WQ_XC_i and WQ_YC_j

(1.2.2) If any of the weight is not found, go to previous step

Else

Rel $(C_i \rightarrow C_j)$ $Q_X \rightarrow Q_Y$ = WQ_XC_i X WQ_YC_j X Confidence ($Q_X \rightarrow Q_Y$)

(1.2.3) If more than one relationship between any 2 concepts,

Rel $(C_i \rightarrow C_j)$ = max (Rel $(C_i \rightarrow C_j)$ $Q_X \rightarrow Q_Y$)

(1.2.4) Confidence $(C_i \rightarrow C_j)$ = Confidence $(Q_X \rightarrow Q_Y)$

Step 2: Frame Concept-Concept Matrix CC

For all Concepts $C_i \rightarrow C_j$, $[1 \leq i \leq P$ and $1 \leq j \leq P]$

(2.1) CC_{ij} = Minimum Non-Zero Value(QC_i , QC_j) where $i \neq j$

Step 3: Formulate Concept – Relationship Map

[Let μ = Min (CC_{ij}) , N_i be the number of quizzes with concept C_i,
N_j be the number of quizzes with concept C_j]

For all Concepts Relationship in Rel $(C_i \rightarrow C_j)$

(3.1) if $\left(\frac{N_i}{N_j}\right) \times CC_{ij} \geq \mu$ and Rel $(C_i \rightarrow C_j) \geq \mu$ then,

Add edge $C_i \rightarrow C_j$

4 Discussions and Results

This section gives an illustrative example how Three-phase concept map design is functioning in an efficient manner. Let 10 learners take up 5 quizzes on part of their learning system. Assume that their performance is as below in Grade Matrix G.

$$G = \begin{bmatrix} 12 & 12 & 12 & 2 & 2 & 2 & 20 & 10 & 10 & 10 \\ 18 & 14 & 16 & 8 & 8 & 10 & 5 & 6 & 5 & 9 \\ 20 & 18 & 14 & 12 & 12 & 8 & 5 & 6 & 5 & 4 \\ 20 & 9 & 4 & 6 & 6 & 2 & 4 & 1 & 1 & 0 \\ 7 & 7 & 7 & 20 & 20 & 20 & 1 & 5 & 5 & 5 \end{bmatrix}.$$

Domain experts have given the Weightage for each concept with respect to each quiz. The conceptual weight relationship in the form of Quiz-Concept Matrix QC is as follows. Each row represents the Quizzes and each column represents the Concepts.

$$QC = \begin{bmatrix} 0 & 0 & 0 & 1 & 0 \\ 0.6 & 0 & 0.4 & 0 & 0 \\ 1 & 0 & 0 & 0 & 0 \\ 0 & 0.6 & 0.4 & 0 & 0 \\ 0 & 0.2 & 0 & 0.7 & 0.1 \end{bmatrix}.$$

The result of fuzzification on the score of sample learner data is as follows:

Table 2. Fuzzification of Learners Performance

Student Id	Q1			Q3			Q5		
	Low	Mid	High	Low	Mid	High	Low	Mid	High
S1	0.0	0.0	0.7	0.0	0.0	1.0	0.2	0.8	0.0
S4	1.0	0.0	0.0	0.0	0.0	0.7	0.0	0.0	1.0
S7	0.0	0.0	1.0	0.5	0.3	0.0	1.0	0.0	0.0
S10	0.0	0.5	0.3	0.7	0.0	0.0	0.5	0.3	0.0

As per the Item Analysis, item which is having discrimination value less than 0.5 is not differentiating the high and low performers well. Hence, quiz Q4 is to be discarded from investigation which has discrimination 0.33. By the end of first phase, pruned Quiz-Concept matrix which will improve the efficiency of analysis, because of removal of inappropriate data from focus. To find grade fuzzy association rules of test items from the testing data, Look Ahead Fuzzy Mining Algorithm is applied. The Candidate_1 Item Set C1 is framed and the support value is computed by summing up learners' fuzzification results of the quiz [9] and Large_1 Item set L1 is generated by discarding item set that is less than 2. Then L2 is constructed from C2 by eliminating those rules which are having support less than minimum support value 1.75.

Table 3. Large_2 Item Set L2

Item Set	Support	Item Set	Support
Q1.L ∩ Q3.H	2.4	Q2.L ∩ Q3.L	2.0
Q1.L ∩ Q5.H	2.7	Q2.L ∩ Q5.L	1.8
Q1.H ∩ Q2.H	2.1	Q2.H ∩ Q3.H	3.0
Q1.H ∩ Q3.H	2.1	Q3.L ∩ Q5.L	1.8
Q1.H ∩ Q5.L	2.5		

The item set in L2 which supports the minimum confidence of 0.75 alone are taken for the further analysis. The corresponding prerequisite relationship (PR) can be developed from the mined rules. Large_3 Item Set is found which comply with min support for this level as 1.64.

Table 4. Large_3 Item Set L3

Item Set	Support	Item Set	Support
Q1.H ∩ Q2.H ∩ Q3.H	2.1	Q2.L ∩ Q3.L ∩ Q5.L	1.8
Q1.H ∩ Q3.H ∩ Q2.H	2.1	Q2.L ∩ Q5.L ∩ Q3.L	1.8

The combinations of each item set in L3 are framed and confidence is found. The item set which supports the minimum confidence of 0.8 alone is taken for the further study. The Table 5 obviously shows the mined rules, the Prerequisite relation with their confidence level.

Table 5. Prerequisite Relationship of Quizzes with Mined Rules [L3]

Rule Type	Mined Rules	Prerequisite Relation	Confidence
L-L-L	Q2.L ∩ Q3.L ∩ Q5.L	Q2 → Q3 → Q5	0.9
	Q2.L ∩ Q5.L ∩ Q3.L	Q2 → Q5 → Q3	1.0
H-H-H	Q1.H ∩ Q2.H ∩ Q3.H	Q1 → Q2 → Q3	1.0
	Q1.H ∩ Q3.H ∩ Q2.H	Q1 → Q3 → Q2	1.0

As per the steps in phase 2, cycle detection and redundant edge checking is done and removed. In both the cases, a single edge with maximum confidence is alone considered. The final and efficient Quiz Relationship map without redundancy and cycle as per the proposed algorithm is in Fig 2. Hence, the number of quiz relationship to be considered for further analysis is condensed which will give efficient computation later.

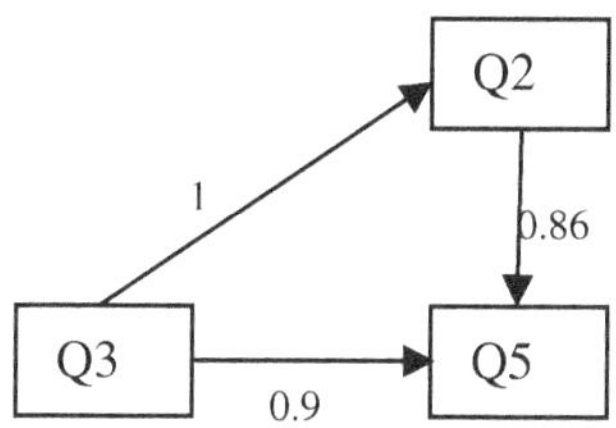

Fig. 1. Efficient Quiz Relationship Map

After get rid of from redundant and cycle, Prerequisite Relationship is as follows:

Table 6. Prerequisite Relation with Max Confidence

Prerequisite Relation	Confidence
Q2 → Q5	0.86
Q3 → Q2	1.00
Q3 → Q5	0.90

In Phase 3, Relevance Degree between all the concepts has to be found. The Relevance degree between concepts is computed by multiplying weight of specific concept in specific quiz in both antecedent and consequent part and confidence of prerequisite relation. If more than one relevance degree present, the one with high value is taken. Concept-Concept Matrix is constructed to find the impact of one concept over other. μ = 0.1, which is the minimum non-zero value in CC. For each concept-concept relation, relative Quiz-Concept value Ret (Ci → Cj) is calculated by dividing the number of quizzes which have concept as per the rule.

Table 7. Relevance Degree of Concept Relation

Concept Relation	Relevance Degree	Confidence	Relative Quiz Concept Value
C1 → C2	0.18	0.90	0.40
C1 → C3	0.40	1.00	0.80
C1 → C4	0.63	0.90	0.60
C1 → C5	0.09	0.90	0.20
C3 → C2	0.07	0.86	0.20
C3 → C4	0.24	0.86	0.02
C3 → C5	0.03	0.86	0.10

If Ret (Ci → Cj) x $CC_{ij} \geq \mu$ and Conf (Ci → Cj) $\geq \mu$, then an edge Ci → Cj is added in the concept relationship map. While formulating this map, no need to check redundant or cycle edge since, they were eliminated in the second phase itself.

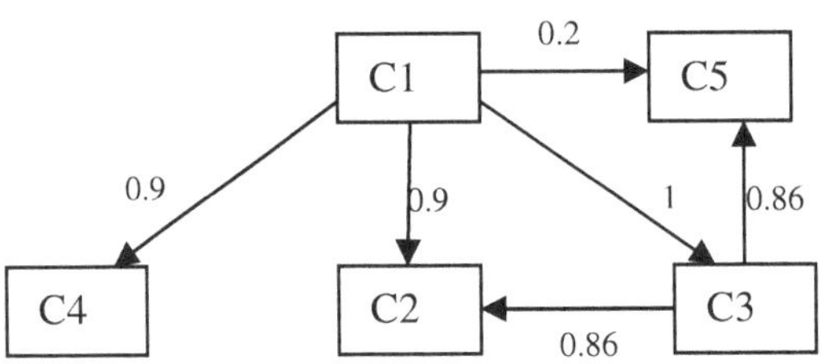

Fig. 2. Concepts-Relationship Map

The created concept map can provide the proper guidance over learning in an adaptive manner. For example, relationship of concept-pair (C1,C3) and (C3,C5) in Fig. 2 represents that if students do not learn concept C1 well, their learning performance of concept C3 are most likely bad and thereby to C5 also. Therefore, teachers can modify their teaching strategies to enhance students' learning performance of concept C1 for getting high performance of concept C3, hence C5.

5 Conclusion and Future Enhancements

The concept map is often used to provide teachers for further analyzing and refining the teaching strategies and to generate adaptive learning guidance in adaptive learning environment. However, creating the concept map of a course is difficult and time consuming. Therefore, in this study, Three-Phase Concept Map Formulation approach is proposed to automatically construct a concept map of a course. Phase 1 is used to preprocess the testing records. Fuzzy set theory is used to transform numeric grade into symbolic form. Norm Referencing in Item Analysis is applied to find Item Discrimination, thereby unrelated quizzes are removed. Phase 2 is used to construct and transform the mined association rules into prerequisite relationships between quizzes which are non-redundant and non-cyclic. Since, the proposed algorithm develops 3Large Item Sets, the additional overhead in the next phase is reduced much. In Phase 3, the relevance degree between concepts in each quiz is found which forms the basis for the construction of concept map. In all the phases, steps are taken to proceed in an efficient and resourceful manner. Thus, the created concept map can be used to develop adaptive learning system and refine the learning strategies of learners.

As a further enhancement to this study, while constructing the Questions-relationship, other fuzzy association rules which involves Medium grade can be considered and impact of it in the relation can be analyzed.

References

1. Bai, S.M., Chen, S.M.: A New Method for Automatically Constructing Concept Maps Based on Data Mining Techniques. In: Proceedings of the Seventh International Conference on Machine Learning and Cybernetics, pp. 3078–3083 (2008)
2. Chen, S.M., Bai, S.M.: Using data mining techniques to automatically construct concept maps for adaptive learning systems. Expert Systems with Applications 37, 4496–4503 (2010)
3. Chen, S.M., Sue, P.J.: A New Method to Construct Concept Maps for Adaptive Learning Systems. In: Proceedings of the Ninth International Conference on Machine Learning and Cybernetics, pp. 2489–2494 (2010)
4. Chu, H.C., Hwang, G.J., Huang, Y.M.: An Enhanced Learning Diagnosis Model Based on Concept-Effect Relationships with Multiple Knowledge Levels. Innovations in Education and Teaching International 47(1), 53–67 (2010)
5. Erdogdu, B.: Computer Based Testing – Evaluation of Question Classification for Computer Adaptive Testing, A Master Thesis submitted to the Graduate School of Natural and Applied Sciences, Istanbul, December 6 (2009)
6. Lee, C.H., Lee, G.G., Leu, Y.H.: Application of automatically constructed concept map of learning to conceptual diagnosis of e-learning. Expert Systems with Application 36(2), 1675–1684 (2009)
7. Tsai, C.-J., Tseng, S.S., Lin, C.-Y.: A Two-Phase Fuzzy Mining and Learning Algorithm for Adaptive Learning Environment. In: Alexandrov, V.N., Dongarra, J., Juliano, B.A., Renner, R.S., Tan, C.J.K. (eds.) ICCS-ComputSci 2001. LNCS, vol. 2074, pp. 429–438. Springer, Heidelberg (2001)
8. Tseng, S.S., Sue, S.P.C., Su, J.M., Weng, J.F., Tsai, W.N.: A new approach for constructing the concept map. Computers & Education 49, 691–707 (2007)
9. Hwang, G.J.: A conceptual map model for developing intelligent tutoring system. Computers and Education 40(3), 217–235 (2003)
10. Al-Sarem, M., Bellafkih, M., Ramdani, M.: Mining Concepts Relationship Based on Numeric Grades. IJCSI, International Journal of Computer Science Issues 8(4/2) (July 2011)

Formal Specification of Trusted Neighbor Information Base of OLSR Routing Protocol of Adhoc Network Using Z Language

Amandeep Verma[1] and Manpreet Singh Gujral[2]

[1] Punjabi University Regional Centre for IT and Management, Mohali
[2] University College of Engineering, Punjabi University, Patiala
{vaman71,msgchd}@gmail.com

Abstract. Nodes in an ad-hoc network lack the protection offered by firewalls in infrastructure-based networks. Trust based system aids to improvise this situation. A few works exists that handle the formal description of ad hoc networks. But describing correct specifications, reusing specifications, and constructing specifications repository are significant issues on software development to product safety and high quality software systems. In order to deal with such issues, we propose a formal specification of the Trusted Neighbor Information Base of OLSR routing protocol of ad hoc network using "Z" language. Z is a state-oriented formal specification language based on set theory and predicate logic. Specification languages are situated between natural and program languages. These types of languages enable to eliminate internal ambiguity, which is characteristic for natural languages. The Z notation is used to for formal specification of this part of the protocol. Finally, the formal specifications is verified and proved using Z Eves tool.

Keywords: Ad hoc Networks, Formal Specification, OLSR, Z Specification Language, Z Eves.

1 Introduction

Ad hoc networks are illustrated by multi-hop wireless connectivity and recurrently changing network topology which have made them infrastructure less. The wireless links in this network are very error prone and can go down frequently due to mobility of nodes, interference and less infrastructure. A routing protocol is needed whenever a packet needs to be transmitted to a destination via number of nodes and numerous routing protocols have been proposed for such kind of ad hoc networks. Trust based systems can provide protection against threats. Within the realm of network security, the interpretation of the concept of trust is as a relation among entities that participate in various protocols. Trust relations are based on evidence created by the previous interactions of entities within a protocol. Trust influences decisions like routing, access control, choice of public keys, etc. Instead of the shortest path, it could be looking for the most trusted path between two nodes. This paper is in the direction of building trust oriented security framework of ad hoc networks.

P.V. Krishna, M.R. Babu, and E. Ariwa (Eds.): ObCom 2011, Part I, CCIS 269, pp. 560–570, 2012.

One way to improve the quality of software is to change the way in which software is documented: at the design stage, during development, and after release. Important information is hidden amongst irrelevant detail, and design flaws are discovered too late, making them expensive or impossible to correct. There is an alternative. Formal methods, based upon elementary mathematics, can be used to produce precise, unambiguous documentation, in which information is structured and presented at an appropriate level of abstraction. This documentation can be used to support the design process, and as a guide to subsequent development, testing, and maintenance. Whatever the discipline, the use of mathematics can be expensive, but it is experience that it can actually reduce costs.

A good specification should be abstract and complete, clear and unambiguous, concise and comprehensible, easy to maintain and cost effective. Above all, it should be useful. The usage of mathematics results abstraction over confusion, precision over ambiguity and reason over doubt. The production of a formal specification helps us to understand requirements and clarify intentions.

Formal specification language creates mathematic basis for formal method. This method shows what specification has to say. Language shows in detail how reality involved in specification can be expressed. Languages like VDM, Z, B, EVES, LOTOS should be included to this language group. Software pack Z/EVES enables writing, developing and analyzing of "Z" language specification. Z/EVES consist of two parts. First part is virtual server, which insures syntactic propriety revision and activities for execution of theorems and paragraphs logic validation. Second part is graphical interface, which enables work with specification. Transcription from informal specification to "Z" language is realized by schema design.

The paper is giving the specifications in "Z" language for building the trusted neighbor information base of the OLSR routing protocol of ad hoc network. The novelty of the work is to give the abstract representation of the procedures used in building the information base include the trust attribute in the information base that are going to be used in making routing decisions. The intended readers are researchers interested in building abstract models and to use trust for security purposes.

The paper is organized as follows. The section 2 is about the review of literature. The section 3 gives an overview of the protocol under study and the specification language used. The section 4 lists down the specification(s). The last section 5 concludes the paper.

2 Review of Literature

There are a number of routing protocols exists for ad hoc networks and every protocol has some significance on one aspect or the other. In order to select a routing protocol for formal verification a study comprising the performance analysis of routing protocols [7] namely – DSR, AODV, OLSR and GRP has been done for common applications: email and ftp in a simulated environment. The observation is that, the OLSR protocol has the better response over others.

An exhaustive review of the formal verification of adhoc network routing protocols [6] using the variety of formal specification languages, modeling techniques and verifying tools are quoted in early work.

In order to demonstrate the methodology for formal verification of routing protocols of ad hoc network [1], a case study of OLSR protocol using PROMELA specification language and SPIN model checker is depicted. The OLSR protocol is also a subject of case study in the description of testing methodology for an ad hoc routing protocol [3].

3 The Protocol and Specification Language

The protocol under study is OLSR and the specification language used for formal specification is the “Z” language.

3.1 OLSR Protocol

Optimized Link State Routing (OLSR) [5] is proposed by IETF's MANET Group at 2003. Although, OLSR has newer and more precise narratives, with the purpose of to congregate our intents, agreed to its minimalism, we use the original version [5]. The Optimized Link State Routing Protocol (OLSR) is developed for mobile ad hoc networks. It operates as a table driven, proactive protocol, i.e., exchanges topology information with other nodes of the network regularly. Each node selects a set of its neighbor nodes as "multipoint relays" (MPR). In OLSR, only nodes, selected as such MPRs, are responsible for forwarding control traffic, intended for diffusion into the entire network. A node selects MPRs from among its one hop neighbors with "symmetric", i.e., bi-directional, linkages. The MPR nodes are chosen among the 1-hop neighbors in such a way that they are the minimum set that covers all the 2-hop neighbors. As a proactive routing protocol, OLSR makes a target for various attacks. In OLSR, each node is injecting topological information into the network through the transmission of HELLO messages and, for some nodes, TC messages. If some nodes (malicious or malfunctioning) inject invalid network traffic, network integrity may be compromised.

3.2 The Z Notation

The Z (pronounced Zed) language [4] [8] is a formal specification language named after Zermelo–Fraenkel set theory, is a formal specification language used for describing and modeling computing systems. Z was developed in Paris, France and Oxford, England. “Z” language is a formal specification language, which is used for description and functions modeling of computer systems. This language enables to write formal specification of computer programs and to formulate evidences of system behavior.

The Z notation is based upon set theory and mathematical logic. The set theory used includes standard set operators, set comprehensions, Cartesian products, and power sets.

The mathematical logic is a first-order predicate calculus. A characteristic feature of Z is the use of types. As well as providing a useful link to programming practice, this notion of types means that an algorithm can be written to check the type of every object in a specification. The other main ingredient in Z is a way of decomposing a specification into small pieces called schemas. By splitting the specification into schemas, we can present it piece by piece. Each piece can be linked with a commentary which explains informally the significance of the formal mathematics. In Z, schemas are used to describe both static and dynamic aspects of a system.

4 The Specification(s)

In order to develop a trust oriented framework for ad hoc network using OLSR routing protocol the approach that we are using is depicted in the Figure 1. This paper is in the direction of building an abstract model--- specification for trusted neighbor information base, an important component of the protocol under study.

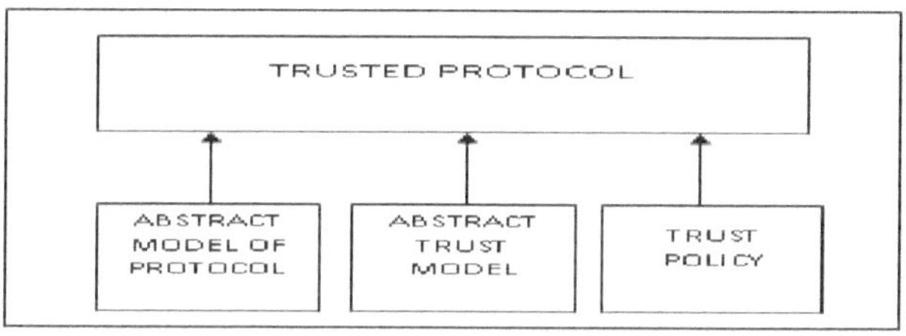

Fig. 1. A General Abstract Trust Oriented Framework

The terminology used in the specification of OLSR protocol is as –

main_address	The main address of a node, which will be used in OLSR control traffic as the "originator address" of all messages emitted.
neighbor node	A node X is a neighbor node of node Y if node Y can hear node X.
2-hop neighbor	A node heard by a neighbor.
multipoint relay (MPR)	A node which is selected by its 1-hop neighbor, node X, to "re-transmit" all the broadcast messages that it receives from X, provided that the message is not a duplicate, and that the time to live field of the message is greater than one.
multipoint relay selector (MPR selector, MS)	A node which has selected its 1-hop neighbor, node X, as its multipoint relay, will be called a multipoint relay selector of node X.

The neighborhood information base stores information about neighbors, 2-hop neighbors, MPRs and MPR selectors [5].

Neighbor Set	A node records a set of "neighbor tuples" (N_neighbor_main_addr, N_willingness), describing neighbors.
2-hop Neighbor Set	A node records a set of "2-hop tuples" (N_neighbor_main_addr, N_2hop_addr, N_time), describing symmetric links between its neighbors and the symmetric 2-hop neighborhood.
MPR Set	A node maintains a set of neighbors which are selected as MPR. Their main addresses are listed in the MPR Set.
MPR Selector Set	A node records a set of MPR-selector tuples (MS_main_addr, MS_time), describing the neighbors which have selected this node as a MPR.

The specification(s) for trusted neighbor information base in "Z" language is as follows:-

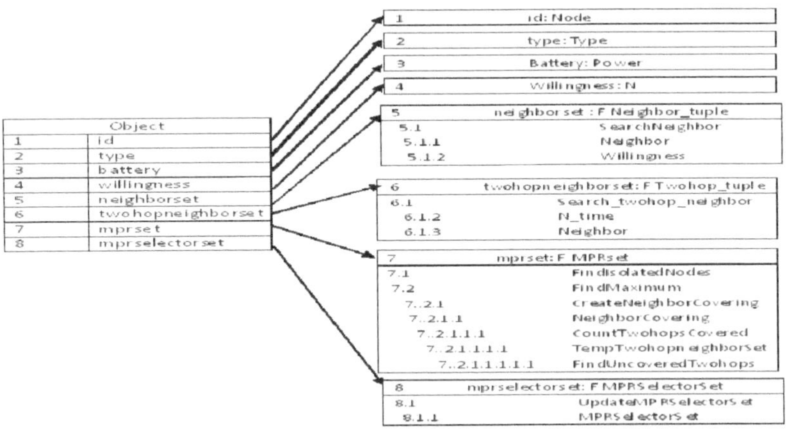

Fig. 2. Structured Diagram of Specifications

The identifier of an object in ad hoc network is denoted by *Node* as given below. Four types of nodes are assumed, i.e., source, destination, internal and nil. The power of battery is assumed dead, low or normal denoted by *Dead, Low and Normal* respectively [2]. The Status, Connectivity, Network and AdhocNetwork schema(s) given in [2] represents the status of link, connections among objects, the network and adhoc network.

[*Node*] *Type* ::= *Source* | *Destination* | *Internal* | *Nil*

The Trust as in Figure 3 can be any value from 0 to 10 where 0 indicates complete distrust and 10 signifies the full trust in the node.

```
┌─ Trust ──────────────────────────
│ N_trust: ℕ
├──────────────
│ N_trust ≤ 10
└──────────────────────────────────
```

Fig. 3. Trust Configuration

The willingness as in Figure 4 that is from 1 to 7 indicates the willingness of node to participate where 1 is the lower level and 7 is the upper level of willingness.

```
┌─ Willingness ────────────────────
│ N_willingness: ℕ
├──────────────
│ N_willingness ≤ 7
└──────────────────────────────────
```

Fig. 4. Node's Willingness Configuration

The specification for neighbor's node main_addr is in Figure 5. This is the main address of the neighbor. It's of type Node.

```
┌─ Neighbor ───────────────────────
│ N_neighbor_main_addr: Node
└──────────────────────────────────
```

Fig. 5. Neighbhour Address

The structure of the neighbor tuple forming Neighbor Set is in Figure 6. Its first member is of type Neighbor, second indicates the willingness of that neighbor to participate in communication and the third component is about the trust on neighbor.

```
┌─ Neighbor_tuple ─────────────────
│ N_neighbor_tuple: Neighbor × Willingness × Trust
└──────────────────────────────────
```

Fig. 6. Structure of Neighbor Tuple

The specification for 2-hop-neighbor main_addr is in Figure 7. This will give the main address of the twohop neighbor of the node. It is of type Node.

```
┌─ TwoHopNeighbor ─────────────────
│ N_2hop_addr: Node
└──────────────────────────────────
```

Fig. 7. TwoHop Neighbor Configuration

To indicate the time at which the connection get Expired as in Figure 8. At the end of time the tuple Expires and must be removed.

```
N_time ::= Live | Expired
```

Fig. 8. Node Connection Time

The structure of the twohop tuple for 2-hop Neighbor Set is in Figure 9. The members are neighbor, twohop neighbor, validity time and trust on twohop neighbor.

Twohop_tuple
$N\_twohop\_tuple: Neighbor \times TwoHopNeighbor \times N\_time \times Trust$

Fig. 9. Structure of TwoHop Tuple

The specification of the MPRSet is in Figure 10. It gives the address of the node which is MPR and the trust of the object on that MPR.

MPRSet
$N\_mpr\_tuple: Node \times Trust$

Fig. 10. Structure of MPR Set

The specification of the MPRSelectorSet is in Figure 11. It gives the address of the Node that selects the object on hand as MPR. The time indicates the time at which tuple expires.

MPRSelectorSet
$MS\_main\_addr: Node$
$MS\_time: \mathbb{N}$

Fig. 11. Structure of MPR Selector Set

The specifications of the object with basic attributes and the attributed required for neighbor information base is given in Figure 12. The id gives the main address of the Object. The willingness is about that node in the participation of communication. The attributes for holding neighbor information base also specified.

Object
$id: Node$
$type: Type$
$willingness: \mathbb{N}$
$neighborset: \mathbb{F}\ Neighbor\_tuple$
$twohopneighborset: \mathbb{F}\ Twohop\_tuple$
$mprset: \mathbb{F}\ MPRSet$
$mprselectorset: \mathbb{F}\ MPRSelectorSet$

Fig. 12. An Object

The network is considered as a graph. The procedure SearchNeighbor as in Figure 13 is to find neighbors and accordingly update the neighborset of that object, a component of the neighbor information base. The invariants are i) host and neighbor should be adhoc network objects ii) should be different iii) they are connected.

```
SearchNeighbor
ΞConnectivity
ΔObject
host_object?: Object
adhoc: Network
────────────
∃o: Object; n: Neighbor_tuple | o ∈ adhoc . objects
   ∧ host_object? ∈ adhoc . objects ∧ host_object? ≠ o ∧ (host_object?, o) = connection
 • n . N_neighbor_tuple . 1 . N_neighbor_main_addr = o . id ∧ n . N_neighbor_tuple . 2 .
N_willingness = o . willingness ⇒ host_object? . neighborset = host_object? . neighborset ∪ {n}
```

Fig. 13. Search Neighbor and Add to Neighborset

The procedure Search_twohop_neighbor is to find the twohop neighbors is given in Figure 14. The invariants are i) the twohop is an object of ad hoc network ii) host, neighbor and twohop neighbors have connections iii) All of these are different.

```
Search_twohop_neighbor
ΞConnectivity
adhoc: Network
host?: Object
neighbor?: Object
twohop_neighbor_id!: Node
twohop_neighbor_willingness!: ℕ
────────────
∃o: Object; t: Twohop_tuple | o ∈ adhoc . objects ∧ (host?, neighbor?) = connection
   ∧ (neighbor?, o) = connection
     ∧ host? . id ≠ neighbor? . id ∧ host? . id ≠ o . id ∧ neighbor? . id ≠ o . id
 • t . N_twohop_tuple . 1 . N_neighbor_main_addr = neighbor? . id
   ∧ t . N_twohop_tuple . 2 . N_2hop_addr = o . id ∧ t . N_twohop_tuple . 3 = Live
   ⇒ host? . twohopneighborset = host? . twohopneighborset ∪ {t}
```

Fig. 14. Search Twohop Neighbor and Add to Twohopneighborset

The specification of the UpdateMPRSelector is given in Figure 15. The invariants are i) the identity of the receiving object and the identity of the MPR of the announced MPR is same.

```
UpdateMPRSelector
adhoc: Network
host?: Object
mpr?: Node
────────────
∃o: Object; m: MPRSelectorSet |    | o ∈ adhoc . objects ∧ o = host? ∧ host? . id = mpr?
•m . MS_main_addr = mpr? ∧ m . MS_time = 5 ⇒ host? . mprselectorset = host? . mprselectorset ∪ {m}
```

Fig. 15. Updation of MPR Selector Set

The MPR Selection procedure involves all following procedures. The FindIsolatedNodes given in Figure 16 searches the isolated twohops, add the neighbors through which connected into the MPRSet of the object; partial MPRs.

$$
\begin{array}{l}
\textit{FindIsolatedNodes} \\
\hline
\Delta Object \\
host?: Object \\
isolated\_2hop\_nodes!: \mathbb{F}\ Node \\
trust: Trust \\
\hline
\exists x: \mathbb{F}\ Twohop\_tuple \bullet \forall ob1: Object; ob2: Object; y: Twohop\_tuple; m: MPRSet \\
\quad \mid x = host?\ .\ twohopneighborset \wedge y \in x \wedge (ob1, ob2) \neq connection \\
\quad \wedge\ ob1\ .\ id = y\ .\ N\_twohop\_tuple\ .\ 2\ .\ N\_2hop\_addr \\
\qquad \bullet\ m\ .\ N\_mpr\_tuple = (y\ .\ N\_twohop\_tuple\ .\ 1\ .\ N\_neighbor\_main\_addr, trust) \\
\qquad\quad \Rightarrow host?\ .\ mprset = host?\ .\ mprset \cup \{m\} \\
\qquad \wedge\ isolated\_2hop\_nodes! = \{y\ .\ N\_twohop\_tuple\ .\ 2\ .\ N\_2hop\_addr\}
\end{array}
$$

Fig. 16. Search of Isolated TwoHop Nodes

The OtherthanPartialMprs procedure shown in Figure 17 finds the neighbors that are not selected as MPRs by the FindIsolatedNodes procedure. The invariant is the others should be equal to the set difference between all neighbor identities and neighbor selected as MPR by the above procedure.

$$
\begin{array}{l}
\textit{OtherthanPartialMprs} \\
\hline
others!: \mathbb{F}\ Node \\
host?: Object \\
\hline
\exists x: \mathbb{F}\ Neighbor\_tuple; neighbor\_ids: \mathbb{F}\ Node; mpr\_ids: \mathbb{F}\ Node; t: \mathbb{F}\ MPRSet \\
\bullet\ \forall y: Neighbor\_tuple; m: MPRSet \mid x = host?\ .\ neighborset \wedge y \in x \wedge t = host?\ .\ mprset \wedge m \in t \\
\bullet\ neighbor\_ids = \{y\ .\ N\_neighbor\_tuple\ .\ 1\ .\ N\_neighbor\_main\_addr\} \\
\quad \wedge\ mpr\_ids = \{m\ .\ N\_mpr\_tuple\ .\ 1\} \ \Rightarrow others! = neighbor\_ids \setminus mpr\_ids
\end{array}
$$

Fig. 17. Search Neighbors other than MPR

The procedure FindUncoveredTwohops of Figure 18 is to find the twohop nodes still not covered by any of the MPR. The invariants is the set difference between the twohopneighborset and the set of tuples of twohopneighborset whose twohopneighbors are given by isolated_hops- one of the output of FindIsolatedNodes.

$$
\begin{array}{l}
\textit{FindUncoveredTwohops} \\
\hline
host?: Object \\
isolated\_2hops?: \mathbb{F}\ Node \\
temptwohopset!: \mathbb{F}\ Twohop\_tuple \\
\hline
\exists x: \mathbb{F}\ Twohop\_tuple \bullet \forall y: Twohop\_tuple \mid x = host?\ .\ twohopneighborset \wedge y \in x \\
\quad \wedge\ y\ .\ N\_twohop\_tuple\ .\ 2\ .\ N\_2hop\_addr \in isolated\_2hops? \\
\quad \bullet\ temptwohopset! = host?\ .\ twohopneighborset \setminus \{y\}
\end{array}
$$

Fig. 18. Search TwoHop Neighbors not covered by MPR

The specification of the tuple for NeighborCovering is given in Figure 19. The components are the identity of the neighbor, the number of twohops covered by that neighbor and the set of identities of twohop neighbors covered by it.

```
NeighborCovering
covered_by_neighbors: Node × ℕ × 𝔽 Node
```

Fig. 19. Structure of Neighbor Covering

The procedure FindNeighborCovering given in Figure 20 is to find the neighbor covering of uncovered twohops given by the above procedure.

```
FindNeighborCovering
host?: Object
neighbor_covering!: NeighborCovering
──────────
∃x: 𝔽 Twohop_tuple; z: Neighbor
  • ∀y: Twohop_tuple | x = host? . twohopneighborset ∧ y ∈ x
      ∧ z ∈ {y . N_twohop_tuple . 1} ∧ z = y . N_twohop_tuple . 1
    • neighbor_covering! . covered_by_neighbors
       = (z . N_neighbor_main_addr,
         # {y . N_twohop_tuple . 2 . N_2hop_addr},
         {y . N_twohop_tuple . 2 . N_2hop_addr})
```

Fig. 20. Search Covering by Neighbor

The procedure given below in Figure 21, Remove2hopNeighbors is to find the twohopneighborset without the twohop neighbors that are covered by any of the entry of the MPRSet of the given object. This removal is only in the temporary set not on the original set of twohopneighborset, as required for the MPR Selection algorithm.

```
Remove2hopNeighbors
host?: Object
modi_2hop_set?: 𝔽 Twohop_tuple
reduced_2hop_set!: 𝔽 Twohop_tuple
twohop_nodes?: 𝔽 Node
──────────
∃x, z: 𝔽 Twohop_tuple
  • ∀y: Node; t: Twohop_tuple | x = modi_2hop_set?
      ∧ x ⊆ host? . twohopneighborset ∧ y ∈ twohop_nodes?
      ∧ t . N_twohop_tuple . 2 . N_2hop_addr ∈ twohop_nodes?
      ∧ z = {t} • reduced_2hop_set! = x \ z
```

Fig. 21. Removal of TwoHop Neighbors

The procedure FindMaximum given in Figure 22, is to find the neighbor with maximum covering of twohop neighbors and then update the MPRSet. So they can be removed from consideration in MPR Selection. This procedure gets repeated till all twohop nodes get covered by any of the selected MPR.

```
FindMaximum
ΔObject
host?: Object
covering_neighbors?: 𝔽 NeighborCovering
twohop_covered!: 𝔽 Node
reduced_covering_neighbors!: 𝔽 NeighborCovering
trust: Trust
─────────────────────
∀y: NeighborCovering • ∃x: NeighborCovering; m: MPRSet
    | x ∈ covering_neighbors? ∧ {y} ⊆ covering_neighbors?
     ∧ x ∉ {y} ∧ x . covered_by_neighbors . 2 ⩾ y . covered_by_neighbors . 2
    • m . N_mpr_tuple = (x . covered_by_neighbors . 1, trust)
     ∧ twohop_covered! = x . covered_by_neighbors . 3
     ⇒ host? . mprset = host? . mprset ∪ {m}
      ∧ reduced_covering_neighbors! = covering_neighbors? \ {x}
```

Fig. 22. Select MPR from Neighbor Covering Tuples

5 Conclusions

The analysis is by invariants rather than exhaustive functional analysis. In this approach, invariants are checked that describe properties in order to detect behaviors that violate them. The invariants are given under the form of a logical formula.

References

[1] Camara, D., Loureiro, A.A.F., Filali, F.: Methodology for Formal Verification of Routing Protocols for Ad Hoc Wireless Networks. In: IEEE Conference on Global Communications, pp. 705–709 (2007)
[2] Ahmed, S., Ramani, A.K., Zafar, N.A.: Verifying Route Request Procedure of AODV Using Graph Theory And Formal Methods. International Journal On Applications Of Graph Theory In Wireless Ad Hoc Networks And Sensor Network 2(2), 1–13 (2011)
[3] Maag, S., Zaidi, F.: Testing Methodology for an Ad Hoc Routing Protocol. In: ACM International Workshop on Performance Monitoring, Measurement, and Evaluation of Heterogeneous Wireless and Wired Networks, pp. 48–55 (2006)
[4] Spivey, J.M.: The Z Notation: A Reference Manual. Prentice-Hall (1989)
[5] Clausen, T., Jacquet, P.: Optimized Link State Routing Protocol (OLSR). IETF INTERNET DRAFT, RFC 3626 (2003)
[6] Amandeep, V.: Formal Verification of Ad Hoc Network Routing Protocols. International Journal of Advanced Research in Computer Science 2(4), 526–530 (2011)
[7] Amandeep, V., Singh, G.M.: Performance Analysis of Routing Protocols for Ad hoc Networks. International Journal of Computer Science and Emerging Technologies 2(4), 484–487 (2011)
[8] Jim, W., Jim, D.: UsingZ: Specification, Refinement and Proof, `http://www.cs.cmu.edu/~15819/zedbook.pdf`

Vertical Handover Based on Voice Activity in Heterogeneous Network

G. Kalaivani[1] and S. Usha[2]

[1] M.E. Computer and Communication, Sri Sairam Engineering College, Chennai-44
vanicseamies@gmail.com
[2] Department of Information Technology, Sri Sairam Engineering College, Chennai-44
usha_sakthivel@yahoo.co.in

Abstract. A heterogeneous network consists of multiple access networks interworking together. Vertical handover is the technique that allows for seamless connectivity among these networks. This vertical handover when used specifically during the off periods of the VoIP (Voice over Internet Protocol) connection, then the QoS can be improved. This paper provides such a method in which we derive a simplified two-state Markov model from the six-state Brady model in which both the talk-spurt period and mutual silence period characteristics are obtained. Then the handover execution time and packet loss time are taken as parameters to analyze the performance. The result is that decrease in VoIP packet loss time. However vertical handover procedure increases within the allowable limit.

Keywords: Heterogeneous network, vertical handover, Voice over Internet Protocol, seamless connectivity.

1 Introduction

The heterogeneous networks are made possible by the acceptance of several architectures by a particular network operator. Thus it allows them to communicate with each other even more common. Heterogeneous itself means containing dissimilar constituents. Providing seamless connection in that requires mobility management. Mobility management is one of the major functions of a GSM or a UMTS network that track where the subscribers are, allow calls, SMS to be delivered and other mobile phone services. One of the key techniques for it is vertical handover which refers to a network node changing the type of connectivity it uses to access a supporting infrastructure, usually to support node mobility [1].

2 Related Work

The Third Generation Partnership Project (3GPP) The Third Generation Partnership Project 2 (3GPP2) defined the standards for 3G and WLAN interworking. It is hindered by several problems, including QoS support and scalability [2][3]. In vertical

P.V. Krishna, M.R. Babu, and E. Ariwa (Eds.): ObCom 2011, Part I, CCIS 269, pp. 571–575, 2012.

handover apart from L2 handover, L3 connection setup procedure, authentication and IP registration with new access network (AN) are also performed. This vertical handover results in longer handover latency and service disruption time, which lead to packet loss of ongoing service and deteriorate QoS [4][5].

The fast handover [6] introduced thus by IETF (Internet Engineering Task Force) using mobileIP protocol in both IPV4 and IPv6 networks uses a pre-registration or post- registration technique [7]. This reduces handover latency as it separates L2 and L3 handovers and performs L3 handover before or after L2 handover as it requires more time. The Context Transfer Protocol [8] and a smooth handover procedure [9] supporting pre authentication are suggested to minimize the signalling procedures. However it is difficult to apply a soft handover technique for the vertical handover as service disruption is inevitable when MN changes the physical air interface.

With efficient signalling procedures, the fast handover mechanisms adopt buffering and forwarding functions to reduce packet loss during a handover. The buffering is but limited by the available storage space in the network agent due to which buffered packets may be dropped by buffer overflow. Also the forwarding function is only effective for a small number of hops as multiple hops on a wired network cause propagation delay.

3 Proposed Work

Let us take a VoIP telephony service as an application model for the proposed scheme. VoIP is vulnerable to service disruption and uses a service-suppression scheme to prevent bandwidth wastage [10]-[12]. The vertical handover depend on various parameters like received signal strength (RSS), minimum bandwidth, access cost, application type, delay required by the application, battery status of the MN, and user's preference[14]. In reality the MN prefers WLAN than 3G networks due to its low cost and high bandwidth, so let us assume that the vertical handover decision depends on RSS from only WLAN channel. Thus RSS_H and RSS_L represents the threshold values for initiation of downward (3G to WLAN) and upward (WLAN to 3G) vertical handover. RSS_{min} is minimum signal strength to maintain a connection with WLAN.

We also assume that preregistration technique is applied for vertical handover execution. The MN cannot receive or transmit during entire L2 handover time and some of the reregistration times until the buffered packets are forwarded to the MN which we call as service-disruption time., The maximum time duration that an MN can wait during the handover procedure is called *margin time.* Here the scheme waits for the start of a mutual silence period during the pre determined margin time. This reduces the packet loss as no packets will be transmitted during the mutual silence period.

The initiation of mutual silence period is recognised by the *silence insertion descriptor* (SID) frame which is sent by sender's VoIP codec at the beginning of silence period to generate artificial noise at the receiving side's decoder during the silent period. The SID frame is smaller in size and hence MN and AN can identify the silence period by easily checking the size information in received packet's header.

When the MN recognizes the beginning of a mutual silence period during the margin time, it starts the detachment procedure with the serving AN and the attachment procedure with the target AN. This operation reduces the packet loss of a

VoIP call because of the absence of VoIP packet transmission during the service disruption caused by the detachment and attachment procedures. After the detachment and attachment procedures are completed, the MN performs the post-operation (i.e. re-registration) and completes its handover procedure. In the case where there is no mutual silence period during the margin time, the MN starts detachment procedure immediately after the margin time is expired, so as not to excessively increase the total handover time.

A Wait and Execute algorithm to explain this concept proposed here. It sets a waiting time for which the handover is delayed and it does not exceed the margin time.

```
loop
if RSS> RSS_H or RSS< RSS_L    then
execute preregistration
set waiting time t=0;
while t < margin time
if mutual silence occurs then
execute L2 handover
break;
else
t= t + δ; /* δ is time increment */
end if
end while
execute reregistration
end if
end loop
```

The basic concept of the proposed algorithm is here extended to traffic whose transmission rate is not fixed but varies by aligning the service disruption with the time when the lowest transmission rate starts. This operation will mitigate the detrimental effect of service disruption on the QoS of the application.

4 Implementation and Result

For the simulation, we set the pre-operation and post-operation times to 1 and 0.1s respectively. The service disruption time (T_d) is varied from 0.1 to 0.4 s, which are regarded as reasonable values for a vertical handover scenario [13]. The VoIP codec under consideration supporting the silence suppression functionality is G.729B, which generates a voice packet every 20ms. Let us assume that a packet buffering is not used in the network agent. So packet loss occurs if packets are transmitted during the service disruption time.

The graph shows relation between the average packet loss time and the handover execution time. As the margin time increases, the handover execution time increases, but the packet loss time decreases, and vice versa. It is seen that both the packet loss time and the handover execution time converge as the margin time goes to infinity. Compared with the traditional handover where the margin time is not applied (i.e. $Tm = 0$), for just $Tm = 0.6$, the packet loss time significantly decreases, while the handover execution time increases by the waiting time of 0.34 s.

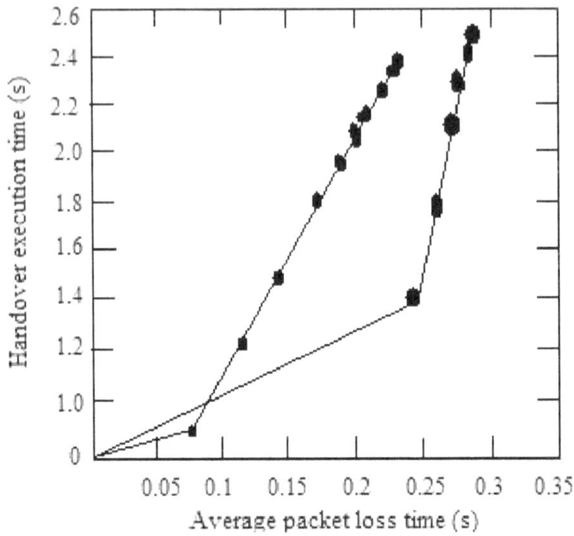

Fig. 1. Shows the relation between handover execution time and average packet loss time. It can be seen the packet loss reduces when margin time (T_m) is set.

Similarly the service disruption time when increases, the packet loss automatically increases. By setting the margin time the reduction in packet loss can be seen. This will in turn improve the Quality of Service of the established connection. The following graph provides a proof for this improved performance.

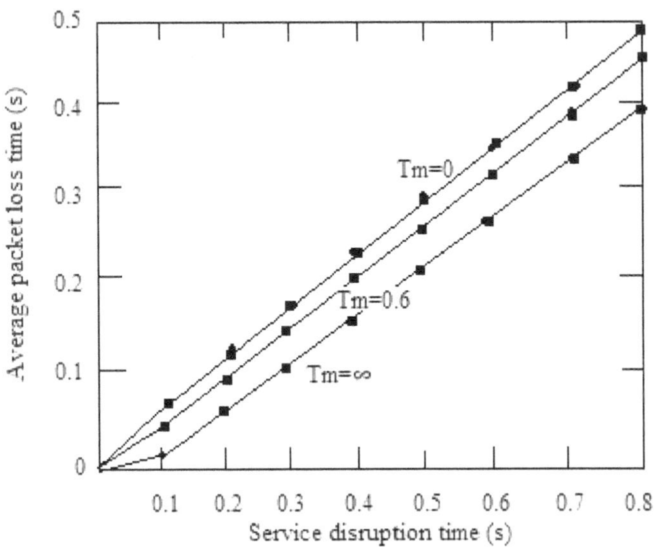

Fig. 2. Shows the relation between service disruption time and the average packet loss time. It can be seen how the packet loss reduces here with appropriate margin time (T_m) being set.

5 Conclusion

The algorithm introduced a margin time to align the mutual silence period and where there is lowest transmission rate with the service disruption time. This reduces the packet loss and the QoS of the communication network is also improved. Though vertical handover latency increases it is tolerable for a seamless connection between heterogeneous networks.

References

1. Choi, H.-H., Song, O., Park, Y.-K., Lee, J.-R.: Performance Evaluation of Opportunistic Vertical Handover Considering On-Off Characteristics of VoIP Traffic. IEEE Transactions on Vehicular Technology 59(6) (July 2010)
2. Third Generation Partnership Project, Requirement on 3GPP System to Wireless Local Area Network (WLAN) Interworking, TS 22.234 (v8.0.0) (March 2007)
3. Third Generation Partnership Project 2, 3GPP2-WLAN Interworking, S.R0087-A(v1.0) (February 2006)
4. Naser, N., Hasswa, A., Hassanein, H.: Handoffs in fourth generation heterogeneous networks. IEEE Communication Magazine 44(10), 96–103 (2006)
5. McNair, J., Zhu, F.: Vertical handoffs in fourth-generation multi network environments. IEEE Wireless Communication 11(3), 8–15 (2004)
6. El Malki, K., Calhoun, P.R., Hiller, T., Kempf, J., McCann, P.J., Singh, A., Soliman, H., Thalanany, S.: Low Latency Handoff in Mobile IPv4, IETF, draft-ietf-mobileip-lowlatency-handoffs-v4-1 (May 2001)
7. Koodli, G.: Fast Handovers for MobileIPv6, IETF RFC 4068 (July 2005)
8. Loughney, J., Nakhjiri, M., Perkins, C., Koodli, R.: Context Transfer Protocol (CXTP), IETF RFC 4067 (July 2005)
9. Choi, H.H., Song, O., Cho, D.H.: Seamless handoff scheme based on pre-registration and pre-authentication for UMTS-WLAN interworking. Wireless Pers. Commun. 41(3), 345–364 (2007)
10. ITU-T Recommendation G.723.1 Annex A: Dual Rate Speech Coder for Multimedia Communications Transmitting at 5.3 and 6.3 kbit/s, ANNEX A: Silence Compression Scheme (November 1996)
11. ITU-T Recommendation G.729 Annex B: A Silence Compression Scheme for G.729 Optimized for Terminals Conforming to RecommendationV.70 (October 1996)
12. Estepa, A., Estepa, R., Vozmediano, J.: A new approach for VoIP traffic characterization. IEEE Commun. Lett. 8(10), 644–646
13. Fathi, H., Chakraborty, S.S., Prasad, R.: Optimization of mobile IPv6-based handovers to support VoIP services in wireless heterogeneous networks. IEEE Trans. Veh. Technol. 56(1), 260–270 (2007)
14. Stevens-Navarro, E., Lin, Y., Wong, W.S.: An MDP-based vertical handoff decision algorithm for heterogeneous wireless networks. IEEE Trans. Veh. Technol. 57(2), 1243–1254 (2008)

Cross-Layer Scheme to Solve Hidden Device Problem in WPANs with Increased Transmission Range

M.L. Mathivathani[1] and S. Usha[2]

[1] ME Computer and Communication, Sri Sai Ram Engineering College, Chennai 44
mathivathani.ml@gmail.com
[2] Department of Information Technology, Sri Sai Ram Engineering College, Chennai 44
usha_sakthivel@yahoo.co.in

Abstract. Wireless Personal Area Networks(WPANs) is one of the promising candidates for interconnections between Wireless Sensor Network. The standard IEEE 802.15.4 is designed specifically to achieve low power transmissions in low rate and short distance WPAN. Previous studies indicate that the probability of any two devices in an infrastructure network unheard of each other is around 41%. The unheard devices are called hidden terminal problem which results in low utilization of bandwidth and unfairness in channel access. A Cross-layer scheme is used in order to overcome the hidden terminal problem and the transmission range is increased. The performance graph experimentally proves that the goodput is increased with the reduced power consumption and with the increase in transmission range the Energy Efficiency is compared with the nodal density.

Keywords: Hidden device problem (HDP), Goodput, Wireless Personal Area Networks (WPANs), Cross-Layer Scheme, Transmission Range.

1 Introduction

Wireless sensor is networked and scalable, consumes very little power, is smart and software programmable, capable of fast data acquisition, reliable and accurate over the long term, costs little to purchase and install, and requires no real maintenance. IEEE 802.15.4 is a standard which specifies the physical layer and media access control for low-rate Wireless Personal Area Networks (LR-WPANs).

Hidden nodes in a Wireless Sensor Networks refer to nodes that are out of range of other nodes or a collection of nodes. Take a physical star topology with an access point with many nodes surrounding it in a circular fashion. Each node is within communication range of the AP, but the nodes cannot communicate with each other, as they do not have a physical connection to each other. In a WSNs, it is likely that the node at the far edge of the access points range, which is known as A, can see the access point, but it is unlikely that the same node can see a node on the opposite end of the access point's range, B. These nodes are known as hidden. The problem is when nodes A and B start to send packet simultaneously to the access point [9].

P.V. Krishna, M.R. Babu, and E. Ariwa (Eds.): ObCom 2011, Part I, CCIS 269, pp. 576–582, 2012.

2 Related Work

It is assumed that the devices have the same transmission radius and are randomly located in the network the probability of any two devices having a hidden device relationship can be as large 41%[10].

In wireless network, the HDP is solved by RTS/CTS handshake mechanism. But the medium access control (MAC) of wireless network does not have a mechanism to control HDP. From Previous studies the solution for HDP is out-of-band busy tone approach [3], [9]. In this approach the busy tone signals are send in control channel while receiving data packets in data channel. The other devices hearing the busy tone will not transmit their signals which solves HDP. But additional channel and transceiver is needed for each device resulting in extra power consumption which is not suitable for LR-WPANs.

The transmission range is divided into the carrier sense range and Interference range. The range in which the signal from one device can be sensed by any other devices is known as carrier sense range and the range that the device could not sense the received signal if any other devices within the range transmitting signals at the same time is known as the interference range. The carrier sensing range is larger than the interference range to resolve the HDP [11][12].The HDP cannot be prevented if there are obstructers between the devices and reduces the spatial reuse.

Devices with smaller transmission power are use to solve the HDP which reduces the carrier sense range and Interference range[5][13].Since the transmission power is low for the standard IEEE 802.15.4 again reducing the power, the reliable communication quality is not maintained.

Zig Zag decoding is used where it does not avoids hidden terminal problem completely but it overcomes the HDP by data retransmissions to collide again and recover the collided data [2].Frequent retransmissions spoil the battery life of the sensors.

The devices are separated into mutually exclusive groups based with their hidden device relationships. Each group is scheduled to transmit at specific time interval so that no two device transmit signals at the same time to solve HDP[6].For this method number of devices required is large in number and due to the movement of the nodes the topology changes, again scheduling process should be done. The complexity increases as the number of devices increases.

The receiver of the collided signals detects frame length and source address, from the collided frame to allocate dedicated time or bandwidth to the respective devices [8]. But, detection of these two fields from the corrupted frame in the MAC layer is very difficult due to the severe frame damage in the physical (PHY) layer.

In this paper, we propose a cross-layer scheme to overcome the hidden terminal problem in low power. The hidden terminal is detected in PHY layer and then schedule the detected address in the MAC layer [14] ,with the increased transmission range and data rate of 250Kb/s.

3 Proposed Scheme

Cross-Layer Scheme consists of operations in both PHY and MAC layers. The address of the devices which cause collision of signals are detected in the PHY layer. Verification of the detected address is done in the MAC layer and separate time slots are scheduled for the detected address ie to the hidden device pair, to overcome the Hidden Device Problem.

3.1 Address Detection in the PHY Layer

The main features of PHY layer in IEEE 802.15.4 standard is energy detection(ED).A Aforementioned energy detection is used that is it stores the energy of all the devices at each coordinator. Whenever the signal is received at the node ,the energy is calculated. If the calculated energy is less the previously mentioned energy then the coordinator concludes that collision of signals have occurred and sends a negative acknowledgement (NACK) to the devices which cause the collision. Acknowledgement(ACK) is send if the received signal is not the collided signal. Address of the devices receiving the NACK is detected from the source address field in the frames using the detected preamble locations. In the frame first eight continuous bits consists of data symbols and located at the beginning of the frame. Then the source address field starts from the twenty third symbol after the end of the preamble sequence. The co- ordinator correlates the chip sequences of the preamble to the received signal. If the peak correlation value is observed then the co-ordinator asserts that a preamble sequence is found.The address detected in the PHY layer is send to the MAC address.

3.2 Verification of Detected Address in the MAC Layer

The main function MAC layer to divide the active period into contention access period (CAP) and contention free period (CFP).CFP is composed of several guaranteed time slots (GTSs).The co-ordinator can allocate the GTSs to the devices for data transmissions per the requests. To verify the detected addresses send by the PHY layer the co-ordinator schedules each hidden devices, according to the flag received by the devices. The two possible cases followed are, If a NACK frame is received then the collision has occurred and the device is allowed to send in the GTS. If no NACK frame is received then the collision has not occurred and the device is not forced to sent in the GTS. If the coordinator has send a NACK flag and no device is allocated in the GTS then the coordinator concludes that the detected address in the PHY layer is incorrect. Then the procedure is repeated until it finds the correct hidden device.

3.3 Time Allocation Algorithm MAC Layer

If the verified address is correct in the MAC layer the coordinator allocates the hidden devices in the Hidden Device Address List(AL).The three types of subperiods available are contention access period (CAP),guaranteed time slots(GTS),Inactive period. The devices which do not cause any hidden device problem are allocated to CAP and the devices which causing the hidden device problem are allocated to GTS and Inactive period(INA) using Time Allocation algorithm diagrammatically represented in Fig-1. Consider the parameters List, the Hidden Device Address List size denoted as AL_{size} and its threshold value $Size_{threshold}$,Hidden device(HD) which cause the HDP denoted as HD_{severe} and its threshold value $Severe_{threshold}$.

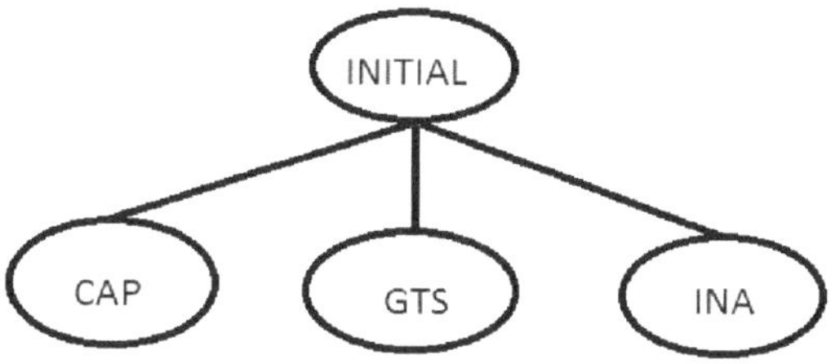

Fig. 1. State Diagram of Time Allocation Algorithm

Time allocation algorithm:

1) $AL_{size}<Size_{threshold}$, $HD_{severe}\{i\}<Severe_{threshold}$ The coordinator allocates the devices to Inactive period since the HDP is not severe.
2) $AL_{size}<Size_{threshold}$,$HD_{severe}\{i\}>Severe_{threshold}$ and
$AL_{size}>Size_{threshold}$, $HD_{severe}\{i\}<Severe_{threshold}$ The coordinator allocates the device which cause more hidden device problem to the GTS (ie) with the largest severeness and rest to Inactive period.
3) $AL_{size}>Size_{threshold}$,$HD_{severe}\{i\}>Severe_{threshold}$ The coordinator allocates the most seven of the device which has largest severeness value to transmit in the GTS and rest in Inactive period.
4) $AL_{size}=Size_{threshold}$, $HD_{severe}\{i\}=Severe_{threshold}$ The coordinator divides the hidden devices equally and allocates half in GTS and another in Inactive period.

Hidden Device Problem is solved by using Cross-Layer scheme to allocate Time slots for the pair of hidden devices.

3.4 Increased Transmission Range

Transmission range is increased using the optimum energy efficiency. Consider the source is located at center of the circle with the radius r, the destination may be present inside the circle or on the circle or outside the circle. If the destination node is present outside the circle then the packets are routed from the source node using number of neighbor node which is known as routers. All the nodes are assumed to know their locations of neighbor and destination nodes. Based on this assumption, transmission strategy is designed as:

1) If the destination node is present inside the circle then the source node transmits directly.
2) If the destination node is present outside the circle

(a) If the nearest neighbor node of the destination is present then the source node sends the packet through the neighbor node.
(b) If the destination does not have any neighbor node due to the mobility nature of the sensor nodes then the transmission is postponed until the neighbor is found.

The transmission range is increased by using optimum transmission range by multihop transmission using the intermediate routers.

4 Implementation and Results

Initially consider N number of devices and are randomly distributed .Consider a circle with radius r and the coordinator is placed at the center of the circle with area of $\pi*25^2m^2$.Assuming that the arrival process of packets at the destination follows the poisson distribution with the arrival rate of n. The transmission range of all devices is assumed to be within the radius and if not then the optimum transmission range is used. The moving direction of each devices is randomly selected .When the boundary is reached, the device reselects a direction. The moving speed of the devices are randomly selected from 0-1m/s . All the device maintains a FIFO buffer of frames and the mean frame length is assumed to be 60 bytes excluding PHY and MAC implemented using JAVA. First, we compare the different performance metrics for Cross-Layer Scheme and IEEE 802.15.4 standard with 50 devices, and Fig-2 shows the effect of the traffic load on good put. We observe that the good put of Cross-Layer Scheme outperforms IEEE 802.15.4 standard. The probability of HDP is decreased by Cross-Layer scheme because the hidden devices are properly separated into suitable sub periods.

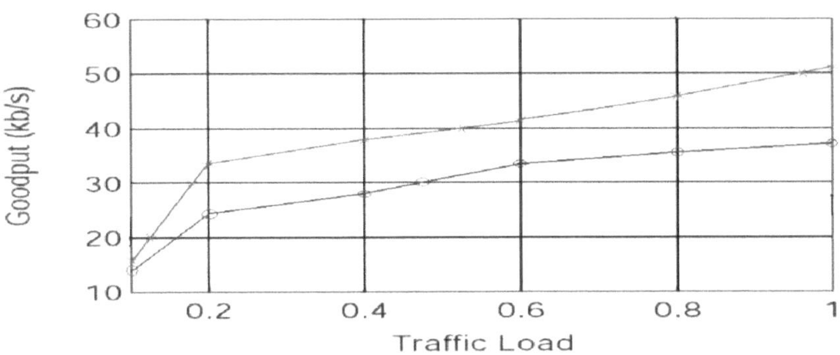

Fig. 2. This graph shows the relation between goodput and traffic load.Cross-Layer Scheme outperforms IEEE 802.15.4 where Cross-Layer Scheme is indicated by green line and IEEE 802.15.4 is indicated by blue line.

The nodal density is assumed for each node and the graph is drawn for Distance-Energy Efficiency versus Transmission Range in Fig-3.The radius r is assumed to be 100meters and the path loss parameter is assumed to be 2.

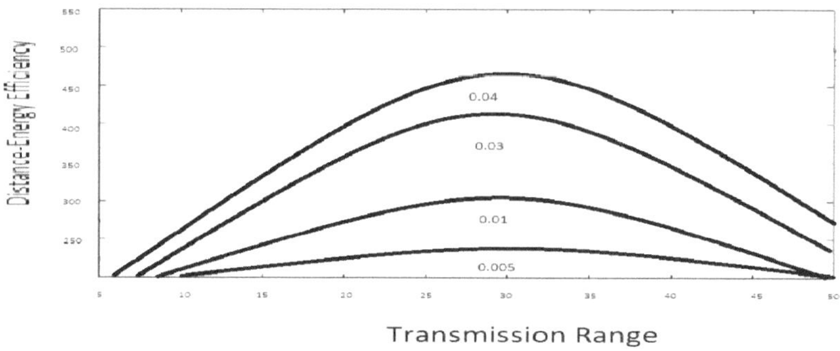

Fig. 3. This graph shows the relation between Distance-Energy Efficiency and the Transmission range for different nodal densities

5 Conclusion

The cross -layer scheme, has proposed in this paper to solve the HDP in IEEE 802.15.4 WPANs with increased transmission range. The proposed scheme detects the hidden devices address in the PHY layer and the address is verified in the MAC layer .The proposed cross-layer scheme significantly reduces the hidden device problem and increases the transmission range with effective enhancement in goodput . Therefore CL-DNA is a simple and efficient approach for enhancing IEEE 802.15.4 protocol in wireless sensor network. The optimum transmission range also shows that the distance-energy efficiency with higher nodal density is higher.

References

1. Data Sheet for CC2420 2.4 GHz IEEE 802.15.4/Zigbee RF Transceiver, `http://focus.ti.com/docs/toolsw/folders/print/cc2430dk.html`
2. Gollakota, S., Katabi, D.: Zigzag decoding: Combating hidden terminals in wireless networks. In: Proc. ACM SIGCOMM, pp. 159–170 (2008)
3. Haas, Z.J., Deng, J.: Dual busy tone multiple access (DBTMA)—A multiple access control scheme for ad hoc networks. IEEE Trans. Commun. 50(6), 975–985 (2002)
4. IEEE 802.15 Working Group, Standard for Part 15.4: Wireless Medium Access Control Layer (MAC) and Physical Layer (PHY) Specifications for Low Rate Wireless Personal Area Networks (LR-WPANs), IEEE Std 802.15.4 (October 2003)
5. Jung, E.S., Vaidya, N.H.: A power control MAC protocol for ad hoc networks. In: Proc. ACM Int. Conf. Mobile Computing Networking (MOBICOM), pp. 36–47 (2002)
6. Koubaa, A., Severino, R., Alves, M., Tovar, E.: Improving quality-of-service in wireless sensor networks by mitigating hidden-node collisions. IEEE Trans. Ind. Informat. (Special Issue on Real-Time and Embedded Networked Systems) 5(3), 299–313 (2009)
7. Hwang, L.-J., Sheu, S.-T., Shih, Y.-Y., Cheng, Y.-C.: Grouping strategy for solving hidden-node problem in IEEE 802.15.4 LRWPANs. In: Proc. IEEE WICON, pp. 26–32 (July 2005)
8. Sheu, S.-T., Shih, Y.-Y., Lee, W.-T.: CSMA/CF protocol for IEEE 802.15.4 WPANs. IEEE Trans. Veh. Technol. 58(3), 1501–1516 (2009)

9. Tobagi, F.A., Kleinrock, L.: Packet switching in radio channels: Part II—The hidden terminal problem in carrier sense multiple-access and the busy-tone solution. IEEE Trans. Commun. 23(12), 1417–1433 (1975)
10. Tseng, Y.-C., Ni, S.-Y., Shih, E.-Y.: Adaptive approaches to relieving broadcast storms in a wireless multihop mobile Ad Hoc network. IEEE Trans. Comput. 52(5), 545–557 (2003)
11. Yang, X., Vaidya, N.H.: On the physical carrier sense in wireless ad hoc networks. In: Proc. IEEE Infocom, pp. 2525–2535 (March 2005)
12. Zhai, H., Fang, Y.: Physical carrier sensing and spatial reuse in multirate and multihop wireless ad hoc networks. In: Proc. IEEE Infocom, pp. 1–12 (April 2006)
13. Zhu, J., Guo, X., Yang, L.L., Steven, W.: A single-channel solution for transmission power control in wireless ad hoc networks. In: Proc. ACM Int. Symp. Mobile Ad Hoc Networking Computing (MOBIHOC), pp. 210–221 (2004)
14. Tseng, H.-W., Yang, S.-C., Yeh, P.-C., Pang, A.-C.: A Cross-Layer Scheme for Solving Hidden Device Problem in IEEE 802.15.4 Wireless Sensor Networks. IEEE Sensors Journal 11(2) (February 2011)
15. Deng, J., Han, Y.S., Chen, P.-N., Varshney, P.K.: Optimum Transmission Range for Wireless Adhoc Networks

Road Detection Using a New Method for Vanishing Point Detection Based on Hough Transform

Binu B.

Dept of CSE, Viswajyothi College of Engineering and Technology, Vazhakulam
binu_cs2005@yahoo.co.in

Abstract. Given an image of the road that is not clear. The computer must determine where the road in that image. Here this road detection process is mainly divided into two steps. 1) Detection of the vanishing point associated with the road. 2) Segmentation of the road area. A new method for detecting the vanishing point based on twice Hough transform is presented in this paper. The first Hough transform is used to detect the straight lines in the image. Then it uses a coordinate transform to translate the points in a circle to points in a line. Finally a Hough transform is used again for the detection of a line. From the parameters of the line the position of the vanishing point can be calculated. Then OCR based road segmentation is used to find the two most dominant edges of the road based on the detected vanishing point.

Keywords: Hough Transform, Vanishing point Detection, Orientation Consistency Ratio, Coordinate Transform.

1 Introduction

There are several methods for road detection. Given an image of the road that is not clear, the computer must determine where the road in that image. This paper presents a framework for segmenting the road area based on the detected vanishing point associated with the road area. Here a new algorithm for the vanishing point detection is used, which is based on the Hough transform. The Hough transform is applied two times [2]. After detecting the vanishing point we must perform the segmentation of the road area based on the detected vanishing point. To segment the road area a vanishing point constrained group of edges are detected based on the orientation consistency ratio, and two most dominant edges are selected as the road borders by combining the color cue. Road segmentation accuracy can be improved by combining OCR and color features.

2 Related Works

Several methods are proposed for the road detection. A road image can be classified into either structured or unstructured. For structured road color cue, steerable filters etc. are utilized to find the two most dominant edges [4]. But these methods work

P.V. Krishna, M.R. Babu, and E. Ariwa (Eds.): ObCom 2011, Part I, CCIS 269, pp. 583–587, 2012.

only when the road have noticeable markings or boarders. Segmenting the road area based on the color cues have also been proposed, but they do not work well, when there is little color difference between road and off road regions.

One of the most popular algorithms for the detection of the vanishing point is based on the construction of the Gaussian sphere [3]. But this results in very heavy computations. Another method for the vanishing point detection requires no priori information, but uses complex probabilistic models. Our method is based on simple 2D geometry of the image space. It performs the automatic detection of the vanishing points.

3 Vanishing Point Detection

The different steps in the vanishing point detection are as shown in Fig.1.

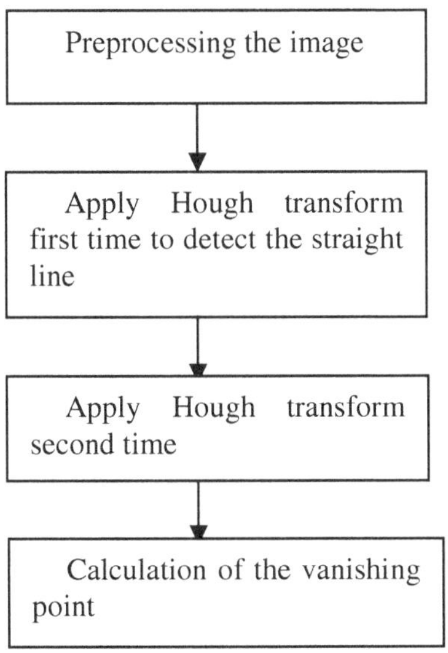

Fig. 1. Steps in Algorithm

Using Hough transform, the straight lines that meet the vanishing point in an image can be mapped to a circle. This extraction of circle helps in detecting the vanishing point. But this is a very complex operation. To reduce the complexity we use a coordinate transform and translate the points in the circle to points in a line. By detecting the straight line we can easily compute the vanishing point. The Hough transform is applied again to find the straight line.

Using the Hough transform a straight line can be described as

$$\lambda = x \cos \theta + y \sin \theta \tag{1}$$

where λ is the length of the perpendicular from the origin to the line, and θ is the angle made by the perpendicular to the x-axis.

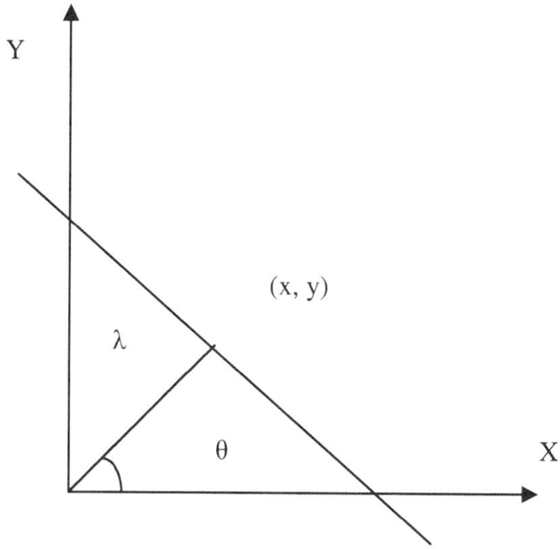

Fig. 2. Normal Straight Line Parameterization

By using the transform {X, Y} => {λ, θ}, the straight line can be mapped to a point in the parameter space. From this we can map the straight line meeting the vanishing point (X_v,Y_v) in image space to a circle in parameter space, which is given by

$$\left[X - \frac{X_v}{2}\right]^2 + \left[Y - \frac{Y_v}{2}\right]^2 = \left[\frac{X_v}{2}\right]^2 + \left[\frac{Y_v}{2}\right]^2 \tag{2}$$

But the detection of a circle is more difficulty than detection of a straight line and high computational complexity. To avoid this we uses a transform {x, y} => {k/λ1, θ}, where k represents a constant. Thus we can rewrite the equation (1) as

$$K/\lambda = X_v \mathrm{Cos}\theta + Y_v \mathrm{Sin}\,\theta \tag{3}$$

This is similar to the cartesian coordinate system. After this transformation, infinite vanishing points project to origin of coordinate. These straight lines meet a vanishing point project to a straight line in coordinate space. We translate the straight line of coordinate space to a polar parameter space by means of Hough transform.

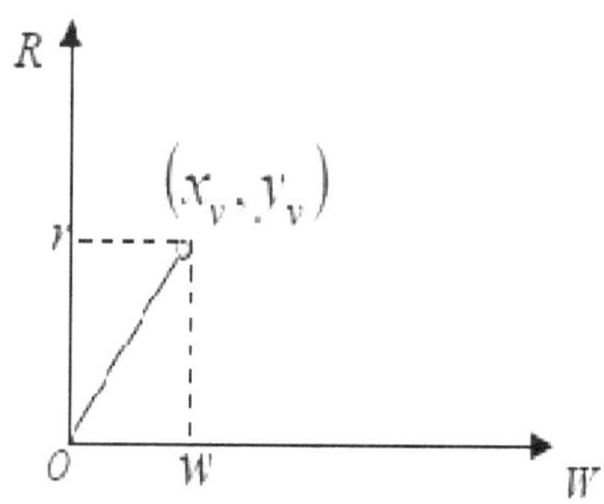

Fig. 3. Parameter coordinates of the straight line

Thus we can easily compute the vanishing point using the Hough transform, which is given by

$$x_{v=}\frac{k}{r\sqrt{1+tan^2 w}} \tag{4}$$

$$y_{v=}\frac{k \tan w}{r\sqrt{1+tan^2 w}} \tag{5}$$

4 Road Segmentation

After estimating the vanishing point, perform segmentation of the road area based on the detected vanishing point. Here to segment the road area a vanishing point constrained group of dominant edges are detected based on the orientation consistency ratio. The segmentation accuracy is improved by combining the OCR and color features [1]. The initial vanishing point estimation is considered as a constraint to find the first edge. i.e. we extend a set of imaginary rays from the initially estimated vanishing point and for each ray compute the sum of OCRs of each ray and the color difference between the two neighboring regions of each ray. The first dominant edge is selected as the ray that maximizes the product of the above measure.

$$b = arg_i \max (diff(A1, A2) \times \textstyle\sum_{j=i-1}^{i+1} OCR_j) \tag{6}$$

Where A1 and A2 are the two neighboring regions of the ith ray and diff (A1, A2) is the color difference of A1 and A2. Based on the detected edge, we can update the initial vanishing point. From this updated vanishing point the second edge of the road can also easily computed.

5 Conclusions

A framework for segmenting the general road region is proposed. Here new method for detecting the vanishing point is used which is based on twice Hough transform. The straight line in the image is detected by first Hough Transform and using a coordinate transform, points in a circle were translated to points in a line. Finally, for detection of the line, Hough Transform was used again. Thus, the positions of vanishing points can be calculated by corresponding to the line parameters in pole coordinate. The proposed algorithm is highly effective and can acquire the vanishing point easily.

References

1. Kong, H., Audibert, J.-Y., Ponce, J.: General Road Detection from a Single Image. Proc. IEEE Transactions on Image Processing 19(8) (August 2010)
2. Chen, X., Jia, R.: A New Vanishing point Detection Algorithm based on Hough Transform. In: Third International Joint Conference on Computational Science and Optimization (2010)

3. Almansa, A., Desolneux, A., Vamech, S.: Vanishing point detection without any a priori information. IEEE Trans. on PAMI 25(4), 502–507 (2003)
4. Magee, M.J., Aggarwal, J.K.: Determining vanishing points from perspedctive images. Computer Vision, Graphics and Image Processing 26, 256–267 (1984)
5. Lutton, E., Maitre, H., Lopez-Krahe, J.: Contribution to the Determination of Vanishing Points Using Hough Transform. IEEE Transaction on Pattern Analysis and Machine Intelligence 16, 430–438 (1994)

Stock Price Prediction Using Support Vector Regression

Abirami R. and Vijaya M.S.

PSGR Krishnammal College for Women, Coimbatore - 4
rr.abirami@gmail.com, msvijaya@grgsact.com

Abstract. Forecasting stock price is an important task as well as difficult problem. Stock price prediction depends on various factors and their complex relationships. Prediction of stock price is an important issue in finance. Stock price prediction is the act of trying to determine the future value of a company stock. The successful prediction of a stock future price could yield significant profit. Hence an efficient automated prediction system is highly essential for stock forecasting. This paper demonstrates the applicability of support vector regression, a machine learning technique, for predicting the stock price by learning the historic data. The stock data for the period of four years is collected and trained with various parameter settings. The performance of the trained model is evaluated by 10-fold cross validation for its predictive accuracy. It has been observed that the support vector regression model with RBF kernel shows better performance when compared with other models.

Keywords: Linear regression, Machine learning, Stock price prediction, Support vector regression.

1 Introduction

A stock market is a public entity for the trading of company stock or shares and derivatives at an agreed price. These are securities listed on a stock exchange as well as those only traded privately. A stock market is a platform to buy and sell stocks. The stock market is driven by supply and demand. The number of shares or stock dictates the supply and the number of shares that investors want to buy dictates the demand. The stock market will climb and climb faster than almost any other traditional investment. The stock market is really just a big, automated superstore where everyone goes to buy and sell the stock. The main players in the stock market are the exchanges. Exchanges are where the sellers are matched with buyers to both facilitate trading and to help set the price of the shares. Among the stock market basics, the share is the smallest unit of ownership in a company.

The size of a share varies from company to company. It can even vary within one company. If the person owns a share in a company, the shareholders are a part of the owners in that company. The total sum of an owner's stock is called stock portfolio. If a company issues dividends, or profits, to the shareholders, owners will receive

P.V. Krishna, M.R. Babu, and E. Ariwa (Eds.): ObCom 2011, Part I, CCIS 269, pp. 588–597, 2012.

money based on the number of shares they owned. Every year, a company issues corporate results and basic stock information for their stockholders to review. Stock market allows corporations looking to expand to raise capital from investors in the primary market and facilitate trade between buyers and sellers of stock in the secondary market. Stock exchange is the efficient way to create a favorable climate for an active and growing for new issues. Hence it is extremely significant, to predict the stock value more accurately in order to facilitate the financial growth of a company [1].

Traditionally, statistical algorithms and time series analysis have been used to predict the stock market. Currently machine learning technology is being employed in computational finance since machine learning deals with techniques that allow computers automatically learn to make accurate predictions based on past observations. In [2] time series analysis system has been used for learning the model and to predict the stock market movement. H.watanabe, B. Chakra borty and G. Chakra borty, developed a stock price trend prediction model based on neural networks and time series analysis for forecasting the stock trends [3]. Vatsal H Shan investigated the application of yale and weka system for stock price prediction. In [5] genetic algorithm has been employed to select the set of most informative input features from all the technical indicators for generating the model.

In this paper, machine learning algorithm namely support vector regression is used for modeling the prediction task. In machine learning, training set is used to fit a model that can be used to predict a 'response' value from one or more 'predictors'. The model is used to forecast the stock value. Training the features of historical data creates the learned model. The process of closing stock price prediction is described in the following section and the various experiments carried out to discover the performance of the models are demonstrated in the rest of this paper. The linear regression and support vector regression algorithms are applied for training the dataset and predict the future stock price.

2 Proposed Stock Price Prediction System

The proposed stock prediction system is based on support vector regression, a supervised learning in order to predict the closing price based on the historical values. The historical data are collected from Aditya Birla money limited, Erode. The historical stock data include opening price of the stock, previous closing price, highest price of stock, lowest price of stock, last price of the stock in a day and average price; these are all the input parameters or predictors. The input parameters are applied to learn the model, which is then used to predict the closing price of the stock.

Opening price

The price at which, a stock first trades upon the opening of an exchange on a given trading day. This is normally determined by the price at which a stock was sold on the previous day. The opening price of shares serves as a benchmark to the company for the day. The calculation of opening price is differs depending on the stock exchange. Opening price is calculated by a special list that looks the book of orders or calculated by supply and demand method. The opening price is one of the attributes for forecasting the future stock price.

Previous closing price

Previous closing price is the stock price of last transaction in the previous day. It is used for the purpose of market verification. The previous closing price is used to calculate the future stock price. The future price prediction is based on technical indicators and sometimes the previous closing price of a stock becomes the current day opening price.

Highest price

The highest price of stocks can make easy to trade profitable. There will be higher demand for the stock with the highest price. The highest historical price level reached by shares, commodity or index during the trading time is called as the highest price of the company. Highest price is also one of important attribute to predict the future stock price.

Lowest price

The lowest price of stocks can make it much more difficult to trade profitable. The lowest price shares are avoided when acquiring a share as it can result in liquidity problems because the share price can easily drop. The stock exchange has limits to open the market because; the increase or decrease in the stock trade depends on the current trading day. If the stock gaps, up or down more than $5/8^{th}$, the stock cannot enter for the trade.

Last Price

The last price is different from the closing price because the last price in this instance represents the last transaction that occurred in the trading day. Last price is a stock price at which the stock was sold from seller to buyer.

Average price

The average price per share is determined by dividing the total cost of the shares by the number of shares purchased. The average price per share can seem complicated to determine if an investor has purchased different quantities of a stock at different prices. The average price reduces the range into a single value, which can be compared to any point, to determine if the actual value is higher or lower than the expected value.

Closing price

The closing price generally refers to the last price at which a stock trades during a regular trading session. The closing price represents the most up to date valuation of a stock until trading on the next day. It is the end of trading session and final procedure in a sale in which documents is signed and recorded. In that time the ownership of the property is transferred. Some time market centers are offered after-hours trading.

Financial publications and market data vendors use the last trade in after-hours markets as the closing price for the day. This parameter is called 'response value' which is to be predicted once the model is learnt.

Price Earning (P/E Ratio)

Price earnings ratio, the most widely used investment measure, is calculated on the previous day's closing share price divided by the earning per share basis. PE ratio is used to appraise a company's profit performance. Where a company's prospects are considered by the stock market is to be good, and then the company's share price will be rise.

The data set with 970 stock records is prepared for training. The learned model is generated through implementing support vector regression. The learned SVR model is used for predicting the future stock price of the company. The architecture of the automated stock prediction system is shown in Figure 1.

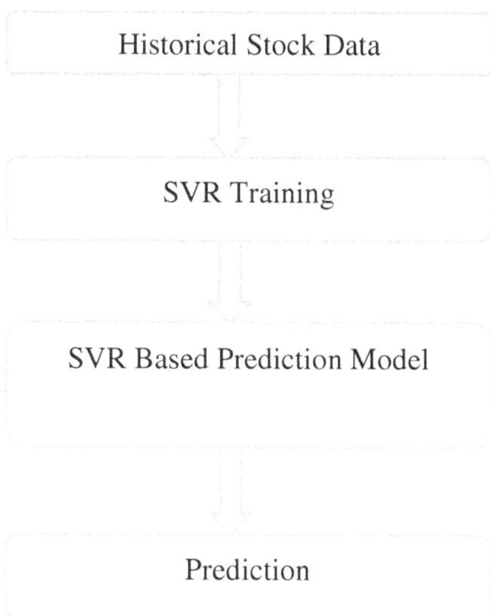

Fig. 1. Proposed SVR based stock price prediction model

3 Methodology

Modeling of stock properties by deciphering the functional relationship between the demand and supply properties is one of the most fascinating topics in forecasting stock market research. By and large, there are essentially three distinguished modeling tools for predicting the stock price namely mathematical models, statistical regression models and machine learning. Mathematical models are very appealing as they are based on the theories of basic sciences and give good understanding about the mechanics of the process. However, the prediction accuracy of mathematical models is not very encouraging due to the assumptions used while building the model.

Statistical regression models are very easy to develop and data coefficient analysis give an indication about the relative importance of various inputs. To counteract this problem, stock researchers have proposed various models relating to price and movement direction. This study employs data driven methodology to generate the predictive model for determining the stock price. Support vector machines (SVMs), based on supervised learning theory, and are gaining applications in the areas of machine learning and pattern recognition because of the high accuracy and good generalization capability. This study briefly introduces the SVM regression algorithms, and presents the SVR model for forecasting stock price.

3.1 Support Vector Regression

Support vector regression is the natural extension of large margin kernel methods used for classification to regression analysis. It retains all the properties that characterize maximal margin algorithms of support vector machines such as duality, sparseness, kernel and convexity. It has become a powerful technique for predicting data analysis with many applications in varied areas of study like biological contexts, drug discovery, civil engineering, stock market prediction, image compression etc., [7] [8]. The problem of regression is that of finding a function, which approximates mapping from an input domain to the real numbers on the basis of a training sample. This refers to the difference between the hypothesis output and its training value as the residual of the output, an indication of the accuracy to fit at the prediction point. To decide how to measure the importance of this accuracy, as small residuals may be inevitable even need to avoid large ones. The loss function determines this prediction measure.

Support vector regression performs linear regression in the feature space using ε insensitive loss function.

$$L\varepsilon(y, f(x,w)) = \begin{cases} 0 & if\,|y - f(x,w)| \le \varepsilon \\ |y - (x,w)| - \varepsilon & otherwise \end{cases} \tag{1}$$

Empirical risk is:

$$R_{emp}(w) = \frac{1}{n}\sum_{i=1}^{n} L\varepsilon(Yi, f(Xi, W)) \tag{2}$$

SVM regression performs linear regression in the high dimension feature space using ε insensitive loss and, at the same time, tries to reduce model complexity by minimizing $\|w\|^2$. This can be done by using slack variables.

$$\xi_i, \xi_i^*, i = 1, \ldots, n. \tag{3}$$

To measure the deviation of training samples outside ε- insensitive zone, thus SVM regression is formulated as minimization of the following functional:

Min

$$\frac{1}{2}\|w\|^2 + C\sum_{i=1}^{n}(\xi_i + \xi_i^*) \tag{4}$$

Such that

$$\begin{cases} y_i - f(x_i, w) \le \xi + \xi_i \\ f(x_i, w) - y_i \le \xi + \xi_i \\ \xi_i, \xi_i^* \ge 0, i = 1, \dots, n \end{cases} \tag{5}$$

This optimization problem can transformed into the dual problem and its solution is given by

$$f(x) = \sum_{i=1}^{n_{sv}}(\alpha_i - \alpha_i^*)K(X_i, X) \tag{6}$$

Where n_{sv}, the number of support vectors and the kernel function is is

$$K(X_i, X) = \varphi(X_i)T\varphi(X) \tag{7}$$

It is well known that SVM generalization performance (estimation accuracy) depends on a good setting of meta-parameters c, ε and the kernel parameters. Selecting a particular kernel type and kernel function parameters is usually based on application-domain knowledge and also should reflect distribution of input (x) values of the training data. Parameter c determines the trade-off between the model and the degree to which deviations larger than ε are tolerated in optimization formulation [9].

3.2 Evaluation Parameters

Generally, the performance of the prediction techniques is evaluated using predictor accuracy. Predictor accuracy measures how far off the predicted value is from the actual known value. The loss function measures the error between actual value y_i and the predicted value y'. The average loss over the set of test cases determines the generalization error of the model and the generalization error can be computed using the following basic parameter.

MEAN ABSOLUTE ERROR

$$\frac{\sum_{i=1}^{d}|y_i - y_i'|}{d} \tag{8}$$

RELATIVE ABSOLUTE ERROR

$$\frac{\sum_{i=1}^{d}|y_i - y_i'|}{\sum_{i=1}^{d}|y_i - \bar{Y}|} \tag{9}$$

MEAN SQUARD ERROR

$$\frac{\sum_{i=1}^{d}(y_i - y_i')}{d} \tag{10}$$

RELATIVE SQUARED ERROR

$$\frac{\sum_{i=1}^{d}|y_i - y_i'|}{\sum_{i=1}^{d}|y_i - \bar{Y}|} \tag{11}$$

The mean squared-error exaggerates the presence of outliers in the training data and commonly used as a measure of performance evaluation. Another important measure is correlation coefficient, which measures the degree of the correlation between the actual and the predicted values. The higher correlation coefficient value is better in the model.

4 Exprements and Results

The data analysis and the prediction of closing price of stock have been carried out using LIBSVM tool for support vector regression. LIBSVM is simple, easy to use and efficient software for classification and regression [10]. The experiment is also carried out in WEKA environment for training the dataset using linear regression. The weka open source, portable, GUI-based workbench is a collection of state-of-the-art machine learning algorithms and data pre-processing tools [11]. To facilitate training, the historical data are collected from Aditya Birla Money limited, Erode. The training dataset consisting of 970 instances with 7 attributes is prepared and converted into the format as required by LIBSVM and WEKA.

Optimization problem of support vector regression with linear, polynomial, RBF kernels is implemented using LIBSVM with parameter c- regulation parameter, d-degree of polynomial and g- gamma. The support vector regression is trained with ‘d’ as 2 in case of polynomial SVR, ‘g’ as 2 in case of SVR with RBF kernel and ‘ε’ as 3 in case of epsilon parameter. The performance of the trained models are evaluated using 10 fold cross validation for its prediction accuracy based on mean squared error and correlation coefficient with the threshold 2.

The performances of the support vector regression and linear regression were evaluated based on the two estimators, the mean squared error and correlation coefficient. The mean squared error is generalization error between actual value and predicted value. The correlation coefficient measures the degree of the correlation between the actual and the estimated values. The result of the performance analysis is summarized in Table 1, Figure 2, Figure 3 and Figure 4.

Table 1. Performance of the models

Evaluation Criteria	SUPPORT VECTOR REGRESSION			Linear Regression
	Linear	Polynomial	RBF	
Mean Squared Error	1.41789	2.57416	0.55132	0.6604
Correlation Coefficient	0.86417	0.83416	0.98599	0.93499
Accuracy	89%	86%	94%	92%

Figure 2 shows the comparative analysis based on mean squared error of the models and it is observed that prediction model based on support vector regression with RBF kernel has lower mean squared error than statistical model.

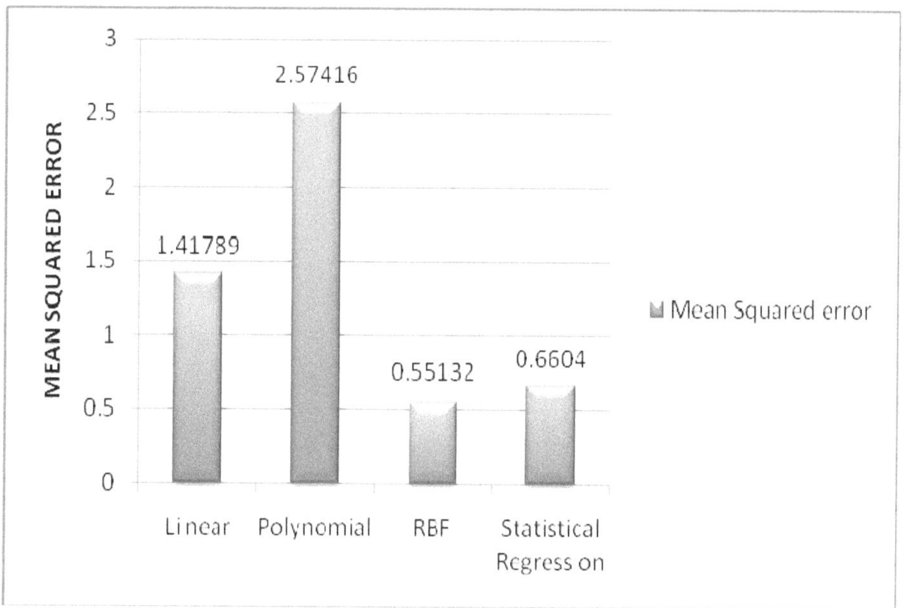

Fig. 2. Comparison based on Mean Squared Error

Figure 3 shows the performance analysis of the models based on correlation coefficient between the actual and the predicted values of the closing price.

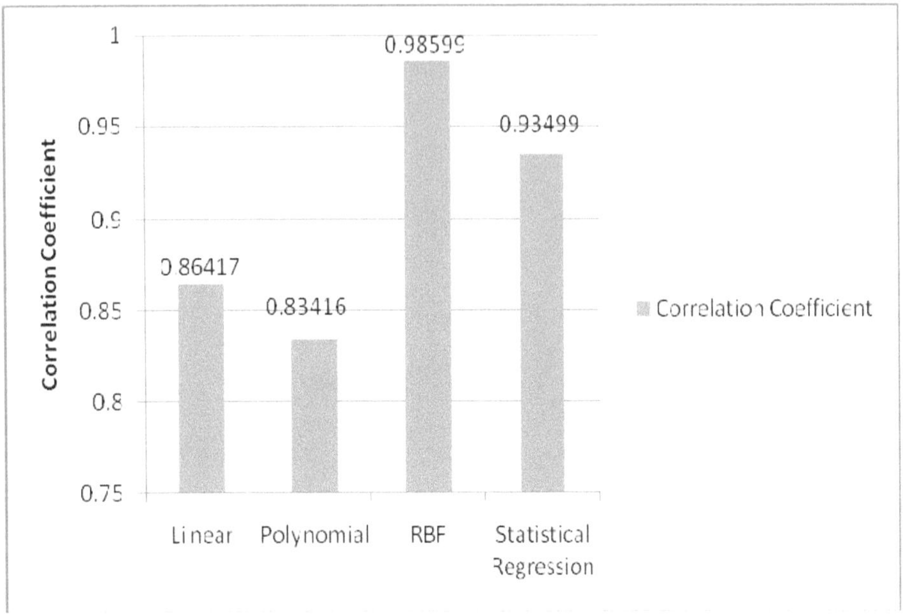

Fig. 3. Comparison based on Correlation coefficient

The comparative results show that prediction model based on support vector regression with RBF kernel has higher correlation coefficient than the statistical model.

From the above results, it is concluded that support vector regression with RBF kernel significantly reduce the mean squared error and improves the correlation

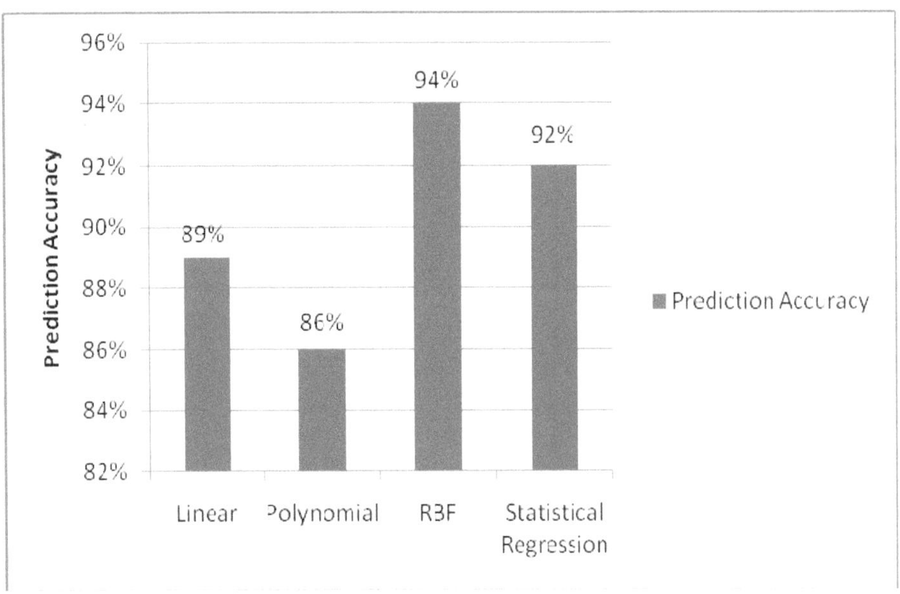

Fig. 4. Accuracy Prediction

coefficient. Figure 4 depicts the comparison of the models based on the prediction accuracy. The prediction accuracy is computed as the ratio of number of correctly predicted instances in the test dataset and the total number of test cases. The total number of cases that have approximately same stock price between actual and predicted values with *threshold T=2* is taken as the number of correctly predicted instances.

From the results it has been observed that stock prediction model based on SVR with RBF kernel produce higher accuracy than statistical regression model.

5 Conclusion

This paper demonstrates the applicability of a supervised learning algorithm namely support vector regression, for forecasting the stock price. The SVR model and linear regression model have been implemented using the dataset collected from a financial services company. The experiments have been carried on the historical data with 970 instances under various parameter settings. The performance of the models has been analysed based on the evaluation criteria such as predictive accuracy, mean squared error and correlation coefficient. It has been observed that the stock prediction model based on SVR with *RBF kernel* shows more efficiency in forecasting the stock value. Finally it is concluded that support vector regression can be well adopted for modelling the stock value prediction.

References

[1] Senthamarai Kannan, K., Sailapathi Sekar, P.: 'Financial Stock Market Forecasting using Data Mining Techniques. In: IMECS (2010)

[2] Huang, W., Nakamori, Y.: Forecasting stock market movement direction with support vector machine. Elsevier (2004)

[3] Watanabe, H., Chakra borty, B., Chakra borty, G.: Soft computing Approach for Stock Price Trend Forecasting from Multivariate Time Series. IEEE (2007)

[4] Shah, V.H.: Machine-learning techniques for stock prediction (spring 2007)

[5] Choudhry, R., Grag, K.: A Hybrid Machine Learning System for Stock Market Forecasting. World Academy of Science, Engineering and Technology (2008)

[6] Witten, L.H., Frank, E.: Data Mining – Practical machine Learning Tools and Techniques, 2nd edn. Elsevier (2005)

[7] Cristianiniand, N., Shawe-Taylor, J.: An Introduction to Support Vector Machines and other Kernel-based learning methods. Cambridge University Press (2000)

[8] Gunn, S.R.: Support Vector Machines for Classifications and Regression Technical Report, University of Southampton (1997)

[9] Soman, K.P., Loganathan, R., Ajay, V.: Machine Learning with SVM and other Kernel Methods. PHI, India (2009)

[10] LIBSVM software, `http://www.csie.ntn.edu.tw/~cjlin/libsvm`

[11] Witten, I.H., Frank, E., Trigg, L., Hall, M., Holmes, G., Cunningham, S.J.: Weka: Practical Machine Learning Tools and Techniques with java implementations. weka software, `http://www.cs.waikato.ac.nz/ml/weka`

[12] Han, J., Kambar, M.: Data Mining: Concepts and Techniques. Morgan Kaufmann Publishers (2001)

Modeling and Simulation of Content-Based Video Streaming Using ns2

Sankar Padmanabhan[1], Krithika Parameswaran[1], Anandhi Natarajan[1], Angel Regi Chelladurai Vijayakumari[1], and Chellamuthu Chinnagounder[2]

[1] Department of ECE, Jerusalem College of Engineering, Chennai, India
sanp_1@yahoo.com
[2] Department of EEE, RMK Engineering College, Chennai, India
malgudi60@gmail.com

Abstract. In this paper, a simulation program for content based video streaming, using ns2 is presented. It is based on publish and subscribe system. The tags or messages are sent to several nodes which are designated as publishers and subscribers and video is streamed based on the content in the routing process. Simulations for different test scenarios are carried out to evaluate the performances like delay, jitter, throughput and PSNR for video streaming.

Keywords: content aware networking, content based routing, content characterization, tag.

1 Introduction

As critical applications are deployed over the Internet, it is becoming necessary for the service or content routers to ensure that the clients are receiving their service or content at a satisfactory level. This issue has prompted a series of activities in the area of Publisher-subscribe system. One emerging technology in this area is content-aware networking, where new generations of routers are specifically designed to address the unique requirements of Web traffic. These content-based routers can route traffic flows based on some attributes of the content being requested such as URL or cookie values. Content-based routers provide flexibility in defining policies for prioritizing traffic and for balancing load and content among servers so that service level agreements can be met. One way of deploying content networking technologies is to interpose a content router between a client and the web server or server cluster. The content router is used as a load balancer for the back-end servers and capable of making optimal decisions [1]. This has the disadvantage of lack of scalability and a single point of failure. The servers select the most appropriate server site depending on the geographical locations of the clients, servers, and network and server load status [2]. The problem of lack of scalability and expressiveness can be improved by using an event notification service. The content based networking can be implemented by

P.V. Krishna, M.R. Babu, and E. Ariwa (Eds.): ObCom 2011, Part I, CCIS 269, pp. 598–606, 2012.

using event notification service. An event notification services is an application-independent infrastructure that supports the construction of event-based systems. The two primary services that should be provided by the infrastructure are notification selection (i.e., determining which notifications match which subscriptions) and notification delivery (i.e., routing and matching notifications from publishers to subscribers). Numerous event notification services have been developed for local-area networks, generally based on a centralized server to select and deliver event notifications. Scalable Internet event notification service (SIENA), have been designed to exhibit both expressiveness and scalability [3].

Antonio Carzaniga et al explains the communication in a content based network through the combined broadcast and content based routing scheme [4]. In a content based communication, the flow of messages from senders to receivers is driven by the content of the messages, rather than by explicit addresses assigned by senders and receivers. A routing protocol for such a content based networking was proposed by George M.P [5]. He has explained the routing protocol with the help of a theoretical model. Another routing mechanism realizing a content based network service over a generic point-to-point network has been also described by Antonio Carzaniga et al [6]. He has also designed principled method for mapping the core concepts and functionalities of generic addressing and routing schemes onto the established infrastructure of network architectures [7]. The publish/subscribe system is an example of a content based networking. A compilation of the main algorithms for routing messages in distributed content- based publish-subscribe systems proposed and published in [8]. The discussion in this paper was focused on the content-based routing problem in respect to optimality, complexity and applicability. The Publish/subscribe paradigm is useful for content diffusion in the Internet. The building of a distributed publish/subscribe infrastructure amounts to define a service model (or interface) and providing an implementation for it. The purpose is to reduce the size of routing table and notification matching time [9].Antonio Carzinga has laid out a set of requirements for a benchmark suite for distributed publish/subscribe services, and its primary components [10].

Video streaming refers to real-time transmission of stored video. There are two modes for transmission of stored video over the Internet, the download mode and the streaming mode (i.e., video streaming). Due to its real-time nature, video streaming typically has bandwidth, delay and loss requirements which can be efficiently overcome as explained by Dapeng Wu et al [11]. When the video data streams through content based network, there are issues to be solved regarding, matching and routing. The Dynamic and flexible video streaming needs to be adopted for better granularity [12] [13]. If video streaming has to be carried out over the publish/subscribe network, the substrings or tags associated with the videos are to be matched for proper retrieval of the video content through the network. In this paper, content-based routing, using NS2 is presented. The content-based routing is performed by examining the content carried by the traffic. The content based scheme is simulated where content is examined only once and the subsequent forwarding operations are based on the tags sent by the subscriber. The rest of the paper is organized as follows. The Section II presents the overall architecture for content-based routing technique in NS2. The Section III gives the various UML diagrams representing the content based simulation in NS2. The simulation of content based video streaming; its scenarios and results are explained in Section IV and V respectively. The Section VI gives discussion and conclusion.

2 Overall Architecture

A typical content based streaming scheme is represented in Fig. 1. There are two types of nodes on the network - Publisher and Subscriber. Each node is connected to an access point (router) on the network. Nodes use these access points to advertise the content in which they are interested. These access points are also used to subscribe to the content it is interested in. The network is responsible for selecting the content that is of interest to a client and deliver it.

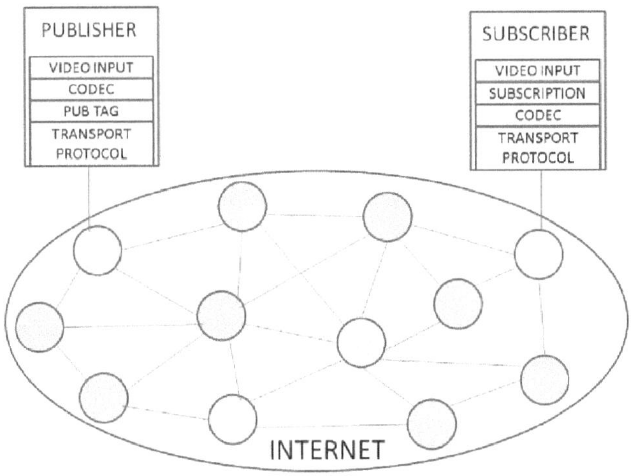

Fig. 1. The content based Architecture

In a content-based networking for video streaming, the nodes can either be a publisher or a subscriber. The publishers hold tags corresponding to the videos they possess. The publishers then publish their tags which are then multicast in the network using routers. These tags reach the subscribers who are connected with the network. The subscribers send their video tags that are multicast in the network so that it reaches the publishers. The publisher holding the corresponding video, streams the video to the subscriber. In the simulation using ns2 content is examined only once and subsequent forwarding operation is based on the tags sent by the subscriber.

3 UML Diagrams

The various UML diagrams describing the simulation process of the content based video streaming using ns2 [13] [14] are described as follows.

3.1 Class Diagram

The class diagram is a type of static structure diagram that describes the structure of a system by showing the system's classes and their relationship between the classes. In Fig. 2 the super class is the 'Agent'. The sub classes derived from Agent are Tags, mvsUDP, mvsSink, UDP, NULL [15]. The Flooding class is further inherited from the Tags class. In Fig.3, the super class is the 'Application'. The sub class Traffic is derived from it.

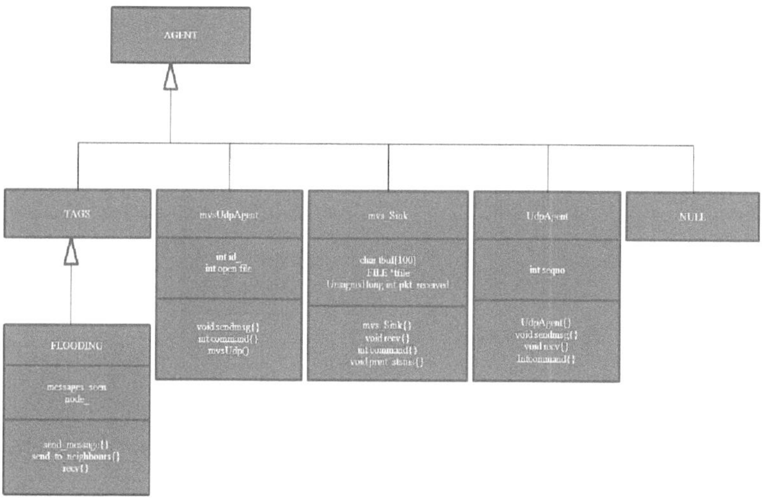

Fig. 2. The Class Diagram (Agent)

Furthermore the two other sub classes derived from the Traffic are mvs and CBR.The various classes are incorporated to perform the simulation.

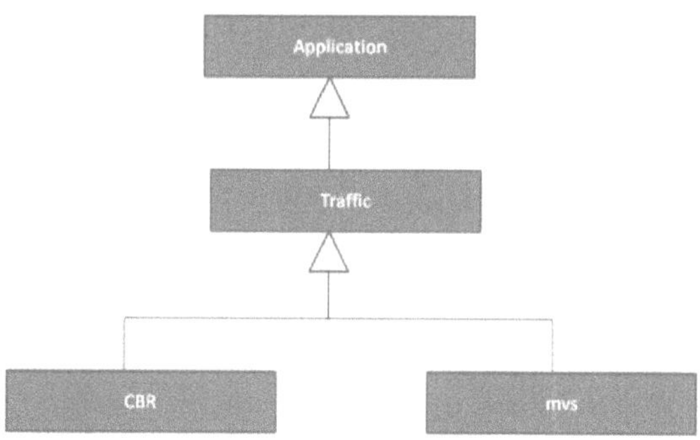

Fig. 3. The Class Diagram (Application)

3.2 Sequence Diagram

Sequence diagram is used to represent or model the flow of messages, events and actions between the objects or components of the system. The time is represented in vertical direction showing the sequence of interactions of the header elements, which are displayed horizontally at the top of the diagram. The sequence diagram is shown in Fig. 4.

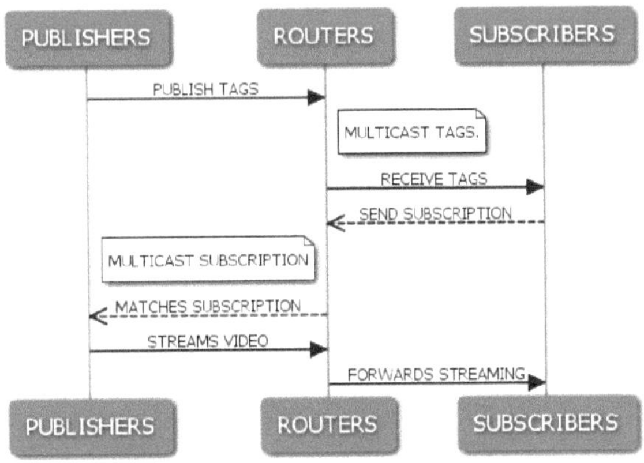

Fig. 4. The Sequence Diagram

The objects in the sequence diagram are publishers, subscribers and routers. The separator is an interface or boundary between the object. The messages represent the interaction between the objects. The Fig.4 depicts how the publish/subscribe operations take place between the objects.

4 Simulation of Content Based Video Streaming

The authors have developed simulation environment using network simulator (NS2), ffmpeg codec and its service utilities to study the performance of video traffic under different scheduling algorithms [12]. Here the simulation is carried out using NS2 simulator with video streaming environment. It consists of a network with 26 nodes. The nodes are labeled as publisher (P), subscriber (S) or router (R). There are 5 publisher nodes and 6 subscriber nodes, remaining being router nodes. The publisher nodes publish the tags corresponding with their videos. The tags are multicast over the network through the routers, which in turn reach the subscribers. The routers are updated when tags reach them. The subscriber nodes subscribe for the videos using the corresponding tags that were published through the routers. The publishers verify the tag from the subscriber and if it is matched with the tags of videos published, the required video is streamed to the subscriber node.

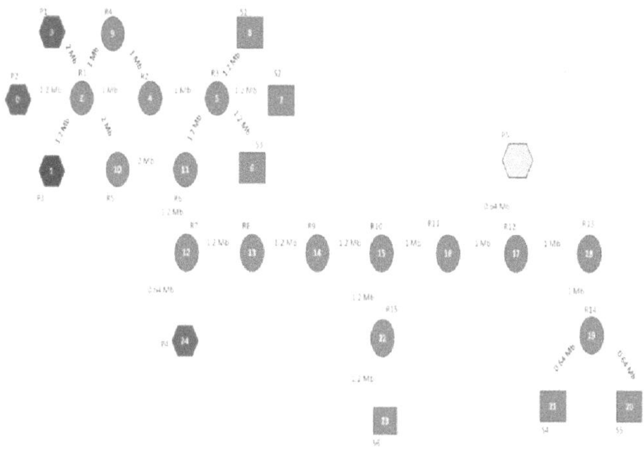

Fig. 5. Simulation Environment

5 Discussion of Simulation Scenarios

The content in the publish/subscribe system can be of different types. The various types of content and the relationship between the publish/subscribe system provides us with various cases that are as described below.

When a subscriber request for a video, the publisher streams the video to the subscriber. Initially the publisher multicasts its tag for the video which it posses. The subscriber which is in need of the video sends its request for the video to the publisher. The corresponding publisher streams the corresponding video. The subscriber nodes may request for a CBR (constant bit rate) file which is sent to the subscriber by the publisher nodes. Publisher which contains the CBR file publishes its tag in the network. The subscriber who is interested in the CBR file sends subscription to the publisher which verifies and sends the CBR file to the corresponding subscriber. It might be required for a publisher to stream a video to multiple subscribers. The publisher streams the video to two or more subscribers. The subscribers can be of different distances from the publishers. A single subscriber may subscribe for multiple videos from different publishers. The various subscriptions are made to different publishers depending on the need and availability of videos. Another important case is the link failure between the nodes. The router node searches for the shortest path and the content flow is carried through it. The same is applicable for multiple link failures. The simulation environment is shown in Fig 5. The simulation is carried out for the streaming of three different videos akiyo, flower and water. The network quality of service (Qos) parameters such as delay, jitter, PSNR and throughput are evaluated and the results have been plotted.

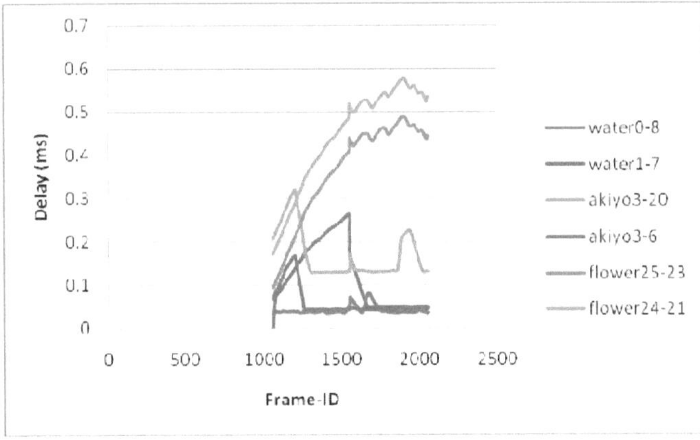

Fig. 6. Delay for publishers streaming video to subscribers

There are lots of videos moving from various publishers to subscribers in the network. The average delay experienced by the three videos in various subscriptions is given in Table-1

Table 1. Average delay experienced in network by various publishers and subscribers

Pub/sub video	0-8	1-7	3-6	3-20	25-23	24-21	1-23
Water	0.1189	0.0955	----	----	----	----	0.2570
Akiyo	----	----	0.0720	0.1637	----	----	----
Flower	----	----	----	----	0.1811	0.2763	----

5.1 Jitter

Jitter is the variance of the inter-packet or inter-frame arrival time. The frame time is determined by the time at which the last segment of a segmented frame is received. It can also be defined as the fluctuation or variation of end-to-end delay from one packet/frame to the next. The jitter experienced by a subscriber when the video is streamed from the publisher is shown in Fig.7.

5.2 Throughput

Throughput is a measure of amount of data transferred over a specific period of time. The smallest unit is bit per second. The Fig. 8 shows the throughput of all the videos that is streamed from publishers to subscribers in the content based streaming.

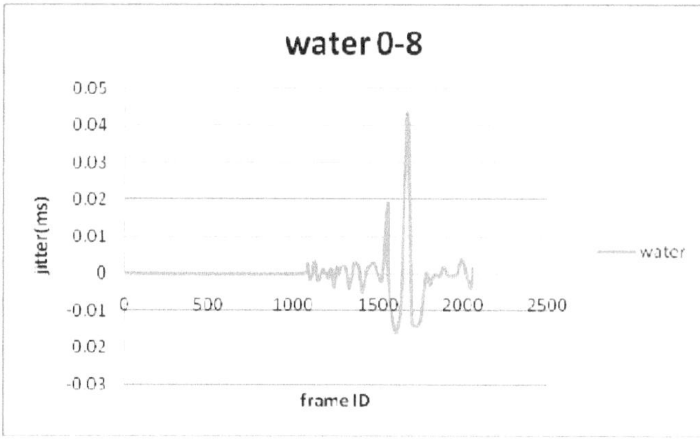

Fig. 7. Jitter for publisher-2 streaming water video to subscriber-1

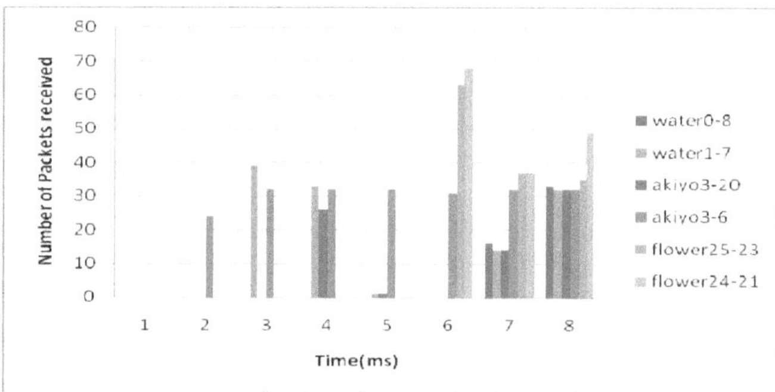

Fig. 8. Throughput of all streaming videos from Publisher to Subscriber

5.3 Peak Signal to Noise Ratio

The Peak signal to noise ratio (PSNR) is the ratio between the maximum power of the original signal (data from the original video) and the power of the interfering noise that is introduced in the process. As the signal quality can vary over a dynamic range, the PSNR values are normally given in a decibel scale. The average PSNR values for all the three videos under consideration are given in Table-2.

Table 2. Average PSNR for the videos

Parameter/ Videos	Average PSNR
Water	27.72556
Akiyo	33.6532
Flower	23.63392

6 Discussion of Simulation Scenarios

A simulation environment for video streaming is presented. The design and implementation of simulation program carried out in NS2 is explained using Agent class and Application class diagram and sequence diagram. Different test scenarios for video streaming to assess quality of service are described. The performance parameters like delay, jitter, PSNR and throughput are evaluated for different scenarios of video streaming. It is seen from the results that the simulation program designed and implemented using NS2 is an useful tool to study content based video streaming.

References

1. Pai, V., Aron, M., Banga, G., Svendsen, M., Druschel, P., Zwaenepoel, W., Nahum, E.: Locality Aware Request Distribution in Cluster-based Network Servers. In: 8th ACM Conference on Architectural Support for Programming Languages and Operating Systems, pp. 205–216 (October 1998)
2. Tang, W., Du, F., Mutka, M.W., Ni, L.M., Esfaha-Nian, A.: Supporting Global Replicated Services by a Routing-Metric-Aware DNS. In: Second International Workshop on Advanced Issues of E-Commerce and Web Based Information Systems, pp. 67–74 (June 2000)
3. Carzaniga, A., Rosenblumz, D.S., Wolf, A.L.: Interfaces and Algorithms for aWide-Area Event Notification Service, Technical Report, CU-CS-902-00 (January 2000)
4. Carzaniga, A., et al.: A Routing Scheme for Content-Based Networking. In: Proceedings of IEEE INFOCOM 2004, Hong Kong, China, vol. 2, pp. 918–928 (2004)
5. George, M.P.: A Routing Protocol for Content Based Networks
6. Carzaniga, A., et al.: Fast Forwarding for Content-Based Networking", Technical report, CU-CS-922-01 (November 2001)
7. Carzaniga, A., Rosenblumz, D.S., Wolf, A.L.: Content-Based Addressing and Routing: A General Model and its Application, CU-CS-902-00, Tech report (January 2000)
8. Martins, L.: Routing Algorithms for Content-based Publish/Subscribe Systems. Journal of IEEE Communications Surveys Tutorials 12(1), 39–58 (2010)
9. Liang, Y.H., ChangGuo, G., Peng, Z.: The subscription-cover-based routing algorithm in content-based publish/subscribe. International Journal of Pervasive Computing and Communications 5(1), 25–41 (2009)
10. Carzaniga, A., Wolf, A.L.: A Benchmark Suite for Distributed Publish/Subscribe Systems, Technical Report, CU-CS-927-02 (April 2002)
11. Marchand-Maillet, S.: Content based video retrieval: an overview, Technical report, Vision, Switzerland No: 0.06, October 06 (2000)
12. Sankar, P., Chellamuthu, C.: Study and simulation of Virtual clock Scheduling Algorithm for Video Streaming. International Journal of Computer Theory and Engineering 1(5), 509–524 (2009)
13. `http://www.isi.edu/nsnam/ns/`
14. Fall, K., Varadhan, K.: The NS Manual (2005)
15. `http://ffmpeg.sourceforge.net/index.php`

A Solution to Prevent Resource Flooding Attacks in 802.11 WLAN

Arockiam L., Vani B., Sivagowry S., and Persia A.

{larockiam,balasundaramvani,persia_paradise}@yahoo.co.in, sivagowry@ymail.com

Abstract. Wireless Local Area Network (WLAN) is more popular today. providing a secure network is the most challenging task. To strengthen WLAN security, many high security protocols have been developed. But those solutions are found to be ineffective in preventing Denial of Service (DoS) attacks. In this paper, the major DoS Attacks called as the Resource Flooding attacks such as the Association Request Flooding (AssRF), Authentication Request Flooding (AuthRF), Deauthentication Request Flooding (DeAuthRF), Dissociation Request Flooding (DissRF) are studied with an experimental setup. The Management Frames (MF) are mostly susceptible to attacks since they are sent unencrypted. Management Frames with Authentication and Integrity (MFIA) was developed to protect MF. But it was found that MFIA protect MF from only Man-in-the-middle attack, MAC address spoofing, etc. It doesn't mean to be an effective solution to prevent the Resource Flooding attacks. But Letter Envelop Protocol (LEP) based on "factorization" provides security to the MF. In this paper, we propose a solution which combines LEP along with Traffic Pattern Filtering (TPF) to protect MF and also to detect and prevent Resource Flooding attacks. The solutions are implemented and the performance of the WLAN is analyzed based on the throughput.

Keywords: WLAN Security, Denial of Service, MAC Spoofing, AuthRF, AssRF, DissRF, DeauthRF, LEP, TPF.

1 Introduction

The exponential growth in the deployment of IEEE 802.11based Wireless LAN (WLAN) in enterprises and homes make WLAN an attractive target for attackers. Wireless Local Area Networks (WLAN) are popular than Wired LAN because they are easy to install, cheap and flexible. Providing security for data transferring in a wireless medium is a challenging task. Hackers can steal the data by pretending themselves as legal users by Medium Access Control (MAC) Address Spoofing. Security Attacks on WLAN are crypto attacks and Denial of Service attacks. Crypto attacks can be resolved [18] but Denial of Service (DoS) attack cannot be easily resolved.

Management Frames are easily susceptible to attacks. No strong security protocols are there to encrypt and protect Management Frames [16]. Number of studies has

P.V. Krishna, M.R. Babu, and E. Ariwa (Eds.): ObCom 2011, Part I, CCIS 269, pp. 607–616, 2012.

been taken place to avoid DoS attacks [3, 5] and different security protocols were also proposed and implemented over WLAN. Wired Equivalent Protocol (WEP) [1, 16], Wi-Fi Protected Access (WPA) [2], Robust Secure Network (RSN), Extensible Authentication Protocol (EAP), Temporal Key Integrity Protocol (TKIP) are the protocols so far available. None of them provide specific solution to avoid DoS attacks [4, 6]. The attacks such as Authentication Request Flooding (AssRF), Association Request Flooding (AssRF), Deauthentication Request Flooding (DeAuthRF) and Disassociation Request Flooding (DissRF) are referred as Resource Flooding Attacks. The name is given to these attacks because when the attack happens, the legitimate client will be totally disconnected from using the resources allowed by the Access Point (AP). Letter Envelop Protocol (LEP) [18] is a valid solution to defend against the Resource Flooding attacks in the initial state itself. But the LEP can prevent only slow attacks. In order to prevent the vigorous attacks, we propose a solution which combines Traffic Pattern Filtering (TPF) [4] with LEP. The NS-2 tool is used to prove the throughput variations.

In this paper, Section 2 presents the background work. Section 3 describes the various Resource Flooding attacks. Section 4 describes how Letter Envelop Protocol (LEP) and Traffic Pattern Filtering (TPF) are used to avoid Resource Flooding Attacks. In Section 5, we discuss the LEP and TPF and also analyze the performance of WLAN based on the throughput.

2 Related Work

Thuc D. Nguyen et al., [17] developed a light weight solution to defend against attacks on Management Frames. It is based on the factorization problem.

Mina Malekzade et al., [13] developed an experimental framework to measure the possible attacks using unprotected EAP frames against wireless communication.

Chibiao Liu et al., [6] present a solution to detect and resolve AuthRF and AssRF attacks based on an experimental framework. It quantifies both the attacks against TCP and wireless voice over communication.

Manish Garg et al., [1] discusses launching of DoS attacks, how to create threats in security and the effect of DoS on WLAN. It is shown that the attacks can be easily done and the difficult task is to prevent those attacks.

3 DoS Attacks

DoS attacks which come under Resource Flooding Attacks are listed below:

1. Authentication Request Flooding (AuthRF)
2. Association Request Flooding(AssRF)
3. Deauthentication Request Flooding(DeAuthRF)
4. Disassociation Request Flooding (DissRF)

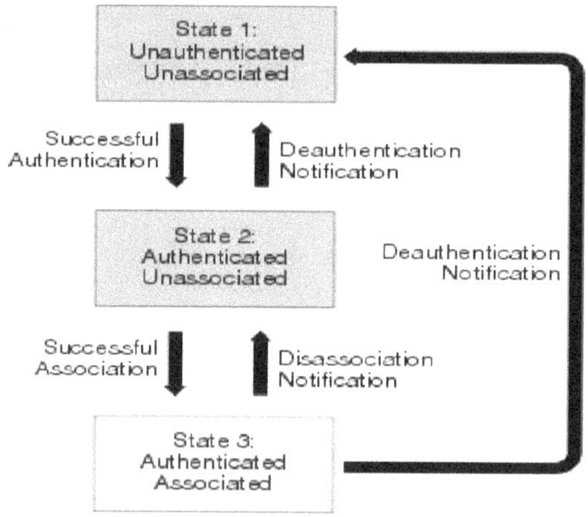

Fig. 1. Authentication process

The Fig 1 shows how a client moves from the unauthenticated to authenticated state. The state 1 shows that client is neither authenticated nor disassociated. In state 2, client moves from unauthenticated to authenticated state after successful authentication. After successful association, it moves to the 3rd state. The reverse procedure is followed to deauthenticate the client when it sends deauthentication frame to the AP.

3.1 Authentication Request Flooding

When the legitimate AP receives the authentication request, with a faked source MAC address, it reserves buffer for authentication request and sends out an authentication response to faked wireless client. AP authentication buffer is used to hold the information of a client during authentication process. Since the faked wireless client doesn't exist, the AP cannot receive the acknowledgement for the transmitted authentication response frame. A lot of AP's resources are consumed in processing the authentication request from faked client and the AP has only little resource to serve for the existing clients. Hence, the legitimate client suffers due to loss of communication.

3.2 Association Request Flooding

When the AP receives an association request from faked source MAC address, it checks its buffer and found that faked wireless client does not present in the authenticated table. It sends deauthentication frame to client which is not received by the client. Hence it keeps on sending deauthenticate frame to the faked client which makes the communication slower or stop with the associated clients.

To prevent both AuthRF and AssRF attacks, the AP has to distinguish whether the request is from the legitimate client or and the hacker.

After crossing the 2 states in Fig 1, the client will be communicating with the AP. The attacker will hack the client's MAC Address and send it to the AP. The AP will disconnect the client from its network as shown in Fig 2.

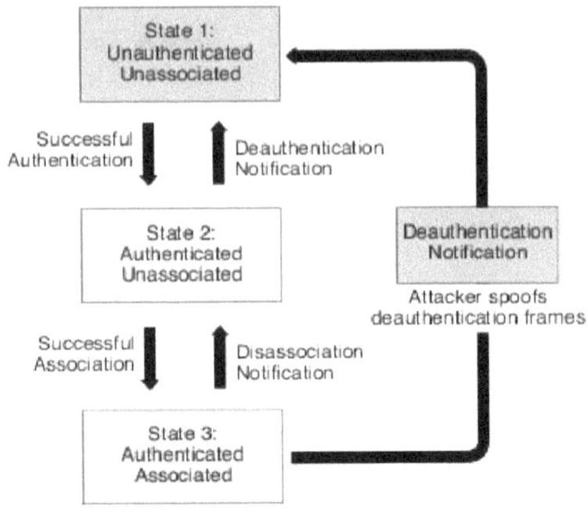

Fig. 2. Sending Deauthentication Frame by the faked Client

3.3 Disassociation Request Flooding

Dissociation Request Flooding is done by sending spoofed dissociation frames targeting the wireless clients. An attacker would repeatedly spoof the disassociation frames to keep the client out of service.

3.4 Deauthentication Request Flooding

In Deauthentication Request Flooding, an attacker transmits the spoofed frame with the source address to the AP. When the AP receives such frames, it will disconnect the client from the network.

Many attacking tools are available to do these kinds of attacks. Of all these attacks, DeauthRF is found to be the worst attack [8] since this attack will disconnect the client from the whole network. This is shown in the Fig 3 given below.

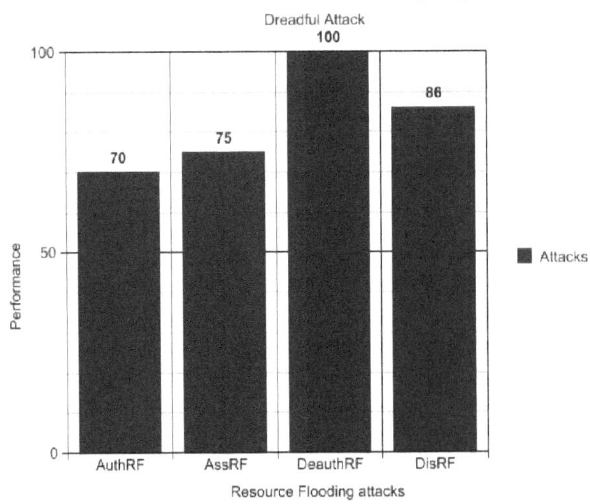

Fig. 3. The most dreadful Attack

4 Solution to Resource Flooding Attacks

Management Frames are sent unauthenticated during data transfer in the WLAN. So they are easily susceptible to attacks. The main focus in the solution is to protect the Management Frames (MF). Letter Envelop Protocol (LEP) [17] is proposed to prevent Resource Flooding attacks. It works based on the factorization problem. The Letter Envelop protocol works as follows:

- The client randomly generates two prime numbers p1 and q1. It then computes N1=p1*q1. In the same way, AP generates p2, q2 and computes N2.
- During the authentication, the client sends an "envelop" containing N1 to the AP. The AP stores it and sends it N2 to the client. The N2 sent by AP is common for all clients.
- When the client wants to disconnect, it will send the deauthentication frame to the AP, along with the p1. The AP will compute p1/N1 and find whether it corresponds with the N1 which was already stored.
- If it is correct, the client will be disconnected. Otherwise, the frame will be rejected assuming that it is from the hacker.
- Similar procedure is followed for AP when it wants to disconnect from the client.

This solution is found to be effective in preventing Resource Flooding attacks because even though the hacker can spoof the MAC address, nothing will happen to the legitimate client. The authentication is progressed based on the LEP. The hacker can generate prime numbers and communicate with AP. But the hacker cannot generate the same prime numbers as the client. It will take long time to generate the same number as the legitimate client. When the attack is vigorous, this protocol is not enough to save the client from the attackers.

In the case of vigorous attacks, we propose the combination of Traffic Pattern Filtering (TPF) with LEP. AP uses TPF along with LEP. The TPF will work as follows:

- If a request is received more than 5 times at a particular time from a client, it infers that the request is from the hacker and ignores it [4].
- Since the hacker continuously sends request, AP is unable to process the request from the legitimate clients.

TPF is employed to prevent continuous Resource Flooding request from the attacker.

5 Performance Evaluations

To evaluate the performance of LEP and TPF, we have implemented LEP in both real time and in simulation environment using NS-2. The solution is validated by measuring the throughput before and after implementing the LEP.

5.1 Test Bed for Real Time Environment

The experimental setup consists of one AP, one target client and one attacker. Configuration requirements are as follows:

- One PC (CPU: Intel i3, RAM 2 GB, HDD 80GB) as Wireless Client.
- One PC (CPU: Intel i5, RAM 2 GB, HDD 80GB) as Attacker.

At the initial stage, when a client wants to communicate with AP, it needs authentication. In the LEP, it has to generate N1, by using p1 and q1, and send it along with authentication frame. The N1 will be stored by the AP. AP again sends N2 by using p2 and q2 to the client. After storing N2, client and AP will start communication. Client moves to the state of association from authentication. When the client wants to deauthenticate or disassociate, it sends p1 to AP along with the frame. AP checks p1/N1, and after confirmation it sends response to the client. The attacker cannot guess the prime number generated by the client. Spoofing 'p' can be easily detected. Because only the client or AP which generates the "envelop" N can prove that they are the legitimate owner of p.

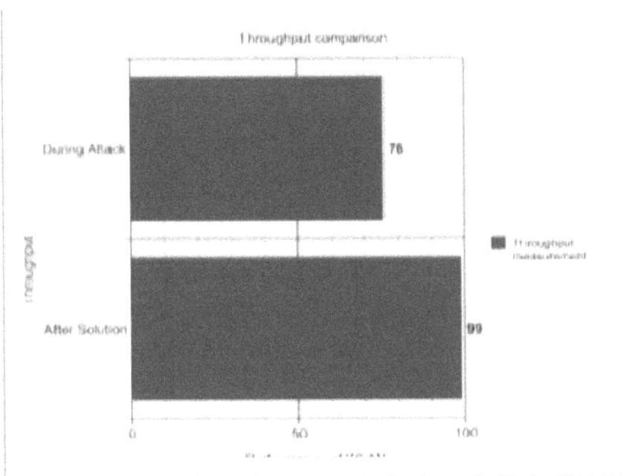

Fig. 4. Comparing the throughput during the attack and after solution

The above Fig 4 shows the comparison of throughput during the attack. It is observed that the throughput is dropped during the Resource Flooding attack. But after implementing the solution it is found that there is no chance for decrease or drop in throughput.

5.2 Simulation in NS-2

We set up a simulation environment to show the performance of our solution. The attacks which are taken for simulation are AuthRF, AssRF, DeAuthRF and DissRF. The simulations [14] are built on Network Simulator NS-2. NS version2 is a discrete-event driven and object-oriented network simulator [18, 19]. The description of the working in NS2 is given in section 6.

6 Result and Discussion

This section discusses the experimental results of the existing and proposed solution to avoid Resource Flooding attacks. It also shows how far the LEP at authentication level prevents the Resource Flooding attack when compared with LEP at association level.

It is observed that LEP at association level can prevent Resource Flooding attacks. But the attacker can do his work at the authentication level itself. Because authentication process is carried out by using "open shared" or "pre shared key" authentication [13]. It is not a secure authentication. If the communication is stopped or hacked at the authentication level, the Resource Flooding attacks are very easy to make. To overcome this, this paper proposes the method of using LEP at the authentication level itself. So, from the initial state itself, we are securing the network from attacks.

Even though the attacker can hack and send the request as legitimate client to AP, the communication of the client with the AP won't collapse. AP already maintains a table which contains 'N' generated by the legitimate clients. The hacker will spoof the client's MAC address and sends request to the AP pretending to be a legitimate client. But the hacker cannot generate the same 'N' which is already generated by the client. The AP will have the 'N' which is already generated by the particular client. So in that case hacker can't deny the resources or services of the client. Because he is unable to guess the 'N' generated by the client. And in the case of continuous Request Flooding attack, TPF is invoked to prevent the network from going down.

LEP invoked at association level can prevent the Request Flooding Attacks. But before association the client has to authenticate it. Since the authentication frame is sent unencrypted, it can be easily attacked. Hence, implementing LEP along with association frame is effective only for a certain level. The hacker need not wait for the association frame to attack. He can do his work with the authentication frame and deny the resources to the client. But, when the LEP is sent along with authentication frame, there is no such possibility of spoofing the frame. So, comparing with each other, it is observed that the LEP sent along with authentication frame is most effective than LEP sent with association frame.

The Fig 5 shows us the comparison taken between the LEP which is imposed in the association level and in the authentication level. It is found that LEP send along with Authentication Frame is most effective in preventing Resource Flooding attacks. The simulation also gives the same result.

The simulation scenario is set by taking AP as one node, client as one node and attacker as another node. At the start of the simulation, AP and client are in communication. At that time, attacker will hack the MAC address of client and start the attack. During the attack, the throughput is found to drop because the attacker will permanently stop the communication. This is observed through the graph generated by NS2 by taking time/second in X axis and throughput/bytes along Y axis.

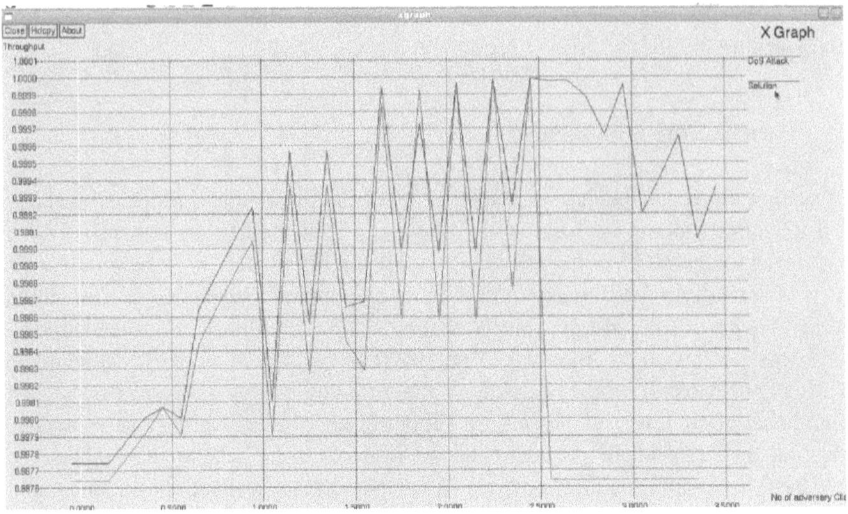

Fig. 5. Throughput comparison before and after the solution

After implementing the solution the attacker cannot do the attack because the client authentication is based on the prime number generated by it. Hence, LEP along with TPF can easily identify the intruder and block him. So, the drop level of throughput during the attack is prevented. It can be easily proved by the graph obtained from the simulation as shown in Fig 5.

The Fig 6 shows that the LEP when employed for slow Resource Flooding attack works well. And when LEP is employed with TPF, it prevents vigorous Resource Flooding attacks.

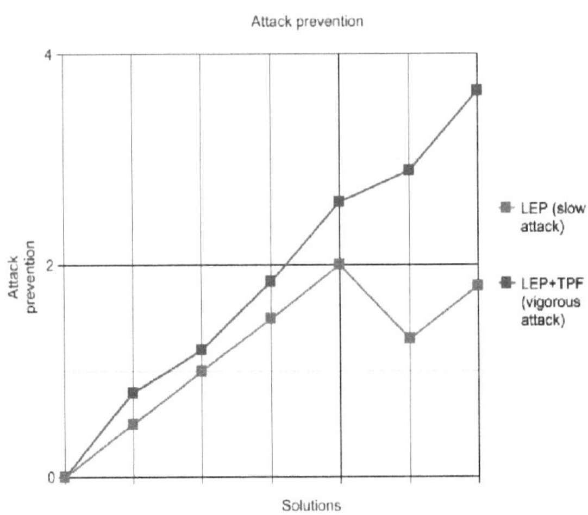

Fig. 6. Comparing the solutions

7 Conclusion

Letter Envelop Protocol is found to be the most effective solution to prevent Resource Flooding attacks. Since it is engaged along with Authentication Frame itself the hacker cannot disconnect the AP from the client and vice versa. There is a possibility of spoofing AP's MAC address and send the request as AP to Client. But in LEP, hacker cannot do the same. It is because the client will store the 'N' generated by the AP before it starts its communication. It is also observed that LEP is effective in preventing Resource Flooding attacks when there are slow attacks. But during the case of vigorous DoS attacks, we have implemented Traffic Patten Filtering (TPF) along with LEP and found better results in preventing Resource Flooding attacks.

References

1. Gupta, A., Garg, M.: DoS Attacks on IEEE 802.11 Wireless Networks and its Proposed Solutions (April 2010), http://ssrn.com/abstract
2. Lashkari, A.H., Danesh, M.M.S., Samadi, B.: A Survey on Wireless Security protocols (WEP,WPA and WPA2/802.11i), pp. 48–52. IEEE Explore (2009) ISBN: 978-1-4244-4519-6
3. Arockiam, L., Vani, B.: A Survey of Denial of Service Attacks and its Countermeasures on Wireless Network. International Journal on Computer Science and Engineering 02(05), 1563–1571 (2010)
4. Arockiam, L., Vani, B.: A Comparative Study of the Available Solution to Miinimize the Denial of Service Attacks in WLAN. International Journal of Computing Application and Technology 2(3), 619–625 (2011)
5. Aslam, B., Islam, M., Khan, S.: 802.11 Disassociation DoS Attack and Its Solutions: A Survey. In: Proceedings of the First Mobile Computing and Wireless Communication International Conference, Amman, Jordan, pp. 221–226 (September 2006)
6. Liu, C., Yu, J.: A Solution to Wireless LAN Authentication and Association DoS Attacks. IAENG International Journal of Computer Science 34(1) (August 2007)
7. Liu, C.: 802.11 Disassociation Denial of Service (DoS) attacks (2005), http://www.mnlab.cs.depaul.edu/seminar/spr
8. Liu, C., Yu, J.T.: Review and Analysis of Wireless LAN Security Attacks and Solutions. Journal of International Engineering Consortium 59 (2006)
9. Liu, C., Yu, J.T.: An Analysis of DoS Attacks on Wireless LAN. In: IASTED International Conferences on Wireless Networks and Emerging Technologies (WNET 2006), Banff, Canada (2006)
10. Ferreri, F., Bernaschi, M., Valcamonici, L.: Access points vulnerabilities to DoS attacks in 802.11 networks. Wireless Netw. 14, 159–169 (2008)
11. Bellardo, J., Savage, S.: 802.11 denial-of-service attacks: real vulnerabilities and practical solutions. In: USENIX Security Symposium (2003)
12. Malekzadeh, M., Ghani, A.A.A., Subramaniam, S., Desa, J.: An Experimental of DoS Attack and Its Impact on Throughput of IEEE 802.11 Wireless Networks. International Journal of Computer Science and Network Security 8(8), 1–5 (2008)
13. Malekzadeh, M., et al.: Security Improvement for Management Frames in IEEE 802.11 Wireless Networks. International Journal of Computer Science and Network Security 7(6), 276–284 (2007)

14. Malekzadeh, M., Ghani, A.A.A., Subramanian, S., Desa, J.: Validating Reliability of OMNeT++ Wireless Networks DoS Attacks: Simulation vs. Test Bed. International Journal of Network Security 13(1), 13–21 (2011)
15. Cam-Winget, N., Housley, R., Wagner, D., Walker, J.: Security flaws in 802.11 data link protocols. Communications of the ACM 46(5) (May 2003)
16. Prodanovic, R., Simic, D.: A Survey of Wireless Security. Journal of Computing and Information Technology, CIT 15(3), 237–255 (2007)
17. Wong, S.: The Evolution of Wireless Security in 802.11 Networks: WEP, WPA and 802.11 Standards, GSEC Practical v1.4b (May 2003)
18. Nguyen, T.D.: A lightweight solution for defending against Deauthentication/disassociation attaks on 802.11 networks, pp. 1–6. IEEE (August 2008)
19. The ns Manual, the VINT Project (January 6, 2009), http://www.scribd.com/doc/52291274/Network-Simulator-2-Manual
20. http://www.isi.edu/nsnam/ns/nsdocumentation.Html

Enhancement of Orchestration Algorithms for Compiler Optimization

J. Andrews[1] and T. Sasikala[2]

[1] Department of CSE, Sathyabama University, Chennai, India
andrews_593@yahoo.com
[2] SRR Engineering College, Chennai, India
sasi_madhu2k2@yahoo.co.in

Abstract. Applying the right compiler optimizations to a particular program can have a significant impact on program performance. But achieving this target involves lot of complication because arriving at the compiler configuration for a particular problem is a complex process. The performance of the program measured by time and memory depends on the machine architecture, problem domain and the settings of the compiler. *Due* to the non-linear interaction of compiler optimizations however, determining the best setting is nontrivial. There have been several proposed techniques that search the space of compiler options to find good solutions; however such approaches can be expensive. This paper proposes a different approach using an effective orchestration algorithm strategy. We show that such an approach which outperforms existing orchestration algorithms. In this paper, it is proposed to study the classification of problems, identification of ideal objective functions for different tasks and the ordering of objective function for optimization. In this paper we proposed an automated framework to select the compiler options for a particular problem from large set options. Many previous works consider only limited set of options. For this framework, we implemented compiler optimization selection algorithms such as branch and bound strategy and advanced combined elimination algorithm and evaluated its efficiencies to improve tuning time. Using our technique we achieve better improvement over the highest optimization setting of the MiBench benchmark suite on Intel core duo processor.

Keywords: Compiler optimization. Advanced combined elimination, Branch and Bound.

1 Introduction

Modern compiler provides a larger set of optimization techniques, from which the user select the best set of optimization techniques. But selecting the best set of options is not easy, especially for average users who do not have in depth understanding of the compiler options. Each optimization tries to improve the performance of the application, although they are not always effective .Through command line flags, the user can decide which optimizations are to be applied in a given compilation run, but clearly it is not a long term solution. As compiler options get increasingly numerous and complex, the problem must find an automated solution.

P.V. Krishna, M.R. Babu, and E. Ariwa (Eds.): ObCom 2011, Part I, CCIS 269, pp. 617–627, 2012.

Automatically selecting the best set of compiler optimizations for a particular program is a difficult task and there has been much previous work on automatically searching for the best optimization settings. This previous work is based on iteratively enabling certain optimizations, running the compiled program and, based on its performance, deciding on a new optimization setting. Pan *et al* introduce a new algorithm called *combined Elimination* (CE) that was shown to outperform all previous search-based techniques in finding good optimization settings with considerably fewer evaluations. However, these pure search or "orchestration" approaches do not use prior knowledge of the hardware, compiler, or program and instead attempt to obtain this knowledge online. Thus, every time a new program is optimized, the system starts with no prior knowledge.

In this paper we have consider GCC Version (4.3.2).GCC provides three levels of optimization techniques [1]. To obtain the best performance a user usually applies the highest optimization level –O3.In this level the compiler perform the most extensive code analysis and expects the compiler generated code to deliver the highest performance. . In this paper we proposed an automated framework to select the compiler options for a particular problem from large set options. Many previous works consider only limited set of options. For this framework, we implemented compiler optimization selection algorithms such as branch and bound strategy and advanced combined elimination algorithm. Efficiency was evaluated to improve its tuning time.

2 GCC Compiler Optimizations

Compilers usually have some form of optimization routines implemented into the code generation process in order to help reduce code discrepancies when converted from high level programming languages into machine codes. Implementing a large set of different optimization options, GCC offers 54 different optimization routines which yield more than 2^{54} different optimization settings .These large 54 optimization options are grouped into 5 general optimization flags pre-selected to provide ease of choice for developers. The general optimization flags implemented in GCC are as following.

- O0 (Level 0)

No optimization.

- O1 (Level 1)

The compiler tries to reduce code size and execution time, without performing any optimizations that take a great deal of compilation time.

- O2 (Level 2)

The 2nd level optimization enables all optimization invoked by the 1st level optimization flag and a few other optimization sets tailored to increase the performance of the code. In this optimization level, GCC performs nearly all supported optimizations that do not involve a space-speed tradeoff.

- Os (Level 2.5)

Optimizes for code size over performance.

This special optimization level (-Os or size) enables all -O2 optimizations that do not increase code size.

- O3 (Level 3)

The 3rd and highest level optimization level enables even more optimizations by putting emphasis on speed over size. This includes optimizations enabled at -O2 and rename register. Although optimization level 3 (-O3) can produce faster code, the increase in the size of the binary image can have adverse effects on its speed.

3 Problem Statement

Given a set of "n" ON-OFF optimization options{F_1,F_2...Fn),find the best combination of flags that minimizes application execution time, using branch and bound strategy and advanced combined elimination algorithm. In this paper a novel performance tuning algorithm advanced combined elimination algorithm proposed which picks best set of options which improves tuning time. The results were compared with branch and bound strategy algorithm.

3.1 Advanced Combined Elimination (ACE) Algorithm

Let S be the Set of available Optimization functions.

Let B represents selected compiler options set.

i) S= {F1, F2...Fn} and B= {F1=1, F2=1...Fn=1}

ii) Compile the program with baseline configuration and measure the program performance. Calculate RIP (Fi) for each optimization. Check if RIP (Fi) has already computed, if so use the pre computed value. If RIP (Fi) <0, then

iii) If RIP (Fi) <0, then

Store Ni, where i=1, 2,..j .Elements in N are sorted in an increasing order. Eliminate N_1 from S and set N_1 to 0 in B.For each k=2 to j, compute RIP (Nk), if RIP (Nk) <0, then remove Nk from S and set Nk to 0.

Else

B represents the selected compiler option set

iv) Repeat steps ii and iii

v) Stop

3.2 Branch and Bound Strategy Algorithm

Let S be the Set of available Optimization functions such as {F1, F2,....Fn}

Let B be the set having appropriate settings which is either ON or OFF

i). Initialization.

ii) Initialize default individual setting of flag for each function in set B

iii) Calculate RIP_UB

iv) While (s<> empty) repeat step v

v) For each Fx in S, x=1 to n

Compute RIP (Fx=0)
Find A, the option in S with most negative RIP.
Find the subset S' from S, of those functions whose RIP<
(50%of RIP_UB)
If S' set is empty then return;
Else
For all the elements in S'
Set respective flag off in B; Remove it from S
if RIP (F_A=0)<RIP_UB
RIP_UB=RIP (F_A=0)

vi) Result Ready;
vii) Stop

4 Experimental Setup

In this paper we have considered GCC Version (4.3.2).GCC provides three levels of optimization techniques. Previous work considered only limited set of optimization techniques. This paper proposes larger set of optimization techniques.

Table 1. List of Optimization Techniques

Level-01 Optimization Techniques	
fcprop-registers	fdefer-pop
fdelayed-branch	fguess-branch-probability
fip-conversion	fip-conversion2
floop-optimize	fmerge-constants
fomit-frame-pointer	ftree-ccp
ftree-ch	ftree-copyrename
ftree-dce	ftree-dominator-opts
ftree-dse	ftree-fre
ftree-lrs	ftree-sra
ftree-ter	
Level-02 Optimization Techniques	
falign-functions	falign-jumps
falign-labels	falign-loops
fcaller-saves	fcross-jumping
fdelete-null-pointer-checks	fexpensive-optimizations
fforce-mem	fgcse
fgcse-lm	fgcse-sm
foptimize-sibling-calls	fpeephole2
fregmove	freorder-blocks
freorder-functions	frerun-cse-after-loop
frerun-loop-opt	fsched-interblock
fsched-spec	fschedule-insns
fschedule-insns2	fstrength-reduce
fstrict-aliasing	fthread-jumps
ftree-pre	funit-at-a-time
fweb	
Level-03 Optimization Techniques	
fgcse-after-reload	finline-functions
funswitch-loops	

4.1 MiBenchMark Programs

The Mibench benchmark suite programs were used to experiment the proposed algorithm. These benchmark suite are comparable with SPEC benchmark suite.

Basicmath: The basic math test performs simple mathematical calculations that often don't have dedicated hardware support in embedded processors. For example, cubic function solving, integer square root and angle conversions from degrees to radians are all necessary calculations for calculating road speed or other vector values. The input data is a fixed set of constants.

qsort: The *sort* test sorts a large array of strings into ascending order using the well known quick sort algorithm. Sorting of information is important for systems so that priorities can be made, output can be better interpreted, data can be organized and the overall run-time of programs reduced. The small data set is a list of words; the large data set is a set of three-tuples representing points of data.

dijkstra: The Dijkstra benchmark constructs a large graph in an adjacency matrix representation and then calculates the shortest path between every pair of nodes using repeated applications of Dijkstra's algorithm. Dijkstra's algorithm is a well known solution to the shortest path problem and completes in O (n^2) time.

patricia: A Patricia trie is a data structure used in place of full trees with very sparse leaf nodes. Branches with only a single leaf are collapsed upwards in the trie to reduce traversal time at the expense of code complexity. Often, Patricia tries are used to represent routing tables in network applications. The input data for this benchmark is a list of IP traffic from a highly active web server for a 2 hour period. The IP numbers are disguised.

Stringsearch: This benchmark searches for given words in phrases using a case insensitive comparison Algorithm.

4.2 Metrics Used for Evaluation

Relative Improvement Percentage (RIP), RIP (Fi), which is the relative difference of the execution times of the two versions with and without Fi.

$$\mathbf{RIP(Fi)=T(Fi=0)-T(Fi=1)/T(Fi=1)} \qquad \mathbf{(4.1)}$$

If Fi=1 then Fi is ON, else OFF

The baseline of this approach switches on all optimizations.

T_B=T(Fi=1)=T(F1=1,F2=1,...Fn=1),Where T_B represents base time.

$$\mathbf{RIP(Fi=0)=(T(Fi=0)-\ T_B/\ T_B)\ X100\%} \quad \mathbf{(4.2)}$$

If RIP (Fi=0) <0, the optimization of Fi has a negative effect, so it is better to turn off the function.

Tuning time
It is the time taken by each probe, to determine the effect of individual options in a set of candidate options.

NTT- Normalized Tuning Time. It is the time taken comparison of execution for computing time needed to check effect of individual optimization settings on option on basic setting, for a single probe.

Architecture used for testing was Intel Core2 Duo processor at 2.80Ghz.With 4GB RAM, using ubuntu operating system with 2MB L2 cache. And the compiler was GCC 4.3.2

Table 2. RIP Values for Quicksort Program

Optimization Techniques	RIP(%)
fauto-inc-dec	4.59
fcprop-registers	2.002
fdce	3.69
fdefer-pop	3.80
fdelayed-branch	2.27
fdse	1.10
fguess-brach	1.60
fif-conversion2	2.16
fipa-pure-const	1.93
fipa-reference	1.32
fmerge-constants	1.66
fsplit-wide-types	1.155
ftree-builtin-call	0.80
ftree-ccp	2.36
ftree-ch	3.56
ftree-dce	-1.01
ftree-dominator-opts	4.04
ftree-dse	1.49
ftree-fre	2.40
ftree-sra	1.719
ftree-ter	1.984
funit-at-a-time	1.970
falign-labels	0.711
falign-loops	1.93
fcaller-saves	2.54
fcrossjumping	1.37

Table 2. (*Continued*)

fcse-follow-jumps	3.23
fcse-skip-blocks	-4.54
fdelete-null-pointer	1.99
fexpensive-optimization	3.55
fgcse	1.29
fgcse-lm	1.736
fgcse-sm	1.951
foptimize-sibling	4.46
fpeephole2	1.05
fregmove	1.588
freorder-blocks	1.621
freorder-functions	4.452
frerun-cse-after	0.625
frerun-loop-opt	-1.96
fsched-interblock	-7.61
fsched-spec	2.51
fschedule-insns	3.36
fschedule-insns2	0.78
fstrength-reduce	2.33
fstrict-aliasing	0.819
fthread-jumps	-2.19
ftree-pre	-6.811
funit-at-a-time	-4.67
fweb	4.80
finline-functions	3.12
funswitch-loops	- 4.32
fbounds-check	- 3.52
fdefault-inline	1.595
ffloat-store	1.893
fforce-addr	-2.75
ffunction-cse	0.955
fmath-errno	2.70
funsafe-math-optimization	3.02

Table 2 shows the set of Relative improvement percentage values of each and every optimization techniques under different levels for a quick sort program. Some techniques have higher negative impact while some techniques have positive impact. Higher negative values eliminated at each iteration, while keeping only positive values.

4.3 Performance and Results Comparison

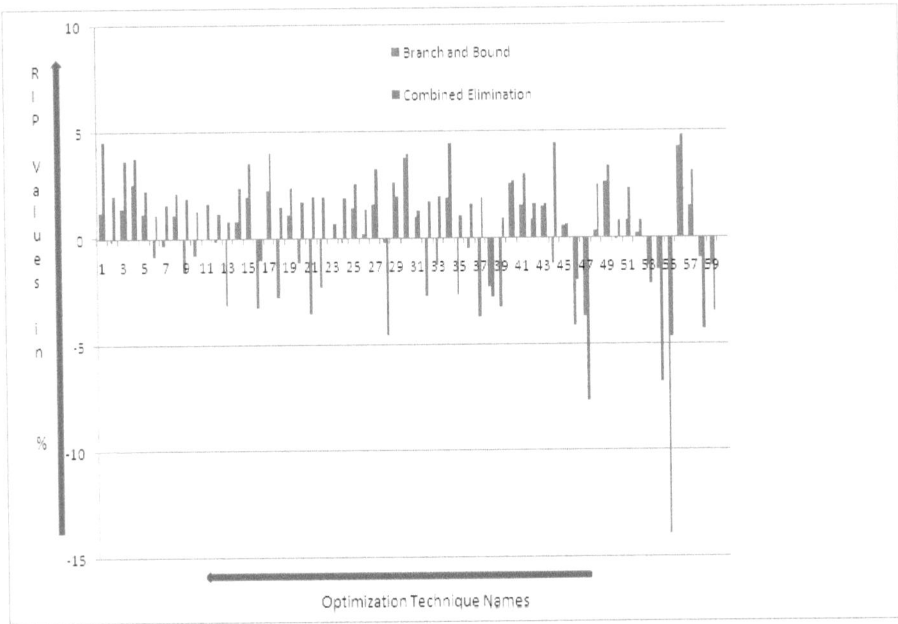

Fig. 1. RIP values for Qsort

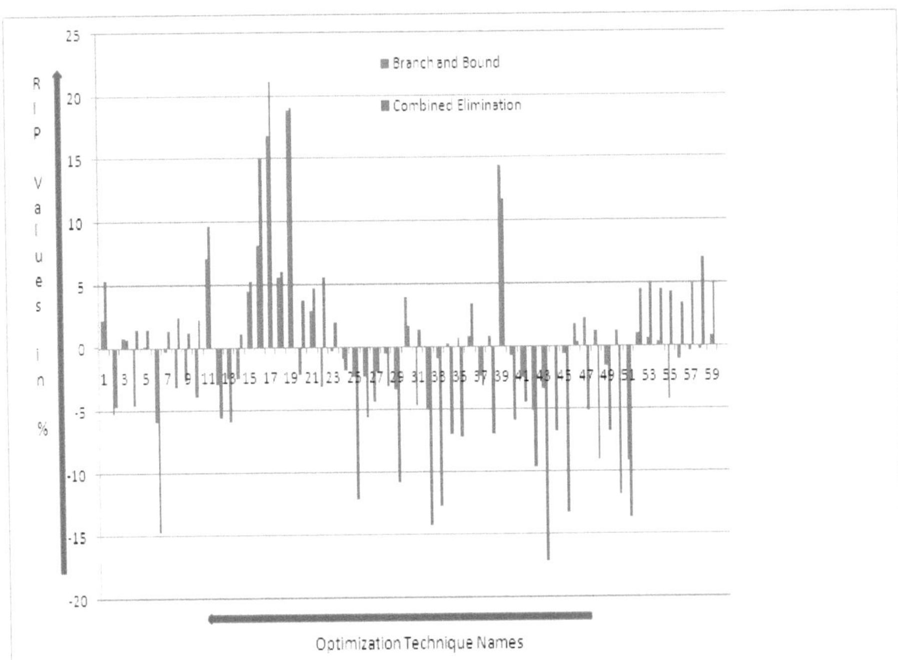

Fig. 2. RIP values for Dijkstra

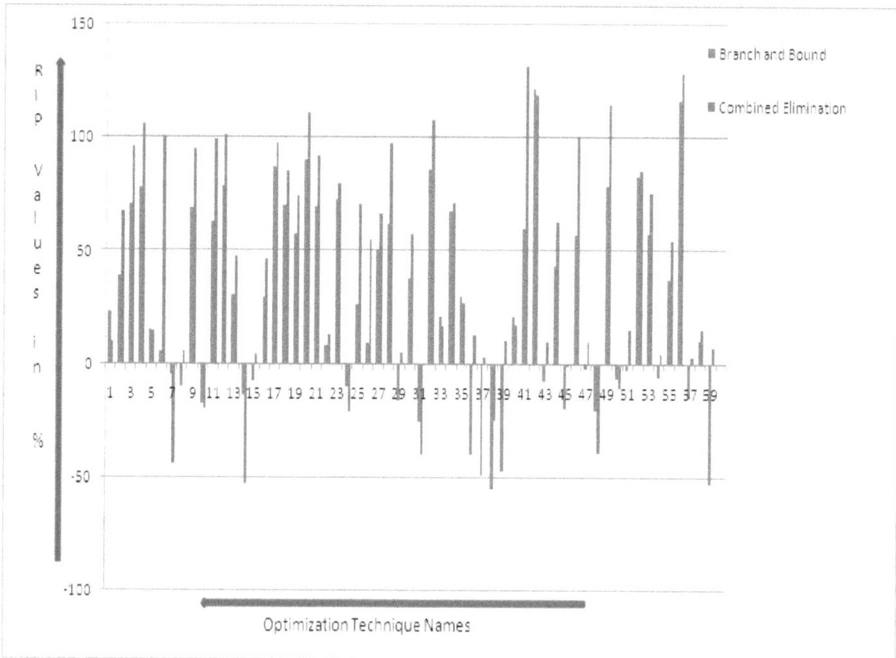

Fig. 3. RIP values for Patricia

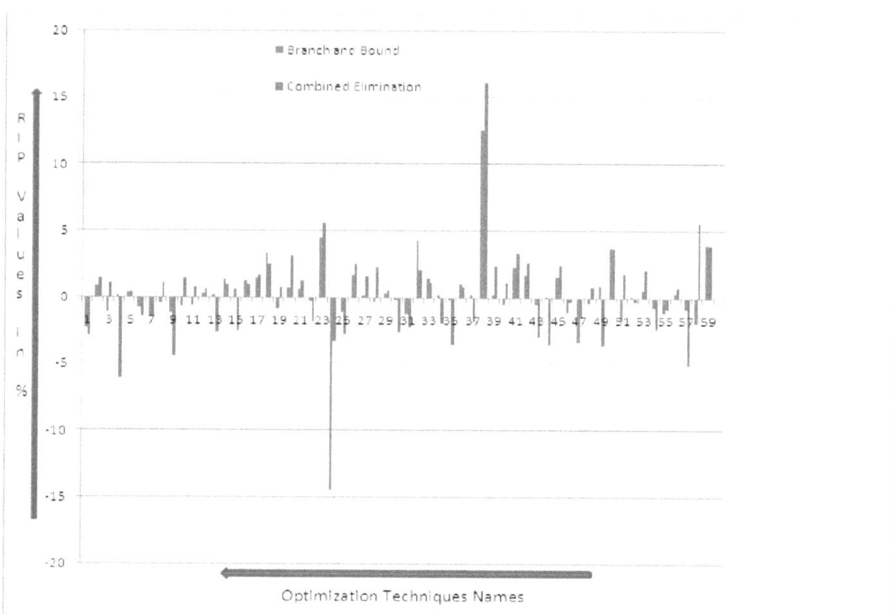

Fig. 4. RIP values for Basicmath

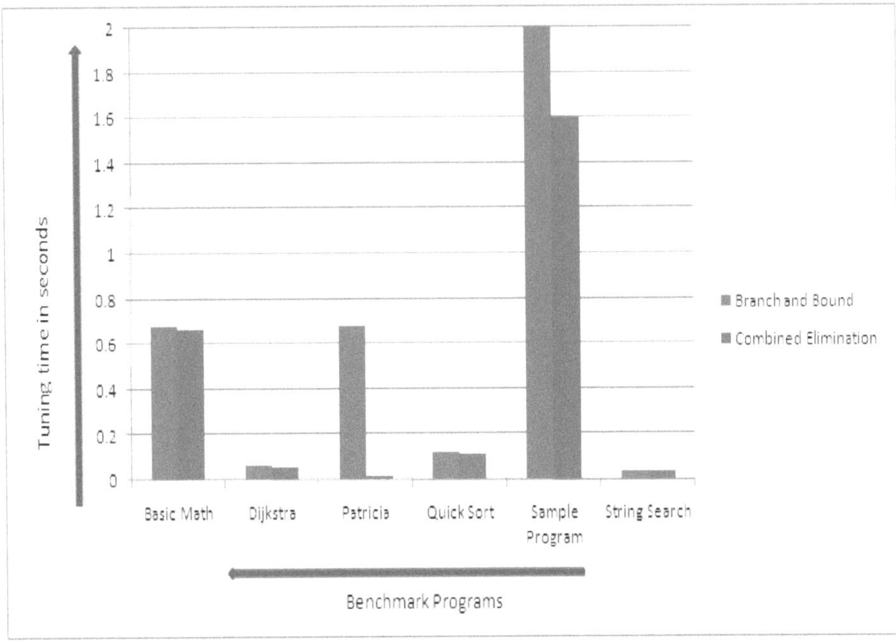

Fig. 5. Comparison of tuning time

5 Conclusions and Future Work

It is found that the new proposed Advanced Combined Elimination strategy works better when compared to branch and bound strategy for most of the bench mark programs. Advanced Combined elimination gives least tuning time for most of the benchmark programs. All levels of optimization techniques applied for the bench mark programs.

In this research, the impact of compiler optimization was measured on the over all program performance, and not on individual code segments. However the ultimate goal of tuning the options on the basis of individual code sections, a more fine grained will be of interest. In future we devise an efficient optimization strategy to improve tuning time. In this research, we have found that significant performance gain could be had by optimizing the algorithm and supporting libraries by issuing specific and generic optimization flags to the compiler during the algorithm's compilation stages. Specific architectural optimizations following the target architecture of the system also have a large impact on the execution speed which in turn affects the entire system performance. By implementing a proper optimization sequences according to the correct target architecture will help increase the system processing speed and help the system to deliver better performance.

References

1. GCC online documentation, http://gcc.gnu.org/onlinedocs/
2. Hung, S.-H., Tu, C.-H., Lin, H.-S., Chen, C.-M.: An Automatic Compiler Optimizations Selection Framework for Embedded Applications. In: Proc. of Int. Conference on Embedded Software and Systems, pp. 381–387 (2009)
3. Pan, Z., Eigenmann, R.: Fast and effective orchestration of compiler optimizations for automatic performance tuning. In: Proc.of the Int. Symp. on Code Generation and Optimization, pp. 319–332 (2006)
4. Agakov, F., Bonilla, E., Cavzos, J., Williams, C.K.I.: Using machine learning to focus iterative optimization, pp. 295–305 (2006)
5. Pan, Z., Eigenmann, R.: Compiler optimization orchestration for peak performance. In: Proc. of the Int. Symp. on Code Generation and Optimization, pp. 319–332 (2004)
6. Tritafyllis, S., Vacharajani, M.: Compiler optimization space exploration. In: Proc. of the Int. Symp. on Code Generation and Optimization, pp. 204–215 (2003)
7. Chow, K., Wu, Y.: Feed back directed selection and characterization of compiler optimization (2001)
8. Von Hagen, W.: The definitive guide to GCC, 2nd edn. Apress Publications (2006)
9. Gough, B.J.: An introduction to GCC for gcc and g++, revised edn. (2005)
10. http://www.networktheroy.co.uk

Development of Sensor Node to Measure Soil Moisture

Kapil Mundada, Pramod Kanjalkar, and Jayant Kulkarni

Department of Instrumentation Engineering,
Vishwakarma Institute of Technology, Pune37, Maharashtra, India
kapilmundada1711@gmail.com, {pmkanjalkar,vitjvk}@yahoo.com

Abstract. The Soil moisture is a vital parameter which decides the quality of a crop. A sensor node prototype is developed to measure soil moisture, analyse it and transmit it over long distance for further processing. Sensor node is a combination of a sensor, signal conditioning circuit, controller and communication module. A low power processor ARM7 is used as a controller. It periodically scans the clock and depending upon the time set by the user the sensor data is checked and accordingly process is carried out. As crops are watered only upon requirement, over and under irrigation is avoided which saves power and water resources. The sensor data is communicated by using RF transmitter (433MHz) to a receiver or base station for logging and display. The hardware architecture is designed to establish the link between a sensor and a controller. The long-time smooth and proper running of the system in the field proved its high reliability and practicability. As an explorative wireless sensor network in irrigation management, this paper gives a methodology to establish large-scale remote intelligent irrigation system.

Keywords: Soil moisture, Sensor Node, ARM, RTC, RF Communication.

1 Introduction

Wireless communication implemented in sensor has applications in a variety of fields such as environmental monitoring, military purposes and gathering, sensing information in inhospitable locations. Connecting sensor, controller and a communication module together is called as a sensor node. Sensor nodes have various energy and computational constraints because of ad-hoc method of deployment. Considerable research has been focused at overcoming these deficiencies through more energy efficient routing, localization algorithms and system design the paper aims at a cost effective, power saving and automated water management system for agriculture. Irregular rainfalls, improper management of available resources, change in soil quality because of changing climatic conditions etc are the major factors behind unpredicted growth in agricultural industry. Factors to consider are plant water requirements, condition of water and its supply, soil type, condition and topography, micro climate concerns and irrigation scheduling constraints. Moisture content of the soil is a major factor determining plant growth, especially in irrigated systems. The basic objective of irrigation scheduling is to minimize water stress of the plant, that of over

P.V. Krishna, M.R. Babu, and E. Ariwa (Eds.): ObCom 2011, Part I, CCIS 269, pp. 628–636, 2012.

irrigation and under irrigation. The decline of soil water content will result in a decrease of photosynthesis and cell expansion of the plant. The project consists of developing a sensor node, which will monitor soil moisture, process the data and then transmit it to a base station. Node consists of a sensor, controller and a wireless transmitter. Moisture is selected as sensing parameters, as it is one of the vital entities which decides the quality of agriculture produce and is the major factor which decide type of crop to be cultivated. Field used for measurement is a black soil, which is most widely used for agriculture purpose. Sensor used is a capacitive sensing probe, due to its considerable advantages over other method such as resistive, conductive, infrared, inductive techniques. The sensor is connected to controller through signal conditioning circuit. The controller used is ARM7 controller because of its low power consumption. Data is transmitted using Radio Frequency (RF) protocol over 100 meter distance. Set point for amount of moisture is taken from user and this set point is compared with process value. The factors considered for development of prototype are: Type of sensor, nature of output, controller, transmission media and its range.

The block schematic of the node is shown in fig 1

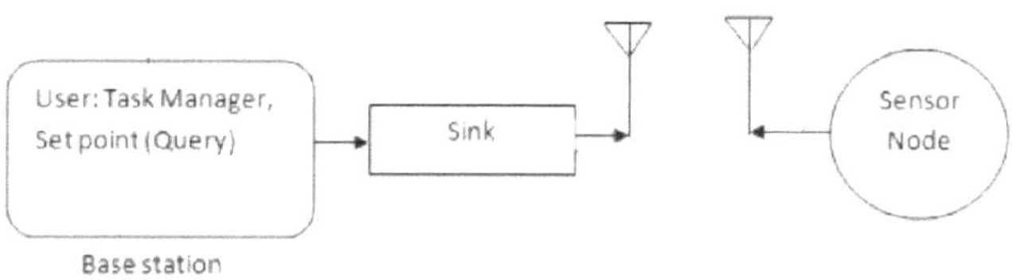

Fig. 1. Schematic of sensor node and base station

Table 1. Water Content in soil for different crops: [Courtesy: College of agricultural, Pune]

Sr.No	Crops	Water Content in Soil
1	Cotton	70-80
2	Onion	75-80
3	Wheat	40-45
4	Sunflower	25-30
5	Sugar Cane	200-225

1.1 Current Methods to Measure Soil Moisture

Gravimetric method: Gravimetric analysis describes a set of methods in analytical chemistry for the quantitative determination of an analyte based on the mass of a solid. A simple example is the measurement of solids suspended in a water sample: A known volume of water is filtered, and the collected solids are weighed.

Tensiometers method: Tensiometers provide a direct measure of the tension at which water is held in soil, and therefore the suction plant roots need to exert in order to extract water. This instrument comprises a water filled tube which is sealed at one end, with a porous ceramic filter at the other end. The specifications of this filter are such that, when buried in soil, it will allow water to flow freely through it, but not air.

The suction of the water within the tube provides a direct measure of the suction at which water is being held in the surrounding soil.

1.2 Need for the Node Development to Measure Soil Moisture

Moisture content of the soil is a major factor determining plant growth, especially in irrigated systems. The basic objective of irrigation scheduling is to minimize water stress of the plant, that of over irrigation, and under irrigation. The decline of soil water content will result in a decrease of photosynthesis and cell expansion of the plant. The ability to accurately measure soil water content, plant size and condition is an integral mechanism in the process of developing an irrigation scheduling program that allows a better understanding of plant and soil water relations. The major drawback in the current method for checking moisture content is that it takes more time, as a farmer needs to take his sample and go to the lab for testing, then he could able to decide about the crop production depending on the results. As moisture content can change due to climatic conditions for every season farmer needs to follow the same procedure. Thus sometimes farmer does not follow the procedure and he decides about moisture content and crop based on his experience which causes improper water management. Remedy to this basic drawback is to check the soil moisture at the field itself so that time can be saved. Sensor node forms the solution for this.

No other climatic occurrence affects the lives of so many people around the world than the monsoon. Economies that are dependent on agriculture critically depend on the rains. India primarily depends on the rains for its agricultural produce as ninety-five percent of all rice is produced during monsoon. The impact of an abnormal monsoon can be tremendous and the damages can cost in millions.

Rain fall Survey: The moisture content of the field is not monitored and it is manually observed by the farmers which are prone to errors. Also the water requirement is different for different crops. Hence this results in poor yield of crops due to inappropriate water supplyIf you have more than one surname, please make sure that the Volume Editor knows how you are to be listed in the author index.

2 Block Diagram of a Sensor Node

Field: Field used is black soil, which is easily available and mostly used for agricultural purpose.

Sensing Probe: A capacitive sensing probe is the sensing element due to its considerable advantages over other method such as resistive, conductive, infrared, inductive techniques. Capacitive Moisture Sensor gives change in capacitance with change in moisture content. Here moisture acts as a dielectric medium and gives a linear relation between moisture and capacitance. Capacitance probe gives output in current signal 4-20 mA for the change in moisture.

Signal conditioning: Signal conditioning circuit is very important part of sensor node configuration, as it converts the sensor output in the required format. Here current to voltage converter is used. Impedance matching is also carried out by using this circuit. By changing the resistors zero and span adjustments can be performed.

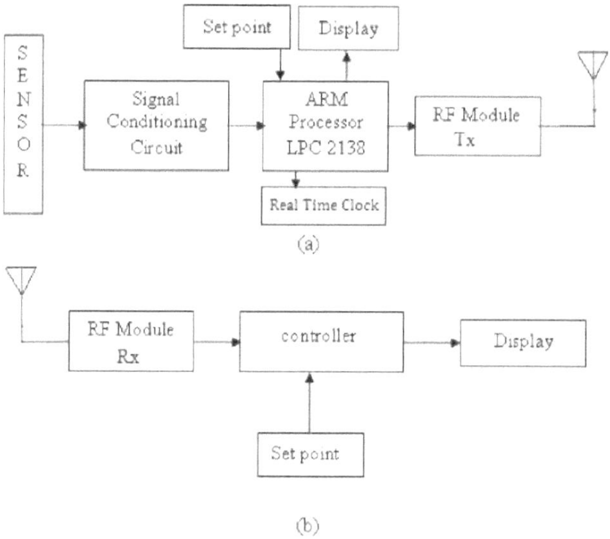

Fig. 2. Block diagram of a sensor node, a) Node, b) Base station

Controller: Controller is the heart of the process. Any micro controller available in the market can be used but to serve the purpose of power saving the controller which consumes less should be used thus ARM controller is used; ARM LPC 2138 controller is used. It is 32 bit processor. It consumes less power, it has Real Time Clock facility, it has 2 eight channel ADC's thus we can interface 16 analog inputs to the controller.

Wireless Communication: The actual field is always located at far distance from the base station because it is not always possible for user to be present at the field specially when the field is hazardous in nature at that time it is essential to transmit the data from field to the base station. Here the field is a soil at land and user is sitting at a base station. The data gathered from the process is to be transmitted for that reason available recourses are RF communication, Blue tooth etc. As these are under the ISM band so free to use by domestic or industry personnel. In this paper communication media used is RF communication, because of its low cost and simplicity for communication. It works in ISM band (Industrial Scientific and Medical) which available for free use. The frequency is 433MHz and the range in which the data can be transmitted is 100 meter distance.

3 Hardware Description

Sensor Node

It consists of a Sensor, Controller, wireless transreceiver and a power source which can be installed in small area. Connecting many sensor nodes together forms a network, which can monitor larger area. Figure 4 shows a sensor node system schematic. It consists of a power source to drive a sensor, a sensor for measurement, a processor, which is heart of a node and a radio communication module to communicate with the base station or other node. Selection of processor depends on area of application, speed required, memory etc. Sensors are used to actually sense the physical parameter. Data from sensor is given to processor for further processing. Node uses radio communication mode to transmit and receive the data. Power reduction is the main objective of the node design thus selection of the components to save the power is vital task.

Properties of a proposed sensor node

Power consumption: 1W
Cost: 8000/- INR
Transmission range: 100 meter, using RF transmitter
Hardware of the model consists of following parts:
1. Sensor
2. Signal conditioning circuit
3. Controller
4. Communication
5. Display

Sensor

The sensor used in the project to measure soil moisture is a capacitive sensor. The operating principle for capacitive sensor is $C = \varepsilon_0\varepsilon_r A/d$, Where, C= capacitance, ε_0 = permeability of air, (Constant), ε_r= dielectric constant, A= area between the plates (cm^2), d= distance between plates (cm). As area, distance and permeability of air are constants change in capacitance is directly proportional to the change in dielectric constant. The dielectric constant of materials or mixtures containing water increases markedly with moisture content because the dielectric constant of water (about 80) is 10 to 30 times higher than the common materials in which it is adsorbed or mixed, as discussed in more detail below. A capacitor with a mixture as the dielectric will display a significant and proportional capacitance increase with moisture content. The dielectric constant of soil, and other materials; which are mixtures of particles and water (including organic materials such as grain and wood), changes in desired manner. The results are summarized in following figures 3 and 4. The dielectric constant (ε) increases with water content (by volume), but depends upon particle size. Soil conductivity is due mostly to the salt concentration (as well as water content) of the soil. Because of the various soil-dependent parameters, the curves relating dielectric constant (and thus capacitance and frequency shift) to moisture content will vary with soil type so that calibrations for specific soils will be needed for high accuracy.[1][2][6] Other types of moisture sensors are: Resistive, Inductive moisture sensors.[6]

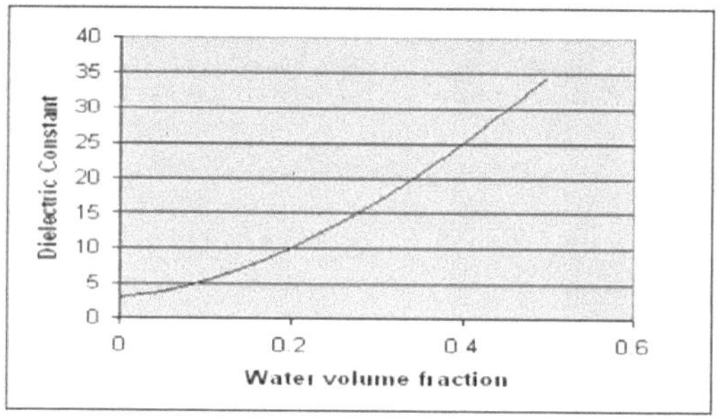

Fig. 3. Dependence of Dielectric Constant of a Mixture on Water Content [2]

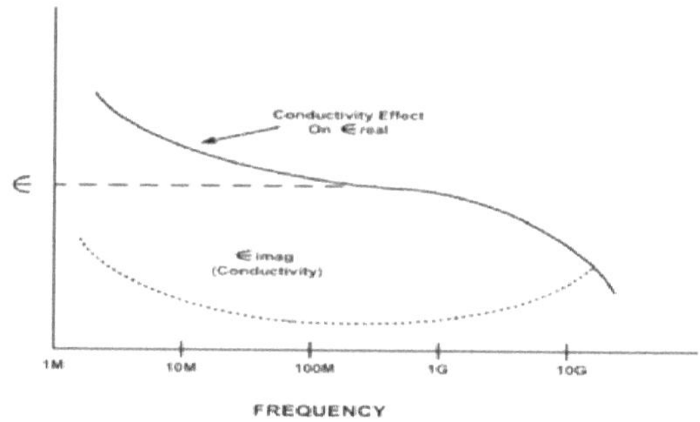

Fig. 4. Typical Dependence of Dielectric Constant on Frequency [2]

ARM Controller

It requires less power. It has feature as in built 10 bit analog to digital converter, RTC, Power down mode, Thumb mode etc. [7][8]

Signal Conditioning Circuit

The output of the capacitive probe is available in the 4 to 20 mA current signals. That is for 0 % moisture it gives 4 mA and for 100 % moisture it gives 20 mA. As the input to ADC is in the standard voltage form the output of probe is converted using I - V converter. Thus now the output which is calibrated in terms of percentage of change in moisture is shown as change in voltage 0 V to 2 V; i.e. for 0 % moisture it gives 0 V and for 100 % moisture it gives 2 V.

Display

16*2 LCD is used to display Set point, Sensor data, and RTC data.

Data transmission

For radio communication RF module is used. RF communication works by creating electromagnetic waves at a source and being able to pick up those electromagnetic waves at a particular destination. These electromagnetic waves travel through the air at near the speed of light. The wavelength of an electromagnetic signal is inversely proportional to the frequency; the higher the frequency, the shorter the wavelength. The RF transreceiver used works satisfactorily over 100 meter distance.

4 Testing and Results

Test Results of Sensor Node: Results are taken under changing moisture conditions. Initially probe was installed in complete dry soil to take 0% reading then slowly water is added in the soil which intern increases moisture content giving change in Capacitance.

Fig. 5. Sensor installed in Soil for Moisture Measurement

Fig. 6. LCD displaying Soil Moisture

Table 2. Result for Capacitive sensor for black soil

Sr.No	Water level (cm)	Current (mA)
1	00	4
2	6	5.5
3	8	7.3
4	9	9
5	11	10.3
6	15	12
7	18	13.6
8	21	15
9	24	16.5
10	26	18
11	28	20

Table 3. Result for Capacitive sensor for black soil

Sr. No	Current (mA)	Output voltage
1	4	0
2	9	0.8
3	12	1.1
4	15	1.5
5	18	1.6
6	20	2

Power Consumption: Power consumption is calculated in 2 parts, Sensor node and base station. The total power is 1W respectively. Power can be reduced using low power components. Using blue tooth transmission media power can be reduced.

Transmission: Sensor data is transmitted using RF module. Data is getting transferred without loss within 100 meter distance.

5 Conclusion

After successful implementation of this project following conclusions are drawn: Sensor node prototype is designed using low power processor ARM. Soil moisture measurement is carried out at the field itself, this saves the time and improves the accuracy of the data.

Data is transmitted using RF transmitter within 100meter distance. By using a keyboard set point for moisture can be entered from base station also. It provides 2 way communications.

As RTC is used the crops are watered only if required; this saves water sources and electricity. Also over irrigation and under irrigation is avoided.

Irregular rain fall which causes main defect in agricultural development this cause is handled by implementation of these kinds of ideas.

References

1. Wobschall, D., Lakshmanan, D.: Wireless Soil Moisture Sensor Based on Fringing Capacitance. In: Proceeding of the IEEE International Conference on Sensors 2005, Irvine, Orange County, California, USA, October 30-November 3, pp. 8–11 (2005)
2. Jackson, T., Mansfield, K., Saafi, M., Colman, T., Romine, P.: Measuring soil temperature and moisture using wireless MEMS sensors. Elesvier Journal of Measurement 41, 381–390 (2008)
3. Bogena, H.R., Huisman, J.A., Rosen-baum, U., Weuthen, A., Vereecken, H.: Evaluation of the ZigBee based wire-less soil moisture sensor network SoilNet. In: Proceeding of Deutsche Bodenkundliche Gesellschaft German Soil Science Society, Kommissionen, Kiel, May 29-30, pp. 561–564 (2008)
4. Park, S., Kim, J.W., Shin, K.-Y., Kim, D.: A Nano Operating System for Wireless Sensor Networks. In: Proceeding of the IEEE International Conference on Advanced Communication Technology (ICACT 2006), Phoenix Park, Korea, February 20-22, pp. 345–348 (2006)
5. Morais, R., Valente, A., Couto, C., Correia, J.H.: A wireless RF CMOS mixed-signal interface for soil moisture measurements. Elsevier Journal of Sensors and Actuators 1(114), 376–384 (2004)
6. Liptak, B.: Handbook of Analytical Instrumentation. CRC Press, Washington
7. Sloss, A., Symes, D., Wright, C.: ARM System Developer's Guide Designing and Optimizing Software. Elsevier Inc. (2004)
8. ARM user manual: Philips Semiconductors

Localization of Sensor Nodes Using Flooding in Wireless Sensor Networks

Basavaraj K. Madagouda, R. Sumathi, and A.H. Shanthakumara

Department of Computer Science and Engineering,
Siddaganga Institute of Technology,
Tumkur, Karnataka, India
basavarajmadagouda@gmail.com,
{rsumathi,shanthakumara}@sit.ac.in

Abstract. The accuracy of localization is a significant criterion to evaluate the practical utility of localization algorithm in wireless sensor networks (*WSNs*). In localization algorithms, one of the main methods to improve localization accuracy is to increase the number of anchor nodes. The number of anchor nodes is always limited because of the hardware constraint, such as cost, energy consumption and so on. In this paper, we propose a novel localization algorithm in which the sensor nodes get localized with the help of virtual anchor nodes. In this scheme VAN gets localized with the help of minimum number of anchor nodes. The objectives to improve the localization accuracy maximize the localization ratio and minimize the cost which incur to deployment of more number of anchor nodes and proposed algorithm is simulated using MAT Lab to evaluate its performance.

Keywords: Flooding, Anchor node, Localization, Sensor networks.

1 Introduction

Wireless sensor networks [1] are a significant technology attracting considerable research interest. Recent advances in wireless communications and electronics have enabled the development of low-cost, low-power and multi-functional sensors that are small in size and communicate in short distances. Wireless sensor network consists of many sensor nodes which have capabilities of sensing, processing and communication. A specific sensor node is called sink node which collects interested data from sensor nodes.

Wireless Sensor Network [2] refers to a group of inexpensive sensors linked by wireless medium, the sensors are provided with sense, computation and wireless communication capability. WSNs usually are arranged at special scout region, and sense special physics information in the region. Sensor nodes are often deployed by random bestrewing (airplane bestrewing for example), and only a few of nodes assembled with Global Positioning System (GPS [3]) which can capture their position after bestrewing, but most of the nodes cannot acquire such information. Due to its

P.V. Krishna, M.R. Babu, and E. Ariwa (Eds.): ObCom 2011, Part I, CCIS 269, pp. 637–646, 2012.

powerful function and low energy cost, the WSN has been widely used in various domains [4], such as national defense and military affair, environment inspection, traffic management, long distance control of dangerous region etc. The localization of sensor nodes has become a hot topic in WSNs. At present, many localization algorithms for sensor networks have been proposed. Most of the WSN includes a small number of anchor nodes, which know their positions beforehand by either using GPS or by manual configuration. Other majority of nodes are unknown position nodes, called unknowns. By using the anchor nodes which knows their location, we can assist the unknowns to be located. But for the existence of various errors, the location precision will be restricted, and some nodes cannot be located.

In this paper, we provide an overview of on-demand techniques, which detects the location of anchor nodes and its location information and other nodes gets localized using the any of the existing localization algorithm techniques can be used for localization of a node [8, 9]. So the improvement of localization precision with lower cost, less energy consumption and less hardware support has become more and more important.

The outline of this paper is as follows. In Section 2 a few localization methods using are being discussed. A proposed technique for on-demand localization of the static sensor nodes is discussed in Section 3. Section 4 shows the simulation and results. Section 5 concludes the paper.

2 Related Works

Localization algorithms are divided into two subsections, which are presented by range-based and range-free, according to whether need to measure the range between nodes. For the former, it is required to measure the real ranges between nodes and its neighbors, and use them to calculate the coordinates of nodes. For the latter, instead of real ranges, it uses estimate factors to calculate the coordinates of nodes.

2.1 Range-Based Localization Algorithms

Time of Arrival (TOA) [10] technology is used to measure range through signal propagation time. The most typical application of TOA technology is GPS. The Time Difference of Arrival (TDOA) [11] technique has been proposed as a localization solution by using two different signals (such as ultrasound and RF). By registering the time difference of signal arrival, it uses the propagating velocity to translate the time difference into distance.

Angle of Arrival (AOA) [12] technology has been proposed to utilize array antennas or combined multi-receivers to obtain the propagation direction of signal. Based on the directions, it gets the range between neighbors.

Received Signal Strength Indicator (RSSI) [13] technology is used to calculate range via signal strength with theoretical or empirical models. The main error source of this technology is the complexity of signal propagation models caused by environment influence. The combination of RSSI and other location algorithm will make a better scheme.

2.2 Range-Free Localization Algorithms

Centroid algorithm [14] is a simple range-free localization algorithm. The node receives signals of anchors in its communication area and makes its coordinates as the centroid of these anchors.

DV-Hop algorithm [15] is the most basic scheme, and it first employs a classical distance vector exchange so that all nodes in the network get distances, in hops, to the anchors. Once an anchor gets distances to other anchors, it estimates an average size for one hop, which is then deployed as a correction to the entire network. When receiving the correction, an arbitrary node may then have estimate distances to anchors, in meters, which can be used to estimate the coordinates of nodes.

Amorphous algorithm [16] is similar to DV-hop, but it assumes to know the network density in advance, and uses offline hop-distance estimations. In APIT [17], the network area is isolated into some triangular regions by anchors. A node's presence inside or outside of these triangular regions allows a node to narrow down the area in which it can potentially reside.

3 Network Model and Definitions

3.1 WSN Model

Consider a WSN as shown in fig. 1 which consists of several nodes scattered randomly. The nodes are of two types: anchor nodes and sensor nodes. Anchor nodes are the nodes which have priori information about their location before deployment. These nodes are equipped with a more powerful GPS system and which localizes with ease. The network model consists of several sensor nodes and few anchor nodes populated. After localization, these nodes act as base stations and send radio waves incessantly which are of low range ranging between 50-100 meters. Each anchor node has a specific ID stored in its memory which is sent along with the radio signals. On the other hand sensor nodes are the nodes whose location is unknown. The sensor nodes are GPS less nodes which localize themselves with the help of the anchors in their

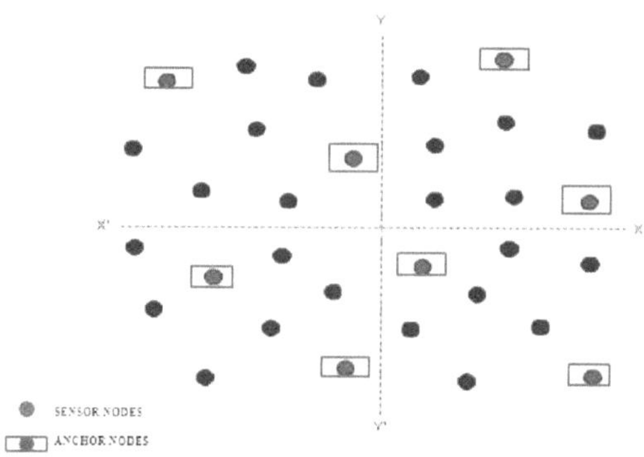

Fig. 1. A typical Wireless Sensor Network

proximity or with the help of the other neighboring sensor nodes. This model has very few anchor nodes and many sensor nodes which are light weighted and less expensive than the anchor nodes.

Query message - A message sent to a node to find out the value of one of the node's properties. The properties are the x co-ordinate and y co-ordinate of the node.

Virtual Anchor Node – The sensor nodes which localize using the location of anchor nodes are called Virtual anchor node (VAN).

A data table – Each sensor node contain a data table which stores the information about location of each anchor node. Fields of data table includes anchor node ID, X co-ordinate and y co-ordinate of the anchor node and the distance from each anchor node with its hop count.

TTL [Time to Live] – The amount of time required to send and receive a request and response message is known as TTL. To find TTL, we consider parameters s and d where s denotes speed of network and d is the hop count distance, TTL = d/s.

Hop count limit - It specifies a limit on the number of hops a query message is allowed to broadcast in the network.

3.2 Overview

In fig. 2, some nodes have their location information and other nodes don't have their location information. To finding location of sensor nodes is known as localization. To find location of sensor nodes, broadcasts a query message to its neighboring nodes for location information of anchor nodes. If any anchor node is in its broadcasting range it replies to that query message and using any range based free algorithm, sensor node gets localized. Sensor nodes which get localized stores all anchor node information in its data table as shown in Table.1 and it acts as a virtual anchor node for the other which are not localized.

Reminder set of sensor nodes which do not have localization inform, once again broadcast a query message. If any Virtual anchor node gets a query message then it replies all anchor nodes information which has stored in its table. A node localized using anchor nodes information and it acts as VAN for other sensor nodes.

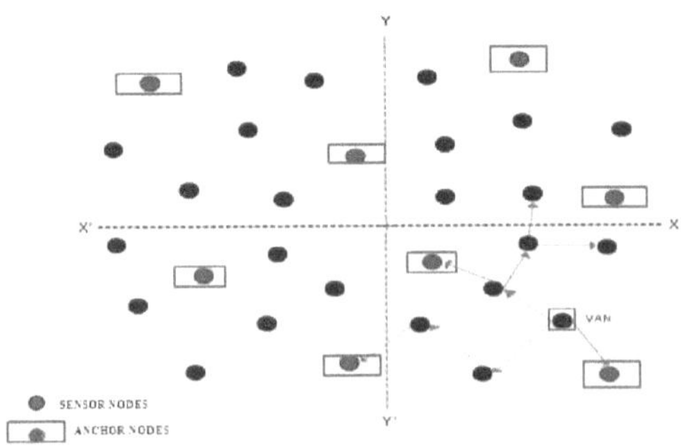

Fig. 2. Flooding query message for localizing a node

Table 1. Structure of Data Table

Anchor Node ID	X co-ordinates	Y co-ordinates	Hop Distance (d)
1	36.7	15.9	2
3	65.2	45.4	1
4	70.3	10.6	3
.	.	.	.
.	.	.	.
N	83.39	9.84	10

Sensor node which has been localized stores all information about anchor nodes with the hop distance in its table. Any virtual anchor node receives a query message sent by other sensor nodes to get information about the anchor nodes. Virtual anchor node sends all anchor nodes' information which is stored in its data table with adding the hop distance (between source node to VAN) to each node in its data table. The sensor node gets localized using the information from the virtual anchor node and it also stores all anchor node information in its data table.

3.3 Localization Scheme : Two Phases

3.3.1 Localization Using Flooding Technique

In wireless sensor network the sensor nodes localize using the information about the anchor nodes, broadcasting the query message in all directions to its neighbor nodes in its transmission range as shown in above figure.3. Sensor node sends the query message using flooding scheme, other nodes receive same query message multiple times from different paths.

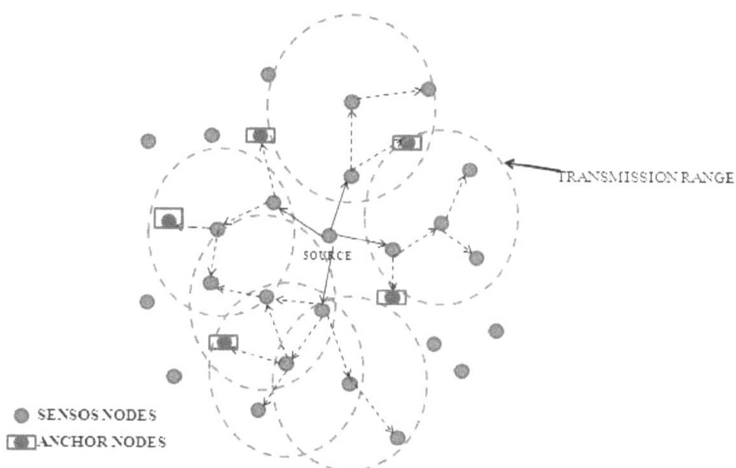

Fig. 3. Localization using flooding technique

The amount of consumption energy to broadcast is given by:

$$E_{total} = (E_{rx} * \text{the average number of neighbors} + E_{tx}) * N \quad (1)$$

As equation (1) [6] means, the total energy directly depends on the number of all nodes (N) and *the average number of neighbors*. So, the total energy consumed for one broadcast is big so that it can rapidly reduce network's lifetime. The life time of nodes become less and also decreases the network life time.

3.3.2 Localization Using Virtual Anchor Nodes

Using On-demand technique the sensor nodes obtain the information about anchor nodes. Sensor node broadcasts a query message to its neighbor nodes which are in its radio frequency range by setting TTL and the hop count. Each sensor node contains a memory to store the information about the query message received from the sensor nodes. Once it receives the message, it decreases the hop count which is set by the source node in network.

The sensor node which receives a query message broadcasts the same message to its neighbor nodes which are in its radio frequency range. The received node in turn sends the query message to its neighbor nodes. Every node checks its memory when a new message is received and it discards if the same message is received twice.

In two conditions the sensor node does not get localized. First condition is if the hop count value becomes zero and the source node does not get any information about minimum three anchor nodes information. Then the source node re-broadcasts the query message by increasing the hop count value. Second condition is when the Time to live becomes zero then the broadcasting of query message will be stopped.

When an anchor node receives the query message, it sends its location information to the node from which it received in the same path. After receiving information about anchor nodes, sensor node stores all anchor nodes information in its data table. If a sensor node get minimum three anchor nodes information, then it calculates its location using information about anchor nodes and also it stores forwarding time (t_F) and backward time (t_B).

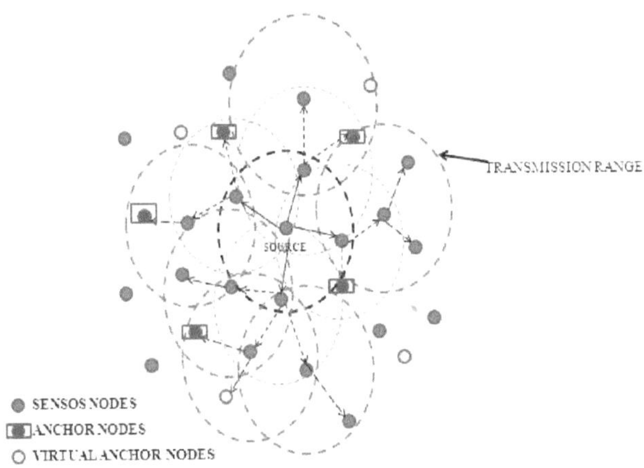

Fig. 4. Localization using Virtual Anchor Nodes

When a sensor node gets localized it acts as Virtual Anchor Node (VAN). Upon receiving query message by virtual anchor node (VAN), it renders all anchor node information from its table to sensor node. Sensor node updates the hop count values and stores all information in its data table. A sensor node can localize using anchor node information from VAN. With this mechanism we can reduce the communication cost of sensor nodes, energy consumption of sensor nodes and also minimize the network lifetime.

Type	Sensor ID	Path	TTL	Query message	Hop Count Limit

Fig. 5. Format of request packets

The request packet format of query message send by the sensor node is shown fig. 5. The fields of packet are type, sensor node ID, path, TTL (time to leave), query message and hop counts. First field Type indicates that the message is request message or response message. If Type value is 0, then its request message. Also the packet contains the sensor node ID which has broadcast a query message, TTL value. Path field contains the path in which the query message is sent. The hop count limit is value to broadcast the query message from a source node to it other nodes.

Type	Anchor ID	Path	TTL	Query message	Hop Count Limit

Fig. 6. Format of response packet

The response packet format sent by the anchor node is shown in fig. 6. The fields of packet are type, sensor node ID, path, TTL, query message and hop counts. If Type value is 1, then its response message and the packet contain the anchor node ID which has responding a query message, TTL value. The anchor node sends its information in same path in which path it received that query message. The hop count is value to find the distance from source node to anchor node.

4 Simulation and Results

The WSN is simulated using MatLab/Simulink. The simulated network model consists of 500 sensor nodes of which 50 are anchor nodes populated over a 100X100 grid area. The nodes are distributed randomly and uniformly over the deployment area. A scatter plot graph depicting the deployed nodes is shown in fig. 7.

The following metrics are used to measure the performance of the proposed scheme: localization error, localization ratio and energy efficiency ratio. Localization error defines the amount of error involved in the location information of the dislocated node. Localization ratio is defined as the ratio of the number of nodes which successfully get localized to the number of nodes deployed in network. Energy efficiency ratio is defined as the ratio of the total energy is used by nodes to get localized to the total amount of energy in the network.

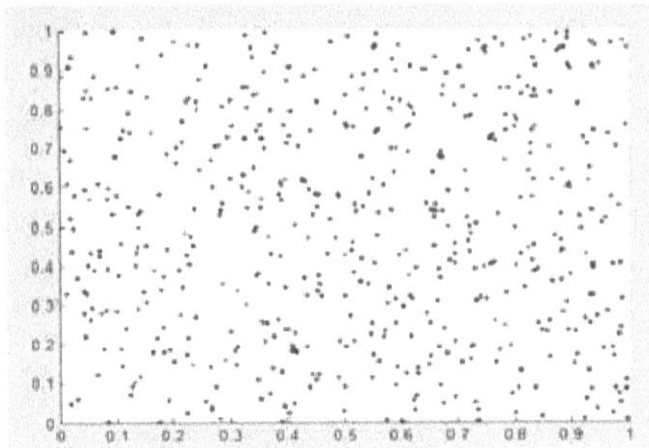

Fig. 7. Snapshot of Matlab/Simulink

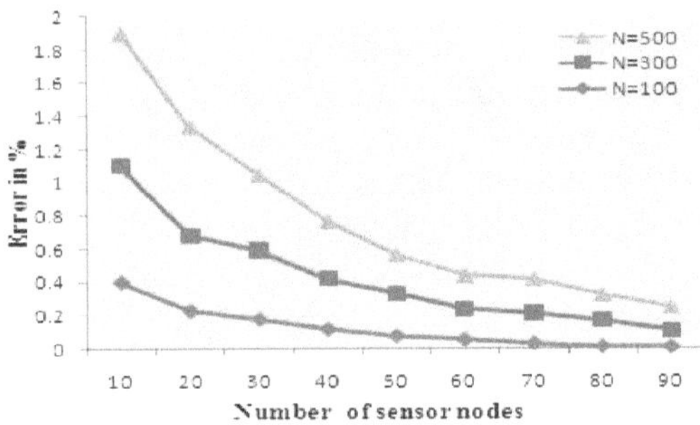

Fig. 8. Localization error

Fig. 8 shows a graph plotted for localization error. The x-axis represents the number of nodes dislocated and the y-axis represents the localization error in percentage. It depicts that, when the total number of nodes deployed (N) in an application increases the error decreases. The localization error [18] is calculated using

$$\text{Localization error} = \frac{\sum (x_e - x_l)^2 + (y_e - y_l)^2}{\text{No of sensor nodes}} \tag{2}$$

Where (x_e, y_e) is the estimated location of sensor node and (x_l, y_l) is the true location of sensor node.

Fig. 9 shows a graph plotting the number of nodes in the x-axis and the localization ratio in the y-axis. It shows that the ratio of the nodes getting localized with the total number of nodes deployed in the application.

Fig. 10 shows a graph plotting the number of nodes in the x-axis and the energy in the y-axis. It shows that the ratio of the energy consumed by the nodes getting localized with the total energy in the network in the application.

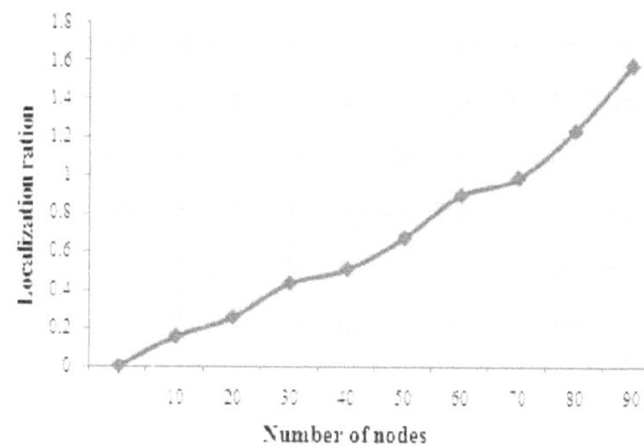

Fig. 9. Localization ratio

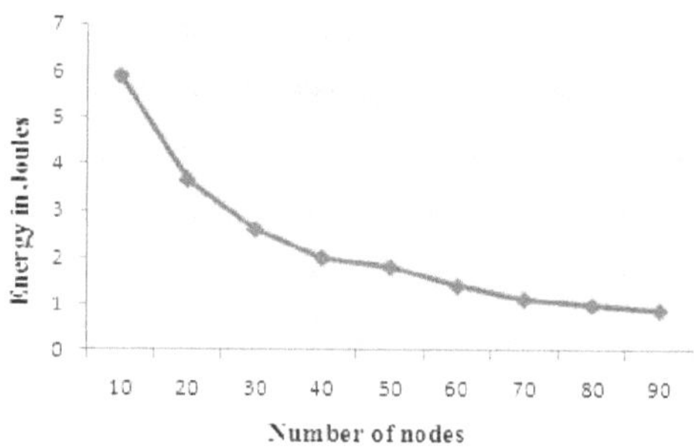

Fig. 10. Energy efficiency ratio

5 Conclusion

Precision is an important criterion for any wireless sensor network to work adeptly. In the paper we show an on- demand flooding technique to reduce the number of broadcasts and localizing other sensor nodes with lower cost, less energy consumption and less hardware support. Also our technique efficiently identifies the location of anchor nodes and virtual anchor nodes information to localize sensor nodes with minimum number of broadcasts. Then it helps the node to trigger the localization algorithm and gets localized on demand. Thus the location information of the sensor nodes is accurate and the WSN operates without any flaw.

References

[1] Chong, C.-Y., Kumar, S.: Sensor networks: evolution, opportunities, and challenges. Proceedings of the IEEE 91(8), 1247–1256 (2003)

[2] Potdar, V., Sharif, A., Chang, E.: Wireless Sensor Networks: A Survey. In: International Conference on Advanced Information Networking and Applications Workshops (2009)

[3] Hofmann-Wellenhof, B., Lichtenegger, H., Collins, J.: Global Positioning System: Theory and Practice, 4th edn. Springer, Heidelberg (1997)

[4] Arampatzis, T., Lygeros, J., Manesis, S.: A Survey of Applications of Wireless Sensors and Wireless Sensor Networks. In: Proceedings of the 13th Mediterranean Conference on Control and Automation Limassol, Cyprus (2005)

[5] Liu, P., Zhang, X., Tian, S., Zhao, Z., Sun, P.: A Novel Virtual Anchor Node-based Localization Algorithm for Wireless Sensor Networks. In: Proceedings of the Sixth International Conference on Networking (2007)

[6] Yu, N., Wan, J.: On Demand Localization Algorithm for Wireless Sensor Networks

[7] Son, J., Byun, T.-Y.: A Routing Scheme with Limited Flooding for Wireless Sensor Networks. International Journal of Future Generation Communication and Networking 3(3) (September 2010)

[8] Alippi, C., Vanini, G.: A RSSI-based and calibrated centralized localization technique for Wireless Sensor Networks. In: Proceedings of the Fourth Annual IEEE International Conference on Pervasive Computing and Communications Workshops (PERCOMW 2006) (2006)

[9] Peng, R., Sichitiu, M.L.: Angle of Arrival Localization for Wireless Sensor Networks. In: Third Annual IEEE Communications Society Conference on Sensor and Ad Hoc Communications and Networks, Reston, VA (September 2006)

[10] Lorincz, K., Welsh, M.: MoteTrack: A Robust, Decentralized Approach to RF-Based Location Tracking. In: Strang, T., Linnhoff-Popien, C. (eds.) LoCA 2005. LNCS, vol. 3479, pp. 63–82. Springer, Heidelberg (2005)

[11] Ni, H., Ren, G., Chang, Y.: A TDOA Location Scheme in OFDM Based WMANs. IEEE Transactions on Consumer Electronics (2008)

[12] Peng, R., Sichitiu, M.L.: Angle of Arrival Localization for Wireless Sensor Networks. In: Third Annual IEEE Communications Society Conference on Sensor and Ad Hoc Communications and Networks, Reston, VA (September 2006)

[13] Alippi, C., Vanini, G.: A RSSI-based and calibrated centralized localization technique for Wireless Sensor Networks. In: Proceedings of the Fourth Annual IEEE International Conference on Pervasive Computing and Communications Workshops, PERCOMW 2006 (2006)

[14] Deng, B., Huang, G., Zhang, L., Liu, H.: Improved Centroid Localization Algorithm in WSNs. In: Proceedings of 3rd International Conference on Intelligent System and Knowledge Engineering (2008)

[15] Lee, B.-T., Kim, S.: Scalable DV-Hop Localization for Wireless Sensor Networks. In: Proceedings of APCC 2008 (2008)

[16] Nagpal, R.: Organizing a global coordinate system from local information- on an amorphous computer, A.I. Memo 1666, MIT A.I. Laboratory (August 1999)

[17] Wang, J.Z., Jin, H.: Improvement on APIT Localization Algorithms for Wireless Sensor Networks. In: Proceedings of International Conference on Networks Security, Wireless Communications and Trusted Computing (2009)

[18] Yadav, V., Mishra, M.K., Sngh, A.K., Gore, M.M.: Localization Scheme For Three Dimensional Wireless Sensor Networks Using GPS Enabled Mobile Sensor Nodes. International Journal of Next-Generation Networks (IJNGN) 1(1) (December 2009)

A Packet Classification and Node-Level Certification Mechanism for Intrusion Detection in MANET

S.P. Manikandan[1], R. Manimegalai[2], V. Rakesh[1], and V. Vaishnavi[1]

[1] Department of Computer Science and Engineering, P.B. College of Engineering, Chennai, India
[2] Department of Computer Science and Engineering, Velammal Engineering College, Chennai, India

Abstract. Security has been the most important aspect in the world of networks, especially in Mobile ad-hoc networks. In particular, the emphasis is laid on intrusion detection and prevention. In this paper, an effective intrusion detection technique based on classification and certification of packets is presented. The certification is done at the node level in MANET. The proposed solution is divided into two phases. In the first phase, the packets are classified using C-SVM algorithm and NSL-KDD dataset. In the second phase, the classified packets are certified at each hop. The proposed solution is efficient in terms of both power and time.

Keywords: Mobile Ad-Hoc Network (MANET), Intrusion Detection System (IDS), Dynamic Source Routing (DSR), Classification Support Vector Machine (C-SVM), NSL-KDD.

1 Introduction

Mobile Ad-Hoc networks (MANET) are wireless communication networks whose applications have increased drastically over the last one decade. The tremendous growth is due to various advantages it possesses when compared to an infrastructure based network. MANET is quite famous for being highly flexible. This flexible nature is due to its dynamic topology. The nodes in such networks have the liberty to enter and leave the network at any point of time. MANET has been widely used in various applications in the form of mobile nodes. It is also used in ubiquitous computing and sensor networks. In spite of all these advantages, there exist few security related issues that prevent the extensive use of MANET. Thus, in order tap the advantages of MANET further, we need to address some security threats that are prevalent. It is not feasible to address all security issues simultaneously, but we can aim to correct some errors, and enhance performance of existing security systems. Intrusions into the network such as malicious packets, unauthorized access of nodes, and illegal transmission of packets are few types of attacks on MANET. In this work, the focus is given to detection of malicious packets into the network.

In order to safeguard the systems and the data that is transmitted, several intrusion detection and prevention techniques have been proposed. However, the prevention

P.V. Krishna, M.R. Babu, and E. Ariwa (Eds.): ObCom 2011, Part I, CCIS 269, pp. 647–653, 2012.

mechanisms are time and power consuming. It is therefore better to detect the intrusions well before they enter into the network. There are numerous ways in which security can be exploited in MANET. Certain features of MANET such as dynamic nature of topology make it difficult to ensure that security has not been compromised. The following attacks have been considered in this work: Denial of Service (DoS), User to Root (U2R), Root to Location (R2L) and probe attacks.

In this paper, a packet classification and node level certification technique is discussed. The proposed methodology makes use of Support Vector Machine (SVM) algorithm and the NSL-KDD dataset for classification of incoming packets. In addition, a certification algorithm is implemented at the node level. TCP data sets are used for experimentation. The authenticity of packet is guaranteed by the combined process of classification and certification.

The rest of the paper is organized as follows: Section 2 presents the related work, while the system architecture and the implementation techniques are discussed in Section 3. The classification simulation details are also provided in Section 3. Section 4 summarizes the paper and gives directions for future work.

2 Related Work

A lot of active research has been going on in the area of intrusion detection in MANET. Ganapathy et al. have proposed a classification technique using the enhanced SVM [1]. The proposed solution in [1] achieves very good accuracy. A three phase technique is proposed in [2] with interesting features such as power check and certification using a modified Dynamic Source Routing (DSR). It [2] tries to mitigate the problems of overhearing technique by introducing an additional phase of authentication in between the route establishment and the packet transmission. A Detailed Analysis of the KDD Data Set has been done in [3] and a new data set NSL-KDD is proposed by Mhabod et al. The NSL-KDD consists of carefully selected records from the complete KDD set and prevents many shortcomings of KDD data set. NSL-KDD [3] along with C-SVM (Classification SVM) forms the basis of the proposed solution in this work.

Combining SVM with decision tree can be effective for classification problem because it reduces the training and testing time drastically with more efficiency. In [4], a decision tree based IDS algorithm called, tree structured multiclass SVM, is proposed using SVM. An efficient attribute reduction algorithm based on a new measure, relative discernibility degree, is presented in [5]. It [5] defines a simplified consistent decision table that reduces the inefficiencies of other attribute reduction algorithms. A new learning approach for network intrusion detection using naïve Bayesian classifier and ID3 algorithm is presented in [6]. Effective attributes are identified from the training dataset. These attributes are used to build a classifier for network intrusion detection using data mining algorithms in [6]. The proposed solution in [6] achieves high classification rates and reduces false positives. Chen et al. proposed an intrusion detection system called ExWatchdog in [7]. It [7] discovers all malicious nodes that can partition the network by falsely reporting other nodes as misbehaving. It protects the network from malicious nodes with less overhead. A detailed discussion on testing and evaluation of IDS is presented by John McHugh in [8].

3 Two Phase Classification and Certification Algorithm

In this section, the proposed solution is discussed in detail. As already mentioned earlier, the proposed methodology contains two phases. The first phase involves classification of packets using the C-SVM algorithm [3]. This algorithm classifies the packets into two types and gives the output as either 1 for good packets or -1 for bad packets. This output is given as input to the certification algorithm in the second phase. During the second phase, the packets are certified and the certificate is attached to the packet before sending it to the next node if the packet is good. Otherwise, the packet is discarded. Thus, after completion of both the phases, we get classified and certified packets as output.

The processes involved in proposed solution are depicted in Figure. 1. It shows a number of nodes in MANET, with their range represented as circles. At each node, training is done using the C-SVM with the help of NSL-KDD training data. Based on the training the current packet is classified and certified at that particular node. Each node might have different learning levels. A packet which clears all of them and certified will be attributed as a good packet or non-malicious packet.

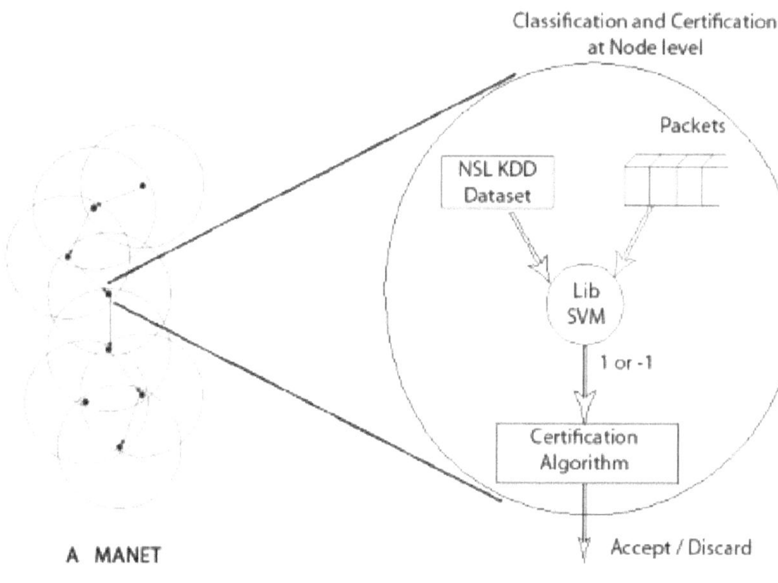

Fig. 1. System Architecture of Intrusion Detection System (IDS) in MANET

3.1 Classification of Packets

Packets, as they enter into the MANET can be routed to any of the nodes present in it. In such a case, there exists a possibility of malicious packet intruding all the security mechanisms provided. Hence, it is better to implement the algorithm at every node of the MANET. The classification is done here using the C-SVM algorithm, which is pre-processed by the Tuple Reduction Technique and attribute selection. It classifies the packet using a tree classifier and we use the NSL-KDD dataset as sample input to the algorithm. Thus, the training dataset values are classified and are compared with the values of the incoming packets. These are given as inputs to the C-SVM algorithm (a binary classifier) and the output is either 1(good packet) or -1(bad packet). The tree classifying algorithm, classifies the packets based on attribute selected, the derived attributes form the subsets of the tree Thus, all the incoming packets are classified. The table below shows the true negatives and false positives achieved while using NSL-KDD and C-SVM in unison. This combined with certification at each node increases the reliability of the system as a whole. The samples are increased for each test by fifty and even for large number of intrusions the false positive seems to be very low. The true negatives are less in number even after increasing the samples in successive tests.

Table 1. Classification of Intrusions

Num of Intrusions	Num of Intruders Captured	True Negative	False Positive
50	48	2	0
100	97	3	0
150	145	4	1
200	194	5	1

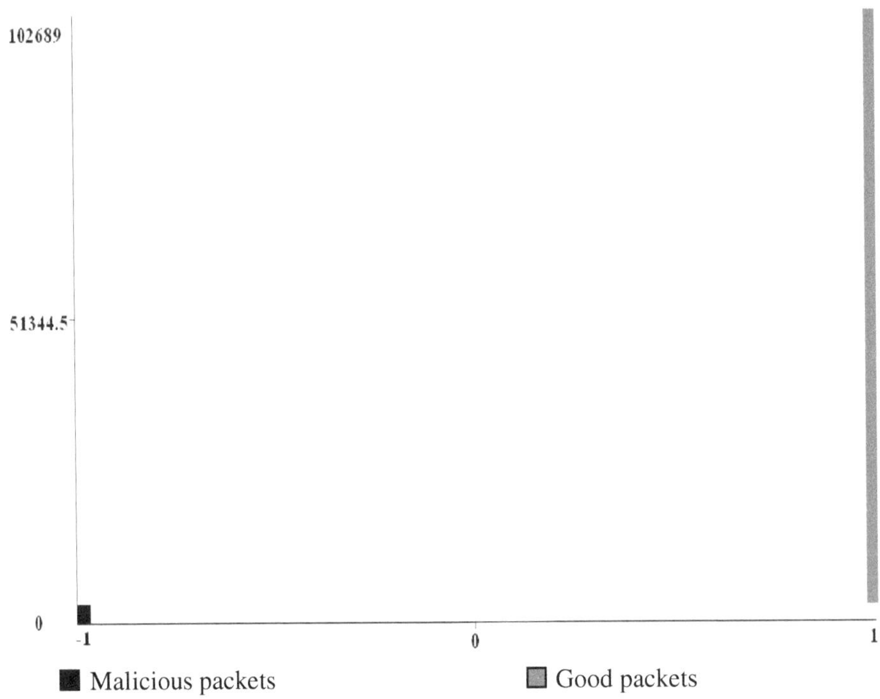

Fig. 2. Classification Graph Showing Good and Bad Packets

The simulation results are shown in Figure 2. From the Figure 2, it can be seen that only very few bad packets were able to intrude the network. The proposed methodology successfully detects most of the malicious nodes and protects the network. The X axis represents the type of packet (1 for good packet and -1 for bad packet). The Y axis represents the number of packets entering in to the network. The number of malicious packets entering into the network is almost negligible and it should be noted that some of them even could be true negatives. This substantiates that the accuracy and efficiency levels of the system are good.

3.2 Certification of Packets

The output of the Lib-SVM (C-SVM) is given to the certification algorithm, which is implemented at node level. The binary values are read and the algorithm only proceeds if it sees a value of 1 for a packet. In this case, the certificate is appended to the packet, else it is discarded. The algorithm of this process is given below.

Algorithm: Two Phase Intrusion Detection

Input: The Current packet to be certified

1. A global variable is used to represent the certificate number implying the number of nodes that have certified the incoming packet. This is initialized to a value of 001.

    Initialize global variable CertNum=001

2. Pass the current packet as an argument to the certify function.

    function certify(cur_packet)

    2.1 This packet is first given as input to the C-SVM which classifies them and the binary output is stored in a variable.

    val= C-SVM(cur_packet)

    2.2 If the output from the SVM algorithm is 1, then it's classified as a good packet. Hence, the packet is certified at this node and so the certificate is appended to the packet and is forwarded to the next node for further certification along the path that it is routed. Increment the *certificate* number.

    if val==1
    {
    Append certificate and forward the packet for certification
    Increment certificate number
    }

    2.3 Else if the output of the SVM algorithm is -1, then it is considered to be a bad packet and is discarded.

    else (if val == -1)
    {
    Discard Packet
    }

3. If the certificate number reaches the maximum limit of 500, we re-initialize the counter to 0.

if (CertNum==500)
{
CertNum=0
}

4. A timer is also set such that if the timeout value exceeds 60 seconds, the certificate number is re-initialized to 0

If timeout_val=60 seconds
CertNum=0

Output: If the packet is good, it is accepted, else it is discarded.

After the completion of this phase, each packet has its own certificate appended and then it is transmitted. The process of certification is done at every node to ensure that there has been no malicious intrusion in between the nodes of MANET during transmission. Both the phases, classification and certification, work in unison. The entire process is given as flowchart in Figure 3.

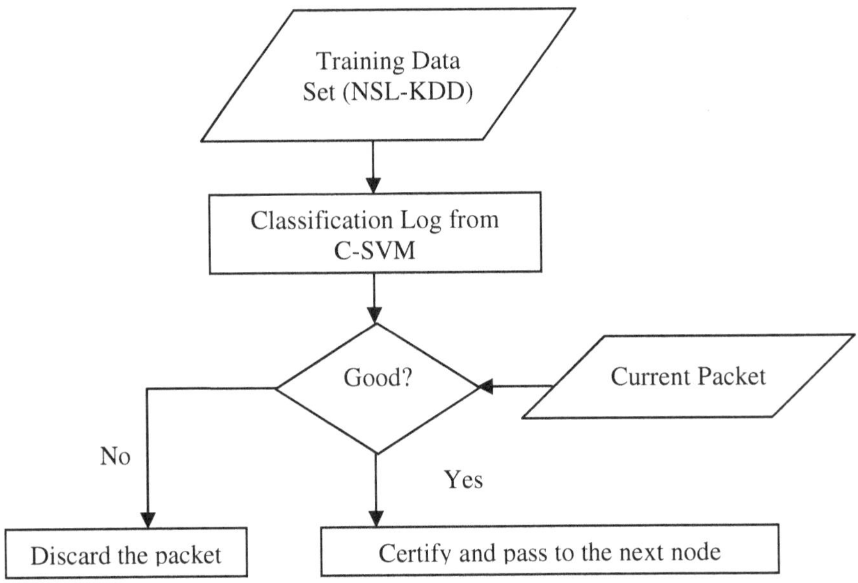

Fig. 3. Two Phase Intrusion Detection System

4 Conclusions

In this paper, a combination of classification followed by a certification mechanism for packet that intrudes the functioning of MANET is presented. The proposed methodology provides 97% accuracy. It identifies and discards the intruding malicious packets effectively. Moreover, the certification mechanism done at node level reduces the possibility of errors. Future work could be using alternatives to SVM, which may yield better results. The NSL-KDD still suffers problems suggested by McHugh [8]. Among the issues raised, the most important seemed to be that no validation was ever performed to show that the dataset actually looked like real network traffic just like KDD99. Indeed, even a cursory examination of the data showed that the data rates were far below what will be experienced in a real medium sized network. Thus better alternatives to it should be looked into for better training sets.

References

1. Ganapathy, S., Yogesh, P., Kannan, A.: An Intelligent Intrusion Detection System for Mobile Ad-Hoc Networks Using Classification Techniques. In: Das, V.V., Thankachan, N., Debnath, N.C. (eds.) PEIE 2011. CCIS, vol. 148, pp. 117–122. Springer, Heidelberg (2011)
2. Arya, K.V., Vashistha, P., Gupta, V.: Phase Technique for Intrusion Detection in Mobile Ad Hoc Network. In: Cherifi, H., Zain, J.M., El-Qawasmeh, E. (eds.) DICTAP 2011, Part I. CCIS, vol. 166, pp. 675–684. Springer, Heidelberg (2011)
3. Tavallaee, M., Bagheri, E., Lu, W., Ghorbani, A.A.: A Detailed Analysis of the KDD CUP 99 Data Set. In: IEEE Symposium on Computational Intelligence for Security and Defense Applications (CISDA 2009), pp. 1–6 (July 2009)
4. Snehal, A., Devale, P.R., Garje, G.V.: Intrusion Detection System using Support Vector Machine and Decision Tree. In: The Proceedings of International Conference of Networking and Information Technology (ICNIT 2010), Philippines, June 11-12, pp. 59–63 (2010)
5. Teng, S., Wu, J., Sun, J., Zhou, S., Liu, G.: An Efficient Attribute Reduction Algorithm. In: The Proceedings of 2nd International Conference on Advanced Computer Control (ICACC 2010), China, March 27-29, pp. 471–475 (2010)
6. Farid, D.M., Dormont, J., Harbi, N., Hoa, N.H., Rahman, M.Z.: Adaptive Network Intrusion Detection Learning: Attribute Selection and Classification. In: International Conference on Computer Systems Engineering, Version 1-19, Bangkok, pp. 810–816 (July 2010)
7. Chen, Y., Nasser, N.: Enhanced Intrusion Detection System for Discovering Malicious Nodes in Mobile Ad-hoc Networks. In: The Proceedings of IEEE International Conference on Communications, Scotland, p. 2 (June 2007)
8. McHugh, J.: Testing Intrusion Detection Systems: a Critique of the 1998 and 1999 DARPA Intrusion Detection System Evaluations as Performed by Lincoln Laboratory. ACM Transactions on Information and System Security, 262–294 (2000)

MEDINFO CLOUD-A Cloud Based Solution to Ensure Secure Access to Health Related Information

Sankari Senthil*, Ramya R., and Saranya B.

Department of Information Technology, Sri Sairam Engineering College, Chennai, India

Abstract. Healthcare facilities require health care workers, adequate infrastructure and information working in harmony to provide services in medically-underserved areas and communities. There has been constant pursuance across the globe to use computing powers to the fullest especially in the healthcare industry where most of the data is fragmented in paperwork.. The current mechanism to provide updates on the latest medicine available is disintegrated and does not penetrate to the grassroots level .All healthcare facilities must be alerted about hazardous medicines instantly to delimit its usage. Organ transplantation is increasing precipitously with the development in healthcare services and the search for a rare blood group has often been in vain. The lack of a proficient system to locate medicines and apt organ and blood donors is a hitch that puts many lives in jeopardy. It is important for all this information to be available as and when required by the hospitals or patients. With the help of IaaS(Infrastructure as a service),our system typically delivers a platform virtualization environment as a service for selective access to information to maximize security. The servers with information are utilized by clients as a fully outsourced service. The internet based computing makes it client centred approach which enables secured access to the data. The main objectives of the project is 1) To provide hospitals with information that can help locate blood and organ donors of specified criteria.2)Supports tracking of organ and blood donations.3)Geographical location based on availability of medicines 4)provide centralized updation of the best medicines available in the market.5)To instantly demarcate the usage of hazardous medicine. There is tremendous promise for cloud computing infrastructure in the healthcare industry and is an ideal tool to leverage computing power at low cost. The project is realistic and can be implemented all over the world.

Keywords: Blood and Organ donor information, cloud computing, centralized medicine database, security, virtualization.

1 Introduction

The rapid developments in the medical field over the years have greatly improved the quality of diagnosis and treatment of dreadful diseases thereby successfully prolonging human lives. To facilitate accurate diagnosis quite a large number of

* Corresponding author.

P.V. Krishna, M.R. Babu, and E. Ariwa (Eds.): ObCom 2011, Part I, CCIS 269, pp. 654–660, 2012.

medical inspection instruments and equipments have been developed .However, the tremendous growth of information technology over the last decade brought new opportunities to integrate the software technology into medical services .The service of cloud computing is most needed in the medical field.[8] There has been constant pursuance across the globe to use computing powers to the fullest. Cloud computing is a product of those efforts. [9]

"Cloud computing" denotes the use of internet based computers for a variety of IT related services such as computing ,storage ,network ,system security ,application ,infrastructure and platform.Cloud computing can remove large capital expenditure from consumer's perspective and gives them liberty to use the best technology on rental basis .[2]It enables convenient, on demand network access to a shared pool of configurable computing resources .The cloud computing system can be divided into two sections front end, the side the client sees and back end, which is the actual "cloud" section of the system and a central server administers the system by monitoring the traffic. Cloud has the attributes and potential to support a global outsourcing environment with better scalability and elasticity - to meet the business-IT demand in this unpredictable global economy [5].

This paper concentrates on real world solutions for medical issues. Med-Info acts as a centralized mechanism to streamline data and ensure efficient flow of information between pharmacies, hospitals, blood banks and pharmaceutical manufacturers. It will aid research and prove to be an effective tool in times of emergency. Enormous computing power is needed to store the humongous amount of data hence cloud computing is needed to provide storage and analysis services .Processing enormous data stored is something cloud is good at due to its distributed architecture that allows for optimum load balancing and seamless transfer of information.

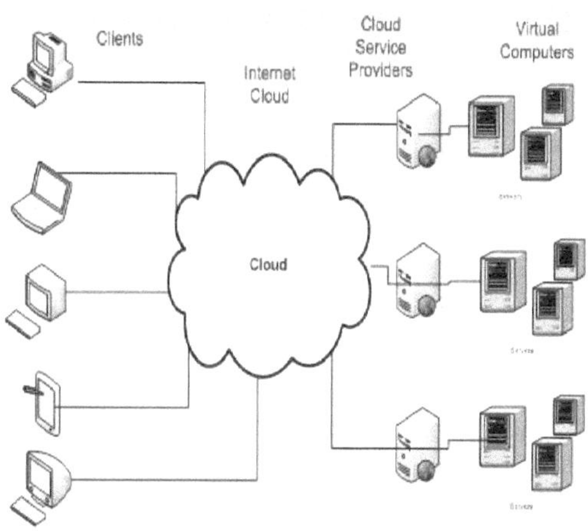

2 Related Work

As far as we know, there is no similar project in India focused on using cloud computing technology to enable medical information sharing such as organ donor availability, availability of medicine in pharmacies and blood in banks and to integrate various Medicare applications. Nevertheless, there are some medical related projects that utilize the computing to support healthcare.

3 MedInfo Cloud

Our project can be divided into three components namely (1)Med-Info architecture (2)Resources in MedInfo (3)Geographic location based search and (4) Security.

3.1 Architecture of Medinfo Cloud

MedInfo delivers Infrastructure as a service (IaaS).Cloud infrastructure services or "Infrastructure as a service" delivers computer infrastructure, typically a platform virtualization environment as a service. Rather than purchasing servers, software data centre space or network equipment, clients instead buy those resources as a fully outsourced service.[10] The service is typically billed on a utility computing basis and amount of resources consumed (and therefore the cost) will typically reflect the level of activity. It is an evolution of virtual private server offerings.[7] Med Info provides an effective mechanism for information sharing between hospitals, pharmacies ,pharmaceutical manufactures and patients. The resources connected to Med info cloud are (1)Blood banks (2)Hospitals with possible organ donors (3)Pharmacies (4)Pharmaceutical manufactures.

Here, the main Med Info cloud is hybrid one which enables customized security and control settings. Based on utility and the sensitivity of the data, the services is made available in public and community type cloudlets. This type of cloud model can be implemented from cloud service providers like Google or Microsoft.

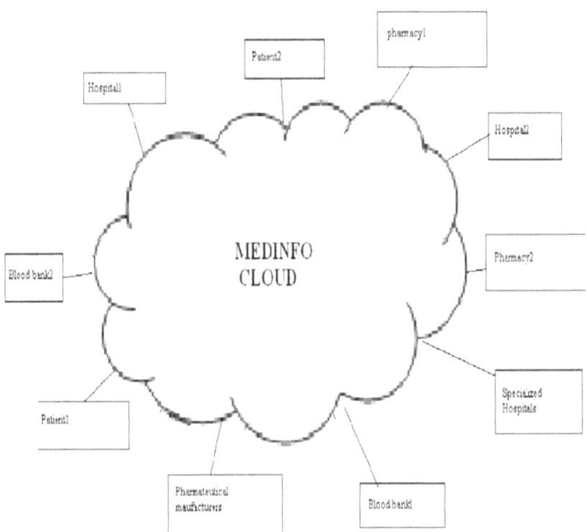

3.2 Resources in Medinfo

The MedInfo Cloud is divided into three cloudlets namely (1)E-Pharm (2)Bloodline (3)Organ Cloud.

3.2.1 E-Pharm

E-Pharm cloud connects hospitals, clinics, pharmacies, pharmaceutical manufacturers and general users. The current mechanism to provide updates on the latest medicine available is disintegrated and does not penetrate to the grassroots level. Using E-Pharm, a centralized mechanism is established where all hospitals, clinics and pharmacies are brought to notice about the up to date developments. Also, healthcare facilities are alerted about hazardous medicines instantly to delimit its usage. In the civic domain, E-Pharm serves as a location based search for medicines eliminating the need to enquire manually. This can be accessed via smart phones also, this effectively reduces the time consumed.

3.2.2 Bloodline Cloud

Rare blood groups are difficult to find in times of emergencies. Although link ups are available between certain hospitals and blood banks, there is an absence of a centralized system to ensure efficient flow of information between them. Bloodline Cloud will provide a centralized mechanism to streamline data transfer between blood banks and hospitals. This will also bring about digitalization of this network , allowing faster and better access to information.

3.2.3 Organ Cloud

Currently, Organ donor information is fragmented and there is a need to reach out in a patient centric fashion. Organ cloud provides a platform between patients and hospitals specialized in performing organ transplantations. It includes current availability of organs with their respective donor details to facilitate inquiries to match the criteria. Research laboratories can also avail this data to aid them.

3.3 Geographic Location Based Search

The Our system will provide an effective mechanism to provide a location based query search to the users since it is vital in the healthcare industry to provide information that will be accessible in reality. there exist various available geographic sources to derive web location, such as place name, postal code, phone number, hyperlink, and languages, etc. In our approach, different types of location are calculated according to different algorithms and geographic sources. Figure 1 shows the workflow of our novel location detection system by the three location types. We first utilize the extracted address segments to acquire the provider location. Then all extracted geographic references will be used to compute the content location. The serving location is estimated based on the content locations computed in the above step, plus the geographic information carried from inbound Hyperlinks and/or from user logs. Figure 1. The flowchart of location detection system by location type. Computing Provider Location Challenges of calculating the provider location of a web resource include: 1) accurately recognizing and extracting address strings from the web content, and then 2) correctly estimating whether extracted address strings are the provider location. Some simple rule such as address string templates, initializations, abbreviations and so on can facilitate this reorganization process. After an address string is recognized and extracted, we employ Support Vector Machine [13] to learn whether the string is a provider location in the binary classification setting. The following features were found be useful to our determination process: URL, title, anchor text, page content, referred frequency, hierarchical level, and even the spatial position of extracted address strings on the page. Computing Content and Serving Location Since it is common that multiple geographic references may coexist in a given web page, the key problem is to estimate the representative location. Here, we use the similar algorithm in [14,15] to calculate content location. The basic idea is to utilize various extracted geographic references to deduce the location focus. The algorithm of calculating serving location is similar to that of content location, the difference lies in the input data and iterative procedure of the algorithm of calculating serving location. First, serving location is initialized to obtained content location. Then, based on the serving location value of the previous iteration and the serving locations of other sites that have inbound hyperlinks to the site of interest, serving location can be further refined using the above content location algorithm.

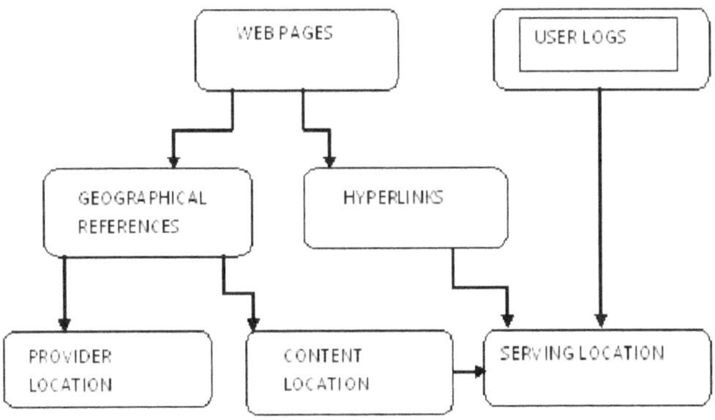

Fig. 1. Algorithm for location based search

4 Security

The biggest concerns about cloud computing are security and privacy. It refers to a broad set of policies, technologies, and controls deployed to protect data, applications, and the associated infrastructure of cloud computing. As cloud computing application adoption becomes pervasive throughout the enterprise, concerns around cloud data privacy, residency and security continue to grow.[4] Many organizations are uncomfortable with storing their data and applications on systems they do not control. Migrating workloads to shared infrastructure increases the potential for unauthorized exposure. To reassure the customers it should offer high degree of security. Privacy is another matter. If a client can log in from any location to access data and applications, it's possible that client's privacy could be compromised.[6]

In MedInfo cloud we have sensitive information about the organ donors, the availability of organs and the hospital information. The providers must ensure that all critical data are masked and only authorized users have access to data in its entirety. One way is to use authentication techniques such as user names and passwords. Another is to employ authorization format that is each user can access only the data and applications relevant to his or her job. To be protected ,data from one customer must be segregated from the other and must be stored securely when it is at rest and must be securely moved from one location to another. Cloud providers have systems to prevent data leaks. Cloud homogeneity makes security auditing simpler and enables automated security management [7].The massive cloud systems can be reduced to simple primitives and can be replicated thousands of times to prevent data loss.

The organ-cloud uses community cloud infrastructure shared by several organizations which can only access the donor details which is highly critical. [12]The donor details cannot be accessed by unauthorized users .Only the major hospitals performing organ transplantation can access the details to avoid illegal use of them. The Bloodline cloud adopts public cloud architecture which can be accessed not only by a particular community but various donors, blood banks, local hospitals and clinics can access them to check the availability of blood. The E-Pharm cloud is also public connecting all the pharmacies in the locality. Each cloud will have an identity management system. A backup for the data stored in these cloud will be created but the organization should check only if the authorized person can access the backup in case of emergency.

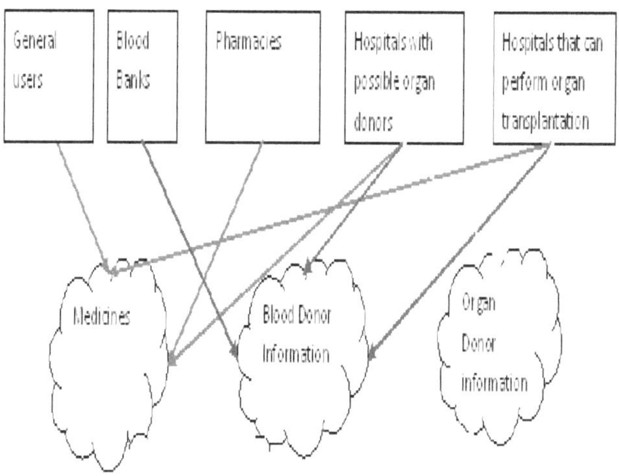

5 Conclusion and Future Work

MedInfo cloud is a viable project that can be implemented in real time. It will provide the users faster, secure, economical access to data. The project will also digitalize the healthcare industry and will definitely benefit it in a tremendous way.The project is currently on experimental stages in PS cloud labs, Chennai.

Acknowledgments. We wish to acknowledge Ms.T.Sheela, HOD, and other staffs of the department of information technology, Sri Sairam engineering college and other contributors for developing this paper on cloud computing.

References

1. http://www.salesforce.com/cloudcomputing
2. http://www.nist.gov/public_affairs/contact.htm
3. http://www.Cloudsecurity.org
4. http://www.Cloudslam10.com/sites/default/files/cloud_computing.pdf
5. http://www.En.wikipedia.org/wiki/cloud_computing#privacy
6. http://www.csrc.nist.gov/groups/SNS/cloud-computing/index.html
7. http://www.wipro.com/resource-center/library/pdf/ims/mit_cloudcomputing.pdf
8. http://www.en.wikipedia.org/wiki/Health_care_industry
9. http://www.frost.com/prod/servlet/market-insight-top.pag?docid=135578323
10. http://www.computerworld.com/s/article/9141024/Cloud_computing_Which_IT_projects_are_right_for_the_cloud_
11. http://www.wipro.com/cloudcomputing/
12. Hearst, M.A.: Trends and controversies: support vector machines. IEEE Intelligent Systems 13(4), 18–28 (1998)
13. Amitay, E., Har'EI, N., Sivan, R., Soffer, A.: Web-awhere: geotagging web content. In: 27th Annual International ACM SIGIR Conference, Sheffield, UK (July 2004)
14. Ding, J., Gravano, L., Shivakumar, N.: Computing geographic scopes of web resource. In: 26th International Conference on VLDB, Cairo, Egypt (September 2000)

A Service Oriented Modeling and Analysis for Building Intrusion Detection Systems

Rama Rao K.V.S.N.[1] and Manas Ranjan Patra[2]

[1] Bandari Srinivas Inst. of Technology, Hyderabad
[2] Berhampur University, Orissa
kvsnramarao@yahoo.co.in, mrpatra12@gmail.com

Abstract. Now-a-days all the major business activities of an enterprise are driven by complex networks. Despite the fact that diversified networking technologies are implemented, the networks have become leaky. Also hackers, displeased employees, unethical firms and terrorist organizations are influencing networks and trying to penetrate into the enterprise network to gather sensitive information. Hence networks are becoming more vulnerable and as a result attacks on networks are intensifying. Although firewalls and routers are deployed, they are self deficient. Intrusion detection systems monitor and inspect the packets traversing over a network ensuring deep packet analysis. But as the attacks are becoming more and more sophisticated, IDS available today are unable to address challenges that surround different types of attacks, since they are designed to handle specific types of attacks only. It is evident that no single technique can guarantee protection against future attacks. Hence there is a need for integrated architecture which can provide robust protection against a complete spectrum of threats. In this paper, we propose our architecture and service oriented modeling based on the service oriented paradigm for building intrusion detection systems.

Keywords: Attack, Intrusion Detection system, SOA, modeling, analysis, service identification.

1 Introduction

It is evident that, today every organization is executing all its major business activities using complex networks. Hence it has become essential for every organization to provide security to its network. So Network and its protection has itself become a business. Diversified technologies such as encryption techniques, distributed data storage systems etc are implemented to protect their networks. But still they are leaky as the business partners interact with network through various channels such as e-commerce, CRM and VPN. Also hackers with little expertise have influenced the leading networks to a greater extent. Added to this, displeased employees, unethical firms and terrorist organizations are trying to penetrate into the enterprise network and gather sensitive information.

Hence networks are becoming more vulnerable and as a result attacks on networks are intensifying. Although firewalls and routers are deployed they are deficient on their own. On the other hand, Intrusion detection systems monitor and inspect the

P.V. Krishna, M.R. Babu, and E. Ariwa (Eds.): ObCom 2011, Part I, CCIS 269, pp. 661–670, 2012.

packets traversing over a network ensuring deep packet analysis when compared to Firewall or router. There are wide varieties of IDS available today, but they are unable to address challenges that surround different types of attacks. Most of these IDS are designed to handle specific types of attacks. With the growing use of Internet, attackers have become active in identifying the flaws in operating systems, underlying network protocols, and different software implementations and are able to make sophisticated attacks on information resources. It is evident that no single technique can guarantee protection against future attacks. Thus, there is a need for a suitable development strategy to build systems to deal with the ever growing network intrusion threats. In this paper, we discuss an architectural model based on the service oriented approach to build intrusion detection systems.

2 Intrusion Detection Systems

An Intrusion Detection System (IDS)[1][2] is a software tool that is used to determine if a computer network has experienced an unauthorized intrusion. If any intrusion is detected, the IDS system will send out an alert or warning which would be further investigated. An IDS has three types of detection methodologies such as signature based detection [3], anomaly based detection [3][5] and Stateful protocol analysis[6][7].

2.1 Generic IDS Model

According to CIDF [8] model, IDS consists of three vital units such as Data Collection unit, Detection Unit and Response Unit. Many of the models are proposed using various techniques which are in line with generic model. {9][10][11][12] have proposed different approaches to IDS modeling.

But as discussed earlier, no single technique can guarantee comprehensive protection against complete spectrum of threats. IDS today are facing the following challenges.

2.2 Major Challenges in IDS [13]

Most of the IDS available today are focusing on only one type of detection i.e. on signature detection or anomaly detection or denial of service detection. Therefore, network security administrators tend to buy solutions from separate vendors and integrate them. Many IDS only detects threats, but there is a strong need to prevent the attacks also. Other IDS use innovative mechanisms of alerting new threats, but suffer from several wrong alerts or false positives. Moreover, current IDS products are designed to support one security policy, even though they monitor different administrative domains like finance, HR, marketing functions.

Concisely, one can state that many of the IDS implementations are not designed to co-operate. To overcome these challenges, there is a need for suitable development architecture to build Intrusion Detection systems that can deal with the ever growing network intrusion threats. Service oriented architecture is gaining importance now-a-days and is proving to be excellent architecture for complex systems. Hence the following factors motivated to apply SOA to IDS modeling.

2.3 Motivation of Applying Service Oriented Architecture to IDS

1) IDS is a software intensive system which should be of high quality and high capability. To deliver these characteristics, robust architectural support is needed. SOA is proved to be the best architecture which will assure these characteristics.
2) IDS may have concerns such as agility, complexity, concurrency, data integrity, distribution, evolvability, flexibility, functionality, performance, reliability. To address these concerns, SOA is the best choice.
3) One of the characteristic of architecture states that "*An architecture is present in every system.* " IDS is also a system which is composed of several components/services. Hence certainly it will have architecture. To meet the present days complicated security threats, SOA can be chosen as a promising architecture.
4) SOA can be used in enterprises as a competent architecture to cope with the flexibility of multi-site and multi-organization rules in the era of globalization to deal with multiple stake holders.Also SOA provides high scalability and interoperability

3 Service Oriented Architecture

A service is a function or some processing logic or business processing that is well-defined, self-contained, and does not depend on the context or state of other services. Examples of Services are Loan Processing Services, which can be self-contained unit for process the Loan Applications. In SOA paradigm [15], service providers register/publish their service in a public registry. This registry is used by consumers to find services that match certain criteria. If the registry has such a service, it provides the consumer with a contract and an endpoint address for that service. W3C defines SOA as [16] *"A set of components which can be invoked, and whose interface descriptions can be published and discovered"*. Hence a service-oriented architecture is an information technology approach or strategy in which applications make use of services available.

Our proposed architecture for IDS is presented in the next section for which service modeling will be carried out.

4 Proposed IDS Architecture

Our architecture is designed for multi-site IDS for a multi-business scenario, shown in Figure 1.

The functionality of the components in the architecture is explained below.

Pre Processor: The pre processor will perform two tasks.

(a) Packet flow identification [4] will identify the type of packet flow based on entropy. Flow can be text or binary or encrypted. Encrypted text flows will have highest entropy and plain text flows will have lowest entropy where as binary flows entropy will stand in between.

(b) Splitting the traffic flow into administrative domains i.e. HR, Marketing and Finance etc based on destination address.

Cache: The proposed solution contains a Cache component that collects network packets.

XML Format Conversion: Sampler and Packet Analyzer components together are considered as XML format conversion module.

Sampler: The Sampler randomly/heuristically picks up sample packet windows (series of contiguous packets) and sends them to the Network Packet Analyzer component. The sampling can be done in a random fashion or by using a heuristic.
Network Packet Analyzer: The Analyzer analyze the packets and convert them into a standard XML format by stripping the network and DLL headers. This metadata is sent for processing to the next component i.e. the "Rules Engine".

Business Rules Engine: The Rules engine application facilitates the XML packet to be checked for anomalies against suspicious activities and pre-defined business rules. The Rules engine should be SOA enabled to allow the organization to implement and customize the rules based on the location of the IDS on the network. For example in a large enterprise, HR may need a different set of rules implemented as against the finance and there may be some organizational rules applicable to all departments. The rules engine upon detecting anomaly will automatically forward to alert agent component or manual intervention component.

Alert Agent: If directed to alert agent component then the alerts are audited, logged, and mailed to concerned authorities.

Manual Intervention: This application may flag to either further analyze or release the associated packets to the verifier.

Verifier: The Verifier component checks the packets against attacks picked from a local signature database. This DB is pre-populated from external and publicly known signatures and other IDS instance detected signatures. These signatures are also batch mode synchronized between IDS instances through the Updater and Digester service component. Whenever the verifier component detects a known signature match, it immediately discards the packet and the payload. In case of innocuous packets it can inform the cache to release them. For packets that have matched a possible known attack, the packets and the payload can be sent into the heuristic and acute scanner. Since the signatures are hashed, comparing them in the verifier against new XMLs and network packet payloads becomes easy and quick to achieve the "fast Ethernet" speeds that this architecture claims.

Heuristic and Acute Scanner: This will perform further analysis to detect newer form of attacks or decisively declare a packet/source as safe. This can over a period of time detect new attacks and recover from false alarms. Thus if a payload was marked as possibly harmful, a fuzzy logic AI agent running in the heuristic scanner can verify the safety or the hostility of the payload to a pre-determined degree of threshold (say 25% to 80%) before declaring and publishing it to other instances through the Master

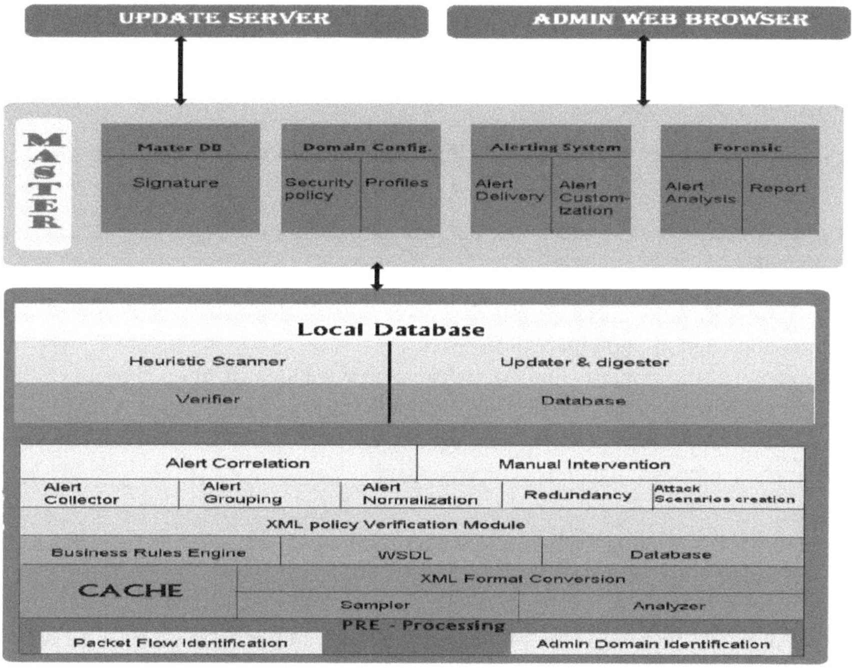

Fig. 1. Proposed IDS architecture

DB and also updating the local DB.

Updater and Digester: The updater listens for updates on a daily basis from the Master DB, which is connected on the cloud and sends web-service based publish notices to all instances. The updater then picks up these XMLs and their packet payloads and digests them using fast and compressive hashing algorithms that compact this information and store it in the local signature DB. The updater and digester component in conjunction with the Business Rules engine thus ensures that over a period of time the IDS learns to detect unknown attacks and thus can prevent them as well making it a true IDS.

Master Database: It is kept updated through SOA components about attacks detected or false alarms nullified at the distributed locations. The Master Database on the next day updates all IDS instances local databases.

Block and Persist: This component fires whenever the Manual intervention module marks a XML cum payload pair as suspicious or malicious or if the alerter escalates a known business rule violation. The component simply publishes the packet to be updated into the local DB via the Updater and Digester service and to the MasterDB which runs a similar Updater and Digester service.

For this architecture, service modeling can be performed as follows.

5 Service Modeling and Analysis for IDS

SOMA (Service oriented modeling and architecture) [17] is a modeling and design technique that provides regulatory steps for developing a service-based IT solution. SOMA is a 3 phase approach.

Service identification phase: uses various techniques to identify an exhaustive list of candidate services.

Service specification phase: which consist detailed design of services and components.

Realization phase: focuses on making architectural decisions, justifying the most practical approach to implement the services.

The scope of this paper is limited to discuss service identification phase.

Service Identification is the first step in modeling a service oriented solution. There exists several approaches [18][19] for service identification. We propose our service identification approach which is comprehensive.

5.1 Service Modeling and Analysis Methodology

Our methodology has two important phases

a) Preliminary Phase: In this phase, project goal and project scope are specified. This will assist in understanding client view and initial requirements. In addition to this, relevant stake holders should be identified and can be categorized into two types such as external partners and internal partners. Active involvement of these stake holders should be ensured and their requests should be considered. There must be effective communication between project team and stake holders. At this stage the business architecture should be understood well. Then the next phase commences.

b) Service Analysis Phase: This phase is further sub divided into three sub phases.

- **Service Modeling:** It comprises six steps.
  - **Value Chain Analysis:** Initially value chain analysis is done which is the best preferred approach to start with. This facilitates to understand critical functions of the enterprise capture functional domains and their interactions and identify high level service candidates.
  - **Overall workflow:** The overall workflow is depicted which assists in further in-depth understanding of overall system functionality.
  - **Business Use cases:** Now use cases are drawn to find out any left out critical functions and core services. When an actor utilizes the system, a use case is executed. The collection of all related use cases is the system functionality and we can extract core service from this functionality.
  - **Functional Processes:** Each Core function identified in the previous steps is collection of several functional processes. Further each functional process is further broken down into processes and sub processes.

- **Process workflow:** Each Functional process will have workflow. The workflow depicts chain of activities linked to one another in a chronological manner. Swim lane diagrams can be used to capture each role and its interaction with various activities.

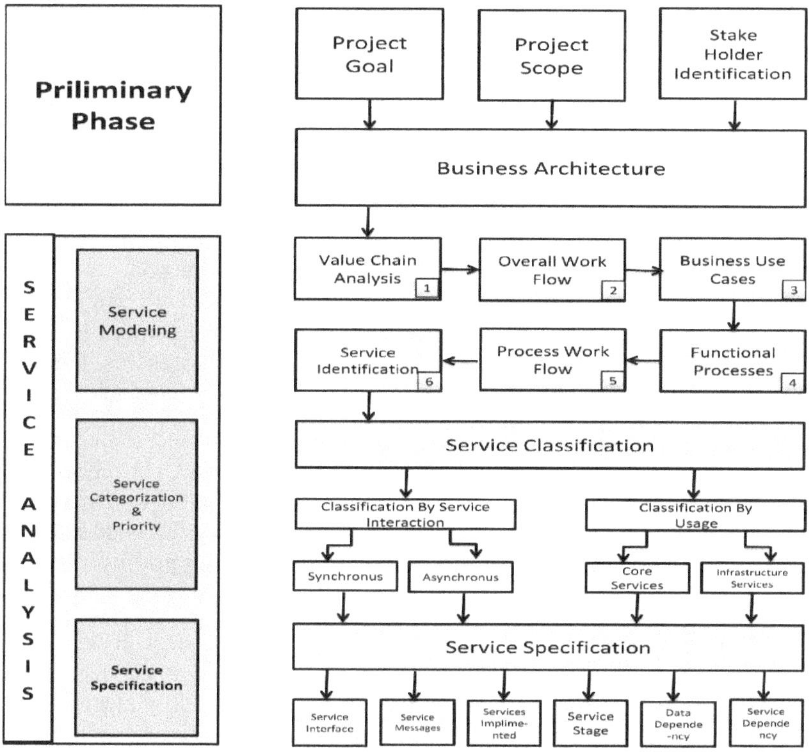

Fig. 2. Service Modeling and analysis methodology

- **Service Identification:** Lastly in the service identification step, we identify several services. If process has a collection of activities, it can be called as process service. All activities related to one swim lane can be combined and considered as candidate service. If the role is outside the organization it can referred as a partner service. If it is atomic unit of business logic, it can be considered as task service.

- **Service Categorization and priority:** After identifying the services, they are classified according to their interaction and usage.
  - **Classification by service interaction** : It is of two types.
    - **Synchronous services:** In this kind of services, consumer invokes a service, and gets actual response from the service. These services in general have less latency and involve no human interactions within the service. Infrastructural services such as data accesses and business queries are few examples of this kind. These services are more fine grained.

        - **Asynchronous services:** In this kind of services, consumer invokes a service but gets a reference code for his request instead of actual response. This reference code becomes a unique id for this service request and service returns the actual response with higher latency because these services generally involve human interactions and/or interactions with other systems and/or complex logic. Services defined at business processes level are of this kind. These services are coarse grained.
    - **Classification by usage:** It is of two types
        - **Core/Process centric services:** These are common business services that represent process logic and are used by multiple higher-level services. These are fine-grained services serving specific business function.
        - **Infrastructural services:** These are more of a support services and provide a common infrastructure for high level services. Services such as basic data access, logging, audit, data transformation, Gateways, Adapters, Facades etc., are few of a kind of this type.
    - **Priority of services:** All independent services get higher priority. Dependant services get lower priority than those services on which it is dependant. Prepare a service inventory list with summary of service details in the descending order of their priority
- **Service Specification:** The next step is service specification and its goal is to express the high level design idea behind the component. It will also help the business team to understand internal details such as key features, business rules implemented, constraints, and limitations. Key elements of Service in SOA are interface, contract, and implementation. As part of the high level design, these need to be captured to help the designers and build a team in the later phases. The service specification will contain interface details, dependencies and invocation methodology.

5.2 Application of above Methodology to IDS for Service Identification

After preliminary analysis, the first step is to perform value chain analysis for IDS.

From the value chain, we can capture the critical functions. The critical functions identified for IDS are Pre-Processing, Sampler &Analyzer, Detection, Alerting and Event Recording. These are referred as Process services or core services. Each of these Process service is associated with one or more functional processes which will be the candidate services. These functional processes are further broken down into sub processes and tasks. These will become the infrastructural or task services. The table 1 below shows service modeling and service categorization for IDS depicting core services, candidate services and task services

Table 1. IDS service modeling and service categorization

Process Service/Core Services	Functional Process/Candidate services	Task services/Infrastructural services
Pre-Processing	• Stream Collection • Flow verification • Domain verification	• Check flow • Maintain flow • Notification • Domain maintenance • …
Sampling & Analyzing	• Sampling • Analyzing	• Perform sampling • Maintain sampled data • Header conversion • Payload conversion • …
Detection	• Business Rules verification • Signature verification • Anomaly detection	• Check Business rule • Add rule • Update existing rule • Context sensitive detection • Use third party rules • Check signature • Stateful detection • Update rule • Specify signature • …
Alerting	• Alert collector • Alert grouping • Alert normalization • Redundancy elimination • Attack scenario construction	• Collect alerts • Maintain alerts • Group alerts on a condition • Apply normal form • Eliminate duplicates • Construct attack graph • Attack specification language • ..
Event Recording	• Heuristic scanner • Updater & Digester • Prevention	• Calculate threshold value • ….

6 Conclusion

Network is the business today. As these networks accessed by through various channels, they are becoming leaky and vulnerable. Though deep packet analysis is performed by IDS, they are unable to address all types of attacks. To provide comprehensive protection we have proposed our architecture. To the proposed architecture SOA paradigm is applied to perform modeling and analysis. Hence this paper has presented a comprehensive solution to model IDS with the proposed architecture and using SOA modeling.

References

[1] NSA Glossary of Terms in Security and Intrusion Detection (June 2003), http://www.sans.org/resources/glossary.php
[2] Amoroso, E.: Intrusion Detection - An Introduction to Internet Surveillance, Correlation, Trace Back, Traps, and Response. Intrusion.Net Books (1999) ISBN 0-9666700-7-8
[3] Bace, R.G.: Intrusion Detection. Macmillan Technical Publishing (2000) ISBN 1-57870-185-6
[4] Khakpour, A.R., Liu, A.X.: Iustitia: An Information Theoretical Approach to High-speed Flow Nature Identification
[5] Patcha, A., Park, J.-M.: An overview of anomaly detection techniques: Existing solutions and latest technological trends. Journal of Computer Networks 51(12) (August 2007)
[6] http://secret-epedemiology-statistic.org.ua/1587052091/ch01lev1sec2.html
[7] http://www.scribd.com//Intrusion-Detection-and-Prevention-Systems
[8] Lundin, E., Jonsson, E.: Survey of Intrusion Detection Research. Technical Report nr. 02-04, Department of Computer Engineering, Chalmers University of Technology, Göteborg, Sweden (2002)
[9] Kim, J., Bentley, P.: Artificial Immune Model for Network Intrusion Detection
[10] Denning, D.E.: An Intrusion-Detection Model
[11] Paek, S.-H., Oh, Y.-K., Yun, J., Lee, D.-H.: The Architecture of Host-based Intrusion Detection Model Generation System for the Frequency Per System Call. In: 2006 International Conference on Hybrid Information Technology, ICHIT 2006. IEEE (2006)
[12] Berqia, A., Nacsimento, G.: A Distributed Approach For Intrusion Detection Systems. IEEE (2004)
[13] Gong, F.: Next generation Intrusion detection systems. McAfee Network Protection solutions
[14] http://www.omg.org
[15] Web Services Architecture W3C Working Draft, http://www.w3.org/TR/2002/WD-ws-arch-20021114
[16] http://www.w3.org/TR/ws-arch/
[17] Arsanjani, A.: Chief Architect, SOA and Web services Center of Excellence, IBM, Software Group, Service-oriented modeling and architecture How to identify, specify, and realize services for your SOA
[18] Inaganti, S., Behara, G.K.: Service Identification: BPM and SOA Handshake
[19] Dwivedi, V., Kulkarni, N.: A Model Driven Service Identification Approach For Process Centric Systems. In: IEEE Congress on Services, Part II (2008)

Centralized Parallel Form of Pattern Matching Algorithm in Packet Inspection by Efficient Utilization of Secondary Memory in Network Processor

N. Kannaiya Raja[1], K. Arulanandam[2], and B. RajaRajeswari[1]

[1] CSE Dept., Arulmigu Meenakshi Amman College of Engg, Thiruvannamalai Dt, Near Kanchipuram,
Kanniya13@hotmail.co.in, rajeswari019@gmail.com
[2] CSE Department, Ganadipathy Tulsi's Jain Engineering College, Vellore

Abstract. The Network detection engine have capable of inspecting the packet and find out increasing number of network worms and virus . The high level of network providing packet inspection in detection system and the network equipments applies the predefined pattern to identify and manage the monitor packet over the network. Therefore consequently the emerging high level network equipments need to contribute pattern matching and packet inspection. However, searching for patterns at multiple offsets in entire content of network packet requires more processing power than most general purpose processor can provide. We present a novel architecture for programmable centralized parallel pattern matching algorithm for efficient packet inspection with network processor . We mapped our centralized multi parallel pattern matching algorithm [CNMPPMA] for filter packet in parallel. The simulation result reveals that CNMPPMA significantly improves the matching performance.

Keywords: Intrusion detection, Network Security, Pattern matching, Packet payload, Packet inspection.

1 Introduction

Now – a – days network services are tremendously increased by the fast emerging technologies. Many of the companies shares their information by providing the network service over the internet. Hence the Network Intrusion Detection System (NIDS) has introduced to control and analyses the packets. Network Intrusion Detection System (NIDS) that contains the detection engine that provide in-depth packet inspection. There are several algorithms are developed to design the detection engine. But most of the algorithm provide low – layer detection which inspect only packet header that contains only specified fields. High layer network equipment have able to inspect the packet payload that contains the entire up –to – date information of the packet . The number of patterns is typically a few thousands, and the lengths of the patterns are varied. The patterns may appear anywhere in any packet payload. Consequently, the emerging high-layer network equipment needs a pattern detection engine capable of

P.V. Krishna, M.R. Babu, and E. Ariwa (Eds.): ObCom 2011, Part I, CCIS 269, pp. 671–680, 2012.

in-depth packet inspection, which searches the entire packet headers and payloads for pattern matching. Network equipment then employs the detection results to manage network systems intelligently. For instance, Snort is an open- source network-based intrusion detection system(NIDS) and is adopted for detecting anomalous intruder behavior with a set of patterns and generating logs and alerts from predefined actions[1]. The pattern matching is considered as the most resource-intensive task in the Snort detection engine [2].

This study proposes a Centralized Multi Parallel Pattern matching algorithm (CNMPPMA) for fast packet inspection, which simultaneously searches the packet payload for a set of patterns for the multiple nodes. This study contributes modifications to the Hierarchical Matching Algorithm (HMA) [9] and introduces the idea of a sampling window and a Safety Shift Strategy in addition. CNMPPMA is a multi-tier and cluster-wise matching algorithm and can perform fast skippable payload scan. Based on the occurrence frequency of grams, this study discovers a small set of signatures from the patterns themselves to narrow the searching domain. Consequently, the proposed CNMPPMA is a very cost-effective and efficient mechanism for real-life network detection systems. The rest of this paper is organized as follows: Section 2 presents previously proposed pattern matching algorithms and the fundamental definitions. Section 3 then describes the proposed CNMPPMA in detail. Next, Section 4 draws up the Conclusion.

2 Related Work

2.1 Previous Work

Multipattern matching is one of the well-studied classical problems in computer science. The most notable algorithm Aho-Corasick and Commentz - Walter algorithms which can be considered as the extension of well-known KMP and Boyer-Moore single pattern matching algorithms, respectively[3],[13]. Both these algorithms are suitable only for software implementation and suffer from throughput limitations. The hardware-based techniques make use of commodity search technologies such as ternary content addressable memory (TCAM) or reconfigurable logic/FPGAs. Some of the FPGA-based techniques make use of the on-chip logic resources to compile patterns into parallel state-machines or combinatorial logic. Therefore, scalability with pattern set size is the primary concern with purely FPGA-based approaches.

A Simple Multi pattern matching algorithm

In a multipattern matching, we are given a set of strings $S = \{ s_1, s_2, s_3, \ldots, s_n \}$and streaming data T (which is alternatively called text). We would like to find out all the occurrences of any of the strings in S in T. We preprocess the string in S and build a machine. We feed the streaming data to this machine then reports matching strings whenever one is found. Basically, string matching can be abstracted as a longest prefix matching (LPM) problem.The same hash table lookup (HTP) procedure can be repeated for each prefix in this window. Thus, by looking up all the prefixes of a window and forwarding this window by a byte in each iteration, we ensure that we scan the entire input to look for the predefined strings with fixed lengths.

3 The Centralized Muti Parallel Pattern Matching Algortithm (CNMPPMA)

In the Centralized Multi Parallel Pattern Matching Algorithm(CNMPPMA) is a centralized system based on a multi-tier and cluster-wise architecture as shown in Fig.1. In the Fig.1. ,the Centralized Network Intrusion Detection System(CNIDS) is constructed to monitor the packets that arrives from 'n' number of nodes. The Internet traffic is made of streams of fragmented packets consisting header and payload. One such attack uses overlapping fragmented IP packets. Such attacks can be eliminated by normalizing the packets. Packet normalization produces consistently clean network traffic without abnormalities . Fig.1 shows an effective deep packet inspection steps which begins with packet normalization followed by static and dynamic inspections. Static inspection step classifies the incoming packets using the header information, while dynamic inspection searches through the payload of the packet to find the patterns defined in the attack signature database.

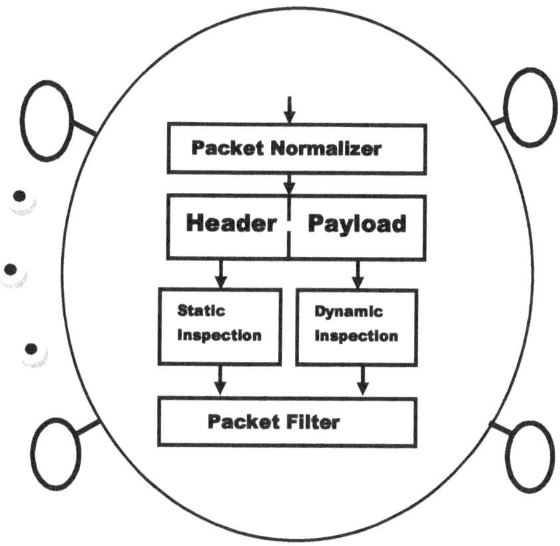

Fig. 1. Block Diagram of CNMPPMA

CNMPPMA comprises two small index tables, namely the first table (H^1) and the second table (H^2).These two tables act as filters to avoid unnecessary external memory accesses and pattern comparisons and, thereby, pass the innocuous packets quickly in the online matching process. The second-table procedure activates only after the first-table procedure gets a match. Using H_2 , which indicates a small subset of patterns that are similar to the input packet, CNMPPMA compares only a few selected patterns of P with the suspected substrings of the packet, rather than comparing all patterns with all substrings of the packet. However, frequently accessing the external memory (to read patterns or tables) significantly decreases the matching efficiency due to the external memory access latency being very long and indeterminable.

3.1 CGS Algorithm

The Common Gram Searching (CGS) algorithm is presented in Fig.3.A bitmap vector V and a matrix R are temporary memories, Vector V records the occurrence of each B_1-gram in a pattern; R is used for recording frequency, where i ≠j, indicates the number of concurrent occurrences of two grams g_i and g_j in P;and r_{ii} records the frequency of the B_1-gram are defined in Fig.2, g_i occurring in distinct patterns. In the CGS algorithm, each pattern is first transferred into a set of grams, and the occurrence of each B_1-gram is recorded in the bitmap V, where B_1 is predefined and depends on the available on-chip memory space. Matrix R is then derived from V (as shown in line 4 of Fig. 3). Second, the largest occurrence frequency is found, and its corresponding gram g_f is selected as one of F. The elements of R relating to g_f are subtracted accordingly to renew R. CGS is repeated until all elements on the diagonal of R become zero. Fig. 4 plots the pattern spectrum of the Snort patterns with different gram sizes. The pattern spectrum indicates the occurrence frequency of grams of patterns.

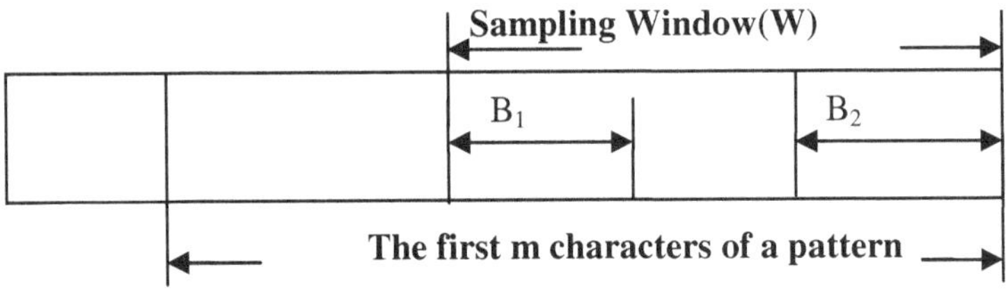

Fig. 2. Sampling Window

CGS Algorithm

Input: Given a set of patterns P, the parameters : W,B_2,$B_1$and m.

Output: A set of frequent – common grams F.

1 Initialize : F, R ,V = 0;

2 **For** each pattern p_i of P, $0 \le i \le p$ /* build a matrix R */

3 Transfer the first W- B_2 bytes of the sampling window of the pattern p_i into B_1-grams and set the element of a vector V .

4 Read V. For each $v_j = 1$, set the elements of matrix R: $r_{jk} = r_j + v_k$.

5 **while** (r_{ii} != 0) **do**

6 Find a frequent – common gram g_k , where $r_{ff} = \max \{ r_{ii} \}$;

7 Add this gram into **F: F= F + { g.f }** ;

8 **For** $0 \le i \le p$ **do** /* refresh the diagonal of R */

9 $r_{ii} = r_{ii} - r_{ji}$ if $r_{ii} > r_{ji}$ otherwise $r_{ii} = 0$;

10 **Return ;**

Fig. 3. The CGS Algorithm

Fig. 4a shows the distribution of 2-grams of patterns, and Fig. 4b is the distribution of 1-gram of patterns. As shown in the figures, they are not normally distributed and have several peaks, which mean that some grams obviously occur more frequent than others.

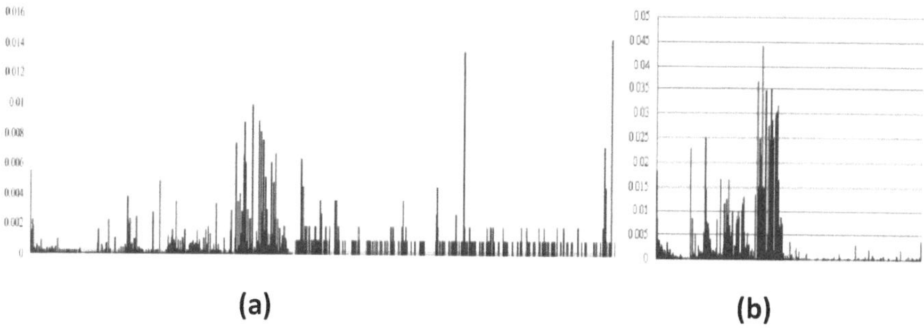

Fig. 4. The pattern spectrum when |P|= 1,200. (a) Spectrum of 2-grams. (b) Spectrum of 1-gram.

3.2 Cluster Balancing Strategy (CBS)

Most packets are innocent in general situations. Even a harmful packet may contain only few patterns. Therefore, comparing all of the patterns in the large P with each input packet is time consuming. If the patterns in P can be distributed into different small clusters based on their similarity, then only the pattern in each cluster that is most similar to the suspected packet needs to be compared, thus improving the efficiency of the matching process. First, the method of clustering a set P based on the similarity of patterns is described. Then, a CBS is adopted to balance the cluster size. A second-tier table (H_2) for online matching can be constructed based on the clusters.Two common grams are employed as a pair of clustering pivots, called a pivot pair, say (a,b) where the first pivot is a frequent-common gram, and the second pivot is the substring following the frequent-common gram.To lower the worst matching time, CBS is adopted to balance the size of all clusters. The CBS is given as follows :

1. First, read one pattern at a time from P and scan the pattern.
2. According to CGS, for any given, there exists a B_1- gram $g \in F$ where B_1 is the length of a frequent common gram.To balance the cluster size, CBS finds the smallest $n_{a,b}$, given by $n_{x,y}$, among all available pivot pairs (a,b)'s of p_i for all $a \in F$ and 'a,b' $\subset p_i$.
3. After grouping p_i into the smallest cluster $p_{x,y}$, the corresponding $n_{x,y}$, is also incremented.

3.3 Safety Shift Strategy

This section presents a safety shift strategy to derive the values of the shift fields of H^1 and H^2. H^1 and H^2 can use the same strategy to derive their safety shifts, respectively. The proposed strategy helps CNMPPMA to speed up the online matching process, since certain characters can be skipped unhesitatingly. The basic concept of the safety shift strategy is that: if x is not a gram of any pattern, and any suffix of x is not any prefix of any pattern in P, then it is safe to shift m when x is scanned; otherwise, the number of safety shifts is the offset between the rightmost occurrence position of x and the position of the frequent common gram nearest to x. Two parameters are needed to derive the safety shifts, namely W and m, as shown in Fig. 2. Assume that $B \leq W \leq m$, and define the safety shifts in which the values associated with the table that carries the address for the gram. The safety shifts are related with the link pointer for the frequent gram obtained from CGS are given as input to the table of multi-tier of various hierarchy table of each entry , (H (x). shift) as follows:

1. *Initially , all shift fields of the table H are set as*
   If m>W, then H(x).shift=m-W+q,
   Else H(x).shift= r;
2. *Scanning every pattern p, for each* i^{th} *B- gram of each pattern* $p^B[i]$*,*
   where $1 \leq i \leq m\text{-}W$*,set* $x[i] \leftarrow p^B$ *if the entry H(x) exists:*
   If the current H(x).shift $>m - W - i + 1$*, then, update, as*
   $H(x).shift = m - W - i + 1;$
3. *For each ith B-gram of each* $p^B[i]$*, where m-W<i/, B+ 1, set* $x \leftarrow p^B[i]$
   if the entry H(x) exists:
   If $x \in F$, then
   H(x).shift=0;
   Else If the current H(x).shift > r, then update the entry:
   H(x).shift=r;

3.4 Table Construction

The result of CGS, F, is used to construct the small table H^1,which is stored in the on-chip memory. A direct index table of entries is used for H^1 to achieve fast lookup. Fig.5 shows an example of CNMPPMA, which has five patterns: "actress," "teacher," "firefighter," "farmer," and "architect," where the alphabet set comprises the 26 English letters. Fig. 5a demonstrates the CGS. According to the CGS (lines 2-4 of Fig. 3), after scanning the first W - B_2 characters of the sampling window of every pattern (the underlined characters of the patterns in Fig. 5a), the matrix R is obtained and shown in the figure. In the first run, the maximum value on the diagonal of R is three, and thus the corresponding gram "e" is added into F. After refreshing the elements on the diagonal of R (lines 8 and 9 of Fig. 3), CGS finds that the maximum value on the diagonal of R is two in the second run, and the corresponding gram is "h".CGS stops while all elements on the diagonal of R are zero, and gets F ={'e','h'}. Fig. 5b displays the logical architecture of the tables of CNMPPMA . Initially, since $B_1 = 1$,

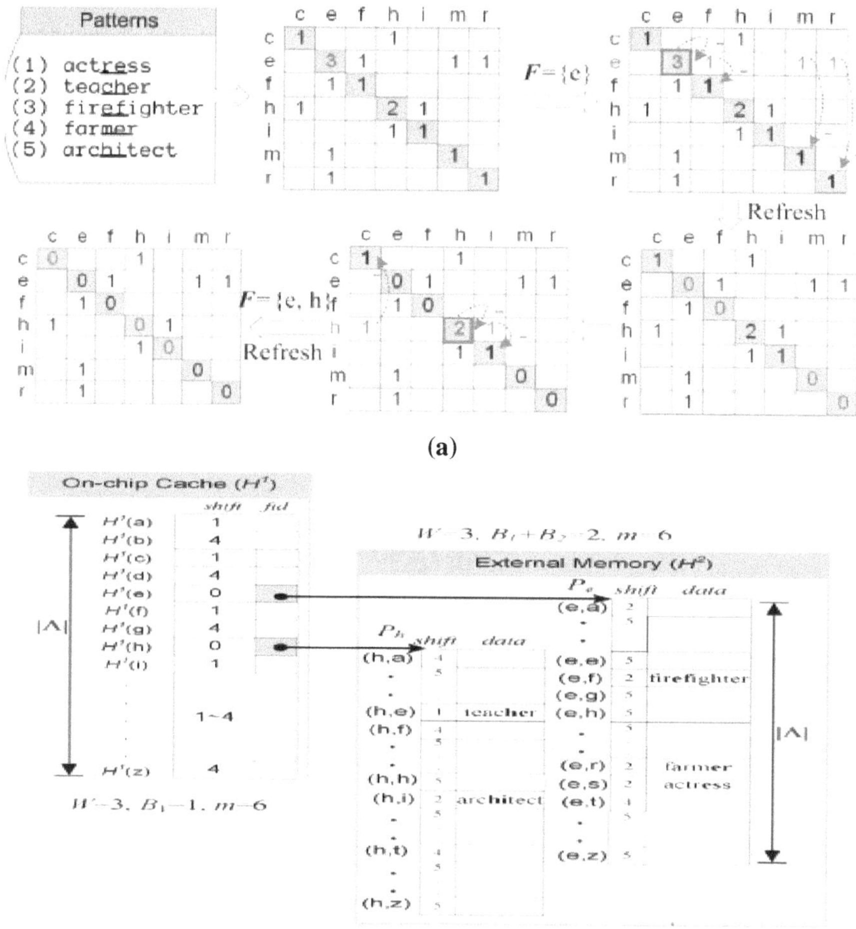

(a)

(b)

Fig. 5. An Example of CNMPPMA, where B1=1,B2=1,m=6,W=3, and F={e,h}. (a)An example of GFGS.(b)The architecture of the hierarchical hash tables.

H^1.shift = 4.When scanning the pattern “actress,” the shift fields of H^1(‘a’), H^1(‘c’), and H^1(‘t’) are updated to 3, 2, and 1, respectively (the second safety shift strategy); the shift fields of H^1(‘r’) and H^1(‘s’) are both updated to 1, while the H^1(‘e’).shift is updated to 0, because ‘e’$\in$ F (the third strategy).

3.5 The Online Multi-tier and Cluster-Wise Matching

The previous sections presented the offline stage of CNMPPMA, which builds two index tables H^1 and H^2, holding the indexing and pattern information in the cache memory and external memory, respectively. These two tables are regarded as the two-tier filters and indices for the online matching. The detection engine then returns the search results of matched patterns P^M. As a hierarchical matching, the online matching procedure of CNMPPMA is divided into two tiers: Tier-1 Matching and Tier-2 Matching. The hierarchical architecture is applied to decrease the number of external memory accesses. Based on the Safety Shift Strategy, CNMPPMA never skips any frequent common gram. Consequently, no patterns in the payload T are missed. An example is provided to demonstrate the online matching of CNMPPMA. Assume that the H^1 and H^2 tables have been built as Fig.5, where W = 3 and M =6. Assume that the input T is "kangaroo" as given in Fig 6. The scan runs from left to right. Because the pointer goes beyond [T]-B_1 after the shift, CNMPPMA completes scanning the input T. This example only requires one on-cache table lookup.

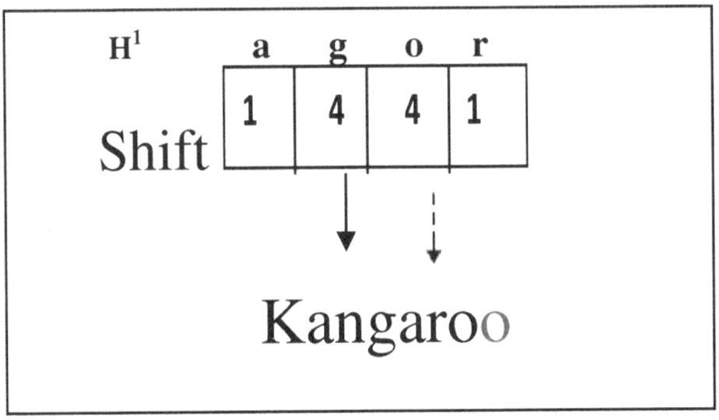

Fig. 6. An example of matching process with input "kangaroo"

By only checking T with the embedded table H^1, CNMPPMA can know that T contains no pattern. Considering another example where T = 'iamanactress' as shown in Fig. 7, the first scanned B_1-gram is "a". Thus, the matching process stays in the Multi - Tier Matching, and the next B_1-gram "n" is read after shifting one character. Similarly, staying in the Multi - Tier Matching, and the next B1-gram "n" is read after shifting one character. Similarly, staying in the Multi - Tier Matching, in order after

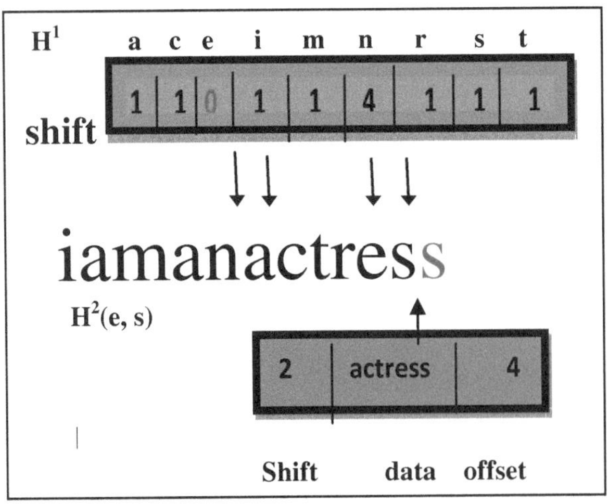

Fig. 7. An example of matching process with input "iamanactress"

shifting. Since the pointer goes beyond |T| - B_l after shifting two characters, the matching process for the input T is finished. In this case, H^1 is checked four times, and H^2 is fetched only once for the string T of 12 characters. CNMPPMA thus significantly reduces the latency caused by memory accesses.

4 Conclusion

The most important component of in-depth packet inspection is an efficient multipattern matching algorithm. This study proposes a CNMPPMA for packet inspection. CNMPPMA applies the common grams obtained by the proposed CGS to narrow the searching scope and to quickly filter out the innocent packets. The hierarchical matching significantly reduces the average number of external memory accesses to only 6 percent to 19 percent, thus improving the matching performance. Particularly, CNMPPMA is very simple and can be easily implemented in both software-based and hardware-based platforms. This study also discusses and evaluates current multipattern matching algorithms for NIDSs. CNMPPMA also works well for the systems with larger minimum pattern size, such as virus detection systems. In conclusion, CNMPPMA facilitates the creation of efficient and cost-effective pattern detection engines for packet inspection.

References

[1] Snort (2008), http://www.snort.org
[2] Antonatos, S., Anagnostakis, K.G., Markatos, E.P.: Generating Realistic Workloads for Network Intrusion Detection Systems. In: Proc. Fourth Int'l ACM Workshop Software and Performance, WOSP (2004)
[3] Horspool, R.N.: Practical Fast Searching in Strings. Software Practice and Experience 10(6), 501–506 (1980)
[4] Aho, A.V., Corasick, M.J.: Efficient String Matching: An Aid to Bibliographic Search. Comm. ACM 18(6), 330–340 (1975)
[5] Fisk, M., Varghese, G.: Fast Content-Based Packet Handling for Intrusion Detection, UCSD Technical Report CS2001-0670 (May 2001)
[6] Erdogan, O., Cao, P.: Hash-AV: Fast Virus Signature Scanning by Cache-Resident Filters. In: Proc. IEEE Global Telecomm. Conf. (GLOBECOM 2005) (November 2005)
[7] Lakshmanamurthy, S., Liu, K.-Y., Pun, Y., Huston, L., Naik, U.: Network Processor Performance Analysis Methodology. Intel. Technology J. 6 (August 2002)
[8] Tuck, N., Sherwood, T., Calder, B., Varghese, G.: Deterministic Memory-Efficient String Matching Algorithms for Intrusion Detection. In: Proc. IEEE INFOCOM (March 2004)
[9] Sheu, T.-F., Huang, N.-F., Lee, H.-P.: A Novel Hierarchical Matching Algorithm for Intrusion Detection Systems. In: Proc. IEEE Global Telecomm. Conf, GLOBECOM 2005 (November 2005)
[10] Wu, S., Manber, U.: A Fast Algorithm for Multi-Pattern Searching, Technical Report TR94-17, Dept. Computer Science, Univ. of Arizona (May 1994)
[11] Markatos, E., Antonatos, S., Polychronakis, M., Anagnostakis, K.: Exclusion-Based Signature Matching for Intrusion Detection. In: Proc. IASTED Int'l Conf. Comm. and Computer Networks, CCN 2002 (October 2002)

[12] Liu, R.-T., Huang, N.-F., Chen, C.-H., Kao, C.-N.: A Fast String Matching Algorithm for Network Processor-Based Intrusion Detection System. ACM Trans. Embedded Computing Systems 3(3) (August 2004)
[13] Boyer, R.S., Moor, J.S.: A Fast String Searching Algorithm. Comm. ACM 20(10), 762–772 (1977)
[14] Sheu, T.-F., Huang, N.-F., Lee, H.-P.: A Time- and Memory-Efficient String Matching Algorithm for Intrusion Detection Systems. In: Proc. IEEE Global Telecomm. Conf. (GLOBECOM 2006) (November 2006)
[15] Coit, C.J., Staniford, S., McAlerney, J.: Towards Faster StringMatching for Intrusion Detection or Exceeding the Speed of Snort. In: Proc. Second DARPA Information Survivability Conf. and Exposition (DISCEX) (2001)
[16] Antonatos, S., Polychronakis, M., Akritidis, P., Anagnostakis, K.G., Markatos, E.P.: Piranha: Fast and Memory-Efficient Pattern Matching for Intrusion Detection. In: Proc. 20th IFIP Int'l Information Security Conf. (SEC 2005 (May 2005)
[17] Li, S., Torresen, J., Soraasen, O.: Exploiting Reconfigurable Hardware for Network Security. In: Proc. 11th Ann. IEEE Symp. Field-Programmable Custom Computing Machines (FCCM) (2003)
[18] Kim, S., Kim, Y.: A Fast Multiple String-Pattern Matching Algorithm. In: Proc. 17th AoM/IAoM Int'l Conf. Computer Science (August 1999)

Effective Use of Interbank Network Services by Using Transaction Counter in ATMs

Rajesh Vemulakonda[1] and Raja Yasodhar Kapalavayi[2]

[1] Mother Teresa Institute of Science and Technology, Sathupalli, Khammam District, A.P, India
raj.vvv2v2@gmail.com
[2] SRK Institute of Technology, Vijayawada, Krishna District, A.P, India
yasodhar.raja1@gmail.com

Abstract. To make banking more comfortable, Banks make the Interbank Networks, by that the usage of ATMs of the non native users also increases. Interbank Network provides so many services, in them the effective one is usage of non native ATM service up to certain times without paying the surcharge, which is better service and not fulfilling due to missing of some elementary representation. This paper informs the problem along with the solution, which is in the form of Transaction counter.

Keywords: Interbank Network, ATM, Transaction, Transaction Counter, Surcharge.

1 Introduction

An interbank network [1] is a computer network that connects the ATMs[2] of different banks and permits these ATMs to interact with the ATM cards of non-native banks. Interbank network is also known as an ATM consortium or ATM network. While interbank networks provide capabilities for all ATM cards within the same network to use other banks' ATMs that belong to the same network, the services vary. Interbank networks are convenient because people can access the ATMs of other banks who are members of the network when their own bank's ATM is unavailable. Such is especially convenient for travelers traveling abroad. Credit cards and debit cards are used to withdraw cash from Automated Teller Machines (ATMs). In order for a card transaction to be approved, the ATM, retailer, must submit the request, and the bank that issued the card must authorize the cash withdrawal. Furthermore, this approval must be provided in real-time since the customer is waiting for it. The information concerning the request must be rapidly gathered from the servicing network to which the devices are connected, sent to the issuing bank for authorization/approval, and the response rapidly returned in order for the system to complete the transaction. A card transaction is captured by such devices as an ATM. The information concerning the request must be rapidly gathered from the servicing network to which the devices are connected, sent to the issuing bank for

P.V. Krishna, M.R. Babu, and E. Ariwa (Eds.): ObCom 2011, Part I, CCIS 269, pp. 681–686, 2012.

authorization/approval, and the response rapidly returned in order for the system to complete the transaction. A major provider offers interbank transaction-switching services for just this purpose. It uses a redundant network of powerful, Non Stop computers to implement an authorization and message switch that gathers the customer transactions from the servicing network, routes them to the appropriate issuing banks for authorization, and then returns the authorization or rejection responses back to the servicing network for delivery to the origination point. Thousands of banks connect hundreds of thousands of ATM devices to the provider's network to service their transaction services. When a user makes a transaction with a card, that card is read via the ATM's device, and the amount is entered. The withdrawal details are transmitted to the provider's switch, which forwards this information to the bank that issued the credit or debit card. The bank authorizes or rejects the transaction and returns a response through the provider's ATM. The transaction can be rejected for many reasons, such as exceeding a daily limit, exceeding the account's balance limit, an expired card, or a card with a credit hold.

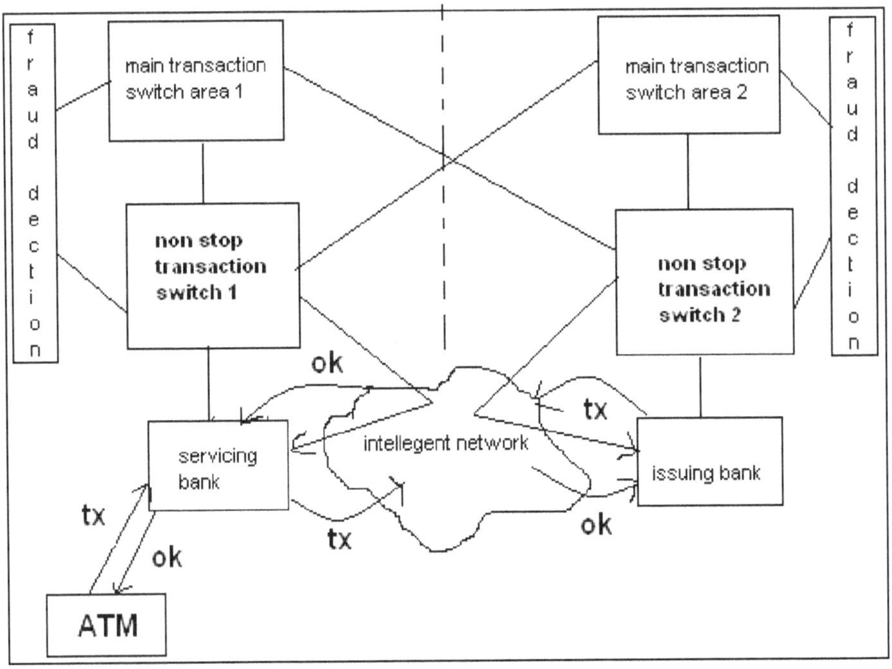

Fig. 1. Usage of non native bank ATM services by using Interbank Networking

The provider's switch also routes ATM transactions for many tens of thousands of ATM devices for authorization. ATMs are controlled by a servicing bank. If a servicing bank receives an ATM request involving a card that the bank did not issue, the request details are sent to the provider's switch, which handles the request in the same way that it handles POS transactions. The data is sent to the issuing bank, and the authorize/reject response is returned via the servicing bank to the ATM. The transaction will be maintained on the native bank's database.

1.1 Transactions

In some cases, it is the Contact Volume Editor that checks all the pdfs. In such cases, the authors are not involved in the checking phase. A transaction usually means a sequence of information exchange and related work that is treated as a unit for the purposes of satisfying a request and for ensuring database integrity.ATM machines are connected to interbank networks, which are computer networks connecting different banks around the world. The interbank networks allow banks to electronically share account information about customers. This enables customers to use ATMs from different banks to access funds in their accounts. The largest interbank networks operate as well. Before a transaction can be processed, the ATM machines must receive authorization from the customer's native bank, such as confirmation that the customer has sufficient funds in his account to permit cash withdrawal. Interbank networks allow this authorization process to take place in seconds. After completion of each transaction, they are stored in respective bank's database.

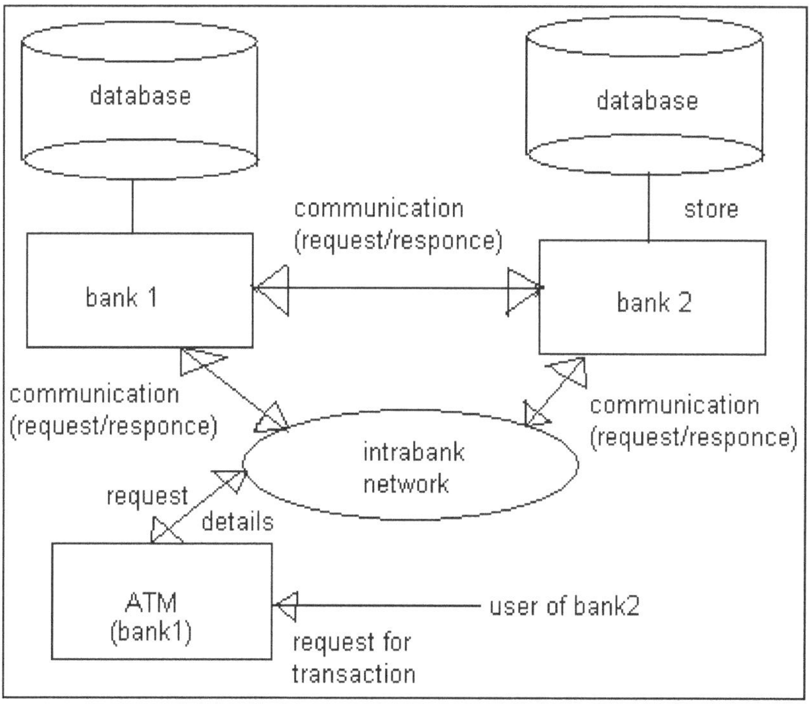

Fig. 1.1. Transaction storing in non native bank environment

1.2 Problem for the User

When an user entered to make transactions the ATM of any bank, whether native or non native bank, providing the transaction services directly, without informing the number of transactions he/she made previously. By that the user got confuses and may lose his/her surcharge amount from the .so there is a deficiency in the interbank network by which the intension of providing services to user is failing. The main intension that makes banks together is to provide maximum free and flexible services to the users of the community. We have availability of huge amount of ATM machines nearby, If the information about the transaction from that particular bank is not available, Having other ATMs available , The user may lose the surcharge amount by exceeding the limited number of transactions provided by that particular bank.**1.3 Copyright Forms**

The copyright form may be downloaded from the For Authors section of the LNCS Webpage: www.springer.com/lncs. Please send your signed copyright form to the Contact Volume Editor, either as a scanned pdf or by fax or by courier. One author may sign on behalf of all of the other authors of a particular paper. Digital signatures are acceptable.

2 Transaction Counter

The solution for that is making a screen that is available to the user when he/she accessing the ATM and which should be kept it as the first one, which is visible to the user when he/she make authentified. After completion of every transaction successful the count for that transaction is maintained at the native banks ATM , even though the transaction is done from non native bank ATM. The interbank network acts as a intermediate thing and distributes the money from one bank to other bank. Gives the result to the native bank, in the database of native bank the results are maintained. When the transaction details are needed to others, it brought from the belonging banks database. So in the transaction counter mechanism, It requires to gather the results from the native bank, When the user using the non native bank's ATM . The result i.e.) number of transactions are showed to the user and if he/she has availability of transactions from the limited transactions provide, Then they make the transactions from the same bank otherwise, to not to lose the surcharge they make the transactions at the nearby ATM, If available. In this process the user enters into ATM and enters the authentication details, Which are checked by the current bank by consulting native bank through the interbank network, If everything is o.k. then the non current banks allows him/her to make transactions and at the end it gives results to native bank through interbank network, For transaction counter, interbank network takes the information regarding transactions from the native bank database, Which contains the account of the user. So this process involves the presenting of information clearly to the user, Even though the limited transactions vary from one bank to other bank, Transaction counter also keep track of this and shows those details also. Taking the transaction details will be done by the interbank network, because information now a day's information is passed in the form of electronic data there may not be any delay.

To provide this information may be useful to the user and he/she also can use the interbank network services effectively. It will become the very handful tool to the customers who want to use the interbank network effectively it makes them to feel to use bank services freely without any other thought and creates an user friendly environment which provides enjoyable facilities to the user. The main intension to create transaction counter is, it's the best service created by interbank network that all banks combining their ATM services to robust service but this is failing due to unindicted service conditions. So many people got confused and they are not using this service purely, I also one of them got confused that how many times I used particular bank's ATM service so avoid this types of problem I thought the design and transaction counter produced by this.

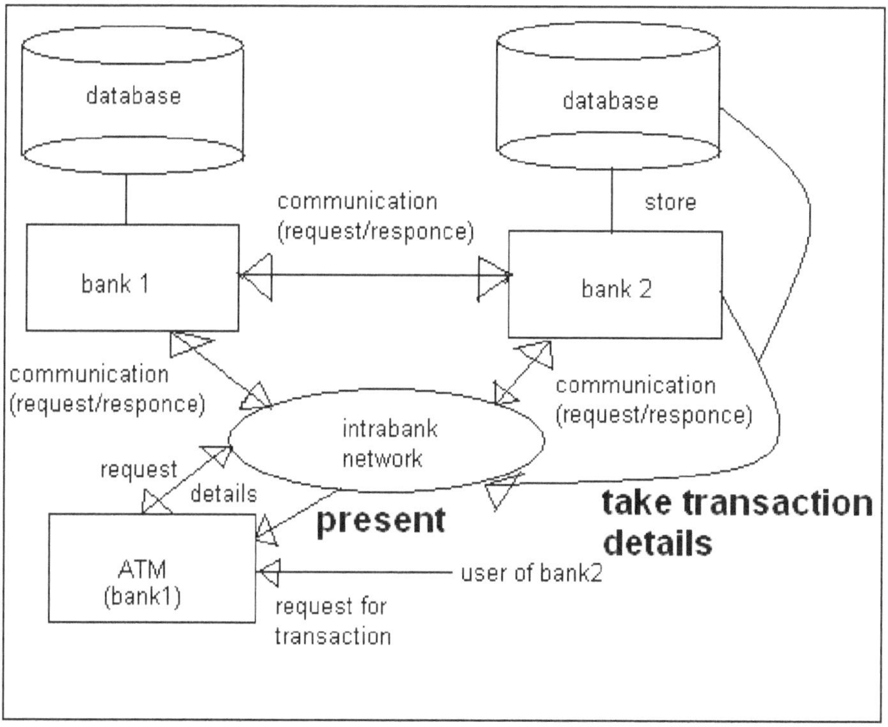

Fig. 2. Taking the transaction details and representing them as transaction counter

2.1 Fields

There are some information fields available in transaction counter regarding the number of the current transaction, Total number of transactions provided by the current bank which he/she is using and the remaining number of transactions, Which are provided by that particular bank. Every time he/she using that bank's ATM the transaction counters increments the values and shows the number of that transaction. It is also provided that if the limited transactions are exceeded then it gives the choice whether to continue or to quit the services, If user want to quit the transaction will not be counted.

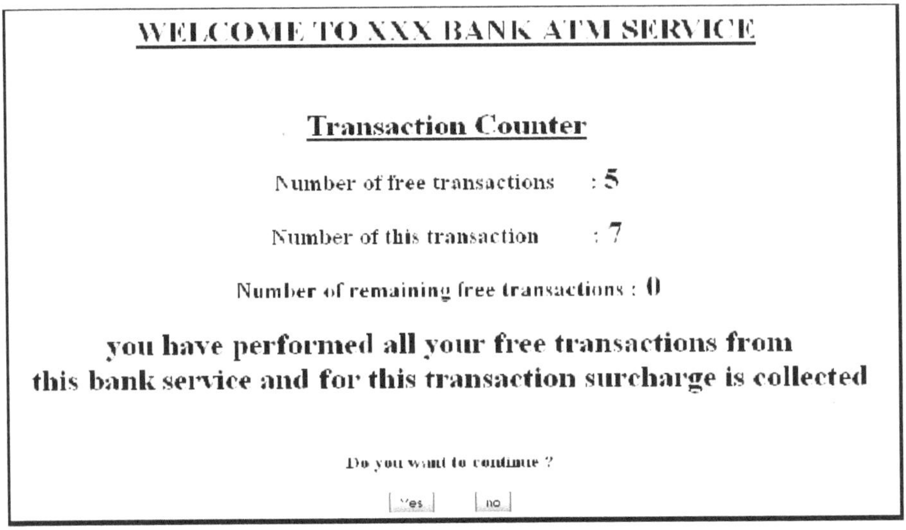

Fig. 2.1. Transaction counter showing all the information

References

1. Soramäkia, K., Bechb, M.L., Arnoldb, J., Glassc, R.J., Beyelerc, W.E.: The topology of interbank payment flows
2. Kaya, N., ErkÍp, F.: Invasion of Personal Space Under the Condition of Short-Term Crowding: A Case Study on an Automatic Teller Machine

Performance Analysis of Case Based Word Sense Disambiguation with Minimal Features Using Neural Network

P. Tamilselvi[1] and S.K. Srivatsa[2]

[1] Sathyabama University, Chennai, India
nagas_67@hotmail.com
[2] St. Joseph College of Engineering, Chennai, India
profsks@rediffmail.com

Abstract. In this paper, the performance of case based word sense disambiguation attained by two different set of knowledge features, such as bigram and trigram are analyzed for identifying the best for word sense disambiguation. To uncover the ambiguous of a word, so many knowledge features like part of features (PoS), collocation, bag of words, noun-verb relation etc. Here, ambiguity of a word is removed with only two and three elements referred as bigram and trigram. Two different representations of bigram, pre-bigram and post-bigram and three different forms of trigram, pre-trigram, in-trigram and post-trigram are considered for disambiguation. Relevant knowledge features are represented as vector form using their respective PoS, and also their cases are represented as vector form. For bigram, the vector size is 1×2 and for trigram 1×3. Feed forward back propagation network with single layer defined with 8 hidden neurons for bigram and 20 hidden neurons for trigram are designed based on their performance. Actually, ten different distance-measuring functions are used for selecting the minimal distance cases from case bases. Finally, the performance of different distance metric functions with bigram and trigram are compared and analyzed.

Keywords: Word Sense disambiguation, bigram, trigram, neural network, case based reasoning, distance measuring functions.

1 Introduction

In this paper, we deal with the problem of word sense disambiguation (WSD), assigning an appropriate sense to an ambiguous word in a given context. Many methods have been proposed to deal with this problem, including supervised learning algorithms (Leacock et al., 1998, Hwee Tou Ng et al., 2007), semi-supervised learning algorithms (Yarowsky, 1995, Zheng-Yu Niu et al., 2005), and unsupervised learning algorithms (Sch¨utze, 1998). Past research has shown that supervised learning is one of the most successful approaches for WSD. In supervised learning approach, large text corpuses with ambiguous word tied with its correct sense are used to serve as a case (training) data.

P.V. Krishna, M.R. Babu, and E. Ariwa (Eds.): ObCom 2011, Part I, CCIS 269, pp. 687–696, 2012.

We did a comparative study on open lexical databases WordNet, Semcor and Sensval 2 (P.Tamilselvi et al., 2010(C)). From the study, it was inferred that Semcor is an enriched data set, tagged with WordNet annotation. Semcor has collection of documents represented in XML form. For our convenience, XML lexical information is refined and only ambiguous words are extracted (as cases) from them and maintained as row in a 26 decentralized form (P.Tamilselvi et al., 2009), based on the starting alphabets. Each word is represented as "{[word] [sense_form] [sense_tag] [assigned weight of left three words] [assigned weight of word] [assigned weight of right three words]}". All PoSs in Semcor are categorized into seventeen types based on their action and weights are assigned from 0.01 to 0.17 for word vectorization.

Our disambiguation system takes a document (paragraph) as input, and split it into sentences. The system will take one sentence at a time and tokenize it to words and convert them to morphologically individual words. Now, parsing is done using Hidden Markov Model (P.Tamilselvi et al., 2010(J)) and all input words are tied with their PoS tag. Next, number of senses of words falling in noun, verb, adjective and adverb PoS categories is isolated from the input list to find the number of senses using WordNet (Fellbaum, 1998) and that is also attached with the PoS tagged words. Poly-sense words are isolated and referred as amb_words. Main goal of the system is making disambiguation with minimum features (bigram and trigram). Two different bigrams, post-bigram (l1 + w) & pre-bigram (w + r1) and three different trigrams, pre-trigram (W + r1 + r2), in-trigram (l1 + W + r1) and post-trigram (l2 + l1 + W) features are used to represent the vector form of the input ambiguous word and also cases from distributed case bases. Neural network is used to extract the sense from cases with the help of vectors. To derive the numeric values of vectors, weights of PoS of three types of trigram features are used. As part of our supervised sense disambiguation evaluation, we accomplished a long English lexical sentence for word sense disambiguation (WSD) using bigram and trigram features.

2 Related Work

(Jun Fu Cai et al.,2007) used, local features such as part of speech of neighboring words, eleven collocation features and syntactic patterns and global features such as single words in surrounding context (bag-of-words) as used by (Lee and Ng, 2002). Sense of a word was identified using topic features and achieved 73.6% as overall disambiguation accuracy performance using Bayes network. For supervised learning, the Open Mind Word Expert (OMWE) project (Chklovski et al.,, 2002) was developed to collect sense-tagged data from Internet users. Data gathered through the OMWE project were used in the SENSEVAL-3 English lexical sample task. In that task, WordNet-1.7.1 was used as the sense inventory for nouns and adjectives, while Wordsmyth was used as the sense inventory for verbs.

(Hwee Tou Ng et al., 2007) used two different parallel corpora for disambiguation. The first corpus was the Chinese English News Magazine Parallel Text, which is an English-Chinese parallel corpus available from the Linguistic Data Consortium (LDC) and the second one from the URL pairs given by the STRAND Bilingual Databases.3 STRAND developed by (Resnik and Smith, 2003) that acquired document pairs in parallel translation automatically from the Web. Three different teams were involved to make the disambiguation process based on supervised learning concept. CITYU-HIF team used Naïve Baye's classifier with text features part of speech of the words, single words in the surrounding context classifier, HIT-IR-WSD team used support vector machine with a linear kernel function with text features POS of surrounding words, local collocations, single words in the surrounding context and syntactic relations and the third team PKU used support vector machine with maximum entropy classifier with POS of surrounding words, local collocations and single words in the surrounding context.

(Zheng-Yu Niu et al., 2005) used three types of features to capture contextual information: part-of-speech of neighboring words with position information, unordered single words in topical context, and local collocations. They used semi-supervised label propagation algorithm for feature clustering to make disambiguation. Two distance measuring metrics were applied, cosine similarity and Jensen-Shannon (JS) divergence.

3 Distance metrics

(Ido Dagan et al., 1997) compared several similarity measuring methods such as KL-Divergence, Total Divergence to the average, L1 norm and confusion probability for finding the similarity between the words for disambiguation and weight affecting parameters were fine tuned in first three methods to get the correct sense of the given word. In this paper, different distance measuring functions (table-1) are used for collecting most similar cases for disambiguation. The function may endow with one or more cases, referred as case set Ci, i=1,2,..10. From the case set more similar case or the best case for the input word is identified using neural network.

4 Neural Network Architecture

Because neural network is a good classifier, it is used to select the best similar case from the case set. Trainable cascade feed-forward back-propagation network with single hidden layer designed with 8 neurons and with sigmoid activation function is used for disambiguation process. To select the best network for bigram and trigram, five different networks namely, feed-forward back propagation network (M1), Elman back propagation network (M2), trainable cascade forward back propagation network (M3), pattern recognition network (M4) and feed forward back propagation network with feedback from output to input (M5) were taken with single layer.

Network performance is tested with different hidden neurons, from 2 to 20 with rising of 2 neurons at a time. More than 500 sentences were taken from Semcor as test data with the condition, training data should not be taken for testing. Disambiguation performance result is given in table-2. From the table, it is clear that the network architecture M3 produced better performance for bigram features , not having much difference between post-bigram and pre-bigram (without using case-based technique) (P.Tamilselvi et al., 2011(C)). And M4 produced better accuracy with 78.6% for trigram features (P.Tamilselvi et al., 2011(J)).

Table 1. Different Distance Measuring Metrics

S.No	Notation used	Distance metric name	Mathematical Representation	Description
1	F1	Euclidean	$D_E = \sqrt{\sum_{i=1}^{n}(x_i - y_i)^2}$	Euclidean distance
2	F2	Standardized Euclidean	$D_{SE} = \sqrt{\sum_{i=1}^{n} W_i (X_i - Y_i)^2}$	Standardized Euclidean distance. Each coordinate difference between rows in X and the query matrix is scaled by dividing by the corresponding element of the standard deviation computed from X
3	F3	City_block	$D_C = \sum_{i=1}^{n} \lvert X_i - Y_i \rvert$	City block distance.
4	F4	Chebechev	$D_{Ch} = \max_i(\lvert X_i - Y_i \rvert)$	Chebychev distance (maximum distance or L∞ Norm distance)
5	F5	Minkowski	$D_M = \sqrt[\lambda]{\sum_{i=1}^{n} \lvert X_i - Y_i \rvert^{\lambda}}$	Minkowski distance. The default exponent is 2.
6	F6	Cosine	$D_{Co} = \frac{\sum_{i=1}^{n} X_i \times Y_i}{\sqrt{\sum_{i=1}^{n}(X_i)^2} \times \sqrt{\sum_{i}^{n}}}$	1 minus the cosine of the included angle between observations (treated as vectors).
7	F7	Correlation	$D_{Cr} = \frac{dcov(X,Y)}{\sqrt{dvar(X) - dvar}}$	One minus the sample linear correlation between observations (treated as sequences of values).
8	F8	Spearman	$D_S = \frac{\sum_{i=1}^{n}(X_i - \bar{X}_i)(}{\sqrt{\sum_{i=1}^{n}(X_i - \bar{X}_i)^2 \sum_{i=1}^{n}}}$	One minus the sample Spearman's rank correlation between observations (treated as sequences of values).
9	F9	Hamming	$D_H = \frac{\#(X_i \neq Y_i)}{n}$	Hamming distance, which is the percentage of coordinates that differ.
10	F10	Jaccard	$D_J = \frac{\lvert X \cup Y \rvert - \lvert X \cap Y \rvert}{\lvert X \cup Y \rvert}$	One minus the Jaccard coefficient, which is the percentage of nonzero coordinates that differ.

5 Result

In this paper, the disambiguation performance is shown using a single sentence (Fig.1) with length 22 with 14 ambiguous words. After pre-disambiguation process, all ambiguous words are collected and listed as "word-position word PoS number_of_senses" (Fig.2). Handling string as such for disambiguation process is not easy. Next step in our disambiguation process is framing vector form for each ambiguous word (table-3) using weight assignment process. Words are taken one by one and their relevant cases (in vector form) in the case set are used to train the network. Finally, the vector value of the ambiguous word is simulated in the trained network to get the best similar case.

Table 2. Overall Disambiguation performance in % (without using case-based technique)

Network Type	Post bigram	Pre Bigram	Pre-trigram	In-trigram	Post-trigram
M1	69.1	70.6	71.4	69.9	67.9
M2	68.5	63.6	75.7	71.6	67.9
M3	***70.6***	***71.3***	75.7	70.3	67.9
M4	68.5	65.7	**78.6**	**78.2**	**76.4**
M5	58	65	57.1	72.4	72.4

The Fulton County Grand Jury said Friday an investigation of Atlanta's recent primary election produced no evidence that any irregularities took place.

Fig. 1. Sample Sentence

Disambiguation accuracy of the distance metrics are measured based on the number of words sensed correctly (table-4). From the table, it is visible that F8 (spearman distance metric) produced high disambiguation with pre-bigram feature. This is not only for this sentence, while testing this disambiguation system with more than 500 sentences (which are not taken as cases) from Brown Corpus, spearman produced better result with pre-bigram features. Fig.3 and Fig.4 project the disambiguation performance based on Noun and verb respectively. Out of two adjectives, only one is sensed (with 50% of accuracy) by almost all function cases.

Disambiguation time is measured using 'tic-toc' command, with the condition of not assigning any other task to CPU. Still, the disambiguation time is not unique, each word is processed 5 times (no changes in sense identification) and the average of that is considered as disambiguation time (Fig.5). Even thought the time taken by F8 is not very less, by seeing the disambiguation accuracy, we recommend spearman metric (F8) with pre-bigram for disambiguation than other metrics.

Table 3. Vector Form of ambiguous words

Ambiguous words	Post-bigram	Pre-Bigram	Pre-trigram	In-trigram	Post-trigram
county	0.1400	**0.1400**	**0.1400**	0.1400	0.0200
	0.1400	0.1400	0.1400	**0.1400**	0.1400
			0.1400	0.1400	**0.1400**
Grand	0.1400	**0.1600**	**0.1600**	0.1400	0.1400
	0.1600	0.1400	0.1400	**0.1600**	0.1400
			0.1500	0.1400	**0.1600**
Jury	0.1400	**0.1400**	**0.1400**	0.1400	0.1400
	0.1400	0.1500	0.1500	**0.1400**	0.1400
			0.1400	0.1500	**0.1500**
Say	0.1400	**0.1500**	**0.1500**	0.1400	0.1400
	0.1500	0.1400	0.1400	**0.1500**	0.1400
			0.0200	0.1400	**0.1500**
Investigation	0.0200	**0.1400**	**0.1400**	0.0200	0.1400
	0.1400	0.1200	0.1200	**0.1400**	0.0200
			0.1400	0.1200	**0.1400**
Atlanta	0.1200	**0.1400**	**0.1400**	0.1200	0.1400
	0.1400	0.1600	0.1600	**0.1400**	0.1200
			0.1400	0.1600	**0.1400**
recent	0.1400	**0.1600**	**0.1600**	0.1400	0.1200
	0.1600	0.1400	0.1400	**0.1600**	0.1400
			0.1400	0.1400	**0.1600**
Primary	0.1600	**0.1400**	**0.1400**	0.1600	0.1400
	0.1400	0.1400	0.1400	**0.1400**	0.1600
			0.1500	0.1400	**0.1400**
Election	0.1400	**0.1400**	**0.1400**	0.1400	0.1600
	0.1400	0.1500	0.1500	**0.1400**	0.1400
			0.0200	0.1500	**0.1400**
Produce	0.1400	**0.1500**	**0.1500**	0.1400	0.1400
	0.1500	0.0200	0.0200	**0.1500**	0.1400
			0.1400	0.0200	**0.1500**
Evidence	0.0200	**0.1400**	**0.1400**	0.0200	0.1500
	0.1400	0.1200	0.1200	**0.1400**	0.0200
			0.0200	0.1200	**0.1400**
irregularity	0.0200	**0.1400**	**0.1400**	0.0200	0.1500
	0.1400	0.1500	0.1500	**0.1400**	0.0200
			0.1500	0.1500	**0.1400**
Take	0.0200	**0.1500**	**0.1500**	0.0200	0.1500
	0.1500	0.1500	0.1500	**0.1500**	0.0200
			0.0001	0.1500	**0.1500**
place	0.0200	**0.1500**	**0.1500**	0.0200	0.1500
	0.1500	0.0001	0.0001	**0.1500**	0.0200
			0.0001	0.0001	**0.1500**

3	county	NN	2
4	grand	JJ	8
5	jury	NN	2
6	say	VB	11
9	investigation	NN	2
11	atlanta	NN	2
12	recent	JJ	3
13	primary	NN	3
14	election	NN	4
15	produce	VB	7
17	evidence	NN	3
20	irregularity	NN	4
21	take	VB	42
22	place	VB	16

Fig. 2. List of Ambiguous words

Table 4. Number of words sensed correctly

Distance Metrics	Post-Bigram	Pre-Bigram	Pre-Trigram	In-Trigram	Post-Trigram
F1	9	10	8	9	6
F2	8	8	9	8	6
F3	9	8	8	9	8
F4	9	8	8	10	8
F5	9	9	8	9	6
F6	8	9	7	10	8
F7	7	10	9	7	7
F8	9	12	10	8	7
F9	9	10	9	9	11
F10	10	10	9	11	8
Maximum Words Identified	10	12	10	11	11

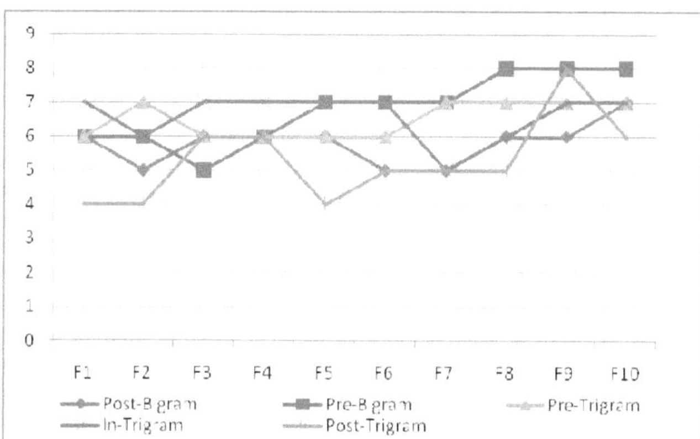

Fig. 3. Noun Disambiguation

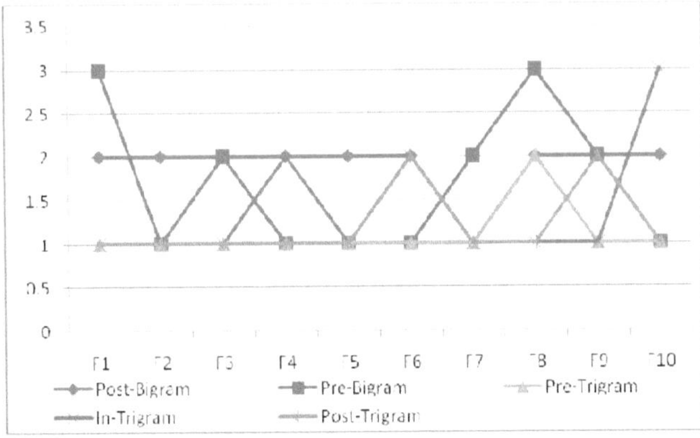

Fig. 4. Verb Disambiguation

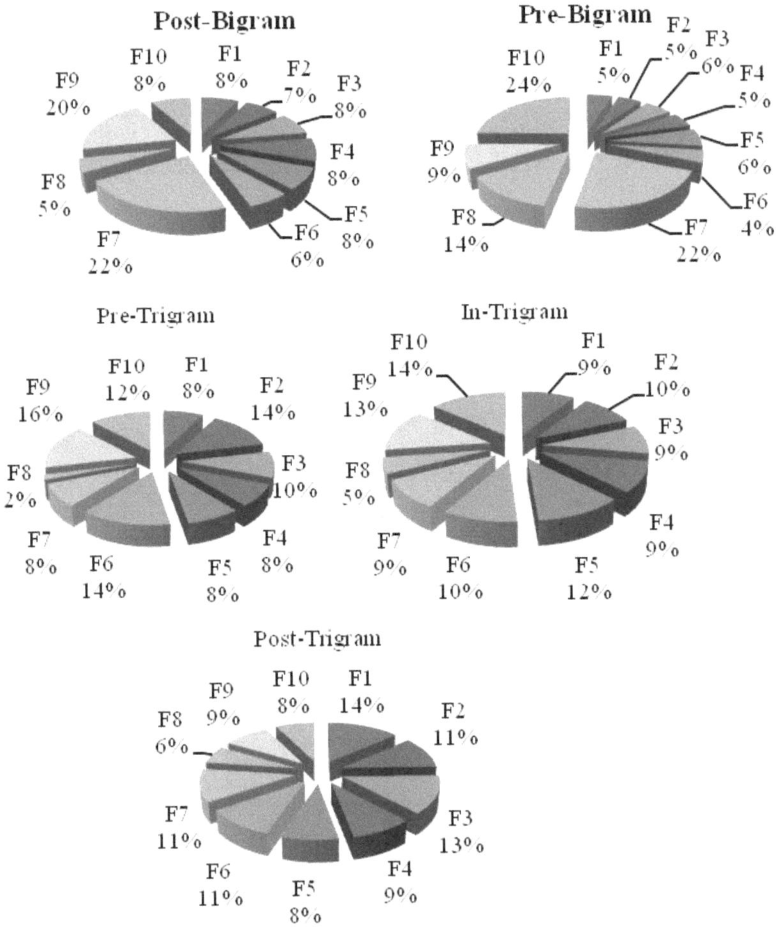

Fig. 5. Disambiguation Time

6 Conclusion

In this paper we showed that word sense disambiguation is achieved with minimum two features, ambiguous word together with either left or right of it. Disambiguation with case based technique produced higher accuracy than without using it. Spearman distance metric with pre-bigram generates better accuracy by disambiguating 12 out of 14 words, nearly, 85.71% for the ambiguous words in the sentence. Neural network is fine tuned to produce a better similar case for the current word. In general, overall disambiguation accuracy performance varies from 43% to 86%. It is very interesting to view better disambiguation accuracy with minimal features

References

1. Chklovski, T., Mihalcea, R.: Building a sense tagged corpus with Open Mind Word Expert. In: Proceedings of ACL 2002 Workshop on Word Sense Disambiguation: Recent Successes and Future Directions, Philadelphia, USA, pp. 116–122 (2002)
2. Dagan, I., Lee, L., Pereira, F.: Similarity-Based Methods For Word Sense Disambiguation. In: Proceedings of the 35th Annual Meeting of the Association for Computational Linguistics and Eighth Conference of the European Chapter of the Association for Computational Linguistics, USA
3. Yarowsky, D.: Unsupervised Word Sense Disambiguation Rivaling supervised methods. In: Proceedings of the 33rd Annual Meeting on Association for Computational Linguistics, ACL (1995)
4. Ng, H.T., Chan, Y.S.: English Lexical Sample Task via English-Chinese Parallel Text. In: Proceedings of the 4th International Workshop on Semantic Evaluations, SemEval, pp. 54–58 (2007)
5. Cai, J.F., Lee, W.S., Teh, Y.W.: Improving Word Sense Disambiguation Using Topic Features. In: Proceedings of the 2007 Joint Conference on Empirical Methods in Natural Language Processing and Computational Natural Language Learning, pp. 1015–1023. Association for Computational Linguistics (2007)
6. Lee, Y.K., Ng, H.T.: An Empirical Evaluation of Knowledge Sources and Learning Algorithms for Word Sense Disambiguation. In: Proc. of EMNLP (2002)
7. Resnik, P., Smith, N.A.: The web as a parallel corpus. Computational Linguistics 29(3), 349–380 (2003)
8. Niu, Z.-Y., Ji, D.-H., Tan, C.L.: Word Sense Disambiguation Using Label Propagation Based Semi-Supervised Learning. In: Proceedings of the 43rd Annual Meeting of the ACL, pp. 395–402 (2005)
9. 2005 Association for Computational Linguistics, Ann Arbor (2005)
10. Leacock, C., Chodorow, M., and Miller, G. A., Using corpus statistics and WordNet relations for sense identification. Computational Linguistics 24(1) (1998)
11. Schütze, H.: Automatic Word Sense Discrimination. Computational Linguistics 24(1) (1998)
12. Tamilselvi, P., Srivatsa, S.K.: A Study on Lexicographical Information using open source lexical databases. In: Proceeding of NCRTCSE 2010, National Conference on Recent Trends in Computer Science and Engineering, India (2010)

13. Tamilselvi, P., Srivatsa, S.K.: Decentralized E-Dictionary (DED) for NLP task. In: Proceedings of ICMCS International Conference on Mathematics and Computer Science, India (2009)
14. Tamilselvi, P., Srivatsa, S.K.: Part-Of-Speech Tag Assignment Using Hidden Markov Model. International Journal of Highly Reliable Electronic System 3(2) (2010)
15. Fellbaum, C. (ed.): WordNet: An Electronic Lexical Database. MIT Press (1998)
16. WordNet, http:/wordnet.princeton.edu\papers
17. Decadt, B., Hoste, V., Daelmans, W.: GAMBL, Genetic Algorithm Optimization of Memory-Based WSD. In: Proc. of Senseval-3 (2004)
18. Mihalcea, R., Faruque, E.: Sense-learner: Minimally Supervised Word Sense Disambiguation for All Words in Open Text. In: Proc. of Senseval-3 (2004)
19. Tamilselvi, P., Srivatsa, S.K.: Word Sense Disambiguation using Cascade Feed-Forward Back Propagation Network. In: Proceeding of NC4T, India (2011)
20. Tamilselvi, P., Srivatsa, S.K.: Trigram based word sense disambiguation using Neural Network (in press). International Journal of Artificial Intelligent Systems and Machine Learning 3(8) (2011)

Performance Evaluation of EAP-TLS Authentication Protocol for UMTS-WiMAX Interworking

R. Narmadha and S. Malarkan

Sathyabama University, Chennai
narmadha1109@gmail.com

Abstract. With the wide application of mobile technology in wireless transmission, the interworking of various networks turns into a new trend. UMTS-WiMAX interworking is being widely considered by mobile service providers because of its advantages for both users and service providers.Generally authentication methods are different for various wireless networks. In this paper, cost analysis are to realize efficient authentication in wireless networks based on the user mobility ,encryption and transmission time. This paper analyses a strong password based EAP-TLS authentication protocol which uses PKI for mutual authentication and satisfy the entire requirement for UMTS-WiMAX interworking authentication.

Keywords: UMTS, WiMAX,EAP-TLS, MATLAB.

1 Introduction

The 3G/UMTS mobile technology provide wide area coverage and complete subscriber management with a data rate of up to 2 Mbps but at a high cost. World wide interoperability for microwave access (WiMAX)/IEEE 802.16 provide high data rates for users without breaking the connection,mobile streaming media services,mobile TV unified communication and voice over IP(VOIP) .But is subject to low bit rate over long distance and speed of connectivity problem.Mainly sharing of user bandwidth have a range of 2-12 Mbit/s.The Integration [10]of WiMAX and UMTS systems will provide a convenient and attractive way for the user to access network and can eliminate their stand-alone defects. The users are able to access low cost high speed WiMAX mobile network while entering into a new network.However while integrating. UMTS-WIMAX, there are still some problems that should be considered in terms of authentication and security.

One of the most widely used security mechanism is authentication.Authentication is the main factor used in the design of a wireless network that protect the supplicant and user from various attacks ,fraud and loss of credentials. Since different networks implement different authentication protocols to get access to the core networks, for example, GERAN by GSM authentication [3], UMTS by UMTS AKA [4], LTE by EPS AKA [5], WLAN and EAP-TLS which is a recommendation of IEEE802.16e provides strongest security.In this paper, to mitigate the deterioration of network

P.V. Krishna, M.R. Babu, and E. Ariwa (Eds.): ObCom 2011, Part I, CCIS 269, pp. 697–702, 2012.

performance during authentication.Analyze EAP-TLS authentication protocol to locally authorize UMTS-WiMAX domain roaming users for efficient authentication which is based on[8] authentication, authorization and accounting (AAA) architecture. Additionally, by considering the traffic load and mobility patterns of a mobile user (Mu)and the message transmission time between the MU and its home AAA server.

The rest of this paper is organized as follows. Chapter 2 provides the interworking architecture of UMTS-WiMAX . In chapter 3, the knowledge of authentication protocol .In chapter 4, firstly the system model to analysis the impact of authentication is explained. Then, quantitatively analyze these authentication time and cost with concern of the message transmission time between the MU and its home server. Chapter 5 states a conclusion and further work.

2 UMTS-WiMAX Authentication Architecture

WiMAX-3G cellular interworking framework, [1][2]the following architectural considerations will be outlined.UMTS network includes Packet Data Switching Node (PDSN) of the CDMA2000 home network (MIP Home Agent HA) or Foreign Agent (FA).Direct end to end communications may be established and comprises of link layer registration . UMTS network interface uses code division multiple access(CDMA), WiMAX [3] network interface uses orthogonal frequency division multiple access(OFDMA).Both the networks are based on [4]AAA (Authentication, Authorization,Accounting) servers using RADIUS or Diameter Protocol.Visiting AAA servers (FA)allow users to authenticate even when it is not on their home network.Both UMTS-WiMAX networks use Mobile IP to manage mobility. UMTS uses Mobile IP for authentication and Home Agent authenticates using RADIUS.

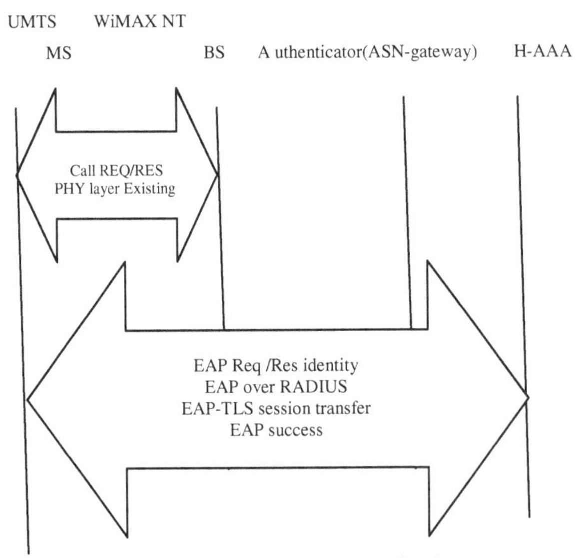

Fig. 1. WIMAX-3G Authentication

WiMAX uses EAP-TLS authentication and ASN-GW authenticates using RADIUS . EAP-TLS provides strong mutual authentication, it relies on certificates on both the User equipment and the subscriber terminal.WiMAX[5] subscriber on a UMTS network and Mobile IP authentication exist between MS and PDSN.Interworking achieved through new Mobile IP authentication extensions and RADIUS authentication between PDSN.when a UMTS network subscriber roams on a WiMAX network,Uses EAP authentication framework to authenticate MS to AN-GW. EAP over RADIUS authentication used between ASN-GW and AAA server.

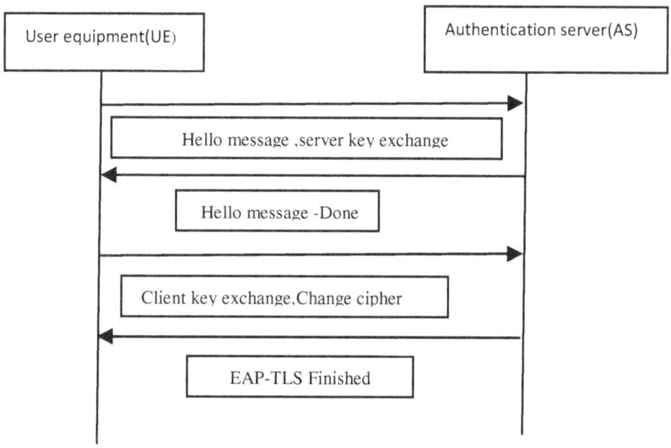

Fig. 2. Message flow of EAP-TLS

2.1 Authentication Protocols

Network security in terms of protection for network resources, information secrecy, and data integrity is affected greatly by the authentication service.Authentication protocols are one of the most widely used security mechanisms for UMTS-WiMAX networks.The authentication is a process to identify an User equipment(UE), authorize resources to an UE, and compromise secret credentials for secure communications [7]. Due to high computation complexity , public/private key based authentication mechanism consume more time and power. In order to achieve efficient authentication, [9]authentication protocol EAP-TLS is based on symmetric keys based on Public key infrastructure.The authentication message transmission and encryption/decryption of credentials increase the overhead of communications thus influence authentication delay and cost.

Authentication delay affects the QoS of real-time applications of mobile users.

When an MU firstly starts the authentication in UMTS network , an initial authentication procedure shown in Fig. 3. However, at this time, there is no authentication message transferred.

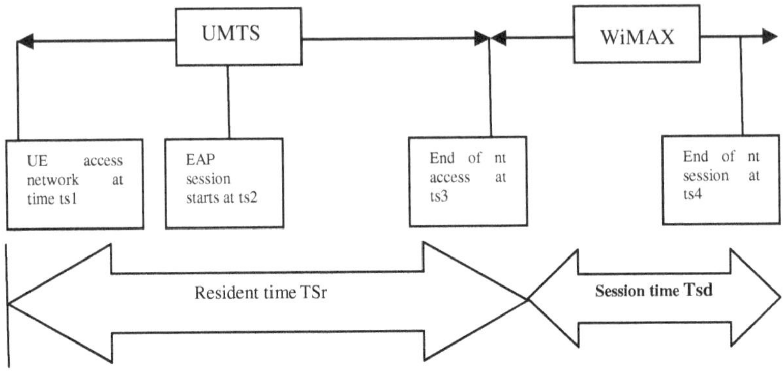

Fig. 3. Timing diagram of UMTS-WiMAX

3 Performance Evaluation of Authentication Time and Cost

The mean authentication time and cost per call in a WiMAX network domain as metrics of authentication latency and cost which is mostly used of analyzing the performance of authentication protocols.

Table 1. Performance evaluation of authentication time parameters

Symbol	Description
S1,S2,S3	Message including a random numbers
e1,f1	UE calculates Commitment pair for encryption with the value of S
β	Number of arrival calls- Average rate
TSd	Call duration time
$1/\Omega$	Exponential distribution with mean
L	UMTS network authentications
B	Boundaries during a call duration time
Ai	Number of authentication request
Yi	Authentication time
A_{call}	Number of calls in a FN
$Z_{UE\text{-}AS}$	Transmission time between UE and AS
$Z_{AS\text{-}HA}$	Transmission time between AS and HA
$Z_{ENR/DR}$	Encryption and decryption time
Z_C, Z_o	Pair generation and starting time

The mean authentication[11] time per call in network domain is given by,

$$M_{AT} = (A_1Y_1 + A_2Y_2 + A_3Y_3) / A_{call} \tag{1}$$

Assume user equipment crosses the network boundaries, the number of authentication signal in inter and intra network can be expressed as,

$$A_1 = \beta / (\beta + \Omega) * 2 \quad (2)$$

$$A_3 = \beta (M + 1) / 2 * \Omega \quad (3)$$

And in one network domain, the number of calls can be obtained by:

$$A_{call} = \beta (M + 1) / \Omega \quad (4)$$

Where the the number of session authentication A_2 equals A_{call}.

To calculate different type of authentications time ,a set of parameters which defined in the table 1

$$Y_i = \overline{f_i} \bullet \overline{Z_t} \quad (5)$$

The authentication messages were transferred from UE to AS through an access point(AP).For authentication message the random number generation to the UE by server. The parameters to evaluate the mean authentication time and cost per call are shown in Table 2.

Similarly mean authentication cost [11]per call defined by mean authentication cost during each call, including the processing load for cryptographic techniques and signaling load.

$$M_{AU} = (A_1 B_1 + A_2 B_2 + A_3 B_3) / A_{cal} \quad (6)$$

The maximum authentication message size is 3000 bytes ,the transmission delay is about 50 milliseconds.

Table 2. Performance evaluation for authentication time and cost

Parameters for evaluation	
$Z_{UE\text{-}AS}$	4
$Z_{AS\text{-}HA}$	2
$Z_{ENR/DR}$	8
Z_C, Z_o	1,1
β	0.01 to 0.1ms
M	100-120
Ω	0.1 -0.3ms

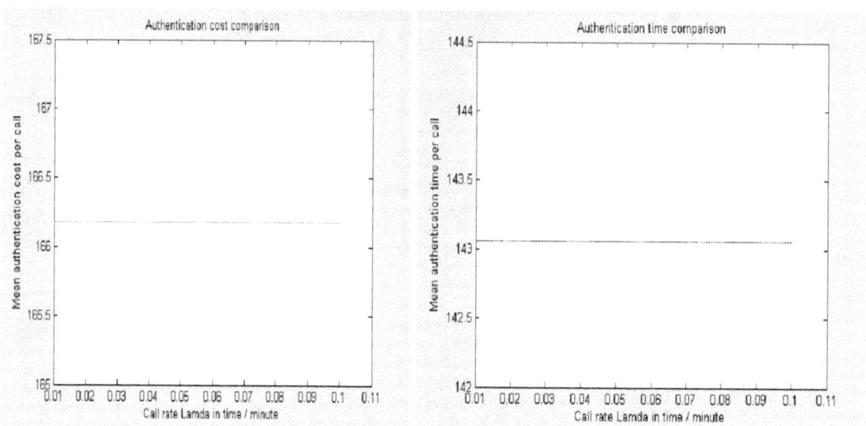

Fig. 4. Analysis of authentication cost and time using MATLAB

4 Conclusion and Future Work

From Fig. 4 , reveals the effect of call rate on the mean authentication time per call and mean authentication cost per call In this paper, a efficient EAP –TLS authentication protocol implementation in UMTS –WiMAX architecture was analyzed. Additionally with the help of strong password based EAP-TLS authentication protocol which supports end to end authentication , prevents password-sniffing .The comparative study shows that the protocol is more promising since it provides strong security,high efficiency and easy deployment.

References

1. Munasinghe, K.S., Jamalipour, A.: Interworked WiMAX-3G Cellular Data Networks: An Architecture for Mobility Management and Performance Evaluation. IEEE Transactions on Wireless Communications 8(4) (April 2009)
2. Khan, M.M.A., Ismail, M.F.B., Dimyati, K.: Interworking between WiMAX and UMTS to provide seamless services. International Journal of the Physical Sciences 5(6), 852–864 (2010)
3. Lin, M., Choi, H., la Porta, T.: CDMA2000-WiMAX Interworking. Sprint Avanced Technology lab
4. Nakhjiri, M., Nakhjiri, M.: AAA and Network Security for Mobile Access:Radius, Diameter, EAP, PKI and IP Mobility. John Wiley and Sons (October 2005)
5. WiMAX End-to-End Network Systems Architecture - 3GPP/ WiMAX Interworking, Release 1. WiMAX Forum (2006)
6. Liang, W., Wang, W.: On performance analysis of challenge/response based authentication in wireless networks. Computer Network 48(2), 267–288 (2005)
7. Cagalj, M., Capkun, S., Hubaux, J.: Key agreement in peer-to-peer wireless networks. Proceedings of the IEEE, Special Issue on Securityand Cryptography 94(2), 467–478 (2006)
8. Hess, A., Schafer, G.: Performance evaluation of AAA/ mobile IP authentication. In: Proc. of 2nd Polish-German Teletraffic Symposium (September 2002)
9. Li, J., Jing, H., Wang, G., Yang, K.: Authentication Protocols for Mobile IP Networks. In: Innovative Computing Information and Control, ICICIC 2008, Grad. Sch. of Syst. & Inf. Eng., Univ. of Tsukuba, Tsukuba (2008)
10. Li, J., Li, R., Kato, J.: Future Trust Management Framework for Mobile Ad Hoc Networks. IEEE Communication Magazine 46(4), 108–114 (2008)
11. Jing, H., Li, J., Yang, K., Chen, H.: A Novel Commitment-based Authentication Protocol Based on AAA Architecture for Mobile IP Networks. In: Proceedings of IEEE Wireless Communications and Networking Conference 2007 (IEEE WCNC 2007), CD-ROM, Hong Kong, March 11-15, 5 pages (2007)

Tiny SPU: Implementation and Analysis of Secure Program Update for Clustered Wireless Sensor Networks

M.B. Nirmala, A.S. Majunath, and B.G. Yogesh

Dept. of Computer Science and Engineering
Siddaganga Institute of Technology, Tumkur,
Karnataka, India
{nirmalamb,asmanju}@sit.ac.in, yogeshbgv@gmail.com

Abstract. This paper presents the design, implementation and evaluation of Secure Program Update for Clustered wireless sensor networks. Tiny SPU follows an approach based on Deluge, an open source code dissemination protocol, and provides confidentiality along with authentication. The scheme is resilient to malicious program image injection by the compromised nodes. We implement our scheme in TinyOS and evaluate the performance in terms of end-to-end latency and power consumption.

Keywords: Clustered Sensor Networks, Key Computation, program image, TinyOS, nesC.

1 Introduction

Wireless sensor networks (WSN) technology has received lot of attention in recent years in the research community. Security in wireless sensor networks has an increasing demand for monitoring application in military and civilian operations. WSN is composed of large number of sensor nodes with limited power, computation, storage and communication capabilities.

After the deployment of WSN, updating the program image for sensor nodes is subsequently essential to provide new functionalities and for bug fixes [1]. The scheme proposed by Deluge [3] and [4, 5] developed the program image update protocols. These protocols aim at providing reliable code update with low end-to-end latency and low resource consumption. But updating the program image securely is more important especially for military service applications. For example, in environmental monitoring applications adversary should not gain any information about the new program image transmitted to sensor nodes. This is because in wireless broadcast medium an attacker can easily inject or corrupt the packet. Authors of [6, 7, 8, 9] discuss code dissemination protocols which ensure authentication and integrity, but does not provide confidentiality. Authors of [10] are the first to provide a protocol for confidential code dissemination. They also use digital signature to overcome denial of service attack which is an expensive operation in WSN with respect to power consumption.

P.V. Krishna, M.R. Babu, and E. Ariwa (Eds.): ObCom 2011, Part I, CCIS 269, pp. 703–713, 2012.

This paper aims at explanation of implementation details and analysis of an efficient secure program update scheme for clustered wireless sensor networks. Our proposed scheme has two phases, one is key computation phase and the other is network program update phase. In key computation phase keys are calculated dynamically when required based on broadcast encryption scheme. No key is communicated, rather they are computed based on cryptographic information. Each node need to store only one key at a time. Code is distributed to sensor nodes securely using this key. In the network program update phase the code is disseminated confidentially. The scheme also provides authentication where the node is certain about the originator of the program image. The node should be able to verify the integrity of each packet and at the same time data freshness should also be ensured.

Rest of the paper is organized as follows. Related work is discussed in more detail in Section 2. Our scheme is explained in detail in Section 3. Section 4 gives the implementation details. Section 5 provides the performance evaluation of our scheme and comparison with multi-hop scheme. Finally conclusion is given in Section 6.

2 Related Work

In this section we review the literature on secure network programming and also focus on the review of key distribution techniques used in sensor networks. Existing network reprogramming protocols employ Deluge [3], the program is divided into pages, pages are further divided into packets. To authenticate the sender of the code, hashing is applied on the last page as in [8] and the hashed value is attached to previous page. This process is applied recursively until the first page is found. Similar approach is followed in [7]. Here instead of pages, packets are hashed. In both the protocols each node has to verify the first packet/page with its base station's public key and then authenticate each packet or page by the hashed value sent with the previous one. This needs the packet or pages to be verified in-order. Deng et al. [9] have proposed a similar protocol on secure code distribution where it allows packets to be verified out-of-order by adapting a Merkle tree for hashing followed by all packets. This scheme does not fully eliminate the ordering requirements. In addition, it requires greater memory to store the hash tree. In our scheme we fully eliminate the ordering requirement. One way key chain for multi-hop program update is proposed in [6]. All the above protocols provide authentication and integrity of the network programming, but none of them provide confidentiality. In confidential deluge [10] authors proposed a confidential and DOS resistant protocol using digital signatures. But signature verification incurs computational overhead and additional power consumption in sensor nodes. secure program update scheme.

3 Secure Program Update

We consider a set S of N sensor nodes $s_1, s_2, \ldots s_N$ in a set C of m cluster nodes $c_1, c_2, \ldots, c_m$. Our new scheme follows the cluster based approach where every sensor node should belong to any one cluster group. The non-compromised nodes with in a cluster will be able to compute the common key based on the cryptographic information sent by the cluster heads and get the information about the program image. If any sensor node compromises with the outside eavesdropper, then he may compute key and decrypt all messages. To learn about the node compromise, mobile agents are used. Mobile agents are the secure mobile nodes which will be roaming around a group of sensor nodes and Mobile agent studies the energy consumptions of the sensor nodes. If energy consumption of any node is comparatively high then it is communicating with an outsider. Outsider may be a sensor node or a computer system or a human. Mobile agent gives the information to the cluster heads about the sensor nodes compromise. Once the cluster head knows about the node compromise, it computes the new common key for rest of the nodes. The compromised node will not be able to compute the new common key and hence will not get any information about the program update.

Distributing the program image to the sensor nodes in clustered-based WSN consists of two main phases. First phase is the key computation phase and the second phase is the Network program update phase. Base station Generates a random strings R_i for i = 1, . . . ,N each of length L, $0 \leq L \leq A$, where A is the composite number. Base station assigns one unique random string R_i to each node S_i for i = 1, . . . , N before deployment of sensor nodes. This random string is used to secure the individual key.

Algorithms

1). Algorithm 1: Key Computation and Network Program update at Base Station:

1. Chooses two prime numbers P and Q and computes random hard to factor composite $A = P.Q$
2. Chooses a secret value g of high index. Node c_i is assigned key $k_i = g^{h_i} \oplus R_i$, where h_i, h_j are relatively prime for all c_i, $c_j \in C$, $i \neq j$ with $i, j = 1$ *to* m.
3. A common key for the nodes in C is computed as $K = g^{h_C} \bmod A$ where $h_C = \prod_{i \in C} h_i$
4. Divides the program image into pages, pages into packets - $p_0, p_1, \ldots, p_n$ of M bytes each
5. Finds $Hash(p_i)$ and Packet $p_i \,||\, Hash(p_i)$.
6. Encrypts with Key K $P'_i = E_K(p_i \,||\, Hash(p_i))$
7. The packet p'_i is broadcast to Cluster heads.

2). Algorithm 2: Key Computation and Network Program update at Cluster Heads

1. Every cluster head $c_i \in C$ can computes K by evaluating

$$k_i^{\prod_{c_j \in C - \{c_i\}} h_j} \bmod A.$$

2. Receives the packet p'_i from base station.
3. Decrypts p_i with the key K $(p_i \parallel Hash(p_i)) \leftarrow D_K(p'_i)$
4. Computes $Hash(p_i)$ compares with the received hash value. If both are same then the packet p_i is stored otherwise discarded.
5. Cluster head chooses a random hard to factor composite $A = P.Q$ where P and Q are primes
6. It chooses a secret value g of high index. User s_i is assigned key $k_i = g^{h}{}_i \oplus R_i$, where h_i, h_j are relatively prime for all s_i, $s_j \in S$, $i \neq j$ with $i, j = 1$ to m.
7. A common key for a non-compromised nodes S is taken as the value $K = g^{h_s} \bmod A$ where $h_s = \prod_{i \in s} h_i$
8. Find $Hash(p_i)$. Packet $p_i \parallel Hash(p_i)$.
9. Encrypt with Key K $P'_i = E_K(p_i \parallel Hash(p_i))$
10. The packet p'_i is broadcast to Sensor nodes.

3). Algorithm 3: Key Computation and Network Program update at Sensor nodes

1. Sensor node s_i receives the secret value k_i and computes $k_i = g^{h_i} \oplus R_i$,
2. Computes the common key

$$K = k_i^{\prod_{s_j \in S - \{s_i\}} h_j} \bmod A$$

3. Packet p'_i is received from cluster head
4. Decrypts p'_i with the key K $(p_i \parallel Hash(p_i)) \leftarrow D_K(p'_i)$
5. Computes $Hash(p_i)$ compare with the received hash value. If both are same then the packet is stored otherwise it is discarded.

4 Implementation Details

We implemented this scheme on the TinyOS platform. The code is written in NesC language. The code is tested on TOSSIM simulator which creates the simulated WSN considering PC as the Motes. It is done by creating Configuration file, Module file and Make file. The configuration file and module file are of .nc. Appropriate header files (.h files) are also created and included in the above files. The following are the details of the implementation:

A. Configuration

The following is the configuration of our component.

```
configuration Ring
{
}
implementation
{
components Main, RingM, TimerC, GenericComm as Comm, LedsC;
```

```
Main.StdControl -> RingM.StdControl;
Main.StdControl -> Comm;
Main.StdControl -> TimerC;
RingM.Timer -> TimerC.Timer[unique("Timer")];
RingM.SendMsg -> Comm.SendMsg[AM_SIMPLEMSG];
RingM.ReceiveMsg -> Comm.ReceiveMsg[AM_SIMPLEMSG];
RingM.Leds -> LedsC;
   }
```

B. Module

In the implementation of our scheme we use some of the existing modules of TinyOS

```
module RingM
{
        provides interface StdControl;
        uses interface SendMsg;
        uses interface ReceiveMsg;
        uses interface Timer;
        uses interface Leds;
}
implementation
{
//Here code is written for network programming, key computation, Sending
and receiving the data.
}
```

C. Topology: In our scheme we follow the clustered approach, where in we have one base station, Cluster heads based on the total number of the sensor nodes and sensor nodes belong to only one particular cluster.

The number of the cluster head is depending upon the total number of the sensor nodes. Suppose we have N nodes, if N is a multiple of 10 then we have $N/10$ Cluster heads else $(N/10)+1$ Cluster heads. Each of the Cluster will be having the 9 sensor nodes belong to them. 0th sensor node is always considered to be the Trusted Base station. Every i^{th} node, such that $i \in N$ and (i is multiple of 10) plus 1 is considered to be the cluster heads. All the jth node belongs to i^{th} cluster such that $i=(j-(j\%10))+1$ if j is not a multiple of 10 else $i=j-9$.

For example: Suppose N=20, then network consists of 0th node as base station, set {1,11} as cluster heads and {2,3,4,5,6,7,8,9,10} as sensor nodes belong to cluster head 1 and {12,13,14,15,16,17,18,19} as sensor nodes belong to cluster head 11 as shown in the Figure *1*.

D. Network Programming

In this phase base station has the binary program image. The size of the program image can be varied. This program image is divided into packets as per the deluge protocol. In our implementation each packet consists of *48 bytes*. For the division the 48 *bytes* of data is read from the file and stored in the packets at the base station with the sequence number and length of the packet also being stored. The packet format is shown below.

```
typedef struct packets
{
uint8_t seqno;
uint8_t len;
uint8_t data[48];
}packet;
```

E. Format of the Packet Being Transmitted

The first byte of the packet is dedicated to indicate the address of the sender that is source address. For example: *0* in case of base station. Second byte is reserved for the sequence number of the packet. Length of the actual data in the packet is stored at the *64th byte*. Sequence number and the length are not encrypted for the purpose that they needed at the receiver before decrypting the data in order to verify the source and also duplication of the packet. *3rd byte to 50th byte* is used for storing the encrypted data. From *51st byte to 63rd* byte encrypted Hashed value of the data is stored as shown in Fig 1.

Source addr	Seq num	Encrypted data	Encrypted hash value	Length
1byte	1byte	48bytes	13bytes	1byte

Fig. 1. Format of the packet

In the implementation, while sending above packets are copied to the AM sampling message of type 50.

F. Key Computation and De-computation

In our scheme the keys used for Encryption at the sender side is not transmitted in air instead they are computed dynamically at the receiver side based on the cryptographic message exchanged between them. Whenever the system boots up the base station will perform the key computation and as well the cluster heads. The information is stored in respective packet. Packet format is as follows

Packet format at the Key computer:

```
typedef struct keydata
{
    uint16_t A;
    uint8_t g;
    uint8_t R[10];
    uint8_t h[10];
    uint32_t k[10];
    uint8_t cnodes;
};
```

G. Communication

The TinyOS provides the interface called GenericComm for communication between the nodes. This interface provides the function for sending and receiving the data. General format is

```
Result SendMsg.send(destinationID,sizeofData,pointerToData)
```

destinationID : ID of the receiver
sizeofData : Size of the actual data to be sent in bytes.
pointerToData: Pointer to the buffer where data is copied for sending. In the following shown code *msgc* and *msgb* are used as buffer at cluster head and base station respectively. The buffers should be of the type *TOS_Msg*. **Base station broadcasts the packets to cluster heads using following code:**

```
task void BSend()
{
if((call    SendMsg.send(TOS_BCAST_ADDR,    sizeof(msgb.data),&msgb))!=
SUCCESS)
dbg(DBG_USR1, "SEND MSG FAIL\n");
}
```

Cluster head broadcasts the packets to the sensor nodes belong to that cluster using the following code:

```
task void CCast()
{
if((call    SendMsg.send(TOS_BCAST_ADDR,    sizeof(msgc.data),&msgc))!=
SUCCESS)
dbg(DBG_USR1, "SEND MSG FAIL\n");
}
```

The following event signifies the success full receive of the packet:

```
event result_t SendMsg.sendDone(TOS_MsgPtr msg, result_t success)
{
      return SUCCESS;
}
```

The following event signifies the receiving of the packets and control will be with the receiver:

```
event TOS_MsgPtr ReceiveMsg.receive(TOS_MsgPtr m)
{
     Retuen m;
}
```

Note:
TOS_BCAST_ADDR is set to ffff which signifies the broadcast address in TinyOS.

H. Demonstration of Node Compromise

Whenever the node compromise occurs with an outsider, the node which has compromised is identified by the cluster head and it will re compute the key excluding the node which compromised. For the purpose of demonstration we have considered a sensor node belong to cluster one will compromise with an outsider. We can change the node *id* from *2* to 10. The cluster head *1* will recompute the key excluding the node compromised and sends the cryptographic information. Every sensor nodes belong to that cluster will re compute the key even compromised node tries to re compute but it fails in getting the common key. The broadcasted packets will also be received whenever it decrypts the packet using wrong key it gets the wrong updates.

5 Experimental Results

The experiment is carried out in TOSSIM Simulator, on TinyOS platform using internal clocks for recording end to end latency and TinyViz Power profiling for recording the Electric energy consumed. Readings for 5KB,10KB,20KB... are taken by varying the number of nodes. The various graphs are also plotted results are compared with the multi hop protocol. The following snapshots shows the working of our scheme for 30 nodes

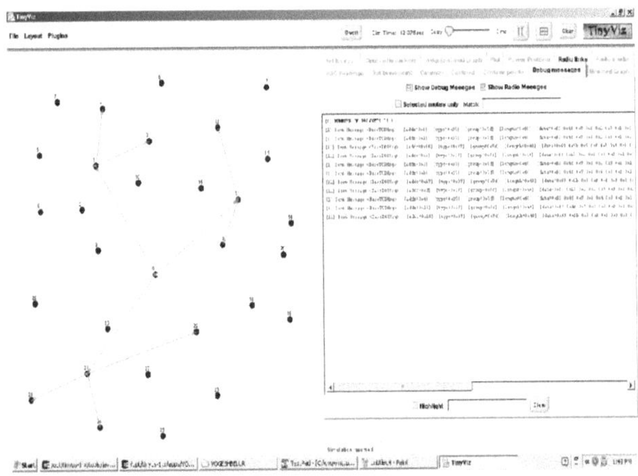

Fig. 2. Base Station Sending Cryptographic Information to Cluster heads and Cluster heads to Sensor nodes

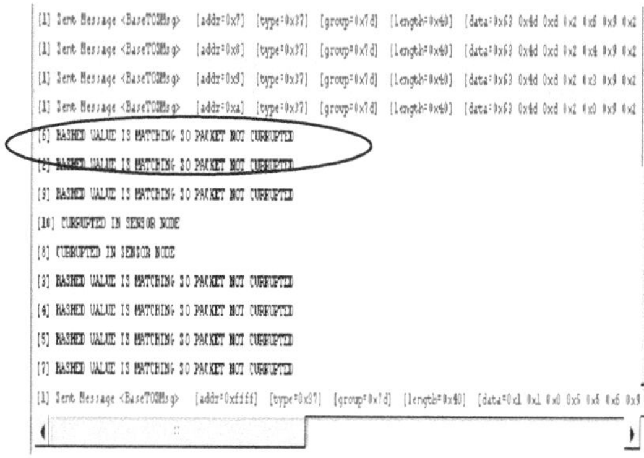

Fig. 3. Compromised nodes can't decrypt the further packets

The figure 4 shows the time required for the transfer of the program image of size of 20KB from base station to the Sensor nodes. In this Experiment, we varied the number of nodes from 10 to 70 for both multi hops and cluster approach. We recorded the time. We can observe that the latency occurred in Multi hop is greatly reduced in cluster based approach. Figure 5 shows the time required for dissemination of images of various size having 40 nodes. This experiment is also carried out for both multi hop and Cluster based approach.

We can observe that time taken by multi hop approach is greatly reduced in Cluster based approach.

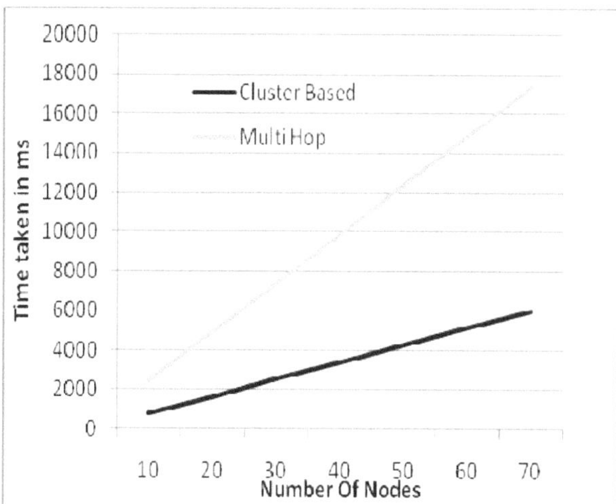

Fig. 4. End to End Latency for Program size 20KB

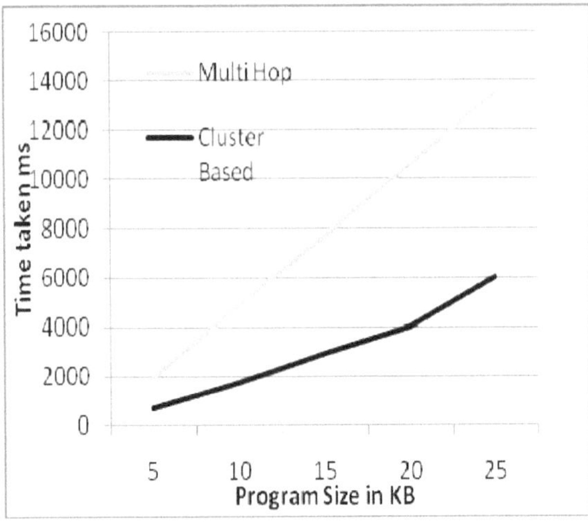

Fig. 5. . End to End latency with varying program size and number of nodes 40

6 Conclusion

In this scheme we considered cluster approach for WSN, where sensor nodes are two hop distances away from the base station. We have showed how security can be imposed for dissemination of packets in terms of confidentiality, authentication. We also dealt with ordering of messages. In real world, security issues are so important that organizations spend more money on security. We say that our scheme gives efficiency in terms of computation power, energy consumption and even storage also comparable to, multi hop approach.

We also compared our scheme with multi hop scheme, analysed that our proposed scheme gives better performance. In terms of end-to-end latency, the time consumed to reach the end nodes is very less. Also the electric energy consumed by each sensor is in the order of 10^{-4}AS. However sensor nodes can withstand 2 to 4 AH. Thus we have developed an efficient protocol for program image update dissemination.

Our developed scheme is resilient against node compromise. The compromised nodes are eliminated from further communications. In our scheme we also dealt with what way the security should be provided whenever a node goes compromised with an outsider. We demonstrated by compromising a node within first cluster. This applies for every cluster and no matter how many nodes compromise with an outsider.

References

1. Akyildiz, F., Su, W., Sankarasubramaniam, Y., Cayirci, E.: A Survey on Sensor Networks. IEEE Communications Magazine 40(8), 102–114 (2002)
2. Fiat, A., Naor, M.: Broadcast Encryption. In: Stinson, D.R. (ed.) CRYPTO 1993. LNCS, vol. 773, pp. 480–491. Springer, Heidelberg (1994)

3. Hui, J.W., Culler, D.: The Dynamic Behavior of a Data Dissemination Protocol for Network Programming at Scale. In: SenSys 2004, pp. 81–94. ACM Press, New York (2004)
4. Stathopoulos, T., Heidemann, J., Estrin, D.: A Remote Code Update Mechanism for Wireless Sensor Networks. Technical report CENS-TR-30, University of California, Los Angeles, Center for Embedded Networked Computing (November 2003)
5. Wang, L.: MNP: Mulltihop Network reProgramming service for sensor Networks. In: SenSys 2004, pp. 285–286. ACM Press (2004)
6. Tan, H., Jha, S., Ostry, D., Zic, J., Sivaraman, V.: Secure Multi-hop Network Programming with multiple one-way Key Chains. In: WiSec 2008: Proceedings of the First ACM Conference on Wireless Network Security, pp. 183–193. ACM, New York (2008)
7. Dutta, P.K., Hui, J.W., Chu, D.C., Cullar, D.E.: Securing the deluge network programming system. In: IPSN 2006, pp. 326–333. ACM Press, New York (2006)
8. Lanigan, P.E., Gandhi, R., Narasimhan, P.: Sluice: Secure Disseeemination of code updates in sensor networks. In: 26th IEEE International Conference on Distributed Computing Systems (ICDCS 2006), pp. 53–63 (July 2006)
9. Deng, J., Han, R., Mishra, S.: Secure Code Distribution in Dynamically Programmable Wireless Sensor Networks. In: IPSN 2006, pp. 292–300. ACM Press, New York (2006)
10. Tan, H., Ostry, D., Zic, J., Jha, S.: A Confidentail and DOS-Resistant Multi-hop code Dissemination Protocol for Wireless Sensor Networks. In: Wisec 2009, Zurich Switzerland, pp. 245–252. ACM Press (2004)

Secured Routing Using Quantum Cryptography

M. Vijay Anand[1] and C. Jayakumar[2]

[1] Aksheyaa College of Engineering
[2] RMK Engineering College
{prof.vijay,cjayakumar2007}@gmail.com

Abstract. This protocol is used to maintain security in networks for secure communication by overcoming some of the drawbacks in existing security protocols. Integration of both classical and quantum cryptography techniques takes place. Quantum cryptography is used for secure optical transmission which employs quantum mechanisms to distribute session keys Classical cryptography provides convenient techniques that enable efficient key verification and user authentication. This protocol used both implicit user authentication and explicit mutual authentication. A Trust centre is used to generate a secret key and public key by using RSA algorithm and it will develop the random key for each session of transmitting data these key develop a QUIBIT values which develop Session key. By using these keys user translate the messages between the other users securely. Error rate gets reduced when compared to the existing quantum cryptography protocol. Bayesian filtering method is integrated to reduce the external noise. The merits of this new protocol are,

- Secures against attacks as man-in-the-middle, eavesdropping and replay.
- Online guessing attacks can be avoided.
- Efficiency is more since the proposed protocol contain the fewest number of communication rounds.
- Two parties can share and use a long-term secret key by a trusted center.
- Error due to noise gets reduced.

Keywords: quantum cryptography, classical cryptography, RSA, session key, Bayesian Filtering, noise, error rate, eavesdropping.

1 Introduction

Today's (symmetrical) cryptography algorithms rest upon secure key transmission. In general this key has to be transmitted through the internet (or some public channel) and an eavesdropper (Eve) can easily intercept the communication, catch the key and the whole encoding is for nothing. And what's worse: Alice and Bob never know that they have another listener. One solution to key distribution is to use asymmetrical algorithms like RSA to encode the symmetric key. RSA uses a public key for encoding and a private (secret) key for decoding. This way, the secret key doesn't have to be sent through the internet. It's as difficult for Eve to compute the inverse RSA algorithm as it is to factor large integers or discrete logarithms (prohibitively difficult with current technology). Symmetrical algorithms would be safer, if only the key transmission problem weren't there. And that's where quantum cryptography comes in.

P.V. Krishna, M.R. Babu, and E. Ariwa (Eds.): ObCom 2011, Part I, CCIS 269, pp. 714–725, 2012.

In optical communications, optical signals suffer distortions from the linear and nonlinear properties of matter. In dense wavelength division multiplexing (DWDM), accurate optical power loss and distortion estimation is critical to network engineering as it influences the selection of path during set up, protection, or dynamic wavelength re-assignment Link engineering assures that the optical signal arrives at the receiver at an expected quality and bit error rate (BER) that meets performance requirements [17].

Today, QC is limited in terms of bit-rate, distance, and extension from dedicated point-to-point links to multi-user networks. The goal of the Chair research program is to conduct leading edge research into high bit-rate and long-distance quantum cryptography and to investigate the building of a quantum secured communication network to the benefit of the Albertan and ultimately Canadian society. This includes the:

- Development of high-speed, point-to-point quantum cryptographic systems based on attenuated laser pulses and operating on widely available standard telecommunication fibres over distances.
- Integration of quantum cryptographic systems with secure encoding algorithm for the building of complete, quantum secured communication systems.
- Extension of point-to-point system to networks.
- Development of versatile and robust quantum communication primitives like sources of entangled photons and quantum teleportation units.
- Development of a quantum memory as needed for a quantum repeater. [13]

Conventional data transmission uses electrical signals to represent a binary '1' or '0'. QC uses the polarization, or phase states of individual photons of light to represent the binary digits. Scientists claim that QC theoretically offers absolute security through the basic laws in quantum physics. Two approaches are possible. The first of these relies upon the 'uncertainty principle', which states that a single photon cannot be detected and its polarization (or phase state) measured simultaneously. In other words the superposition of a pair of quantum 'observables' cannot be measured without interfering with the measurement of the other. Moreover, under the 'no cloning' theorem it is not possible to clone a photon so that one can be measured and the other passed on to the recipient. By the use of suitable protocols, involving additional communication over a conventional public communications channel, any attempt to intercept the data may therefore be detected. The first provably secure QC protocol, known as BB84, was proposed by C H Bennett and G Brassard of IBM, in 1984. [10]

Bayesian filtering: Owing to analytical intractability, sequential Monte Carlo methods provide an appealing means of addressing the Bayesian filtering task. For the variance minimizing importance function p(Xt|Xit−1, Yt), we have the weight recursion wit = wit−1p(Yt|Xit−1) and hence must find p(Yt|Xit−1) =ZVk,mp(Yt|Xt)p(Xt|Xit−1)dXt. In the case of filtering on the Stiefel manifold considered here, this integral cannot in general be evaluated analytically and must be approximated. Hence, we choose as importance function p(Xt|Xit−1), providing the simple weight recursion wit = wit−1p(Yt|Xit).This requires only that we sample each particle Xit = p(Xt|Xit−1),a von Mises-Fisher distribution, and evaluate p(Yt|Xit), a matrixGaussian distribution.[5]

Use of low-noise detectors can both increase the secret bit rate of long-distance quantum key distribution (QKD) and dramatically extend the length of a fiber optic link over which secure key can be distributed. [12]

Authentication can be accomplished in many ways. The importance of selecting an environment appropriate Authentication Method is perhaps the most crucial decision in designing secure systems. Authentication protocols are capable of simply authenticating the connecting party or authenticating the connecting party as well as authenticating itself to the connecting party. [15]

2 Related Work

BB84 and Ekert91 protocols: Benett und Brassard proposed a protocol for a secret key exchange between Alice and Bob in 1984 (BB84). Alice wants to send the key to Bob. She has two bases with polarized Photons She chooses an arbitrary basis for her bits and sends them over the Quantum Channel to Bob. Bob measures in an arbitrary chosen basis, too. If he has no detection he deletes this register. Then he sends this information and information on what bases he chose over a public channel to Alice and keeps the outcome of each measurement secret. After Alice gets Bob's info, she can compare it to her own chosen bases and select the coincidences. She sends the information on the coinciding bases back to Bob and he just looks in his protocol, checks whether he had 0 or 1 for this register and the result forms the key. Now, they can use the key and encrypt the message. The key should be as long as the plaintext and be used only once (one-time-pad). Eve can wiretap the public channel, but that won't do her any good. She gets information on the bases and not on the outcome of the measurement. In case Eve attempts to measure part of the Quantum Channel she betrays herself by a high Quantum Bit Error Rate (QBER) and Alice and Bob are warned. Two parties using BB84 know that Eve is listening and will not use this key for transmitting the actual message.

Researchers built SARG04 when they noticed that by using the four states of BB84 with a different information encoding they could develop a new protocol which would be more robust when attenuated laser pulses are used instead of single-photon sources. SARG04 was defined by Scarani et al in 2004.

3 Proposed Work

Principle: Integration of quantum cryptography for secure optical transmission and classical cryptography for identity and authentication. In existing quantum cryptography, communication rounds are more and identity of the user is not specified.

Assumptions:

- Number of users are 5.
- Any user can communicate with any other user at any point of time.
- Trusted center should approve based on the number of requests.

Possible Combinations: Consider 5 users are there in an authenticated community and the authentication between those users will be done by using a trusted center (TC). Each and every user can communicate through trusted center for getting a key. Between each user communication channel was available to transmit message after authentication, so the number of communication channel will be n (n-1). (i.e.) 5(5-1).

A1→A2	A2→A1	A3→A1	A4→A1	A5→A1
A1→A3	A2→A3	A3→A2	A4→A2	A5→A2
A1→A4	A2→A4	A3→A4	A4→A3	A5→A3
A1→A5	A2→A5	A3→A5	A4→A5	A5→A4

Out of 5 users, the possible communication channels are 4 per user. Therefore for n number of users then n (n-1) channels are required. This is applicable for one time communication among the users. Number of session keys for one time communication is n (n-1). M number of times if communication among the users, irrespective of time then Total number of communications among the users at any point of time is M(n(n-1)). Session key generation is done by the trusted center.

Table 1. Distance Specification for each user

User	Distance between user and trust center
User1	50
User2	35
User3	20
User4	15
User5	65

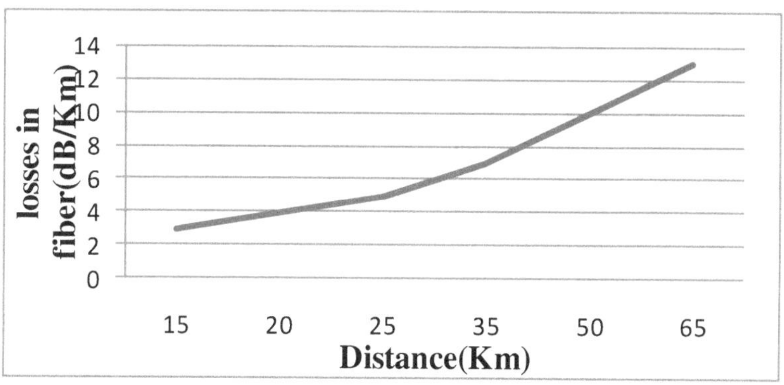

Fig. 1. Graph ranging between distance and losses in fiber

Step1:
Trusted center maintain a log record for each user (password or facial or RFID or any Biometrics). Through comparison user authentication is done. For each and every user, a private key and public key was created at the time of registration by using RSA algorithm.

1. Choose two large prime numbers P and Q.
2. Compute N=P*Q.
3. Choose e(less than N) such that e and (P-1)(Q-1) are relatively prime(having no common factor other than 1), Public key is (N,e).
4. Choose d such that (e*d) mod [(P-1)(Q-1)] is equal to 1, Private key is (N,d).

Private Key and public key will be known to the trusted center and the corresponding user. All user information is stored in trusted center.

Table 2. Private and public key generation using RSA algorithm

User	P	Q	N=P*Q	A=(P-1)(Q-1)	e<N	d {(e*d)modA=1}
User1	5	11	55	40	3	27
User2	11	3	33	20	3	7
User3	47	71	3337	3220	79	1019
User4	7	17	119	96	5	77
User5	137	131	17947	17680	3	11787

Step 2:
If number of requests are <=1, no problem for TC to approve for communication. Else Select user according to the time of request.

Source id	time units	Destination id

Request packet:
The trusted center gives response based on First-In-First-out basis.

Step3:
Creation of session key: Trusted center creates a session key and distribute to both the source and destination. A random number is generated by using Random () function.

Random number generation: Shennon entropy based random number generation.

- All bits are random
- Uncertainty
- Zero entropy

Table 3. Random numbers for user1

x_n	P1	P2	N	$B=P1*x_n+P2$	SK=BmodN
28	9	15	55	267	47
47	9	15	55	438	53
53	9	15	55	492	52
52	9	15	55	483	43
43	9	15	55	402	17

This session key is unique for each communication between users. The session key gets encrypted by using the public key of source and destination by using the formula,

$$C=P^e \bmod N$$

Where P is the session key and C is the encrypted key. These encrypted session key should be converted into quibits and send to the corresponding user.

Table 4. Encryption of session key for user1

Session Key(SK)	Public Key	N	ESK=(SK)^e mod N	Binary value of ESK
47	3	55	38	100110
53	3	55	47	101111
52	3	55	28	11100
43	3	55	32	100000
17	3	55	18	10010

Step4:

Generation of Quibits: 4 types of polarizing filters,

1. Vertical represents 0
2. Horizontal represents 1
3. Down left to upper right '/' represents 1
4. Down right to upper left'\' represents 0

Single photon is separated from the light source by using any one of the polarizing filter. This will be done in TC. Based on the private key of sender and receiver these quibits will be passed through the quantum channel. The quibits passed through the beam splitter and avalanche photodiode is used to capture the photon. In trusted center a laser diode is used to produce photon by passing it through the polarizing filter. If the encrypted session key contains 'n' number of bits then 'n' number of photons should be generated. The polarizing filter for polarization of photon will be selected based on the ith bit of the private key of the user and the ith bit of the session key of the same user. If number of bits in private key is m and number of bits in encrypted session key is n, where m<n,

(i.e.) private key bits are 1, 2, 3… m, Public key bits are 1, 2…m, m+1…n

Till mth bit the corresponding values will be taken and for (m+1) th bit the first bit of private key will be considered and so on.

For example, private key is, 11000100, Encrypted session key is, 1000011111

Private key	1	1	0	0	0	1	0	0	1	1
Session key	1	0	0	0	0	1	1	1	1	1
Basis	D	D	R	R	R	D	R	R	D	Ê
Polarizing filter	/	\	|	|	|	/	_	_	/	/
Quibits	/	\	|	|	|	/	_	_	/	/

Table 5. Creating quibits for user1 for different session

Binary value of ESK	Binary value of Secret Key(e)	Quibit Basis	Quibit Values
100110	11011	D D R D Ê	/ \ I / / \
101111	11011	D D R D Ê	/ \ - / / /
11100	11011	D D R D Ê	/ / - \ \
100000	11011	D D R D Ê	/ \ I \ \ \
10010	11011	D D R D Ê	/ \ I / \

Table 6. Selection of quibit basis

Bit Value of SK	Bit Value of Secret Key	Quibit basis	Quibit Value
0	1	D(Diagonal)	\
1	1	D(Diagonal)	/
0	0	R(Rectilinear)	I
1	0	R(Rectilinear)	_

These quibits will pass through the quantum channel to the corresponding user. The packet consists of

Step5:

Decrypting the session key: In both sender and receiver the quibits are converted based on the photon direction. Thus session key was known. In the user, polarizing beam splitters (PBS) were used which is of rectilinear basis and diagonal basis. Avalanche photodiode (APD) is used to separate '0' and '1' in quibit.

Quibits	/	\	I	I	I	/	_	_	/	/
Polarizing filter	D	D	R	R	R	D	R	R	D	Ê
Result bits	/	\	I	I	I	/	_	_	/	/
Binary value	1	0	0	0	0	1	1	1	1	1

Which is the encrypted session key; this will be converted into its decimal value,

$$512 + 0 + 16 + 8 + 4 + 2 + 1 = 543$$

Decrypting the session key will be done by,

P=c^d mod N

This value gives the session key and the binary value is calculated.

Table 7. Receiving Quibits and decrypting the session key

Quibit Basis	Quibit Values	ESK Binary Value	ESK	SK=$(ESK)^d$ mod N
D D R D Ê	/ \ I / / \	100110	38	47
D D R D Ê	/ \ - / / /	101111	47	53
D D R D Ê	/ / - \ \	11100	28	52
D D R D Ê	/ \ I \ \ \	100000	32	43
D D R D Ê	/ \ I / \	10010	18	17

Step6:

Security checks and Transfer messages: Users do a security check with the trust center by adding their Bits (0+1+0+0+0+1...) and both must have an either odd or even result. This key is used for encrypting the messages to be transformed. Similarly, the session key was identified by receiver and it will use that key for decrypting the messages received during that session.

Quantum bit error rate: 2 parameters are considered,

1. Data rate
2. Transmission length

$$R_{raw} = \tfrac{1}{2}\, V\, \mu\, \eta_t\, \eta_d$$

Where, ½ is incompatibility, V is pulse rate, μ is average number of photons per pulse,

η_t is transfer efficiency, η_d is detector efficiency.

Table 8. Calculating Raw rate

User	Pulse Rate(V)	Mean number of photons(μ)	Transmitter Efficiency(η_t)	Receiver Efficiency(η_d)	R_{raw}= ½ V μ η_t η_d
User1	10^6	0.02	0.01	0.00003	0.003
User2	10^6	0.02	0.03	0.00006	0.018
User3	10^6	0.02	0.1	0.00019	0.19
User4	10^6	0.02	0.25	0.00035	0.875
User5	10^6	0.02	0.002	0.000018	0.00036

Table 9. Calculation of Transmitter and Receiver Efficiency

User	Losses in fiber(L_f) dB/Km	Length of the fiber(l)	Internal losses in dB	$\eta_t = 10^{-L_f l + L_B / 10}$	Receiver Efficiency (η_d)= $1/4\pi l^2$
User1	0.2	50	10	0.01	0.00003
User2	0.2	35	7	0.03	0.00006
User3	0.2	20	4	0.1	0.00019
User4	0.2	15	3	0.25	0.00035
User5	0.2	65	13	0.002	0.000018

$$\eta_t = 10^{-L_f l + L_b / 10}$$

Where, L_f is losses in fiber in dB/km,
l is length of the fiber,
L_B is internal losses in dB.

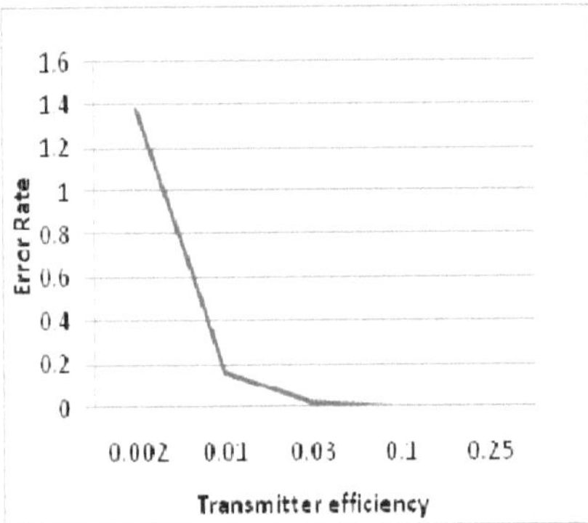

Fig. 2. Variation of Error Rate

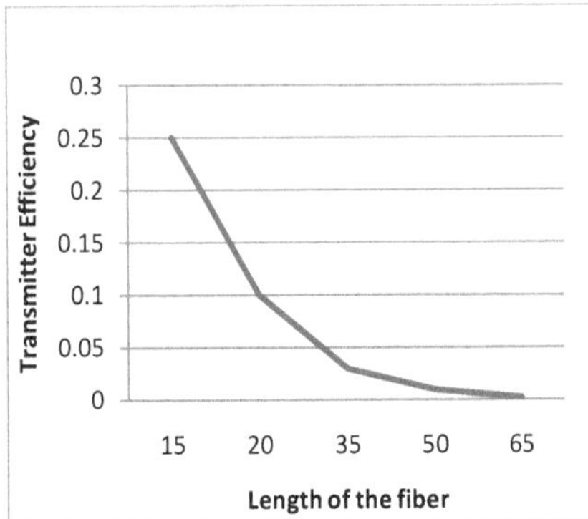

Fig. 3. Variation in Transmitter Efficiency

Two factors cause errors in raw key,

1. Imperfect detector
2. Dark count

Imperfect detector, $R_{opt} = R_{raw} * P_{opt}$.
P_{opt} is probability of wrong detection of polarization. Here P_{opt} is nil.
$R_{det} = ¼\ V\ P_{dark}$
P_{dark} is probability to get a dark count (photon detection when there are no photons)
$Q_{BER} = R_{wrong}/ (R_{wrong} + R_{right}) = R_{error}/R_{raw} = (R_{opt} + R_{det})/ R_{raw} = ¼\ VP_{dark}/ ½\ V\mu\ \eta_t\ \eta_d$
$= P_{dark}/ 2\mu\ \eta_t\ \eta_d = Q_{BERopt} + Q_{BERdet} = P_{opt} + (P_{dark}/2\mu\ \eta_t\ \eta_d)$

Table 10. Calculating Bit Error Rate

User	P_{opt}	P_{dark}	$C=2\mu\eta_t\eta_d$	$Q_{BER}= P_{opt} + (P_{dark}/C)$
User1	NIL	2	$12*10^{-9}$	$0.16*10^{9}$
User2	NIL	2	$72*10^{-9}$	$0.027*10^{9}$
User3	NIL	2	$760*10^{-9}$	$0.002*10^{9}$
User4	NIL	2	$3500*10^{-9}$	$0.0005*10^{9}$
User5	NIL	2	$1.44*10^{-9}$	$1.38*10^{9}$

Error rate based on dark count

P_{dark}	Q_{BER}
1	$0.08*10^{9}$
2	$0.16*10^{9}$
3	$0.25*10^{9}$
4	$0.33*10^{9}$

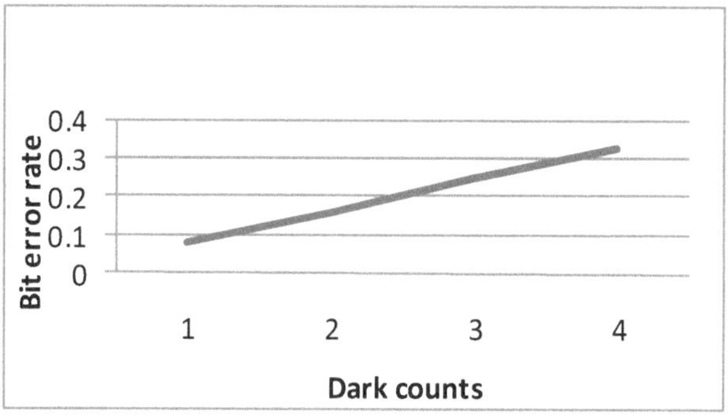

Fig. 4. Increase in error rate with respect to dark counts

Bits lost due to error correction, $r_{ec} = Q_{BER}$ (½ - $\log_2 Q_{BER}$)

Fraction of bits lost due to privacy amplification, rpa = 1 + $\log_2$ ((1 + 4 Q_{BER} – 4$Q_{BER}{}^{2)}$/ 2)

$$\text{Final bit rate} = (1 - r_{ec})\,(1 - r_{pa})\,R_{raw}$$

Noise accumulation over distance, if transmission length l increases then transfer rate η will decrease. Receiver efficiency = 1/ $4\pi r^2$, where r is the distance

Error classification:

1. Photon wrong detector
2. Detect dark counts
3. Uncorrelated photons due to imperfect photon sources.

Randomization of phase angle θ,

1 pulse = 1 state (+ive pulse and –ive pulse)

Photon number Eigen states and number of photons per signal is calculated by using Poisson distribution, $f(x) = e^{-\lambda} \lambda^x / x!$

λ=mean number of successes in a given time period

x= number of success we are interested in

e=base of natural log function (ln) ≈271828

Noise:

- Bayesian filter is used to reduce the noise.
- For error free common key, 2D parity check scheme is used in both sides confirmation.
- Any row or column that has different parities is discarded which occurred due to noise.
- To maintain privacy, diagonals of the matrix are discarded.
- For error correction, partial information of the key is used.

Uncertainty → variation from actual of bits. Variation with respect to amplitude, frequency and phase. Only using phase splitter, phase angle variation is due to noise which in turn related to uncertainty. (i.e.) either 0 may be represented as 1 or 1 may be represented as 0.

Beam splitter equations:

- If η =0, zero transmission, 100% reflection.
- If η=1, 100% transmission, zero reflection.

$\hat{g}=\sqrt{n}\,\hat{a} + \sqrt{(1-\eta)}\,\hat{c}$ $\hat{h}=\sqrt{(1-\eta)}\,\hat{a} - \sqrt{n}\,\hat{c}$

$\hat{a}$ is signal, $\hat{c}$ is noise, variance $(\hat{c})^2 = 1$

Two aspects, 1. Quality→ entropy

2. Quantity → number of bits

If any one bit varies there is entropy. Entropy data must be incorporated at a particular position of the key bits. No bit variation → zero entropy

Error rate is reduced in this protocol by reducing the number of bits to be transmitted and by selecting the basis correctly by the receiver.

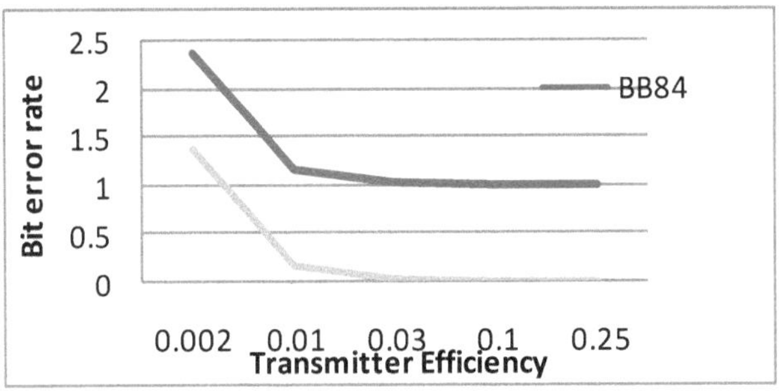

Fig. 5. Comparing the efficiency of BB84 and SRP protocol

4 Conclusion and Future Work

This work demonstrates the advantages of combining classical cryptography with quantum cryptography. Compared with classical third-party key distribution protocols, the proposed Quantum Key Distribution Protocol (QKDP) easily resists replay and passive attacks. Compared with other QKDP, the proposed schemes efficiently achieve key verification and user authentication and preserve a long-term secret key between the Trust Center and each user. Additionally, the proposed QKDP have fewer communication rounds than other protocols. Although the requirement of the quantum channel can be costly in practice, it may not be costly in the future. Moreover, the proposed QKDP have been shown secure under the random oracle model. By combining the advantages of classical cryptography with quantum cryptography, this work presents a new direction in designing QKDP. Quantum bit error rate is reduced comparing with the existing quantum cryptography protocol by improving the transmitter efficiency. The motivation of the project is sending the information between source to destination in secure manner and also becomes the protection of attackers due to communication. In that condition the trust center can generate the key for new users become register. The entire communication makes through trust center, the trust center can match both the source key and destination key. Thus identification and authentication of users takes place.

Quantum repeaters can be used in the future to overcome the distance problem in sending quibits through large networks. Collision of data in wireless medium can be avoided to send high quality of data. By overcoming these problems, the whole data itself can be sending as Quibits in the future which is going to be the next generation data transmission.

References

1. Hammond, A., Citrano, A.: MagiQ Technologies Announces New., Next Generation Quantum Cryptography Solution. MagiQ Technologies, Inc. PR 617/ 661-8300 x201 617/ 758-4140 (March 28, 2005)
2. Clifford Neuman, B., Ts'o, T.: Kerberos: An Authentication Service for Computer Networks. IEEE Communications Magazine (September 1994) 0163-6804/94
3. Blumenthal, D.J.: Photon Statistics and Basics of Propagation in Dielectric Media, ECE 228A (Fall 2007)
4. Stipčević, M.: Institut Ruder Bołković CARNet, New directions in Quantum Cryptography Users Conference (2004)
5. Tompkins, F., Wolfe, P.J.: Bayesian filtering on the stiefel manifold. Harvard University
6. García-Mata, G., Frahm, K.M.: Shor's factorization algorithm with a single control qubit and imperfections, Université de Toulouse, France (December 12, 2008)
7. Smith, G., Smolin, J.A.: Additive extensions of a quantum channel, IBM TJ Watson Research Center, 978-1-4244-2270-8/08 ©2008 IEEE
8. Imai, H., Hagiwara, M.: Error-correcting codes and cryptography. Springer, Heidelberg (2008)
9. Jim, A.-F.: Security Implications of Quantum Technologies. University of Idaho, Moscow
10. Scholz, M. Quantum Key Distribution via BB84 (November 27, 2007)
11. Gisin, N., Ribordy, G., Tittel, W., Zbinden, H.: Quantum cryptography, University of Geneva, Switzerland (February 1, 2008)
12. Hiskett, P.A., Rosenberg, D., Peterson, C.G., Hughes, R.J., Nam, S., Lita, A.E., Miller, A.J., Nordholt, J.E.: Long-distance quantum key distribution in optical fibre, Contribution of an agency of the U.S. government
13. Tittel, W.: Quantum Cryptography and Communication. Icore research report 6 (Fall 2007)
14. Goel, R.: Research Directions in Quantum Cryptography. In: International Conference on Information Technology (ITNG 2007), Howard University, 0-7695-2776-0/07 © 2007
15. Duncan, R.: An Overview of Different Authentication Methods and Protocols (October 23, 2001)
16. Levitan, S.P., Marchand, P.J., Rempel, M.A., Chiarulli, D.M., McCormick, F.B.: Computer-Aided Design of Free-Space Optoelectronic Interconnection (FSOI) Systems, University of California, San Diego
17. Kartalopoulos, S.V., Williams: Factors affecting the signal quality in optical data transmission and estimation method for BER and SNR, 0-7695-2108-8/04 © 2004 IEEE
18. Nguyen, T.M.T., Sfaxi, M.A., Ghernaouti-Hélie, S.: Integration of Quantum Cryptography in 802.11 Networks University of Lausanne, Switzerland, 0-7695-2567-9/06 © 2006 IEEE
19. Zhao, Y., Qi, B., Ma, X., Lo, H.-K., Qian, L.: Experimental Decoy State Quantum Key Distribution Over 15km, Center for Quantum Information and Quantum Control, University of Toronto, Canada (March 25, 2005)

Green Technology and Monetization of Clonization Model: The Chinese and Indian Options for Nigeria

Ezendu Ariwa[1] and Ijeoma Chichebe Ezeasor[2]

[1] London Metropolitan University, UK
[2] Institute of Development Studies,
University of Nigeria, Enugu campus, Nigeria
e.ariwa@londonmet.ac.uk

Abstract. China and India have successfully penetrated the Nigerian market. Their competitive strategies make them the biggest rivals of domestic industries and other exporters. However, close interactions between the markets have offered the option of technology cloning. The option of technology cloning as the paper suggests is based on a revolutionary concept through which technology is genetically transferred from one country to another based not on structured or previously thought out plans but driven by close interactions with the market; and executed through the efforts of the entrepreneur who adopts the technology solely for his personal gains. The paper is structured into five sections. The first section discusses the concept of technology cloning; section two reviews Nigeria's past efforts at industrialisation; section three looks at the Nigeria's movement towards the East; section four discusses existing case studies; while section five discusses the options available.

Keywords: China, India, Green Technology, Nigeria.

1 Introduction

Technology involves the use of specialised knowledge to transform ideas, natural resources, human resources and capital into functional products and services. Technological advancement is the singular factor with the capability of bridging the resource endowment gap between nations. Economic growth and sustainable human development depends on the transformative attribute of technology, also the classification of countries into the developed, emerging or developing categories also depends on the country's technological capacity, transformation and supremacy.

The successful transformation of the Chinese and Indian economy as an outcome of their technological success buttress the fact that technological advancement is still the ultimate to route to development. China and India has both created a niche for themselves in a highly competitive market as the producers of standard products at affordable cost. Although both countries technological success was propelled by the state supported industrialisation policies and plan, the same cannot be said of the Nigerian state masterminded industrialisation plans and policies. The successes of

P.V. Krishna, M.R. Babu, and E. Ariwa (Eds.): ObCom 2011, Part I, CCIS 269, pp. 726–742, 2012.

these two countries serve as an inspiration to other yet to emerge countries like Nigeria, were a new phase of industrialisation is currently going on.

The option of technology cloning as the paper suggests is based on a revolutionary concept through which technology is genetically transferred from one location/country to another based not on structured or previously thought out plans but driven by close interactions with the market; and executed through the efforts of the entrepreneur who adopts the technology solely for his personal gains. However, the gains go beyond the personal profits of the entrepreneur. The gain outwardly improves industrialisation.

During Nigeria's economic golden pre-SAP years (1970-1986), Chinese (Taiwanese) and India products were generally perceived as counterfeit not because they actually are but because of the existence of the colonial perception ascribing superiority and power to the West. However with the continuous devaluation of the *naira* (the Nigerian currency) and contraction of household income, products of Asian origin crept into the market as competitive alternatives to the original.

With the emergence of China and India as major contenders in the global economic and political arena, concerns have been raised on the impact of Chinese and Indian business practices and economic association with Africa especially as it relates to their exports to Africa (Idun-Arkhurst and Laing, 2007; Broadman, 2007; Jenkins and Edwards 2005; Goldstein et al. 2006; Ezeasor, 2008). Very few analysis and comments are complimentary (Brautigam, 2007; Mochizuki, 2000) while most predict doom for Africans manufacturing industries. Unfortunately, the disastrous state of the textile industry both in Nigerian and other African is a nearby example to such predictions.

The Chinese and Indians have long lasting economic relationships with Nigeria which spans through aid, investment and trade. The uncertainty and tensions surrounding both countries economic relations are not unfounded. But are their options in this relationship? Are their opportunities for survival and growth?

The Nigeria auto parts and pharmaceutical industry give a clear illustration of successful options created from the relationship. Close economic relations fostered by trade interactions between the Ibos and their Chinese and Indian partners is successfully driving industrialisation especially in the South Eastern part of Nigeria.

This study is based on the author's field discussions and first hand observations. The author being first of all is a Nigerian of Ibo origin and secondly, a native of Nnewi town but that does not mean that the researcher is biased as there are several similar studies on the subject. Ethnic Chinese from China and Taiwan are recognised as one people united by one culture.

This paper is generally aimed at sparking academic, trade and professional debates on the challenges, options and opportunities created by the trade domination of the Chinese and Indians not only in Nigeria but the whole of Africa. This study reviews innovative technological options created by this trade interaction. The *technology cloning* option is based on a revolutionary trend by which technology is innovatively adopted and transferred through the sole efforts of the entrepreneur.

The paper is structured into five sections. The first section discusses the concept of technology cloning; section two reviews Nigeria's past efforts at industrialisation; section three looks at the Nigeria's movement towards the East; section four discusses existing case studies; while section five discusses the options available.

2 The Concept of Technology Cloning

Technology refers to specialized knowledge used to transform inputs (raw material, labour, and capital) into outputs (products and services) or simply, knowledge or idea put to practical use (Massaquoi, 1995; 62). It involves the process of transforming science based knowledge into practical, viable, market demand driven products. It can be altered to fit into all circumstances and purposes. Access to technology not only improves the competitiveness and growth of low-income developing countries but also improves the citizens' accessibility to goods and services at competitive prices. Technology also forms part of the ideologies of modernity. Contemporary progress is equated with technological advancement and "the rationality and universality of technology substitute for diverse and 'ideological' process of politics" (Fisher, 2005).

The concept of *Technology cloning* is borrowed from the biological practice of genetically reproducing an identical offspring from the cells of the parent. The term "cloning" in the context of technology does not refer to biological cloning rather it refers to a trend were technology is transferred and adopted through close market interactions based on the sole efforts of the entrepreneur.

Biological cloning could be achieved through the processes of:

- asexual reproduction of identical individuals plants descended from the same parent
- mitotic division from an original cell to create new sets of chromosomes
- reproducing a group of DNA molecules through molecular biology techniques (molecular or DNA cloning)
- production of genetically identical animals by 'embryo splitting'
- creation of genetically identical animals by transferring the nucleus of a somatic (body) cell of a parent into an egg from which the nucleus has been removed (nuclear transfer) (Prodiversitas, 2005)

In relation to the practice of biological cloning, *technology cloning* is based on the three basic features of - a *parent* (pre-existing technology), the *transfer of cells* (movement of ideas, skills, innovation, products) from one location to another and the *creation/reproduction* of an offspring (replicated technology). These basic characteristics provide the opportunity for technology to be transferred from one advanced country to a less developed one.

A special feature of technology cloning is its ability to create young cloned off springs which are identical to the parent but possess special genetic strains (which the parent does not possess and have no need for) that fortifies it against environmental challenges which were not envisaged. These special strains make it possible for the cloned off springs to withstand hash and difficult situations in which it might find in its physically adopted environment.

Hughes (1983) likened physical environmental constraints to "reverse salient". Reverse salient is of military origin and customarily refers to a section of an advancing battle line that is continuous with other sections of the front but has fallen behind. It also refers to an extremely complex situation in which individuals, groups, material forces, and historical factors have idiosyncratic causal roles; and to delays in the growth of systems and other enterprises as they evolve toward a goal. *Reverse salient* include:

organisational, financial and physical reverse salients. In contemporary terms they are referred to as "drag", "emergent friction," "systemic inefficiency," "bottlenecks," and "technical imbalance" (Oyeyinka, 1995).

Reverse salient constraints in the evolution of the Nigerian technology system include:

- Poor ancillarization (shortages and long lead times for the delivery of spare parts and consumables);
- Lack of coordination of production, distribution, and services;
- Inadequate provision of utilities, such as those for power, transportation, and communications; and
- Lack of human resources with the broad and specific kinds of knowledge needed to define and execute projects.

For technology adopted or transferred into Nigeria, realities include:

- Power fluctuations, outages and shortages which are alien challenges in the parent country.
- Unskilled and untrained labour who blindly take charge of sophisticated technology
- Non-existent maintenance process and culture
- Low quality consumables which are used as a substitute for recommended ones
- Unavailability of spare parts

3 Nigeria's Efforts at Industrialisation

Nigeria's contact with modern industrialisation came as a result of formal trade contacts with European industrial trade merchants. Prior to this era, pre-colonial industrialisation in Nigeria was characterised by subsistence traditional hereditary hand-craft technology. Industrial production was limited to local crafts that directly suited the domestic and economic needs of the people. A distinctive feature of local industries was its proximity to source of raw materials. Technical expertise was limited to the production of brass, bronze, clay and wooden artefacts and tools, textile weaving and dyeing and calabash carving, iron works and raffia embroidery (Ajayi, 2007: 141).

Trade relations with the Europeans brought about the need for conversion of these raw materials from their natural state to preserve-able and transportable states. Local waste and quality processing industries began to spring up. Conversion into storable and transportable states gave birth to indirect services industries which specialised in the finishing operations like printing, publishing, baking and furniture works (Onyemelukwe 1983; Ajayi, 2007). Industries were step up purely to cater for the needs and demands of the European administrators, merchants and missionaries). According to Onyemelukwe (1983) 47 industrial establishments in the country in the pre-1947 period, 21 (44.71 percent) were engaged in processing activities while the remaining 26 (55.3 percent) establishments were engaged in the finishing aspects of manufacturing. Out of the 26, as many as 15 (31.9 percent) establishments were small printing works and bakeries.

The two distinctive characteristics of this era was the change in scene after World War II. The demand for traditional industrial raw materials increased tremendously following the post-war reconstruction needs and global resumption of full-scale activity in trade and industry triggering a sharp rise in the income of indigenous businessmen bring about the growth in the number of manufacturing establishments (Adegbola 1983; Onyemelukwe 1983; Ajayi, 2007: 142). Nigeria's economic transformation was constrained by low level technological capability and the small size of available indigenous skilled labour. Inadequate technological base subsequently limited industrial capability to assembly-type import substitution. The gradual assumption of political decision-making power by Nigerians during the 1950s enhanced the substitution of capital goods import or raw material imports for consumer goods (Ajayi, 2007: 142).

Industrialisation in Nigeria has since then gone past the pre-colonial and colonial growth stages. Early post colonial era was characterised by an enthusiastic incline to import substitution in favour of export-oriented processing of raw materials. Import substitution policy was meant for foreign exchange savings and reduction of dependence on foreign trade; however, it resulted in the mere assemblage of imported goods instead of local manufacturing. As at Nigeria's independence in 1960, there were only about 150 plants of medium and large-scale size in the industrial sector. Five years after independence, the number of medium and large scale firms had risen to 380 as a result of the intensification of the process of import substitution and the establishment of firms to undertake domestic manufacture of goods hitherto imported, though still largely dominated by low technology light industries. The manufacturing sector was dominated by food, beverages and tobacco; the engineering sector was dominated by metal, furniture and fixtures, structural metal products and fabricated metals while the manufacture of agricultural and special industrial machinery and equipment, household apparatus, and transport equipment contributed a low share of value added goods (Teriba et al. 1981; Ajayi, 2007:143).

However, the economic growth witnessed in this era was nipped by the political crisis that led to a civil war from 1967-1970. As a part of the reconstruction efforts, a technologically biased indigenous development plan was initiated. The Second National Development Plan, 1970-74, which had the objectives of a united, strong and self-reliant nation; a great and dynamic society; a just and egalitarian society; a land of bright and full employment for all citizens; and a free and democratic society, had as its major policy thrust:

- To promote even development and fair distribution of industries in all parts of the country;
- To ensure a rapid expansion and diversification of the industrial sector of the economy;
- To increase the incomes realised from manufacturing activity;
- To create more employment opportunities;
- To promote the establishment of industries which catered for overseas markets in order to earn foreign exchange;
- To continue the programme of import-substitution, as well as raise the level of intermediate and capital goods production;

- To initiate schemes designed to promote indigenous manpower development in the industrial sector; and
- To raise the proportion of indigenous ownership of industrial investments.

To attain these goals, government had from time to time initiated policies meant to increase industrial capacity. Throughout the changing scenes of growth (from the high industrial growth rates of the 1970s to the 1980s period of economic recession) Nigeria's industrial sector experienced major changes in production techniques, labour skills and relations; market arrangements and management practices (Olukoshi, 1996) which unfortunately did not lead to successfully industrialisation. The oil crisis of the early 1980s had critical implications on the industrial sector. Sharp reductions in foreign exchange earnings deeply affected the importation of essential raw materials, machinery and spare parts (Olukoshi, 1991).

Since the pre-SAP (1975-1985) and SAP periods (1986-1996), there has been a steady decline in manufacturing capacity utilisation. Form 1975- 1985, the average Nigerian manufacturing capacity utilisation rate decreased from 76.6 percent to 38.3 percent. In 1986, it decreased from 38.8 percent to 32.46 percent in 1996. The manufacturing sector in 1992 was reported to be "on the verge of collapse with returns to manufacturing activity being "dismally low" in relation to other sectors (Thompson, 1992:35). Nevertheless the decline had linkages with the structural adjustment economic liberalisation programmes which generally affected the manufacturing sector in other Sub-Saharan African countries (Bennell, 1998: 4). The factor of SAP deserves to be mentioned because of conflicting reports on the impact of structural adjustment policies on industrialisation. While World Bank economists were of the opinion that industrial restructuring was successful under structural reform, economists outside the confine of the World Bank and citizens who had firsthand experience felt otherwise (Stoneman, 1994:10). However, from 1997 to 2007, there has been a steady increase of capacity utilisation from 30.4 percent to 53.38 percent (CBN, 2008).

In summary, Nigeria's State driven attempts at industrialisation was grossly characterised by:

- An assembly of plants with little or no back ward linkage in the economy because the bulk of the inputs (materials, spare parts and machinery) were imported (Olukoshi, 1996; Olukoshi, 1991). PHCN (previously NEPA the monopoly State controlled electricity provider) have had several components of its system kept idle for long periods as a result of unavailability of spare parts and consumables (Oyeyinka, 1995).
- Long recessions and economic stabilisation programmes of the 1980s triggered by oil crisis and depleted foreign reserve exposed the structural weakness of import-substitution industrialisation (Olukoshi, 1996)
- Wide-ranged collapse of social and physical infrastructure compounded industrial problems. Instability in electricity power supply resulted in the use of mainly diesel powered generators as alternative energy sources. State-owned industry like the Ajaokuta Steel Company had to build its own power

plant. Also, the collapse of the railways systems contributed to the demise of the State run Nigerian Coal Corporation (Oyeyinka, 1995).

- Subsequent to the protracted fuel crisis in the 1990s, high production costs made it practically impossible for local manufactured goods to compete with imported ones.
- Misguided efforts were made to promote industrialisation without regard to comparative advantage or stage of development (Bennell, 1998).
- Reliance on conventional investment analysis and decisions which overemphasised the importance of capital-embodied resources as the vehicle of technological development. The State embarked on huge capital spending, investing in gigantic industrial complexes which were economically unviable (Ogbu, et al, 1995). In some cases like that of the adoption of the Nigerian Coal Corporation's KOPEX Project money was committed to the project before prefeasibility studies and detailed studies on technology adopted (Oyeyinka, 1995)
- Choice of industrial location was based on political consideration instead of economic viability and geographically feasibility. For example, Ajaokuta Steel Mill was politically sited in a land locked area. If that industry had been located near the sea port, transportation of exports would have been more competitive and economically. Moreover, rail way lines were constructed specifically for the complex at huge costs.
- The State practically *transplanted* industrial prototype complexes from foreign countries into Nigeria without given due consideration to technological capabilities (Ogbu, et al, 1995). There are instances of basic industrial parts abandoned over years at sea ports because there were no means of transporting them to the site. Whole systems of machineries were also abandoned because installation and operation information manuals were in languages which could not be translated.

Labour capability needed for operation, modification of existing system, commencement of systems based on existing technologies and innovating new systems based on information from pre-existing systems was not readily available. Human resources were rarely trained for start-up, maintenance and basic engineering needs. Industries were left at the hands of poor managers who had limited skill and organisational competency. Contributions were not made on basic technical features. Hence technologies were adopted by the book without alterations that could suit the physical environment.

4 Movement towards the East

It is no longer in contention that the Asians have taken over both the domestic and industrial markets in Nigeria. With the devaluation of the naira as a result of dwindling oil prices and economic reformation under the Structural Adjustment Policies (SAP), the demand for imported goods gradually moved from the West to the East.

Cutting cost became priority and traders began scouting for cheaper innovative options. Just before the current economic crisis, cost was not a major criterion for choice. Choice was all about quality, innovation, and creating market niche. To us in the developing world, cost really mattered. It mattered on the options between life and death. The cost of basic items had life threatening impacts on people. It didn't matter if drugs administered even on children were counterfeit, people had no options.

The effect of devaluation also had devastating impacts on industries motor vehicles, pharmaceuticals and chemical industries which were all import dependent. Even agro-allied industries which were able to source raw materials locally where not left out. These industries had to reckon with very high interest rates and a general decline in consumer spending power. Average capacity utilization levels stood at 45 per cent for the good performers and as low as 10 per cent for industries that had problems diversifying their sources of raw materials (Olukoshi, 1996).

4.1 Nigeria's Economic Relations with China and India China

Nigeria's unofficially trade links with china was established in 1957 through Chan Hiang-Kang a commercial officer in the Chinese Embassy in Cairo Egypt. However, ambassadorial diplomatic ties were established in 1971 while economic, scientific and technical corporation agreement was signed in 1972. From 1999 to 2006 there has been a high level of diplomatic visits in different levels at each side (see *Ogunkola, et al, 2008* for list of Chinese leaders who have visited Nigeria and list of selected agreements between Nigeria and China).

China's FDI in Nigeria increased from an average of $0.55 million in 1999-2000 to about $5.5 million in 2006. In terms of magnitude of FDI, China ranked 5th from the Asia-Pacific region behind India, Singapore, Hong Kong and Japan.

Chinese economic interests in Nigeria cover both the private and public sector. China has over 30 solely owned companies or joint ventures in Nigeria which are actively involved in oil and gas, construction, technology, consultancy services and education sectors. FDI in the private sector encompass the agro-allied industry, manufacturing and communications sector by joint venture or by wholly foreign ownership by the Chinese or in partnership with other foreign investors (Ogunkola, et al, 2008: 5).

In 2005, the official recording of FDI from China hit $1.88 million. From 2006 onwards there has been a steady increase in Chinese investment mainly because of oil and gas activities which obviously is the main interest of the Chinese. The Chinese state controlled China National Overseas Oil Company Limited (CNOOC) invested $2.3 billion for 45% stake in OPL 246 an offshore deepwater Nigerian oil field. Other interests of the Chinese in the public sector include construction of infrastructure not only as grants but as competitively tendered contracts such as in the case of the 2005 contract for the expansion the CDMA network for the state telecommunications outfit NITEL in Borno State and the construction of the Nigerian Communications Commission (NCC) building in Abuja by the Chinese Civil Engineering and Construction Company (CCECC) (Momoh, 2009). However, Trade stands out in all Chinese economic dealings in with Nigeria.

Trade Data based on the Standard International Trade Classification Revision 3 (SITC Rev. 3) show that in 2000, four broad commodities totalling US$307.7 million were exported from Nigeria to China. The main export was *Mineral Fuel and*

Lubricants representing US$273.7 million of total exports followed by *Crude materials excluding food and fuel* totalling US$33.3 million while the remaining broad commodities exported *Beverage and Live animals* and *Manufactured Goods* were represented by insignificant values of US$0.1 million and US$0.2 million respectively. In terms of significance, percentage of Nigeria's exports in 2000 to China relation to world exports, show that Nigeria exported more C*rude materials excluding food and fuel* to China as this constituted 61.1% while *Mineral Fuel and lubricants* which constituted the main exports in terms of value was a paltry 1.4% of Nigeria's total world exports. In effect, out of US$20.3 billion total Nigeria's exports, only 1.5% was exported to China (Ogunkola et al, 2008: 7-8).

However, the position of Nigeria's exports to china improved in 2005. Nigeria's total exports increased from US$20.3 billion in 2000 to US$44.4 billion in 2005. The composition of exports to China in 2005 was not very different from that of 2000 but experienced some repositioning of certain broad products. Thus, *mineral fuel and lubricants* still ranked first followed in ranking by *crude materials excluding food and fuel.* However, manufactured goods, which ranked last in 2000, displaced *food and live animals* while two broad products; *chemicals, and miscellaneous manufactures*, featured in 2005. Also, exports of *crude materials excluding food and fuel* reduced between 2000 and 2005. The proportion of Nigeria's exports destined for China reduced in 2005 even when the absolute value showed an increase. Nigeria's export to China in 2005 was 1.2% of its total exports which represented a reduction pared to 2000.

Nigeria's total imports increased from US$5.3 billion in 1996 through US$5.8billion in 2000 to US$17.7billion in 2005 (Table 3.2). The dramatic increase of Nigeria's total imports between 2000 and 2005 was also reflected in the country's imports from China which rose phenomenally from as little as US$252million in 2000 to US$2.3billion in 2005.

Nigeria imports almost all of the broad categories of products from China. In 2005, imports of machinery and transport equipment ranked first followed by manufactured goods, miscellaneous manufactures, chemicals and food and live animals. In trend terms, the composition of Nigeria's imports changed. In 1996 for example, chemical products imports ranked second only to machinery and transport equipment while in 2000, manufactured products replaced chemicals in second place. Machinery and transport equipment imports thus ranked highest in all the reference years.

This picture altered when China's share of Nigeria's total import is considered. While that share rose successively from 1996 to 2005 from 3.5% to 13%, not all broad categories of goods imported from China maintained such consistent increase. This is especially the case of mineral fuels/lubricants, and animal/ vegetable oil/fat/wax. Furthermore, when the broad categories are considered, Nigeria imported more of miscellaneous manufactures from China relative to the rest of the world. This rose from 7.8% in 1996 to 30.6% in 2005. China's share of Nigeria's imports also rose consecutively in food and live animals, as well as beverages and tobacco (both minimally); crude materials excluding food and fuel, manufactured goods, machinery and transport equipment, and miscellaneous manufactures (all four substantially). Thus, in terms of stakeholders' analysis, countries which hitherto exported these products to Nigeria have lost their market share in Nigeria to China as Nigeria increasingly look towards China for the importation of these products (Ogunkola, et al 2008: 8-9).

Table 1. China's Share of Nigeria's Imports (US$ million)

		1996		2000		2005		1996	2000	2005
SITC R. 3	Product Name	World	China	World	China	World	China	China's share of Nigeria's imports		
0	Food & live animals	885.9	3.5	1098.0	12.7	2140.6	29.8	0.4	1.2	1.4
1	Beverages and tobacco	10.8	0.0	34.2	0.3	69.4	0.7	0.0	0.9	1.0
2	Crude mater.ex food/fuel	121.9	1.8	94.0	1.8	120.4	8.9	1.5	1.9	7.4
3	Mineral fuel/lubricants	70.9	0.0	100.8	0.3	2396.7	1.0	0.0	0.3	0.04
4	Animal/veg oil/fat/wax	37.2	0.0	23.3	0.05	64.4	0.04	0.1	0.2	0.1
5	Chemicals/products n.e.s	981.3	59.6	1176.5	46.3	2085.5	174.6	6.1	3.9	8.4
6	Manufactured goods	1031.5	30.7	1095.5	53.8	3297.8	566.0	3.0	4.9	17.2
7	Machinery/transp equipmt	1876.7	66.2	1955.1	98.1	6600.0	1229.7	3.5	5.0	18.6
8	Miscellaneous manuf arts	296.1	23.2	238.4	39.4	948.7	290.1	7.8	16.5	30.6
9	Commodities nes	0.0	0.0	0.0	0.0	0.0	0.0	0.0	0.0	0.0
	Total Imports	5312.1	185.1	5815.8	252.7	17723.5	2300.8	3.5	4.3	13.0

Source: World Integrated Trade Solution (WITS) database, 2007 culled from Ogunkola et al (2008: 9)

India

Nigeria and India are traditionally related as both countries were colonies of the British Empire. India established its Nigerian diplomatic mission in 1958, two years before Nigeria's 1960s independence. After the 1962 State visit of the Indian Prime Minister Jawaharlal Nehru, diplomatic relations between the two States have immensely improved with Nigeria's return to democratic rule in 1999. In 2007, Dr. Manmohan Singh became the first Indian leader to visits Nigeria after 45 years (see High Commission of India, 2007 for details on bilateral visits and trade visits).

Nigeria and India are also culturally and politically similar; both countries have very diverse religious and ethnic populations and are each the largest democracies in their respective regions. Contrary to the moral support maintained by some African states regarding the 1962 Sino-Indian border conflict, Nigeria under Sir Abubakar Tafawa Balewa vehemently and openly supported India's position and called for a total condemnation of China's action against India (see Kura, 2009 for details on Nigeria's political and socio-cultural relations with Nigeria)

In terms of economic interests, India's investments in Nigeria include manufacturing, trading and services, pharmaceutical, plastics, engineering and Information Communication Technology. Indian's main imports from Nigeria include: Crude oil, Metal Scrap, Wood, Cashew nuts, Iron and Steel, Cotton and Gum Arabic while Nigeria imports more pharmaceuticals from India than another African country.

Nigeria's trade with India increased from US$293.71 million to US$875 million and substantially climbed to US$875 million. Between April and September 2006, Nigeria's exports to India amounted to US$3.9 billion and climbed to US$6-7.9 billion in 2007. Crude oil accounts for 96% India's exports from Nigeria at an average of 40,000 barrels per day. 20% of all India's crude requirements are imported from Nigeria (This Day, 2007).

Oil is of great significance to indo-Nigerian economic relations. In its formative years, the balance of trade was in favour of India because of the volume of Nigeria's imports from India. However, due to India's technological development vis-à-vis its increasing volume of crude oil imports from Nigeria, the balance of trade between the two countries has increasingly shifted in favour of Nigeria (Kura, 2009:21).

Table 2. India-Nigeria Trade

	1998–1999	**1999–2000**	**2000–2001**	**2001–2002**	**2002–2003**
Indian exports to Nigeria	248.09	293.71	384.66	563.15	449.09
Indian Imports from Nigeria	1177.73	2928.39	2704.18	2485.00	78.13 2389.00*
Total	**1425.82**	**3222.11**	**3088.84**	**3048.15**	**2916.21****

Source: *Kura, (2009)*

India historically has substantial investments in Nigeria. K. Chellaram and Sons (Nigeria) a private trading company was set up in Nigeria in 1923. Indian publicly owned companies also in the banking, machine tool manufacturing and consultancy services sector. The Indo-Nigerian Mercantile Bank was opened towards the end of 1981 with an upfront capital investment of USD3 million with 40% of the capital provided by the Indian State Bank (ARB, 1981). Similarly, the Hindustan Machine Tools Company (HMT) is a partner in Nigerian Machine Tool Ltd., which produces machine tools for Nigeria. In addition, USD5 million in aid was provided to Nigeria by Indian authorities in order to enhance the revitalisation of the Nigerian machine tools industry at Osogbo (Kura, 2009).

5 Case Studies

Trade relations between Nigerian traders of Ibo origin with their Chinese and Indian counter-parts offer good examples of how commerce transforms to industrialisation. The Ibos of eastern Nigeria are well known for their entrepreneurial capabilities (Olutayo, 1999) and are economically visible all over Nigeria and the West African Coast. They are mainly associated with trading activities and were actively engaged in 19th century trading with the Europeans. They were selected as a case study because of their success in transforming their trading relationship with the Chinese (Taiwanese) and Indians into manufacturing ventures (Brautigam, 1998, Zeng, 2006: 10; UNCTAD 1998:7).

Auto-parts Industry

The transformation of the ethnic town of Nnewi to a metropolitan industrial cluster provides a good case for study. The people of Nnewi were previously associated mainly with retail and whole sale trading, export, import and transportation. However, currently they are mainly acknowledged and respected for their technical capabilities. Their foray into trading and technical skills acquisition as against agro-production is directly linked to scarcity of fertile land.

The domination of Nnewi indigenes in the Nigerian mass transportation sector (the Odimegwu- Ojukwus' – Ojukwu Transport company, the Ilodibes'- Ekene di Chukwu Transport and the Ubajiaka's – Izuchukwu Transport) and the growing demand for auto spare parts brought about the large concentration of Nnewi people in the auto parts trading. The current location of the auto parts market in Nnewi town came as a result of disagreements between the Nnewi people and the indigenes of Onitsha over land and market lease after the Nigeria civil war. The refusal of the Nnewi traders to renew their land lease facilitated the movement of the auto parts market from Onitsha to Nnewi.

Auto parts trade relations first started with the Europeans who dominated the automobile industry and whose cars were in use as at then. Asian contact came with the importation of Toyota cars and the subsequent importation of spare parts form Japan. Nnewi traders' contacts with the Asians started with the Japanese who supplied them with Toyota spare parts. Subsequently with the devaluation of the naira, traders sourced for cheaper auto spare part brands.

First attempts at innovation came with the entrance of the Taiwanese with their counterfeit copies of the original which came at reduced costs. The Taiwanese came into the scene with marketing innovations which strongly favoured the Nnewi traders. Instead of merely supplying the traders with counterfeit copies in similar packaging with the original, the Taiwanese manufactured spare parts for the traders in their own trade names. This marketing strategy became successful instantly. Traders competed among themselves for an opportunity to introduce products which could dominate the market in their own trade names.

Competition was driven more by ego than for the economic growth of the town. Traders intensified their efforts in search of fresh avenues to produce and market auto parts identified with their brand names. Wealthy merchants not satisfied with trading alone scouted the whole of Asia looking for technical assistance. Armed with technical support from the Chinese, trading outfits diversified into manufacturing.

Closer interactions with small and medium scale of factories of Taiwanese origin changed the mindset of the traders whose perceptions of industries were based on publicly owned gigantic, capital intensive and techno managerial tasking firms. Motivated by the Taiwanese small scale industrial model, Nnewi traders invested in machineries which were assembled in Nnewi with the help of their Chinese technical partners.

With the help of the Chinese, Nnewi town has transformed into a successful industrial cluster which has split over not only to neighbouring towns but to the whole of the Southeast. Nnewi auto parts industry is currently made up of auto-related firms that manufacture spare parts for motorcars, bicycles and motorcycles; assemble motor cycle and bicycle, manufacture tubes and tyres; fabricate vehicle body and consumables like lubricants. Most importantly the first made-in-Nigeria car is been expected in the near future from Innonson Technical Nnewi.

One may wish to ask what makes the Chinese trade relationship special. The relationship is definitely special because it is the close market interactions with the Chinese that steered the industrialisation of Nnewi and its subsequent transformation into a prosperous multi-ethnic town. Similar interactions with the Germans through Mercedes Benz or the Japanese through Toyota could not propel that drive. In comparison, all pervious state motor assembling industries established under the import-substitution era were all unsuccessful. The last surviving industry, Anambra Motor Manufacturing Company (ANAMCO) is right now on the verge of collapse. (See Brautigam, 2007 and 1998 and Zeng, 2006 for similar studies on the Chinese and the Nnewi industrial cluster).

Pharmaceutical industry

India's industrial presence in Nigeria predates that of the Chinese. Trade and technical relations span a wide category of goods and sectors. However, the pharmaceutical industry stands out in this relationship. Indians emergence in Outward Foreign Direct Investment (OFDI) can be traced to its Nigerian joint ventures - first with India's largest pharmaceutical company Ranbaxy in 1977, and the other with Unique Pharmaceutical Laboratories in 1982 (Pradhan, 2008:7).

Early interactions with the Indian pharmaceutical companies and Nigeria were limited to joint ventures which were motivated by "matching regulatory requirements with that of India" and the "occurrence of diseases which were more or less similar" (Dixit and Yadav 2008: 14). However, from the late 1980s to date, interactions have been more export based. The reason for this been the devaluation of the naira and the need for alternative sources of cheaper drugs.

Unlike the United States and Europe, where drug importation and distribution regulations are strict, regulations are still relatively loose. In Nigeria, drugs are merchandise that can be purchased from the open market in spite of recent efforts made by the National Food and Drug Administration and Control Agency (NAFDAC) to sanitize and regulate the importation and distribution of drugs.

Trading in pharmaceuticals is controlled by the Ibos. Patent medicine dealership is openly ascribed to the Ibos. All over the country, Ibos dominate the trade and distribution of drugs. For any Ibo visitor to an alien city or village, his first point of contact with his Ibo brothers is from the patent medicine stores. In fact, previously in the northern parts of Nigeria, they were used as embassies or post office addresses. Ibos domination of the domestic trading and distribution of drugs made automatically lead to their dominance in the drug distribution business.

The Ibo trader's interactions with the Indian market was also encouraged with the level of technological advancement which the Indians had attained (Mehrota et al, 1991:256; UNIDO, 1975) and its lenient bureaucratic policies. Unlike the developed countries that required certain standardisation, custom requirements and trade registration, the Indian required less. While traders were required to meet certain satisfactory trade and marketing requirements like registration as sole distributors for the Nigerian, West African or African markets, the Indians entertained all market demands.

However, the indulgence guaranteed by this lenient trade regime directly affected the proliferation of Nigeria with sub-standard drugs. The drug market was dominated with Indian drugs form smaller pharmaceutical companies which contained non-active ingredients. The traders simply placed orders for drugs exclusively for the Nigerian market on their personal prescriptions and standards. Newton et al (2006) projected that up to 36% of the drugs labelled as containing artesunate (an effective anti-malarial) contain no active ingredient. In 2002, WHO estimated the total percentage of fake or adulterated drugs in Nigeria much higher, at 70% (Bate, 2008: 6).

Eventually, when the NAFDAC began clamping down on adulterated drugs from the year 2000, Indian companies simply modified their market to fit in to the new regulations. It was required that Nigerian bound drugs should first of all be registered with NAFDAC for certification and onward issuance of NADFAC numbers. This became the basic requirement for any drug, food or cosmetics product to be sold in Nigeria. Unlike, other developed countries who hesitated in complying with the regulation, the Indians quickly complied. That singular action ended the U.S. dominance of the Nigerian drug market.

Since the introduction of the new regulatory regime, local drug importers have been encouraged to domestically manufacture drugs. Based on their previous trade relations with the Indians, most machinery, ingredients and technical expertise was imported from India. These new companies have also started innovating new drugs based on locally sourced materials. However, unlike the Nnewi auto parts industrial cluster, these new industries are scattered all over Nigeria. But they are predominantly located in the Lagos-Ogun industrial axis and the South Eastern parts of the country.

6 Options

Chinese and Indian economic interactions in Nigeria as well as other African countries are based on unequal footing. There are no doubts that local production in Africa will completely collapse if protection measures are not put in place. Trade liberalisation has devastating effects in Africa where cheap imports continuously stamp out local production. However, the greatest threat comes from the Chinese and Indians whose products are averagely cheaper than other imports but can easily be mistaking for the original product which they copy.

As debates continue to mount on the effects cheap Chinese and Indian imports have on African industries, efforts should also be channelled into researching resultant innovative options available. After all trading is an intermediary between innovation, industrialisation and technological advancement.

As observed from the cases above, Nigeria has the chances of taking full advantage of opportunities which trade interactions avail. Cloning technology can play a positive role in nurturing low-tech industrial development. Cloning technology could provide options which can:

- Transform local scientific knowledge into innovative complex technology
- Generate a successful phase of industrialisation driven by the private sector
- Generate innovative ideas and knowledge

- Transform Nigeria from an oil dependent economy to a multi-product economy
- Spur resultant innovations which will transform the existing import dependent market to an equally competitive export driven
- Provide employment for the restive youths
- Lower the prices of basic goods
- Increase peoples accessibility to basic products
- Expand household incomes
- Revitalise the idle industrial parks
- Offer renewed hope for improving the competitiveness and growth of the economy

Conclusion

Nigeria's efforts at industrialisation were based on the priority attached to it by the State. Most efforts were channelled to huge capital intensive project which would help the State tap into mineral resources. Distinctions were not made between political and economic decisions. Industries were allocated to political regions without giving considerations to physical infrastructure and human resource available. Choice of technology was mainly based on the political whims of the state policy analysts without having good consideration for feasibility and viability of the technology adopted. However, form what was deduced from the cases of the private sector, technology is adopted based on cost and practicality through market interactions.

Technological advancement is the key to industrial, economic and sustainable development. Cloning technologies from market rivals can turn around the economic platform on which low-income developing countries operate. However, for cloned technology to be effective and sustainable in any given environment, necessary alterations must be made.

References

1. Adegbola, K.: Manufacturing Industries. In: Oguntoyinbo, J.S. (ed.) A Geography of Nigerian Development, 2nd edn., pp. 326–338. Heinemann Educational Books Ltd., Ibadan (1983)
2. Ajayi, D.D.: Recent Trends and Patterns in Nigeria's Industrial Development. Africa Development, Council for the Development of Social Science Research in Africa (CODESRIA) XXXII(2), 139–155 (2007)
3. Bate, R.: Local Pharmaceutical Production in Developing Countries: How Economic Protectionism Undermines Access to Quality Medicines. In: Campaign for Fighting Diseases Discussion Paper no. 1. International Policy Network, London (2008)
4. Brautigam, D.: Chinese Aid and African Development. Macmillan Press (1998)
5. Brautigam, D.: Flying Geese or Hidden Dragon? Chinese Business and African Industrial Development, Draft chapter, prepared for The Politics of Contemporary China-Africa Relations (March 2007)
6. Bennell, P.: Industrial Restructuring in Africa during the 1990s: Outcomes and Prospects, African Development Report (1998)
7. Broadman, H.: Africa's Silk Road: China and India's New Economic Frontier. World Bank, Washington (2007)

8. Central Bank of Nigeria (CBN). Statistical Bulletin, Golden Jubilee Edition. CBN, Abuja
9. Dixit, M.R., Yadav, S.: Motivations, Capability Handicaps and Firm Responses in the Early Phase of Internationalization from Emerging Economies: A study in the Indian Pharmaceutical Industry, W.P. No.2008-02-05. Indian Institute of Management, Ahmedabad, India (2008)
10. Ezeasor, I.C.: The Impact of China's Economic Interest in Africa. Department of Finance, University of Nigeria, Enugu (2008) (unpublished work)
11. Fisher, E.: Upgrading Market Legitimation: Revisiting Habermas's 'Technlogy as Ideology' in Neoliberal Times', Fast Capitalism (2005), http://www.uta.edu/huma/agger/fastcapitalism/2_2/fisher.html (retrieved September 6, 2009)
12. Goldstein, A., Pinaud, N., Reisen, H., Chen, X.: The Rise of China and India. What's in it for Africa? OECD Development Centre Studies, Paris (2006)
13. High Commission of India, Basic Facts about Nigeria. Indian High Commission, Abuja (2007)
14. Hughes, T.P.: The Evolution of Large Technological Systems. In: Bigker, et al. (eds.), The Social Construction of Technological System: New Directions in the Sociology and History of Technology (1983)
15. Idun-Arkhurst, I., Laing, J.: The Impact of Chinese Presence in Africa. Africa Practice, London (2007)
16. Jenkins, R., Edwards, C.: The Effect of China and India's growth and Trade Liberalisation on Poverty in Africa. Department for International Development (DFID), London (2005)
17. Kura, S.B.: Nigeria-India Economic, Political and Socio-Cultural Relations: Critical Reflections for Continuous Mutual Co-Operation. IJAPS 5(1), 1–31 (2009)
18. Mehrotra, N.N., Tandon, S., Dhawan, B.N.: Recent Developments in the Drugs and Pharmaceuticals in India. In: Srivastava, U.S. (ed.) Glimpses of Science in India, pp. 256–269. Malhotra Publishing House, New Delhi (1991)
19. Mochizuki, K.: Chinese Business as an Emergent Actor in Nigerian Economy (2001), http://www.ide.go.jp/English/Publish/Download/Ars/1863ra00000072zq-att/1863ra000000732n.pdf
20. Momoh, S.: How tidy is Nigeria-China relations? BusinessDay Monday (January 12, 2009), http://www.businessdayonline.com/index.php
21. Newton, P.N., Green, M.D., Fernández, F.M., Day, N.P.J., White, N.J.: Counterfeit Anti-Infective Drugs. The Lancet Infectious Diseases 6(9), 602–613 (2006)
22. Ogbu, O.M., Oyeyinka, B.O., Mlawa, H. M. (eds.): Technology Policy and Practice in Africa. International Development Research Centre (IDRC), Ottawa Canada (1995)
23. Ogunkola, O.E., Bankole, A.S., Adewuyi, A.: China-Nigeria Economic Relations, AERC Scoping Studies on China-Africa Relations, Revised Report submitted to the African Economic Research Consortium (AERC) (February 2008)
24. Olukoshi, A.: An Assessment of the Economic Recovery Programme of the Nigerian State on the Manufacturing Sector: A Kano Case Study, Final Report to the Social Science Council of Nigeria, Ibadan (July 1991)
25. Olukoshi, A.: Economic Crisis, Structural Adjustment And The Coping Strategies of Manufacturers In Kano, Nigeria, Discussion Papers 77, United Nations Research Institute For Social Development (UNRISD) (September 1996)
26. Olutayo, O.A.: The Igbo Entrepreneur in the Political Economy of Nigeria. African Study Monographs 20(3), 147–174 (1999)

27. Onyemelukwe, J.O.C.: Structural and Locational Characteristics of Manufacturing. In: Oguntoyinbo, J.S., Areola, O.O., Filani, M. (eds.) A Geography of Nigerian Development, 2nd edn., pp. 296–310. Heinemann Educational Books Ltd., Ibadan (1983)
28. Oyeyinka, B.O.: Management of Technological Change in Africa: The Coal Industry in Nigeria. In: Ogbu, O.M., Oyeyinka, B.O., Mlawa, H.M. (eds.) Technology Policy and Practice in Africa. International Development Research Centre (IDRC), Ottawa (1995)
29. Pradhan, J.P.: Overcoming Innovation Limits through Outward FDI: The Overseas Acquisition Strategy of Indian Pharmaceutical Firms, MPRA Paper No. 12362 (2008), http://mpra.ub.uni-muenchen.de/12362/
30. ProDiversitas, What is Cloning Useful for? (2009), http://www.prodiversitas.bioetica.org/clonacion2.htm
31. Stoneman, C.: Policy Reform or Industrialisation? The Choice in Zimbabwe. In: Adhikari, R., Kirkpatrick, C., Weiss, J. (eds.) Industrial & Trade Policy Reform in Developing Countries. Manchester University Press (1992)
32. Teriba, O., Edosien, E.C., Kayode, M.O.: The Structure of the Nigerian Economy. In: Teriba, O., Edosien, E.C., Kayode, M.O. (eds.) The Structure of Manufacturing Industry in Nigeria, pp. 13–28. University of Ibadan Press, Ibadan (1981)
33. United Nations Conference on Trade and Development (UNCTAD). Selected Policy Issues, Measures and Programmes on Inter-Firm Partnerships, TD/B/COM.3/EM.4/2, Trade and Development Board, UNCTAD, Geneva (1998)
34. United Nations Industrial Development Organisation (UNIDO). The Steps Involved in Establishing a Pharmaceutical Industry in Developing Countries. UNIDO, Vienna (1975)
35. Zeng, D.Z.: Knowledge, Technology, and Cluster-Based Growth in Africa: Findings from 11 Case Studies of Enterprise Clusters in Africa. In: Zeng, D.Z. (ed.) Knowledge, Technology, and Cluster-based Growth in Africa. The World Bank. WBI Development Studies Washington, DC (2006)

Emitted Sound Amplitude Analysis Using Hilbert Huang Transformation for Cutting Tool Flank Wear Prediction

Emerson Raja Joseph[1], Loo Chu Kiong[2], Lim Way Soong[3], and S. Purushothaman[4]

[1] Faculty of Engineering and Technology, Multimedia University, Malaysia
emerson.raja@mmu.edu.my
[2] Faculty of Information Science and Technology, Multimedia University, Malaysia
ckloo@mmu.edu.my
[3] Faculty of Engineering and Technology, Multimedia University, Malaysia
wslim@mmu.edu.my
[4] Udaya School of Engineering, Kanyakumari district-629204, India
dr.purushothaman.s@gmail.com

Abstract. In this paper, the relationship between emitted sound amplitude and tool flank wear was investigated during turning operation by using Hilbert Huang Transform (HHT). For this purpose, a series of experiments using carbide insert cutting tools and stainless steel work pieces were conducted in a conventional turning machine. The emitted sounds from fresh, slightly worn and severely worn tools were recorded at the sampling rate of 44100/sec using a highly sensitive directional microphone. Each recorded multi-component sound signal was decomposed into several intrinsic mode functions (IMFs) using Empirical mode decomposition (EMD). The instantaneous frequencies with time and their amplitudes were obtained by applying Hilbert transform on each IMF. From the marginal spectrums produced using selected IMFs it was observed that there was an increase in sound amplitude with increasing tool wears. Hence it can be concluded that cutting tool flank wear prediction is possible using emitted sound by HHT.

Keywords: Tool flank wear, emitted sound, HHT, EMD, marginal spectrum.

1 Introduction

Choosing suitable machining methods and tooling systems is important to achieve dimensional accuracy and surface quality of the work piece during turning operation. From an economic point of view, maximum tool life is also another requirement besides these requirements. In addition, cutting conditions, cutter geometry, tool and work piece material, chip formation, and tool wear are parameters that affect production performance significantly. The most important one among these parameters that influence production performance is the tool wear [1, 2]. Tool flank wear can be measured visually by using tool makers microscope. However, in practice, tool life is estimated by Taylor equation [3] instead of making cumbersome measurements. Indirect method of tool condition monitoring is based on the acquisition of measured

P.V. Krishna, M.R. Babu, and E. Ariwa (Eds.): ObCom 2011, Part I, CCIS 269, pp. 743–752, 2012.

values of process variables (such as cutting force, temperature, vibration, spindle motor current, acoustic emission, surface roughness and emitted sound) and the relationship between tool wear and these values [1]. Ghani et al. [4] presented a study of tool life, surface finish and vibration, while turning nodular cast iron using ceramic tool. They concluded that surface finish was found to be almost constant with the progression of the flank wear under different cutting conditions. They also observed that, the vibration during cutting decreases as the speed increases and at low depth of cut, the vibration remains almost constant with the increase of flank wear. Ming-Chyuan et al. [5] used audible sound generated from the cutting process as a source for monitoring tool flank wear during turning and concluded that the asperity height is found to decrease as tool wear increases. Delio, Tlusty, and Smith [6] concluded that audible sound is a good method for detecting chatter during the milling process. Andrews et al. [7, 8] applied SVD analysis on the audible sound generated from the cutting process and concluded that the tool flank wear can be predicted from this audible sound.

Sound monitoring is one technology that has not been extensively investigated for tool wear monitoring, even though it is extensively used by machine tool operators for decision making [1, 5]. One major issue related to application of this technology in industry is the ability to protect the sensor from the hazardous machining environment. Cutting fluids or metal chips may damage the sensor. This can be prevented by protecting the sensor with gauze, for example. Noise from adjacent machines, motors, conveyors, etc. or processes may contaminate the signals. This effect can be reduced by using noise cancellation methods in the signal processing algorithm or by using HHT analysis as used in this paper. In this paper, emitted sound is investigated as a basis for tool flank wear monitoring and HHT analysis is done on this sound signal to study the relationship between the sound signal generated from the cutting process and the progression of tool wear.

Traditional data analysis methods such as Fourier analysis are all based on linear and stationary assumptions, i.e. the signal to be processed must be linear and temporarily stationary; otherwise, resulting Fourier spectrum will make little physical sense [9]. In addition, it represents the global rather than any local properties of the signal because it employs a convolution integral through which the signal is decomposed in terms of sine and cosine functions covering uniformly the whole data span [10]. On the other hand, the time-frequency analysis such wavelet transform can generate both time and frequency information of a signal simultaneously through mapping one dimensional signal to a two-dimensional time-frequency plane. However, the wavelet transform still has some inevitable deficiencies, including the interference terms, border distortion and energy leakage, all of which will generate a lot of small undesired spikes all over the frequency scales and make the results confusing and difficult to interpret [11]. Hence, new methods are needed to analyze the data from non-linear and non-stationary processes.

The Hilbert-Huang Transform (HHT) derived from the principles of Empirical Mode Decomposition (EMD) and the Hilbert Transform is considered as a new method. It is a two step process, first, the given multi-component signal is decomposed into a set of complete and almost orthogonal components called intrinsic mode function (IMF) by using EMD process. Since the IMF is almost mono-component it can determine all the instantaneous frequencies from nonlinear and non-stationary signal. Secondly the local energy of each instantaneous frequency can be derived through the Hilbert Transform [9, 10]. It seems that the HHT has the potential of becoming a perfect tool for analyzing non-stationary and nonlinear data [12]. Yuping Zhang [13] successfully applied this new signal processing technique in analyzing vibration signals and faults diagnosis of roller bearing. An attempt is also made here to investigate the possibility of using HHT for tool flank wear monitoring.

2 Research Methodology

Given below are the four major steps used in this research work.

1. Recording the emitted sound signal during turning operation with fresh, slightly and severely worn tools by using an ICP microphone.
2. Decomposing each multi-component sound signal into mono-component IMFs by using EMD.
3. Obtaining the local energy (amplitude) of each instantaneous frequency found in IMF by applying Hilbert Transform.
4. Plotting the energy found in all the IMFs and constructing the marginal spectrums on selected IMFs for final analysis.

The following sub sections explain the principle behind Hilbert Huang Transform, Empirical Mode Decomposition and Marginal Spectrum.

2.1 Hilbert Huang Transform

The physically meaningful way to describe the system is in terms of the instantaneous frequency, which will reveal the intra wave frequency modulations [10]. The easiest way to extract or compute the instantaneous frequency of a mono-component signal is by using Hilbert Transform. For an arbitrary signal or time series $x(t)$, its Hilbert transform $y(t)$ is defined as

$$y(t) = \frac{P}{\pi} \int_{-\infty}^{+\infty} \frac{x(\tau)}{t - \tau} d\tau \qquad (1)$$

where P is the Cauchy principal value of the singular transform. From Eq.(1), it can be seen that the Hilert transform is defined as the convolution of the signal $x(t)$ with $1/t$. Therefore, the Hilbert transform is capable of identifying the local properties of $x(t)$. Coupling the $x(t)$ and $y(t)$, we can have the analytic signal $z(t)$ of $x(t)$, as

$$z(t) = x(t) + iy(t) = a(t)e^{i\varphi(t)} \qquad (2)$$

with

$$a(t) = \left[x^2(t) + y^2(t)\right]^{1/2}, \varphi(t) = \arctan(y(t)/x(t)). \qquad (3)$$

where $a(t)$ is the instantaneous amplitude of $x(t)$, which can reflect how the energy of the $x(t)$ varies with time, and the $\Phi(t)$ is the instantaneous phase of $x(t)$. The controversial instantaneous frequency $\omega(t)$ is defined as the time derivative of the instantaneous phase $\phi(t)$, as follows:

$$\omega(t) = d\varphi(t) / d(t). \tag{4}$$

Because the instantaneous frequency is defined through differentiation rather than integration it appears to be local and can describe intra-wave frequency modulation. Therefore Eq. (4) is useful in extracting instantaneous frequencies from any non-stationary signals. However, Eq. (4)is only valid in obtaining the instantaneous frequency of a signal in a given time frame if the signal is mono-component within the time frame. If the inspected signal is multi-component within the defined time frame, the result of the instantaneous frequency will be distorted [10]. Unfortunately, in almost all of the practical applications, the inspected signals are hardly mono-component but multi-component. Therefore to make the instantaneous frequency applicable, the key is the ability to decompose the signal into some individual mono-component signals. The Empirical Mode Decomposition provides such decomposition ability.

2.2 Empirical Mode Decomposition

The data, depending on its complexity, may have many different coexisting modes of oscillation at the same time. Each of these oscillatory modes is represented by an Intrinsic Mode Function (IMF) with the following definitions [10].

(a) In the whole data set, the number of extrema and the number of zero-crossings must either equal or differ at most by one, and
(b) At any point, the mean value of the envelope defined by the local maxima and the envelope defined by the local minima is zero.

To extract the IMF from a given data set, the sifting process is implemented as follows [10]. First, identify all the local maxima, and then connect all of the local maxima by a cubic spline line as the upper envelope. Then, repeat the procedure for the local minima to produce the lower envelope. The upper and lower envelopes should cover all the data between them. Their mean is designated $m_1(t)$, and the difference between the data and $m_1(t)$ is $h_1(t)$, i.e.

$$x(t) - m_1(t) = h_1(t) \tag{5}$$

The sifting process has to be repeated as many times as it is required to reduce the extracted signal to an IMF. In the subsequent sifting process steps $h_1(t)$ is treated as the data; then:

$$h_1(t) - m_{11}(t) = h_{11}(t) \tag{6}$$

where $m_{11}(t)$ is the mean of the upper and lower envelops of $h_1(t)$. This process can be repeated up to k times; $h_{1k}(t)$ is then given by

$$h1_{(k-1)}(t) - m_{1k}(t) = h_{1k}(t) \tag{7}$$

After each processing step, checking must be done on whether the number of zero crossings equals the number of extrema. The resulting time series is the first IMF, and then it is designated as $c_1(t) = h_{1k}(t)$. The first IMF component from the data contains the highest oscillation frequencies found in the original data x(t) .

This first IMF is subtracted from the original data, and this difference, is called a residue $r_1(t)$ by:

$$x(t) - c_1(t) = r_1(t) \tag{8}$$

The residue $r_1(t)$ is taken as if it was the original data and we apply to it again the sifting process. The process of finding more intrinsic modes $c_i(t)$ continues until the last mode is found. The final residue will be a constant or a monotonic function.

$$x(t) = \sum_{j=1}^{n} c_j(t) + r_n(t) \tag{9}$$

Thus, one achieves a decomposition of the data into n-empirical IMF modes, plus a residue, $r_n(t)$, which can be either the mean trend or a constant.

2.3 Marginal Spectrum

Eq. (2) enables us to represent the amplitude and the instantaneous frequency, in a three-dimensional plot, in which the amplitude is the height in the time-frequency plane. This time-frequency distribution is designated as the Hilbert spectrum $H(\omega,t)$:

$$H(\omega,t) = \mathrm{Re}\sum_{i=1}^{n} a_i(t) e^{j\int w_i(t)dt} \tag{10}$$

With the Hilbert spectrum defined, the marginal spectrum, $h(\omega)$, can be defined as

$$h(\omega) = \int_0^T H(\omega,t)dt \tag{11}$$

where T is the total data length.

The Hilbert spectrum offers a measure of amplitude contribution from each frequency and time, while the marginal spectrum offers a measure of the total amplitude contribution from each frequency [6, 9]. Therefore, local marginal spectrum of each IMF component is given as

$$h_i(\omega) = \int_0^T H_i(\omega,t)dt \tag{12}$$

The local marginal $h_i(\omega)$ spectrum offers a measure of the total amplitude contribution from the frequency. According to marginal spectrum, the characteristic amplitude of the tool flank wear can be easily recognized and thereby the condition of the tool wear can easily be determined.

3 Experimental Set-Up

The photography of actual experimental setup is shown in Fig. 1. In the present experiment, the noise due to the machining was recorded by a microphone, and in contrast with the accelerometer, the position of the microphone can be arbitrary [14]. A PCB 130D20 microphone is mounted on the side of the coolant pipe and facing towards the tool tip to capture the emitted sound. The microphone is connected to the computer through a specially designed signal conditioner. GoldWave software is used to record the captured sound with sampling frequency set to 44100Hz.

A series of machining experiments were conducted on a conventional lathe (EME Turning machine) with Carbide Insert NM6 and stainless steel work piece with a diameter of 25mm. First, the free running sound for the spindle rotational speed of 570 rev/min was recorded, without the machining operation. Keeping the spindle rotational speed at 570 rev/min, the sound emitted due to machining with a fresh tool was recorded separately for the depth of cut of 0.5 mm and 1 mm. This recording process was repeated separately for slightly worn tool with 0.2mm flank wear and severely worn tool with 0.4mm flank wear [15]. A constant feed rate of 0.5 mm/rotation was maintained throughout the experiment. The 12 second long sound signal is split into 12 one second sound signals for the subsequent signal processing using HHT. Each one second signal contains 44100 sampling data. The matlab *waveread* function was used to digitize the sound signals.

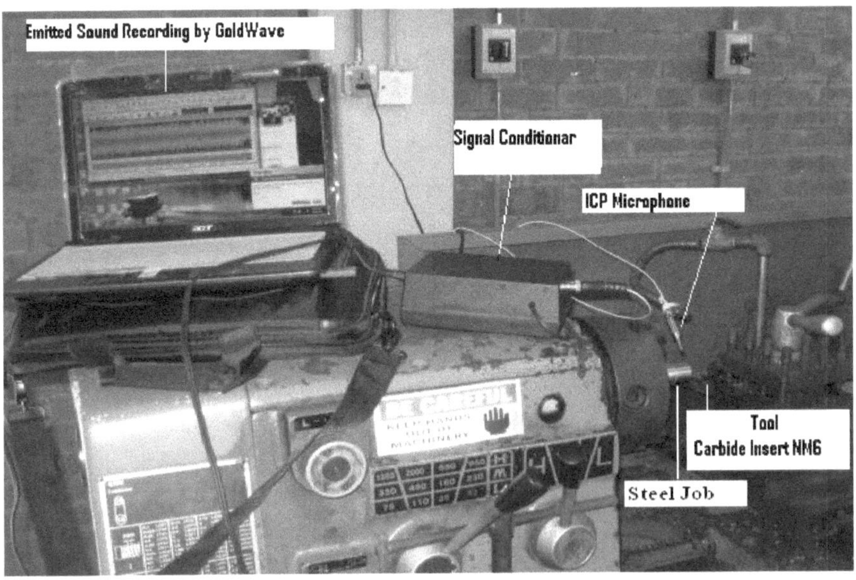

Fig. 1. The experimental setup

Table 1. The details of the experiments conducted

Exp. number	Name	Various cutting conditions		
		Tool flank wear(mm)	Spindle Speed (rev/min)	Depth of cut (mm)
1	Free run	NA	570	NA
2	Fresh-1	0.0	570	0.5
3	Fresh-2	0.0	570	1.0
4	Slightly worn-1	0.2	570	0.5
5	Slightly worn-2	0.2	570	1.0
6	Severely worn-1	0.4	570	0.5
7	Severely worn-2	0.4	570	1.0

4 Results and Discussion

A sample of the recorded multi-component sound signal of severely worn tool is shown in Fig. 2(a). It contains various components such as sound emitted from machine rotational parts and the much needed sound emitted due to the contact between the tool flank face and the surface of the work piece. In addition to these components, it also contains the harmonics of the fundamental signals of this kind. The several mono-component signals obtained from the EMD process on this signal is shown in the form of 13 IMFs and the residue in Fig. 2(b). The instantaneous frequencies and amplitudes were then obtained by applying Hilbert transform on the IMFs. Average amplitude of each IMF for free run, fresh tool, slightly and severely worn tool sound signals were calculated for 0.5 mm depth of cut and line graphs were generated to compare these amplitude values. Fig. 3 shows such a comparison of turning operations with spindle speed 570 rev/min and 0.5 mm depth of cut. Similar results, which are not shown in this paper for want of space, were also obtained from signals of 1mm depth of cut. From Fig. 3, it is very clear that IMF3 to IMF7 are representing the sound signal and its harmonics emitted due to the contact of the tool flank face with the surface of the work piece. Out of these five IMFs, more energy in the form of amplitude is found in IMF6, hence it is appropriate to perform further marginal spectral analysis on IMF6. The marginal spectrum of IMF6 for fresh, slightly and severely worn tool sound signals were obtained as shown in Fig. 4. The maximum amplitude of sound emitted with the fresh, slightly and severely worn tool bit insert is measured as 0.4166, 0.4555 and 0.6198 respectively. These findings show that the increase of sound pressure amplitude is co-related to the increase in tool flank wear. This is also found true for signals collected at different cutting conditions. It is also clearly viewed from Fig. 5. the plot of the average amplitude found in fresh, slightly and severely worn tool sound signal of IMF3 through IMF7. Even though the relation is not linear, this difference is sufficient to train any suitable neural network classifier to classify the state of the wear.

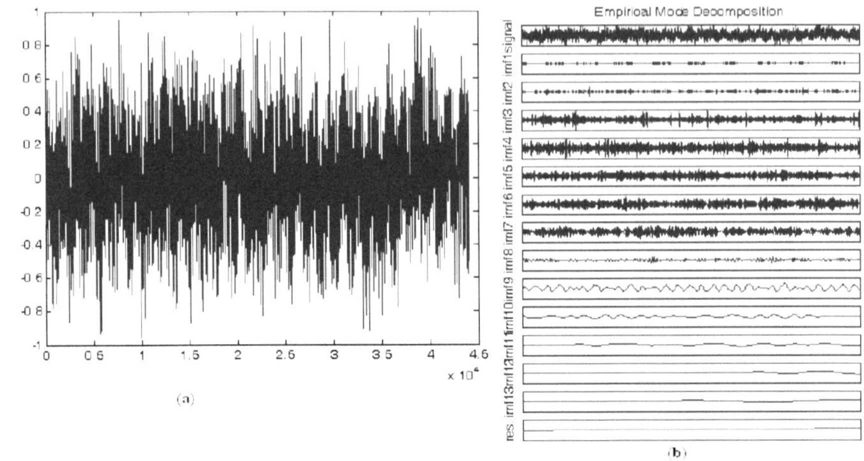

Fig. 2. The original multi-component sound signal of worn tool (a) and its EMD (b)

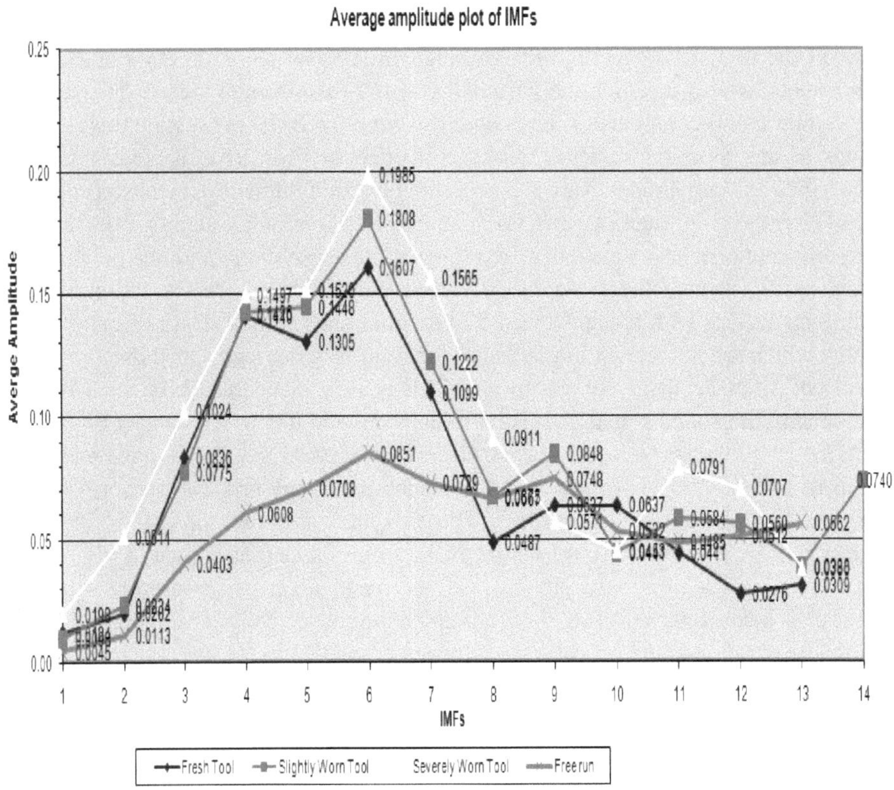

Fig. 3. Comparison of the average amplitude found in the IMFs of free run, fresh tool, slightly and severely worn tool sound signals with spindle speed 570 rev/min and 0.5 mm depth of cut

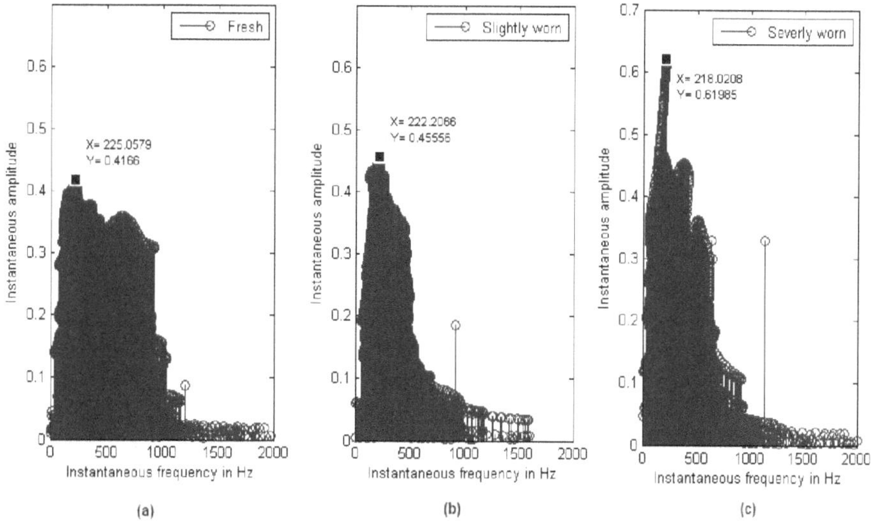

Fig. 4. Marginal spectrum of IMF6 for (a) fresh l (b) slightly worn and (c) severely worn tool sound signal collected at spindle speed 570 rev/min and 0.5 mm depth of cut

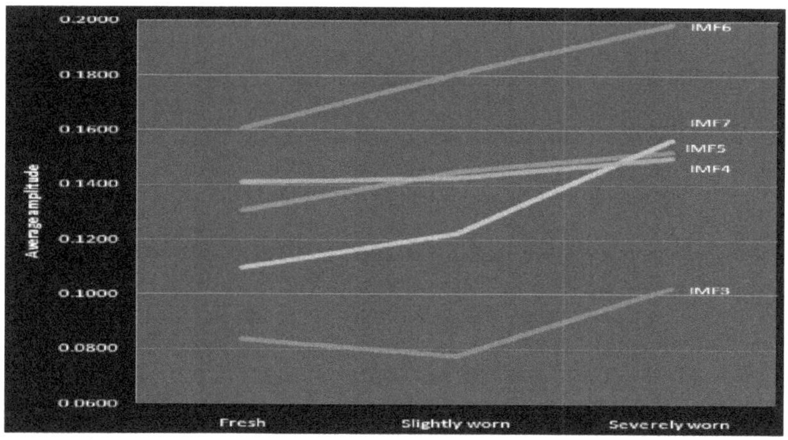

Fig. 5. Plot of the average amplitude found in fresh, slightly and severely worn tool sound signal of IMF3, IMF4, IMF5, IMF6 and IMF7

5 Conclusion

It is observed that out of the 13 IMFs, the considerable difference from the free run signal is found only in the 3rd, 4th, 5th, 6th and 7th IMFs. It implies that these five IMFs are corresponding to the sound and its harmonics emitted from the tool bit and others are corresponding to the sound emitted from other components of the machine. It is found that the emitted sound amplitude increases with the progression of tool wear. Hence it can be concluded that cutting tool flank wear prediction is possible using emitted sound by HHT.

References

1. Dimla Snr, D.E.: Sensor signals for tool-wear monitoring in metal cutting operations-a review of methods. International Journal of Machine Tools & Manufacture 40, 1073–1098 (2000)
2. Sick, B.: On-line and indirect tool wear monitoring in turning with artificial neural networks: A review of more than a decade of research. Mechanical Systems and Signal Processing 16(4), 487–546 (2002)
3. Axinte, D.A., et al.: Reliable tool life measurements in turning—an application to cutting fluid efficiency evaluation. International Journal of Machine Tool Manufacturing 41, 1003–1014 (2001)
4. Ghani, A.K., et al.: Study of tool life, surface roughness and vibration in machining nodular cast iron with ceramic tool. Journal of Material Processing Technology 127, 17–22 (2002)
5. Lu, M.-C., Kannatey-Asibu, E.: Analysis of Sound Signal Generation Due to Flank Wear in Turning. Journal of Manufacturing Science and Engineering 124(4), 799 (10 pages) (2002), doi:10.1115/1.1511177
6. Delio, T., Tlusty, J., Smith, S.: Use of Audio Signals for Chatter Detection and Control. ASME J. Eng. Ind. 114, 146–157
7. Samraj, A., Sayeed, S., Raja, J.E., Hossen, J., Rahman, A.: Dynamic Clustering Estimation of Tool Flank Wear in Turning Process using SVD Models of the Emitted Sound Signals. World Academy of Science, Engineering and Technology 80, 1322–1326 (2011)
8. Raja, E., Sayeed, S., Samraj, A., Kiong, L.C., Soong, L.W.: Tool Flank Wear Condition Monitoring during Turning Process by SVD Analysis on Emitted Sound Signal. European Journal of Scientific Research 49(4), 503–509 (2011) ISSN 1450-216X
9. Peng, Z.K., Tse, P.W., Chu, F.L.: An improved Hilbert-Hung transform and its application in vibration signal analysis. Journal of Sound and Vibration 286(1-2), 187–205
10. Huang, N.E., Shen, Z., Long, S.R., Wu, M.L.C., Shih, H.H., Zheng, Q.N., Yen, N.C., Tung, C.C., Liu, H.H.: The empirical mode decomposition and the Hilbert spectrum for nonlinear and non-stationary time series analysis. Proceeding of the Royal Society of London Series A—Mathematical Physical and Engineering Sciences, 903–995 (1998)
11. Peng, Z.K., Tse, P.W., Chu, F.L.: A comparison study of improved Hilbert-Huang transform and wavelet transform: Application to fault diagnosis for rolling bearing. Mechanical Systems and Signal Processing 19(5), 974–988
12. Sun, L., Shen, M., Chan, F.H.Y.: A method for estimating the instantaneous frequency of non-stationary heart sound signals. In: Proceedings of the 2003 International Conference on Neural Networks and Signal Processing, vol. 1, pp. 798–801 (2003)
13. Zhang, Y.: Hilbert-Huang Transform and Marginal Spectrum for Detection of Bearing Localized Defects. In: Proceedings of the 6th World Congress on Intelligent Control and Automation, Dalian, China, June 21-23, pp. 5457–5461 (2006)
14. Kopac, J., Sali, S.: Tool wear monitoring during the turning process. Journal of Material Processing and Technology 113(1-3), 312–316 (2001)
15. Altina, A., Nalbantb, M., Taskesenb, A.: The effects of cutting speed on tool wear and tool life when machining Inconel 718 with ceramic tools. ScienceDirect: Materials & Design 28(9), 2518–2522 (2007)

A Survey on Cellular Automata and Its Applications

Debasis Das

Department of Computer Science and Engineering,
Indian Institute of Technology Patna, Patna-800013, Bihar, India
ddas@iitp.ac.in
http://www.iitp.ac.in

Abstract. A Cellular Automata (CA) is a computing model of complex system using simple rule. CA divides the problem space into number of cell and each cell can be one or several final state. Cells are affected by neighbors to the simple rule. This paper provides a survey of available literature of some methodologies employed by researchers to utilize the cellular automata for modeling purpose. The literature survey introduces the different type of cellular automata being used for modeling and also tries to present the different fields in which CA have been applied.

Keywords: Cellular Automata, Simple Rule, State, Cells.

1 Introduction

Von Neumann and Ulam, who first proposed the concept of Cellular Automata. The simple structure of CA has attracted researchers from various disciplines. Its application had been proposed in different branches of science. A large number of research papers are published every year. Specialized International Conference and special issues of various journals on CA have been initiated in the last decades. Now several universities have also started offering course on cellular automata. Furthermore, more than hundred books and research papers are authored on CA and can be found on the website www.amazon.com and www.ieee.org respectively.

The popularity of CA can be traced to their simplicity and it is used for the modeling of complex system using simple rule. Cellular automata can be viewed as a simple model of a spatially extended decentralized system made up of a number of individual component is called cell and each individual cell communicates between themselves using the simple rules. Each individual cell is in a specific state which changes over time depending on the state of its local neighbors. The overall structure can be viewed as parallel processing devices.

1.1 Concept of Cellular Automata

Cellular automata are a collection of cells that each adapts one of a finite number of states. Single cells change in states by following a local rule that depends on the environment of the cell. The environment of a cell is usually taken to be a small

P.V. Krishna, M.R. Babu, and E. Ariwa (Eds.): ObCom 2011, Part I, CCIS 269, pp. 753–762, 2012.

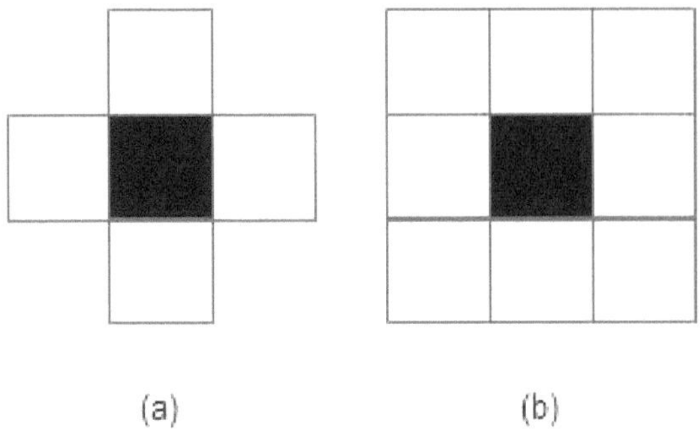

Fig. 1. (a) Von Neumann Neighborhood (b)Moore Neighborhood

number of neighboring cells. Fig. 1. shows two typical neighborhood options (a) Von Neumann Neighborhood (b) Moore Neighborhood. A CA consists of a of a regular uniform n-dimensional lattice (or array), as depicted in Fig. 1. At each site of the lattice (cell), a physical quantity takes values. This physical quantity is the global state of the CA, and the value of this quantity at each cell is its local state. Each cell is restricted to the local neighborhood interactions only, and consequently it is incapable of immediate global communication. The neighborhood of the cell is taken to be the cell itself and some or all of the immediately adjacent cells.

A cellular automaton evolves in discrete steps, with the next value of one site determined by its previous value and that of a set of sites called the neighbor sites. The extent of the neighborhood can vary, depending among other factors upon the dimensionality of the cellular automaton under consideration. The width of the neighborhood of the cell j is the width of the neighborhood at the *jth* side of the array. Classical examples for cell neighborhood are presented in Fig. 1.(a) with 3 cells for one-dimensional cellular automata respective 5 for bi-dimensional cellular automata, case in which are considerate the direct neighbors for establishment of the next state of a one cell and in Fig. 1.(b) with 3 cells for one-dimensional cellular automata respective 9 cells for bi-dimensional cellular automata, case in which are considerate the direct and the diagonal neighbors. The state of each cell is updated simultaneously at discrete time steps, based on the states in its neighborhood at the preceding time step. The algorithm used to compute the next cell state is referred to as the CA local rule.

Typically, a cellular automaton consists of a graph where each node is a finite state automaton (FSA) or cell. This graph is usually in the form of a two dimensional lattice whose cells evolve according to a global update function applied uniformly over all the cells. As arguments, this update function takes the cells present state and the states of the cells in its interaction neighborhood as shown in Fig. 2.

CA is a bio-inspired paradigm highly addressing the soft computing and hardware for large class of applications including information security. They are a particular class of dynamical systems that enable to describe the evolution of complex systems with simple rules, without using partial differential equations. Typically, a cellular automaton consists of graph where each node is a Finite State Automaton (FSA) or cell. This graph is usually in the form of a two dimensional lattice whose cells evolve according to a global update function applied uniformly over all the cells. As

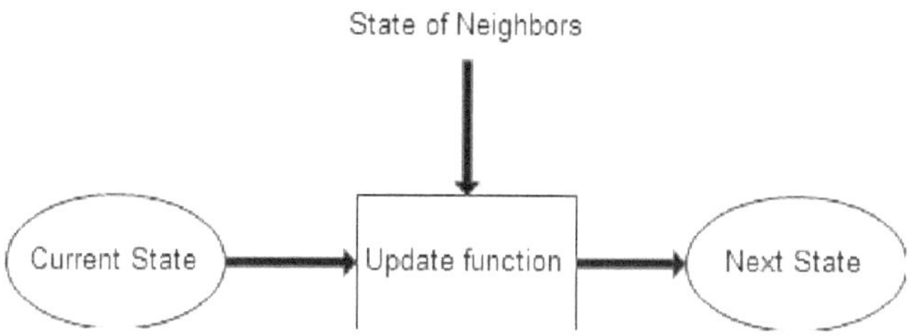

Fig. 2. State Transition Depend on Neighbourhood State

arguments, this update function takes the cells present state and the states of the cells in its interaction with neighborhood. The cells evolve in discrete time steps according to some deterministic rule that depends only on local neighbors. In effect, each cell consists of a storage element (D flip-flop) and a combinational logic implementing the next-state functions (see Fig. 3). The combinational logic is called the rule of the CA. The algorithm used to compute the next cell state is referred to as the CA local rule. The state of each cell is updated simultaneously at discrete time steps based on the states in its neighborhood at the preceding time step.

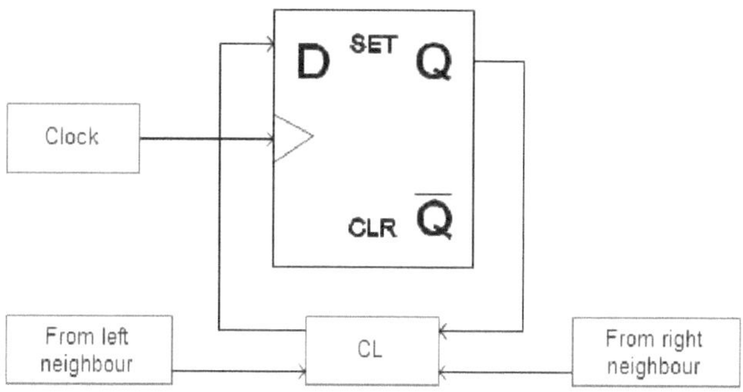

Fig. 3. A typical CA cell

This paper has been laid out as follows. The section 2 discusses about different type of cellular automata structure, section 3 represents varieties of applications of Cellular Automata, section 4 discusses about some advantages of CA in various research fields and section 5 deals with conclusion.

2 Types of Cellular Automata

This section describes different variations of CA which have been proposed by different authors to ease the design and modelling of complex systems.

2.1 Linear CA

The Linear Cellular Automata have been explored by Nandi et al. [21]. If the rule of CA involves only XOR logic then it is called the linear rules. A CA with all the cells having linear rules is called linear CA. In linear CA, the next state function applied at each cell follows the operation of Galois Field (GF()) [19], [20]. The linear CA are also termed as GF(q) CA where q is a prime number. The GF(2), CA the most popular variant of GF(q) CA [19], [20] has attracted considerable attention in recent years since it can be applied in the field of VLSI design and test. There have been several attempts to characterize GF(q) CA through a suitable algebraic tools. It has been characterized using dipolynomials [33], but hybrid CA cannot be represented by dipolynomials. CA state transition behavior has also been represented on arbitrary graphs and its behavior has been studied based on graph theoretic properties. There are some abstract realizations of linear CA in which the cell space is termed as an Abelian group and the state space is represented by a commutative ring [34].

2.2 Complement CA

The Complement Cellular Automata have been explored by Nandi et al. [21]. If the rule of CA involves only XNOR logic then it is called the complement rules. A CA with all the cells having Complements rules is called Complement CA.

2.3 Additive CA

The Additive Cellular Automata have been explored by Nandi et al. [21]. A CA having a combination of XOR and XNOR rules is called Additive CA. They matrix algebraic tools that characterize Additive CA and help develop its applications in the field of VLSI testing. The Additive CA schemes based on easily testable FSM, bit-error correcting code, byte error correcting code, and characterization of 2D cellular automata. The Additive CA used in universal pattern generation, data encryption, and synthesis of easily testable combinational logic. The new characterizations of additive CA behavior, Additive CA-based tools for fault diagnosis, and a wide variety of applications to solve real-life problems. Das et al. [16] has shown that a three neighborhood additive CA can be represented by a tri diagonal matrix a matrix which has the elements of its diagonal and two off-diagonals as non-zero properties of CA with varying (non-uniform) neighborhoods.

2.4 Uniform CA

The Uniform Cellular Automata have been explored by Nandi et al. [21]. If all the cells obey the same rule, then the CA said to be a Uniform CA.

2.5 Hybrid CA

The Hybrid Cellular Automata have been explored by Anghelescu et al. [10]. If all the cells obey different rules, then the CA said to be a Hybrid CA. The hybrid CA has been especially applied in a linear/additive variant in which the rule set can be analyzed through matrix algebra [18].

2.6 Null Boundary CA

The Null Boundary Cellular Automata have been explored by Kundu et al. [4]. A CA said to be a null boundary CA if both the left and right neighbor of the leftmost and rightmost terminal cell is connected to logic 0. One-dimensional (1D) CA over finite fields are studied in which each interior (local) cell is updated to contain the sum of the previous values of its two nearest (left & right) neighbors' along with its own cell value. Boundary cells are updated according to null boundary conditions. For a given initial configuration, the CA evolves through state transitions to an attracting cycle which is defined as attractor/basin. The number of cycles can be determined from the minimal polynomial and characteristic polynomial of the updated matrix which is formed by the linear CA. Chaudhuri et al. [8] represented a detailed theoretical study. But, in case of non-linear CA, matrix cannot be formed since it does not follow any regular mathematics.

2.7 Periodic Boundary CA

The Periodic Boundary Cellular Automata have been explored Anghelescu et al. [22]. In Periodic Boundary CA the rightmost cell as the left neighbor of leftmost cell and similarly, the leftmost cell is considered as the right neighbor of rightmost cell forming a structure like a circular linked list.

2.8 Programmable CA

The Programmable Cellular Automata have been Anghelescu et al. [10]. A CA is called Programmable CA[7] if it employs some control signals. By specifying values of control signal at run time, programmable CA can implement various function dynamically.

2.9 Reversible CA

The Reversible Cellular Automata have been explored by Seredynski et al. [25]. A CA is said to be reversible CA[7] in the sense that the CA will always return to its initial state. The interesting property of being the reversible which means not only forward but also reverse iteration is possible. Using reversible rule it is always possible to return to an initial state of CA at any point. One rule is used for forward iteration and another rule, reversible to the first one, is used for backward iteration. This type of CA is used in cryptography [3].

2.10 Non-linear CA

The Non-Linear Cellular Automata have been explored by Das et al. [23]. Non linear CA uses all possible logic available in CA. Das et al. [23] establishes the non-linear CA as a powerful pattern recognizer.

2.11 Generalized Multiple Attractor CA

The special class of CA, referred to as GMACA [27], is employed for the design of desired CA models, evolved through an efficient implementation of genetic algorithm, are found to be at the edge of chaos. Cellular automata are mathematical idealizations of complex systems in discrete space and time.

2.12 Fuzzy CA

The Fuzzy Cellular Automata have been explored by Maji et al. [24]. Fuzzy CA means CA employed with fuzzy logic. Application of fuzzy CA in pattern recognition. A special class of CA referred to as Fuzzy CA (FCA) [29] is employed to design the pattern classifier. Simple CA can handle only the binary patterns but Fuzzy Cellular Automata assumes each cell a state and a rational value in (0, 1).

3 CA Applications

Wolfram in his recent book 'A New Kind of Science' [1], explored the reason behind the widespread appeal of cellular automata in a large number of application domains. One another book Automata-2008, theory and applications of Cellular Automata [2], book discuss the different application of cellular automata. The broad application fields are presented as follows:

3.1 CA for Parallel Computing

In machine design, the application of CA was proposed for building parallel multipliers [28], prime number sieves, parallel processing computers [30], and also for sorting machines . According to Toffoli et al. [35] the CA can be used as a fault tolerant computing machine. Two dimensional CA have been used extensively for image processing and pattern recognition [27]. The MPP (Massively Parallel Processor) of Goodyear Aerospace Corporation was one of the fastest computers of the early 1980s. CA based machines termed as CAMs (CA Machines) have been developed by Toffoli et al. [35]. These CAMs operate in autonomous mode. The structure of such machines having a high degree of parallelism (with local and uniform interconnection) is ideally suited for simulation of complex systems [32]. A CAM can achieve simulation performance of at least several orders of magnitude higher than that can be achieved with a conventional computer at comparable cost. CAMs were developed as a result of over a decade of machine and modeling research by the Information Mechanics Group at MIT. Since the publication of Von Neumanns seminal work in the late 1950s, the study of artificial self replicating structures has produced a plethora of results. The studies have raised the possibility of using such self replicating machine to perform computations. Das et al. [16] describes CA as a self eplicating structure and can be used to solve the NP-complete problem known as satisfybility. Recently, researchers have started exploring the cellular automaton as a typical computing device it has been presented as a nano meter scale classical computer.

3.2 CA for Modeling Physical & Biological System

It is from the physicists the drive for developing cellular automata as an alternative to differential equations in modeling laws of physics began. This has resulted in investigation of CA models for physical systems with an emphasis on spin systems, models for various forms of regular, dendrites, and random growth based on two-dimensional CA, models for pattern formation in reaction diffusion systems, modeling of hydro dynamical systems [1], [12] etc. CA have been also used to model different chemical processes: the absorption desorption phenomenon important for analyzing poisoning of a surface during heterogeneous catalysis, the inter-diffusion of atoms of two materials, the driven diffusion system where the external field biases the movement of each species in opposite direction, the solidification process with special analysis of the phase transformation of the substance from liquid to solid, alloy formation etc.

3.3 CA for VLSI Design

Due to the simplicity, regularity, modularity and cascadable structure with local neighborhood, additive CA are ideally suited for VLSI implementation [16]. The 64 cells are connected as a MASH cascade in a chain or ring topology on a two-dimensional (2D) grid and can be rearranged, for use in various VLSI applications that require a parallel supply of random analog vectors, such as analog encryption and secure communications, analog built in self test, stochastic neural networks and simulated annealing optimization and learning.

3.4 Pattern Recognition

There have been quite a few works on pattern recognition [27], [17], [31] based on syntactic approach. A finite CA can be thought of as a language acceptor by considering initial configuration as the input string and acceptance or rejection is determined by a specific cell of the CA. The advent of neural net with the seminal work of Hopfield [37] popularized the use of machine intelligence techniques in recognizing patterns.

3.5 CA Games

Cellular automata have been used to model different games, the most famous one proposed by Berlekamp et al. [26]. They have illustrated how extremely simple CA rules can be used to characterize highly complex system behavior such as the game of life. The game was originally proposed by Conway and made popular through Martin Gardner [36]. There are different variations of the game of life like games of proto life which provides a model for the emergence of a crystalline precursor to life from an initial random periodic soup. Besides the game of life, there are other games which have been modeled through CA. Notable among these are the games which provide insights into the synchronization problems for example, the firing squad, firing mob, and queen bee.

4 Advantages of CA in Various Research Fields

4.1 Sequential Fault Convergence

In hardware implementation [28] of CA, the experimental result shows that CA produces better sequential fault convergence than the linear feedback shift register by applying the linear hybrid cellular automata rules [13].

4.2 Memorizing Capacity

The memorizing capacity of a hybrid 3-neighborhood CA [14] is better than that of Hopfield network. The Hopfield network is the model of neural network known for it association capacity.

4.3 Simulation Performance

A cellular automata machine can achieve simulation performance of at least several orders of magnitude higher than that can be achieved with a conventional computer at compactable cost.

4.4 Theoretical Framework

A theoretical framework to study CA evolution based on graph theoretic formulation a graph named as RVG (Rule Vector Graph) can be derived from the rule vector of a CA employing linear and non-linear rules. CA evolution can be characterized from the study of RVG properties.

4.5 Soft Computing

A soft computing tool for CA synthesis a methodology is under development for evolution of SOCA (Self Organizing CA) to realize a given global behavior.

4.6 Modeling Tools

Modeling tools based on the CA theory developed, a general methodology is under development to build a CA based model to simulate a system. The modeling tool enables design of a program to be executed on PCA (Programmable CA) [10] to simulate the given system environment.

4.7 Pattern Recognition

Pattern recognition in the current Cyber Age, has got wide varieties of applications. CA based Pattern Classification [9] or Clustering methodologies [24] are under development based on the theoretical framework .

4.8 CA-Encompression

CA-Encompression (Encryption + Compression), in the current cyber age, large volume of different classes of data - text, image, graphics, video, audio, voice, custom data files -are stored and/or transferred over communication links. Compression and security of such data files are of major concern. Solutions to these problems lie in the development of high speed low cost software/hardware for data compression and data encryption. CA-Encompression technology is being developed as a single integrated operation for both compression and encryption of specific classes of data files such as medical image, voice data, video conference, DNA sequence, Protein sequence etc. Both lossy and lossless encompression are under development based on CA model.

4.9 CA Compression

Standalone CA Compression or CA-encryption technology instead of a single integrated operation of compression and encryption, if a user demands only compression or only encryption, it can be supported using standalone packages (software/hardware version) [15].

4.10 CA Based AES

CA based AES (Advanced Encryption System), as AES is the most popular security package, CA based implementation of AES algorithm [5], [6], [7], [11] in underway for development of low cost, high speed hardwired version of AES, is under development.

5 Conclusion

This paper reports a detailed survey of the various modeling applications of CA. The survey also provides a vivid sketch of the different theoretical developments which have taken place over the years in the CA research field. These developments have established the immense potential of CA in modeling different applications, thus spreading the appeal of cellular automata over a wide cross-section of researchers. The extensive references in support of the different developments of CA research provided with the paper should be of great help to CA researchers in the future.

References

1. Wolfram, S.: A new kind of science. Wolfram Media, Inc. (2002)
2. Adamatzky, A., Alonso-Sanz, R., Lawniczak, A., Juarez Martinez, G., Morita, K., Worsch, T. (eds.): AUTOMATA-2008 Theory and Application of Cellular Automata (2008)
3. Seredynski, M., Bouvary, P.: Block Cipher Based On Reversible Cellular Automata. New Generation Computing 23, 245–258 (2005)
4. Kundu, A., Pal, A.R., Sarkar, T., Banarjee, M., Guha, S.K., Mukhopadhayay, D.: Comparative Study on Null Boundary and Periodic Boundary Neighbourhood Mulriple Attractor Cellular Automata for Classification. IEEE 2008 (2008)
5. Guan, P.: Cellular Automaton Public Key Cryptosystem. Complex System 1, 51–56 (1987)
6. Wolfram, S.: Cryptography with Cellular Automata. In: Williams, H.C. (ed.) CRYPTO 1985. LNCS, vol. 218, pp. 429–432. Springer, Heidelberg (1986)
7. Das, D., Ray, A.: A Parallel Encryption Algorithm for Block Ciphers Based on Reversible Programmable Cellular Automata. Journal of Computer Science and Engineering 1(1), 82–90 (2010)
8. Pal Chaudhuri, P., Roy Chowdhury, D., Nandi, S., Chattopadhyay, S.: Additive Cellular Automata Theory and Applications, vol. 1. IEEE Computer Society Press, USA (1997)
9. Ganguly, N.: Cellular Automata Evolution: Theory and Applications in Pattern Classification. Ph.D thesis, B.E. College (2003)
10. Anghelescu, P., Ionita, S., Safron, E.: Block Encryption Using Hybrid Additive Cellular Automata. In: 7th International Conference on Hybrid Intelligent Systems. IEEE (2007)
11. Nandi, S., Kar, B.K., Pal Chaudhuri, P.: Theory and Application of Cellular Automata in Cryptography. IEEE Transaction on Computers 43 (December 1994)
12. Ganguly, N., Sarkar, B., Deutsch, A., Canright, G., Chaudhuri, P.: A Survey on Cellular Automata. Project BISON, IST 2001 (2001)
13. Anghelescu, P., Ionita, S., Safron, E.: FPGA Implementation of Hybrid Additive Programmable Cellular Automata. In: Eight International Conference on Hybrid Intelligent Systems. IEEE (2008)
14. Maleki, F., Mohades, A., Mehdi Hashemi, S., Shiri, M.E.: An Image Encryption System By Cellular Automata with Memory. In: The Third International Conference on Availability, Reliability and Security. IEEE (2008)
15. Standaert, F., Rouvroy, G., Quisquater, J., Legat, J.: A methodology to Implement Block Ciphers in Reconfigurable Hardware and its Application to First and Compact AES Rijndael. In: FPGA 2003, California, pp. 281–291 (2003)
16. Das, A.K.: Additive Cellular Automata : Theory and Application as a Built-in Self-test Structure. Ph.D thesis, I.I.T. Kharagpur, India (1990)

17. Das, A.K., Pal Chaudhuri, P.: An Efficient On-Chip Deterministic Test Pattern Generation Scheme. Euromicro Journal, Microprocessing & Microprogramming, 195–204 (1989)
18. Das, A.K., Pal Chaudhuri, P.: Efficient Characterization of Cellular Automata. Proc. IEE (Part E) 137(1), 81–87 (1990)
19. Das, A.K., Pal Chaudhuri, P.: Vector Space Theoretic Analysis of Additive Cellular Automata and Its Applications for Pseudo-Exhaustive Test Pattern Generation. IEEE Trans. on Computers 42(3), 340–352 (1993)
20. Das, A.K., Sanyal, A., Pal Chaudhuri, P.: On Characterization of Cellular Automata with Matrix Algebra. Information Science 61(3), 251 (1991)
21. Maji, P., Shaw, C., Ganguly, N., Sikdar, B.K., Pal Chaudhuri, P.: Theory and Applications of Cellular Automata for Pattern Classification. Fundamenta Informaticae 58, 321–354 (2003)
22. Anghelescu, P., Ionita, S., Sofron, E.: Programmable Cellular Automata Based Encryption Algorithm. IEEE (2008)
23. Das, S.: Theory and Applications of Nonlinear Cellular Automata In: VLSI Design. Ph.D Thesis, B.E. College (2006)
24. Maji, P., Pal Chaudhuri, P.: FMACA: A Fuzzy Cellular Automata Based Pattern Classifier. In: Lee, Y., Li, J., Whang, K.-Y., Lee, D. (eds.) DASFAA 2004. LNCS, vol. 2973, pp. 494–505. Springer, Heidelberg (2004)
25. Seredynski, M., Bouvry, P.: Block Cipher Based on Reversible Cellular Automata. New Generation Computer (2005)
26. Berlekamp, E.R., Conway, J.H., Guy, R.K.: Winning ways for your Mathematical Plays, vol. 2. Academic Press (1984)
27. Ganguly, N., Maji, P., Das, A., Sikdar, B.K., Pal Chaudhuri, P.: Characterization of Non-linear Cellular Automata Model for Pattern Recognition. In: Pal, N.R., Sugeno, M. (eds.) AFSS 2002. LNCS (LNAI), vol. 2275, pp. 214–220. Springer, Heidelberg (2002)
28. Bidlo, M., Vasicek, Z.: Gate Level Evolutionary Development Using Cellular Automata. IEEE (2008)
29. Mraz, M., Zimic, N., Lapanja, I., Bajec, I.: Fuzzy Cellular Automata: From Theory to Applications. IEEE (2000)
30. Manning, F.B.: An Approach to Highly Integrated, Computer-maintained Cellular Arrays. IEEE Trans. on Computers C-26, 536–552 (1977)
31. de Oliveira, P.P.B., Kari, J. : Automata 2009. In: 15th International Workshop on Cellular Automata and Discrete Complex Systems, Mackenzie (2009)
32. Hortencius, P.D., McLeod, R.D., Pries, W., Miller, D.M., Card, H.C.: Cellular Automata based Pseudo-random Number Generators for Built-in Self-Test. IEEE Trans. on CAD 8(8), 842–859 (1989)
33. Martin, O., Odlyzko, A.M., Wolfram, S.: Algebraic Properties of Cellular Automata Comm. Math. Phys. 93, 219–258 (1984)
34. Aso, H., Honda, N.: Dynamical Characteristics of Linear Cellular Automata. Journal Computer System Science 30, 291–317 (1985)
35. Toffoli, T.: CAM: A High-Performance Cellular Automata Machine. Physica D 10, 195–204 (1984)
36. Gardner, M.: The Fantastic Combinations of John Conways New Solitaire Game of Life. Sci. Am. 223, 120–123 (1970)
37. Hopfield, J.J.: Neural Networks and Physical System with Emergent Collective Computational Abilities. Proceedings of National Academic of Sciences 79, 2554–2558 (1982)

Extraction of Domain-Specific Concepts to Create Expertise Profiles

Gagandeep Kaur, S.K. Jain, Saurabh Parmar, and Anand Kumar

Computer Engineering Department
National Institute of Technology Kurukshetra, 136119, India
{deep.gagan102,anandncst777}@gmail.com,
{skj_nith,saurabh_1only1}@yahoo.co.in

Abstract. This work is an attempt to identify the domain specific concepts automatically that are useful in various NLP applications. Concept extraction in ontology building is one of the most important aspects. By implementing the methodology discussed, one can easliy capture the knowledgeable topics that represents a particular domain. The topics captured are utilized for producing experts profile. A list of experts and their expertise topics can be a valuable source of information to find out the expert's interests. By automatically identifying the expertise topics, the manual intervention for filtering is reduced as the manual recognition is more subjective and labor-intensive. Thus, by finding the expertise topics in an efficient way the ontology construction process also becomes easy as concept extraction is one of the important steps in ontology learning.

Keywords: Concept extraction, natural language processing, ontology learning.

1 Introduction

As the size of Web is expanding rapidly locating relevant information becomes increasingly difficult. With the emergence of machine translation and natural language interface in the area of computational linguistics, management of lexical units which are specific to an application domain or certain sublanguage is increasing. Therefore, it becomes a matter of concern for computational linguistics to extract domain specific lexical units. In these circumstances the need for tools that adequately and efficiently extract information from the Web is becoming important. Extracting and indentifying concepts from texts is now a well-known and widely explored step in the ontology learning process and terminology building process. Ontologies provide a common layer which plays a major role in supporting information exchange and sharing by extending syntactic interoperability to semantic interoperability in the semantic Web. Semantic Web uses ontologies as an important mechanism to add structure to the data, but building domain specific ontologies is still an intricate, laborious and error-prone process since most of the information available currently is unstructured or free-textDefining the process that retrieves a set of domain concepts and their taxonomic relations is the beginning of a more complex task which is the building of ontologies. So one of the fundamental research problems related to

P.V. Krishna, M.R. Babu, and E. Ariwa (Eds.): ObCom 2011, Part I, CCIS 269, pp. 763–771, 2012.

ontology learning is the extraction of concepts from text. Ontology learning is a technology that automatically or semi-automatically obtains terms from existing data sources to build ontology, including extraction of concepts, obtaining constraints and properties. Among them, concept extraction in ontology building is one of the most important aspects [1]. Thus the evolution of rapid and economical solutions for ontology learning from text is a crucial factor for the success and large scale adoption of the Semantic Web.

2 Problem Statement

To examine the notion we focus on the problem of extracting concepts from research papers or scientific publications to find Expertise (knowledgeable) topics and then these topics are assigned to the authors of the papers. The extertise topics shows the area of interest of the authors of specific domain. The interested ontological concepts are person's knowledge and skills. To improve proficiency most of the organizations facilitate the identification of experts among its workforce. It is necessary to keep up to date information regarding the competencies in any organization. Some of the Text based approaches are used in specialist domains, where the database is created about the competencies of expert witnesses [2]. The identification and management of experts and their knowledge in certain competency areas is known as Competency Management. The human effort required for competency management can be reduced by automatically identifying the experts and expertise topics from text. The automatic identification of competency coverage and structure, e.g. from publications, is therefore of increasing importance, as this allows for a sustainable, dynamic and time-critical approach to competency management [3].

Concept extraction, aims at extracting domain specific concepts from a corpus of a certain academic or technical domain. Concept extraction (also called term extraction/acquisition tools or term extractors) makes use of corpora to identify terms and provide end-users with lists of topics found in the texts they contain. More precisely, they aim at finding terms or set of terms that are likely to be concepts in the subject field a specific corpus deals with. The end results are the expertise topics that are useful for conceptualizing knowledge domain and building domain ontology.

3 Present Work

Information retrieval techniques are already being used where users look for domain experts in a collection of documents by giving a query with the topics of interest [4,5]. Some of the approaches make use of ontologies for competency management, building inference services [6,7] but these methods can only be applied for domains where an ontology of skills already exists. An approach to build an ontology of competencies has been proposed in [8], making use of an already built domain ontology, but this cannot be applied for domains where an ontology is not defined or where new concepts are introduced often. Expertise should be analysed on several levels (knowledge, ability, centrality, and context). In [3] an approach based on text genre specific lexico-syntactic patterns from scientific publications is investigated, but only a short list of context patterns manually identified is considered. In this work, an automatic method is purposed to identify context patterns that will increase the number of expertise topics that are considered.

4 Natural Language Processing Techniques

As the term extraction is an important problem in NLP, in order to better understand and organize the work produced in the field, it can be useful to comprehend the NLP. Three mainstream approaches in NLP are identified to extract and recognize terms: Statistical, Pattern based and hybrid.

4.1 Pattern-Based Approach

These approaches are based on linguistic or lexicographic knowledge, as well as existing human knowledge regarding the contents of the text that is to be processed. They rely on linguistic features, namely grammatical, morphological and/or syntactic information. This knowledge is mined from corpora by using predefined or discovered patterns. Lexico-syntactic patterns combine lexical representations and syntactical information with regular expressions, whereas the lexico-semantic patterns also employ semantic information. Authors in [9,10,11] describe an approach to term extraction based on linguistic knowledge. In [12] a simple *regular expression* is supposed to be sufficient to identify the candidate term forms.Extraction of the candidate terms from a domain corpus is usually carried out by *parser,* able to perform a shallow linguistic analysis using Part of Speech (POS) tagging techniques in [13].

Within a linguistic approach framework, other techniques can be applied in order to refine the terminology like *stop list* removal. The end of the process is a list of good concept candidates likely to constitute the final terminology. However, a further analysis step is needed. In pure linguistic approaches this process takes the form of a human expert manual validation.

4.2 Statistical Method

These are commonly used for NLP applications. These approaches are data-driven and are solely based on quantitative methods to find statistical relations. They learn from text and do not require any pre-built language models. One of the problems with syntactic methods for terminology discovery is that more terms are selected as candidates than should be. Further filtering must be done by statistical methods. Studies show that 50-80% of terms run through statistical filters are not candidates to be selected as vocabulary [14] . Many of the statistical studies also revolve around noun phrases. Mutual Information [15] and the Dice Factor[16] are two statistical measures designed to eliminate poor candidates.

The statistical approach is efficient because it is based on a raw corpus and does not require a POS tagged corpus, it is not language-dependent. However, it bears some limits as: relying on frequency alone has the disadvantage of excluding low-frequent words that may be interesting. The results need to be filtered in order to exclude the strings that are not relevant for a given terminological project. So far we have been comparing statistical approaches and linguistic approaches. However, some extraction programs exist which combine the two techniques.

4.3 Hybrid Approach

Recent terminology extraction systems combine linguistic and statistical techniques in structured hybrid approaches. Linguistic analysis is carried out before the application of statistical measures, to be helpful in selecting all linguistic admissible candidates over which will be applied numerical tests. One of the first systems using an hybrid approach is presented in[17]and [12], where noun phrases are firstly extracted as term candidates and then selected according to the frequency of their noun elements. Justeson and Katz found that when they examined noun phrases, certain patterns in these noun phrases were more likely to contain appropriate terms than other patterns. frequency filters. In this research, the hybrid approach is used which incorporate the linguistic approach to match the required pattern and statistical approach to measure the frequency count of the initial concept candidates. In the subsequent sections, a methodology to locate interesting terminology is described which further leads to expertise topics extraction in the text corpus.

5 Methodology

Concept extraction is the process of identifying concepts from a raw document collection. The raw document collection can be web pages retrieved by search engines, documents collected during legal discovery, or documents from a specific domain. There is no limit on the size of the corpus. Corpus can range from a few hundred documents to hundreds of millions of documents. In this research, the input is technical research papers. The two main steps in the *concept extraction* are, namely *concept mining* and *concept filtering*.

5.1 Concept Mining

Concept mining is used to extract all possible concept candidates from a corpus. It mainly consists of tokenization of text corpus, *Part-of-Speech tagging*, *n-gram identification* in order to get concepts that are likely to be the expertise topics.

Part-of-Speech Tagging. A first basic step of any natural language processing application is *tokenization*. The sentences in the text file are divided into tokens. Tokens are often defined to be space delimited alphanumeric strings. To find out concept candidates each document in a corpus is split into sentences; and each sentence is parsed by a *part-of-speech (POS) tagger*. Part-of-speech (POS) tagging, verb predicate extraction and topic centroid extraction are common techniques to extract concepts from text. Here, *Stanford nlp POS* is used for tagging the sentence, i.e. a grammatical category is associated with each word. This tagger tags the input according to the standard Penn Treebank Tag Set [13]. There are some other taggers also discussed in [18,19,20].

K-gram Sequence Generator. In order to allow complex term extraction, words appearing frequently together in a corpus are identified. These are known as coocurrents. Once the tokens are identified, sequence of n tokens is assembled into k-grams. Having tokenized a given corpus of text and from that constructed n-grams, frequency of each unique n-gram is calculated. This technique aims at detecting sequences of two or more lexical units whose co-occurrence is higher than a given level or threshold. Therefore, the procedure is based on a threshold frequency below which words are not extracted.

The noun phrase is often the desired concept, which usually occurs frequently in daily language. Conversely, the joint occurrence of the verb/adjective and the noun phrase is usually much less frequent. So we are interested in noun sequences only. An *k-gram sequence generator* is used that scans through the parsed sentence to identify noun sequences, i.e., sequences of words tagged only with NN (singular noun), NNP (proper noun), NNS (plural nouns), or NNPS (plural proper noun).

As a result, the n-gram generator produces a collection of noun sequences with various lengths. We only consider nouns phrases upto length three, namely unigrams, bigrams, trigrams where unigram is one-word nouns, bigram is two consecutive nouns, and trigram is three consecutive nouns. A pre-processing step extracts k-grams and annotates them with the frequency of their occurrence in the corpus. The nominal unigrams, nominal bigrams, and nominal trigrams are the initial concept candidates identified by *concept mining*. After the candidate concepts are extracted the relevant concepts are obtained and these concepts are evaluated in terms of *precision and recall*.

5.2 Concept Filtering

Concept filtering removes errors generated during concept mining. In concept mining, a part-of-speech tagger is employed to recognize nouns. Notice that this concept extraction technique depends heavily on the quality of the POS tagging. Tagging errors may cause extraction programs to extract candidate terms that are not proper terminological units. Tagging errors can be increased when documents have spelling, capitalization, punctuation and grammar errors, which are common in public comments and emails. POS tagging error, especially the false positive error, is one of the major error sources in *concept mining*.Very often, the whole set of candidate terms automatically extracted by term extractors is not of interest to the end-users i.e. terminologists - who need to filter the list. The presence of unwanted, uninteresting elements is called *Noise*. Noise is typical of linguistically-based approaches, and is often due to POS tagging errors.

The corpus that is being used in the experiment consists of the five research papers from computer science domain. To find out the Concepts, the first step is to prepare the input. The research papers are converted into the text file and all the punctuation marks are removed as the tagger incorrectly identify the terms with punctuation marks and it also take more time to tag the input. In the pre-processing step, the text files are given to tagger to find their grammatical category. After tagging, the patterns that are noun phrases in this case are identified i.e., total number of terms in each research paper that constitute 1-word, 2-word and 3-word nouns are identified. The following patterns are identified:

Unigram Noun. NN, NNP, NNS, NNPS

Bigram Noun. NN NN, NNP NNP, NNS NNS, NNPS NNPS, NN NNS

Trigram Noun. NN NN NN, NNP NNP NNP, NNS NNS NNS, NNPS NNPS NNPS

The above thirteen patterns are recognized in this work. As, the number of terms that are being identified are very large in number and they also contain the terms that are not of our interest, so they should not be considered. To remove the irrelavant ones, the terms having frequency greater than or equal to 1, 2, 4 and 5 are collected.In this experiment we have choosen frequency 5 threshold to get the desired concepts. These resulted terms are the concept candidates and remaining terms are discarded.

6 Results

By applying the above methodology the total number of terms calculated in each paper is given in the table 1. This table also contains the total number of unigram, bigram and trigram identified.

Table 1. Total number of terms in all papers

Paper number	Number of terms	Number of Unigram	Number of Bigram	Number of Trigram
Paper 1	1027	416	122	11
Paper 2	1137	682	269	64
Paper 3	1121	643	170	37
Paper 4	928	492	146	25
Paper 5	1190	663	207	41

Table 2. Values of precision, recall, F1-measure in paper 1

	Freq>=1	Freq>=2	Freq>=4	Freq>=5
Precision	0.048	0.020	0.010	0.010
Recall	0.164	0.212	0.244	0.289
F1-measure	0.075	0.037	0.020	0.020

The Expertise topics recognised are given in table 3. The outcome in the form of expertise topics are evaluated in terms of precision, recall and F1-measure. *Precision* is calculated by the ratio of real concepts retrieved when the frequency threshold is set to a specific count and the total number of concepts in one paper. Precision for all the papers can also be calculated in the same way. *Recall* is calculated as the ratio of number of real concept candidates retrieved when the frequency threshold is set to particular count and concepts candidates retrieved at that particular count. Precision is a measure of exactness or fidelity, whereas recall is a measure of completeness. *F1-measure* is a collective measure of precision and recall.

Table 3. Expertise topics

Author name	Expertise Topics
S.K. Jain	entity, relationship, tabletype, database, abstraction, schema, entity type, tabletype relationship, part entity, semantics, attributes
Darshan Singh	computing, grid, resource, scheduling, resource broker, grid resource broker, grid resource
R.M. Sharma	delay, Delivery, protocol, network, node, route, packet, Delivery Ratio, MANET, AODV, DSR, AntHocNet, AntNet, data packet
V.K. Ranga	message, node, exclusion algorithm, model checker, message handler, SPIN, Promela, request
Jitender Saini	packet, delay, bandwidth, protocol, transmission, congestion, network, TCP, HTTP, MultiTCP

$$Precision = \frac{number\ of\ correct\ concept\ candidates}{number\ of\ returned\ concept\ candidates}$$

$$Recall = \frac{number\ of\ correct\ concept\ candidates}{concepts\ identified\ according\ to\ frequency}$$

$$F1 - measure = \frac{2 * Precision * Recall}{Precision + Recall}$$

The values for precision, recall and F1-measure in paper 1 are shown in table 2. Similarly all the values are calculated in other 4 papers also.

6.1 Performance Evaluation

The values of precision, recall and F1-measure are calculated at frequencies >=1, >=2, >=4, >=5. The precision values shows that at freq>=1, it is highest and at freq>=5, it is the lowest. This shows as we move from low frequency to high frequency the precision decreases. Now, the values of recall shows that at freq>= 1, it is lowest and at freq>=5, it is highest. This demonstrates as we move from low to high frequency, recall increases. Thus, the precision and recall both are inversely proportion. If one is decreasing, another will be increasing. A low threshold increases precision and reduces recall while a high threshold decreases precision and increases recall. Hence, there is a trade-off between precision and recall. By varying the cut off value, the relation between precision and recall can be obtained.

The F1-measure is a weighted harmonic mean that combines Recall (R) and Precision (P) with an equal weight. The results shows F1-measure is decreased as the frequency threshold increases.

The ground truth of concept extraction is generated by extracting concepts manually. Given the fact that it is very time-consuming for domain experts to look through the corpus and obtain all the real terms, we can calculate recall in two steps. In first step, frequency threshold of 3 can be used to get all the candidate terms instead of all the terms. Second, we count the number of real terms in this candidate term list. Now recall can be calculated as the ratio of the number of terms after step2 to the number of terms after step1 [21].

By analysing the results some of the interesting facts emerged like in every paper nominal unigram noun have the highest count and the trigram nouns are the lowest in number. So this study reveals that unigram nouns are most frequently occurred in the text in comparison with the bigram and trigram nouns. As the number of k in k-gram increases, the frequency of occurrence of noun phrases decreases. Thus, most of the concepts that are recognised in this work are unigram or bigram nouns. It is concluded that the group of candidate terms of lower frequency have lower quality than groups of candidate terms of higher frequency; and the most frequent strings recovered from technical texts are almost always valid technical terms.

The concept candidates recognised by the system further require refinement, that is done manually. In ideal cases this refinement is performed by the experts of that specific domain. But in this work, as the papers are from computer science domain the filtration is carried out by the author to create expertise profiles.

7 Conclusion and Future Work

This work is an attempt to identify the important or domain specific concepts automatically that are useful in various NLP applications. By implementing the methodology discussed in this work, one can easliy capture the knowledgeable topics that represents a particular domain. The topics captured are utilized for producing experts profile. A list of experts and their expertise topics can be a valuable source of information to find out the expert's interests.

By automatically identifying the expertise topics, the manual intervention for filtering is reduced. As the manual recognition is more subjective and labor-intensive. Thus, by finding the expertise topics in an efficient way the ontology construction process also becomes easy as concept extraction is one of the important steps in ontology learning. Analysis of results shows that precision and recall measures are inversely proportion in nature. So there is a tradeoff between the two.

The work presented in this dissertation extends to following directions.The topics that are recognized may not contain all the topics that should have been in the list. Thus, other patterns can also be identified in addition to already recognized patterns so that the precision and recall can be improved by extracting more number of expertise topics.Furthermore, the scoring method can also be applied to the final expertise topics so that the topics having more weight or score are considered more important. This can further reduce the manual verification task as more of the topics are filtered by scoring methods. The terms having more frequency can be sorted so that higher weight or score can be assigned to them.

References

1. Yang, Q., Cai, K.-M., Li, Y., Liu, R.-Q.: An Area Concept Extraction Algorithm Based on Association Rule. In: Proceedings of International Conference of Information Science and Management Engineering, vol. 2, pp. 562–564 (2010)
2. Dozier, C., Jackson, P., Guo, X., Chaudhary, M., Arumainayagam, Y.: Creation of an Expert Witness Database through Text Mining. In: Proceedings of the 9th International Conference on Artificial Intelligence and Law, pp. 177–184 (2003)

3. Paul, B., Thomas, E.: Topic extraction from scientific literature for competency management. In: Proceedings of the 3rd ExpertFinder Workshop Personal Identification and Collaborations: Knowledge Mediation and Extraction at the 7th International Semantic Web Conference (PICKME 2008), Karlsruhe, Germany (2008)
4. Serdyukov, P., Rode, H., Hiemstra, D.: Exploiting sequential dependencies for expert finding. In: Proceedings of the 31st Annual International ACM SIGIR Conference on Research and Development in Information Retrieval, pp. 795–796 (2008)
5. Craswell, N., Hawking, D., Vercoustre, A.M., Wilkins, P.: P@noptic expert: Searching for experts not just for documents. In: Ausweb 2001, pp. 21–25 (2001)
6. Sure, Y., Maedche, A., Staab, S.: Leveraging corporate skill knowledge- from proper to ontoproper. In: Proceedings of the Third International Conference on Practical Aspects of Knowledge Management, pp. 30–31 (2000)
7. Kunzmann, C., Schmidt, A.: Ontology-based competence management for healthcare training planning: A case study. In: 6th International Conference on Knowledge Management, IKNOW 2006 (2006)
8. Posea, V., Harzallah, M.: Building a competence ontology. In: Proceedings of the Workshop Enterprise Modelling and Ontology of the International Conference on Practical Aspects of Knowledge Management, PAKM 2004 (2004)
9. Basili, R., Bordoni, L., Pazienza, M.T.: Extracting terminology from corpora. In: Proceedings of the 2nd International Conference on Terminology, Standardization and Technology Transfer (1997)
10. Basili, R., Pazienza, M.T., Zanzotto, F.M.: Customizable modular lexicalized parsing. In: Proceedings of the 6th International Workshop on Parsing Technology (2000)
11. Evans, D.A., Zhai, C.: Noun-phrase analysis in unrestricted text for information retrieval. In: Proceedings of the 34th Conference on Association for Computational Linguistics, Santa Cruz, California, pp. 17–24 (1996)
12. Justeson, J., Katz, S.: Technical Terminology: some linguistic properties and an algorithm for identification in text. Natural Language Engineering, 9–27 (1995)
13. Marcus, M.P., Beatrice, S., Ann, M.M.: Building a Large Annotated Corpus of English: The Penn Treebank. In: International Conference on Computational Linguistics, vol. 19(2), pp. 313–330 (1993)
14. Basili, R., Missikoff, M., Velardi, M.: Identification of relevant terms to support the construction of Domain Ontologies. In: ACL Workshop on HLT, Toulouse, France (2001)
15. Fano, R.M.: Transmission of Information: A Statistical Theory of Communications. MIT Press (1961)
16. Smadja, F., McKeown, K., Hatzivassiloglou, V.: Translating collocations for bilingual lexicons: a statistical approach. Computational Linguistics, 1–38 (1996)
17. Earl, L.L.: Experiments in Automatic Extracting and Indexing. Information Storage and Retrieval 6(X), 273–288 (1970)
18. Brill, E.: Some advances in transformation-based part-of-speech tagging. In: Proceedings of the 15th International Conference on Computational Linguistic, pp. 1034–1038 (1994)
19. Schmid, H.: Probabilistic part-of-speech tagging using decision trees. In: Proceedings of the International Conference on New Methods in Language Processing, pp. 44–49 (1994)
20. Schmid, H.: Improvements in part-of-speech tagging with an application to German. In: Proceedings of the ACL SIGDAT Workshop, pp. 47–50 (1995)
21. Frantzi, K., Ananiadou, S., Mima, H.: Automatic recognition of multi-word terms. International Journal of Digital Libraries 3(2), 117–132 (2000)

Inter and Intra Cluster Load Balancing Strategies for Cluster Based Video-on-Demand Systems

Vinay A. and Prateek Saxena

Department of Information Science and Enigneering, P E S Institute of Technology, Bangalore, Karnataka, India
a.vinay@pes.edu

Abstract. Video-on-Demand (VoD) has been an active area of research for the past few years in the multimedia research community. Significant research efforts have been directed towards reduction of network bandwidth requirements, improvement of server utilization, and minimization of start-up latency. Server load and network bandwidth are the major performance issues in streaming video over the Internet. Thus, load balancing among servers is one of the major challenges. This paper presents a novel load balancing strategy for cluster based hybrid Video-on-Demand (VoD) systems. The architecture used for load balancing contains peer servers in different levels of hierarchy. The simulation results of the proposed technique illustrates that the load on the servers in a group is balanced up to 90% and the rejection rate is reduced.

Keywords: Video-on-Demand (VoD) systems, load balancing, clustering, replication, intra-cluster load balancing, inter-cluster load balancing.

1 Introduction

Video-on-demand (VoD) systems have evolved as one of the most popular types of multimedia service on the Internet over the past decade. Video news clips, full-length movies, TV shows, video lectures, videos made and shared by common people are watched by millions of users every day over Internet. VoD systems exert enormous pressure on both the video servers and the network because of their high bandwidth and stringent delay requirements. The video servers' throughput and the network traffic volume grow linearly with the number of clients and further lead to imbalance in the load. The net effect is on the performance of the overall system in terms of long delays or even request rejections. Hence appropriate techniques for load balancing among servers is utmost important in the current scenario mainly for achieving high throughput, availability, and scalability. In this direction, this paper presents a novel load balancing strategy for cluster based hybrid Video-on-Demand (VoD) systems [1, 2, 3, 4 and 5].

The rest of the paper is organized as follows; section 2 describes related work; section 3 deals with proposed system; section 4 illustrates simulation results and section 5 concludes the work carried out.

P.V. Krishna, M.R. Babu, and E. Ariwa (Eds.): ObCom 2011, Part I, CCIS 269, pp. 772–781, 2012.

2 Related Work

Liang-Teh Lee et al proposed a load balanced PC-Cluster for the VOD server system has been proposed. Two-Tier model is used in the systematic architecture, and PC-Cluster are used as storage system of the VOD server. The load balancing mechanism is based on the Least-Connection-First algorithm. Furthermore, a video placement strategy is also proposed in this paper to share and balance the loads among video servers in the cluster. Accompany with the dynamically adjusted files in each video level, a dynamically cyclical video replacement mechanism has been proposed to replicate and allocate video files for improving load balance of the system [6].

H S Guruprasad et al proposes a load balancing algorithm for a distributed VoD architecture using agents. The proposed approach groups a set of local proxy servers into a Local Proxy Server Group [LPG] for load balancing among the proxy servers. However the proposed algorithm always uses maximum number of channels between the proxy servers in a LPG and also between the CMS and the proxy servers of a LPG by allocating more channels to the more popular videos [7].

Yitzhak Birk work focuses on load-balancing for the purpose of providing throughput that is independent of viewing choices. At the inter-disk level, data striping is the obvious solution, but may lead to a quadratic growth of RAM buffer requirements with system size. At the intra-disk level, multi-zone recording results in variable disk throughput. Deterministic schemes for solving each problem are discussed, as well as their joint operation. Finally, efficient staging of data from tertiary storage devices to disk is shown to be possible [8].

Anant Nimkar et al proposes a greedy video placement and disk load balancing algorithms to minimize the static and dynamic loads of disks respectively. The proposed greedy video placement along with round robin DLB improves the performance of the VoD system by 10% as compared to random video placement along with round robin DLB. The proposed DLB using the variance minimization algorithm along with random video placement evenly distributes the load among disks continuously except at startup time of the VoD server [9].

Pushpendra Kumar Chandra et al propose an algorithm for a wide variety of workload conditions including I/O intensive and memory intensive loads. However, the CPU requirements of the system is minimum as the tasks which arrive are mostly video fetch tasks which require negligible system interaction but a lot of I/O consumption. The proposed load balancing algorithm tries to achieve the effective usage of global disk resources in the VOD cluster [10].

3 Proposed System

3.1 System Model

The proposed system model for VoD system is illustrated in Figure 1. The architecture is a cluster based hybrid architecture consisting of server peer at various levels and client server model in the base level or level 0 in the architecture. The components of the architecture are Multimedia Server (MS), Global Server Group

(GSG), Intermediate Server Group (ISG), Local Server Group (LSG), Local Coordinator (LC), Intermediate Coordinator (IC), Global Coordinator (GC) and Clients. The MS consists of high end data storage with all the video files. The GSG and ISG consist of a set of intermediate peer servers and are associated with ISG and LSG through respective coordinators. The peer servers in turn consist of subset of the videos that are stored on MS.

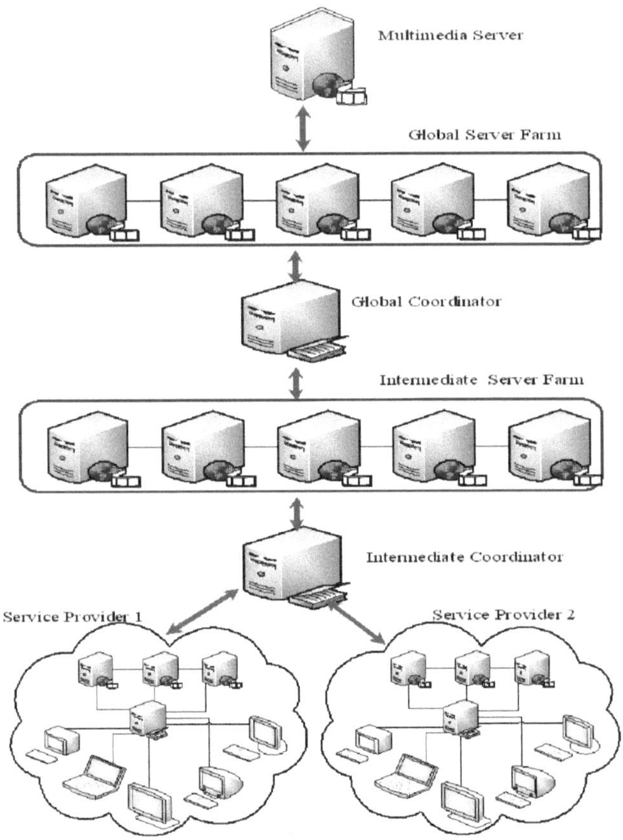

Fig. 1. Hybrid Video-on-Demand (VoD) System Model

Each cloud in the figure represents service provider regions i.e. cluster. The client sends request to LC, if the requested movie / video are available among the servers of the LSG, then the LC forwards request to the server in the LSG and the server streams video to the client. If the video request cannot be satisfied by the servers of LSG, the LC forwards it to next level in the hierarchy. Similar set of actions are performed at the ISG and GSG levels. The servers in the LSG, ISG and GSG are classified strong cluster server and weak cluster server based on the popularity of the video that they contain. The servers in the LSG contain highly popular videos. The popularity decrease as one moves up in the hierarchy. The MS contains all video files. Either in servers of LSG, ISG or GSG, the popularity of a video is the measured through the hit rate of the video. Table 1 lists the various nomenclatures used in the algorithms to represent various system components.

Table 1. Nomenclatures Used

SG	:	Server Group
S_i	:	Server in a server group
C_i	:	Client
W_i	:	Weight of a server S_i in SG
V_{req}	:	Video Request
W	:	Vector containing server id with their weights
SBW_i	:	Total available bandwidth in server S_i
SSP_i	:	Processing speed of the server S_i
SAL_i	:	Access latency
SMZ_i	:	Memory size
S_c	:	Strong cluster group
S_w	:	Weak cluster group
SPS_i	:	Super Peer Server in SG
λ	:	Threshold value for W_i
W_{avg}	:	Average workload
W_{th}	:	Workload threshold (5% of W_{avg})
SPS_{LK}	:	List of kth super peer server

3.2 Clustering

Let us consider a collection of N server nodes that are part of a server group (Local, Intermediate and Global). It is assumed that each server always stores one copy of its own content item which it serves to clients and that it has additional storage space to store *k* replicated content items from other server which it can also serve. Each video is associated with an authoritative *origin server* (OS) in the network. The video copy located at the origin server is called the *origin copy* and a video copy at any remaining server is called a *replica*. The servers in the server group are grouped into strong and weak clusters based on their weight vector which comprises the following parameters: available capacity, processing speed, memory and access latency.

Procedure for clustering

Create_Cluster()

{

1. for each S_i in *SG* calculate weight W_i of server as
   $W_i = (SBW_i + SSP_i + SMZ_i) / SAL_i$
2. $W = \{S_i, W_i\}$ in descending order of weights.
3. for each S_i *in W*
   if $W_i \geq \lambda$
      append S_i into S_c
   else
      append S_i into S_w

}

3.3 Replication

The videos are classified as Class I and Class II, based on their popularity. The most frequently accessed videos are ranked as Class I and the less frequently accessed videos as Class II. Then more copies of Class I videos are replicated in strong clusters (servers having high weights). Routing is performed hierarchically by broadcasting the request to the strong clusters.

Procedure for replica placement

```
Create_Replica()
{
   1. for each V_req arriving from C_i,
           Identify V_req € C_I or C_II
   2. if V_req € C_I
          Assign V_req to S_c
       else
          Assign V_req to S_w]
   3. if Replica of V_req
          Serve request
      else
          If SBW_i && SSP_i && SMZ_i available
          Create replica
      else
              Put V_req into Queue
}
```

3.4 Load Balancing

A typical Video-on-Demand (VoD) system has a number of servers working independently with each other. Some of them are linked by communication channel, while some are not. Each server possesses an initial load i.e. video request, which represents the amount of work to be performed. Each server may have a different processing capacity. To minimize the time to perform all tasks or to serve all the incoming video requests from the clients, an efficient load balancing algorithm is required. Thus, the VoD systems need efficient load balancing of the requests mainly for achieving high throughput, availability, and scalability. A number of load balancing algorithms for VoD system as stated in related work have been proposed. The current ubiquitous environments are quite different from those assumed by the classical load balancing algorithms. An effective load balancing scheme requires correct and timely knowledge on the global system state (e.g., the workload distribution, video popularity, execution time, etc.). However, the global state of a large-scale VoD system swiftly and dynamically changes, and it is very difficult to accurately model the system using a typical approach.

The proposed load balancing implements intra-cluster and inter-cluster load balancing through the replication of videos. Balancing the load within a particular cluster is called as intra-cluster load balancing and balancing the load among the clusters is called as inter-cluster load balancing. Thus complete load balancing across the system is achieved. The proposed load balancing algorithm is also a dynamic load balancing algorithm because it makes decision at run-time for both intra-cluster and inter-cluster. The load balancing is achieved through replication strategy. Every cluster monitor called Super Peer Server (SPS) observes its server availability over a period of time. A video will be replicated only under the following circumstances:

- if the disk space at the server having the required video is very low.
- if the disk space of the server is larger than that of the requested video

The servers periodically checks the popularity of the video on a weekly basis and removes the less popular ones to utilize disk space for storing other videos that are more popular. However, the original copy is stored at the server in which replication was done first.

3.4.1 Intra-Cluster Load Balancing

The Super Peer Server (SPS) receives the information periodically regarding the current loads W_i and available disk space SMZ_i of the servers. Based on W_i the tracker SPS creates a sorted list SPS_L of the servers. For instance consider that are n servers in the list. Among the last [n/2] servers in the list, the servers whose corresponding values of SMZ_i less than the threshold MZ_{Th} are deleted. Thus, load balancing is achieved by replicating the hot video from the first server in the list to the last server and the second server to the second last server and so on. If the load difference between the servers exceeds a threshold λ, then the video is replicated.

Procedure for Intra-Cluster Load Balancing

IntraCluster_Loadbalancing()
{
1. for each S_i in S_c and S_w,
   Periodically communicate W_i and SMZ_i to SPS.
2. SPS appends W_i and SMZ_i to its list SPS_L
3. for each last (n/2) S_i in S_c / S_w
   if $SMZ_i < MZ_t$
   Delete S_i from SPS_L
4. for each remaining S_i in SPS_L
   if $W_i(S_i) - W_i(S_{i+1}) > \lambda$
   Replicate videos from first half of SPS_L to last half (ascending to descending order)
}

3.4.2 Inter-Cluster Load Balancing

Inter-cluster load balancing is necessary in order to prevent load imbalance among the clusters. Here, the load current loads W_i ΣSPS_i is exchanged from the SPS with their neighbouring SPS periodically. The SPS_k checks whether its load exceeds the average load of the set SPS_i of its neighbouring cluster leaders by more than workload threshold W_{th} of the average load. If it exceeds, then it determines the hot video which should be moved. It sends a message about the disk space requirements SMZ of each video to each SPS_i to transfer some part of its load to them. Each SPS_i check the available disk space in each of their cluster servers. They send a message to SPS_k about the total loads and their available disk space if the space limits are satisfied. Then, SPS_k arranges the servers which are ready in SPS_i to the list SPS_{LK} so that the first element of the SPS_{LK} is the least loaded cluster. The hot videos are assigned to the willing servers in RR fashion. Once the new videos are received all SPSi sort the list SPS_{LI} in descending order of load of its servers and performs intra-cluster load balancing.

Procedure for Inter-Cluster Load Balancing

InterCluster_Loadbalancing()
{
1. for each SPS_i in the network
   Periodically communicates W_i and SMZ_i to each other.
2. for each SPS_i in the network
   Compute the average load W_{avg} of the ΣSPS_i
3. for each SPS_i in the network
   if $W_i > (W_{avg} + W_{th})$
   {
      Calculate the exceeded W_i and SMZ_i
      Broadcast the new SMZ_i to all remaining SPS.
      Collect the W_i and SMZ_i information from the responding SPS_i and sort in ascending order.
   }
4. Do until W_i of heavily loaded SPS_i is equal to W_{avg}
   for each SPS_i in the new list created
   {
      Transfer videos starting from to the first SPS_i
      Each SPS_i performs intra-cluster load balancing.
   }
}

4 Results and Discussions

The simulation of the proposed load balancing strategy yielded in the results as depicted in the following graphs. The simulation experiments were conducted for the server of LSG1 and LSG2 (Service Provider Servers). To illustrate that the load among the servers of LSG1 are balanced a graph depicting the load on all three servers is drawn (figure 2). Figure 3 illustrate that the load among the servers of LSG2 are balanced. The intra-cluster and inter-cluster load balancing algorithms yielded in results depicted in figure 4. The load on the servers of LSG1 and LSG2 are balanced up to 90%. Slight variations in the load are due to unavailability of bandwidth or video replication time. The delay between request arrival time and response start-up time is illustrated in figure 5. Here, there is an acceptable amount of delay as load increases exponentially in the systems.

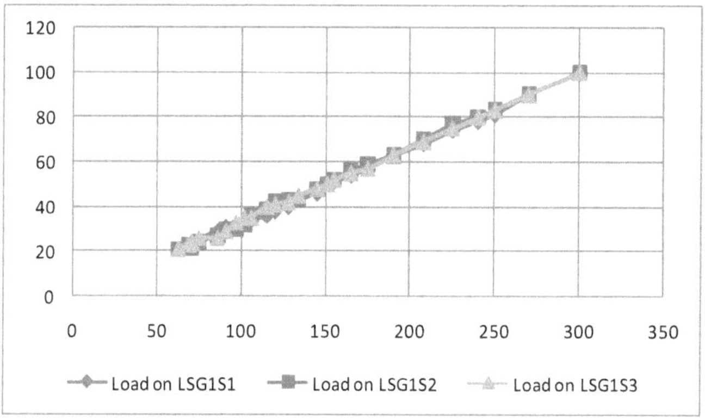

Fig. 2. Load balanced among servers of LSG1

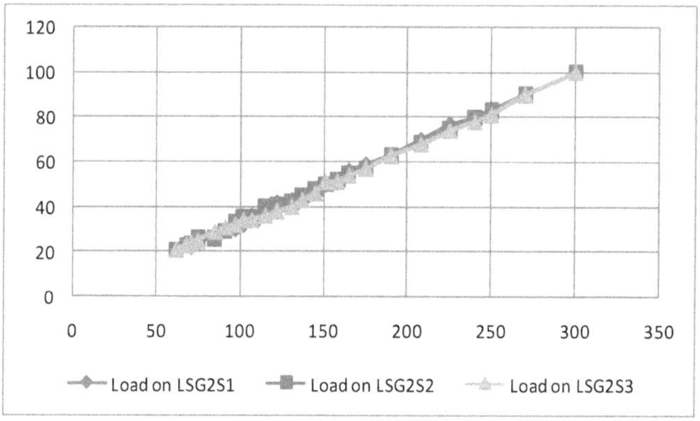

Fig. 3. Load balanced among servers of LSG2

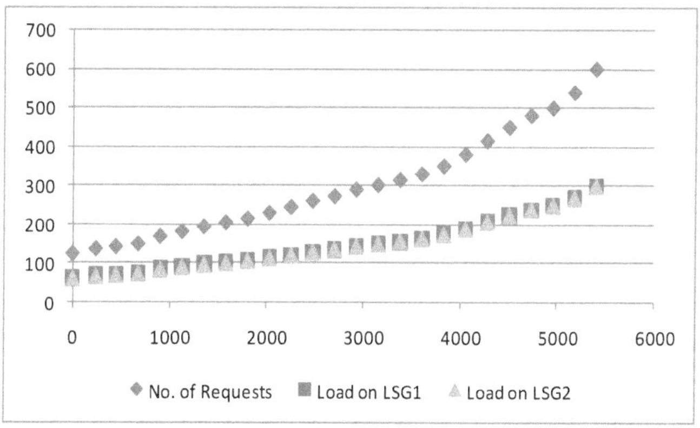

Fig. 4. Load balanced between LSG1 and LSG2

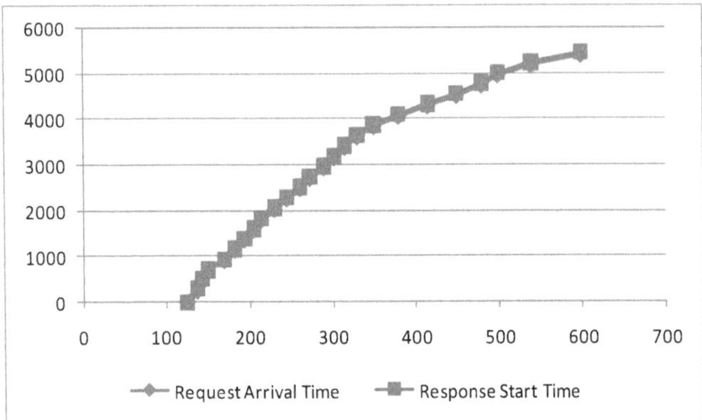

Fig. 5. Request Arrival Vs. Response Start-up Time

Figure 6 and 7 depicts the total number of request being successfully served and rejected by the system respectively. Around 8% of the total requests are rejected because of non-availability of resources for serving them.

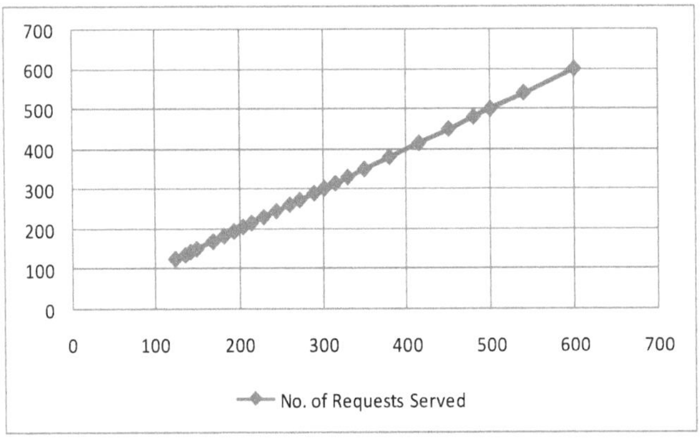

Fig. 6. Total number of requests served

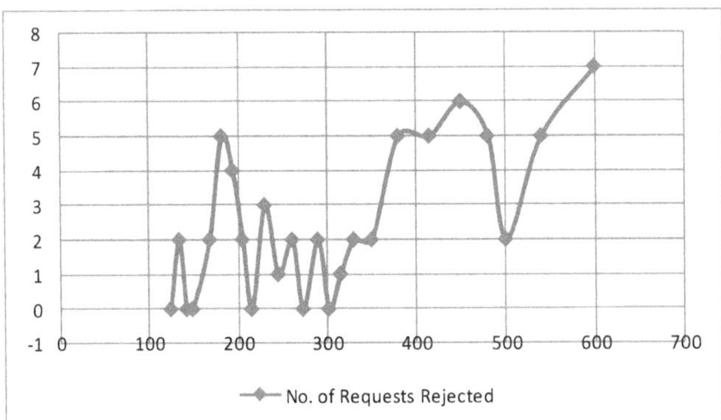

Fig. 7. Number of requests rejected

5 Conclusions and Future Work

This paper proposed a novel load balancing strategy for cluster based hybrid VoD systems. The usage of efficient hybrid architecture will good replication strategy, intra-cluster and inter-cluster load balancing strategies, use of coordinator (tracker) nodes, peer servers at various levels in the system hierarchy increases the system performance. Thus the system has features like availability and reliability. Simulation of the proposed strategy yielded in fruitful results. Load among the servers of cluster (service provider's region is considered as a cluster) was up to 90%. Future work includes improving the system model to reduce the number of servers in the used in the architecture. The proposed load balancing strategy can be modified to provide system wide load balancing rather than just at the server groups. Pricing strategy for inter-cluster routing among different service providers can also be a novel strategy. Finally, the rejection rate must be reduced.

Acknowledgement. The authors extend their heartfelt sincere gratitude to PES Management for all the support extended in carrying out this research work.

References

1. Ligang, D., Bharadwaj, V., Ko, C.C.: Efficient Movie Retrieval Strategies for Movie-On-Demand Multimedia Services On Distributed Networks. The Proceedings of Multimedia Tools Applications 20(2), 99–133 (2003)
2. Fischbach, K., Schoder, D., Schmitt, C.: Core Concepts in Peer-to-Peer Networking, ch. 1, pp. 1–27. Idea Group Inc. (2005)
3. Ghose, D., Kim, H.J.: Scheduling video streams in video-on-demand systems: A survey. In: The Proceedings of Multimedia Tools and Applications, ch. 11, pp. 167–195 (2000)
4. de la Paix, N.-D., Namur: Video-on-Demand over Internet : A Survey of Existing Systems and Solutions (2008)
5. Miao, Z., Ortega, A.: Proxy Caching for Efficient Video Services over the Internet. In: The Proceedings of Ninth International Packet Video Workshop (PVW 1999), pp. 20–26 (1999)
6. Lee, L.-T., Chang, H.-Y., Tao, D.-F., Yang, S.-L.: A Load Balanced PC-Cluster for Video-On-Demand Server Systems. The Proccedings of International Journal of Grid and Distributed Computing, 63–70 (2005)
7. Jaiphakdee, W., Srinilta, C.: Dynamic Load Balancing of Short Videos in Heterogeneous Storage Environment. In: The Proceedings of the International MultiConference of Engineers and Computer Scientist, vol. I, pp. 1–5 (2010)
8. Guruprasad, H.S., Maheshappa, H.D.: Dynamic Load Balancing Architecture for Distributed VoD using Agent Technology. The Proceedings of International Journal of Computer Science & Security (IJCSS) 2(5), 13–22 (2008)
9. Nimkar, A., Mandal, C., Reade, C.: Video Placement and Disk Load Balancing Algorithm for VoD Proxy Server. In: The Proceedings of 3rd IEEE International Conference on Internet Multimedia Services Architecture and Applications, pp. 141–146 (2009)
10. Chandra, P.K., Sahoo, B.: Performance Analysis of Load Balancing Algorithms for cluster of Video on Demand Servers. In: The Proceedings of IEEE International Advance Computing Conference, pp. 408–412 (2009)

Symlet2 Based Wavelet Filter Bank for Uncorrelated Digital Signal Recovery: Some Advantages over Matched Filter

Amit Kumar Ahuja and Ram Chakka

Meerut Institute of Engineering and Technology,
Meerut, India
amit123ahuja@gmail.com, ramchakka@yahoo.com
http://www.miet.ac.in/dep-ec.htm
http://www.miet.ac.in/director-research.htm

Abstract. Presence of noise in communication channels presents difficulty in signal recovery at the receiver. In this paper a methodology is developed for signal recovery using a wavelet filter bank (WFB), with applicability to baseband receivers. Uncorrelated test signals, useful in many practical applications, are conceived and used for the experimentation. This test signal is polar Non-Return-to-Zero (NRZ) line coded and transmitted through AWGN channel. Though we have considered the Symlet2 based WFB for this study, the methodology is suitable for any other filter bank too. The performance of the WFB-receiver in terms of Bit Error Rate (BER) is compared with that of a conventional matched filter based baseband receiver (MF-receiver). The results show that the WFB-receiver performs better than the conventional MF-receiver for certain input parameter ranges. Appropriate selection of the WFB and the use of adaptive filtering for improvised signal recovery come under future prospects of this research.

Keywords: performance, QoS, bit error rate, wavelet filter, matched filter, baseband receiver.

1 Introduction

Transmitters, communication channels and receivers are main components of communication systems. Noise is the primary source of signal corruption in baseband communication systems and it reduces the quality of received signal and hence the quality-of-service (QoS). Many ways exist to minimize the effect of the output errors. For example, one way is by increasing the Signal-to-Noise-Ratio (SNR_i) at the receiver input, by increasing the signal strength. Being important communication resources, transmitted power cannot be increased beyond a point since this may result in its improper utilization and many other problems too. For example, the effect of increased transmitted power on human body is still intensely researched and being debated in context of cellular networks [1]. Also, increasing transmitted power is not favourable to green technologies. This clearly

P.V. Krishna, M.R. Babu, and E. Ariwa (Eds.): ObCom 2011, Part I, CCIS 269, pp. 782–791, 2012.

shows that transmitting signals of low intensity (hence at low SNR levels) effectively is not only very important but also very essential. Another solution is the use of error detecting and correcting codes at the transmitter which interleave with original bits. These extra bits help further in signal recovery even if some bits get corrupted by noise. The result is reduction in average transmitted power per bit but at the cost of reduced utilization of the channel capacity. In the above two solutions, savings in one of the communication resources is usually achieved at the cost of the other. Use of proper filtering at the receiver end is the third and a highly promising solution of minimizing the effect of noise [2][3]. For a given SNR_i (input Signal-to-Noise Ratio, also referred as SNR in this paper), receivers are designed to optimize the SNR_o (output Signal-to-Noise-Ratio) and thus the Bit-Error-Rate (BER). The advantage gained by the third method over the other two methods is that, for given optimized B.W. and average transmitted power per bit, improvement or optimization in received signal quality can still be achieved. That is how the optimum design of communication receiver has become very important and attracted the attention of researchers. The third approach is used here for the BER improvement at the receiver output.

For transmitting through communication channel, bits need to be represented using suitable line codes. A wide variety of line codes have been mentioned in the literature and their choice may lead to efficient spectral shaping and efficient clock recovery at the receivers [2][3]. In some of these line codes, upon converting bits into electrical form, the statistical properties of bits to be transmitted remain unchanged. In other words, for example if bits are uncorrelated before line coding, the use of some of the line codes does not introduce any correlation among the bits. NRZ line coding comes under such codes. Such signal is simulated by conceiving uncorrelated (past-independent) $\boldsymbol{r_0}$-$\boldsymbol{r_1}$ test signals. Upon polar NRZ line coding and passing through AWGN (Additive White Gaussian Noise) environment, the transmitted bits are recovered using matched filter based baseband receiver (MF-receiver) and wavelet filter bank based baseband receiver (WFB-receiver), independently. In classical receivers (baseband or passband), the use of matched filter (MF) optimizes SNR_o for a given SNR_i. The block diagram of classical baseband receiver is shown in Fig. 1. For optimum detection, the impulse response of MF matches with the shape of transmitted

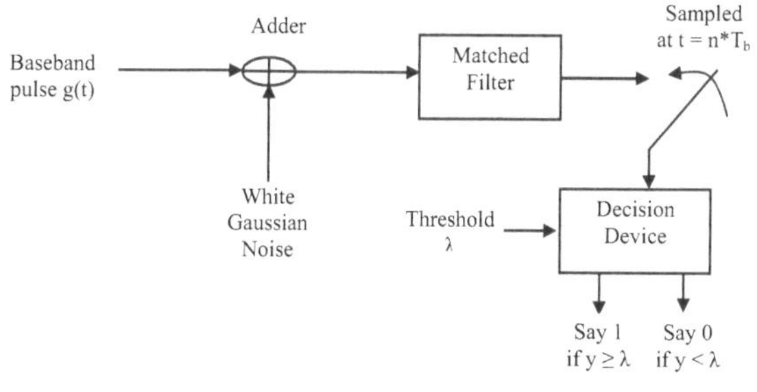

Fig. 1. Block diagram of classical digital baseband receiver using MF

noiseless pulse. In digital baseband receivers, the MF is practically implemented using integrate-and-dump filter. It can be proved that if MF output is sampled at sampling instants $t = n * T_b$, where n is non-zero positive integer and T_b is the bit duration, the SNR_o gets optimized [2][4][5]. The sampled output of the MF is compared with judiciously selected optimum threshold (λ) in decision device. The decision device takes decision of bit 1 if output sampled value is greater than and equal to λ, else it produces bit 0. Decision device makes a random decision like flipping a coin if sampled value of MF output is exactly equal to λ.

In performance analysis of classical digital baseband receivers, the signal to be transmitted is assumed to be corrupted by AWGN. For a given independent probability of bit generation r_0 for bit 0 and r_1 ($r_0 + r_1 = 1.0$) for bit 1 in the transmitted binary signal, bit duration T_b, power spectral density $N_0/2$ of the white noise, and peak amplitude A of the transmitted pulse, the optimum threshold λ_{opt} is given by following relation [2]:

$$\lambda_{opt} = \frac{N_0}{4AT_b} \ln\left(\frac{r_0}{r_1}\right) \tag{1}$$

Let p_{e0} and p_{e1} represents the respective probabilities of bit error when bit 0 and bit 1 are transmitted. Then for the special case of $r_0 = r_1 = 0.5$ and $p_{e0} = p_{e1}$, the average probability of bit error at the output of classical baseband receiver using MF can be derived as [2][3]:

$$p_e = \frac{1}{2}\boldsymbol{erfc}\left(\sqrt{\frac{E_b}{N_0}}\right) \tag{2}$$

Where $\boldsymbol{erfc}(.)$ is the complementary error function as defined in [2] and E_b is the bit energy. It is evident from (2) that, for a digital baseband receiver using MF, the average probability of bit error is a function of bit energy to the power spectral density ratio (E_b/N_0). Also;

$$p_e = \frac{1}{2}\boldsymbol{erfc}\left(\sqrt{\frac{SNR_i}{2}}\right) \tag{3}$$

where $SNR_i = 2E_b/N_0$ as given in [6]. The reduction in BER would lead to reduced B.W. requirement, for a given SNR_i [3], and therefore, any effort to further reduce BER is highly beneficial.

In this paper, a WFB based baseband receiver (WFB-receiver) is conceived, implemented, and its performance is evaluated and compared with that of conventional matched filter based baseband receiver (MF-receiver), with respect to BER. The WFB-receiver is found to perform better than the MF-receiver for some range of values of r_0. While for other ranges, the MF-receiver dominates the WFB-receiver, in performance. So this phenomenon gives rise to the possibility of exploiting the goodness of both these receivers in an adaptive way. In this paper, the emphasis has been laid mainly on the development of the required methodology for implementing the WFB at the receiver, and for performance comparisons with MF. For the purpose of experimentation, we have chosen Symlet2 wavelet filter bank, rather as a sample only, looking at its previous applications [7][8][9]. The important aspects of choosing appropriate WFB for maximizing the improvement would be the scope for further research.

2 Wavelet Filtering

There are many application areas of Wavelet Transform (WT) [10][11][12] and these are increasing day by day. One of the widely explored application areas, in context to WT, is noise filtering.

The history of WT can be seen from [12][13][14]. In the framework of noise suppression, noisy signal can be analyzed using either Continuous-Wavelet-Transform (CWT) or Discrete-Wavelet-Transform (DWT). Being faster, DWT is more effective than CWT.

For the signal de-noising using WT, the noisy signal is passed through the first stage of half band Low-Pass-Filter (LPF) and half band High-Pass-Filter (HPF). It was explained by Strang and Nguyen [15] that, the retrieval using decomposed signal is possible with less distortion if the wavelet decomposition and wavelet reconstruction filters are Quadrature-Mirror-Filters (QMF's). So the LPF and HPF need to be QMF's having their band in the range $0 - \pi/2$ and $\pi/2 - 0$ respectively. The process of signal decomposition and reconstruction is shown in Fig. 2 and further details can be held from [10][12].

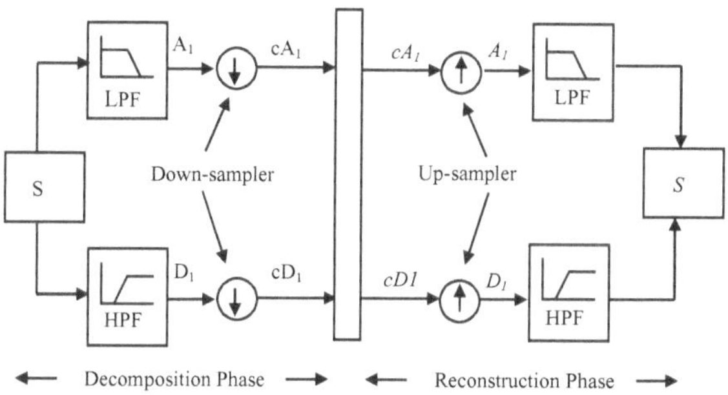

Fig. 2. Signal decomposition and synthesis using WFB at the receiver

3 Test Signal Conceived and Used

In this paper, the uncorrelated test signals r_0-r_1 are conceived and used in the experimentation. More categories are indeed possible but, because of page limitation, we have limited our analysis to this type of test signals only. The MATLAB software has been used for the generation of test signals.

3.1 Uncorrelated r_0-r_1 Signals

Since the digital data stream that is transmitted for a number of applications is often uncorrelated, the performance evaluation using these test signals becomes

very important. In this type of test signal, binary bits 0 and 1 are generated with probabilities that are independent of past generated bits. The $\boldsymbol{r_0}$-$\boldsymbol{r_1}$ signals are generated with following rules: r_0 = Probability of generation of bit 0; r_1= Probability of generation of bit 1. Also, note that $r_0+r_1 = 1.0$.
Obviously, r_0 is approximately equal to $\left(\frac{\text{No. of 0 bits in the binary data stream}}{\text{Total no. of bits in the binary data stream}}\right)$, and, r_1 is approximately equal to $\left(\frac{\text{No. of 1 bits in the binary data stream}}{\text{Total no. of bits in the binary data stream}}\right)$

Since the generation of the present bit in no way depends on the past bits, this class of signal is termed here as uncorrelated $\boldsymbol{r_0}$-$\boldsymbol{r_1}$ or past-independent signals. Bit streams are generated corresponding to a range of r_0 values that lie between 0.0 and 1.0. Since, source coding of bits after A/D conversion changes the proportion of number of 1's and 0's in the stream to be transmitted, the value of r_0 may be smaller or larger than 0.5. For example, in the interest of establishing strong clock signal, more 1's than 0's are produced in $\mu - 255$ PCM based codec [6]. The value of r_0 for T_1 voice line is normally somewhat smaller than 0.5 and depends on the amplitude of voice signals. The value of r_0 remains approximately equal to 0.35 for low-level signals that are in first encoding segment. On the other hand, for full scale sine wave, r_0 remains somewhat more than 0.5. Also, when a signal in the limited window is considered, the range of r_0 can become even wider, especially when the window is small. After transmitting through AWGN channel, the NRZ line coded bits are recovered at the receivers (one is MF-receiver and other is WFB-receiver) separately.

4 Simulation and Numerical Results

The simulation of MF-receiver and Symlet2 based WFB-receiver are carried out using MATLAB 7.6.0 (R2008a) version, on Intel(R) Xeon (R) CPU W3503 @ 2.40GHz, 64 bit processor based workstation. A signal length of 150000 bits is used for BER calculation at any given SNR at each simulation run. We find this sufficiently accurate when the Batch Means Method is applied.

4.1 Implementation Details

Aim of this paper is to develop a methodology for signal recovery at the receiver using a WFB and to check for improvements over MF, for any input parameter range. For this purpose, Symlet2 wavelet filter has been selected, as an example. However, as mentioned already, the selection of appropriate WFB for optimizing the signal recovery is a topic that has tremendous scope of further research.

Impulse responses corresponding to Symlet2 WFB are given as:

h_1 = [-0.12941 0.22414 0.83652 0.48296](For decomposition low pass filter);
h_2 = [-0.48296 0.83652 -0.22414 -0.12941](For decomposition high pass filter);
h_3 = [0.48296 0.83652 0.22414 -0.12941](For reconstruction low pass filter);
h_4 = [-0.12941 -0.22414 0.83652 -0.48296](For reconstruction high pass filter);

The approximate and detail coefficients are obtained after decomposition of noisy signal up to the first stage (as shown in Fig. 2). These coefficients correspond to the outputs of first stage LPF (given by h_1) and HPF (given by h_2) respectively. Approximation coefficients are neglected and the detail coefficients, after down-sampling and up-sampling respectively, are applied at the input of QMF corresponding to HPF (given by h_4) which is placed at the other side of the receiver. The output signal of QMF is compared with judiciously chosen threshold λ (given by (1) for $\boldsymbol{r_0}$-$\boldsymbol{r_1}$ signal) in a decision device.

Decision device produces bit 1 if sample value at its input is greater than and equal to λ. Otherwise, bit 0 is produced at its output. The improvement of WFB-receiver over MF-receiver is indicated by BER-Reduction-Factor ($BERRF$), which is defined as:

$$BERRF = \frac{BER_w}{BER_m} \tag{4}$$

Where BER_w denotes the Bit-Error-Rate at the output of the WFB-receiver, and BER_m is that of MF-receiver. Improvement of WFB-receiver over MF-receiver is indicated by $BERRF \leq 1.0$.

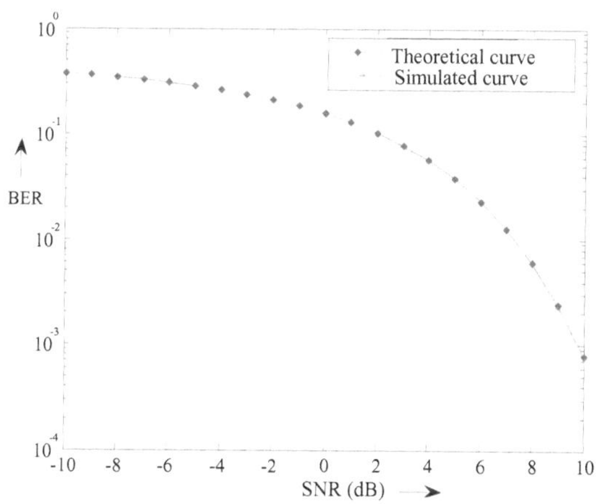

Fig. 3. Simulated and theoretical BER vs. SNR curve for MF-receiver

Fig. 3 shows the comparison (BER vs. SNR curve) between simulation result and the result based on theoretical expression (3), for the case of the MF-receiver. This result is generated using past independent test signal with $r_0 = r_1 = 0.5$. The mean square error (MSE) between theoretical expression given by (3) and the simulated curve is 6.2×10^{-4} which is very small.

4.2 Simulation Results

Test signals corresponding to different r_0, r_1 values are generated. The value of r_0 is varied between 0 and 1.0. The corresponding test signals are generated and applied at the inputs of the MF-receiver and the WFB-receiver, separately after passing through AWGN channel. BER vs. r_0 curve for WFB-receiver and MF-receiver at high noisy condition is shown in Fig. 4.

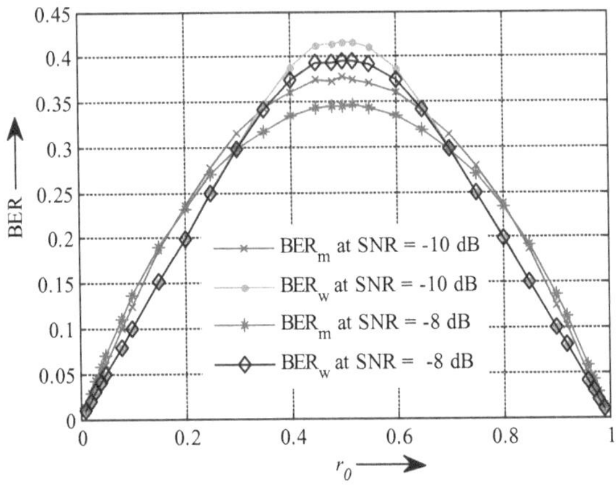

Fig. 4. Comparison of WFB-receiver and MF-receiver in terms of BER vs. r_0 curve at high noisy conditions

From the results, shown in Fig. 4, following conclusions can be drawn:

1. BER is low at lower values of r_0 and it increases with increase in r_0. BER curve reaches at its maximum at $r_0 = 0.5$.
2. BER curve is symmetrical about $r_0 = 0.5$. This is quite intuitive since $r_0 = 0.5$ corresponds to random generation of bit 0 and bit 1.
3. At $SNR = -10$ dB, for $r_0 \leq 0.35$ and $r_0 \geq 0.65$, the WFB-receiver performs better than the MF-receiver since BER_w (BER at the output of WFB-receiver) is smaller than BER_m (BER at the output of MF-receiver). If we define favourable range as the range of values of r_0 for which $BERRF \leq 1.0$, the favourable range at $SNR = -10$ dB is 70%.
4. Similarly in the range $r_0 \leq 0.3$ and $r_0 \geq 0.6$, at $SNR = -8$ dB, the performance of WFB-receiver is better than the MF-receiver and favourable range is 60%.
5. Comparing the BER vs. r_0 curves for $SNR = -10$ dB and $SNR = -8$ dB, it is clear that the favourable range is decreasing with increase in SNR value.

$BERRF$ vs. r_0 curve for SNR's ranging from -10 dB to -2 dB (high noisy conditions) and that for higher values of SNR's are shown in the left portion and right portion respectively of Fig. 5. Obviously, cases in which $BERRF \leq 1.0$ corresponds to better performance of the WFB-receiver over the MF-receiver.

Following conclusions can be drawn from Fig. 5:

1. For all SNR levels, $BERRF$ vs. r_0 curves are symmetrical about $r_0 = 0.5$. This is quite understandable since BER vs. r_0 curve for WFB-receiver and MF-receiver is symmetrical as discussed already.
2. It is clear that the favourable range depends upon the SNR levels. For $SNR = -10$ dB, there is much wider favourable range of r_0 compared to the case of higher SNR's.

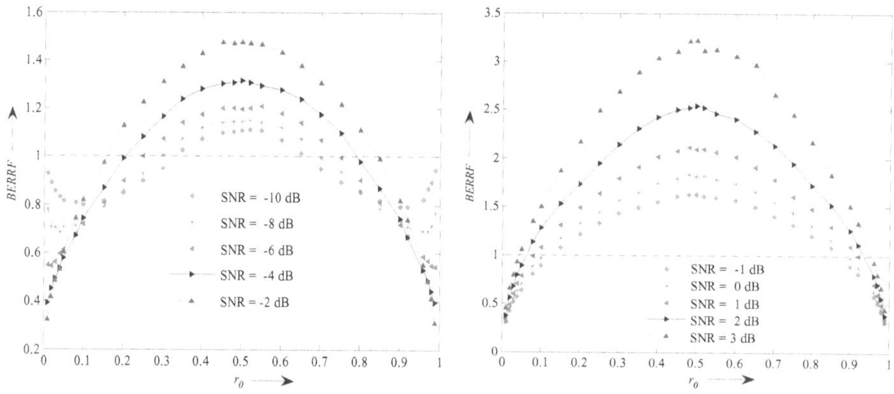

Fig. 5. $BERRF$ vs. r_0 performance curve for high noisy conditions

3. At very low and very high values of r_0, high improvement with up to 70% reduction in BER is observed.
4. For a given r_0, with r_0 in the range $r_0 \leq 0.3$ and $r_0 \geq 0.6$, $BERRF$ is increasing with decrease in SNR.
5. Higher improvement at low SNR indicates the potential applicability of WFB-receivers at high noisy conditions.
6. As seen in the left portion of Fig. 5, a reverse trend in improvement (lower improvement corresponding to higher SNR) is observed for the range $r_0 \leq$ 0.1 and $r_0 \geq 0.9$.
7. It is important to note that the improvement of the WFB over MF may indeed be much higher than what is presented here if more appropriate WFB be used. Though this is our guess, however, finding the most appropriate wavelet filter is a very important topic for future research.

5 Analysis of Numerical Results

For the case of r_0-r_1 signals, in the low and high ranges of r_0, especially at low SNR's, $BERRF$ is less than 1.0, which indicates that the WFB-receiver performs better than MF-receiver. It is important to see the possible reasons behind these improvements. Following is the brief reasoning which can be verified using some suitable methodology, not covered in this paper.

In MF-receiver, because of implementation of MF as an integrate-and-dump filter, there is no effect of past bits on the present bits. This effect is known as interference. In WFB-receiver, the wavelet filter (Symlet2) used is of order 4 (as given in section 4.1). So this would cause finite interference on the present bit from the previous bit. It appears that, at the low and high range of r_0, and especially at high-noisy conditions, this interference is helping in bit recovery in WFB-receiver. This is an interesting discovery which can be used for advantage. We consider and call this phenomenon as 'constructive interference'. Likewise for the other values of r_0, the interference from previous bit seems to produce more errors in WFB-receiver compared to MF-receiver so, the interference being 'destructive' in nature. Quantitative analysis of constructive and destructive interferences can be a good topic for future research. Here, we are thus using the interference connected with the WFB to our advantage of more accurate signal extraction which is possible only in the limited range of r_0.

6 Conclusion

Recovery of the noisy signal in baseband and other communication systems with low BER, especially at high noisy conditions, is the important area of research today. In this paper, a new methodology has been proposed and used for signal recovery using a WFB (Wavelet Filter Bank). Uncorrelated (past-independent) $\boldsymbol{r_0}$-$\boldsymbol{r_1}$ test signals having their importance in many practical applications is considered for the performance analysis study. The $\boldsymbol{r_0}$-$\boldsymbol{r_1}$ signals after passing through AWGN channel, are recovered using two receivers separately, one is the classical MF-receiver (matched filter based baseband receiver), and the other is a WFB-receiver (Wavelet filter based baseband receiver). In the conventional receiver, the MF is implemented as an integrate-and-dump filter, while a standard de-noising procedure using WT (Wavelet Transform) is used for the signal recovery in the WFB-receiver. The purpose of this paper is to develop the required methodology for employing any given WFB, and to demonstrate the possible advantages over conventional MF. Though different types of WFB's exist, we have chosen Symlet2 filter bank, as an example. Since appreciable improvement is seen in the WFB-receiver, the results are encouraging especially at low and high values of r_0 and at low SNR conditions.

The results clearly show that there exist the possibilities of developing an appropriate adaptive scheme in which the goodness of both the receivers can be exploited. In other words, for low and high values of r_0, the adaptive filter scheme could switch to WFB mode, and for value of r_0 near 0.5 it could work in MF mode. Since maximum improvement of approximately 70% in BER is observed, corresponding to low and high values of r_0, this research may lead to a methodology for the significant reduction in B.W. requirement.

Although an important aspect of choosing the most appropriate WFB is not concentrated upon in this paper, the methodologies developed here in can be used for other WFB's and is the important topic for further research. Additional improvements in the WFB-receivers are indeed possible by a number of ways such as, right tuning of the threshold, and selecting more appropriate classes of WFB's which could give better performance over wider favourable range of r_0.

References

1. IARC Monographs on the Evaluation of Carcinogenic Risks to Humans, Non-Ionizing Radiation, PART II: Radiofrequency Electromagnetic Fields (Includes Mobile Telephones, Microwaves and Radars), Lyon, France, vol. 102 (2011)

2. Hykins, S.: Communication Systems, 4th edn., pp. 247–259. John Wiley and Sons Inc. (2004)
3. Lathi, B.P.: Modern Digital and Analog Communication Systems, 3rd edn. The Oxford Series in Electrical and Computer Engineering, pp. 717–722. Oxford University Press (2007)
4. Reiger, S.: Error Probabilities of Binary Data Transmission in the Presence of Random Noise. IRE Convention Record, pt. 9, 72–79 (1953)
5. Arthur, E.: Optimum Detection of Digital Signal in Presence of White Noise-A Geometric Interpretation and Study of Three Basic Data Transmission Systems. IRE Transaction on Information Theory (1962)
6. Bellamy, J.C.: Digital Telephony, 3rd edn., pp. 173–175, 597–600 . John-Wiley and Sons, Inc. (2005)
7. Anoaba, O.A.: Noise Analysis in Mobile Radio Environment using Pathlets and Symlet2 Wavelets. In: IEEE Int. Conf. on TENCON, p. 1318 (2010)
8. Aktas, M., Turkmenaglu, V.: Wavelet based Switching Faults Detection in Direct Torque Control Induction Motor Drives. IET Journal of Sci. Meas. Techno. 4(6), 303–310 (2010)
9. Tse, N.C.F.: Practical Applications of Wavelet to Power Quality Analysis. In: Power Engg. Society General Meeting, p. 5 (2006)
10. Tang, Y.T., Wickershauser, V., Yuen, P.C., Li, C.-H. (eds.): WAA 2001. LNCS, vol. 2251. Springer, Heidelberg (2001)
11. Chen, K.H., Chiueh, T.D.: A 1.8V 165mW Discrete Wavelet Multi-Tone Baseband Receiver for Cognitive Radio Applications. In: Solid-State Circuits Conf., Dig. of Tech. Papers, IEEE Int., pp. 578–623 (2007)
12. Wavelet Toolbox, MATLAB help, `http://www.mathworks.com/products/wavelet`
13. Mallat, S.: A Theory for Multiresolution Signal Decomposition: The Wavelet Representation. IEEE Trans. Pattern Anal. Machine Intell. 31, 674–693 (1989)
14. Pathak, R.S.: The Wavelet Transform. Atlantis Studies in Mathematics for Engineering and Science, vol. 4 (2009)
15. Strang, G., Nguyen, T.: Wavelets and Filter Banks. Wellesley-Cambridge Press (1996)
16. Ali, N.K.: Subband and Wavelet Transform: Design and Applications. Springer, Heidelberg (1996)

Iterative Relaxed Median Filter for Impulse Noise Removal and Validation of FCM Clustering Using Cluster Error Index in Median Filtered MR Images

R. Vijayarajan[1] and S. Muttan[2]

[1] Anna University Chennai, Tamil Nadu, India
[2] Centre for Medical Electronics, Department of ECE, Anna University Chennai, India
viraj2k@gmail.com, muthan_s@annauniv.edu

Abstract. Impulse noise removal is a complex procedure in MR images and hence in this paper, Iterative relaxed median filter is proposed to improve Peak signal to noise ratio of the filtered image and validation of Fuzzy C-Means clustering (FCM) over median filtered MR images is carried out using Cluster Error Index (CEI). For comparative analysis, median filtering methods such as standard median filter (SMF), adaptive median filter (AMF), hybrid median filter (HMF) and relaxed median filter (RMF) are used. Elaborate analysis of noise removal of median filtering methods and effect of these median filtering methods over FCM Clustering is done based on different validity measures.

Keywords: FCM, Standard median, Adaptive median, Hybrid median, Relaxed median, Validity measures, Cluster Error Index.

1 Introduction

Medical images are more vulnerable to noises particularly impulse noise which is introduced during image acquisition, transmission and storage. Removing noises is highly complex because it requires the balance between the gained improvement and the introduced degradation by a particular filter. Among the non-linear statistical filters, the standard median filter and its modifications provide balancing performance in suppression of impulse noise [1,2,3]. These filtering methods adapt to the local properties and structures in the image. Despite its effectiveness in smoothing noise, it removes fine details of the image [4,5,6]. To preserve the fine details and to restore the image, other median filtering techniques such as adaptive median, hybrid median, relaxed median filtering methods have been used.

Image segmentation plays an important role in the analysis and applications of medical image processing . The main purpose of medical image segmentation is to extract interesting regions which contain important diagnostic information in order to provide credibility basis for clinic diagnose and pathology research. Fuzziness and in-homogeneity are inevitable in medical images compared with ordinary images

P.V. Krishna, M.R. Babu, and E. Ariwa (Eds.): ObCom 2011, Part I, CCIS 269, pp. 792–801, 2012.

because of its imaging principle and human body tissues' high complexity and diversity. Meanwhile, the rapid development of medical imaging technology makes it possible to obtain various complex and massive medical image data, which all put forward higher requirements for medical image segmentation. Segmentation of medical images is quiet complex due to the poor image contrast and artifacts which result in missing or diffused organ or tissue boundaries.

Many image processing techniques have been proposed for brain MR images segmentation, most popularly thresholding, region growing, edge detection and clustering.

Rajapakse et.al [7] classified different methods of Image Segmentation as four main categories. The classical methods such as thresholding, region growing, edge based techniques and the statistical methods such as the maximum-likelihood-classifier (MLC). These methods are basically supervised and depend on the prior model and its parameters. In unsupervised methods such as clustering, the n-dimensional vectors of the input image are evaluated on the basis of the pixel values of a limited region. Similar vectors will be associated to pixels belonging to the same region while different ones will be associated to corresponding regions.

Among the clustering algorithms, FCM clustering is most popular for medical image segmentation because of its robustness. A conventional FCM does not use spatial information in the image. Its advantages include a straightforward implementation, fairly robust behaviour, applicability to multichannel data, and the ability to model uncertainty within the data. A major disadvantage of its use in imaging applications, however, is that FCM does not incorporate information about spatial context, causing it to be sensitive to noise and other imaging artifacts. Since medical images include considerable uncertainty and unknown noise, this generally leads to further difficulties with clustering. Spatial operations performed on local neighbourhood of input pixels are used for image enhancement thus can contribute to the performance of FCM algorithm. The advantages [8] of spatial information into FCM are the following (i) Regions are more homogeneous (ii) It reduces the spurious blobs. (iii) It is less sensitive to noise than other techniques.

The non-linear spatial filtering methods discussed above not only remove impulse noise but also provide neighborhood information. Clustering performance of FCM algorithm changes with respect to the filtering methods applied to the images. Neighborhood information given by the spatial filtering methods effectively reduces local minima problem in FCM clustering algorithm. In this paper, performance of FCM algorithm is analyzed for the images which are corrupted by impulse noise and restored by various median filtering methods. Performance analysis of those filtering methods with respect to medical images is also carried out.

The remaining sections of this paper are organized as follows. Section 2 gives a brief on various median filtering methods and proposed method. Section 3 is about FCM algorithm and the steps involved for performance analysis. Section 4 gives performance measures for both filtering and clustering. Performance analysis, simulation and results are given in Section 5. This is followed by a conclusion.

2 Filtering Methods

2.1 Existing Methods

2.1.1 Standard Median Filtering

This filter uses the median value of all the pixels in the filtering window as a replacement for the central pixel value. This provides very good noise removal but results in loss of fine details [9, 10, 11]. The small filtering window leads to poor elimination of noise and big one results in loss of fine details.

Let Xi and Yi be the input and the output at location i of the filter, then the standard median filter is given by

$$Y_i = med\{W_i\} = med\{X_{i+r}: r\epsilon W\} \tag{1}$$

Where med {.} denotes the median operator and $[W_i]_{(r)}$, r=1,...,2N+1, the rth order statistic of the samples inside the window W_i is

$$[Wi]_{(1)} \leq [Wi]_{(2)} \leq \ldots \leq [Wi]_{(2N+1)} \tag{2}$$

2.1.2 Adaptive Median Filter

This filter uses adaptively altered window size to detect noise pixels so the fine details are highly preserved and at the same time noise pixels also contribute in sorting the pixels in the window

The adaptive median filtering works in two levels [12, 13]

(i) if $W_{min} < W_{med} < W_{max}$, go to level (ii)
Else increase the window size
If window size $\leq S_{max}$, repeat level (i)
Else output W_{med}

(ii) If $W_{min} < W_i < W_{max}$, output W_I
Else output W_{med}

Where S_{max} denotes the maximum allowed size of the adaptive filter window W_i

2.1.3 Hybrid Median Filter

In this filter [14], three median values are calculated in the NXN window: MR is the median of horizontal and vertical R pixels, and MD is the median of diagonal D pixels. The filtered value is the median of the two median values and the central pixel C: median (MR, MD and C). For N=3;

$$\begin{vmatrix} D & R & D \\ R & C & R \\ D & R & D \end{vmatrix} \tag{3}$$

2.1.4 Relaxed Median Filter

Let $\{X_i\}$ be a m-dimensional sequence, where the index i Є Z_m. A sliding window is defined as a subset

$W Є Z_m$ of odd size 2N + 1. Given a sliding window W,define $W_i = \{ X_i \}$: r Є W to be the window located at position i.

Let X_i and Y_i be the input and the output at location i, respectively, then the standard median (SM) filter is given by

$$Y_i = med\{W_i\} = med\{X_{i+r}: r \in W\}; \tag{4}$$

where med{.} denotes the median operator.

Denoted by $[W_i]_{(r)}$, r = 1,...,2N+1, the r th order statistic of the samples inside the window W_i.

$$[W_i]_{(1)} \leq [W_i]_{(2)} \leq [W_i]_{(3)} \leq \ldots \leq [W_i]_{(2N+1)}.$$

The relaxed median filter works as follows [15]: Lower (l) and Upper (u) bounds, define a sublist inside the $[W_i](.)$, which contains the gray levels which are good enough not to be impulse noise. If the input belongs to the sublist, then it remains unfiltered, otherwise the standard median filter is output.

Let m = N + 1 and l, u such that $1 \leq l \leq m \leq u \leq 2N+1$. The relaxed median filter with bounds l and u is defined as

$$Y_i = \text{Relaxedmedian}_{lu}\{W_i\} \begin{cases} X_i \text{ if } X_i \epsilon [[W_i]_l, [W_i]_u] \\ [W_i]_m \text{ otherwise} \end{cases} \tag{5}$$

where [Wi](m) is the median value of the samples inside the window Wi.

2.2 Proposed Method

Iterative relaxed median filter (IRMF)

Iterations are applied to filtering methods to maximize the outcomes. Relaxed median filter results in better noise removal with respect to other median filtering methods. Performance of this filter can be improved further by doing iterative filtering of the input image.

Steps involved

Relaxed median filter is applied to the input image which is corrupted by impulse noise.

1. Peak signal to noise ratio is calculated between filtered image and the original image.
2. Filtered image is subjected to filtering again.
3. PSNR is calculated for the new filtered image.
4. Check the following condition

If $[PSNR(i) - PSNR(i-1)] < 0$ (6)

Stop and PSNR is given by PSNR = PSNR(i-1)

or

if Number of iterations = Max. No. of iterations (7)

Stop and PSNR is given by PSNR = PSNR(i)

5. If the conditions 6 & 7 are not satisfied, repeat steps 3-5

where PSNR(i) is peak signal to noise ratio between newly filtered image and the original image.

3 FCM Clustering Algorithm

FCM is an unsupervised clustering algorithm [16, 17, 18] which allows one piece input vector to two or more clusters. It is based on minimization of the given objective function

$$J_m = \sum_{i=1}^{N} \sum_{j=1}^{c} u_{ij}^m \left\|x_i - c_j\right\|^2 \quad (8)$$

where m is any real value greater than one and set to two by Bezdek[16]. u_{ij} is the degree of membership of x_i in the cluster j. x_i is the ith of d-dimensional data. C_j is the centre of the cluster j and II*II is any norm showing the similarity between any measured data and the centre.

Fuzzy portioning is done through an iterative optimization of the objective function with the updating of membership of u_{ij} and the C_j cluster centres

$$u_{ij} = \frac{1}{\sum_{k=1}^{c}\left(\frac{\|x_i - c_j\|}{\|x_i - c_k\|}\right)^{\frac{2}{m-1}}} \quad (9)$$

$$c_j = \frac{\sum_{i=1}^{N} u_{ij}^m . x_i}{\sum_{i=1}^{N} u_{ij}^m} \quad (10)$$

Termination of iteration is given by

$$max_{ij}\{\left|u_{ij}^{k+1} - u_{ij}^{k}\right|\} < \varepsilon \quad (11)$$

Where ε is a termination criterion which lies between 0 and 1. k is the iteration steps.

Simulation Steps

1. For MR brain image corrupted by impulse noise of different probability densities, apply median filtering methods by considering a window of size (mxn)
2. Replace each pixel value by its spatially modified and filtered value and apply FCM algorithm.

FCM Algorithm

3. Initialize U=[u_j] matrix, U(0)
4. At k-step, determine the centres vectors C(k)=[c_j] with U(k)

$$c_j = \frac{\sum_{i=1}^{N} u_{ij}^m . x_i}{\sum_{i=1}^{N} u_{ij}^m} \quad (12)$$

5. Update U(k), U(k+1)$u_{ij} = \frac{1}{\sum_{k=1}^{c}\left(\frac{\|x_i - c_j\|}{\|x_i - c_k\|}\right)^{\frac{2}{m-1}}}$ (13)

If $\|U(k+1) - U(k)\| < \varepsilon$, then stop the iterations otherwise go to step 2.

4 Validity Functions

4.1 Validity Functions for Noise Removal

The median filtering methods are evaluated and compared in terms of Peak signal-to-noise ratio (PSNR) and mean absolute error (MAE). These quantitative measures are defined [8] as

$$PSNR = \frac{255^2}{\frac{1}{mn}\sum_{i=1}^{m}\sum_{j=1}^{n}(I(i,j)-I_O(i,j))^2} \quad (14)$$

$$MAE = \frac{1}{mn}\sum_{i=1}^{m}\sum_{j=1}^{n}|(I(i,j)-I_O(i,j))| \quad (15)$$

Where I(i,j) and Io(i,j) are the pixel values of restored and original images respectively at the location (i, j).

4.2 Cluster Error Index (CEI) and Average Cluster Error Index (ACEI)

Quality of a partition provided by clustering algorithms is evaluated by a function called Cluster Error Index (CEI) and Average Cluster Error Index (ACEI) which are calculated by the following steps

(i) Let x(i) be the original image and y(i) be the filtered output of image with impulse noise. Where i=1,2,...,N. N is number of pixels in the input image.

(ii) Let $x_r(i)$ and $y_r(i)$ be the clustered regions of x(i) and y(i) respectively. Where r=1,...,C. C is number of clusters which is taken as 3 here.

(iii) Find out number of pixels in $x_r(i)$ and $y_r(i)$ denoted as N_r and M_r respectively.

(iv) Calculate CEI

$$CEI = \frac{|N_r - M_r|}{N}; r = 1, \ldots, C \quad (16)$$

Average CEI of all the clusters

$$ACEI = \frac{\sum_{r=1}^{C}\frac{|N_r - M_r|}{N}}{C} \quad (17)$$

5 Simulation and Results

Median filtering methods mentioned above with a window size of 3x3 are taken for analysis. MR brain image was subjected to various impulse noise probability densities ranging from 10% to 90%. Fig. 5 shows the input image and the image with 30% impulse noise. Filtering was done for all noise densities. To analyze the performance of noise removal, quantitative performance measures such as PSNR and MAE have been tabulated in table 1 and table 2. Analysing fig.1 and fig.2, it is evident that IRMF shows better noise removing capability at mid and higher noise probability densities.

Furthermore IRMF shows remarkable improvement in terms of MAE. Even up to a noise probability density of 60%, MAE of IRMF is very less as compared to other methods. At lower noise probability densities particularly 10% and 20%, proposed method shows considerable improvement interms of both PSNR and MAE. Among all the filters analysed, AMF results in very poor noise removing ability.

Validation of clustering is done by Cluster Error Index. Higher CEI shows poor clustering. Smaller ACEI shows superior clustering performance among all gray values. CEI and ACEI are tabulated in table 3 and table 4. Fig.3 clearly shows that HMF & RMF lead to poor clustering whereas SMF & IRMF lead to remarkable clustering performance. From fig.4, effect of all median filtering methods on clustering at lower gray values is very high; meanwhile SMF & IRMF result in very small CEI at mid and higher gray values.

Clustered regions of all filtered images are given in fig.6 – fig.10. From the figures, it is obvious that AMF leads to poor clustering for all gray values. Other methods achieved better noise removal and clustering. Over all, IRMF shows higher noise removal, edge smoothing and preservation of most of the details of the image.

Table 1. PSNR for different noise densities

Noise Probability Density (%)	10	20	30	40	50	60	70	80	90
SMF	31.202	27.4305	22.1932	18.1053	14.1387	11.3508	8.9577	6.993	5.4778
AMF	24.6791	19.3578	15.8549	13.5781	11.3811	9.7454	8.152	6.6682	5.4161
HMF	28.9216	27.2477	24.4256	19.8656	15.9341	12.6294	9.6087	7.38	5.6126
RMF	28.78	27.6733	25.8306	23.1825	19.322	15.9918	12.1374	8.9501	6.375
IRMF	31.3238	29.0595	28.0223	26.7768	24.9884	22.3304	17.3055	11.5893	7.5656

Table 2. MAE for different noise densities

Noise Probability Density (%)	10	20	30	40	50	60	70	80	90
SMF	49.3039	117.4992	392.4269	1005.9	2507.3	4764.3	8266.3	12995	18420
AMF	221.3971	753.8752	1688.8	2852.8	4731.2	6895.2	9951.4	14004	18684
HMF	83.3535	122.5504	234.7026	670.6929	1658.3	3549.2	7115.6	11887	17857
RMF	86.115	111.1102	169.8309	312.4859	760.118	1636.4	3975.1	8280.8	14982
IRMF	47.9401	80.7471	102.5291	136.5838	206.1769	380.2	1209.3	4509.8	11390

Table 3. Cluster wise Cluster Error Index

	SMF	AMF	HMF	RMF	IRMF
MCR	0.279331	0.368301	0.709211	0.709851	0.278529

Table 4. Average Cluster Error Index

	SMF	AMF	HMF	RMF	IRMF
Cluster1	0.767885	0.904787	0.769023	0.765381	0.761251
Cluster2	0.045656	0.114627	0.674883	0.672704	0.045623
Cluster3	0.024454	0.08549	0.683728	0.691467	0.028714

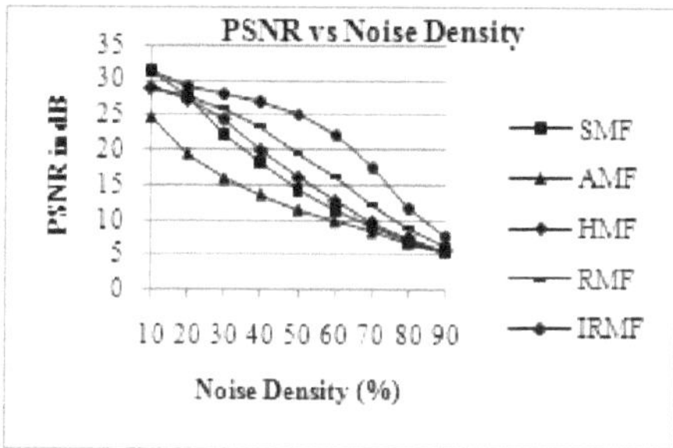

Fig. 1. PSNR performance index

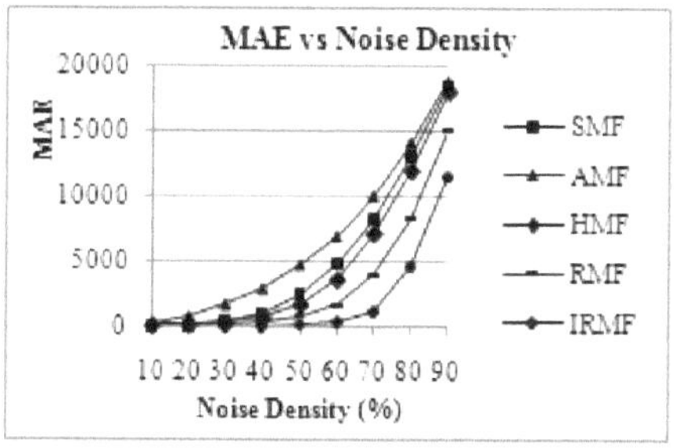

Fig. 2. MAE performance index

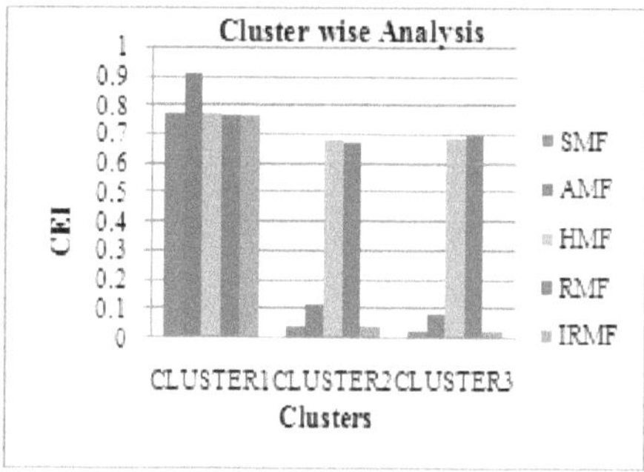

Fig. 3. Cluster wise Cluster Error Index

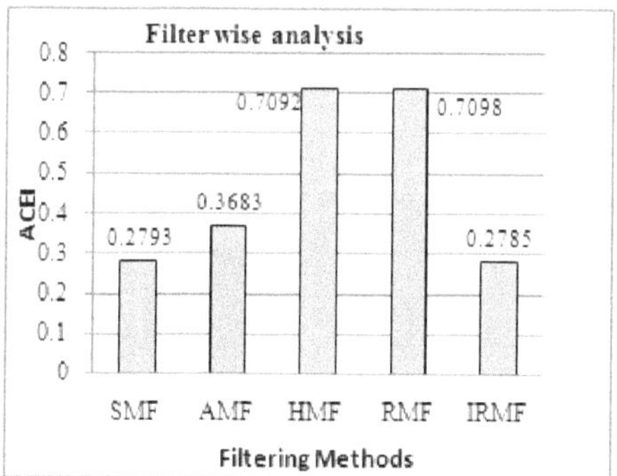

Fig. 4. Filter wise Cluster Error Index

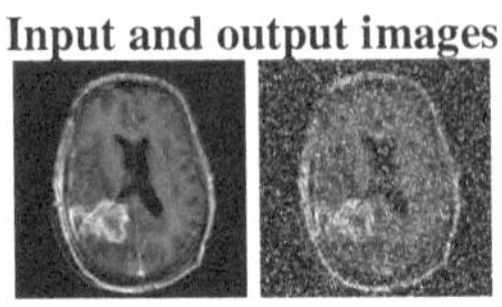

(a) (b)

Fig. 5. (a) MR Brain Image (b) Image with 30% Impulse noise

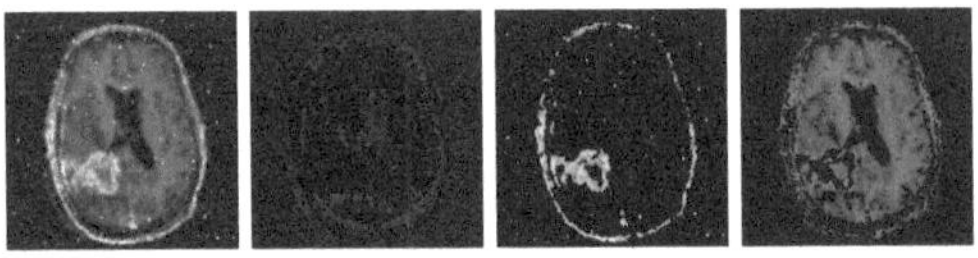

(a) (b) (c) (d)

Fig. 6. (a) SMF (b)-(d) Clustered Regions

(a) (b) (c) (d)

Fig. 7. (a) AMF (b)-(d) Clustered Regions

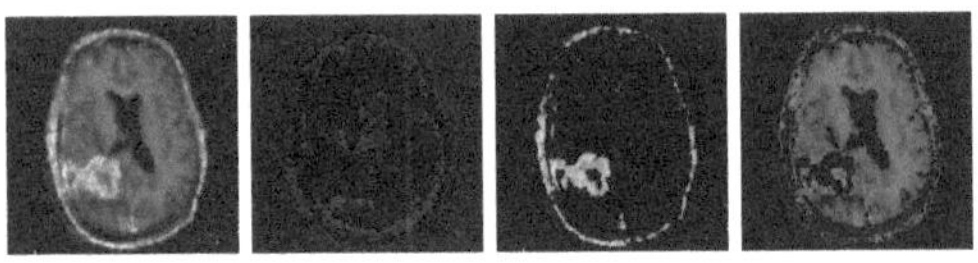

(a) (b) (c) (d)

Fig. 8. (a) HMF (b)-(d) Clustered Regions

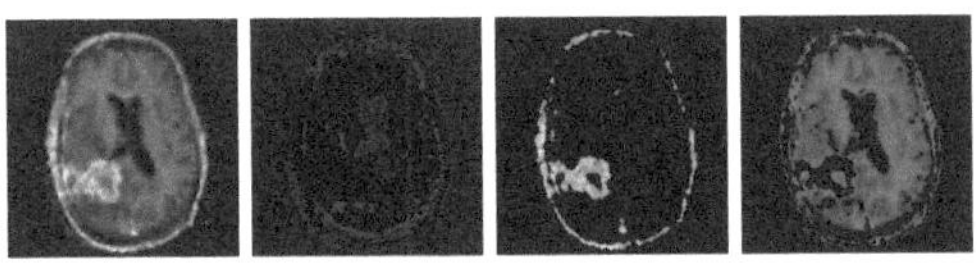

(a) (b) (c) (d)

Fig. 9. (a) RMF (b)-(d) Clustered Regions

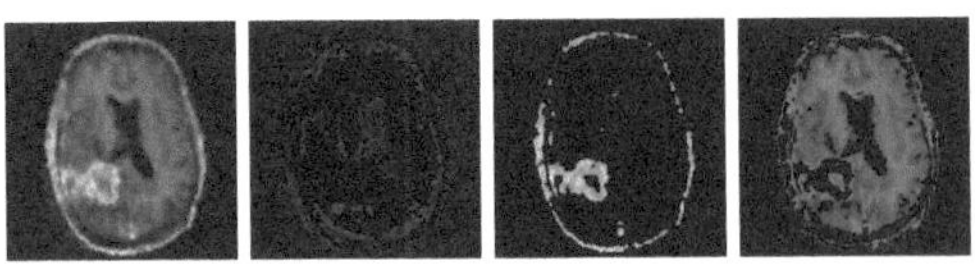

(a) (b) (c) (d)

Fig. 10. (a) IRMF (b)-(d) Clustered Regions

6 Conclusion

Based on the tabulation and analysis, among the above mentioned median filtering methods, it is proved that IRMF results in improved noise removal in terms of PSNR and MAE than other methods but not preservation of edges. Even though adaptive median filtering is good for other imageries, it shows poor performance for the image taken for analysis. The proposed Iterative relaxed median filtering also leads to reasonable clustering performance as compared to other methods.

References

[1] Bessdok, E.: Impulsive noise suppression from images by using Anfis Interpolant and Lilliefest. EURASIP Journal on Applied Signal Processing 16, 2423–2433 (2004)

[2] Wang, Z., Zhang, D.: Progressive switching median filter for the removal of impulse noise from highly corrupted images. IEEE Trans. on Circuits and Systems II: Analog and Digital Signal Processing 46(1), 78–80 (1999)

[3] Chen, T., Wu, H.R.: Adaptive impulse detection using center weighted median filters. IEEE Signal Processing Letters 8(1), 1–3 (2001)

[4] Pok, G., et al.: Selective removal of impulse noise based on homogeneity level information. IEEE Transactions on Image Processing 12(1) (2003)

[5] Arce, G.R., McLoughlin, M.P.: Theoretical analysis of the Max/Median filter. IEEE Transactions on Acoust., Speech, Signal Processing ASSP-35, 60–69 (1987)

[6] Gabbouj, M., et al.: An overview of median and stack filtering. Circuits Syst. Signal Process. 11, 7–45 (1992)

[7] Rajapakse, J.C., et al.: Statistical Approach to Segmentation of Single-Channel Cerebral MR Images. IEEE Trans. on Medical Imaging 16(2) (1997)

[8] Chuang, K.-S., et al.: Fuzzy c-means clustering with spatial information for image segmentation. Journal on Computerized Medical Imaging and Graphics (30), 9–15 (2006)

[9] Pan, M.-S., et al.: An Adaptive median filter algorithm based on B-Spline function. International Journal on Automation and Computing 8(1), 92–99 (2011)

[10] Chan, R.H., et al.: Salt and pepper noise removal by median-type noise detectors and detail-preserving regularization. IEEE Trans. on Image Processing 14(10), 1479–1485 (2005)

[11] Toprak, A., Guler, I.: Suppression of impulse noise in medical images with the use of fuzzy adaptive median filter. Journal of Medical Systems 30(6), 465–471 (2006)

[12] Jain, A.K.: Fundamentals of Digital Image Processing, 2nd edn. Eastern Economy Edition, India

[13] Gonzalez, R.C., et al.: Digital Image Processing using MATLAB, 2nd edn. Pearson Education, India (2005)

[14] `http://www.mathworks.com`

[15] Hamza, A.B., et al.: Removing Noise and Preserving Details with Relaxed Median Filters. Journal of Mathematical Imaging and Vision 11, 161–177 (1999)

[16] Xie, X.L., Beni, G.A.: Validity measure for fuzzy clustering. IEEE Trans. Pattern Analysis and Machine Intelligence 13(8) (1991)

[17] Bezdek, J.C.: Cluster validity with fuzzy sets. Journal of Cybernetics 3, 58–73 (1974)

[18] Alata, M., et al.: Optimizing of Fuzzy C-Means Clustering algorithm using GA. World Academy of Science, Engineering and Technology, 39 (2008)

Author Index

Kolibri 360 GmbH
Ferdinand-Jühlke-Straße 7
99095 Erfurt, Deutschland
produktsicherheit@kolibri360.de